MW01014115

ELLWOOD TABLES

for
Real Estate Appraising
and
Financing

by
L. W. Ellwood, M.A.I.

Fourth Edition
Containing both Explanatory Text
and Tables

Published for the

American Institute of Real Estate Appraisers
of the National Association of Realtors

Ballinger Publishing Company • Cambridge, Massachusetts
A Subsidiary of J.B. Lippincott Company

FOR EDUCATIONAL PURPOSES ONLY

Library of Congress Cataloging in Publication Data

Ellwood, L W

Ellwood tables for real estate appraising and financing.

Includes index.

1. Real property–Valuation–Problems, exercises, etc. 2. Real estate business–Finance–Problems, exercises, etc. I. American Institute of Real Estate Appraisers. II. Title. III. Title: Tables for real estate appraising and financing.

HD1387,E39 1977 333.3'32'076 77–4874

ISBN 0–88410–587–3

"All values are anticipations of the future."

JUSTICE OLIVER WENDELL HOLMES

IN MEMORIAM

In life's fields of endeavor, from time to time, there appear giants who mightily affect the actions and thoughts of participants in their callings, leaving deep imprints in the sands of progress. Just such a man was L.W. "Pete" Ellwood. Certainly, he was not a titan in physical stature but, surely, he was in the realms of intellect and wisdom. Over the past 25 years, his writings and teachings have had more widespread and powerful influence on real estate appraisers and investors than the efforts of any other individual.

"Pete" Ellwood recognized and demonstrated the relevance of investment analysis as a part of the appraisal process. He saw clearly that the broad economy in which the appraiser functions is one involving intense competition for capital; and to be successful in securing funds, real estate situations must appear financially attractive against the array of other investment opportunities. In this economic climate, "Pete" Ellwood's most significant contribution to real estate appraisal was his effort to bring investment analysis in the realty field to the same level of thoroughness and sophistication existing in other investment areas. Through his teachings, appraisers' thoughts and opinions are now more clearly understood by reason of being expressed in commonly used terms and forms.

Ellwood Tables for Real Estate Appraising and Financing–Explanatory Text and Tables represents a large part of "Pete" Ellwood's contributions to real estate appraisal education. A generation of deeply appreciative students came to maturity and understanding through study of "The Red Book" and its accompanying tables, and future generations will profit equally. The continuing outstanding merit and usefulness of its material stems from solid foundations in basic economic principles: The principles of anticipation, change, contribution, substitution, supply and demand, etc. In logical and concise steps, these principles have been arranged in procedures and programs representing the implementation of the best wisdom in real estate investment analysis. It is amazing to realize that in this small text volume, one will find explicitly or implicitly all the concepts appraisers are currently discussing: Discounted cash flow, internal rates of return, equity yields, impact of financing on yields, tax considerations, etc. The applicability of "Pete" Ellwood's teaching continues unimpaired; the only effect of passing time is variation of the data input employed in his analytical procedures. The extraordinary merit and value of "The Red Book" is that it says so very much in so few words.

What sort of a man was "Pete" Ellwood? Having had the privilege of teaching and working with him in appraisal education, I feel particularly qualified to comment. "Pete" was an intellectual genius. He presented the rare combination of philosophic depth and intensely practical application. With his impressive attainments, he remained sincerely humble, devoting his time, without stint or complaint, to the problems of all who sought his help. He never rested on his laurels but pushed on ever to investigate new fields. If any attribute could be said to match his intellectual qualities, it was a fine sense of humor that was the delight of his many students. Very few men have exhibited a more sincere love and concern for family than that quietly evidenced by "Pete". Mildred, Russell, Dick and Tom can be justly proud. A multitude of grateful students, appraisers and investors will remember, with respect and affection, L.W. "Pete" Ellwood.

JAMES E. GIBBONS, MAI

FOREWORD

The now famous Ellwood Tables were first published in 1959 by their formulator, L.W. Ellwood, and in the years that followed the publication gained wide acceptance. The American Institute of Real Estate Appraisers published the Second Edition in 1967 and the Third Edition in 1970. Other publications of a similar nature appeared with elaborations and variations on the original Ellwood theme. Computers, and even pocket calculators, were programmed with Ellwood's formulas to solve mortgage-equity problems automatically without reference to tables. Thus, Ellwood's influence transcended his own readership, and the Ellwood Tables became a classic.

This Fourth Edition of the Ellwood Tables preserves the classic nature of the work. The complete text and composition of the Third Edition have been retained, but a new table of contents, an index and a table of annual mortgage constants for monthly payment mortgages have been added to facilitate use as a reference source. The tables remain unchanged except for the addition of technical notes and expansion of the Analyses of Selected Capitalization Rates and the Basic Capitalization Rate Tables. The scope of these supplementary tabulations has been shifted upward to cover a range of interest rates in line with today's market.

Parts I and II, formerly published in separate volumes, have been combined in a single volume. No attempt has been made to edit the work or to reconcile the terminology and symbols with more recent publications. The Fourth Edition is therefore faithful to the original style and format but includes new features for increased utility.

Ellwood's original "Explanatory Text," Part I, was written to assist in use of tables presented in Part II. Part I was not written as a conventional textbook, with progressive lessons to accompany a course of instruction on applied mathematics of finance and mortgage-equity techniques. Few are likely to have the mathematical background and interest in reading through Part I with complete understanding without the benefit of collateral instruction.

The Analyses of Selected Capitalization Rates and the Basic Capitalization Rate Tables were updated for this edition by the author's son, C. Russell Ellwood, MAI, who also prepared the newly added tables of mortgage constants. Mr. Ellwood's contribution will be welcomed by the many analysts who will be spared the time of making these calculations.

The author of this work, the late L.W. Ellwood, MAI, contributed much more than a book and a set of tables. He contributed new thinking and new techniques at a time when they were needed. He provided leadership, guidance, and inspiration to students and colleagues. It is hoped that this latest edition of his work will become a fitting tribute by inspiring more new thinking in the Ellwood tradition.

William T. Van Court, MAI
1977 President
American Institute of Real Estate Appraisers

CONTENTS

PART II—TABLES

Prologue

EXPERIENCE and JUDGMENT

I believe experience can teach lessons which may lead to sound judgment. I believe sound judgment is vital in selecting the critical factors for appraisal. But, I also believe the bright 17 year old high school student in elementary astronomy can do a better job estimating the distance to the moon than the old man of the mountains who has looked at the moon for 80 years. So, I find it difficult to accept the notion that dependable valuation of real estate is nothing more than experience and judgment.

I would not give a red cent for an appraisal by the "expert" who beats his breast and shouts; "I don't have to give reasons. I've had 40 years experience in this business. And, this property is worth so much because I *say so".*

After all, value is expressed as a number. And, no man lives who, through experience, has all numbers so filed in the convolutions of his brain that he can be relied upon to choose the right one without explicable analysis and calculation.

L.W.E.

I

THE CAPITALIZATION PROCESS

Chapter Three of the American Institute of Real Estate Appraisers' basic text: "The Appraisal of Real Estate," defines and discusses the ten principles of real property value.

Two of these principles cover the motivation for purchase and the basis for price negotiation.

1. *The Principle of Anticipation:*

   People buy real estate because they anticipate that ownership will provide them with certain future benefits.

2. *The Principle of Substitution:*

   Price is generally determined by the buyer's notion concerning the price at which he believes he could acquire substitute investments which would provide him with comparable benefits.

The other eight principles pertain to conditions the prudent buyer considers in estimating the nature, quality and magnitude of future benefits of ownership.

Value is therefore specifically defined as *the present worth of all rights to future benefits arising from ownership.*

To find value in dollars, according to this definition, the phrase "present worth" dictates that future benefits be estimated in dollars and discounted to present worth at rates of investment yield which will attract purchase capital.

This is the capitalization process. And, since future benefits must be expressed in dollars, it follows that the process applies in particular to the valuation of properties that produce dollar benefits in the form of rent and the proceeds of resale.

Other approaches are more applicable to properties in which the benefits of ownership are amenities of an aesthetic or emotional nature.

The first requirement for success in teaching any subject is mutual agreement between the text and the student as to the precise meaning of words and phrases. For this reason, semantics is especially important in a text on capitalization because it involves the use of language which may be interpreted in numerous ways.

SEMANTICS:

The following definitions are presented to avoid misunderstanding as to the specific meaning of various terminology.

Cash Market Value:

As used here, "cash market value" contemplates a transaction in which the seller would receive all cash in exchange for a clear and merchantable title to his property. This does not mean, however, that the buyer would not pledge such title to a financial institution as security for borrowing a major part of the purchase capital. The objective of the seller is to obtain the maximum amount of cash for his property. The buyer's source of funds is of no concern to him. The fact that mortgage money is available to typical buyers not only makes the real estate market what it is but the available amount, rate and term have a significant influence on the amount of cash the seller may obtain for good title. Therefore, realistic application of the capitalization process requires provision for normal composition and sources of purchase capital.

Equity:

The amount or value of a property or properties above the total of liens or charges. When property is held free and clear, the owner is said to have a 100% equity. If 75% of purchase price is financed by mortgage, the buyer is said to acquire a 25% equity. Capital invested in any equity position whether it represents 100% or any fraction of value is known as risk or venture capital because there are no guarantees with regard to yield or recapture.

Dividend Rate or Income Yield:

This is the ratio of net, annual cash flow income collected by the owner to his cash investment in the property.

Investment Yield:

This is the total yield produced by both income and resale expressed as an annual rate of yield. In other words, it is the rate of interest at which the total present value of both income and reversion is equal to the cost of investment.

Depreciation and Book Depreciation:

"Depreciation" means total, actual decline in the market value of a property (including both land and improvements) from time of purchase to time of resale.

"Book Depreciation" means arbitrary, periodic reserves or allowances as set up against historical costs of wearing assets for purposes of cost accounting and income tax calculations. Since it pertains to historic costs only and is not affected by the movement of market values, it normally bears little relation to what actually happens in the market with regard to a given parcel of real estate.

Recapture of Purchase Capital:

This phrase is not to be confused with or considered as synonymous with depreciation.

In actual experience, recapture of purchase capital is usually accomplished by mortgage amortization and by sale of the equity position. Recapture of the mortgage component occurs according to terms of a periodic installment contract without regard to fluctuations in market value.

Appreciation:

This means increase in market value.

Simultaneous Occurrence of Depreciation, Recapture and Appreciation:

The following type of experience, which is not unusual, illustrates why it is essential to treat these three factors as separate amounts in realistic application of the capitalization process.

Smith purchased an income property for $150,000 and sold it ten years later for $135,000. He paid $50,000 cash and borrowed $100,000 on an installment mortgage contract. Amortization amounted to $35,000 reducing the loan balance to $65,000 and leaving Smith $70,000 as his share of the $135,000 proceeds of sale. During the term of ownership, depreciation amounted to 10 per cent, recapture by mortgage amortization amounted to 23⅓ per cent and the value of Smith's equity investment of $50,000 appreciated 40 per cent to $70,000.

The average net cash flow income produced by the property was $11,450 per year. The mortgage interest rate was 5 per cent. The composite capitalization rate was:

$$\frac{d}{v} = \frac{11{,}450}{150{,}000} = .0763 \text{ or } 7.63\%$$

The income distribution was:

Mortgage interest, \$100,000 at 5%	\$ 5,000
Mortgage amortization, \$35,000 × .00644 × 12	2,705
Smith's average dividend	3,745
Total Income	\$11,450

On a \$50,000 investment, Smith collected income at \$3,745 per year for ten years and a reversion of \$70,000 at the end of that time. His average "dividend rate" was:

$$\frac{3{,}745}{50{,}000} = .0749 \text{ or } 7.49\%$$

His "investment yield" was 10 per cent as proved by the use of 10 per cent, ten years income and reversion factors as follows:

Income; \$3.745 × 6.144567*	\$23,012
Reversion deferred 10 years; \$70,000 × .385543*	26,988
Value of equity investment at time of purchase	\$50,000

*Multipliers from 10% Compound Interest Table at 10 years. Cols. 5 & 4.

Thus, an over-all capitalization rate of .0763 provided for mortgage requirements, capital recapture, depreciation in property value and a 10% yield to the buyer.

Annuities:

An annuity is commonly thought of as a series of equal annual payments. The word is used here in a broader sense. The time interval between payments must be equal throughout the series but does not have to be a year. It may be a month, a quarter year, a half year or any other period of time. A common type is the "ordinary annuity" or "annuity in arrears" as represented by the series of payments in a level installment amortized mortgage contract where each payment is received at the end of each period. The "annuity in advance" or "annuity due" as represented by the series of payments provided by a lease requiring payment of rent at the beginning of each period will also be encountered. There will be problems involving declining annuities, increasing annuities and fluctuating annuities. In short, each type of periodic income stream may be considered as an annuity of one kind or another. Equal time intervals between payments is the only required characteristic. They can all be stabilized by formula to an equivalent "ordinary annuity."

Coefficients:

A coefficient is any quantity to be used as a multiplier of another quantity. Standard coefficients for general and repeated use in the solution of various types of financial and engineering problems are precomputed and presented in tables.

A primary table is the "Table of Mortgage Coefficients." The six factors in standard "Compound Interest Tables" may also be used as coefficients or multipliers.

The Sinking Fund Factor:

The sinking fund factor in combination with effective interest or yield rate is the most useful of all compound interest functions. It is used to calculate investment yield in the analysis of a composite capitalization rate.

It is used to determine the effect of depreciation or appreciation on present value. The periodic installment per dollar of mortgage money is the sinking fund factor for the full amortization term plus the effective interest rate. One or more sinking fund factors are integral parts of all capitalization rates except those pertaining to perpetuities. Sinking fund factors comprise Column No. 3 of the compound interest tables and applicable ones are included with the other tables.

Reciprocals:

When one is divided by any number, the quotient is called the reciprocal of the given number. Since $1/4 = .25$ the reciprocal of 4 is .25. When any quantity is multiplied by the reciprocal of a given number, the product of multiplication will equal the quotient found when the same quantity is divided by the given number; i.e.;

$$16 \times .25 = 4$$

And

$$16 \div 4 = 4$$

The reciprocals of any two numbers are related to each other in reverse of the order in which the same numbers are related to each other; i.e.,

$$8 \div 4 = 2$$

whereas

$$1/4 \div 1/8$$

or

$$.25 \div .125 = 2$$

Complements:

The complement of any fraction is the difference between the fraction and the whole number 1. The complement of 75% is 25% because $1 - .75 = .25$. If 30% of a mortgage loan is amortized, the unamortized balance will be the original amount multiplied by 70% which is the complement of 30%. If we call the total value of a property "V" in which \$50,000 is allocated to land, the fraction of total value allocated to the building will be the complement of $\frac{\$50,000}{V}$ or $1 - \frac{50,000}{V} =$ fraction of "V" allocated to building.

If "V" happens to be \$400,000 in this case, we will have:

$$1 - \frac{50,000}{400,000} = 1 - .125 = .875 \text{ or } 87\tfrac{1}{2}\%.$$

In other words, 87½% of total value is allocated to the building.

Income Projection Term:

The existence of market value presupposes a market in which properties are bought and sold. If the tenure of ownership were total useful life, there would be no sales of improved income properties; hence, no market and no standards of comparison.

All commonly accepted definitions of market value contemplate a sale, at time of appraisal, *to one buyer.* It follows then that the projection term for appraisal should not attempt to cover more than one typical or optimum term of ownership.

As with any other form of investment, the timing of resale of income real estate has a very significant influence upon the yield. The investment yield may be raised two or three percentage points above the dividend yield if appreciation attributable to mortgage amortization, or any other cause, is taken advantage of during the first half dozen years. On the other hand, if the same property with the same dividend yield is held forty or fifty years, it will require several hundred times as much appreciation to produce the same investment yield.

Optimum terms of ownership have tended to become shorter in recent years because of changes in the monetary side of the market and the ever increasing impact of income taxes on take-home income.

Public records pertaining to many thousands of conventional income properties indicate that on the average this type of real estate changes hands or recasts its financing within ten years of purchase.

Aside from the obvious fact that a more reliable short term projection can be made than one purporting to cover total useful life, there are numerous other advantages.

The short projection will produce the same total value as a longer one, regardless of the capitalization technique so long as we assume the same income stream, the same rate of value change and the same rate of interest. In other words, any value loss due to the shorter income stream will be offset by a gain in the present value of the reversion. Thus, a five-year projection will produce the same value as a fifty-year projection when all other assumptions implicit in each projection are equal.

The short term projection offers a better chance for accuracy not only because the estimate of periodic income can be based on current facts and well-remembered experience but also because total value will not be attributable to income alone. A substantial portion of it will be due to residual value at the end of the projection. The law of compensating errors favors short projections.

The normal net cash flow income stream produced by landlord-serviced properties is one which fluctuates irregularly up and down from year to year. It does not follow a straight line path in either direction. A reasonably reliable estimate of average, annual net cash flow for a term of ten years or less can be treated as a level annuity with no significant error in the result. This has been proved by numerous case history tests pertaining to actual year by year earning records of office buildings, apartment projects, shopping centers, etc.

The most supportable over-all capitalization rate is one derived from comparable sales. It is relatively easy to test or analyze any over-all rate and interpret it in terms of probable yield to the equity investor when the projection is limited to ten years. It is virtually impossible to make such analyses when the projection is presumed to cover the total useful life of any structure which represents an appropriate use for its site at time of appraisal.

Therefore, projections in numerous examples of the uses of the various tables are confined to ten years. Longer projections are generally used only in cases involving long-term leases to financially responsible tenants. Since the duration of a specific income stream is fixed by contract, in such cases, it is advisable to employ the stipulated facts in preference to assumptions.

Composite Capitalization Rate and Overall Capitalization Rate

These are synonymous terms. They both mean the same thing.

STANDARD SYMBOLS:

Symbols, usually in the form of letters of the alphabet, are used to represent specific amounts or quantities. This avoids endless, time-consuming repetition in defining the factors presented in the statement of problems and in writing the equations by which they are solved.

Remember that each symbol dictates the use of a given number, and to solve any problem, all you need to do is substitute the proper number for each symbol and perform the operations in arithmetic indicated by the formula.

Standard symbols in common use are identified as follows:

Y is the equity yield rate.

I is the *annual* mortgage interest rate.

i is the *effective* mortgage interest rate. It is the quotient found by dividing the annual mortgage interest rate by the number of installments per year. If installments are payable monthly; i = I ÷ 12. If installments are payable quarterly; i = I ÷ 4; etc. Note: Y, I and i are interest rates and may be interchangeable in compound interest formulas.

f is the annual mortgage requirement per dollar of mortgage money including both interest and the provision for recapture or amortization. It is 12 times the monthly installment per dollar; etc. With interest at 5¼% per annum, the monthly installment including interest and provision for full amortization in 20 years or 240 months is quoted at $6.74 per month for each $1,000 of loan. The monthly requirement per dollar is 6.74 ÷ 1,000 = .00674, and "f" in this case is 12 × .00674 = .08088. Obviously, "f" varies with each change in the mortgage interest rate and each change in the amortization term.

M is the ratio of mortgage money to appraised value or to assumed total purchase price. If we assume 75 per cent of purchase price will be borrowed as mortgage money: M = .75. And, of course, "M" can be any ratio from zero to 100 per cent.

C is the mortgage coefficient used in calculating a composite capitalization rate. When employed with equity yield "Y" and mortgage ratio "M," it provides for all ingredients of the composite capitalization rate except depreciation or appreciation in over-all property value. Table "C" presents a large selection of precomputed coefficients with auxiliary factors for depreciation or appreciation. Tables "Ca," "Cp" and "Cy" are used for problems outside the scope of Table "C."

P is the fraction of mortgage money which will be recaptured, amortized or "Paid Off" during the income projection term.

Sm is the amount to which one dollar will grow including interest compounded at the effective mortgage interest rate over the entire term required for full amortization of a mortgage.*

Sp is the amount to which one dollar will grow including interest compounded at the effective mortgage interest rate during the term of the income projection.*

$1/S_{\overline{n}|}$ is the symbol for a sinking fund factor at a given rate of interest for a given length of time. In most problems this will be at rate "Y" for a stated income projection term.

*Note: Factors represented generally by symbol "S^n" comprise Column No. 1 of the compound interest tables. This factor is sometimes called "the future worth of one dollar including interest."

r is the basic capitalization rate which includes all the ingredients except provision for depreciation or appreciation during the income projection term. Since the mortgage component of purchase capital enjoys a secured position involving much less risk and management burden than the equity position, it will normally command a much lower interest rate than the prospective equity yield rate "Y." The equation for the basic rate is: the equity yield "Y" less the product of mortgage ratio "M" multiplied by mortgage coefficient "C," i.e.*

$$r = Y - MC$$

*Note: "r" is also used to represent the ratio of progression in the formula for the sum of a geometric progression.

J adjustment factor to provide for gradual increases or declines in income. Table Cy.

dep is the total amount of depreciation in over-all market value of property during the income projection term. Depreciation *increases* the over-all capitalization rate.

app is the total amount of appreciation in over-all market value of property during the income projection term. Appreciation *decreases* the over-all capitalization rate.

R is the over-all capitalization rate including depreciation or appreciation.

d is the projected average, net cash flow income per year before mortgage installments.

ed is the equity dividend rate, i.e., the ratio of cash flow to equity investment after mortgage installments.

V is the present market value or assumed purchase price, i.e.,

$$\frac{d}{R} = V \text{ and, by transposition } \frac{d}{V} = R$$

COMMON FORMULAS:

Common formulas in which these symbols are used follow. The next two chapters contain explanations and derivations.

Unless otherwise stipulated, the sinking fund factor is at equity yield "Y" for the income projection term in years.

For Estimating Market Value, "V":

$$r = Y - MC$$
$$R = r + \text{dep } 1/S_{\overline{n|}}$$
$$R = r - \text{app } 1/S_{\overline{n|}}$$
$$V = \frac{d}{R}$$

For Computing Mortgage Coefficient, "C":

$$C = Y + P\ 1/S_{\overline{n|}} - f$$

For Computing "P" the Fraction of Mortgage Amortized During the Income Projection Term:

$$P = \left(\frac{f}{I} - 1\right)(Sp - 1)$$

"Sp" the amount to which one dollar will grow in any number of periods is in Column No. 1 of the compound interest tables. Caution should be exercised in selecting this factor on the basis of the frequency of mortgage installments. In other words, use the monthly table where installments are monthly, the quarterly table when installments are quarterly, etc.

Example:

Compute "P" for 10 years where the annual requirement "f" is 7.56% including interest at 5¼% per annum and where installments are payable; (a) monthly, (b) quarterly, (c) semi-annually.

Solutions:

$$\text{Constant Multiplier} = \frac{f}{I} - 1 = \frac{.0756}{.0525} - 1 = .44$$

Sp — 1 from 5¼% compound interest tables at 10 years; Col. No. 1.

(a) Monthly; .688524 and $P = .44 \times .688524 = .30295$
(b) Quarterly; .684695 and $P = .44 \times .684695 = .30127$
(c) Semi-Annually; .679049 and $P = .44 \times .679049 = .29879$

Note:

Since monthly installments will accelerate equity value build-up without increasing the mortgage requirement, monthly installments are usually assumed in computing the composite capitalization rate. "Sp — 1" factors for from 1 to 40 years on a monthly basis are presented in Table "Cp."

To Compute the Annual Requirement "f" for Any Desired Amount of "P":

$$f = \left(1 + \frac{P}{Sp - 1}\right) I$$

Example:

A lease will expire in 9 years. A mortgage commitment for $200,000 is to be 50 per cent amortized by the end of the lease term with interest at 5½ per cent per annum by monthly installments. Compute the monthly installment.

Solution:

P = .50; Sp — 1 at 5½%, 9 years monthly = .6386 from Table Cp.

$$f = \left(1 + \frac{.50}{.6386}\right).055 = 1.782963 \times .055 = .098063$$

Annual Requirements: $200,000 × .098063 = $19,612.58

Monthly Installment: $19,612.58/12 = $1,634.38

To Calculate Value Change: (depreciation or appreciation in over-all property value) which must occur during any income projection term for realization of any selected equity yield, "Y."

The basic rate "r" will increase as the equity yield "Y" increases. When the composite rate "R" is greater than "r," a decline in property value must occur to compensate for the difference in the two rates.

Thus: $\text{dep.} = \dfrac{R - r}{1/S_{\overline{n}|}}$

When equity yield "Y" is high enough to make basic rate "r" greater than composite rate "R," an increase in property value must occur to compensate for the difference.

Thus: $\text{app} = \dfrac{r - R}{1/S_{\overline{n}|}}$

Note: The above two formulas provide a practical method for analyzing any composite capitalization rate derived from market experience and interpreting it in terms of yield prospects for any equity investment. They are used in making the graphic analysis which shows value changes which must occur at any time during a projection for any yield within a selected range. For instruction and demonstration, see: "Problems Involving Use of Table C; (4) Estimating Prospects for Equity Yield."

For Calculating the Full Amortization Term when "f" and "I" are stated:

$$Sm = \frac{f}{f - I}$$

"Sm" is the amount to which one dollar will grow with interest at the effective rate "i" or the future worth of one dollar with interest for the full amortization term. This is in Column No. 1 of the Compound Interest Tables.

Example:

The annual constant mortgage requirement is 8 per cent including interest at 5½%. How long will it take to fully amortize the mortgage if installments are paid monthly?

Solution:

Stated factors: f = .08, I = .055

$$Sm = \frac{.08}{.08 - .055} = \frac{.08}{.025} = 3.2$$

Refer to 5½% Monthly Compound Interest Table. Reading down the first column, the nearest factor below 3.2 is 3.165659 at 21 years, and:

$$\frac{3.2}{3.165659} = 1.0108479$$

The nearest factor above this quotient is at three months. Answer: 21 years and 3 months.

To Stabilize the Declining Income Stream Implicit in the Straight Line Depreciation Technique to the Equivalent Ordinary Annuity:

$$\frac{d\,(Y + Nk\ 1/S_{\overline{n|}})}{Y + k} = \text{ordinary annuity}$$

In which:

d = first year income

N = Projection term in years

k = Annual straight-line depreciation rate

Example:

First year income "d" is $19,000. Yield rate "Y" is 7%. Projection term "N" is 10 years. Straight line depreciation rate "k" is 2½%. Sinking fund factor at 7% 10 years is .0724.

Straight Line Valuation: $\frac{19{,}000}{.07 + .025} = \$200{,}000$

Annual Recapture at 2½%: $200,000 × .025 = $ 5,000

Annual Income Decline: $ 5,000 × .07 = $ 350

Income will be $19,000 the first year and decline $350 each year thereafter.

Problem:

What ordinary annuity has the same present value as the first ten years of this declining income stream?

Solution:

$$19{,}000\left(\frac{.07 + 10 \times .025 \times .0724}{.07 + .025}\right) = \frac{19{,}000 \times .0881}{.095} = \$17.619$$

Arithmetic Check:

Total depreciation in ten years would be 25 per cent of \$200,000 or \$50,000. Reversion deferred 10 years would be \$150,000. Present value of income and reversion discounted 10 years at 7% must equal straight-line valuation of \$200,000.

Income,	$17,619 × 7.023582	$123,748
Reversion,	$150,000 × .508349	76,252
Total		$200,000

Note: Coefficients are from Columns 5 and 4 of 7% Annual Compound Interest Table.

GEOMETRIC AND ARITHMETIC PROGRESSIONS:

The capitalization process and the analysis of investments for prospective yields involve two types of quantitative series. Since each one may include a large number of quantities, formulae by which the sum or total of the series can be calculated are good time savers.

Geometric Progression:—

This is any series in which all preceding or all succeeding quantities are related to each other by a constant multiplier called the "ratio of progression." The series of quantities whose sum comprises the Inwood Annuity Coefficient represents this type. While this can normally be found in a precomputed table, there are other geometric progressions which are not tabulated. An example would be the present value of a series of income tax deductions where reserves for depreciation are accumulated by any declining balance method. Another would be the total book depreciation which will be accrued by the declining balance method at any point in time.

The formula for the sum of a geometric progression is:

$$\frac{ar^n - a}{r - 1} = \text{sum}$$

in which

a = The smallest quantity in the series
r = The ratio of progression
n = The number of quantities in the series

Although derivation and uses of this formula are discussed in the next chapter, a word of caution is appropriate here: Make sure any series in question is in fact a geometric progression before application of the formula. This can be done by dividing several adjoining quantities to see if the ratio is constant.

Arithmetic Progression:—

This is any series of quantities in which there is a constant difference between quantities. Examples are: the income stream implicit in the straight line depreciation capitalization technique and income tax deductions where reserves for depreciation are accrued by sum of the years digits method.

The formula for the sum of any arithmetic progression is:

$$\frac{n}{2}(a + L) = \text{sum}$$

in which

n = Number of quantities in the series
a = Smallest quantity in the series
L = Largest quantity in the series

The following series is an arithmetic progression:

$$2 + 5 + 8 + 11 + 14 + 17 = 57$$

The constant difference is 3

$n = 6, \quad a = 2, \quad L = 17$

$$\frac{6}{2}(2 + 17) = 3 \times 19 = 57$$

II

CONSTRUCTION AND USE OF COMPOUND INTEREST TABLES

To understand the income approach, the appraiser must understand the arithmetic of compound interest. The reason this branch of arithmetic has remained a mystery, shunned by many people, is not because it is complex or hard to understand. Rather, it is because manual application is a tedious, time-consuming, and mentally exhausting process.

The electric calculator has eliminated this obstacle. Its use in conjunction with tables of pre-computed functions makes it possible to combine pertinent facts with realistic assumptions and solve problems in minutes which would otherwise consume many hours.

The critical factors in the income approach by any technique are amount, time, and investment yield. Although it should be obvious that every valid technique will produce the same result so long as these factors are equal, this is not always clear to the novice. Specific assumptions as to amount, time, and yield are implicit in each technique. These assumptions change more or less surreptitiously when a switch is made from one technique to another. The appraiser cannot make an intelligent selection of technique unless he knows exactly what the assumptions are and how they affect his result. Moreover, he cannot do a professional job with integrity unless he *believes* the assumptions implicit in the technique he selects. Otherwise, the appraisal will not be the result of his own judgment applied to pertinent facts. Instead it will be the product of a formula which may not be plausible in the light of relevant facts.

Every capitalization technique is a process for discounting anticipated future profits to present market value at yields which will attract purchase capital. The arithmetic of the process is the arithmetic of discount at compound interest. The objective of this chapter is to clarify this branch of arithmetic. The student appraiser will find the income approach by any technique readily understandable if he will take the time needed to absorb this subject.

There are two general classes of problems pertaining to the investment of capital for profit in the form of interest at a periodic rate. The first class concerns the amount to which a single sum or a series of future periodic installments will grow with the accumulation of interest at a fixed rate per period. The second class pertains to the present worth of a single sum to be collected at a specific future date or a series of future periodic installments for a specific number of periods when discounted from date of collection to the present time at a fixed rate of interest per period.

In each class there are three problem types. Hence there are six basic formulas. Since direct application of the formulas to each problem would consume a great deal of time, the formulas are employed for the compilation of standard tables. Each table presents six precomputed functions of one dollar at selected rates of interest for various periods of time. In other words, a lump sum of one dollar, or a series of one dollar installments, is assumed for calculation of each tabulated function. When the desired function for one dollar is known, it can be applied to any number of dollars by multiplication or division.

Thus a comprehensive, compound interest table presents six standard functions of one dollar. And since many problems involve the use of two or more of them it is most convenient to have them arranged in six columns on the same page for each effective interest rate. The "effective" interest rate is the quotient of the annual or "nominal" rate when divided by the number of conversion periods or installments per year. The user is, therefore, cautioned to select the appropriate conversion frequency. Do not use a monthly table when dealing with annual collections or annual compounding. The compound interest tables which supplement this text present functions computed for monthly, quarterly, semi-annual and annual collections or conversions for all nominal interest rates from 3 per cent to 12 per cent. The more speculative rates; i.e. from 13 per cent to 30 per cent, are presented on the basis of annual collections or conversions only.

The columns on each page are numbered from 1 to 6 and the identity of the function in each column with its formula and standard symbol is as follows:

FUTURE VALUES:

Column No.		*Formula*	*Standard Symbol*
1.	The amount to which an investment or deposit of one dollar will grow in a given number of time periods, including the accumulation of interest at the effective rate per period. This factor is commonly known as the *Future Worth of One Dollar with Interest.*	$(1+i)^n$	$= S^n$
2.	The total accumulation of principal and interest of a series of deposits or installments of 1 dollar per period for a given number of periods with interest at the effective rate per period. This factor is commonly known as the *Future Worth of One Dollar per Period with Interest.*	$\frac{S^n - 1}{i}$	$= s_{\overline{n}\rceil}$
3.	The level periodic investment or deposit required to accumulate one dollar in a given number of periods including the accumulation of interest at the effective rate. This is commonly known as the *Sinking Fund Factor.*	$\frac{i}{S^n - 1}$	$= 1/s_{\overline{n}\rceil}$

PRESENT VALUES:

Column No.		*Formula*	*Standard Symbol*
4.	The present value of one dollar to be collected at a given future time when discounted at the effective interest rate for the number of periods from now to the date of collection. This is called the *Reversion Factor.*	$\frac{1}{S^n}$	$= V^n$
5.	The present value of a series of future installments or payments of one dollar per period for a given number of periods when discounted at the effective interest rate. This factor is commonly known as the *Inwood Ordinary Annuity Coefficient.*	$\frac{1 - V^n}{i}$	$= a_{\overline{n}\rceil}$
6.	The level periodic installment which will pay interest and provide full amortization or recapture of an investment of one dollar in a given number of periods with interest at a given rate per period. Its most common application is as the periodic mortgage installment per dollar, and is in fact the *Ordinary Annuity which has a Present Value of One Dollar.*	$\frac{i}{1 - V^n}$	$= 1/a_{\overline{n}\rceil}$

Although the functions in columns 2, 3, 5, and 6 are computed on the basis of level periodic income, specific inter-relationships provide methods by which declining and increasing income streams can be readily converted or stabilized to a level income of equal value.

Please notice that S^n or its reciprocal V^n is the key factor in each formula. The only other quantities are "1" which represents 1 dollar and "i" which represents the "effective" interest rate. Thus, calculation of the quantity S^n is the only one involving more than elementary arithmetic. Let us start the explanation by presenting the equation for it as follows:

$$S^n = (\text{BASE})^{\text{EXPONENT}}$$

In which:

S^n Equals the value to which one dollar will grow in a given length of time including the accumulation of interest at a given rate. Col. No. 1 Compound Interest Table.

The Base is one dollar plus the interest on one dollar for one interest conversion period of time; i.e. $(1 + i)$.

An interest conversion period is the time interval for which each interest collection or each interest accumulation is to be calculated.

In the United States, the interest rate is usually quoted as an annual rate called the "Nominal Rate."

The rate used in the base, however, is called the "Effective Rate."

The "Effective Rate" is found by dividing the annual or Nominal Rate by the number of interest conversion periods per year.

Rule For Determining The Base

The Base is always one dollar plus the interest on one dollar at the "effective rate" for one conversion period.

Assume for example an annual or nominal rate of 6%

If interest is to be converted annually, the interest on one dollar for 1 year is 6 cents and the base is 1.06. The "effective rate" is 6%.

If interest is to be converted semi-annually, the interest on one dollar for ½ year is 3 cents and the base is 1.03. The "effective rate" is 3%.

If interest is to be converted quarterly, the interest on one dollar for ¼ year is 1½ cents and the base is 1.015. The "effective rate" is 1½%.

If interest is to be converted monthly, the interest on one dollar for 1/12th year is one half cent and the base is 1.005. The "effective rate" is ½ of one per cent.

The Exponent

The "Exponent" is the total number of conversion periods for which interest is to be accumulated at the effective rate. It is the number of times the base must be multiplied by itself to produce the sum "S^n"

Assuming a total term of 20 years with 6% as the nominal rate, each base with its exponent and resulting sum would be as follows:

Conversion	*Base & Exponent*		*Col. 1 at 20 Years S^n*
Annually	1.06^{20}	=	3.207135
Semi-Annually	1.03^{40}	=	3.262038
Quarterly	1.015^{80}	=	3.290663
Monthly	1.005^{240}	=	3.310204

Please note that although the annual interest rate is the same in all of the above examples, the value to which one dollar will grow changes with each variation in the frequency of conversion. The difference is not great with regard to one dollar but would be quite substantial if the original investment were a million dollars.

The formula in which the base and its exponent are usually written is:

$$(1 + i)^n$$

In which "i" is the effective rate of interest written as a decimal fraction of one dollar and "n" is the exponent.

The Rule Of Exponents:

In a problem such as our last example where:

$$(1 + i)^n = 1.005^{240}$$

It would take a long time to multiply 1.005 by itself 240 times. This can be cut down to 9 steps however, by employing the rule of exponents as follows:

	WHICH EQUALS
$1.005 \times 1.005 = 1.005^{2}$	$1.005 \times 1.005 = 1.010025$
$1.005^{2} \times 1.005^{2} = 1.005^{4}$	$1.010025 \times 1.010025 = 1.020151$
$1.005^{4} \times 1.005^{4} = 1.005^{8}$	$1.020151 \times 1.020151 = 1.040707$
$1.005^{2} \times 1.005^{8} = 1.005^{10}$	$1.010025 \times 1.040707 = 1.051140$
$1.005^{10} \times 1.005^{10} = 1.005^{20}$	$1.051140 \times 1.051140 = 1.104896$
$1.005^{20} \times 1.005^{20} = 1.005^{40}$	$1.104896 \times 1.104896 = 1.220795$
$1.005^{40} \times 1.005^{40} = 1.005^{80}$	$1.220795 \times 1.220795 = 1.490338$
$1.005^{80} \times 1.005^{80} = 1.005^{160}$	$1.490338 \times 1.490338 = 2.221110$
$1.005^{80} \times 1.005^{160} = 1.005^{240}$	$1.490338 \times 2.221110 = 3.310204$

It should be noted that the exponent of the multiplier is added to that of the multiplicand in each step to determine the exponent of their product. Thus, if we know that:

$$1.005^{80} = 1.490338 \text{ and } 1.005^{160} = 2.221110$$

We also know that $80 + 160 = 240$ and, therefore:

$$1.005^{240} = 1.490338 \times 2.221110 = 3.310204$$

In multiplication, when exponents of a common base are added, their total is the exponent of the product.

In division, when numerator and denominator are expressed as a common base with exponents, the exponent of the quotient is found by subtracting the exponent of the denominator from that of the numerator. This is an important rule to remember because its use is required quite frequently in the capitalization process. To clarify it more emphatically, let us use the number "2" as a common base.

$2 \times 2 = 2^2 = 4$

$2 \times 2 \times 2 = 2^3 = 8$

$2 \times 2 \times 2 \times 2 \times 2 = 2^5 = 32$

$2^2 \times 2^3 = 2^5$ and $4 \times 8 = 32$

$2^5 \div 2^3 = 2^2 = 4$ and $32 \div 8 = 4$

Exercises:

(a) How many months will it take for an investment to double in value if the nominal rate is 6% and conversion occurs monthly?

We know that $1.005^{n} = 2$

By reading down the "amount of 1" column (Col. 1) we find the nearest number below 2 is 1.931613 which appears at 11 years or 132 months. Next, we divide 2 by this number.

$$\frac{(1+i)^{n}}{(1+i)^{132}} = \frac{2}{1.931613} = 1.035404$$

The nearest number to this quotient appears in the same column at 7 months. Since $132 + 7 = 139$, we know it will take approximately 139 months for the investment to double in value.

In other words, we find that:

$$1.005^{132} \times 1.005^{7} = 1.005^{139}$$

and

$$1.005^{139} = 1.931613 \times 1.035529 = 2.000 +$$

(b) Find the value to which one dollar will grow in 12½ years at 6% interest per annum converted quarterly.
(Col. 1)

At 12 years, we find 2.043478. At 2 quarters which is ½ year, we find 1.030225.

Since our base is 1.015 and 12½ years is 50 quarter years, we know:

$$1.015^{50} = 2.043478 \times 1.030225 = 2.105242$$

The Present Value of Future Collections:

In exercise (b) we found that 1 dollar will grow to 2.105242 in 12½ years at 6% per annum compounded quarterly. Obviously then \$10,000 in the same span of time and at the same rate would grow to:

$$2.105242 \times \$10,000 = \$21,052.42$$

Now, suppose a contract calls for payment of \$100,000 in a lump sum 12½ years from today. The owner of this contract sells it on the basis of 6% interest per annum compounded quarterly. How much does he receive for the contract?

It is plain that he will receive the amount which will grow to $100,000 in 12½ years at 6% per annum compounded quarterly. And, this will be $100,000 divided by the amount to which 1 dollar will grow in 12½ years at the same rate, i.e.

$$\frac{\$100{,}000}{2.105242} = \$47{,}500.48$$

In other words, $47,500.48 × 2.105242 = $100,000. So the present value of $100,000 deferred 12½ years and discounted at 6% per annum compounded quarterly is $47,500.48. Moreover, the present value of 1 dollar deferred 12½ years at the same rate is:

$$\frac{1}{2.105242} = .4750048$$

Thus, the quantity .4750048 is the present value of each dollar deferred 12½ years at 6% per annum compounded quarterly and the present value of any given number of dollars discounted for the same length of time at the same rate is the product of the given number of dollars multiplied by .4750048; i.e.

$$\$100{,}000 \times .4750048 = \$47{,}500.48$$

In any case, where one is divided by a given quantity, the quotient is called the *"Reciprocal"* of the given quantity.

In this exercise .4750048 is the reciprocal of 2.105242. The amount $100,000 is called a *"Reversion."*

When $100,000 was divided by the base 1.015, converted 50 times, the quotient was $47,500.48. The same result was obtained by employing the reciprocal of the base converted 50 times as a multiplier of $100,000.

The present value of each dollar of any future reversion can, therefore, be represented by the following formula:

$$\mathbf{V^n = \frac{1}{(BASE)^{EXPONENT}}}$$

In which:

$\mathbf{V^n}$ symbolizes the present value of each dollar of any reversion deferred "n" conversion periods. Column No. 4 Compound Interest Table.

Development of the Annuity Coefficient:

Let us now assume an effective rate of 25% in which case the base will be 1.25.

The present value of one dollar reversion deferred 1 period is:

$$\frac{1}{1.25} = .80 \text{ or } 80 \text{ cents}$$

The present value of a one dollar reversion deferred 2 periods is:

$$\frac{1}{1.25 \times 1.25} = \frac{1}{1.5625} = .64 \text{ or } 64 \text{ cents}$$

The present value of a one dollar reversion deferred 3 periods is:

$$\frac{1}{1.25 \times 1.25 \times 1.25} = \frac{1}{1.953125} = .512 \text{ or } 51.2 \text{ cents}$$

The present value of a one dollar reversion deferred 4 periods is:

$$\frac{1}{1.25 \times 1.25 \times 1.25 \times 1.25} = \frac{1}{2.44140625} = .4096 \text{ or } 40.96 \text{ cents}$$

An income stream of one dollar per period for four periods would comprise a series of 4 reversions of one dollar each. And the present value of the entire series can be summed up by employing the above factors as follows:

Present Value of 1st dollar	.80
Present Value of 2nd dollar	.64
Present Value of 3rd dollar	.512
Present Value of 4th dollar	.4096
Total Value of Series	2.3616

Since each item in this summation is the reciprocal of the base converted according to its respective exponent, it is apparent that the present value of the series can be expressed in this form:

$$\frac{1}{1.25} + \frac{1}{1.25^2} + \frac{1}{1.25^3} + \frac{1}{1.25^4} = 2.3616$$

or

$$.80 + .64 + .512 + .4096 = 2.3616$$

The series of 4 quantities left of the equal sign is what is known as a "geometric progression." In every series of this type, the ratio of progression will be the base. In other words, if we start with the smallest quantity .4096 and read from right to left, each quantity will be 1.25 times its predecessor. Therefore:

$$.4096 \times 1.25 = .512; \ .512 \times 1.25 = .64 \text{ and } .64 \times 1.25 = .80$$

Obviously, this is a very simple series involving only 4 reversions. However, if we had a 20-year, monthly conversion series, we would have 240 reversions and although the same method for determining total present value could be employed, it would be a very long process.

A quick method is provided by the following formula which produces the sum of any geometric progression regardless of the number of quantities in the series.

$$\frac{ar^n - a}{r - 1} = T$$

In which:

	In the Example
a = Smallest quantity in the series;	$\frac{1}{1.25^4} = .4096$
r = Ratio of progression, i.e., the base;	1.25
n = Number of quantities in series;	4
T = Total of the series	

Substituting these quantities for the symbols;

$$\frac{\dfrac{1 \times 1.25^4}{1.25^4} - \dfrac{1}{1.25^4}}{1.25 - 1} = T$$

$$\frac{1 \times 1.25^4}{1.25^4} = 1 \qquad \text{and, } \frac{1}{1.25^4} = .4096 = V^n$$

$$1.25 - 1 = .25 = i$$

So it boils down to:

$$\frac{1 - .4096}{.25} = \frac{.5904}{.25} = 2.3616$$

Therefore, the formula for the present value of any ordinary annuity of one dollar per period for any number of periods (i.e., the Inwood coefficient) is:

$$\frac{1 - V^n}{i} = a_{\overline{n|}}$$

An easy way to remember it is that it is the complement of the reversion factor divided by the interest rate.

$a_{\overline{n}|}$ is merely a standard symbol for the present value of an ordinary annuity of one dollar per period for "n" periods, where "i" is the effective interest rate.

It is commonly known as the "Inwood Coefficient" for an ordinary annuity. Column No. 5 Compound Interest Tables.

Now let us assume an income stream of $10,000 per period for four periods. We wish to know its present value at an effective rate of 25%. Since the present value of one dollar per period is 2.3616, the present value of $10,000 per period is:

$$\$10{,}000 \times 2.3616 = \$23{,}616$$

And the distribution of each $10,000 collection can be tabulated in this way:

Period	*Balance at Beginning of Period*	*Interest at 25% A*	*Principal Recapture B*	*Balance after Payment*
1	$23,616	$ 5,904	$ 4,096	$19,520
2	19,520	4,880	5,120	14,400
3	14,400	3,600	6,400	8,000
4	8,000	2,000	8,000	0
	Totals	$16,384	$23,616	

The amount in column (A) is always 25% of the unrecaptured balance shown in the first column.

The amount in column (B) is always what is left from $10,000 after payment of interest.

The Future Worth of $1 per Period with Interest:

Notice that each succeeding amount from top to bottom in column "B" increases at the rate of 25% over its predecessor, i.e.

$$4096 \times 1.25 = 5120;\ 5120 \times 1.25 = 6400;\ 6400 \times 1.25 = 8000$$

Another way to compute the total recapture would be:

$$4096(1 + 1.25 + 1.25^2 + 1.25^3)$$

which equals:

$$4096(1 + 1.25 + 1.5625 + 1.953125)$$

which equals:

$$\$4096 \times 5.765625 = 23{,}616$$

The series inside the parentheses is another geometric progression

$$1 + 1.25 + 1.25^2 + 1.25^3$$

In which:

"a," the smallest quantity is, 1
"r," the ratio is our base; 1.25
"n," the number of quantities is; 4

Thus, by formula:

$$\frac{ar^n - a}{r - 1} = \text{total}$$

We have:

$$\frac{(1 \times 1.25^4) - 1}{1.25 - 1} \qquad \text{which equals } \frac{2.441040625 - 1}{1.25 - 1}$$

which equals:

$$\frac{1.44140625}{.25} = 5.765625$$

The quantity 5.765625 is the total amount of principal and interest which would be accumulated if we deposited one dollar at the end of each period for 4 periods in an account which earned interest at the effective rate of 25%.

Hence, the progressive growth of principal recapture, as shown in Column "B" of our tabulation is precisely the same as if we deposited \$4,096 at the end of each period for 4 periods with interest accumulating at the 25% effective rate. So if we multiply \$4,096 by the accumulation of one dollar per period, the product is the original investment:

$$\$4{,}096 \times 5.765625 = \$23{,}616$$

This is exactly the manner in which the mortgage part of purchase capital is recaptured whenever part of the purchase price is financed by borrowing on a level installment basis.

The Sinking Fund Installment:

In our example, the first payment in reduction of principal is \$4096. We call this the "Sinking Fund Installment" because the growth and accumulation of a sinking fund is the same as that of one dollar per period deposited in an interest bearing account.

.The sinking fund installment in an amortizing mortgage loan is that portion of the first periodic payment which is applied to reduction of principal.

The sinking fund installment is found by subtracting the first interest payment from the total periodic payment; i.e.

$$\$10{,}000 - \$5{,}904 = \$4{,}096$$

The formula which produced 5.765625 in our example was

$$\frac{(1 \times 1.25^4) - 1}{1.25 - 1} \quad \text{which equals} \quad \frac{1.25^4 - 1}{.25}$$

The same formula expressed in symbols is:

$$\frac{(1 + i)^n - 1}{i} = s_{\overline{n|}}$$

In which:

$s_{\overline{n|}}$ is a standard symbol for the accumulation of one dollar per period for any given number of periods including interest. $(1 + i)$ is the base and, of course, "n" is the number of installments in the series. (Column No. 2 Compound Interest Tables.)

If we know the amount of the sinking fund installment we can calculate the total amount of capital which will be recaptured at any time by multiplying the sinking fund installment by the accumulation of one dollar per period at the effective rate for the number of periods stated in the problem.

Example:

$200,000 of purchase price is financed by mortgage with interest at 5% per annum. Level quarterly installments of interest and principal are based on 7% per annum.

How much purchase capital will be recaptured by mortgage amortization at the end of 8 years?

Solution:

Annual 7% less 5% interest = 2%. Quarterly sinking fund installment is:

$$\frac{\$200{,}000 \times .02}{4} = \frac{4000}{4} = \$1000$$

Find $s_{\overline{n}|}$ for 8 years in column 2 of 5% quarterly table.

Answer:

$1000 × 39.050441 = $39,050.44.

$1/s_{\overline{n}|}$ The Sinking Fund Factor:

This function of 1 dollar is the periodic sinking fund installment required to accumulate 1 dollar in a given number of periods including the accumulation of interest at a given rate per period.

It was previously demonstrated that 4 periodic installments of 1 dollar each with interest accumulated at an effective rate of 25% would grow to 5.765625. It follows then, that the periodic installment or deposit required to accumulate 1 dollar including interest at 25% in 4 periods is 1 dollar divided by 5.765625, i.e.

$$\frac{1}{5.76525} = .173442$$

If a sinking fund installment of .173442 is required to recapture an investment of 1 dollar, the sinking fund installment required to recapture $23,616 is $23,616 times .173442, i.e.

$$\$23{,}616 \times .173442 = \$4096$$

Thus, the sinking fund factor is the reciprocal of the future worth of 1 dollar per period with interest and is represented as such by the symbol: $1/s_{\overline{n}|}$

The formula as developed for $s_{\overline{n}|}$ is:

$$\frac{(1+i)^n - 1}{i} \text{ or } \frac{s^n - 1}{i} = s_{\overline{n}|}$$

The formula for its reciprocal is the inversion of that formula; i.e.

$$\frac{i}{(1+i)^n - 1} \text{ or } \frac{i}{s^n - 1} = 1/s_{\overline{n}|}$$

This factor comprises Column No. 3 of the compound interest tables. It has several very important uses. For one; the level periodic installment required to pay interest on and recapture each dollar of any investment is the sum of the effective interest rate and the sinking fund factor. With interest at 25% and the 4 year sinking fund factor at .173442, the combination is:

$$.25 + .173442 = .423442$$

It was found that the present value of $10,000 per period for 4 periods at 25% was $23,616. Conversely, the periodic installment required to pay interest on and recapture $23,616 in 4 periods would be:

$$\$23{,}616 \times .423442 = \$10{,}000$$

In most cases sinking fund recapture occurs at a lower rate of interest than the investment yield rate. This happens when purchase capital is composed of mortgage and equity money where the mortgage installments provide for recapture at a lower rate of interest than the prospective yield to equity. It may also happen in certain types of contracts where a recapture fund called the "depreciation reserve account" or "replacement reserve account" is required to be accumulated and held as a cash reserve. In this case, a level periodic sinking fund installment might be deposited in trust with a savings institution which would agree to credit and accumulate interest on it at a fixed contract or "safe rate." The technique involving recapture by this process is the same as used, for example, in the Hoskold Sinking Fund Method. It is appropriate to demonstrate the mechanics of it in discussing applications of the sinking fund factor.

Assume an investment of $100,000. The yield is to be 25 per cent and recapture is to be accomplished by depositing four level sinking fund installments in an account which will accumulate at 10 per cent interest. We have found that: $1.10^4 = 1.4641$

Thus:

$$s_{\overline{n}|} = \frac{(1+i)^n - 1}{i} = \frac{1.4641 - 1}{.10} = \frac{.4641}{.10} = 4.641$$

and $1/S_{\overline{n}|} = 1/4.641 = .215471$

Interest plus sinking fund per dollars is:

$$.25 + .215471 = .465471$$

Required periodic income is:

$$\$100{,}000 \times .465471 = \$46{,}547.10$$

Income distribution is:

Income per period	$46,547.10
Less Investment Yield; $100,000 × .25	25,000.00
Sinking Fund Installment	$21,547.10

Accumulation of Sinking Fund at 10%

$$\$21{,}547.10 \times 4.641 = \$100{,}000$$

The sinking fund factor will also be used later to reflect influence of future property value declines and increases on over-all capitalization rates and for interpreting comparative values in terms of probable yield to the buyer.

$1/a_{\overline{n|}}$ The Ordinary Annuity Which Has a Present Value of 1 Dollar:

If 1 dollar per period for 4 periods at 25% has a present value of 2.3616, it is apparent that the level annuity which has a present value of 1 dollar is 1 dollar divided by 2.3616; i.e.

$$\frac{1}{2.3616} = .423442$$

Thus, we find that the total periodic installment required for interest and recapture is not only the sum of the interest rate and the sinking fund factor at that rate but it is also the reciprocal of the Inwood Ordinary Annuity Coefficient. The formula for this coefficient is:

$$\frac{1 - V^n}{i} = a_{\overline{n|}}$$

The formula for its reciprocal is the inversion of that formula:

$$\frac{i}{1 - V^n} = 1/a_{\overline{n|}}$$

This function is presented in column No. 6 of the compound interest tables. A common application of it is to calculate the periodic installment which will provide for interest and recapture in a level installment mortgage loan.

Important Relationships of Compound Interest Functions:

Since the 1st column function "S^n" is a key quantity in all formulas for the other 5 functions, it follows that the functions are all specifically related to each other. It is important to learn and remember a few of these relationships.

It has just been demonstrated that:

$$1/{}^{a}\overline{n|} \text{ is equal to } i + 1/{}^{s}\overline{n|}$$

$$.423442 = .25 + .173442$$

It is therefore apparent that:

$$1/{}^{a}\overline{n|} - 1/{}^{s}\overline{n|} = i; \quad .423442 - .173442 = .25$$

We found that, $1.25^4 = 2.44140625$

Other relationships are:

$${}^{a}\overline{n|}(1 + i)^{n} = {}^{s}\overline{n|}; \qquad 2.3616 \times 2.44140625 = 5.765625$$

$$1/{}^{s}\overline{n|}(1 + i)^{n} = 1/{}^{a}\overline{n|}; \quad .173442 \times 2.44140625 = .423442$$

Therefore:

$$\frac{1/{}^{a}\overline{n|}}{1/{}^{s}\overline{n|}} = (1 + i)^{n}, \frac{.423442}{.173442} = 2.44140 \text{ etc.}$$

And, since $1/{}^{a}\overline{n|} - i = 1/{}^{s}\overline{n|}$

$$\frac{1/{}^{a}\overline{n|}}{1/{}^{a}\overline{n|} - i} = (1 + i)^{n}$$

To Review and Remember:

1. $\mathbf{1/{}^{a}\overline{n|} - 1/{}^{s}\overline{n|} = i}$
2. $\mathbf{{}^{a}\overline{n|}\,(1 + i)^{n} = {}^{s}\overline{n|}}$
3. $\mathbf{\dfrac{1/{}^{a}\overline{n|}}{1/{}^{a}\overline{n|} - i} = (1 + i)^{n}}$

To Compute Fraction of Purchase Capital Recaptured by Mortgage Amortization:

When the sinking fund installment per dollar is multiplied by the future worth of 1 per period with interest for any given number of periods (i.e. $s_{\overline{n}|}$) the product is the fraction of investment recaptured by amortization in the given number of periods.

Assume, for example, a mortgage component of purchase capital is to be fully amortized by "n" monthly installments of interest and amortization. A key lease expires in 8 years or 96 months and the fraction of mortgage to be amortized (call it "P" for "paid off") at lease termination is to be calculated.

The calculation expressed in basic formulas would be:

$$\left(\frac{i}{(1+i)^{n}-1}\right)\left(\frac{(1+i)^{96}-1}{i}\right)=P$$

Since numerator "i" in the multiplicand is the same as denominator "i" in the multiplier, they cancel out and the equation can be condensed to:

$$\frac{(1+i)^{96}-1}{(1+i)^{n}-1}=P$$

If the reciprocal of the denominator is used as a multiplier, the equation can be written as:

$$\left(\frac{1}{(1+i)^{n}-1}\right)\times[(1+i)^{96}-1]=P$$

Now assume monthly installments are based on a constant annual requirement of 9% including interest at 6% per annum.

Thus;

$$1/a_{\overline{n}|}=\frac{.09}{12} \text{ and } i=\frac{.06}{12}$$

By relationship you have memorized:

$$\frac{1/a_{\overline{n}|}}{1/a_{\overline{n}|}-i}=(1+i)^{n}$$

Thus;

$$\frac{\frac{.09}{12}}{\frac{.09}{12}-\frac{.06}{12}}=(1+i)^{n}=\frac{.0075}{.0075-.005}=\frac{.0075}{.0025}=3$$

Since the number of installments per year, "12" is a common denominator, it can be omitted without affecting the result; i.e.

$$(1+i)^n = \frac{.09}{.09-.06} = \frac{.09}{.03} = 3$$

Call the annual mortgage requirement per dollar "f" and the nominal interest rate "I." The amount to which 1 dollar will grow with interest at effective rate "i" during the full amortization term; i.e. $(1+i)^n$ is always:

$$\frac{f}{f-I} = (1+i)^n$$

In the above example:

$$(1+i)^n = 3 \text{ and } (1+i)^n - 1 = 2$$

The reciprocal of $(1+i)^n - 1$, in this case is:

$$\frac{1}{2} = .50$$

This reciprocal in any case where "f" and "I" are known is:

$$\frac{f}{I} - 1 \text{ Thus; } \frac{.09}{.06} - 1 = 1.50 - 1 = .50$$

Call the amount to which 1 dollar will grow with interest in any income projection term "Sp." And, we have the formula:

$$\left(\frac{f}{I} - 1\right)(Sp - 1) = P$$

In the 6% *monthly* compound interest table (Column No. 1) $(1+i)^n$ at 8 years or $(1+i)^{96}$ is 1.614143.

Therefore; Sp − 1 is .614143 and;

$$P = \left(\frac{f}{I} - 1\right)(Sp - 1) = .50 \times .614143 = .307071$$

Suppose Mortgage is $160,000, the amount recaptured in 8 years will be:

$$P = \$160{,}000 \times .307071 = \$49{,}131$$

Arithmetic Check:

Level monthly installment; $160,000 × .0075	$1200.00
Interest, 1st month, $160,000 × .005	800.00
Sinking fund installment	$ 400.00

$s_{\overline{n}|}$ at 8 years, Col. 2 in 6% *Monthly* compound interest table is 122.828542. Thus;

$$P = \$400 \times 122.828542 = \$49{,}131$$

When purchase capital is composed of equity and mortgage money, the fraction of mortgage recaptured (P) during an income projection term is a key factor in the composite capitalization rate. It is therefore, important to remember this formula for "P"

$$\left(\frac{f}{I} - 1\right)(Sp - 1) = P$$

The Annuity In Advance:

Most real estate leases provide for payment of each installment of rent at the *beginning* of each period. The income stream provided by this type of contract is commonly known as the "annuity in advance" or "annuity due."

The "ordinary annuity" or "annuity in arrears" is represented by the series of payments provided by the level installment amortized mortgage contract where each installment is paid at the *end* of each period.

To convert the ordinary annuity coefficient to the "annuity in advance" coefficient, we must move each installment forward one period so each payment will be one period closer to the point of beginning. In other words, each installment will be subject to discount for one less period than each installment in the ordinary annuity. This conversion is accomplished by multiplying the ordinary annuity coefficient by its base.

The progression for an ordinary annuity of one dollar per period for 4 periods with interest at an effective rate of 25% is:

$$\frac{1}{1.25} + \frac{1}{1.25^2} + \frac{1}{1.25^3} + \frac{1}{1.25^4}$$

If we multiply this through by the base 1.25 we have:

$$\frac{1.25}{1.25} + \frac{1.25}{1.25^2} + \frac{1.25}{1.25^3} + \frac{1.25}{1.25^4}$$

And, by the rule of exponents, this equals:

$$1 + \frac{1}{1.25} + \frac{1}{1.25^2} + \frac{1}{1.25^3}$$

Or:

$$1 + .80 + .64 + .512 = 2.952$$

We found that the coefficient for the ordinary annuity for 4 periods at 25% effective rate is 2.3616. If we multiply it by the base;

$$1.25 \times 2.3616 = 2.952$$

The present value of $10,000 per period for 4 periods at an effective rate of 25% with each installment paid at the beginning of each period would be:

$$\$10{,}000 \times 2.952 = \$29{,}520$$

The distribution of each $10,000 collection can be tabulated as follows:

Period	*Balance at Beginning Of Period*	*Interest at 25% A*	*Principal Recapture B*	*Balance After Payment*
1	$29,520	0	$10,000	$19,520
2	19,520	$ 4,880	5,120	14,400
3	14,400	3,600	6,400	8,000
4	8,000	2,000	8,000	0
		$10,480	$29,520	

Notice that the entire amount of the first installment is applied to principal recapture. The reason for this is that since this payment is received at the beginning of the series, no time has elapsed for the accrual of interest. In effect, the buyer of the income stream is only out of pocket $19,520 at the point of beginning because he gets $10,000 back at the same time he pays $29,520 for the right to collect the series.

Exercise:

What is the present value of income from a 25 year net lease at $40,000 per year payable $10,000 quarterly in advance at a nominal rate of 6%.

Solution:

Quarterly Table at 6%, Col. 5. The ordinary coefficient at 25 years is 51.624704. The base is 1.015.

$$\$10{,}000 \times 1.015 \times 51.624704 = \$523{,}991$$

The Declining Annuity:

When provision for recapture of investment capital is made on the basis of straight line depreciation, it is automatically assumed that the income stream will also decline in a straight line. Although constant periodic declines in values and income are not compatible with experience, provision for them is a safety factor which may protect against contingencies that do occur from time to time in market behavior and operating performance.

To facilitate the analysis of income real estate from the viewpoint of an equity investor, however, it is usually desirable to stabilize the income to an ordinary annuity of equal value.

To illustrate the principle of declining annuity valuation, let us visualize a 4 year income stream starting at $10,000 and declining at the rate of $562.50 per year. It can be diagrammed as set forth below:

	Year 1	*Year 2*	*Year 3*	*Year 4*
	$ 562.50			
	562.50	562.50		
	562.50	562.50	562.50	
	562.50	562.50	562.50	562.50
	7750.00	7750.00	7750.00	7750.00
Total	$10,000.00	$9437.50	$8875.00	$8312.50

Reading the lines horizontally, the entire income stream is equivalent to 1 ordinary annuity of $7750 for 4 years plus 4 ordinary annuities of $562.50 from 1 to 4 years. Thus, $7750 multiplied by the Inwood coefficient for 4 years plus $562.50 multiplied by the total of all Inwood coefficients from 1 to 4 will produce the present value of the series. The addition of 4 coefficients is simple enough but if the declining annuity ran 40 or 50 years, it would involve the addition of a long column of coefficients. Therefore, a short-cut is desirable. Let us use 25% as the interest rate and write the series of 4 coefficients by formula:

$$\frac{1-\frac{1}{1.25^1}}{.25}+\frac{1-\frac{1}{1.25^2}}{.25}+\frac{1-\frac{1}{1.25^3}}{.25}+\frac{1-\frac{1}{1.25^4}}{.25}$$

Since the interest rate .25 is a common denominator, the series is equal to:

$$\frac{1-\frac{1}{1.25}+1-\frac{1}{1.25^2}+1-\frac{1}{1.25^3}+1-\frac{1}{1.25^4}}{.25}$$

The numerator now comprises 4 positive quantities of 1 or a total of 4 (which is the number of annuities) less the progression for the Inwood coefficient. In other words, we have:

$$\frac{4-\left(\frac{1}{1.25}+\frac{1}{1.25^2}+\frac{1}{1.25^3}+\frac{1}{1.25^4}\right)}{.25}=\frac{4-2.3616}{.25}$$

which equals; $\frac{1.6384}{.25}=6.5536$

The total value of the declining annuity is therefore:

$$\begin{aligned}(\$7750 \times 2.3616) &+ (\$562.50 \times 6.5536)\\ &= \$18,302.40 + \$3686.40\\ &= \$21,988.80\end{aligned}$$

Arithmetic Check:

Year	*Income*	V^n	*Present Value*
1	10,000.00 ×	.80	$ 8,000.00
2	9,437.50 ×	.64	6,040.00
3	8,875.00 ×	.512	4,544.00
4	8,312.50 ×	.4096	3,404.80
Total Present Value:			$21,988.80

Therefore, where:

d = 1st period income

k = decline per period

N = number of periods

The present value of the declining annuity is:

$$(d-kN)\,a_{\overline{n}|}+\frac{k\,(N-a_{\overline{n}|})}{i}=V$$

The equivalent ordinary annuity is:

$$\frac{V}{a_{\overline{n}|}}$$

When the formula for V is divided through by the Inwood coefficient it boils down to:

$$d - \frac{k\,(1 - N\,1/s_{\overline{n|}})}{i} = \frac{V}{a_{\overline{n|}}};\ \text{i.e.}\ \frac{\$21{,}988.80}{2.3616} = \$9310.98$$

In which, $1/s_{\overline{n|}}$ is the sinking fund factor at rate i for N periods. In this case the sinking fund factor is .173442

$$\$10{,}000 - \$562.50\,\frac{(1 - 4 \times .173442)}{.25} =$$

$$\$10{,}000 - \$689.02 = \$9310.98$$

$$\$9310.98 \times 2.3616 = \$21{,}988.80$$

When straight line depreciation is quoted at a percentage rate per year, call the depreciation rate "k" and compute the amount to be subtracted from 1st year income "d" as follows:

$$\frac{dk\,(1 - N\,1/s_{\overline{n|}})}{i}$$

Say 1st year net income "d" is $50,000, the depreciation rate "k" is 2½%, the interest "i" is 10% and the income projection term "N" is 10 years. $1/s_{\overline{n|}}$ for 10 years at 10% (Col. 3 Compound Interest Table) is .062745. The multiplier of $50,000 is:

$$.025\,\frac{(1 - 10 \times .062745)}{.10} = .025\,\frac{(.37255)}{.10} = .0931375$$

1st year income	$50,000.00
Less adjustment for decline; $50,000 × .0931375	4,656:88
Level annuity of equal value	45,343.12

If gross rent with present occupancy is $93,000, a vacancy allowance of 5% would provide a safety factor equal to that implicit in the 2½% depreciation rate, i.e., $93,000 × .05 = $4650.

The Increasing Annuity:

A 4 period annuity starting at $100 and increasing $100 per period can be diagrammed for valuation as follows. The underscored installments $100 are added to produce a constant annuity for the 1st step. Their present value is then subtracted leaving the present value of actual installments to be received.

Period	1	2	3	4
	100	100	100	100
	100	100	100	100
	100	100	100	100
	100	100	100	100
	100	100	100	100

Using reversion factors with interest at 25% we would have:

Present Value 1st installment 100 × .80	$ 80.00
Present Value 2nd installment 200 × .64	128.00
Present Value 3rd installment 300 × .512	152.60
Present Value 4th installment 400 × .4096	163.84
Total Present Value of the Series	$525.44

Formula:

Call periodic increase "h"; Number of Installments "N"; First Installment "d."

$$(d + hN)a_{\overline{n|}} - h\frac{(N - a_{\overline{n|}})}{i} = \text{Present Value}$$

By formula for present value of the 4 period straight line increasing annuity:

$100 + (4 \times 100) = 500$

500×2.3616	$1,180.80
Less $100 \dfrac{(4 - 2.3616)}{.25} = 100 \times 6.5536$	655.36
	$ 525.44

Exercise:

What is the present value at 6% effective of a 40 period straight line increasing annuity which starts at $4,000 the first period and increases $100 each period thereafter?

Solution:

If we multiply $100 by 40 and add the $4,000 product to our $4,000 initial period installment the total is $8,000. And, the present value of the entire income stream will be the present value of $8,000 per period for 40 periods less the present value of 40 annuities of $100 each for terms of 1 to 40 periods. (Factor from column 5 at 40 periods 15.046297.)

$8,000 × 15.046297		$120,370
Less $100 $\frac{(40 - 15.046297)}{.06}$	= 100 × 415.89505	41,590
Present Value of the Increasing Annuity........		$ 78,780

Other Variable Annuities:

Many complicated problems can be divided into two or more simple problems. This is especially true in the valuation of future income streams which are expected to increase or decline.

Step up and step down leases are not uncommon.

Valuation of such income streams can usually be simplified by dividing them into ordinary annuities.

(A) What is the present value at 6% of the income provided by a net lease as follows assuming rent is payable monthly in advance?

1st 3 years........	$6,000 per year
Next 5 years........	$7,200 per year
Last 12 years	$8,100 per year

Solution:

The total term is 240 months:
The highest rent is $675.00 per month.
The middle term rent is $600.00 per month.
The first term rent is $500.00 per month.
The entire stream is equal to a 240 monthly annuity at $675.00 *less* 2 annuities for 36 and 96 months at $100.00 and $75.00 respectively.

Problems of this type can usually be visualized most clearly by diagram. A suggested method is to surround areas representing annuities to be received by solid lines and those to be subtracted by dotted lines.

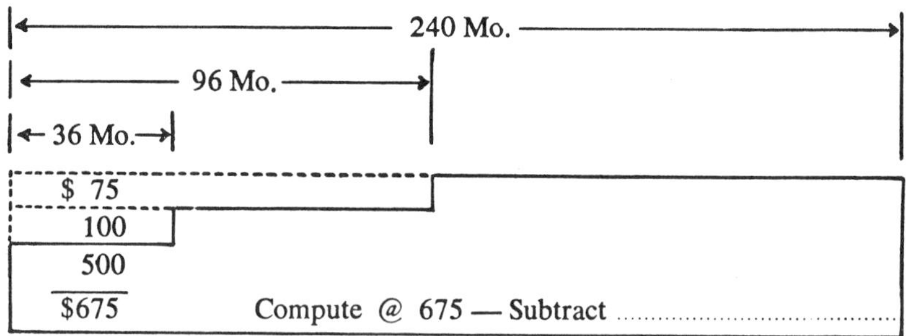

	240 months	\$675 × 139.580771		\$94,217.02
Less	36 months	100 × 32.871016	\$3,287.10	
and	96 months	75 × 76.095218	5,707.14	8,994.24
	Value as ordinary annuities			\$85,222.78
	Times Base			1.005
	Value as Annuities in advance			\$85,648.89

(B) A property is leased at \$48,000 net per year payable \$4,000 monthly in advance for 25 years with 2 renewal options. The 1st option is for 15 years with rental at \$3,500 monthly in advance. The 2nd option is for 10 years with rental at \$3,000 monthly in advance.

What is the value of this income at 6% if both options are exercised by the tenant?

Solution:

This is the equivalent of 1 annuity of \$3,000 per month for 600 months, plus 2 annuities of \$500 per month for 480 and 300 months.

600 months; \$3,000 × 189.967874	\$569,903.62
480 months; 181.747584	
300 months; 155.206864	
336.954448 × 500	168,477.22
Value as ordinary annuity	\$738,380.84
Times Base	1.005
Value as annuity in advance	\$742,072.74

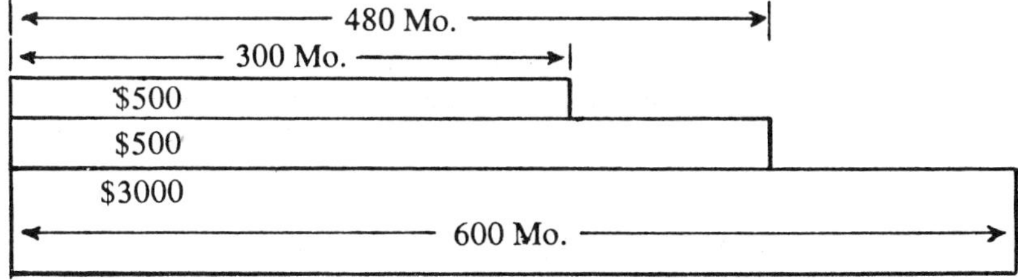

(C) What is the value at 6% of an annuity in advance of \$6,000 per month for 10 years starting 5 years from today?

Solution:

This is equivalent to a monthly annuity in advance of $6,000 for 15 years or 180 months less one of the same amount for 60 months.

	180 months;	118.503514	
Less	60 months;	51.725561	
		66.777953 × $6,000	$400,667.72
	Times base		1.005
Value as annuity in advance			$402,671.06

The effect of subtracting the 60 month factor from that for 180 months is that of deferring a 10 year factor 60 months. Another method would be to multiply the 10 year column 5 factor by the 5 year column 4 factor and the base.

$$90.073453 \times .741372 \times 1.005 \times \$6{,}000 = \$402{,}671$$

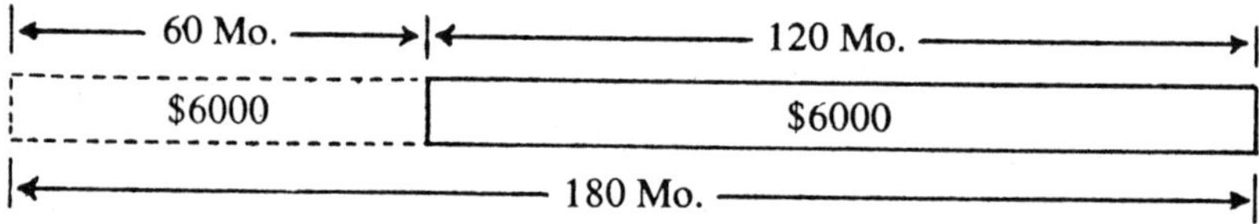

(D) A property is leased for 20 years at a net rental of $42,000 per year payable $3,500 monthly in advance. A buyer can borrow $400,000 of the purchase price at 5%. He has the choice of two 20 year amortization plans.

(1) He can pay level monthly installments of $2,640 which will fully amortize the loan in 20 years.

(2) Or he can make constant quarterly payments of $5,000 each in reduction of principal and pay interest each quarter on the unpaid balance. This will reduce the total installment $62.50 each quarter.

The total 20 year interest payment under plan (1) will be $233,600.

Under plan (2) it will be $202,500.

Which plan will produce the greatest value for the equity position on the basis of an 8% equity yield?

Solution:

Factors from column 5. 240 month annuity adjusted in payment in advance:

at 8% $3,500 × 1.00666666 + = 3523.33			
Plan (1)		$3,523.33	
Less ordinary annuity		2,640.00	
119.554291 ×		$ 883.33	
= Value of Equity Income			$105,606

Plan (2)

In this case the mortgage installments will be a straight line declining annuity starting at $10,000 and declining $62.50 each quarter to the 80th quarter. This is equivalent to an 80 quarter ordinary annuity of $5,000 per quarter plus 80 ordinary annuities of $62.50 for from 1 to 80 quarters.

Present value of total income stream at 8%:		
$3,523.33 × 119.554291		$421,229
Less $5,000 × 39.744514	$198,723	
62.50 × 2012.7743	125,798	324,521
Value of Equity Income		$ 96,708

It is noteworthy that despite the larger mortgage interest obligation in Plan (1), this plan produces a greater equity value than Plan (2). The reason is that several years must pass before residual income to equity in Plan (2) catches up with the level equity annuity provided by Plan (1). And, since present dollars are worth so much more than future dollars, the aggregate interest advantage of Plan (2) is more than offset by the time advantage to equity in Plan (1).

The multiplier 2012.7743 by which we determine the present value of the series of $62.50 drops in quarterly mortgage installments is the total of all Inwood ordinary annuity coefficients from 1 period to 80 periods at the effective quarterly rate of 2%, i.e. 8% divided by 4.

The formula by which this multiplier is calculated is as follows:

$$\frac{80 - 39.744514}{.02} = \frac{40.255486}{.02} = 2012.7743$$

The factor 39.744514 is in column 5 at 80 quarters.

USE OF THE RULE OF EXPONENTS FOR TABULAR EXPANSION:

The future worth of one dollar with interest "S^n" (Column No. 1) and its reciprocal "V^n" (Column No. 4) can be expanded by direct application of the rule of exponents. Use of this rule with the formula for each function facilitates tabular expansion. Each monthly compound interest table, for example, presents each function for each of the first eleven months. After that, they are presented by the year for 1 to 50 years. This provides on one page all quantities needed to find any function for any number of months from 1 to 600. Assume for instance, we wish the six functions at a nominal rate of 6 per cent converted monthly for nineteen years and seven months. Needed factors from Columns 1 and 4 of the 6% *monthly* compound interest table are:

Column No. 1 at 7 months 1.035529; at 19 years 3.117899

7 months + 228 months = 235 months

$(1.005)^{235} = 1.035529 \times 3.117899 = 3.228675$

Column No. 4 at 7 months, .965690; at 19 years, .320729

$$\frac{1}{(1.005)^{235}} = .965690 \times .320729 = .309725$$

$$\text{Complement} = 1 - .309725 = .690275$$

Future worth of 1 per period:

$$\frac{S^n - 1}{i} = \frac{2.228675}{.005} = 444.735$$

Sinking Fund Factor:

$$\frac{i}{S^n - 1} = \frac{1}{444.735} = .002243$$

Inwood Coefficients:

$$\frac{1 - V^n}{i} = \frac{.690275}{.005} = 138.055$$

Monthly Installment Factor:

$$\frac{i}{1 - V^n} = \frac{1}{138.055} = .007243.$$

or $i + 1/S_{\overline{n|}} = .005 + .002243 = .007243$

For Expansion Beyond Scope of Table:

The same rule applies for expansion to a greater number of periods than shown by the table. For example, a ninety-nine year ground lease provides net rent at $54,000 per year payable $13,500 quarterly in advance. What is the present value of this income stream at 6% per annum? Factors from 6% *quarterly* compound interest table Column No. 4 at 39 years, .098016; at 60 years, .028064. 156 quarters + 240 quarters = 396 quarters.

$$\frac{1}{(1.015)^{396}} = .098016 \times .028064 = .0027507$$

Complement = 1 − .0027507 = .9972493
Inwood Ordinary Coefficient:

$$\frac{1 - V^n}{i} = \frac{.9972493}{.015} = 66.483287$$

Answer:

$$\$13{,}500 \times 1.015 \times 66.483287 = \$910{,}987.$$

It is noteworthy that the quarterly in advance feature makes present value of income before reversion greater than would be produced by the common practice of treating long term lease income as a perpetuity which assumes a 100 per cent reversion.

$$\frac{54000}{.06} \text{ or } \frac{13500}{.015} = \$900{,}000$$

AMORTIZATION AND DEPRECIATION SCHEDULES

There are occasions when it is desirable to know the amount of capital which will be recaptured through mortgage amortization each year. A schedule of this type is sometimes compiled in conjunction with one showing annual depreciation allowances under various methods permitted by Internal Revenue Service. This is done to determine the extent to which amortization installments may be sheltered against income taxes by allowable deductions.

Example:

Appraised Value or Purchase Price:

Land	$ 100,000
Building	900,000
Total	$1,000,000

Assumed Purchase Capital Structure:

75% Mortgage (5%, 20 yrs. Monthly)	$ 750,000
25% Cash Equity	250,000
Total	$1,000,000

Problem:

Prepare an annual schedule showing amortization and depreciation based on 30 year building life, 150% declining balance basis. Carry schedule to the year in which amortization will exceed the allowance for depreciation.

Solution:

The monthly installment per dollar of mortgage with interest at 5% and full amortization in 20 years by level monthly installments is .0066 (Col. 6 at 20 years).

Monthly installment $750,000 × .0066	$4,950
Less: 1st interest payment:	
$\frac{750{,}000 \times .05}{12} = \frac{37500}{12}$	3,125
Sinking fund installment	$1,825

Amortization, 1st year (2nd column at 1 year times sinking fund installment).

$$12.278855 \times 1825 = \$22{,}408.91$$

The construction of the 1st year multiplier is:

$$1 + S + S^2 + S^3 + S^4 \text{ etc. to } S^{11}$$

The 2nd year multiplier will be the series of 12 quantities from S^{12} to S^{23} inclusive.

If we multiply the 2nd column factor at 1 year by the 1st column factor at 1 year we will have our 2nd year multiplier.

S^{12} $(1 + S + S^2 + S^3$ etc. to $S^{11})$ which will equal:

$$S^{12} + S^{13} + S^{14} \text{ etc. to } S^{23}$$

The 3rd year multiplier will be the series of 12 quantities from S^{24} to

S^{35}. Thus, if we multiply our 2nd year multiplier by the 1st column factor at 1 year, we will have the 3rd year multiplier:

$$S^{12} (S^{12} + S^{13} + S^{14} \text{ etc. to } S^{23}) = S^{24} + S^{25} + S^{26} \text{ etc. to } S^{35}$$

Now, it is apparent that if we continue to use S^{12} as a constant multiplier of the product for each preceding year, we can produce a schedule showing the amount of amortization each year. S^{12} the 1st column factor at 1 year is 1.051162.

1st year amortization as computed	....	$22,408.91
2nd year	1.051162 × $22,408.91	23,555.39
3rd year	1.051162 × 23,555.39 ...	24,760.53
4th year	1.051162 × 24,760.53	26,027.33

And, so on.

The allocation to building is $900,000. The 30 year life straight line depreciation rate would be 3⅓%. The 150% declining balance rate would start at 1½ times 3⅓% or 5% and the amount of depreciation for each succeeding year would be 5% of the undepreciated balance. In other words, the depreciation allowance will decline at the rate of 5% per year. The 1st year depreciation allowance will be 5% of $900,000 which is $45,000 and we must use 0.95 as a constant multiplier to determine the allowance for each succeeding year. Therefore, the schedule would be as set forth below:

Year	*A* *Amortization*	*B* *Depreciation*	*B-A* *Surplus* *Shelter*	
1	$ 22,408.91	$ 45,000.00	$22,591.09	
2	23,555.39	42,750.00	19,194.61	
3	24,760.53	40,612.50	15,851.97	
4	26,027.33	38,581.87	12,554.54	
5	27,358.93	36,652.78	9,293.85	Total
6	28,758.66	34,820.13	6,061.47	surplus
7	30,230.00	33,079.12	2,849.12	$88,396.65
8	31,776.63	31,425.16	Deficit 351.47	
	$214,876.38	$302,921.56	$88,045.18	

The tabulation shows that not only will all amortization payments be sheltered against income taxes during the 1st 7 years but the owner would also realize over \$88,000 of surplus shelter for other income during this period. If he retains ownership beyond 7 years, he will be liable for a rather rapidly increasing amount of tax on amortization installment unless he refinances. It is apparent that the optimum term of ownership in this case would be something less than 8 years.

Computing the Amortization for a Specific Period

The sinking fund installment in the foregoing example is \$1,825. Starting with 1 to represent the 1st or sinking fund installment, the series of succeeding installments will grow as follows:

Installment No.	1	2	3	4	5 etc.
Amount	1	S	S^2	S^3	S^4 etc.

Since the exponent at each period is 1 less than the position of the installment in the series, we can calculate the amount of principal in any periodic installment by using the column 1 factor at 1 period less as a multiplier of the sinking fund installment. In other words, the sinking fund installment multiplied by S^{68} would produce the amount of principal in the 69th periodic payment.

Since S^{68} is the product of S^8 and S^{60} Col. 1 the 69th amortization installment in our example would be as follows:

$$\$1{,}825 \times 1.033824 \times 1.283359 = \$2{,}421.35$$

Amortization which will occur in any year can be calculated by multiplying the 1st year amortization by the column 1 factor at 1 year less than the year for which amortization is to be determined. First year amortization in our example is \$22,408.91. If we wish to know the amount of amortization to be paid during the 7th year, we multiply this by the column 1 factor at 6 years.

$$1.349018 \times \$22{,}408.91 = \$30{,}230$$

The reason for this is that the 1st year series of quantities is represented as follows:

$$1 + S + S^2 + S^3 \text{ etc. to } S^{11}$$

The 7th year will be the 12 quantities:

$$S^{72} + S^{73} + S^{74} \text{ etc. to } S^{83}$$

The 1st column factor at 6 years is S^{72}. Thus, by multiplying the 1st year we have:

$$S^{72}\,(1 + S + S^2 + S^3 \text{ etc. to } S^{11}) = S^{72} + S^{73} + S^{74} \text{ etc. to } S^{83}$$

III

INVESTMENT YIELDS AND CAPITALIZATION RATES

The combination of debenture and risk capital which supplies the monetary requirements of the real estate market presents two completely different problems with regard to the determination of investment yield.

The interest rate or yield and the provision for recapture are specifically stipulated by contract with regard to the mortgage or debenture money involved in market transactions.

A directly opposite set of conditions presents itself with regard to the equity or risk component of purchase capital. Both recapture and interest rate are entirely speculative at the time of investment. In fact, the interest or yield rate is never known until the complete investment experience is a matter of history. It cannot be calculated until *after* the property has been bought, operated over a span of time and then resold.

Consequently, it is incorrect to say that buyers demand this or that yield. The only plausible and supportable opinion is that "good prospects" for a yield of Y% or better would probably attract a buyer.

The yield on equity investment will be significantly influenced by the source of recapture, and this in turn will be determined by the relative magnitudes of periodic income and proceeds of resale or "reversion."

1. If reversion is less than original investment, part of the recapture must be taken from periodic income leaving only the remainder income as yield producing profit.
2. If the reversion is equal to the original investment, all of the recapture will be in the reversion and all of the periodic income will be yield producing profit.
3. If the reversion is greater than the original investment, all of the recapture will be in the reversion and the balance of the reversion plus all of the periodic income will be yield producing profit.
4. If the aggregate total of reversion and all periodic income is equal to or less than the original investment, there will be no profit and no yield.

Obviously, one of these sets of conditions will occur. Which one, when and to what extent is never known at time of purchase.

The equity position may represent 100% of value as in the all-cash-out-of-pocket market transaction. Or, it may be very thin with virtually all purchase capital in the form of mortgage money.

Obviously, the risk of equity investment increases as it gets thinner. A relatively small decline in the market will wipe out a 5% equity, whereas the 100% equity will survive so long as the property retains any value at all.

Since risk is a prime factor in determining the market attractiveness of any prospective yield, it follows that the prospective yield to equity must increase as the ratio of mortgage to value increases; which is to say that the availability of a large amount of mortgage money does not necessarily increase market value. If there is an increase in value, it will be more attributable to keen competition between mortgage investors driving interest rates down, plus the fact that plenty of cheap money will increase the number of prospective buyers.

Many buyers who are capable of paying all cash out of pocket are attracted to the fractional equity by leverage and by income tax shelter. A 10% increase in property value appreciates the value of a 25% equity by 40%.

When mortgage installments are paid from property income, the value of the equity position increases to any extent that mortgage amortization exceeds decline in over-all market value of the property. Thus, "appreciation" in equity value can occur simultaneously with "depreciation" in property value. And, since equity yield is properly defined as the interest rate at which the total present value of equity income and equity reversion is equal to the cost of the investment, it is clear that equity value build-up by reason of mortgage amortization may have a significant influence on equity yield.

Assume the following circumstances, for example:

A property is purchased for $400,000, of which $300,000 is financed by mortgage in which monthly installments are based on 8% per annum including interest at 5½%. The equity investment is $100,000. This property is resold 10 years after purchase for $340,000. The equity reversion can be calculated in this manner:

Sp − 1 at 10 years from Col. 1. 5½% *Monthly* Table = .731076

$$P = \left(\frac{.08}{.055} - 1\right).731076 = .454545 \times .731076 = .332307$$

Selling Price (Property Reversion)		$340,000
Original Mortgage	$300,000	
Less Amortization, $300,000 × .332307	99,692	
Unamortized balance at time of sale		$200,308
Reversion to Equity		$139,692

Despite 15% decline in property value, the value of equity increases almost 40%.

Exercise:

With purchase price and depreciation as above:

(a) What stabilized annual cash flow income would provide for mortgage requirements and give the buyer a 10% yield on his $100,000 investment?

(b) What composite capitalization rate is indicated by the answer to (a)?

(c) Allocate the composite capitalization rate to the mortgage and equity components of purchase capital.

Solution:

(a) Mortgage Requirement $300,000 at 8%		$24,000
Equity Investment	$100,000	
Less Pres. Val. Reversion $139,692 × .385543	53,857	
Required Pres. Val. Equity Income	$ 46,143	
Multiply by Instal. factor Col. 6	.162745	*7,510
Total Annual Income Requirement		$31,510

(b) Indicated Composite Capitalization Rate:

$$\frac{31{,}510}{400{,}000} = .078775$$

*Use of the installment factor as a multiplier produces the ordinary annuity which has a present value of $46,143.

(c) Allocation:

Mortgage Money, 75% at .08	.060000
Equity dividend rate, $\frac{7510}{100{,}000} = .0751$	
Equity money, 25% at .0751	.018775
Composite	.078775

Symbol "Y"

Symbols "I" and "i" have been used to represent nominal and effective interest rates respectively up to this point in the text. A new symbol, "Y," is now introduced to represent equity yield and to distinguish the interest rate on risk capital from that on debenture capital. This makes no difference in rules pertaining to the relationship of compound interest functions.

$(1+Y)^n$ is the base to the "n"th power.

$$a_{\overline{n}|}\,(1+Y)^n = s_{\overline{n}|} \text{ at } Y$$

$$1/a_{\overline{n}|} - 1/s_{\overline{n}|} = Y$$

The composite capitalization rate by which periodic income is divided to calculate present value of income and reversion is equal to the periodic income per dollar of value. In other words, if a present value of 1 dollar is assumed with periodic income, called "d," and the composite capitalization rate, called "R," the equation is:

$$\frac{d}{R} = 1$$

In this case "d" and "R" are equal to each other and, therefore, "R" can be used to represent both the income per dollar of value and the composite rate by which income is divided to determine present value.

Now, consider a situation in which property is bought for 1 dollar, held for a term of years and resold for 1 dollar. In other words, there is no change in value from time of purchase to time of reversion.

Present value of income is: $R\,a_{\overline{n}|}$

Present value of reversion is: $\dfrac{1}{(1+Y)^n}$

and:

$$R\,a_{\overline{n}|} + \frac{1}{(1+Y)^n} = 1$$

By transposition:

$$R\,a_{\overline{n}|} = 1 - \frac{1}{(1+Y)^n}$$

and:

$$R = \frac{1}{a_{\overline{n}|}} - \frac{1}{a_{\overline{n}|}\,(1+Y)^n}$$

Remember:

$$a_{\overline{n|}}\,(1+Y)^{n} = s_{\overline{n|}} \text{ and } \frac{1}{a_{\overline{n|}}} - \frac{1}{s_{\overline{n|}}} = Y$$

Therefore:

$$R = \frac{1}{a_{\overline{n|}}} - \frac{1}{s_{\overline{n|}}} \text{ which equals "Y"}$$

When there is no change in value, the composite capitalization rate is the investment yield rate.

Assume an income of \$8,000 per year for 10 years and yield "Y" = 8%

$$\text{Value} = \frac{8000}{.08} = \$100{,}000$$

Present Value of income and reversion at 8%:

Income; 10 years \$8000 × 6.710081	\$ 53,681
Reversion deferred 10 years \$100,000 × .463193	46,319
Present value Income and Reversion	\$100,000

Of all the basic principles of real property valuation, none is more valid than the principle of change. Market values fluctuate irregularly up and down over the years for many reasons. After several years of ownership, it would be a coincidence indeed for equity reversion to be the same as its original cost. The professional appraiser recognizes this and is profoundly concerned with community, neighborhood and economic trends as indicators of future changes in value.

Remembering that the projection of periodic income is the numerator in the equation for value, and the appropriate composite rate or denominator must reflect the influence of future value changes, the question is; how to provide for them in composite rate development?

Assume it is decided to provide for a certain amount of value decline or increase over a given projection term. Call the total fraction of decline "dep" and total fraction of increase "app."

In case of decline, present value of the reversion will be:

$$\frac{1-\text{dep}}{(1+Y)^{n}} \text{ or } \frac{1}{(1+Y)^{n}} - \frac{\text{dep}}{(1+Y)^{n}}$$

In case of increase, present value of the reversion will be:

$$\frac{1+\text{app}}{(1+Y)^{n}} \text{ or } \frac{1}{(1+Y)^{n}} + \frac{\text{app}}{(1+Y)^{n}}$$

And derivations for composite rates are:

$$R\, a_{\overline{n}|} + \frac{1}{(1+Y)^n} - \frac{dep}{(1+Y)^n} = 1$$

$$R\, a_{\overline{n}|} = 1 - \frac{1}{(1+Y)^n} + \frac{dep}{(1+Y)^n}$$

$$R = \frac{1}{a_{\overline{n}|}} - \frac{1}{s_{\overline{n}|}} + \frac{dep}{s_{\overline{n}|}}$$

Since:

$$1/a_{\overline{n}|} - 1/s_{\overline{n}|} = Y;$$

$$R = Y + dep\ 1/s_{\overline{n}|}$$

In case of increase:

$$R\, a_{\overline{n}|} + \frac{1}{(1+Y)^n} + \frac{app}{(1+Y)^n} = 1$$

Proceeding with transposition the same as above, the resulting equation is:

$$R = Y - app\ 1/s_{\overline{n}|}$$

Check this with Y at 8% and value change at 20% in a 10-year projection. The 10-year sinking fund factor at 8% (Col. 3) is .069029.

With 20% decline:

$$R = .08 + .20 \times .069029 = .08 + .0138058 = .0938058$$

Income: \$9,380.58; Value: $\frac{\$9{,}380.58}{.0938058} = \$100{,}000$

Present Value Income and Reversion at 8%.

Income: \$9,380.58 × 6.710081	\$ 62,945
Reversion, depreciated 20%: \$80,000 × .463193	37,055
	\$100,000

With 20% increase:

$$R = .08 - .20 \times .069029 = .08 - .0138058 = .0661942$$

Income: \$6,619.42; Value: $\frac{\$6{,}619.42}{.0661942} = \$100{,}000$

Income: \$6,619.42 × 6.710081	\$ 44,417
Reversion, 20% appreciation: \$120,000 × .463193	55,583
	\$100,000

The appraiser's function with regard to income real estate is that of analyzing his subject as an investment opportunity and setting a price in which the prospects for yield to the buyer will have market attractiveness. The most explicable and supportable process is to start with a price selected from market experience and test it for yields within a considerable range of future market conditions. When the test reveals that a substantial amount of depreciation can occur without reducing the yield below a reasonably satisfactory limit and that it requires no more than a steady market or modest appreciation to make the yield exceptionally attractive, the appraisal will be persuasive. If the test indicates poor prospects, the price must be adjusted accordingly.

A significant factor in yield calculation is the average, annual rate of profit per dollar of investment. Each of the preceding three examples involves an investment of $100,000 and a yield of 8%. The average annual rate of profit in each case is calculated as follows:

(1) No change in value:

Income 10 years at $8,000	$ 80,000
Reversion	100,000
Total collection	$180,000
Cost of Investment	100,000
Profit	$ 80,000
Average profit per year: $80,000/10	$ 8,000

Average, annual rate of profit:

$$\frac{8,000}{100,000} = .08 \text{ or } 8\%$$

The average annual rate of profit is *equal* to the 8% yield.

(2) 20% decline in value:

Income 10 years at $9,380.58	$ 93,805.80
Reversion	80,000.00
Total collection	$173,805.80
Cost of investment	100,000.00
Profit	$ 73,805.80
Average profit per year: $73,805.80/10	$ 7,380.58

Average, annual rate of profit:

$$\frac{7,380.58}{100,000} = .0738058$$

The average annual rate of profit is *less* than the 8% yield.

(3) 20% increase in value:

Income 10 years at $6,619.42	$ 66,194.20
Reversion	120,000.00
Total collection	$186,194.20
Cost of investment	100,000.00
Profit	$ 86,194.20
Average profit per year: $86,194.20/10	$ 8,619.42

Average, annual rate of profit:

$$\frac{8{,}619.42}{100{,}000} = .0861942$$

The average annual rate of profit is *greater* than the 8% yield.

Summary of Rules:

(1) To calculate composite rate "R" when *depreciation* is to be provided for:

$$Y + \text{dep}\ {}^{1/s}\overline{n|} = R$$

(2) To calculate composite rate "R" when *appreciation* is to be provided for:

$$Y - \text{app}\ {}^{1/s}\overline{n|} = R$$

(3) When reversion is equal to the cost of investment (i.e. no change in value), investment yield is equal to the average, annual rate of profit per dollar of investment.

(4) When reversion is less than the cost of investment (i.e. depreciation occurs), the average rate of profit per dollar of investment is less than the investment yield.

(5) When reversion is greater than the cost of investment (i.e. appreciation occurs) the average rate of profit per dollar of investment is greater than the investment yield.

Yield Calculations:

Investment yield calculations will illustrate practical applications of these rules.

The yield on any capital investment is the rate of interest at which the present value of income and reversion is equal to the amount invested.

Since yield can rarely be determined by direct computation because of more than one unknown factor, it is usually done by closely bracketing the answer by use of 2 trial rates and interpolating for actual yield. This can be done most accurately by employing the compound interest functions which introduce the smallest error when subjected to straight line interpolation. If the difference between corresponding functions at 6% and 7% were according to a straight line, the corresponding function at 6½% would be one half the sum of the 6% and 7% functions. Although this is not the case because changes occur according to logarithmic curves, the differentials are much smaller with regard to some functions than others.

This is demonstrated by the following tabulation based on 6%, 7% and 6½% functions at 9 years: Annual Compounding.

COLUMN:	*1.*	*2.*	*3.*	*4.*	*5.*	*6.*
YIELD:						
6%	1.689479	11.491316	.087022	.591898	6.801692	.147022
7%	1.838459	11.977989	.083486	.543934	6.515232	.153486
TOTALS:	3.527938	23.469305	.170508	1.135752	13.316924	.300508
÷ BY 2,	1.763969	11.734653	.085254	.567876	6.658462	.150254
6½%	1.762570	11.731852	.085238	.567353	6.656104	.150238
DIFFERENCES:	.001399	.002801	.000016	.000523	.002358	.000016

Notice that in Columns 3 and 6 there is no differential error by direct interpolation until we reach the 5th decimal place. It is therefore apparent that the error by direct or straight line interpolation will be of little significance where we can use these functions in yield calculations. The third column or sinking fund factor is used in every case where the equity reversion is either greater or less than the equity investment.

Use of the sinking fund factor in yield calculation is demonstrated in this computation for bond yield.

A $1,000 bond bearing interest at 3% payable annually is offered at $800 nine years before maturity.

What is the yield if bought for $800, held to maturity and collected at face amount?

Solution:

Interest dividend as % of \$800 = 30/800 = .0375 or 3.75%. (Cap. rate is .0375.)

Appreciation 9 yrs. \$1,000 — \$800 = \$200; 200/800 = .25 or 25%.

Interest Collection, 9 yrs. 9 × 30	\$ 270
Principal Collection	1,000
Total Collection	\$1,270
Investment	800
Profit	\$ 470

Average profit per year, 470/9 = \$52.22+ as a % of investment, $\frac{52.22}{800} = 6.5275\%$.

REF: "When reversion is greater than capital investment, yield will be *less* than average annual rate of profit per dollar of investment." Since reversion in this case is 25% greater than investment, we know the yield will be less than the average profit of 6.5275%. We can therefore start with 6% as a trial rate in the formula which would be used to find "R" = .0375.

$$Y - .25 \times 1/s_{\overline{n}|} = .0375$$

.06 — .25 × .087022 = .06 — .021756 =	.038244;	Target;	.037500
.05 — .25 × .090690 = .05 — .022673 =	.027327;		.027327
.01 Differences;	.010917		.010173

And, By Interpolation:

$$Y = .05 + \frac{.01 \times .010173}{.010917} = .05 + .009318 = .059318 \text{ or, } 5.9318\%$$

This answer is correct to 6 decimal places; price of the bond would probably be quoted to yield 5.93% or 5.932%.

Sinking fund factors for 6% and 5% are from Col. 3 at 9 years.

The same principle is applicable to equity investment yield.

(A) *Example:*

Jim Higgins purchased an apartment building for \$600,000. He borrowed \$450,000 at 5½% interest to be fully amortized in 25 years by level monthly installments. His cash equity investment was \$150,000. He resold the property 8 years later for \$525,000. Net cash flow income produced by the property during the 8 year term of ownership averaged \$49,500 per year as if free and clear. Compute the equity yield.

Solution:

Annual Mortgage Requirement, "f" = .0738

Sp — 1 at 5½% 8 years monthly table = .551147

$$P = \left(\frac{.0738}{.055} - 1\right) \times .551147 = .188392;\ \text{complement};\ .811608$$

Purchase Capital:		*Income*	
Mortgage	\$450,000 × .0738	\$33,210	*Equity Cap.*
Equity	150,000	16,290	*Rate*
Cash to Seller	\$600,000	\$49,500	.1086

Property reversion deferred 8 years	\$525,000
Less mortgage balance, \$450,000 × .811608	365,224
Reversion to Equity	\$159,776

Equity appreciates \$9776/150000 = .0651733.

Income 8 years at \$16,290	\$130,320
Reversionary profit	9,776
Total profit	\$140,096
Average profit per year \$140096/8	\$ 17,512

Average rate of profit, 17512/150000 = .1167. Equity Cap. rate; 16290/150000 = .1086; (Target.) Since reversion is slightly greater than investment, yield will be slightly less than .1167. Start bracketing at .12%

Y		
.12 — .0651733 × .081302 =	.1147013	.1086000
.11 — .0651733 × .084321 =	.1045046	.1045046
.01 *Differences*	.0101967	.0040954

By Interpolation:

$$Y = .11 + \frac{.01 \times 40954}{101967} = .114016+.\ \text{Say}\ 11.4\%$$

(B) *Influence of Financing:*

Assume the \$600,000 purchase price was paid as a 100% cash equity investment. Compute yield with income and resale the same as above.

Income 8 years at \$49,500	\$396,000
Proceeds of resale	525,000
Total collection	\$921,000
Cost of Investment	600,000
Profit	\$321,000

Average profit per year, \$321,000/8 = \$40,125

Average rate of profit 40125/600000 = .066875

Composite cap. rate, target, $\frac{49500}{600,000} = .0825$

Depreciation $\frac{75,000}{600000} = .125$

Since reversion is less than investment, average rate of profit is less than yield. Start bracketing at 7½ % for target .0825

Y		
.075 + .125 × .095727 =	.0869658	.0825000
.070 + .125 × .097468 =	.0821835	.0821835
.005 *Differences*	47823	3165

By interpolation:

$$Y = .070 + \frac{.005 \times 3165}{47823} = .07033 \text{ Say } 7.03\%$$

(C) *Influence of Recapture Term:*

Now assume all conditions the same as in the first example except that the 75% or \$450,000 mortgage is to be fully amortized in 15 years instead of 25 years. The annual mortgage requirement per dollar, "f," in this case, would be .09816 and the yield on Higgins' \$150,000 equity investment could be calculated as follows:

$$P = \left(\frac{.09816}{.055} - 1\right) \times .551147 = .4325, \text{ Complement } .5675$$

Purchase Capital		*Income*
Mortgage	\$450,000 × .09816	\$ 44,172
Equity	150,000	5,328
Cash to Seller	\$600,000	\$ 49,500

Property reversion deferred 8 years	\$525,000
Less mortgage balance; \$450,000 × .5675	255,375
Reversion to Equity	\$269,625
Equity Income; 8 years 8 × 5328	42,624
Total Equity collection	\$312,249
Cost of Investment	150,000
Equity Profit	\$162,249
Average profit per year, 162,249/8	\$ 20,281
Average rate of profit, 20281/150000	.1352

Equity appreciates .... 269625 — 150000 = $119,625
119,625/150000 = .7975

Equity capitalization rate and target; 5328/150000; .03552
With reversion so much greater than investment, average rate of profit is substantially greater than yield. Start bracketing at 11%

Y			
.11 — .7975 × .084321 =		.0427541	.0355200
.10 — .7975 × .087444 =		.0302635	.0302635
.01	*Differences*	124906	52565

By interpolation:

$$Y = .10 + \frac{.01 \times 52565}{124906} = .1042083; \text{ Say } 10.42\%$$

Thus, 3 sets of conditions produce 3 different yields to the buyer. And yet, there was no change in total value, no change in the composite capitalization rate and no change in the amount of decline or depreciation which occurred during the term of ownership. It is obvious, moreover, that these are only 3 of an infinite variety of conditions which would cause changes in the investment yield without modification of the over-all purchase price or capitalization rate.

This generates a question as to just what guide lines appraisers do have for selection of appropriate capitalization rates. The only answer lies in the market. And this starts with knowledge of the money market. The majority of the capital used for the purchase of conventional income property is mortgage money. When the appraiser knows 75% of acceptable appraisal can be borrowed by a typical buyer at a given rate of interest with provision for recapture over a given term of years, he has a factual capitalization rate pertaining to 75% of his appraisal.

The objective of the appraisal is to make a reasonable estimate of cash market value, and the point is that facts pertaining to the availability of mortgage money provide the valid and supportable place of beginning for selection of the capitalization rate.

Band of Investment Interest Rate Selection:

A plausible method for selection of a composite interest rate is based on the "band of investment theory."

It starts with the prevailing mortgage interest rate and available ratio of mortgage to value. An attractive "prospective" equity yield is combined with this to form the composite interest rate.

Assume, for example, 75% mortgage money is available at 5½% and the appraiser judges that good prospects for double this rate, or 11%, would attract a buyer for the 25% equity position. The composite interest rate would be calculated as follows:

Mortgage Money, 75% at .055	.04125
Equity Money, 25% at .110	.02750
Composite Interest Rate	.06875

If a stabilized annual income of $41,250, after provision for recapture, is capitalized at this composite rate, distributions of capital and income would be as set forth below:

Valuation; $41250/.06875 = $600,000

Distribution:

Mortgage	75%;	$450,000	at 5½%	$24,750
Equity	25%;	150,000	at 11%	16,500
Totals;		$600,000		$41,250

If the 5½% and 11% rate combination could be established by comparable sales as reflecting the market with 75% and 25% mortgage and equity ratios, it could be used as a standard of comparison for calculating the relative equity rate with any other equity to value ratio and any other mortgage interest rate.

This system would at least provide a means for explaining the source of an equity yield rate. Despite the fact that the actual, ultimate yield is unknown, the appraiser needs an explicable "prospective yield" to start with.

The relationship of mortgage and composite rate in this example is:

$$.06875/.055 = 1.25$$

If the differential addition .25 is combined with any equity ratio, "E" and any mortgage interest rate "I," the comparable equity yield "Y" can be calculated by formula:

$$\frac{(.25 + E)}{E} I = Y$$

Examples with "I" at 5½%:

Mortgage	*E*		*Y*
0%	1.00;	$\frac{(.25 + 1)\ .055}{1} = 1.25 \times .055,$	.06875
40%	.60;	$\frac{(.25 + .60)\ .055}{.60} = 1.41⅔ \times 055,$	.07792
66⅔%	.33⅓;	$\frac{(.25 + .33⅓)\ .055}{.33⅓} = 1.75 \times .055,$	.09625
75%	.25;	$\frac{(.25 + .25)\ .055}{.25} = 2 \times .055,$	.1100
90%	.10;	$\frac{(.25 + .10)\ .055}{.10} = 3.5 \times .055,$	.1925

Examples with "I" at 6%:

(Multipliers of "I" do not change)

Mortgage	*E*		*Y*
0%	1.00	1.25 × .06	.075
40%	.60	1.41⅔ × .06	.085
66⅔%	.33⅓	1.75 × .06	.1050
75%	.25	2 × .06	.12
90%	.10	3.5 × .06	.21

Advantages of this method are:

(a) The composite interest rate by band of investment calculation will always be the same regardless of mortgage and equity ratios:

Mortgage 40% at .055	.02200
Equity 60% at .07792	.04675
Composite Interest Rate	.06875

Mortgage 90% at .055	.04950
Equity 10% at .1925	.01925
Composite Interest Rate	.06875

Mortgage 40% at .06	.024
Equity 60% at .085	.051
Composite Interest Rate	.075

Mortgage 90% at .06	.054
Equity 10% at .21	.021
Composite Interest Rate	.075

(b) Any mortgage position should always be superior to that of equity because the rate is fixed by contract and burden of management is the responsibility of the equity owner. Therefore, the composite interest rate should always exceed the prevailing mortgage interest rate.

(c) The risk of equity investment increases as its ratio to value declines. Prospective yield should increase accordingly.

A formula of this type accomplishes conditions (b) and (c) without permitting the mortgage ratio to affect the over-all interest rate. This is as it should be because the fact that a majority of purchase capital can be borrowed does not in any way affect a property's future performance. It only determines how earnings are to be distributed.

INCOME PROJECTION & VALUATION

Following is the actual cash flow income stream produced by a typical apartment project over a 10 year period. It is noteworthy that year to year fluctuation runs quite high in several places. This is characteristic of individual performance of multiple occupancy properties because nonrecurring replacement and maintenance expenditures decrease net income substantially in years of their occurrence and result in corresponding increases in years when nothing more than operating expenses are incurred.

Year		Year		Year	
1.	$41887	4.	40803	7.	37914
2.	38782	5.	31706	8.	40727
3.	48036	6.	$51048	9.	37563
				10.	40908

Now let us assume:

(a) This property was purchased at the beginning of the 10 year period for $513000.

(b) The purchase capital structure was:

Cash equity investment	$171000
Mortgage at 5% interest to be fully amortized in 20 years by level installments of $2257.20 per month	342000
Total cash to seller	$513000

(c) The property was sold at the end of the 10 year period for $436,000 indicating about 15% depreciation in value during the term of ownership.

The distribution of income would be as follows:

Year	Mortgage Interest	Mortgage Amortization	Equity Dividend	Total
1	$ 16867.94	$ 10218.46	$ 14800.60	$ 41887
2	16345.14	10741.26	11695.60	38782
3	15795.60	11290.80	20949.60	48036
4	15217.94	11868.46	13716.60	40803
5	14610.73	12475.67	4619.60	31706
6	13972.45	13113.95	23961.60	51048
7	13301.51	13784.89	10827.60	37914
8	12596.25	14490.15	13640.60	40727
9	11854.90	15231.50	10476.60	37563
10	11075.63	16010.77	13821.6Q	40908
Totals	$141638.09	$129225.91	$138510.00	$409374
Averages (pennies dropped)			$13851	$40937

This is graphically presented by Plate I showing the types of annuities involved.

PLATE I

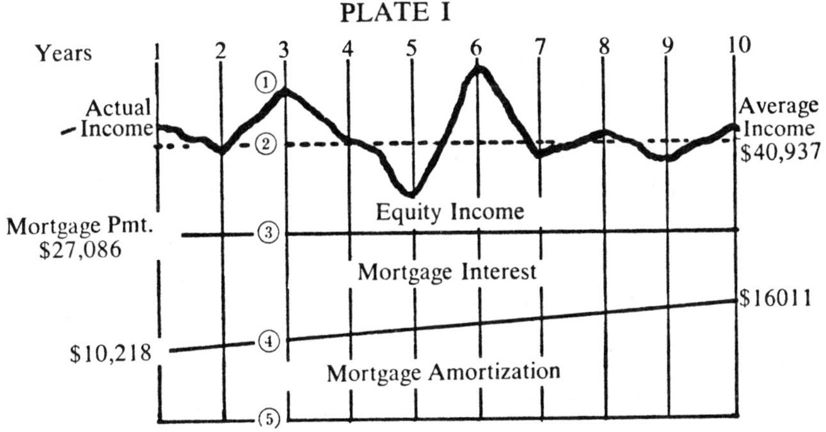

Vertical Distance Between Lines	Represents	Type Annuity
1 and 3	Actual Equity Income	Fluctuating
2 and 3	Average Equity Income	Ordinary
3 and 5	Total Annual Mortgage Installments	Ordinary
3 and 4	Mortgage Interest	Decreasing
4 and 5	Mortgage Amortization	Increasing

The actual yield on the equity investment of $171000 in this case would be slightly more than 10% as will be seen by the following calculations in which we discount each equity dividend at 10% and add the amount of the equity reversion discounted at 10%.

Year	Equity Dividend	$\frac{1}{1.10^n}$	Present Value
1	14800.60	.9091	13455.23
2	11695.60	.8264	9665.24
3	20949.60	.7513	15739.43
4	13716.60	.6830	9368.44
5	4619.60	.6209	2868.31
6	23961.60	.5645	13526.32
7	10827.60	.5132	5556.72
8	13640.60	.4665	6363.34
9	10476.60	.4241	4443.13
10	13821.60	.3855	5328.23
Present Value all equity dividends at 10%			$86314.39

Selling Price of Property		$436000
Less mortgage balance;		
Original amount	$342000	
10 Year amortization	129226	
Mortgage Balance	$212774	212774
Equity Reversion; (appreciation 30.54%)		$223226
Discount 10 years at 10%		× .3855
Present Value Equity Reversion		$ 86053.62
Present Value Equity Income		86314.39
Present Value of Equity at 10% Yield		$172368+
Value of Mortgage		342000
Value of Property with equity yield at 10%		$514368

Now we can determine the error introduced by treating the average equity dividend as an ordinary annuity. We know that when a market transaction is partially financed by the modern type of mortgage the aggregate payment of interest and amortization will comprise an ordinary annuity. Therefore, the only income in question is the residual income to equity. This is a rather wildly fluctuating annuity. First, let us see what its actual value amounts to as a fraction of computed value of the property.

$$\frac{86314}{514368} = .1678 \text{ or } 16.78\%$$

If we omit equity income entirely from consideration, the error will be 16.78% and any method by which we attribute value to it will reduce that margin of error. If we treat its average as an ordinary annuity, we have:

Present value equity income $13851 × 6.1446	$ 85109
Present value equity reversion	86054
Mortgage	342000
Total Value	$513163

$$\text{Fraction correct } \frac{513163}{514368} = .9976 \qquad 99.76\%$$

Numerous tests of this type have been conducted against recorded performance of typical, multiple occupancy, investment properties. Clinical material included operating records and market transactions in landlord service apartment and office buildings where year to year variations in the earning stream were substantial. The results proved that no significant error was involved in treating average annual income as an ordinary annuity in a comparatively short term projection.

The term of the income projection should be related to the definition of market value and experience as to the average frequency at which the ownership of property changes hands.

Market value as defined by the courts is: "the highest price estimated in terms of money which a property will bring if exposed for sale in the open market allowing a reasonable time to find a purchaser who buys with knowledge of all the uses to which it is adapted and for which it is capable of being used."

Obviously, this contemplates one sale to one well-informed purchaser. Therefore, it covers no more than one term of ownership and the potential benefits which would effect the determination of price would be those one purchaser would anticipate during his term of ownership.

A 10 year projection is recommended for most cases. It is a matter of common knowledge based on general observation that most properties of ordinary investment types change hands several times in the course of a half century. Transfer records indicate 10 years as adequate coverage for the typical term of ownership. There is no way of rationalizing, stabilizing or estimating average income on a total useful life basis. First, because there is no reliable method of predicting total useful life. Secondly, because it probably will encompass future price level plateaus which are far beyond the reach of an appraiser's telescope. Finally, because it is quite certain to exceed the term of ownership of one purchaser as contemplated by all commonly accepted definitions of market value. An estimate of rentals and a budget of expenses with intelligent allowances for vacancies and replacements can be based on contemporary fact and well remembered experience in a 10 year projection.

The appraiser has a much better chance for reliable estimate in a comparatively short projection than in one based on the very nebulous concept of total useful life. The 10 year projection gives him a definite basis for calculating a specific average.

Exceptions to the 10 year norm can always be made when income is fixed for longer terms by leases at equitable rents to financially strong tenants or where the rate of neighborhood transition or other conditions indicate a shorter projection.

The figures in the foregoing example should give us information for development of a formula for finding a composite capitalization rate, including the influence of the mortgage component of the purchase capital structure. Based on purchase price and total average annual income, the composite capitalization rate should be:

$$\frac{40937}{513000} = .0798 \text{ or } 7.98\% \text{ (rounded)}$$

The Mortgage Coefficient Method:

A variation of the band of investment rate calculation is accomplished by using the difference between equity and mortgage rates as a coefficient of mortgage ratios.

In explanation; Call;

Y = Equity yield rate

I = Mortgage interest rate

M = Mortgage to value ratio

C = Coefficient

r = Composite interest rate

$$Y - I = C$$

and:

$$Y - MC = r$$

This will produce the same composite interest rates but offers an advantage in facilitating adjustment for mortgage amortization and consequent equity value build-up. To illustrate; first *with interest rates only:*

Y = .11; I = .055; M = .75

Y − I = C; .1100 − .055 = .055

Y − MC = r

Y	.11000
Less MC; .75 × .055	.04125
Composite Interest Rate	.06875

Y = .1050; I = .06; M = .66⅔

Y − I = C .1050 − .06 = .045

Y − MC = r

Y	.105
Less MC; .66⅔ × .045	.030
Composite Interest Rate	.075

Equity yield "Y" can be adjusted to reflect any equity value build-up by reason of mortgage amortization and the mortgage interest "I" can be adjusted to cover the cost of amortization or recapture. *When adjusted "I" is subtracted from adjusted "Y," the remainder is a coefficient "C" which can be used with any mortgage ratio "M," to produce a comprehensive, composite rate "r."*

Call the fraction of mortgage to be amortized "P."

$$Y + P\ 1/s_{\overline{n}|} = \text{Adjusted "Y"}$$

The sinking fund factor is at rate "Y" for the income projection term.

Adjusted "I" is the annual mortgage requirement per dollar of mortgage including both interest and amortization. This combination is represented by symbol "f."

Thus, the subtraction of adjusted "I" (now called "f") from adjusted "Y" is as follows:

$$\mathbf{C = Y + P1/s_{\overline{n}|} - f}$$

The coefficient "C" is employed in the same manner as when interest rates only are involved. And, since it can be calculated for any combination of rates, amortization requirement and income projection term, this formula has been employed to compile tables of pre-computed coefficients and capitalization rates. The scopes of the tables are such that the appraiser can usually find the desired combination and thus eliminate the need for involved calculations.

Nevertheless, it must be repeated that tables are only working tools. They do not supplant judgment. Therefore, a requisite for intelligent use is knowledge of how they are computed. Without such knowledge, the appraiser is unable to explain what he assumes and *believes* when he uses them.

For this reason, detailed calculation of a composite rate by use of functions from standard compound interest tables is presented here:

1. Mortgage money to help finance purchase of a group of retail shops is available up to 75% of appraisal to be amortized in 25 years by monthly installments including interest at 5½% per annum.

2. Net cash flow income is projected 10 years at an average of $32,250 per year.
3. Allow for 15% over-all value decline in 10 years and appraise the property to yield 11% on a 25% equity.

Solution:

Reference; 5½% monthly compound interest table; Column 6; monthly installment at 25 years is .006141. In practice this is rounded to $6.15 per month per $1000 to avoid dealing in fractions of a cent. The annual requirement is 12 × $6.15 = $73.80 per $1000 or .0738 per dollar; i.e. "f" = .0738. In Column 1, at 10 years, Sp — 1 = .731076.

In Column 3 of 11% compound interest table, sinking fund factor at 10 years is .0598.

Calculation of fraction amortized in 10 years;

$$P = \left(\frac{.0738}{.055} - 1\right) \times .731076 = .249895$$

Calculation of mortgage coefficient by formula:

$$C = Y + P\ 1/s_{\overline{n}|} - f$$

Equity Yield Y	.1100000
Plus, $P\ 1/s_{\overline{n}|}$, .249895 × .0598	.0149437
Adjusted "Y"	.1249437
Less "f" (adjusted I)	.0738000
Mortgage Coefficient "C"	.0511437
Rounded to	.0511

Calculation of basic capitalization rate by formula.

$$r = Y - M.C.$$

Equity yield "Y"	.110000
Less M.C., .75 × .0511	.038325
*Basic rate, before depreciation	.071675
Add for depreciation by formula:	
$R = r + dep\ 1/s_{\overline{n}|}$; .15 × .0598	.008970
Composite Capitalization Rate; "R"	.080645

Valuation; $32250/.080645 = $399,901

Say, $400,000

This can be checked for mathematical validity by computing present value of indicated equity income and reversion at 11% and comparing the result with the assumed equity investment.

Arithmetic Check

Purchase Capital				*Income Distribution*
Mortgage, 75%,	$300,000	at .0738		$ 22,140
Equity, 25%,	100,000	.1011		$ 10,110
Cash to Seller;	$400,000			$ 32,250
Original Price				$400,000
Less 15% depreciation				60,000
Property Reversion, deferred 10 years				$340,000
Original mortgage			$300,000	
Less 10 yr. amortization; × .249895			74,968	225,032
Equity Reversion, deferred 10 years				$114,968
Present Value Equity income and reversion at 11%.				
Income,	$ 10,110 × 5.889230			$ 59,540
Reversion,	114,968 × .352184			40,490
Total				$100,030
Investment				100,000
Rounding surplus				$ 30

Obviously, the appraiser does not know what value change will occur in 10 years. His physical summation indicates a building value of $240,000. Bulletin "F" indicates depreciation at 2½% per year or 25% in 10 years would be allowable as income tax shelter. 25% of $240,000 is $60,000 or 15% of over-all value. He believes the prospect of an 11% yield after this deduction would be attractive. Moreover, the income to equity at about 10% after mortgage charges compares favorably with other market transactions. He therefore concludes his appraisal presents a price at which the property would find a ready market.

This process is merely a variation of the band of investment method of composite rate selection with adjustment for capital recapture as provided by typical mortgage contracts. Application is made practical by use of tables which eliminate the need for lengthy calculations.*

*75% Mortgage, Capitalization Rate Table at 25 yr. amortization, 5½% interest, 10 year projection, 11% equity yield, shows this basic rate as pre-computed at .0717. The sinking fund factor .0598 for use in the depreciation adjustment is in the right hand column. Thus, by tabular reference, the value calculation would be condensed to:

Basic rate; "r"	.07170
Add depreciation; .15 × .0598	.00897
Composite Cap. Rate. "R"	.08067

Valuation: 32250/.08067 = $399,777 Say: $400,000

REVIEW OF THE 100% EQUITY TECHNIQUES

Prior to general adoption of the long-term, level installment, amortized mortgage method of financing market transactions, the income approach to value contemplated purchase on the basis of a 100% cash-out of-pocket equity investment.

Assumptions implicit in the several techniques employed under this concept vary as to the nature and duration of the income stream and in the method by which purchase capital will be recaptured. Each variation will have a significant influence on the investment yield whenever a specific overall capitalization rate is applied to a given annual income. In other words, if we capitalize $8500 at an overall rate of 8½%, the valuation will be $100,000 by every technique but the investment yield will change as we move from one technique to another.

And, since the prospect for yield is not only the motivation for purchase but also the only basis by which an appraisal can be intelligently tested for plausibility and market attractiveness, a clear understanding of yield as the critical component of each technique is important.

Capitalization in Perpetuity:

Assumes a steady income and no change in value. The overall capitalization rate is the investment yield rate. The present value of income and reversion is always the same regardless of the income projection term; to wit:

5 Year Projection; Yield 8½%

Income 5 Years	$ 8,500 × 3.940642+	$ 33,495.50
Reversion deferred 5 years	$100,000 × .665045	66,504.50
Total Present Value		$100,000.00

100 Year Projection; Yield 8½%

Income 100 Years	$ 8,500 × 11.761336+	$ 99,971.40
Reversion deferred 100 years	$100,000 × .000286	28.60
Total Present Value		$100,000.00

Straight Line Depreciation Process:

Assumes declining income and declining value on a straight line basis. Total projection term is called "useful life" or "economic life." The useful life term in years is normally an arbitrary decision based on nature and condition of the physical property. The assumed annual depreciation rate is the reciprocal of useful life in years. The difference between the overall capitalization rate and the depreciation rate is the investment yield rate.

Or, to put it another way, the overall capitalization rate is the sum of investment yield and depreciation rates.

With useful life projected at 40 years, the depreciation rate is the reciprocal of 40 which is 2½%. The difference between an overall capitalization rate of 8½% and a depreciation rate of 2½% is 6% which is the investment yield rate.

If we start with income at $8500 the first year and present value at $100,000, depreciation at 2½% of $100,000 will amount to $2500 per year. Thus, it is assumed that $2500 will be extracted from income each year to offset the straight line decline in value and provide full recapture of $100,000 in 40 years.

Each $2500 extraction will reduce capital remaining in the investment by that amount. It is, therefore, assumed that income will decline 6% of $2500 or $150 each year.

In summary, our assumptions are; (1) that value of the property is now $100,000; (2) that this value will decline $2500 per year; (3) that income will start at $8500 and decline at the rate of $150 per year.

The 40 year straight line declining annuity is equivalent to one ordinary annuity of $2500 per year for 40 years and 40 ordinary annuities of $150 per year from 1 to 40 years. The present value of this income stream discounted at 6% is $100,000 calculated as follows:

Inwood Ordinary Annuity Coefficient at 6% for 40 years is 15.046297 (Col. 5 annual compound interest table).

The sum of all Inwood Ordinary Coefficients from 1 to 40 years is;

$$\frac{40 - 15.046297}{.06} = \frac{24.953703}{.06} = 415.89505$$

$$\begin{aligned} \$2500 \times 15.046297 &= \$\ 37{,}615.74+ \\ 150 \times 415.89505 &= \underline{\quad 62{,}384.26-} \\ \text{Total Present Value....} &\ \$100{,}000.00 \end{aligned}$$

The appraiser should also understand any projection of less than 40 years will also have a present value of $100,000 so long as he assumes the 6% investment yield rate, 2½% annual value decline with income starting at $8,500 declining $150 per year.

Assume a 10 year projection for example. Value decline at $2500 per year will amount to $25,000 leaving a reversion of $75,000 deferred 10 years.

The straight line declining annuity will be equivalent to one 10 year ordinary annuity of $7,000, i.e. $8,500—(10 × 150), plus 10 ordinary annuities of $150 per year for from 1 to 10 years.

The 6% reversion factor at 10 years is .558395 (Col. 4 annual compound interest table). The ordinary annuity coefficient at 10 years is 7.360087. The sum of these coefficients from 1 to 10 is:

$$\frac{10 - 7.360087}{.06} = \frac{2.639913}{.06} = 43.99855$$

Present Value of Income and Reversion discounted at 6%;

$ 7,000 ×	7.360087 =	$ 51,520.60
150 ×	43.99855 =	6,599.78
75,000 ×	.558395 =	41,879.62
Total Present Value....		$100,000.00

The Inwood Ordinary Annuity Technique:

Assumes a steady income and recapture of purchase capital on the basis of a sinking fund installment accumulating over assumed useful life at the investment yield rate. With overall capitalization rate at 8½% and a 40 year useful life projection, the investment yield would be the interest rate at which .085 would appear at 40 years in column No. 6 of the compound interest table. In other words, it is the yield at which an ordinary annuity of 8½ cents per year for 40 years has a present value of 1 dollar. This can be calculated by interpolation of the 8½% and 8% Column 6 factors as follows:

Interest rate	Col. 6 40 Yrs.	Target
.085	.088382	.085000
.080	.083860	.083860
.005	4522	1140

By Interpolation;

$$\text{Yield} = 08 + \frac{.005 \times 1140}{4522} = .08 + .00126+ = .08126+$$

Investment yield would be slightly over 8⅛%. Any projection less than 40 years will have the same present value at this yield rate if the sinking fund accumulation for the smaller projection term is treated as depreciation and subtracted from original value to determine the reversion.

Hoskold Sinking Fund Technique:

Assumes a steady income and a dual interest rate. A level periodic sinking fund installment is taken from income and deposited in an account on which interest will accumulate at a contract or "safe rate" to provide recapture of purchase capital during the useful life projection. The overall capitalization rate is the sum of the investment yield rate (known as the "speculative" rate) and the sinking fund requirement per dollar of investment.

Assume for example, a savings institution agrees to accumulate interest at 4% on a level annual sinking fund deposit for a term of 40 years. Column 3 of the 4% annual compound interest table at 40 years shows the sinking fund factor at .010523. If the overall capitalization rate is 8½%, the investment yield or "speculative" rate will be .085 less .010523 or .074477 i.e., 7.4477%.

The Hoskold overall capitalization rate for any dual rate and time combination is always the sinking fund factor at the "safe rate" plus the yield or "speculative rate."

IV

TABLE C — MORTGAGE COEFFICIENTS

Precomputed by formula: $C = Y + P\ 1/s_{\overline{n|}} - f$

Use; $r = Y - MC$; and $R = r + dep\ 1/s_{\overline{n|}}$; etc.

Scope:

Mortgage amortization terms; 10 to 30 years by 5 year increments.

Mortgage interest rates, 3¼% to 12% by ¼% increments.

Income Projection Terms, 5 years to full amortization by 5 year increments.

Equity Yields; 4% to 30% by 1% increments.

Instructions for Finding Desired Coefficient "C":

1. Find the amortization term at top of table.
2. Find pages on which mortgage interest rate appears.
3. Find desired projection bracket.
4. Read across on Equity Yield line to coefficient in interest rate column.

Supplementary Data:

Right hand column contains the sinking fund factors.

Immediately below the interest rate at the top of each column is the annual mortgage requirement, "f" per dollar of mortgage.

On the next line below, is the monthly mortgage requirement per dollar; "f/12."

The unrecaptured mortgage balance per original dollar at the end of the projection term is at the top of each projection bracket.

Positive Mortgage Coefficients:

Although the normal application of the mortgage coefficient is in the equation:

$$r = Y - MC$$

A rare exception occurs when equity yield "Y" is *less* than mortgage interest rate "I." Obviously, this would cause the basic rate "r" to be greater than "Y." In other words, if "Y" were 4% and "I" were 6%, the mortgage rate would cause the basic rate "r" to exceed 4%. In such cases, the effect of the coefficient is positive. Please note that positive coefficients in Table C are underlined and printed in light face italics or followed by minus signs. When they are used, the equation is:

$$r = Y + MC$$

Problems Involving Use of Table C:

(1) Ten-year projection of cash flow income is stabilized at $24,342 per year. Mortgage money to help finance purchase is available up to 70 per cent of acceptable appraisal with interest at 5½ per cent to be fully amortized in twenty years.
Allow for a 15 per cent decline in over-all property value in ten years, and appraise this property to yield 10 per cent on the equity investment.

Solution:

Table reference, 20 year amortization, I = 5½%, 10 year bracket; C = .0404; sinking fund factor, same line, equals .0628.

Y	.10000
Less MC; .70 × .0404	.02828
Basic Rate	.07172
Add depreciation; .15 × .0628	.00942
Composite Cap Rate	.08114

$$\text{Appraisal; } \frac{d}{R} = \frac{24342}{.08114} = \$300{,}000$$

(2) Prospective purchaser of an office building has commitment for a $900,000 loan at 5¼% to be amortized in 25 years. Land value has been established at $250,000. Book depreciation on building will be reserved at 2½% per year. Ten year projection of income has been stabilized at $94,000 per year.

Appraise this property to yield 11 per cent on equity after book depreciation on building; i.e., 25 per cent in 10 years.

Solution:

$$\text{Stated factors: } M = \frac{900{,}000}{V};\ Y = .11$$

$$\text{Depreciation} = \left(1 - \frac{250{,}000}{V}\right) \times .25;\ R = \frac{\$94{,}000}{V}$$

Table reference: 25 year amortization, "I" 5¼%, 10 year bracket, "Y" at 11 per cent; $C = .0533$; $1/S_{\overline{n}|} = .0598$

$$MC = \frac{\$900{,}000 \times .0533}{V} = \frac{\$47{,}970}{V}$$

$$\text{"dep"} = \left(1 - \frac{\$250{,}000}{V}\right) .25 \times .0598 = .01495 - \frac{\$3{,}737}{V}$$

$$Y - MC + \text{dep } 1/S_{\overline{n}|} = R$$

Substitution of quantities:

$$.11 - \frac{47{,}970}{V} + .01495 - \frac{3{,}737}{V} = \frac{94{,}000}{V}$$

By gathering and transposition:

$$.11 + .01495 = \frac{\$94{,}000 + \$47{,}970 + \$3{,}737}{V} \text{ or } .12495 = \frac{\$145{,}707}{V}$$

$$\text{And } V = \frac{145{,}707}{.12495} = \$1{,}166{,}122$$

Appraised Value, say: $1,166,000

(3) *Triple Rate Structure*

Ten Year Income Projection stabilized at $18,720 per year; 60 per cent, first mortgage available at 5½% per cent, 20 year amortization; 25%, second mortgage available at 7 per cent, 10 year amortization. Allow for 20 per cent depreciation in 10 years and appraise to yield 15 per cent on equity.

Solution:

Coefficients from Table C; 10 years at 15 per cent.

First Mortgage .0855
Second Mortgage .0598
Sinking Fund Factor .0493

Y		.15000
Less MC, first mtg. .60 × .0855	.05130	
MC, second mtg. .25 × .0598	.01495	.06625
Basic Rate		.08375
Plus dep. .20 × .0493		.00986
Composite Rate		.09361

$$\text{Appraisal; } \frac{18{,}720}{.09361} = \$199{,}979, \text{ Say } \$200{,}000$$

(4) *Estimating Prospects for Equity Yield:*

The yield on equity investment will be a product of three conditions:

(1) Net cash flow income to equity after mortgage installments.
(2) Time interval from date of purchase to date of reversion.
(3) Amount of cash reversion to equity.

Although the time interval and the amount of reversion are very important, it is obvious that neither of them can be reliably predicted. The only things we know about them are: (a) the shorter the time interval is, the greater the impact of any value change on yield; and (b) optimum opportunity for reversion will probably occur within the first ten years after purchase.

Therefore, the most plausible and explicable procedure is to derive an over-all or composite capitalization rate, "R" from the best available market date, select a range of yields from high to low and calculate the value changes which must occur at any time during the projection for any yield within the range. When this test reveals that a substantial amount of depreciation can occur without reducing the yield below a reasonably satisfactory limit and that it requires no more than a steady market or a modest amount of appreciation to make the yield exceptionally attractive, it provides convincing evidence that the appraisal presents a price at which the property could be sold.

The amount of any decline or increase in over-all property value during any projection period for realization of any yield "Y" is the quotient of the difference between "R" and "r" when divided by the sinking fund factor at "Y" for the projection period.

When "R" is greater than "r," the quotient will be "depreciation." And when "r" is greater than "R," the quotient will be "appreciation."

Example:

To explain this clearly, let us move slowly, step by step, through a simple demonstration.

Suppose a review of recent sales indicates that by comparison our subject of appraisal should sell at about 6.7 times gross rent.

We wish to interpret this in terms of probable yield to equity.

After allowance for vacancies, expenses and cost of appurtenances which may have to be replaced within 10 years, we find that net cash flow income, before mortgage installments, should average about 55 per cent of gross rent.

If we call gross rent "G," we can derive the indicated over-all capitalization rate "R" as follows:

$$R = \frac{d}{V}; \ .55\ G = d \text{ and } 6.7\ G = V$$

Therefore,

$$R = \frac{.55\ G}{6.7\ G}$$

The "G's" cancel out, and we have:

$$R = \frac{.55}{6.7} = .082089, \text{ Say } .0821$$

The money market informs us that a typical buyer could obtain mortgage funds up to 70 per cent of acceptable appraisal with full amortization in twenty years by level monthly installments including interest at 5½ per cent per annum. Acceptability of the appraisal will hinge on whether or not prospects for equity yield are sufficient to attract a prudent buyer.

In this case, we will select an equity yield range of 15% to 6%, and our first step is to calculate the value change, which must occur in five years for the 15 per cent yield.

Referring to the "C" Table, twenty year amortization, 4¾ per cent to 6 per cent, moving down the 5½ per cent interest column to the 15 per cent equity yield line in the five year projection bracket, we find the mortgage coefficient "C" is .0909. On the same line, in the right-hand column, we find the applicable sinking fund factor is .1483. So we now know:

$$Y = .15;\ M = .70;\ C = .0909;\ 1/S_{\overline{n|}} = .1483$$

and

"R" to be tested is .0821

Substituting these quantities for symbols, we have:

$$r = .15 - (.70 \times .0909) = .15 - .06363 = .08637$$

Since "r" is greater than "R," appreciation is required and is calculated:

$$\text{app.} = \frac{.08637 - .0821}{.1483} = \frac{.00427}{.1483} = .0288$$

The property value must increase 2.88 per cent in five years for an equity yield of 15 per cent.

Referring to the 6 per cent equity yield line in the same column and same bracket of the same table, we find the mortgage coefficient "C" is .0055, and the applicable sinking fund factor in the right-hand column is .1774.

Again substituting quantities for symbols and proceeding as before,

$$r = .06 - (.70 \times .0055) = .06 - .00385 = .05615$$

Since "r" is now less than "R," depreciation is required and is calculated:

$$\text{dep} = \frac{.0821 - .05615}{.1774} = \frac{.02595}{.1774} = .1463$$

If the property value declines 14.63 per cent in five years, equity yield will be 6 per cent.

Next let us move down to the 10 year projection bracket of the same table. In the 5½ per cent interest rate column on the 15 per cent equity yield line, we find "C" is .0855 and the applicable sinking fund factor in the right-hand column is .0493. Therefore,

$$r = .15 - (.70 \times .0855) = .15 - .05985 = .09015$$

Again "r" is greater than "R," and we calculate required appreciation:

$$\text{app} = \frac{.09015 - .0821}{.0493} = \frac{.00805}{.0493} = .1633$$

Property value would have to increase about 16⅓ per cent in ten years for an equity yield of 15 per cent. It is noteworthy that the required increase in 10 years is almost six times as much as that for five years for the same yield.

On the 6 per cent equity yield line in the 10 year bracket, we find "C" is .0052 and the applicable sinking fund factor is .0759. The calculation of required value change is:

$$r = .06 - (.70 \times .0052) = .06 - .00364 = .05636$$

Again "r" is less than "R," and the required decline in value is:

$$\text{dep} = \frac{.0821 - .05636}{.0759} = \frac{.02574}{.0759} = .3391$$

Equity yield will be 6 per cent if the value of the property declines 33.91 per cent in 10 years.

In recapitulation we have:

	REQUIRED VALUE CHANGES	
Equity Yield	*In 5 Years*	*In 10 Years*
6%	14.63% dep.	33.91% dep.
15%	2.88% app.	16.33% app.

The Effect of Book Depreciation:

Let us assume that a normal book depreciation allowance would be based on a 40 year building life and that 80 per cent of the appraisal would be allocated to the building. The book depreciation rate on the building would be 2½ per cent per year or 25 per cent in 10 years. If there were no offsetting change in land value and if market value of the property should actually decline according to book depreciation, the over-all property value decline in 10 years would be 80 per cent of 25 per cent or 20 per cent.

The result of these calculations can be used in drawing a graph which will cover the market value change, which must occur at any time during the 10 year period for any equity yield from 6 per cent to 15 per cent.

The graphic analysis form is a block of ½ inch squares. A heavy horizontal line near the center represents appraised value or assumed purchase price. The scales are:

horizontal 1″ = 2 years
vertical 1″ = 20%

Therefore, each half inch in a horizontal direction represents one year. Each half inch in a vertical direction above the appraised value line represents 10 per cent appreciation and each half inch below it represents 10 per cent depreciation.

A draftsman's or ship curve (designated as #60 by some manufacturers and obtainable from an artists or drafting supply store) can be used in plotting value changes on the graph. A modification of such a curve, with reference points for depreciation and appreciation graduated at 20 points to the inch, can also be prepared (see Technical Notes, page 136 for instructions and pattern for making an appropriately sized curve).

In our example we would refer to the recapitulation of required value changes at five years. Placing the scale on the five year vertical where "Purchase Price" coincides with "Appraised Value," we measure down to 14.63% depreciation and mark the point with a circled dot. We then measure up the same vertical to 2.88% appreciation and mark that point with a circled dot.

Next we place our scale on the 10 year vertical, refer to the required 10 year value changes, measure down to 33.91% depreciation and mark that point with a circled dot. Then measure up the same vertical to 16.33% appreciation and mark that point.

Now we have three reference points for drawing each yield line. The first one is at the point of beginning on the Appraised Value level. Place the curve so that its edge coincides with that point and 14.63% depreciation on the five year vertical and 33.91% depreciation on the 10 year vertical. Hold the curve firmly and draw a line along its edge. The position of this line in relation to the depreciation lines on the form will indicate the amount of value decline the property will have to suffer at any time during 10 years for an equity yield of 6%.

PLATE II

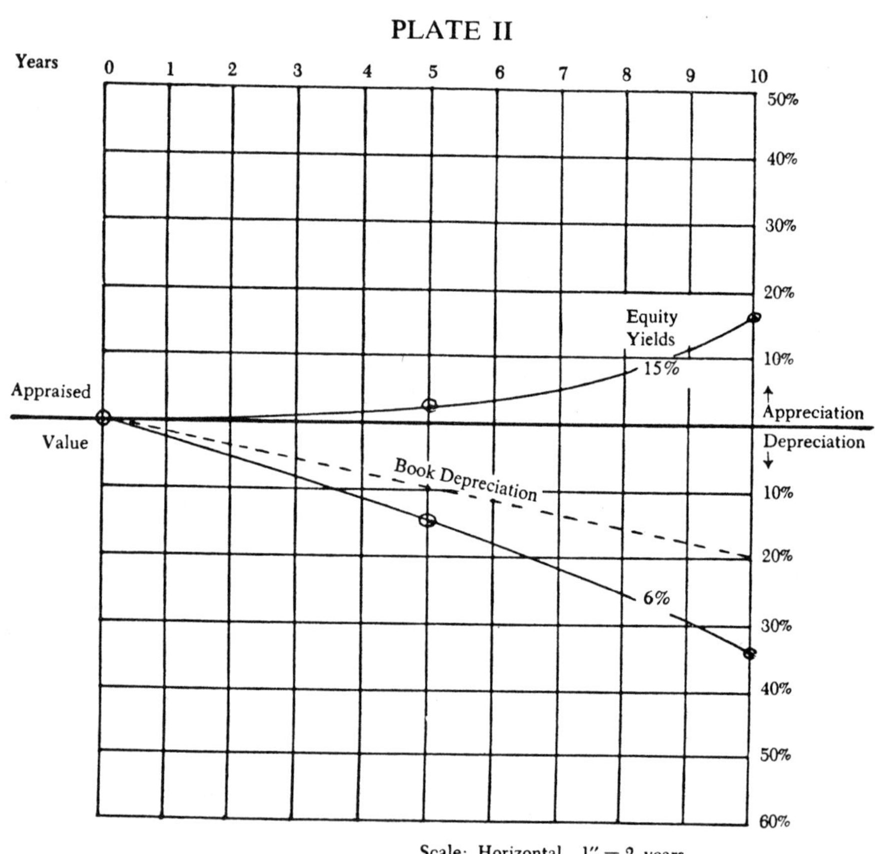

Scale: Horizontal 1″ = 2 years
Vertical 1″ = 20%

Now turn the curve over, place its edge where it touches the appraised value level at the point beginning, the 2.88% appreciation point on the 5 year vertical and 16.33% appreciation point on the 10 year vertical. Draw a line along the edge of the curve. The position of this line in relation to the appreciation lines on the form will indicate the value increase which must occur at any time during 10 years for equity yield of 15 per cent.

An approximation of the value change required for any yield from 6% to 15% can be judged by visual interpolation of distances between the 6% and 15% curves at any point.

Now place the straight edge of the scale from the appraised value level at the point of beginning to the 20 per cent depreciation point on the 10 year vertical. Draw a straight dotted line which will indicate the yield level if the property should be sold at "book value" at any time. At first glance, we can see that equity yield will be substantially better than 6 per cent in this event. (See Plate I.)

Finally, to make the graphic analysis so it can be read quickly and interpolated at a glance, we would calculate required value changes for intermediate yields. Say 9 per cent and 12 per cent and draw these curves on the form.

To expedite the entire process in practical application, we would select three or four yields at the start, enter all the needed factors from the "C" table, and make the calculations in tabular form, as set forth below:

5 Years.		*"r"*	*dif.*		
"Y"	"C"	*Y — .70C*	*.0821 — "r"*	$1/S_{\overline{n}\vert}$	*Change %*
.06	.0055	.05615	.02595	÷ .1774	14.63 dep.
.09	.0338	.06634	.01576	÷ .1671	9.43 dep.
.12	.0623	.07639	.00571	÷ .1574	3.63 dep.
.15	.0909	.08637	.00427+	÷ .1483	2.88 app.

10 Years		*"r"*	*dif.*		
"Y"	"C"	*Y — .70C*	*.0821 — "r"*	$1/S_{\overline{n}\vert}$	*Change %*
.06	.0052	.05636	.02574	÷ .0759	33.91 dep.
.09	.0315	.06795	.01415	÷ .0658	21.50 dep.
.12	.0583	.07919	.00291	÷ .0570	5.10 dep.
.15	.0855	.09015	.00805+	÷ .0493	16.33 app.

The graph is completed by adding the 9% and 12% yield curves. (See Plate III.)

PLATE III

ANALYSIS OF 0821 CAPITALIZATION RATE

Prospects for yield on equity investment assuming purchase at appraised value 70% financed by 20 year level payment loan @ 5½% interest.

Equity Yield Will be:	If Property Value: in 5 Years	in 10 Years
6%	Declines, 14.63%	Declines, 33.91%
9%	" 9.43%	" 21.50%
12%	" 3.63%	" 5.10%
15%	Increases; 2.88%	Increases; 16.33%

Dotted line locates book depreciation at 2½% per yr. on building.

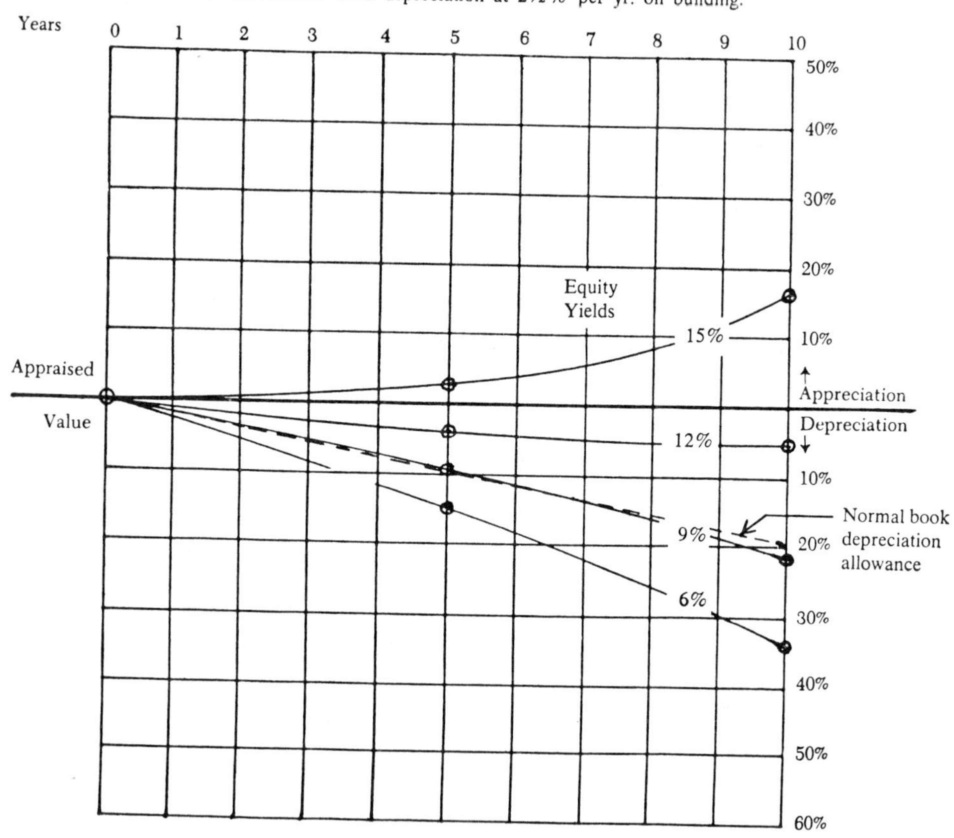

Scale: Horizontal 1″ = 2 years
Vertical 1″ = 20%

Value changes which must occur at any time during the first 10 years for a considerable range of yields can be judged by noting the positions of the yield curves in relation to depreciation and appreciation levels.

In this example, the space interval from one yield curve to the next represents three percentage points. Thus to judge the value decline which must occur at any time for an equity yield of 10 per cent, we would locate a point at one third the distance from the 9 per cent curve to the 12 per cent curve. For instance, at 9 years, this would be at about the 15 per cent depreciation level.

For any yield from 6% to 15%, we judge required value changes either by the location of a captioned curve or by visual interpolation of spaces between captioned curves.

Required value changes for yields of several percentage points outside the 6% to 15% range can be judged by extrapolation. At five years, for example, the distance from the 15% yield curve to the 10% appreciation level is about the same as the distance from the 12% yield curve to the 15% yield curve. The difference from 12% to 15% is 3%, and 3% added to 15% equals 18%.

Hence we know the equity investor would realize a yield of about 18% if he purchased the property at appraised value and sold it five years later at 10% above that price.

Obviously, we can go on indefinitely reading the graph and speculating as to possibilities under an endless variety of future market conditions.

A primary advantage of the graphic analysis as an exhibit in the appraisal report is that it provides the appraisal reviewer with a quick and specific method for judging the quality of the appraisal as an estimate of market value.

Having satisfied himself as to the property description and income projection, a look at the graph will give him an immediate impression as to whether or not the subject has market appeal at appraised value. If it clearly indicates a very attractive investment opportunity, there is no question in his mind as to the validity of the appraisal. On the other hand, if it reveals poor prospects for an equity yield substantially in excess of the mortgage interest rate, he knows the appraisal is too high. A summary of the valuation and interpretation of the analysis might appear in the report about as follows:

Let us say gross annual rent with full occupancy would be $74,700 and the 10 year budget for expenses and contingencies averages $33,600 per year leaving $41,100 as projected average cash flow:

Valuation:

$41,100/.0821 = $500,609; Round to $500,000

Allocation:

Land	$100,000	
Improvements	400,000	80%
Total	$500,000	

Assumed Composition of Purchase Capital & Income Distribution:

	Capital		*Income*
Mortgage Money, 70%	$350,000	× .08256	$28,896*
Equity Investment, 30%	150,000		12,204
Total Cash to Seller	$500,000		$41,100

Indicated Average Equity Dividend:

12,204/150,000 = 8.14%

* The annual requirement "f" per dollar of mortgage money is immediately below the interest rate in the "C" table. In this case "f" = .08256.

Investment Analysis:

"Income imputed to the mortgage component of purchase capital provides for full recapture of 70% of the total valuation in 20 years with interest at 5½%. This reduction in debt should result in a substantial build-up of equity value.

For accounting purposes, a typical buyer would probably take a depreciation deduction of 2½% per year against the allocation to improvement. It is common knowledge, however, that actual market values move both up and down. They never move at a fixed annual rate in either direction over long spans of time. It is not unusual for increasing land values, increasing construction costs and other economic forces to surpass the effect of age to the extent that property of the subject type is resold at a substantial profit several years after purchase. This could easily happen in this case.

Since there is no reliable way to predict either a specific decline or increase in the future value of the property, we have not made any specific allowances for depreciation or appreciation. Instead, we have made an analysis which shows prospects for yield on the equity investment in case of either decline or increase in value.

Among other things, this shows the equity yield would be from about 13% to 14% if the property were purchased at appraised value and resold at the same price any time within 10 years. It would be about 9% with pretty good tax shelter if market value should actually decline according to the normal accounting deduction for depreciation. Since properties of the subject type usually sell for more than book depreciated value, the prospect is excellent for a yield of 10% or better. We believe this would be sufficient to attract a well informed and prudent buyer. It is therefore our opinion that $500,000 represents a sound and obtainable market value for the subject."

AUXILIARY TABLES Ca, Cp, and Cy

These tables supplement the table of pre-computed mortgage coefficients. They present factors to aid in the calculation of mortgage coefficients outside the scope of Table "C."

Table "Ca": Annual Constant Financing:

To simplify the determination of periodic installments, some financial institutions quote mortgage requirements on the basis of rounded over-all annual rates covering interest and amortization. An example would be 7½ per cent including interest at 5½ per cent. In this case, the annual cost of a $100,000 loan would be $7,500, and monthly installments would be one-twelfth of $7,500 or $625. Full amortization terms generally are in years and fractions thereof. At 7½ per cent with interest at 5½ per cent it would take about 24 years and 2 months for full recapture.

Table "Ca" presents factors which will be helpful in calculating capitalization rates where the availability of mortgage money is quoted on the basis of a rounded annual constant rate.

Scope:

Mortgage interest rates, 4 per cent to 12 per cent by ¼ per cent increments.

Annual constants "f" from 1 per cent above mortgage interest rate increasing by ¼ per cent increments to point where full amortization occurs in about ten years.

Arrangements:

Each tabular page pertains to one mortgage interest rate shown at the top of the page. This is the index to the desired table.

First Column, "f," the annual constant.

Second Column, full amortization term in years and months.

Next four columns, "P," fraction of mortgage amortized in 5, 10, 15, and 20 years.

Last column, constant multiplier of (Sp — 1) to compute "P," fraction amortized in any given number of periods. See Table "Cp" for (Sp — 1).

Sinking Fund Factors for 5, 10, 15, and 20 years with various equity yields are shown at the bottom of each page.

Table Cp:

This table presents mortgage components for from 1 to 40 years with interest rates from 3 per cent to 12% per cent.

The first column of each pair, captioned S — 1, is (Sp — 1) for calculating the fraction of mortgage amortized.

The second column presents the annual requirement "f" per dollar of mortgage based on monthly installment financing.

Table Cy:

Despite more than two decades of an inflation minded real estate market, the phrase "net income before depreciation" became so firmly established in appraisal education and in the minds of many practitioners that only the heretic would dare an allowance for "appreciation."

Since future depreciation and appreciation are imponderables which cannot be predicted with any degree of certainty, the question is, "Why be so presumptuous as to try?" It seems more plausible to obtain an overall capitalization rate from the best available market information and test it for plus and minus value changes which would produce a broad range of investment yields.

There is no question of the propriety of projecting income for a comparatively short term on a stabilized or average basis by allowing for vacancies and other contingencies. But, what about the month-to-month or year-to-year lease situation where the landlord has a waiting list with no vacancies? Contingent allowances at the point of beginning may unduly penalize the property. We have no way of knowing when vacancies will occur nor do we know that they will not be offset by rental increases between now and when they do occur.

Table Cy has been recalculated to include both the sinking fund factor and an income adjustment factor indicated by symbol "J" in the right-hand column under each equity yield rate.

Combined use of both factors facilitates investment analysis where the value to be tested is the result of capitalizing the actual net cash flow income before debt service as it is at time of appraisal. In other words, there are no contingent allowances or other efforts to project income on a stabilized or average basis.

The analysis will show decreases and increases in net cash flow income as well as corresponding decreases and increases in overall property value that would produce any selected group of equity yields. In other words, yield curves on the graphic analysis form will present changes in *both* income and property value.

Rules for use of adjustment factor "J" are as follows:

For analysis of a given cap. rate "R" to show changes in both income and value for any equity yield:

$$\frac{r - R}{RJ + 1/s_{\overline{n}|}} = \text{dep. or app.}$$

Note: If quotient is negative, it will represent the decline in both income and value for the selected yield. If it is positive, it will represent the increase in both income and value for the selected yield.

To compute overall cap. rate "R" for any given change in income and value, i.e., (depreciation or appreciation) with any equity yield:

$$\frac{r + \text{dep. } 1/s_{\overline{n}|}}{1 - \text{dep. J}} = R$$

$$\frac{r - \text{app. } 1/s_{\overline{n}|}}{1 + \text{app. J}} = R$$

Formula for calculating "J" is:

$$1/s_{\overline{n}|}\left(\frac{N}{1 - V^n} - \frac{1}{Y}\right) = J$$

N = Projection years

$1/s_{\overline{n}|}$ and V^n are at equity yield Y for N years

The reader will probably have little need for this formula because Table Cy covers equity yields from 3% to 30% and for from 1 to 40 years.

In the following example, basic rates "r" and sinking fund factors were obtained from the 25-year amortization, 75% mortage capitalization rate table. "J" factors are from Table Cy. The arithmetic by use of any calculating machine is expedited by entering all these factors on a form at the start.

Auxiliary Table "Cy"

Subject:—

60-unit garden apartment project, 3 years old. Well located in a growing neighborhood. Has had practically 100% occupancy since completion.

Salient Facts:—

1.	Gross annual rent 100% occupancy	$192,540
2.	Audited collection, last 12 months	$191,896
3.	Audited expenses, last 12 months	72,464
	Net Income, last 12 months	$119,432

4. Apartments are rented on a year-to-year basis. We do not know what rent and expenses will be next year or any year thereafter.
5. A purchaser can finance 75% of acceptable appraisal by mortgage to be amortized in 25 years by level monthly installments including interest based on 9¼% per annum. The annual constant is .10284 per dollar.
6. Our best advice from brokers is that this property can be sold with the prospect of a 12% cash flow dividend to the equity investor after debt service.

Problem:—

Capitalize current income on the basis of #5 and #6 and analyze the result for 5- and 10-year income and value changes for equity yields of 8%, 12%, 16% and 20%.

Solution:—

Mortgage .75 × .10284 = .07713
Equity .25 × .12000 = .03000
Overall cap. rate, R .10713

Capitalized Value: 119432/.10713 = $1,114,832+
say $1,114,000

Adjustment for R, 119,432/1,114,000 = .10721

Distribution:

Purchase Capital			*Income*
Mortgage	$ 835,500	× .10284	$ 85,087.32
Equity Investment	278,500	× .12332	34,344.68
	$1,114,000		$119,432.00

Auxiliary Table "Cy"

FUTURE INCOME AND VALUE CHANGES FOR INDICATED YIELDS

R .10721

Y	Projection yrs. 5	Projection yrs. 10
8%	r 088766 $1/s_{\overline{n}\rceil}$ .1705 R .107210 XJ .5375 = .0576 −018444 ÷ .2281 = Change −.0808	r 088374 $1/s_{\overline{n}\rceil}$ .0690 R .10721 XJ .4230 = .0453 −.018836 ÷ .1143 = Change −.1648
12%	r .099406 $1/s_{\overline{n}\rceil}$ .1574 R .10721 XJ .5077 = .0544 −007804 ÷ .2118 = Change −.0368	r .099902 $1/s_{\overline{n}\rceil}$ .0570 R .10721 XJ .3655 = .0392 .007308 ÷ .0962 = Change −0760
16%	r .109995 $1/s_{\overline{n}\rceil}$ .1454 R .10721 XJ .4789 = .0513 +.002785 ÷ .1967 = Change + 0142	r .111180 $1/s_{\overline{n}\rceil}$ .0469 R .10721 XJ .3133 = .0336 +.00397 ÷ .0805 = Change +.0493
20%	r .120536 $1/s_{\overline{n}\rceil}$ .1344 R .10721 XJ .4514 = .0484 +.013326 ÷ .1828 = Change +.0729	r .122243 $1/s_{\overline{n}\rceil}$ .0325 R .10721 XJ .2668 = .0286 +.015033 ÷ .0671 = Change +.2240
	r ____ $1/s_{\overline{n}\rceil}$ ____ R ____ XJ ____ ____ ____ ÷ ____ = Change ____	r ____ $1/s_{\overline{n}\rceil}$ ____ R ____ XJ ____ ____ ____ ÷ ____ = Change ____
	r ____ $1/s_{\overline{n}\rceil}$ ____ R ____ XJ ____ ____ ____ ÷ ____ = Change ____	r ____ $1/s_{\overline{n}\rceil}$ ____ R ____ XJ ____ ____ ____ ÷ ____ = Change ____

PLATE IV

ANALYSIS OF .10721 CAPITALIZATION RATE

Prospects for yield on equity investment assuming purchase at appraised value 75% financed by 25-year level payment loan at 9¼% interest.

Yield curves below and above the central "appraised value" line indicate declines and increases in net cash flow income before mortgage payments as well as declines and increases in overall property values which would result in the equity yield written on each curve.

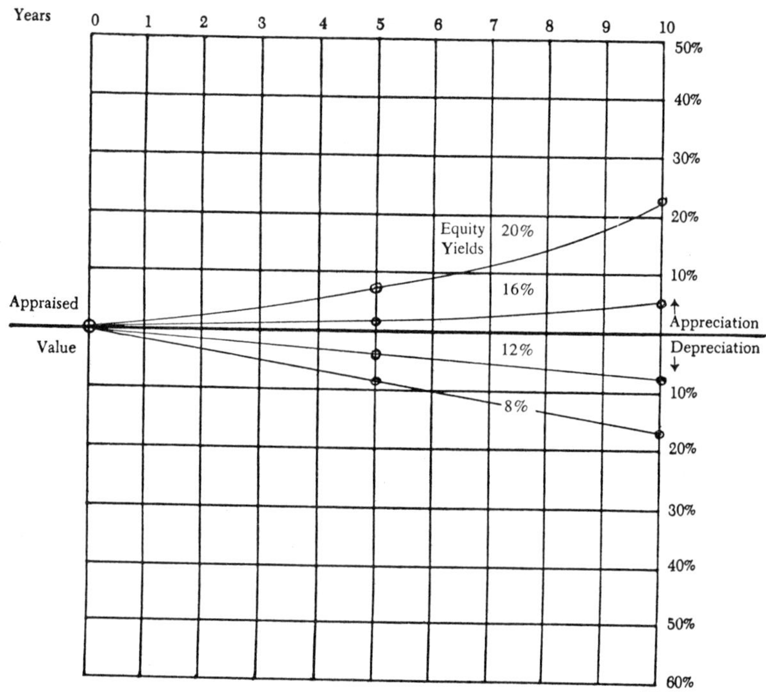

It is apparent that yield to equity will be 15% or better if earnings of the property remain at about the current level.

OTHER PROBLEMS INVOLVING USE OF AUXILIARY TABLES Ca, Cp, and Cy

1. Stabilized income projected 10 years at $17,120 per year. Mortgage money to help finance purchase is available to 75 per cent of acceptable appraisal with monthly installments based on 8 per cent annual constant including interest at 5¾ per cent.

   Allow for 15 per cent property value decline in 10 years, and appraise this property to yield 12 per cent on equity.

Solution:

From Table Ca at I = 5¾ %

Formulas:

$$Y + P\ 1/S_{\overline{n}|} - f = C$$
$$Y - MC + dep\ 1/S_{\overline{n}|} = R$$
$$d/R = V$$

Equity Yield, "Y"	.1200
Plus P $1/S_{\overline{n}|}$; .303140 × .0570	.01728
Adjusted "Y"	.13728
Less "f" (adjusted I)	.08000
Mortgage coefficient, "C"	.05728
Equity Yield, "Y"	.12000
Less MC; .75 × .05728	.04296
Basic rate, "r"	.07704
Plus dep $1/S_{\overline{n}|}$; .15 × .0570	.00855
Over-all capitalization rate "R"	.08559

Valuation, over-all rate called .0856

$$V = 17120/.0856 = \$200{,}000$$

2. A supermarket lease providing a net annual income of $21,000 per year will expire in 17 years. Mortgage money is available at 75 per cent of acceptable appraisal on 7¾ per cent annual constant basis including interest at 5½ per cent. Allow for 40 per cent property value decline in 17 years, and appraise to yield 10 per cent on equity.

Solution:

Tables Ca, Cp, and Cy

Formulas:

$$(f/I - 1)\ (Sp - 1) = P$$

Other formulas same as last problem. Sp − 1 at 5½ %, 1.5418, $1/S_{\overline{n}|}$ 17 years from Table, Cy = .0247 (f/I − 1) from Table Ca = .409091

$$P = .409091 \times 1.5418 = .630736$$

Equity Yield, "Y"	.10000
Plus P $1/S_{\overline{n}|}$; .630736 × .0247	.01558
Adjústed "Y"	.11558
Less "f"	.07750
Mortgage coefficient "C"	.03808
Equity Yield, "Y"	.10000
Less MC, .75 × .03808	.02856
Basic rate "r"	.07144
Plus dep $1/S_{\overline{n}|}$, .40 × .0247	.00988
Over-all Cap. rate, "R"	.08132

Valuation:

$21,000/.08132 = $258,239
Say $258,000

3. A single occupant retail store property is offered for sale subject to the unexpired term of an existing lease, and the unamortized balance of an existing mortgage.

   The unexpired terms of the lease is 12 years. It produces $38,000 per year in net cash flow. The present balance of the mortgage is $416,972, and the required monthly installment is $2,500 including interest at 4½ per cent per annum.

   Price this property to yield 10 per cent on the equity investment after allowance for a decline of 25 per cent in value of the property in 12 years.

Solution:

Tables Cp and Cy

Quantities provided by the statement of the problem are:

Income projection terms, 12 years,

$$Y = .10;\ I = .045;\ M = \frac{\$416{,}972}{V}$$

$$f = \frac{2{,}500 \times 12}{416{,}972} = \frac{30{,}000}{416{,}972} = .071947$$

$$\frac{f}{I} - 1 = \frac{.071947}{.045} - 1 = .5988$$

$$dep = .25;\quad R = \frac{\$38{,}000}{V}$$

By substitution in the equation:

$$Y - MC + \text{dep } 1/S_{\overline{n}|} = R$$

$$.10 - \frac{416{,}972 \times C}{V} + .25\ 1/S_{\overline{n}|} = \frac{38{,}000}{V}$$

Compute the mortgage coefficient, "C," add for depreciation, and write an equation in which the only unknown quantity is "V."

Factors needed for these computations are:

> Sp — 1 at 4½%, 12 years (Table Cp) = .7143
> Sinking fund factor at 10 per cent, 12 years (Table Cy) = .0468
> $P = (f/I - 1)(Sp - 1) = .5988 \times .7143 = .4277$

Calculation for "C";

Equity yield, "Y"	.1000
Plus P $1/S_{\overline{n}|}$; .4277 × .0468	.0200
Adjusted "Y"	.1200
Less Mortgage factor "f"	.071947
Mortgage Coefficient, "C"	.048053

Thus:

$$MC = \frac{416{,}972 \times .048053}{V} = \frac{\$20{,}037}{V}$$

The depreciation requirement is:

$$\text{dep } 1/S_{\overline{n}|} = .25 \times .0468 = .0117$$

Hence, the equation is:

$$.10 - \frac{\$20{,}037}{V} + .0117 = \frac{\$38{,}000}{V}$$

And by transposition:

$$.10 + .0117 = \frac{38{,}000 + 20{,}037}{V}; \text{ or } .1117 = \frac{\$58{,}037}{V}$$

and

$$V = \frac{58{,}037}{.1117} \text{ which equals } \$519{,}579$$

In practice we would omit some of the explanatory steps, calculate "P" and "C" and proceed as follows:

Income	$38,000
Adjustment for mortgage, 416,972 × .048053	20,037
Adjusted amount to be capitalized	$58,037

Equity "Y"	.1000
Depreciation .25 × .0468	.0117
Adjusted cap. rate	.1117

$$\text{Valuation: } \frac{58,037}{.1117} = \$519,579, \text{ Say } \$519,600$$

Arithmetic Check:

	Capital	*Income*
Mortgage	$416,972	$30,000
Equity Investment	102,628	8,000
Totals	$519,600	$38,000

If this arithmetic is correct, the present value of the equity dividend of $8,000 per year for 12 years plus the present value of the assumed equity reversion deferred 12 years at 10 per cent should approximate $102,628. Assumed property reversion, depreciated 25%:

$519,600 × .75 (assumed property reversion)	$389,700

Mortgage balance:

1 − P = 1 − .4277 = .5723; $416,972 × .5723	238,633
Assumed Equity Reversion	$151,067

Present value income and reversion discounted 12 years at 10%.

Income, $8,000 × 6.813692	$ 54,509
Reversion, $151,067 × .318631	48,135
	$102,644
Investment	102,628
Decimal rounding difference	16

This example illustrates the seller's advantage in being able to offer property subject to a favorable existing mortgage. If the mortgage condition were ignored in this case, appraisal by conventional methods in a period of high interest rates would reduce the indicated value of the owner's equity by a very substantial amount.

ADJUSTMENTS FOR DISCOUNTED MORTGAGE FINANCING

When purchase capital includes a discounted mortgage, the equity buyer must pay interest and amortization installments on more money than he actually receives. In effect, this increases the mortgage interest rate and retards purchase capital recapture through amortization. It also decreases the actual ratio of mortgage money to property value.

If we call the mortgage discount "k," we can calculate the mortgage coefficient of the capitalization rate by use of this formula:

$$C = Y - \frac{f - 1/s_{\overline{n|}}\,(P - k)}{1 - k}$$

Symbols "f" and "P" represent the quantities we would use if there were no discount. The discount "k" is expressed as a decimal fraction, i.e. 15% would be written .15 and 1 — k would be .85.

The ratio of mortgage money to value must be adjusted as follows:

$$M\,(1 - k) = \text{adjusted "M"}$$

Example:

Compute the overall capitalization rate for a 15% equity yield in the following situation.

1st Mortgage 60% of "V" at 5¼% interest to be amortized in 20 years.

2nd Mortgage 30% of "V" before discount at 6% interest to be amortized in 15 years. This mortgage to be sold at 15% discount.

Allow for 20% depreciation in a 10 year projection.

Solution:

1st mortgage coefficient from Table C; .0874. Sinking fund factor at Y = 15% same page .0493.

2nd mortgage factors before adjustment, Table C, 15 year amortization.

$$\begin{aligned} f &= .10128 \\ P &= 1 - .436255 = .563745 \\ 1 - k &= 1 - .15 = .85 \\ P - k &= .563740 - .15 = .413745 \end{aligned}$$

2nd mortgage coefficient by formula.

$$C = .15 - \frac{.10128 - (.0493 \times .413745)}{.85}$$

which equals

$$.15 - \frac{.080882}{.85} = .15 - .095155 = .054845$$

adjusted "M" = .30 × .85 = .255

Calculation for overall capitalization rate:

Y		.150000
Less M.C. 1st mtg. 60 × .0874	.052440	
Less M.C. 2nd mtg. .255 × .054845	.013985	.066425
Basic cap. rate		.083575
Plus depreciation .20 × .0493		.009860
Overall Capitalization Rate		.093435

Arithmetic Check:
Assume income at $93,435 and value of $1,000,000.

	Capital		Income
1st Mtg.	$ 600,000	× .08088	$ 48,528
2nd Mtg.	255,000	300,000 × .10128	30,384
Equity	145,000		14,523
	$1,000,000		$ 93,435

Assumed Reversion after 20% depreciation		$800,000
1st Mtg. balance; $600,000 × .627803	$376,682	
2nd Mtg. balance; $300,000 × .436255	130,877	507,559
Assumed Equity Reversion; 10 years		$292,441

Present Value Equity Income and Reversion at 15%.
Multipliers from columns 5 and 4 compound interest table.

Income $14,523 × 5.018769	$ 72,887
Reversion $292,441 × .247185	72,287
Total	$145,174
Assumed Investment	145,000
Rounding difference	$ 174

V

BASIC CAPITALIZATION RATE TABLES WITH 75% and 66⅔% MORTGAGE FINANCING

These tables were computed by use of mortgage coefficients from Table C.

With exception of the few rate combinations requiring use of positive coefficients, basic formula Y — MC was used to produce basic rate "r" as presented by the tables.* In other words:

The 75% Table presents "r" as calculated by formula;

$$r = Y - .75C$$

The 66⅔% Table presents "r" as calculated by formula;

$$r = Y - .66\tfrac{2}{3}C$$

* Note: Rate combinations involving positive coefficients were calculated as; $r = Y + .75C$ and $r = Y + .66\tfrac{2}{3}C$.

Scope of the 75% Table:

Mortgage amortization terms, 10 years to 30 years by 5 year increments.
Mortage interest rates, 3¼% to 12% by ¼% increments.

Income projection terms, 5 years to full amortization term by 5 year increments.

Equity yields, 5% to 20% by 1% increments.

Instructions for Finding Desired Rate "r":

1. Find amortization term at top of table.
2. Find pages on which mortgage interest rate appears.
3. Find desired income projection term bracket.
4. Read across on Equity Yield line to basic Capitalization Rate in mortgage interest rate column.

Supplementary Data:

Right hand column contains the sinking fund factors.

Immediately below the interest rate at the top of each column is the annual mortgage requirement "f" per dollar of mortgage.

The "coverage minimum rate" on the line below "f" is the lowest capitalization rate which can be used to produce a value in which projected income is sufficient to pay required mortgage installments. The unrecaptured mortgage balance per original dollar at the end of the projection term is at the top of each projection bracket.

Scope of the 66⅔% Table:

Scope of this table and supplementary data are the same as those of the 75% Table except that equity yields range from 4% to 15% by 1% increments.

Purchase Capital Structures:

Use of the 75% Table assumes purchase capital would be a combination of 75% mortgage money and a 25% cash equity investment.

Use of the 66⅔% Table assumes purchase capital would be a combination of 66⅔% mortgage money and a 33⅓% cash equity investment.

The basic reason for assuming specific mortgage and equity ratios should be kept in mind.

The margin of security for every real estate mortgage investment is the actual cash market value of the equity above the mortgage. The mortgage loan is never in jeopardy so long as the equity position can be sold for a substantial amount of cash.

Purchase capital and income are therefore, distributed to mortgage and equity with market attractiveness of the equity position as a primary objective.

This does not mean however, that the validity of the appraisal hinges on actual commitment of mortgage money in the amount and at the terms assumed in the appraisal. The fact that appraised value and income are specifically allocated to mortgage and equity provides information by which a prospective mortgage investor can evaluate the effect of any alternative amount and terms he may wish to consider.

A statement in the appraisal report covering this point will eliminate questions concerning it.

Problems Involving Use of The 75% Table:

(1) Net Income of a garden apartment is projected 10 years at an average of $21,800 per year. A typical buyer could borrow 75% of acceptable appraisal at 6% interest to be fully amortized in 20 years.
Allow for a 15% value decline in 10 years and appraise the property to yield 12% on a 25% equity investment.

Solution:

Basic rate from 75% Table	.07940
Adjust for "dep" $1/s_{\overline{n}|}$, .15 × .0570	.00855
Overall Cap. Rate, "R"	.08795

Appraisal:

$21,800/.08795 = $247,868
Say $248,000

(2) Net income from a super-market is projected on the basis of a 15 year lease at $18,400 per year. A 75% mortgage is available at 5¾% to be fully amortized in 20 years. Present market value of land is established at $90,000. Allow for 45% building depreciation in 15 years and appraise this property to yield 11% on equity.

Solution:

Basic rate from 75% Table (15 year bracket)		.0770
Sinking fund factor, same table		.0291
Income		$ 18,400
Less land requirement, $90,000 × .0770		6,930
Income imputed to building		$ 11,470
Basic rate	.0770	
Depreciation, .45 × .0291	.0131	
Overall Bldg. Cap. Rate	.0901	

Building Residual Valuation:

$11,470/.0901, $127,303 Rounded	$127,000
Add Land Value	90,000
Appraised Value	$217,000

(3) Make an analysis of the above appraisal showing overall changes in property value which must occur in 5 years and 10 years for equity yields of 7%, 10%, 13% and 16%.

Solution:

Overall Cap. Rate to be tested:

$$R = \frac{18,400}{217,000} = .0848$$

Distribution:

	Capital		Income
Mortgage 75%	$162,750 × .08436		$13,730
Equity 25%	54,250	.0861 div.	4,670
Cash to Seller..............	$217,000		$18,400

Basic Cap. Rate "r" from 5 year and 10 year brackets.

	5 Year Projection				*10 Year Projection*			
Equity Yield	*r*	*dif.*	$1/s_{\overline{n}\rvert}$	*% Change*	*r*	*dif.*	$1/s_{\overline{n}\rvert}$	*% Change*
7%	.0606	.0242	.1739	13.92 dep.	.0612	.0236	.0724	32.60 dep.
10%	.0693	.0155	.1638	9.46 dep.	.0713	.0135	.0628	21.50 dep.
13%	.0778	.0070	.1543	4.54 dep.	.0811	.0037	.0543	6.81 dep.
16%	.0864	.0016+	.1454	1.10 app.	.0906	.0058+	.0469	12.37 app.

Book depreciation on the building was allowed at 45% in 15 years or 3% per year. The commensurate amount in 10 years would be 30%. The ratio of building allocation to overall valuation is:

$$127000/217000 = .5853$$

a 30% decline in building value with no offsetting change in land value would cause a decline of 17.56% in overall property value; i.e.

$$.5853 \times .30 = .17559 \qquad \text{Say:} \quad 17.56\%$$

Suggestion to Students:

Use the above tabulation and book depreciation to draw a graphic analysis.

The Income Projection; Special Treatments:—

The importance of the income projection cannot be over-emphasized. The chapters on *Gross Income Estimates* and *Analysis of Expense* in the basic text, "The Appraisal of Real Estate" * treat this subject in such comprehensive fashion that the only need for addition pertains to the nature and philosophy of short term projections.

A study of performance records of typical rental properties will reveal income streams which fluctuate irregularly up and down from year to year. Net income will be up in years of high occupancy when nothing more than regular expenses are incurred. It will be down when there are substantial vacancies and when non-recurring expenses are involved in the replacement of worn-out equipment, appurtenances, etc.

Since there is no way to pin-point either the timing or the magnitude of the peaks and valleys of the fluctuating income stream, the best that can be done is to make adequate allowances for them on an average annual basis and thus project the equivalent of a level stream. If this is done on a reasonably reliable basis in a short projection, the arithmetic error due to time and magnitude of fluctuations will not be significant.

The analysis of prospects for equity investment yield normally shows that a substantial drop in market value can occur in conjunction with the lower level of yield rates selected for analysis. Naturally this generates questions concerning the propriety of the level income assumption.

Say the analysis indicates a market value decline of 20% can be suffered in conjunction with an equity yield rate of 8%. Does it not seem logical to expect that the decline in value would be accompanied by a commensurate decline in income?

Herein lies the importance of adequate allowance for income fluctuation. A 7% vacancy allowance, for instance, does not mean that exactly 7% of the rent roll will be lost every year by reason of vacancies. A property may enjoy virtually full occupancy for several years and then encounter a period of competition when vacancies amount to 20% or more. Naturally the net income will be down in such periods and so will the reversionary value of the property. However, this does not invalidate the projection or the analysis so long as the 7% annual allowance for vacancy is sufficient to cover average occupancy for the projection term.

In some special situations, however, the appraiser is confronted with problems in which the projection of an average income level for terms of 5 to 10 years is so highly speculative that he wishes to avoid it. Even though he knows the odds against error can be cushioned by use of exceptionally high yield rates, he would prefer to make an analysis which starts with income as he finds it at time of appraisal and allows for gradual decline or increase over the projection term.

This is a comparatively simple matter when the over-all capitalization rate is abstracted from market data. The differences between overall rate "R" and basic rates "r" are merely treated as straight line depreciation or

*** "The Appraisal of Real Estate"; The American Institute of Real Estate Appraisers. Chicago, Illinois, U.S.A.**

appreciation rates. In other words, they are not modified by the use of sinking fund factors as divisors. Here are some examples:—

(a) A furnished apartment building, rented on a month to month basis, is currently earning $50,000 per year. Market transactions indicate an overall capitalization rate of 12½%. Mortgage money is available to a typical buyer up to 75% of acceptable appraisal at 6¾% interest with full amortization in 15 years.

The high overall capitalization rate obviously indicates that buyers demand a hedge against declining income and value. The value indicated by this rate is:—

$$\$50{,}000/.125 = \$400{,}000$$

The required equity investment would be $100,000.

This is tested for yields of 12%, 16% and 20% with tabulation showing changes in value and income in a 10 year projection. Basic rates "r" are from the 75% Mortgage Table.

R = .125; Mortgage Recapture, 10 years; $165,175
Mortgage Balance, 10 years $134,825

Equity Yield	*"r"*	*Dep. Rate*	*10 Yr. Dep.*	*Property Reversion*	*Equity Reversion*	*10 Yr. Income Decline*
12%	.0862	3.88%	$155,200	$244,800	$109,975	$18,624
16%	.1003	2.47%	98,800	301,200	166,375	15,808
20%	.1138	1.12%	44,800	355,200	220,375	8,960

1. The depreciation rate is the difference between the overall rate .125 and basic rate "r".
2. 10 year depreciation is the value $400,000 multiplied by 10 times the depreciation rate.
3. Property reversion is $400,000 less 10 year depreciation.
4. Equity reversion is property reversion less the 10 year mortgage balance.
5. The 10 year income decline is 10 year depreciation times the equity yield rate.

In each case the present value of equity reversion plus the present value of the declining income stream to equity, both discounted 10 years at the equity yield rate will equal the equity investment of $100,000. In this example, annual mortgage requirement "f" is .1062 and $300,000 times .1062 is $31,860. First year income to equity is $50,000 less $31,860 or $18,140. The analysis provides for annual decline equal to one tenth of the 10 year income decline.

If graphic analysis is desired, it can be accomplished by use of basic rates from the 5 and 10 year projection brackets. Differences "R" and "r"

*Note: See also text on use of Table Cy

are multiplied by 5 and 10 respectively to find value changes at 5 and 10 years. The graph is then drawn in the regular manner.

(b) One of the most challenging problems has to do with the appraisal of property which comes on the rental market before there is sufficient demand to fill it. This may occur as the result of a building boom extending beyond current needs to a point where it will probably require several years for demand to catch up with supply.

If the property is basically sound as to location, design and construction, it is simply a matter of time coupled with a good long range program of aggressive promotion aimed at gradually increasing occupancy and earnings until capacity is reached.

Such properties have the same attraction for buyers who can afford to wait as common stocks in "growth industries" have for Wall Street investors.

The question the appraiser must answer is; what price has market attractiveness when an otherwise desirable property is suffering from an exceptionally high percentage of vacancy? He may reel quite certain that good management could achieve a high percentage of occupancy during the next 5 to 10 years but a stabilized income projection based on this notion would be very difficult to support. The experienced appraiser knows that qualified reviewers are skeptical of valuation based on capitalization of income substantially in excess of current performance unless it can be documented by fact.

It is much more persuasive to start with contemporary conditions and make the analysis to determine what progressive program of renting must be accomplished over a period of years to produce attractive yields.

A case in point might be as follows:—

About 8 months after completion a 198 unit apartment house is only about 65% rented. There are 69 vacant apartments. Current operating condition is as set forth below;

Gross rent with full occupancy	$487,600
Budget for expenses and taxes	198,800
Net rent capacity	$288,800
Rent value of vacancies;	
69 @ $2446 average	168,774
Current net income;	$120,026
Say	$120,000

75% of purchase price can be financed at 6% interest with full recapture in 25 years.

If current income is capitalized at an overall rate of 6%, distribution of purchase capital and current income would be as follows:—

Purchase Price 120,000/.06 = $2,000,000

	Capital		*Income*
Mortgage	$1,500,000	× .0774	$116,100
Equity Investment	500,000		3,900
Assumed Purchase Price	$2,000,000		$120,000

The following tabulation indicates the average annual rental increase, total occupancy ratio and reversionary property value which must be achieved during the next 5 years for equity yields of 14%, 17% and 20%.

Tested Overall rate; "R" = .06
Basic rates "r" from 75% Table.

Y	*r*	*App. Rate*	*Ann. Rent Increase*	*Assumed Occ. End of 5 Yr.*	*Promotion Allowance*	*Required Property Reversion*
14%	.0816	.0216	$ 6,048	80%	$41,000	$2,216,000
17%	.0898	.0298	10,132	85%	45,000	2,298,000
20%	.0979	.0379	15,160	95%	68,620	2,379,000

1. The annual appreciation rate is the difference betwen "r" and "R" at .06.
2. Annual rent increase is the appreciation rate times "Y" times "V" at $2,000,000. This is the amount by which net rent (or its averaged equivalent) must be increased each year for 5 years to realize equity yield "Y".
3. It would not be plausible to omit promotional expense as a requirement for obtaining increased occupancy. Assumed occupancy at the end of 5 years is therefore, rounded to several percentage points above the occupancy actually required for 5 times the needed annual rent increase.
4. The promotion allowance is the difference between the required 5 year rent increase and that which must occur to reach assumed occupancy at the end of 5 years. In other words, this amount or its equivalent in concessions could be spent to obtain the assumed occupancy.
5. The required property reversion reflects the addition of 5 times the appreciation rate as applied to assumed purchase price at $2,000,000. If assumed occupancy were achieved in 5 years, there seems little doubt that this reversionary value could be realized.

Present value of equity reversion plus that of the increasing equity income stream will equal the assumed investment of $500,000 when discounted at the respective yield rates.

Obviously, an analysis of this type is quite speculative but so are the yield rates. There is considerable cushion in them for errors which could drop the ultimate yield by several percentage points and still make the investment reasonably successful. The prospects should be especially attractive to a buyer in a high income tax bracket.

Land Speculation

Anticipation of profit from future increases in value has always been a popular incentive for speculation in vacant, non-income producing land.

The value to which the purchase price must increase in any specific length of time for realization of any given yield is a relatively simple calculation when the buyer pays all cash out of pocket (100% equity) and when a reasonably reliable estimate of average annual taxes can be made. The formula is:—

$$\text{Purchase Price } [(1 + Y)^n + s_{\overline{n|}}t] = \text{Appreciated Value}$$

In which:
n = projection term in years
t = average effective tax rate
$s_{\overline{n|}}$ = Future worth of 1 per period at "Y" for n years. (Col. 2 compound interest table)

Assume a purchase price of $100,000 and average tax of 2½%. What value is needed after 5 years of ownership for a yield of 10%?

"Solution"—

In the 10% compound interest table at 5 years, we find 1.61051 in Col. 1 and 6.1051 in Col. 2

$$1.61051 + (.025 \times 6.1051) = 1.7631375$$

Value in 5 years must be:—

$$\$100{,}000 \times 1.7631375 = \$176{,}314$$

However, many sales of land are made on the basis of a down payment with the seller taking back an installment mortgage contract. In this case, the problem becomes a little more sophisticated, especially if the buyer prudently assumes that taxes will probably increase progressively with the increase in value.

Solution is simplified by use of basic rate "r" as found by formula $r = Y - MC$. The required amount of appreciation for yield "Y" on the equity investment may be calculated as follows:—

$$\text{App.} = \frac{r + t}{1/s_{\overline{n}|}\left(1 + \frac{t}{Y}\right) - \frac{t}{nY}}$$

"Examples"

(a) A tract of land is purchased for $100,000. The seller takes back a $75,000 mortgage to be amortized in 15 years by level periodic installments including interest at 5¾%. Taxes are now 2% of $100,000 or $2,000 and are expected to increase proportionately as the value of the land increases. How much appreciation must occur in 5 years for a yield of 10% on the buyer's equity investment?

Solution

Stated factors are:

$$t = .02,\ Y = .10,\ n = 5 \text{ years}$$
$$M = .75$$

In the 75% mortgage table, 15 year amortization, 5¾% interest, 10% yield 5 year projection we find;

$$r = .0698 \text{ and } 1/s_{\overline{n}|} = .1638$$

$$\text{App} = \frac{.0698 + .02}{.1638\left(1 + \frac{.02}{.10}\right) - \frac{.02}{5 \times .10}}$$

which equals:

$$\frac{.0898}{.1638 \times 1.2 - .04} = \frac{.0898}{.15656} = .57358$$

The property would have to be worth $157358 in 5 years. The mortgage balance at that time would be $56707 leaving an equity reversion of $100,651. In addition to his $25000 downpayment the buyer would pay mortgage installments amounting to $7479 per year plus taxes. Taxes are calculated to start at $2000 and increase $229 per year:

Arithmetic Check;

Reversion deferred 5 years at 10%, $100,651 × .620921, $62,496.
Less present value of mortgage payments and taxes at 10%.

	Brought forward;			\$62,496
	\$10,624 × 3.790787	=	\$40,273.	
Less	$229 \frac{(5-3.790787)}{.10}$	=	2,769	37,504
Present Value of Equity at 10%				\$24,992
Penny dropping differential				8
				\$25,000

(b) An 80 acre tract is in the direction of community expansion. The growth rate indicates that this tract will be ripe for residential sub-division development within 5 years. Sub-dividers are currently paying \$5000 to \$8000 per acre for raw land where new, middle income housing is in demand. It is plausible to expect that the subject tract will command a price of not less than \$6,000 per acre within 5 years. The tract would be worth \$480,000 at \$6,000 per acre. The present owner is willing to sell at present discounted value on the basis of a 25% cash down payment. He will take back a 75% mortgage to be amortized in 10 years by level, periodic installments including interest at 6%. Prepayment privilege without charge after 5 years.

Problem:

Assume a resale price of \$480,000 in 5 years and an effective real estate tax rate of 2¼%. Compute present value on the basis of a 15% yield to the equity investor.

Solution:

Calculate required appreciation, add 1 and use the sum as a divisor of \$480,000.

Basic rate "r" from 75% mortgage table is .0901. The sinking fund factor from the same table at 5 years 15% is .1483. Effective tax rate "t" is quoted at .0225. Thus, we have:

$$\text{App.} = \frac{.0901 + .0225}{.1483\left(1 + \frac{.0225}{.15}\right) - \frac{.0225}{5 \times .15}} = \frac{.1126}{.140545}$$

which equals, .801168, Say .8012

Divisor = 1.8012

Present value: $\frac{\$480,000}{1.8012}$ = \$266,489

Called \$266,500

Time is the most critical factor in valuation of land for future potential use. A value growth from $266,500 to $480,000 in 5 years, in this case, produces a yield of 15% on the buyer's downpayment and interim payments. But, if he should have to wait 10 years for the same appreciation in value, the investment would be unwise. He would do better by depositing the same amounts in a bank paying 3% interest on savings accounts.

Failure to make adequate allowances for time and interim carrying charges is a rather common reason for wide divergencies in land valuation.

TABULATED ANALYSES OF SELECTED CAPITALIZATION RATES

Each of the basic capitalization rate tables is supplemented by one in which each column is headed by a selected overall capitalization rate. Value changes in indicated projection terms for realization of specific equity yields have been calculated, rounded to the nearest percentage and shown under each capitalization rate.

Value declines or depreciation are indicated by minus signs. Value increases or appreciation are indicated by plus signs. In other words; "— 16" means that 16% depreciation in overall property value during the indicated projection term would produce the equity yield shown in the left hand column whereas, "+ 16" means that 16% appreciation in overall property value would be needed for realization of the indicated yield.

Each page of these tables is calculated for one mortgage interest rate shown at the top of the page. The page is divided into 4 amortization term brackets; i.e., 15, 20, 25 and 30 years.

The table for 75% mortgage financing shows depreciation and appreciation with equity yields at 6%, 9%, 12% and 15% and, for 5 and 10 year income projection terms.

The table for 66⅔% mortgage financing shows depreciation and appreciation for equity yields of 5%, 10% and 15%. The income projection terms are 5 years, 10 years and full mortgage amortization term.

Blank spaces occur on the 5% and 10% equity yield lines in the full amortization projection brackets when 100% depreciation is reached. When reliable long-term leases justify income projection equal to or exceeding the full amortization term, equity yield will exceed the rate on the line where blanks occur. The letter "m" appears on the 15% equity yield line in several places. This indicates that 1000% or more appreciation would be needed for realization of the 15% yield.

These analysis tables provide data for quickly judging market attractiveness of values produced by a considerable range of overall capitalization rates. Frequently the capitalization rate derived from market data or one close enough to it will be found in the appropriate table. Tabulated factors can be used for preparation of the graphic analysis in such cases.

Correlation of Classical Approaches to Value:

The concept of correlation as an arbitrary selection from among several independent approaches to value not only disregards the meaning of the word. It also falsely implies that the cost approach, comparison approach and capitalization approach can each be accomplished without integration of factors common to all. Value is always the product of anticipated future benefits and no method of measuring it can be sound without employing this fact as the central theme regardless of what we may choose to call the approach.

The proper capitalization rate is said to be determined by the market. If this is so, correlation becomes an accomplished fact by selection of the proper capitalization rate because *"the market"* is a very broad term. Among other things, it reflects: (1) the ability and willingness of buyers and tenants to pay the cost of creating and operating improved real estate; (2) prices at which the inventory of standing stock changes hands; (3) rates and terms for borrowed purchase capital; (4) potential yield from competitive investment opportunities. These are diverse but interdependent components of the market. If we weave them all into a single overall approach we will achieve correlation in the result.

An application of this principle is demonstrated in the following example. It involves use of the capitalization rate analysis table with mortgage at 66⅔% of value.

Exercise:

In the process of appraising a 24 family apartment house our investigation has developed the following summary of information and assumptions:

(a) The building is about 8 years old. It has been well managed. It is in a popular neighborhood and in harmony with its surroundings. The area is well built up. New apartment buildings are now under construction in several remaining sites. Subject will be in excellent competitive position so far as any new construction is concerned.

(b) Estimated cost of comparable land by market comparisons		$ 30,000
Current reproduction cost of subject building	$314,600	
Allowances for accrued wear and tear:		
Structure	$ 11,400	
Mechanical appurtenances	23,600	
Equipment	14,600	
Total physical depreciation	$ 49,600	
Net building: 314600 — 49600		$265,000
Total Physical Summation		$295,000
(c) Present gross annual rent, 100% occupancy		$ 45,850
(d) Estimated average, annual net rent, 10 year projection		$ 24,300

(f) Records reveal 5 sales of competitive properties within the past 12 months. These are in scattered locations and vary in number of units but compete with subject as to tenant accommodations and rent. The ratio of net to gross income will approximate that of the subject in each case. Gross income multipliers found by dividing selling prices by gross rent range from 6.28 to 7.35. The composite for the 5 properties is 6.48. The lowest multiplier pertains to a larger building and the highest pertains to a sale subject to the balance of a high ratio 4% mortgage.

(g) Mortgage money is available for purchase of subject property up to ⅔rds of value at 5½% with full amortization by level installments in 20 years.

1. Select a correlated capitalization rate based on the physical summation and comparative sales.

2. Analyze the selected rate to show the prospects for yield on the equity investment.

Solution:

The rate indicated by the physical summation or cost approach is found by dividing the net income by the summation, to wit:

$$24300/295000 = .0824 \text{ (rounded)}$$

Rates indicated by comparative sales are found by dividing the net income ratio by gross multiplier as set forth below:

Net income ratio, 24300/45850 = .53

Ratio Low multiplier	$\frac{.53}{6.28}$	= .0844
High multiplier	$\frac{.53}{7.35}$	= .0721
Composite multiplier	$\frac{.53}{6.48}$	= .0818

The range of capitalization rates indicated by sales is .0721 to .0844. If we use one lower than .0824, the resulting valuation will be higher than the physical summation and, since a carefully prepared summation based on current costs of duplication is wisely considered the upper limit in a case of this type, we should select our rate accordingly. .0824 is well within the range indicated by sales and it is obvious that valuation based on this rate will be supported by both cost and market data. In other words, it will be correlated so far as these 2 approaches are concerned.

Let us now turn to 66⅔% Mortgage Cap. Rate Analysis Table captioned, "Mortgage Interest Rate 5½%."

The nearest capitalization rate to .0824 on the top line of this table is .0825. Valuation based on this rate is:

24300/.0825 = $294,500 (rounded)

Moving down the .0825 column into the 20 years amortization section of the table we find the following factors for graphic analysis.

Yield	5 Years		10 Years	
5%	17%	depreciation	38%	depreciation
10%	7%	"	15%	"
15%	5%	appreciation	21%	appreciation

with appraisal at $294,500, assumed purchase capital and income distribution would be as follows (rounded):

	Capital		*Income*	
Mortgage Money	$196,000	× .08256	$16,182	
Equity Investment	98,500	average dividend	8,118	.0824 +
Totals	$294,500		$24,300	

This is a correlated appraisal supported by the cost approach and market comparison. The gross multiplier is 6.42 which is close to the composite of the 5 comparative sales. The capitalization approach provides for mortgage interest and amortization at the prevailing rate and terms. Graphic analysis of the capitalization rate reveals excellent prospects for an attractive yield on the equity investment.

PLATE V

ANALYSIS OF .0825 CAPITALIZATION RATE

Prospects for yield on equity investment assuming purchase at appraised value 66⅔ % financed by 20 year level payment loan @ 5½ % interest.

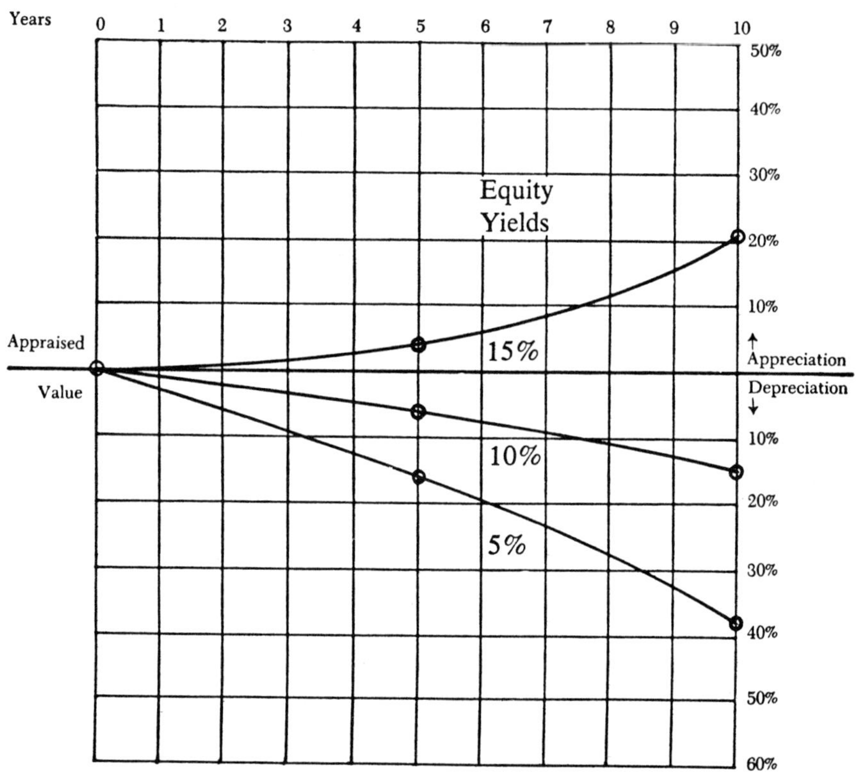

Assuming a typical purchaser would resell at some time within 10 years, our graph shows everything that must occur in the market at any point within 10 years to produce any equity yield from 5% to 15%. Reading the yield curves and interpolating between them we can see many potentials such as:

If the property is resold at the purchase price, the yield will be 12% or more.

If it is sold in 7 years at 10% below purchase price, the yield will be 10%.

If it is sold in 5 years at 5% above purchase price, the yield will be 15%.

If total value (land and building) depreciates 20% in 10 years, the yield will be a little over 9%. If it depreciates 25%, the yield will be about 8%. It can depreciate 38% (which is substantially more than the assumed equity investment) and still produce an equity yield of 5%. Any such decline in the market for this class of property is quite certain to be temporary. Competent management does not sell under such conditions.

VI

THE PURCHASE AND LEASEBACK TABLES

Although the real estate market is, in general, an installment market financed by the combination of mortgage and equity money, there is an exception which is growing in popularity. This is the purchase and lease transaction which in most instances is consummated on an all cash basis.

Despite its all cash nature, the philosophy and economics of purchase-leaseback are little different than those of the level periodic installment, full-amortization mortgage investment. Imagine if you will this type of mortgage investment at 100% of purchase price and you have the most important, initial characteristic of the typical purchase-leaseback transaction. The essential differences are that the investor receives a warranty deed rather than a deed in trust; the periodic installments are called rent instead of interest and principal and, he owns the residual property at the end of the lease term. He can then take possession of it, occupy it, dispose of it by sale or lease it as he chooses. This, of course, is a very important advantage if the property is readily marketable and the lease is for a comparatively short term. When the lease with options for extension exceeds 40 years it will make very little difference except in event of excessive inflation.

One other difference which has a minor effect on the arithmetic of valuation is that rent installments are usually paid in advance, i.e., at the beginning of each installment period instead of at its end. In other words, the income stream from a typical purchase-leaseback investment is an annuity due, whereas the level installment mortgage contract provides an income stream in the form of an ordinary annuity. Assuming equal capital investment and rate the annuity due installment and the total annual requirement are a little less than those of the ordinary annuity because each installment is subject to discount for one less period.

The common philosophy then of the purchase-lease investor is: "I will buy the property and lease it to its present owner at a rent which will provide full recovery of my investment, plus a return during the lease term. Of course, I will not have the margin of security represented by equity in a mortgage investment but I will own the property and anything I can get out of it upon expiration of the initial lease term will increase my yield over and above the rate upon which the initial lease is based."

The owner who sells releases capital which has been tied up in the property but retains possession under the lease. In many cases, the initial lease term with its options for extension will reserve the right of possession and use to the original owner for a period of 50 years or longer.

Typical buyers are life insurance companies and pension trusts who are interested primarily in long-term income at a fixed rate of return commensurate with that obtainable from well secured mortgage investments. The prospect for improving this yield through lease extensions and eventual sale of the residual property adds a bit of speculative glamour and provides protection against long-range inflation.

Institutional buyers normally are not in position to or, at least, do not wish to provide real estate management. Consequently, the leases are usually written on an absolutely net basis with the tenant providing all management and paying all the bills.

Although type, quality and condition of the real estate are afforded due consideration, the financial responsibility of the tenant and his prospects for continued success for a long period of future years are of great importance. He will be subjected to the same investigation and be expected to meet the same qualifications as if he were applying for long-term debenture financing.

Having met specifications as to type of property and credit of tenant, valuation of the real estate is usually a comparatively simple matter. Ordinarily, it can be accomplished by dividing the periodic net rent by the rent factor per dollar which will amortize the investment during the initial lease term at the rate of return on which it is based. (Initial term is the duration of the lease exclusive of options for extension.) If inspection of the property indicates that this will produce a value substantially in excess of a well supported physical summation, it is wise to include the physical summation.

Sometimes a prospective seller will seek to raise additional capital through sale and leaseback of his real estate at a rental substantially in excess of that warranted by replacement cost of the real estate. When there is evidence of this in the proposed lease, it is well to note it in the appraisal report. In connection with special purpose property, however, keep replacement cost in mind as distinguished from what the property would bring if offered for sale or lease in the open market. It might include special features which may not contribute to its open market value but may be costly and quite essential to the seller's operation.

Set forth below is a summary of some of the advantages of this type of transaction to sellers and buyers:

To Sellers:

Releases capital tied up in nonliquid, fixed assets for use as working capital or retirement of debt.

Provides capital for expansion or other operations without creating debt.

In cases where a large proportion of value is in the land, there may be a tax advantage as rent is a deductible expense, whereas only building depreciation is deductible when the property is owned free and clear.

To buyers:

Provides long-term, fixed income at a favorable rate of return.

Involves a minimum of management burden.

Lease renewals or extensions increase the yield above the rate upon which the initial lease term rental is based.

Provides a long-range hedge against inflations.

Although the influence of the reversion on yield was not given much thought in the early days of institutional purchase-lease investment, some of the investors are now becoming very much aware of this feature. The earlier reversion occurs the greater its impact on investment yield. For this reason a great deal of attention is now being given to the initial lease term. When a transaction involves property of a readily marketable type, some institutions will quote a much lower initial term yield rate on a 15 year lease than they will on a 25 or 30 year lease.

Two tables are presented as aids in solution of purchase-leaseback problems.

The first table presents periodic rent factors and annual capitalization rates for initial lease terms of 10 years to 50 by 1 year increments. The yield rate at which rent without reversion or renewals will fully amortize the investment during the initial lease term is shown at the top of each set of 4 columns. These rates range from 3% to 12¼% by ¼th of 1% increments. The 4 columns in each set present the monthly and quarterly rent per dollar of purchase price. These assume payment of rent at the beginning of each month or quarter and have been adjusted to reflect it. The annual rental requirement is at the right of each periodic rent factor. It is 12 times the monthly factor and 4 times the quarterly factor. It is captioned CAP. RATE as it can be used as a divisor of annual rent to determine value. And, of course, it can also be used as a multiplier of purchase price to determine the annual rent requirement.

The second table is captioned "PURCHASE-LEASEBACK INVESTMENT YIELD CHARACTERISTICS." It shows investment yields with reversions computed at from 5% to 100% of the original investment by 5% increments.

This table is presented as an aid in negotiating options for repurchase at the end of initial lease terms or for extension of leases beyond initial terms.

Initial lease term in years is shown at the top of each page. Residual values of the property at the end of the initial term as percentages of original investment are listed as reversions in the left hand column. The rate of return at which the initial term rent will fully amortize the investment is in bold type on the zero reversion line in each column. The annual rent as a percentage of original investment is shown at top of each column. This is the monthly rent factor multiplied by 12.

Problems Involving Use of the Table of Purchase-Leaseback Rent Factors and Capitalization Rates

(1) A large metropolitan area department store organization occupies its main store under a 30 year net lease with 3, 10-year renewal options. Rent during the initial 30 year term is $510,000 net per annum, payable $42,500 monthly in advance. 8 years of the initial term have expired and 22 years remain.

Title to the fee is held by an individual subject to a mortgage in which the present balance is approximately $4,000,000. Amortization requirements on this mortgage have now reached a point where they will exceed the depreciation allowance on the building. The fee owner is in a top income tax bracket. Unless he disposes of this property he will have to pay a tax on the difference between the depreciation allowance and amortization. Every dollar of the excess will cost him about $1.70. The mortgage can be paid in full.

A pension fund offers to buy the property free and clear on a 4¾% basis with full recovery during the balance of the initial term.

What is the amount of this offer?

Solution:

Turn to the 4¾% columns in Table IV.

Find the capitalization rate in the monthly section on the 22 year line. It is .073068. Divide the annual rent, $510,000 by this factor.

Offering price = $510,000/.073068 = $6,979,800.

(2) To finance an expansion program a national retail food chain will buy locations, build supermarkets and offer to sell them on a leaseback basis. Cost is budgeted at $16,000,000.

Two offers are received from insurance companies on a 5½% basis and both with 25 year initial lease terms. One will require rent monthly in advance. The other will accept rent quarterly in advance.

What is the annual rent requirement in each offer? Explain the difference.

Solution:

In the 5½% columns of Table IV, we find that when rent is paid monthly in advance with the initial lease term at 25 years, the capitalization rate or annual requirement is .073356, whereas when paid quarterly in advance it is .072848. Thus we have:

Annual rent; paid monthly—$16,000,000 × .073356	$1,173,696
Annual rent, paid quarterly—$16,000,000 × .072848	1,165,568
Difference per year	$ 8,128

The difference is caused by the fact that when rent is paid monthly in advance the discount applicable to each installment is computed for 1 month. It is computed for 3 months when rent is paid quarterly in advance. The tenants choice in this situation probably would depend on his preference as to cash position. If it is profitable for him to have money tied up in advance rentals, he will select the quarterly proposition. On the other hand, if he can do better by using the money to take advantage of merchandise discounts, etc., he will elect to pay rent monthly.

(3) In negotiating transactions of this type, brokers are sometimes impressed by quotation of a low rate of return in conjunction with a comparatively short initial term. Assume, for example, a third proposition in the foregoing case from a pension trust quoting the rate of return at 4½% with an initial term of 15 years, rent to be paid monthly in advance.

What would the annual rent be and under what conditions might the tenant consider this the best offer?

Solution:

At 4½% monthly, 15 years, Table IV shows the capitalization rate or annual requirement at .091464.

Annual rent payable monthly in advance, $16,000,000 × .091464 = $1,463,424.

This is $289,728 more per year than the 5½%, 25 year monthly proposal. However, the 25 year offer involves a total rent obligation of $29,342,400 while the 15 year proposition involves $21,951,360. The difference is over $7,390,000. Despite much higher annual rent during the initial term, the shorter term might be the most desirable because of the much lower aggregate commitment. If attractive extension options can be worked out, the 15 year lease might be accepted in preference to the 25 year proposition.

(4) The central headquarters of a corporation is on land valued at $6,000,000. Depreciation has been taken at $250,000 per year on the building for 29 years as a tax deduction. The cost of the building was $10,000,000. It has been maintained in first class condition and retains its prestige as one of the most desirable office buildings in its area but its book value is now down to $2,750,000. A well supported appraisal for present market value indicates that the property could now be sold for $15,000,000. The owning corporation offers to sell it on a leaseback basis for $15,000,000.

An offer to buy the property for $15,000,000 with a 25 year leaseback based on 5¼% return is received. This offer includes 2 options: one for repurchase at the end of 25 years at $7,500,000; the other grants 3, 10-year lease extension at 60% of the initial term rent.

Assume the following conditions and make a comparative analysis indicating how the corporation would fare by accepting this offer.

(a) Present book value of the property is $8,750,000 of which $6,000,000 is allocated to land.

(b) Seller would have to pay 25% capital gain tax on the differential between $8,750,000 and $15,000,000.

(c) Corporate income tax is 52%. Deduction for depreciation is $250,000 per year. This will continue 11 years when the present building will be written off.

(d) Rent under the leaseback arrangement will be payable monthly in advance.

Solution:

Selling Price	$15,000,000
Book Value	8,750,000
Capital Gain	$ 6,250,000
Capital Gain Tax at 25%	1,562,500
Net Asset Gain to corporation	$ 4,687,500

Proceeds of Sale		$15,000,000
Capital Gain Tax		1,562,500
Cash addition to working capital		$13,437,500
Current Assets increase	$13,437,500	
Fixed Assets decline	8,750,000	

Assuming 5¼% as the minimum rate of return at which the owner is justified in having capital tied up in company occupied real estate, present annual cost of occupancy is:

$8,750,000 @ 5¼%	$459,375
Plus depreciation	250,000
Present cost, owner occupancy	$709,375

Of this amount $250,000 is deductible from corporate earnings for 11 more years. At 52% the tax saving is $130,000.

Annual rent requirement, 25 years, 5¼%, payable monthly, Table IV (cap. rate) .071604.

Annual leaseback rent requirement:

$15,000,000 × .071604	$1,074,060
Present depreciation deduction	250,000
Gain in deduction for taxes	$ 824,060
Gain in tax saving at 52%	428,511
Net comparative cost of occupancy— $1,074,060 − $428,511	$ 645,549

This all boils down to the condition that if this transaction is consummated the corporation will be paying out $645,549 more cash per year than it does in its present situation. As an offset to this, it will increase its cash working capital $13,437,500. Decision should rest on whether or not it is reasonable to expect that this change in the capital structure of the corporation will increase its overall operating profit by more than $645,549 per year.

Problems Involving Use of Purchase-Leaseback Investment Yield Table

(1) A warehouse is purchased subject to a net lease which will fully amortize the investment in 15 years at 3¾%. The seller wants an option to repurchase at the end of 15 years and the buyer is willing to grant such an option at a price to yield 7% on the investment.

What price is quoted for repurchase?

Solution:

Turn to "Lease Term 15 years" table.

In column where 3.75 appears on the zero reversion line, read down to the reversion bracket in which 7% would occur. In this case 6.84% appears on the 50% reversion line and 7.06% is on the 55% reversion line. A 5% difference in reversion produces 22 basis points difference in yield. Mental interpolation indicates that sale of the property at the end of 15 years for 54% of the original investment will result in a yield of slightly more than 7%. Quote 54% of original investment as the repurchase price.

(2) A property is purchased subject to a 25 year net lease which will fully amortize the investment at 5%. The lessee wants an option for an additional 25 years at a reduced rental. The lessor is willing to grant such option on the basis of a 6¼% investment yield with no allowance for residual value at the end of 50 years.

Compute the extension rent as a percentage of original investment.

Solution:

Turn to "Lease Term 25 Years" table.

In 5.00% zero reversion column 6.27% yield appears at 55% reversion. The annual rent factor required for full amortization in 25 years at 6.25% is 7.875%. Multiply this factor by 55%.

$$.55 \times .07875 = .0433$$

If rent is paid at the rate of 4.33% per year computed against the original investment during the 25 year extension period, the yield will slightly exceed 6¼% before allowance for 50 year residual.

Example:

Original Investment $1,000,000

Rent per month 1st 25 years @ 5.00%

$$\frac{1000000 \times .06986}{12} \quad \$ \quad 5,821.67$$

Rent per month next 25 years

$$\frac{1000000 \times .0433}{12} \quad \$ \quad 3,608.33$$

The value of this 50 year income stream at 6¼% is $1,002,830.60.

(3) A property is purchased subject to a 20 year net lease which will completely amortize the investment at 4¾%. The lessee wants an option for 3 ten year extensions with reductions at the beginning of

each extension period. The lessor is willing to grant this on the basis of a 6½% yield before allowance for the 50 year residual.

Quote the monthly rent on a \$2,000,000 investment for the initial lease term and each of the 10 year extensions with the 2nd extension 10% less than the 1st extension and the 3rd extension 20% less than the 1st extension.

Solution:

Refer to "Lease Term 20 Years" table.

Rent during initial term

$\frac{2000000 \times .07725}{12}$ .... per mo. \$12,875

Table shows 6.40% yield with 45% reversion and 6.55% yield with 50% reversion. The differential is 3 basis points in yield for each 1% increase in reversion. Thus, a reversion of .483 would produce a yield of approximately 6½% and the value of the extension rents should equal 48.3% of the original investment at 6½%.

Reversion \$2,000,000 × .483 = \$966,000

Call 1st extension rent, d; 2nd extension rent, .90d; 3rd extension rent, .80d and solve for d at 6½% converted monthly as an annuity due. In effect, we have .80d for 360 months, plus .10d for 120 months and 240 months.

Therefore,

$$.80d \times 159.0678 + .10d\,(88.5455 + 134.8515) = \$966.000$$

$$149.59394d = \$966,000$$

$$d = \frac{966000}{149.59394} = 6457.48$$

Monthly Rent 1st extension	\$6,457.48
Monthly Rent 2nd extension—6457.48 × .90	5,811.73
Monthly Rent 3rd extension—6457.48 × .80	5,165.98

Long Range Residuals

After customary allowances for depreciation, residual values removed 40 or more years from date of investment add little to the yield. And, since the actual amount recoverable through liquidation in the distant future can be nothing more than a rough guess, it seems more prudent to consider it as a feature which adds speculative glamour to the investment rather than one whose effect on yield can be measured mathematically at the point of beginning.

In problems 2 and 3 residuals deferred 50 years at 100% of the original investment would increase the yield about 30 basis points and, of course, any fraction of 100% would reduce this differential proportionately.

Problems Involving Use of Standard Compound Interest Tables

(1) There is a type of problem in this field which is becoming increasingly common and where the services of competent appraisers are in demand. This has to do with cases where the initial lease terms are of such short duration that analyses of the reversionary potentials are required for determination of acceptable prices.

The following situation represents this type of assignment. Eight years ago a district office building was crccted and leased to Standard Oil Co. The initial lease term was 25 years with 2 renewal options for 10 years each. Net rent is $173,450 per annum, payable $43,362.50 quarterly in advance. Income tax shelter by use of the double declining balance method has been reduced to a point where the owner finds his take home net unsatisfactory. He wants to sell.

Although the unexpired balance of the initial lease term is only 17 years, the trustee of a pension fund is willing to buy on the basis of reasonably certain prospects for a yield of 5¾% or better. Full recapture at 5¾% in 17 years from lease income alone would require purchase at about $1,900,000 which is substantially below an acceptable price for the property.

An appraiser is assigned the job of investment analysis and price recommendation. His investigation produces the following initial information and reasoning.

The site comprises about 2½ acres on a broad avenue convenient to the central business district. The street was formerly one of fine mansions on large plots. For several years it has been in transition to professional offices, insurance company branches and district headquarters of large corporations. Most recent sales of comparable sites and asking prices for the few remaining parcels indicate a current land value of $400,000 for the subject site. There are good reasons to expect that this will increase during the next 17 years; at least, it seems perfectly safe to assume that it will not decline.

The improvement is a very attractive, modern, reinforced concrete, centrally air conditioned office building. It cost about $2,000,000 to build and could not be reproduced today for less than $2,325,000.

The tenant has been an excellent housekeeper. Physically, it provides a convenient, comfortable and pleasant place in which to work.

It will last as long as the present quality of maintenance is employed. In all probability its useful life will be terminated by economic conditions rather than physical durability. In this case, it is likely that the land value will have increased to a point where more intensive development is warranted.

If the tenant does not exercise the renewal option at the end of 17 years, the owner will come into possession of a vacant building. Of all reversionary prospects, this is probably the least desirable. It is not likely to happen if prices and rents continue to increase In this event, the tenant would probably take advantage of the renewal option and profit by subletting if he no longer needs the space for his own use. Renewal options give rights of possession to the present tenant for the next 37 years. Thus, a present buyer should expect to have to wait at least that long before he could realize any benefit from inflation.

If the property is vacated in 17 years, it may take some time to find another tenant. However, the building is one which could be subdivided for multiple occupancy without prohibitive cost. Thus, there is every reason to believe that it will have substantial value even if vacated upon expiration of the initial lease term. On the basis of this reasoning, the appraiser decides that a 50% decline from present value of the improvement represents a maximum plausible allowance for depreciation. This should cover any physical deterioration which may occur during the next 17 years and provide for remodelling and re-renting.

The appraiser prices the property to yield 5¾% on the basis of a 17 year projection with 50% decline in improvement value. This price is then subjected to analysis for higher yields within the range of reasonable assumptions as to other income terms and reversionary possibilities.

The annual rent is adjusted to reflect the quarterly payment in advance feature by using the quarterly payment base at 5¾% as a multiplier.

$$\$173{,}450 \times 1.014375 = \$175{,}943$$

The quarterly sinking fund factor at 5¾% (Col. 3 at 17 years), is multiplied by 4 for use in the provision for depreciation on an annual basis.

$$.008769 \times 4 = .035076$$

Adjusted income	$ 175,943
Less land requirement $400,000 × .0575	23,000
Income imputed to building	$ 152,943

Minimum Yield Rate	.057500
Plus adjustment for 50% depreciation;	
.50 × .035076	.017538
Cap. Rate applicable to building	.075038
Building Residual Valuation: $152,943/.075038	$2,038,207
Add Land Value	400,000
Total	$2,438,207
Rounded to	$2,438,000

The appraiser starts his analysis by assuming purchase at $2,438,000 allocated as follows:

Land	$ 400,000	.1641
Improvement	2,038,000	.8359
Total	$2,438,000	1.0000

Assumed 17 year Reversion:

Land	$ 400,000
Improvement 50% depreciated	1,019,000
Total	$1,419,000

Present Value of 17 year income and assumed reversion at 5¾% converted quarterly (factors from Cols. 5 and 4; 5¾% quarterly compound interest table):

Income: $43,362.50 × 1.014375 × 43.208482	$1,900,561
Assumed Reversion: $1,419,000 × .378878	537,628
Total	$2,438,189

Reversionary requirements for other investment yields under various possibilities:

I. Assuming termination of Lease at end of 17 years

	A	*B*	*C*	*D*	
Yield	*Present Val. of Income*	*Required Present Value of Reversion*	*Required Reversion*	*Equivalent Building Depreciation*	
6%	$1,868,095	$569,905	$1,568,532	$869,468	42.66%
6¼%	1,836,458	601,542	1,726,379	711,621	34.92%
6½%	1,805,625	632,375	1,892,399	545,601	26.77%
7%	1,746,276	691,724	2,250,470	187,530	9.20%

II. Assuming one 10 year Renewal Option Exercised. Income Stream continues 27 years. Reversion deferred 27 years.

6½%	$2,236,269	$201,731	$1,150,358	$1,287,642	63.18%
6¾%	2,184,206	253,794	1,546,603	891,397	43.74%
7%	2,134,057	303,943	1,979,289	458,711	22.51%

III. Assuming both 10 year Renewal Options Exercised. Income Stream continues 37 years. Reversion deferred 37 years.

6¾%	$2,393,440	$ 44,560	$ 530,329	$1,907,671	93.61%
7%	2,327,793	110,207	1,436,491	1,101,509	49.14%
				Appreciation	
7½%	2,205,309	232,691	3,637,371	1,199,371	49.20%

Column "B" in these tabulations is the difference between the assumed purchase price $2,438,000 and the present value of income as shown in Column "A." Since this difference must represent the present value of reversion at the end of each income projection, it must be multiplied by the value to which 1 dollar will grow at the stated yield rate over the projection term (Col. 1 quarterly tables). The product of this multiplication shown in Column "C" is the residual value the property must have at the end of the income projection to produce the corresponding yield. The difference between this required reversion and $2,438,000 shown in Column "D" is the amount of value decline or depreciation the property must suffer. It is also expressed as a percentage of $2,038,000 allocated to the improvement.

The analysis indicates a probable yield range of 6% to 7% with almost certainty that it will not fall below 5¾%. The property can suffer some loss in value over each income projection and still produce a yield of 7%. Its value would have to increase about 49% over the next 37 years for a yield of 7½%. Of course, this is not impossible either, in the light of what has happened to property values during the past 37 years.

To Calculate Required Reversion:

(2) The amount of reversionary value required for any selected investment yield can be calculated by use of the following formula:

$V\,[(1+i)^n - d(1+i)s_{\overline{n}|}] =$ Required Reversion

In which:

$V =$ Purchase Price

$(1 + i) =$ The base; i.e., 1 plus effective yield rate or "Y" divided by number of rent installments per year.

$n =$ Number of rent installments in lease term.

$d =$ Periodic rent per dollar of purchase price.

$s_{\overline{n|}} =$ Future worth of 1 dollar per period at rate "i" for "n" periods (Col. 2, compound interest table).

Exercise:

A lease which will expire in 16 years provides rent at $6,573 payable monthly in advance. A prospective buyer is considering purchase at $1,000,000. What reversion at the end of 16 years will give him a yield of 6½%?

Solution:

$$d = 6573/1{,}000{,}000 = .006573$$

From 6½% *monthly* compound interest table:

(Col. 1) Base $= 1.005417$ at 16 years $(1 + i)^{192} = 2.821288$

(Col. 2) $s_{\overline{n|}}$ at 16 years $= 336.237757$

Multiplier of V equals:

$$2.821288 - (.006573 \times 1.005417 \times 336.237757)$$

which equals;

$$2.821288 - 2.222027 = .599261$$

Required Reversion:

$$\$1{,}000{,}000 \times .599261 = \$599261$$

Part II

The Tables

TECHNICAL NOTES

Although great care was taken in the original Ellwood Tables to assure accuracy in all computations, there is no warranty of a uniform degree of precision. Calculations from the original tables are preserved in their original form in this edition. The possibility of typographical or computational errors is acknowledged.

Because of variations in computing routines and rounding systems, some differences can be observed between the numbers in these tables and the corresponding numbers in other tables. For high precision work, the analyst is advised to compute the required factor using the appropriate formula.

The numbers shown for the annual requirement (f) in the C, Cp, and r tables will often be slightly higher than the corresponding "annual constants" found in some other tables. The numbers have been up-rounded by adding 1 to the last digit of the monthly Installment to Amortize $1 (Column 6 Compound Interest Tables) and multiplying the result by 12 to obtain the annual requirement (f). This system of up-rounding insures that the loan will be repaid within the specified term and compensates for any deficiency resulting from half-rounding or down-rounding.

For annual constants (f) accurate to six decimal places, see "Annual Constant Tables," page 311. These Annual Constant Tables are new with the current edition and may be at variance with some calculated annual constants for monthly payment mortgages reported in the original tables. Effort has been made in the new tables to achieve higher precision than that reflected in the original works wherever possible.

Tables C, Ca, Cp and r presume direct reduction loans with level monthly payments. For other loan types the factors should be calculated (see preceding material for formulas and explanations).

Graphic Analysis

Earlier in this text mention was made of use of a draftsman's or ship curve in producing a graphic illustration of value changes (see page 85). The pattern shown below is a modification of such a standard curve, having one side a straight edge for scaling rates of appreciation and depreciation (20 to the inch). Readers can produce this curve by using the scale drawing as a pattern. Each square in the grid represents one inch and the pattern must be enlarged accordingly.

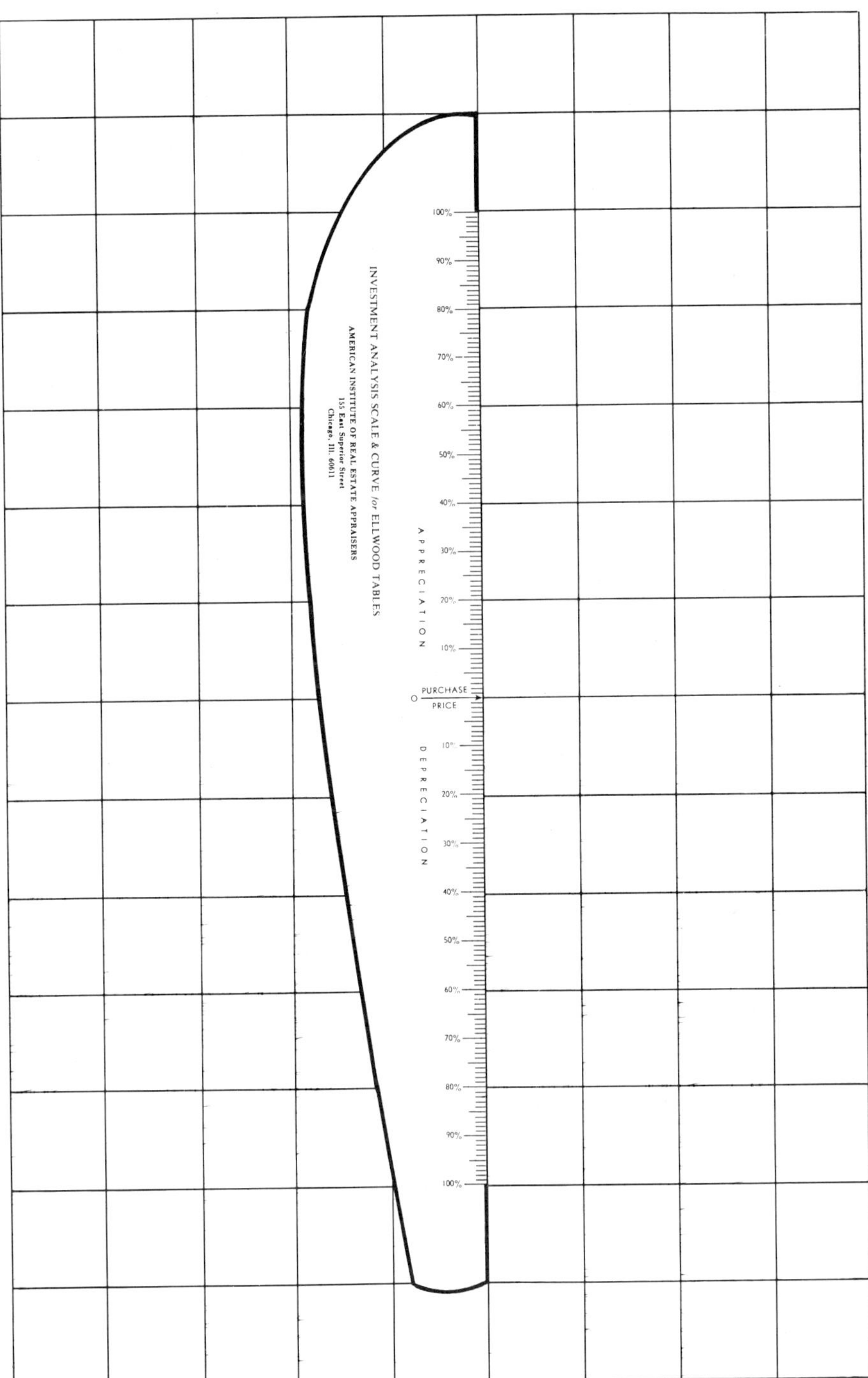

Scale: One square equals one square inch

These tables were compiled to save the appraiser's time. Each one is designed for solution of specific types of problems. Although it may be possible to use factors from several tables for solution of a given problem, the user is well advised to familiarize himself with the scope and applications of each table. This will enable him to select those involving the minimum number of steps.

In general, the objectives are to provide factors for professional analysis and appraisal of income real estate and to give prospective equity and mortgage investors information needed for intelligent decision. A broad classification of problems types to which the tables are most applicable may be summarized as follows:

Investment Analysis:

The appraisal of property for the price obtainable in the market is a comparative process in which the standards of comparison must be found in market experience. Real estate is unique as a market commodity in that no two parcels are exactly alike. Even though the details of market transactions pertaining to properties similar to the subject of appraisal may be known, prices may have been substantially affected by special terms or other extraneous circumstances which could not apply to the appraisal subject.

Thus, while the appraiser starts with standards of comparison based upon market experience, he must usually make quantitative and qualitative adjustments to properly reflect the differences.

Of all appraisal approaches, only capitalization has a common denominator as the standard of comparison. Capitalization is the process of discounting anticipated future profits to present market value. Each dollar of profit produced by any one investment is exactly like each dollar of profit produced at the same time by every other investment. Given apparent equality as to management burdens and the risks involved in profit projection, the ratio of expected earnings to obtainable price will tend to be equal with regard to various types of properties.

The sole motivation for the purchase of income real estate is expectation of profit. And, since this form of investment is normally one of considerable duration, profit is measured by the year and expressed as an annual rate of investment yield. An investment yielding 10 per cent is one in which the profit is equal to 10 cents each year on each dollar of capital remaining in the investment from year to year.

Profit from income real estate usually arises from two sources, i.e. (1) Income produced by the property during the term of ownership and;

(2) The proceeds of resale at the end of the term of ownership. This is called the "reversion." Thus, capitalization usually consists of discounting the periodic installments of a projected income stream and a lump sum reversion to present value at yields which will attract purchase capital. The critical factors are amount, time and rate. Although there are several well-known techniques, they will all produce the same result so long as there are no changes in these critical factors.

The final step in the process usually consists of dividing stabilized annual income by a composite rate or multiplying such income by the reciprocal of the composite rate; i.e.

$$\frac{\text{income}}{\text{composite rate}} = \text{Value}$$

$$\frac{\$16{,}000}{.08} = \$200{,}000$$

Reciprocal $= \frac{1}{.08} = 12.5$

And; $12.5 \times \$16{,}000 = \$200{,}000$

Since the numerator is income only, it is obvious that the composite rate must be a combination of several ingredients which will reflect not only the value of income and reversion at attractive yields but also provision for recapture of purchase capital. There can be no profit until purchase capital has been recovered.

In the majority of market transactions in income real estate, purchase capital is a combination of cash equity investment by the buyer and mortgage money usually supplied by others at a contract rate of interest and with provisions for amortization or recapture by means of level periodic installments over a specific term of years. The level, periodic installment includes both interest and principal amortization. The unpaid mortgage balance becomes progressively smaller at a constantly accelerating rate as the periodic mortgage installments are paid. And, since the value of the equity is the difference between the unpaid mortgage balance and the value of the property as a whole, the declining mortgage balance tends to increase the value of the equity. The mortgage installments are normally paid from rent produced by the property. Thus, the equity value build up by reason of mortgage amortization becomes profit to the equity investor. In some cases, profit from this source exceeds the net income to equity after expenses and mortgage installments. It, therefore, has a significant influence on equity investment yield.

Assuming a typical purchase capital structure, the composite capitalization rate should include the following ingredients.

1. Available ratio of mortgage money to justifiable purchase price, i.e., appraised value.
2. Mortgage interest rate available to a typical buyer at time of appraisal.
3. Maximum available mortgage amortization term.
4. Income projection term in years.
5. Proportion of purchase capital to be recaptured by mortgage amortization during the income projection term.
6. Decline or increase in property value during the income projection term.
7. Prospective yield that will attract equity investment.

There is no need for conjecture as to mortgage ratio, interest rate and amortization as these are factual market data available to the appraiser. Obviously, the most critical factor in the list is the prospective yield that will attract a buyer. Moreover it is also apparent that this factor is so deeply buried among the other ingredients that it can only be revealed by analysis of the over-all rate derived from market experience.

The tables provide a practical and reasonably simple method for testing any over-all rate or any price and interpreting it in terms of probable yield to the buyer. When this test clearly shows that the subject of appraisal would represent an attractive investment opportunity at the price indicated by market comparison, the appraisal will be persuasive. On the other hand, if it reveals poor prospects for a yield commensurate with those obtainable from alternative investment opportunities, it is easy to make appropriate adjustments. In either case, this technique has the advantage of minimum conjecture. There is no question concerning the source of the over-all capitalization rate.

Calculation of a Composite Rate:

The tables present precomputed capitalization rates for cases involving 75 per cent and 66⅔ per cent mortgage financing with standard amortization terms and a broad range of interest rates. They include all ingredients except provision for depreciation or appreciation. Auxiliary factors for making these provisions are presented in each table.

When a purchase capital structure involves any other ratio of mortgage to value or any special time factors, the table of mortgage coefficients or its auxiliary tables are used for quick calculations of the composite rate. These tables are also used where the ratio of mortgage to value is unknown as in appraisals subject to the unamortized balance of an existing mortgage.

Purchase-Leaseback Problems:

Rent and capitalization rates in the purchase-leaseback tables assume 100 per cent cash-out-of-pocket equity purchase without mortgage financing.

Compound Interest Problems:

The six standard compound interest functions with rates up to 30 per cent and with monthly, quarterly, semi-annual and annual compounding for a full range of mortgage rates are arranged in six columns on each page.

These tables are usable for solution of a wide variety of problems involving future values, present value, investment recapture, income stabilization, installment financing, amount amortized at any interim period, etc.

Income Tax Shelter:

Book depreciation allowances and methods permitted by Internal Revenue Service are of substantial interest to many prospective buyers of income real estate. The appraiser or counsellor can make comparative schedules to show the extent to which equity income and mortgage amortization may be sheltered by such allowances for any term of years. This is simplified by use of constant multipliers from the compound interest tables.

Feasibility Studies:

Problems in this category generally involve the question of whether a proposed project will justify its cost. Starting with a reliable estimate of cost, the required rent schedule can be calculated to meet any desired program of financing. Tabulated factors for use in such calculations will depend on whether financing is to be accomplished by combination of equity and mortgage or by sale and leaseback. In either case, prudent decision will often hinge on whether or not the required rents appear to be obtainable in the light of current competition.

Problems Pertaining to Assessed Values:

The validity of assessed valuation against which real estate taxes are imposed on income real estate can be tested by dividing stabilized income before real estate taxes by the sum of the effective tax rate and a supportable composite capitalization rate.

The effective tax rate is the product of the official tax rate and the equalization factor established as a matter of policy by taxing authorities or as determined by a sampling of actual, arms-length market transactions where the ratio of assessed valuation to selling price can be calculated.

If, for example, assessed value is supposed to be 40 per cent of full, fair cash market value and the official tax rate is 7 per cent, the effective tax rate for application to full value is 40% of 7% or 2.8%. Assessed value would be too high in this case if the tax bill exceeds 2.8% of full value as indicated by the test.

6-FUNCTION COMPOUND INTEREST TABLES

Annual Rates	Increment	Compounding Frequency	— Term — Years	Periods
3%-12%	¼ %	Monthly	50	600
3%-12%	¼ %	Quarterly	60	240
3%-12%	¼ %	Semi-annually	60	120
3%-12%	¼ %	Annually	60	60
13%-20%	1%	Annually	30	30
21%-30%	1%	Annually	25	25

Intermediate Functions and Tabular Expansions:

Col. 1, the amt. of 1 and Col. 4, reversion factor, are expandable by multiplication. Col. 2 is an accumulation of Col. 1. Col. 3 is reciprocal of Col. 2. Col. 5 is the accumulation of Col. 4. Col. 6 is reciprocal of Col. 5. These relationships facilitate calculation of intermediate functions and expansion of the table. Example: find 6 monthly functions for 5 years, 7 months with interest at 9% per annum.

Col.

1. Col. 1 at 7 mo. × Col. 1 at 5 yrs: 1.053696 × 1.565681 = 1.649752
2. Col. 2 at 7 mo. + (Col. 1 at 7 mo. × Col. 2 at 5 yrs.)
   7.159483 + (1.053696 × 75.424136) = 86.633593
3. $\dfrac{1}{86.633593} = .011543$
4. Col. 4 at 7 mo. × Col. 4 at 5 yrs: .949040 × .638699 = .606151
5. Col. 5 at 7 mo. + (Col. 4 at 7 mo. × Col. 5 at 5 yrs.)
   6.794637 + (.949040 × 48.173373) = 52.513095
6. $\dfrac{1}{52.513095} = .019043$

Expansion:

A 99-year lease provides rent at $40,000 per year payable $10,000 quarterly in advance. What is the present value of this income stream at 9%?

[Col. 5 at 39 yrs. + (Col. 4 at 39 yrs. × Col. 5 at 60 yrs.)] × Base
[43.062979 + (.031083 × 44.231326)] 1.0225 = 45.437672
10000 × 45.437672 = $454,377

3% MONTHLY COMPOUND INTEREST TABLE 3%

EFFECTIVE RATE = 1/4% BASE = 1.0025

MONTHS	1 AMOUNT OF 1 AT COMPOUND INTEREST $S^n = (1+i)^n$	2 ACCUMULATION OF 1 PER PERIOD $S_{\overline{n}\mid} = \frac{S^n - 1}{i}$	3 SINKING FUND FACTOR $1/S_{\overline{n}\mid} = \frac{i}{S^n - 1}$	4 PRES. VALUE REVERSION OF 1 $V^n = \frac{1}{S^n}$	5 PRESENT VALUE ORD. ANNUITY 1 PER PERIOD $a_{\overline{n}\mid} = \frac{1 - V^n}{i}$	6 INSTALMENT TO AMORTIZE 1 $1/a_{\overline{n}\mid} = \frac{i}{1 - V^n}$	n MONTHS
1	1.002500	1.000000	1.000000	.997506	.997506	1.002500	1
2	1.005006	2.002500	.499376	.995019	1.992525	.501876	2
3	1.007519	3.007506	.332501	.992537	2.985062	.335001	3
4	1.010038	4.015025	.249064	.990062	3.975124	.251564	4
5	1.012563	5.025063	.199002	.987593	4.962718	.201502	5
6	1.015094	6.037625	.165628	.985130	5.947848	.168128	6
7	1.017632	7.052719	.141789	.982674	6.930522	.144289	7
8	1.020176	8.070351	.123910	.980223	7.910745	.126410	8
9	1.022726	9.090527	.110005	.977779	8.888524	.112505	9
10	1.025283	10.113253	.098880	.975340	9.863864	.101380	10
11	1.027846	11.138536	.089778	.972908	10.836772	.092278	11
YEARS							
1	1.030416	12.166383	.082194	.970482	11.807254	.084694	12
2	1.061757	24.702818	.040481	.941835	23.265980	.042981	24
3	1.094051	37.620560	.026581	.914034	34.386465	.029081	36
4	1.127328	50.931208	.019634	.887053	45.178695	.022134	48
5	1.161617	64.646713	.015469	.860869	55.652358	.017969	60
6	1.196948	78.779387	.012694	.835458	65.816858	.015194	72
7	1.233355	93.341920	.010713	.810797	75.681321	.013213	84
8	1.270868	108.347387	.009230	.786863	85.254603	.011730	96
9	1.309523	123.809259	.008077	.763637	94.545300	.010577	108
10	1.349354	139.741419	.007156	.741096	103.561753	.009656	120
11	1.390395	156.158171	.006404	.719220	112.312057	.008904	132
12	1.432686	173.074254	.005778	.697990	120.804068	.008278	144
13	1.476262	190.504855	.005249	.677386	129.045412	.007749	156
14	1.521164	208.465626	.004787	.657391	137.043485	.007297	168
15	1.567432	226.972690	.004406	.637986	144.805471	.006906	180
16	1.615107	246.042664	.004064	.619154	152.338338	.006564	192
17	1.664232	265.692670	.003764	.600878	159.648848	.006264	204
18	1.714851	285.940350	.003497	.583141	166.743566	.005997	216
19	1.767010	306.803882	.003259	.565928	173.628860	.005759	228
20	1.820755	328.301998	.003046	.549223	180.310914	.005546	240
21	1.876135	350.454000	.002853	.533011	186.795726	.005353	252
22	1.933199	373.279777	.002679	.517277	193.089119	.005179	264
23	1.992000	396.799821	.002520	.502008	199.196742	.005020	276
24	2.052588	421.035250	.002375	.487190	205.124079	.004875	288
25	2.115020	446.007823	.002242	.472809	210.876453	.004742	300
26	2.179350	471.739961	.002120	.458852	216.459027	.004620	312
27	2.245637	498.254766	.002007	.445308	221.876814	.004507	324
28	2.313940	525.576044	.001903	.432163	227.134678	.004403	336
29	2.384321	553.728325	.001806	.419407	232.237340	.004306	348
30	2.456842	582.736885	.001716	.407027	237.189381	.004216	360
31	2.531569	612.627767	.001632	.395012	241.995247	.004132	372
32	2.608570	643.427810	.001554	.383352	246.659252	.004054	384
33	2.687912	675.164665	.001481	.372036	251.185585	.003981	396
34	2.769667	707.866827	.001413	.361054	255.578309	.003913	408
35	2.853909	741.563657	.001349	.350397	259.841368	.003849	420
36	2.940714	776.285408	.001288	.340054	263.978589	.003788	432
37	3.030158	812.063254	.001231	.330016	267.993687	.003731	444
38	3.122323	848.929318	.001178	.320274	271.890267	.003678	456
39	3.217292	886.916698	.001128	.310820	275.671828	.003628	468
40	3.315149	926.059501	.001080	.301646	279.341763	.003580	480
41	3.415982	966.392870	.001035	.292742	282.903369	.003535	492
42	3.519883	1007.953017	.000992	.284100	286.359843	.003492	504
43	3.626943	1050.777255	.000952	.275714	289.714289	.003452	516
44	3.737260	1094.904033	.000913	.267576	292.969717	.003413	528
45	3.850932	1140.372970	.000877	.259677	296.129051	.003377	540
46	3.968062	1187.224888	.000842	.252012	299.195128	.003342	552
47	4.088755	1235.501852	.000809	.244573	302.170700	.003309	564
48	4.213118	1285.247206	.000778	.237354	305.058438	.003278	576
49	4.341264	1336.505612	.000748	.230348	307.860936	.003248	588
50	4.473308	1389.323092	.000720	.223548	310.580709	.003220	600

3% QUARTERLY COMPOUND INTEREST TABLE 3%

EFFECTIVE RATE = 3/4% BASE = 1.0075

QUARTERS	1 AMOUNT OF I AT COMPOUND INTEREST $S^n = (1+i)^n$	2 ACCUMULATION OF I PER PERIOD $S_{\overline{n}\rceil} = \frac{S^n - 1}{i}$	3 SINKING FUND FACTOR $1/S_{\overline{n}\rceil} = \frac{i}{S^n - 1}$	4 PRES. VALUE REVERSION OF I $V^n = \frac{1}{S^n}$	5 PRESENT VALUE ORD. ANNUITY 1 PER PERIOD $a_{\overline{n}\rceil} = \frac{1 - V^n}{i}$	6 INSTALMENT TO AMORTIZE I $1/a_{\overline{n}\rceil} = \frac{i}{1 - V^n}$	n QUARTERS
1	1.007500	1.000000	1.000000	.992556	.992556	1.007500	1
2	1.015056	2.007500	.498132	.985167	1.977723	.505632	2
3	1.022669	3.022556	.330846	.977833	2.955556	.338346	3
YEARS							
1	1.030339	4.045225	.247205	.970554	3.926110	.254705	4
2	1.061599	8.213180	.121756	.941975	7.736613	.129256	8
3	1.093807	12.507586	.079951	.914238	11.434913	.087451	12
4	1.126992	16.932282	.059059	.887318	15.024313	.066559	16
5	1.161184	21.491219	.046531	.861190	18.508020	.054031	20
6	1.196414	26.188471	.038185	.835831	21.889146	.045685	24
7	1.232712	31.028233	.032229	.811220	25.170713	.039729	28
8	1.270111	36.014830	.027766	.787333	28.355650	.035266	32
9	1.308645	41.152716	.024300	.764149	31.446805	.031800	36
10	1.348349	46.446482	.021530	.741648	34.446938	.029030	40
11	1.389256	51.900856	.019268	.719810	37.358730	.026768	44
12	1.431405	57.520711	.017385	.698614	40.184782	.024885	48
13	1.474833	63.311068	.015795	.678043	42.927618	.023295	52
14	1.519578	69.277100	.014435	.658077	45.589689	.021935	56
15	1.565681	75.424137	.013258	.638700	48.173374	.020758	60
16	1.613183	81.757670	.012231	.619893	50.680979	.019731	64
17	1.662125	88.283357	.011327	.601639	53.114746	.018827	68
18	1.712553	95.007028	.010526	.583924	55.476849	.018026	72
19	1.764510	101.934689	.009810	.566730	57.769398	.017310	76
20	1.818044	109.072531	.009168	.550042	59.994440	.016668	80
21	1.873202	116.426928	.008589	.533845	62.153965	.016089	84
22	1.930033	124.004453	.008064	.518126	64.249900	.015564	88
23	1.988589	131.811873	.007587	.502869	66.284119	.015087	92
24	2.048921	139.856164	.007150	.488062	68.258439	.014650	96
25	2.111084	148.144512	.006750	.473690	70.174623	.014250	100
26	2.175132	156.684322	.006382	.459742	72.034383	.013882	104
27	2.241124	165.483223	.006043	.446205	73.839382	.013543	108
28	2.309118	174.549075	.005729	.433066	75.591230	.013229	112
29	2.379175	183.889979	.005438	.420314	77.291494	.012938	116
30	2.451357	193.514277	.005168	.407937	78.941693	.012668	120
31	2.525729	203.430569	.004916	.395925	80.543300	.012416	124
32	2.602358	213.647713	.004681	.384267	82.097746	.012181	128
33	2.681311	224.174838	.004461	.372952	83.606420	.011961	132
34	2.762660	235.021346	.004255	.361970	85.070670	.011755	136
35	2.846477	246.196929	.004062	.351311	86.491805	.011562	140
36	2.932837	257.711570	.003880	.340967	87.871092	.011380	144
37	3.021817	269.575556	.003710	.330927	89.209765	.011210	148
38	3.113496	281.799485	.003549	.321182	90.509020	.011049	152
39	3.207957	294.394279	.003397	.311725	91.770018	.010897	156
40	3.305284	307.371189	.003253	.302546	92.993884	.010753	160
41	3.405564	320.741807	.003118	.293637	94.181713	.010618	164
42	3.508886	334.518080	.002989	.284991	95.334565	.010489	168
43	3.615342	348.712313	.002868	.276599	96.453470	.010368	172
44	3.725029	363.337187	.002752	.268454	97.539428	.010252	176
45	3.838043	378.405769	.002643	.260549	98.593409	.010143	180
46	3.954486	393.931519	.002539	.252877	99.616355	.010039	184
47	4.074462	409.928308	.002439	.245431	100.609179	.009939	188
48	4.198078	426.410427	.002345	.238204	101.572769	.009845	192
49	4.325444	443.392599	.002255	.231190	102.507985	.009755	196
50	4.456675	460.889997	.002170	.224383	103.415663	.009670	200
51	4.591887	478.918252	.002088	.217775	104.296614	.009588	204
52	4.731201	497.493470	.002010	.211363	105.151624	.009510	208
53	4.874742	516.632245	.001936	.205139	105.981458	.009436	212
54	5.022638	536.351674	.001864	.199099	106.786856	.009364	216
55	5.175020	556.669375	.001796	.193236	107.568539	.009296	220
56	5.332026	577.603499	.001731	.187546	108.327205	.009231	224
57	5.493796	599.172747	.001669	.182024	109.063531	.009169	228
58	5.660473	621.396389	.001609	.176664	109.778176	.009109	232
59	5.832207	644.294278	.001552	.171462	110.471777	.009052	236
60	6.009152	667.886870	.001497	.166413	111.144954	.008997	240

3% SEMI-ANNUAL COMPOUND INTEREST TABLE 3%

EFFECTIVE RATE = 1½% BASE = 1.015

HALF YEARS	1 AMOUNT OF 1 AT COMPOUND INTEREST $s^n = (1+i)^n$	2 ACCUMULATION OF 1 PER PERIOD $s_{\overline{n}\vert} = \frac{s^n - 1}{i}$	3 SINKING FUND FACTOR $1/s_{\overline{n}\vert} = \frac{i}{s^n - 1}$	4 PRES. VALUE REVERSION OF 1 $v^n = \frac{1}{s^n}$	5 PRESENT VALUE ORD. ANNUITY 1 PER PERIOD $a_{\overline{n}\vert} = \frac{1 - v^n}{i}$	6 INSTALMENT TO AMORTIZE 1 $1/a_{\overline{n}\vert} = \frac{i}{1 - v^n}$	n HALF YEARS
1	1.015000	1.000000	1.000000	.985222	.985222	1.015000	1
YEARS							
1	1.030225	2.015000	.496278	.970662	1.955883	.511278	2
2	1.061364	4.090903	.244445	.942184	3.854385	.259445	4
3	1.093443	6.229551	.160525	.914542	5.697187	.175525	6
4	1.126493	8.432839	.118584	.887711	7.485925	.133584	8
5	1.160541	10.702722	.093434	.861667	9.222185	.108434	10
6	1.195618	13.041211	.076680	.836387	10.907505	.091680	12
7	1.231756	15.450382	.064723	.811849	12.543382	.079723	14
8	1.268986	17.932370	.055765	.788031	14.131264	.070765	16
9	1.307341	20.489376	.048806	.764912	15.672561	.063806	18
10	1.346855	23.123667	.043246	.742470	17.168639	.058246	20
11	1.387564	25.837580	.038703	.720688	18.620824	.053703	22
12	1.429503	28.633521	.034924	.699544	20.030405	.049924	24
13	1.472710	31.513969	.031732	.679021	21.398632	.046732	26
14	1.517222	34.481479	.029001	.659099	22.726717	.044001	28
15	1.563080	37.538681	.026639	.639762	24.015838	.041639	30
16	1.610324	40.688288	.024577	.620993	25.267139	.039577	32
17	1.658996	43.933092	.022762	.602774	26.481729	.037762	34
18	1.709140	47.275969	.021152	.585090	27.660684	.036152	36
19	1.760798	50.719885	.019716	.567924	28.805052	.034716	38
20	1.814018	54.267894	.018427	.551262	29.915845	.033427	40
21	1.868847	57.923141	.017264	.535089	30.994050	.032264	42
22	1.925333	61.688868	.016210	.519391	32.040622	.031210	44
23	1.983526	65.568414	.015251	.504153	33.056490	.030251	46
24	2.043478	69.565219	.014375	.489362	34.042554	.029375	48
25	2.105242	73.682828	.013572	.475005	34.999688	.028572	50
26	2.168873	77.924892	.012833	.461069	35.928742	.027833	52
27	2.234428	82.295171	.012151	.447542	36.830539	.027151	54
28	2.301963	86.797543	.011521	.434412	37.705879	.026521	56
29	2.371540	91.435999	.010937	.421667	38.555538	.025937	58
30	2.443220	96.214652	.010393	.409296	39.380269	.025393	60
31	2.517066	101.137740	.009888	.397288	40.180804	.024888	62
32	2.593144	106.209628	.009415	.385632	40.957853	.024415	64
33	2.671522	111.434814	.008974	.374318	41.712105	.023974	66
34	2.752269	116.817931	.008560	.363337	42.444228	.023560	68
35	2.835456	122.363753	.008172	.352677	43.154872	.023172	70
36	2.921158	128.077197	.007808	.342330	43.844667	.022808	72
37	3.009450	133.963331	.007465	.332287	44.514224	.022465	74
38	3.100411	140.027372	.007141	.322538	45.164138	.022141	76
39	3.194120	146.274700	.006836	.313075	45.794985	.021836	78
40	3.290663	152.710852	.006548	.303890	46.407324	.021548	80
41	3.390123	159.341538	.006276	.294975	47.001697	.021276	82
42	3.492590	166.172636	.006018	.286321	47.578633	.021018	84
43	3.598153	173.210204	.005773	.277920	48.138643	.020773	86
44	3.706907	180.460482	.005541	.269767	48.682222	.020541	88
45	3.818949	187.929900	.005321	.261852	49.209855	.020321	90
46	3.934376	195.625082	.005112	.254170	49.722007	.020112	92
47	4.053293	203.552850	.004913	.246713	50.219134	.019913	94
48	4.175804	211.720235	.004723	.239475	50.701675	.019723	96
49	4.302017	220.134479	.004543	.232449	51.170060	.019543	98
50	4.432046	228.803043	.004371	.225629	51.624704	.019371	100
51	4.566004	237.733615	.004206	.219010	52.066009	.019206	102
52	4.704012	246.934114	.004050	.212585	52.494366	.019050	104
53	4.846190	256.412697	.003900	.206348	52.910157	.018900	106
54	4.992667	266.177771	.003757	.200294	53.313749	.018757	108
55	5.143570	276.237994	.003620	.194417	53.705500	.018620	110
56	5.299034	286.602288	.003489	.188714	54.085758	.018489	112
57	5.459198	297.279842	.003364	.183177	54.454860	.018364	114
58	5.624202	308.280125	.003244	.177803	54.813133	.018244	116
59	5.794193	319.612892	.003129	.172587	55.160895	.018129	118
60	5.969323	331.288192	.003019	.167523	55.498454	.018019	120

ANNUAL COMPOUND INTEREST TABLE

EFFECTIVE RATE = 3% BASE = 1.03

YEARS	1 AMOUNT OF 1 AT COMPOUND INTEREST $S^n = (1+i)^n$	2 ACCUMULATION OF 1 PER PERIOD $S_{\overline{n}\vert} = \frac{S^n - 1}{i}$	3 SINKING FUND FACTOR $1/S_{\overline{n}\vert} = \frac{i}{S^n - 1}$	4 PRES. VALUE REVERSION OF 1 $V^n = \frac{1}{S^n}$	5 PRESENT VALUE ORD. ANNUITY 1 PER PERIOD $a_{\overline{n}\vert} = \frac{1 - V^n}{i}$	6 INSTALMENT TO AMORTIZE 1 $1/a_{\overline{n}\vert} = \frac{i}{1 - V^n}$	n YEARS
1	1.030000	1.000000	1.000000	.970874	.970874	1.030000	1
2	1.060900	2.030000	.492611	.942596	1.913470	.522611	2
3	1.092727	3.090900	.323530	.915142	2.828611	.353530	3
4	1.125509	4.183627	.239027	.888487	3.717098	.269027	4
5	1.159274	5.309136	.188355	.862609	4.579707	.218355	5
6	1.194052	6.468410	.154598	.837484	5.417191	.184598	6
7	1.229874	7.662462	.130506	.813092	6.230283	.160506	7
8	1.266770	8.892336	.112456	.789409	7.019692	.142456	8
9	1.304773	10.159106	.098434	.766417	7.786109	.128434	9
10	1.343916	11.463879	.087231	.744094	8.530203	.117231	10
11	1.384234	12.807796	.078077	.722421	9.252624	.108077	11
12	1.425761	14.192030	.070462	.701380	9.954004	.100462	12
13	1.468534	15.617790	.064030	.680951	10.634955	.094030	13
14	1.512590	17.086324	.058526	.661118	11.296073	.088526	14
15	1.557967	18.598914	.053767	.641862	11.937935	.083767	15
16	1.604706	20.156881	.049611	.623167	12.561102	.079611	16
17	1.652848	21.761588	.045953	.605016	13.166118	.075953	17
18	1.702433	23.414435	.042709	.587395	13.753513	.072709	18
19	1.753506	25.116868	.039814	.570286	14.323799	.069814	19
20	1.806111	26.870374	.037216	.553676	14.877475	.067216	20
21	1.860295	28.676486	.034872	.537549	15.415024	.064872	21
22	1.916103	30.536780	.032747	.521893	15.936917	.062747	22
23	1.973587	32.452884	.030814	.506692	16.443608	.060814	23
24	2.032794	34.426470	.029047	.491934	16.935542	.059047	24
25	2.093778	36.459264	.027428	.477606	17.413148	.057428	25
26	2.156591	38.553042	.025938	.463695	17.876842	.055938	26
27	2.221289	40.709634	.024564	.450189	18.327031	.054564	27
28	2.287928	42.930923	.023293	.437077	18.764108	.053293	28
29	2.356566	45.218850	.022115	.424346	19.188455	.052115	29
30	2.427262	47.575416	.021019	.411987	19.600441	.051019	30
31	2.500080	50.002678	.019999	.399987	20.000428	.049999	31
32	2.575083	52.502759	.019047	.388337	20.388766	.049047	32
33	2.652335	55.077841	.018156	.377026	20.765792	.048156	33
34	2.731905	57.730177	.017322	.366045	21.131837	.047322	34
35	2.813862	60.462082	.016539	.355383	21.487220	.046539	35
36	2.898278	63.275944	.015804	.345032	21.832252	.045804	36
37	2.985227	66.174223	.015112	.334983	22.167235	.045112	37
38	3.074783	69.159449	.014459	.325226	22.492462	.044459	38
39	3.167027	72.234233	.013844	.315754	22.808215	.043844	39
40	3.262038	75.401260	.013262	.306557	23.114772	.043262	40
41	3.359899	78.663298	.012712	.297628	23.412400	.042712	41
42	3.460696	82.023196	.012192	.288959	23.701359	.042192	42
43	3.564517	85.483892	.011698	.280543	23.981902	.041698	43
44	3.671452	89.048409	.011230	.272372	24.254274	.041230	44
45	3.781596	92.719861	.010785	.264439	24.518713	.040785	45
46	3.895044	96.501457	.010363	.256737	24.775449	.040363	46
47	4.011895	100.396501	.009961	.249259	25.024708	.039961	47
48	4.132252	104.408396	.009578	.241999	25.266707	.039578	48
49	4.256219	108.540648	.009213	.234950	25.501657	.039213	49
50	4.383906	112.796867	.008865	.228107	25.729764	.038865	50
51	4.515423	117.180773	.008534	.221463	25.951227	.038534	51
52	4.650886	121.696197	.008217	.215013	26.166240	.038217	52
53	4.790412	126.347082	.007915	.208750	26.374990	.037915	53
54	4.934125	131.137495	.007626	.202670	26.577660	.037626	54
55	5.082149	136.071620	.007349	.196767	26.774428	.037349	55
56	5.234613	141.153768	.007084	.191036	26.965464	.037084	56
57	5.391651	146.388381	.006831	.185472	27.150936	.036831	57
58	5.553401	151.780033	.006588	.180070	27.331005	.036588	58
59	5.720003	157.333434	.006356	.174825	27.505831	.036356	59
60	5.891603	163.053437	.006133	.169733	27.675564	.036133	60

3 ¼% MONTHLY COMPOUND INTEREST TABLE 3 ¼%

EFFECTIVE RATE = 13/48% **BASE = 1.00270833+**

MONTHS	1 AMOUNT OF 1 AT COMPOUND INTEREST $s^n = (1+i)^n$	2 ACCUMULATION OF 1 PER PERIOD $s_{\overline{n}\vert} = \frac{s^n - 1}{i}$	3 SINKING FUND FACTOR $1/s_{\overline{n}\vert} = \frac{i}{s^n - 1}$	4 PRES. VALUE REVERSION OF 1 $v^n = \frac{1}{s^n}$	5 PRESENT VALUE ORD. ANNUITY 1 PER PERIOD $a_{\overline{n}\vert} = \frac{1 - v^n}{i}$	6 INSTALMENT TO AMORTIZE 1 $1/a_{\overline{n}\vert} = \frac{i}{1 - v^n}$	n MONTHS
1	1.002708	1.000000	1.000000	.997299	.997299	1.002708	1
2	1.005424	2.002708	.499324	.994605	1.991904	.502032	2
3	1.008147	3.008132	.332432	.991919	2.983823	.335140	3
4	1.010877	4.016279	.248987	.989240	3.973063	.251695	4
5	1.013615	5.027157	.198920	.986568	4.959630	.201628	5
6	1.016360	6.040772	.165542	.983903	5.943533	.168250	6
7	1.019113	7.057132	.141701	.981245	6.924779	.144409	7
8	1.021873	8.076245	.123820	.978595	7.903374	.126528	8
9	1.024641	9.098119	.109913	.975952	8.879326	.112621	9
10	1.027416	10.122759	.198787	.973316	9.852641	.101495	10
11	1.030198	11.150175	.089685	.970687	10.823328	.092393	11
YEARS							
1	1.032989	12.180374	.082099	.968065	11.791393	.084807	12
2	1.067065	24.762560	.040384	.937150	23.206228	.043092	24
3	1.102266	37.759813	.026483	.907222	34.256529	.029191	36
4	1.138628	51.185827	.019537	.878250	44.953940	.022245	48
5	1.176190	65.054745	.015372	.850203	55.309728	.018080	60
6	1.214991	79.381177	.012597	.823052	65.334803	.015305	72
7	1.255071	94.180218	.010618	.796767	75.039728	.013326	84
8	1.296474	109.467457	.009135	.771323	84.434726	.011843	96
9	1.339243	125.258999	.007983	.746690	93.529694	.010691	108
10	1.383423	141.571480	.007064	.722845	102.334214	.009772	120
11	1.429060	158.422086	.006312	.699761	110.857562	.009020	132
12	1.476202	175.828568	.005687	.677414	119.108716	.008395	144
13	1.524900	193.809265	.005160	.655781	127.096370	.007868	156
14	1.575204	212.383117	.004708	.634838	134.828938	.007416	168
15	1.627168	231.569694	.004318	.614565	142.314566	.007026	180
16	1.680846	251.389207	.003978	.594939	149.561140	.006686	192
17	1.736294	271.862536	.003678	.575939	156.576295	.006386	204
18	1.793572	293.011250	.003413	.557547	163.367420	.006121	216
19	1.852739	314.857629	.003176	.539741	169.941671	.005884	228
20	1.913859	337.424687	.002964	.522505	176.305973	.005672	240
21	1.976994	360.736199	.002772	.505818	182.467031	.005480	252
22	2.042212	384.816722	.002599	.489665	188.431336	.005307	264
23	2.109581	409.691627	.002441	.474028	194.205170	.005149	276
24	2.179173	435.387117	.002297	.458890	199.794617	.005005	288
25	2.251061	461.930264	.002165	.444235	205.205564	.004873	300
26	2.325320	489.349029	.002044	.430048	210.443713	.004752	312
27	2.402029	517.672299	.001932	.416315	215.514582	.004640	324
28	2.481268	546.929911	.001828	.403020	220.423512	.004536	336
29	2.563122	577.152688	.001733	.390149	225.175675	.004441	348
30	2.647675	608.372470	.001644	.377690	229.776078	.004352	360
31	2.735018	640.622145	.001561	.365628	234.229567	.004269	372
32	2.825242	673.935690	.001484	.353952	238.540834	.004192	384
33	2.918443	708.348199	.001412	.342648	242.714420	.004120	396
34	3.014718	743.895925	.001344	.331706	246.754723	.004052	408
35	3.114169	780.616318	.001281	.321113	250.665998	.003989	420
36	3.216901	818.548062	.001222	.310858	254.452367	.003930	432
37	3.323022	857.731117	.001166	.300931	258.117818	.003874	444
38	3.432643	898.206764	.001113	.291321	261.666213	.003821	456
39	3.545881	940.017641	.001064	.282017	265.101290	.003772	468
40	3.662854	983.207797	.001017	.273011	268.426668	.003725	480
41	3.783687	1027.822733	.000973	.264293	271.645849	.003681	492
42	3.908505	1073.909448	.000931	.255852	274.762226	.003639	504
43	4.037440	1121.516496	.000892	.247682	277.779081	.003600	516
44	4.170630	1170.694029	.000854	.239772	280.699593	.003562	528
45	4.308212	1221.493856	.000819	.232115	283.526839	.003527	540
46	4.450334	1273.969494	.000785	.224702	286.263796	.003493	552
47	4.597144	1328.176224	.000753	.217526	288.913348	.003461	564
48	4.748797	1384.171154	.000722	.210580	291.478287	.003430	576
49	4.905453	1442.013274	.000693	.203855	293.961315	.003401	588
50	5.067276	1501.763519	.000666	.197345	296.365047	.003374	600

3¼% QUARTERLY COMPOUND INTEREST TABLE 3¼%

EFFECTIVE RATE = 13/16% BASE = 1.008125

QUARTERS	1 AMOUNT OF 1 AT COMPOUND INTEREST $S^n = (1+i)^n$	2 ACCUMULATION OF 1 PER PERIOD $S_{\overline{n}\rvert} = \frac{S^n - 1}{i}$	3 SINKING FUND FACTOR $1/S_{\overline{n}\rvert} = \frac{i}{S^n - 1}$	4 PRES. VALUE REVERSION OF 1 $V^n = \frac{1}{S^n}$	5 PRESENT VALUE ORD. ANNUITY 1 PER PERIOD $a_{\overline{n}\rvert} = \frac{1 - V^n}{i}$	6 INSTALMENT TO AMORTIZE 1 $1/a_{\overline{n}\rvert} = \frac{i}{1 - V^n}$	n QUARTERS
1	1.008125	1.000000	1.000000	.991940	.991940	1.008125	1
2	1.016316	2.008125	.497977	.983946	1.975886	.506102	2
3	1.024574	3.024441	.330640	.976016	2.951902	.338765	3
YEARS							
1	1.032898	4.049015	.246974	.968150	3.920052	.255099	4
2	1.066879	8.231235	.121488	.937314	7.715248	.129613	8
3	1.101977	12.551042	.079675	.907460	11.389566	.087800	12
4	1.138230	17.012964	.058779	.878557	14.946855	.066904	16
5	1.175676	21.621676	.046250	.850574	18.390844	.054375	20
6	1.214354	26.382005	.037905	.823483	21.725139	.046030	24
7	1.254304	31.298942	.031950	.797255	24.953236	.040075	28
8	1.295568	36.377636	.027489	.771862	28.078517	.035614	32
9	1.338190	41.623411	.024025	.747278	31.104256	.032150	36
10	1.382214	47.041763	.021258	.723477	34.033624	.029383	40
11	1.427687	52.638369	.018998	.700434	36.869691	.027123	44
12	1.474655	58.419093	.017118	.678125	39.615427	.025243	48
13	1.523169	64.389994	.015530	.656526	42.273711	.023655	52
14	1.573278	70.557326	.014173	.635615	44.847328	.022298	56
15	1.625036	76.927553	.012999	.615371	47.338973	.021124	60
16	1.678497	83.507349	.011975	.595771	49.751259	.020100	64
17	1.733717	90.303608	.011074	.576795	52.086712	.019199	68
18	1.790753	97.323453	.010275	.558424	54.347780	.018400	72
19	1.849666	104.574238	.009563	.540638	56.536832	.017688	76
20	1.910516	112.063562	.008924	.523419	58.656162	.017049	80
21	1.973369	119.799271	.008347	.506748	60.707990	.016472	84
22	2.038289	127.789471	.007825	.490607	62.694467	.015950	88
23	2.105346	136.042534	.007351	.474981	64.617674	.015476	92
24	2.174608	144.567110	.006917	.459853	66.479625	.015042	96
25	2.246149	153.372128	.006520	.445207	68.282273	.014645	100
26	2.320043	162.466816	.006155	.431027	70.027506	.014280	104
27	2.396368	171.860704	.005819	.417298	71.717152	.013944	108
28	2.475205	181.563634	.005508	.404007	73.352982	.013633	112
29	2.556634	191.585773	.005220	.391139	74.936711	.013345	116
30	2.640743	201.937623	.004952	.378681	76.469997	.013077	120
31	2.727619	212.630031	.004703	.366620	77.954447	.012828	124
32	2.817353	223.674200	.004471	.354943	79.391617	.012596	128
33	2.910039	235.081703	.004254	.343638	80.783012	.012379	132
34	3.005774	246.864493	.004051	.332693	82.130091	.012176	136
35	3.104659	259.034915	.003860	.322097	83.434265	.011985	140
36	3.206797	271.605724	.003682	.311838	84.696900	.011807	144
37	3.312294	284.590090	.003514	.301906	85.919320	.011639	148
38	3.421263	298.001618	.003356	.292290	87.102806	.011481	152
39	3.533817	311.854363	.003207	.282980	88.248596	.011332	156
40	3.650073	326.162838	.003066	.273967	89.357893	.011191	160
41	3.770154	340.942037	.002933	.265241	90.431859	.011058	164
42	3.894185	356.207446	.002807	.256793	91.471618	.010932	168
43	4.022297	371.975060	.002688	.248614	92.478260	.010813	172
44	4.154624	388.261401	.002576	.240696	93.452840	.010701	176
45	4.291304	405.083533	.002469	.233029	94.396380	.010594	180
46	4.432480	422.459085	.002367	.225607	95.309867	.010492	184
47	4.578301	440.406261	.002271	.218422	96.194259	.010396	188
48	4.728919	458.943868	.002179	.211465	97.050484	.010304	192
49	4.884492	478.091330	.002092	.204730	97.879437	.010217	196
50	5.045183	497.868710	.002009	.198209	98.681987	.010134	200
51	5.211161	518.296731	.001929	.191896	99.458976	.010054	204
52	5.382599	539.396797	.001854	.185784	100.211218	.009979	208
53	5.559677	561.191019	.001782	.179867	100.939500	.009907	212
54	5.742581	583.702233	.001713	.174138	101.644586	.009838	216
55	5.931501	606.954025	.001648	.168591	102.327215	.009773	220
56	6.126637	630.970761	.001585	.163222	102.988102	.009710	224
57	6.328193	655.777606	.001525	.158023	103.627940	.009650	228
58	6.536379	681.400552	.001468	.152990	104.247398	.009593	232
59	6.751415	707.866448	.001413	.148117	104.847126	.009538	236
60	6.973525	735.203025	.001360	.143400	105.427753	.009485	240

3 ¼% SEMI-ANNUAL COMPOUND INTEREST TABLE 3 ¼%

EFFECTIVE = 1-5/8% **BASE = 1.01625**

	1 AMOUNT OF 1 AT COMPOUND INTEREST $S^n = (1+i)^n$	2 ACCUMULATION OF 1 PER PERIOD $S_{\overline{n}\rceil} = \frac{S^n - 1}{i}$	3 SINKING FUND FACTOR $1/S_{\overline{n}\rceil} = \frac{i}{S^n - 1}$	4 PRES. VALUE REVERSION OF 1 $V^n = \frac{1}{S^n}$	5 PRESENT VALUE ORD. ANNUITY 1 PER PERIOD $a_{\overline{n}\rceil} = \frac{1 - V^n}{i}$	6 INSTALMENT TO AMORTIZE 1 $1/a_{\overline{n}\rceil} = \frac{i}{1 - V^n}$	n HALF YEARS
HALF YEARS 1	1.016250	1.000000	1.000000	.984010	.984010	1.016250	1
YEARS 1	1.032764	2.016250	.495970	.968275	1.952285	.512220	2
2	1.066602	4.098561	.243988	.937557	3.842635	.260238	4
3	1.101548	6.249096	.160023	.907814	5.673014	.176273	6
4	1.137639	8.470092	.118062	.879013	7.445325	.134312	8
5	1.174913	10.763856	.092904	.851127	9.161410	.109154	10
6	1.213408	13.132774	.076145	.824125	10.823053	.092395	12
7	1.253164	15.579307	.064188	.797980	12.431980	.080438	14
8	1.294222	18.105999	.055230	.772665	13.989866	.071480	16
9	1.336626	20.715475	.048273	.748152	15.498327	.064523	18
10	1 380420	23.410448	.042716	.724417	16.958934	.058966	20
11	1.425648	26.193719	.038177	.701435	18.373203	.054427	22
12	1.472358	29.068182	.034402	.679183	19.742605	.050652	24
13	1.520598	32.036823	.031214	.657636	21.068563	.047464	26
14	1.570419	35.102730	.028488	.636773	22.352456	.044738	28
15	1.621873	38.269088	.026131	.616571	23.595618	.042381	30
16	1.675012	41.539189	.024074	.597011	24.799341	.040324	32
17	1.729892	44.916431	.022264	.578071	25.964876	.038514	34
18	1.786570	48.404326	.020659	.559732	27.093435	.036909	36
19	1.845106	52.006498	.019228	.541974	28.186191	.035478	38
20	1.905559	55.726693	.017945	.524780	29.244279	.034195	40
21	1.967993	59.568775	.016787	.508132	30.268801	.033037	42
22	2.032472	63.536741	.015739	.492012	31.260819	.031989	44
23	2.099064	67.634712	.014785	.476403	32.221366	.031035	46
24	2.167838	71.866950	.013915	.461289	33.151440	.030165	48
25	2.238865	76.237853	.013117	.446655	34.052008	.029367	50
26	2.312219	80.751965	.012384	.432485	34.924006	.028634	52
27	2.387977	85.413978	.011708	.418764	35.768340	.027958	54
28	2.466217	90.228737	.011083	.405479	36.585887	.027333	56
29	2.547020	95.201247	.010504	.392616	37.377499	.026754	58
30	2.630471	100.336676	.009966	.380160	38.143996	.026216	60
31	2.716656	105.640363	.009466	.368100	38.886177	.025716	62
32	2.805665	111.117821	.008999	.356422	39.604813	.025249	64
33	2.897590	116.774742	.008563	.345114	40.300650	.024813	66
34	2.992526	122.617007	.008155	.334166	40.974412	.024405	68
35	3.090574	128.650688	.007773	.323565	41.626799	.024023	70
36	3.191833	134.882057	.007414	.313300	42.258489	.023664	72
37	3.296411	141.317591	.007076	.303360	42.870139	.023326	74
38	3.404415	147.963980	.006758	.293736	43.462385	.023008	76
39	3.515957	154.828131	.006459	.284418	44.035842	.022709	78
40	3.631154	161.917180	.006176	.275395	44.591106	.022426	80
41	3.750126	169.238494	.005909	.266658	45.128754	.022159	82
42	3.872995	176.799685	.005656	.258198	45.649346	.021906	84
43	3.999890	184.608611	.005417	.250007	46.153423	.021667	86
44	4.130943	192.673389	.005190	.242076	46.641507	.021440	88
45	4.266289	201.002402	.004975	.234396	47.114108	.021225	90
46	4.406070	209.604307	.004771	.226960	47.571715	.021021	92
47	4.550431	218.488046	.004577	.219759	48.014805	.020827	94
48	4.699521	227.662851	.004392	.212788	48.443838	.020642	96
49	4.853497	237.138261	.004217	.206037	48.859260	.020467	98
50	5.012517	246.924124	.004050	.199501	49.261503	.020300	100
51	5.176747	257.030612	.003891	.193171	49.650985	.020141	102
52	5.346359	267.468229	.003739	.187043	50.028111	.019989	104
53	5.521527	278.247824	.003594	.181109	50.393273	.019844	106
54	5.702435	289.380604	.003456	.175364	50.746850	.019706	108
55	5.889270	300.878138	.003324	.169800	51.089210	.019574	110
56	6.082226	312.752378	.003197	.164413	51.420709	.019447	112
57	6.281505	325.015666	.003077	.159198	51.741691	.019327	114
58	6.487312	337.680750	.002961	.154147	52.052490	.019211	116
59	6.699863	350.760793	.002851	.149257	52.353429	.019101	118
60	6.919378	364.269392	.002745	.144522	52.644820	.018995	120

3 ¼% ANNUAL COMPOUND INTEREST TABLE 3 ¼%

EFFECTIVE RATE = 3¼% BASE = 1.0325

YEARS	1 AMOUNT OF I AT COMPOUND INTEREST $S^n = (1+i)^n$	2 ACCUMULATION OF I PER PERIOD $S_{\overline{n}\vert} = \frac{S^n - 1}{i}$	3 SINKING FUND FACTOR $1/S_{\overline{n}\vert} = \frac{i}{S^n - 1}$	4 PRES. VALUE REVERSION OF I $V^n = \frac{1}{S^n}$	5 PRESENT VALUE ORD. ANNUITY 1 PER PERIOD $a_{\overline{n}\vert} = \frac{1-V^n}{i}$	6 INSTALMENT TO AMORTIZE I $1/a_{\overline{n}\vert} = \frac{i}{1-V^n}$	n YEARS
1	1.032500	1.000000	1.000000	.968523	.968523	1.032500	1
2	1.066056	2.032500	.492005	.938037	1.906560	.524505	2
3	1.100703	3.098556	.322731	.908510	2.815070	.355231	3
4	1.136476	4.199259	.238137	.879913	3.694983	.270637	4
5	1.173411	5.335735	.187416	.852216	4.547199	.219916	5
6	1.211547	6.509147	.153630	.825391	5.372590	.186130	6
7	1.250923	7.720694	.129522	.799410	6.172000	.162022	7
8	1.291578	8.971616	.111463	.774247	6.946247	.143963	8
9	1.333554	10.263194	.097436	.749876	7.696123	.129936	9
10	1.376894	11.596748	.086231	.726272	8.422395	.118731	10
11	1.421643	12.973642	.077079	.703411	9.125806	.109579	11
12	1.467847	14.395285	.069467	.681270	9.807076	.101967	12
13	1.515552	15.863132	.063039	.659826	10.466902	.095539	13
14	1.564807	17.378684	.057542	.639056	11.105958	.090042	14
15	1.615663	18.943491	.052789	.618941	11.724899	.085289	15
16	1.668173	20.559155	.048640	.599458	12.324358	.081140	16
17	1.722388	22.227327	.044990	.580589	12.904947	.07749[illegible]	17
18	1.778366	23.949715	.041754	.562314	13.467261	.074254	18
19	1.836163	25.728081	.038868	.544614	14.011875	.071368	19
20	1.895838	27.564244	.036279	.527471	14.539346	.068779	20
21	1.957453	29.460082	.033944	.510868	15.050214	.066444	21
22	2.021070	31.417534	.031829	.494787	15.545002	.064329	22
23	2.086755	33.438604	.029906	.479213	16.024215	.062406	23
24	2.154574	35.525359	.028149	.464129	16.488343	.060649	24
25	2.224598	37.679933	.026539	.449519	16.937863	.059039	25
26	2.296897	39.904531	.025060	.435370	17.373233	.057560	26
27	2.371546	42.201428	.023696	.421666	17.794899	.056196	27
28	2.448622	44.572975	.022435	.408393	18.203292	.054935	28
29	2.528202	47.021596	.021267	.395538	18.598830	.053767	29
30	2.610368	49.549798	.020182	.383088	18.981917	.052682	30
31	2.695205	52.160167	.019172	.371029	19.352947	.051672	31
32	2.782800	54.855372	.018230	.359350	19.712297	.050730	32
33	2.873241	57.638172	.017350	.348039	20.060336	.049850	33
34	2.966621	60.511412	.016526	.337084	20.397420	.049026	34
35	3.063036	63.478033	.015753	.326473	20.723893	.048253	35
36	3.162585	66.541069	.015028	.316197	21.040090	.047528	36
37	3.265369	69.703654	.014346	.306244	21.346335	.046846	37
38	3.371493	72.969023	.013704	.296604	21.642939	.046204	38
39	3.481067	76.340516	.013099	.287268	21.930207	.045599	39
40	3.594201	79.821583	.012528	.278226	22.208433	.045028	40
41	3.711013	83.415784	.011988	.269468	22.477901	.044488	41
42	3.831621	87.126797	.011478	.260986	22.738888	.043978	42
43	3.956149	90.958418	.010994	.252771	22.991659	.043494	43
44	4.084723	94.914566	.010536	.244815	23.236473	.043036	44
45	4.217477	98.999290	.010101	.237109	23.473582	.042601	45
46	4.354545	103.216767	.009688	.229645	23.703227	.042188	46
47	4.496068	107.571312	.009296	.222417	23.925644	.041796	47
48	4.642190	112.067379	.008923	.215416	24.141059	.041423	48
49	4.793061	116.709569	.008568	.208635	24.349694	.041068	49
50	4.948835	121.502630	.008230	.202068	24.551762	.040730	50
51	5.109673	126.451466	.007908	.195707	24.747469	.040408	51
52	5.275737	131.561138	.007601	.189547	24.937016	.040101	52
53	5.447198	136.836875	.007308	.183581	25.120597	.039808	53
54	5.624232	142.284074	.007028	.177802	25.298399	.039528	54
55	5.807020	147.908306	.006761	.172205	25.470604	.039261	55
56	5.995748	153.715326	.006506	.166785	25.637389	.039006	56
57	6.190610	159.711074	.006261	.161535	25.798924	.038761	57
58	6.391805	165.901684	.006028	.156450	25.955374	.038528	58
59	6.599538	172.293489	.005804	.151526	26.106900	.038304	59
60	6.814023	178.893027	.005590	.146756	26.253656	.038090	60

3½% MONTHLY COMPOUND INTEREST TABLE 3½%

EFFECTIVE RATE = 7/24% **BASE = 1.00291666+**

MONTHS	1 AMOUNT OF I AT COMPOUND INTEREST $S^n = (1+i)^n$	2 ACCUMULATION OF I PER PERIOD $S_{\overline{n}\rvert} = \frac{S^n - 1}{i}$	3 SINKING FUND FACTOR $1/S_{\overline{n}\rvert} = \frac{i}{S^n - 1}$	4 PRES. VALUE REVERSION OF I $V^n = \frac{1}{S^n}$	5 PRESENT VALUE ORD. ANNUITY 1 PER PERIOD $a_{\overline{n}\rvert} = \frac{1-V^n}{i}$	6 INSTALMENT TO AMORTIZE I $1/a_{\overline{n}\rvert} = \frac{i}{1-V^n}$	n MONTHS
1	1.002917	1.000000	1.000000	.997092	.997092	1.002917	1
2	1.005842	2.002917	.499272	.994192	1.991284	.502189	2
3	1.008776	3.008759	.332363	.991301	2.982585	.335280	3
4	1.011718	4.017534	.248909	.988418	3.971003	.251826	4
5	1.014669	5.029252	.198837	.985543	4.956546	.201754	5
6	1.017628	6.043921	.165456	.982677	5.939223	.168373	6
7	1.020596	7.061549	.141612	.979819	6.919043	.144529	7
8	1.023573	8.082145	.123730	.976970	7.896013	.126647	8
9	1.026558	9.105718	.109821	.974129	8.870141	.112738	9
10	1.029552	10.132276	.098695	.971296	9.841437	.101612	10
11	1.032555	11.161829	.089591	.968471	10.809908	.092508	11
YEARS							
1	1.035567	12.194384	.082005	965655	11.775563	.084922	12
2	1.072399	24.822485	.040286	.932489	23.146690	.043203	24
3	1.110541	37.899729	.026385	.900462	34.127270	.029302	36
4	1.150039	51.442091	.019439	.869535	44.730719	.022356	48
5	1.190943	65.466113	.015275	839671	54.969988	.018192	60
6	1.233301	79.988927	.012502	.810832	64.857585	.015419	72
7	1.277166	95.028273	.010523	.782984	74.405589	.013440	84
8	1.322591	110.602523	.009041	.756092	83.625663	.011958	96
9	1.369631	126.730702	.007891	.730124	92.529069	.010808	108
10	1.418345	143.432511	.006972	.705047	101.126685	.009889	120
11	1.468791	160.728352	.006222	.680832	109.429012	.009139	132
12	1 521031	178.639354	.005598	.657449	117.446193	.008515	144
13	1.575130	197.187395	.005071	.634868	125.188020	.007988	156
14	1.631152	216.395134	.004621	.613063	132.663952	.007538	168
15	1.689168	236.286033	.004232	.592008	139.883119	.007149	180
16	1.749246	256.884392	.003893	.571675	146.854341	.006810	192
17	1.811462	278.215371	.003594	.552040	153.586134	.006511	204
18	1.875890	300.305028	.003330	.533080	160.086721	.006247	216
19	1.942609	323.180346	.003094	.514772	166.364043	.006011	228
20	2 011702	346.869271	.002883	.497092	172.425768	.005800	240
21	2.083252	371.400738	.002693	.480019	178.279300	.005610	252
22	2.157347	396.804714	.002520	.463532	183.931790	.005437	264
23	2.234077	423.112233	.002363	.447612	189.390144	005280	276
24	2.313537	450.355430	.002220	.432239	194.661028	.005137	288
25	2.395822	478.567584	.002090	.417393	199.750882	.005007	300
26	2.481034	507.783159	.001969	.403058	204.665922	.004886	312
27	2.569277	538.037843	.001859	.389215	209.412154	004776	324
28	2.660658	569.368593	.001756	.375847	213.995374	.004673	336
29	2.755290	601.813684	.001662	.362938	218.421182	.004579	348
30	2.853287	635.412747	.001574	.350473	222.694984	.004491	360
31	2.954770	670.206826	.001492	.338436	226.822000	.004409	372
32	3.059862	706.238425	.001416	.326812	230.807273	.004333	384
33	3.168692	743.551558	.001345	.315588	234.655669	.004262	396
34	3.281393	782.191805	.001278	.304749	238.371891	.004195	408
35	3.398102	822.206369	.001216	.294282	241.960478	004133	420
36	3.518962	863.644128	.001158	.284175	245.425813	.004075	432
37	3.644121	906.555702	.001103	.274415	248.772131	.004020	444
38	3.773731	950 993511	.001052	.264990	252.003517	.003969	456
39	3 907951	997.011836	.001003	.255889	255.123920	.003920	468
40	4.046945	1044.666894	.000957	.247100	258.137152	.003874	480
41	4.190883	1094.016896	.000914	.238613	261.046893	.003831	492
42	4.339940	1145.122128	.000873	.230418	263.856698	.003790	504
43	4.494298	1198.045017	.000835	.222504	266.569999	.003752	516
44	4.654146	1252.850212	.000798	.214862	269.190111	.003715	528
45	4.819680	1309.604661	.000764	.207483	271.720234	.003681	540
46	4.991102	1368.377693	.000731	.200357	274.163459	.003648	552
47	5.168620	1429.241102	.000700	.193475	276.522770	.003617	564
48	5.352452	1492.269238	.000670	.186830	278.801050	.003587	576
49	5.542822	1557.539092	.000642	.180414	281.001082	.003559	588
50	5 739964	1625.130396	.000615	.174217	283.125552	.003532	600

3½% QUARTERLY COMPOUND INTEREST TABLE 3½%

EFFECTIVE RATE = 7/8% BASE = 1.00875

QUARTERS	1 AMOUNT OF 1 AT COMPOUND INTEREST $s^n = (1+i)^n$	2 ACCUMULATION OF 1 PER PERIOD $s_{\overline{n}\vert} = \frac{s^n - 1}{i}$	3 SINKING FUND FACTOR $1/s_{\overline{n}\vert} = \frac{i}{s^n - 1}$	4 PRES. VALUE REVERSION OF 1 $v^n = \frac{1}{s^n}$	5 PRESENT VALUE ORD. ANNUITY 1 PER PERIOD $a_{\overline{n}\vert} = \frac{1 - v^n}{i}$	6 INSTALMENT TO AMORTIZE 1 $1/a_{\overline{n}\vert} = \frac{i}{1 - v^n}$	n QUARTERS
1	1.008750	1.000000	1.000000	.991326	.991326	1.008750	1
2	1.017577	2.008750	.497822	.982727	1.974053	.506572	2
3	1.026480	3.026327	.330434	.974203	2.948256	.339184	3
YEARS							
1	1.035462	4.052807	.246743	.965752	3.914008	.255493	4
2	1.072182	8.249335	.121222	.932678	7.693971	.129972	8
3	1.110203	12.594680	.079399	.900736	11.344479	.088149	12
4	1.149574	17.094120	.058500	.869888	14.869967	.067250	16
5	1.190340	21.753120	.045970	.840096	18.274714	.054720	20
6	1.232552	26.577337	.037626	.811325	21.562858	.046376	24
7	1.276261	31.572631	.031673	.783539	24.738391	.040423	28
8	1.321519	36.745069	.027215	.756705	27.805169	.035965	32
9	1.368383	42.100932	.023752	.730789	30.766918	.032502	36
10	1.416909	47.646724	.020988	.705762	33.627234	.029738	40
11	1.467155	53.389182	.018730	.681591	36.389591	.027480	44
12	1.519184	59.335280	.016853	.658248	39.057344	.025603	48
13	1.573057	65.492238	.015269	.635705	41.633733	.024019	52
14	1.628841	71.867534	.013914	.613933	44.121886	.022664	56
15	1.686603	78.468912	.012744	.592908	46.524827	.021494	60
16	1.746413	85.304388	.011723	.572602	48.845473	.020473	64
17	1.808345	92.382265	.010825	.552992	51.086642	.019575	68
18	1.872472	99.711137	.010029	.534053	53.251057	.018779	72
19	1.938874	107.299906	.009320	.515763	55.341346	.018070	76
20	2.007631	115.157789	.008684	.498100	57.360047	.017434	80
21	2.078825	123.294329	.008111	.481041	59.309613	.016861	84
22	2.152545	131.719406	.007592	.464566	61.192411	.016342	88
23	2.228878	140.443255	.007120	.448656	63.010728	.015870	92
24	2.307919	149.476469	.006690	.433291	64.766771	.015440	96
25	2.389763	158.830020	.006296	.418452	66.462675	.015046	100
26	2.474509	168.515266	.005934	.404121	68.100498	.014684	104
27	2.562260	178.543972	.005601	.390280	69.682229	.014351	108
28	2.653123	188.928316	.005293	.376914	71.209790	.014043	112
29	2.747208	199.680910	.005008	.364006	72.685036	.013758	116
30	2.844630	210.814813	.004743	.351540	74.109758	.013493	120
31	2.945506	222.343548	.004498	.339500	75.485687	.013248	124
32	3.049960	234.281115	.004268	.327873	76.814494	.013018	128
33	3.158118	246.642013	.004054	.316644	78.097792	.012804	132
34	3.270111	259.441254	.003854	.305800	79.337141	.012604	136
35	3.386076	272.694383	.003667	.295327	80.534044	.012417	140
36	3.506153	286.417494	.003491	.285213	81.689957	.012241	144
37	3.630488	300.627256	.003326	.275445	82.806283	.012076	148
38	3.759233	315.340925	.003171	.266012	83.884377	.011921	152
39	3.892543	330.576370	.003025	.256901	84.925549	.011775	156
40	4.030581	346.352097	.002887	.248103	85.931063	.011637	160
41	4.173514	362.687263	.002757	.239606	86.902141	.011507	164
42	4.321515	379.601707	.002634	.231400	87.839962	.011384	168
43	4.474765	397.115973	.002518	.223475	88.745665	.011268	172
44	4.633449	415.251330	.002408	.215822	89.620349	.011158	176
45	4.797761	434.029805	.002304	.208431	90.465078	.011054	180
46	4.967899	453.474203	.002205	.201292	91.280877	.010955	184
47	5.144071	473.608140	.002111	.194399	92.068737	.010861	188
48	5.326491	494.456067	.002022	.187741	92.829614	.010772	192
49	5.515379	516.043305	.001938	.181311	93.564434	.010688	196
50	5.710966	538.396071	.001857	.175102	94.274087	.010607	200
51	5.913488	561.541512	.001781	.169105	94.959437	.010531	204
52	6.123193	585.507738	.001708	.163313	95.621315	.010458	208
53	6.340334	610.323856	.001638	.157720	96.260525	.010388	212
54	6.565175	636.020004	.001572	.152319	96.877844	.010322	216
55	6.797990	662.627391	.001509	.147102	97.474022	.010259	220
56	7.039060	690.178331	.001449	.142064	98.049781	.010199	224
57	7.288680	718.706283	.001391	.137199	98.605822	.010141	228
58	7.547152	748.245896	.001336	.132500	99.142821	.010086	232
59	7.814789	778.833044	.001284	.127963	99.661428	.010034	236
60	8.091918	810.504876	.001234	.123580	100.162274	.009984	240

3½% SEMI-ANNUAL COMPOUND INTEREST TABLE 3½%

EFFECTIVE RATE = 1¾% BASE = 1.0175

HALF YEARS	1 AMOUNT OF 1 AT COMPOUND INTEREST $S^n = (1+i)^n$	2 ACCUMULATION OF 1 PER PERIOD $S_{\overline{n}\vert} = \frac{S^n - 1}{i}$	3 SINKING FUND FACTOR $1/S_{\overline{n}\vert} = \frac{i}{S^n - 1}$	4 PRES. VALUE REVERSION OF 1 $V^n = \frac{1}{S^n}$	5 PRESENT VALUE ORD. ANNUITY 1 PER PERIOD $a_{\overline{n}\vert} = \frac{1 - V^n}{i}$	6 INSTALMENT TO AMORTIZE 1 $1/a_{\overline{n}\vert} = \frac{i}{1 - V^n}$	n HALF YEARS
1	1.017500	1.000000	1.000000	.982801	.982801	1.017500	1
YEARS							
1	1.035306	2.017500	.495663	.965898	1.948699	.513163	2
2	1.071859	4.106230	.243532	.932959	3.830943	.261032	4
3	1.109702	6.268706	.159523	.901143	5.648998	.177023	6
4	1.148882	8.507530	.117543	.870412	7.405053	.135043	8
5	1.189444	10.825399	.092375	.840729	9.101223	.109875	10
6	1.231439	13.225104	.075614	.812058	10.739550	.093114	12
7	1.274917	15.709533	.063656	.784365	12.322006	.081156	14
8	1.319929	18.281677	.054700	.757616	13.850497	.072200	16
9	1.366531	20.944635	.047745	.731780	15.326863	.065245	18
10	1.414778	23.701611	.042191	.706825	16.752881	.059691	20
11	1.464729	26.555926	.037656	.682720	18.130269	.055156	22
12	1.516443	29.511016	.033886	.659438	19.460686	.051386	24
13	1.569983	32.570440	.030703	.636950	20.745732	.048203	26
14	1.625413	35.737880	.027982	.615228	21.986955	.045482	28
15	1.682800	39.017150	.025630	.594248	23.185849	.043130	30
16	1.742213	42.412200	.023578	.573982	24.343859	.041078	32
17	1.803725	45.927115	.021774	.554408	25.462378	.039274	34
18	1.867407	49.566129	.020175	.535502	26.542753	.037675	36
19	1.933338	53.333624	.018750	.517240	27.586285	.036250	38
20	2.001597	57.234134	.017472	.499601	28.594230	.034972	40
21	2.072266	61.272357	.016321	.482563	29.567801	.033821	42
22	2.145430	65.453154	.015278	.466107	30.508172	.032778	44
23	2.221177	69.781559	.014330	.450212	31.416474	.031830	46
24	2.299599	74.262784	.013466	.434858	32.293801	.030966	48
25	2.380789	78.902225	.012674	.420029	33.141209	.030174	50
26	2.464846	83.705466	.011947	.405705	33.959719	.029447	52
27	2.551870	88.678292	.011277	.391869	34.750316	.028777	54
28	2.641967	93.826690	.010658	.378506	35.513951	.028158	56
29	2.735245	99.156859	.010085	.365598	36.251545	.027585	58
30	2.831816	104.675216	.009553	.353130	36.963986	.027053	60
31	2.931797	110.388405	.009059	.341088	37.652130	.026559	62
32	3.035308	116.303306	.008598	.329456	38.316807	.026098	64
33	3.142473	122.427039	.008168	.318221	38.958817	.025668	66
34	3.253422	128.766979	.007766	.307369	39.578934	.025266	68
35	3.368288	135.330758	.007389	.296887	40.177903	.024889	70
36	3.487210	142.126280	.007036	.286762	40.756445	.024536	72
37	3.610330	149.161726	.006704	.276983	41.315259	.024204	74
38	3.737797	156.445567	.006392	.267537	41.855015	.023892	76
39	3.869765	163.986573	.006098	.258414	42.376364	.023598	78
40	4.006392	171.793824	.005821	.249601	42.879935	.023321	80
41	4.147843	179.876720	.005559	.241089	43.366332	.023059	82
42	4.294287	188.244992	.005312	.232868	43.836142	.022812	84
43	4.445903	196.908717	.005078	.224926	44.289931	.022578	86
44	4.602871	205.878326	.004857	.217256	44.728244	.022357	88
45	4.765381	215.164617	.004648	.209847	45.151610	.022148	90
46	4.933629	224.778773	.004449	.202691	45.560539	.021949	92
47	5.107816	234.732369	.004260	.195778	45.955521	.021760	94
48	5.288154	245.037388	.004081	.189102	46.337035	.021581	96
49	5.474859	255.706239	.003911	.182653	46.705537	.021411	98
50	5.668156	266.751768	.003749	.176424	47.061473	.021249	100
51	5.868277	278.187273	.003595	.170408	47.405271	.021095	102
52	6.075464	290.026522	.003448	.164596	47.737344	.020948	104
53	6.289966	302.283771	.003308	.158983	48.058093	.020808	106
54	6.512041	314.973777	.003175	.153562	48.367904	.020675	108
55	6.741957	328.111820	.003048	.148325	48.667149	.020548	110
56	6.979990	341.713718	.002926	.143267	48.956190	.020426	112
57	7.226427	355.795848	.002811	.138381	49.235373	.020311	114
58	7.481565	370.375165	.002700	.133662	49.505036	.020200	116
59	7.745711	385.469223	.002594	.129104	49.765503	.020094	118
60	8.019183	401.096196	.002493	.124701	50.017087	.019993	120

3½% **ANNUAL** COMPOUND INTEREST TABLE 3½%

EFFECTIVE RATE = 3½% BASE = 1.035

YEARS	1 AMOUNT OF I AT COMPOUND INTEREST $S^n = (1+i)^n$	2 ACCUMULATION OF I PER PERIOD $S_{\overline{n}\vert} = \frac{S^n - 1}{i}$	3 SINKING FUND FACTOR $1/S_{\overline{n}\vert} = \frac{i}{S^n - 1}$	4 PRES. VALUE REVERSION OF I $V^n = \frac{1}{S^n}$	5 PRESENT VALUE ORD. ANNUITY 1 PER PERIOD $a_{\overline{n}\vert} = \frac{1 - V^n}{i}$	6 INSTALMENT TO AMORTIZE I $1/a_{\overline{n}\vert} = \frac{i}{1 - V^n}$	n YEARS
1	1.035000	1.000000	1.000000	.966184	.966184	1.035000	1
2	1.071225	2.035000	.491400	.933511	1.899694	.526400	2
3	1.108718	3.106225	.321934	.901943	2.801637	.356934	3
4	1.147523	4.214943	.237251	.871442	3.673079	.272251	4
5	1.187686	5.362466	.186481	.841973	4.515052	.221481	5
6	1.229255	6.550152	.152668	.813501	5.328553	.187668	6
7	1.272279	7.779408	.128544	.785991	6.114544	.163544	7
8	1.316809	9.051687	.110477	.759412	6.873956	.145477	8
9	1.362897	10.368496	.096446	.733731	7.607687	.131446	9
10	1.410599	11.731393	.085241	.708919	8.316605	.120241	10
11	1.459970	13.141992	.076092	.684946	9.001551	.111092	11
12	1.511069	14.601962	.068484	.661783	9.663334	.103484	12
13	1.563956	16.113030	.062062	.639404	10.302738	.097062	13
14	1.618695	17.676986	.056571	.617782	10.920520	.091571	14
15	1.675349	19.295681	.051825	.596891	11.517411	.086825	15
16	1.733986	20.971030	.047685	.576706	12.094117	.082685	16
17	1.794676	22.705016	.044043	.557204	12.651321	.079043	17
18	1.857489	24.499691	.040817	.538361	13.189682	.075817	18
19	1.922501	26.357180	.037940	.520156	13.709837	.072940	19
20	1.989789	28.279682	.035361	.502566	14.212403	.070361	20
21	2.059431	30.269471	.033037	.485571	14.697974	.068037	21
22	2.131512	32.328902	.030932	.469151	15.167125	.065932	22
23	2.206114	34.460414	.029019	.453286	15.620410	.064019	23
24	2.283328	36.666528	.027273	.437957	16.058368	.062273	24
25	2.363245	38.949857	.025674	.423147	16.481515	.060674	25
26	2.445959	41.313102	.024205	.408838	16.890352	.059205	26
27	2.531567	43.759060	.022852	.395012	17.285365	.057852	27
28	2.260172	46.290627	.021603	.381654	17.667019	.056603	28
29	2.711878	48.910799	.020445	.368748	18.035767	.055445	29
30	2.806794	51.622677	.019371	.356278	18.392045	.054371	30
31	2.905031	54.429471	.018372	.344230	18.736276	.053372	31
32	3.006708	57.334502	.017442	.332590	19.068865	.052442	32
33	3.111942	60.341210	.016572	.321343	19.390208	.051572	33
34	3.220860	63.453152	.015760	.310476	19.700684	.050760	34
35	3.333590	66.674013	.014998	.299977	20.000661	.049998	35
36	3.450266	70.007603	.014284	.289833	20.290494	.049284	36
37	3.571025	73.457869	.013613	.280032	20.570525	.048613	37
38	3.696011	77.028895	.012982	.270562	20.841087	.047982	38
39	3.825372	80.724906	.012388	.261413	21.102500	.047388	39
40	3.959260	84.550278	.011827	.252572	21.355072	.046827	40
41	4.097834	88.509537	.011298	.244031	21.599104	.046298	41
42	4.241258	92.607371	.010798	.235779	21.834883	.045798	42
43	4.389702	96.848629	.010325	.227806	22.062689	.045325	43
44	4.543342	101.238331	.009878	.220102	22.282791	.044878	44
45	4.702359	105.781673	.009453	.212659	22.495450	.044453	45
46	4.866941	110.484031	.009051	.205468	22.700918	.044051	46
47	5.037284	115.350973	.008669	.198520	22.899438	.043669	47
48	5.213589	120.388257	.008306	.191806	23.091244	.043306	48
49	5.396065	125.601846	.007962	.185320	23.276564	.042962	49
50	5.584927	130.997910	.007634	.179053	23.455618	.042634	50
51	5.780399	136.582837	.007322	.172998	23.628616	.042322	51
52	5.982713	142.363236	.007024	.167148	23.795765	.042024	52
53	6.192108	148.345950	.006741	.161496	23.957260	.041741	53
54	6.408832	154.538058	.006471	.156035	24.113295	.041471	54
55	6.633141	160.946890	.006213	.150758	24.264053	.041213	55
56	6.865301	167.580031	.005967	.145660	24.409713	.040967	56
57	7.105587	174.445332	.005732	.140734	24.550448	.040732	57
58	7.354282	181.550919	.005508	.135975	24.686423	.040508	58
59	7.611682	188.905201	.005294	.131377	24.817800	.040294	59
60	7.878091	196.516883	.005089	.126934	24.944734	.040089	60

3¾% MONTHLY COMPOUND INTEREST TABLE 3¾%

EFFECTIVE RATE = 5/16% BASE = 1.003125

YEARS	1 AMOUNT OF 1 AT COMPOUND INTEREST $S^n = (1+i)^n$	2 ACCUMULATION OF 1 PER PERIOD $S_{\overline{n}\|} = \frac{S^n - 1}{i}$	3 SINKING FUND FACTOR $1/S_{\overline{n}\|} = \frac{i}{S^n - 1}$	4 PRES. VALUE REVERSION OF 1 $V^n = \frac{1}{S^n}$	5 PRESENT VALUE ORD. ANNUITY 1 PER PERIOD $a_{\overline{n}\|} = \frac{1-V^n}{i}$	6 INSTALMENT TO AMORTIZE 1 $1/a_{\overline{n}\|} = \frac{i}{1-V^n}$	n YEARS
1	1.003125	1.000000	1.000000	.996885	.996885	1.003125	1
2	1.006260	2.003125	.499220	.993779	1.990664	.502345	2
3	1.009404	3.009385	.332294	.990683	2.981347	.335419	3
4	1.012559	4.018789	.248831	.987597	3.968944	.251956	4
5	1.015723	5.031348	.198754	.984520	4.953465	.201879	5
6	1.018897	6.047071	.165369	.981453	5.934918	.168494	6
7	1.022081	7.065968	.141523	.978396	6.913314	.144648	7
8	1.025275	8.088049	.123639	.975348	7.888662	.126764	8
9	1.028479	9.113324	.109729	.972309	8.860971	.112854	9
10	1.031693	10.141803	.098602	.969280	9.830252	.101727	10
11	1.034917	11.173496	.089498	.966261	10.796513	.092623	11
YEARS							
1	1.038151	12.208414	.081911	.963251	11.759763	.085036	12
2	1.077758	24.882594	.040189	.927852	23.087364	.043314	24
3	1.118876	38.040311	.026288	.893754	33.998684	.029413	36
4	1.161563	51.700011	.019342	.860909	44.509021	.022467	48
5	1.205878	65.880847	.015179	.829272	54.633111	.018304	60
6	1.251883	80.602700	.012407	.798796	64.385148	.015532	72
7	1.299644	95.886211	.010429	.769441	73.778805	.013554	84
8	1.349228	111.752808	.008948	.741165	82.827252	.012073	96
9	1.400702	128.224735	.007799	.713928	91.543175	.010924	108
10	1.454141	145.325088	.006881	.687691	99.938794	.010006	120
11	1.509618	163.077842	.006132	.662419	108.025881	.009257	132
12	1.567212	181.507886	.005509	.638076	115.815773	.008634	144
13	1.627003	200.641060	.004984	.614627	123.319392	.008109	156
14	1.689076	220.504190	.004535	.592040	130.547259	.007660	168
15	1.753516	241.125123	.004147	.570283	137.509508	.007272	180
16	1.820415	262.532772	.003809	.549325	144.215898	.006934	192
17	1.889866	284.757150	.003512	.529138	150.675834	.006637	204
18	1.961967	307.829417	.003249	.509693	156.898372	.006374	216
19	2.036819	331.781921	.003014	.490962	162.892236	.006139	228
20	2.114526	356.648243	.002804	.472919	168.665830	.005929	240
21	2.195198	382.463249	.002615	.455540	174.227249	.005740	252
22	2.278947	409.263129	.002443	.438799	179.584290	.005568	264
23	2.365892	437.085461	.002288	.422674	184.744464	.005413	276
24	2.456154	465.969249	.002146	.407141	189.715005	.005271	288
25	2.549859	495.954992	.002016	.392178	194.502882	.005141	300
26	2.647140	527.084730	.001897	.377766	199.114808	.005022	312
27	2.748132	559.402107	.001788	.363884	203.557250	.004913	324
28	2.852976	592.952434	.001686	.350511	207.836435	.004811	336
29	2.961821	627.782750	.001593	.337630	211.958363	.004718	348
30	3.074818	663.941887	.001506	.325222	215.928813	.004631	360
31	3.192127	701.480541	.001426	.313271	219.753352	.004551	372
32	3.313910	740.451344	.001351	.301758	223.437342	.004476	384
33	3.440340	780.908934	.001281	.290669	226.985949	.004406	396
34	3.571594	822.910033	.001215	.279987	230.404146	.004340	408
35	3.707855	866.513528	.001154	.269698	233.696728	.004279	420
36	3.849314	911.780552	.001097	.259787	236.868309	.004222	432
37	3.996171	958.774573	.001043	.250240	239.923337	.004168	444
38	4.148630	1007.561476	.000992	.241043	242.866095	.004117	456
39	4.306905	1058.209662	.000945	.232185	245.700709	.004070	468
40	4.471219	1110.790142	.000900	.223653	248.431153	.004025	480
41	4.641802	1165.376635	.000858	.215434	251.061256	.003983	492
42	4.818893	1222.045674	.000818	.207517	253.594703	.003943	504
43	5.002740	1280.876709	.000781	.199890	256.035049	.003906	516
44	5.193601	1341.952225	.000745	.192545	258.385714	.003870	528
45	5.391743	1405.357851	.000712	.185469	260.649993	.003837	540
46	5.597445	1471.182483	.000680	.178653	262.831062	.003805	552
47	5.810995	1539.518410	.000650	.172088	264.931978	.003775	564
48	6.032692	1610.461441	.000621	.165763	266.955687	.003746	576
49	6.262847	1684.111040	.000594	.159672	268.905027	.003719	588
50	6.501783	1760.570466	.000568	.153804	270.782729	.003693	600

3¾% QUARTERLY COMPOUND INTEREST TABLE 3¾%

EFFECTIVE RATE = 15/16%   BASE = 1.009375

QUARTERS	1 AMOUNT OF 1 AT COMPOUND INTEREST $S^n = (1+i)^n$	2 ACCUMULATION OF 1 PER PERIOD $S_{\overline{n}\vert} = \frac{S^n - 1}{i}$	3 SINKING FUND FACTOR $1/S_{\overline{n}\vert} = \frac{i}{S^n - 1}$	4 PRES. VALUE REVERSION OF 1 $V^n = \frac{1}{S^n}$	5 PRESENT VALUE ORD. ANNUITY 1 PER PERIOD $a_{\overline{n}\vert} = \frac{1 - V^n}{i}$	6 INSTALMENT TO AMORTIZE 1 $1/a_{\overline{n}\vert} = \frac{i}{1 - V^n}$	n QUARTERS
1	1.009375	1.000000	1.000000	.990712	.990712	1.009375	1
2	1.018838	2.009375	.497667	.981510	1.972222	.507042	2
3	1.028389	3.028213	.330228	.972394	2.944617	.339603	3
YEARS							
1	1.038031	4.056602	.246512	.963363	3.907979	.255887	4
2	1.077508	8.267480	.120956	.928068	7.672781	.130331	8
3	1.118486	12.638500	.079123	.894066	11.299650	.088498	12
4	1.161023	17.175753	.058222	.861310	14.793641	.067597	16
5	1.205177	21.885560	.045692	.829754	18.159621	.055067	20
6	1.251011	26.774485	.037349	.799354	21.402281	.046724	24
7	1.298588	31.849338	.031398	.770067	24.526138	.040773	28
8	1.347974	37.117191	.026942	.741854	27.535546	.036317	32
9	1.399238	42.585384	.023482	.714675	30.434697	.032857	36
10	1.452452	48.261537	.020720	.688491	33.227631	.030095	40
11	1.507690	54.153556	.018466	.663267	35.918240	.027841	44
12	1.565028	60.269654	.016592	.638966	38.510272	.025967	48
13	1.624547	66.618350	.015011	.615556	41.007338	.024386	52
14	1.686330	73.208491	.013660	.593004	43.412919	.023035	56
15	1.750462	80.049260	.012492	.571278	45.730366	.021867	60
16	1.817033	87.150188	.011474	.550348	47.962908	.020849	64
17	1.886136	94.521168	.010580	.530184	50.113656	.019955	68
18	1.957867	102.172472	.009787	.510760	52.185606	.019162	72
19	2.032326	110.114759	.009081	.492047	54.181645	.018456	76
20	2.109617	118.359097	.008449	.474020	56.104555	.017824	80
21	2.189847	126.916973	.007879	.456653	57.957015	.017254	84
22	2.273128	135.800310	.007364	.439922	59.741605	.016739	88
23	2.359576	145.021486	.006896	.423805	61.460813	.016271	92
24	2.449313	154.593349	.006469	.408278	63.117034	.015844	96
25	2.542462	164.529237	.006078	.393320	64.712575	.015453	100
26	2.639153	174.842992	.005719	.378909	66.249660	.015094	104
27	2.739522	185.548987	.005389	.365027	67.730430	.014764	108
28	2.843708	196.662137	.005085	.351654	69.156949	.014460	112
29	2.951856	208.197928	.004803	.338770	70.531204	.014178	116
30	3.064117	220.172433	.004542	.326358	71.855110	.013917	120
31	3.180647	232.602335	.004299	.314401	73.130512	.013674	124
32	3.301609	245.504955	.004073	.302883	74.359186	.013448	128
33	3.427171	258.898270	.003863	.291786	75.542845	.013238	132
34	3.557509	272.800941	.003666	.281096	76.683138	.013041	136
35	3.692803	287.232340	.003482	.270797	77.781654	.012857	140
36	3.833243	302.212574	.003309	.260876	78.839923	.012684	144
37	3.979024	317.762516	.003147	.251318	79.859420	.012522	148
38	4.130348	333.903833	.002995	.242110	80.841565	.012370	152
39	4.287428	350.659014	.002852	.233240	81.787727	.012227	156
40	4.450482	368.051406	.002717	.224695	82.699225	.012092	160
41	4.619737	386.105241	.002590	.216463	83.577327	.011965	164
42	4.795428	404.845676	.002470	.208532	84.432259	.011845	168
43	4.977801	424.298821	.002357	.200892	85.238197	.011732	172
44	5.167110	444.491783	.002250	.193532	86.023279	.011625	176
45	5.363619	465.452695	.002148	.186441	86.779597	.011523	180
46	5.567601	487.210765	.002052	.179611	87.508205	.011427	184
47	5.779340	509.796308	.001962	.173030	88.210120	.011337	188
48	5.999132	533.240794	.001875	.166691	88.886318	.011250	192
49	6.227283	557.576889	.001793	.160584	89.537742	.011168	196
50	6.464111	582.838502	.001716	.154700	90.165300	.011091	200
51	6.709945	609.060830	.001642	.149033	90.769865	.011017	204
52	6.965129	636.280410	.001572	.143572	91.352281	.010947	208
53	7.230017	664.535168	.001505	.138312	91.913359	.010880	212
54	7.504979	693.864473	.001441	.133245	92.453881	.010816	216
55	7.790399	724.309190	.001381	.128363	92.974599	.010756	220
56	8.086673	755.911740	.001323	.123660	93.476239	.010698	224
57	8.394214	788.716156	.001268	.119130	93.959501	.010643	228
58	8.713451	822.768144	.001215	.114765	94.425057	.010590	232
59	9.044830	858.115151	.001165	.110560	94.873557	.010540	236
60	9.388810	894.806429	.001118	.106510	95.305625	.010493	240

3 ¾% SEMI-ANNUAL COMPOUND INTEREST TABLE 3 ¾%

EFFECTIVE RATE = 1-7/8% BASE = 1.01875

	1 AMOUNT OF 1 AT COMPOUND INTEREST $S^n = (1+i)^n$	2 ACCUMULATION OF 1 PER PERIOD $S_{\overline{n}\vert} = \frac{S^n - 1}{i}$	3 SINKING FUND FACTOR $1/S_{\overline{n}\vert} = \frac{i}{S^n - 1}$	4 PRES. VALUE REVERSION OF 1 $V^n = \frac{1}{S^n}$	5 PRESENT VALUE ORD. ANNUITY 1 PER PERIOD $a_{\overline{n}\vert} = \frac{1-V^n}{i}$	6 INSTALMENT TO AMORTIZE 1 $1/a_{\overline{n}\vert} = \frac{i}{1-V^n}$	n HALF YEARS
HALF YEARS 1	1.018750	1.000000	1.000000	.981595	.981595	1.018750	1
YEARS							
1	1.037852	2.018750	.495356	.963529	1.945124	.514106	2
2	1.077136	4.113913	.243078	.928388	3.819307	.261828	4
3	1.117907	6.288381	.159023	.894529	5.625137	.177773	6
4	1.160222	8.545156	.117025	.861904	7.365106	.135775	8
5	1.204138	10.887353	.091850	.830470	9.041617	.110600	10
6	1.249716	13.318207	.075085	.800182	10.656983	.093835	12
7	1.297020	15.841072	.063127	.770998	12.213436	.081877	14
8	1.346114	18.459431	.054173	.742879	13.713123	.072923	16
9	1.397067	21.176899	.047221	.715785	15.158114	.065971	18
10	1.449948	23.997228	.041671	.689680	16.550406	.060421	20
11	1.504831	26.924311	.037141	.664527	17.891919	.055891	22
12	1.561791	29.962188	.033375	.640291	19.184505	.052125	24
13	1.620907	33.115053	.030198	.616938	20.429950	.048948	26
14	1.682261	36.387260	.027482	.594438	21.629971	.046232	28
15	1.745937	39.783325	.025136	.572758	22.786227	.043886	30
16	1.812024	43.307936	.023090	.551869	23.900313	.041840	32
17	1.880612	46.965959	.021292	.531742	24.973767	.040042	34
18	1.951796	50.762444	.019700	.512349	26.008071	.038450	36
19	2.025674	54.702631	.018281	.493663	27.004652	.037031	38
20	2.102349	58.791961	.017009	.475658	27.964888	.035759	40
21	2.181926	63.036079	.015864	.458311	28.890102	.034614	42
22	2.264516	67.440843	.014828	.441596	29.781573	.033578	44
23	2.350231	72.012334	.013887	.425490	30.640531	.032637	46
24	2.439191	76.756864	.013028	.409972	31.468162	.031778	48
25	2.531518	81.680981	.012243	.395020	32.265608	.030993	50
26	2.627340	86.791484	.011522	.380613	33.033971	.030272	52
27	2.726789	92.095427	.010858	.366732	33.774310	.029608	54
28	2.830002	97.600133	.010246	.353357	34.487649	.028996	56
29	2.937123	103.313200	.009679	.340469	35.174971	.028429	58
30	3.048297	109.242516	.009154	.328052	35.837226	.027904	60
31	3.163680	115.396266	.008666	.316088	36.475328	.027416	62
32	3.283430	121.782945	.008211	.304560	37.090158	.026961	64
33	3.407713	128.411370	.007787	.293452	37.682564	.026537	66
34	3.536700	135.290691	.007391	.282749	38.253364	.026141	68
35	3.670570	142.430405	.007021	.272437	38.803347	.025771	70
36	3.809507	149.840369	.006674	.262501	39.333271	.025424	72
37	3.953703	157.530811	.006348	.252927	39.843869	.025098	74
38	4.103357	165.512348	.006042	.243703	40.335844	.024792	76
39	4.258675	173.795999	.005754	.234815	40.809876	.024504	78
40	4.419872	182.393199	.005483	.226251	41.266620	.024233	80
41	4.587172	191.315817	.005227	.217999	41.706706	.023977	82
42	4.760803	200.576169	.004986	.210049	42.130742	.023736	84
43	4.941007	210.187041	.004758	.202388	42.539312	.023508	86
44	5.128032	220.161699	.004542	.195007	42.932982	.023292	88
45	5.322136	230.513913	.004338	.187894	43.312294	.023088	90
46	5.523587	241.257975	.004145	.181042	43.677772	.022895	92
47	5.732663	252.408716	.003962	.174439	44.029921	.022712	94
48	5.949654	263.981530	.003788	.168077	44.369226	.022538	96
49	6.174857	275.992394	.003623	.161947	44.696157	.022373	98
50	6.408585	288.457887	.003467	.156041	45.011164	.022217	100
51	6.651160	301.395219	.003318	.150350	45.314682	.022068	102
52	6.902917	314.822249	.003176	.144866	45.607131	.021926	104
53	7.164203	328.757513	.003042	.139583	45.888914	.021792	106
54	7.435380	343.220248	.002914	.134492	46.160420	.021664	108
55	7.716820	358.230421	.002791	.129587	46.422024	.021541	110
56	8.008914	373.808752	.002675	.124861	46.674087	.021425	112
57	8.312064	389.976748	.002564	.120307	46.916957	.021314	114
58	8.626689	406.756727	.002458	.115919	47.150969	.021208	116
59	8.953222	424.171854	.002358	.111692	47.376446	.021108	118
60	9.292116	442.246172	.002261	.107618	47.593700	.021011	120

ANNUAL COMPOUND INTEREST TABLE

3¾%

EFFECTIVE RATE = 3¾% BASE = 1.0375

YEARS	1 AMOUNT OF 1 AT COMPOUND INTEREST $S^n = (1+i)^n$	2 ACCUMULATION OF 1 PER PERIOD $S_{\overline{n}\mid} = \frac{S^n - 1}{i}$	3 SINKING FUND FACTOR $1/S_{\overline{n}\mid} = \frac{i}{S^n - 1}$	4 PRES. VALUE REVERSION OF 1 $V^n = \frac{1}{S^n}$	5 PRESENT VALUE ORD. ANNUITY 1 PER PERIOD $a_{\overline{n}\mid} = \frac{1 - V^n}{i}$	6 INSTALMENT TO AMORTIZE 1 $1/a_{\overline{n}\mid} = \frac{i}{1 - V^n}$	n YEARS
1	1.037500	1.000000	1.000000	.963855	.963855	1.037500	1
2	1.076406	2.037500	.490798	.929017	1.892873	.528298	2
3	1.116771	3.113906	.321140	.895438	2.788311	.358640	3
4	1.158650	4.230678	.236369	.863073	3.651384	.273869	4
5	1.202100	5.389328	.185552	.831878	4.483262	.223052	5
6	1.247179	6.591428	.151712	.801810	5.285072	.189212	6
7	1.293948	7.838607	.127574	.772829	6.057900	.165074	7
8	1.342471	9.132554	.109498	.744895	6.802796	.146998	8
9	1.392813	10.475025	.095465	.717971	7.520767	.132965	9
10	1.445044	11.867838	.084261	.692020	8.212787	.121761	10
11	1.499233	13.312882	.075115	.667008	8.879795	.112615	11
12	1.555454	14.812116	.067512	.642899	9.522694	.105012	12
13	1.613784	16.367570	.061096	.619662	10.142356	.098596	13
14	1.674301	17.981354	.055613	.597264	10.739620	.093113	14
15	1.737087	19.655654	.050876	.575676	11.315296	.088376	15
16	1.802228	21.392742	.046745	.554869	11.870165	.084245	16
17	1.869811	23.194969	.043113	.534813	12.404978	.080613	17
18	1.939929	25.064781	.039897	.515483	12.920461	.077397	18
19	2.012677	27.004710	.037031	.496851	13.417312	.074531	19
20	2.088152	29.017387	.034462	.478892	13.896204	.071962	20
21	2.166458	31.105539	.032149	.461583	14.357787	.069649	21
22	2.247700	33.271996	.030055	.444899	14.802686	.067555	22
23	2.331989	35.519696	.028153	.428819	15.231505	.065653	23
24	2.419438	37.851685	.026419	.413319	15.644824	.063919	24
25	2.510167	40.271123	.024832	.398380	16.043204	.062332	25
26	2.604298	42.781290	.023375	.383981	16.427185	.060875	26
27	2.701960	45.385588	.022033	.370102	16.797286	.059533	27
28	2.803283	48.087548	.020795	.356725	17.154011	.058295	28
29	2.908406	50.890831	.019650	.343831	17.497842	.057150	29
30	3.017471	53.799237	.018588	.331403	17.829245	.056088	30
31	3.130627	56.816709	.017600	.319425	18.148670	.055100	31
32	3.248025	59.947335	.016681	.307879	18.456549	.054181	32
33	3.369826	63.195360	.015824	.296751	18.753301	.053324	33
34	3.496194	66.565186	.015023	.286025	19.039326	.052523	34
35	3.627302	70.061381	.014273	.275687	19.315013	.051773	35
36	3.763326	73.688682	.013571	.265722	19.580735	.051071	36
37	3.904450	77.452008	.012911	.256118	19.836853	.050411	37
38	4.050867	81.356458	.012292	.246861	20.083714	.049792	38
39	4.202775	85.407326	.011709	.237938	20.321652	.049209	39
40	4.360379	89.610100	.011159	.229338	20.550990	.048659	40
41	4.523893	93.970479	.010642	.221049	20.772039	.048142	41
42	4.693539	98.494372	.010153	.213059	20.985097	.047653	42
43	4.869547	103.187911	.009691	.205358	21.190455	.047191	43
44	5.052155	108.057458	.009254	.197935	21.388391	.046754	44
45	5.241610	113.109612	.008841	.190781	21.579172	.046341	45
46	5.438171	118.351223	.008449	.183885	21.763057	.045949	46
47	5.642102	123.789394	.008078	.177239	21.940296	.045578	47
48	5.853681	129.431496	.007726	.170833	22.111129	.045226	48
49	6.073194	135.285177	.007392	.164658	22.275787	.044892	49
50	6.300939	141.358371	.007074	.158707	22.434493	.044574	50
51	6.537224	147.659310	.006772	.152970	22.587463	.044272	51
52	6.782370	154.196534	.006485	.147441	22.734904	.043985	52
53	7.036709	160.978904	.006212	.142112	22.877016	.043712	53
54	7.300585	168.015613	.005952	.136975	23.013992	.043452	54
55	7.574357	175.316199	.005704	.132024	23.146016	.043204	55
56	7.858396	182.890556	.005468	.127252	23.273268	.042968	56
57	8.153086	190.748952	.005242	.122653	23.395921	.042742	57
58	8.458826	198.902037	.005028	.118220	23.514141	.042528	58
59	8.776032	207.360864	.004823	.113947	23.628088	.042323	59
60	9.105134	216.136896	.004627	.109828	23.737916	.042127	60

4% MONTHLY COMPOUND INTEREST TABLE 4%

EFFECTIVE RATE = 1/3% BASE = 1.00333333+

MONTHS	1 AMOUNT OF 1 AT COMPOUND INTEREST $S^n = (1+i)^n$	2 ACCUMULATION OF 1 PER PERIOD $S_{\overline{n}\vert} = \frac{S^n - 1}{i}$	3. SINKING FUND FACTOR $1/S_{\overline{n}\vert} = \frac{i}{S^n - 1}$	4 PRES. VALUE REVERSION OF 1 $V^n = \frac{1}{S^n}$	5 PRESENT VALUE ORD. ANNUITY 1 PER PERIOD $a_{\overline{n}\vert} = \frac{1-V^n}{i}$	6 INSTALMENT TO AMORTIZE 1 $1/a_{\overline{n}\vert} = \frac{i}{1-V^n}$	n MONTHS
1	1.003333	1.000000	1.000000	.996678	.996678	1.003333	1
2	1.006678	2.003333	.499168	.993367	1.990044	.502501	2
3	1.010033	3.010011	.332225	.990066	2.980111	.335558	3
4	1.013400	4.020044	.248753	.986777	3.966888	.252086	4
5	1.016778	5.033445	.198671	.983499	4.950386	.202004	5
6	1.020167	6.050223	.165283	.980231	5.930618	.168616	6
7	1.023568	7.070390	.141435	.976975	6.907592	.144768	7
8	1.026980	8.093958	.123549	.973729	7.881321	.126882	8
9	1.030403	9.120938	.109638	.970494	8.851815	.112971	9
10	1.033838	10.151341	.098509	.967270	9.819085	.101842	10
11	1.037284	11.185179	.089404	.964056	10.783141	.092737	11
YEARS							
1	1.040742	12.222463	.081817	.960853	11.743994	.085150	12
2	1.083143	24.942888	.040092	.923239	23.028251	.043425	24
3	1.127272	38.181562	.026191	.887097	33.870766	.029524	36
4	1.173199	51.959601	.019246	.852371	44.288834	.022579	48
5	1.220997	66.298978	.015083	.819003	54.299069	.018416	60
6	1.270742	81.222564	.012312	.786942	63.917437	.015645	72
7	1.322514	96.754159	.010335	.756136	73.159278	.013668	84
8	1.376395	112.918536	.008856	.726536	82.039332	.012189	96
9	1.432472	129.741474	.007708	.698094	90.571761	.011041	108
10	1.490833	147.249804	.006791	.670766	98.770175	.010124	120
11	1.551571	165.471451	.006043	.644508	106.647648	.009376	132
12	1.614785	184.435477	.005422	.619278	114.216745	.008755	144
13	1.680574	204.172125	.004898	.595035	121.489536	.008231	156
14	1.749043	224.712875	.004450	.571741	128.477623	.007783	168
15	1.820302	246.090487	.004064	.549360	135.192149	.007397	180
16	1.894464	268.339056	.003727	.527854	141.643824	.007060	192
17	1.971647	291.494066	.003431	.507190	147.842938	.006764	204
18	2.051975	315.592447	.003169	.487335	153.799377	.006502	216
19	2.135575	340.672633	.002935	.468258	159.522641	.006268	228
20	2.222582	366.774625	.002726	.449927	165.021859	.006059	240
21	2.313133	393.940051	.002538	.432314	170.305801	.005871	252
22	2.407374	422.212240	.002368	.415390	175,382894	.005701	264
23	2.505454	451.636280	.002214	.399129	180.261236	.005547	276
24	2.607530	482.259102	.002074	.383505	184.948607	.005407	288
25	2.713765	514.129545	.001945	.368492	189.452484	.005278	300
26	2.824328	547.298438	.001827	.354067	193.780049	.005160	312
27	2.939396	581.818684	.001719	.340206	197.938204	.005052	324
28	3.059151	617.745337	.001619	.326888	201.933581	.004952	336
29	3.183786	655.135698	.001526	.314091	205.772553	.004859	348
30	3.313498	694.049400	.001441	.301796	209.461241	.004774	360
31	3.448495	734.548506	.001361	.289982	213.005530	.004694	372
32	3.588992	776.697608	.001288	.278630	216.411072	.004621	384
33	3.735213	820.563929	.001219	.267722	219.683299	.004552	396
34	3.887391	866.217432	.001154	.257242	222.827429	.004487	408
35	4.045770	913.730929	.001094	.247172	225.848476	.004427	420
36	4.210601	963.180200	.001038	.237496	228.751260	.004371	432
37	4.382147	1014.644110	.000986	.228199	231.540409	.004319	444
38	4.560682	1068.204739	.000936	.219265	234.220373	.004269	456
39	4.746492	1123.947510	.000890	.210682	236.795425	.004223	468
40	4.939871	1181.961329	.000846	.202434	239.269672	.004179	480
41	5.141129	1242.338719	.000805	.194510	241.647061	.004138	492
42	5.350587	1305.175978	.000766	.186895	243.931383	.004099	504
43	5.568578	1370.573323	.000730	.179579	246.126282	.004063	516
44	5.795450	1438.635057	.000695	.172549	248.235257	.004028	528
45	6.031566	1509.469732	.000662	.165794	250.261674	.003995	540
46	6.277301	1583.190320	.000632	.159304	252.208762	.003965	552
47	6.533048	1659.914398	.000602	.153068	254.079629	.003935	564
48	6.799214	1739.764334	.000575	.147076	255.877258	.003908	576
49	7.076225	1822.867480	.000549	.141318	257.604516	.003882	588
50	7.364521	1909.356375	.000524	.135786	259.264157	.003857	600

4% QUARTERLY COMPOUND INTEREST TABLE 4%

EFFECTIVE RATE = 1% BASE = 1.01

QUARTERS	1 AMOUNT OF 1 AT COMPOUND INTEREST $S^n = (1+i)^n$	2 ACCUMULATION OF 1 PER PERIOD $S_{\overline{n}|} = \frac{S^n - 1}{i}$	3 SINKING FUND FACTOR $1/S_{\overline{n}|} = \frac{i}{S^n - 1}$	4 PRES. VALUE REVERSION OF 1 $V^n = \frac{1}{S^n}$	5 PRESENT VALUE ORD. ANNUITY 1 PER PERIOD $a_{\overline{n}|} = \frac{1 - V^n}{i}$	6 INSTALMENT TO AMORTIZE 1 $1/a_{\overline{n}|} = \frac{i}{1 - V^n}$	n QUARTERS
1	1.010000	1.000000	1.000000	.990099	.990099	1.010000	1
2	1.020100	2.010000	.497512	.980296	1.970395	.507512	2
3	1.030301	3.030100	.330022	.970590	2.940985	.340022	3
YEARS							
1	1.040604	4.060401	.246281	.960980	3.901966	.256281	4
2	1.082857	8.285671	.120690	.923483	7.651678	.130690	8
3	1.126825	12.682503	.078849	.887449	11.255077	.088849	12
4	1.172579	17.257864	.057945	.852821	14.717874	.067945	16
5	1.220190	22.019004	.045415	.819544	18.045553	.055415	20
6	1.269735	26.973465	.037073	.787566	21.243387	.047073	24
7	1.321291	32.129097	.031124	.756836	24.316443	.041124	28
8	1.374941	37.494068	.026671	.727304	27.269589	.036671	32
9	1.430769	43.076878	.023214	.698925	30.107505	.033214	36
10	1.488864	48.886373	.020456	.671653	32.834686	.030456	40
11	1.549318	54.931757	.018204	.645445	35.455454	.028204	44
12	1.612226	61.222608	.016334	.620260	37.973959	.026334	48
13	1.677689	67.768892	.014756	.596058	40.394194	.024756	52
14	1.745810	74.580982	.013408	.572800	42.719992	.023408	56
15	1.816697	81.669670	.012244	.550450	44.955038	.022244	60
16	1.890462	89.046187	.011230	.528971	47.102874	.021230	64
17	1.967222	96.722220	.010339	.508331	49.166901	.020339	68
18	2.047099	104.709931	.009550	.488496	51.150391	.019550	72
19	2.130220	113.021975	.008848	.469435	53.056486	.018848	76
20	2.216715	121.671522	.008219	.451118	54.888206	.018219	80
21	2.306723	130.672274	.007653	.433515	56.648453	.017653	84
22	2.400385	140.038494	.007141	.416600	58.340015	.017141	88
23	2.497850	149.785019	.006676	.400344	59.965573	.016676	92
24	2.599273	159.927293	.006253	.384723	61.527703	.016253	96
25	2.704814	170.481383	.005866	.369711	63.028879	.015866	100
26	2.814640	181.464012	.005511	.355285	64.471479	.015511	104
27	2.928926	192.892579	.005184	.341422	65.857790	.015184	108
28	3.047852	204.785193	.004883	.328100	67.190007	.014883	112
29	3.171607	217.160694	.004605	.315298	68.470242	.014605	116
30	3.300387	230.038690	.004347	.302995	69.700522	.014347	120
31	3.434396	243.439584	.004108	.291172	70.882797	.014108	124
32	3.573846	257.384608	.003885	.279811	72.018940	.013885	128
33	3.718959	271.895856	.003678	.268892	73.110752	.013678	132
34	3.869963	286.996319	.003484	.258400	74.159961	.013484	136
35	4.027099	302.709922	.003303	.248318	75.168230	.013303	140
36	4.190616	319.061559	.003134	.238628	76.137157	.013134	144
37	4.360771	336.077139	.002976	.229317	77.068277	.012976	148
38	4.537836	353.783620	.002827	.220369	77.963065	.012827	152
39	4.722091	372.209054	.002687	.211771	78.822939	.012687	156
40	4.913826	391.382636	.002555	.203507	79.649261	.012555	160
41	5.113347	411.334741	.002431	.195567	80.443339	.012431	164
42	5.320970	432.096982	.002314	.187936	81.206434	.012314	168
43	5.537023	453.702253	.002204	.180602	81.939752	.012204	172
44	5.761848	476.184785	.002100	.173555	82.644457	.012100	176
45	5.995802	499.580198	.002002	.166783	83.321664	.012002	180
46	6.239256	523.925558	.001909	.160276	83.972447	.011909	184
47	6.492594	549.259438	.001821	.154022	84.597836	.011821	188
48	6.756220	575.621974	.001737	.148012	85.198824	.011737	192
49	7.030549	603.054936	.001658	.142236	85.776360	.011658	196
50	7.316018	631.601785	.001583	.136686	86.331362	.011583	200
51	7.613078	661.307752	.001512	.131353	86.864707	.011512	204
52	7.922199	692.219899	.001445	.126228	87.377242	.011445	208
53	8.243872	724.387204	.001380	.121302	87.869778	.011380	212
54	8.578606	757.860630	.001320	.116569	88.343095	.011320	216
55	8.926932	792.693212	.001262	.112021	88.797943	.011262	220
56	9.289401	828.940136	.001206	.107650	89.235044	.011206	224
57	9.666588	866.658830	.001154	.103449	89.655089	.011154	228
58	10.059091	905.909055	.001104	.099413	90.058743	.011104	232
59	10.467530	946.752997	.001056	.095534	90.446648	.011056	236
60	10.892554	989.255366	.001011	.091806	90.819416	.011011	240

4% SEMI-ANNUAL COMPOUND INTEREST TABLE 4%

EFFECTIVE RATE = 2%   BASE = 1.02

HALF YEARS	1 AMOUNT OF 1 AT COMPOUND INTEREST $s^n = (1+i)^n$	2 ACCUMULATION OF 1 PER PERIOD $s_{\overline{n}\vert} = \frac{s^n - 1}{i}$	3 SINKING FUND FACTOR $1/s_{\overline{n}\vert} = \frac{i}{s^n - 1}$	4 PRES. VALUE REVERSION OF 1 $v^n = \frac{1}{s^n}$	5 PRESENT VALUE ORD. ANNUITY 1 PER PERIOD $a_{\overline{n}\vert} = \frac{1 - v^n}{i}$	6 INSTALMENT TO AMORTIZE 1 $1/a_{\overline{n}\vert} = \frac{i}{1 - v^n}$	n HALF YEARS
1	1.020000	1.000000	1.000000	.980392	.980392	1.020000	1
YEARS							
1	1.040400	2.020000	.495050	.961169	1.941561	.515050	2
2	1.082432	4.121608	.242624	.923845	3.807729	.262624	4
3	1.126162	6.308121	.158526	.887971	5.601431	.178526	6
4	1.171659	8.582969	.116510	.853490	7.325481	.136510	8
5	1.218994	10.949721	.091327	.820348	8.982585	.111327	10
6	1.268242	13.412090	.074560	.788493	10.575341	.094560	12
7	1.319479	15.973938	.062602	.757875	12.106249	.082602	14
8	1.372786	18.639285	.053650	.728446	13.577709	.073650	16
9	1.428246	21.412312	.046702	.700159	14.992031	.066702	18
10	1.485947	24.297370	.041157	.672971	16.351433	.061157	20
11	1.545980	27.298984	.036631	.646839	17.658048	.056631	22
12	1.608437	30.421862	.032871	.621721	18.913926	.052871	24
13	1.673418	33.670906	.029699	.597579	20.121036	.049699	26
14	1.741024	37.051210	.026990	.574375	21.281272	.046990	28
15	1.811362	40.568079	.024650	.552071	22.396456	.044650	30
16	1.884541	44.227030	.022611	.530633	23.468335	.042611	32
17	1.960676	48.033802	.020819	.510028	24.498592	.040819	34
18	2.039887	51.994367	.019233	.490223	25.488842	.039233	36
19	2.122299	56.114940	.017821	.471187	26.440641	.037821	38
20	2.208040	60.401983	.016556	.452890	27.355479	.036556	40
21	2.297244	64.862223	.015417	.435304	28.234794	.035417	42
22	2.390053	69.502657	.014388	.418401	29.079963	.034388	44
23	2.486611	74.330564	.013453	.402154	29.892314	.033453	46
24	2.587070	79.353519	.012602	.386538	30.673120	.032602	48
25	2.691588	84.579401	.011823	.371528	31.423606	.031823	50
26	2.800328	90.016409	.011109	.357101	32.144950	.031109	52
27	2.913461	95.673072	.010452	.343234	32.838283	.030452	54
28	3.031165	101.558264	.009847	.329906	33.504694	.029847	56
29	3.153624	107.681218	.009287	.317095	34.145227	.029287	58
30	3.281031	114.051539	.008768	.304782	34.760887	.028768	60
31	3.413584	120.679222	.008286	.292947	35.352640	.028286	62
32	3.551493	127.574662	.007839	.281572	35.921415	.027839	64
33	3.694974	134.748679	.007421	.270638	36.468104	.027421	66
34	3.844251	142.212525	.007032	.260129	36.993564	.027032	68
35	3.999558	149.977911	.006668	.250028	37.498619	.026668	70
36	4.161140	158.057019	.006327	.240319	37.984063	.026327	72
37	4.329250	166.462522	.006007	.230987	38.450657	.026007	74
38	4.504152	175.207608	.005708	.222017	38.899132	.025708	76
39	4.686120	184.305996	.005426	.213396	39.330192	.025426	78
40	4.875439	193.771958	.005161	.205110	39.744514	.025161	80
41	5.072407	203.620345	.004911	.197145	40.142747	.024911	82
42	5.277332	213.866607	.004676	.189490	40.525516	.024676	84
43	5.490536	224.526818	.004454	.182132	40.893422	.024454	86
44	5.712354	235.617701	.004244	.175059	41.247041	.024244	88
45	5.943133	247.156656	.004046	.168261	41.586929	.024046	90
46	6.183236	259.161785	.003859	.161728	41.913619	.023859	92
47	6.433038	271.651921	.003681	.155448	42.227623	.023681	94
48	6.692933	284.646659	.003513	.149411	42.529434	.023513	96
49	6.963328	298.166384	.003354	.143609	42.819525	.023354	98
50	7.244646	312.232306	.003203	.138033	43.098352	.023203	100
51	7.537330	326.866491	.003059	.132673	43.366351	.023059	102
52	7.841838	342.091897	.002923	.127521	43.623944	.022923	104
53	8.158648	357.932410	.002794	.122569	43.871534	.022794	106
54	8.488258	374.412879	.002671	.117810	44.109510	.022671	108
55	8.831183	391.559160	.002554	.113235	44.338245	.022554	110
56	9.187963	409.398150	.002443	.108838	44.558097	.022443	112
57	9.559157	427.957835	.002337	.104612	44.769413	.022337	114
58	9.945347	447.267332	.002236	.100550	44.972523	.022236	116
59	10.347139	467.356932	.002140	.096645	45.167746	.022140	118
60	10.765163	488.258152	.002048	.092892	45.355389	.022048	120

4% ANNUAL COMPOUND INTEREST TABLE 4%

EFFECTIVE RATE = 4% BASE = 1.04

YEARS	1 AMOUNT OF 1 AT COMPOUND INTEREST $S^n = (1+i)^n$	2 ACCUMULATION OF 1 PER PERIOD $S_{\overline{n}\mid} = \frac{S^n - 1}{i}$	3 SINKING FUND FACTOR $1/S_{\overline{n}\mid} = \frac{i}{S^n - 1}$	4 PRES. VALUE REVERSION OF 1 $V^n = \frac{1}{S^n}$	5 PRESENT VALUE ORD. ANNUITY 1 PER PERIOD $a_{\overline{n}\mid} = \frac{1-V^n}{i}$	6 INSTALMENT TO AMORTIZE 1 $1/a_{\overline{n}\mid} = \frac{i}{1-V^n}$	n YEARS
1	1.040000	1.000000	1.000000	.961538	.961538	1.040000	1
2	1.081600	2.040000	.490196	.924556	1.886095	.530196	2
3	1.124864	3.121600	.320349	.888996	2.775091	.360349	3
4	1.169859	4.246464	.235490	.854804	3.629895	.275490	4
5	1.216653	5.416323	.184627	.821927	4.451822	.224627	5
6	1.265319	6.632975	.150762	.790315	5.242137	.190762	6
7	1.315932	7.898294	.126610	.759918	6.002055	.166610	7
8	1.368569	9.214226	.108528	.730690	6.732745	.148528	8
9	1.423312	10.582795	.094493	.702587	7.435332	.134493	9
10	1.480244	12.006107	.083291	.675564	8.110896	.123291	10
11	1.539454	13.486351	.074149	.649581	8.760477	.114149	11
12	1.601032	15.025805	.066552	.624597	9.385074	.106552	12
13	1.665074	16.626838	.060144	.600574	9.985648	.100144	13
14	1.731676	18.291911	.054669	.577475	10.563123	.094669	14
15	1.800944	20.023588	.049941	.555265	11.118387	.089941	15
16	1.872981	21.824531	.045820	.533908	11.652296	.085820	16
17	1.947900	23.697512	.042199	.513373	12.165669	.082199	17
18	2.025817	25.645413	.038993	.493628	12.659297	.078993	18
19	2.106849	27.671229	.036139	.474642	13.133939	.076139	19
20	2.191123	29.778079	.033582	.456387	13.590326	.073582	20
21	2.278768	31.969202	.031280	.438834	14.029160	.071280	21
22	2.369919	34.247970	.029199	.421955	14.451115	.069199	22
23	2.464716	36.617889	.027309	.405726	14.856842	.067309	23
24	2.563304	39.082604	.025587	.390121	15.246963	.065587	24
25	2.665836	41.645908	.024012	.375117	15.622080	.064012	25
26	2.772470	44.311745	.022567	.360689	15.982769	.062567	26
27	2.883369	47.084214	.021239	.346817	16.329586	.061239	27
28	2.998703	49.967583	.020013	.333477	16.663063	.060013	28
29	3.118651	52.966286	.018880	.320651	16.983715	.058880	29
30	3.243398	56.084938	.017830	.308319	17.292033	.057830	30
31	3.373133	59.328335	.016855	.296460	17.588494	.056855	31
32	3.508059	62.701469	.015949	.285058	17.873551	.055949	32
33	3.648381	66.209527	.015104	.274094	18.147646	.055104	33
34	3.794316	69.857909	.014315	.263552	18.411198	.054315	34
35	3.946089	73.652225	.013577	.253415	18.664613	.053577	35
36	4.103933	77.598314	.012887	.243669	18.908282	.052887	36
37	4.268090	81.702246	.012240	.234297	19.142579	.052240	37
38	4.438813	85.970336	.011632	.225285	19.367864	.051632	38
39	4.616366	90.409150	.011061	.216621	19.584485	.051061	39
40	4.801021	95.025516	.010523	.208289	19.792774	.050523	40
41	4.993061	99.826536	.010017	.200278	19.993052	.050017	41
42	5.192784	104.819598	.009540	.192575	20.185627	.049540	42
43	5.400495	110.012382	.009090	.185168	20.370795	.049090	43
44	5.616515	115.412877	.008665	.178046	20.548841	.048665	44
45	5.841176	121.029392	.008262	.171198	20.720040	.048262	45
46	6.074823	126.870568	.007882	.164614	20.884654	.047882	46
47	6.317816	132.945390	.007522	.158283	21.042936	.047522	47
48	6.570528	139.263206	.007181	.152195	21.195131	.047181	48
49	6.833349	145.833734	.006857	.146341	21.341472	.046857	49
50	7.106683	152.667084	.006550	.140713	21.482185	.046550	50
51	7.390951	159.773767	.006259	.135301	21.617485	.046259	51
52	7.686589	167.164718	.005982	.130097	21.747582	.045982	52
53	7.994052	174.851306	.005719	.125093	21.872675	.045719	53
54	8.313814	182.845359	.005469	.120282	21.992957	.045469	54
55	8.646367	191.159173	.005231	.115656	22.108612	.045231	55
56	8.992222	199.805540	.005005	.111207	22.219819	.045005	56
57	9.351910	208.797761	.004789	.106930	22.326749	.044789	57
58	9.725987	218.149672	.004584	.102817	22.429567	.044584	58
59	10.115026	227.875659	.004388	.098863	22.528430	.044388	59
60	10.519627	237.990685	.004202	.095060	22.623490	.044202	60

4¼% MONTHLY COMPOUND INTEREST TABLE 4¼%

EFFECTIVE RATE = 17/48% BASE = 1.00354166+

MONTHS	1 AMOUNT OF 1 AT COMPOUND INTEREST $S^n = (1+i)^n$	2 ACCUMULATION OF 1 PER PERIOD $S_{\overline{n}\rvert} = \frac{S^n - 1}{i}$	3 SINKING FUND FACTOR $1/S_{\overline{n}\rvert} = \frac{i}{S^n - 1}$	4 PRES. VALUE REVERSION OF 1 $V^n = \frac{1}{S^n}$	5 PRESENT VALUE ORD. ANNUITY 1 PER PERIOD $a_{\overline{n}\rvert} = \frac{1 - V^n}{i}$	6 INSTALMENT TO AMORTIZE 1 $1/a_{\overline{n}\rvert} = \frac{i}{1 - V^n}$	n MONTHS
1	1.003542	1.000000	1.000000	.996471	.996471	1.003542	1
2	1.007096	2.003542	.499116	.992954	1.989425	.502658	2
3	1.010663	3.010638	.332156	.989450	2.978875	.335698	3
4	1.014242	4.021300	.248676	.985958	3.964833	.252218	4
5	1.017834	5.035542	.198588	.982478	4.947311	.202130	5
6	1.021439	6.053377	.165197	.979011	5.926322	.168739	6
7	1.025057	7.074816	.141346	.975556	6.901878	.144888	7
8	1.028687	8.099872	.123459	.972113	7.873991	.127001	8
9	1.032330	9.128559	.109546	.968682	8.842673	.113088	9
10	1.035986	10.160890	.098417	.965264	9.807936	.101959	10
11	1.039656	11.196876	.089311	.961857	10.769793	.092853	11
YEARS							
1	1.043338	12.236532	.081723	.958462	11.728256	.085265	12
2	1.088554	25.003367	.039995	.918650	22.969348	.043537	24
3	1.135729	38.323487	.026094	.880492	33.743513	.029636	36
4	1.184949	52.220871	.019149	.843918	44.070145	.022691	48
5	1.236302	66.720536	.014988	.808864	53.967834	.018530	60
6	1.289880	81.848584	.012218	.775266	63.454397	.015760	72
7	1.345781	97.632246	.010243	.743063	72.546911	.013785	84
8	1.404104	114.099936	.008764	.712198	81.261745	.012306	96
9	1.464955	131.281299	.007617	.682615	89.614585	.011159	108
10	1.528442	149.207262	.006702	.654261	97.620468	.010244	120
11	1.594682	167.910096	.005956	.627084	105.293807	.009498	132
12	1.663791	187.423468	.005336	.601037	112.648413	.008878	144
13	1.735896	207.782504	.004813	.576071	119.697527	.008355	156
14	1.811126	229.023855	.004366	.552143	126.453838	.007908	168
15	1.889616	251.185758	.003981	.529208	132.929509	.007523	180
16	1.971508	274.308107	.003646	.507226	139.136195	.007188	192
17	2.056949	298.432526	.003351	.486157	145.085071	.006893	204
18	2.146092	323.602442	.003090	.465963	150.786845	.006632	216
19	2.239099	349.863164	.002858	.446608	156.251781	.006400	228
20	2.336136	377.261967	.002651	.428057	161.489717	.006193	240
21	2.437379	405.848171	.002464	.410277	166.510082	.006006	252
22	2.543009	435.673235	.002295	.393235	171.321913	.005837	264
23	2.653218	466.790850	.002142	.376901	175.933872	.005684	276
24	2.768202	499.257031	.002003	.361245	180.354262	.005545	288
25	2.888170	533.130223	.001876	.346240	184.591039	.005418	300
26	3.013336	568.471401	.001759	.331858	188.651831	.005301	312
27	3.143927	605.344185	.001652	.318074	192.543948	.005194	324
28	3.280178	643.814952	.001553	.304862	196.274395	.005095	336
29	3.422333	683.952954	.001462	.292198	199.849889	.005004	348
30	3.570650	725.830445	.001378	.280061	203.276866	.004920	360
31	3.725393	769.522810	.001300	.268428	206.561494	.004842	372
32	3.886843	815.108704	.001227	.257278	209.709686	.004769	384
33	4.055290	862.670185	.001159	.246591	212.727111	.004701	396
34	4.231037	912.292873	.001096	.236349	215.619198	.004638	408
35	4.414401	964.066095	.001037	.226531	218.391156	.004579	420
36	4.605711	1018.083050	.000982	.217122	221.047973	.004524	432
37	4.805312	1074.440976	.000931	.208103	223.594432	.004473	444
38	5.013563	1133.241327	.000882	.199459	226.035118	.004424	456
39	5.230839	1194.589950	.000837	.191174	228.374424	.004379	468
40	5.457532	1258.597283	.000795	.183233	230.616560	.004337	480
41	5.694049	1325.378547	.000755	.175622	232.765564	.004297	492
42	5.940816	1395.053958	.000717	.168327	234.825303	.004259	504
43	6.198278	1467.748943	.000681	.161335	236.799485	.004223	516
44	6.466897	1543.594363	.000648	.154634	238.691665	.004190	528
45	6.747157	1622.726750	.000616	.148211	240.505248	.004158	540
46	7.039564	1705.288554	.000586	.142054	242.243500	.004128	552
47	7.344642	1791.428398	.000558	.136154	243.909548	.004100	564
48	7.662942	1881.301346	.000532	.130498	245.506393	.004074	576
49	7.995037	1975.069182	.000506	.125078	247.036909	.004048	588
50	8.341523	2072.900703	.000482	.119882	248.503851	.004024	600

4 ¼% QUARTERLY COMPOUND INTEREST TABLE 4 ¼%

EFFECTIVE RATE = 1-1/16% BASE = 1.010625

QUARTERS	1 AMOUNT OF 1 AT COMPOUND INTEREST $S^n = (1+i)^n$	2 ACCUMULATION OF 1 PER PERIOD $s_{\overline{n}\vert} = \frac{S^n - 1}{i}$	3 SINKING FUND FACTOR $1/s_{\overline{n}\vert} = \frac{i}{S^n - 1}$	4 PRES. VALUE REVERSION OF 1 $V^n = \frac{1}{S^n}$	5 PRESENT VALUE ORD. ANNUITY 1 PER PERIOD $a_{\overline{n}\vert} = \frac{1 - V^n}{i}$	6 INSTALMENT TO AMORTIZE 1 $1/a_{\overline{n}\vert} = \frac{i}{1 - V^n}$	n QUARTERS
1	1.010625	1.000000	1.000000	.989487	.989487	1.010625	1
2	1.021363	2.010625	.497358	.979084	1.968571	.507983	2
3	1.032215	3.031988	.329817	.968791	2.937361	.340442	3
YEARS							
1	1.043182	4.064203	.246051	.958605	3.895967	.256676	4
2	1.088229	8.303907	.120425	.918924	7.630661	.131050	8
3	1.135221	12.726690	.078575	.880886	11.210759	.089200	12
4	1.184242	17.340459	.057669	.844422	14.642660	.068294	16
5	1.235381	22.153460	.045140	.809467	17.932499	.055765	20
6	1.288727	27.174297	.036799	.775960	21.086156	.047424	24
7	1.344377	32.411944	.030853	.743839	24.109269	.041478	28
8	1.402430	37.875764	.026402	.713048	27.007241	.037027	32
9	1.462990	43.575524	.022949	.683532	29.785252	.033574	36
10	1.526165	49.521412	.020193	.655237	32.448269	.030818	40
11	1.592068	55.724056	.017946	.628114	35.001051	.028571	44
12	1.660817	62.194543	.016079	.602113	37.448161	.026704	48
13	1.732535	68.944441	.014504	.577189	39.793974	.025129	52
14	1.807349	75.985813	.013160	.553296	42.042683	.023785	56
15	1.885394	83.331247	.012000	.530393	44.198308	.022625	60
16	1.966810	90.993872	.010990	.508438	46.264701	.021615	64
17	2.051741	98.987386	.010102	.487391	48.245557	.020727	68
18	2.140340	107.326078	.009317	.467216	50.144416	.019942	72
19	2.232764	116.024852	.008619	.447875	51.964672	.019244	76
20	2.329180	125.099258	.007994	.429336	53.709580	.018619	80
21	2.429759	134.565516	.007431	.411564	55.382257	.018056	84
22	2.534681	144.440548	.006923	.394527	56.985695	.017548	88
23	2.644134	154.742004	.006462	.378196	58.522759	.017087	92
24	2.758313	165.488300	.006043	.362540	59.996197	.016668	96
25	2.877423	176.698644	.005659	.347533	61.408642	.016284	100
26	3.001676	188.393075	.005308	.333147	62.762620	.015933	104
27	3.131295	200.592497	.004985	.319357	64.060550	.015610	108
28	3.266511	213.318716	.004688	.306137	65.304753	.015313	112
29	3.407566	226.594480	.004413	.293465	66.497452	.015038	116
30	3.554712	240.443521	.004159	.281317	67.640780	.014784	120
31	3.708213	254.890593	.003923	.269672	68.736781	.014548	124
32	3.868341	269.961520	.003704	.258509	69.787413	.014329	128
33	4.035384	285.683243	.003500	.247808	70.794554	.014125	132
34	4.209641	302.083864	.003310	.237550	71.760005	.013935	136
35	4.391422	319.192699	.003133	.227717	72.685492	.013758	140
36	4.581054	337.040330	.002967	.218290	73.572668	.013592	144
37	4.778873	355.658660	.002812	.209254	74.423120	.013437	148
38	4.985235	375.080970	.002666	.200592	75.238368	.013291	152
39	5.200509	395.341977	.002529	.192289	76.019869	.013154	156
40	5.425078	416.477898	.002401	.184329	76.769020	.013026	160
41	5.659344	438.526514	.002280	.176699	77.487161	.012905	164
42	5.903727	461.527236	.002167	.169385	78.175574	.012792	168
43	6.158663	485.521179	.002060	.162373	78.835490	.012685	172
44	6.424607	510.551233	.001959	.155652	79.468090	.012584	176
45	6.702035	536.662137	.001863	.149208	80.074503	.012488	180
46	6.991444	563.900567	.001773	.143032	80.655814	.012398	184
47	7.293349	592.315212	.001688	.137111	81.213062	.012313	188
48	7.608292	621.956861	.001608	.131436	81.747242	.012233	192
49	7.936834	652.878501	.001532	.125995	82.259311	.012157	196
50	8.279564	685.135404	.001460	.120779	82.750183	.012085	200
51	8.637093	718.785230	.001391	.115780	83.220735	.012016	204
52	9.010061	753.888127	.001326	.110987	83.671809	.011951	208
53	9.399135	790.506843	.001265	.106393	84.104210	.011890	212
54	9.805010	828.706835	.001207	.101989	84.518713	.011832	216
55	10.228412	868.556384	.001151	.097767	84.916057	.011776	220
56	10.670096	910.126722	.001099	.093720	85.296954	.011724	224
57	11.130854	953.492158	.001049	.089840	85.662083	.011674	228
58	11.611508	998.730206	.001001	.086121	86.012098	.011626	232
59	12.112918	1045.921731	.000956	.082556	86.347625	.011581	236
60	12.635980	1095.151087	.000913	.079139	86.669262	.011538	240

4 ¼% SEMI-ANNUAL COMPOUND INTEREST TABLE 4 ¼%

EFFECTIVE RATE = 2-1/8% BASE = 1.02125

HALF YEARS	1 AMOUNT OF 1 AT COMPOUND INTEREST $s^n = (1+i)^n$	2 ACCUMULATION OF 1 PER PERIOD $s_{\overline{n}\vert} = \frac{s^n - 1}{i}$	3 SINKING FUND FACTOR $1/s_{\overline{n}\vert} = \frac{i}{s^n - 1}$	4 PRES. VALUE REVERSION OF 1 $v^n = \frac{1}{s^n}$	5 PRESENT VALUE ORD. ANNUITY 1 PER PERIOD $a_{\overline{n}\vert} = \frac{1 - v^n}{i}$	6 INSTALMENT TO AMORTIZE 1 $1/a_{\overline{n}\vert} = \frac{i}{1 - v^n}$	n HALF YEARS
1	1.021250	1.000000	1.000000	.979192	.979192	1.021250	1
YEARS							
1	1.042952	2.021250	.494743	.958817	1.938009	.515993	2
2	1.087748	4.129316	.242171	.919331	3.796206	.263421	4
3	1.134468	6.327926	.158030	.881470	5.577878	.179280	6
4	1.183196	8.620971	.115996	.845169	7.286175	.137246	8
5	1.234016	11.012505	.090806	.810362	8.924120	.112056	10
6	1.287019	13.506759	.074037	.776990	10.494610	.095287	12
7	1.342298	16.108146	.062080	.744991	12.000424	.083330	14
8	1.399952	18.821266	.053131	.714310	13.444223	.074381	16
9	1.460082	21.650918	.046187	.684893	14.828563	.067437	18
10	1.522795	24.602109	.040647	.656687	16.155892	.061897	20
11	1.588201	27.680058	.036127	.629643	17.428559	.057377	22
12	1.656417	30.890210	.032373	.603713	18.648813	.053623	24
13	1.727563	34.238243	.029207	.578850	19.818814	.050457	26
14	1.801764	37.730079	.026504	.555012	20.940631	.047754	28
15	1.879153	41.371895	.024171	.532155	22.016249	.045421	30
16	1.959865	45.170132	.022139	.510239	23.047570	.043389	32
17	2.044045	49.131510	.020354	.489226	24.036418	.041604	34
18	2.131839	53.263035	.018775	.469078	24.984543	.040025	36
19	2.223405	57.572016	.017370	.449761	25.893621	.038620	38
20	2.318904	62.066074	.016112	.431238	26.765261	.037362	40
21	2.418505	66.753158	.014981	.413479	27.601005	.036231	42
22	2.522383	71.641561	.013958	.396450	28.402331	.035208	44
23	2.630723	76.739928	.013031	.380124	29.170655	.034281	46
24	2.743717	82.057278	.012187	.364469	29.907339	.033437	48
25	2.861564	87.603016	.011415	.349459	30.613683	.032665	50
26	2.984473	93.386952	.010708	.335068	31.290938	.031958	52
27	3.112661	99.419318	.010058	.321269	31.940302	.031308	54
28	3.246354	105.710783	.009460	.308038	32.562924	.030710	56
29	3.385790	112.171476	.008907	.295352	33.159904	.030157	58
30	3.531215	119.116005	.008395	.283189	33.732299	.029645	60
31	3.682886	126.253473	.007921	.271526	34.281122	.029171	62
32	3.841072	133.697507	.007480	.260344	34.807342	.028730	64
33	4.006052	141.461274	.007069	.249622	35.311891	.028319	66
34	4.178118	149.558507	.006686	.239342	35.795661	.027936	68
35	4.357575	158.003528	.006329	.229485	36.259509	.027579	70
36	4.544740	166.811276	.005995	.220035	36.704254	.027245	72
37	4.739943	175.997331	.005682	.210973	37.130683	.026932	74
38	4.943531	185.577942	.005389	.202285	37.539551	.026639	76
39	5.155864	195.570054	.005113	.193954	37.931580	.026363	78
40	5.377316	205.991344	.004855	.185966	38.307465	.026105	80
41	5.608280	216.860244	.004611	.178308	38.667869	.025861	82
42	5.849165	228.195980	.004382	.170965	39.013431	.025632	84
43	6.100395	240.018604	.004166	.163924	39.344762	.025416	86
44	6.362417	252.349028	.003963	.157173	39.662448	.025213	88
45	6.635693	265.209063	.003771	.150700	39.967051	.025021	90
46	6.920706	278.621457	.003589	.144494	40.259109	.024839	92
47	7.217961	292.609934	.003418	.138543	40.539140	.024668	94
48	7.527984	307.199238	.003255	.132838	40.807638	.024505	96
49	7.851322	322.415175	.003102	.127367	41.065079	.024352	98
50	8.188549	338.284661	.002956	.122122	41.311917	.024206	100
51	8.540260	354.835765	.002818	.117092	41.548590	.024068	102
52	8.907078	372.097766	.002687	.112270	41.775517	.023937	104
53	9.289650	390.101196	.002563	.107647	41.993098	.023813	106
54	9.688655	408.877902	.002446	.103213	42.201718	.023696	108
55	10.104798	428.461097	.002334	.098963	42.401747	.023584	110
56	10.538815	448.885420	.002228	.094887	42.593538	.023478	112
57	10.991474	470.187001	.002127	.090980	42.777430	.023377	114
58	11.463575	492.403517	.002031	.087233	42.953750	.023281	116
59	11.955953	515.574267	.001940	.083640	43.122808	.023190	118
60	12.469480	539.740238	.001853	.080196	43.284903	.023103	120

4 ¼% ANNUAL COMPOUND INTEREST TABLE 4 ¼%

EFFECTIVE RATE = 4¼% BASE = 1.0425

YEARS	1 AMOUNT OF 1 AT COMPOUND INTEREST $S^n = (1+i)^n$	2 ACCUMULATION OF 1 PER PERIOD $s_{\overline{n}\vert} = \frac{S^n - 1}{i}$	3 SINKING FUND FACTOR $1/s_{\overline{n}\vert} = \frac{i}{S^n - 1}$	4 PRES. VALUE REVERSION OF 1 $V^n = \frac{1}{S^n}$	5 PRESENT VALUE ORD. ANNUITY 1 PER PERIOD $a_{\overline{n}\vert} = \frac{1-V^n}{i}$	6 INSTALMENT TO AMORTIZE 1 $1/a_{\overline{n}\vert} = \frac{i}{1-V^n}$	n YEARS
1	1.042500	1.000000	1.000000	.959233	.959233	1.042500	1
2	1.086806	2.042500	.489596	.920127	1.879360	.532096	2
3	1.132996	3.129306	.319560	.882616	2.761976	.362060	3
4	1.181148	4.262302	.234615	.846634	3.608610	.277115	4
5	1.231347	5.443450	.183707	.812119	4.420729	.226207	5
6	1.283679	6.674796	.149817	.779011	5.199740	.192317	6
7	1.338235	7.958475	.125652	.747253	5.946993	.168152	7
8	1.395110	9.296710	.107565	.716789	6.663782	.150065	8
9	1.454402	10.691820	.093529	.687568	7.351350	.136029	9
10	1.516214	12.146223	.082330	.659537	8.010887	.124830	10
11	1.580654	13.662437	.073193	.632650	8.643537	.115693	11
12	1.647831	15.243091	.065603	.606858	9.250395	.108103	12
13	1.717864	16.890922	.059203	.582118	9.832513	.101703	13
14	1.790873	18.608786	.053738	.558387	10.390900	.096238	14
15	1.866986	20.399660	.049020	.535623	10.926523	.091520	15
16	1.946332	22.266645	.044910	.513787	11.440309	.087410	16
17	2.029052	24.212978	.041300	.492841	11.933151	.083800	17
18	2.115286	26.242029	.038107	.472749	12.405900	.080607	18
19	2.205186	28.357316	.035264	.453477	12.859376	.077764	19
20	2.298906	30.562501	.032720	.434989	13.294366	.075220	20
21	2.396610	32.861408	.030431	.417256	13.711622	.072931	21
22	2.498466	35.258018	.028362	.400246	14.111868	.070862	22
23	2.604651	37.756483	.026486	.383929	14.495796	.068986	23
24	2.715348	40.361134	.024776	.368277	14.864073	.067276	24
25	2.830750	43.076482	.023215	.353263	15.217336	.065715	25
26	2.951057	45.907233	.021783	.338862	15.556198	.064283	26
27	3.076477	48.858290	.020467	.325047	15.881245	.062967	27
28	3.207228	51.934767	.019255	.311796	16.193041	.061755	28
29	3.343535	55.141995	.018135	.299085	16.492125	.060635	29
30	3.485635	58.485530	.017098	.286892	16.779017	.059598	30
31	3.633775	61.971165	.016137	.275196	17.054213	.058637	31
32	3.788210	65.604939	.015243	.263977	17.318190	.057743	32
33	3.949209	69.393149	.014411	.253215	17.571405	.056911	33
34	4.117050	73.342358	.013635	.242892	17.814298	.056135	34
35	4.292025	77.459408	.012910	.232990	18.047288	.055410	35
36	4.474436	81.751433	.012232	.223492	18.270780	.054732	36
37	4.664599	86.225869	.011597	.214381	18.485160	.054097	37
38	4.862845	90.890468	.011002	.205641	18.690801	.053502	38
39	5.069516	95.753313	.010444	.197257	18.888059	.052944	39
40	5.284970	100.822829	.009918	.189216	19.077275	.052418	40
41	5.509581	106.107799	.009424	.181502	19.258777	.051924	41
42	5.743739	111.617381	.008959	.174103	19.432879	.051459	42
43	5.987848	117.361119	.008521	.167005	19.599884	.051021	43
44	6.242331	123.348967	.008107	.160197	19.760081	.050607	44
45	6.507630	129.591298	.007717	.153666	19.913747	.050217	45
46	6.784204	136.098928	.007348	.147401	20.061148	.049848	46
47	7.072533	142.883133	.006999	.141392	20.202540	.049499	47
48	7.373116	149.955666	.006669	.135628	20.338168	.049169	48
49	7.686473	157.328782	.006356	.130099	20.468266	.048856	49
50	8.013148	165.015255	.006060	.124795	20.593061	.048560	50
51	8.353707	173.028403	.005779	.119707	20.712769	.048279	51
52	8.708740	181.382110	.005513	.114827	20.827596	.048013	52
53	9.078861	190.090850	.005261	.110146	20.937742	.047761	53
54	9.464713	199.169711	.005021	.105656	21.043397	.047521	54
55	9.866963	208.634424	.004793	.101348	21.144746	.047293	55
56	10.286309	218.501387	.004577	.097217	21.241962	.047077	56
57	10.723477	228.787696	.004371	.093253	21.335216	.046871	57
58	11.179225	239.511173	.004175	.089452	21.424667	.046675	58
59	11.654342	250.690398	.003989	.085805	21.510472	.046489	59
60	12.149651	262.344740	.003812	.082307	21.592779	.046312	60

4½% MONTHLY COMPOUND INTEREST TABLE 4½%

EFFECTIVE RATE = 3/8% BASE = 1.00375

MONTHS	1 AMOUNT OF I AT COMPOUND INTEREST $S^n = (1+i)^n$	2 ACCUMULATION OF I PER PERIOD $S_{\overline{n}\vert} = \frac{S^n - 1}{i}$	3 SINKING FUND FACTOR $1/S_{\overline{n}\vert} = \frac{i}{S^n - 1}$	4 PRES. VALUE REVERSION OF I $V^n = \frac{1}{S^n}$	5 PRESENT VALUE ORD. ANNUITY 1 PER PERIOD $a_{\overline{n}\vert} = \frac{1 - V^n}{i}$	6 INSTALMENT TO AMORTIZE I $1/a_{\overline{n}\vert} = \frac{i}{1 - V^n}$	n MONTHS
1	1.003750	1.000000	1.000000	.996264	.996264	1.003750	1
2	1.007514	2.003750	.499064	.992542	1.988806	.502814	2
3	1.011292	3.011264	.332086	.988834	2.977640	.335836	3
4	1.015085	4.022556	.248598	.985140	3.962779	.252348	4
5	1.018891	5.037641	.198506	.981459	4.944239	.202256	5
6	1.022712	6.056532	.165111	.977792	5.922031	.168861	6
7	1.026547	7.079244	.141258	.974139	6.896170	.145008	7
8	1.030397	8.105791	.123369	.970500	7.866670	.127119	8
9	1.034261	9.136188	.109455	.966874	8.833544	.113205	9
10	1.038139	10.170449	.098324	.963262	9.796806	.102074	10
11	1.042032	11.208588	.089217	.959663	10.756470	.092967	11
YEARS							
1	1.045940	12.250620	.081629	.956078	11.712548	.085379	12
2	1.093990	25.064031	.039898	.914085	22.910656	.043648	24
3	1.144248	38.466089	.025997	.873937	33.616921	.029747	36
4	1.196814	52.483834	.019053	.835551	43.852944	.022803	48
5	1.251796	67.145552	.014893	.798852	53.639380	.018643	60
6	1.309303	82.480827	.012124	.763765	62.995976	.015874	72
7	1.369452	98.520602	.010150	.730219	71.941611	.013900	84
8	1.432365	115.297241	.008673	.698146	80.494336	.012423	96
9	1.498167	132.844596	.007528	.667482	88.671407	.011278	108
10	1.566993	151.198074	.006614	.638165	96.489324	.010364	120
11	1.638980	170.394707	.005869	.610136	103.963863	.009619	132
12	1.714275	190.473230	.005250	.583337	111.110104	.009000	144
13	1.793028	211.474157	.004729	.557716	117.942468	.008479	156
14	1.875399	233.439862	.004284	.533220	124.474740	.008034	168
15	1.961555	256.414669	.003900	.509800	130.720101	.007650	180
16	2.051669	280.444934	.003566	.487408	136.691154	.007316	192
17	2.145922	305.579145	.003272	.466000	142.399945	.007022	204
18	2.244505	331.868017	.003013	.445533	147.857995	.006763	216
19	2.347617	359.364596	.002783	.425964	153.076316	.006533	228
20	2.455466	388.124363	.002576	.407255	158.065437	.006326	240
21	2.568270	418.205348	.002391	.389367	162.835426	.006141	252
22	2.686256	449.668249	.002224	.372265	167.395908	.005974	264
23	2.809662	482.576549	.002072	.355915	171.756084	.005822	276
24	2.938737	516.996652	.001934	.340282	175.924751	.005684	288
25	3.073743	552.998007	.001808	.325336	179.910323	.005558	300
26	3.214950	590.653259	.001693	.311047	183.720840	.005443	312
27	3.362644	630.038387	.001587	.297385	187.363991	.005337	324
28	3.517123	671.232860	.001490	.284323	190.847127	.005240	336
29	3.678699	714.319800	.001400	.271835	194.177277	.005150	348
30	3.847698	759.386147	.001317	.259896	197.361160	.005067	360
31	4.024461	806.522833	.001240	.248481	200.405200	.004990	372
32	4.209344	855.824971	.001168	.237567	203.315540	.004918	384
33	4.402720	907.392041	.001102	.227132	206.098052	.004852	396
34	4.604980	961.328092	.001040	.217156	208.758350	.004790	408
35	4.816532	1017.741957	.000983	.207618	211.301802	.004733	420
36	5.037803	1076.747464	.000929	.198499	213.733541	.004679	432
37	5.269239	1138.463674	.000878	.189781	216.058472	.004628	444
38	5.511307	1203.015116	.000831	.181445	218.281288	.004581	456
39	5.764495	1270.532040	.000787	.173476	220.406474	.004537	468
40	6.029315	1341.150680	.000746	.165856	222.438316	.004496	480
41	6.306301	1415.013527	.000707	.158572	224.380916	.004457	492
42	6.596011	1492.269621	.000670	.151607	226.238194	.004420	504
43	6.899031	1573.074847	.000636	.144948	228.013895	.004386	516
44	7.215971	1657.592250	.000603	.138581	229.711604	.004353	528
45	7.547471	1745.992368	.000573	.132495	231.334747	.004323	540
46	7.894201	1838.453572	.000544	.126675	232.886597	.004294	552
47	8.256859	1935.162427	.000517	.121111	234.370287	.004267	564
48	8.636178	2036.314071	.000491	.115792	235.788811	.004241	576
49	9.032922	2142.112603	.000467	.110706	237.145030	.004217	588
50	9.447893	2252.771501	.000444	.105844	238.441681	.004194	600

4 ½% QUARTERLY COMPOUND INTEREST TABLE 4 ½%

EFFECTIVE RATE = 1-1/8% BASE = 1.01125

QUARTERS	1 AMOUNT OF 1 AT COMPOUND INTEREST $S^n = (1+i)^n$	2 ACCUMULATION OF 1 PER PERIOD $S_{\overline{n}\vert} = \frac{S^n - 1}{i}$	3 SINKING FUND FACTOR $1/S_{\overline{n}\vert} = \frac{i}{S^n - 1}$	4 PRES. VALUE REVERSION OF 1 $V^n = \frac{1}{S^n}$	5 PRESENT VALUE ORD. ANNUITY 1 PER PERIOD $a_{\overline{n}\vert} = \frac{1-V^n}{i}$	6 INSTALMENT TO AMORTIZE 1 $1/a_{\overline{n}\vert} = \frac{i}{1-V^n}$	n QUARTERS
1	1.011250	1.000000	1.000000	.988875	.988875	1.011250	1
2	1.022627	2.011250	.497203	.977874	1.966749	.508453	2
3	1.034131	3.033877	.329611	.966995	2.933745	.340861	3
YEARS							
1	1.045765	4.068008	.245821	.956238	3.889982	.257071	4
2	1.093625	8.322188	.120161	.914391	7.609730	.131411	8
3	1.143674	12.771061	.078302	.874375	11.166693	.089552	12
4	1.196015	17.423538	.057394	.836110	14.567995	.068644	16
5	1.250751	22.288935	.044865	.799520	17.820448	.056115	20
6	1.307991	27.376998	.036527	.764531	20.930567	.047777	24
7	1.367852	32.697916	.030583	.731073	23.904579	.041833	28
8	1.430451	38.262347	.026135	.699080	26.748442	.037385	32
9	1.495916	44.081434	.022685	.668487	29.467851	.033935	36
10	1.564377	50.166832	.019933	.639232	32.068253	.031183	40
11	1.635971	56.530730	.017689	.611258	34.554854	.028939	44
12	1.710841	63.185871	.015826	.584508	36.932637	.027076	48
13	1.789138	70.145585	.014256	.558928	39.206362	.025506	52
14	1.871018	77.423812	.012916	.534468	41.380584	.024166	56
15	1.956645	85.035127	.011760	.511079	43.459656	.023010	60
16	2.046191	92.994775	.010753	.488713	45.447744	.022003	64
17	2.139835	101.318696	.009870	.467326	47.348828	.021120	68
18	2.237765	110.023563	.009089	.446874	49.166717	.020339	72
19	2.340177	119.126808	.008394	.427318	50.905051	.019644	76
20	2.447275	128.646665	.007773	.408618	52.567311	.019023	80
21	2.559275	138.602198	.007215	.390736	54.156827	.018465	84
22	2.676400	149.013347	.006711	.373636	55.676782	.017961	88
23	2.798886	159.900964	.006254	.357285	57.130220	.017504	92
24	2.926977	171.286853	.005838	.341649	58.520052	.017088	96
25	3.060930	183.193818	.005459	.326698	59.849062	.016709	100
26	3.201014	195.645707	.005111	.312401	61.119912	.016361	104
27	3.347509	208.667457	.004792	.298730	62.335146	.016042	108
28	3.500708	222.285149	.004499	.285657	63.497199	.015749	112
29	3.660918	236.526055	.004228	.273156	64.608398	.015478	116
30	3.828460	251.418698	.003977	.261202	65.670968	.015227	120
31	4.003670	266.992905	.003745	.249771	66.687038	.014995	124
32	4.186898	283.279866	.003530	.238840	67.658642	.014780	128
33	4.378512	300.312201	.003330	.228388	68.587726	.014580	132
34	4.578895	318.124022	.003143	.218393	69.476152	.014393	136
35	4.788449	336.751003	.002970	.208836	70.325698	.014220	140
36	5.007593	356.230450	.002807	.199697	71.138066	.014057	144
37	5.236765	376.601375	.002655	.190958	71.914883	.013905	148
38	5.476426	397.904577	.002513	.182601	72.657704	.013763	152
39	5.727056	420.182722	.002380	.174610	73.368018	.013630	156
40	5.989155	443.480428	.002255	.166968	74.047247	.013505	160
41	6.263249	467.844356	.002137	.159662	74.696752	.013387	164
42	6.549887	493.323301	.002027	.152674	75.317832	.013277	168
43	6.849643	519.968292	.001923	.145993	75.911733	.013173	172
44	7.163118	547.832693	.001825	.139604	76.479643	.013075	176
45	7.490939	576.972311	.001733	.133495	77.022700	.012983	180
46	7.833762	607.445507	.001646	.127653	77.541992	.012896	184
47	8.192275	639.313310	.001564	.122066	78.038558	.012814	188
48	8.567195	672.639547	.001487	.116724	78.513394	.012737	192
49	8.959273	707.490961	.001413	.111616	78.967449	.012663	196
50	9.369295	743.937354	.001344	.106732	79.401634	.012594	200
51	9.798082	782.051719	.001279	.102061	79.816818	.012529	204
52	10.246492	821.910391	.001217	.097594	80.213833	.012467	208
53	10.715423	863.593199	.001158	.093323	80.593473	.012408	212
54	11.205816	907.183624	.001102	.089239	80.956500	.012352	216
55	11.718651	952.768968	.001050	.085334	81.303639	.012300	220
56	12.254956	1000.440530	.001000	.081600	81.635587	.012250	224
57	12.815805	1050.293785	.000952	.078029	81.953009	.012202	228
58	13.402322	1102.428578	.000907	.074614	82.256539	.012157	232
59	14.015680	1156.949325	.000864	.071349	82.546786	.012114	236
60	14.657109	1213.965218	.000824	.068226	82.824331	.012074	240

4½% SEMI-ANNUAL COMPOUND INTEREST TABLE 4½%

EFFECTIVE RATE = 2¼% BASE = 1.0225

HALF YEARS	1 AMOUNT OF I AT COMPOUND INTEREST $S^n = (1+i)^n$	2 ACCUMULATION OF I PER PERIOD $S_{\overline{n}\rvert} = \frac{S^n - 1}{i}$	3 SINKING FUND FACTOR $1/S_{\overline{n}\rvert} = \frac{i}{S^n - 1}$	4 PRES. VALUE REVERSION OF I $V^n = \frac{1}{S^n}$	5 PRESENT VALUE ORD. ANNUITY 1 PER PERIOD $a_{\overline{n}\rvert} = \frac{1 - V^n}{i}$	6 INSTALMENT TO AMORTIZE I $1/a_{\overline{n}\rvert} = \frac{i}{1 - V^n}$	n HALF YEARS
1	1.022500	1.000000	1.000000	.977995	.977995	1.022500	1
YEARS							
1	1.045506	2.022500	.494438	.956474	1.934470	.516938	2
2	1.093083	4.137036	.241719	.914843	3.784740	.264219	4
3	1.142825	6.347797	.157535	.875024	5.554477	.180035	6
4	1.194831	8.659162	.115485	.836938	7.247185	.137985	8
5	1.249203	11.075708	.090288	.800510	8.866216	.112788	10
6	1.306050	13.602222	.073517	.765667	10.414779	.096017	12
7	1.365483	16.243708	.061562	.732341	11.895939	.084062	14
8	1.427621	19.005398	.052617	.700466	13.312631	.075117	16
9	1.492587	21.892763	.045677	.669978	14.667661	.068177	18
10	1.560509	24.911520	.040142	.640816	15.963712	.062642	20
11	1.631522	28.067650	.035628	.612925	17.203352	.058128	22
12	1.705767	31.367403	.031880	.586247	18.389036	.054380	24
13	1.783390	34.817316	.028721	.560730	19.523113	.051221	26
14	1.864545	38.424222	.026025	.536324	20.607828	.048525	28
15	1.949393	42.195264	.023699	.512980	21.645330	.046199	30
16	2.038103	46.137912	.021674	.490652	22.637674	.044174	32
17	2.130849	50.259976	.019897	.469296	23.586826	.042397	34
18	2.227816	54.569619	.018325	.448870	24.494666	.040825	36
19	2.329196	59.075377	.016928	.429333	25.362991	.039428	38
20	2.435189	63.786176	.015677	.410646	26.193522	.038177	40
21	2.546005	68.711346	.014554	.392772	26.987904	.037054	42
22	2.661864	73.860642	.013539	.375677	27.747710	.036039	44
23	2.782996	79.244262	.012619	.359325	28.474444	.035119	46
24	2.909640	84.872872	.011782	.343685	29.169548	.034282	48
25	3.042046	90.757618	.011018	.328726	29.834396	.033518	50
26	3.180479	96.910157	.010319	.314418	30.470307	.032819	52
27	3.325210	103.342674	.009677	.300733	31.078539	.032177	54
28	3.476528	110.067912	.009085	.287643	31.660298	.031585	56
29	3.634732	117.099190	.008540	.275123	32.216735	.031040	58
30	3.800135	124.450435	.008035	.263149	32.748953	.030535	60
31	3.973065	132.136208	.007568	.251695	33.258006	.030068	62
32	4.153864	140.171731	.007134	.240740	33.744902	.029634	64
33	4.342891	148.572921	.006731	.230261	34.210605	.029231	66
34	4.540519	157.356417	.006355	.220239	34.656039	.028855	68
35	4.747141	166.539618	.006005	.210653	35.082085	.028505	70
36	4.963166	176.140711	.005677	.201484	35.489587	.028177	72
37	5.189021	186.178714	.005371	.192715	35.879352	.027871	74
38	5.425154	196.673509	.005085	.184327	36.252153	.027585	76
39	5.672032	207.645883	.004816	.176304	36.608727	.027316	78
40	5.930145	219.117569	.004564	.168630	36.949781	.027064	80
41	6.200004	231.111288	.004327	.161290	37.275990	.026827	82
42	6.482143	243.650796	.004104	.154270	37.588001	.026604	84
43	6.777121	256.760930	.003895	.147555	37.886432	.026395	86
44	7.085522	270.467657	.003697	.141133	38.171873	.026197	88
45	7.407958	284.798126	.003511	.134990	38.444890	.026011	90
46	7.745066	299.780720	.003336	.129114	38.706024	.025836	92
47	8.097515	315.445117	.003170	.123495	38.955792	.025670	94
48	8.466003	331.822341	.003014	.118119	39.194689	.025514	96
49	8.851259	348.944831	.002866	.112978	39.423187	.025366	98
50	9.254046	366.846502	.002726	.108061	39.641740	.025226	100
51	9.675163	385.562811	.002594	.103357	39.850781	.025094	102
52	10.115444	405.130828	.002468	.098859	40.050723	.024968	104
53	10.575760	425.589313	.002350	.094556	40.241962	.024850	106
54	11.057023	446.978787	.002237	.090440	40.424877	.024737	108
55	11.560186	469.341615	.002131	.086504	40.599831	.024631	110
56	12.086247	492.722092	.002030	.082739	40.767170	.024530	112
57	12.636247	517.166527	.001934	.079137	40.927226	.024434	114
58	13.211275	542.723336	.001843	.075693	41.080315	.024343	116
59	13.812471	569.443140	.001756	.072398	41.226740	.024256	118
60	14.441024	597.378862	.001674	.069247	41.366793	.024174	120

4 ½% ANNUAL COMPOUND INTEREST TABLE 4 ½%

EFFECTIVE RATE = 4½% BASE = 1.045

YEARS	1 AMOUNT OF I AT COMPOUND INTEREST $S^n = (1+i)^n$	2 ACCUMULATION OF I PER PERIOD $S_{\overline{n}|} = \frac{S^n - 1}{i}$	3 SINKING FUND FACTOR $1/S_{\overline{n}|} = \frac{i}{S^n - 1}$	4 PRES. VALUE REVERSION OF I $V^n = \frac{1}{S^n}$	5 PRESENT VALUE ORD. ANNUITY 1 PER PERIOD $a_{\overline{n}|} = \frac{1 - V^n}{i}$	6 INSTALMENT TO AMORTIZE I $1/a_{\overline{n}|} = \frac{i}{1 - V^n}$	n YEARS
1	1.045000	1.000000	1.000000	.956938	.956938	1.045000	1
2	1.092025	2.045000	.488998	.915730	1.872668	.533998	2
3	1.141166	3.137025	.318773	.876297	2.748964	.363773	3
4	1.192519	4.278191	.233744	.838561	3.587526	.278744	4
5	1.246182	5.470710	.182792	.802451	4.389977	.227792	5
6	1.302260	6.716892	.148878	.767896	5.157872	.193878	6
7	1.360862	8.019152	.124701	.734828	5.892701	.169701	7
8	1.422101	9.380014	.106610	.703185	6.595886	.151610	8
9	1.486095	10.802114	.092574	.672904	7.268790	.137574	9
10	1.552969	12.288209	.081379	.643928	7.912718	.126379	10
11	1.622853	13.841179	.072248	.616199	8.528917	.117248	11
12	1.695881	15.464032	.064666	.589664	9.118581	.109666	12
13	1.772196	17.159913	.058275	.564272	9.682852	.103275	13
14	1.851945	18.932109	.052820	.539973	10.222825	.097820	14
15	1.935282	20.784054	.048114	.516720	10.739546	.093114	15
16	2.022370	22.719337	.044015	.494469	11.234015	.089015	16
17	2.113377	24.741707	.040418	.473176	11.707191	.085418	17
18	2.208479	26.855084	.037237	.452800	12.159992	.082237	18
19	2.307860	29.063562	.034407	.433302	12.593294	.079407	19
20	2.411714	31.371423	.031876	.414643	13.007936	.076876	20
21	2.520241	33.783137	.029601	.396787	13.404724	.074601	21
22	2.633652	36.303378	.027546	.379701	13.784425	.072546	22
23	2.752166	38.937030	.025682	.363350	14.147775	.070682	23
24	2.876014	41.689196	.023987	.347703	14.495478	.068987	24
25	3.005434	44.565210	.022439	.332731	14.828209	.067439	25
26	3.140679	47.570645	.021021	.318402	15.146611	.066021	26
27	3.282010	50.711324	.019719	.304691	15.451303	.064719	27
28	3.429700	53.993333	.018521	.291571	15.742874	.063521	28
29	3.584036	57.423033	.017415	.279015	16.021889	.062415	29
30	3.745318	61.007070	.016392	.267000	16.288889	.061392	30
31	3.913857	64.752388	.015443	.255502	16.544391	.060443	31
32	4.089981	68.666245	.014563	.244500	16.788891	.059563	32
33	4.274030	72.756226	.013745	.233971	17.022862	.058745	33
34	4.466362	77.030256	.012982	.223896	17.246758	.057982	34
35	4.667348	81.496618	.012270	.214254	17.461012	.057270	35
36	4.877378	86.163966	.011606	.205028	17.666041	.056606	36
37	5.096860	91.041344	.010984	.196199	17.862240	.055984	37
38	5.326219	96.138205	.010402	.187750	18.049990	.055402	38
39	5.565899	101.464424	.009856	.179665	18.229656	.054856	39
40	5.816365	107.030323	.009343	.171929	18.401584	.054343	40
41	6.078101	112.846688	.008862	.164525	18.566109	.053862	41
42	6.351615	118.924789	.008409	.157440	18.723550	.053409	42
43	6.637438	125.276404	.007982	.150661	18.874210	.052982	43
44	6.936123	131.913842	.007581	.144173	19.018383	.052581	44
45	7.248248	138.849965	.007202	.137964	19.156347	.052202	45
46	7.574420	146.098214	.006845	.132023	19.288371	.051845	46
47	7.915268	153.672633	.006507	.126338	19.414709	.051507	47
48	8.271456	161.587902	.006189	.120898	19.535607	.051189	48
49	8.643671	169.859357	.005887	.115692	19.651298	.050887	49
50	9.032636	178.503028	.005602	.110710	19.762008	.050602	50
51	9.439105	187.535665	.005332	.105942	19.867950	.050332	51
52	9.863865	196.974769	.005077	.101380	19.969330	.050077	52
53	10.307739	206.838634	.004835	.097014	20.066345	.049835	53
54	10.771587	217.146373	.004605	.092837	20.159181	.049605	54
55	11.256308	227.917959	.004388	.088839	20.248021	.049388	55
56	11.762842	239.174268	.004181	.085013	20.333034	.049181	56
57	12.292170	250.937110	.003985	.081353	20.414387	.048985	57
58	12.845318	263.229280	.003799	.077849	20.492236	.048799	58
59	13.423357	276.074597	.003622	.074497	20.566733	.048622	59
60	14.027408	289.497954	.003454	.071289	20.638022	.048454	60

4 ¾% MONTHLY COMPOUND INTEREST TABLE 4 ¾%

EFFECTIVE RATE = 19/48% BASE = 1.00395833+

MONTHS	1 AMOUNT OF I AT COMPOUND INTEREST $S^n = (1+i)^n$	2 ACCUMULATION OF I PER PERIOD $S_{\overline{n}\rvert} = \frac{S^n - 1}{i}$	3 SINKING FUND FACTOR $1/S_{\overline{n}\rvert} = \frac{i}{S^n - 1}$	4 PRES. VALUE REVERSION OF I $V^n = \frac{1}{S^n}$	5 PRESENT VALUE ORD. ANNUITY 1 PER PERIOD $a_{\overline{n}\rvert} = \frac{1 - V^n}{i}$	6 INSTALMENT TO AMORTIZE I $1/a_{\overline{n}\rvert} = \frac{i}{1 - V^n}$	n MONTHS
1	1.003958	1.000000	1.000000	.996057	.996057	1.003958	1
2	1.007932	2.003958	.499012	.992130	1.988187	.502970	2
3	1.011922	3.011891	.332017	.988218	2.976406	.335975	3
4	1.015928	4.023813	.248521	.984322	3.960728	.252479	4
5	1.019949	5.039740	.198423	.980441	4.941169	.202381	5
6	1.023986	6.059689	.165025	.976576	5.917745	.168983	6
7	1.028040	7.083676	.141170	.972725	6.890470	.145128	7
8	1.032109	8.111715	.123278	.968890	7.859360	.127236	8
9	1.036194	9.143824	.109363	.965070	8.824430	.113321	9
10	1.040296	10.180018	.098232	.961265	9.785695	.102190	10
11	1.044414	11.220314	.089124	.957475	10.743170	.093082	11
YEARS							
1	1.048548	12.264728	.081535	.953700	11.696870	.085493	12
2	1.099453	25.124882	.039801	.909543	22.852173	.043759	24
3	1.152829	38.609370	.025900	.867432	33.490985	.029858	36
4	1.208796	52.748501	.018958	.827269	43.637218	.022916	48
5	1.267481	67.574057	.014799	.788967	53.313680	.018757	60
6	1.329014	83.119362	.012031	.752437	62.542120	.015989	72
7	1.393535	99.419359	.010058	.717600	71.343283	.014016	84
8	1.461188	116.510686	.008583	.684375	79.736951	.012541	96
9	1.532126	134.431761	.007439	.652688	87.741991	.011397	108
10	1.606507	153.222866	.006526	.622468	95.376397	.010484	120
11	1.684500	172.926240	.005783	.593648	102.657329	.009741	132
12	1.766279	193.586170	.005166	.566162	109.601153	.009124	144
13	1.852028	215.249097	.004646	.539949	116.223478	.008604	156
14	1.941940	237.963712	.004202	.514949	122.539188	.008160	168
15	2.036217	261.781074	.003820	.491107	128.562480	.007778	180
16	2.135071	286.754718	.003487	.468369	134.306892	.007445	192
17	2.238724	312.940780	.003195	.446683	139.785338	.007153	204
18	2.347409	340.398120	.002938	.426002	145.010132	.006896	216
19	2.461371	369.188455	.002709	.406278	149.993016	.006667	228
20	2.580865	399.376500	.002504	.387467	154.745193	.006462	240
21	2.706161	431.030111	.002320	.369527	159.277343	.006278	252
22	2.837539	464.220438	.002154	.352418	163.599655	.006112	264
23	2.975296	499.022084	.002004	.336101	167.721843	.005962	276
24	3.119740	535.513277	.001867	.320540	171.653173	.005825	288
25	3.271197	573.776040	.001743	.305699	175.402482	.005701	300
26	3.430006	613.896379	.001629	.291545	178.978197	.005587	312
27	3.596526	655.964475	.001524	.278046	182.388357	.005482	324
28	3.771130	700.074888	.001428	.265173	185.640626	.005386	336
29	3.954210	746.326768	.001340	.252895	188.742314	.005298	348
30	4.146179	794.824079	.001258	.241186	191.700394	.005216	360
31	4.347467	845.675832	.001182	.230019	194.521515	.005140	372
32	4.558527	898.996330	.001112	.219369	197.212017	.005070	384
33	4.779834	954.905425	.001047	.209212	199.777949	.005005	396
34	5.011885	1013.528788	.000987	.199526	202.225078	.004945	408
35	5.255201	1074.998191	.000930	.190288	204.558904	.004888	420
36	5.510330	1139.451803	.000878	.181477	206.784674	.004836	432
37	5.777845	1207.034501	.000828	.173075	208.907391	.004786	444
38	6.058347	1277.898197	.000783	.165062	210.931826	.004741	456
39	6.352467	1352.202174	.000740	.157419	212.862529	.004698	468
40	6.660866	1430.113452	.000699	.150131	214.703840	.004657	480
41	6.984237	1511.807158	.000661	.143180	216.459899	.004619	492
42	7.323307	1597.466920	.000626	.136550	218.134652	.004584	504
43	7.678838	1687.285282	.000593	.130228	219.731863	.004551	516
44	8.051629	1781.464135	.000561	.124198	221.255124	.004519	528
45	8.442518	1880.215172	.000532	.118448	222.707857	.004490	540
46	8.852385	1983.760362	.000504	.112964	224.093329	.004462	552
47	9.282149	2092.332452	.000478	.107734	225.414653	.004436	564
48	9.732778	2206.175487	.000453	.102746	226.674799	.004411	576
49	10.205284	2325.545360	.000430	.097988	227.876601	.004388	588
50	10.700729	2450.710388	.000408	.093452	229.022759	.004366	600

4 ¾% QUARTERLY COMPOUND INTEREST TABLE 4 ¾%

EFFECTIVE RATE = 1-3/16%   BASE = 1.011875

QUARTERS	1 AMOUNT OF I AT COMPOUND INTEREST $S^n = (1+i)^n$	2 ACCUMULATION OF I PER PERIOD $S_{\overline{n}\vert} = \frac{S^n - 1}{i}$	3 SINKING FUND FACTOR $1/S_{\overline{n}\vert} = \frac{i}{S^n - 1}$	4 PRES. VALUE REVERSION OF I $V^n = \frac{1}{S^n}$	5 PRESENT VALUE ORD. ANNUITY 1 PER PERIOD $a_{\overline{n}\vert} = \frac{1-V^n}{i}$	6 INSTALMENT TO AMORTIZE I $1/a_{\overline{n}\vert} = \frac{i}{1-V^n}$	n QUARTERS
1	1.011875	1.000000	1.000000	.988264	.988264	1.011875	1
2	1.023891	2.011875	.497049	.976666	1.964931	.508924	2
3	1.036050	3.035766	.329406	.965205	2.930135	.341281	3
YEARS							
1	1.048353	4.071816	.245591	.953877	3.884013	.257466	4
2	1.099044	8.340515	.119897	.909882	7.588885	.131772	8
3	1.152185	12.815618	.078030	.867916	11.122878	.089905	12
4	1.207897	17.507105	.057120	.827885	14.493874	.068995	16
5	1.266302	22.425439	.044592	.789701	17.709391	.056467	20
6	1.327531	27.581587	.036256	.753278	20.776600	.048131	24
7	1.391721	32.987051	.030315	.718535	23.702341	.042190	28
8	1.459015	38.653883	.025871	.685394	26.493139	.037746	32
9	1.529562	44.594723	.022424	.653782	29.155218	.034299	36
10	1.603521	50.822819	.019676	.623628	31.694514	.031551	40
11	1.681056	57.352060	.017436	.594864	34.116692	.029311	44
12	1.762339	64.197010	.015577	.567428	36.427153	.027452	48
13	1.847554	71.372931	.014011	.541256	38.631049	.025886	52
14	1.936888	78.895829	.012675	.516292	40.733295	.024550	56
15	2.030542	86.782480	.011523	.492479	42.738580	.023398	60
16	2.128724	95.050473	.010521	.469765	44.651376	.022396	64
17	2.231654	103.718246	.009642	.448098	46.475949	.021517	68
18	2.339561	112.805130	.008865	.427431	48.216368	.020740	72
19	2.452685	122.331391	.008175	.407716	49.876514	.020050	76
20	2.571280	132.318274	.007558	.388911	51.460090	.019433	80
21	2.695608	142.788050	.007003	.370974	52.970627	.018878	84
22	2.825948	153.764070	.006503	.353864	54.411494	.018378	88
23	2.962591	165.270811	.006051	.337542	55.785904	.017926	92
24	3.105840	177.333935	.005639	.321974	57.096923	.017514	96
25	3.256017	189.980345	.005264	.307124	58.347474	.017139	100
26	3.413454	203.238244	.004920	.292958	59.540347	.016795	104
27	3.578504	217.137201	.004605	.279446	60.678201	.016480	108
28	3.751535	231.708211	.004316	.266558	61.763574	.016191	112
29	3.932932	246.983770	.004049	.254263	62.798887	.015924	116
30	4.123101	262.997946	.003802	.242536	63.786449	.015677	120
31	4.322464	279.786451	.003574	.231350	64.728461	.015449	124
32	4.531467	297.386729	.003363	.220679	65.627026	.015238	128
33	4.750577	315.838029	.003166	.210501	66.484146	.015041	132
34	4.980280	335.181502	.002983	.200792	67.301734	.014858	136
35	5.221091	355.460286	.002813	.191531	68.081612	.014688	140
36	5.473545	376.719606	.002654	.182697	68.825520	.014529	144
37	5.738207	399.006874	.002506	.174270	69.535118	.014381	148
38	6.015665	422.371794	.002368	.166233	70.211986	.014243	152
39	6.306539	446.866473	.002238	.158566	70.857636	.014113	156
40	6.611478	472.545539	.002116	.151252	71.473507	.013991	160
41	6.931162	499.466261	.002002	.144276	72.060972	.013877	164
42	7.266303	527.688675	.001895	.137622	72.621342	.013770	168
43	7.617649	557.275722	.001794	.131274	73.155866	.013669	172
44	7.985984	588.293385	.001700	.125219	73.665736	.013575	176
45	8.372129	620.810841	.001611	.119444	74.152090	.013486	180
46	8.776945	654.900606	.001527	.113935	74.616011	.013402	184
47	9.201335	690.638708	.001448	.108680	75.058536	.013323	188
48	9.646245	728.104847	.001373	.103667	75.480650	.013248	192
49	10.112668	767.382579	.001303	.098886	75.883295	.013178	196
50	10.601644	808.559501	.001237	.094325	76.267369	.013112	200
51	11.114263	851.727442	.001174	.089974	76.633728	.013049	204
52	11.651669	896.982674	.001115	.085825	76.983190	.012990	208
53	12.215060	944.426124	.001059	.081866	77.316534	.012934	212
54	12.805693	994.163599	.001006	.078090	77.634503	.012881	216
55	13.424884	1046.306020	.000956	.074489	77.937807	.012831	220
56	14.074015	1100.969674	.000908	.071053	78.227122	.012783	224
57	14.754533	1158.276469	.000863	.067776	78.503092	.012738	228
58	15.467956	1218.354209	.000821	.064650	78.766334	.012696	232
59	16.215875	1281.336877	.000780	.061668	79.017435	.012655	236
60	16.999959	1347.364933	.000742	.058824	79.256954	.012617	240

4¾% SEMI-ANNUAL COMPOUND INTEREST TABLE 4¾%

EFFECTIVE RATE = 2-3/8% BASE = 1.02375

HALF YEARS	1 AMOUNT OF 1 AT COMPOUND INTEREST $S^n = (1+i)^n$	2 ACCUMULATION OF 1 PER PERIOD $S_{\overline{n}\vert} = \frac{S^n - 1}{i}$	3 SINKING FUND FACTOR $1/S_{\overline{n}\vert} = \frac{i}{S^n - 1}$	4 PRES. VALUE REVERSION OF 1 $V^n = \frac{1}{S^n}$	5 PRESENT VALUE ORD. ANNUITY 1 PER PERIOD $a_{\overline{n}\vert} = \frac{1 - V^n}{i}$	6 INSTALMENT TO AMORTIZE 1 $1/a_{\overline{n}\vert} = \frac{i}{1 - V^n}$	n HALF YEARS
1	1.023750	1.000000	1.000000	.976801	.976801	1.023750	1
YEARS							
1	1.048064	2.023750	.494132	.954140	1.930941	.517882	2
2	1.098438	4.144770	.241268	.910383	3.773330	.265018	4
3	1.151234	6.367734	.157042	.868633	5.531226	.180792	6
4	1.206567	8.697543	.114975	.828798	7.208506	.138725	8
5	1.264559	11.139333	.089772	.790789	8.808866	.113522	10
6	1.325339	13.698484	.073001	.754524	10.335834	.096751	12
7	1.389040	16.380639	.061048	.719922	11.792775	.084798	14
8	1.455803	19.191709	.052106	.686906	13.182902	.075856	16
9	1.525775	22.137890	.045171	.655405	14.509277	.068921	18
10	1.599110	25.225677	.039642	.625348	15.774825	.063392	20
11	1.675970	28.461876	.035135	.596670	16.982335	.058885	22
12	1.756523	31.853619	.031394	.569306	18.134469	.055144	24
13	1.840949	35.408384	.028242	.543198	19.233766	.051992	26
14	1.929433	39.134004	.025553	.518287	20.282649	.049303	28
15	2.022169	43.038694	.023235	.494519	21.283431	.046985	30
16	2.119363	47.131058	.021217	.471840	22.238317	.044967	32
17	2.221228	51.420118	.019448	.450201	23.149412	.043198	34
18	2.327989	55.915328	.017884	.429555	24.018725	.041634	36
19	2.439882	60.626596	.016494	.409856	24.848171	.040244	38
20	2.557152	65.564306	.015252	.391060	25.639578	.039002	40
21	2.680059	70.739343	.014136	.373126	26.394692	.037886	42
22	2.808874	76.163114	.013130	.356015	27.115177	.036880	44
23	2.943880	81.847572	.012218	.339688	27.802620	.035968	46
24	3.085375	87.805249	.011389	.324110	28.458537	.035139	48
25	3.233670	94.049276	.010633	.309246	29.084374	.034383	50
26	3.389094	100.593416	.009941	.295064	29.681510	.033691	52
27	3.551987	107.452094	.009306	.281533	30.251261	.033056	54
28	3.722710	114.640429	.008723	.268622	30.794884	.032473	56
29	3.901639	122.174263	.008185	.256303	31.313576	.031935	58
30	4.089167	130.070205	.007688	.244549	31.808482	.031438	60
31	4.285709	138.345657	.007228	.233334	32.280690	.030978	62
32	4.491698	147.018862	.006802	.222633	32.731244	.030552	64
33	4.707587	156.108935	.006406	.212423	33.161135	.030156	66
34	4.933853	165.635915	.006037	.202681	33.571311	.029787	68
35	5.170994	175.620800	.005694	.193386	33.962677	.029444	70
36	5.419533	186.085599	.005374	.184518	34.336095	.029124	72
37	5.680018	197.053379	.005075	.176056	34.692388	.028825	74
38	5.953022	208.548315	.004795	.167982	35.032341	.028545	76
39	6.239149	220.595744	.004533	.160278	35.356704	.028283	78
40	6.539028	233.222222	.004288	.152928	35.666192	.028038	80
41	6.853320	246.455579	.004058	.145915	35.961487	.027808	82
42	7.182718	260.324986	.003841	.139223	36.243240	.027591	84
43	7.527949	274.861012	.003638	.132838	36.512071	.027388	86
44	7.889773	290.095699	.003447	.126746	36.768574	.027197	88
45	8.268987	306.062627	.003267	.120934	37.013314	.027017	90
46	8.666429	322.796990	.003098	.115388	37.246830	.026848	92
47	9.082972	340.335674	.002938	.110096	37.469637	.026688	94
48	9.519537	358.717340	.002788	.105047	37.682226	.026538	96
49	9.977084	377.982502	.002646	.100230	37.885066	.026396	98
50	10.456624	398.173627	.002511	.095633	38.078604	.026261	100
51	10.959211	419.335219	.002385	.091247	38.263266	.026135	102
52	11.485956	441.513923	.002265	.087063	38.439459	.026015	104
53	12.038017	464.758626	.002152	.083070	38.607572	.025902	106
54	12.616613	489.120564	.002044	.079261	38.767976	.025794	108
55	13.223019	514.653435	.001943	.075626	38.921023	.025693	110
56	13.858571	541.413520	.001847	.072158	39.067052	.025597	112
57	14.524670	569.459803	.001756	.068848	39.206384	.025506	114
58	15.222785	598.854105	.001670	.065691	39.339326	.025420	116
59	15.954454	629.661216	.001588	.062678	39.466172	.025338	118
60	16.721290	661.949042	.001511	.059804	39.587200	.025261	120

4¾% ANNUAL COMPOUND INTEREST TABLE 4¾%

EFFECTIVE RATE = 4¾% BASE = 1.0475

YEARS	1 AMOUNT OF 1 AT COMPOUND INTEREST $S^n = (1+i)^n$	2 ACCUMULATION OF 1 PER PERIOD $S_{\overline{n}\vert} = \frac{S^n - 1}{i}$	3 SINKING FUND FACTOR $1/S_{\overline{n}\vert} = \frac{i}{S^n - 1}$	4 PRES. VALUE REVERSION OF 1 $V^n = \frac{1}{S^n}$	5 PRESENT VALUE ORD. ANNUITY 1 PER PERIOD $a_{\overline{n}\vert} = \frac{1 - V^n}{i}$	6 INSTALMENT TO AMORTIZE 1 $1/a_{\overline{n}\vert} = \frac{i}{1 - V^n}$	n YEARS
1	1.047500	1.000000	1.000000	.954654	.954654	1.047500	1
2	1.097256	2.047500	.488400	.911364	1.866018	.535900	2
3	1.149376	3.144756	.317990	.870037	2.736055	.365490	3
4	1.203971	4.294132	.232876	.830585	3.566640	.280376	4
5	1.261160	5.498103	.181881	.792921	4.359561	.229381	5
6	1.321065	6.759263	.147945	.756965	5.116526	.195445	6
7	1.383816	8.080328	.123757	.722640	5.839166	.171257	7
8	1.449547	9.464144	.105662	.689871	6.529036	.153162	8
9	1.518400	10.913691	.091628	.658588	7.187624	.139128	9
10	1.590524	12.432091	.080437	.628723	7.816348	.127937	10
11	1.666074	14.022615	.071313	.600213	8.416561	.118813	11
12	1.745213	15.688690	.063740	.572996	8.989557	.111240	12
13	1.828110	17.433902	.057360	.547013	9.536570	.104860	13
14	1.914946	19.262013	.051916	.522208	10.058778	.099416	14
15	2.005906	21.176958	.047221	.498528	10.557306	.094721	15
16	2.101186	23.182864	.043135	.475922	11.033228	.090635	16
17	2.200992	25.284050	.039551	.454341	11.487568	.087051	17
18	2.305540	27.485042	.036383	.433738	11.921306	.083883	18
19	2.415053	29.790582	.033568	.414070	12.335376	.081068	19
20	2.529768	32.205635	.031050	.395293	12.730669	.078550	20
21	2.649932	34.735402	.028789	.377368	13.108037	.076289	21
22	2.775803	37.385334	.026748	.360256	13.468293	.074248	22
23	2.907654	40.161137	.024900	.343920	13.812213	.072400	23
24	3.045768	43.068791	.023219	.328324	14.140538	.070719	24
25	3.190442	46.114559	.021685	.313436	14.453974	.069185	25
26	3.341988	49.305000	.020282	.299223	14.753197	.067782	26
27	3.500732	52.646988	.018994	.285655	15.038852	.066494	27
28	3.667017	56.147720	.017810	.272701	15.311553	.065310	28
29	3.841200	59.814736	.016718	.260335	15.571888	.064218	29
30	4.023657	63.655936	.015709	.248530	15.820418	.063209	30
31	4.214781	67.679593	.014776	.237260	16.057679	.062276	31
32	4.414983	71.894374	.013909	.226501	16.284180	.061409	32
33	4.624694	76.309357	.013105	.216231	16.500410	.060605	33
34	4.844367	80.934051	.012356	.206425	16.706836	.059856	34
35	5.074475	85.778419	.011658	.197065	16.903901	.059158	35
36	5.315512	90.852894	.011007	.188129	17.092029	.058507	36
37	5.567999	96.168406	.010398	.179598	17.271627	.057898	37
38	5.832479	101.736405	.009829	.171454	17.443081	.057329	38
39	6.109522	107.568884	.009296	.163679	17.606759	.056796	39
40	6.399724	113.678406	.008797	.156257	17.763016	.056297	40
41	6.703711	120.078131	.008328	.149171	17.912187	.055828	41
42	7.022137	126.781842	.007888	.142407	18.054594	.055388	42
43	7.355689	133.803980	.007474	.135949	18.190543	.054974	43
44	7.705084	141.159669	.007084	.129784	18.320328	.054584	44
45	8.071076	148.864753	.006718	.123899	18.444227	.054218	45
46	8.454452	156.935829	.006372	.118281	18.562508	.053872	46
47	8.856038	165.390280	.006046	.112917	18.675425	.053546	47
48	9.276700	174.246319	.005739	.107797	18.783222	.053239	48
49	9.717343	183.523019	.005449	.102909	18.886131	.052949	49
50	10.178917	193.240362	.005175	.098242	18.984373	.052675	50
51	10.662416	203.419279	.004916	.093787	19.078160	.052416	51
52	11.168881	214.081695	.004671	.089534	19.167695	.052171	52
53	11.699402	225.250576	.004440	.085474	19.253169	.051940	53
54	12.255124	236.949978	.004220	.081599	19.334768	.051720	54
55	12.837242	249.205102	.004013	.077898	19.412666	.051513	55
56	13.447011	262.042344	.003816	.074366	19.487032	.051316	56
57	14.085744	275.489356	.003630	.070994	19.558026	.051130	57
58	14.754817	289.575100	.003453	.067774	19.625800	.050953	58
59	15.455671	304.329917	.003286	.064701	19.690502	.050786	59
60	16.189815	319.785589	.003127	.061767	19.752269	.050627	60

5% MONTHLY COMPOUND INTEREST TABLE 5%

EFFECTIVE RATE = 5/12% BASE = 1.00416666+

MONTHS	1 AMOUNT OF 1 AT COMPOUND INTEREST $S^n = (1+i)^n$	2 ACCUMULATION OF 1 PER PERIOD $S_{\overline{n}\vert} = \frac{S^n - 1}{i}$	3 SINKING FUND FACTOR $1/S_{\overline{n}\vert} = \frac{i}{S^n - 1}$	4 PRES. VALUE REVERSION OF 1 $V^n = \frac{1}{S^n}$	5 PRESENT VALUE ORD. ANNUITY 1 PER PERIOD $a_{\overline{n}\vert} = \frac{1 - V^n}{i}$	6 INSTALMENT TO AMORTIZE 1 $1/a_{\overline{n}\vert} = \frac{i}{1 - V^n}$	n MONTHS
1	1.004167	1.000000	1.000000	.995851	.995851	1.004167	1
2	1.008351	2.004167	.498960	.991718	1.987569	.503127	2
3	1.012552	3.012517	.331948	.987603	2.975173	.336115	3
4	1.016771	4.025070	.248443	.983506	3.958678	.252610	4
5	1.021008	5.041841	.198340	.979425	4.938103	.202507	5
6	1.025262	6.062848	.164939	.975361	5.913463	.169106	6
7	1.029534	7.088110	.141081	.971313	6.884777	.145248	7
8	1.033824	8.117644	.123188	.967283	7.852060	.127355	8
9	1.038131	9.151467	.109272	.963269	8.815329	.113439	9
10	1.042457	10.189599	.098139	.959272	9.774602	.102306	10
11	1.046800	11.232055	.089031	.955292	10.729894	.093198	11
YEARS							
1	1.051162	12.278855	.081441	.951328	11.681222	.085608	12
2	1.104941	25.185921	.039705	.905025	22.793898	.043872	24
3	1.161472	38.753336	.025804	.860976	33.365701	.029971	36
4	1.220895	53.014885	.018863	.819071	43.422956	.023030	48
5	1.283359	68.006083	.014705	.779205	52.990706	.018872	60
6	1.349018	83.764259	.011938	.741280	62.092777	.016105	72
7	1.418036	100.328653	.009967	.705201	70.751835	.014134	84
8	1.490585	117.740513	.008493	.670877	78.989441	.012660	96
9	1.566847	136.043196	.007351	.638225	86.826108	.011518	108
10	1.647010	155.282280	.006440	.607161	94.281350	.010607	120
11	1.731274	175.505671	.005698	.577609	101.373733	.009865	132
12	1.819849	196.763730	.005082	.549496	108.120917	.009249	144
13	1.912956	219.109392	.004564	.522751	114.539704	.008731	156
14	2.010826	242.598300	.004122	.497308	120.646077	.008289	168
15	2.113704	267.288945	.003741	.473103	126.455243	.007908	180
16	2.221845	293.242810	.003410	.450076	131.981666	.007577	192
17	2.335519	320.524524	.003120	.428170	137.239108	.007287	204
18	2.455008	349.202023	.002864	.407331	142.240661	.007031	216
19	2.580611	379.346717	.002636	.387505	146.998780	.006803	228
20	2.712640	411.033670	.002433	.368645	151.525313	.006600	240
21	2.851424	444.341789	.002251	.350702	155.831531	.006418	252
22	2.997308	479.354014	.002086	.333633	159.928159	.006253	264
23	3.150656	516.157530	.001937	.317394	163.825396	.006104	276
24	3.311850	554.843985	.001802	.301946	167.532948	.005969	288
25	3.481290	595.509712	.001679	.287250	171.060047	.005846	300
26	3.659400	638.255975	.001567	.273269	174.415476	.005734	312
27	3.846622	683.189218	.001464	.259968	177.607590	.005631	324
28	4.043422	730.421330	.001369	.247315	180.644338	.005536	336
29	4.250291	780.069928	.001282	.235278	183.533282	.005449	348
30	4.467744	832.258641	.001202	.223827	186.281617	.005369	360
31	4.696323	887.117429	.001127	.212933	188.896185	.005294	372
32	4.936595	944.782896	.001058	.202569	191.383497	.005225	384
33	5.189161	1005.398638	.000995	.192709	193.749748	.005162	396
34	5.454648	1069.115596	.000935	.183330	196.000829	.005102	408
35	5.733719	1136.092435	.000880	.174407	198.142346	.005047	420
36	6.027066	1206.495936	.000829	.165918	200.179632	.004996	432
37	6.335423	1280.501414	.000781	.157843	202.117759	.004948	444
38	6.659555	1358.293153	.000736	.150160	203.961554	.004903	456
39	7.000270	1440.064865	.000694	.142852	205.715609	.004861	468
40	7.358417	1526.020172	.000655	.135899	207.384290	.004822	480
41	7.734888	1616.373117	.000619	.129284	208.971754	.004786	492
42	8.130620	1711.348689	.000584	.122992	210.481953	.004751	504
43	8.546598	1811.183392	.000552	.117006	211.918649	.004719	516
44	8.983858	1916.125828	.000522	.111311	213.285417	.004689	528
45	9.443489	2026.437318	.000493	.105893	214.585663	.004660	540
46	9.926636	2142.392554	.000467	.100739	215.822623	.004634	552
47	10.434501	2264.280279	.000442	.095836	216.999379	.004609	564
48	10.968350	2392.404012	.000418	.091171	218.118860	.004585	576
49	11.529512	2527.082798	.000396	.086734	219.183853	.004563	588
50	12.119383	2668.652007	.000375	.082512	220.197012	.004542	600

5% QUARTERLY COMPOUND INTEREST TABLE 5%

EFFECTIVE RATE = 1¼% BASE = 1.0125

QUARTERS	1 AMOUNT OF I AT COMPOUND INTEREST $s^n = (1+i)^n$	2 ACCUMULATION OF I PER PERIOD $s_{\overline{n}\rvert} = \frac{s^n - 1}{i}$	3 SINKING FUND FACTOR $1/s_{\overline{n}\rvert} = \frac{i}{s^n - 1}$	4 PRES. VALUE REVERSION OF I $v^n = \frac{1}{s^n}$	5 PRESENT VALUE ORD. ANNUITY 1 PER PERIOD $a_{\overline{n}\rvert} = \frac{1 - v^n}{i}$	6 INSTALMENT TO AMORTIZE I $1/a_{\overline{n}\rvert} = \frac{i}{1 - v^n}$	n QUARTERS
1	1.012500	1.000000	1.000000	.987654	.987654	1.012500	1
2	1.025156	2.012500	.496894	.975461	1.963115	.509394	2
3	1.037971	3.037656	.329201	.963418	2.926534	.341701	3
YEARS							
1	1.050945	4.075627	.245361	.951524	3.878058	.257861	4
2	1.104486	8.358888	.119633	.905398	7.568124	.132133	8
3	1.160755	12.860361	.077758	.861509	11.079312	.090258	12
4	1.219890	17.591164	.056847	.819746	14.420292	.069347	16
5	1.282037	22.562979	.044320	.780009	17.599316	.056820	20
6	1.347351	27.788084	.035987	.742197	20.624235	.048487	24
7	1.415992	33.279384	.030049	.706219	23.502518	.042549	28
8	1.488131	39.050441	.025608	.671984	26.241274	.038108	32
9	1.563944	45.115506	.022165	.639409	28.847267	.034665	36
10	1.643619	51.489557	.019421	.608413	31.326933	.031921	40
11	1.727354	58.188337	.017186	.578920	33.686395	.029686	44
12	1.815355	65.228388	.015331	.550856	35.931481	.027831	48
13	1.907839	72.627097	.013769	.524153	38.067734	.026269	52
14	2.005034	80.402736	.012437	.498745	40.100431	.024937	56
15	2.107181	88.574508	.011290	.474568	42.034592	.023790	60
16	2.214532	97.162593	.010292	.451563	43.874992	.022792	64
17	2.327353	106.188201	.009417	.429673	45.626178	.021917	68
18	2.445920	115.673621	.008645	.408844	47.292474	.021145	72
19	2.570529	125.642280	.007959	.389025	48.877995	.020459	76
20	2.701485	136.118795	.007347	.370167	50.386657	.019847	80
21	2.839113	147.129040	.006797	.352223	51.822185	.019297	84
22	2.983753	158.700206	.006301	.335148	53.188125	.018801	88
23	3.135761	170.860868	.005853	.318902	54.487850	.018353	92
24	3.295513	183.641059	.005445	.303443	55.724570	.017945	96
25	3.463404	197.072342	.005074	.288733	56.901339	.017574	100
26	3.639849	211.187886	.004735	.274737	58.021064	.017235	104
27	3.825282	226.022551	.004424	.261419	59.086509	.016924	108
28	4.020162	241.612973	.004139	.248746	60.100305	.016639	112
29	4.224971	257.997654	.003876	.236688	61.064957	.016376	116
30	4.440213	275.217058	.003633	.225214	61.982847	.016133	120
31	4.666421	293.313711	.003409	.214297	62.856242	.015909	124
32	4.904154	312.332304	.003202	.203909	63.687298	.015702	128
33	5.153998	332.319805	.003009	.194024	64.478068	.015509	132
34	5.416570	353.325577	.002830	.184619	65.230505	.015330	136
35	5.692519	375.401494	.002664	.175669	65.946467	.015164	140
36	5.982526	398.602077	.002509	.167153	66.627722	.015009	144
37	6.287308	422.984621	.002364	.159051	67.275953	.014864	148
38	6.607617	448.609342	.002229	.151340	67.892760	.014729	152
39	6.944244	475.539523	.002103	.144004	68.479668	.014603	156
40	7.298021	503.841671	.001985	.137023	69.038124	.014485	160
41	7.669821	533.585681	.001874	.130381	69.569509	.014374	164
42	8.060563	564.845011	.001770	.124061	70.075135	.014270	168
43	8.471211	597.696857	.001673	.118047	70.556250	.014173	172
44	8.902779	632.222352	.001582	.112324	71.014042	.014082	176
45	9.356334	668.506759	.001496	.106879	71.449643	.013996	180
46	9.832996	706.639689	.001415	.101698	71.864128	.013915	184
47	10.333941	746.715313	.001339	.096768	72.258520	.013839	188
48	10.860408	788.832603	.001268	.092078	72.633794	.013768	192
49	11.413695	833.095572	.001200	.087614	72.990876	.013700	196
50	11.995169	879.613534	.001137	.083367	73.330649	.013637	200
51	12.606267	928.501369	.001077	.079326	73.653950	.013577	204
52	13.248498	979.879811	.001021	.075480	73.961580	.013521	208
53	13.923447	1033.875745	.000967	.071821	74.254296	.013467	212
54	14.632781	1090.622520	.000917	.068340	74.532824	.013417	216
55	15.378253	1150.260278	.000869	.065027	74.797849	.013369	220
56	16.161704	1212.936303	.000824	.061875	75.050027	.013324	224
57	16.985067	1278.805378	.000782	.058875	75.289980	.013282	228
58	17.850377	1348.030176	.000742	.056021	75.518302	.013242	232
59	18.759771	1420.781655	.000704	.053306	75.735556	.013204	236
60	19.715494	1497.239482	.000668	.050722	75.942278	.013168	240

5% SEMI-ANNUAL COMPOUND INTEREST TABLE 5%

EFFECTIVE RATE = 2½%   BASE = 1.025

HALF YEARS	1 AMOUNT OF 1 AT COMPOUND INTEREST $S^n = (1+i)^n$	2 ACCUMULATION OF 1 PER PERIOD $S_{\overline{n}\rceil} = \frac{S^n - 1}{i}$	3 SINKING FUND FACTOR $1/S_{\overline{n}\rceil} = \frac{i}{S^n - 1}$	4 PRES. VALUE REVERSION OF 1 $V^n = \frac{1}{S^n}$	5 PRESENT VALUE ORD. ANNUITY 1 PER PERIOD $a_{\overline{n}\rceil} = \frac{1 - V^n}{i}$	6 INSTALMENT TO AMORTIZE 1 $1/a_{\overline{n}\rceil} = \frac{i}{1 - V^n}$	n HALF YEARS
1	1.025000	1.000000	1.000000	.975610	.975610	1.025000	1
YEARS							
1	1.050625	2.025000	.493827	.951814	1.927424	.518827	2
2	1.103813	4.152516	.240818	.905951	3.761974	.265818	4
3	1.159693	6.387737	.156550	.862297	5.508125	.181550	6
4	1.218403	8.736116	.114467	.820747	7.170137	.139467	8
5	1.280085	11.203382	.089259	.781198	8.752064	.114259	10
6	1.344889	13.795553	.072487	.743556	10.257765	.097487	12
7	1.412974	16.518953	.060537	.707727	11.690912	.085537	14
8	1.484506	19.380225	.051599	.673625	13.055003	.076599	16
9	1.559659	22.386349	.044670	.641166	14.353364	.069670	18
10	1.638616	25.544658	.039147	.610271	15.589162	.064147	20
11	1.721571	28.862856	.034647	.580865	16.765413	.059647	22
12	1.808726	32.349038	.030913	.552875	17.884986	.055913	24
13	1.900293	36.011708	.027769	.526235	18.950611	.052769	26
14	1.996495	39.859801	.025088	.500878	19.964889	.050088	28
15	2.097568	43.902703	.022778	.476743	20.930293	.047778	30
16	2.203757	48.150278	.020768	.453771	21.849178	.045768	32
17	2.315322	52.612885	.019007	.431905	22.723786	.044007	34
18	2.432535	57.301413	.017452	.411094	23.556251	.042452	36
19	2.555682	62.227297	.016070	.391285	24.348603	.041070	38
20	2.685064	67.402554	.014836	.372431	25.102775	.039836	40
21	2.820995	72.839808	.013729	.354485	25.820607	.038729	42
22	2.963808	78.552323	.012730	.337404	26.503849	.037730	44
23	3.113851	84.554034	.011827	.321146	27.154170	.036827	46
24	3.271490	90.859582	.011006	.305671	27.773154	.036006	48
25	3.437109	97.484349	.010258	.290942	28.362312	.035258	50
26	3.611112	104.444494	.009574	.276923	28.923081	.034574	52
27	3.793925	111.756996	.008948	.263579	29.456829	.033948	54
28	3.985992	119.439694	.008372	.250879	29.964858	.033372	56
29	4.187783	127.511329	.007842	.238790	30.448407	.032842	58
30	4.399790	135.991590	.007353	.227284	30.908656	.032353	60
31	4.622529	144.901164	.006901	.216332	31.346728	.031901	62
32	4.856545	154.261786	.006482	.205908	31.763691	.031482	64
33	5.102407	164.096289	.006094	.195986	32.160563	.031094	66
34	5.360717	174.428663	.005733	.186542	32.538311	.030733	68
35	5.632103	185.284114	.005397	.177554	32.897857	.030397	70
36	5.917228	196.689122	.005084	.168998	33.240078	.030084	72
37	6.216788	208.671509	.004792	.160855	33.565809	.029792	74
38	6.531513	221.260504	.004520	.153104	33.875844	.029520	76
39	6.862170	234.486817	.004265	.145726	34.170940	.029265	78
40	7.209568	248.382713	.004026	.138705	34.451817	.029026	80
41	7.574552	262.982087	.003803	.132021	34.719160	.028803	82
42	7.958014	278.320556	.003593	.125659	34.973620	.028593	84
43	8.360888	294.435534	.003396	.119605	35.215819	.028396	86
44	8.784158	311.366333	.003212	.113841	35.446348	.028212	88
45	9.228856	329.154253	.003038	.108356	35.665768	.028038	90
46	9.696067	347.842687	.002875	.103135	35.874616	.027875	92
47	10.186931	367.477223	.002721	.098165	36.073400	.027721	94
48	10.702644	388.105758	.002577	.093435	36.262606	.027577	96
49	11.244465	409.778612	.002440	.088933	36.442694	.027440	98
50	11.813716	432.548654	.002312	.084647	36.614105	.027312	100
51	12.411786	456.471430	.002191	.080569	36.777257	.027191	102
52	13.040132	481.605296	.002076	.076686	36.932546	.027076	104
53	13.700289	508.011564	.001968	.072991	37.080354	.026968	106
54	14.393866	535.754649	.001867	.069474	37.221039	.026867	108
55	15.122556	564.902228	.001770	.066126	37.354944	.026770	110
56	15.888135	595.525404	.001679	.062940	37.482398	.026679	112
57	16.692472	627.698877	.001593	.059907	37.603710	.026593	114
58	17.537528	661.501133	.001512	.057021	37.719177	.026512	116
59	18.425366	697.014628	.001435	.054273	37.829080	.026435	118
60	19.358150	734.325993	.001362	.051658	37.933687	.026362	120

5% ANNUAL COMPOUND INTEREST TABLE 5%

EFFECTIVE RATE = 5% BASE = 1.05

YEARS	1 AMOUNT OF I AT COMPOUND INTEREST $s^n = (1+i)^n$	2 ACCUMULATION OF I PER PERIOD $s_{\overline{n}\vert} = \frac{s^n - 1}{i}$	3 SINKING FUND FACTOR $1/s_{\overline{n}\vert} = \frac{i}{s^n - 1}$	4 PRES. VALUE REVERSION OF I $v^n = \frac{1}{s^n}$	5 PRESENT VALUE ORD. ANNUITY 1 PER PERIOD $a_{\overline{n}\vert} = \frac{1 - v^n}{i}$	6 INSTALMENT TO AMORTIZE I $1/a_{\overline{n}\vert} = \frac{i}{1 - v^n}$	n YEARS
1	1.050000	1.000000	1.000000	.952381	.952381	1.050000	1
2	1.102500	2.050000	.487805	.907029	1.859410	.537805	2
3	1.157625	3.152500	.317209	.863838	2.723248	.367209	3
4	1.215506	4.310125	.232012	.822702	3.545951	.282012	4
5	1.276282	5.525631	.180975	.783526	4.329477	.230975	5
6	1.340096	6.801913	.147017	.746215	5.075692	.197017	6
7	1.407100	8.142008	.122820	.710681	5.786373	.172820	7
8	1.477455	9.549109	.104722	.676839	6.463213	.154722	8
9	1.551328	11.026564	.090690	.644609	7.107822	.140690	9
10	1.628895	12.577893	.079505	.613913	7.721735	.129505	10
11	1.710339	14.206787	.070389	.584679	8.306414	.120389	11
12	1.795856	15.917127	.062825	.556837	8.863252	.112825	12
13	1.885649	17.712983	.056456	.530321	9.393573	.106456	13
14	1.979932	19.598632	.051024	.505068	9.898641	.101024	14
15	2.078928	21.578564	.046342	.481017	10.379658	.096342	15
16	2.182875	23.657492	.042270	.458112	10.837770	.092270	16
17	2.292018	25.840366	.038699	.436297	11.274066	.088699	17
18	2.406619	28.132385	.035546	.415521	11.689587	.085546	18
19	2.526950	30.539004	.032745	.395734	12.085321	.082745	19
20	2.653298	33.065954	.030243	.376889	12.462210	.080243	20
21	2.785963	35.719252	.027996	.358942	12.821153	.077996	21
22	2.925261	38.505214	.025971	.341850	13.163003	.075971	22
23	3.071524	41.430475	.024137	.325571	13.488574	.074137	23
24	3.225100	44.501999	.022471	.310068	13.798642	.072471	24
25	3.386355	47.727099	.020952	.295303	14.093945	.070952	25
26	3.555673	51.113454	.019564	.281241	14.375185	.069564	26
27	3.733456	54.669126	.018292	.267848	14.643034	.068292	27
28	3.920129	58.402583	.017123	.255094	14.898127	.067123	28
29	4.116136	62.322712	.016046	.242946	15.141074	.066046	29
30	4.321942	66.438848	.015051	.231377	15.372451	.065051	30
31	4.538039	70.760790	.014132	.220359	15.592811	.064132	31
32	4.764941	75.298829	.013280	.209866	15.802677	.063280	32
33	5.003189	80.063771	.012490	.199873	16.002549	.062490	33
34	5.253348	85.066959	.011755	.190355	16.192904	.061755	34
35	5.516015	90.320307	.011072	.181290	16.374194	.061072	35
36	5.791816	95.836323	.010434	.172657	16.546852	.060434	36
37	6.081407	101.628139	.009840	.164436	16.711287	.059840	37
38	6.385477	107.709546	.009284	.156605	16.867893	.059284	38
39	6.704751	114.095023	.008765	.149148	17.017041	.058765	39
40	7.039989	120.799774	.008278	.142046	17.159086	.058278	40
41	7.391988	127.839763	.007822	.135282	17.294368	.057822	41
42	7.761588	135.231751	.007395	.128840	17.423208	.057395	42
43	8.149667	142.993339	.006993	.122704	17.545912	.056993	43
44	8.557150	151.143006	.006616	.116861	17.662773	.056616	44
45	8.985008	159.700156	.006262	.111297	17.774070	.056262	45
46	9.434258	168.685164	.005928	.105997	17.880067	.055928	46
47	9.905971	178.119422	.005614	.100949	17.981016	.055614	47
48	10.401270	188.025393	.005318	.096142	18.077158	.055318	48
49	10.921333	198.426663	.005040	.091564	18.168722	.055040	49
50	11.467400	209.347996	.004777	.087204	18.255925	.054777	50
51	12.040770	220.815395	.004529	.083051	18.338977	.054529	51
52	12.642808	232.856165	.004294	.079096	18.418073	.054294	52
53	13.274949	245.498974	.004073	.075330	18.493403	.054073	53
54	13.938696	258.773922	.003864	.071743	18.565146	.053864	54
55	14.635631	272.712618	.003667	.068326	18.633472	.053667	55
56	15.367412	287.348249	.003480	.065073	18.698545	.053480	56
57	16.135783	302.715662	.003303	.061974	18.760519	.053303	57
58	16.942572	318.851445	.003136	.059023	18.819542	.053136	58
59	17.789701	335.794017	.002978	.056212	18.875754	.052978	59
60	18.679186	353.583718	.002828	.053536	18.929290	.052828	60

5¼% MONTHLY COMPOUND INTEREST TABLE 5¼%

EFFECTIVE RATE = 7/16% BASE = 1.004375

MONTHS	1 AMOUNT OF 1 AT COMPOUND INTEREST $S^n = (1+i)^n$	2 ACCUMULATION OF 1 PER PERIOD $S_{\overline{n}\vert} = \frac{S^n - 1}{i}$	3 SINKING FUND FACTOR $1/S_{\overline{n}\vert} = \frac{i}{S^n - 1}$	4 PRES. VALUE REVERSION OF 1 $V^n = \frac{1}{S^n}$	5 PRESENT VALUE ORD. ANNUITY 1 PER PERIOD $a_{\overline{n}\vert} = \frac{1 - V^n}{i}$	6 INSTALMENT TO AMORTIZE 1 $1/a_{\overline{n}\vert} = \frac{i}{1 - V^n}$	n MONTHS
1	1.004375	1.000000	1.000000	.995644	.995644	1.004375	1
2	1.008769	2.004375	.498909	.991307	1.986951	.503284	2
3	1.013183	3.013144	.331879	.986989	2.973940	.336254	3
4	1.017615	4.026327	.248365	.982690	3.956630	.252740	4
5	1.022067	5.043942	.198258	.978409	4.935039	.202633	5
6	1.026539	6.066009	.164853	.974147	5.909186	.169228	6
7	1.031030	7.092548	.140993	.969904	6.879090	.145368	7
8	1.035541	8.123578	.123098	.965679	7.844770	.127473	8
9	1.040071	9.159118	.109181	.961473	8.806242	.113556	9
10	1.044621	10.199190	.098047	.957285	9.763527	.102422	10
11	1.049192	11.243811	.088938	.953115	10.716641	.093313	11
YEARS							
1	1.053782	12.293003	.081347	.948963	11.665604	.085722	12
2	1.110456	25.247146	.039608	.900531	22.735831	.043983	24
3	1.170179	38.897988	.025708	.854570	33.241067	.030083	36
4	1.233113	53.282998	.018768	.810956	43.210146	.023143	48
5	1.299432	68.441661	.014611	.769567	52.670433	.018986	60
6	1.369318	84.415585	.011846	.730290	61.647896	.016221	72
7	1.442963	101.248617	.009877	.693019	70.167175	.014252	84
8	1.520568	118.986962	.008404	.657649	78.251656	.012779	96
9	1.602347	137.679308	.007263	.624085	85.923530	.011638	108
10	1.688524	157.376963	.006354	.592233	93.203853	.010729	120
11	1.779336	178.133996	.005614	.562007	100.112611	.009989	132
12	1.875032	200.007381	.005000	.533324	106.668766	.009375	144
13	1.975875	223.057158	.004483	.506105	112.890314	.008858	156
14	2.082141	247.346595	.004043	.480275	118.794333	.008418	168
15	2.194123	272.942365	.003664	.455763	124.397029	.008039	180
16	2.312127	299.914723	.003334	.432502	129.713780	.007709	192
17	2.436477	328.337705	.003046	.410429	134.759180	.007421	204
18	2.567516	358.289329	.002791	.389482	139.547077	.007166	216
19	2.705602	389.851808	.002565	.369604	144.090615	.006940	228
20	2.851114	423.111776	.002363	.350740	148.402263	.006738	240
21	3.004452	458.160529	.002183	.332839	152.493859	.006558	252
22	3.166037	495.094269	.002020	.315852	156.376631	.006395	264
23	3.336313	534.014376	.001873	.299732	160.061238	.006248	276
24	3.515746	575.027679	.001739	.284435	163.557794	.006114	288
25	3.704830	618.246755	.001617	.269918	166.875896	.005992	300
26	3.904082	663.790235	.001507	.256142	170.024652	.005882	312
27	4.114051	711.783129	.001405	.243069	173.012705	.005780	324
28	4.335313	762.357171	.001312	.230664	175.848256	.005687	336
29	4.568474	815.651181	.001226	.218891	178.539090	.005601	348
30	4.814175	871.811443	.001147	.207720	181.092591	.005522	360
31	5.073090	930.992110	.001074	.197118	183.515769	.005449	372
32	5.345931	993.355624	.001007	.187058	185.815276	.005382	384
33	5.633445	1059.073167	.000944	.177511	187.997422	.005319	396
34	5.936422	1128.325123	.000886	.168452	190.068199	.005261	408
35	6.255694	1201.301579	.000832	.159854	192.033289	.005207	420
36	6.592137	1278.202847	.000782	.151696	193.898086	.005157	432
37	6.946675	1359.240011	.000736	.143954	195.667710	.005111	444
38	7.320280	1444.635506	.000692	.136607	197.347018	.005067	456
39	7.713979	1534.623732	.000652	.129635	198.940619	.005027	468
40	8.128851	1629.451694	.000614	.123019	200.452887	.004989	480
41	8.566036	1729.379683	.000578	.116740	201.887973	.004953	492
42	9.026734	1834.681988	.000545	.110782	203.249817	.004920	504
43	9.512208	1945.647649	.000514	.105128	204.542157	.004889	516
44	10.023793	2062.581254	.000485	.099763	205.768539	.004860	528
45	10.562891	2185.803768	.000457	.094671	206.932330	.004832	540
46	11.130984	2315.653421	.000432	.089839	208.036725	.004807	552
47	11.729629	2452.486634	.000408	.085254	209.084755	.004783	564
48	12.360471	2596.678995	.000385	.080903	210.079297	.004760	576
49	13.025240	2748.626293	.000364	.076774	211.023080	.004739	588
50	13.725762	2908.745604	.000344	.072856	211.918695	.004719	600

5 ¼% QUARTERLY COMPOUND INTEREST TABLE 5 ¼%

EFFECTIVE RATE = 1-5/16% BASE = 1.013125

QUARTERS	1 AMOUNT OF 1 AT COMPOUND INTEREST $s^n = (1+i)^n$	2 ACCUMULATION OF 1 PER PERIOD $s_{\overline{n}\rvert} = \frac{s^n - 1}{i}$	3 SINKING FUND FACTOR $1/s_{\overline{n}\rvert} = \frac{i}{s^n - 1}$	4 PRES. VALUE REVERSION OF 1 $v^n = \frac{1}{s^n}$	5 PRESENT VALUE ORD. ANNUITY 1 PER PERIOD $a_{\overline{n}\rvert} = \frac{1-v^n}{i}$	6 INSTALMENT TO AMORTIZE 1 $1/a_{\overline{n}\rvert} = \frac{i}{1-v^n}$	n QUARTERS
1	1.013125	1.000000	1.000000	.987045	.987045	1.013125	1
2	1.026422	2.013125	.496125	.974258	1.961303	.509865	2
3	1.039894	3.039547	.328996	.961636	2.922939	.342121	3
YEARS							
1	1.053543	4.079441	.245132	.949178	3.872118	.258257	4
2	1.109952	8.377307	.119370	.900940	7.547449	.132495	8
3	1.169382	12.905291	.077488	.855153	11.035993	.090613	12
4	1.231994	17.675717	.056575	.811692	14.347245	.069700	16
5	1.297958	22.701563	.044050	.770441	17.490214	.057175	20
6	1.367454	27.996506	.035719	.731286	20.473452	.048844	24
7	1.440671	33.574955	.029784	.694121	23.305077	.042909	28
8	1.517809	39.452089	.025347	.658845	25.992795	.038472	32
9	1.599076	45.643901	.021909	.625361	28.543919	.035034	36
10	1.684695	52.167238	.019169	.593579	30.965390	.032294	40
11	1.774898	59.039853	.016938	.563413	33.263799	.030063	44
12	1.869931	66.280445	.015087	.534779	35.445399	.028212	48
13	1.970052	73.908718	.013530	.507601	37.516127	.026655	52
14	2.075534	81.945430	.012203	.481804	39.481617	.025328	56
15	2.186663	90.412448	.011060	.457318	41.347218	.024185	60
16	2.303743	99.332813	.010067	.434076	43.118006	.023192	64
17	2.427092	108.730798	.009197	.412016	44.798800	.022322	68
18	2.557045	118.631976	.008429	.391076	46.394174	.021554	72
19	2.693956	129.063290	.007748	.371201	47.908468	.020873	76
20	2.838197	140.053124	.007140	.352336	49.345803	.020265	80
21	2.990162	151.631383	.006595	.334430	50.710091	.019720	84
22	3.150263	163.829573	.006104	.317434	52.005044	.019229	88
23	3.318937	176.680887	.005660	.301301	53.234185	.018785	92
24	3.496641	190.220294	.005257	.285989	54.400859	.018382	96
25	3.683861	204.484637	.004890	.271454	55.508241	.018015	100
26	3.881105	219.512732	.004556	.257659	56.559344	.017681	104
27	4.088909	235.345470	.004249	.244564	57.557029	.017374	108
28	4.307840	252.025936	.003968	.232135	58.504009	.017093	112
29	4.538494	269.599518	.003709	.220337	59.402863	.016834	116
30	4.781497	288.114037	.003471	.209140	60.256035	.016596	120
31	5.037511	307.619872	.003251	.198511	61.065848	.016376	124
32	5.307233	328.170102	.003047	.188422	61.834505	.016172	128
33	5.591396	349.820646	.002859	.178846	62.564098	.015984	132
34	5.890774	372.630417	.002684	.169757	63.256612	.015809	136
35	6.206182	396.661485	.002521	.161130	63.913930	.015646	140
36	6.538478	421.979241	.002370	.152941	64.537844	.015495	144
37	6.888565	448.652576	.002229	.145168	65.130048	.015354	148
38	7.257397	476.754073	.002098	.137790	65.692156	.015223	152
39	7.645978	506.360199	.001975	.130788	66.225697	.015100	156
40	8.055364	537.551516	.001860	.124141	66.732123	.014985	160
41	8.486669	570.412899	.001753	.117832	67.212811	.014878	164
42	8.941068	605.033769	.001653	.111843	67.669070	.014778	168
43	9.419797	641.508332	.001559	.106159	68.102141	.014684	172
44	9.924158	679.935841	.001471	.100764	68.513202	.014596	176
45	10.455524	720.420860	.001388	.095643	68.903373	.014513	180
46	11.015340	763.073556	.001310	.090782	69.273715	.014435	184
47	11.605131	808.009991	.001238	.086169	69.625236	.014363	188
48	12.226501	855.352443	.001169	.081790	69.958891	.014294	192
49	12.881140	905.229735	.001105	.077633	70.275590	.014230	196
50	13.570831	957.777591	.001044	.073687	70.576194	.014169	200
51	14.297449	1013.139000	.000987	.069943	70.861520	.014112	204
52	15.062973	1071.464605	.000933	.066388	71.132346	.014058	208
53	15.869485	1132.913120	.000883	.063014	71.389408	.014008	212
54	16.719179	1197.651751	.000835	.059812	71.633406	.013960	216
55	17.614369	1265.856662	.000790	.056772	71.865003	.013915	220
56	18.557489	1337.713445	.000748	.053887	72.084830	.013873	224
57	19.551106	1413.417633	.000708	.051148	72.293486	.013833	228
58	20.597925	1493.175224	.000670	.048549	72.491537	.013795	232
59	21.700793	1577.203250	.000634	.046081	72.679522	.013759	236
60	22.862711	1665.730360	.000600	.043739	72.857955	.013725	240

5 ¼% SEMI-ANNUAL COMPOUND INTEREST TABLE 5 ¼%

EFFECTIVE RATE = 2-5/8%   BASE = 1.02625

HALF YEARS	1 AMOUNT OF I AT COMPOUND INTEREST $S^n = (1+i)^n$	2 ACCUMULATION OF I PER PERIOD $S_{\overline{n}\vert} = \frac{S^n - 1}{i}$	3 SINKING FUND FACTOR $1/S_{\overline{n}\vert} = \frac{i}{S^n - 1}$	4 PRES. VALUE REVERSION OF I $V^n = \frac{1}{S^n}$	5 PRESENT VALUE ORD. ANNUITY 1 PER PERIOD $a_{\overline{n}\vert} = \frac{1 - V^n}{i}$	6 INSTALMENT TO AMORTIZE I $1/a_{\overline{n}\vert} = \frac{i}{1 - V^n}$	n HALF YEARS
1	1.026250	1.000000	1.000000	.974421	.974421	1.026250	1
YEARS							
1	1.053189	2.026250	.493523	.949497	1.923919	.519773	2
2	1.109207	4.160274	.240369	.901545	3.750674	.266619	4
3	1.168205	6.407805	.156060	.856014	5.485173	.182310	6
4	1.230341	8.774881	.113962	.812783	7.132074	.140212	8
5	1.295781	11.267858	.088748	.771735	8.695803	.114998	10
6	1.364703	13.893435	.071976	.732760	10.180558	.098226	12
7	1.437290	16.658664	.060029	.695754	11.590330	.086279	14
8	1.513738	19.570973	.051096	.660616	12.928903	.077346	16
9	1.594252	22.638184	.044173	.627253	14.199875	.070423	18
10	1.679049	25.868538	.038657	.595575	15.406659	.064907	20
11	1.768356	29.270711	.034164	.565497	16.552498	.060414	22
12	1.862413	32.853843	.030438	.536938	17.640468	.056688	24
13	1.961473	36.627558	.027302	.509821	18.673492	.053552	26
14	2.065802	40.601994	.024629	.484073	19.654346	.050879	28
15	2.175680	44.787826	.022327	.459626	20.585664	.048577	30
16	2.291403	49.196298	.020327	.436414	21.469947	.046577	32
17	2.413280	53.839253	.018574	.414374	22.309572	.044824	34
18	2.541641	58.729162	.017027	.393447	23.106793	.043277	36
19	2.676828	63.879162	.015655	.373576	23.863753	.041905	38
20	2.819206	69.303084	.014429	.354710	24.582484	.040679	40
21	2.969157	75.015500	.013331	.336796	25.264916	.039581	42
22	3.127084	81.031754	.012341	.319787	25.912884	.038591	44
23	3.293410	87.368008	.011446	.303637	26.528128	.037696	46
24	3.468584	94.041280	.010634	.288302	27.112300	.036884	48
25	3.653074	101.069497	.009894	.273742	27.666970	.036144	50
26	3.847378	108.471539	.009219	.259917	28.193627	.035469	52
27	4.052016	116.267289	.008601	.246791	28.693687	.034851	54
28	4.267539	124.477687	.008034	.234327	29.168492	.034284	56
29	4.494526	133.124788	.007512	.222493	29.619319	.033762	58
30	4.733585	142.231821	.007031	.211256	30.047377	.033281	60
31	4.985360	151.823248	.006587	.200587	30.453817	.032837	62
32	5.250527	161.924834	.006176	.190457	30.839730	.032426	64
33	5.529798	172.563715	.005795	.180838	31.206154	.032045	66
34	5.823922	183.768467	.005442	.171706	31.554073	.031692	68
35	6.133691	195.569189	.005113	.163034	31.884420	.031363	70
36	6.459937	207.997581	.004808	.154800	32.198084	.031058	72
37	6.803534	221.087027	.004523	.146982	32.495908	.030773	74
38	7.165408	234.872689	.004258	.139559	32.778690	.030508	76
39	7.546529	249.391597	.004010	.132511	33.047191	.030260	78
40	7.947922	264.682752	.003778	.125819	33.302132	.030028	80
41	8.370665	280.787230	.003561	.119465	33.544197	.029811	82
42	8.815893	297.748289	.003359	.113432	33.774038	.029609	84
43	9.284802	315.611492	.003168	.107703	33.992271	.029418	86
44	9.778652	334.424821	.002990	.102264	34.199482	.029240	88
45	10.298769	354.238814	.002823	.097099	34.396229	.029073	90
46	10.846551	375.106694	.002666	.092195	34.583040	.028916	92
47	11.423469	397.084518	.002518	.087539	34.760416	.028768	94
48	12.031072	420.231321	.002380	.083118	34.928834	.028630	96
49	12.670994	444.609281	.002249	.078920	35.088746	.028499	98
50	13.344952	470.283882	.002126	.074935	35.240583	.028376	100
51	14.054757	497.324091	.002011	.071150	35.384751	.028261	102
52	14.802317	525.802543	.001902	.067557	35.521638	.028152	104
53	15.589638	555.795737	.001799	.064145	35.651613	.028049	106
54	16.418836	587.384241	.001702	.060906	35.775023	.027952	108
55	17.292139	620.652908	.001611	.057830	35.892200	.027861	110
56	18.211891	655.691105	.001525	.054909	36.003460	.027775	112
57	19.180565	692.592950	.001444	.052136	36.109101	.027694	114
58	20.200761	731.457570	.001367	.049503	36.209406	.027617	116
59	21.275221	772.389362	.001295	.047003	36.304646	.027545	118
60	22.406830	815.498278	.001226	.044629	36.395076	.027476	120

5¼% ANNUAL COMPOUND INTEREST TABLE 5¼%

EFFECTIVE RATE = 5¼%   BASE = 1.0525

YEARS	1 AMOUNT OF 1 AT COMPOUND INTEREST $S^n = (1+i)^n$	2 ACCUMULATION OF 1 PER PERIOD $S_{\overline{n}|} = \frac{S^n - 1}{i}$	3 SINKING FUND FACTOR $1/S_{\overline{n}|} = \frac{i}{S^n - 1}$	4 PRES. VALUE REVERSION OF 1 $V^n = \frac{1}{S^n}$	5 PRESENT VALUE ORD. ANNUITY 1 PER PERIOD $a_{\overline{n}|} = \frac{1 - V^n}{i}$	6 INSTALMENT TO AMORTIZE 1 $1/a_{\overline{n}|} = \frac{i}{1 - V^n}$	n YEARS
1	1.052500	1.000000	1.000000	.950119	.950119	1.052500	1
2	1.107756	2.052500	.487211	.902726	1.852844	.539711	2
3	1.165913	3.160256	.316430	.857697	2.710541	.368930	3
4	1.227124	4.326170	.231151	.814914	3.525455	.283651	4
5	1.291548	5.553294	.180073	.774265	4.299719	.232573	5
6	1.359354	6.844842	.146095	.735643	5.035363	.198595	6
7	1.430720	8.204196	.121889	.698949	5.734311	.174389	7
8	1.505833	9.634916	.103789	.664084	6.398396	.156289	8
9	1.584889	11.140749	.089761	.630959	7.029355	.142261	9
10	1.668096	12.725638	.078582	.599486	7.628840	.131082	10
11	1.755671	14.393734	.069475	.569583	8.198423	.121975	11
12	1.847844	16.149405	.061922	.541171	8.739595	.114422	12
13	1.944856	17.997249	.055564	.514177	9.253772	.108064	13
14	2.046961	19.942105	.050145	.488529	9.742301	.102645	14
15	2.154426	21.989065	.045477	.464161	10.206462	.097977	15
16	2.267533	24.143491	.041419	.441008	10.647469	.093919	16
17	2.386579	26.411025	.037863	.419010	11.066479	.090363	17
18	2.511874	28.797603	.034725	.398109	11.464588	.087225	18
19	2.643748	31.309478	.031939	.378251	11.842839	.084439	19
20	2.782544	33.953225	.029452	.359383	12.202223	.081952	20
21	2.928628	36.735769	.027221	.341457	12.543679	.079721	21
22	3.082381	39.664397	.025212	.324425	12.868104	.077712	22
23	3.244206	42.746778	.023394	.308242	13.176346	.075894	23
24	3.414527	45.990984	.021743	.292866	13.469212	.074243	24
25	3.593789	49.405511	.020241	.278258	13.747470	.072741	25
26	3.782463	52.999300	.018868	.264378	14.011848	.071368	26
27	3.981043	56.781763	.017611	.251190	14.263038	.070111	27
28	4.190047	60.762806	.016457	.238661	14.501699	.068957	28
29	4.410025	64.952853	.015396	.226756	14.728455	.067896	29
30	4.641551	69.362878	.014417	.215445	14.943901	.066917	30
31	4.885233	74.004429	.013513	.204699	15.148599	.066013	31
32	5.141707	78.889662	.012676	.194488	15.343087	.065176	32
33	5.411647	84.031369	.011900	.184787	15.527874	.064400	33
34	5.695758	89.443016	.011180	.175569	15.703443	.063680	34
35	5.994786	95.138774	.010511	.166812	15.870255	.063011	35
36	6.309512	101.133560	.009888	.158491	16.028745	.062388	36
37	6.640761	107.443071	.009307	.150585	16.179331	.061807	37
38	6.989401	114.083833	.008765	.143074	16.322404	.061265	38
39	7.356345	121.073234	.008259	.135937	16.458341	.060759	39
40	7.742553	128.429579	.007786	.129156	16.587498	.060286	40
41	8.149037	136.172132	.007344	.122714	16.710212	.059844	41
42	8.576861	144.321169	.006929	.116593	16.826804	.059429	42
43	9.027147	152.898030	.006540	.110777	16.937581	.059040	43
44	9.501072	161.925176	.006176	.105251	17.042833	.058676	44
45	9.999878	171.426248	.005833	.100001	17.142834	.058333	45
46	10.524872	181.426126	.005512	.095013	17.237847	.058012	46
47	11.077427	191.950998	.005210	.090274	17.328121	.057710	47
48	11.658992	203.028425	.004925	.085771	17.413891	.057425	48
49	12.271089	214.687418	.004658	.081492	17.495384	.057158	49
50	12.915322	226.958507	.004406	.077427	17.572811	.056906	50
51	13.593376	239.873829	.004169	.073565	17.646376	.056669	51
52	14.307028	253.467205	.003945	.069896	17.716272	.056445	52
53	15.058147	267.774233	.003734	.066409	17.782681	.056234	53
54	15.848700	282.832380	.003536	.063097	17.845778	.056036	54
55	16.680757	298.681080	.003348	.059949	17.905727	.055848	55
56	17.556496	315.361837	.003171	.056959	17.962686	.055671	56
57	18.478212	332.918333	.003004	.054118	18.016804	.055504	57
58	19.448319	351.396546	.002846	.051418	18.068222	.055346	58
59	20.469355	370.844864	.002697	.048854	18.117076	.055197	59
60	21.543997	391.314220	.002555	.046417	18.163492	.055055	60

5 ½% MONTHLY COMPOUND INTEREST TABLE 5 ½%

EFFECTIVE RATE = 11/24%   BASE = 1.00458333+

MONTHS	1 AMOUNT OF I AT COMPOUND INTEREST $S^n = (1+i)^n$	2 ACCUMULATION OF I PER PERIOD $S_{\overline{n}\mid} = \frac{S^n - 1}{i}$	3 SINKING FUND FACTOR $1/S_{\overline{n}\mid} = \frac{i}{S^n - 1}$	4 PRES. VALUE REVERSION OF I $V^n = \frac{1}{S^n}$	5 PRESENT VALUE ORD. ANNUITY 1 PER PERIOD $a_{\overline{n}\mid} = \frac{1 - V^n}{i}$	6 INSTALMENT TO AMORTIZE I $1/a_{\overline{n}\mid} = \frac{i}{1 - V^n}$	n MONTHS
1	1.004583	1.000000	1.000000	.995438	.995438	1.004583	1
2	1.009188	2.004583	.498857	.990896	1.986334	.503440	2
3	1.013813	3.013771	.331810	.986375	2.972709	.336393	3
4	1.018460	4.027584	.248288	.981875	3.954583	.252871	4
5	1.023128	5.046044	.198175	.977395	4.931979	.202758	5
6	1.027817	6.069172	.164767	.972936	5.904914	.169350	6
7	1.032528	7.096989	.140905	.968497	6.873411	.145488	7
8	1.037260	8.129516	.123009	.964078	7.837489	.127592	8
9	1.042014	9.166777	.109090	.959680	8.797169	.113673	9
10	1.046790	10.208791	.097955	.955301	9.752470	.102538	10
11	1.051588	11.255581	.088845	.950943	10.703413	.093428	11
YEARS							
1	1.056408	12.307170	.081253	.946604	11.650017	.085836	12
2	1.115998	25.308560	.039512	.896059	22.677971	.044095	24
3	1.178949	39.043331	.025613	.848213	33.117077	.030196	36
4	1.245451	53.552852	.018673	.802922	42.998777	.023256	48
5	1.315704	68.880823	.014518	.760050	52.352835	.019101	60
6	1.389920	85.073412	.011755	.719466	61.207425	.016338	72
7	1.468322	102.179391	.009787	.681049	69.589216	.014370	84
8	1.551147	120.250281	.008316	.644684	77.523453	.012899	96
9	1.638644	139.340512	.007177	.610261	85.034035	.011760	108
10	1.731076	159.507582	.006269	.577675	92.143582	.010852	120
11	1.828723	180.812232	.005531	.546830	98.873509	.010114	132
12	1.931877	203.318633	.004918	.517631	105.244085	.009501	144
13	2.040850	227.094572	.004403	.489992	111.274498	.008986	156
14	2.155970	252.211660	.003965	.463828	116.982912	.008548	168
15	2.277584	278.745549	.003588	.439062	122.386520	.008171	180
16	2.406057	306.776159	.003260	.415618	127.501597	.007843	192
17	2.541778	336.387915	.002973	.393425	132.343550	.007556	204
18	2.685154	367.670007	.002720	.372418	136.926963	.007303	216
19	2.836618	400.716655	.002496	.352532	141.265640	.007079	228
20	2.996626	435.627393	.002296	.333709	145.372649	.006879	240
21	3.165659	472.507372	.002116	.315890	149.260361	.006699	252
22	3.344227	511.467671	.001955	.299023	152.940485	.006538	264
23	3.532867	552.625637	.001810	.283056	156.424106	.006393	276
24	3.732149	596.105236	.001678	.267942	159.721715	.006261	288
25	3.942672	642.037427	.001558	.253635	162.843246	.006141	300
26	4.165069	690.560553	.001448	.240092	165.798099	.006031	312
27	4.400012	741.820766	.001348	.227272	168.595176	.005931	324
28	4.648207	795.972457	.001256	.215137	171.242900	.005839	336
29	4.910402	853.178730	.001172	.203649	173.749246	.005755	348
30	5.187388	913.611886	.001095	.192775	176.121764	.005678	360
31	5.479997	977.453946	.001023	.182482	178.367599	.005606	372
32	5.789112	1044.897201	.000957	.172738	180.493516	.005540	384
33	6.115664	1116.144786	.000896	.163515	182.505917	.005479	396
34	6.460635	1191.411294	.000839	.154784	184.410864	.005422	408
35	6.825066	1270.923425	.000787	.146519	186.214095	.005370	420
36	7.210053	1354.920665	.000738	.138695	187.921041	.005321	432
37	7.616757	1443.656010	.000693	.131289	189.536843	.005276	444
38	8.046402	1537.396726	.000650	.124279	191.066367	.005233	456
39	8.500282	1636.425154	.000611	.117643	192.514222	.005194	468
40	8.979765	1741.039565	.000574	.111361	193.884766	.005157	480
41	9.486294	1851.555050	.000540	.105415	195.182130	.005123	492
42	10.021395	1968.304478	.000508	.099787	196.410219	.005091	504
43	10.586681	2091.639491	.000478	.094458	197.572734	.005061	516
44	11.183853	2221.931568	.000450	.089415	198.673175	.005033	528
45	11.814710	2359.573142	.000424	.084640	199.714856	.005007	540
46	12.481153	2504.978783	.000399	.080121	200.700917	.004982	552
47	13.185188	2658.586445	.000376	.075843	201.634325	.004959	564
48	13.928936	2820.858786	.000355	.071793	202.517894	.004938	576
49	14.714637	2992.284563	.000334	.067960	203.354284	.004917	588
50	15.544659	3173.380101	.000315	.064331	204.146013	.004898	600

5½% QUARTERLY COMPOUND INTEREST TABLE 5½%

EFFECTIVE RATE = 1-3/8% BASE = 1.01375

QUARTERS	1 AMOUNT OF 1 AT COMPOUND INTEREST $S^n = (1+i)^n$	2 ACCUMULATION OF 1 PER PERIOD $S_{\overline{n}\vert} = \frac{S^n - 1}{i}$	3 SINKING FUND FACTOR $1/S_{\overline{n}\vert} = \frac{i}{S^n - 1}$	4 PRES. VALUE REVERSION OF 1 $V^n = \frac{1}{S^n}$	5 PRESENT VALUE ORD. ANNUITY 1 PER PERIOD $a_{\overline{n}\vert} = \frac{1 - V^n}{i}$	6 INSTALMENT TO AMORTIZE 1 $1/a_{\overline{n}\vert} = \frac{i}{1 - V^n}$	n QUARTERS
1	1.013750	1.000000	1.000000	.986436	.986436	1.013750	1
2	1.027689	2.013750	.496586	.973057	1.959493	.510336	2
3	1.041820	3.041439	.328792	.959859	2.919352	.342542	3
YEARS							
1	1.056145	4.083259	.244902	.946840	3.866192	.258652	4
2	1.115442	8.395771	.119108	.896506	7.526857	.132858	8
3	1.178068	12.950409	.077218	.848847	10.992921	.090968	12
4	1.244211	17.760766	.056304	.803722	14.274728	.070054	16
5	1.314067	22.841200	.043781	.760996	17.382073	.057531	20
6	1.387845	28.206874	.035452	.720542	20.324232	.049202	24
7	1.465765	33.873802	.029521	.682238	23.109985	.043271	28
8	1.548060	39.858899	.025089	.645970	25.747647	.038839	32
9	1.634975	46.180028	.021654	.611630	28.245091	.035404	36
10	1.726771	52.856056	.018919	.579116	30.609770	.032669	40
11	1.823720	59.906908	.016693	.548330	32.848742	.030443	44
12	1.926112	67.353629	.014847	.519181	34.968691	.028597	48
13	2.034254	75.218444	.013295	.491581	36.975942	.027045	52
14	2.148466	83.524828	.011972	.465448	38.876488	.025722	56
15	2.269092	92.297573	.010835	.440705	40.676001	.024585	60
16	2.396489	101.562861	.009846	.417277	42.379851	.023596	64
17	2.531040	111.348348	.008981	.395095	43.993124	.022731	68
18	2.673145	121.683238	.008218	.374091	45.520636	.021968	72
19	2.823228	132.598379	.007542	.354205	46.966945	.021292	76
20	2.981737	144.126349	.006938	.335375	48.336367	.020688	80
21	3.149146	156.301554	.006398	.317546	49.632991	.020148	84
22	3.325955	169.160334	.005912	.300666	50.860687	.019662	88
23	3.512690	182.741067	.005472	.284682	52.023117	.019222	92
24	3.709909	197.084288	.005074	.269548	53.123753	.018824	96
25	3.918201	212.232807	.004712	.255219	54.165879	.018462	100
26	4.138188	228.231836	.004382	.241652	55.152606	.018132	104
27	4.370526	245.129128	.004079	.228805	56.086877	.017829	108
28	4.615908	262.975115	.003803	.216642	56.971483	.017553	112
29	4.875067	281.823062	.003548	.205125	57.809063	.017298	116
30	5.148777	301.729222	.003314	.194221	58.602117	.017064	120
31	5.437854	322.753011	.003098	.183896	59.353013	.016848	124
32	5.743161	344.957176	.002899	.174120	60.063990	.016649	128
33	6.065610	368.407990	.002714	.164864	60.737172	.016464	132
34	6.406162	393.175445	.002543	.156100	61.374568	.016293	136
35	6.765835	419.333464	.002385	.147801	61.978079	.016135	140
36	7.145702	446.960120	.002237	.139944	62.549508	.015987	144
37	7.546896	476.137870	.002100	.132505	63.090559	.015850	148
38	7.970615	506.953798	.001973	.125461	63.602848	.015723	152
39	8.418123	539.499881	.001854	.118791	64.087904	.015604	156
40	8.890757	573.873258	.001743	.112476	64.547174	.015493	160
41	9.389927	610.176522	.001639	.106497	64.982029	.015389	164
42	9.917123	648.518025	.001542	.100836	65.393768	.015292	168
43	10.473918	689.012204	.001451	.095475	65.783618	.015201	172
44	11.061974	731.779922	.001367	.090400	66.152743	.015117	176
45	11.683046	776.948825	.001287	.085594	66.502246	.015037	180
46	12.338989	824.653727	.001213	.081044	66.833170	.014963	184
47	13.031759	875.037012	.001143	.076736	67.146501	.014893	188
48	13.763425	928.249057	.001077	.072656	67.443176	.014827	192
49	14.536169	984.448682	.001016	.068794	67.724079	.014766	196
50	15.352300	1043.803625	.000958	.065137	67.990050	.014708	200
51	16.214252	1106.491039	.000904	.061674	68.241881	.014654	204
52	17.124598	1172.698026	.000853	.058396	68.480325	.014603	208
53	18.086055	1242.622192	.000805	.055291	68.706093	.014555	212
54	19.101493	1316.472236	.000760	.052352	68.919860	.014510	216
55	20.173943	1394.468578	.000717	.049569	69.122263	.014467	220
56	21.306605	1476.844009	.000677	.046934	69.313905	.014427	224
57	22.502860	1563.844393	.000639	.044439	69.495361	.014389	228
58	23.766279	1655.729396	.000604	.042076	69.667169	.014354	232
59	25.100632	1752.773266	.000571	.039840	69.829845	.014321	236
60	26.509903	1855.265646	.000539	.037722	69.983873	.014289	240

SEMI-ANNUAL COMPOUND INTEREST TABLE

5 ½%

EFFECTIVE RATE = 2¾% BASE = 1.0275

HALF YEARS	1 AMOUNT OF I AT COMPOUND INTEREST $s^n = (1+i)^n$	2 ACCUMULATION OF I PER PERIOD $s_{\overline{n}|} = \frac{s^n - 1}{i}$	3 SINKING FUND FACTOR $1/s_{\overline{n}|} = \frac{i}{s^n - 1}$	4 PRES. VALUE REVERSION OF I $v^n = \frac{1}{s^n}$	5 PRESENT VALUE ORD. ANNUITY 1 PER PERIOD $a_{\overline{n}|} = \frac{1 - v^n}{i}$	6 INSTALMENT TO AMORTIZE I $1/a_{\overline{n}|} = \frac{i}{1 - v^n}$	n HALF YEARS
1	1.027500	1.000000	1.000000	.973236	.973236	1.027500	1
YEARS							
1	1.055756	2.027500	.493218	.947188	1.920424	.520718	2
2	1.114621	4.168046	.239921	.897166	3.739428	.267421	4
3	1.176768	6.427940	.155571	.849785	5.462367	.183071	6
4	1.242381	8.813838	.113458	.804906	7.094314	.140958	8
5	1.311651	11.332765	.088240	.762398	8.640076	.115740	10
6	1.384784	13.992137	.071469	.722134	10.104204	.098969	12
7	1.461994	16.799786	.059525	.683997	11.491008	.087025	14
8	1.543509	19.763979	.050597	.647874	12.804573	.078097	16
9	1.629570	22.893445	.043681	.613659	14.048767	.071181	18
10	1.720428	26.197398	.038172	.581251	15.227252	.065672	20
11	1.816353	29.685566	.033686	.550554	16.343500	.061186	22
12	1.917626	33.368222	.029969	.521478	17.400797	.057469	24
13	2.024546	37.256209	.026841	.493938	18.402256	.054341	26
14	2.137427	41.360975	.024177	.467852	19.350826	.051677	28
15	2.256602	45.694608	.021884	.443144	20.249301	.049384	30
16	2.382421	50.269868	.019893	.419741	21.100326	.047393	32
17	2.515256	55.100228	.018149	.397574	21.906407	.045649	34
18	2.655498	60.199910	.016611	.376577	22.669918	.044111	36
19	2.803558	65.583931	.015248	.356690	23.393106	.042748	38
20	2.959874	71.268145	.014032	.337852	24.078101	.041532	40
21	3.124905	77.269290	.012942	.320010	24.726921	.040442	42
22	3.299138	83.605035	.011961	.303109	25.341475	.039461	44
23	3.483086	90.294039	.011075	.287102	25.923574	.038575	46
24	3.677290	97.355996	.010272	.271939	26.474931	.037772	48
25	3.882322	104.811701	.009541	.257578	26.997170	.037041	50
26	4.098785	112.683108	.008874	.243975	27.491829	.036374	52
27	4.327318	120.993396	.008265	.231090	27.960364	.035765	54
28	4.568593	129.767034	.007706	.218886	28.404155	.035206	56
29	4.823321	139.029857	.007193	.207326	28.824508	.034693	58
30	5.092251	148.809140	.006720	.196377	29.222662	.034220	60
31	5.376176	159.133680	.006284	.186006	29.599789	.033784	62
32	5.675932	170.033877	.005881	.176183	29.956999	.033381	64
33	5.992400	181.541829	.005508	.166878	30.295344	.033008	66
34	6.326514	193.691420	.005163	.158065	30.615821	.032663	68
35	6.679257	206.518427	.004842	.149717	30.919372	.032342	70
36	7.051667	220.060621	.004544	.141810	31.206893	.032044	72
37	7.444842	234.357876	.004267	.134321	31.479229	.031767	74
38	7.859938	249.452292	.004009	.127227	31.737183	.031509	76
39	8.298179	265.388316	.003768	.120508	31.981514	.031268	78
40	8.760854	282.212873	.003543	.114144	32.212941	.031043	80
41	9.249326	299.975505	.003334	.108116	32.432146	.030834	82
42	9.765034	318.728514	.003137	.102406	32.639775	.030637	84
43	10.309496	338.527121	.002954	.096998	32.836438	.030454	86
44	10.884315	359.429624	.002782	.091875	33.022715	.030282	88
45	11.491183	381.497572	.002621	.087023	33.199155	.030121	90
46	12.131889	404.795946	.002470	.082427	33.366276	.029970	92
47	12.808317	429.393350	.002329	.078074	33.524572	.029829	94
48	13.522461	455.362213	.002196	.073951	33.674508	.029696	96
49	14.276423	482.779002	.002071	.070046	33.816525	.029571	98
50	15.072422	511.724449	.001954	.066346	33.951042	.029454	100
51	15.912804	542.283785	.001844	.062842	34.078455	.029344	102
52	16.800042	574.546995	.001741	.059524	34.199140	.029241	104
53	17.736750	608.609081	.001643	.056380	34.313450	.029143	106
54	18.725684	644.570341	.001551	.053403	34.421724	.029051	108
55	19.769758	682.536666	.001465	.050582	34.524280	.028965	110
56	20.872046	722.619851	.001384	.047911	34.621419	.028884	112
57	22.035793	764.937924	.001307	.045381	34.713429	.028807	114
58	23.264426	809.615495	.001235	.042984	34.800579	.028735	116
59	24.561563	856.784119	.001167	.040714	34.883126	.028667	118
60	25.931024	906.582688	.001103	.038564	34.961315	.028603	120

5 ½% ANNUAL COMPOUND INTEREST TABLE 5 ½%

EFFECTIVE RATE = 5½% BASE = 1.055

YEARS	1 AMOUNT OF I AT COMPOUND INTEREST $S^n = (1+i)^n$	2 ACCUMULATION OF I PER PERIOD $S_{\overline{n}\rceil} = \frac{S^n - 1}{i}$	3 SINKING FUND FACTOR $1/S_{\overline{n}\rceil} = \frac{i}{S^n - 1}$	4 PRES. VALUE REVERSION OF I $V^n = \frac{1}{S^n}$	5 PRESENT VALUE ORD. ANNUITY 1 PER PERIOD $a_{\overline{n}\rceil} = \frac{1 - V^n}{i}$	6 INSTALMENT TO AMORTIZE I $1/a_{\overline{n}\rceil} = \frac{i}{1 - V^n}$	n YEARS
1	1.055000	1.000000	1.000000	.947867	.947867	1.055000	1
2	1.113025	2.055000	.486618	.898452	1.846320	.541618	2
3	1.174241	3.168025	.315654	.851614	2.697933	.370654	3
4	1.238825	4.342266	.230294	.807217	3.505150	.285294	4
5	1.306960	5.581091	.179176	.765134	4.270284	.234176	5
6	1.378843	6.888051	.145179	.725246	4.995530	.200179	6
7	1.454679	8.266894	.120964	.687437	5.682967	.175964	7
8	1.534687	9.721573	.102864	.651599	6.334566	.157864	8
9	1.619094	11.256260	.088839	.617629	6.952195	.143839	9
10	1.708144	12.875354	.077668	.585431	7.537626	.132668	10
11	1.802092	14.583498	.068571	.554911	8.092536	.123571	11
12	1.901207	16.385591	.061029	.525982	8.618518	.116029	12
13	2.005774	18.286798	.054684	.498561	9.117079	.109684	13
14	2.116091	20.292572	.049279	.472569	9.589648	.104279	14
15	2.232476	22.408663	.044626	.447933	10.037581	.099626	15
16	2.355263	24.641140	.040583	.424581	10.462162	.095583	16
17	2.484802	26.996403	.037042	.402447	10.864609	.092042	17
18	2.621466	29.481205	.033920	.381466	11.246074	.088920	18
19	2.765647	32.102671	.031150	.361579	11.607654	.086150	19
20	2.917757	34.868318	.028679	.342729	11.950382	.083679	20
21	3.078234	37.786076	.026465	.324862	12.275244	.081465	21
22	3.247537	40.864310	.024471	.307926	12.583170	.079471	22
23	3.426152	44.111847	.022670	.291873	12.875042	.077670	23
24	3.614590	47.537998	.021036	.276657	13.151699	.076036	24
25	3.813392	51.152588	.019549	.262234	13.413933	.074549	25
26	4.023129	54.965981	.018193	.248563	13.662495	.073193	26
27	4.244401	58.989109	.016952	.235605	13.898100	.071952	27
28	4.477843	63.233510	.015814	.223322	14.121422	.070814	28
29	4.724124	67.711354	.014769	.211679	14.333101	.069769	29
30	4.983951	72.435478	.013805	.200644	14.533745	.068805	30
31	5.258069	77.419429	.012917	.190184	14.723929	.067917	31
32	5.547262	82.677498	.012095	.180269	14.904198	.067095	32
33	5.852362	88.224760	.011335	.170871	15.075069	.066335	33
34	6.174242	94.077122	.010630	.161963	15.237033	.065630	34
35	6.513825	100.251364	.009975	.153520	15.390552	.064975	35
36	6.872085	106.765189	.009366	.145516	15.536068	.064366	36
37	7.250050	113.637274	.008800	.137930	15.673999	.063800	37
38	7.648803	120.887324	.008272	.130739	15.804738	.063272	38
39	8.069487	128.536127	.007780	.123924	15.928662	.062780	39
40	8.513309	136.605614	.007320	.117463	16.046125	.062320	40
41	8.981541	145.118923	.006891	.111339	16.157464	.061891	41
42	9.475525	154.100464	.006489	.105535	16.262999	.061489	42
43	9.996679	163.575989	.006113	.100033	16.363032	.061113	43
44	10.546497	173.572669	.005761	.094818	16.457851	.060761	44
45	11.126554	184.119165	.005431	.089875	16.547726	.060431	45
46	11.738515	195.245719	.005122	.085190	16.632915	.060122	46
47	12.384133	206.984234	.004831	.080748	16.713664	.059831	47
48	13.065260	219.368367	.004559	.076539	16.790203	.059559	48
49	13.783849	232.433627	.004302	.072549	16.862751	.059302	49
50	14.541961	246.217476	.004061	.068767	16.931518	.059061	50
51	15.341769	260.759438	.003835	.065182	16.996699	.058835	51
52	16.185566	276.101207	.003622	.061783	17.058483	.058622	52
53	17.075773	292.286773	.003421	.058563	17.117045	.058421	53
54	18.014940	309.362546	.003232	.055509	17.172555	.058232	54
55	19.005762	327.377486	.003055	.052616	17.225170	.058055	55
56	20.051079	346.383247	.002887	.049873	17.275043	.057887	56
57	21.153888	366.434326	.002729	.047273	17.322316	.057729	57
58	22.317352	387.588214	.002580	.044808	17.367124	.057580	58
59	23.544806	409.905566	.002440	.042472	17.409596	.057440	59
60	24.839770	433.450372	.002307	.040258	17.449854	.057307	60

5¾% MONTHLY COMPOUND INTEREST TABLE 5¾%

EFFECTIVE RATE = 23/48% **BASE = 1.00479166+**

MONTHS	1 AMOUNT OF 1 AT COMPOUND INTEREST $S^n = (1+i)^n$	2 ACCUMULATION OF 1 PER PERIOD $S_{\overline{n}\vert} = \frac{S^n - 1}{i}$	3 SINKING FUND FACTOR $1/S_{\overline{n}\vert} = \frac{i}{S^n - 1}$	4 PRES. VALUE REVERSION OF 1 $V^n = \frac{1}{S^n}$	5 PRESENT VALUE ORD. ANNUITY 1 PER PERIOD $a_{\overline{n}\vert} = \frac{1 - V^n}{i}$	6 INSTALMENT TO AMORTIZE 1 $1/a_{\overline{n}\vert} = \frac{i}{1 - V^n}$	n MONTHS
1	1.004792	1.000000	1.000000	.995231	.995231	1.004792	1
2	1.009606	2.004792	.498805	.990485	1.985716	.503597	2
3	1.014444	3.014398	.331741	.985762	2.971478	.336533	3
4	1.019305	4.028842	.248210	.981061	3.952539	.253002	4
5	1.024189	5.048147	.198092	.976382	4.928921	.202884	5
6	1.029097	6.072336	.164681	.971726	5.900647	.169473	6
7	1.034028	7.101432	.140817	.967092	6.867739	.145609	7
8	1.038982	8.135460	.122919	.962480	7.830219	.127711	8
9	1.043961	9.174443	.108998	.957890	8.788110	.113790	9
10	1.048963	10.218403	.097863	.953322	9.741432	.102655	10
11	1.053989	11.267367	.088752	.948776	10.690208	.093544	11
YEARS							
1	1.059040	12.321356	.081160	.944252	11.634460	.085952	12
2	1.121565	25.370163	.039416	.891611	22.620316	.044208	24
3	1.187782	39.189369	.025517	.841905	32.993728	.030309	36
4	1.257909	53.824459	.018579	.794970	42.788838	.023371	48
5	1.332176	69.323602	.014425	.750652	52.037886	.019217	60
6	1.410827	85.737812	.011663	.708804	60.771314	.016455	72
7	1.494122	103.121114	.009697	.669289	69.017867	.014489	84
8	1.582335	121.530724	.008228	.631978	76.804687	.013020	96
9	1.675755	141.027233	.007091	.596746	84.157405	.011883	108
10	1.774692	161.674813	.006185	.563478	91.100219	.010977	120
11	1.879469	183.541423	.005448	.532065	97.655982	.010240	132
12	1.990433	206.699034	.004838	.502403	103.846272	.009630	144
13	2.107948	231.223866	.004325	.474395	109.691463	.009117	156
14	2.232401	257.196640	.003888	.447948	115.210793	.008680	168
15	2.364201	284.702843	.003512	.422976	120.422429	.008304	180
16	2.503783	313.833007	.003186	.399396	125.343525	.007978	192
17	2.651606	344.683011	.002901	.377130	129.990277	.007693	204
18	2.808156	377.354394	.002650	.356106	134.377980	.007442	216
19	2.973950	411.954690	.002427	.336253	138.521075	.007219	228
20	3.149531	448.597782	.002229	.317508	142.433199	.007021	240
21	3.335479	487.404275	.002052	.299807	146.127228	.006844	252
22	3.532405	528.501898	.001892	.283093	149.615321	.006684	264
23	3.740958	572.025917	.001748	.267311	152.908958	.006540	276
24	3.961823	618.119587	.001618	.252409	156.018980	.006410	288
25	4.195728	666.934620	.001499	.238338	158.955623	.006291	300
26	4.443444	718.631683	.001392	.225051	161.728552	.006184	312
27	4.705784	773.380933	.001293	.212504	164.346895	.006085	324
28	4.983612	831.362569	.001203	.200658	166.819270	.005995	336
29	5.277844	892.767432	.001120	.189471	169.153813	.005912	348
30	5.589447	957.797627	.001044	.178909	171.358210	.005836	360
31	5.919447	1026.667193	.000974	.168935	173.439714	.005766	372
32	6.268930	1099.602808	.000909	.159517	175.405178	.005701	384
33	6.639047	1176.844529	.000850	.150624	177.261071	.005642	396
34	7.031015	1258.646588	.000795	.142227	179.013500	.005587	408
35	7.446125	1345.278226	.000743	.134298	180.668234	.005535	420
36	7.885743	1437.024583	.000696	.126811	182.230719	.005488	432
37	8.351316	1534.187628	.000652	.119742	183.706098	.005444	444
38	8.844376	1637.087164	.000611	.113066	185.099227	.005403	456
39	9.366547	1746.061870	.000573	.106763	186.414691	.005365	468
40	9.919546	1861.470425	.000537	.100811	187.656820	.005329	480
41	10.505194	1983.692682	.000504	.095191	188.829703	.005296	492
42	11.125419	2113.130920	.000473	.089884	189.937198	.005265	504
43	11.782262	2250.211170	.000444	.084873	190.982953	.005236	516
44	12.477885	2395.384615	.000417	.080142	191.970409	.005209	528
45	13.214577	2549.129076	.000392	.075674	192.902815	.005184	540
46	13.994763	2711.950584	.000369	.071455	193.783241	.005161	552
47	14.821012	2884.385046	.000347	.067472	194.614585	.005139	564
48	15.696042	3067.000010	.000326	.063710	195.399583	.005118	576
49	16.622733	3260.396530	.000307	.060159	196.140818	.005099	588
50	17.604137	3465.211149	.000289	.056805	196.840731	.005081	600

5¾% QUARTERLY COMPOUND INTEREST TABLE 5¾%

EFFECTIVE RATE = 1-7/16% BASE = 1.014375

QUARTERS	1 AMOUNT OF 1 AT COMPOUND INTEREST $s^n=(1+i)^n$	2 ACCUMULATION OF 1 PER PERIOD $s_{\overline{n}\vert}=\frac{s^n-1}{i}$	3 SINKING FUND FACTOR $1/s_{\overline{n}\vert}=\frac{i}{s^n-1}$	4 PRES. VALUE REVERSION OF 1 $v^n=\frac{1}{s^n}$	5 PRESENT VALUE ORD. ANNUITY 1 PER PERIOD $a_{\overline{n}\vert}=\frac{1-v^n}{i}$	6 INSTALMENT TO AMORTIZE 1 $1/a_{\overline{n}\vert}=\frac{i}{1-v^n}$	n QUARTERS
1	1.014375	1.000000	1.000000	.985829	.985829	1.014375	1
2	1.028957	2.014375	.496432	.971858	1.957687	.510807	2
3	1.043748	3.043332	.328587	.958086	2.915773	.342962	3
YEARS							
1	1.058752	4.087080	.244673	.944508	3.860281	.259048	4
2	1.120955	8.414282	.118846	.892096	7.506349	.133221	8
3	1.186813	12.995716	.076948	.842592	10.950092	.091323	12
4	1.256541	17.846317	.056034	.795836	14.202735	.070409	16
5	1.330365	22.981899	.043513	.751674	17.274885	.057888	20
6	1.408526	28.419205	.035187	.709962	20.176556	.049562	24
7	1.491279	34.175964	.029260	.670565	22.917209	.043635	28
8	1.578895	40.270941	.024832	.633354	25.505779	.039207	32
9	1.671658	46.724010	.021402	.598209	27.950705	.035777	36
10	1.769870	53.556208	.018672	.565013	30.259959	.033047	40
11	1.873854	60.789809	.016450	.533660	32.441068	.030825	44
12	1.983946	68.448397	.014610	.504046	34.501144	.028985	48
13	2.100506	76.556941	.013062	.476076	36.446904	.027437	52
14	2.223914	85.141877	.011745	.449658	38.284690	.026120	56
15	2.354573	94.231192	.010612	.424705	40.020495	.024987	60
16	2.492909	103.854521	.009629	.401138	41.659977	.024004	64
17	2.639372	114.043237	.008769	.378878	43.208482	.023144	68
18	2.794439	124.830558	.008011	.357854	44.671058	.022386	72
19	2.958618	136.251654	.007339	.337996	46.052473	.021714	76
20	3.132442	148.343759	.006741	.319240	47.357232	.021116	80
21	3.316478	161.146296	.006206	.301525	48.589587	.020581	84
22	3.511327	174.701006	.005724	.284793	49.753557	.020099	88
23	3.717624	189.052078	.005290	.268989	50.852937	.019665	92
24	3.936041	204.246302	.004896	.254062	51.891310	.019271	96
25	4.167290	220.333213	.004539	.239964	52.872062	.018914	100
26	4.412126	237.365258	.004213	.226648	53.798391	.018588	104
27	4.671346	255.397966	.003915	.214071	54.673317	.018290	108
28	4.945796	274.490128	.003643	.202192	55.499691	.018018	112
29	5.236370	294.703988	.003393	.190972	56.280209	.017768	116
30	5.544016	316.105448	.003164	.180375	57.017415	.017539	120
31	5.869737	338.764282	.002952	.170365	57.713712	.017327	124
32	6.214594	362.754362	.002757	.160912	58.371370	.017132	128
33	6.579712	388.153901	.002576	.151982	58.992534	.016951	132
34	6.966282	415.045709	.002409	.143549	59.579228	.016784	136
35	7.375563	443.517458	.002255	.135583	60.133366	.016630	140
36	7.808891	473.661972	.002111	.128059	60.656754	.016486	144
37	8.267677	505.577530	.001978	.120953	61.151099	.016353	148
38	8.753418	539.368184	.001854	.114241	61.618011	.016229	152
39	9.267696	575.144098	.001739	.107902	62.059014	.016114	156
40	9.812190	613.021910	.001631	.101914	62.475545	.016006	160
41	10.388673	653.125111	.001531	.096259	62.868961	.015906	164
42	10.999026	695.584446	.001438	.090917	63.240547	.015813	168
43	11.645239	740.538341	.001350	.085872	63.591513	.015725	172
44	12.329417	788.133358	.001269	.081107	63.923003	.015644	176
45	13.053792	838.524666	.001193	.076606	64.236098	.015568	180
46	13.820725	891.876552	.001121	.072355	64.531819	,015496	184
47	14.632717	948.362956	.001054	.068340	64.811130	.015429	188
48	15.492416	1008.168036	.000992	.064548	65.074942	.015367	192
49	16.402622	1071.486771	.000933	.060966	65.324114	.015308	196
50	17.366305	1138.525593	.000878	.057583	65.559459	.015253	200
51	18.386607	1209.503064	.000827	.054387	65.781745	.015202	204
52	19.466852	1284.650588	.000778	.051369	65.991696	.015153	208
53	20.610564	1364.213161	.000733	.048519	66.189996	.015108	212
54	21.821471	1448.450176	.000690	.045826	66.377292	.015065	216
55	23.103521	1537.636264	.000650	.043283	66.554195	.015025	220
56	24.460894	1632.062193	.000613	.040882	66.721282	.014988	224
57	25.898015	1732.035813	.000577	.038613	66.879096	.014952	228
58	27.419569	1837.883059	.000544	.036470	67.028153	.014919	232
59	29.030517	1949.949018	.000513	.034447	67.168939	.014888	236
60	30.736111	2068.599051	.000483	.032535	67.301912	.014858	240

5 ¾% SEMI-ANNUAL COMPOUND INTEREST TABLE 5 ¾%

EFFECTIVE RATE = 2-7/8% BASE = 1.02875

HALF YEARS	1 AMOUNT OF I AT COMPOUND INTEREST $S^n = (1+i)^n$	2 ACCUMULATION OF I PER PERIOD $s_{\overline{n}\vert} = \frac{S^n - 1}{i}$	3 SINKING FUND FACTOR $1/s_{\overline{n}\vert} = \frac{i}{S^n - 1}$	4 PRES. VALUE REVERSION OF I $V^n = \frac{1}{S^n}$	5 PRESENT VALUE ORD. ANNUITY 1 PER PERIOD $a_{\overline{n}\vert} = \frac{1 - V^n}{i}$	6 INSTALMENT TO AMORTIZE I $1/a_{\overline{n}\vert} = \frac{i}{1 - V^n}$	n HALF YEARS
1	1.028750	1.000000	1.000000	.972053	.972053	1.028750	1
YEARS							
1	1.058327	2.028750	.492914	.944888	1.916941	.521664	2
2	1.120055	4.175830	.239473	.892813	3.728236	.268223	4
3	1.185384	6.448142	.155083	.843608	5.439707	.183833	6
4	1.254523	8.852990	.112956	.797115	7.056855	.141706	8
5	1.327695	11.398104	.087734	.753185	8.584878	.116484	10
6	1.405135	14.091666	.070964	.711675	10.028689	.099714	12
7	1.487092	16.942335	.059024	.672453	11.392929	.087774	14
8	1.573829	19.959273	.050102	.635393	12.681982	.078852	16
9	1.665625	23.152179	.043192	.600375	13.899994	.071942	18
10	1.762775	26.531316	.037691	.567287	15.050878	.066441	20
11	1.865592	30.107546	.033214	.536023	16.138334	.061964	22
12	1.974406	33.892366	.029505	.506482	17.165859	.058255	24
13	2.089566	37.897941	.026387	.478568	18.136754	.055137	26
14	2.211443	42.137148	.023732	.452193	19.054141	.052482	28
15	2.340429	46.623613	.021448	.427272	19.920970	.050198	30
16	2.476938	51.371758	.019466	.403724	20.740025	.048216	32
17	2.621409	56.396846	.017731	.381474	21.513941	.046481	34
18	2.774307	61.715030	.016204	.360450	22.245205	.044954	36
19	2.936123	67.343406	.014849	.340585	22.936167	.043599	38
20	3.107377	73.300065	.013643	.321815	23.589049	.042393	40
21	3.288619	79.604156	.012562	.304079	24.205949	.041312	42
22	3.480433	86.275943	.011591	.287321	24.788851	.040341	44
23	3.683435	93.336872	.010714	.271486	25.339627	.039464	46
24	3.898277	100.809641	.009920	.256524	25.860050	.038670	48
25	4.125650	108.718271	.009198	.242386	26.351790	.037948	50
26	4.366285	117.088184	.008541	.229028	26.816430	.037291	52
27	4.620956	125.946285	.007940	.216405	27.255463	.036690	54
28	4.890480	135.321049	.007390	.204479	27.670299	.036140	56
29	5.175725	145.242610	.006885	.193210	28.062273	.035635	58
30	5.477607	155.742862	.006421	.182561	28.432645	.035171	60
31	5.797097	166.855558	.005993	.172500	28.782604	.034743	62
32	6.135222	178.616419	.005599	.162993	29.113277	.034349	64
33	6.493068	191.063251	.005234	.154010	29.425726	.033984	66
34	6.871787	204.236064	.004896	.145523	29.720954	.033646	68
35	7.272595	218.177201	.004583	.137503	29.999913	.033333	70
36	7.696780	232.931478	.004293	.129924	30.263497	.033043	72
37	8.145707	248.546320	.004023	.122764	30.512555	.032773	74
38	8.620818	265.071922	.003773	.115998	30.747886	.032523	76
39	9.123640	282.561406	.003539	.109605	30.970248	.032289	78
40	9.655791	301.070992	.003321	.103565	31.180355	.032071	80
41	10.218980	320.660178	.003119	.097857	31.378883	.031869	82
42	10.815018	341.391934	.002929	.092464	31.566469	.031679	84
43	11.445821	363.332902	.002752	.087368	31.743717	.031502	86
44	12.113416	386.553611	.002587	.082553	31.911197	.031337	88
45	12.819950	411.128704	.002432	.078003	32.069446	.031182	90
46	13.567694	437.137178	.002288	.073704	32.218974	.031038	92
47	14.359051	464.662637	.002152	.069642	32.360261	.030902	94
48	15.196565	493.793562	.002025	.065804	32.493762	.030775	96
49	16.082928	524.623593	.001906	.062178	32.619905	.030656	98
50	17.020990	557.251834	.001795	.058751	32.739096	.030545	100
51	18.013766	591.783168	.001690	.055513	32.851718	.030440	102
52	19.064447	628.328595	.001592	.052454	32.958134	.030342	104
53	20.176411	667.005593	.001499	.049563	33.058684	.030249	106
54	21.353231	707.938486	.001413	.046831	33.153693	.030163	108
55	22.598692	751.258854	.001331	.044250	33.243466	.030081	110
56	23.916796	797.105951	.001255	.041812	33.328291	.030005	112
57	25.311781	845.627151	.001183	.039507	33.408442	.029933	114
58	26.788130	896.978426	.001115	.037330	33.484175	.029865	116
59	28.350589	951.324844	.001051	.035273	33.555734	.029801	118
60	30.004182	1008.841102	.000991	.033329	33.623350	.029741	120

5 ¾% ANNUAL COMPOUND INTEREST TABLE 5 ¾%

EFFECTIVE RATE = 5¾% BASE = 1.0575

YEARS	1 AMOUNT OF I AT COMPOUND INTEREST $S^n = (1+i)^n$	2 ACCUMULATION OF I PER PERIOD $S_{\overline{n}\vert} = \frac{S^n - 1}{i}$	3 SINKING FUND FACTOR $1/S_{\overline{n}\vert} = \frac{i}{S^n - 1}$	4 PRES. VALUE REVERSION OF I $V^n = \frac{1}{S^n}$	5 PRESENT VALUE ORD. ANNUITY 1 PER PERIOD $a_{\overline{n}\vert} = \frac{1-V^n}{i}$	6 INSTALMENT TO AMORTIZE I $1/a_{\overline{n}\vert} = \frac{i}{1-V^n}$	n YEARS
1	1.057500	1.000000	1.000000	.945626	.945626	1.057500	1
2	1.118306	2.057500	.486027	.894209	1.839836	.543527	2
3	1.182609	3.175806	.314881	.845588	2.685424	.372381	3
4	1.250609	4.358415	.229441	.799611	3.485035	.286941	4
5	1.322519	5.609024	.178284	.756133	4.241167	.235784	5
6	1.398564	6.931543	.144268	.715019	4.956187	.201768	6
7	1.478981	8.330107	.120046	.676141	5.632328	.177546	7
8	1.564023	9.809088	.101946	.639377	6.271705	.159446	8
9	1.653954	11.373110	.087927	.604612	6.876317	.145427	9
10	1.749056	13.027064	.076763	.571737	7.448054	.134263	10
11	1.849627	14.776120	.067677	.540650	7.988703	.125177	11
12	1.955980	16.625747	.060148	.511253	8.499956	.117648	12
13	2.068449	18.581728	.053816	.483454	8.983410	.111316	13
14	2.187385	20.650177	.048426	.457167	9.440576	.105926	14
15	2.313160	22.837562	.043788	.432309	9.872886	.101288	15
16	2.446167	25.150722	.039760	.408803	10.281688	.097260	16
17	2.586821	27.596888	.036236	.386575	10.668263	.093736	17
18	2.735563	30.183710	.033130	.365555	11.033819	.090630	18
19	2.892858	32.919273	.030377	.345679	11.379498	.087877	19
20	3.059198	35.812131	.027923	.326883	11.706381	.085423	20
21	3.235101	38.871329	.025726	.309109	12.015490	.083226	21
22	3.421120	42.106430	.023749	.292302	12.307792	.081249	22
23	3.617834	45.527550	.021965	.276408	12.584200	.079465	23
24	3.825860	49.145384	.020348	.261379	12.845580	.077848	24
25	4.045846	52.971243	.018878	.247167	13.092747	.076378	25
26	4.278483	57.017090	.017539	.233728	13.326474	.075039	26
27	4.524495	61.295573	.016314	.221019	13.547494	.073814	27
28	4.784654	65.820068	.015193	.209002	13.756495	.072693	28
29	5.059772	70.604722	.014163	.197637	13.954132	.071663	29
30	5.350708	75.664493	.013216	.186891	14.141024	.070716	30
31	5.658374	81.015202	.012343	.176729	14.317753	.069843	31
32	5.983731	86.673576	.011538	.167120	14.484873	.069038	32
33	6.327795	92.657307	.010792	.158033	14.642906	.068292	33
34	6.691643	98.985102	.010103	.149440	14.792346	.067603	34
35	7.076413	105.676745	.009463	.141315	14.933660	.066963	35
36	7.483307	112.753158	.008869	.133631	15.067291	.066369	36
37	7.913597	120.236464	.008317	.126365	15.193656	.065817	37
38	8.368629	128.150061	.007803	.119494	15.313150	.065303	38
39	8.849825	136.518690	.007325	.112997	15.426146	.064825	39
40	9.358690	145.368514	.006879	.106853	15.532999	.064379	40
41	9.896814	154.727204	.006463	.101043	15.634041	.063963	41
42	10.465881	164.624018	.006074	.095549	15.729590	.063574	42
43	11.067669	175.089899	.005711	.090353	15.819943	.063211	43
44	11.704060	186.157568	.005372	.085440	15.905384	.062872	44
45	12.377044	197.861628	.005054	.080795	15.986178	.062554	45
46	13.088724	210.238672	.004756	.076402	16.062580	.062256	46
47	13.841325	223.327396	.004478	.072247	16.134828	.061978	47
48	14.637201	237.168721	.004216	.068319	16.203147	.061716	48
49	15.478841	251.805922	.003971	.064604	16.267751	.061471	49
50	16.368874	267.284763	.003741	.061092	16.328842	.061241	50
51	17.310084	283.653637	.003525	.057770	16.386612	.061025	51
52	18.305414	300.963721	.003323	.054629	16.441241	.060823	52
53	19.357975	319.269135	.003132	.051658	16.492899	.060632	53
54	20.471059	338.627110	.002953	.048849	16.541749	.060453	54
55	21.648145	359.098169	.002785	.046193	16.587942	.060285	55
56	22.892913	380.746314	.002626	.043682	16.631624	.060126	56
57	24.209256	403.639227	.002477	.041307	16.672930	.059977	57
58	25.601288	427.848482	.002337	.039061	16.711991	.059837	58
59	27.073362	453.449770	.002205	.036937	16.748927	.059705	59
60	28.630080	480.523132	.002081	.034928	16.783856	.059581	60

6% MONTHLY COMPOUND INTEREST TABLE 6%

EFFECTIVE RATE = 1/2% BASE = 1.005

MONTHS	1 AMOUNT OF I AT COMPOUND INTEREST $S^n = (1+i)^n$	2 ACCUMULATION OF I PER PERIOD $S_{\overline{n}\vert} = \frac{S^n - 1}{i}$	3 SINKING FUND FACTOR $1/S_{\overline{n}\vert} = \frac{i}{S^n - 1}$	4 PRES. VALUE REVERSION OF I $V^n = \frac{1}{S^n}$	5 PRESENT VALUE ORD. ANNUITY 1 PER PERIOD $a_{\overline{n}\vert} = \frac{1-V^n}{i}$	6 INSTALMENT TO AMORTIZE I $1/a_{\overline{n}\vert} = \frac{i}{1-V^n}$	n MONTHS
1	1.005000	1.000000	1.000000	.995025	.995025	1.005000	1
2	1.010025	2.005000	.498753	.990075	1.985099	.503753	2
3	1.015075	3.015025	.331672	.985149	2.970248	.336672	3
4	1.020151	4.030100	.248133	.980248	3.950496	.253133	4
5	1.025251	5.050251	.198010	.975371	4.925866	.203010	5
6	1.030378	6.075502	.164595	.970518	5.896384	.169595	6
7	1.035529	7.105879	.140729	.965690	6.862074	.145729	7
8	1.040707	8.141409	.122829	.960885	7.822959	.127829	8
9	1.045911	9.182116	.108907	.956105	8.779064	.113907	9
10	1.051140	10.228026	.097771	.951348	9.730412	.102771	10
11	1.056396	11.279167	.088659	.946615	10.677027	.093659	11
YEARS							
1	1.061678	12.335562	.081066	.941905	11.618932	.086066	12
2	1.127160	25.431955	.039321	.887186	22.562866	.044321	24
3	1.196681	39.336105	.025422	.835645	32.871016	.030422	36
4	1.270489	54.097832	.018485	.787098	42.580318	.023485	48
5	1.348850	69.770031	.014333	.741372	51.725561	.019333	60
6	1.432044	86.408856	.011573	.698302	60.339514	.016573	72
7	1.520370	104.073927	.009609	.657735	68.453042	.014609	84
8	1.614143	122.828542	.008141	.619524	76.095218	.013141	96
9	1.713699	142.739900	.007006	.583533	83.293424	.012006	108
10	1.819397	163.879347	.006102	.549633	90.073453	.011102	120
11	1.931613	186.322629	.005367	.517702	96.459599	.010367	132
12	2.050751	210.150163	.004759	.487626	102.474743	.009759	144
13	2.177237	235.447328	.004247	.459298	108.140440	.009247	156
14	2.311524	262.304766	.003812	.432615	113.476990	.008812	168
15	2.454094	290.818713	.003439	.407482	118.503514	.008439	180
16	2.605457	321.091337	.003114	.383810	123.238025	.008114	192
17	2.766156	353.231110	.002831	.361513	127.697486	.007831	204
18	2.936766	387.353195	.002582	.340511	131.897876	.007582	216
19	3.117899	423.579854	.002361	.320729	135.854246	.007361	228
20	3.310204	462.040895	.002164	.302096	139.580771	.007164	240
21	3.514371	502.874129	.001989	.284546	143.090806	.006989	252
22	3.731129	546.225867	.001831	.268015	146.396926	.006831	264
23	3.961257	592.251446	.001688	.252445	149.510979	.006688	276
24	4.205579	641.115782	.001560	.237779	152.444121	.006560	288
25	4.464970	692.993963	.001443	.223966	155.206864	.006443	300
26	4.740359	748.071876	.001337	.210954	157.809106	.006337	312
27	5.032734	806.546875	.001240	.198699	160.260171	.006240	324
28	5.343142	868.628484	.001151	.187156	162.568843	.006151	336
29	5.672696	934.539150	.001070	.176283	164.743393	.006070	348
30	6.022575	1004.515043	.000996	.166042	166.791614	.005996	360
31	6.394034	1078.806895	.000927	.156396	168.720844	.005927	372
32	6.788405	1157.680906	.000864	.147310	170.537996	.005864	384
33	7.207098	1241.419694	.000806	.138752	172.249581	.005806	396
34	7.651617	1330.323306	.000752	.130691	173.861732	.005752	408
35	8.123551	1424.710299	.000702	.123099	175.380226	.005702	420
36	8.624594	1524.918875	.000656	.115947	176.810503	.005656	432
37	9.156540	1631.308097	.000613	.109212	178.157689	.005613	444
38	9.721296	1744.259174	.000573	.102867	179.426611	.005573	456
39	10.320884	1864.176825	.000536	.096891	180.621815	.005536	468
40	10.957454	1991.490735	.000502	.091262	181.747584	.005502	480
41	11.633285	2126.657088	.000470	.085960	182.807952	.005470	492
42	12.350801	2270.160207	.000440	.080966	183.806718	.005440	504
43	13.112571	2422.514283	.000413	.076263	184.747461	.005413	516
44	13.921326	2584.265226	.000387	.071832	185.633552	.005387	528
45	14.779963	2755.992612	.000363	.067659	186.468166	.005363	540
46	15.691559	2938.311769	.000340	.063729	187.254293	.005340	552
47	16.659380	3131.875972	.000319	.060026	187.994750	.005319	564
48	17.686894	3337.378791	.000300	.056539	188.692191	.005300	576
49	18.777783	3555.556574	.000281	.053254	189.349115	.005281	588
50	19.935955	3787.191086	.000264	.050161	189.967874	.005264	600

6% QUARTERLY COMPOUND INTEREST TABLE 6%

EFFECTIVE RATE = 1½% **BASE = 1.015**

QUARTERS	1 AMOUNT OF 1 AT COMPOUND INTEREST $s^n = (1+i)^n$	2 ACCUMULATION OF 1 PER PERIOD $s_{\overline{n}\vert} = \frac{s^n - 1}{i}$	3 SINKING FUND FACTOR $1/s_{\overline{n}\vert} = \frac{i}{s^n - 1}$	4 PRES. VALUE REVERSION OF 1 $v^n = \frac{1}{s^n}$	5 PRESENT VALUE ORD. ANNUITY 1 PER PERIOD $a_{\overline{n}\vert} = \frac{1 - v^n}{i}$	6 INSTALMENT TO AMORTIZE 1 $1/a_{\overline{n}\vert} = \frac{i}{1 - v^n}$	n QUARTERS
1	1.015000	1.000000	1.000000	.985222	.985222	1.015000	1
2	1.030225	2.015000	.496278	.970662	1.955883	.511278	2
3	1.045678	3.045225	.328383	.956317	2.912200	.343383	3
YEARS							
1	1.061364	4.090903	.244445	.942184	3.854385	.259445	4
2	1.126493	8.432839	.118584	.887711	7.485925	.133584	8
3	1.195618	13.041211	.076680	.836387	10.907505	.091680	12
4	1.268986	17.932370	.055765	.788031	14.131264	.070765	16
5	1.346855	23.123667	.043246	.742470	17.168639	.058246	20
6	1.429503	28.633521	.034924	.699544	20.030405	.049924	24
7	1.517222	34.481479	.029001	.659099	22.726717	.044001	28
8	1.610324	40.688288	.024577	.620993	25.267139	.039577	32
9	1.709140	47.275969	.021152	.585090	27.660684	.036152	36
10	1.814018	54.267894	.018427	.551262	29.915845	.033427	40
11	1.925333	61.688868	.016210	.519391	32.040622	.031210	44
12	2.043478	69.565219	.014375	.489362	34.042554	.029375	48
13	2.168873	77.924892	.012833	.461069	35.928742	.027833	52
14	2.301963	86.797543	.011521	.434412	37.705879	.026521	56
15	2.443220	96.214652	.010393	.409296	39.380269	.025393	60
16	2.593144	106.209628	.009415	.385632	40.957853	.024415	64
17	2.752269	116.817931	.008560	.363337	42.444228	.023560	68
18	2.921158	128.077197	.007808	.342330	43.844667	.022808	72
19	3.100411	140.027372	.007141	.322538	45.164138	.022141	76
20	3.290663	152.710852	.006548	.303890	46.407324	.021548	80
21	3.492590	166.172636	.006018	.286321	47.578633	.021018	84
22	3.706907	180.460482	.005541	.269767	48.682222	.020541	88
23	3.934376	195.625082	.005112	.254170	49.722007	.020112	92
24	4.175804	211.720235	.004723	.239475	50.701675	.019723	96
25	4.432046	228.803043	.004371	.225629	51.624704	.019371	100
26	4.704012	246.934114	.004050	.212585	52.494366	.019050	104
27	4.992667	266.177771	.003757	.200294	53.313749	.018757	108
28	5.299034	286.602288	.003489	.188714	54.085758	.018489	112
29	5.624202	308.280125	.003244	.177803	54.813133	.018244	116
30	5.969323	331.288192	.003019	.167523	55.498454	.018019	120
31	6.335622	355.708115	.002811	.157838	56.144153	.017811	124
32	6.724398	381.626531	.002620	.148712	56.752520	.017620	128
33	7.137031	409.135393	.002444	.140114	57.325714	.017444	132
34	7.574984	438.332297	.002281	.132013	57.865769	.017281	136
35	8.039812	469.320827	.002131	.124381	58.374599	.017131	140
36	8.533164	502.210922	.001991	.117190	58.854012	.016991	144
37	9.056789	537.119271	.001862	.110414	59.305706	.016862	148
38	9.612546	574.169720	.001742	.104031	59.731286	.016742	152
39	10.202406	613.493716	.001630	.098016	60.132260	.016630	156
40	10.828462	655.230772	.001526	.092349	60.510052	.016526	160
41	11.492934	699.528962	.001430	.087010	60.866001	.016430	164
42	12.198182	746.545446	.001340	.081979	61.201371	.016340	168
43	12.946705	796.447029	.001256	.077240	61.517352	.016256	172
44	13.741161	849.410750	.001177	.072774	61.815063	.016177	176
45	14.584368	905.624513	.001104	.068567	62.095562	.016104	180
46	15.479316	965.287752	.001036	.064602	62.359844	.016036	184
47	16.429182	1028.612139	.000972	.060867	62.608847	.015972	188
48	17.437335	1095.822336	.000913	.057348	62.843453	.015913	192
49	18.507352	1167.156788	.000857	.054033	63.064495	.015857	196
50	19.643029	1242.868576	.000805	.050909	63.272757	.015805	200
51	20.848395	1323.226308	.000756	.047965	63.468978	.015756	204
52	22.127726	1408.515076	.000710	.045192	63.653855	.015710	208
53	23.485562	1499.037466	.000667	.042579	63.828043	.015667	212
54	24.926719	1595.114631	.000627	.040118	63.992161	.015627	216
55	26.456311	1697.087432	.000589	.037798	64.146789	.015589	220
56	28.079765	1805.317645	.000554	.035613	64.292478	.015554	224
57	29.802839	1920.189250	.000521	.033554	64.429743	.015521	228
58	31.631647	2042.109783	.000490	.031614	64.559073	.015490	232
59	33.572677	2171.511794	.000461	.029786	64.680925	.015461	236
60	35.632816	2308.854371	.000433	.028064	64.795732	.015433	240

SEMI-ANNUAL COMPOUND INTEREST TABLE

EFFECTIVE RATE = 3% **BASE = 1.03**

HALF YEARS	1 AMOUNT OF I AT COMPOUND INTEREST $S^n = (1+i)^n$	2 ACCUMULATION OF I PER PERIOD $S_{\overline{n}\vert} = \frac{S^n - 1}{i}$	3 SINKING FUND FACTOR $1/S_{\overline{n}\vert} = \frac{i}{S^n - 1}$	4 PRES. VALUE REVERSION OF I $V^n = \frac{1}{S^n}$	5 PRESENT VALUE ORD. ANNUITY 1 PER PERIOD $a_{\overline{n}\vert} = \frac{1 - V^n}{i}$	6 INSTALMENT TO AMORTIZE I $1/a_{\overline{n}\vert} = \frac{i}{1 - V^n}$	n HALF YEARS
1	1.030000	1.000000	1.000000	.970874	.970874	1.030000	1
YEARS							
1	1.060900	2.030000	.492611	.942596	1.913470	.522611	2
2	1.125509	4.183627	.239027	.888487	3.717098	.269027	4
3	1.194052	6.468410	.154598	.837484	5.417191	.184598	6
4	1.266770	8.892336	.112456	.789409	7.019692	.142456	8
5	1.343916	11.463879	.087231	.744094	8.530203	.117231	10
6	1.425761	14.192030	.070462	.701380	9.954004	.100462	12
7	1.512590	17.086324	.058526	.661118	11.296073	.088526	14
8	1.604706	20.156881	.049611	.623167	12.561102	.079611	16
9	1.702433	23.414435	.042709	.587395	13.753513	.072709	18
10	1.806111	26.870374	.037216	.553676	14.877475	.067216	20
11	1.916103	30.536780	.032747	.521893	15.936917	.062747	22
12	2.032794	34.426470	.029047	.491934	16.935542	.059047	24
13	2.156591	38.553042	.025938	.463695	17.876842	.055938	26
14	2.287928	42.930923	.023293	.437077	18.764108	.053293	28
15	2.427262	47.575416	.021019	.411987	19.600441	.051019	30
16	2.575083	52.502759	.019047	.388337	20.388766	.049047	32
17	2.731905	57.730177	.017322	.366045	21.131837	.047322	34
18	2.898278	63.275944	.015804	.345032	21.832252	.045804	36
19	3.074783	69.159449	.014459	.325226	22.492462	.044459	38
20	3.262038	75.401260	.013262	.306557	23.114772	.043262	40
21	3.460696	82.023196	.012192	.288959	23.701359	.042192	42
22	3.671452	89.048409	.011230	.272372	24.254274	.041230	44
23	3.895044	96.501457	.010363	.256737	24.775449	.040363	46
24	4.132252	104.408396	.009578	.241999	25.266707	.039578	48
25	4.383906	112.796867	.008865	.228107	25.729764	.038865	50
26	4.650886	121.696197	.008217	.215013	26.166240	.038217	52
27	4.934125	131.137495	.007626	.202670	26.577660	.037626	54
28	5.234613	141.153768	.007084	.191036	26.965464	.037084	56
29	5.553401	151.780033	.006588	.180070	27.331005	.036588	58
30	5.891603	163.053437	.006133	.169733	27.675564	.036133	60
31	6.250402	175.013391	.005714	.159990	28.000343	.035714	62
32	6.631051	187.701707	.005328	.150806	28.306478	.035328	64
33	7.034882	201.162741	.004971	.142149	28.595040	.034971	66
34	7.463307	215.443551	.004642	.133989	28.867038	.034642	68
35	7.917822	230.594064	.004337	.126297	29.123421	.034337	70
36	8.400017	246.667242	.004054	.119047	29.365088	.034054	72
37	8.911578	263.719277	.003792	.112214	29.592881	.033792	74
38	9.454293	281.809781	.003548	.105772	29.807598	.033548	76
39	10.030060	301.001997	.003322	.099700	30.009990	.033322	78
40	10.640891	321.363019	.003112	.093977	30.200763	.033112	80
41	11.288921	342.964026	.002916	.088582	30.380586	.032916	82
42	11.976416	365.880536	.002733	.083497	30.550086	.032733	84
43	12.705780	390.192660	.002563	.078704	30.709855	.032563	86
44	13.479562	415.985393	.002404	.074186	30.860454	.032404	88
45	14.300467	443.348904	.002256	.069928	31.002407	.032256	90
46	15.171366	472.378852	.002117	.065914	31.136212	.032117	92
47	16.095302	503.176724	.001987	.062130	31.262336	.031987	94
48	17.075506	535.850186	.001866	.058563	31.381219	.031866	96
49	18.115404	570.513463	.001753	.055202	31.493279	.031753	98
50	19.218632	607.287733	.001647	.052033	31.598905	.031647	100
51	20.389047	646.301556	.001547	.049046	31.698469	.031547	102
52	21.630740	687.691320	.001454	.046231	31.792317	.031454	104
53	22.948052	731.601722	.001367	.043577	31.880777	.031367	106
54	24.345588	778.186267	.001285	.041075	31.964160	.031285	108
55	25.828234	827.607810	.001208	.038717	32.042756	.031208	110
56	27.401174	880.039126	.001136	.036495	32.116840	.031136	112
57	29.069905	935.663509	.001069	.034400	32.186672	.031069	114
58	30.840262	994.675416	.001005	.032425	32.252495	.031005	116
59	32.718434	1057.281149	.000946	.030564	32.314540	.030946	118
60	34.710987	1123.699571	.000890	.028809	32.373023	.030890	120

6% ANNUAL COMPOUND INTEREST TABLE 6%

EFFECTIVE RATE = 6% BASE = 1.06

YEARS	1 AMOUNT OF I AT COMPOUND INTEREST $S^n = (1+i)^n$	2 ACCUMULATION OF I PER PERIOD $S_{\overline{n}\rvert} = \frac{S^n - 1}{i}$	3 SINKING FUND FACTOR $1/S_{\overline{n}\rvert} = \frac{i}{S^n - 1}$	4 PRES. VALUE REVERSION OF I $V^n = \frac{1}{S^n}$	5 PRESENT VALUE ORD. ANNUITY 1 PER PERIOD $a_{\overline{n}\rvert} = \frac{1 - V^n}{i}$	6 INSTALMENT TO AMORTIZE I $1/a_{\overline{n}\rvert} = \frac{i}{1 - V^n}$	n YEARS
1	1.060000	1.000000	1.000000	.943396	.943396	1.060000	1
2	1.123600	2.060000	.485437	.889996	1.833393	.545437	2
3	1.191016	3.183600	.314110	.839619	2.673012	.374110	3
4	1.262477	4.374616	.228591	.792094	3.465106	.288591	4
5	1.338226	5.637093	.177396	.747258	4.212364	.237396	5
6	1.418519	6.975319	.143363	.704961	4.917324	.203363	6
7	1.503630	8.393838	.119135	.665057	5.582381	.179135	7
8	1.593848	9.897468	.101036	.627412	6.209794	.161036	8
9	1.689479	11.491316	.087022	.591898	6.801692	.147022	9
10	1.790848	13.180795	.075868	.558395	7.360087	.135868	10
11	1.898299	14.971643	.066793	.526788	7.886875	.126793	11
12	2.012196	16.869941	.059277	.496969	8.383844	.119277	12
13	2.132928	18.882138	.052960	.468839	8.852683	.112960	13
14	2.260904	21.015066	.047585	.442301	9.294984	.107585	14
15	2.396558	23.275970	.042963	.417265	9.712249	.102963	15
16	2.540352	25.672528	.038952	.393646	10.105895	.098952	16
17	2.692773	28.212880	.035445	.371364	10.477260	.095445	17
18	2.854339	30.905653	.032357	.350344	10.827603	.092357	18
19	3.025600	33.759992	.029621	.330513	11.158116	.089621	19
20	3.207135	36.785591	.027185	.311805	11.469921	.087185	20
21	3.399564	39.992727	.025005	.294155	11.764077	.085005	21
22	3.603537	43.392290	.023046	.277505	12.041582	.083046	22
23	3.819750	46.995828	.021278	.261797	12.303379	.081278	23
24	4.048935	50.815577	.019679	.246979	12.550358	.079679	24
25	4.291871	54.864512	.018227	.232999	12.783356	.078227	25
26	4.549383	59.156383	.016904	.219810	13.003166	.076904	26
27	4.822346	63.705766	.015697	.207368	13.210534	.075697	27
28	5.111687	68.528112	.014593	.195630	13.406164	.074593	28
29	5.418388	73.639798	.013580	.184557	13.590721	.073580	29
30	5.743491	79.058186	.012649	.174110	13.764831	.072649	30
31	6.088101	84.801677	.011792	.164255	13.929086	.071792	31
32	6.453387	90.889778	.011002	.154957	14.084043	.071002	32
33	6.840590	97.343165	.010273	.146186	14.230230	.070273	33
34	7.251025	104.183755	.009598	.137912	14.368141	.069598	34
35	7.686087	111.434780	.008974	.130105	14.498246	.068974	35
36	8.147252	119.120867	.008395	.122741	14.620987	.068395	36
37	8.636087	127.268119	.007857	.115793	14.736780	.067857	37
38	9.154252	135.904206	.007358	.109239	14.846019	.067358	38
39	9.703507	145.058458	.006894	.103056	14.949075	.066894	39
40	10.285718	154.761966	.006462	.097222	15.046297	.066462	40
41	10.902861	165.047684	.006059	.091719	15.138016	.066059	41
42	11.557033	175.950545	.005683	.086527	15.224543	.065683	42
43	12.250455	187.507577	.005333	.081630	15.306173	.065333	43
44	12.985482	199.758032	.005006	.077009	15.383182	.065006	44
45	13.764611	212.743514	.004700	.072650	15.455832	.064700	45
46	14.590487	226.508125	.004415	.068538	15.524370	.064415	46
47	15.465917	241.098612	.004148	.064658	15.589028	.064148	47
48	16.393872	256.564529	.003898	.060998	15.650027	.063898	48
49	17.377504	272.958401	.003664	.057546	15.707572	.063664	49
50	18.420154	290.335905	.003444	.054288	15.761861	.063444	50
51	19.525364	308.756059	.003239	.051215	15.813076	.063239	51
52	20.696885	328.281422	.003046	.048316	15.861393	.063046	52
53	21.938698	348.978308	.002866	.045582	15.906974	.062866	53
54	23.255020	370.917006	.002696	.043001	15.949976	.062696	54
55	24.650322	394.172027	.002537	.040567	15.990543	.062537	55
56	26.129341	418.822348	.002388	.038271	16.028814	.062388	56
57	27.697101	444.951689	.002247	.036105	16.064919	.062247	57
58	29.358927	472.648790	.002116	.034061	16.098980	.062116	58
59	31.120463	502.007718	.001992	.032133	16.131113	.061992	59
60	32.987691	533.128181	.001876	.030314	16.161428	.061876	60

6 ¼ % MONTHLY COMPOUND INTEREST TABLE 6 ¼ %

EFFECTIVE RATE = 25/48% BASE = 1.00520833+

MONTHS	1 AMOUNT OF I AT COMPOUND INTEREST $S^n = (1+i)^n$	2 ACCUMULATION OF I PER PERIOD $S_{\overline{n}\vert} = \frac{S^n - 1}{i}$	3 SINKING FUND FACTOR $1/S_{\overline{n}\vert} = \frac{i}{S^n - 1}$	4 PRES. VALUE REVERSION OF I $V^n = \frac{1}{S^n}$	5 PRESENT VALUE ORD. ANNUITY 1 PER PERIOD $a_{\overline{n}\vert} = \frac{1 - V^n}{i}$	6 INSTALMENT TO AMORTIZE I $1/a_{\overline{n}\vert} = \frac{i}{1 - V^n}$	n MONTHS
1	1.005208	1.000000	1.000000	.994819	.994819	1.005208	1
2	1.010444	2.005208	.498701	.989664	1.984483	.503909	2
3	1.015707	3.015652	.331603	.984536	2.969019	.336811	3
4	1.020997	4.031359	.248055	.979435	3.948454	.253263	4
5	1.026314	5.052355	.197927	.974360	4.922815	.203135	5
6	1.031660	6.078670	.164510	.969312	5.892126	.169718	6
7	1.037033	7.110329	.140640	.964290	6.856416	.145848	7
8	1.042434	8.147362	.122739	.959293	7.815709	.127947	8
9	1.047864	9.189797	.108816	.954323	8.770032	.114024	9
10	1.053321	10.237660	.097679	.949378	9.719410	.102887	10
11	1.058807	11.290981	.088566	.944459	10.663869	.093774	11
YEARS							
1	1.064322	12.349788	.080973	.939565	11.603434	.086181	12
2	1.132781	25.493938	.039225	.882783	22.505621	.044433	24
3	1.205643	39.483542	.025327	.829433	32.748938	.030535	36
4	1.283193	54.372984	.018391	.779306	42.373205	.023599	48
5	1.365730	70.220141	.014241	.732209	51.415834	.019449	60
6	1.453576	87.086616	.011483	.687958	59.911975	.016691	72
7	1.547073	105.037974	.009520	.646382	67.894656	.014728	84
8	1.646583	124.143995	.008055	.607318	75.394907	.013263	96
9	1.752495	144.478951	.006921	.570615	82.441884	.012129	108
10	1.865218	166.121887	.006020	.536130	89.062980	.011228	120
11	1.985192	189.156937	.005287	.503730	95.283933	.010495	132
12	2.112884	213.673643	.004680	.473287	101.128925	.009888	144
13	2.248788	239.767308	.004171	.444684	106.620678	.009379	156
14	2.393434	267.539364	.003738	.417810	111.780540	.008946	168
15	2.547384	297.097770	.003366	.392560	116.628567	.008574	180
16	2.711237	328.557426	.003044	.368835	121.183606	.008252	192
17	2.885628	362.040624	.002762	.346545	125.463363	.007970	204
18	3.071237	397.677522	.002515	.325602	129.484476	.007723	216
19	3.268785	435.606650	.002296	.305924	133.262573	.007504	228
20	3.479039	475.975448	.002101	.287436	136.812344	.007309	240
21	3.702817	518.940841	.001927	.270065	140.147585	.007135	252
22	3.940989	564.669846	.001771	.253743	143.281263	.006979	264
23	4.194480	613.340223	.001630	.238409	146.225558	.006838	276
24	4.464277	665.141168	.001503	.224000	148.991916	.006711	288
25	4.751427	720.274043	.001388	.210463	151.591091	.006596	300
26	5.057048	778.953164	.001284	.197744	154.033185	.006492	312
27	5.382326	841.406633	.001188	.185793	156.327693	.006396	324
28	5.728527	907.877223	.001101	.174565	158.483533	.006309	336
29	6.096996	978.623321	.001022	.164015	160.509086	.006230	348
30	6.489166	1053.919937	.000949	.154103	162.412225	.006157	360
31	6.906561	1134.059768	.000882	.144790	164.200349	.006090	372
32	7.350804	1219.354338	.000820	.136040	165.880409	.006028	384
33	7.823621	1310.135209	.000763	.127818	167.458935	.005971	396
34	8.326850	1406.755271	.000711	.120093	168.942063	.005919	408
35	8.862448	1509.590111	.000662	.112836	170.335560	.005870	420
36	9.432497	1619.039473	.000618	.106016	171.644840	.005826	432
37	10.039213	1735.528818	.000576	.099609	172.874996	.005784	444
38	10.684953	1859.510969	.000538	.093590	174.030807	.005746	456
39	11.372228	1991.467876	.000502	.087934	175.116767	.005710	468
40	12.103711	2131.912491	.000469	.082619	176.137098	.005677	480
41	12.882243	2281.390758	.000438	.077626	177.095765	.005646	492
42	13.710853	2440.483739	.000410	.072935	177.996496	.005618	504
43	14.592760	2609.809869	.000383	.068527	178.842792	.005591	516
44	15.531392	2790.027363	.000358	.064386	179.637942	.005566	528
45	16.530400	2981.836773	.000335	.060495	180.385037	.005543	540
46	17.593665	3185.983712	.000314	.056839	181.086983	.005522	552
47	18.725322	3403.261753	.000294	.053404	181.746506	.005502	564
48	19.929768	3634.515512	.000275	.050176	182.366172	.005483	576
49	21.211687	3880.643931	.000258	.047144	182.948388	.005466	588
50	22.576061	4142.603778	.000241	.044295	183.495418	.005449	600

6¼% QUARTERLY COMPOUND INTEREST TABLE 6¼%

EFFECTIVE RATE = 1-9/16% BASE = 1.015625

QUARTERS	1 AMOUNT OF 1 AT COMPOUND INTEREST $S^n = (1+i)^n$	2 ACCUMULATION OF 1 PER PERIOD $S_{\overline{n}\rvert} = \frac{S^n - 1}{i}$	3 SINKING FUND FACTOR $1/S_{\overline{n}\rvert} = \frac{i}{S^n - 1}$	4 PRES. VALUE REVERSION OF 1 $V^n = \frac{1}{S^n}$	5 PRESENT VALUE ORD. ANNUITY 1 PER PERIOD $a_{\overline{n}\rvert} = \frac{1 - V^n}{i}$	6 INSTALMENT TO AMORTIZE 1 $1/a_{\overline{n}\rvert} = \frac{i}{1 - V^n}$	n QUARTERS
1	1.015625	1.000000	1.000000	.984615	.984615	1.015625	1
2	1.031494	2.015625	.496124	.969467	1.954083	.511749	2
3	1.047611	3.047119	.328179	.954553	2.908635	.343804	3
YEARS							
1	1.063980	4.094730	.244216	.939867	3.848503	.259841	4
2	1.132054	8.451442	.118323	.883350	7.465584	.133948	8
3	1.204483	13.086897	.076412	.830232	10.865159	.092037	12
4	1.281546	18.018929	.055497	.780308	14.060309	.071122	16
5	1.363539	23.266514	.042980	.733386	17.063325	.058605	20
6	1.450779	28.849840	.034662	.689285	19.885761	.050287	24
7	1.543600	34.790387	.028744	.647836	22.538476	.044369	28
8	1.642360	41.111012	.024324	.608880	25.031676	.039949	32
9	1.747438	47.836032	.020905	.572266	27.374952	.036530	36
10	1.859239	54.991319	.018185	.537854	29.577321	.033810	40
11	1.978194	62.604403	.015973	.505512	31.647255	.031598	44
12	2.104759	70.704574	.014143	.475114	33.592718	.029768	48
13	2.239422	79.322994	.012607	.446544	35.421194	.028232	52
14	2.382700	88.492823	.011300	.419692	37.139719	.026925	56
15	2.535146	98.249338	.010178	.394455	38.754905	.025803	60
16	2.697345	108.630077	.009206	.370735	40.272964	.024831	64
17	2.869922	119.674977	.008356	.348442	41.699739	.023981	68
18	3.053540	131.426532	.007609	.327489	43.040717	.023234	72
19	3.248906	143.929953	.006948	.307796	44.301058	.022573	76
20	3.456771	157.233345	.006360	.289287	45.485612	.021985	80
21	3.677936	171.387891	.005835	.271892	46.598935	.021460	84
22	3.913251	186.448046	.005363	.255542	47.645311	.020988	88
23	4.163621	202.471753	.004939	.240176	48.628765	.020564	92
24	4.430010	219.520659	.004555	.225733	49.553081	.020180	96
25	4.713443	237.660356	.004208	.212159	50.421815	.019833	100
26	5.015010	256.960635	.003892	.199401	51.238310	.019517	104
27	5.335871	277.495748	.003604	.187411	52.005707	.019229	108
28	5.677261	299.344702	.003341	.176141	52.726958	.018966	112
29	6.040493	322.591555	.003100	.165549	53.404838	.018725	116
30	6.426965	347.325745	.002879	.155594	54.041956	.018504	120
31	6.838163	373.642433	.002676	.146238	54.640761	.018301	124
32	7.275670	401.642867	.002490	.137444	55.203559	.018115	128
33	7.741168	431.434773	.002318	.129179	55.732514	.017943	132
34	8.236450	463.132770	.002159	.121412	56.229662	.017784	136
35	8.763419	496.858810	.002013	.114111	56.696914	.017638	140
36	9.324104	532.742648	.001877	.107249	57.136070	.017502	144
37	9.920662	570.922339	.001752	.100800	57.548817	.017377	148
38	10.555387	611.544773	.001635	.094738	57.936745	.017260	152
39	11.230722	654.766238	.001527	.089041	58.301346	.017152	156
40	11.949266	700.753018	.001427	.083687	58.644022	.017052	160
41	12.713782	749.682040	.001334	.078655	58.966093	.016959	164
42	13.527212	801.741549	.001247	.073925	59.268796	.016872	168
43	14.392685	857.131834	.001167	.069480	59.553297	.016792	172
44	15.313531	916.065998	.001092	.065302	59.820690	.016717	176
45	16.293293	978.770779	.001022	.061375	60.072003	.016647	180
46	17.335741	1045.487423	.000956	.057684	60.308205	.016581	184
47	18.444884	1116.472608	.000896	.054216	60.530203	.016521	188
48	19.624991	1191.999437	.000839	.050955	60.738852	.016464	192
49	20.880601	1272.358484	.000786	.047891	60.934954	.016411	196
50	22.216546	1357.858917	.000736	.045011	61.119264	.016361	200
51	23.637964	1448.829681	.000690	.042305	61.292491	.016315	204
52	25.150325	1545.620769	.000647	.039761	61.455301	.016272	208
53	26.759446	1648.604567	.000607	.037370	61.608321	.016232	212
54	28.471520	1758.177285	.000569	.035123	61.752140	.016194	216
55	30.293133	1874.760483	.000533	.033011	61.887310	.016158	220
56	32.231292	1998.802693	.000500	.031026	62.014352	.016125	224
57	34.293455	2130.781144	.000469	.029160	62.133755	.016094	228
58	36.487556	2271.203597	.000440	.027407	62.245977	.016065	232
59	38.822036	2420.610302	.000413	.025759	62.351452	.016038	236
60	41.305876	2579.576072	.000388	.024210	62.450584	.016013	240

6 ¼% SEMI-ANNUAL COMPOUND INTEREST TABLE 6 ¼%

EFFECTIVE RATE = 3-1/8% BASE = 1.03125

HALF YEARS	1 AMOUNT OF 1 AT COMPOUND INTEREST $s^n = (1+i)^n$	2 ACCUMULATION OF 1 PER PERIOD $s_{\overline{n}\vert} = \frac{s^n - 1}{i}$	3 SINKING FUND FACTOR $1/s_{\overline{n}\vert} = \frac{i}{s^n - 1}$	4 PRES. VALUE REVERSION OF 1 $v^n = \frac{1}{s^n}$	5 PRESENT VALUE ORD. ANNUITY 1 PER PERIOD $a_{\overline{n}\vert} = \frac{1-v^n}{i}$	6 INSTALMENT TO AMORTIZE 1 $1/a_{\overline{n}\vert} = \frac{i}{1-v^n}$	n HALF YEARS
1	1.031250	1.000000	1.000000	.969697	.969697	1.031250	1
YEARS							
1	1.063477	2.031250	.492308	.940312	1.910009	.523558	2
2	1.130982	4.191437	.238582	.884187	3.706014	.269832	4
3	1.202773	6.488745	.154113	.831412	5.394820	.185363	6
4	1.279121	8.931878	.111959	.781787	6.982824	.143209	8
5	1.360315	11.530093	.086730	.735124	8.476044	.117980	10
6	1.446664	14.293234	.069963	.691246	9.880137	.101213	12
7	1.538493	17.231769	.058032	.649987	11.200422	.089282	14
8	1.636151	20.356832	.049124	.611191	12.441903	.080374	16
9	1.740008	23.680264	.042229	.574710	13.609283	.073479	18
10	1.850458	27.214656	.036745	.540407	14.706984	.067995	20
11	1.967919	30.973399	.032286	.508151	15.739166	.063536	22
12	2.092835	34.970734	.028595	.477821	16.709739	.059845	24
13	2.225681	39.221805	.025496	.449301	17.622381	.056746	26
14	2.366960	43.742721	.022861	.422483	18.480549	.054111	28
15	2.517207	48.550608	.020597	.397266	19.287495	.051847	30
16	2.676990	53.663684	.018635	.373554	20.046276	.049885	32
17	2.846916	59.101320	.016920	.351257	20.759768	.048170	34
18	3.027629	64.884119	.015412	.330291	21.430672	.046662	36
19	3.219812	71.033990	.014078	.310577	22.061532	.045328	38
20	3.424195	77.574233	.012891	.292039	22.654737	.044141	40
21	3.641551	84.529629	.011830	.274608	23.212535	.043080	42
22	3.872704	91.926529	.010878	.258218	23.737040	.042128	44
23	4.118530	99.792959	.010021	.242805	24.230237	.041271	46
24	4.379960	108.158723	.009246	.228313	24.693997	.040496	48
25	4.657985	117.055517	.008543	.214685	25.130077	.039793	50
26	4.953658	126.517049	.007904	.201871	25.540127	.039154	52
27	5.268099	136.579167	.007322	.189822	25.925703	.038572	54
28	5.602500	147.279993	.006790	.178492	26.288264	.038040	56
29	5.958127	158.660070	.006303	.167838	26.629185	.037553	58
30	6.336329	170.762516	.005856	.157820	26.949757	.037106	60
31	6.738537	183.633184	.005446	.148400	27.251195	.036696	62
32	7.166276	197.320837	.005068	.139542	27.534640	.036318	64
33	7.621167	211.877335	.004720	.131214	27.801168	.035970	66
34	8.104932	227.357830	.004398	.123382	28.051787	.035648	68
35	8.619405	243.820974	.004101	.116017	28.287447	.035351	70
36	9.166536	261.329141	.003827	.109092	28.509041	.035077	72
37	9.748396	279.948667	.003572	.102581	28.717409	.034822	74
38	10.367190	299.750096	.003336	.096458	28.913339	.034586	76
39	11.025264	320.808451	.003117	.090701	29.097575	.034367	78
40	11.725110	343.203519	.002914	.085287	29.270815	.034164	80
41	12.469380	367.020149	.002725	.080196	29.433714	.033975	82
42	13.260893	392.348576	.002549	.075410	29.586890	.033799	84
43	14.102649	419.284765	.002385	.070909	29.730923	.033635	86
44	14.997837	447.930771	.002232	.066676	29.866359	.033482	88
45	15.949848	478.395126	.002090	.062697	29.993711	.033340	90
46	16.962289	510.793254	.001958	.058954	30.113462	.033208	92
47	18.038997	545.247904	.001834	.055435	30.226065	.033084	94
48	19.184051	581.889617	.001719	.052127	30.331948	.032969	96
49	20.401788	620.857220	.001611	.049015	30.431510	.032861	98
50	21.696823	662.298352	.001510	.046090	30.525130	.032760	100
51	23.074063	706.370024	.001416	.043339	30.613161	.032666	102
52	24.538725	753.239215	.001328	.040752	30.695939	.032578	104
53	26.096359	803.083501	.001245	.038320	30.773775	.032495	106
54	27.752867	856.091732	.001168	.036032	30.846966	.032418	108
55	29.514523	912.464742	.001096	.033882	30.915788	.032346	110
56	31.388004	972.416117	.001028	.031859	30.980502	.032278	112
57	33.380406	1036.173000	.000965	.029958	31.041354	.032215	114
58	35.499280	1103.976950	.000906	.028170	31.098573	.032156	116
59	37.752652	1176.084862	.000850	.026488	31.152377	.032100	118
60	40.149060	1252.769936	.000798	.024907	31.202970	.032048	120

6 ¼% ANNUAL COMPOUND INTEREST TABLE 6 ¼%

EFFECTIVE RATE = 6¼% BASE = 1.0625

YEARS	1 AMOUNT OF I AT COMPOUND INTEREST $S^n = (1+i)^n$	2 ACCUMULATION OF I PER PERIOD $s_{\overline{n\|}} = \frac{S^n - 1}{i}$	3 SINKING FUND FACTOR $1/s_{\overline{n\|}} = \frac{i}{S^n - 1}$	4 PRES. VALUE REVERSION OF I $V^n = \frac{1}{S^n}$	5 PRESENT VALUE ORD. ANNUITY 1 PER PERIOD $a_{\overline{n\|}} = \frac{1 - V^n}{i}$	6 INSTALMENT TO AMORTIZE I $1/a_{\overline{n\|}} = \frac{i}{1 - V^n}$	n YEARS
1	1.062500	1.000000	1.000000	.941176	.941176	1.062500	1
2	1.128906	2.062500	.484848	.885813	1.826990	.547348	2
3	1.199463	3.191406	.313341	.833706	2.660696	.375841	3
4	1.274429	4.390869	.227745	.784665	3.445361	.290245	4
5	1.354081	5.665298	.176513	.738508	4.183869	.239013	5
6	1.438711	7.019380	.142463	.695067	4.878936	.204963	6
7	1.528631	8.458091	.118230	.654180	5.533116	.180730	7
8	1.624170	9.986722	.100133	.615699	6.148815	.162633	8
9	1.725681	11.610892	.086126	.579481	6.728297	.148626	9
10	1.833536	13.336572	.074982	.545394	7.273691	.137482	10
11	1.948132	15.170108	.065919	.513312	7.787003	.128419	11
12	2.069890	17.118240	.058417	.483117	8.270121	.120917	12
13	2.199258	19.188130	.052116	.454699	8.724819	.114616	13
14	2.336712	21.387388	.046757	.427952	9.152771	.109257	14
15	2.482756	23.724100	.042151	.402778	9.555549	.104651	15
16	2.637928	26.206856	.038158	.379085	9.934635	.100658	16
17	2.802799	28.844784	.034668	.356786	10.291421	.097168	17
18	2.977974	31.647583	.031598	.335799	10.627220	.094098	18
19	3.164097	34.625557	.028880	.316046	10.943266	.091380	19
20	3.361853	37.789655	.026462	.297455	11.240721	.088962	20
21	3.571969	41.151508	.024300	.279958	11.520678	.086800	21
22	3.795217	44.723477	.022360	.263490	11.784168	.084860	22
23	4.032418	48.518695	.020611	.247990	12.032158	.083111	23
24	4.284445	52.551113	.019029	.233402	12.265560	.081529	24
25	4.552222	56.835558	.017595	.219673	12.485233	.080095	25
26	4.836736	61.387780	.016290	.206751	12.691984	.078790	26
27	5.139032	66.224516	.015100	.194589	12.886573	.077600	27
28	5.460222	71.363549	.014013	.183143	13.069716	.076513	28
29	5.801486	76.823771	.013017	.172370	13.242086	.075517	29
30	6.164079	82.625256	.012103	.162230	13.404316	.074603	30
31	6.549333	88.789335	.011263	.152687	13.557003	.073763	31
32	6.958667	95.338668	.010489	.143706	13.700709	.072989	32
33	7.393583	102.297335	.009775	.135252	13.835961	.072275	33
34	7.855682	109.690918	.009117	.127296	13.963258	.071617	34
35	8.346663	117.546601	.008507	.119808	14.083066	.071007	35
36	8.868329	125.893263	.007943	.112761	14.195827	.070443	36
37	9.422600	134.761592	.007421	.106128	14.301955	.069921	37
38	10.011512	144.184192	.006936	.099885	14.401840	.069436	38
39	10.637231	154.195704	.006485	.094009	14.495849	.068985	39
40	11.302058	164.832935	.006067	.088479	14.584329	.068567	40
41	12.008437	176.134994	.005677	.083275	14.667603	.068177	41
42	12.758964	188.143431	.005315	.078376	14.745980	.067815	42
43	13.556400	200.902395	.004978	.073766	14.819746	.067478	43
44	14.403675	214.458795	.004663	.069427	14.889172	.067163	44
45	15.303904	228.862470	.004369	.065343	14.954515	.066869	45
46	16.260398	244.166374	.004096	.061499	15.016014	.066596	46
47	17.276673	260.426772	.003840	.057882	15.073896	.066340	47
48	18.356465	277.703445	.003601	.054477	15.128373	.066101	48
49	19.503744	296.059911	.003378	.051272	15.179645	.065878	49
50	20.722728	315.563655	.003169	.048256	15.227901	.065669	50
51	22.017899	336.286384	.002974	.045418	15.273318	.065474	51
52	23.394018	358.304283	.002791	.042746	15.316064	.065291	52
53	24.856144	381.698300	.002620	.040232	15.356296	.065120	53
54	26.409653	406.554444	.002460	.037865	15.394161	.064960	54
55	28.060256	432.964097	.002310	.035638	15.429799	.064810	55
56	29.814022	461.024353	.002169	.033541	15.463340	.064669	56
57	31.677398	490.838375	.002037	.031568	15.494908	.064537	57
58	33.657236	522.515773	.001914	.029711	15.524619	.064414	58
59	35.760813	556.173009	.001798	.027964	15.552583	.064298	59
60	37.995864	591.933822	.001689	.026319	15.578902	.064189	60

6 ½ % MONTHLY COMPOUND INTEREST TABLE 6 ½ %

EFFECTIVE RATE = 13/24% BASE = 1.00541666+

MONTHS	1 AMOUNT OF I AT COMPOUND INTEREST $S^n = (1+i)^n$	2 ACCUMULATION OF I PER PERIOD $S_{\overline{n\rvert}} = \frac{S^n - 1}{i}$	3 SINKING FUND FACTOR $1/S_{\overline{n\rvert}} = \frac{i}{S^n - 1}$	4 PRES. VALUE REVERSION OF I $V^n = \frac{1}{S^n}$	5 PRESENT VALUE ORD. ANNUITY 1 PER PERIOD $a_{\overline{n\rvert}} = \frac{1 - V^n}{i}$	6 INSTALMENT TO AMORTIZE I $1/a_{\overline{n\rvert}} = \frac{i}{1 - V^n}$	n MONTHS
1	1.005417	1.000000	1.000000	.994613	.994613	1.005417	1
2	1.010863	2.005417	.498649	.989254	1.983867	.504066	2
3	1.016338	3.016279	.331534	.983924	2.967791	.336951	3
4	1.021843	4.032618	.247978	.978624	3.946415	.253395	4
5	1.027378	5.054461	.197845	.973351	4.919766	.203262	5
6	1.032943	6.081839	.164424	.968107	5.887873	.169841	6
7	1.038538	7.114782	.140552	.962892	6.850765	.145969	7
8	1.044164	8 153321	.122649	.957704	7.808469	.128066	8
9	1.049820	9.197485	.108725	.952545	8.761014	.114142	9
10	1.055506	10.247304	.097587	.947413	9.708426	.103004	10
11	1.061224	11.302811	.088474	.942309	10.650735	.093891	11
YEARS							
1	1.066972	12.364034	.080880	.937232	11.587967	.086297	12
2	1.138429	25.556111	.039130	.878404	22.448578	.044547	24
3	1.214672	39.631685	.025232	.823268	32.627489	.030649	36
4	1.296020	54.649927	.018298	.771593	42.167488	.023715	48
5	1.382817	70.673968	.014149	.723161	51.108680	.019566	60
6	1.475427	87.771168	.011393	.677770	59.488649	.016810	72
7	1.574239	106.013400	.009433	.635227	67.342623	.014850	84
8	1.679669	125.477348	.007970	.595355	74.703617	.013387	96
9	1.792160	146.244833	.006838	.557986	81.602576	.012255	108
10	1.912184	168.403155	.005938	.522962	88.068500	.011355	120
11	2.040246	192.045460	.005207	.490137	94.128569	.010624	132
12	2.176885	217.271135	.004603	.459372	99.808259	.010020	144
13	2.322675	244.186219	.004095	.430538	105.131446	.009512	156
14	2.478229	272.903857	.003664	.403514	110.120506	.009081	168
15	2.644201	303.544768	.003294	.378186	114.796412	.008711	180
16	2.821288	336.237757	.002974	.354448	119.178820	.008391	192
17	3.010235	371.120257	.002695	.332200	123.286152	.008112	204
18	3.211836	408.338902	.002449	.311348	127.135674	.007866	216
19	3.426938	448.050149	.002232	.291806	130.743570	.007649	228
20	3.656447	490.420932	.002039	.273490	134.125004	.007456	240
21	3.901326	535.629365	.001867	.256323	137.294192	.007284	252
22	4.162605	583.865490	.001713	.240234	140.264455	.007130	264
23	4.441382	635.332077	.001574	.225155	143.048281	.006991	276
24	4.738830	690.245477	.001449	.211023	145.657372	.006866	288
25	5.056198	748.836530	.001335	.197777	148.102694	.006752	300
26	5.394821	811.351534	.001233	.185363	150.394528	.006650	312
27	5,756122	878.053283	.001139	.173728	152.542508	.006556	324
28	6.141620	949.222172	.001053	.162823	154.555663	.006470	336
29	6.552936	1025.157374	.000975	.152603	156.442456	.006392	348
30	6.991798	1106.178096	.000904	.143025	158.210819	.006321	360
31	7.460052	1192.624927	.000838	.134047	159.868185	.006255	372
32	7.959665	1284.861262	.000778	.125633	161.421520	.006195	384
33	8.492739	1383.274835	.000723	.117748	162.877356	.006140	396
34	9.061513	1488.279347	.000672	.110357	164.241812	.006089	408
35	9.668380	1600.316206	.000625	.103430	165.520624	.006042	420
36	10.315889	1719.856381	.000581	.096938	166.719166	.005998	432
37	11.006763	1847.402383	.000541	.090853	167.842479	.005958	444
38	11.743906	1983.490377	.000504	.085151	168.895283	.005921	456
39	12.530417	2128.692436	.000470	.079806	169.882005	.005887	468
40	13.369603	2283.618946	.000438	.074797	170.806792	.005855	480
41	14.264990	2448.921171	.000408	.070102	171.673532	.005825	492
42	15.220343	2625.293993	.000381	.065702	172.485868	.005798	504
43	16.239677	2813.478829	.000355	.061578	173.247215	.005772	516
44	17.327278	3014.266752	.000332	.057712	173.960774	.005749	528
45	18.487718	3228.501814	.000310	.054090	174.629544	.005727	540
46	19.725875	3457.084595	.000289	.050695	175.256337	.005706	552
47	21.046953	3700.975989	.000270	.047513	175.843787	.005687	564
48	22.456507	3961.201241	.000252	.044531	176.394364	.005669	576
49	23.960461	4238.854260	.000236	.041735	176.910382	.005653	588
50	25.565137	4535.102216	.000221	.039116	177.394011	.005638	600

6 ½ % QUARTERLY COMPOUND INTEREST TABLE 6 ½ %

EFFECTIVE RATE = 1-5/8%   BASE = 1.01625

QUARTERS	1 AMOUNT OF 1 AT COMPOUND INTEREST $S^n = (1+i)^n$	2 ACCUMULATION OF 1 PER PERIOD $s_{\overline{n}\vert} = \frac{S^n - 1}{i}$	3 SINKING FUND FACTOR $1/s_{\overline{n}\vert} = \frac{i}{S^n - 1}$	4 PRES. VALUE REVERSION OF 1 $V^n = \frac{1}{S^n}$	5 PRESENT VALUE ORD. ANNUITY 1 PER PERIOD $a_{\overline{n}\vert} = \frac{1 - V^n}{i}$	6 INSTALMENT TO AMORTIZE 1 $1/a_{\overline{n}\vert} = \frac{i}{1 - V^n}$	n QUARTERS
1	1.016250	1.000000	1.000000	.984010	.984010	1.016250	1
2	1.032764	2.016250	.495970	.968275	1.952285	.512220	2
3	1.049546	3.049014	.327975	.952792	2.905078	.344225	3
YEARS							
1	1.066602	4.098561	.243988	.937557	3.842635	.260238	4
2	1.137639	8.470092	.118062	.879013	7.445325	.134312	8
3	1.213408	13.132774	.076145	.824125	10.823053	.092395	12
4	1.294222	18.105999	.055230	.772665	13.989866	.071480	16
5	1.380420	23.410448	.042716	.724417	16.958934	.058966	20
6	1.472358	29.068182	.034402	.679183	19.742605	.050652	24
7	1.570419	35.102730	.028488	.636773	22.352456	.044738	28
8	1.675012	41.539189	.024074	.597011	24.799341	.040324	32
9	1.786570	48.404326	.020659	.559732	27.093435	.036909	36
10	1.905559	55.726693	.017945	.524780	29.244279	.034195	40
11	2.032472	63.536741	.015739	.492012	31.260819	.031989	44
12	2.167838	71.866950	.013915	.461289	33.151440	.030165	48
13	2.312219	80.751965	.012384	.432485	34.924006	.028634	52
14	2.466217	90.228737	.011083	.405479	36.585887	.027333	56
15	2.630471	100.336676	.009966	.380160	38.143996	.026216	60
16	2.805665	111.117821	.008999	.356422	39.604813	.025249	64
17	2.992526	122.617007	.008155	.334166	40.974412	.024405	68
18	3.191833	134.882057	.007414	.313300	42.258489	.023664	72
19	3.404415	147.963980	.006758	.293736	43.462385	.023008	76
20	3.631154	161.917180	.006176	.275395	44.591106	.022426	80
21	3.872995	176.799685	.005656	.258198	45.649346	.021906	84
22	4.130943	192.673389	.005190	.242076	46.641507	.021440	88
23	4.406070	209.604307	.004771	.226960	47.571715	.021021	92
24	4.699521	227.662851	.004392	.212788	48.443838	.020642	96
25	5.012517	246.924124	.004050	.199501	49.261503	.020300	100
26	5.346359	267.468229	.003739	.187043	50.028111	.019989	104
27	5.702435	289.380604	.003456	.175364	50.746850	.019706	108
28	6.082226	312.752378	.003197	.164413	51.420709	.019447	112
29	6.487312	337.680750	.002961	.154147	52.052490	.019211	116
30	6.919378	364.269392	.002745	.144522	52.644820	.018995	120
31	7.380219	392.628880	.002547	.135497	53.200164	.018797	124
32	7.871754	422.877155	.002365	.127036	53.720831	.018615	128
33	8.396025	455.140015	.002197	.119104	54.208986	.018447	132
34	8.955214	489.551632	.002043	.111667	54.666659	.018293	136
35	9.551646	526.255119	.001900	.104694	55.095754	.018150	140
36	10.187801	565.403117	.001769	.098157	55.498055	.018019	144
37	10.866325	607.158435	.001647	.092027	55.875235	.017897	148
38	11.590039	651.694724	.001534	.086281	56.228862	.017784	152
39	12.361955	699.197202	.001430	.080893	56.560409	.017680	156
40	13.185281	749.863421	.001334	.075842	56.871252	.017584	160
41	14.063441	803.904092	.001244	.071106	57.162686	.017494	164
42	15.000089	861.543958	.001161	.066666	57.435922	.017411	168
43	15.999119	923.022732	.001083	.062503	57.692096	.017333	172
44	17.064686	988.596092	.001012	.058601	57.932274	.017262	176
45	18.201222	1058.536742	.000945	.054941	58.157454	.017195	180
46	19.413453	1133.135553	.000883	.051511	58.368574	.017133	184
47	20.706420	1212.702764	.000825	.048294	58.566511	.017075	188
48	22.085501	1297.569280	.000771	.045279	58.752088	.017021	192
49	23.556431	1388.088042	.000720	.042451	58.926077	.016970	196
50	25.125327	1484.635499	.000674	.039800	59.089201	.016924	200
51	26.798714	1587.613172	.000630	.037315	59.242140	.016880	204
52	28.583552	1697.449324	.000589	.034985	59.385529	.016839	208
53	30.487262	1814.600741	.000551	.032801	59.519964	.016801	212
54	32.517763	1939.554630	.000516	.030752	59.646005	.016766	216
55	34.683498	2072.830649	.000482	.028832	59.764175	.016732	220
56	36.993475	2214.983066	.000451	.027032	59.874966	.016701	224
57	39.457300	2366.603062	.000423	.025344	59.978840	.016673	228
58	42.085219	2528.321194	.000396	.023761	60.076227	.016646	232
59	44.888163	2700.810013	.000370	.022278	60.167533	.016620	236
60	47.877787	2884.786866	.000347	.020887	60.253138	.016597	240

6½% SEMI-ANNUAL COMPOUND INTEREST TABLE 6½%

EFFECTIVE RATE = 3¼% BASE = 1.0325

HALF YEARS	1 AMOUNT OF 1 AT COMPOUND INTEREST $S^n = (1+i)^n$	2 ACCUMULATION OF 1 PER PERIOD $S_{\overline{n}\vert} = \frac{S^n - 1}{i}$	3 SINKING FUND FACTOR $1/S_{\overline{n}\vert} = \frac{i}{S^n - 1}$	4 PRES. VALUE REVERSION OF 1 $V^n = \frac{1}{S^n}$	5 PRESENT VALUE ORD. ANNUITY 1 PER PERIOD $a_{\overline{n}\vert} = \frac{1 - V^n}{i}$	6 INSTALMENT TO AMORTIZE 1 $1/a_{\overline{n}\vert} = \frac{i}{1 - V^n}$	n HALF YEARS
1	1.032500	1.000000	1.000000	.968523	.968523	1.032500	1
YEARS							
1	1.066056	2.032500	.492005	.938037	1.906560	.524505	2
2	1.136476	4.199259	.238137	.879913	3.694983	.270637	4
3	1.211547	6.509147	.153630	.825391	5.372590	.186130	6
4	1.291578	8.971616	.111463	.774247	6.946247	.143963	8
5	1.376894	11.596748	.086231	.726272	8.422395	.118731	10
6	1.467847	14.395285	.069467	.681270	9.807076	.101967	12
7	1.564807	17.378684	.057542	.639056	11.105958	.090042	14
8	1.668173	20.559155	.048640	.599458	12.324358	.081140	16
9	1.778366	23.949715	.041754	.562314	13.467261	.074254	18
10	1.895838	27.564244	.036279	.527471	14.539346	.068779	20
11	2.021070	31.417534	.031829	.494787	15.545002	.064329	22
12	2.154574	35.525359	.028149	.464129	16.488343	.060649	24
13	2.296897	39.904531	.025060	.435370	17.373233	.057560	26
14	2.448622	44.572975	.022435	.408393	18.203292	.054935	28
15	2.610368	49.549798	.020182	.383088	18.981917	.052682	30
16	2.782800	54.855372	.018230	.359350	19.712297	.050730	32
17	2.966621	60.511412	.016526	.337084	20.397420	.049026	34
18	3.162585	66.541069	.015028	.316197	21.040090	.047528	36
19	3.371493	72.969023	.013704	.296604	21.642939	.046204	38
20	3.594201	79.821583	.012528	.278226	22.208433	.045028	40
21	3.381621	87.126797	.011478	.260986	22.738888	.043978	42
22	4.084723	94.914566	.010536	.244815	23.236473	.043036	44
23	4.354545	103.216767	.009688	.229645	23.703227	.042188	46
24	4.642190	112.067379	.008923	.215416	24.141059	.041423	48
25	4.948835	121.502630	.008230	.202068	24.551762	.040730	50
26	5.275737	131.561138	.007601	.189547	24.937016	.040101	52
27	5.624232	142.284074	.007028	.177802	25.298399	.039528	54
28	5.995748	153.715326	.006506	.166785	25.637389	.039006	56
29	6.391805	165.901684	.006028	.156450	25.955374	.038528	58
30	6.814023	178.893027	.005590	.146756	26.253656	.038090	60
31	7.264132	192.742530	.005188	.137663	26.533456	.037688	62
32	7.743974	207.506879	.004819	.129133	26.795918	.037319	64
33	8.255511	223.246505	.004479	.121131	27.042117	.036979	66
34	8.800840	240.025832	.004166	.113626	27.273061	.036666	68
35	9.382190	257.913538	.003877	.106585	27.489695	.036377	70
36	10.001942	276.982839	.003610	.099981	27.692905	.036110	72
37	10.662633	297.311787	.003363	.093785	27.883524	.035863	74
38	11.366967	318.983589	.003135	.087974	28.062332	.035635	76
39	12.117826	342.086948	.002923	.082523	28.230060	.035423	78
40	12.918284	366.716429	.002727	.077410	28.387395	.035227	80
41	13.771617	392.972841	.002545	.072613	28.534981	.035045	82
42	14.681319	420.963654	.002376	.068114	28.673422	.034876	84
43	15.651112	450.803434	.002218	.063893	28.803285	.034718	86
44	16.684965	482.614318	.002072	.059934	28.925102	.034572	88
45	17.787112	516.526510	.001936	.056220	29.039370	.034436	90
46	18.962061	552.678815	.001809	.052737	29.146557	.034309	92
47	20.214624	591.219205	.001691	.049469	29.247103	.034191	94
48	21.549926	632.305428	.001582	.046404	29.341419	.034082	96
49	22.973434	676.105654	.001479	.043529	29.429891	.033979	98
50	24.490973	722.799158	.001384	.040831	29.512881	.033884	100
51	26.108754	772.577060	.001294	.038301	29.590728	.033794	102
52	27.833401	825.643103	.001211	.035928	29.663752	.033711	104
53	29.671971	882.214490	.001134	.033702	29.732251	.033634	106
54	31.631990	942.522771	.001061	.031614	29.796506	.033561	108
55	33.721481	1006.814791	.000993	.029655	29.856779	.033493	110
56	35.948995	1075.353700	.000930	.027817	29.913317	.033430	112
57	38.323651	1148.420033	.000871	.026094	29.966352	.033371	114
58	40.855168	1226.312854	.000815	.024477	30.016101	.033315	116
59	43.553907	1309.350983	.000764	.022960	30.062768	.033264	118
60	46.430915	1397.874298	.000715	.021537	30.106542	.033215	120

6½% ANNUAL COMPOUND INTEREST TABLE 6½%

EFFECTIVE RATE = 6½% BASE = 1.065

YEARS	1 AMOUNT OF 1 AT COMPOUND INTEREST $S^n = (1+i)^n$	2 ACCUMULATION OF 1 PER PERIOD $s_{\overline{n}\vert} = \frac{S^n - 1}{i}$	3 SINKING FUND FACTOR $1/s_{\overline{n}\vert} = \frac{i}{S^n - 1}$	4 PRES. VALUE REVERSION OF 1 $V^n = \frac{1}{S^n}$	5 PRESENT VALUE ORD. ANNUITY 1 PER PERIOD $a_{\overline{n}\vert} = \frac{1 - V^n}{i}$	6 INSTALMENT TO AMORTIZE 1 $1/a_{\overline{n}\vert} = \frac{i}{1 - V^n}$	n YEARS
1	1.065000	1.000000	1.000000	.938967	.938967	1.065000	1
2	1.134225	2.065000	.484262	.881659	1.820626	.549262	2
3	1.207950	3.199225	.312576	.827849	2.648476	.377576	3
4	1.286466	4.407175	.226903	.777323	3.425799	.291903	4
5	1.370087	5.693641	.175635	.729881	4.155679	.240635	5
6	1.459142	7.063728	.141568	.685334	4.841014	.206568	6
7	1.553987	8.522870	.117331	.643506	5.484520	.182331	7
8	1.654996	10.076856	.099237	.604231	6.088751	.164237	8
9	1.762570	11.731852	.085238	.567353	6.656104	.150238	9
10	1.877137	13.494423	.074105	.532726	7.188830	.139105	10
11	1.999151	15.371560	.065055	.500212	7.689042	.130055	11
12	2.129096	17.370711	.057568	.469683	8.158725	.122568	12
13	2.267487	19.499808	.051283	.441017	8.599742	.116283	13
14	2.414874	21.767295	.045940	.414100	9.013842	.110940	14
15	2.571841	24.182169	.041353	.388827	9.402669	.106353	15
16	2.739011	26.754010	.037378	.365095	9.767764	.102378	16
17	2.917046	29.493021	.033906	.342813	10.110577	.098906	17
18	3.106654	32.410067	.030855	.321890	10.432466	.095855	18
19	3.308587	35.516722	.028156	.302244	10.734710	.093156	19
20	3.523645	38.825309	.025756	.283797	11.018507	.090756	20
21	3.752682	42.348954	.023613	.266476	11.284983	.088613	21
22	3.996606	46.101636	.021691	.250212	11.535196	.086691	22
23	4.256386	50.098242	.019961	.234941	11.770137	.084961	23
24	4.533051	54.354628	.018398	.220602	11.990739	.083398	24
25	4.827699	58.887679	.016981	.207138	12.197877	.081981	25
26	5.141500	63.715378	.015695	.194496	12.392373	.080695	26
27	5.475697	68.856877	.014523	.182625	12.574998	.079523	27
28	5.831617	74.332574	.013453	.171479	12.746477	.078453	28
29	6.210672	80.164192	.012474	.161013	12.907490	.077474	29
30	6.614366	86.374864	.011577	.151186	13.058676	.076577	30
31	7.044300	92.989230	.010754	.141959	13.200635	.075754	31
32	7.502179	100.033530	.009997	.133295	13.333929	.074997	32
33	7.989821	107.535710	.009299	.125159	13.459089	.074299	33
34	8.509159	115.525531	.008656	.117520	13.576609	.073656	34
35	9.062255	124.034690	.008062	.110348	13.686957	.073062	35
36	9.651301	133.096945	.007513	.103613	13.790570	.072513	36
37	10.278636	142.748247	.007005	.097289	13.887859	.072005	37
38	10.946747	153.026883	.006535	.091351	13.979210	.071535	38
39	11.658286	163.973630	.006099	.085776	14.064986	.071099	39
40	12.416075	175.631916	.005694	.080541	14.145527	.070694	40
41	13.223119	188.047990	.005318	.075625	14.221152	.070318	41
42	14.082622	201.271110	.004968	.071010	14.292162	.069968	42
43	14.997993	215.353732	.004644	.066676	14.358837	.069644	43
44	15.972862	230.351725	.004341	.062606	14.421443	.069341	44
45	17.011098	246.324587	.004060	.058785	14.480228	.069060	45
46	18.116820	263.335685	.003797	.055197	14.535426	.068797	46
47	19.294413	281.452504	.003553	.051828	14.587254	.068553	47
48	20.548550	300.746917	.003325	.048665	14.635919	.068325	48
49	21.884205	321.295467	.003112	.045695	14.681615	.068112	49
50	23.306679	343.179672	.002914	.042906	14.724521	.067914	50
51	24.821613	366.486351	.002729	.040287	14.764808	.067729	51
52	26.435018	391.307963	.002556	.037829	14.802637	.067556	52
53	28.153294	417.742981	.002394	.035520	14.838157	.067394	53
54	29.983258	445.896275	.002243	.033352	14.871509	.067243	54
55	31.932170	475.879533	.002101	.031316	14.902825	.067101	55
56	34.007761	507.811702	.001969	.029405	14.932230	.066969	56
57	36.218265	541.819463	.001846	.027610	14.959840	.066846	57
58	38.572452	578.037728	.001730	.025925	14.985766	.066730	58
59	41.079662	616.610180	.001622	.024343	15.010109	.066622	59
60	43.749840	657.689842	.001520	.022857	15.032966	.066520	60

6 ¾% MONTHLY COMPOUND INTEREST TABLE 6 ¾%

EFFECTIVE RATE = 9/16% BASE = 1.005625

MONTHS	1 AMOUNT OF I AT COMPOUND INTEREST $S^n = (1+i)^n$	2 ACCUMULATION OF I PER PERIOD $S_{\overline{n}\rvert} = \frac{S^n - 1}{i}$	3 SINKING FUND FACTOR $1/S_{\overline{n}\rvert} = \frac{i}{S^n - 1}$	4 PRES. VALUE REVERSION OF I $V^n = \frac{1}{S^n}$	5 PRESENT VALUE ORD. ANNUITY 1 PER PERIOD $a_{\overline{n}\rvert} = \frac{1 - V^n}{i}$	6 INSTALMENT TO AMORTIZE I $1/a_{\overline{n}\rvert} = \frac{i}{1 - V^n}$	n MONTHS
1	1.005625	1.000000	1.000000	.994406	.994406	1.005625	1
2	1.011282	2.005625	.498598	.988844	1.983251	.504223	2
3	1.016970	3.016970	.331465	.983313	2.966564	.337090	3
4	1.022691	4.033877	.247900	.977813	3.944377	.253525	4
5	1.028443	5.056567	.197763	.972343	4.916720	.203388	5
6	1.034228	6.085010	.164338	.966905	5.883625	.169963	6
7	1.040046	7.119239	.140464	.961496	6.845121	.146089	7
8	1.045896	8.159284	.122560	.956118	7.801239	.128185	8
9	1.051779	9.205180	.108634	.950770	8.752009	.114259	9
10	1.057695	10.256960	.097495	.945452	9.697461	.103120	10
11	1.063645	11.314655	.088381	.940163	10.637624	.094006	11
YEARS							
1	1.069628	12.378300	.080787	.934905	11.572529	.086412	12
2	1.144104	25.618475	.039034	.874046	22.391738	.044659	24
3	1.223766	39.780537	.025138	.817150	32.506666	.030763	36
4	1.308974	54.928673	.018205	.763957	41.963157	.023830	48
5	1.400115	71.131543	.014058	.714227	50.804074	.019683	60
6	1.497602	88.462585	.011304	.667734	59.069488	.016929	72
7	1.601877	107.000353	.009346	.624268	66.796860	.014971	84
8	1.713412	126.828866	.007885	.583631	74.021215	.013510	96
9	1.832714	148.037998	.006755	.545639	80.775298	.012380	108
10	1.960322	170.723878	.005857	.510120	87.089720	.011482	120
11	2.096815	194.989330	.005128	.476914	92.993102	.010753	132
12	2.242812	220.944334	.004526	.445869	98.512201	.010151	144
13	2.398974	248.706532	.004021	.416845	103.672031	.009646	156
14	2.566010	278.401755	.003592	.389710	108.495979	.009217	168
15	2.744676	310.164594	.003224	.364342	113.005911	.008849	180
16	2.935782	344.139015	.002906	.340625	117.222266	.008531	192
17	3.140194	380.479004	.002628	.318452	121.164156	.008253	204
18	3.358840	419.349272	.002385	.297722	124.849446	.008010	216
19	3.592709	460.925996	.002170	.278342	128.294841	.007795	228
20	3.842862	505.397622	.001979	.260223	131.515956	.007604	240
21	4.110432	552.965715	.001808	.243283	134.527391	.007433	252
22	4.396633	603.845877	.001656	.227447	137.342795	.007281	264
23	4.702762	658.268719	.001519	.212641	139.974930	.007144	276
24	5.030205	716.480912	.001396	.198799	142.435724	.007021	288
25	5.380448	778.746299	.001284	.185858	144.736331	.006909	300
26	5.755077	845.347097	.001183	.173760	146.887180	.006808	312
27	6.155792	916.585171	.001091	.162449	148.898018	.006716	324
28	6.584407	992.783405	.001007	.151874	150.777960	.006632	336
29	7.042865	1074.287164	.000931	.141988	152.535525	.006556	348
30	7.533245	1161.465863	.000861	.132745	154.178682	.006486	360
31	8.057770	1254.714634	.000797	.124104	155.714876	.006422	372
32	8.618816	1354.456125	.000738	.116025	157.151071	.006363	384
33	9.218926	1461.142410	.000684	.108473	158.493776	.006309	396
34	9.860821	1575.257041	.000635	.101411	159.749077	.006260	408
35	10.547409	1697.317238	.000589	.094810	160.922664	.006214	420
36	11.281804	1827.876235	.000547	.088638	162.019855	.006172	432
37	12.067333	1967.525785	.000508	.082868	163.045625	.006133	444
38	12.907556	2116.898846	.000472	.077474	164.004621	.006097	456
39	13.806282	2276.672444	.000439	.072431	164.901191	.006064	468
40	14.767585	2447.570748	.000409	.067716	165.739399	.006034	480
41	15.795822	2630.368349	.000380	.063308	166.523043	.006005	492
42	16.895652	2825.893769	.000354	.059187	167.255675	.005979	504
43	18.072062	3035.033221	.000329	.055334	167.940616	.005954	516
44	19.330382	3258.734622	.000307	.051732	168.580971	.005932	528
45	20.676317	3498.011889	.000286	.048365	169.179641	.005911	540
46	22.115966	3753.949539	.000266	.045216	169.739341	.005891	552
47	23.655855	4027.707599	.000248	.042273	170.262606	.005873	564
48	25.302964	4320.526868	.000231	.039521	170.751810	.005856	576
49	27.064757	4633.734539	.000216	.036948	171.209169	.005841	588
50	28.949220	4968.750213	.000201	.034543	171.636755	.005826	600

6 ¾% QUARTERLY COMPOUND INTEREST TABLE 6 ¾%

EFFECTIVE RATE = 1-11/16% BASE = 1.016875

QUARTERS	1 AMOUNT OF 1 AT COMPOUND INTEREST $S^n = (1+i)^n$	2 ACCUMULATION OF 1 PER PERIOD $s_{\overline{n}\vert} = \frac{S^n - 1}{i}$	3 SINKING FUND FACTOR $1/s_{\overline{n}\vert} = \frac{i}{S^n - 1}$	4 PRES. VALUE REVERSION OF 1 $V^n = \frac{1}{S^n}$	5 PRESENT VALUE ORD. ANNUITY 1 PER PERIOD $a_{\overline{n}\vert} = \frac{1 - V^n}{i}$	6 INSTALMENT TO AMORTIZE 1 $1/a_{\overline{n}\vert} = \frac{i}{1 - V^n}$	n QUARTERS
1	1.016875	1.000000	1.000000	.983405	.983405	1.016875	1
2	1.034035	2.016875	.495817	.967085	1.950491	.512692	2
3	1.051484	3.050910	.327771	.951037	2.901527	.344646	3
YEARS							
1	1.069228	4.102394	.243760	.935254	3.836782	.260635	4
2	1.143248	8.488788	.117802	.874701	7.425148	.134677	8
3	1.222393	13.178843	.075879	.818068	10.781183	.092754	12
4	1.307017	18.193580	.054964	.765101	13.919930	.071839	16
5	1.397499	23.555477	.042453	.715564	16.855456	.059328	20
6	1.494245	29.288567	.034143	.669234	19.600919	.051018	24
7	1.597688	35.418547	.028234	.625904	22.168626	.045109	28
8	1.708293	41.972892	.023825	.585380	24.570084	.040700	32
9	1.826554	48.980981	.020416	.547479	26.816059	.037291	36
10	1.953003	56.474225	.017707	.512032	28.916616	.034582	40
11	2.088205	64.486211	.015507	.478880	30.881172	.032382	44
12	2.232767	73.052850	.013689	.447875	32.718530	.030564	48
13	2.387337	82.212539	.012164	.418877	34.436928	.029039	52
14	2.552607	92.006334	.010869	.391756	36.044067	.027744	56
15	2.729318	102.478133	.009758	.366392	37.547151	.026633	60
16	2.918263	113.674872	.008797	.342670	38.952916	.025672	64
17	3.120289	125.646738	.007959	.320483	40.267664	.024834	68
18	3.336300	138.447391	.007223	.299733	41.497288	.024098	72
19	3.567265	152.134207	.006573	.280327	42.647299	.023448	76
20	3.814219	166.768532	.005996	.262177	43.722852	.022871	80
21	4.078269	182.415960	.005482	.245202	44.728767	.022357	84
22	4.360599	199.146628	.005021	.229326	45.669554	.021896	88
23	4.662474	217.035524	.004608	.214478	46.549429	.021483	92
24	4.985248	236.162830	.004234	.200592	47.372336	.021109	96
25	5.330366	256.614280	.003897	.187604	48.141963	.020772	100
26	5.699376	278.481541	.003591	.175458	48.861760	.020466	104
27	6.093932	301.862626	.003313	.164098	49.534953	.020188	108
28	6.515802	326.862334	.003059	.153473	50.164560	.019934	112
29	6.966877	353.592720	.002828	.143536	50.753403	.019703	116
30	7.449179	382.173594	.002617	.134243	51.304120	.019492	120
31	7.964870	412.733062	.002423	.125551	51.819181	.019298	124
32	8.516262	445.408098	.002245	.117422	52.300894	.019120	128
33	9.105825	480.345157	.002082	.109820	52.751418	.018957	132
34	9.736202	517.700836	.001932	.102709	53.172773	.018807	136
35	10.410218	557.642570	.001793	.096059	53.566847	.018668	140
36	11.130896	600.349386	.001666	.089840	53.935406	.018541	144
37	11.901464	646.012705	.001548	.084023	54.280102	.018423	148
38	12.725378	694.837199	.001439	.078583	54.602481	.018314	152
39	13.606329	747.041711	.001339	.073495	54.903988	.018214	156
40	14.548266	802.860231	.001246	.068737	55.185973	.018121	160
41	15.555412	862.542950	.001159	.064286	55.449700	.018034	164
42	16.632281	926.357378	.001079	.060124	55.696353	.017954	168
43	17.783699	994.589544	.001005	.056231	55.927036	.017880	172
44	19.014827	1067.545280	.000937	.052591	56.142783	.017812	176
45	20.331183	1145.551588	.000873	.049186	56.344561	.017748	180
46	21.738668	1228.958109	.000814	.046001	56.533275	.017689	184
47	23.243590	1318.138688	.000759	.043023	56.709771	.017634	188
48	24.852695	1413.493050	.000707	.040237	56.874840	.017582	192
49	26.573195	1515.448595	.000660	.037632	57.029220	.017535	196
50	28.412801	1624.462307	.000616	.035195	57.173606	.017491	200
51	30.379760	1741.022810	.000574	.032917	57.308643	.017449	204
52	32.482887	1865.652550	.000536	.030785	57.434937	.017411	208
53	34.731609	1998.910146	.000500	.028792	57.553054	.017375	212
54	37.136005	2141.392885	.000467	.026928	57.663523	.017342	216
55	39.706852	2293.739403	.000436	.025185	57.766840	.017311	220
56	42.455674	2456.632551	.000407	.023554	57.863468	.017282	224
57	45.394791	2630.802449	.000380	.022029	57.953840	.017255	228
58	48.537377	2817.029763	.000355	.020603	58.038360	.017230	232
59	51.897518	3016.149202	.000332	.019269	58.117408	.017207	236
60	55.490274	3229.053260	.000310	.018021	58.191338	.017185	240

6 ¾% SEMI-ANNUAL COMPOUND INTEREST TABLE 6 ¾%

EFFECTIVE RATE = 3-3/8% BASE = 1.03375

HALF YEARS	1 AMOUNT OF 1 AT COMPOUND INTEREST $S^n = (1+i)^n$	2 ACCUMULATION OF 1 PER PERIOD $S_{\overline{n}\vert} = \frac{S^n - 1}{i}$	3 SINKING FUND FACTOR $1/S_{\overline{n}\vert} = \frac{i}{S^n - 1}$	4 PRES. VALUE REVERSION OF 1 $V^n = \frac{1}{S^n}$	5 PRESENT VALUE ORD. ANNUITY 1 PER PERIOD $a_{\overline{n}\vert} = \frac{1 - V^n}{i}$	6 INSTALMENT TO AMORTIZE 1 $1/a_{\overline{n}\vert} = \frac{i}{1 - V^n}$	n HALF YEARS
1	1.033750	1.000000	1.000000	.967352	.967352	1.033750	1
YEARS							
1	1.068639	2.033750	.491703	.935770	1.903122	.525453	2
2	1.141989	4.207095	.237694	.875665	3.684005	.271444	4
3	1.220375	6.529616	.153148	.819421	5.350501	.186898	6
4	1.304140	9.011552	.110969	.766789	6.909958	.144719	8
5	1.393655	11.663847	.085735	.717538	8.369251	.119485	10
6	1.489314	14.498192	.068974	.671450	9.734812	.102724	12
7	1.591539	17.527085	.057055	.628323	11.012664	.090805	14
8	1.700781	20.763877	.048161	.587965	12.208438	.081911	16
9	1.817521	24.222841	.041283	.550200	13.327407	.075033	18
10	1.942274	27.919224	.035818	.514860	14.374505	.069568	20
11	2.075590	31.869323	.031378	.481791	15.354347	.065128	22
12	2.218056	36.090553	.027708	.450845	16.271253	.061458	24
13	2.370301	40.601525	.024630	.421887	17.129266	.058380	26
14	2.532997	45.422126	.022016	.394789	17.932169	.055766	28
15	2.706859	50.573608	.019773	.369432	18.683501	.053523	30
16	2.892656	56.078683	.017832	.345703	19.386575	.051582	32
17	3.091205	61.961621	.016139	.323498	20.044490	.049889	34
18	3.303382	68.248359	.014652	.302720	20.660147	.048402	36
19	3.530123	74.966612	.013339	.283276	21.236260	.047089	38
20	3.772428	82.146000	.012173	.265081	21.775369	.045923	40
21	4.031363	89.818175	.011134	.248055	22.279851	.044884	42
22	4.308072	98.016960	.010202	.232122	22.751930	.043952	44
23	4.603774	106.778502	.009365	.217213	23.193687	.043115	46
24	4.919773	116.141428	.008610	.203261	23.607070	.042360	48
25	5.257462	126.147017	.007927	.190206	23.993901	.041677	50
26	5.618329	136.839380	.007308	.177989	24.355886	.041058	52
27	6.003966	148.265657	.006745	.166557	24.694620	.040495	54
28	6.416073	160.476223	.006231	.155859	25.011597	.039981	56
29	6.856466	173.524910	.005763	.145848	25.308215	.039513	58
30	7.327087	187.469247	.005334	.136480	25.585781	.039084	60
31	7.830011	202.370711	.004941	.127714	25.845519	.038691	62
32	8.367456	218.294996	.004581	.119511	26.088574	.038331	64
33	8.941790	235.312310	.004250	.111834	26.316017	.038000	66
34	9.555547	253.497677	.003945	.104651	26.528851	.037695	68
35	10.211430	272.931270	.003664	.097929	26.728016	.037414	70
36	10.912333	293.698766	.003405	.091639	26.914387	.037155	72
37	11.661346	315.891724	.003166	.085753	27.088788	.036916	74
38	12.461770	339.607986	.002945	.080245	27.251987	.036695	76
39	13.317134	364.952109	.002740	.075091	27.404704	.036490	78
40	14.231209	392.035830	.002551	.070268	27.547612	.036301	80
41	15.208026	420.978552	.002375	.065755	27.681341	.036125	82
42	16.251891	451.907875	.002213	.061531	27.806480	.035963	84
43	17.367405	484.960158	.002062	.057579	27.923581	.035812	86
44	18.559488	520.281119	.001922	.053881	28.033162	.035672	88
45	19.833394	558.026477	.001792	.050420	28.135703	.035542	90
46	21.194739	598.362641	.001671	.047182	28.231659	.035421	92
47	22.649526	641.467442	.001559	.044151	28.321451	.035309	94
48	24.204168	687.530916	.001454	.041315	28.405476	.035204	96
49	25.865520	736.756143	.001357	.038662	28.484103	.035107	98
50	27.640905	789.360144	.001267	.036178	28.557681	.035017	100
51	29.538151	845.574834	.001183	.033855	28.626533	.034933	102
52	31.565622	905.648048	.001104	.031680	28.690962	.034854	104
53	33.732256	969.844631	.001031	.029645	28.751253	.034781	106
54	36.047607	1038.447607	.000963	.027741	28.807671	.034713	108
55	38.521881	1111.759428	.000899	.025959	28.860466	.034649	110
56	41.165986	1190.103302	.000840	.024292	28.909870	.034590	112
57	43.991581	1273.824627	.000785	.022732	28.956100	.034535	114
58	47.011122	1363.292506	.000734	.021272	28.999361	.034484	116
59	50.237921	1458.901375	.000685	.019905	29.039843	.034435	118
60	53.686205	1561.072748	.000641	.018627	29.077726	.034391	120

ANNUAL COMPOUND INTEREST TABLE

6¾%

EFFECTIVE RATE = 6¾% BASE = 1.0675

YEARS	1 AMOUNT OF 1 AT COMPOUND INTEREST $S^n = (1+i)^n$	2 ACCUMULATION OF 1 PER PERIOD $S_{\overline{n}\rvert} = \frac{S^n - 1}{i}$	3 SINKING FUND FACTOR $1/S_{\overline{n}\rvert} = \frac{i}{S^n - 1}$	4 PRES. VALUE REVERSION OF 1 $V^n = \frac{1}{S^n}$	5 PRESENT VALUE ORD. ANNUITY 1 PER PERIOD $a_{\overline{n}\rvert} = \frac{1 - V^n}{i}$	6 INSTALMENT TO AMORTIZE 1 $1/a_{\overline{n}\rvert} = \frac{i}{1 - V^n}$	n YEARS
1	1.067500	1.000000	1.000000	.936768	.936768	1.067500	1
2	1.139556	2.067500	.483676	.877535	1.814303	.551176	2
3	1.216476	3.207056	.311812	.822046	2.636349	.379312	3
4	1.298588	4.423533	.226064	.770067	3.406416	.293564	4
5	1.386243	5.722121	.174760	.721374	4.127790	.242260	5
6	1.479815	7.108364	.140679	.675760	4.803551	.208179	6
7	1.579702	8.588179	.116439	.633031	5.436581	.183939	7
8	1.686332	10.167881	.098349	.593003	6.029584	.165849	8
9	1.800159	11.854213	.084358	.555506	6.585091	.151858	9
10	1.921670	13.654372	.073237	.520381	7.105471	.140737	10
11	2.051383	15.576042	.064201	.487476	7.592947	.131701	11
12	2.189851	17.627425	.056730	.456652	8.049600	.124230	12
13	2.337666	19.817276	.050461	.427777	8.477377	.117961	13
14	2.495459	22.154942	.045137	.400728	8.878105	.112637	14
15	2.663902	24.650401	.040567	.375389	9.253494	.108067	15
16	2.843715	27.314303	.036611	.351653	9.605146	.104111	16
17	3.035666	30.158019	.033159	.329417	9.934563	.100659	17
18	3.240574	33.193685	.030126	.308587	10.243151	.097626	18
19	3.459312	36.434259	.027447	.289075	10.532225	.094947	19
20	3.692816	39.893571	.025067	.270796	10.803021	.092567	20
21	3.942081	43.586387	.022943	.253673	11.056695	.090443	21
22	4.208172	47.528468	.021040	.237633	11.294327	.088540	22
23	4.492223	51.736640	.019329	.222607	11.516934	.086829	23
24	4.795448	56.228863	.017784	.208531	11.725465	.085284	24
25	5.119141	61.024311	.016387	.195345	11.920811	.083887	25
26	5.464683	66.143452	.015119	.182993	12.103804	.082619	26
27	5.833549	71.608135	.013965	.171422	12.275226	.081465	27
28	6.227314	77.441684	.012913	.160583	12.435809	.080413	28
29	6.647657	83.668998	.011952	.150429	12.586238	.079452	29
30	7.096374	90.316655	.011072	.140917	12.727155	.078572	30
31	7.575380	97.413030	.010266	.132007	12.859162	.077766	31
32	8.086718	104.988409	.009525	.123660	12.982821	.077025	32
33	8.632571	113.075127	.008844	.115840	13.098662	.076344	33
34	9.215270	121.707698	.008216	.108516	13.207177	.075716	34
35	9.837300	130.922967	.007638	.101654	13.308831	.075138	35
36	10.501318	140.760268	.007104	.095226	13.404057	.074604	36
37	11.210157	151.261586	.006611	.089205	13.493262	.074111	37
38	11.966843	162.471743	.006155	.083564	13.576826	.073655	38
39	12.774605	174.438586	.005733	.078280	13.655107	.073233	39
40	13.636890	187.213190	.005342	.073331	13.728437	.072842	40
41	14.557380	200.850080	.004979	.068694	13.797131	.072479	41
42	15.540004	215.407461	.004642	.064350	13.861481	.072142	42
43	16.588954	230.947464	.004330	.060281	13.921762	.071830	43
44	17.708708	247.536418	.004040	.056469	13.978231	.071540	44
45	18.904046	265.245127	.003770	.052899	14.031130	.071270	45
46	20.180069	284.149173	.003519	.049554	14.080684	.071019	46
47	21.542224	304.329242	.003286	.046420	14.127104	.070786	47
48	22.996324	325.871466	.003069	.043485	14.170589	.070569	48
49	24.548576	348.867789	.002866	.040736	14.211325	.070366	49
50	26.205605	373.416365	.002678	.038160	14.249485	.070178	50
51	27.974483	399.621970	.002502	.035747	14.285232	.070002	51
52	29.862761	427.596453	.002339	.033487	14.318718	.069839	52
53	31.878497	457.459213	.002186	.031369	14.350087	.069686	53
54	34.030295	489.337710	.002044	.029386	14.379473	.069544	54
55	36.327340	523.368006	.001911	.027527	14.407000	.069411	55
56	38.779436	559.695346	.001787	.025787	14.432787	.069287	56
57	41.397048	598.474782	.001671	.024156	14.456944	.069171	57
58	44.191349	639.871830	.001563	.022629	14.479572	.069063	58
59	47.174265	684.063178	.001462	.021198	14.500770	.068962	59
60	50.358527	731.237443	.001368	.019858	14.520628	.068868	60

7% MONTHLY COMPOUND INTEREST TABLE 7%

EFFECTIVE RATE = 7/12% **BASE = 1.00583333+**

	1 AMOUNT OF 1 AT COMPOUND INTEREST $S^n = (1+i)^n$	2 ACCUMULATION OF 1 PER PERIOD $S_{\overline{n}\rvert} = \frac{S^n - 1}{i}$	3 SINKING FUND FACTOR $1/S_{\overline{n}\rvert} = \frac{i}{S^n - 1}$	4 PRES. VALUE REVERSION OF 1 $V^n = \frac{1}{S^n}$	5 PRESENT VALUE ORD. ANNUITY 1 PER PERIOD $a_{\overline{n}\rvert} = \frac{1 - V^n}{i}$	6 INSTALMENT TO AMORTIZE 1 $1/a_{\overline{n}\rvert} = \frac{i}{1 - V^n}$	n MONTHS
MONTHS							
1	1.005833	1.000000	1.000000	.994200	.994200	1.005833	1
2	1.011701	2.005833	.498546	.988435	1.982635	.504379	2
3	1.017602	3.017534	.331396	.982702	2.965337	.337229	3
4	1.023538	4.035136	.247823	.977003	3.942340	.253656	4
5	1.029509	5.058675	.197680	.971337	4.913677	.203513	5
6	1.035514	6.088184	.164253	.965704	5.879381	.170086	6
7	1.041555	7.123698	.140377	.960103	6.839484	.146210	7
8	1.047631	8.165253	.122470	.954535	7.794019	.128303	8
9	1.053742	9.212883	.108544	.948999	8.743018	.114377	9
10	1.059889	10.266625	.097403	.943495	9.686513	.103236	10
11	1.066071	11.326514	.088288	.938024	10.624537	.094006	11
YEARS							
1	1.072290	12.392585	.080693	.932583	11.557120	.086526	12
2	1.149806	25.681032	.038939	.869712	22.335099	.044772	24
3	1.232926	39.930101	.025044	.811079	32.386464	.030877	36
4	1.322054	55.209236	.018113	.756399	41.760201	.023946	48
5	1.417625	71.592902	.013968	.705405	50.501993	.019801	60
6	1.520106	89.160943	.011216	.657849	58.654444	.017049	72
7	1.629994	107.998981	.009259	.613499	66.257285	.015092	84
8	1.747826	128.198821	.007800	.572139	73.347569	.013633	96
9	1.874177	149.858909	.006673	.533568	79.959850	.012506	108
10	2.009661	173.084807	.005778	.497596	86.126354	.011611	120
11	2.154940	197.989707	.005051	.464050	91.877134	.010884	132
12	2.310721	224.694984	.004450	.432765	97.240216	.010283	144
13	2.477763	253.330788	.003947	.403590	102.241738	.009780	156
14	2.656881	284.036676	.003521	.376381	106.906075	.009354	168
15	2.848947	316.962296	.003155	.351007	111.255958	.008988	180
16	3.054897	352.268111	.002839	.327343	115.312587	.008672	192
17	3.275736	390.126186	.002563	.305275	119.095732	.008396	204
18	3.512539	430.721025	.002322	.284694	122.623831	.008155	216
19	3.766461	474.250468	.002109	.265501	125.914077	.007942	228
20	4.038739	520.926657	.001920	.247602	128.982507	.007753	240
21	4.330700	570.977073	.001751	.230910	131.844073	.007584	252
22	4.643766	624.645636	.001601	.215342	134.512723	.007434	264
23	4.979464	682.193905	.001466	.200825	137.001461	.007299	276
24	5.339430	743.902343	.001344	.187286	139.322418	.007177	288
25	5.725418	810.071688	.001234	.174660	141.486903	.007067	300
26	6.139309	881.024421	.001135	.162885	143.505467	.006968	312
27	6.583120	957.106332	.001045	.151904	145.387946	.006878	324
28	7.059015	1038.688211	.000963	.141663	147.143515	.006796	336
29	7.569311	1126.167651	.000888	.132112	148.780729	.006721	348
30	8.116497	1219.970986	.000820	.123206	150.307568	.006653	360
31	8.703240	1320.555373	.000757	.114900	151.731473	.006590	372
32	9.332398	1428.411012	.000700	.107154	153.059383	.006533	384
33	10.007037	1544.063544	.000648	.099930	154.297770	.006481	396
34	10.730447	1668.076607	.000599	.093193	155.452669	.006432	408
35	11.506152	1801.054585	.000555	.086910	156.529709	.006388	420
36	12.337932	1943.645551	.000514	.081051	157.534139	.006347	432
37	13.229842	2096.544429	.000477	.075587	158.470853	.006310	444
38	14.186229	2260.496380	.000442	.070491	159.344418	.006275	456
39	15.211752	2436.300430	.000410	.065739	160.159089	.006243	468
40	16.311411	2624.813370	.000381	.061307	160.918839	.006214	480
41	17.490564	2826.953925	.000354	.057174	161.627369	.006187	492
42	18.754959	3043.707236	.000329	.053319	162.288132	.006162	504
43	20.110756	3276.129663	.000305	.049725	162.904348	.006138	516
44	21.564564	3525.353925	.000284	.046372	163.479022	.006117	528
45	23.123469	3792.594629	.000264	.043246	164.014953	.006097	540
46	24.795066	4079.154185	.000245	.040331	164.514754	.006078	552
47	26.587503	4386.429154	.000228	.037612	164.980859	.006061	564
48	28.509516	4715.917056	.000212	.035076	165.415542	.006045	576
49	30.570471	5069.223664	.000197	.032711	165.820919	.006030	588
50	32.780413	5448.070836	.000184	.030506	166.198968	.006017	600

7% QUARTERLY COMPOUND INTEREST TABLE 7%

EFFECTIVE RATE = 1¾% BASE = 1.0175

QUARTERS	1 AMOUNT OF I AT COMPOUND INTEREST $S^n = (1+i)^n$	2 ACCUMULATION OF I PER PERIOD $S_{\overline{n}\rvert} = \frac{S^n - 1}{i}$	3 SINKING FUND FACTOR $1/S_{\overline{n}\rvert} = \frac{i}{S^n - 1}$	4 PRES. VALUE REVERSION OF I $V^n = \frac{1}{S^n}$	5 PRESENT VALUE ORD. ANNUITY 1 PER PERIOD $a_{\overline{n}\rvert} = \frac{1 - V^n}{i}$	6 INSTALMENT TO AMORTIZE I $1/a_{\overline{n}\rvert} = \frac{i}{1 - V^n}$	n QUARTERS
1	1.017500	1.000000	1.000000	.982801	.982801	1.017500	1
2	1.035306	2.017500	.495663	.965898	1.948699	.513163	2
3	1.053424	3.052806	.327567	.949285	2.897984	.345067	3
YEARS							
1	1.071859	4.106230	.243532	.932959	3.830943	.261032	4
2	1.148882	8.507530	.117543	.870412	7.405053	.135043	8
3	1.231439	13.225104	.075614	.812058	10.739550	.093114	12
4	1.319929	18.281677	.054700	.757616	13.850497	.072200	16
5	1.414778	23.701611	.042191	.706825	16.752881	.059691	20
6	1.516443	29.511016	.033886	.659438	19.460686	.051386	24
7	1.625413	35.737880	.027982	.615228	21.986955	.045482	28
8	1.742213	42.412200	.023578	.573982	24.343859	.041078	32
9	1.867407	49.566129	.020175	.535502	26.542753	.037675	36
10	2.001597	57.234134	.017472	.499601	28.594230	.034972	40
11	2.145430	65.453154	.015278	.466107	30.508172	.032778	44
12	2.299599	74.262784	.013466	.434858	32.293801	.030966	48
13	2.464846	83.705466	.011947	.405705	33.959719	.029447	52
14	2.641967	93.826690	.010658	.378506	35.513951	.028158	56
15	2.831816	104.675216	.009553	.353130	36.963986	.027053	60
16	3.035308	116.303306	.008598	.329456	38.316807	.026098	64
17	3.253422	128.766979	.007766	.307369	39.578934	.025266	68
18	3.487210	142.126280	.007036	.286762	40.756445	.024536	72
19	3.737797	156.445567	.006392	.267537	41.855015	.023892	76
20	4.006392	171.793824	.005821	.249601	42.879935	.023321	80
21	4.294287	188.244992	.005312	.232868	43.836142	.022812	84
22	4.602871	205.878326	.004857	.217256	44.728244	.022357	88
23	4.933629	224.778773	.004449	.202691	45.560539	.021949	92
24	5.288154	245.037388	.004081	.189102	46.337035	.021581	96
25	5.668156	266.751768	.003749	.176424	47.061473	.021249	100
26	6.075464	290.026522	.003448	.164596	47.737344	.020948	104
27	6.512041	314.973777	.003175	.153562	48.367904	.020675	108
28	6.979990	341.713718	.002926	.143267	48.956190	.020426	112
29	7.481565	370.375165	.002700	.133662	49.505036	.020200	116
30	8.019183	401.096196	.002493	.124701	50.017087	.019993	120
31	8.595434	434.024811	.002304	.116341	50.494809	.019804	124
32	9.213094	469.319643	.002131	.108541	50.940504	.019631	128
33	9.875138	507.150729	.001972	.101264	51.356319	.019472	132
34	10.584756	547.700319	.001826	.094475	51.744258	.019326	136
35	11.345366	591.163764	.001692	.088142	52.106188	.019192	140
36	12.160633	637.750450	.001568	.082233	52.443854	.019068	144
37	13.034484	687.684809	.001454	.076720	52.758882	.018954	148
38	13.971130	741.207404	.001349	.071576	53.052790	.018849	152
39	14.975081	798.576080	.001252	.066778	53.326994	.018752	156
40	16.051176	860.067214	.001163	.062301	53.582815	.018663	160
41	17.204598	925.977042	.001080	.058124	53.821486	.018580	164
42	18.440904	996.623085	.001003	.054227	54.044156	.018503	168
43	19.766049	1072.345685	.000933	.050592	54.251897	.018433	172
44	21.186419	1153.509637	.000867	.047200	54.445711	.018367	176
45	22.708854	1240.505953	.000806	.044036	54.626532	.018306	180
46	24.340690	1333.753739	.000750	.041083	54.795230	.018250	184
47	26.089789	1433.702221	.000697	.038329	54.952619	.018197	188
48	27.964576	1540.832905	.000649	.035760	55.099456	.018149	192
49	29.974083	1655.661895	.000604	.033362	55.236448	.018104	196
50	32.127992	1778.742385	.000562	.031126	55.364257	.018062	200
51	34.436678	1910.667320	.000523	.029039	55.483497	.018023	204
52	36.911264	2052.072253	.000487	.027092	55.594743	.017987	208
53	39.563672	2203.638408	.000454	.025276	55.698531	.017954	212
54	42.406679	2366.095960	.000423	.023581	55.795361	.017923	216
55	45.453982	2540.227554	.000394	.022000	55.885699	.017894	220
56	48.720261	2726.872075	.000367	.020525	55.969981	.017867	224
57	52.221252	2926.928691	.000342	.019149	56.048612	.017842	228
58	55.973821	3141.361182	.000318	.017865	56.121972	.017818	232
59	59.996045	3371.202584	.000297	.016668	56.190413	.017797	236
60	64.307303	3617.560166	.000276	.015550	56.254267	.017776	240

7% SEMI-ANNUAL COMPOUND INTEREST TABLE 7%

EFFECTIVE RATE = 3½% BASE = 1.035

HALF YEARS	1 AMOUNT OF I AT COMPOUND INTEREST $S^n = (1+i)^n$	2 ACCUMULATION OF I PER PERIOD $S_{\overline{n}\vert} = \frac{S^n - 1}{i}$	3 SINKING FUND FACTOR $1/S_{\overline{n}\vert} = \frac{i}{S^n - 1}$	4 PRES. VALUE REVERSION OF I $V^n = \frac{1}{S^n}$	5 PRESENT VALUE ORD. ANNUITY 1 PER PERIOD $a_{\overline{n}\vert} = \frac{1 - V^n}{i}$	6 INSTALMENT TO AMORTIZE I $1/a_{\overline{n}\vert} = \frac{i}{1 - V^n}$	n HALF YEARS
1	1.035000	1.000000	1.000000	.966184	.966184	1.035000	1
YEARS							
1	1.071225	2.035000	.491400	.933511	1.899694	.526400	2
2	1.147523	4.214943	.237251	.871442	3.673079	.272251	4
3	1.229255	6.550152	.152668	.813501	5.328553	.187668	6
4	1.316809	9.051687	.110477	.759412	6.873956	.145477	8
5	1.410599	11.731393	.085241	.708919	8.316605	.120241	10
6	1.511069	14.601962	.068484	.661783	9.663334	.103484	12
7	1.618695	17.676986	.056571	.617782	10.920520	.091571	14
8	1.733986	20.971030	.047685	.576706	12.094117	.082685	16
9	1.857489	24.499691	.040817	.538361	13.189682	.075817	18
10	1.989789	28.279682	.035361	.502566	14.212403	.070361	20
11	2.131512	32.328902	.030932	.469151	15.167125	.065932	22
12	2.283328	36.666528	.027273	.437957	16.058368	.062273	24
13	2.445959	41.313102	.024205	.408838	16.890352	.059205	26
14	2.620172	46.290627	.021603	.381654	17.667019	.056603	28
15	2.806794	51.622677	.019371	.356278	18.392045	.054371	30
16	3.006708	57.334502	.017442	.332590	19.068865	.052442	32
17	3.220860	63.453152	.015760	.310476	19.700684	.050760	34
18	3.450266	70.007603	.014284	.289833	20.290494	.049284	36
19	3.696011	77.028895	.012982	.270562	20.841087	.047982	38
20	3.959260	84.550278	.011827	.252572	21.355072	.046827	40
21	4.241258	92.607371	.010798	.235779	21.834883	.045798	42
22	4.543342	101.238331	.009878	.220102	22.282791	.044878	44
23	4.866941	110.484031	.009051	.205468	22.700918	.044051	46
24	5.213589	120.388257	.008306	.191806	23.091244	.043306	48
25	5.584927	130.997910	.007634	.179053	23.455618	.042634	50
26	5.982713	142.363236	.007024	.167148	23.795765	.042024	52
27	6.408832	154.538058	.006471	.156035	24.113295	.041471	54
28	6.865301	167.580031	.005967	.145660	24.409713	.040967	56
29	7.354282	181.550919	.005508	.135975	24.686423	.040508	58
30	7.878091	196.516883	.005089	.126934	24.944734	.040089	60
31	8.439208	212.548798	.004705	.118495	25.185870	.039705	62
32	9.040291	229.722586	.004353	.110616	25.410974	.039353	64
33	9.684185	248.119577	.004030	.103261	25.621110	.039030	66
34	10.373941	267.826894	.003734	.096395	25.817275	.038734	68
35	11.112825	288.937865	.003461	.089986	26.000397	.038461	70
36	11.904336	311.552464	.003210	.084003	26.171343	.038210	72
37	12.752223	335.777788	.002978	.078418	26.330923	.037978	74
38	13.660500	361.728561	.002765	.073204	26.479892	.037765	76
39	14.633469	389.527678	.002567	.068336	26.618957	.037567	78
40	15.675738	419.306787	.002385	.063793	26.748776	.037385	80
41	16.792242	451.206913	.002216	.059551	26.869963	.037216	82
42	17.988269	485.379125	.002060	.055592	26.983092	.037060	84
43	19.269484	521.985253	.001916	.051896	27.088699	.036916	86
44	20.641953	561.198653	.001782	.048445	27.187285	.036782	88
45	22.112176	603.205027	.001658	.045224	27.279316	.036658	90
46	23.687116	648.203305	.001543	.042217	27.365227	.036543	92
47	25.374230	696.406585	.001436	.039410	27.445427	.036436	94
48	27.181510	748.043144	.001337	.036790	27.520294	.036337	96
49	29.117513	803.357517	.001245	.034344	27.590183	.036245	98
50	31.191408	862.611657	.001159	.032060	27.655425	.036159	100
51	33.413016	926.086172	.001080	.029928	27.716330	.036080	102
52	35.792858	994.081659	.001006	.027939	27.773185	.036006	104
53	38.342204	1066.920126	.000937	.026081	27.826259	.035937	106
54	41.073128	1144.946512	.000873	.024347	27.875805	.035873	108
55	43.998561	1228.530327	.000814	.022728	27.922057	.035814	110
56	47.132359	1318.067399	.000759	.021217	27.965233	.035759	112
57	50.489361	1413.981750	.000707	.019806	28.005539	.035707	114
58	54.085466	1516.727600	.000659	.018489	28.043164	.035659	116
59	57.937703	1626.791523	.000615	.017260	28.078288	.035615	118
60	62.064316	1744.694750	.000573	.016112	28.111077	.035573	120

7% ANNUAL COMPOUND INTEREST TABLE 7%

EFFECTIVE RATE = 7%   BASE = 1.07

YEARS	1 AMOUNT OF I AT COMPOUND INTEREST $S^n = (1+i)^n$	2 ACCUMULATION OF I PER PERIOD $s_{\overline{n}\vert} = \frac{S^n - 1}{i}$	3 SINKING FUND FACTOR $1/s_{\overline{n}\vert} = \frac{i}{S^n - 1}$	4 PRES. VALUE REVERSION OF I $V^n = \frac{1}{S^n}$	5 PRESENT VALUE ORD. ANNUITY 1 PER PERIOD $a_{\overline{n}\vert} = \frac{1-V^n}{i}$	6 INSTALMENT TO AMORTIZE I $1/a_{\overline{n}\vert} = \frac{i}{1-V^n}$	n YEARS
1	1.070000	1.000000	1.000000	.934579	.934579	1.070000	1
2	1.144900	2.070000	.483092	.873439	1.808018	.553092	2
3	1.225043	3.214900	.311052	.816298	2.624316	.381052	3
4	1.310796	4.439943	.225228	.762895	3.387211	.295228	4
5	1.402552	5.750739	.173891	.712986	4.100197	.243891	5
6	1.500730	7.153291	.139796	.666342	4.766540	.209796	6
7	1.605781	8.654021	.115553	.622750	5.389289	.185553	7
8	1.718186	10.259803	.097468	.582009	5.971299	.167468	8
9	1.838459	11.977989	.083486	.543934	6.515232	.153486	9
10	1.967151	13.816448	.072378	.508349	7.023582	.142378	10
11	2.104852	15.783599	.063357	.475093	7.498674	.133357	11
12	2.252192	17.888451	.055902	.444012	7.942686	.125902	12
13	2.409845	20.140643	.049651	.414964	8.357651	.119651	13
14	2.578534	22.550488	.044345	.387817	8.745468	.114345	14
15	2.759032	25.129022	.039795	.362446	9.107914	.109795	15
16	2.952164	27.888054	.035858	.338735	9.446649	.105858	16
17	3.158815	30.840217	.032425	.316574	9.763223	.102425	17
18	3.379932	33.999033	.029413	.295864	10.059087	.099413	18
19	3.616528	37.378965	.026753	.276508	10.335595	.096753	19
20	3.869684	40.995492	.024393	.258419	10.594014	.094393	20
21	4.140562	44.865177	.022289	.241513	10.835527	.092289	21
22	4.430402	49.005739	.020406	.225713	11.061241	.090406	22
23	4.740530	53.436141	.018714	.210947	11.272187	.088714	23
24	5.072367	58.176671	.017189	.197147	11.469334	.087189	24
25	5.427433	63.249038	.015811	.184249	11.653583	.085811	25
26	5.807353	68.676470	.014561	.172195	11.825779	.084561	26
27	6.213868	74.483823	.013426	.160930	11.986709	.083426	27
28	6.648838	80.697691	.012392	.150402	12.137111	.082392	28
29	7.114257	87.346529	.011449	.140563	12.277674	.081449	29
30	7.612255	94.460786	.010586	.131367	12.409041	.080586	30
31	8.145113	102.073041	.009797	.122773	12.531814	.079797	31
32	8.715271	110.218154	.009073	.114741	12.646555	.079073	32
33	9.325340	118.933425	.008408	.107235	12.753790	.078408	33
34	9.978114	128.258765	.007797	.100219	12.854009	.077797	34
35	10.676581	138.236878	.007234	.093663	12.947672	.077234	35
36	11.423942	148.913460	.006715	.087535	13.035208	.076715	36
37	12.223618	160.337402	.006237	.081809	13.117017	.076237	37
38	13.079271	172.561020	.005795	.076457	13.193473	.075795	38
39	13.994820	185.640292	.005387	.071455	13.264928	.075387	39
40	14.974458	199.635112	.005009	.066780	13.331709	.075009	40
41	16.022670	214.609570	.004660	.062412	13.394120	.074660	41
42	17.144257	230.632240	.004336	.058329	13.452449	.074336	42
43	18.344355	247.776496	.004036	.054513	13.506962	.074036	43
44	19.628460	266.120851	.003758	.050946	13.557908	.073758	44
45	21.002452	285.749311	.003500	.047613	13.605522	.073500	45
46	22.472623	306.751763	.003260	.044499	13.650020	.073260	46
47	24.045707	329.224386	.003037	.041587	13.691608	.073037	47
48	25.728907	353.270093	.002831	.038867	13.730474	.072831	48
49	27.529930	378.998999	.002639	.036324	13.766799	.072639	49
50	29.457025	406.528929	.002460	.033948	13.800746	.072460	50
51	31.519017	435.985955	.002294	.031727	13.832473	.072294	51
52	33.725348	467.504971	.002139	.029651	13.862124	.072139	52
53	36.086122	501.230319	.001995	.027711	13.889836	.071995	53
54	38.612151	537.316442	.001861	.025899	13.915735	.071861	54
55	41.315001	575.928593	.001736	.024204	13.939939	.071736	55
56	44.207052	617.243594	.001620	.022621	13.962560	.071620	56
57	47.301545	661.450646	.001512	.021141	13.983701	.071512	57
58	50.612653	708.752191	.001411	.019758	14.003459	.071411	58
59	54.155539	759.364844	.001317	.018465	14.021924	.071317	59
60	57.946427	813.520383	.001229	.017257	14.039181	.071229	60

7¼ % MONTHLY COMPOUND INTEREST TABLE 7¼ %

EFFECTIVE RATE = 29/48% BASE = 1.00604167

	1 AMOUNT OF I AT COMPOUND INTEREST $S^n = (1+i)^n$	2 ACCUMULATION OF I PER PERIOD $S_{\overline{n}\vert} = \frac{S^n - 1}{i}$	3 SINKING FUND FACTOR $1/S_{\overline{n}\vert} = \frac{i}{S^n - 1}$	4 PRES. VALUE REVERSION OF I $V^n = \frac{1}{S^n}$	5 PRESENT VALUE ORD. ANNUITY 1 PER PERIOD $a_{\overline{n}\vert} = \frac{1 - V^n}{i}$	6 INSTALMENT TO AMORTIZE I $1/a_{\overline{n}\vert} = \frac{i}{1 - V^n}$	n MONTHS
MONTHS							
1	1.006041	1.000000	1.000000	.993994	.993994	1.006041	1
2	1.012119	2.006041	.498494	.988025	1.982019	.504535	2
3	1.018234	3.018161	.331327	.982091	2.964111	.337369	3
4	1.024386	4.036396	.247745	.976193	3.940305	.253787	4
5	1.030575	5.060782	.197597	.970331	4.910637	.203639	5
6	1.036801	6.091358	.164166	.964504	5.875141	.170208	6
7	1.043065	7.128160	.140288	.958712	6.833853	.146330	7
8	1.049367	8.171226	.122380	.952954	7.786808	.128422	8
9	1.055707	9.220594	.108452	.947231	8.734040	.114494	9
10	1.062085	10.276301	.097311	.941543	9.675583	.103352	10
11	1.068502	11.338387	.088195	.935889	10.611472	.094237	11
YEARS							
1	1.074958	12.406890	.080600	.930268	11.541741	.086642	12
2	1.155535	25.743780	.038844	.865399	22.278661	.044886	24
3	1.242152	40.080381	.024949	.805054	32.266881	.030991	36
4	1.335261	55.491628	.018020	.748916	41.558609	.024062	48
5	1.435350	72.058077	.013877	.696693	50.202412	.019919	60
6	1.542942	89.866319	.011127	.648112	58.243471	.017169	72
7	1.658598	109.009436	.009173	.602918	65.723816	.015215	84
8	1.782924	129.587488	.007716	.560876	72.682547	.013758	96
9	1.916569	151.708036	.006591	.521765	79.156036	.012633	108
10	2.060232	175.486703	.005698	.485382	85.178120	.011740	120
11	2.214663	201.047778	.004973	.451535	90.780275	.011015	132
12	2.380671	228.524868	.004375	.420049	95.991785	.010417	144
13	2.559122	258.061594	.003875	.390758	100.839889	.009916	156
14	2.750949	289.812342	.003450	.363510	105.349928	.009492	168
15	2.957156	323.943073	.003086	.338162	109.545477	.009128	180
16	3.178819	360.632185	.002772	.314582	113.448463	.008814	192
17	3.417098	400.071450	.002499	.292645	117.079290	.008541	204
18	3.673238	442.467015	.002260	.272239	120.456933	.008301	216
19	3.948577	488.040480	.002049	.253255	123.599049	.008090	228
20	4.244556	537.030055	.001862	.235595	126.522062	.007903	240
21	4.562721	589.691804	.001695	.219167	129.241248	.007737	252
22	4.904735	646.300988	.001547	.203884	131.770823	.007588	264
23	5.272385	707.153501	.001414	.189667	134.124006	.007455	276
24	5.667594	772.567415	.001294	.176441	136.313099	.007336	288
25	6.092428	842.884644	.001186	.164138	138.349542	.007228	300
26	6.549106	918.472733	.001088	.152692	140.243984	.007130	312
27	7.040015	999.726776	.001000	.142045	142.006322	.007041	324
28	7.567723	1087.071484	.000919	.132140	143.645770	.006961	336
29	8.134987	1180.963403	.000846	.122925	145.170897	.006888	348
30	8.744772	1281.893299	.000780	.114354	146.589676	.006821	360
31	9.400265	1390.388730	.000719	.106379	147.909520	.006760	372
32	10.104893	1507.016793	.000663	.098961	149.137330	.006705	384
33	10.862338	1632.387097	.000612	.092061	150.279523	.006654	396
34	11.676561	1767.154947	.000565	.085641	151.342071	.006607	408
35	12.551816	1912.024764	.000523	.079669	152.330523	.006564	420
36	13.492679	2067.753776	.000483	.074114	153.250051	.006525	432
37	14.504067	2235.155970	.000447	.068946	154.105458	.006489	444
38	15.591267	2415.106347	.000414	.064138	154.901219	.006455	456
39	16.759962	2608.545498	.000383	.059666	155.641488	.006425	468
40	18.016260	2816.484519	.000355	.055505	156.330138	.006396	480
41	19.366728	3040.010295	.000328	.051634	156.970765	.006370	492
42	20.818426	3280.291182	.000304	.048034	157.566723	.006346	504
43	22.378939	3538.583116	.000282	.044684	158.121123	.006324	516
44	24.056427	3816.236177	.000262	.041568	158.636865	.006303	528
45	25.859655	4114.701635	.000243	.038670	159.116643	.006284	540
46	27.798051	4435.539556	.000225	.035973	159.562966	.006267	552
47	29.881746	4780.426941	.000209	.033465	159.978166	.006250	564
48	32.121631	5151.166497	.000194	.031131	160.364412	.006235	576
49	34.529413	5549.696060	.000180	.028960	160.723727	.006221	588
50	37.117679	5978.098720	.000167	.026941	161.057983	.006208	600

7¼ % QUARTERLY COMPOUND INTEREST TABLE 7¼ %

EFFECTIVE RATE = 1-13/16% BASE = 1.018125

QUARTERS	1 AMOUNT OF 1 AT COMPOUND INTEREST $S^n = (1+i)^n$	2 ACCUMULATION OF 1 PER PERIOD $S_{\overline{n}\vert} = \frac{S^n - 1}{i}$	3 SINKING FUND FACTOR $1/S_{\overline{n}\vert} = \frac{i}{S^n - 1}$	4 PRES. VALUE REVERSION OF 1 $V^n = \frac{1}{S^n}$	5 PRESENT VALUE ORD. ANNUITY 1 PER PERIOD $a_{\overline{n}\vert} = \frac{1 - V^n}{i}$	6 INSTALMENT TO AMORTIZE 1 $1/a_{\overline{n}\vert} = \frac{i}{1 - V^n}$	n QUARTERS
1	1.018125	1.000000	1.000000	.982198	.982198	1.018125	1
2	1.036579	2.018125	.495509	.964712	1.946910	.513634	2
3	1.055367	3.054704	.327364	.947538	2.894448	.345489	3
YEARS							
1	1.074495	4.110070	.243305	.930670	3.825118	.261430	4
2	1.154540	8.526320	.117284	.866146	7.385039	.135409	8
3	1.240547	13.271558	.075349	.806096	10.698150	.093474	12
4	1.332962	18.370293	.054436	.750209	13.781563	.072561	16
5	1.432261	23.848859	.041931	.698197	16.651201	.060056	20
6	1.538957	29.735550	.033630	.649791	19.321887	.051755	24
7	1.653601	36.060770	.027731	.604741	21.807413	.045856	28
8	1.776787	42.857188	.023333	.562814	24.120617	.041458	32
9	1.909148	50.159905	.019936	.523794	26.273446	.038061	36
10	2.051370	58.006638	.017239	.487479	28.277019	.035364	40
11	2.204187	66.437914	.015052	.453682	30.141684	.033177	44
12	2.368388	75.497277	.013246	.422228	31.877071	.031371	48
13	2.544821	85.231519	.011733	.392955	33.492143	.029858	52
14	2.734398	95.690912	.010450	.365711	34.995242	.028575	56
15	2.938097	106.929479	.009352	.340356	36.394131	.027477	60
16	3.156970	119.005262	.008403	.316759	37.696034	.026528	64
17	3.392149	131.980631	.007577	.294798	38.907676	.025702	68
18	3.644847	145.922601	.006853	.274360	40.035314	.024978	72
19	3.916370	160.903178	.006215	.255338	41.084773	.024340	76
20	4.208120	176.999733	.005650	.237636	42.061473	.023775	80
21	4.521604	194.295402	.005147	.221160	42.970458	.023272	84
22	4.858441	212.879511	.004697	.205827	43.816423	.022822	88
23	5.220371	232.848045	.004295	.191557	44.603737	.022420	92
24	5.609262	254.304134	.003932	.178277	45.336466	.022057	96
25	6.027125	277.358596	.003605	.165917	46.018395	.021730	100
26	6.476115	302.130500	.003310	.154414	46.653045	.021435	104
27	6.958554	328.747787	.003042	.143708	47.243695	.021167	108
28	7.476931	357.347930	.002798	.133745	47.793395	.020923	112
29	8.033925	388.078640	.002577	.124472	48.304985	.020702	116
30	8.632413	421.098636	.002375	.115842	48.781105	.020500	120
31	9.275485	456.578457	.002190	.107811	49.224216	.020315	124
32	9.966462	494.701348	.002021	.100337	49.636606	.020146	128
33	10.708914	535.664204	.001867	.093380	50.020405	.019992	132
34	11.506674	579.678589	.001725	.086906	50.377595	.019850	136
35	12.363864	626.971827	.001595	.080881	50.710021	.019720	140
36	13.284911	677.788175	.001475	.075273	51.019400	.019600	144
37	14.274570	732.390088	.001365	.070055	51.307330	.019490	148
38	15.337955	791.059571	.001264	.065198	51.575297	.019389	152
39	16.480556	854.099639	.001171	.060678	51.824686	.019296	156
40	17.708275	921.835878	.001085	.056471	52.056785	.019210	160
41	19.027454	994.618130	.001005	.052556	52.272792	.019130	164
42	20.444904	1072.822296	.000932	.048912	52.473824	.019057	168
43	21.967948	1156.852284	.000864	.045521	52.660918	.018989	172
44	23.604450	1247.142087	.000802	.042365	52.835040	.018927	176
45	25.362864	1344.158030	.000744	.039428	52.997091	.018869	180
46	27.252271	1448.401178	.000690	.036694	53.147907	.018815	184
47	29.282430	1560.409922	.000641	.034150	53.288266	.018766	188
48	31.463825	1680.762759	.000595	.031783	53.418895	.018720	192
49	33.807723	1810.081282	.000552	.029579	53.540467	.018677	196
50	36.326230	1949.033392	.000513	.027528	53.653610	.018638	200
51	39.032353	2098.336742	.000477	.025620	53.758909	.018602	204
52	41.940069	2258.762447	.000443	.023844	53.856908	.018568	208
53	45.064396	2431.139069	.000411	.022190	53.948112	.018536	212
54	48.421469	2616.356890	.000382	.020652	54.032993	.018507	216
55	52.028627	2815.372516	.000355	.019220	54.111990	.018480	220
56	55.904500	3029.213816	.000330	.017888	54.185509	.018455	224
57	60.069107	3258.985226	.000307	.016647	54.253931	.018432	228
58	64.543957	3505.873463	.000285	.015493	54.317610	.018410	232
59	69.352160	3771.153644	.000265	.014419	54.376874	.018390	236
60	74.518550	4056.195876	.000247	.013419	54.432029	.018372	240

7¼ % SEMI-ANNUAL COMPOUND INTEREST TABLE 7¼ %

EFFECTIVE RATE = 3-5/8%   BASE = 1.03625

HALF YEARS	1 AMOUNT OF I AT COMPOUND INTEREST $S^n = (1+i)^n$	2 ACCUMULATION OF I PER PERIOD $S_{\overline{n}\vert} = \frac{S^n - 1}{i}$	3 SINKING FUND FACTOR $1/S_{\overline{n}\vert} = \frac{i}{S^n - 1}$	4 PRES. VALUE REVERSION OF I $V^n = \frac{1}{S^n}$	5 PRESENT VALUE ORD. ANNUITY 1 PER PERIOD $a_{\overline{n}\vert} = \frac{1 - V^n}{i}$	6 INSTALMENT TO AMORTIZE I $1/a_{\overline{n}\vert} = \frac{i}{1 - V^n}$	n HALF YEARS
1	1.036250	1.000000	1.000000	.965018	.965018	1.036250	1
YEARS							
1	1.073814	2.036250	.491099	.931260	1.896278	.527349	2
2	1.153077	4.222804	.236809	.867245	3.662206	.273059	4
3	1.238190	6.570756	.152189	.807631	5.306743	.188439	6
4	1.329586	9.092020	.109987	.752114	6.838236	.146237	8
5	1.427728	11.799389	.084750	.700414	8.264453	.121000	10
6	1.533114	14.706600	.067997	.652267	9.592632	.104247	12
7	1.646280	17.828404	.056090	.607430	10.829511	.092340	14
8	1.767798	21.180641	.047213	.565675	11.981368	.083463	16
9	1.898287	24.780320	.040355	.526791	13.054046	.076605	18
10	2.038407	28.645706	.034909	.490579	14.052988	.071159	20
11	2.188870	32.796412	.030491	.456857	14.983262	.066741	22
12	2.350439	37.253499	.026843	.425452	15.849590	.063093	24
13	2.523935	42.039581	.023787	.396207	16.656366	.060037	26
14	2.710237	47.178943	.021196	.368971	17.407684	.057446	28
15	2.910290	52.697663	.018976	.343608	18.107356	.055226	30
16	3.125111	58.623741	.017058	.319989	18.758933	.053308	32
17	3.355788	64.987248	.015388	.297993	19.365721	.051638	34
18	3.603492	71.820470	.013924	.277509	19.930798	.050174	36
19	3.869480	79.158081	.012633	.258433	20.457031	.048883	38
20	4.155103	87.037311	.011489	.240668	20.947091	.047739	40
21	4.461808	95.498138	.010471	.224124	21.403464	.046721	42
22	4.791152	104.583494	.009562	.208718	21.828467	.045812	44
23	5.144806	114.339476	.008746	.194371	22.224254	.044996	46
24	5.524565	124.815587	.008012	.181010	22.592835	.044262	48
25	5.932356	136.064983	.007349	.168567	22.936080	.043599	50
26	6.370247	148.144742	.006750	.156980	23.255730	.043000	52
27	6.840461	161.116157	.006207	.146189	23.553407	.042457	54
28	7.345383	175.045045	.005713	.136140	23.830622	.041963	56
29	7.887575	190.002081	.005263	.126782	24.088781	.041513	58
30	8.469789	206.063157	.004853	.118067	24.329195	.041103	60
31	9.094979	223.309766	.004478	.109951	24.553082	.040728	62
32	9.766316	241.829417	.004135	.102393	24.761579	.040385	64
33	10.487208	261.716078	.003821	.095354	24.955744	.040071	66
34	11.261311	283.070655	.003533	.088800	25.136563	.039783	68
35	12.092554	306.001500	.003268	.082696	25.304951	.039518	70
36	12.985155	330.624964	.003025	.077011	25.461765	.039275	72
37	13.943642	357.065986	.002801	.071717	25.607799	.039051	74
38	14.972879	385.458727	.002594	.066787	25.743795	.038844	76
39	16.078088	415.947251	.002404	.062196	25.870443	.038654	78
40	17.264877	448.686257	.002229	.057921	25.988385	.038479	80
41	18.539268	483.841863	.002067	.053940	26.098219	.038317	82
42	19.907726	521.592446	.001917	.050232	26.200503	.038167	84
43	21.377196	562.129554	.001779	.046779	26.295757	.038029	86
44	22.955134	605.658870	.001651	.043563	26.384462	.037901	88
45	24.649546	652.401261	.001533	.040569	26.467070	.037783	90
46	26.469029	702.593899	.001423	.037780	26.544000	.037673	92
47	28.422815	756.491459	.001322	.035183	26.615641	.037572	94
48	30.520819	814.367417	.001228	.032765	26.682358	.037478	96
49	32.773684	876.515434	.001141	.030512	26.744489	.037391	98
50	35.192843	943.250849	.001060	.028415	26.802348	.037310	100
51	37.790570	1014.912276	.000985	.026462	26.856231	.037235	102
52	40.580045	1091.863324	.000916	.024643	26.906410	.037166	104
53	43.575424	1174.494441	.000851	.022949	26.953139	.037101	106
54	46.791903	1263.224897	.000792	.021371	26.996656	.037042	108
55	50.245803	1358.504909	.000736	.019902	27.037182	.036986	110
56	53.954650	1460.817925	.000685	.018534	27.074922	.036935	112
57	57.937262	1570.683081	.000637	.017260	27.110068	.036887	114
58	62.213846	1688.657830	.000592	.016074	27.142797	.036842	116
59	66.806103	1815.340774	.000551	.014969	27.173277	.036801	118
60	71.737333	1951.374702	.000512	.013940	27.201662	.036762	120

7¼ % ANNUAL COMPOUND INTEREST TABLE 7¼ %

EFFECTIVE RATE = 7¼% BASE - 1.0725

YEARS	1 AMOUNT OF I AT COMPOUND INTEREST $S^n = (1+i)^n$	2 ACCUMULATION OF I PER PERIOD $S_{\overline{n}\vert} = \frac{S^n - 1}{i}$	3 SINKING FUND FACTOR $1/S_{\overline{n}\vert} = \frac{i}{S^n - 1}$	4 PRES. VALUE REVERSION OF I $V^n = \frac{1}{S^n}$	5 PRESENT VALUE ORD. ANNUITY 1 PER PERIOD $a_{\overline{n}\vert} = \frac{1 - V^n}{i}$	6 INSTALMENT TO AMORTIZE I $1/a_{\overline{n}\vert} = \frac{i}{1 - V^n}$	n YEARS
1	1.072500	1.000000	1.000000	.932401	.932401	1.072500	1
2	1.150256	2.072500	.482509	.869371	1.801772	.555009	2
3	1.233650	3.222756	.310293	.810603	2.612375	.382793	3
4	1.323089	4.456406	.224396	.755807	3.368182	.296896	4
5	1.419013	5.779496	.173025	.704715	4.072897	.245525	5
6	1.521892	7.198509	.138918	.657077	4.729974	.211418	6
7	1.632229	8.720401	.114674	.612659	5.342633	.187174	7
8	1.750566	10.352630	.096594	.571244	5.913877	.169094	8
9	1.877482	12.103196	.082623	.532628	6.446505	.155123	9
10	2.013599	13.980677	.071527	.496623	6.943128	.144027	10
11	2.159585	15.994276	.062522	.463052	7.406180	.135022	11
12	2.316155	18.153861	.055085	.431750	7.837930	.127585	12
13	2.484076	20.470016	.048852	.402564	8.240495	.121352	13
14	2.664172	22.954093	.043565	.375351	8.615846	.116065	14
15	2.857324	25.618264	.039035	.349978	8.965824	.111535	15
16	3.064480	28.475588	.035118	.326320	9.292143	.107618	16
17	3.286655	31.540069	.031706	.304261	9.596404	.104206	17
18	3.524937	34.826724	.028714	.283693	9.880097	.101214	18
19	3.780495	38.351661	.026074	.264516	10.144612	.098574	19
20	4.054581	42.132156	.023735	.246635	10.391247	.096235	20
21	4.348538	46.186738	.021651	.229962	10.621209	.094151	21
22	4.663808	50.535276	.019788	.214417	10.835626	.092288	22
23	5.001934	55.199084	.018116	.199923	11.035549	.090616	23
24	5.364574	60.201017	.016611	.186408	11.221957	.089111	24
25	5.753505	65.565591	.015252	.173807	11.395764	.087752	25
26	6.170634	71.319096	.014021	.162058	11.557822	.086521	26
27	6.618005	77.489731	.012905	.151103	11.708925	.085405	27
28	7.097811	84.107736	.011890	.140889	11.849814	.084390	28
29	7.612402	91.205547	.010964	.131365	11.981178	.083464	29
30	8.164301	98.817949	.010120	.122484	12.103663	.082620	30
31	8.756213	106.982251	.009347	.114205	12.217867	.081847	31
32	9.391039	115.738464	.008640	.106484	12.324352	.081140	32
33	10.071889	125.129503	.007992	.099286	12.423638	.080492	33
34	10.802101	135.201392	.007396	.092575	12.516213	.079896	34
35	11.585253	146.003492	.006849	.086317	12.602529	.079349	35
36	12.425184	157.588746	.006346	.080482	12.683011	.078846	36
37	13.326010	170.013930	.005882	.075041	12.758052	.078382	37
38	14.292146	183.339940	.005454	.069969	12.828021	.077954	38
39	15.328326	197.632085	.005060	.065239	12.893259	.077560	39
40	16.439630	212.960411	.004696	.060829	12.954088	.077196	40
41	17.631503	229.400041	.004359	.056717	13.010805	.076859	41
42	18.909787	247.031544	.004048	.052883	13.063687	.076548	42
43	20.280747	265.941331	.003760	.049308	13.112995	.076260	43
44	21.751101	286.222078	.003494	.045975	13.158970	.075994	44
45	23.328055	307.973178	.003247	.042867	13.201837	.075747	45
46	25.019339	331.301234	.003018	.039969	13.241806	.075518	46
47	26.833242	356.320573	.002806	.037267	13.279073	.075306	47
48	28.778652	383.153815	.002610	.034748	13.313821	.075110	48
49	30.865104	411.932466	.002428	.032399	13.346220	.074928	49
50	33.102824	442.797570	.002258	.030209	13.376429	.074758	50
51	35.502779	475.900394	.002101	.028167	13.404596	.074601	51
52	38.076730	511.403173	.001955	.026263	13.430858	.074455	52
53	40.837293	549.479903	.001820	.024487	13.455346	.074320	53
54	43.797997	590.317196	.001694	.022832	13.478178	.074194	54
55	46.973351	634.115192	.001577	.021289	13.499467	.074077	55
56	50.378919	681.088544	.001468	.019850	13.519316	.073968	56
57	54.031391	731.467463	.001367	.018508	13.537824	.073867	57
58	57.948667	785.498854	.001273	.017257	13.555081	.073773	58
59	62.149945	843.447521	.001186	.016090	13.571171	.073686	59
60	66.655816	905.597467	.001104	.015002	13.586173	.073604	60

7½% MONTHLY COMPOUND INTEREST TABLE 7½%

EFFECTIVE RATE = 5/8% BASE = 1.00625

MONTHS	1 AMOUNT OF I AT COMPOUND INTEREST $s^n = (1+i)^n$	2 ACCUMULATION OF I PER PERIOD $s_{\overline{n}\vert} = \frac{s^n - 1}{i}$	3 SINKING FUND FACTOR $1/s_{\overline{n}\vert} = \frac{i}{s^n - 1}$	4 PRES. VALUE REVERSION OF I $v^n = \frac{1}{s^n}$	5 PRESENT VALUE ORD. ANNUITY 1 PER PERIOD $a_{\overline{n}\vert} = \frac{1 - v^n}{i}$	6 INSTALMENT TO AMORTIZE I $1/a_{\overline{n}\vert} = \frac{i}{1 - v^n}$	n MONTHS
1	1.006250	1.000000	1.000000	.993789	.993789	1.006250	1
2	1.012539	2.006250	.498442	.987616	1.981405	.504692	2
3	1.018867	3.018789	.331259	.981482	2.962887	.337509	3
4	1.025235	4.037656	.247668	.975386	3.938273	.253918	4
5	1.031643	5.062892	.197516	.969327	4.907600	.203766	5
6	1.038091	6.094535	.164081	.963307	5.870907	.170331	6
7	1.044579	7.132626	.140201	.957324	6.828231	.146451	7
8	1.051108	8.177205	.122291	.951377	7.779608	.128541	8
9	1.057677	9.228312	.108362	.945468	8.725076	.114612	9
10	1.064287	10.285989	.097220	.939596	9.664672	.103470	10
11	1.070939	11.350277	.088104	.933760	10.598432	.094354	11
YEARS							
1	1.077633	12.421216	.080507	.927960	11.526392	.086757	12
2	1.161292	25.806723	.038750	.861110	22.222423	.045000	24
3	1.251446	40.231382	.024856	.799076	32.147913	.031106	36
4	1.348599	55.775864	.017929	.741510	41.358371	.024179	48
5	1.453294	72.527105	.013788	.688092	49.905308	.020038	60
6	1.566117	90.578789	.011040	.638522	57.836524	.017290	72
7	1.687699	110.031871	.009088	.592523	65.196376	.015338	84
8	1.818720	130.995147	.007634	.549837	72.026024	.013884	96
9	1.959912	153.585857	.006511	.510227	78.363665	.012761	108
10	2.112065	177.930342	.005620	.473470	84.244743	.011870	120
11	2.276030	204.164753	.004898	.439362	89.702148	.011148	132
12	2.452724	232.435809	.004302	.407710	94.766402	.010552	144
13	2.643135	262.901621	.003804	.378339	99.465827	.010054	156
14	2.848329	295.732572	.003381	.351083	103.826706	.009631	168
15	3.069452	331.112276	.003020	.325791	107.873427	.009270	180
16	3.307741	369.238599	.002708	.302321	111.628623	.008958	192
17	3.564530	410.324767	.002437	.280542	115.113294	.008687	204
18	3.841254	454.600560	.002200	.260332	118.346930	.008450	216
19	4.139460	502.313599	.001991	.241577	121.347616	.008241	228
20	4.460817	553.730725	.001806	.224174	124.132131	.008056	240
21	4.807122	609.139496	.001642	.208025	126.716051	.007892	252
22	5.180311	668.849794	.001495	.193039	129.113825	.007745	264
23	5.582472	733.195558	.001364	.179132	131.338864	.007614	276
24	6.015854	802.536650	.001246	.166227	133.403610	.007496	288
25	6.482880	877.260872	.001140	.154252	135.319613	.007390	300
26	6.986163	957.786129	.001044	.143140	137.097587	.007294	312
27	7.528517	1044.562771	.000957	.132828	138.747476	.007207	324
28	8.112976	1138.076110	.000879	.123259	140.278507	.007129	336
29	8.742807	1238.849131	.000807	.114380	141.699242	.007057	348
30	9.421534	1347.445425	.000742	.106140	143.017628	.006992	360
31	10.152952	1464.472331	.000683	.098494	144.241037	.006933	372
32	10.941152	1590.584340	.000629	.091398	145.376312	.006879	384
33	11.790542	1726.486752	.000579	.084814	146.429802	.006829	396
34	12.705873	1872.939621	.000534	.078704	147.407398	.006784	408
35	13.692263	2030.762007	.000492	.073034	148.314569	.006742	420
36	14.755228	2200.836555	.000454	.067773	149.156387	.006704	432
37	15.900715	2384.114432	.000419	.062890	149.937560	.006669	444
38	17.135129	2581.620647	.000387	.058360	150.662458	.006637	456
39	18.465374	2794.459783	.000358	.054155	151.335134	.006608	468
40	19.898889	3023.822175	.000331	.050254	151.959350	.006581	480
41	21.443691	3270.990564	.000306	.046634	152.538598	.006556	492
42	23.108420	3537.347278	.000283	.043274	153.076118	.006533	504
43	24.902387	3824.381956	.000261	.040157	153.574914	.006511	516
44	26.835624	4133.699883	.000242	.037264	154.037777	.006492	528
45	28.918944	4467.030963	.000224	.034579	154.467295	.006474	540
46	31.163996	4826.239402	.000207	.032088	154.865871	.006457	552
47	33.583338	5213.334125	.000192	.029777	155.235733	.006442	564
48	36.190500	5630.480018	.000178	.027632	155.578951	.006428	576
49	39.000063	6080.010030	.000164	.025641	155.897443	.006414	588
50	42.027739	6564.438226	.000152	.023794	156.192991	.006402	600

7½% QUARTERLY COMPOUND INTEREST TABLE 7½%

EFFECTIVE RATE = 1-7/8% BASE = 1.01875

QUARTERS	1 AMOUNT OF 1 AT COMPOUND INTEREST $s^n = (1+i)^n$	2 ACCUMULATION OF 1 PER PERIOD $s_{\overline{n}\rvert} = \frac{s^n - 1}{i}$	3 SINKING FUND FACTOR $1/s_{\overline{n}\rvert} = \frac{i}{s^n - 1}$	4 PRES. VALUE REVERSION OF 1 $v^n = \frac{1}{s^n}$	5 PRESENT VALUE ORD. ANNUITY 1 PER PERIOD $a_{\overline{n}\rvert} = \frac{1-v^n}{i}$	6 INSTALMENT TO AMORTIZE 1 $1/a_{\overline{n}\rvert} = \frac{i}{1-v^n}$	n QUARTERS
1	1.018750	1.000000	1.000000	.981595	.981595	1.018750	1
2	1.037852	2.018750	.495356	.963529	1.945124	.514106	2
3	1.057311	3.056602	.327161	.945795	2.890919	.345911	3
YEARS							
1	1.077136	4.113913	.243078	.928388	3.819307	.261828	4
2	1.160222	8.545156	.117025	.861904	7.365106	.135775	8
3	1.249716	13.318207	.075085	.800182	10.656983	.093835	12
4	1.346114	18.459431	.054173	.742879	13.713123	.072923	16
5	1.449948	23.997228	.041671	.689680	16.550406	.060421	20
6	1.561791	29.962188	.033375	.640291	19.184505	.052125	24
7	1.682261	36.387260	.027482	.594438	21.629971	.046232	28
8	1.812024	43.307936	.023090	.551869	23.900313	.041840	32
9	1.951796	50.762444	.019700	.512349	26.008071	.038450	36
10	2.102349	58.791961	.017009	.475658	27.964888	.035759	40
11	2.264516	67.440843	.014828	.441596	29.781573	.033578	44
12	2.439191	76.756864	.013028	.409972	31.468162	.031778	48
13	2.627340	86.791484	.011522	.380613	33.033971	.030272	52
14	2.830002	97.600133	.010246	.353357	34.487649	.028996	56
15	3.048297	109.242516	.009154	.328052	35.837226	.027904	60
16	3.283430	121.782945	.008211	.304560	37.090158	.026961	64
17	3.536700	135.290691	.007391	.282749	38.253364	.026141	68
18	3.809507	149.840369	.006674	.262501	39.333271	.025424	72
19	4.103357	165.512348	.006042	.243703	40.335844	.024792	76
20	4.419872	182.393199	.005483	.226251	41.266620	.024233	80
21	4.760803	200.576169	.004986	.210049	42.130742	.023736	84
22	5.128032	220.161699	.004542	.195007	42.932982	.023292	88
23	5.523587	241.257975	.004145	.181042	43.677772	.022895	92
24	5.949654	263.981530	.003788	.168077	44.369226	.022538	96
25	6.408585	288.457887	.003467	.156041	45.011164	.022217	100
26	6.902917	314.822249	.003176	.144866	45.607131	.021926	104
27	7.435380	343.220248	.002914	.134492	46.160420	.021664	108
28	8.008914	373.808752	.002675	.124861	46.674087	.021425	112
29	8.626689	406.756727	.002458	.115919	47.150969	.021208	116
30	9.292116	442.246172	.002261	.107618	47.593700	.021011	120
31	10.008871	480.473126	.002081	.099911	48.004727	.020831	124
32	10.780914	521.648749	.001917	.092757	48.386319	.020667	128
33	11.612509	566.000490	.001767	.086114	48.740585	.020517	132
34	12.508250	613.773341	.001629	.079947	49.069481	.020379	136
35	13.473085	665.231192	.001503	.074222	49.374824	.020253	140
36	14.512343	720.658289	.001388	.068907	49.658301	.020138	144
37	15.631765	780.360802	.001281	.063972	49.921477	.020031	148
38	16.837535	844.668535	.001184	.059391	50.165807	.019934	152
39	18.136313	913.936672	.001094	.055138	50.392640	.019844	156
40	19.535273	988.547881	.001012	.051189	50.603229	.019762	160
41	21.042143	1068.914291	.000936	.047524	50.798737	.019686	164
42	22.665247	1155.479833	.000865	.044120	50.980245	.019615	168
43	24.413550	1248.722683	.000801	.040961	51.148754	.019551	172
44	26.296711	1349.157901	.000741	.038028	51.305196	.019491	176
45	28.325130	1457.340277	.000686	.035304	51.450435	.019436	180
46	30.510014	1573.867394	.000635	.032776	51.585273	.019385	184
47	32.863430	1699.382931	.000588	.030429	51.710455	.019338	188
48	35.398379	1834.580217	.000545	.028250	51.826673	.019295	192
49	38.128864	1980.206063	.000505	.026227	51.934568	.019255	196
50	41.069967	2137.064885	.000468	.024349	52.034736	.019218	200
51	44.237934	2306.023148	.000434	.022605	52.127731	.019184	204
52	47.650265	2488.014153	.000402	.020986	52.214067	.019152	208
53	51.325810	2684.043192	.000373	.019483	52.294220	.019123	212
54	55.284871	2895.193100	.000345	.018088	52.368633	.019095	216
55	59.549317	3122.630239	.000320	.016793	52.437717	.019070	220
56	64.142705	3367.610939	.000297	.015590	52.501854	.019047	224
57	69.090408	3631.488437	.000275	.014474	52.561398	.019025	228
58	74.419757	3915.720355	.000255	.013437	52.616678	.019005	232
59	80.160189	4221.876748	.000237	.012475	52.667999	.018987	236
60	86.343415	4551.648779	.000220	.011582	52.715645	.018970	240

7½% SEMI-ANNUAL COMPOUND INTEREST TABLE 7½%

EFFECTIVE RATE = 3¾% BASE = 1.0375

HALF YEARS	1 AMOUNT OF I AT COMPOUND INTEREST $s^n = (1+i)^n$	2 ACCUMULATION OF I PER PERIOD $s_{\overline{n}\vert} = \frac{s^n - 1}{i}$	3 SINKING FUND FACTOR $1/s_{\overline{n}\vert} = \frac{i}{s^n - 1}$	4 PRES. VALUE REVERSION OF I $v^n = \frac{1}{s^n}$	5 PRESENT VALUE ORD. ANNUITY 1 PER PERIOD $a_{\overline{n}\vert} = \frac{1-v^n}{i}$	6 INSTALMENT TO AMORTIZE I $1/a_{\overline{n}\vert} = \frac{i}{1-v^n}$	n HALF YEARS
1	1.037500	1.000000	1.000000	.963855	.963855	1.037500	1
YEARS							
1	1.076406	2.037500	.490798	.929017	1.892873	.528298	2
2	1.158650	4.230678	.236369	.863073	3.651384	.273869	4
3	1.247179	6.591428	.151712	.801810	5.285072	.189212	6
4	1.342471	9.132554	.109498	.744895	6.802796	.146998	8
5	1.445044	11.867838	.084261	.692020	8.212787	.121761	10
6	1.555454	14.812116	.067512	.642899	9.522694	.105012	12
7	1.674301	17.981354	.055613	.597264	10.739620	.093113	14
8	1.802228	21.392742	.046745	.554869	11.870165	.084245	16
9	1.939929	25.064781	.039897	.515483	12.920461	.077397	18
10	2.088152	29.017387	.034462	.478892	13.896204	.071962	20
11	2.247700	33.271996	.030055	.444899	14.802686	.067555	22
12	2.419438	37.851685	.026419	.413319	15.644824	.063919	24
13	2.604298	42.781290	.023375	.383981	16.427185	.060875	26
14	2.803283	48.087548	.020795	.356725	17.154011	.058295	28
15	3.017471	53.799237	.018588	.331403	17.829245	.056088	30
16	3.248025	59.947335	.016681	.307879	18.456549	.054181	32
17	3.496194	66.565186	.015023	.286025	19.039326	.052523	34
18	3.763326	73.688682	.013571	.265722	19.580735	.051071	36
19	4.050867	81.356458	.012292	.246861	20.083714	.049792	38
20	4.360379	89.610100	.011159	.229338	20.550990	.048659	40
21	4.693539	98.494372	.010153	.213059	20.985097	.047653	42
22	5.052155	108.057458	.009254	.197935	21.388391	.046754	44
23	5.438171	118.351223	.008449	.183885	21.763057	.045949	46
24	5.853681	129.431496	.007726	.170833	22.111129	.045226	48
25	6.300939	141.358371	.007074	.158707	22.434493	.044574	50
26	6.782370	154.196534	.006485	.147441	22.734904	.043985	52
27	7.300585	168.015613	.005952	.136975	23.013992	.043452	54
28	7.858396	182.890556	.005468	.127252	23.273268	.042968	56
29	8.458826	198.902037	.005028	.118220	23.514141	.042528	58
30	9.105134	216.136896	.004627	.109828	23.737916	.042127	60
31	9.800823	234.688606	.004261	.102032	23.945807	.041761	62
32	10.549667	254.657782	.003927	.094790	24.138941	.041427	64
33	11.355727	276.152729	.003621	.088061	24.318366	.041121	66
34	12.223376	299.290023	.003341	.081810	24.485054	.040841	68
35	13.157318	324.195151	.003085	.076003	24.639911	.040585	70
36	14.162620	351.003187	.002849	.070608	24.783776	.040349	72
37	15.244732	379.859524	.002633	.065596	24.917429	.040133	74
38	16.409525	410.920666	.002434	.060940	25.041594	.039934	76
39	17.663315	444.355073	.002250	.056615	25.156946	.039750	78
40	19.012903	480.344078	.002082	.052596	25.264110	.039582	80
41	20.465608	519.082868	.001926	.048862	25.363668	.039426	82
42	22.029308	560.781543	.001783	.045394	25.456158	.039283	84
43	23.712485	605.666258	.001651	.042172	25.542083	.039151	86
44	25.524267	653.980445	.001529	.039178	25.621909	.039029	88
45	27.474480	705.986139	.001416	.036397	25.696069	.038916	90
46	29.573702	761.965392	.001312	.033814	25.764965	.038812	92
47	31.833318	822.221810	.001216	.031414	25.828970	.038716	94
48	34.265582	887.082196	.001127	.029184	25.888432	.038627	96
49	36.883687	956.898320	.001045	.027112	25.943673	.038545	98
50	39.701831	1032.048832	.000969	.025188	25.994993	.038469	100
51	42.735299	1112.941313	.000899	.023400	26.042670	.038399	102
52	46.000543	1200.014485	.000833	.021739	26.086963	.038333	104
53	49.515272	1293.740592	.000773	.020196	26.128112	.038273	106
54	53.298548	1394.627959	.000717	.018762	26.166340	.038217	108
55	57.370891	1503.223751	.000665	.017430	26.201855	.038165	110
56	61.754385	1620.116941	.000617	.016193	26.234848	.038117	112
57	66.472806	1745.941501	.000573	.015044	26.265500	.038073	114
58	71.551744	1881.379844	.000532	.013976	26.293976	.038032	116
59	77.018745	2027.166523	.000493	.012984	26.320431	.037993	118
60	82.903458	2184.092215	.000458	.012062	26,345007	.037958	120

7½% ANNUAL COMPOUND INTEREST TABLE 7½%

EFFECTIVE RATE = 7½% BASE = 1.075

YEARS	1 AMOUNT OF I AT COMPOUND INTEREST $S^n = (1+i)^n$	2 ACCUMULATION OF I PER PERIOD $s_{\overline{n}\|} = \frac{S^n - 1}{i}$	3 SINKING FUND FACTOR $1/s_{\overline{n}\|} = \frac{i}{S^n - 1}$	4 PRES. VALUE REVERSION OF I $V^n = \frac{1}{S^n}$	5 PRESENT VALUE ORD. ANNUITY 1 PER PERIOD $a_{\overline{n}\|} = \frac{1 - V^n}{i}$	6 INSTALMENT TO AMORTIZE I $1/a_{\overline{n}\|} = \frac{i}{1 - V^n}$	n YEARS
1	1.075000	1.000000	1.000000	.930233	.930233	1.075000	1
2	1.155625	2.075000	.481928	.865333	1.795565	.556928	2
3	1.242297	3.230625	.309538	.804961	2.600526	.384538	3
4	1.335469	4.472922	.223568	.748801	3.349326	.298568	4
5	1.435629	5.808391	.172165	.696559	4.045885	.247165	5
6	1.543302	7.244020	.138045	.647962	4.693846	.213045	6
7	1.659049	8.787322	.113800	.602755	5.296601	.188800	7
8	1.783478	10.446371	.095727	.560702	5.857304	.170727	8
9	1.917239	12.229849	.081767	.521583	6.378887	.156767	9
10	2.061032	14.147087	.070686	.485194	6.864081	.145686	10
11	2.215609	16.208119	.061697	.451343	7.315424	.136697	11
12	2.381780	18.423728	.054278	.419854	7.735278	.129278	12
13	2.560413	20.805508	.048064	.390562	8.125840	.123064	13
14	2.752444	23.365921	.042797	.363313	8.489154	.117797	14
15	2.958877	26.118365	.038287	.337966	8.827120	.113287	15
16	3.180793	29.077242	.034391	.314387	9.141507	.109391	16
17	3.419353	32.258035	.031000	.292453	9.433960	.106000	17
18	3.675804	35.677388	.028029	.272049	9.706009	.103029	18
19	3.951489	39.353192	.025411	.253069	9.959078	.100411	19
20	4.247851	43.304681	.023092	.235413	10.194491	.098092	20
21	4.566440	47.552532	.021029	.218989	10.413480	.096029	21
22	4.908923	52.118972	.019187	.203711	10.617191	.094187	22
23	5.277092	57.027895	.017535	.189498	10.806689	.092535	23
24	5.672874	62.304987	.016050	.176277	10.982967	.091050	24
25	6.098340	67.977862	.014711	.163979	11.146946	.089711	25
26	6.555715	74.076201	.013500	.152539	11.299485	.088500	26
27	7.047394	80.631916	.012402	.141896	11.441381	.087402	27
28	7.575948	87.679310	.011405	.131997	11.573378	.086405	28
29	8.144144	95.255258	.010498	.122788	11.696165	.085498	29
30	8.754955	103.399403	.009671	.114221	11.810386	.084671	30
31	9.411577	112.154358	.008916	.106252	11.916638	.083916	31
32	10.117445	121.565935	.008226	.098839	12.015478	.083226	32
33	10.876253	131.683380	.007594	.091943	12.107421	.082594	33
34	11.691972	142.559633	.007015	.085529	12.192950	.082015	34
35	12.568870	154.251606	.006483	.079562	12.272511	.081483	35
36	13.511536	166.820476	.005994	.074011	12.346522	.080994	36
37	14.524901	180.332012	.005545	.068847	12.415370	.080545	37
38	15.614268	194.856913	.005132	.064044	12.479414	.080132	38
39	16.785339	210.471181	.004751	.059576	12.538989	.079751	39
40	18.044239	227.256520	.004400	.055419	12.594409	.079400	40
41	19.397557	245.300759	.004077	.051553	12.645962	.079077	41
42	20.852374	264.698315	.003778	.047956	12.693918	.078778	42
43	22.416302	285.550689	.003502	.044610	12.738528	.078502	43
44	24.097524	307.966991	.003247	.041498	12.780026	.078247	44
45	25.904839	332.064515	.003011	.038603	12.818629	.078011	45
46	27.847702	357.969354	.002794	.035910	12.854539	.077794	46
47	29.936279	385.817055	.002592	.033404	12.887943	.077592	47
48	32.181500	415.753334	.002405	.031074	12.919017	.077405	48
49	34.595113	447.934835	.002232	.028906	12.947922	.077232	49
50	37.189746	482.529947	.002072	.026889	12.974812	.077072	50
51	39.978977	519.719693	.001924	.025013	12.999825	.076924	51
52	42.977400	559.698670	.001787	.023268	13.023093	.076787	52
53	46.200705	602.676070	.001659	.021645	13.044737	.076659	53
54	49.665758	648.876776	.001541	.020135	13.064872	.076541	54
55	53.390690	698.542534	.001432	.018730	13.083602	.076432	55
56	57.394992	751.933224	.001330	.017423	13.101025	.076330	56
57	61.699616	809.328216	.001236	.016208	13.117233	.076236	57
58	66.327087	871.027832	.001148	.015077	13.132309	.076148	58
59	71.301619	937.354919	.001067	.014025	13.146334	.076067	59
60	76.649240	1008.656538	.000991	.013046	13.159381	.075991	60

7¾ % MONTHLY COMPOUND INTEREST TABLE 7¾ %

EFFECTIVE RATE = 31/48% BASE = 1.00645833

MONTHS	1 AMOUNT OF I AT COMPOUND INTEREST $S^n = (1+i)^n$	2 ACCUMULATION OF I PER PERIOD $S_{\overline{n}\vert} = \frac{S^n - 1}{i}$	3 SINKING FUND FACTOR $1/S_{\overline{n}\vert} = \frac{i}{S^n - 1}$	4 PRES. VALUE REVERSION OF I $V^n = \frac{1}{S^n}$	5 PRESENT VALUE ORD. ANNUITY 1 PER PERIOD $a_{\overline{n}\vert} = \frac{1 - V^n}{i}$	6 INSTALMENT TO AMORTIZE I $1/a_{\overline{n}\vert} = \frac{i}{1 - V^n}$	n MONTHS
1	1.006458	1.000000	1.000000	.993583	.993583	1.006458	1
2	1.012958	2.006458	.498390	.987207	1.980790	.504848	2
3	1.019500	3.019416	.331189	.980872	2.961663	.337648	3
4	1.026084	4.038917	.247591	.974578	3.936241	.254049	4
5	1.032711	5.065001	.197433	.968324	4.904566	.203891	5
6	1.039381	6.097713	.163995	.962111	5.866677	.170454	6
7	1.046093	7.137094	.140113	.955937	6.822614	.146571	7
8	1.052849	8.183188	.122201	.949803	7.772417	.128660	8
9	1.059649	9.236037	.108271	.943708	8.716126	.114729	9
10	1.066492	10.295687	.097128	.937652	9.653778	.103586	10
11	1.073380	11.362180	.088011	.931635	10.585414	.094469	11
YEARS							
1	1.080312	12.435560	.080414	.925657	11.511072	.086872	12
2	1.167076	25.869859	.038655	.856842	22.166384	.045113	24
3	1.260807	40.383105	.024762	.793142	32.029555	.031221	36
4	1.362066	56.061955	.017837	.734178	41.159475	.024295	48
5	1.471458	73.000019	.013698	.679597	49.610656	.020156	60
6	1.589635	91.298431	.010953	.629074	57.433556	.017411	72
7	1.717304	111.066442	.009003	.582308	64.674883	.015461	84
8	1.855225	132.422082	.007551	.539017	71.377873	.014009	96
9	2.004224	155.492857	.006431	.498946	77.582547	.012889	108
10	2.165189	180.416516	.005542	.461853	83.325951	.012001	120
11	2.339082	207.341868	.004822	.427517	88.642377	.011281	132
12	2.526941	236.429676	.004229	.395735	93.563567	.010687	144
13	2.729887	267.853612	.003733	.366315	98.118905	.010191	156
14	2.949133	301.801300	.003313	.339082	102.335588	.009771	168
15	3.185987	338.475428	.002954	.313874	106.238793	.009412	180
16	3.441863	378.094965	.002644	.290540	109.851824	.009103	192
17	3.718289	420.896466	.002375	.268940	113.196255	.008834	204
18	4.016916	467.135484	.002140	.248947	116.292052	.008599	216
19	4.339527	517.088095	.001933	.230439	119.157702	.008392	228
20	4.688047	571.052552	.001751	.213308	121.810311	.008209	240
21	5.064558	629.351054	.001588	.197450	124.265720	.008047	252
22	5.471308	692.331685	.001444	.182771	126.538587	.007902	264
23	5.910725	760.370479	.001315	.169183	128.642484	.007773	276
24	6.385434	833.873672	.001199	.156606	130.589974	.007657	288
25	6.898267	913.280127	.001094	.144963	132.392681	.007553	300
26	7.452287	999.063953	.001000	.134186	134.061372	.007459	312
27	8.050803	1091.737334	.000915	.124211	135.606008	.007374	324
28	8.697387	1191.853593	.000839	.114977	137.035812	.007297	336
29	9.395901	1300.010488	.000769	.106429	138.359320	.007227	348
30	10.150514	1416.853789	.000705	.098517	139.584438	.007164	360
31	10.965732	1543.081123	.000648	.091193	140.718475	.007106	372
32	11.846423	1679.446155	.000595	.084413	141.768207	.007053	384
33	12.797844	1826.763070	.000547	.078138	142.739898	.007005	396
34	13.825678	1985.911449	.000503	.072329	143.639353	.006961	408
35	14.936059	2157.841510	.000463	.066952	144.471938	.006921	420
36	16.135619	2343.579792	.000426	.061974	145.242628	.006885	432
37	17.431519	2544.235269	.000393	.057367	145.956024	.006851	444
38	18.831496	2761.005992	.000362	.053102	146.616384	.006820	456
39	20.343910	2995.186218	.000333	.049154	147.227650	.006792	468
40	21.977791	3248.174163	.000307	.045500	147.793474	.006766	480
41	23.742893	3521.480325	.000283	.042117	148.317234	.006742	492
42	25.649756	3816.736528	.000262	.038986	148.802057	.006720	504
43	27.709765	4135.705638	.000241	.036088	149.250835	.006700	516
44	29.935219	4480.292117	.000223	.033405	149.666251	.006681	528
45	32.339406	4852.553364	.000206	.030922	150.050783	.006664	540
46	34.936681	5254.712033	.000190	.028623	150.406729	.006648	552
47	37.742551	5689.169265	.000175	.026495	150.736213	.006634	564
48	40.773768	6158.519065	.000162	.024525	151.041202	.006620	576
49	44.048432	6665.563748	.000150	.022702	151.323518	.006608	588
50	47.586093	7213.330716	.000138	.021014	151.584846	.006596	600

7¾ % QUARTERLY COMPOUND INTEREST TABLE 7¾ %

EFFECTIVE RATE = 1-15/16% BASE = 1.019375

QUARTERS	1 AMOUNT OF I AT COMPOUND INTEREST $S^n = (1+i)^n$	2 ACCUMULATION OF I PER PERIOD $S_{\overline{n}\vert} = \frac{S^n - 1}{i}$	3 SINKING FUND FACTOR $1/S_{\overline{n}\vert} = \frac{i}{S^n - 1}$	4 PRES. VALUE REVERSION OF I $V^n = \frac{1}{S^n}$	5 PRESENT VALUE ORD. ANNUITY 1 PER PERIOD $a_{\overline{n}\vert} = \frac{1 - V^n}{i}$	6 INSTALMENT TO AMORTIZE I $1/a_{\overline{n}\vert} = \frac{i}{1 - V^n}$	n QUARTERS
1	1.019375	1.000000	1.000000	.980993	.980993	1.019375	1
2	1.039125	2.019375	.495203	.962348	1.943341	.514578	2
3	1.059258	3.058500	.326958	.944057	2.887398	.346333	3
YEARS							
1	1.079782	4.117759	.242851	.926113	3.813511	.262226	4
2	1.165928	8.564039	.116767	.857686	7.345254	.136142	8
3	1.258948	13.365050	.074822	.794314	10.616048	.094197	12
4	1.359389	18.549094	.053911	.735625	13.645173	.073286	16
5	1.467843	24.146729	.041413	.681272	16.450486	.060788	20
6	1.584950	30.190952	.033123	.630935	19.048524	.052498	24
7	1.711399	36.717392	.027235	.584317	21.454601	.046610	28
8	1.847938	43.764523	.022850	.541144	23.682900	.042225	32
9	1.995369	51.373884	.019465	.501160	25.746558	.038840	36
10	2.154563	59.590332	.016781	.464131	27.657739	.036156	40
11	2.326457	68.462302	.014607	.429838	29.427709	.033982	44
12	2.512066	78.042091	.012814	.398079	31.066901	.032189	48
13	2.712482	88.386171	.011314	.368666	32.584979	.030689	52
14	2.928888	99.555518	.010045	.341426	33.990891	.029420	56
15	3.162559	111.615973	.008959	.316200	35.292925	.028334	60
16	3.414873	124.638631	.008023	.292837	36.498755	.027398	64
17	3.687317	138.700256	.007210	.271200	37.615491	.026585	68
18	3.981497	153.883740	.006498	.251162	38.649714	.025873	72
19	4.299148	170.278587	.005873	.232604	39.607523	.025248	76
20	4.642140	187.981440	.005320	.215418	40.494562	.024695	80
21	5.012498	207.096654	.004829	.199501	41.316060	.024204	84
22	5.412403	227.736911	.004391	.184761	42.076860	.023766	88
23	5.844213	250.023880	.004000	.171109	42.781448	.023375	92
24	6.310473	274.088938	.003648	.158467	43.433976	.023023	96
25	6.813933	300.073945	.003333	.146758	44.038290	.022708	100
26	7.357559	328.132076	.003048	.135915	44.597954	.022423	104
27	7.944557	358.428730	.002790	.125872	45.116266	.022165	108
28	8.578386	391.142498	.002557	.116572	45.596281	.021932	112
29	9.262783	426.466222	.002345	.107959	46.040830	.021720	116
30	10.001783	464.608129	.002152	.099982	46.452533	.021527	120
31	10.799740	505.793058	.001977	.092595	46.833816	.021352	124
32	11.661361	550.263784	.001817	.085753	47.186927	.021192	128
33	12.591723	598.282456	.001671	.079417	47.513948	.021046	132
34	13.596310	650.132133	.001538	.073549	47.816807	.020913	136
35	14.681045	706.118459	.001416	.068115	48.097288	.020791	140
36	15.852322	766.571462	.001305	.063082	48.357046	.020680	144
37	17.117045	831.847501	.001202	.058421	48.597610	.020577	148
38	18.482670	902.331366	.001108	.054105	48.820401	.020483	152
39	19.957247	978.438545	.001022	.050107	49.026730	.020397	156
40	21.549467	1060.617674	.000943	.046405	49.217814	.020318	160
41	23.268718	1149.353185	.000870	.042976	49.394779	.020245	164
42	25.125133	1245.168153	.000803	.039801	49.558669	.020178	168
43	27.129656	1348.627391	.000741	.036860	49.710450	.020116	172
44	29.294102	1460.340771	.000685	.034137	49.851016	.020060	176
45	31.631232	1580.966820	.000633	.031614	49.981196	.020008	180
46	34.154822	1711.216606	.000584	.029278	50.101758	.019959	184
47	36.879747	1851.857925	.000540	.027115	50.213411	.519915	188
48	39.822072	2003.719831	.000499	.025112	50.316815	.019874	192
49	42.999139	2167.697518	.000461	.023256	50.412579	.019836	196
50	46.429679	2344.757605	.000426	.021538	50.501267	.019801	200
51	50.133912	2535.943824	.000394	.019947	50.583402	.019769	204
52	54.133674	2742.383181	.000365	.018473	50.659469	.019740	208
53	58.452544	2965.292597	.000337	.017108	50.729915	.019712	212
54	63.115980	3205.986076	.000312	.015844	50.795156	.019687	216
55	68.151473	3465.882462	.000289	.014673	50.855577	.019664	220
56	73.588705	3746.513791	.000267	.013589	50.911533	.019642	224
57	79.459728	4049.534330	.000247	.012585	50.963355	.019622	228
58	85.799150	4376.730326	.000228	.011655	51.011348	.019603	232
59	92.644342	4730.030535	.000211	.010794	51.055795	.019586	236
60	100.035653	5111.517590	.000196	.009996	51.096958	.019571	240

7¾ % SEMI-ANNUAL COMPOUND INTEREST TABLE 7¾ %

EFFECTIVE RATE = 3-7/8% BASE = 1.03875

HALF YEARS	1 AMOUNT OF I AT COMPOUND INTEREST $S^n = (1+i)^n$	2 ACCUMULATION OF I PER PERIOD $S_{\overline{n}\rvert} = \frac{S^n - 1}{i}$	3 SINKING FUND FACTOR $1/S_{\overline{n}\rvert} = \frac{i}{S^n - 1}$	4 PRES. VALUE REVERSION OF I $V^n = \frac{1}{S^n}$	5 PRESENT VALUE ORD. ANNUITY 1 PER PERIOD $a_{\overline{n}\rvert} = \frac{1-V^n}{i}$	6 INSTALMENT TO AMORTIZE I $1/a_{\overline{n}\rvert} = \frac{i}{1-V^n}$	n - HALF YEARS
1	1.038750	1.000000	1.000000	.962696	.962696	1.038750	1
YEARS							
1	1.079002	2.038750	.490497	.926783	1.889478	.529247	2
2	1.164244	4.238564	.235929	.858926	3.640614	.274679	4
3	1.256221	6.612168	.151236	.796038	5.263536	.189986	6
4	1.355465	9.173289	.109012	.737754	6.767633	.147762	8
5	1.462549	11.936743	.083775	.683738	8.161603	.122525	10
6	1.578092	14.918515	.067031	.633676	9.453511	.105781	12
7	1.702764	18.135851	.055139	.587280	10.650829	.093889	14
8	1.837285	21.607361	.046281	.544281	11.760483	.085031	16
9	1.982434	25.353127	.039443	.504430	12.788890	.078193	18
10	2.139049	29.394813	.034020	.467497	13.742001	.072770	20
11	2.308037	33.755799	.029625	.433269	14.625327	.068375	22
12	2.490376	38.461310	.026000	.401546	15.443979	.064750	24
13	2.687119	43.538564	.022968	.372146	16.202691	.061718	26
14	2.899406	49.016929	.020401	.344898	16.905852	.059151	28
15	3.128464	54.928093	.018206	.319646	17.557530	.056956	30
16	3.375617	61.306248	.016312	.296242	18.161493	.055062	32
17	3.642296	68.188287	.014665	.274552	18.721236	.053415	34
18	3.930043	75.614018	.013225	.254450	19.239997	.051975	36
19	4.240523	83.626394	.011958	.235820	19.720775	.050708	38
20	4.575531	92.271760	.010838	.218554	20.166351	.049588	40
21	4.937005	101.600123	.009843	.202552	20.579304	.048593	42
22	5.327036	111.665441	.008955	.187722	20.962022	.047705	44
23	5.747880	122.525936	.008162	.173977	21.316718	.046912	46
24	6.201972	134.244426	.007449	.161239	21.645444	.046199	48
25	6.691937	146.888696	.006808	.149434	21.950102	.045558	50
26	7.220610	160.531882	.006229	.138492	22.232453	.044979	52
27	7.791050	175.252901	.005706	.128352	22.494131	.044456	54
28	8.406555	191.136905	.005232	.118955	22.736651	.043982	56
29	9.070686	208.275769	.004801	.110245	22.961413	.043551	58
30	9.787284	226.768630	.004410	.102173	23.169719	.043160	60
31	10.560495	246.722456	.004053	.094693	23.362773	.042803	62
32	11.394791	268.252665	.003728	.087759	23.541693	.042478	64
33	12.294997	291.483795	.003431	.081334	23.707512	.042181	66
34	13.266321	316.550220	.003159	.075379	23.861191	.041909	68
35	14.314381	343.596932	.002910	.069860	24.003618	.041660	70
36	15.445240	372.780377	.002683	.064745	24.135616	.041433	72
37	16.665438	404.269359	.002474	.060004	24.257950	.041224	74
38	17.982033	438.246020	.002282	.055611	24.371327	.041032	76
39	19.402642	474.906891	.002106	.051539	24.476403	.040856	78
40	20.935481	514.464027	.001944	.047766	24.573786	.040694	80
41	22.589417	557.146240	.001795	.044269	24.664038	.040545	82
42	24.374016	603.200413	.001658	.041027	24.747683	.040408	84
43	26.299601	652.892938	.001532	.038023	24.825203	.040282	86
44	28.377311	706.511250	.001415	.035239	24.897047	.040165	88
45	30.619163	764.365493	.001308	.032659	24.963631	.040058	90
46	33.038125	826.790312	.001209	.030268	25.025340	.039959	92
47	35.648188	894.146788	.001118	.028052	25.082531	.039868	94
48	38.464451	966.824531	.001034	.025998	25.135535	.039784	96
49	41.503202	1045.243930	.000957	.024095	25.184657	.039707	98
50	44.782020	1129.858584	.000885	.022330	25.230183	.039635	100
51	48.319870	1221.157927	.000819	.020695	25.272376	.039569	102
52	52.137215	1319.670062	.000758	.019180	25.311480	.039508	104
53	56.256136	1425.964809	.000701	.017776	25.347720	.039451	106
54	60.700459	1540.657006	.000649	.016474	25.381307	.039399	108
55	65.495890	1664.410067	.000601	.015268	25.412435	.039351	110
56	70.670168	1797.939813	.000556	.014150	25.441284	.039306	112
57	76.253221	1942.018618	.000515	.013114	25.468021	.039265	114
58	82.277345	2097.479873	.000477	.012154	25.492800	.039227	116
59	88.777384	2265.222811	.000441	.011264	25.515764	.039191	118
60	95.790936	2446.217702	.000409	.010439	25.537048	.039159	120

7¾% ANNUAL COMPOUND INTEREST TABLE 7¾%

EFFECTIVE RATE = 7¾% BASE = 1.0775

YEARS	1 AMOUNT OF I AT COMPOUND INTEREST $S^n = (1+i)^n$	2 ACCUMULATION OF I PER PERIOD $S_{\overline{n}\vert} = \frac{S^n - 1}{i}$	3 SINKING FUND FACTOR $1/S_{\overline{n}\vert} = \frac{i}{S^n - 1}$	4 PRES. VALUE REVERSION OF I $V^n = \frac{1}{S^n}$	5 PRESENT VALUE ORD. ANNUITY 1 PER PERIOD $a_{\overline{n}\vert} = \frac{1 - V^n}{i}$	6 INSTALMENT TO AMORTIZE I $1/a_{\overline{n}\vert} = \frac{i}{1 - V^n}$	n YEARS
1	1.077500	1.000000	1.000000	.928074	.928074	1.077500	1
2	1.161006	2.077500	.481348	.861322	1.789396	.558848	2
3	1.250984	3.238506	.308784	.799371	2.588767	.386284	3
4	1.347936	4.489490	.222742	.741875	3.330642	.300242	4
5	1.452401	5.837426	.171308	.688515	4.019157	.248808	5
6	1.564962	7.289827	.137177	.638993	4.658151	.214677	6
7	1.686246	8.854788	.112933	.593033	5.251184	.190433	7
8	1.816930	10.541034	.094867	.550379	5.801563	.172367	8
9	1.957742	12.357964	.080919	.510792	6.312355	.158419	9
10	2.109467	14.315707	.069853	.474053	6.786409	.147353	10
11	2.272951	16.425174	.060882	.439957	7.226365	.138382	11
12	2.449105	18.698125	.053481	.408312	7.634678	.130981	12
13	2.638910	21.147229	.047288	.378944	8.013622	.124788	13
14	2.843426	23.786140	.042041	.351688	8.365310	.119541	14
15	3.063791	26.629566	.037552	.326393	8.691703	.115052	15
16	3.301235	29.693357	.033678	.302917	8.994620	.111178	16
17	3.557081	32.994592	.030308	.281129	9.275750	.107808	17
18	3.832755	36.551673	.027359	.260909	9.536659	.104859	18
19	4.129793	40.384428	.024762	.242143	9.778802	.102262	19
20	4.449852	44.514221	.022465	.224727	10.003528	.099965	20
21	4.794716	48.964073	.020423	.208563	10.212091	.097923	21
22	5.166306	53.758788	.018602	.193562	10.405653	.096102	22
23	5.566695	58.925094	.016971	.179640	10.585293	.094471	23
24	5.998114	64.491789	.015506	.166719	10.752012	.093006	24
25	6.462967	70.489903	.014186	.154728	10.906740	.091686	25
26	6.963847	76.952870	.012995	.143599	11.050338	.090495	26
27	7.503546	83.916718	.011917	.133270	11.183609	.089417	27
28	8.085070	91.420264	.010938	.123685	11.307293	.088438	28
29	8.711663	99.505334	.010050	.114789	11.422082	.087550	29
30	9.386817	108.216997	.009241	.106532	11.528614	.086741	30
31	10.114296	117.603815	.008503	.098870	11.627484	.086003	31
32	10.898154	127.718110	.007830	.091759	11.719243	.085330	32
33	11.742760	138.616264	.007214	.085159	11.804402	.084714	33
34	12.652824	150.359024	.006651	.079034	11.883436	.084151	34
35	13.633418	163.011849	.006135	.073349	11.956785	.083635	35
36	14.690008	176.645267	.005661	.068073	12.024858	.083161	36
37	15.828484	191.335275	.005226	.063177	12.088036	.082726	37
38	17.055191	207.163759	.004827	.058633	12.146669	.082327	38
39	18.376969	224.218951	.004460	.054416	12.201085	.081960	39
40	19.801184	242.595919	.004122	.050502	12.251587	.081622	40
41	21.335775	262.397103	.003811	.046870	12.298456	.081311	41
42	22.989298	283.732879	.003524	.043499	12.341955	.081024	42
43	24.770969	306.722177	.003260	.040370	12.382325	.080760	43
44	26.690719	331.493145	.003017	.037466	12.419791	.080517	44
45	28.759249	358.183864	.002792	.034771	12.454562	.080292	45
46	30.988091	386.943113	.002584	.032270	12.486833	.080084	46
47	33.389668	417.931205	.002393	.029949	12.516782	.079893	47
48	35.977368	451.320873	.002216	.027795	12.544577	.079716	48
49	38.765614	487.298241	.002052	.025796	12.570373	.079552	49
50	41.769949	526.063854	.001901	.023941	12.594314	.079401	50
51	45.007120	567.833803	.001761	.022219	12.616533	.079261	51
52	48.495172	612.840923	.001632	.020621	12.637153	.079132	52
53	52.253547	661.336094	.001512	.019137	12.656291	.079012	53
54	56.303197	713.589641	.001401	.017761	12.674052	.078901	54
55	60.666695	769.892839	.001299	.016484	12.690535	.078799	55
56	65.368364	830.559534	.001204	.015298	12.705833	.078704	56
57	70.434412	895.927897	.001116	.014198	12.720031	.078616	57
58	75.893079	966.362309	.001035	.013176	12.733207	.078535	58
59	81.774793	1042.255388	.000959	.012229	12.745436	.078459	59
60	88.112339	1124.030181	.000890	.011349	12.756785	.078390	60

8% MONTHLY COMPOUND INTEREST TABLE 8%

EFFECTIVE RATE = 2/3%   BASE = 1.00666666+

MONTHS	1 AMOUNT OF 1 AT COMPOUND INTEREST $S^n = (1+i)^n$	2 ACCUMULATION OF 1 PER PERIOD $S_{\overline{n}\vert} = \frac{S^n - 1}{i}$	3 SINKING FUND FACTOR $1/S_{\overline{n}\vert} = \frac{i}{S^n - 1}$	4 PRES. VALUE REVERSION OF 1 $V^n = \frac{1}{S^n}$	5 PRESENT VALUE ORD. ANNUITY 1 PER PERIOD $a_{\overline{n}\vert} = \frac{1 - V^n}{i}$	6 INSTALMENT TO AMORTIZE 1 $1/a_{\overline{n}\vert} = \frac{i}{1 - V^n}$	n MONTHS
1	1.006667	1.000000	1.000000	.993377	.993377	1.006667	1
2	1.013378	2.006667	.498339	.986799	1.980176	.505006	2
3	1.020134	3.020044	.331121	.980264	2.960440	.337788	3
4	1.026935	4.040178	.247514	.973772	3.934212	.254181	4
5	1.033781	5.067113	.197351	.967323	4.901535	.204018	5
6	1.040673	6.100893	.163910	.960917	5.862452	.170577	6
7	1.047610	7.141566	.140025	.954553	6.817005	.146692	7
8	1.054595	8.189176	.122112	.948232	7.765237	.128779	8
9	1.061625	9.243771	.108181	.941952	8.707189	.114848	9
10	1.068703	10.305396	.097037	.935714	9.642903	.103704	10
11	1.075827	11.374099	.087919	.929517	10.572420	.094586	11
YEARS							
1	1.083000	12.449926	.080322	.923361	11.495782	.086989	12
2	1.172888	25.933190	.038561	.852596	22.110544	.045228	24
3	1.270237	40.535558	.024670	.787255	31.911805	.031337	36
4	1.375666	56.349915	.017746	.726921	40.961913	.024413	48
5	1.489846	73.476856	.013610	.671210	49.318433	.020277	60
6	1.613502	92.025325	.010867	.619770	57.034522	.017534	72
7	1.747422	112.113308	.008920	.572272	64.159261	.015587	84
8	1.892457	133.868583	.007470	.528414	70.737970	.014137	96
9	2.049530	157.429536	.006352	.487917	76.812497	.013019	108
10	2.219640	182.946036	.005466	.450523	82.421481	.012133	120
11	2.403869	210.580392	.004749	.415996	87.600600	.011416	132
12	2.603389	240.508387	.004158	.384115	92.382799	.010825	144
13	2.819469	272.920391	.003664	.354677	96.798498	.010331	156
14	3.053484	308.022575	.003247	.327495	100.875783	.009914	168
15	3.306921	346.038223	.002890	.302396	104.640592	.009557	180
16	3.581394	387.209151	.002583	.279221	108.116871	.009250	192
17	3.878648	431.797246	.002316	.257822	111.326733	.008983	204
18	4.200574	480.086130	.002083	.238063	114.290596	.008750	216
19	4.549220	532.382969	.001878	.219818	117.027313	.008545	228
20	4.926803	589.020419	.001698	.202971	119.554291	.008365	240
21	5.335725	650.358749	.001538	.187416	121.887606	.008205	252
22	5.778588	716.788131	.001395	.173053	124.042099	.008062	264
23	6.258207	788.731119	.001268	.159790	126.031475	.007935	276
24	6.777636	866.645339	.001154	.147544	127.868388	.007821	288
25	7.340176	951.026401	.001051	.136237	129.564522	.007718	300
26	7.949407	1042.411050	.000959	.125796	131.130667	.007626	312
27	8.609204	1141.380579	.000876	.116155	132.576785	.007543	324
28	9.323764	1248.564531	.000801	.107253	133.912075	.007468	336
29	10.097631	1364.644698	.000733	.099033	135.145030	.007400	348
30	10.935730	1490.359462	.000671	.091443	136.283493	.007338	360
31	11.843390	1626.508488	.000615	.084435	137.334707	.007282	372
32	12.826386	1773.957818	.000564	.077964	138.305356	.007231	384
33	13.890969	1933.645368	.000517	.071989	139.201617	.007184	396
34	15.043913	2106.586907	.000475	.066472	140.029189	.007142	408
35	16.292550	2293.882508	.000436	.061378	140.793337	.007103	420
36	17.644824	2496.723552	.000401	.056674	141.498922	.007068	432
37	19.109335	2716.400303	.000368	.052330	142.150433	.007035	444
38	20.695401	2954.310116	.000338	.048320	142.752012	.007005	456
39	22.413109	3211.966325	.000311	.044617	143.307487	.006978	468
40	24.273386	3491.007874	.000286	.041197	143.820391	.006953	480
41	26.288065	3793.209733	.000264	.038040	144.293988	.006931	492
42	28.469961	4120.494198	.000243	.035125	144.731288	.006910	504
43	30.832954	4474.943112	.000223	.032433	145.135074	.006890	516
44	33.392074	4858.811111	.000206	.029947	145.507915	.006873	528
45	36.163600	5274.539965	.000190	.027652	145.852182	.006857	540
46	39.165161	5724.774109	.000175	.025533	146.170065	.006842	552
47	42.415850	6212.377465	.000161	.023576	146.463585	.006828	564
48	45.936345	6740.451660	.000148	.021769	146.734611	.006815	576
49	49.749039	7312.355752	.000137	.020101	146.984865	.006804	588
50	53.878184	7931.727602	.000126	.018560	147.215941	.006793	600

8% QUARTERLY COMPOUND INTEREST TABLE 8%

EFFECTIVE RATE = 2% BASE = 1.02

QUARTERS	1 AMOUNT OF 1 AT COMPOUND INTEREST $s^n = (1+i)^n$	2 ACCUMULATION OF 1 PER PERIOD $s_{\overline{n}\vert} = \frac{s^n - 1}{i}$	3 SINKING FUND FACTOR $1/s_{\overline{n}\vert} = \frac{i}{s^n - 1}$	4 PRES. VALUE REVERSION OF 1 $v^n = \frac{1}{s^n}$	5 PRESENT VALUE ORD. ANNUITY 1 PER PERIOD $a_{\overline{n}\vert} = \frac{1-v^n}{i}$	6 INSTALMENT TO AMORTIZE 1 $1/a_{\overline{n}\vert} = \frac{i}{1-v^n}$	n QUARTERS
1	1.020000	1.000000	1.000000	.980392	.980392	1.020000	1
2	1.040400	2.020000	.495050	.961169	1.941561	.515050	2
3	1.061208	3.060400	.326755	.942322	2.883883	.346755	3
YEARS							
1	1.082432	4.121608	.242624	.923845	3.807729	.262624	4
2	1.171659	8.582969	.116510	.853490	7.325481	.136510	8
3	1.268242	13.412090	.074560	.788493	10.575341	.094560	12
4	1.372786	18.639285	.053650	.728446	13.577709	.073650	16
5	1.485947	24.297370	.041157	.672971	16.351433	.061157	20
6	1.608437	30.421862	.032871	.621721	18.913926	.052871	24
7	1.741024	37.051210	.026990	.574375	21.281272	.046990	28
8	1.884541	44.227030	.022611	.530633	23.468335	.042611	32
9	2.039887	51.994367	.019233	.490223	25.488842	.039233	36
10	2.208040	60.401983	.016556	.452890	27.355479	.036556	40
11	2.390053	69.502657	.014388	.418401	29.079963	.034388	44
12	2.587070	79.353519	.012602	.386538	30.673120	.032602	48
13	2.800328	90.016409	.011109	.357101	32.144950	.031109	52
14	3.031165	101.558264	.009847	.329906	33.504694	.029847	56
15	3.281031	114.051539	.008768	.304782	34.760887	.028768	60
16	3.551493	127.574662	.007839	.281572	35.921415	.027839	64
17	3.844251	142.212525	.007032	.260129	36.993564	.027032	68
18	4.161140	158.057019	.006327	.240319	37.984063	.026327	72
19	4.504152	175.207608	.005708	.222017	38.899132	.025708	76
20	4.875439	193.771958	.005161	.205110	39.744514	.025161	80
21	5.277332	213.866607	.004676	.189490	40.525516	.024676	84
22	5.712354	235.617701	.004244	.175059	41.247041	.024244	88
23	6.183236	259.161785	.003859	.161728	41.913619	.023859	92
24	6.692933	284.646659	.003513	.149411	42.529434	.023513	96
25	7.244646	312.232306	.003203	.138033	43.098352	.023203	100
26	7.841838	342.091897	.002923	.127521	43.623944	.022923	104
27	8.488258	374.412879	.002671	.117810	44.109510	.022671	108
28	9.187963	409.398150	.002443	.108838	44.558097	.022443	112
29	9.945347	447.267332	.002236	.100550	44.972523	.022236	116
30	10.765163	488.258152	.002048	.092892	45.355389	.022048	120
31	11.652559	532.627934	.001877	.085818	45.709097	.021877	124
32	12.613104	580.655213	.001722	.079283	46.035869	.021722	128
33	13.652830	632.641484	.001581	.073245	46.337756	.021581	132
34	14.778262	688.913096	.001452	.067667	46.616652	.021452	136
35	15.996466	749.823299	.001334	.062514	46.874310	.021334	140
36	17.315089	815.754461	.001226	.057753	47.112345	.021226	144
37	18.742409	887.120471	.001127	.053355	47.332253	.021127	148
38	20.287387	964.369336	.001037	.049292	47.535415	.021037	152
39	21.959720	1047.985992	.000954	.045538	47.723104	.020954	156
40	23.769907	1138.495348	.000878	.042070	47.896500	.020878	160
41	25.729312	1236.465587	.000809	.038866	48.056691	.020809	164
42	27.850234	1342.511724	.000745	.035906	48.204683	.020745	168
43	30.145989	1457.299474	.000686	.033172	48.341405	.020686	172
44	32.630988	1581.549425	.000632	.030646	48.467714	.020632	176
45	35.320831	1716.041568	.000583	.028312	48.584405	.020583	180
46	38.232404	1861.620189	.000537	.026156	48.692209	.020537	184
47	41.383983	2019.199171	.000495	.024164	48.791803	.020495	188
48	44.795355	2189.767728	.000457	.022324	48.883813	.020457	192
49	48.487932	2374.396619	.000421	.020624	48.968816	.020421	196
50	52.484897	2574.244869	.000388	.019053	49.047345	.020388	200
51	56.811341	2790.567042	.000358	.017602	49.119894	.020358	204
52	61.494422	3024.721119	.000331	.016262	49.186918	.020331	208
53	66.563540	3278.177023	.000305	.015023	49.248838	.020305	212
54	72.050517	3552.525843	.000281	.013879	49.306043	.020281	216
55	77.989797	3849.489830	.000260	.012822	49.358891	.020260	220
56	84.418664	4170.933200	.000240	.011846	49.407714	.020240	224
57	91.377477	4518.873841	.000221	.010944	49.452819	.020221	228
58	98.909920	4895.495980	.000204	.010110	49.494490	.020204	232
59	107.063278	5303.163896	.000189	.009340	49.532987	.020189	236
60	115.888735	5744.436759	.000174	.008629	49.568552	.020174	240

8% SEMI-ANNUAL COMPOUND INTEREST TABLE 8%

EFFECTIVE RATE = 4% BASE = 1.04

	1 AMOUNT OF I AT COMPOUND INTEREST $s^n = (1+i)^n$	2 ACCUMULATION OF I PER PERIOD $s_{\overline{n}\vert} = \frac{s^n - 1}{i}$	3 SINKING FUND FACTOR $1/s_{\overline{n}\vert} = \frac{i}{s^n - 1}$	4 PRES. VALUE REVERSION OF I $V^n = \frac{1}{s^n}$	5 PRESENT VALUE ORD. ANNUITY 1 PER PERIOD $a_{\overline{n}\vert} = \frac{1 - V^n}{i}$	6 INSTALMENT TO AMORTIZE I $1/a_{\overline{n}\vert} = \frac{i}{1 - V^n}$	n HALF YEARS
HALF YEARS 1	1.040000	1.000000	1.000000	.961538	.961538	1.040000	1
YEARS							
1	1.081600	2.040000	.490196	.924556	1.886095	.530196	2
2	1.169859	4.246464	.235490	.854804	3.629895	.275490	4
3	1.265319	6.632975	.150762	.790315	5.242137	.190762	6
4	1.368569	9.214226	.108528	.730690	6.732745	.148528	8
5	1.480244	12.006107	.083291	.675564	8.110896	.123291	10
6	1.601032	15.025805	.066552	.624597	9.385074	.106552	12
7	1.731676	18.291911	.054669	.577475	10.563123	.094669	14
8	1.872981	21.824531	.045820	.533908	11.652296	.085820	16
9	2.025817	25.645413	.038993	.493628	12.659297	.078993	18
10	2.191123	29.778079	.033582	.456387	13.590326	.073582	20
11	2.369919	34.247970	.029199	.421955	14.451115	.069199	22
12	2.563304	39.082604	.025587	.390121	15.246963	.065587	24
13	2.772470	44.311745	.022567	.360689	15.982769	.062567	26
14	2.998703	49.967583	.020013	.333477	16.663063	.060013	28
15	3.243398	56.084938	.017830	.308319	17.292033	.057830	30
16	3.508059	62.701469	.015949	.285058	17.873551	.055949	32
17	3.794316	69.857909	.014315	.263552	18.411198	.054315	34
18	4.103933	77.598314	.012887	.243669	18.908282	.052887	36
19	4.438813	85.970336	.011632	.225285	19.367864	.051632	38
20	4.801021	95.025516	.010523	.208289	19.792774	.050523	40
21	5.192784	104.819598	.009540	.192575	20.185627	.049540	42
22	5.616515	115.412877	.008665	.178046	20.548841	.048665	44
23	6.074823	126.870568	.007882	.164614	20.884654	.047882	46
24	6.570528	139.263206	.007181	.152195	21.195131	.047181	48
25	7.106683	152.667084	.006550	.140713	21.482185	.046550	50
26	7.686589	167.164718	.005982	.130097	21.747582	.045982	52
27	8.313814	182.845359	.005469	.120282	21.992957	.045469	54
28	8.992222	199.805540	.005005	.111207	22.219819	.045005	56
29	9.725987	218.149672	.004584	.102817	22.429567	.044584	58
30	10.519627	237.990685	.004202	.095060	22.623490	.044202	60
31	11.378029	259.450725	.003854	.087889	22.802783	.043854	62
32	12.306476	282.661904	.003538	.081258	22.968549	.043538	64
33	13.310685	307.767116	.003249	.075128	23.121810	.043249	66
34	14.396836	334.920912	.002986	.069460	23.263507	.042986	68
35	15.571618	364.290459	.002745	.064219	23.394515	.042745	70
36	16.842262	396.056560	.002525	.059374	23.515639	.042525	72
37	18.216591	430.414775	.002323	.054895	23.627625	.042323	74
38	19.703065	467.576621	.002139	.050754	23.731162	.042139	76
39	21.310835	507.770873	.001969	.046924	23.826888	.041969	78
40	23.049799	551.244977	.001814	.043384	23.915392	.041814	80
41	24.930663	598.266567	.001671	.040111	23.997219	.041671	82
42	26.965005	649.125119	.001541	.037085	24.072872	.041541	84
43	29.165349	704.133728	.001420	.034287	24.142818	.041420	86
44	31.545242	763.631041	.001310	.031701	24.207487	.041310	88
45	34.119333	827.983333	.001208	.029309	24.267278	.041208	90
46	36.903471	897.586774	.001114	.027098	24.322557	.041114	92
47	39.914794	972.869854	.001028	.025053	24.373666	.041028	94
48	43.171841	1054.296034	.000949	.023163	24.420919	.040949	96
49	46.694664	1142.366591	.000875	.021416	24.464607	.040875	98
50	50.504948	1237.623705	.000808	.019800	24.504999	.040808	100
51	54.626152	1340.653799	.000746	.018306	24.542344	.040746	102
52	59.083646	1452.091149	.000689	.016925	24.576871	.040689	104
53	63.904871	1572.621787	.000636	.015648	24.608793	.040636	106
54	69.119509	1702.987724	.000587	.014468	24.638308	.040587	108
55	74.759661	1843.991523	.000542	.013376	24.665595	.040542	110
56	80.860049	1996.501231	.000501	.012367	24.690824	.040501	112
57	87.458229	2161.455731	.000463	.011434	24.714149	.040463	114
58	94.594821	2339.870519	.000427	.010571	24.735715	.040427	116
59	102.313758	2532.843953	.000395	.009774	24.755654	.040395	118
60	110.662561	2741.564020	.000365	.009036	24.774088	.040365	120

8% ANNUAL COMPOUND INTEREST TABLE 8%

EFFECTIVE RATE = 8% BASE = 1.08

YEARS	1 AMOUNT OF I AT COMPOUND INTEREST $S^n = (1+i)^n$	2 ACCUMULATION OF I PER PERIOD $S_{\overline{n}\vert} = \frac{S^n - 1}{i}$	3 SINKING FUND FACTOR $1/S_{\overline{n}\vert} = \frac{i}{S^n - 1}$	4 PRES. VALUE REVERSION OF I $V^n = \frac{1}{S^n}$	5 PRESENT VALUE ORD. ANNUITY 1 PER PERIOD $a_{\overline{n}\vert} = \frac{1-V^n}{i}$	6 INSTALMENT TO AMORTIZE I $1/a_{\overline{n}\vert} = \frac{i}{1-V^n}$	n YEARS
1	1.080000	1.000000	1.000000	.925926	.925926	1.080000	1
2	1.166400	2.080000	.480769	.857339	1.783265	.560769	2
3	1.259712	3.246400	.308034	.793832	2.577097	.388034	3
4	1.360489	4.506112	.221921	.735030	3.312127	.301921	4
5	1.469328	5.866601	.170456	.680583	3.992710	.250456	5
6	1.586874	7.335929	.136315	.630170	4.622880	.216315	6
7	1.713824	8.922803	.112072	.583490	5.206370	.192072	7
8	1.850930	10.636628	.094015	.540269	5.746639	.174015	8
9	1.999005	12.487558	.080080	.500249	6.246888	.160080	9
10	2.158925	14.486562	.069029	.463193	6.710081	.149029	10
11	2.331639	16.645487	.060076	.428883	7.138964	.140076	11
12	2.518170	18.977126	.052695	.397114	7.536078	.132695	12
13	2.719624	21.495297	.046522	.367698	7.903776	.126522	13
14	2.937194	24.214920	.041297	.340461	8.244237	.121297	14
15	3.172169	27.152114	.036830	.315242	8.559479	.116830	15
16	3.425943	30.324283	.032977	.291890	8.851369	.112977	16
17	3.700018	33.750226	.029629	.270269	9.121638	.109629	17
18	3.996019	37.450244	.026702	.250249	9.371887	.106702	18
19	4.315701	41.446263	.024128	.231712	9.603599	.104128	19
20	4.660957	45.761964	.021852	.214548	9.818147	.101852	20
21	5.033834	50.422921	.019832	.198656	10.016803	.099832	21
22	5.436540	55.456755	.018032	.183941	10.200744	.098032	22
23	5.871464	60.893296	.016422	.170315	10.371059	.096422	23
24	6.341181	66.764759	.014978	.157699	10.528758	.094978	24
25	6.848475	73.105940	.013679	.146018	10.674776	.093679	25
26	7.396353	79.954415	.012507	.135202	10.809978	.092507	26
27	7.988061	87.350768	.011448	.125187	10.935165	.091448	27
28	8.627106	95.338830	.010489	.115914	11.051078	.090489	28
29	9.317275	103.965936	.009619	.107328	11.158406	.089619	29
30	10.062657	113.283211	.008827	.099377	11.257783	.088827	30
31	10.867669	123.345868	.008107	.092016	11.349799	.088107	31
32	11.737083	134.213537	.007451	.085200	11.434999	.087451	32
33	12.676050	145.950620	.006852	.078889	11.513888	.086852	33
34	13.690134	158.626670	.006304	.073045	11.586934	.086304	34
35	14.785344	172.316804	.005803	.067635	11.654568	.085803	35
36	15.968172	187.102148	.005345	.062625	11.717193	.085345	36
37	17.245626	203.070320	.004924	.057986	11.775179	.084924	37
38	18.625276	220.315945	.004539	.053690	11.828869	.084539	38
39	20.115298	238.941221	.004185	.049713	11.878582	.084185	39
40	21.724521	259.056519	.003860	.046031	11.924613	.083860	40
41	23.462483	280.781040	.003561	.042621	11.967235	.083561	41
42	25.339482	304.243523	.003287	.039464	12.006699	.083287	42
43	27.366640	329.583005	.003034	.036541	12.043240	.083034	43
44	29.555972	356.949646	.002802	.033834	12.077074	.082802	44
45	31.920449	386.505617	.002587	.031328	12.108401	.082587	45
46	34.474085	418.426067	.002390	.029007	12.137409	.082390	46
47	37.232012	452.900152	.002208	.026859	12.164267	.082208	47
48	40.210573	490.132164	.002040	.024869	12.189136	.082040	48
49	43.427419	530.342737	.001886	.023027	12.212163	.081886	49
50	46.901613	573.770156	.001743	.021321	12.233485	.081743	50
51	50.653742	620.671769	.001611	.019742	12.253227	.081611	51
52	54.706041	671.325510	.001490	.018280	12.271506	.081490	52
53	59.082524	726.031551	.001377	.016925	12.288432	.081377	53
54	63.809126	785.114075	.001274	.015672	12.304103	.081274	54
55	68.913856	848.923201	.001178	.014511	12.318614	.081178	55
56	74.426965	917.837058	.001090	.013436	12.332050	.081090	56
57	80.381122	992.264022	.001008	.012441	12.344491	.081008	57
58	86.811612	1072.645144	.000932	.011519	12.356010	.080932	58
59	93.756540	1159.456755	.000862	.010666	12.366676	.080862	59
60	101.257064	1253.213296	.000798	.009876	12.376552	.080798	60

8 ¼ % MONTHLY COMPOUND INTEREST TABLE 8 ¼ %

EFFECTIVE RATE = 33/48% BASE = 1.006875

MONTHS	1 AMOUNT OF I AT COMPOUND INTEREST $s^n = (1+i)^n$	2 ACCUMULATION OF I PER PERIOD $s_{\overline{n}\vert} = \frac{s^n - 1}{i}$	3 SINKING FUND FACTOR $1/s_{\overline{n}\vert} = \frac{i}{s^n - 1}$	4 PRES. VALUE REVERSION OF I $v^n = \frac{1}{s^n}$	5 PRESENT VALUE ORD. ANNUITY 1 PER PERIOD $a_{\overline{n}\vert} = \frac{1 - v^n}{i}$	6 INSTALMENT TO AMORTIZE I $1/a_{\overline{n}\vert} = \frac{i}{1 - v^n}$	n MONTHS
1	1.006875	1.000000	1.000000	.993171	.993171	1.006875	1
2	1.013797	2.006875	.498287	.986390	1.979562	.505162	2
3	1.020767	3.020672	.331052	.979655	2.959217	.337927	3
4	1.027784	4.041439	.247436	.972966	3.932184	.254311	4
5	1.034850	5.069224	.197268	.966322	4.898506	.204143	5
6	1.041965	6.104075	.163824	.959724	5.858231	.170699	6
7	1.049129	7.146040	.139937	.953171	6.811403	.146812	7
8	1.056341	8.195169	.122023	.946663	7.758066	.128898	8
9	1.063604	9.251511	.108090	.940199	8.698265	.114965	9
10	1.070916	10.315115	.096945	.933779	9.632045	.103820	10
11	1.078278	11.386032	.087826	.927403	10.559449	.094701	11
YEARS							
1	1.085692	12.464311	.080229	.921071	11.480520	.087104	12
2	1.178727	25.996715	.038466	.848372	22.054900	.045341	24
3	1.279735	40.688740	.024576	.781411	31.794659	.031451	36
4	1.389398	56.639757	.017655	.719736	40.765672	.024530	48
5	1.508458	73.957650	.013521	.662928	49.028616	.020396	60
6	1.637721	92.759550	.010780	.610604	56.639378	.017655	72
7	1.778061	113.172625	.008836	.562410	63.649433	.015711	84
8	1.930427	135.334941	.007389	.518019	70.106194	.014264	96
9	2.095850	159.396392	.006273	.477133	76.053332	.013148	108
10	2.275448	185.519721	.005390	.439473	81.531072	.012265	120
11	2.470436	213.881614	.004675	.404786	86.576460	.011550	132
12	2.682133	244.673898	.004087	.372837	91.223624	.010962	144
13	2.911970	278.104839	.003595	.343410	95.503993	.010470	156
14	3.161503	314.400548	.003180	.316305	99.446520	.010055	168
15	3.432419	353.806515	.002826	.291339	103.077868	.009701	180
16	3.726551	396.589262	.002521	.268344	106.422599	.009396	192
17	4.045887	443.038156	.002257	.247164	109.503335	.009132	204
18	4.392588	493.467354	.002026	.227656	112.340913	.008901	216
19	4.768998	548.217938	.001824	.209687	114.954525	.008699	228
20	5.177663	607.660217	.001645	.193137	117.361848	.008520	240
21	5.621349	672.196231	.001487	.177893	119.579165	.008362	252
22	6.103054	742.262475	.001347	.163852	121.621472	.008222	264
23	6.626038	818.332845	.001221	.150919	123.502582	.008096	276
24	7.193837	900.921848	.001109	.139007	125.235219	.007984	288
25	7.810293	990.588079	.001009	.128036	126.831103	.007884	300
26	8.479573	1087.938002	.000919	.117930	128.351025	.007794	312
27	9.206206	1193.630047	.000837	.108622	129.654927	.007712	324
28	9.995106	1308.379069	.000764	.100048	130.901968	.007639	336
29	10.851608	1432.961181	.000697	.092152	132.050583	.007572	348
30	11.781505	1568.219000	.000637	.084878	133.108539	.007512	360
31	12.791088	1715.067352	.000583	.078179	134.082991	.007458	372
32	13.887183	1874.499452	.000533	.072008	134.980533	.007408	384
33	15.077206	2047.593629	.000488	.066325	135.807230	.007363	396
34	16.369204	2235.520618	.000447	.061090	136.568680	.007322	408
35	17.771916	2439.551471	.000409	.056268	137.270029	.007284	420
36	19.294829	2661.066167	.000375	.051827	137.916021	.007250	432
37	20.948245	2901.562927	.000344	.047736	138.511027	.007219	444
38	22.743345	3162.668370	.000316	.043968	139.059068	.007191	456
39	24.692270	3446.148499	.000290	.040498	139.563854	.007165	468
40	26.808204	3753.920644	.000266	.037302	140.028797	.007141	480
41	29.105456	4088.066446	.000244	.034357	140.457045	.007119	492
42	31.599565	4450.845912	.000224	.031646	140.851490	.007099	504
43	34.307399	4844.712726	.000206	.029148	141.214802	.007081	516
44	37.247274	5272.330834	.000189	.026847	141.549440	.007064	528
45	40.439073	5736.592448	.000174	.024728	141.857664	.007049	540
46	43.904383	6240.637638	.000160	.022776	142.141561	.007035	552
47	47.666644	6787.875532	.000147	.020979	142.403050	.007022	564
48	51.751300	7382.007411	.000135	.019323	142.643900	.007010	576
49	56.185980	8027.051730	.000124	.017798	142.865741	.006999	588
50	61.000677	8727.371267	.000114	.016393	143.070072	.006989	600

8 ¼ % QUARTERLY COMPOUND INTEREST TABLE 8 ¼ %

EFFECTIVE RATE = 2-1/16% BASE = 1.020625

QUARTERS	1 AMOUNT OF I AT COMPOUND INTEREST $S^n = (1+i)^n$	2 ACCUMULATION OF I PER PERIOD $S_{\overline{n}\|} = \frac{S^n - 1}{i}$	3 SINKING FUND FACTOR $1/S_{\overline{n}\|} = \frac{i}{S^n - 1}$	4 PRES. VALUE REVERSION OF I $V^n = \frac{1}{S^n}$	5 PRESENT VALUE ORD. ANNUITY 1 PER PERIOD $a_{\overline{n}\|} = \frac{1 - V^n}{i}$	6 INSTALMENT TO AMORTIZE I $1/a_{\overline{n}\|} = \frac{i}{1 - V^n}$	n QUARTERS
1	1.020625	1.000000	1.000000	.979792	.979792	1.020625	1
2	1.041675	2.020625	.494896	.959992	1.939784	.515521	2
3	1.063160	3.062300	.326552	.940592	2.880376	.347177	3
YEARS							
1	1.085088	4.125460	.242397	.921585	3.801961	.263022	4
2	1.177415	8.601946	.116253	.849318	7.305789	.136878	8
3	1.277599	13.459326	.074298	.782718	10.534863	.094923	12
4	1.386306	18.730008	.053390	.721341	13.510727	.074015	16
5	1.504264	24.449160	.040901	.664777	16.253238	.061526	20
6	1.632258	30.654941	.032621	.612648	18.780694	.053246	24
7	1.771143	37.388758	.026746	.564607	21.109958	.047371	28
8	1.921845	44.695539	.022374	.520333	23.256572	.042999	32
9	2.085371	52.624036	.019003	.479531	25.234859	.039628	36
10	2.262810	61.227150	.016333	.441928	27.058017	.036958	40
11	2.455347	70.562283	.014172	.407274	28.738211	.034797	44
12	2.664267	80.691720	.012393	.375338	30.286652	.033018	48
13	2.890963	91.683047	.010907	.345906	31.713672	.031532	52
14	3.136948	103.609599	.009652	.318781	33.028791	.030277	56
15	3.403863	116.550954	.008580	.293784	34.240784	.029205	60
16	3.693490	130.593457	.007657	.270747	35.357739	.028282	64
17	4.007760	145.830804	.006857	.249516	36.387107	.027482	68
18	4.348771	162.364660	.006159	.229950	37.335757	.026784	72
19	4.718798	180.305343	.005546	.211918	38.210018	.026171	76
20	5.120309	199.772556	.005006	.195301	39.015723	.025631	80
21	5.555984	220.896187	.004527	.179986	39.758249	.025152	84
22	6.028729	243.817178	.004101	.165872	40.442549	.024726	88
23	6.541700	268.688462	.003722	.152865	41.073189	.024347	92
24	7.098317	295.675984	.003382	.140878	41.654378	.024007	96
25	7.702296	324.959810	.003077	.129831	42.189992	.023702	100
26	8.357666	356.735327	.002803	.119651	42.683606	.023428	104
27	9.068800	391.214547	.002556	.110268	43.138513	.023181	108
28	9.840443	428.627522	.002333	.101621	43.557748	.022958	112
29	10.677742	469.223878	.002131	.093653	43.944109	.022756	116
30	11.586286	513.274481	.001948	.086309	44.300173	.022573	120
31	12.572136	561.073245	.001782	.079541	44.628316	.022407	124
32	13.641869	612.939092	.001631	.073304	44.930728	.022256	128
33	14.802623	669.218081	.001494	.067556	45.209426	.022119	132
34	16.062143	730.285715	.001369	.062258	45.466269	.021994	136
35	17.428832	796.549448	.001255	.057376	45.702973	.021880	140
36	18.911810	868.451405	.001151	.052877	45.921115	.021776	144
37	20.520971	946.471328	.001057	.048731	46.122151	.021682	148
38	22.267052	1031.129780	.000970	.044909	46.307423	.021595	152
39	24.161702	1122.991619	.000890	.041388	46.478167	.021515	156
40	26.217564	1222.669763	.000818	.038142	46.635521	.021443	160
41	28.448354	1330.829283	.000751	.035151	46.780537	.021376	164
42	30.868957	1448.191839	.000691	.032395	46.914182	.021316	168
43	33.495523	1575.540496	.000635	.029855	47.037346	.021260	172
44	36.345577	1713.724946	.000584	.027514	47.150853	.021209	176
45	39.438136	1863.667183	.000537	.025356	47.255459	.021162	180
46	42.793833	2026.367647	.000493	.023368	47.351862	.021118	184
47	46.435058	2202.911906	.000454	.021535	47.440705	.021079	188
48	50.386107	2394.477897	.000418	.019847	47.522582	.021043	192
49	54.673340	2602.343781	.000384	.018290	47.598039	.021009	196
50	59.325365	2827.896479	.000354	.016856	47.667578	.020979	200
51	64.373219	3072.640919	.000325	.015534	47.731665	.020950	204
52	69.850583	3338.210080	.000300	.014316	47.790726	.020925	208
53	75.794003	3626.375890	.000276	.013194	47.845156	.020901	212
54	82.243134	3939.061042	.000254	.012159	47.895318	.020879	216
55	89.241006	4278.351829	.000234	.011206	47.941546	.020859	220
56	96.834311	4646.512062	.000215	.010327	47.984149	.020840	224
57	105.073712	5045.998172	.000198	.009517	48.023412	.020823	228
58	114.014184	5479.475602	.000182	.008771	48.059596	.020807	232
59	123.715380	5949.836596	.000168	.008083	48.092942	.020793	236
60	134.242027	6460.219491	.000155	.007449	48.123674	.020780	240

8 ¼ % SEMI-ANNUAL COMPOUND INTEREST TABLE 8 ¼ %

EFFECTIVE RATE = 4-1/8% BASE = 1.04125

HALF YEARS	1 AMOUNT OF I AT COMPOUND INTEREST $s^n = (1+i)^n$	2 ACCUMULATION OF I PER PERIOD $s_{\overline{n}\vert} = \frac{s^n - 1}{i}$	3 SINKING FUND FACTOR $1/s_{\overline{n}\vert} = \frac{i}{s^n - 1}$	4 PRES. VALUE REVERSION OF I $V^n = \frac{1}{s^n}$	5 PRESENT VALUE ORD. ANNUITY 1 PER PERIOD $a_{\overline{n}\vert} = \frac{1 - V^n}{i}$	6 INSTALMENT TO AMORTIZE I $1/a_{\overline{n}\vert} = \frac{i}{1 - V^n}$	n HALF YEARS
1	1.041250	1.000000	1.000000	.960384	.960384	1.041250	1
YEARS							
1	1.084202	2.041250	.489896	.922338	1.882722	.531146	2
2	1.175493	4.254376	.235052	.850707	3.619227	.276302	4
3	1.274471	6.653852	.150289	.784639	5.220872	.191539	6
4	1.381784	9.255366	.108045	.723702	6.698129	.149295	8
5	1.498132	12.075933	.082809	.667498	8.060659	.124059	10
6	1.624277	15.133995	.066076	.615658	9.317372	.107326	12
7	1.761044	18.449551	.054202	.567845	10.476485	.095452	14
8	1.909327	22.044282	.045363	.523745	11.545579	.086613	16
9	2.070095	25.941695	.038548	.483070	12.531645	.079798	18
10	2.244400	30.167276	.033149	.445553	13.441131	.074399	20
11	2.433382	34.748658	.028778	.410951	14.279984	.070028	22
12	2.638277	39.715799	.025179	.379035	15.053690	.066429	24
13	2.860424	45.101182	.022172	.349599	15.767308	.063422	26
14	3.101276	50.940022	.019631	.322448	16.425505	.060881	28
15	3.362408	57.270501	.017461	.297406	17.032584	.058711	30
16	3.645528	64.134017	.015592	.274309	17.592517	.056842	32
17	3.952487	71.575451	.013971	.253005	18.108964	.055221	34
18	4.285293	79.643466	.012556	.233356	18.585302	.053806	36
19	4.646121	88.390820	.011313	.215233	19.024647	.052563	38
20	5.037332	97.874716	.010217	.198518	19.429872	.051467	40
21	5.461483	108.157170	.009246	.183100	19.803626	.050496	42
22	5.921349	119.305422	.008382	.168880	20.148353	.049632	44
23	6.419935	131.392375	.007611	.155765	20.466308	.048861	46
24	6.960504	144.497069	.006921	.143668	20.759570	.048171	48
25	7.546589	158.705198	.006301	.132510	21.030056	.047551	50
26	8.182024	174.109673	.005744	.122219	21.279536	.046994	52
27	8.870963	190.811230	.005241	.112727	21.509640	.046491	54
28	9.617912	208.919083	.004787	.103973	21.721875	.046037	56
29	10.427755	228.551647	.004375	.095898	21.917626	.045625	58
30	11.305789	249.837302	.004003	.088450	22.098175	.045253	60
31	12.257754	272.915244	.003664	.081581	22.264703	.044914	62
32	13.289876	297.936384	.003356	.075245	22.418297	.044606	64
33	14.408904	325.064343	.003076	.069402	22.559963	.044326	66
34	15.622156	354.476518	.002821	.064012	22.690627	.044071	68
35	16.937566	386.365245	.002588	.059040	22.811143	.043838	70
36	18.363736	420.939052	.002376	.054455	22.922299	.043626	72
37	19.909991	458.424028	.002181	.050226	23.024823	.043431	74
38	21.586444	499.065298	.002004	.046325	23.119385	.043254	76
39	23.404056	543.128626	.001841	.042728	23.206603	.043091	78
40	25.374714	590.902154	.001692	.039409	23.287047	.042942	80
41	27.511304	642.698289	.001556	.036349	23.361244	.042806	82
42	29.827799	698.855739	.001431	.033526	23.429678	.042681	84
43	32.339347	759.741735	.001316	.030922	23.492798	.042566	86
44	35.062370	825.754426	.001211	.028521	23.551016	.042461	88
45	38.014676	897.325489	.001114	.026306	23.604712	.042364	90
46	41.215572	974.922947	.001026	.024263	23.654238	.042276	92
47	44.685987	1059.054232	.000944	.022378	23.699918	.042194	94
48	48.448617	1150.269503	.000869	.020640	23.742050	.042119	96
49	52.528066	1249.165242	.000801	.019037	23.780911	.042051	98
50	56.951012	1356.388158	.000737	.017559	23.816753	.041987	100
51	61.746376	1472.639410	.000679	.016195	23.849811	.041929	102
52	66.945517	1598.679199	.000626	.014938	23.880303	.041876	104
53	72.582434	1735.331736	.000576	.013777	23.908426	.041826	106
54	78.693988	1883.490629	.000531	.012707	23.934365	.041781	108
55	85.320145	2044.124733	.000489	.011721	23.958289	.041739	110
56	92.504235	2218.284480	.000451	.010810	23.980356	.041701	112
57	100.293236	2407.108749	.000415	.009971	24.000709	.041665	114
58	108.738083	2611.832318	.000383	.009196	24.019481	.041633	116
59	117.894000	2833.793930	.000353	.008482	24.036795	.041603	118
60	127.820859	3074.445057	.000325	.007823	24.052765	.041575	120

8 ¼ % ANNUAL COMPOUND INTEREST TABLE 8 ¼ %

EFFECTIVE RATE = 8¼% BASE = 1.0825

YEARS	1 AMOUNT OF I AT COMPOUND INTEREST $S^n = (1+i)^n$	2 ACCUMULATION OF I PER PERIOD $S_{\overline{n}\rvert} = \frac{S^n - 1}{i}$	3 SINKING FUND FACTOR $1/S_{\overline{n}\rvert} = \frac{i}{S^n - 1}$	4 PRES. VALUE REVERSION OF I $V^n = \frac{1}{S^n}$	5 PRESENT VALUE ORD. ANNUITY 1 PER PERIOD $a_{\overline{n}\rvert} = \frac{1 - V^n}{i}$	6 INSTALMENT TO AMORTIZE I $1/a_{\overline{n}\rvert} = \frac{i}{1 - V^n}$	n YEARS
1	1.082500	1.000000	1.000000	.923788	.923788	1.082500	1
2	1.171806	2.082500	.480192	.853383	1.777171	.562692	2
3	1.268480	3.254306	.307285	.788345	2.565516	.389785	3
4	1.373130	4.522787	.221103	.728263	3.293779	.303603	4
5	1.486413	5.895916	.169609	.672760	3.966540	.252109	5
6	1.609042	7.382330	.135459	.621488	4.588027	.217959	6
7	1.741788	8.991372	.111218	.574123	5.162150	.193718	7
8	1.885486	10.733160	.093169	.530367	5.692517	.175669	8
9	2.041038	12.618646	.079248	.489947	6.182464	.161748	9
10	2.209424	14.659684	.068214	.452607	6.635071	.150714	10
11	2.391701	16.869108	.059280	.418112	7.053183	.141780	11
12	2.589017	19.260809	.051919	.386247	7.439430	.134419	12
13	2.802611	21.849826	.045767	.356810	7.796240	.128267	13
14	3.033826	24.652436	.040564	.329617	8.125857	.123064	14
15	3.284117	27.686263	.036119	.304496	8.430353	.118619	15
16	3.555056	30.970379	.032289	.281289	8.711642	.114789	16
17	3.848348	34.525435	.028964	.259852	8.971494	.111464	17
18	4.165837	38.373784	.026059	.240048	9.211542	.108559	18
19	4.509519	42.539621	.023507	.221753	9.433295	.106007	19
20	4.881554	47.049140	.021254	.204853	9.638148	.103754	20
21	5.284282	51.930694	.019256	.189240	9.827388	.101756	21
22	5.720236	57.214976	.017478	.174818	10.002206	.099978	22
23	6.192155	62.935212	.015889	.161495	10.163701	.098389	23
24	6.703008	69.127367	.014466	.149187	10.312888	.096966	24
25	7.256006	75.830374	.013187	.137817	10.450705	.095687	25
26	7.854626	83.086380	.012036	.127314	10.578018	.094536	26
27	8.502633	90.941007	.010996	.117611	10.695629	.093496	27
28	9.204100	99.443640	.010056	.108647	10.804276	.092556	28
29	9.963439	108.647740	.009204	.100367	10.904643	.091704	29
30	10.785422	118.611178	.008431	.092718	10.997361	.090931	30
31	11.675220	129.396601	.007728	.085651	11.083012	.090228	31
32	12.638425	141.071820	.007089	.079124	11.162136	.089589	32
33	13.681095	153.710245	.006506	.073094	11.235230	.089006	33
34	14.809786	167.391341	.005974	.067523	11.302752	.088474	34
35	16.031593	182.201126	.005488	.062377	11.365129	.087988	35
36	17.354199	198.232719	.005045	.057623	11.422752	.087545	36
37	18.785921	215.586918	.004639	.053231	11.475984	.087139	37
38	20.335759	234.372839	.004267	.049174	11.525158	.086767	38
39	22.013459	254.708598	.003926	.045427	11.570585	.086426	39
40	23.829570	276.722058	.003614	.041965	11.612549	.086114	40
41	25.795509	300.551627	.003327	.038766	11.651316	.085827	41
42	27.923639	326.347137	.003064	.035812	11.687128	.085564	42
43	30.227339	354.270775	.002823	.033083	11.720210	.085323	43
44	32.721094	384.498114	.002601	.030561	11.750772	.085101	44
45	35.420585	417.219209	.002397	.028232	11.779004	.084897	45
46	38.342783	452.639793	.002209	.026081	11.805085	.084709	46
47	41.506063	490.982576	.002037	.024093	11.829177	.084537	47
48	44.930313	532.488639	.001878	.022257	11.851434	.084378	48
49	48.637064	577.418952	.001732	.020560	11.871995	.084232	49
50	52.649621	626.056015	.001597	.018993	11.890988	.084097	50
51	56.993215	678.705636	.001473	.017546	11.908534	.083973	51
52	61.695155	735.698851	.001359	.016209	11.924743	.083859	52
53	66.785006	797.394007	.001254	.014973	11.939716	.083754	53
54	72.294769	864.179012	.001157	.013832	11.953548	.083657	54
55	78.259087	936.473781	.001068	.012778	11.966326	.083568	55
56	84.715462	1014.732868	.000985	.011804	11.978131	.083485	56
57	91.704487	1099.448329	.000910	.010905	11.989035	.083410	57
58	99.270107	1191.152816	.000840	.010074	11.999109	.083340	58
59	107.459891	1290.422924	.000775	.009306	12.008415	.083275	59
60	116.325332	1397.882815	.000715	.008597	12.017011	.083215	60

8 ½ % MONTHLY COMPOUND INTEREST TABLE 8 ½ %

EFFECTIVE RATE = 17/24% BASE = 1.00708333+

MONTHS	1 AMOUNT OF I AT COMPOUND INTEREST $S^n = (1+i)^n$	2 ACCUMULATION OF I PER PERIOD $S_{\overline{n}\vert} = \frac{S^n - 1}{i}$	3 SINKING FUND FACTOR $1/S_{\overline{n}\vert} = \frac{i}{S^n - 1}$	4 PRES. VALUE REVERSION OF I $V^n = \frac{1}{S^n}$	5 PRESENT VALUE ORD. ANNUITY 1 PER PERIOD $a_{\overline{n}\vert} = \frac{1 - V^n}{i}$	6 INSTALMENT TO AMORTIZE I $1/a_{\overline{n}\vert} = \frac{i}{1 - V^n}$	n MONTHS
1	1.007083	1.000000	1.000000	.992966	.992966	1.007083	1
2	1.014217	2.007083	.498235	.985982	1.978949	.505318	2
3	1.021401	3.021300	.330983	.979048	2.957996	.338066	3
4	1.028636	4.042701	.247359	.972161	3.930158	.254442	4
5	1.035922	5.071337	.197187	.965324	4.895482	.204270	5
6	1.043260	6.107259	.163740	.958534	5.854016	.170823	6
7	1.050650	7.150519	.139850	.951792	6.805808	.146933	7
8	1.058092	8.201168	.121934	.945098	7.750906	.129017	8
9	1.065586	9.259260	.108000	.938450	8.689356	.115083	9
10	1.073134	10.324846	.096854	.931850	9.621206	.103937	10
11	1.080736	11.397980	.087735	.925296	10.546501	.094818	11
YEARS							
1	1.088391	12.478716	.080136	.918788	11.465289	.087219	12
2	1.184595	26.060437	.038372	.844171	21.999453	.045455	24
3	1.289302	40.842659	.024484	.775613	31.678112	.031567	36
4	1.403265	56.931495	.017565	.712624	40.570744	.024648	48
5	1.527301	74.442437	.013433	.654750	48.741183	.020516	60
6	1.662300	93.501188	.010695	.601576	56.248080	.017778	72
7	1.809232	114.244559	.008753	.552721	63.145324	.015836	84
8	1.969152	136.821455	.007309	.507833	69.482425	.014392	96
9	2.143207	161.393943	.006196	.466590	75.304875	.013279	108
10	2.332647	188.138416	.005315	.428698	80.654470	.012398	120
11	2.538832	217.246857	.004603	.393882	85.569611	.011686	132
12	2.753242	248.928219	.004017	.361894	90.085581	.011100	144
13	3.007487	283.409926	.003528	.332504	94.234798	.010611	156
14	3.273321	320.939502	.003116	.305500	98.047047	.010199	168
15	3.562653	361.786352	.002764	.280690	101.549693	.009847	180
16	3.877559	406.243691	.002462	.257894	104.767882	.009545	192
17	4.220300	454.630655	.002200	.236950	107.724713	.009283	204
18	4.593337	507.294586	.001971	.217707	110.441412	.009054	216
19	4.999346	564.613530	.001771	.200026	112.937482	.008854	228
20	5.441243	626.998947	.001595	.183782	115.230840	.008678	240
21	5.922199	694.898668	.001439	.168856	117.337949	.008522	252
22	6.445667	768.800107	.001301	.155143	119.273934	.008384	264
23	7.015406	849.233760	.001178	.142543	121.052693	.008261	276
24	7.635504	936.777018	.001067	.130967	122.686994	.008150	288
25	8.310413	1032.058303	.000969	.120331	124.188570	.008052	300
26	9.044978	1135.761586	.000880	.110559	125.568200	.007963	312
27	9.844472	1248.631298	.000801	.101580	126.835786	.007884	324
28	10.714633	1371.477665	.000729	.093330	128.000428	.007812	336
29	11.661710	1505.182533	.000664	.085751	129.070487	.007747	348
30	12.692499	1650.705697	.000606	.078787	130.053644	.007689	360
31	13.814400	1809.091784	.000553	.072388	130.956956	.007636	372
32	15.035467	1981.477761	.000505	.066509	131.786908	.007588	384
33	16.364466	2169.101090	.000461	.061108	132.549457	.007544	396
34	17.810936	2373.308616	.000421	.056145	133.250078	.007504	408
35	19.385261	2595.566229	.000385	.051586	133.893800	.007468	420
36	21.098741	2837.469395	.000352	.047396	134.485244	.007435	432
37	22.963678	3100.754600	.000323	.043547	135.028655	.007406	444
38	24.993459	3387.311823	.000295	.040010	135.527934	.007378	456
39	27.202653	3699.198098	.000270	.036761	135.986666	.007353	468
40	29.607120	4038.652283	.000248	.033776	136.408143	.007331	480
41	32.224120	4408.111132	.000227	.031033	136.795390	.007310	492
42	35.072440	4810.226782	.000208	.028512	137.151189	.007291	504
43	38.172524	5247.885799	.000191	.026197	137.478092	.007274	516
44	41.546628	5724.229893	.000175	.024069	137.778446	.007258	528
45	45.218972	6242.678472	.000160	.022115	138.054408	.007243	540
46	49.215918	6806.953191	.000147	.020319	138.307959	.007230	552
47	53.566158	7421.104663	.000135	.018669	138.540918	.007218	564
48	58.300919	8089.541540	.000124	.017152	138.754957	.007207	576
49	63.454190	8817.062157	.000113	.015759	138.951614	.007196	588
50	69.062963	9608.888981	.000104	.014480	139.132301	.007187	600

8 ½% QUARTERLY COMPOUND INTEREST TABLE 8 ½%

EFFECTIVE RATE = 2-1/8% BASE = 1.02125

QUARTERS	1 AMOUNT OF I AT COMPOUND INTEREST $s^n = (1+i)^n$	2 ACCUMULATION OF I PER PERIOD $s_{\overline{n}\vert} = \frac{s^n - 1}{i}$	3 SINKING FUND FACTOR $1/s_{\overline{n}\vert} = \frac{i}{s^n - 1}$	4 PRES. VALUE REVERSION OF I $v^n = \frac{1}{s^n}$	5 PRESENT VALUE ORD. ANNUITY 1 PER PERIOD $a_{\overline{n}\vert} = \frac{1 - v^n}{i}$	6 INSTALMENT TO AMORTIZE I $1/a_{\overline{n}\vert} = \frac{i}{1 - v^n}$	n QUARTERS
1	1.021250	1.000000	1.000000	.979192	.979192	1.021250	1
2	1.042952	2.021250	.494743	.958817	1.938009	.515993	2
3	1.065114	3.064202	.326349	.938866	2.876876	.347599	3
YEARS							
1	1.087748	4.129316	.242171	.919331	3.796206	.263421	4
2	1.183196	8.620971	.115996	.845169	7.286175	.137246	8
3	1.287019	13.506759	.074037	.776990	10.494610	.095287	12
4	1.399952	18.821266	.053131	.714310	13.444223	.074381	16
5	1.522795	24.602109	.040647	.656687	16.155892	.061897	20
6	1.656417	30.890210	.032373	.603713	18.648813	.053623	24
7	1.801764	37.730079	.026504	.555012	20.940631	.047754	28
8	1.959865	45.170132	.022139	.510239	23.047570	.043389	32
9	2.131839	53.263035	.018775	.469078	24.984543	.040025	36
10	2.318904	62.066074	.016112	.431238	26.765261	.037362	40
11	2.522383	71.641561	.013958	.396450	28.402331	.035208	44
12	2.743717	82.057278	.012187	.364469	29.907339	.033437	48
13	2.984473	93.386952	.010708	.335068	31.290938	.031958	52
14	3.246354	105.710783	.009460	.308038	32.562924	.030710	56
15	3.531215	119.116005	.008395	.283189	33.732299	.029645	60
16	3.841072	133.697507	.007480	.260344	34.807342	.028730	64
17	4.178118	149.558507	.006686	.239342	35.795661	.027936	68
18	4.544740	166.811276	.005995	.220035	36.704254	.027245	72
19	4.943531	185.577942	.005389	.202285	37.539551	.026639	76
20	5.377316	205.991344	.004855	.185966	38.307465	.026105	80
21	5.849165	228.195980	.004382	.170965	39.013431	.025632	84
22	6.362417	252.349028	.003963	.157173	39.662448	.025213	88
23	6.920706	278.621457	.003589	.144494	40.259109	.024839	92
24	7.527984	307.199238	.003255	.132838	40.807638	.024505	96
25	8.188549	338.284661	.002956	.122122	41.311917	.024206	100
26	8.907078	372.097766	.002687	.112270	41.775517	.023937	104
27	9.688655	408.877902	.002446	.103213	42.201718	.023696	108
28	10.538815	448.885420	.002228	.094887	42.593538	.023478	112
29	11.463575	492.403517	.002031	.087233	42.953750	.023281	116
30	12.469480	539.740238	.001853	.080196	43.284903	.023103	120
31	13.563652	591.230659	.001691	.073726	43.589343	.022941	124
32	14.753834	647.239261	.001545	.067779	43.869224	.022795	128
33	16.048453	708.162502	.001412	.062311	44.126527	.022662	132
34	17.456672	774.431634	.001291	.057285	44.363074	.022541	136
35	18.988460	846.515747	.001181	.052664	44.580538	.022431	140
36	20.654658	924.925095	.001081	.048415	44.780460	.022331	144
37	22.467062	1010.214702	.000990	.044510	44.964254	.022240	148
38	24.438501	1102.988299	.000907	.040919	45.133222	.022157	152
39	26.582930	1203.902590	.000831	.037618	45.288559	.022081	156
40	28.915528	1313.671904	.000761	.034583	45.431365	.022011	160
41	31.452807	1433.073252	.000698	.031794	45.562651	.021948	164
42	34.212726	1562.951825	.000640	.029229	45.683346	.021890	168
43	37.214823	1704.226978	.000587	.026871	45.794305	.021837	172
44	40.480348	1857.898737	.000538	.024703	45.896313	.021788	176
45	44.032416	2025.054880	.000494	.022711	45.990092	.021744	180
46	47.896171	2206.878634	.000453	.020878	46.076306	.021703	184
47	52.098962	2404.657052	.000416	.019194	46.155565	.021666	188
48	56.670540	2619.790123	.000382	.017646	46.228431	.021632	192
49	61.643264	2853.800682	.000350	.016222	46.295418	.021600	196
50	67.052335	3108.345191	.000322	.014914	46.357001	.021572	200
51	72.936041	3385.225462	.000295	.013711	46.413617	.021545	204
52	79.336030	3686.401412	.000271	.012605	46.465665	.021521	208
53	86.297605	4014.004938	.000249	.011588	46.513515	.021499	212
54	93.870044	4370.355005	.000229	.010653	46.557505	.021479	216
55	102.106949	4757.974065	.000210	.009794	46.597946	.021460	220
56	111.066626	5179.605906	.000193	.009004	46.635125	.021443	224
57	120.812496	5638.235083	.000177	.008277	46.669304	.021427	228
58	131.413546	6137.108035	.000163	.007610	46.700726	.021413	232
59	142.944817	6679.756072	.000150	.006996	46.729614	.021400	236
60	155.487933	7270.020368	.000138	.006431	46.756171	.021388	240

8 ½% SEMI-ANNUAL COMPOUND INTEREST TABLE 8 ½%

EFFECTIVE RATE = 4¼% BASE = 1.0425

HALF YEARS	1 AMOUNT OF I AT COMPOUND INTEREST $S^n = (1+i)^n$	2 ACCUMULATION OF I PER PERIOD $S_{\overline{n}\rvert} = \frac{S^n - 1}{i}$	3 SINKING FUND FACTOR $1/S_{\overline{n}\rvert} = \frac{i}{S^n - 1}$	4 PRES. VALUE REVERSION OF I $V^n = \frac{1}{S^n}$	5 PRESENT VALUE ORD. ANNUITY 1 PER PERIOD $a_{\overline{n}\rvert} = \frac{1-V^n}{i}$	6 INSTALMENT TO AMORTIZE I $1/a_{\overline{n}\rvert} = \frac{i}{1-V^n}$	n HALF YEARS
1	1.042500	1.000000	1.000000	.959233	.959233	1.042500	1
YEARS							
1	1.086806	2.042500	.489596	.920127	1.879360	.532096	2
2	1.181148	4.262302	.234615	.846634	3.608610	.277115	4
3	1.283679	6.674796	.149817	.779011	5.199740	.192317	6
4	1.395110	9.296710	.107565	.716789	6.663782	.150065	8
5	1.516214	12.146223	.082330	.659537	8.010887	.124830	10
6	1.647831	15.243091	.065603	.606858	9.250395	.108103	12
7	1.790873	18.608786	.053738	.558387	10.390900	.096238	14
8	1.946332	22.266645	.044910	.513787	11.440309	.087410	16
9	2.115286	26.242029	.038107	.472749	12.405900	.080607	18
10	2.298906	30.562501	.032720	.434989	13.294366	.075220	20
11	2.498466	35.258018	.028362	.400246	14.111868	.070862	22
12	2.715348	40.361134	.024776	.368277	14.864073	.067276	24
13	2.951057	45.907233	.021783	.338862	15.556198	.064283	26
14	3.207228	51.934767	.019255	.311796	16.193041	.061755	28
15	3.485635	58.485530	.017098	.286892	16.779017	.059598	30
16	3.788210	65.604939	.015243	.263977	17.318190	.057743	32
17	4.117050	73.342358	.013635	.242892	17.814298	.056135	34
18	4.474436	81.751433	.012232	.223492	18.270780	.054732	36
19	4.862845	90.890468	.011002	.205641	18.690801	.053502	38
20	5.284970	100.822829	.009918	.189216	19.077275	.052418	40
21	5.743739	111.617381	.008959	.174103	19.432879	.051459	42
22	6.242331	123.348967	.008107	.160197	19.760081	.050607	44
23	6.784204	136.098928	.007348	.147401	20.061148	.049848	46
24	7.373116	149.955666	.006669	.135628	20.338168	.049169	48
25	8.013148	165.015255	.006060	.124795	20.593061	.048560	50
26	8.708740	181.382110	.005513	.114827	20.827596	.048013	52
27	9.464713	199.169711	.005021	.105656	21.043397	.047521	54
28	10.286309	218.501387	.004577	.097217	21.241962	.047077	56
29	11.179225	239.511173	.004175	.089452	21.424667	.046675	58
30	12.149651	262.344740	.003812	.082307	21.592779	.046312	60
31	13.204317	287.160403	.003482	.075733	21.747463	.045982	62
32	14.350534	314.130221	.003183	.069684	21.889793	.045683	64
33	15.596250	343.441187	.002912	.064118	22.020754	.045412	66
34	16.950102	375.296529	.002665	.058997	22.141254	.045165	68
35	18.421477	409.917113	.002440	.054284	22.252130	.044940	70
36	20.020577	447.542980	.002234	.049949	22.354150	.044734	72
37	21.758488	488.435008	.002047	.045959	22.448022	.044547	74
38	23.647261	532.876719	.001877	.042288	22.534395	044377	76
39	25.699991	581.176249	.001721	.038911	22.613870	.044221	78
40	27.930910	633.668480	.001578	.035803	22.686997	.044078	80
41	30.355488	690.717364	.001448	.032943	22.754283	.043948	82
42	32.990534	752.718449	.001329	.030312	22.816195	.043829	84
43	35.854319	820.101614	.001219	.027891	22.873161	.043719	86
44	38.966698	893.334060	.001119	.025663	22.925578	043619	88
45	42.349250	972.923540	.001028	.023613	22.973808	.043528	90
46	46.025430	1059.421884	.000944	.021727	23.018185	.043444	92
47	50.020725	1153.428825	.000867	.019992	23.059018	.043367	94
48	54.362837	1255.596156	.000796	.018395	23.096590	.043296	96
49	59.081871	1366.632250	.000732	.016926	23.131161	.043232	98
50	64.210546	1487.306970	.000672	.015574	23.162970	.043172	100
51	69.784423	1618.457011	.000618	.014330	23.192239	.043118	102
52	75.842147	1760.991695	.000568	.013185	23.219170	.043068	104
53	82.425719	1915.899280	.000522	.012132	23.243950	.043022	106
54	89.580787	2084.253812	.000480	.011163	23.266750	.042980	108
55	97.356959	2267.222570	.000441	.010271	23.287730	.042941	110
56	105.808152	2466.074159	.000406	.009451	23.307034	.042906	112
57	114.992961	2682.187309	.000373	.008696	23.324796	.042873	114
58	124.975068	2917.060431	.000343	.008002	23.341139	.042843	116
59	135.823685	3172.322008	.000315	.007362	23.356177	.042815	118
60	147.614030	3449.741886	.000290	.006774	23.370014	.042790	120

8½% ANNUAL COMPOUND INTEREST TABLE 8½%

EFFECTIVE RATE = 8½% BASE = 1.085

YEARS	1 AMOUNT OF 1 AT COMPOUND INTEREST $S^n = (1+i)^n$	2 ACCUMULATION OF 1 PER PERIOD $S_{\overline{n}\vert} = \frac{S^n - 1}{i}$	3 SINKING FUND FACTOR $1/S_{\overline{n}\vert} = \frac{i}{S^n - 1}$	4 PRES. VALUE REVERSION OF 1 $V^n = \frac{1}{S^n}$	5 PRESENT VALUE ORD. ANNUITY 1 PER PERIOD $a_{\overline{n}\vert} = \frac{1 - V^n}{i}$	6 INSTALMENT TO AMORTIZE 1 $1/a_{\overline{n}\vert} = \frac{i}{1 - V^n}$	n YEARS
1	1.085000	1.000000	1.000000	.921659	.921659	1.085000	1
2	1.177225	2.085000	.479616	.849455	1.771114	.564616	2
3	1.277289	3.262225	.306539	.782908	2.554022	.391539	3
4	1.385859	4.539514	.220288	.721574	3.275597	.305288	4
5	1.503657	5.925373	.168766	.665045	3.940642	.253766	5
6	1.631468	7.429030	.134607	.612945	4.553587	.219607	6
7	1.770142	9.060497	.110369	.564926	5.118514	.195369	7
8	1.920604	10.830639	.092331	.520669	5.639183	.177331	8
9	2.083856	12.751244	.078424	.479880	6.119063	.163424	9
10	2.260983	14.835099	.067408	.442285	6.561348	.152408	10
11	2.453167	17.096083	.058493	.407636	6.968984	.143493	11
12	2.661686	19.549250	.051153	.375702	7.344686	.136153	12
13	2.887930	22.210936	.045023	.346269	7.690955	.130023	13
14	3.133404	25.098866	.039842	.319142	8.010097	.124842	14
15	3.399743	28.232269	.035420	.294140	8.304237	.120420	15
16	3.688721	31.632012	.031614	.271097	8.575333	.116614	16
17	4.002262	35.320733	.028312	.249859	8.825192	.113312	17
18	4.342455	39.322995	.025430	.230285	9.055476	.110430	18
19	4.711563	43.665450	.022901	.212244	9.267720	.107901	19
20	5.112046	48.377013	.020671	.195616	9.463337	.105671	20
21	5.546570	53.489059	.018695	.180292	9.643628	.103695	21
22	6.018028	59.035629	.016939	.166167	9.809796	.101939	22
23	6.529561	65.053658	.015372	.153150	9.962945	.100372	23
24	7.084574	71.583219	.013970	.141152	10.104097	.098970	24
25	7.686762	78.667792	.012712	.130094	10.234191	.097712	25
26	8.340137	86.354555	.011580	.119902	10.354093	.096580	26
27	9.049049	94.694692	.010560	.110509	10.464602	.095560	27
28	9.818218	103.743741	.009639	.101851	10.566453	.094639	28
29	10.652766	113.561959	.008806	.093872	10.660326	.093806	29
30	11.558252	124.214725	.008051	.086518	10.746844	.093051	30
31	12.540703	135.772977	.007365	.079740	10.826584	.092365	31
32	13.606663	148.313680	.006742	.073493	10.900078	.091742	32
33	14.763229	161.920343	.006176	.067736	10.967813	.091176	33
34	16.018104	176.683572	.005660	.062429	11.030243	.090660	34
35	17.379642	192.701675	.005189	.057539	11.087781	.090189	35
36	18.856912	210.081318	.004760	.053031	11.140812	.089760	36
37	20.459750	228.938230	.004368	.048876	11.189689	.089368	37
38	22.198828	249.397979	.004010	.045047	11.234736	.089010	38
39	24.085729	271.596808	.003682	.041518	11.276255	.088682	39
40	26.133016	295.682536	.003382	.038266	11.314520	.088382	40
41	28.354322	321.815552	.003107	.035268	11.349788	.088107	41
42	30.764439	350.169874	.002856	.032505	11.382293	.087856	42
43	33.379417	380.934313	.002625	.029959	11.412252	.087625	43
44	36.216667	414.313730	.002414	.027612	11.439864	.087414	44
45	39.295084	450.530397	.002220	.025448	11.465312	.087220	45
46	42.635166	489.825480	.002042	.023455	11.488767	.087042	46
47	46.259155	532.460646	.001878	.021617	11.510384	.086878	47
48	50.191183	578.719801	.001728	.019924	11.530308	.086728	48
49	54.457434	628.910984	.001590	.018363	11.548671	.086590	49
50	59.086316	683.368418	.001463	.016924	11.565595	.086463	50
51	64.108652	742.454733	.001347	.015599	11.581194	.086347	51
52	69.557888	806.563386	.001240	.014377	11.595570	.086240	52
53	75.470308	876.121273	.001141	.013250	11.608821	.086141	53
54	81.885284	951.591582	.001051	.012212	11.621033	.086051	54
55	88.845534	1033.476866	.000968	.011255	11.632288	.085968	55
56	96.397404	1122.322400	.000891	.010374	11.642662	.085891	56
57	104.591183	1218.719804	.000821	.009561	11.652223	.085821	57
58	113.481434	1323.310987	.000756	.008812	11.661035	.085756	58
59	123.127356	1436.792421	.000696	.008122	11.669157	.085696	59
60	133.593181	1559.919777	.000641	.007485	11.676642	.085641	60

8 ¾ % MONTHLY COMPOUND INTEREST TABLE 8 ¾ %

EFFECTIVE RATE = 35/48%   BASE = 1.00729167

MONTHS	1 AMOUNT OF I AT COMPOUND INTEREST $S^n = (1+i)^n$	2 ACCUMULATION OF I PER PERIOD $S_{\overline{n}\rvert} = \frac{S^n - 1}{i}$	3 SINKING FUND FACTOR $1/S_{\overline{n}\rvert} = \frac{i}{S^n - 1}$	4 PRES. VALUE REVERSION OF I $V^n = \frac{1}{S^n}$	5 PRESENT VALUE ORD. ANNUITY 1 PER PERIOD $a_{\overline{n}\rvert} = \frac{1 - V^n}{i}$	6 INSTALMENT TO AMORTIZE I $1/a_{\overline{n}\rvert} = \frac{i}{1 - V^n}$	n MONTHS
1	1.007291	1.000000	1.000000	.992761	.992761	1.007291	1
2	1.014636	2.007291	.498183	.985574	1.978335	.505475	2
3	1.022034	3.021928	.330914	.978440	2.956775	.338206	3
4	1.029487	4.043963	.247282	.971357	3.928133	.254573	4
5	1.036993	5.073450	.197104	.964325	4.892459	.204396	5
6	1.044555	6.110444	.163654	.957345	5.849804	.170945	6
7	1.052171	7.154999	.139762	.950415	6.800219	.147054	7
8	1.059843	8.207171	.121844	.943535	7.743754	.129136	8
9	1.067571	9.267015	.107909	.936704	8.680459	.115201	9
10	1.075356	10.334587	.096762	.929924	9.610383	.104054	10
11	1.083197	11.409943	.087642	.923192	10.533576	.094934	11
YEARS							
1	1.091095	12.493141	.080043	.916509	11.450086	.087335	12
2	1.190490	26.124355	.038278	.839990	21.944202	.045570	24
3	1.298938	40.997316	.024391	.769859	31.562162	.031683	36
4	1.417266	57.225141	.017474	.705583	40.377116	.024766	48
5	1.546373	74.931254	.013345	.646674	48.456109	.020637	60
6	1.687241	94.250319	.010610	.592683	55.860584	.017901	72
7	1.840942	115.329271	.008670	.543199	62.646858	.015962	84
8	2.008644	138.328427	.007229	.497848	68.866545	.014520	96
9	2.191623	163.422710	.006119	.456282	74.566948	.013410	108
10	2.391271	190.802977	.005241	.418187	79.791424	.012532	120
11	2.609106	220.677472	.004531	.383272	84.579707	.011823	132
12	2.846785	253.273409	.003948	.351273	88.968216	.011239	144
13	3.106115	288.838700	.003462	.321945	92.990327	.010753	156
14	3.389069	327.643839	.003052	.295066	96.676631	.010343	168
15	3.697799	369.983966	.002702	.270431	100.055165	.009994	180
16	4.034653	416.181100	.002402	.247852	103.151624	.009694	192
17	4.402193	466.586601	.002143	.227159	105.989559	.009434	204
18	4.803215	521.583832	.001917	.208193	108.590555	.009208	216
19	5.240768	581.591081	.001719	.190811	110.974393	.009011	228
20	5.718180	647.064740	.001545	.174880	113.159203	.008837	240
21	6.239082	718.502775	.001391	.160279	115.161603	.008683	252
22	6.807437	796.448517	.001255	.146898	116.996823	.008547	264
23	7.427566	881.494791	.001134	.134633	118.678819	.008426	276
24	8.104186	974.288424	.001026	.123393	120.220386	.008318	288
25	8.842443	1075.535171	.000929	.113090	121.633246	.008221	300
26	9.647953	1186.005072	.000843	.103648	122.928147	.008134	312
27	10.526841	1306.538319	.000765	.094995	124.114936	.008057	324
28	11.485793	1438.051644	.000695	.087064	125.202640	.007987	336
29	12.532101	1581.545281	.000632	.079795	126.199531	.007923	348
30	13.673723	1738.110588	.000575	.073132	127.113191	.007867	360
31	14.919342	1908.938341	.000523	.067027	127.950570	.007815	372
32	16.278431	2095.327791	.000477	.061430	128.718036	.007768	384
33	17.761329	2298.696538	.000435	.056302	129.421427	.007726	396
34	19.379311	2520.591329	.000396	.051601	130.066090	.007688	408
35	21.144686	2762.699811	.000361	.047293	130.656930	.007653	420
36	23.070878	3026.863361	.000330	.043344	131.198442	.007622	432
37	25.172539	3315.091106	.000301	.039725	131.694743	.007593	444
38	27.465652	3629.575198	.000275	.036409	132.149607	.007567	456
39	29.967658	3972.707474	.000251	.033369	132.566494	.007543	468
40	32.697587	4347.097666	.000230	.030583	132.948576	.007521	480
41	35.676200	4755.593240	.000210	.028029	133.298757	.007501	492
42	38.926153	5201.301059	.000192	.025689	133.619701	.007483	504
43	42.472163	5687.610992	.000175	.023544	133.913851	.007467	516
44	46.341200	6218.221729	.000160	.021579	134.183440	.007452	528
45	50.562690	6797.168893	.000147	.019777	134.430523	.007438	540
46	55.168739	7428.855718	.000134	.018126	134.656977	.007426	552
47	60.194381	8118.086574	.000123	.016612	134.864524	.007414	564
48	65.677838	8870.103489	.000112	.015225	135.054741	.007404	576
49	71.660814	9690.625994	.000103	.013954	135.229079	.007394	588
50	78.188815	10585.894670	.000094	.012789	135.388861	.007386	600

8¾% QUARTERLY COMPOUND INTEREST TABLE 8¾%

EFFECTIVE RATE = 2-3/16% BASE = 1.021875

QUARTERS	1 AMOUNT OF I AT COMPOUND INTEREST $S^n = (1+i)^n$	2 ACCUMULATION OF I PER PERIOD $S_{\overline{n}\rvert} = \frac{S^n - 1}{i}$	3 SINKING FUND FACTOR $1/S_{\overline{n}\rvert} = \frac{i}{S^n - 1}$	4 PRES. VALUE REVERSION OF I $V^n = \frac{1}{S^n}$	5 PRESENT VALUE ORD. ANNUITY 1 PER PERIOD $a_{\overline{n}\rvert} = \frac{1 - V^n}{i}$	6 INSTALMENT TO AMORTIZE I $1/a_{\overline{n}\rvert} = \frac{i}{1 - V^n}$	n QUARTERS
1	1.021875	1.000000	1.000000	.978593	.978593	1.021875	1
2	1.044229	2.021875	.494590	.957645	1.936238	.516465	2
3	1.067071	3.066104	.326147	.937145	2.873383	.348022	3
YEARS							
1	1.090413	4.133175	.241945	.917084	3.790466	.263820	4
2	1.189001	8.640043	.115740	.841042	7.266641	.137615	8
3	1.296502	13.554391	.073777	.771306	10.454583	.095652	12
4	1.413723	18.913061	.052874	.707352	13.378192	.074749	16
5	1.541542	24.756226	.040394	.648701	16.059387	.062269	20
6	1.680918	31.127690	.032126	.594913	18.518266	.054001	24
7	1.832895	38.075218	.026264	.545585	20.773263	.048139	28
8	1.998613	45.650895	.021905	.500347	22.841284	.043780	32
9	2.179314	53.911513	.018549	.458860	24.737832	.040424	36
10	2.376353	62.918999	.015893	.420813	26.477125	.037768	40
11	2.591207	72.740881	.013747	.385921	28.072202	.035622	44
12	2.825486	83.450791	.011983	.353921	29.535021	.033858	48
13	3.080947	95.129018	.010512	.324575	30.876549	.032387	52
14	3.359506	107.863111	.009271	.297663	32.106841	.031146	56
15	3.663249	121.748534	.008214	.272982	33.235122	.030089	60
16	3.994455	136.889382	.007305	.250347	34.269850	.029180	64
17	4.355607	153.399163	.006519	.229589	35.218782	.028394	68
18	4.749411	171.401645	.005834	.210552	36.089032	.027709	72
19	5.178820	191.031790	.005235	.193094	36.887124	.027110	76
20	5.647054	212.436758	.004707	.177083	37.619041	.026582	80
21	6.157622	235.777018	.004241	.162400	38.290270	.026116	84
22	6.714353	261.227546	.003828	.148935	38.905843	.025703	88
23	7.321419	288.979137	.003460	.136586	39.470375	.025335	92
24	7.983371	319.239838	.003132	.125260	39.988098	.025007	96
25	8.705174	352.236505	.002839	.114874	40.462893	.024714	100
26	9.492236	388.216507	.002576	.105349	40.898320	.024451	104
27	10.350459	427.449575	.002339	.096614	41.297643	.024214	108
28	11.286278	470.229831	.002127	.088603	41.663855	.024002	112
29	12.306706	516.877986	.001935	.081257	41.999702	.023810	116
30	13.419395	567.743750	.001761	.074519	42.307702	.023636	120
31	14.632685	623.208449	.001605	.068340	42.590164	.023480	124
32	15.955673	683.687889	.001463	.062674	42.849205	.023338	128
33	17.398276	749.635468	.001334	.057477	43.086768	.023209	132
34	18.971310	821.545579	.001217	.052711	43.304632	.023092	136
35	20.686566	899.957313	.001111	.048341	43.504432	.022986	140
36	22.556905	985.458501	.001015	.044332	43.687665	.022890	144
37	24.596346	1078.690125	.000927	.040656	43.855705	.022802	148
38	26.820181	1180.351118	.000847	.037285	44.009812	.022722	152
39	29.245079	1291.203606	.000774	.034194	44.151141	.022649	156
40	31.889220	1412.078621	.000708	.031359	44.280752	.022583	160
41	34.772426	1543.882332	.000648	.028758	44.399615	.022523	164
42	37.916312	1687.602838	.000593	.026374	44.508623	.022468	168
43	41.344447	1844.317573	.000542	.024187	44.608592	.022417	172
44	45.082530	2015.201388	.000496	.022182	44.700272	.022371	176
45	49.158586	2201.535355	.000454	.020342	44.784351	.022329	180
46	53.603171	2404.716369	.000416	.018656	44.861458	.022291	184
47	58.449604	2626.267629	.000381	.017109	44.932171	.022256	188
48	63.734220	2867.850045	.000349	.015690	44.997021	.022224	192
49	69.496634	3131.274699	.000319	.014389	45.056494	.022194	196
50	75.780047	3418.516416	.000293	.013196	45.111036	.022168	200
51	82.631563	3731.728575	.000268	.012102	45.161055	.022143	204
52	90.102546	4073.259244	.000246	.011098	45.206927	.022121	208
53	98.249005	4445.668792	.000225	.010178	45.248996	.022100	212
54	107.132011	4851.749074	.000206	.009334	45.287576	.022081	216
55	116.818158	5294.544375	.000189	.008560	45.322957	.022064	220
56	127.380061	5777.374213	.000173	.007851	45.355405	.022048	224
57	138.896899	6303.858235	.000159	.007200	45.385162	.022034	228
58	151.455011	6877.943360	.000145	.006603	45.412452	.022020	232
59	165.148542	7503.933353	.000133	.006055	45.437479	.022008	236
60	180.080149	8186.521102	.000122	.005553	45.460431	.021997	240

8 ¾% SEMI-ANNUAL COMPOUND INTEREST TABLE 8 ¾ %

EFFECTIVE RATE = 4-3/8% BASE = 1.04375

HALF YEARS	1 AMOUNT OF I AT COMPOUND INTEREST $S^n = (1+i)^n$	2 ACCUMULATION OF I PER PERIOD $S_{\overline{n}\rvert} = \frac{S^n - 1}{i}$	3 SINKING FUND FACTOR $1/S_{\overline{n}\rvert} = \frac{i}{S^n - 1}$	4 PRES. VALUE REVERSION OF I $V^n = \frac{1}{S^n}$	5 PRESENT VALUE ORD. ANNUITY 1 PER PERIOD $a_{\overline{n}\rvert} = \frac{1 - V^n}{i}$	6 INSTALMENT TO AMORTIZE I $1/a_{\overline{n}\rvert} = \frac{i}{1 - V^n}$	n HALF YEARS
1	1.043750	1.000000	1.000000	.958084	.958084	1.043750	1
YEARS							
1	1.089414	2.043750	.489297	.917925	1.876008	.533047	2
2	1.186823	4.270240	.234179	.842586	3.598043	.277929	4
3	1.292942	6.695810	.149347	.773430	5.178741	.193097	6
4	1.408549	9.338259	.107086	.709951	6.629702	.150836	8
5	1.534493	12.216981	.081853	.651681	7.961575	.125603	10
6	1.671698	15.353101	.065133	.598194	9.184134	.108883	12
7	1.821171	18.769634	.053278	.549097	10.306352	.097028	14
8	1.984010	22.491653	.044461	.504030	11.336463	.088211	16
9	2.161408	26.546473	.037670	.462661	12.282027	.081420	18
10	2.354668	30.963851	.032296	.424688	13.149983	.076046	20
11	2.565209	35.776205	.027952	.389832	13.946702	.071702	22
12	2.794575	41.018850	.024379	.357836	14.678030	.068129	24
13	3.044449	46.730263	.021399	.328467	15.349333	.065149	26
14	3.316666	52.952355	.018885	.301508	15.965540	.062635	28
15	3.613222	59.730790	.016742	.276761	16.531171	.060492	30
16	3.936295	67.115313	.014900	.254046	17.050377	.058650	32
17	4.288255	75.160116	.513305	.233195	17.526970	.057055	34
18	4.671685	83.924237	.011916	.214056	17.964445	.055666	36
19	5.089400	93.471994	.010698	.196487	18.366015	.054448	38
20	5.544464	103.873455	.009627	.180360	18.734626	.053377	40
21	6.040217	115.204952	.008680	.165557	19.072983	.052430	42
22	6.580297	127.549645	.007840	.151969	19.383570	.051590	44
23	7.168668	140.998127	.007092	.139496	19.668665	.050842	46
24	7.809648	155.649093	.006425	.128047	19.930360	.050175	48
25	8.507940	171.610060	.005827	.117537	20.170577	.049577	50
26	9.268670	188.998163	.005291	.107890	20.391078	.049041	52
27	10.097419	207.941006	.004809	.099035	20.593481	.048559	54
28	11.000270	228.577607	.004375	.090907	20.779272	.048125	56
29	11.983849	251.059409	.003983	.083446	20.949814	.047733	58
30	13.055374	275.551401	.003629	.076597	21.106359	.047379	60
31	14.222708	302.233321	.003309	.070310	21.250055	.047059	62
32	15.494418	331.300980	.003018	.064539	21.381957	.046768	64
33	16.879837	362.967697	.002755	.059242	21.503034	.046505	66
34	18.389132	397.465863	.002516	.054380	21.614173	.046266	68
35	20.033378	435.048651	.002299	.049917	21.716190	.046049	70
36	21.824644	475.991868	.002101	.045820	21.809834	.045851	72
37	23.776074	520.595984	.001921	.042059	21.895792	.045671	74
38	25.901990	569.188336	.001757	.038607	21.974695	.045507	76
39	28.217992	622.125528	.001607	.035438	22.047123	.045357	78
40	30.741077	679.796049	.001471	.032530	22.113605	.045221	80
41	33.489762	742.623125	.001347	.029860	22.174632	.045097	82
42	36.484217	811.067826	.001233	.027409	22.230649	.044983	84
43	39.746419	885.632445	.001129	.025159	22.282069	.044879	86
44	43.300308	966.864190	.001034	.023095	22.329268	.044784	88
45	47.171965	1055.359195	.000948	.021199	22.372594	.044698	90
46	51.389802	1151.766898	.000868	.019459	22.412363	.044618	92
47	55.984773	1256.794805	.000796	.017862	22.448869	.044546	94
48	60.990599	1371.213685	.000729	.016396	22.482378	.044479	96
49	66.444016	1495.863221	.000669	.015050	22.513137	.044419	98
50	72.385045	1631.658178	.000613	.013815	22.541371	.044363	100
51	78.857286	1779.595115	.000562	.012681	22.567288	.044312	102
52	85.908237	1940.759694	.000515	.011640	22.591078	.044265	104
53	93.589641	2116.334652	.000473	.010685	22.612916	.044223	106
54	101.957871	2307.608482	.000433	.009808	22.632961	.044183	108
55	111.074339	2515.984882	.000397	.009003	22.651360	.044147	110
56	121.005947	2742.993063	.000365	.008264	22.668250	.044115	112
57	131.825580	2990.298967	.000334	.007586	22.683754	.044084	114
58	143.612640	3259.717495	.000307	.006963	22.697985	.044057	116
59	156.453630	3553.225829	.000281	.006392	22.711048	.044031	118
60	170.442785	3872.977936	.000258	.005867	22.723038	.044008	120

8¾% ANNUAL COMPOUND INTEREST TABLE 8¾%

EFFECTIVE RATE = 8¼%   BASE = 1.0875

YEARS	1 AMOUNT OF I AT COMPOUND INTEREST $S^n = (1+i)^n$	2 ACCUMULATION OF I PER PERIOD $S_{\overline{n}\rvert} = \frac{S^n - 1}{i}$	3 SINKING FUND FACTOR $1/S_{\overline{n}\rvert} = \frac{i}{S^n - 1}$	4 PRES. VALUE REVERSION OF I $V^n = \frac{1}{S^n}$	5 PRESENT VALUE ORD. ANNUITY 1 PER PERIOD $a_{\overline{n}\rvert} = \frac{1 - V^n}{i}$	6 INSTALMENT TO AMORTIZE I $1/a_{\overline{n}\rvert} = \frac{i}{1 - V^n}$	n YEARS
1	1.087500	1.000000	1.000000	.919540	.919540	1.087500	1
2	1.182656	2.087500	.479042	.845554	1.765094	.566542	2
3	1.286139	3.270156	.305796	.777521	2.542616	.393296	3
4	1.398676	4.556295	.219477	.714962	3.257578	.306977	4
5	1.521060	5.954971	.167927	.657436	3.915014	.255427	5
6	1.654153	7.476031	.133761	.604539	4.519553	.221261	6
7	1.798891	9.130183	.109527	.555898	5.075451	.197027	7
8	1.956294	10.929074	.091499	.511171	5.586622	.178999	8
9	2.127470	12.885368	.077607	.470042	6.056664	.165107	9
10	2.313623	15.012838	.066610	.432222	6.488886	.154110	10
11	2.516065	17.326461	.057715	.397446	6.886332	.145215	11
12	2.736221	19.842527	.050397	.365468	7.251800	.137897	12
13	2.975640	22.578748	.044289	.336062	7.587862	.131789	13
14	3.236009	25.554388	.039132	.309023	7.896884	.126632	14
15	3.519160	28.790397	.034734	.284159	8.181043	.122234	15
16	3.827086	32.309557	.030951	.261295	8.442338	.118451	16
17	4.161956	36.136643	.027673	.240272	8.682610	.115173	17
18	4.526127	40.298600	.024815	.220939	8.903549	.112315	18
19	4.922164	44.824727	.022309	.203163	9.106712	.109809	19
20	5.352853	49.746891	.020102	.186816	9.293528	.107602	20
21	5.821228	55.099744	.018149	.171785	9.465313	.105649	21
22	6.330585	60.920971	.016415	.157963	9.623277	.103915	22
23	6.884511	67.251556	.014870	.145254	9.768530	.102370	23
24	7.486906	74.136068	.013489	.133567	9.902097	.100989	24
25	8.142010	81.622973	.012251	.122820	10.024917	.099751	25
26	8.854436	89.764984	.011140	.112938	10.137854	.098640	26
27	9.629199	98.619420	.010140	.103851	10.241705	.097640	27
28	10.471754	108.248619	.009238	.095495	10.337200	.096738	28
29	11.388033	118.720373	.008423	.087811	10.425012	.095923	29
30	12.384486	130.108406	.007686	.080746	10.505758	.095186	30
31	13.468128	142.492891	.007018	.074249	10.580007	.094518	31
32	14.646589	155.961019	.006412	.068275	10.648283	.093912	32
33	15.928166	170.607608	.005861	.062782	10.711064	.093361	33
34	17.321880	186.535774	.005361	.057730	10.768795	.092861	34
35	18.837545	203.857654	.004905	.053085	10.821880	.092405	35
36	20.485830	222.695199	.004490	.048814	10.870695	.091990	36
37	22.278340	243.181029	.004112	.044887	10.915581	.091612	37
38	24.227695	265.459369	.003767	.041275	10.956856	.091267	38
39	26.347618	289.687064	.003452	.037954	10.994810	.090952	39
40	28.653035	316.034682	.003164	.034900	11.029711	.090664	40
41	31.160175	344.687717	.002901	.032092	11.061803	.090401	41
42	33.886691	375.847892	.002661	.029510	11.091313	.090161	42
43	36.851776	409.734582	.002441	.027136	11.118449	.089941	43
44	40.076306	446.586358	.002239	.024952	11.143401	.089739	44
45	43.582983	486.662665	.002055	.022945	11.166346	.089555	45
46	47.396494	530.245648	.001886	.021099	11.187444	.089386	46
47	51.543687	577.642142	.001731	.019401	11.206846	.089231	47
48	56.053760	629.185829	.001589	.017840	11.224686	.089089	48
49	60.958464	685.239590	.001459	.016405	11.241090	.088959	49
50	66.292330	746.198054	.001340	.015085	11.256175	.088840	50
51	72.092909	812.490383	.001231	.013871	11.270046	.088731	51
52	78.401038	884.583292	.001130	.012755	11.282801	.088630	52
53	85.261129	962.984330	.001038	.011729	11.294529	.088538	53
54	92.721478	1048.245459	.000954	.010785	11.305314	.088454	54
55	100.834607	1140.966936	.000876	.009917	11.315232	.088376	55
56	109.657635	1241.801543	.000805	.009119	11.324351	.088305	56
57	119.252678	1351.459178	.000740	.008386	11.332737	.088240	57
58	129.687287	1470.711856	.000680	.007711	11.340447	.088180	58
59	141.034925	1600.399144	.000625	.007090	11.347538	.088125	59
60	153.375481	1741.434070	.000574	.006520	11.354058	.088074	60

9% MONTHLY COMPOUND INTEREST TABLE 9%

EFFECTIVE RATE = 3/4% BASE = 1.0075

MONTHS	1 AMOUNT OF I AT COMPOUND INTEREST $S^n = (1+i)^n$	2 ACCUMULATION OF I PER PERIOD $S_{\overline{n}|} = \frac{S^n - 1}{i}$	3 SINKING FUND FACTOR $1/S_{\overline{n}|} = \frac{i}{S^n - 1}$	4 PRES. VALUE REVERSION OF I $V^n = \frac{1}{S^n}$	5 PRESENT VALUE ORD. ANNUITY 1 PER PERIOD $a_{\overline{n}|} = \frac{1 - V^n}{i}$	6 INSTALMENT TO AMORTIZE I $1/a_{\overline{n}|} = \frac{i}{1 - V^n}$	n MONTHS
1	1.007500	1.000000	1.000000	.992555	.992555	1.007500	1
2	1.015056	2.007500	.498132	.985167	1.977722	.505632	2
3	1.022669	3.022556	.330845	.977833	2.955556	.338345	3
4	1.030339	4.045225	.247205	.970554	3.926110	.254705	4
5	1.038066	5.075564	.197022	.963329	4.889439	.204522	5
6	1.045852	6.113631	.163568	.956158	5.845597	.171068	6
7	1.053696	7.159483	.139674	.949040	6.794637	.147174	7
8	1.061598	8.213179	.121755	.941975	7.736613	.129255	8
9	1.069560	9.274778	.107819	.934963	8.671576	.115319	9
10	1.077582	10.344339	.096671	.928003	9.599579	.104171	10
11	1.085664	11.421921	.087550	.921094	10.520674	.095050	11
YEARS							
1	1.093806	12.507586	.079951	.914238	11.434912	.087451	12
2	1.196413	26.188470	.038184	.835831	21.889146	.045684	24
3	1.308645	41.152716	.024299	.764148	31.446805	.031799	36
4	1.431405	57.520711	.017385	.698614	40.184781	.024885	48
5	1.565681	75.424136	.013258	.638699	48.173373	.020758	60
6	1.712552	95.007027	.010525	.583923	55.476848	.018025	72
7	1.873201	116.426928	.008589	.533845	62.153964	.016089	84
8	2.048921	139.856163	.007150	.488061	68.258438	.014650	96
9	2.241124	165.483222	.006042	.446204	73.839381	.013542	108
10	2.451357	193.514276	.005167	.407937	78.941692	.012667	120
11	2.681311	224.174837	.004460	.372951	83.606419	.011960	132
12	2.932836	257.711569	.003880	.340966	87.871091	.011380	144
13	3.207957	294.394278	.003396	.311724	91.770017	.010896	156
14	3.508885	334.518079	.002989	.284990	95.334563	.010489	168
15	3.838043	378.405768	.002642	.260549	98.593409	.010142	180
16	4.198078	426.410426	.002345	.238204	101.572769	.009845	192
17	4.591886	478.918251	.002088	.217775	104.296613	.009588	204
18	5.022637	536.351673	.001864	.199098	106.786855	.009364	216
19	5.493795	599.172746	.001668	.182023	109.063530	.009168	228
20	6.009151	667.886868	.001497	.166412	111.144953	.008997	240
21	6.572851	743.046850	.001345	.152140	113.047869	.008845	252
22	7.189430	825.257356	.001211	.139093	114.787589	.008711	264
23	7.863848	915.179775	.001092	.127164	116.378106	.008592	276
24	8.601531	1013.537537	.000986	.116258	117.832217	.008486	288
25	9.408414	1121.121935	.000891	.106287	119.161622	.008391	300
26	10.290988	1238.798492	.000807	.097172	120.377014	.008307	312
27	11.256354	1367.513922	.000731	.088838	121.488171	.008231	324
28	12.312278	1508.303747	.000662	.081219	122.504035	.008162	336
29	13.467254	1662.300628	.000601	.074254	123.432775	.008101	348
30	14.730576	1830.743479	.000546	.067886	124.281865	.008046	360
31	16.112405	2014.987432	.000496	.062063	125.058136	.007996	372
32	17.623860	2216.514738	.000451	.056741	125.767833	.007951	384
33	19.277100	2436.946695	.000410	.051875	126.416663	.007910	396
34	21.085425	2678.056691	.000373	.047426	127.009849	.007873	408
35	23.063383	2941.784467	.000339	.043358	127.552164	.007839	420
36	25.226887	3230.251727	.000309	.039640	128.047967	.007809	432
37	27.593344	3545.779207	.000282	.036240	128.501249	.007782	444
38	30.181790	3890.905340	.000257	.033132	128.915658	.007757	456
39	33.013050	4268.406685	.000234	.030291	129.294525	.007734	468
40	36.109901	4681.320260	.000213	.027693	129.640901	.007713	480
41	39.497259	5132.967977	.000194	.025318	129.957571	.007694	492
42	43.202375	5626.983364	.000177	.023146	130.247083	.007677	504
43	47.255056	6167.340803	.000162	.021161	130.511766	.007662	516
44	51.687906	6758.387497	.000147	.019346	130.753748	.007647	528
45	56.536588	7404.878447	.000135	.017687	130.974978	.007635	540
46	61.840110	8112.014707	.000123	.016170	131.177236	.007623	552
47	67.641139	8885.485227	.000112	.014783	131.362146	.007612	564
48	73.986344	9731.512616	.000102	.013516	131.531199	.007602	576
49	80.926774	10656.903210	.000093	.012356	131.685753	.007593	588
50	88.518263	11669.101820	.000085	.011297	131.827052	.007585	600

9% QUARTERLY COMPOUND INTEREST TABLE 9%

EFFECTIVE RATE = 2¼% BASE = 1.0225

	1 AMOUNT OF I AT COMPOUND INTEREST $S^n = (1+i)^n$	2 ACCUMULATION OF I PER PERIOD $S_{\overline{n}\rvert} = \frac{S^n - 1}{i}$	3 SINKING FUND FACTOR $1/S_{\overline{n}\rvert} = \frac{i}{S^n - 1}$	4 PRES. VALUE REVERSION OF I $V^n = \frac{1}{S^n}$	5 PRESENT VALUE ORD. ANNUITY 1 PER PERIOD $a_{\overline{n}\rvert} = \frac{1 - V^n}{i}$	6 INSTALMENT TO AMORTIZE I $1/a_{\overline{n}\rvert} = \frac{i}{1 - V^n}$	n
QUARTERS							QUARTERS
1	1.022500	1.000000	1.000000	.977995	.977995	1.022500	1
2	1.045506	2.022500	.494438	.956474	1.934470	.516938	2
3	1.069030	3.068006	.325945	.935427	2.869897	.348445	3
YEARS							
1	1.093083	4.137036	.241719	.914843	3.784740	.264219	4
2	1.194831	8.659162	.115485	.836938	7.247185	.137985	8
3	1.306050	13.602222	.073517	.765667	10.414779	.096017	12
4	1.427621	19.005398	.052617	.700466	13.312631	.075117	16
5	1.560509	24.911520	.040142	.640816	15.963712	.062642	20
6	1.705767	31.367403	.031880	.586247	18.389036	.054380	24
7	1.864545	38.424222	.026025	.536324	20.607828	.048525	28
8	2.038103	46.137912	.021674	.490652	22.637674	.044174	32
9	2.227816	54.569619	.018325	.448870	24.494666	.040825	36
10	2.435189	63.786176	.015677	.410646	26.193522	.038177	40
11	2.661864	73.860642	.013539	.375677	27.747710	.036039	44
12	2.909640	84.872872	.011782	.343685	29.169548	.034282	48
13	3.180479	96.910157	.010319	.314418	30.470307	.032819	52
14	3.476528	110.067912	.009085	.287643	31.660298	.031585	56
15	3.800135	124.450435	.008035	.263149	32.748953	.030535	60
16	4.153864	140.171731	.007134	.240740	33.744902	.029634	64
17	4.540519	157.356417	.006355	.220239	34.656039	.028855	68
18	4.963166	176.140711	.005677	.201484	35.489587	.028177	72
19	5.425154	196.673510	.005085	.184327	36.252153	.027585	76
20	5.930145	219.117569	.004564	.168630	36.949781	.027064	80
21	6.482143	243.650796	.004104	.154270	37.588001	.026604	84
22	7.085522	270.467657	.003697	.141133	38.171873	.026197	88
23	7.745066	299.780721	.003336	.129114	38.706024	.025836	92
24	8.466003	331.822342	.003014	.118119	39.194689	.025514	96
25	9.254046	366.846503	.002726	.108061	39.641741	.025226	100
26	10.115444	405.130829	.002468	.098859	40.050723	.024968	104
27	11.057023	446.978788	.002237	.090440	40.424877	.024737	108
28	12.086247	492.722093	.002030	.082739	40.767170	.024530	112
29	13.211275	542.723337	.001843	.075693	41.080315	.024343	116
30	14.441024	597.378863	.001674	.069247	41.366793	.024174	120
31	15.785243	657.121907	.001522	.063350	41.628875	.024022	124
32	17.254586	722.426031	.001384	.057956	41.868640	.023884	128
33	18.860700	793.808880	.001260	.053020	42.087987	.023760	132
34	20.616316	871.836281	.001147	.048505	42.288655	.023647	136
35	22.535351	957.126733	.001045	.044375	42.472234	.023545	140
36	24.633017	1050.356302	.000952	.040596	42.640181	.023452	144
37	26.925940	1152.263989	.000868	.037139	42.793826	.023368	148
38	29.432296	1263.657582	.000791	.033976	42.934387	.023291	152
39	32.171951	1385.420060	.000722	.031083	43.062979	.023222	156
40	35.166623	1518.516594	.000659	.028436	43.180620	.023159	160
41	38.440049	1664.002195	.000601	.026015	43.288243	.023101	164
42	42.018177	1823.030078	.000549	.023799	43.386701	.023049	168
43	45.929368	1996.860804	.000501	.021773	43.476775	.023001	172
44	50.204626	2186.872272	.000457	.019918	43.559179	.022957	176
45	54.877839	2394.570637	.000418	.018222	43.634565	.022918	180
46	59.986051	2621.602256	.000381	.016671	43.703531	.022881	184
47	65.569751	2869.766731	.000348	.015251	43.766625	.022848	188
48	71.673202	3141.031179	.000318	.013952	43.824346	.022818	192
49	78.344781	3437.545822	.000291	.012764	43.877151	.022791	196
50	85.637373	3761.661032	.000266	.011677	43.925460	.022766	200
51	93.608784	4115.945962	.000243	.010683	43.969655	.022743	204
52	102.322200	4503.208907	.000222	.009773	44.010087	.022722	208
53	111.846690	4926.519573	.000203	.008941	44.047075	.022703	212
54	122.257752	5389.233400	.000186	.008179	44.080914	.022686	216
55	133.637909	5895.018169	.000170	.007483	44.111871	.022670	220
56	146.077369	6447.883062	.000155	.006846	44.140192	.022655	224
57	159.674735	7052.210453	.000142	.006263	44.166101	.022642	228
58	174.537790	7712.790645	.000130	.005729	44.189804	.022630	232
59	190.784346	8434.859831	.000119	.005242	44.211488	.022619	236
60	208.543186	9224.141613	.000108	.004795	44.231326	.022608	240

9% SEMI-ANNUAL COMPOUND INTEREST TABLE 9%

EFFECTIVE RATE = 4½% BASE = 1.045

HALF YEARS	1 AMOUNT OF I AT COMPOUND INTEREST $S^n = (1+i)^n$	2 ACCUMULATION OF I PER PERIOD $S_{\overline{n}\vert} = \frac{S^n - 1}{i}$	3 SINKING FUND FACTOR $1/S_{\overline{n}\vert} = \frac{i}{S^n - 1}$	4 PRES. VALUE REVERSION OF I $V^n = \frac{1}{S^n}$	5 PRESENT VALUE ORD. ANNUITY 1 PER PERIOD $a_{\overline{n}\vert} = \frac{1 - V^n}{i}$	6 INSTALMENT TO AMORTIZE I $1/a_{\overline{n}\vert} = \frac{i}{1 - V^n}$	n HALF YEARS
1	1.045000	1.000000	1.000000	.956938	.956938	1.045000	1
YEARS							
1	1.092025	2.045000	.488998	.915730	1.872668	.533998	2
2	1.192519	4.278191	.233744	.838561	3.587526	.278744	4
3	1.302260	6.716892	.148878	.767896	5.157872	.193878	6
4	1.422101	9.380014	.106610	.703185	6.595886	.151610	8
5	1.552969	12.288209	.081379	.643928	7.912718	.126379	10
6	1.695881	15.464032	.064666	.589664	9.118581	.109666	12
7	1.851945	18.932109	.052820	.539973	10.222825	.097820	14
8	2.022370	22.719337	.044015	.494469	11.234015	.089015	16
9	2.208479	26.855084	.037237	.452800	12.159992	.082237	18
10	2.411714	31.371423	.031876	.414643	13.007936	.076876	20
11	2.633652	36.303378	.027546	.379701	13.784425	.072546	22
12	2.876014	41.689196	.023987	.347703	14.495478	.068987	24
13	3.140679	47.570645	.021021	.318402	15.146611	.066021	26
14	3.429700	53.993333	.018521	.291571	15.742874	.063521	28
15	3.745318	61.007070	.016392	.267000	16.288889	.061392	30
16	4.089981	68.666245	.014563	.244500	16.788891	.059563	32
17	4.466362	77.030256	.012982	.223896	17.246758	.057982	34
18	4.877378	86.163966	.011606	.205028	17.666041	.056606	36
19	5.326219	96.138205	.010402	.187750	18.049990	.055402	38
20	5.816365	107.030323	.009343	.171929	18.401584	.054343	40
21	6.351615	118.924789	.008409	.157440	18.723550	.053409	42
22	6.936123	131.913842	.007581	.144173	19.018383	.052581	44
23	7.574420	146.098214	.006845	.132023	19.288371	.051845	46
24	8.271456	161.587902	.006189	.120898	19.535607	.051189	48
25	9.032636	178.503028	.005602	.110710	19.762008	.050602	50
26	9.863865	196.974769	.005077	.101380	19.969330	.050077	52
27	10.771587	217.146372	.004605	.092837	20.159181	.049605	54
28	11.762842	239.174267	.004181	.085013	20.333034	.049181	56
29	12.845318	263.229279	.003799	.077849	20.492236	.048799	58
30	14.027408	289.497954	.003454	.071289	20.638022	.048454	60
31	15.318280	318.184003	.003143	.065281	20.771523	.048143	62
32	16.727945	349.509886	.002861	.059780	20.893773	.047861	64
33	18.267334	383.718533	.002606	.054743	21.005722	.047606	66
34	19.948385	421.075231	.002375	.050129	21.108236	.047375	68
35	21.784136	461.869679	.002165	.045905	21.202112	.047165	70
36	23.788821	506.418237	.001975	.042037	21.288077	.046975	72
37	25.977987	555.066375	.001802	.038494	21.366797	.046802	74
38	28.368611	608.191358	.001644	.035250	21.438884	.046644	76
39	30.979233	666.205168	.001501	.032280	21.504896	.046501	78
40	33.830096	729.557698	.001371	.029559	21.565345	.046371	80
41	36.943311	798.740245	.001252	.027068	21.620700	.046252	82
42	40.343019	874.289317	.001144	.024787	21.671390	.046144	84
43	44.055586	956.790791	.001045	.022699	21.717809	.046045	86
44	48.109801	1046.884463	.000955	.020786	21.760316	.045955	88
45	52.537105	1145.269006	.000873	.019034	21.799241	.045873	90
46	57.371832	1252.707386	.000798	.017430	21.834885	.045798	92
47	62.651475	1370.032783	.000730	.015961	21.867526	.045730	94
48	68.416977	1498.155050	.000667	.014616	21.897417	.045667	96
49	74.713050	1638.067768	.000610	.013385	21.924788	.045610	98
50	81.588518	1790.855955	.000558	.012257	21.949853	.045558	100
51	89.096701	1957.704474	.000511	.011224	21.972805	.045511	102
52	97.295825	2139.907228	.000467	.010278	21.993824	.045467	104
53	106.249474	2338.877191	.000428	.009412	22.013071	.045428	106
54	116.027081	2556.157364	.000391	.008619	22.030696	.045391	108
55	126.704474	2793.432747	.000358	.007892	22.046836	.045358	110
56	138.364453	3052.543396	.000328	.007227	22.061616	.045328	112
57	151.097442	3335.498702	.000300	.006618	22.075150	.045300	114
58	165.002184	3644.492971	.000274	.006061	22.087544	.045274	116
59	180.186510	3981.922436	.000251	.005550	22.098893	.045251	118
60	196.768173	4350.403847	.000230	.005082	22.109286	.045230	120

9% ANNUAL COMPOUND INTEREST TABLE 9%

EFFECTIVE RATE = 9%   BASE = 1.09

YEARS	1 AMOUNT OF I AT COMPOUND INTEREST $S^n = (1+i)^n$	2 ACCUMULATION OF I PER PERIOD $s_{\overline{n}\vert} = \frac{S^n - 1}{i}$	3 SINKING FUND FACTOR $1/s_{\overline{n}\vert} = \frac{i}{S^n - 1}$	4 PRES. VALUE REVERSION OF I $V^n = \frac{1}{S^n}$	5 PRESENT VALUE ORD. ANNUITY 1 PER PERIOD $a_{\overline{n}\vert} = \frac{1 - V^n}{i}$	6 INSTALMENT TO AMORTIZE I $1/a_{\overline{n}\vert} = \frac{i}{1 - V^n}$	n YEARS
1	1.090000	1.000000	1.000000	.917431	.917431	1.090000	1
2	1.188100	2.090000	.478469	.841680	1.759111	.568469	2
3	1.295029	3.278100	.305055	.772183	2.531295	.395055	3
4	1.411582	4.573129	.218669	.708425	3.239720	.308669	4
5	1.538624	5.984711	.167092	.649931	3.889651	.257092	5
6	1.667100	7.523335	.132920	.596267	4.485919	.222920	6
7	1.828039	9.200435	.108691	.547034	5.032953	.198691	7
8	1.992563	11.028474	.090674	.501866	5.534819	.180674	8
9	2.171893	13.021036	.076799	.460428	5.995247	.166799	9
10	2.367364	15.192930	.065820	.422411	6.417658	.155820	10
11	2.580426	17.560293	.056947	.387533	6.805191	.146947	11
12	2.812665	20.140720	.049651	.355535	7.160725	.139651	12
13	3.065805	22.953385	.043567	.326179	7.486904	.133567	13
14	3.341727	26.019189	.038433	.299246	7.786150	.128433	14
15	3.642482	29.360916	.034059	.274538	8.060688	.124059	15
16	3.970306	33.003399	.030300	.251870	8.312558	.120300	16
17	4.327633	36.973705	.027046	.231073	8.543631	.117046	17
18	4.717120	41.301338	.024212	.211994	8.755625	.114212	18
19	5.141661	46.018458	.021730	.194490	8.950115	.111730	19
20	5.604411	51.160120	.019546	.178431	9.128546	.109546	20
21	6.108808	56.764530	.017617	.163698	9.292244	.107617	21
22	6.658600	62.873338	.015905	.150182	9.442425	.105905	22
23	7.257874	69.531939	.014382	.137781	9.580207	.104382	23
24	7.911083	76.789813	.013023	.126405	9.706612	.103023	24
25	8.623081	84.700896	.011806	.115968	9.822580	.101806	25
26	9.399158	93.323977	.010715	.106393	9.928972	.100715	26
27	10.245082	102.723135	.009735	.097608	10.026580	.099735	27
28	11.167140	112.968217	.008852	.089548	10.116128	.098852	28
29	12.172182	124.135356	.008056	.082155	10.198283	.098056	29
30	13.267678	136.307539	.007336	.075371	10.273654	.097336	30
31	14.461770	149.575217	.006686	.069148	10.342802	.096686	31
32	15.763329	164.036987	.006096	.063438	10.406240	.096096	32
33	17.182028	179.800315	.005562	.058200	10.464441	.095562	33
34	18.728411	196.982344	.005077	.053395	10.517835	.095077	34
35	20.413968	215.710755	.004636	.048986	10.566821	.094636	35
36	22.251225	236.124723	.004235	.044941	10.611763	.094235	36
37	24.253835	258.375948	.003870	.041231	10.652993	.093870	37
38	26.436680	282.629783	.003538	.037826	10.690820	.093538	38
39	28.815982	309.066463	.003236	.034703	10.725523	.093236	39
40	31.409420	337.882445	.002960	.031838	10.757360	.092960	40
41	34.236268	369.291865	.002708	.029209	10.786569	.092708	41
42	37.317532	403.528133	.002478	.026797	10.813366	.092478	42
43	40.676110	440.845665	.002268	.024584	10.837951	.092268	43
44	44.336960	481.521775	.002077	.022555	10.860505	.092077	44
45	48.327286	525.858735	.001902	.020692	10.881197	.091902	45
46	52.676742	574.186021	.001742	.018984	10.900181	.091742	46
47	57.417649	626.862762	.001595	.017416	10.917597	.091595	47
48	62.585237	684.280411	.001461	.015978	10.933575	.091461	48
49	68.217908	746.865648	.001339	.014659	10.948234	.091339	49
50	74.357520	815.083556	.001227	.013449	10.961683	.091227	50
51	81.049697	889.441077	.001124	.012338	10.974021	.091124	51
52	88.344170	970.490773	.001030	.011319	10.985340	.091030	52
53	96.295145	1058.834943	.000944	.010385	10.995725	.090944	53
54	104.961708	1155.130088	.000866	.009527	11.005252	.090866	54
55	114.408262	1260.091796	.000794	.008741	11.013993	.090794	55
56	124.705005	1374.500057	.000728	.008019	11.022012	.090728	56
57	135.928456	1499.205063	.000667	.007357	11.029369	.090667	57
58	148.162017	1635.133518	.000612	.006749	11.036118	.090612	58
59	161.496598	1783.295535	.000561	.006192	11.042310	.090561	59
60	176.031292	1944.792133	.000514	.005681	11.047991	.090514	60

9 ¼ % MONTHLY COMPOUND INTEREST TABLE 9 ¼ %

EFFECTIVE RATE = 37/48% BASE = 1.00770833

MONTHS	1 AMOUNT OF I AT COMPOUND INTEREST $S^n = (1+i)^n$	2 ACCUMULATION OF I PER PERIOD $S_{\overline{n}\rvert} = \frac{S^n - 1}{i}$	3 SINKING FUND FACTOR $1/S_{\overline{n}\rvert} = \frac{i}{S^n - 1}$	4 PRES. VALUE REVERSION OF I $V^n = \frac{1}{S^n}$	5 PRESENT VALUE ORD. ANNUITY 1 PER PERIOD $a_{\overline{n}\rvert} = \frac{1 - V^n}{i}$	6 INSTALMENT TO AMORTIZE I $1/a_{\overline{n}\rvert} = \frac{i}{1 - V^n}$	n MONTHS
1	1.007708	1.000000	1.000000	.992350	.992350	1.007708	1
2	1.015476	2.007708	.498080	.984759	1.977110	.505788	2
3	1.023303	3.023184	.330777	.977226	2.954337	.338485	3
4	1.031191	4.046488	.247127	.969751	3.924089	.254836	4
5	1.039140	5.077679	.196940	.962333	4.886423	.204648	5
6	1.047150	6.116820	.163483	.954972	5.841395	.171191	6
7	1.055222	7.163970	.139587	.947667	6.789063	.147295	7
8	1.063356	8.219193	.121666	.940418	7.729481	.129374	8
9	1.071552	9.282549	.107729	.933224	8.662706	.115437	9
10	1.079812	10.354102	.096580	.926086	9.588793	.104288	10
11	1.088136	11.433915	.087459	.919002	10.507795	.095167	11
YEARS							
1	1.096524	12.522051	.079859	.911972	11.419768	.087567	12
2	1.202365	26.252783	.038091	.831694	21.834284	.045799	24
3	1.318422	41.308862	.024207	.758482	31.332037	.031916	36
4	1.445682	57.818216	.017295	.691715	39.993728	.025003	48
5	1.585225	75.921122	.013171	.630825	47.892953	.020879	60
6	1.738237	95.771395	.010441	.575295	55.096830	.018149	72
7	1.906019	117.537699	.008507	.524653	61.666569	.016216	84
8	2.089996	141.404977	.007071	.478469	67.657991	.014780	96
9	2.291731	167.576024	.005967	.436351	73.122003	.013675	108
10	2.512939	196.273208	.005094	.397940	78.105033	.012803	120
11	2.755498	227.740364	.004390	.362910	82.649420	.012099	132
12	3.021470	262.244859	.003813	.330964	86.793776	.011521	144
13	3.313115	300.079873	.003332	.301830	90.573315	.011040	156
14	3.632911	341.566878	.002927	.275261	94.020152	.010636	168
15	3.983575	387.058382	.002583	.251030	97.163572	.010291	180
16	4.368086	436.940913	.002288	.228933	100.030286	.009996	192
17	4.789711	491.638314	.002034	.208780	102.644650	.009742	204
18	5.252034	551.615335	.001812	.190402	105.028879	.009521	216
19	5.758983	617.381585	.001619	.173641	107.203230	.009328	228
20	6.314863	689.495868	.001450	.158356	109.186179	.009158	240
21	6.924400	768.570921	.001301	.144416	110.994574	.009009	252
22	7.592772	855.278625	.001169	.131704	112.643781	.008877	264
23	8.325658	950.355716	.001052	.120110	114.147812	.008760	276
24	9.129285	1054.610044	.000948	.109537	115.519447	.008656	288
25	10.010482	1168.927431	.000855	.099895	116.770341	.008563	300
26	10.976735	1294.279205	.000772	.091101	117.911122	.008480	312
27	12.036255	1431.730453	.000698	.083082	118.951483	.008406	324
28	13.198044	1582.449066	.000631	.075768	119.900264	.008340	336
29	14.471974	1747.715663	.000572	.069099	120.765525	.008280	348
30	15.868869	1928.934479	.000518	.063016	121.554622	.008226	360
31	17.400599	2127.645287	.000470	.057469	122.274254	.008178	372
32	19.080177	2345.536487	.000426	.052410	122.930541	.008134	384
33	20.921874	2584.459445	.000386	.047796	123.529056	.008095	396
34	22.941340	2846.444242	.000351	.043589	124.074885	.008059	408
35	25.155734	3133.716897	.000319	.039752	124.572665	.008027	420
36	27.583870	3448.718297	.000289	.036253	125.026629	.007998	432
37	30.246379	3794.124943	.000263	.033061	125.440630	.007971	444
38	33.165885	4172.871670	.000239	.030151	125.818189	.007947	456
39	36.367194	4588.176598	.000217	.027497	126.162511	.007926	468
40	39.877506	5043.568484	.000198	.025076	126.476524	.007906	480
41	43.726649	5542.916684	.000180	.022869	126.762896	.007888	492
42	47.947326	6090.464043	.000164	.020856	127.024058	.007872	504
43	52.575401	6690.862938	.000149	.019020	127.262230	.007857	516
44	57.650197	7349.214831	.000136	.017345	127.479438	.007844	528
45	63.214833	8071.113579	.000123	.015819	127.677527	.007832	540
46	69.316591	8862.692980	.000112	.014426	127.858176	.007821	552
47	76.007316	9730.678916	.000102	.013156	128.022923	.007811	564
48	83.343857	10682.446450	.000093	.011998	128.173170	.007801	576
49	91.388552	11726.082540	.000085	.010942	128.310189	.007793	588
50	100.209754	12870.454700	.000077	.009979	128.435149	.007786	600

9 ¼ % QUARTERLY COMPOUND INTEREST TABLE 9 ¼ %

EFFECTIVE RATE = 2-5/16% BASE = 1.023125

QUARTERS	1 AMOUNT OF I AT COMPOUND INTEREST $S^n = (1+i)^n$	2 ACCUMULATION OF I PER PERIOD $S_{\overline{n}\vert} = \frac{S^n - 1}{i}$	3 SINKING FUND FACTOR $1/S_{\overline{n}\vert} = \frac{i}{S^n - 1}$	4 PRES. VALUE REVERSION OF I $V^n = \frac{1}{S^n}$	5 PRESENT VALUE ORD. ANNUITY 1 PER PERIOD $a_{\overline{n}\vert} = \frac{1 - V^n}{i}$	6 INSTALMENT TO AMORTIZE I $1/a_{\overline{n}\vert} = \frac{i}{1 - V^n}$	n QUARTERS
1	1.023125	1.000000	1.000000	.977398	.977398	1.023125	1
2	1.046785	2.023125	.494285	.955306	1.932704	.517410	2
3	1.070992	3.069910	.325742	.933714	2.866418	.348867	3
YEARS							
1	1.095758	4.140901	.241493	.912610	3.779028	.264618	4
2	1.200686	8.678329	.115230	.832857	7.227807	.138355	8
3	1.315662	13.650253	.073259	.760074	10.375196	.096384	12
4	1.441648	19.098280	.052361	.693651	13.247536	.075486	16
5	1.579698	25.068001	.039891	.633033	15.868861	.063516	20
6	1.730967	31.609372	.031636	.577712	18.261109	.054761	24
7	1.896721	38.777135	.025788	.527226	20.444298	.048913	28
8	2.078348	46.631271	.021445	.481151	22.436699	.044570	32
9	2.277367	55.237506	.018104	.439104	24.254983	.041229	36
10	2.495444	64.667859	.015464	.400730	25.914367	.038589	40
11	2.734404	75.001248	.013333	.365710	27.428738	.036458	44
12	2.996246	86.324145	.011584	.333751	28.810768	.034709	48
13	3.283161	98.731303	.010128	.304584	30.072023	.033253	52
14	3.597551	112.326551	.008903	.277967	31.223056	.032028	56
15	3.942047	127.223657	.007860	.253675	32.273500	.030985	60
16	4.319531	143.547286	.006966	.231507	33.232146	.030091	64
17	4.733162	161.434038	.006194	.211275	34.107016	.029319	68
18	5.186402	181.033595	.005524	.192812	34.905431	.028649	72
19	5.683043	202.509974	.004938	.175962	35.634073	.028063	76
20	6.227242	226.042896	.004424	.160585	36.299038	.027549	80
21	6.823552	251.829291	.003971	.146551	36.905893	.027096	84
22	7.476964	280.084949	.003570	.133744	37.459714	.026695	88
23	8.192946	311.046321	.003215	.122056	37.965137	.026340	92
24	8.977489	344.972504	.002899	.111390	38.426391	.026024	96
25	9.837159	382.147402	.002617	.101655	38.847335	.025742	100
26	10.779149	422.882106	.002365	.092772	39.231494	.025490	104
27	11.811342	467.517498	.002139	.084664	39.582081	.025264	108
28	12.942377	516.427102	.001936	.077266	39.902030	.025061	112
29	14.181717	570.020208	.001754	.070513	40.194019	.024879	116
30	15.539735	628.745302	.001590	.064351	40.460490	.024715	120
31	17.027794	693.093813	.001443	.058728	40.703675	.024568	124
32	18.658348	763.604231	.001310	.053595	40.925608	.024435	128
33	20.445040	840.866610	.001189	.048912	41.128146	.024314	132
34	22.402824	925.527507	.001080	.044637	41.312985	.024205	136
35	24.548081	1018.295391	.000982	.040736	41.481670	.024107	140
36	26.898765	1119.946575	.000893	.037176	41.635614	.024018	144
37	29.474546	1231.331707	.000812	.033928	41.776105	.023937	148
38	32.296979	1353.382896	.000739	.030963	41.904318	.023864	152
39	35.389685	1487.121504	.000672	.028257	42.021327	.023797	156
40	38.778542	1633.666701	.000612	.025787	42.128110	.023737	160
41	42.491912	1794.244823	.000557	.023534	42.225561	.023682	164
42	46.560867	1970.199640	.000508	.021477	42.314497	.023633	168
43	51.019458	2163.003600	.000462	.019600	42.395660	.023587	172
44	55.904997	2374.270147	.000421	.017887	42.469730	.023546	176
45	61.258367	2605.767230	.000384	.016324	42.537328	.023509	180
46	67.124367	2859.432090	.000350	.014898	42.599018	.023475	184
47	73.552085	3137.387478	.000319	.013596	42.655316	.023444	188
48	80.595311	3441.959414	.000291	.012408	42.706695	.023416	192
49	88.312985	3775.696655	.000265	.011323	42.753584	.023390	196
50	96.769690	4141.392021	.000241	.010334	42.796376	.023366	200
51	106.036196	4542.105773	.000220	.009431	42.835427	.023345	204
52	116.190047	4981.191209	.000201	.008607	42.871066	.023326	208
53	127.316213	5462.322737	.000183	.007854	42.903591	.023308	212
54	139.507803	5989.526629	.000167	.007168	42.933273	.023292	216
55	152.866840	6567.214690	.000152	.006542	42.960361	.023277	220
56	167.505115	7200.221206	.000139	.005970	42.985083	.023264	224
57	183.545128	7893.843377	.000127	.005448	43.007643	.023252	228
58	201.121106	8653.885661	.000116	.004972	43.028232	.023241	232
59	220.380130	9486.708337	.000105	.004538	43.047022	.023230	236
60	241.483367	10399.280740	.000096	.004141	43.064170	.023221	240

9¼% SEMI-ANNUAL COMPOUND INTEREST TABLE 9¼%

EFFECTIVE RATE = 4-5/8% BASE = 1.04625

HALF YEARS	1 AMOUNT OF I AT COMPOUND INTEREST $S^n = (1+i)^n$	2 ACCUMULATION OF I PER PERIOD $s_{\overline{n}|} = \frac{S^n - 1}{i}$	3 SINKING FUND FACTOR $1/s_{\overline{n}|} = \frac{i}{S^n - 1}$	4 PRES. VALUE REVERSION OF I $V^n = \frac{1}{S^n}$	5 PRESENT VALUE ORD. ANNUITY 1 PER PERIOD $a_{\overline{n}|} = \frac{1 - V^n}{i}$	6 INSTALMENT TO AMORTIZE I $1/a_{\overline{n}|} = \frac{i}{1 - V^n}$	n HALF YEARS
1	1.046250	1.000000	1.000000	.955795	.955795	1.046250	1
YEARS							
1	1.094639	2.046250	.488699	.913543	1.869338	.534949	2
2	1.198235	4.286155	.233309	.834561	3.577058	.279559	4
3	1.311634	6.738043	.148411	.762408	5.137135	.194661	6
4	1.435766	9.421975	.106135	.696492	6.562332	.152385	8
5	1.571646	12.359912	.080907	.636276	7.864311	.127157	10
6	1.720385	15.575892	.064202	.581265	9.053725	.110452	12
7	1.883201	19.096230	.052366	.531011	10.140306	.098616	14
8	2.061425	22.949730	.043573	.485101	11.132944	.089823	16
9	2.256516	27.167920	.036808	.443161	12.039762	.083058	18
10	2.470071	31.785317	.031461	.404847	12.868180	.077711	20
11	2.703836	36.839700	.027145	.369845	13.624975	.073395	22
12	2.959725	42.372424	.023600	.337869	14.316340	.069850	24
13	3.239830	48.428761	.020649	.308658	14.947932	.066899	26
14	3.546445	55.058263	.018163	.281973	15.524918	.064413	28
15	3.882077	62.315176	.016047	.257594	16.052020	.062297	30
16	4.249473	70.258875	.014233	.235323	16.533550	.060483	32
17	4.651639	78.954359	.012666	.214978	16.973449	.058916	34
18	5.091866	88.472776	.011303	.196392	17.375315	.057553	36
19	5.573755	98.892007	.010112	.179412	17.742438	.056362	38
20	6.101250	110.297303	.009066	.163901	18.077820	.055316	40
21	6.678667	122.781987	.008145	.149730	18.384206	.054395	42
22	7.310730	136.448209	.007329	.136785	18.664103	.053579	44
23	8.002610	151.407789	.006605	.124959	18.919800	.052855	46
24	8.759970	167.783131	.005960	.114156	19.153391	.052210	48
25	9.589005	185.708219	.005385	.104286	19.366787	.051635	50
26	10.496500	205.329720	.004870	.095270	19.561733	.051120	52
27	11.489878	226.808183	.004409	.087033	19.739824	.050659	54
28	12.577270	250.319346	.003995	.079509	19.902519	.050245	56
29	13.767571	276.055585	.003622	.072634	20.051147	.049872	58
30	15.070521	304.227476	.003287	.066355	20.186925	.049537	60
31	16.496781	335.065530	.002984	.060618	20.310965	.049234	62
32	18.058021	368.822067	.002711	.055377	20.424280	.048961	64
33	19.767015	405.773292	.002464	.050589	20.527798	.048714	66
34	21.637746	446.221546	.002241	.046216	20.622367	.048491	68
35	23.685523	490.497784	.002039	.042220	20.708759	.048289	70
36	25.927098	538.964285	.001855	.038570	20.787683	.048105	72
37	28.380814	592.017609	.001689	.035235	20.859782	.047939	74
38	31.066748	650.091851	.001538	.032189	20.925649	.047788	76
39	34.006876	713.662184	.001401	.029406	20.985820	.047651	78
40	37.225255	783.248754	.001277	.026863	21.040790	.047527	80
41	40.748218	859.420932	.001164	.024541	21.091006	.047414	82
42	44.604591	942.801973	.001061	.022419	21.136882	.047311	84
43	48.825928	1034.074118	.000967	.020481	21.178791	.047217	86
44	53.446768	1133.984173	.000882	.018710	21.217077	.047132	88
45	58.504920	1243.349622	.000804	.017093	21.252052	.047054	90
46	64.041771	1363.065314	.000734	.015615	21.284004	.046984	92
47	70.102624	1494.110787	.000669	.014265	21.313193	.046919	94
48	76.737071	1637.558282	.000611	.013032	21.339859	.046861	96
49	83.999395	1794.581512	.000557	.011905	21.364220	.046807	98
50	91.949019	1966.465274	.000509	.010876	21.386474	.046759	100
51	100.650988	2154.615955	.000464	.009935	21.406804	.046714	102
52	110.176503	2360.573038	.000424	.009076	21.425376	.046674	104
53	120.603504	2586.021706	.000387	.008292	21.442343	.046637	106
54	132.017306	2832.806625	.000353	.007575	21.457843	.046603	108
55	144.511301	3102.947038	.000322	.006920	21.472003	.046572	110
56	158.187715	3398.653287	.000294	.006322	21.484938	.046544	112
57	173.158452	3722.344897	.000269	.005775	21.496756	.046519	114
58	189.546005	4076.670378	.000245	.005276	21.507551	.046495	116
59	207.484461	4464.528891	.000224	.004820	21.517413	.046474	118
60	227.120596	4889.093970	.000205	.004403	21.526423	.046455	120

9¼% ANNUAL COMPOUND INTEREST TABLE 9¼%

EFFECTIVE RATE = 9¼% BASE = 1.0925

YEARS	1 AMOUNT OF I AT COMPOUND INTEREST $S^n = (1+i)^n$	2 ACCUMULATION OF I PER PERIOD $S_{\overline{n}\mid} = \frac{S^n - 1}{i}$	3 SINKING FUND FACTOR $1/S_{\overline{n}\mid} = \frac{i}{S^n - 1}$	4 PRES. VALUE REVERSION OF I $V^n = \frac{1}{S^n}$	5 PRESENT VALUE ORD. ANNUITY 1 PER PERIOD $a_{\overline{n}\mid} = \frac{1 - V^n}{i}$	6 INSTALMENT TO AMORTIZE I $1/a_{\overline{n}\mid} = \frac{i}{1 - V^n}$	n YEARS
1	1.092500	1.000000	1.000000	.915332	.915332	1.092500	1
2	1.193556	2.092500	.477897	.837832	1.753164	.570397	2
3	1.303960	3.286056	.304316	.766895	2.520059	.396816	3
4	1.424577	4.590016	.217864	.701963	3.222022	.310364	4
5	1.556350	6.014593	.166262	.642529	3.864551	.258762	5
6	1.700312	7.570943	.132084	.588127	4.452678	.224584	6
7	1.857591	9.271255	.107860	.538332	4.991010	.200360	7
8	2.029418	11.128846	.089857	.492752	5.483762	.182357	8
9	2.217139	13.158264	.075998	.451032	5.934793	.168498	9
10	2.422225	15.375404	.065039	.412844	6.347637	.157539	10
11	2.646281	17.797629	.056187	.377889	6.725526	.148687	11
12	2.891062	20.443909	.048914	.345894	7.071419	.141414	12
13	3.158485	23.334971	.042854	.316608	7.388027	.135354	13
14	3.450645	26.493456	.037745	.289801	7.677828	.130245	14
15	3.769829	29.944100	.033396	.265264	7.943092	.125896	15
16	4.118539	33.713930	.029661	.242805	8.185896	.122161	16
17	4.499503	37.832468	.026432	.222247	8.408143	.118932	17
18	4.915707	42.331972	.023623	.203430	8.611573	.116123	18
19	5.370410	47.247679	.021165	.186206	8.797778	.113665	19
20	5.867173	52.618089	.019005	.170440	8.968218	.111505	20
21	6.409887	58.485263	.017098	.156009	9.124227	.109598	21
22	7.002801	64.895149	.015409	.142800	9.267027	.107909	22
23	7.650560	71.897951	.013909	.130709	9.397736	.106409	23
24	8.358237	79.548511	.012571	.119642	9.517379	.105071	24
25	9.131374	87.906748	.011376	.109513	9.626891	.103876	25
26	9.976026	97.038123	.010305	.100240	9.727132	.102805	26
27	10.898809	107.014149	.009345	.091753	9.818885	.101845	27
28	11.906949	117.912958	.008481	.083985	9.902869	.100981	28
29	13.008341	129.819906	.007703	.076874	9.979743	.100203	29
30	14.211613	142.828248	.007001	.070365	10.050108	.099501	30
31	15.526187	157.039860	.006368	.064407	10.114516	.098868	31
32	16.962359	172.566048	.005795	.058954	10.173470	.098295	32
33	18.531378	189.528407	.005276	.053963	10.227432	.097776	33
34	20.245530	208.059785	.004806	.049394	10.276826	.097306	34
35	22.118242	228.305315	.004380	.045212	10.322037	.096880	35
36	24.164179	250.423556	.003993	.041384	10.363421	.096493	36
37	26.399366	274.587735	.003642	.037880	10.401301	.096142	37
38	28.841307	300.987101	.003322	.034672	10.435973	.095822	38
39	31.509128	329.828408	.003032	.031737	10.467710	.095532	39
40	34.423722	361.337535	.002767	.029050	10.496760	.095267	40
41	37.607916	395.761257	.002527	.026590	10.523350	.095027	41
42	41.086649	433.369174	.002308	.024339	10.547689	.094808	42
43	44.887164	474.455822	.002108	.022278	10.569967	.094608	43
44	49.039226	519.342986	.001926	.020392	10.590359	.094426	44
45	53.575355	568.382212	.001759	.018665	10.609024	.094259	45
46	58.531075	621.957566	.001608	.017085	10.626109	.094108	46
47	63.945199	680.488641	.001470	.015638	10.641747	.093970	47
48	69.860130	744.433841	.001343	.014314	10.656061	.093843	48
49	76.322192	814.293971	.001228	.013102	10.669164	.093728	49
50	83.381995	890.616163	.001123	.011993	10.681157	.093623	50
51	91.094830	973.998158	.001027	.010978	10.692134	.093527	51
52	99.521101	1065.092988	.000939	.010048	10.702182	.093439	52
53	108.726803	1164.614090	.000859	.009197	10.711380	.093359	53
54	118.784033	1273.340893	.000785	.008419	10.719798	.093285	54
55	129.771556	1392.124925	.000718	.007706	10.727504	.093218	55
56	141.775425	1521.896481	.000657	.007053	10.734558	.093157	56
57	154.889651	1663.671906	.000601	.006456	10.741014	.093101	57
58	169.216944	1818.561558	.000550	.005910	10.746924	.093050	58
59	184.869511	1987.778502	.000503	.005409	10.752333	.093003	59
60	201.969941	2172.648013	.000460	.004951	10.757284	.092960	60

9 ½% MONTHLY COMPOUND INTEREST TABLE 9 ½%

EFFECTIVE RATE = 19/24% BASE = 1.00791667

MONTHS	1 AMOUNT OF I AT COMPOUND INTEREST $S^n = (1+i)^n$	2 ACCUMULATION OF I PER PERIOD $S_{\overline{n\vert}} = \frac{S^n - 1}{i}$	3 SINKING FUND FACTOR $1/S_{\overline{n\vert}} = \frac{i}{S^n - 1}$	4 PRES. VALUE REVERSION OF I $V^n = \frac{1}{S^n}$	5 PRESENT VALUE ORD. ANNUITY 1 PER PERIOD $a_{\overline{n\vert}} = \frac{1 - V^n}{i}$	6 INSTALMENT TO AMORTIZE I $1/a_{\overline{n\vert}} = \frac{i}{1 - V^n}$	n MONTHS
1	1.007916	1.000000	1.000000	.992145	.992145	1.007916	1
2	1.015896	2.007916	.498028	.984352	1.976498	.505945	2
3	1.023938	3.023812	.330708	.976621	2.953119	.338624	3
4	1.032044	4.047751	.247050	.968950	3.922069	.254967	4
5	1.040215	5.079795	.196858	.961339	4.883409	.204774	5
6	1.048450	6.120010	.163398	.953788	5.837198	.171315	6
7	1.056750	7.168461	.139499	.946297	6.783495	.147416	7
8	1.065116	8.225211	.121577	.938864	7.722360	.129494	8
9	1.073548	9.290327	.107638	.931490	8.653850	.115555	9
10	1.082047	10.363876	.096488	.924173	9.578024	.104405	10
11	1.090613	11.445923	.087367	.916915	10.494939	.095284	11
YEARS							
1	1.099247	12.536536	.079766	.909713	11.404652	.087683	12
2	1.208345	26.317294	.037997	.827578	21.779615	.045914	24
3	1.328270	41.465759	.024116	.752858	31.217855	.032032	36
4	1.460098	58.117673	.017206	.684885	39.803946	.025123	48
5	1.605009	76.422248	.013085	.623049	47.614827	.021001	60
6	1.764302	96.543509	.010358	.566796	54.720488	.018274	72
7	1.939405	118.661756	.008427	.515621	61.184601	.016343	84
8	2.131886	142.975186	.006994	.469068	67.065089	.014910	96
9	2.343471	169.701664	.005892	.426717	72.414647	.013809	108
10	2.576055	199.080682	.005023	.388190	77.281211	.012939	120
11	2.831722	231.375496	.004321	.353141	81.708388	.012238	132
12	3.112764	266.875491	.003747	.321257	85.735849	.011663	144
13	3.421698	305.898776	.003269	.292252	89.399683	.011185	156
14	3.761293	348.795028	.002867	.265865	92.732722	.010783	168
15	4.134593	395.948629	.002525	.241861	95.764830	.010442	180
16	4.544941	447.782111	.002233	.220024	98.523179	.010149	192
17	4.996016	504.759941	.001981	.200159	101.032486	.009897	204
18	5.491858	567.392683	.001762	.182087	103.315236	.009679	216
19	6.036912	636.241573	.001571	.165647	105.391882	.009488	228
20	6.636061	711.923549	.001404	.150691	107.281036	.009321	240
21	7.294674	795.116779	.001257	.137086	108.999623	.009174	252
22	8.018653	886.566735	.001127	.124709	110.563045	.009044	264
23	8.814485	987.092880	.001013	.113449	111.985310	.008929	276
24	9.689301	1097.596002	.000911	.103206	113.279164	.008827	288
25	10.650941	1219.066291	.000820	.093888	114.456200	.008736	300
26	11.708021	1352.592212	.000739	.085411	115.526965	.008655	312
27	12.870014	1499.370259	.000666	.077699	116.501053	.008583	324
28	14.147332	1660.715673	.000602	.070684	117.387195	.008518	336
29	15.551421	1838.074228	.000544	.064302	118.193328	.008460	348
30	17.094862	2033.035192	.000491	.058497	118.926680	.008408	360
31	18.791485	2247.345562	.000444	.053215	119.593819	.008361	372
32	20.656495	2482.925719	.000402	.048410	120.200724	.008319	384
33	22.706602	2741.886634	.000364	.044040	120.752834	.008281	396
34	24.960178	3026.548797	.000330	.040063	121.255097	.008247	408
35	27.437415	3339.462993	.000299	.036446	121.712010	.008216	420
36	30.160512	3683.433163	.000271	.033155	122.127670	.008188	432
37	33.153870	4061.541545	.000246	.030162	122.505803	.008162	444
38	36.444312	4477.176271	.000223	.027439	122.849793	.008140	456
39	40.061322	4934.061735	.000202	.024961	123.162727	.008119	468
40	44.037311	5436.291983	.000183	.022708	123.447408	.008100	480
41	48.407908	5988.367370	.000166	.020657	123.706385	.008083	492
42	53.212276	6595.234905	.000151	.018792	123.941980	.008068	504
43	58.493466	7262.332571	.000137	.017095	124.156303	.008054	516
44	64.298801	7995.638076	.000125	.015552	124.351276	.008041	528
45	70.680302	8801.722381	.000113	.014148	124.528646	.008030	540
46	77.695151	9687.808598	.000103	.012870	124.690002	.008019	552
47	85.406207	10661.836740	.000093	.011708	124.836788	.008010	564
48	93.882567	11732.534820	.000085	.010651	124.970322	.008001	576
49	103.200185	12909.497090	.000077	.009689	125.091800	.007994	588
50	113.442554	14203.270040	.000070	.008815	125.202311	.007987	600

9½ % QUARTERLY COMPOUND INTEREST TABLE 9½ %

EFFECTIVE RATE = 2-3/8% BASE = 1.02375

QUARTERS	1 AMOUNT OF I AT COMPOUND INTEREST $S^n = (1+i)^n$	2 ACCUMULATION OF I PER PERIOD $S_{\overline{n}\rceil} = \frac{S^n - 1}{i}$	3 SINKING FUND FACTOR $1/S_{\overline{n}\rceil} = \frac{i}{S^n - 1}$	4 PRES. VALUE REVERSION OF I $V^n = \frac{1}{S^n}$	5 PRESENT VALUE ORD. ANNUITY 1 PER PERIOD $a_{\overline{n}\rceil} = \frac{1 - V^n}{i}$	6 INSTALMENT TO AMORTIZE I $1/a_{\overline{n}\rceil} = \frac{i}{1 - V^n}$	n QUARTERS
1	1.023750	1.000000	1.000000	.976801	.976801	1.023750	1
2	1.048064	2.023750	.494132	.954140	1.930941	.517882	2
3	1.072956	3.071814	.325541	.932005	2.862946	.349291	3
YEARS							
1	1.098438	4.144770	.241268	.910383	3.773330	.265018	4
2	1.206567	8.697543	.114975	.828798	7.208506	.138725	8
3	1.325339	13.698484	.073001	.754524	10.335834	.096751	12
4	1.455803	19.191709	.052106	.686906	13.182902	.075856	16
5	1.599110	25.225677	.039642	.625348	15.774825	.063392	20
6	1.756523	31.853619	.031394	.569306	18.134469	.055144	24
7	1.929433	39.134005	.025553	.518287	20.282649	.049303	28
8	2.119363	47.131058	.021217	.471840	22.238317	.044967	32
9	2.327989	55.915328	.017884	.429555	24.018725	.041634	36
10	2.557152	65.564306	.015252	.391060	25.639578	.039002	40
11	2.808874	76.163114	.013130	.356015	27.115177	.036880	44
12	3.085375	87.805249	.011389	.324110	28.458537	.035139	48
13	3.389094	100.593416	.009941	.295064	29.681510	.033691	52
14	3.722710	114.640429	.008723	.268622	30.794884	.032473	56
15	4.089167	130.070205	.007688	.244549	31.808482	.031438	60
16	4.491698	147.018862	.006802	.222633	32.731244	.030552	64
17	4.933853	165.635915	.006037	.202681	33.571311	.029787	68
18	5.419533	186.085599	.005374	.184518	34.336095	.029124	72
19	5.953022	208.548315	.004795	.167982	35.032341	.028545	76
20	6.539028	233.222222	.004288	.152928	35.666192	.028038	80
21	7.182718	260.324985	.003841	.139223	36.243240	.027591	84
22	7.889773	290.095699	.003447	.126746	36.768574	.027197	88
23	8.666429	322.796990	.003098	.115388	37.246830	.026848	92
24	9.519537	358.717339	.002788	.105047	37.682226	.026538	96
25	10.456624	398.173627	.002511	.095633	38.078604	.026261	100
26	11.485956	441.513923	.002265	.087063	38.439459	.026015	104
27	12.616613	489.120563	.002044	.079261	38.767976	.025794	108
28	13.858571	541.413520	.001847	.072158	39.067052	.025597	112
29	15.222785	598.854104	.001670	.065691	39.339326	.025420	116
30	16.721290	661.949042	.001511	.059804	39.587200	.025261	120
31	18.367305	731.254936	.001368	.054445	39.812860	.025118	124
32	20.175351	807.383183	.001239	.049565	40.018298	.024989	128
33	22.161377	891.005364	.001122	.045124	40.205324	.024872	132
34	24.342905	982.859168	.001017	.041080	40.375590	.024767	136
35	26.739179	1083.754903	.000923	.037398	40.530598	.024673	140
36	29.371338	1194.582640	.000837	.034047	40.671714	.024587	144
37	32.262602	1316.320069	.000760	.030996	40.800184	.024510	148
38	35.438477	1450.041121	.000690	.028218	40.917140	.024440	152
39	38.926979	1596.925443	.000626	.025689	41.023616	.024376	156
40	42.758884	1758.268805	.000569	.023387	41.120549	.024319	160
41	46.967995	1935.494530	.000517	.021291	41.208796	.024267	164
42	51.591444	2130.166051	.000469	.019383	41.289134	.024219	168
43	56.670017	2344.000700	.000427	.017646	41.362273	.024177	172
44	62.248516	2578.884865	.000388	.016065	41.428857	.024138	176
45	68.376152	2836.890622	.000352	.014625	41.489474	.024102	180
46	75.106983	3120.294023	.000320	.013314	41.544659	.024070	184
47	82.500385	3431.595166	.000291	.012121	41.594899	.024041	188
48	90.621581	3773.540259	.000265	.011035	41.640636	.024015	192
49	99.542214	4149.145837	.000241	.010046	41.682274	.023991	196
50	109.340978	4561.725381	.000219	.009146	41.720181	.023969	200
51	120.104316	5014.918547	.000199	.008326	41.754691	.023949	204
52	131.927178	5512.723267	.000181	.007580	41.786108	.023931	208
53	144.913862	6059.531027	.000165	.006901	41.814709	.023915	212
54	159.178933	6660.165604	.000150	.006282	41.840748	.023900	216
55	174.848233	7319.925613	.000137	.005719	41.864453	.023887	220
56	192.059993	8044.631263	.000124	.005207	41.886033	.023874	224
57	210.966048	8840.675688	.000113	.004740	41.905680	.023863	228
58	231.733182	9715.081360	.000103	.004315	41.923566	.023853	232
59	254.544598	10675.562020	.000094	.003929	41.939849	.023844	236
60	279.601530	11730.590750	.000085	.003577	41.954673	.023835	240

9½ % SEMI-ANNUAL COMPOUND INTEREST TABLE 9½ %

EFFECTIVE RATE = 4¾% BASE = 1.0475

	1 AMOUNT OF I AT COMPOUND INTEREST $S^n = (1+i)^n$	2 ACCUMULATION OF I PER PERIOD $S_{\overline{n}\vert} = \frac{S^n - 1}{i}$	3 SINKING FUND FACTOR $1/S_{\overline{n}\vert} = \frac{i}{S^n - 1}$	4 PRES. VALUE REVERSION OF I $V^n = \frac{1}{S^n}$	5 PRESENT VALUE ORD. ANNUITY 1 PER PERIOD $a_{\overline{n}\vert} = \frac{1 - V^n}{i}$	6 INSTALMENT TO AMORTIZE I $1/a_{\overline{n}\vert} = \frac{i}{1 - V^n}$	n
HALF YEARS							HALF YEARS
1	1.047500	1.000000	1.000000	.954654	.954654	1.047500	1
YEARS							
1	1.097256	2.047500	.488400	.911364	1.866018	.535900	2
2	1.203971	4.294132	.232876	.830585	3.566640	.280376	4
3	1.321065	6.759263	.147945	.756965	5.116526	.195445	6
4	1.449547	9.464144	.105662	.689871	6.529036	.153162	8
5	1.590524	12.432091	.080437	.628723	7.816348	.127937	10
6	1.745213	15.688690	.063740	.572996	8.989557	.111240	12
7	1.914946	19.262013	.051916	.522208	10.058778	.099416	14
8	2.101186	23.182864	.043135	.475922	11.033228	.090635	16
9	2.305540	27.485042	.036383	.433738	11.921306	.083883	18
10	2.529768	32.205635	.031050	.395293	12.730669	.078550	20
11	2.775803	37.385334	.026748	.360256	13.468293	.074248	22
12	3.045768	43.068791	.023219	.328324	14.140538	.070719	24
13	3.341988	49.305000	.020282	.299223	14.753197	.067782	26
14	3.667017	56.147720	.017810	.272701	15.311553	.065310	28
15	4.023657	63.655936	.015709	.248530	15.820418	.063209	30
16	4.414983	71.894374	.013909	.226501	16.284180	.061409	32
17	4.844367	80.934051	.012356	.206425	16.706836	.059856	34
18	5.315512	90.852894	.011007	.188129	17.092029	.058507	36
19	5.832479	101.736405	.009829	.171454	17.443081	.057329	38
20	6.399724	113.678407	.008797	.156257	17.763016	.056297	40
21	7.022137	126.781842	.007888	.142407	18.054594	.055388	42
22	7.705084	141.159669	.007084	.129784	18.320328	.054584	44
23	8.454452	156.935829	.006372	.118281	18.562508	.053872	46
24	9.276700	174.246319	.005739	.107797	18.783222	.053239	48
25	10.178917	193.240362	.005175	.098242	18.984373	.052675	50
26	11.168881	214.081695	.004671	.089534	19.167695	.052171	52
27	12.255124	236.949978	.004220	.081599	19.334768	.051720	54
28	13.447011	262.042345	.003816	.074366	19.487032	.051316	56
29	14.754817	289.575100	.003453	.067774	19.625801	.050953	58
30	16.189815	319.785589	.003127	.061767	19.752269	.050627	60
31	17.764376	352.934236	.002833	.056292	19.867528	.050333	62
32	19.492073	389.306796	.002569	.051303	19.972570	.050069	64
33	21.387799	429.216815	.002330	.046756	20.068303	.049830	66
34	23.467896	473.008333	.002114	.042611	20.155549	.049614	68
35	25.750295	521.058850	.001919	.038835	20.235063	.049419	70
36	28.254673	573.782580	.001743	.035392	20.307529	.049243	72
37	31.002616	631.634022	.001583	.032255	20.373572	.049083	74
38	34.017814	695.111878	.001439	.029396	20.433761	.048939	76
39	37.326259	764.763352	.001308	.026791	20.488615	.048808	78
40	40.956471	841.188868	.001189	.024416	20.538607	.048689	80
41	44.939744	925.047243	.001081	.022252	20.584168	.048581	82
42	49.310415	1017.061369	.000983	.020280	20.625691	.048483	84
43	54.106161	1118.024443	.000894	.018482	20.663533	.048394	86
44	59.368323	1228.806808	.000814	.016844	20.698021	.048314	88
45	65.142264	1350.363450	.000741	.015351	20.729452	.048241	90
46	71.477756	1483.742236	.000674	.013990	20.758098	.048174	92
47	78.429415	1630.092941	.000613	.012750	20.784204	.048113	94
48	86.057165	1790.677168	.000558	.011620	20.807996	.048058	96
49	94.426763	1966.879214	.000508	.010590	20.829680	.048008	98
50	103.610356	2160.218011	.000463	.009652	20.849441	.047963	100
51	113.687110	2372.360213	.000422	.008796	20.867451	.047922	102
52	124.743892	2605.134571	.000384	.008016	20.883865	.047884	104
53	136.876015	2860.547691	.000350	.007306	20.898824	.047850	106
54	150.188063	3140.801333	.000318	.006658	20.912456	.047818	108
55	164.794791	3448.311392	.000290	.006068	20.924881	.047790	110
56	180.822115	3785.728726	000264	.005530	20.936204	.047764	112
57	198.408195	4155.962006	.000241	.005040	20.946524	.047741	114
58	217.704632	4562.202785	.000219	.004593	20.955929	.047719	116
59	238.877768	5007.953019	.000200	.004186	20.964500	.047700	118
60	262.110124	5497.055251	.000182	.003815	20.972312	.047682	120

ANNUAL COMPOUND INTEREST TABLE

EFFECTIVE RATE = 9½%　　BASE = 1.095

YEARS	1 AMOUNT OF I AT COMPOUND INTEREST $S^n = (1+i)^n$	2 ACCUMULATION OF I PER PERIOD $S_{\overline{n}|} = \frac{S^n - 1}{i}$	3 SINKING FUND FACTOR $1/S_{\overline{n}|} = \frac{i}{S^n - 1}$	4 PRES. VALUE REVERSION OF I $V^n = \frac{1}{S^n}$	5 PRESENT VALUE ORD. ANNUITY 1 PER PERIOD $a_{\overline{n}|} = \frac{1 - V^n}{i}$	6 INSTALMENT TO AMORTIZE I $1/a_{\overline{n}|} = \frac{i}{1 - V^n}$	n YEARS
1	1.095000	1.000000	1.000000	.913242	.913242	1.095000	1
2	1.199025	2.095000	.477327	.834011	1.747253	.572327	2
3	1.312932	3.294025	.303580	.761654	2.508907	.398580	3
4	1.437661	4.606957	.217063	.695574	3.204481	.312063	4
5	1.574239	6.044618	.165436	.635228	3.839709	.260436	5
6	1.723791	7.618857	.131253	.580117	4.419825	.226253	6
7	1.887552	9.342648	.107036	.529787	4.949612	.202036	7
8	2.066869	11.230200	.089046	.483824	5.433436	.184046	8
9	2.263222	13.297069	.075205	.441848	5.875284	.170205	9
10	2.478228	15.560291	.064266	.403514	6.278798	.159266	10
11	2.713659	18.038518	.055437	.368506	6.647304	.150437	11
12	2.971457	20.752178	.048188	.336535	6.983839	.143188	12
13	3.253745	23.723634	.042152	.307338	7.291178	.137152	13
14	3.562851	26.977380	.037068	.280674	7.571852	.132068	14
15	3.901322	30.540231	.032744	.256323	7.828175	.127744	15
16	4.271948	34.441553	.029035	.234085	8.062260	.124035	16
17	4.677783	38.713500	.025831	.213777	8.276037	.120831	17
18	5.122172	43.391283	.023046	.195230	8.471266	.118046	18
19	5.608778	48.513454	.020613	.178292	8.649558	.115613	19
20	6.141612	54.122233	.018477	.162824	8.812382	.113477	20
21	6.725065	60.263845	.016594	.148697	8.961080	.111594	21
22	7.363946	66.988910	.014928	.135797	9.096876	.109928	22
23	8.063521	74.352856	.013449	.124015	9.220892	.108449	23
24	8.829556	82.416378	.012134	.113256	9.334148	.107134	24
25	9.668364	91.245934	.010959	.103430	9.437578	.105959	25
26	10.586858	100.914297	.009909	.094457	9.532034	.104909	26
27	11.592610	111.501156	.008969	.086262	9.618296	.103969	27
28	12.693908	123.093766	.008124	.078778	9.697074	.103124	28
29	13.899829	135.787673	.007364	.071943	9.769018	.102364	29
30	15.220313	149.687502	.006681	.065702	9.834719	.101681	30
31	16.666242	164.907815	.006064	.060002	9.894721	.101064	31
32	18.249535	181.574057	.005507	.054796	9.949517	.100507	32
33	19.983241	199.823593	.005004	.050042	9.999559	.100004	33
34	21.881649	219.806834	.004549	.045700	10.045259	.099549	34
35	23.960406	241.688483	.004138	.041736	10.086995	.099138	35
36	26.236644	265.648889	.003764	.038115	10.125109	.098764	36
37	28.729126	291.885534	.003426	.034808	10.159917	.098426	37
38	31.458393	320.614659	.003119	.031788	10.191705	.098119	38
39	34.446940	352.073052	.002840	.029030	10.220735	.097840	39
40	37.719399	386.519992	.002587	.026512	10.247247	.097587	40
41	41.302742	424.239391	.002357	.024211	10.271458	.097357	41
42	45.226503	465.542133	.002148	.022111	10.293569	.097148	42
43	49.523020	510.768636	.001958	.020193	10.313762	.096958	43
44	54.227707	560.291656	.001785	.018441	10.332203	.096785	44
45	59.379340	614.519364	.001627	.016841	10.349043	.096627	45
46	65.020377	673.898703	.001484	.015380	10.364423	.096484	46
47	71.197313	738.919080	.001353	.014045	10.378469	.096353	47
48	77.961057	810.116393	.001234	.012827	10.391296	.096234	48
49	85.367358	888.077450	.001126	.011714	10.403010	.096126	49
50	93.477257	973.444808	.001027	.010698	10.413707	.096027	50
51	102.357596	1066.922065	.000937	.009770	10.423477	.095937	51
52	112.081568	1169.279661	.000855	.008922	10.432399	.095855	52
53	122.729317	1281.361229	.000780	.008148	10.440547	.095780	53
54	134.388602	1404.090545	.000712	.007441	10.447988	.095712	54
55	147.155519	1538.479147	.000650	.006796	10.454784	.095650	55
56	161.135293	1685.634666	.000593	.006206	10.460990	.095593	56
57	176.443146	1846.769959	.000541	.005668	10.466657	.095541	57
58	193.205245	2023.213105	.000494	.005176	10.471833	.095494	58
59	211.559743	2216.418351	.000451	.004727	10.476560	.095451	59
60	231.657919	2427.978094	.000412	.004317	10.480877	.095412	60

9¾% MONTHLY COMPOUND INTEREST TABLE 9¾%

EFFECTIVE RATE = 13/16% BASE = 1.008125

MONTHS	1 AMOUNT OF I AT COMPOUND INTEREST $S^n = (1+i)^n$	2 ACCUMULATION OF I PER PERIOD $S_{\overline{n}\rvert} = \frac{S^n - 1}{i}$	3 SINKING FUND FACTOR $1/S_{\overline{n}\rvert} = \frac{i}{S^n - 1}$	4 PRES. VALUE REVERSION OF I $V^n = \frac{1}{S^n}$	5 PRESENT VALUE ORD. ANNUITY 1 PER PERIOD $a_{\overline{n}\rvert} = \frac{1 - V^n}{i}$	6 INSTALMENT TO AMORTIZE I $1/a_{\overline{n}\rvert} = \frac{i}{1 - V^n}$	n MONTHS
1	1.008125	1.000000	1.000000	.991940	.991940	1.008125	1
2	1.016316	2.008125	.497976	.983945	1.975886	.506101	2
3	1.024573	3.024441	.330639	.976015	2.951902	.338764	3
4	1.032898	4.049014	.246973	.968149	3.920051	.255098	4
5	1.041290	5.081912	.196776	.960346	4.880398	.204901	5
6	1.049751	6.123203	.163313	.952606	5.833005	.171438	6
7	1.058280	7.172954	.139412	.944929	6.777934	.147537	7
8	1.066878	8.231234	.121488	.937313	7.715248	.129613	8
9	1.075547	9.298113	.107548	.929759	8.645007	.115673	9
10	1.084285	10.373660	.096397	.922265	9.567273	.104522	10
11	1.093095	11.457946	.087275	.914832	10.482106	.095400	11
YEARS 1	1.101977	12.551042	.079674	.907459	11.389566	.087799	12
2	1.214353	26.382005	.037904	.823483	21.725139	.046029	24
3	1.338190	41.623411	.024024	.747277	31.104256	.032149	36
4	1.474655	58.419093	.017117	.678124	39.615427	.025242	48
5	1.625036	76.927552	.012999	.615370	47.338972	.021124	60
6	1.790753	97.323452	.010275	.558424	54.347780	.018400	72
7	1.973369	119.799270	.008347	.506747	60.707990	.016472	84
8	2.174607	144.567109	.006917	.459853	66.479625	.015042	96
9	2.396368	171.860703	.005818	.417298	71.717152	.013943	108
10	2.640743	201.937623	.004952	.378681	76.469996	.013077	120
11	2.910038	235.081703	.004253	.343638	80.783012	.012378	132
12	3.206796	271.605724	.003681	.311837	84.696900	.011806	144
13	3.533816	311.854362	.003206	.282980	88.248596	.011331	156
14	3.894185	356.207446	.002807	.256793	91.471617	.010932	168
15	4.291303	405.083533	.002468	.233029	94.396379	.010593	180
16	4.728918	458.943868	.002178	.211464	97.050483	.010303	192
17	5.211160	518.296731	.001929	.191895	99.458975	.010054	204
18	5.742580	583.702232	.001713	.174137	101.644586	.009838	216
19	6.328193	655.777605	.001524	.158022	103.627939	.009649	228
20	6.973524	735.203025	.001360	.143399	105.427752	.009485	240
21	7.684665	822.728028	.001215	.130129	107.061010	.009340	252
22	8.468326	919.178588	.001087	.118087	108.543126	.009212	264
23	9.331902	1025.464907	.000975	.107159	109.888087	.009100	276
24	10.283543	1142.590010	.000875	.097242	111.108585	.009000	288
25	11.332231	1271.659205	.000786	.088243	112.216138	.008911	300
26	12.487860	1413.890518	.000707	.080077	113.221198	.008832	312
27	13.761337	1570.626185	.000636	.072667	114.133249	.008761	324
28	15.164680	1743.345317	.000573	.065942	114.960898	.008698	336
29	16.711132	1933.677869	.000517	.059840	115.711957	.008642	348
30	18.415287	2143.420004	.000466	.054302	116.393513	.008591	360
31	20.293227	2374.551060	.000421	.049277	117.011997	.008546	372
32	22.362674	2629.252219	.000380	.044717	117.573246	.008505	384
33	24.643157	2909.927090	.000343	.040579	118.082558	.008468	396
34	27.156198	3219.224407	.000310	.036824	118.544738	.008435	408
35	29.925511	3560.063005	.000280	.033416	118.964147	.008405	420
36	32.977232	3935.659376	.000254	.030323	119.344744	.008379	432
37	36.340158	4349.558020	.000229	.027517	119.690121	.008354	444
38	40.046027	4805.664898	.000208	.024971	120.003535	.008333	456
39	44.129809	5308.284282	.000188	.022660	120.287948	.008313	468
40	48.630045	5862.159398	.000170	.020563	120.546040	.008295	480
41	53.589201	6472.517159	.000154	.018660	120.780249	.008279	492
42	59.054079	7145.117508	.000139	.016933	120.992784	.008264	504
43	65.076250	7886.307770	.000126	.015366	121.185649	.008251	516
44	71.712545	8703.082546	.000114	.013944	121.360669	.008239	528
45	79.025591	9603.149752	.000104	.012654	121.519491	.008229	540
46	87.084401	10595.003310	.000094	.011483	121.663617	.008219	552
47	95.965027	11688.003330	.000085	.010420	121.794404	.008210	564
48	105.751273	12892.464460	.000077	.009456	121.913089	.008202	576
49	116.535494	14219.753180	.000070	.008581	122.020790	.008195	588
50	128.419460	15682.395120	.000063	.007786	122.118524	.008188	600

9¾% QUARTERLY COMPOUND INTEREST TABLE 9¾%

EFFECTIVE RATE = 2-7/16% BASE = 1.024375

QUARTERS	1 AMOUNT OF I AT COMPOUND INTEREST $S^n = (1+i)^n$	2 ACCUMULATION OF I PER PERIOD $S_{\overline{n}\mid} = \frac{S^n - 1}{i}$	3 SINKING FUND FACTOR $1/S_{\overline{n}\mid} = \frac{i}{S^n - 1}$	4 PRES. VALUE REVERSION OF I $V^n = \frac{1}{S^n}$	5 PRESENT VALUE ORD. ANNUITY 1 PER PERIOD $a_{\overline{n}\mid} = \frac{1 - V^n}{i}$	6 INSTALMENT TO AMORTIZE I $1/a_{\overline{n}\mid} = \frac{i}{1 - V^n}$	n QUARTERS
1	1.024375	1.000000	1.000000	.976205	.976205	1.024375	1
2	1.049344	2.024375	.493980	.952976	1.929181	.518355	2
3	1.074922	3.073719	.325339	.930300	2.859481	.349714	3
YEARS							
1	1.101123	4.148641	.241043	.908164	3.767645	.265418	4
2	1.212472	8.716806	.114721	.824761	7.189283	.139096	8
3	1.335081	13.746917	.072744	.749018	10.296691	.097119	12
4	1.470089	19.285690	.051852	.680231	13.118725	.076227	16
5	1.618749	25.384560	.039394	.617761	15.681594	.063769	20
6	1.782442	32.100167	.031152	.561028	18.009099	.055527	24
7	1.962688	39.494877	.025320	.509505	20.122854	.049695	28
8	2.161161	47.637364	.020992	.462714	22.042490	.045367	32
9	2.379704	56.603244	.017667	.420220	23.785833	.042042	36
10	2.620347	66.475782	.015043	.381629	25.369074	.039418	40
11	2.885325	77.346662	.012929	.346581	26.806916	.037304	44
12	3.177098	89.316839	.011196	.314753	28.112712	.035571	48
13	3.498376	102.497478	.009756	.285847	29.298588	.034131	52
14	3.852143	117.010984	.008546	.259596	30.375558	.032921	56
15	4.241683	132.992142	.007519	.235755	31.353622	.031894	60
16	4.670616	150.589364	.006641	.214105	32.241865	.031016	64
17	5.142923	169.966072	.005884	.194442	33.048535	.030259	68
18	5.662991	191.302213	.005227	.176585	33.781123	.029602	72
19	6.235651	214.795932	.004656	.160368	34.446433	.029031	76
20	6.866219	240.665409	.004155	.145641	35.050644	.028530	80
21	7.560553	269.150889	.003715	.132265	35.599366	.028090	84
22	8.325100	300.516909	.003328	.120119	36.097695	.027703	88
23	9.166960	335.054759	.002985	.109087	36.550260	.027360	92
24	10.093951	373.085184	.002680	.099069	36.961262	.027055	96
25	11.114683	414.961365	.002410	.089971	37.334520	.026785	100
26	12.238635	461.072197	.002169	.081708	37.673499	.026544	104
27	13.476244	511.845899	.001954	.074205	37.981348	.026329	108
28	14.839004	567.753997	.001761	.067390	38.260924	.026136	112
29	16.339570	629.315697	.001589	.061201	38.514826	.025964	116
30	17.991879	697.102708	.001435	.055581	38.745410	.025810	120
31	19.811274	771.744554	.001296	.050476	38.954818	.025671	124
32	21.814651	853.934416	.001171	.045841	39.144995	.025546	128
33	24.020617	944.435575	.001059	.041631	39.317707	.025434	132
34	26.449657	1044.088493	.000958	.037808	39.474557	.025333	136
35	29.124329	1153.818626	.000867	.034336	39.617003	.025242	140
36	32.069472	1274.645013	.000785	.031182	39.746367	.025160	144
37	35.312437	1407.689741	.000710	.028319	39.863851	.025085	148
38	38.883341	1554.188368	.000643	.025718	39.970545	.025018	152
39	42.815347	1715.501395	.000583	.023356	40.067442	.024958	156
40	47.144968	1893.126899	.000528	.021211	40.155439	.024903	160
41	51.912415	2088.714449	.000479	.019263	40.235355	.024854	164
42	57.161960	2304.080423	.000434	.017494	40.307932	.024809	168
43	62.942356	2541.224878	.000394	.015888	40.373844	.024769	172
44	69.307284	2802.350122	.000357	.014428	40.433703	.024732	176
45	76.315853	3089.881166	.000324	.013103	40.488064	.024699	180
46	84.033151	3406.488248	.000294	.011900	40.537433	.024669	184
47	92.530846	3755.111628	.000266	.010807	40.582268	.024641	188
48	101.887854	4138.988894	.000242	.009815	40.622986	.024617	192
49	112.191073	4561.685030	.000219	.008913	40.659965	.024594	196
50	123.536185	5027.125518	.000199	.008095	40.693547	.024574	200
51	136.028550	5539.632804	.000181	.007351	40.724045	.024556	204
52	149.784182	6103.966429	.000164	.006676	40.751743	.024539	208
53	164.930826	6725.367233	.000149	.006063	40.776897	.024524	212
54	181.609147	7409.606027	.000135	.005506	40.799740	.024510	216
55	199.974032	8163.037190	.000123	.005001	40.820486	.024498	220
56	220.196031	8992.657666	.000111	.004541	40.839327	.024486	224
57	242.462941	9906.171955	.000101	.004124	40.856437	.024476	228
58	266.981552	10912.063670	.000092	.003746	40.871976	.024467	232
59	293.979561	12019.674290	.000083	.003402	40.886088	.024458	236
60	323.707693	13239.289970	.000076	.003089	40.898904	.024451	240

9 ¾ % SEMI-ANNUAL COMPOUND INTEREST TABLE 9 ¾ %

EFFECTIVE RATE = 4-7/8% BASE = 1.04875

	1 AMOUNT OF I AT COMPOUND INTEREST $S^n = (1+i)^n$	2 ACCUMULATION OF I PER PERIOD $S_{\overline{n}\mid} = \frac{S^n - 1}{i}$	3 SINKING FUND FACTOR $1/S_{\overline{n}\mid} = \frac{i}{S^n - 1}$	4 PRES. VALUE REVERSION OF I $V^n = \frac{1}{S^n}$	5 PRESENT VALUE ORD. ANNUITY 1 PER PERIOD $a_{\overline{n}\mid} = \frac{1 - V^n}{i}$	6 INSTALMENT TO AMORTIZE I $1/a_{\overline{n}\mid} = \frac{i}{1 - V^n}$	n HALF YEARS
HALF YEARS 1	1.048750	1.000000	1.000000	.953516	.953516	1.048750	1
YEARS							
1	1.099877	2.048750	.488102	.909193	1.862709	.536852	2
2	1.209728	4.302122	.232443	.826632	3.556271	.281193	4
3	1.330552	6.780553	.147481	.751568	5.096045	.196231	6
4	1.463443	9.506522	.105191	.683320	6.495998	.153941	8
5	1.609607	12.504750	.079970	.621270	7.768824	.128720	10
6	1.770369	15.802432	.063281	.564854	8.926069	.112031	12
7	1.947187	19.429474	.051468	.513561	9.978228	.100218	14
8	2.141665	23.418773	.042701	.466926	10.934843	.091451	16
9	2.355567	27.806510	.035963	.424526	11.804591	.084713	18
10	2.590833	32.632479	.030644	.385976	12.595360	.079394	20
11	2.849597	37.940449	.026357	.350927	13.314321	.075107	22
12	3.134205	43.778560	.022842	.319060	13.967996	.071592	24
13	3.447238	50.199762	.019920	.290087	14.562312	.068670	26
14	3.791537	57.262292	.017463	.263745	15.102660	.066213	28
15	4.170222	65.030203	.015377	.239795	15.593941	.064127	30
16	4.586730	73.573946	.013592	.218020	16.040610	.062342	32
17	5.044837	82.971009	.012052	.198222	16.446719	.060802	34
18	5.548698	93.306618	.010717	.180222	16.815949	.059467	36
19	6.102882	104.674512	.009553	.163857	17.151651	.058303	38
20	6.712417	117.177793	.008534	.148978	17.456869	.057284	40
21	7.382831	130.929858	.007638	.135449	17.734371	.056388	42
22	8.120202	146.055432	.006847	.123150	17.986674	.055597	44
23	8.931220	162.691696	.006147	.111967	18.216066	.054897	46
24	9.823240	180.989534	.005525	.101799	18.424628	.054275	48
25	10.804351	201.114896	.004972	.092555	18.614250	.053722	50
26	11.883453	223.250311	.004479	.084151	18.786654	.053229	52
27	13.070331	247.596534	.004039	.076509	18.943402	.052789	54
28	14.375751	274.374375	.003645	.069562	19.085916	.052395	56
29	15.811551	303.826694	.003291	.063245	19.215489	.052041	58
30	17.390755	336.220610	.002974	.057502	19.333296	.051724	60
31	19.127684	371.849919	.002689	.052280	19.440405	.051439	62
32	21.038091	411.037761	.002433	.047533	19.537788	.051183	64
33	23.139303	454.139549	.002202	.043217	19.626328	.050952	66
34	25.450377	501.546196	.001994	.039292	19.706828	.050744	68
35	27.992273	553.687656	.001806	.035724	19.780018	.050556	70
36	30.788045	611.036826	.001637	.032480	19.846561	.050387	72
37	33.863049	674.113834	.001483	.029531	19.907062	.050233	74
38	37.245174	743.490756	.001345	.026849	19.962069	.050095	76
39	40.965094	819.796807	.001220	.024411	20.012082	.049970	78
40	45.056547	903.724045	.001107	.022194	20.057552	.049857	80
41	49.556640	996.033646	.001004	.020179	20.098894	.049754	82
42	54.506187	1097.562812	.000911	.018347	20.136481	.049661	84
43	59.950078	1209.232363	.000827	.016681	20.170655	.049577	86
44	65.937685	1332.055085	.000751	.015166	20.201726	.049501	88
45	72.523315	1467.144917	.000682	.013789	20.229976	.049432	90
46	79.766694	1615.727058	.000619	.012537	20.255660	.049369	92
47	87.733517	1779.149073	.000562	.011398	20.279012	.049312	94
48	96.496039	1958.893117	.000510	.010363	20.300244	.049260	96
49	106.133732	2156.589378	.000464	.009422	20.319547	.049214	98
50	116.734005	2374.030862	.000421	.008566	20.337098	.049171	100
51	128.392996	2613.189653	.000383	.007789	20.353055	.049133	102
52	141.216447	2876.234804	.000348	.007081	20.367563	.049098	104
53	155.320660	3165.552000	.000316	.006438	20.380753	.049066	106
54	170.833554	3483.765202	.000287	.005854	20.392746	.049037	108
55	187.895822	3833.760445	.000261	.005322	20.403649	.049011	110
56	206.662211	4218.712010	.000237	.004839	20.413563	.048987	112
57	227.302922	4642.111214	.000215	.004399	20.422576	.048965	114
58	250.005156	5107.798076	.000196	.004000	20.430771	.048946	116
59	274.974812	5619.996139	.000178	.003637	20.438222	.048928	118
60	302.438351	6183.350786	.000162	.003306	20.444996	.048912	120

9¾% ANNUAL COMPOUND INTEREST 9¾%

EFFECTIVE RATE = 9¾% BASE = 1.0975

YEARS	1 AMOUNT OF I AT COMPOUND INTEREST $S^n = (1 + i)^n$	2 ACCUMULATION OF I PER PERIOD $S_{\overline{n}\vert} = \frac{S^n - 1}{i}$	3 SINKING FUND FACTOR $1/S_{\overline{n}\vert} = \frac{i}{S^n - 1}$	4 PRES. VALUE REVERSION OF I $V^n = \frac{1}{S^n}$	5 PRESENT VALUE ORD. ANNUITY 1 PER PERIOD $a_{\overline{n}\vert} = \frac{1 - V^n}{i}$	6 INSTALMENT TO AMORTIZE I $1/a_{\overline{n}\vert} = \frac{i}{1 - V^n}$	n YEARS
1	1.097500	1.000000	1.000000	.911162	.911162	1.097500	1
2	1.204506	2.097500	.476758	.830216	1.741377	.574258	2
3	1.321946	3.302006	.302846	.756461	2.497838	.400346	3
4	1.450835	4.623952	.216265	.689258	3.187096	.313765	4
5	1.592292	6.074787	.164615	.628026	3.815122	.262115	5
6	1.747540	7.667079	.130428	.572233	4.387355	.227928	6
7	1.917925	9.414619	.106218	.521397	4.908752	.203718	7
8	2.104923	11.332544	.088241	.475077	5.383828	.185741	8
9	2.310153	13.437468	.074419	.432872	5.816700	.171919	9
10	2.535393	15.747621	.063502	.394416	6.211116	.161002	10
11	2.782594	18.283014	.054696	.359377	6.570493	.152196	11
12	3.053897	21.065608	.047471	.327450	6.897944	.144971	12
13	3.351652	24.119504	.041460	.298360	7.196304	.138960	13
14	3.678438	27.471156	.036402	.271855	7.468159	.133902	14
15	4.037085	31.149594	.032103	.247703	7.715862	.129603	15
16	4.430701	35.186679	.028420	.225698	7.941560	.125920	16
17	4.862695	39.617380	.025241	.205647	8.147207	.122741	17
18	5.336807	44.480075	.022482	.187378	8.334585	.119982	18
19	5.857146	49.816882	.020074	.170732	8.505317	.117574	19
20	6.428218	55.674028	.017962	.155564	8.660881	.115462	20
21	7.054969	62.102246	.016102	.141744	8.802625	.113602	21
22	7.742828	69.157215	.014460	.129152	8.931777	.111960	22
23	8.497754	76.900043	.013004	.117678	9.049455	.110504	23
24	9.326285	85.397797	.011710	.107224	9.156679	.109210	24
25	10.235598	94.724083	.010557	.097698	9.254377	.108057	25
26	11.233569	104.959681	.009527	.089019	9.343396	.107027	26
27	12.328842	116.193250	.008606	.081111	9.424506	.106106	27
28	13.530904	128.522092	.007781	.073905	9.498411	.105281	28
29	14.850167	142.052995	.007040	.067339	9.565751	.104540	29
30	16.298058	156.903163	.006373	.061357	9.627108	.103873	30
31	17.887119	173.201221	.005774	.055906	9.683014	.103274	31
32	19.631113	191.088340	.005233	.050940	9.733953	.102733	32
33	21.545147	210.719453	.004746	.046414	9.780368	.102246	33
34	23.645798	232.264600	.004305	.042291	9.822658	.101805	34
35	25.951264	255.910398	.003908	.038534	9.861192	.101408	35
36	28.481512	281.861662	.003548	.035110	9.896303	.101048	36
37	31.258459	310.343174	.003222	.031991	9.928294	.100722	37
38	34.306159	341.601634	.002927	.029149	9.957443	.100427	38
39	37.651010	375.907793	.002660	.026560	9.984003	.100160	39
40	41.321983	413.558803	.002418	.024200	10.008203	.099918	40
41	45.350877	454.880786	.002198	.022050	10.030253	.099698	41
42	49.772587	500.231663	.001999	.020091	10.050345	.099499	42
43	54.625414	550.004250	.001818	.018306	10.068651	.099318	43
44	59.951392	604.629664	.001654	.016680	10.085331	.099154	44
45	65.796653	664.581056	.001505	.015198	10.100530	.099005	45
46	72.211827	730.377709	.001369	.013848	10.114378	.098869	46
47	79.252480	802.589536	.001246	.012618	10.126996	.098746	47
48	86.979597	881.842016	.001134	.011497	10.138493	.098634	48
49	95.460107	968.821612	.001032	.010476	10.148968	.098532	49
50	104.767468	1064.281720	.000940	.009545	10.158513	.098440	50
51	114.982296	1169.049188	.000855	.008697	10.167210	.098355	51
52	126.193070	1284.031483	.000779	.007924	10.175135	.098279	52
53	138.496894	1410.224553	.000709	.007220	10.182355	.098209	53
54	152.000341	1548.721447	.000646	.006579	10.188934	.098146	54
55	166.820374	1700.721789	.000588	.005994	10.194929	.098088	55
56	183.085361	1867.542163	.000535	.005462	10.200390	.098035	56
57	200.936184	2050.627524	.000488	.004977	10.205367	.097988	57
58	220.527462	2251.563708	.000444	.004535	10.209902	.097944	58
59	242.028889	2472.091169	.000405	.004132	10.214033	.097905	59
60	265.626706	2714.120058	.000368	.003765	10.217798	.097868	60

10% MONTHLY COMPOUND INTEREST TABLE 10%

EFFECTIVE RATE = 5/6%   BASE = 1.00833333

MONTHS	1 AMOUNT OF I AT COMPOUND INTEREST $S^n = (1+i)^n$	2 ACCUMULATION OF I PER PERIOD $s_{\overline{n}\|} = \frac{S^n - 1}{i}$	3 SINKING FUND FACTOR $1/s_{\overline{n}\|} = \frac{i}{S^n - 1}$	4 PRES. VALUE REVERSION OF I $V^n = \frac{1}{S^n}$	5 PRESENT VALUE ORD. ANNUITY 1 PER PERIOD $a_{\overline{n}\|} = \frac{1 - V^n}{i}$	6 INSTALMENT TO AMORTIZE I $1/a_{\overline{n}\|} = \frac{i}{1 - V^n}$	n MONTHS
1	1.008333	1.000000	1.000000	.991735	.991735	1.008333	1
2	1.016736	2.008333	.497925	.983539	1.975274	.506258	2
3	1.025208	3.025069	.330570	.975410	2.950685	.338904	3
4	1.033752	4.050278	.246896	.967349	3.918035	.255229	4
5	1.042366	5.084030	.196694	.959355	4.877390	.205027	5
6	1.051053	6.126397	.163228	.951426	5.828817	.171561	6
7	1.059812	7.177450	.139325	.943563	6.772380	.147658	7
8	1.068643	8.237262	.121399	.935765	7.708146	.129732	8
9	1.077549	9.305906	.107458	.928031	8.636177	.115791	9
10	1.086528	10.383456	.096307	.920362	9.556540	.104640	10
11	1.095583	11.469984	.087184	.912755	10.469295	.095517	11
YEARS							
1	1.104713	12.565568	.079582	.905212	11.374508	.087915	12
2	1.220390	26.446915	.037811	.819409	21.670854	.046144	24
3	1.348181	41.781821	.023933	.741739	30.991235	.032267	36
4	1.489354	58.722491	.017029	.671432	39.428160	.025362	48
5	1.645308	77.437072	.012913	.607788	47.065369	.021247	60
6	1.817594	98.111313	.010192	.550177	53.978665	.018525	72
7	2.007920	120.950418	.008267	.498027	60.236667	.016601	84
8	2.218175	146.181075	.006840	.450820	65.901488	.015174	96
9	2.450447	174.053712	.005745	.408088	71.029355	.014078	108
10	2.707041	204.844978	.004881	.369406	75.671163	.013215	120
11	2.990504	238.860492	.004186	.334391	79.872985	.012519	132
12	3.303648	276.437875	.003617	.302695	83.676528	.011950	144
13	3.649584	317.950100	.003145	.274003	87.119542	.011478	156
14	4.031743	363.809198	.002748	.248031	90.236200	.011082	168
15	4.453919	414.470344	.002412	.224521	93.057438	.010746	180
16	4.920303	470.436373	.002125	.203239	95.611258	.010459	192
17	5.435523	532.262776	.001878	.183974	97.923008	.010212	204
18	6.004693	600.563212	.001665	.166536	100.015632	.009998	216
19	6.633463	676.015596	.001479	.150750	101.909902	.009812	228
20	7.328073	759.368830	.001316	.136461	103.624619	.009650	240
21	8.095418	851.450237	.001174	.123526	105.176801	.009507	252
22	8.943114	953.173772	.001049	.111817	106.581857	.009382	264
23	9.879575	1065.549089	.000938	.101218	107.853729	.009271	276
24	10.914096	1189.691570	.000840	.091624	109.005045	.009173	288
25	12.056944	1326.833392	.000753	.082939	110.047230	.009087	300
26	13.319464	1478.335753	.000676	.075078	110.990629	.009009	312
27	14.714186	1645.702391	.000607	.067961	111.844605	.008940	324
28	16.254954	1830.594505	.000546	.061519	112.617636	.008879	336
29	17.957060	2034.847238	.000491	.055688	113.317391	.008824	348
30	19.837399	2260.487900	.000442	.050409	113.950820	.008775	360
31	21.914633	2509.756088	.000398	.045631	114.524207	.008731	372
32	24.209382	2785.125915	.000359	.041306	115.043244	.008692	384
33	26.744421	3089.330559	.000323	.037390	115.513083	.008657	396
34	29.544911	3425.389403	.000291	.033846	115.938387	.008625	408
35	32.638649	3796.638004	.000263	.030638	116.323378	.008596	420
36	36.056343	4206.761180	.000237	.027734	116.671875	.008571	432
37	39.831913	4659.829611	.000214	.025105	116.987341	.008547	444
38	44.002835	5160.340233	.000193	.022725	117.272903	.008527	456
39	48.610506	5713.260852	.000175	.020571	117.531398	.008508	468
40	53.700662	6324.079483	.000158	.018621	117.765390	.008491	480
41	59.323823	6998.858807	.000142	.016856	117.977204	.008476	492
42	65.535802	7744.296352	.000129	.015258	118.168940	.008462	504
43	72.398257	8567.790939	.000116	.013812	118.342502	.008450	516
44	79.979301	9477.516170	.000105	.012503	118.499611	.008438	528
45	88.354179	10482.501530	.000095	.011318	118.641830	.008428	540
46	97.606016	11592.721980	.000086	.010245	118.770568	.008419	552
47	107.826641	12819.197020	.000078	.009274	118.887103	.008411	564
48	119.117499	14174.100030	.000070	.008395	118.992592	.008403	576
49	131.590658	15670.879080	.000063	.007599	119.088082	.008397	588
50	145.369919	17324.390450	.000057	.006879	119.174520	.008391	600

10% QUARTERLY COMPOUND INTEREST TABLE 10%

EFFECTIVE RATE = 2½% BASE = 1.025

QUARTERS	1 AMOUNT OF 1 AT COMPOUND INTEREST $S^n = (1+i)^n$	2 ACCUMULATION OF 1 PER PERIOD $s_{\overline{n}\rvert} = \frac{S^n - 1}{i}$	3 SINKING FUND FACTOR $1/s_{\overline{n}\rvert} = \frac{i}{S^n - 1}$	4 PRES. VALUE REVERSION OF 1 $V^n = \frac{1}{S^n}$	5 PRESENT VALUE ORD. ANNUITY 1 PER PERIOD $a_{\overline{n}\rvert} = \frac{1 - V^n}{i}$	6 INSTALMENT TO AMORTIZE 1 $1/a_{\overline{n}\rvert} = \frac{i}{1 - V^n}$	n QUARTERS
1	1.025000	1.000000	1.000000	.975610	.975610	1.025000	1
2	1.050625	2.025000	.493827	.951814	1.927424	.518827	2
3	1.076891	3.075625	.325137	.928599	2.856024	.350137	3
YEARS							
1	1.103813	4.152516	.240818	.905951	3.761974	.265818	4
2	1.218403	8.736116	.114467	.820747	7.170137	.139467	8
3	1.344889	13.795553	.072487	.743556	10.257765	.097487	12
4	1.484506	19.380225	.051599	.673625	13.055003	.076599	16
5	1.638616	25.544658	.039147	.610271	15.589162	.064147	20
6	1.808726	32.349038	.030913	.552875	17.884986	.055913	24
7	1.996495	39.859801	.025088	.500878	19.964889	.050088	28
8	2.203757	48.150278	.020768	.453771	21.849178	.045768	32
9	2.432535	57.301413	.017452	.411094	23.556251	.042452	36
10	2.685064	67.402554	.014836	.372431	25.102775	.039836	40
11	2.963808	78.552323	.012730	.337404	26.503849	.037730	44
12	3.271490	90.859583	.011006	.305671	27.773154	.036006	48
13	3.611112	104.444494	.009574	.276923	28.923081	.034574	52
14	3.985992	119.439695	.008372	.250879	29.964858	.033372	56
15	4.399790	135.991590	.007353	.227284	30.908657	.032353	60
16	4.856545	154.261786	.006482	.205908	31.763692	.031482	64
17	5.360717	174.428664	.005733	.186542	32.538311	.030733	68
18	5.917228	196.689123	.005084	.168998	33.240078	.030084	72
19	6.531513	221.260505	.004520	.153104	33.875844	.029520	76
20	7.209568	248.382713	.004026	.138705	34.451817	.029026	80
21	7.958014	278.320556	.003593	.125659	34.973620	.028593	84
22	8.784158	311.366333	.003212	.113841	35.446348	.028212	88
23	9.696067	347.842688	.002875	.103135	35.874616	.027875	92
24	10.702644	388.105759	.002577	.093435	36.262606	.027577	96
25	11.813716	432.548655	.002312	.084647	36.614105	.027312	100
26	13.040132	481.605297	.002076	.076686	36.932546	.027076	104
27	14.393866	535.754651	.001867	.069474	37.221039	.026867	108
28	15.888135	595.525406	.001679	.062940	37.482398	.026679	112
29	17.537528	661.501135	.001512	.057021	37.719177	.026512	116
30	19.358150	734.325996	.001362	.051658	37.933687	.026362	120
31	21.367775	814.711016	.001227	.046799	38.128022	.026227	124
32	23.586026	903.441037	.001107	.042398	38.304081	.026107	128
33	26.034559	1001.382378	.000999	.038410	38.463581	.025999	132
34	28.737282	1109.491294	.000901	.034798	38.608080	.025901	136
35	31.720583	1228.823308	.000814	.031525	38.738989	.025814	140
36	35.013588	1360.543523	.000735	.028560	38.857586	.025735	144
37	38.648450	1505.937994	.000664	.025874	38.965030	.025664	148
38	42.660657	1666.426286	.000600	.023441	39.062368	.025600	152
39	47.089383	1843.575332	.000542	.021236	39.150552	.025542	156
40	51.977868	2039.114732	.000490	.019239	39.230442	.025490	160
41	57.373841	2254.953642	.000443	.017430	39.302818	.025443	164
42	63.329985	2493.199414	.000401	.015790	39.368388	.025401	168
43	69.904454	2756.178168	.000363	.014305	39.427790	.025363	172
44	77.161438	3046.457506	.000328	.012960	39.481606	.025328	176
45	85.171790	3366.871582	.000297	.011741	39.530361	.025297	180
46	94.013719	3720.548769	.000269	.010637	39.574530	.025269	184
47	103.773555	4110.942208	.000243	.009636	39.614545	.025243	188
48	114.546588	4541.863516	.000220	.008730	39.650797	.025220	192
49	126.438000	5017.520012	.000199	.007909	39.683639	.025199	196
50	139.563895	5542.555784	.000180	.007165	39.713393	.025180	200
51	154.052426	6122.097036	.000163	.006491	39.740348	.025163	204
52	170.045054	6761.802144	.000148	.005881	39.764768	.025148	208
53	187.697922	7467.916888	.000134	.005328	39.786892	.025134	212
54	207.183386	8247.335444	.000121	.004827	39.806934	.025121	216
55	228.691692	9107.667692	.000110	.004373	39.825092	.025110	220
56	252.432838	10057.313520	.000099	.003961	39.841542	.025099	224
57	278.638621	11105.544820	.000090	.003589	39.856445	.025090	228
58	307.564901	12262.596050	.000082	.003251	39.869946	.025082	232
59	339.494103	13539.764110	.000074	.002946	39.882178	.025074	236
60	374.737967	14949.518680	.000067	.002669	39.893259	.025067	240

10% SEMI-ANNUAL COMPOUND INTEREST TABLE 10%

EFFECTIVE RATE = 5% BASE = 1.05

HALF YEARS	1 AMOUNT OF I AT COMPOUND INTEREST $S^n = (1+i)^n$	2 ACCUMULATION OF I PER PERIOD $S_{\overline{n}\rvert} = \frac{S^n - 1}{i}$	3 SINKING FUND FACTOR $1/S_{\overline{n}\rvert} = \frac{i}{S^n - 1}$	4 PRES. VALUE REVERSION OF I $V^n = \frac{1}{S^n}$	5 PRESENT VALUE ORD. ANNUITY 1 PER PERIOD $a_{\overline{n}\rvert} = \frac{1 - V^n}{i}$	6 INSTALMENT TO AMORTIZE I $1/a_{\overline{n}\rvert} = \frac{i}{1 - V^n}$	n HALF YEARS
1	1.050000	1.000000	1.000000	.952381	.952381	1.050000	1
YEARS							
1	1.102500	2.050000	.487805	.907029	1.859410	.537805	2
2	1.215506	4.310125	.232012	.822702	3.545951	.282012	4
3	1.340096	6.801913	.147017	.746215	5.075692	.197017	6
4	1.477455	9.549109	.104722	.676839	6.463213	.154722	8
5	1.628895	12.577893	.079505	.613913	7.721735	.129505	10
6	1.795856	15.917127	.062825	.556837	8.863252	.112825	12
7	1.979932	19.598632	.051024	.505068	9.898641	.101024	14
8	2.182875	23.657492	.042270	.458112	10.837770	.092270	16
9	2.406619	28.132385	.035546	.415521	11.689587	.085546	18
10	2.653298	33.065954	.030243	.376889	12.462210	.080243	20
11	2.925261	38.505214	.025971	.341850	13.163003	.075971	22
12	3.225100	44.501999	.022471	.310068	13.798642	.072471	24
13	3.555673	51.113454	.019564	.281241	14.375185	.069564	26
14	3.920129	58.402583	.017123	.255094	14.898127	.067123	28
15	4.321942	66.438847	.015051	.231377	15.372451	.065051	30
16	4.764941	75.298829	.013280	.209866	15.802677	.063280	32
17	5.253348	85.066959	.011755	.190355	16.192904	.061755	34
18	5.791816	95.836323	.010434	.172657	16.546852	.060434	36
19	6.385477	107.709546	.009284	.156605	16.867893	.059284	38
20	7.039989	120.799774	.008278	.142046	17.159086	.058278	40
21	7.761588	135.231751	.007395	.128840	17.423208	.057395	42
22	8.557150	151.143005	.006616	.116861	17.662773	.056616	44
23	9.434258	168.685164	.005928	.105997	17.880066	.055928	46
24	10.401270	188.025393	.005318	.096142	18.077158	.055318	48
25	11.467400	209.347996	.004777	.087204	18.255925	.054777	50
26	12.642808	232.856165	.004294	.079096	18.418073	.054294	52
27	13.938696	258.773922	.003864	.071743	18.565146	.053864	54
28	15.367412	287.348249	.003480	.065073	18.698545	.053480	56
29	16.942572	318.851445	.003136	.059023	18.819542	.053136	58
30	18.679186	353.583718	.002828	.053536	18.929290	.052828	60
31	20.593802	391.876049	.002552	.048558	19.028834	.052552	62
32	22.704667	434.093344	.002304	.044044	19.119124	.052304	64
33	25.031896	480.637912	.002081	.039949	19.201019	.052081	66
34	27.597665	531.953298	.001880	.036235	19.275301	.051880	68
35	30.426426	588.528511	.001699	.032866	19.342677	.051699	70
36	33.545134	650.902683	.001536	.029811	19.403788	.051536	72
37	36.983510	719.670208	.001390	.027039	19.459218	.051390	74
38	40.774320	795.486404	.001257	.024525	19.509495	.051257	76
39	44.953688	879.073761	.001138	.022245	19.555098	.051138	78
40	49.561441	971.228821	.001030	.020177	19.596460	.051030	80
41	54.641489	1072.829775	.000932	.018301	19.633978	.050932	82
42	60.242241	1184.844827	.000844	.016600	19.668007	.050844	84
43	66.417071	1308.341422	.000764	.015056	19.698873	.050764	86
44	73.224821	1444.496418	.000692	.013657	19.726869	.050692	88
45	80.730365	1594.607301	.000627	.012387	19.752262	.050627	90
46	89.005227	1760.104549	.000568	.011235	19.775294	.050568	92
47	98.128263	1942.565265	.000515	.010191	19.796185	.050515	94
48	108.186410	2143.728204	.000466	.009243	19.815134	.050466	96
49	119.275517	2365.510344	.000423	.008384	19.832321	.050423	98
50	131.501258	2610.025154	.000383	.007604	19.847910	.050383	100
51	144.980137	2879.602732	.000347	.006897	19.862050	.050347	102
52	159.840601	3176.812012	.000315	.006256	19.874875	.050315	104
53	176.224262	3504.485244	.000285	.005675	19.886508	.050285	106
54	194.287249	3865.744982	.000259	.005147	19.897060	.050259	108
55	214.201692	4264.033842	.000235	.004668	19.906630	.050235	110
56	236.157366	4703.147310	.000213	.004234	19.915311	.050213	112
57	260.363496	5187.269910	.000193	.003841	19.923184	.050193	114
58	287.050754	5721.015076	.000175	.003484	19.930326	.050175	116
59	316.473456	6309.469122	.000158	.003160	19.936804	.050158	118
60	348.911985	6958.239706	.000144	.002866	19.942679	.050144	120

10% ANNUAL COMPOUND INTEREST TABLE 10%

EFFECTIVE RATE = 10% BASE = 1.10

YEARS	1 AMOUNT OF 1 AT COMPOUND INTEREST $S^n = (1+i)^n$	2 ACCUMULATION OF 1 PER PERIOD $S_{\overline{n}\mid} = \frac{S^n - 1}{i}$	3 SINKING FUND FACTOR $1/S_{\overline{n}\mid} = \frac{i}{S^n - 1}$	4 PRES. VALUE REVERSION OF 1 $V^n = \frac{1}{S^n}$	5 PRESENT VALUE ORD. ANNUITY 1 PER PERIOD $a_{\overline{n}\mid} = \frac{1 - V^n}{i}$	6 INSTALMENT TO AMORTIZE 1 $1/a_{\overline{n}\mid} = \frac{i}{1 - V^n}$	n YEARS
1	1.100000	1.000000	1.000000	.909091	.909091	1.100000	1
2	1.210000	2.100000	.476190	.826446	1.735537	.576190	2
3	1.331000	3.310000	.302115	.751315	2.486852	.402115	3
4	1.464100	4.641000	.215471	.683013	3.169865	.315471	4
5	1.610510	6.105100	.163797	.620921	3.790787	.263797	5
6	1.771561	7.715610	.129607	.564474	4.355261	.229607	6
7	1.948717	9.487171	.105405	.513158	4.868419	.205405	7
8	2.143589	11.435888	.087444	.466507	5.334926	.187444	8
9	2.357948	13.579477	.073641	.424098	5.759024	.173641	9
10	2.593742	15.937425	.062745	.385543	6.144567	.162745	10
11	2.853117	18.531167	.053963	.350494	6.495061	.153963	11
12	3.138428	21.384284	.046763	.318631	6.813692	.146763	12
13	3.452271	24.522712	.040779	.289664	7.103356	.140779	13
14	3.797498	27.974983	.035746	.263331	7.366687	.135746	14
15	4.177248	31.772482	.031474	.239392	7.606080	.131474	15
16	4.594973	35.949730	.027817	.217629	7.823709	.127817	16
17	5.054470	40.544703	.024664	.197845	8.021553	.124664	17
18	5.559917	45.599173	.021930	.179859	8.201412	.121930	18
19	6.115909	51.159090	.019547	.163508	8.364920	.119547	19
20	6.727500	57.274999	.017460	.148644	8.513564	.117460	20
21	7.400250	64.002499	.015624	.135131	8.648694	.115624	21
22	8.140275	71.402749	.014005	.122846	8.771540	.114005	22
23	8.954302	79.543024	.012572	.111678	8.883218	.112572	23
24	9.849733	88.497327	.011300	.101526	8.984744	.111300	24
25	10.834706	98.347059	.010168	.092296	9.077040	.110168	25
26	11.918177	109.181765	.009159	.083905	9.160945	.109159	26
27	13.109994	121.099942	.008258	.076278	9.237223	.108258	27
28	14.420994	134.209936	.007451	.069343	9.306567	.107451	28
29	15.863093	148.630930	.006728	.063039	9.369606	.106728	29
30	17.449402	164.494023	.006079	.057309	9.426914	.106079	30
31	19.194342	181.943425	.005496	.052099	9.479013	.105496	31
32	21.113777	201.137767	.004972	.047362	9.526376	.104972	32
33	23.225154	222.251544	.004499	.043057	9.569432	.104499	33
34	25.547670	245.476699	.004074	.039143	9.608575	.104074	34
35	28.102437	271.024368	.003690	.035584	9.644159	.103690	35
36	30.912681	299.126805	.003343	.032349	9.676508	.103343	36
37	34.003949	330.039486	.003030	.029408	9.705917	.103030	37
38	37.404343	364.043434	.002747	.026735	9.732651	.102747	38
39	41.144778	401.447778	.002491	.024304	9.756956	.102491	39
40	45.259256	442.592556	.002259	.022095	9.779051	.102259	40
41	49.785181	487.851811	.002050	.020086	9.799137	.102050	41
42	54.763699	537.636992	.001860	.018260	9.817397	.101860	42
43	60.240069	592.400692	.001688	.016600	9.833998	.101688	43
44	66.264076	652.640761	.001532	.015091	9.849089	.101532	44
45	72.890484	718.904837	.001391	.013719	9.862808	.101391	45
46	80.179532	791.795321	.001263	.012472	9.875280	.101263	46
47	88.197485	871.974853	.001147	.011338	9.886618	.101147	47
48	97.017234	960.172338	.001041	.010307	9.896926	.101041	48
49	106.718957	1057.189572	.000946	.009370	9.906296	.100946	49
50	117.390853	1163.908529	.000859	.008519	9.914814	.100859	50
51	129.129938	1281.299382	.000780	.007744	9.922559	.100780	51
52	142.042932	1410.429320	.000709	.007040	9.929599	.100709	52
53	156.247225	1552.472252	.000644	.006400	9.935999	.100644	53
54	171.871948	1708.719477	.000585	.005818	9.941817	.100585	54
55	189.059142	1880.591425	.000532	.005289	9.947106	.100532	55
56	207.965057	2069.650567	.000483	.004809	9.951915	.100483	56
57	228.761562	2277.615624	.000439	.004371	9.956286	.100439	57
58	251.637719	2506.377186	.000399	.003974	9.960260	.100399	58
59	276.801490	2758.014905	.000363	.003613	9.963873	.100363	59
60	304.481640	3034.816395	.000330	.003284	9.967157	.100330	60

10 ¼ % MONTHLY COMPOUND INTEREST TABLE 10 ¼ %

EFFECTIVE RATE = 41/48% BASE = 1.00854167

MONTHS	1 AMOUNT OF I AT COMPOUND INTEREST $S^n = (1+i)^n$	2 ACCUMULATION OF I PER PERIOD $S_{\overline{n}\rvert} = \frac{S^n - 1}{i}$	3 SINKING FUND FACTOR $1/S_{\overline{n}\rvert} = \frac{i}{S^n - 1}$	4 PRES. VALUE REVERSION OF I $V^n = \frac{1}{S^n}$	5 PRESENT VALUE ORD. ANNUITY 1 PER PERIOD $a_{\overline{n}\rvert} = \frac{1 - V^n}{i}$	6 INSTALMENT TO AMORTIZE I $1/a_{\overline{n}\rvert} = \frac{i}{1 - V^n}$	n MONTHS
1	1.008541	1.000000	1.000000	.991530	.991530	1.008541	1
2	1.017156	2.008541	.497873	.983133	1.974663	.506415	2
3	1.025844	3.025697	.330502	.974806	2.949470	.339043	3
4	1.034606	4.051542	.246819	.966550	3.916021	.255361	4
5	1.043444	5.086149	.196612	.958364	4.874385	.205154	5
6	1.052356	6.129593	.163142	.950247	5.824633	.171684	6
7	1.061345	7.181950	.139237	.942199	6.766833	.147779	7
8	1.070411	8.243296	.121310	.934220	7.701053	.129852	8
9	1.079554	9.313707	.107368	.926307	8.627361	.115910	9
10	1.088775	10.393262	.096216	.918462	9.545824	.104757	10
11	1.098075	11.482038	.087092	.910683	10.456508	.095634	11
YEARS							
1	1.107455	12.580113	.079490	.902971	11.359479	.088032	12
2	1.226456	26.512025	.037718	.815356	21.616761	.046260	24
3	1.358245	41.940993	.023843	.736243	30.878790	.032384	36
4	1.504196	59.027882	.016941	.664806	39.242135	.025482	48
5	1.665830	77.950845	.012828	.600301	46.793993	.021370	60
6	1.844832	98.907178	.010110	.542054	53.613104	.018652	72
7	2.043068	122.115377	.008188	.489459	59.770564	.016730	84
8	2.262607	147.817416	.006765	.441968	65.330571	.015306	96
9	2.505735	176.281272	.005672	.399084	70.351099	.014214	108
10	2.774990	207.803714	.004812	.360361	74.884489	.013353	120
11	3.073177	242.713406	.004120	.325396	78.978010	.012661	132
12	3.403405	281.374323	.003553	.293823	82.674340	.012095	144
13	3.769119	324.189554	.003084	.265313	86.012021	.011626	156
14	4.174130	371.605502	.002691	.239570	89.025850	.011232	168
15	4.622662	424.116538	.002357	.216325	91.747250	.010899	180
16	5.119390	482.270154	.002073	.195335	94.204596	.010615	192
17	5.669495	546.672675	.001829	.176382	96.423508	.010370	204
18	6.278712	617.995578	.001618	.159268	98.427121	.010159	216
19	6.953392	696.982494	.001434	.143814	100.236327	.009976	228
20	7.700569	784.456959	.001274	.129860	101.869987	.009816	240
21	8.528035	881.331006	.001134	.117260	103.345135	.009676	252
22	9.444416	988.614667	.001011	.105882	104.677151	.009553	264
23	10.459268	1107.426510	.000902	.095608	105.879922	.009444	276
24	11.583170	1239.005295	.000807	.086332	106.965991	.009348	288
25	12.827841	1384.722897	.000722	.077955	107.946680	.009263	300
26	14.206258	1546.098605	.000646	.070391	108.832212	.009188	312
27	15.732794	1724.814960	.000579	.063561	109.631824	.009121	324
28	17.423364	1922.735308	.000520	.057394	110.353849	.009061	336
29	19.295594	2141.923215	.000466	.051825	111.005818	.009008	348
30	21.369004	2384.663989	.000419	.046796	111.594526	.008961	360
31	23.665214	2653.488507	.000376	.042256	112.126112	.008918	372
32	26.208163	2951.199602	.000338	.038156	112.606120	.008880	384
33	29.024365	3280.901284	.000304	.034453	113.039553	.008846	396
34	32.143182	3646.031107	.000274	.031110	113.430931	.008815	408
35	35.597132	4050.396006	.000246	.028092	113.784333	.008788	420
36	39.422227	4498.211992	.000222	.025366	114.103444	.008763	432
37	43.658348	4994.148108	.000200	.022905	114.391595	.008741	444
38	48.349662	5543.375103	.000180	.020682	114.651785	.008722	456
39	53.545082	6151.619368	.000162	.018675	114.886729	.008704	468
40	59.298776	6825.222606	.000146	.016863	115.098876	.008688	480
41	65.670735	7571.207975	.000132	.015227	115.290440	.008673	492
42	72.727393	8397.353306	.000119	.013749	115.463417	.008660	504
43	80.542325	9312.272200	.000107	.012415	115.619609	.008649	516
44	89.197012	10325.503830	.000096	.011211	115.760646	.008638	528
45	98.781689	11447.612410	.000087	.010123	115.887999	.008629	540
46	109.396290	12690.297330	.000078	.009141	116.002994	.008620	552
47	121.151483	14066.515120	.000071	.008254	116.106833	.008612	564
48	134.169833	15590.614580	.000064	.007453	116.200595	.008605	576
49	148.587071	17278.486380	.000057	.006730	116.285261	.008599	588
50	164.553516	19147.728680	.000052	.006077	116.361710	.008593	600

10 ¼ % QUARTERLY COMPOUND INTEREST TABLE 10 ¼ %

EFFECTIVE RATE = 2-9/16% BASE = 1.025625

QUARTERS	1 AMOUNT OF I AT COMPOUND INTEREST $S^n = (1+i)^n$	2 ACCUMULATION OF I PER PERIOD $S_{\overline{n}|} = \frac{S^n - 1}{i}$	3 SINKING FUND FACTOR $1/S_{\overline{n}|} = \frac{i}{S^n - 1}$	4 PRES. VALUE REVERSION OF I $V^n = \frac{1}{S^n}$	5 PRESENT VALUE ORD. ANNUITY 1 PER PERIOD $a_{\overline{n}|} = \frac{1 - V^n}{i}$	6 INSTALMENT TO AMORTIZE I $1/a_{\overline{n}|} = \frac{i}{1 - V^n}$	n QUARTERS
1	1.025625	1.000000	1.000000	.975015	.975015	1.025625	1
2	1.051907	2.025625	.493675	.950655	1.925670	.519300	2
3	1.078862	3.077532	.324936	.926903	2.852573	.350561	3
YEARS							
1	1.106508	4.156393	.240593	.903744	3.756317	.266218	4
2	1.224359	8.755474	.114214	.816754	7.151068	.139839	8
3	1.354763	13.844392	.072231	.738137	10.219054	.097856	12
4	1.499055	19.475318	.051347	.667087	12.991730	.076972	16
5	1.658716	25.705980	.038901	.602876	15.497520	.064526	20
6	1.835382	32.600256	.030675	.544846	17.762114	.056300	24
7	2.030864	40.228823	.024858	.492401	19.808727	.050483	28
8	2.247166	48.669891	.020547	.445005	21.658343	.046172	32
9	2.486506	58.009997	.017238	.402171	23.329923	.042863	36
10	2.751338	68.344895	.014632	.363460	24.840604	.040257	40
11	3.044376	79.780538	.012534	.328475	26.205873	.038159	44
12	3.368625	92.434163	.010819	.296857	27.439727	.036444	48
13	3.727410	106.435496	.009395	.268283	28.554816	.035020	52
14	4.124407	121.928076	.008202	.242459	29.562572	.033827	56
15	4.563688	139.070734	.007191	.219121	30.473325	.032816	60
16	5.049755	158.039215	.006328	.198029	31.296413	.031953	64
17	5.587592	179.027983	.005586	.178968	32.040274	.031211	68
18	6.182713	202.252213	.004944	.161741	32.712535	.030569	72
19	6.841219	227.950001	.004387	.146173	33.320086	.030012	76
20	7.569860	256.384797	.003900	.132103	33.869158	.029525	80
21	8.376108	287.848115	.003474	.119387	34.365378	.029099	84
22	9.268227	322.662515	.003099	.107896	34.813834	.028724	88
23	10.255363	361.184912	.002769	.097510	35.219124	.028394	92
24	11.347637	403.810236	.002476	.088124	35.585402	.028101	96
25	12.556247	450.975481	.002217	.079642	35.916424	.027842	100
26	13.893582	503.164182	.001987	.071976	36.215583	.027612	104
27	15.373354	560.911374	.001783	.065048	36.485947	.027408	108
28	17.010733	624.809081	.001600	.058786	36.730286	.027225	112
29	18.822505	695.512378	.001438	.053128	36.951107	.027063	116
30	20.827244	773.746112	.001292	.048014	37.150672	.026917	120
31	23.045504	860.312332	.001162	.043392	37.331028	.026787	124
32	25.500024	956.098510	.001046	.039216	37.494023	.026671	128
33	28.215970	1062.086642	.000942	.035441	37.641330	.026567	132
34	31.221185	1179.363314	.000848	.032030	37.774457	.026473	136
35	34.546478	1309.130841	.000764	.028947	37.894770	.026389	140
36	38.225940	1452.719593	.000688	.026160	38.003503	.026313	144
37	42.297292	1611.601636	.000621	.023642	38.101769	.026246	148
38	46.802274	1787.405820	.000559	.021366	38.190576	.026184	152
39	51.787071	1981.934482	.000505	.019310	38.270836	.026130	156
40	57.302787	2197.181922	.000455	.017451	38.343369	.026080	160
41	63.405968	2435.354846	.000411	.015771	38.408922	.026036	164
42	70.159184	2698.894992	.000371	.014253	38.468164	.025996	168
43	77.631669	2990.504162	.000334	.012881	38.521704	.025959	172
44	85.900030	3313.171918	.000302	.011641	38.570090	.025927	176
45	95.049035	3670.206236	.000272	.010521	38.613819	.025897	180
46	105.172478	4065.267415	.000246	.009508	38.653339	.025871	184
47	116.374144	4502.405604	.000222	.008593	38.689055	.025847	188
48	128.768872	4986.102326	.000201	.007766	38.721333	.025826	192
49	142.483733	5521.316414	.000181	.007018	38.750504	.025806	196
50	157.659331	6113.534861	.000164	.006343	38.776867	.025789	200
51	174.451245	6768.829061	.000148	.005732	38.800692	.025773	204
52	193.031625	7493.917061	.000133	.005180	38.822224	.025758	208
53	213.590956	8296.232429	.000121	.004682	38.841684	.025746	212
54	236.340012	9184.000468	.000109	.004231	38.859271	.025734	216
55	261.512015	10166.322530	.000098	.003824	38.875164	.025723	220
56	289.365027	11253.269340	.000089	.003456	38.889528	.025714	224
57	320.184596	12455.984230	.000080	.003123	38.902509	.025705	228
58	354.286682	13786.797360	.000073	.002823	38.914241	.025698	232
59	392.020900	15259.352190	.000066	.002551	38.924844	.025691	236
60	433.774097	16888.745260	.000059	.002305	38.934425	.025684	240

10¼% SEMI-ANNUAL COMPOUND INTEREST TABLE 10¼%

EFFECTIVE RATE = 5-1/8% BASE = 1.05125

HALF YEARS	1 AMOUNT OF I AT COMPOUND INTEREST $S^n = (1+i)^n$	2 ACCUMULATION OF I PER PERIOD $S_{\overline{n}\vert} = \frac{S^n - 1}{i}$	3 SINKING FUND FACTOR $1/S_{\overline{n}\vert} = \frac{i}{S^n - 1}$	4 PRES. VALUE REVERSION OF I $V^n = \frac{1}{S^n}$	5 PRESENT VALUE ORD. ANNUITY 1 PER PERIOD $a_{\overline{n}\vert} = \frac{1 - V^n}{i}$	6 INSTALMENT TO AMORTIZE I $1/a_{\overline{n}\vert} = \frac{i}{1 - V^n}$	n HALF YEARS
1	1.051250	1.000000	1.000000	.951249	.951249	1.051250	1
YEARS							
1	1.105127	2.051250	.487508	.904874	1.856122	.538758	2
2	1.221305	4.318141	.231581	.818796	3.535679	.282831	4
3	1.349696	6.823342	.146556	.740907	5.055465	.197806	6
4	1.491585	9.591907	.104255	.670428	6.430680	.155505	8
5	1.648390	12.651521	.079042	.606652	7.675075	.130292	10
6	1.821680	16.032782	.062372	.548944	8.801096	.113622	12
7	2.013187	19.769503	.050583	.496725	9.820003	.101833	14
8	2.224826	23.899053	.041843	.449473	10.741985	.093093	16
9	2.458715	28.462728	.035134	.406717	11.576263	.086384	18
10	2.717191	33.506167	.029845	.368027	12.331178	.081095	20
11	3.002840	39.079805	.025589	.333018	13.014281	.076839	22
12	3.318518	45.239381	.022105	.301339	13.632404	.073355	24
13	3.667383	52.046491	.019214	.272674	14.191726	.070464	26
14	4.052922	59.569210	.016787	.246736	14.697843	.068037	28
15	4.478992	67.882766	.014731	.223265	15.155814	.065981	30
16	4.949853	77.070298	.012975	.202026	15.570220	.064225	32
17	5.470214	87.223684	.011465	.182808	15.945206	.062715	34
18	6.045279	98.444460	.010158	.165418	16.284520	.061408	36
19	6.680798	110.844837	.009022	.149683	16.591557	.060272	38
20	7.383127	124.548824	.008029	.135444	16.869386	.059279	40
21	8.159290	139.693464	.007159	.122560	17.120787	.058409	42
22	9.017048	156.430207	.006393	.110901	17.348272	.057643	44
23	9.964979	174.926427	.005717	.100351	17.554118	.056967	46
24	11.012563	195.367091	.005119	.090805	17.740383	.056369	48
25	12.170276	217.956612	.004588	.082167	17.908929	.055838	50
26	13.449696	242.920892	.004117	.074351	18.061441	.055367	52
27	14.863616	270.509580	.003697	.067278	18.199446	.054947	54
28	16.426177	300.998572	.003322	.060878	18.324323	.054572	56
29	18.153004	334.692767	.002988	.055087	18.437321	.054238	58
30	20.061367	371.929117	.002689	.049847	18.539570	.053939	60
31	22.170350	413.079997	.002421	.045105	18.632092	.053671	62
32	24.501043	458.556927	.002181	.040815	18.715813	.053431	64
33	27.076753	508.814690	.001965	.036932	18.791570	.053215	66
34	29.923239	564.355880	.001772	.033419	18.860120	.053022	68
35	33.068966	625.735923	.001598	.030240	18.922150	.052848	70
36	36.545393	693.568640	.001442	.027363	18.978278	.052692	72
37	40.387284	768.532377	.001301	.024760	19.029068	.052551	74
38	44.633061	851.376794	.001175	.022405	19.075026	.052425	76
39	49.325181	942.930360	.001061	.020274	19.116612	.052311	78
40	54.510568	1044.108637	.000958	.018345	19.154243	.052208	80
41	60.241076	1155.923439	.000865	.016600	19.188293	.052115	82
42	66.574014	1279.492947	.000782	.015021	19.219105	.052032	84
43	73.572711	1416.052892	.000706	.013592	19.246985	.051956	86
44	81.307157	1566.968915	.000638	.012299	19.272214	.051888	88
45	89.854699	1733.750220	.000577	.011129	19.295042	.051827	90
46	99.300814	1918.064671	.000521	.010070	19.315699	.051771	92
47	109.739968	2121.755467	.000471	.009112	19.334391	.051721	94
48	121.276553	2346.859577	.000426	.008246	19.351305	.051676	96
49	134.025941	2595.628107	.000385	.007461	19.366610	.051635	98
50	148.115627	2870.548818	.000348	.006751	19.380459	.051598	100
51	163.686514	3174.370997	.000315	.006109	19.392990	.051565	102
52	180.894314	3510.132958	.000285	.005528	19.404330	.051535	104
53	199.911112	3881.192420	.000258	.005002	19.414591	.051508	106
54	220.927080	4291.260088	.000233	.004526	19.423876	.051483	108
55	244.152384	4744.436759	.000211	.004096	19.432277	.051461	110
56	269.819285	5245.254336	.000191	.003706	19.439879	.051441	112
57	298.184459	5798.721143	.000172	.003354	19.446758	.051422	114
58	329.531566	6410.372014	.000156	.003035	19.452983	.051406	116
59	364.174086	7086.323637	.000141	.002746	19.458616	.051391	118
60	402.458456	7833.335733	.000128	.002485	19.463713	.051378	120

10 ¼ % ANNUAL COMPOUND INTEREST TABLE 10 ¼ %

EFFECTIVE RATE = 10¼%   BASE = 1.1025

YEARS	1 AMOUNT OF I AT COMPOUND INTEREST $S^n = (1+i)^n$	2 ACCUMULATION OF I PER PERIOD $S_{\overline{n}\|} = \frac{S^n - 1}{i}$	3 SINKING FUND FACTOR $1/S_{\overline{n}\|} = \frac{i}{S^n - 1}$	4 PRES. VALUE REVERSION OF I $V^n = \frac{1}{S^n}$	5 PRESENT VALUE ORD. ANNUITY 1 PER PERIOD $a_{\overline{n}\|} = \frac{1 - V^n}{i}$	6 INSTALMENT TO AMORTIZE I $1/a_{\overline{n}\|} = \frac{i}{1 - V^n}$	n YEARS
1	1.102500	1.000000	1.000000	.907029	.907029	1.102500	1
2	1.215506	2.102500	.475624	.822702	1.729732	.578124	2
3	1.340096	3.318006	.301386	.746215	2.475947	.403886	3
4	1.477455	4.658102	.214680	.676839	3.152787	.317180	4
5	1.628895	6.135557	.162984	.613913	3.766700	.265484	5
6	1.795856	7.764452	.128792	.556837	4.323537	.231292	6
7	1.979932	9.560308	.104599	.505068	4.828605	.207099	7
8	2.182875	11.540240	.086653	.458112	5.286717	.189153	8
9	2.406619	13.723114	.072870	.415521	5.702238	.175370	9
10	2.653298	16.129734	.061997	.376889	6.079127	.164497	10
11	2.925261	18.783031	.053240	.341850	6.420977	.155740	11
12	3.225100	21.708292	.046565	.310068	6.731045	.148565	12
13	3.555673	24.933392	.040107	.281241	7.012286	.142607	13
14	3.920129	28.489065	.035101	.255094	7.267379	.137601	14
15	4.321942	32.409194	.030855	.231377	7.498757	.133355	15
16	4.764941	36.731136	.027225	.209866	7.708623	.129725	16
17	5.253348	41.496078	.024099	.190355	7.898978	.126599	17
18	5.791816	46.749426	.021391	.172657	8.071635	.123891	18
19	6.385477	52.541242	.019033	.156605	8.228240	.121533	19
20	7.039989	58.926719	.016970	.142046	8.370286	.119470	20
21	7.761588	65.966708	.015159	.128840	8.499126	.117659	21
22	8.557150	73.728295	.013563	.116861	8.615987	.116063	22
23	9.434258	82.285446	.012153	.105997	8.721984	.114653	23
24	10.401270	91.719704	.010903	.096142	8.818126	.113403	24
25	11.467400	102.120974	.009792	.087204	8.905329	.112292	25
26	12.642808	113.588373	.008804	.079096	8.984426	.111304	26
27	13.938696	126.231182	.007922	.071743	9.056169	.110422	27
28	15.367412	140.169878	.007134	.065073	9.121241	.109634	28
29	16.942572	155.537290	.006429	.059023	9.180264	.108929	29
30	18.679186	172.479862	.005798	.053536	9.233800	.108298	30
31	20.593802	191.159048	.005231	.048558	9.282358	.107731	31
32	22.704667	211.752851	.004722	.044044	9.326402	.107222	32
33	25.031896	234.457518	.004265	.039949	9.366351	.106765	33
34	27.597665	259.489414	.003854	.036235	9.402586	.106354	34
35	30.426426	287.087078	.003483	.032866	9.435452	.105983	35
36	33.545134	317.513504	.003149	.029811	9.465263	.105649	36
37	36.983510	351.058638	.002849	.027039	9.492302	.105349	37
38	40.774320	388.042148	.002577	.024525	9.516827	.105077	38
39	44.953688	428.816469	.002332	.022245	9.539072	.104832	39
40	49.561441	473.770157	.002111	.020177	9.559249	.104611	40
41	54.641489	523.331598	.001911	.018301	9.577550	.104411	41
42	60.242241	577.973086	.001730	.016600	9.594150	.104230	42
43	66.417071	638.215328	.001567	.015056	9.609206	.104067	43
44	73.224821	704.632399	.001419	.013657	9.622863	.103919	44
45	80.730365	777.857220	.001286	.012387	9.635250	.103786	45
46	89.005227	858.587585	.001165	.011235	9.646485	.103665	46
47	98.128263	947.592812	.001055	.010191	9.656676	.103555	47
48	108.186410	1045.721075	.000956	.009243	9.665919	.103456	48
49	119.275517	1153.907485	.000867	.008384	9.674303	.103367	49
50	131.501258	1273.183002	.000785	.007604	9.681907	.103285	50
51	144.980137	1404.684260	.000712	.006897	9.688805	.103212	51
52	159.840601	1549.664396	.000645	.006256	9.695061	.103145	52
53	176.224262	1709.504997	.000585	.005675	9.700736	.103085	53
54	194.287249	1885.729260	.000530	.005147	9.705883	.103030	54
55	214.201692	2080.016508	.000481	.004668	9.710551	.102981	55
56	236.157366	2294.218200	.000436	.004234	9.714786	.102936	56
57	260.363496	2530.375566	.000395	.003841	9.718626	.102895	57
58	287.050754	2790.739061	.000358	.003484	9.722110	.102858	58
59	316.473456	3077.789816	.000325	.003160	9.725270	.102825	59
60	348.911985	3394.263271	.000295	.002866	9.728136	.102795	60

10 ½ % MONTHLY COMPOUND INTEREST TABLE 10 ½ %

EFFECTIVE RATE = 7/8% BASE = 1.00875

	1 AMOUNT OF I AT COMPOUND INTEREST $S^n = (1+i)^n$	2 ACCUMULATION OF I PER PERIOD $S_{\overline{n}\rvert} = \frac{S^n - 1}{i}$	3 SINKING FUND FACTOR $1/S_{\overline{n}\rvert} = \frac{i}{S^n - 1}$	4 PRES. VALUE REVERSION OF I $V^n = \frac{1}{S^n}$	5 PRESENT VALUE ORD. ANNUITY 1 PER PERIOD $a_{\overline{n}\rvert} = \frac{1 - V^n}{i}$	6 INSTALMENT TO AMORTIZE I $1/a_{\overline{n}\rvert} = \frac{i}{1 - V^n}$	n MONTHS
MONTHS							
1	1.008750	1.000000	1.000000	.991325	.991325	1.008750	1
2	1.017576	2.008750	.497822	.982727	1.974052	.506572	2
3	1.026480	3.026326	.330433	.974202	2.948255	.339183	3
4	1.035462	4.052806	.246742	.965752	3.914008	.255492	4
5	1.044522	5.088268	.196530	.957375	4.871383	.205280	5
6	1.053661	6.132791	.163057	.949071	5.820454	.171807	6
7	1.062881	7.186453	.139150	.940838	6.761293	.147900	7
8	1.072181	8.249334	.121221	.932677	7.693970	.129971	8
9	1.081563	9.321516	.107278	.924587	8.618558	.116028	9
10	1.091026	10.403079	.096125	.916567	9.535126	.104875	10
11	1.100573	11.494106	.087001	.908617	10.443743	.095751	11
YEARS							
1	1.110203	12.594680	.079398	.900735	11.344479	.088148	12
2	1.232551	26.577337	.037626	.811324	21.562858	.046376	24
3	1.368383	42.100931	.023752	.730789	30.766917	.032502	36
4	1.519183	59.335279	.016853	.658248	39.057343	.025603	48
5	1.686602	78.468912	.012743	.592907	46.524827	.021493	60
6	1.872472	99.711137	.010028	.534053	53.251056	.018778	72
7	2.078825	123.294328	.008110	.481040	59.309612	.016860	84
8	2.307919	149.476469	.006690	.433290	64.766771	.015440	96
9	2.562259	178.543971	.005600	.390280	69.682229	.014350	108
10	2.844629	210.814813	.004743	.351539	74.109758	.013493	120
11	3.158117	246.642013	.004054	.316644	78.097792	.012804	132
12	3.506153	286.417494	.003491	.285212	81.689957	.012241	144
13	3.892543	330.576370	.003025	.256901	84.925548	.011775	156
14	4.321514	379.601707	.002634	.231400	87.839961	.011384	168
15	4.797760	434.029805	.002303	.208430	90.465078	.011053	180
16	5.326490	494.456067	.002022	.187740	92.829614	.010772	192
17	5.913488	561.541511	.001780	.169104	94.959437	.010530	204
18	6.565175	636.020004	.001572	.152318	96.877844	.010322	216
19	7.288679	718.706283	.001391	.137199	98.605822	.010141	228
20	8.091917	810.504875	.001233	.123580	100.162273	.009983	240
21	8.983674	912.419989	.001095	.111313	101.564226	.009845	252
22	9.973706	1025.566500	.000975	.100263	102.827013	.009725	264
23	11.072843	1151.182148	.000868	.090311	103.964452	.009618	276
24	12.293109	1290.641073	.000774	.081346	104.988984	.009524	288
25	13.647852	1445.468852	.000691	.073271	105.911816	.009441	300
26	15.151892	1617.359187	.000618	.065998	106.743045	.009368	312
27	16.821683	1808.192429	.000553	.059447	107.491762	.009303	324
28	18.675491	2020.056156	.000495	.053546	108.166158	.009245	336
29	20.733594	2255.267994	.000443	.048230	108.773610	.009193	348
30	23.018508	2516.400988	.000397	.043443	109.320766	.009147	360
31	25.555227	2806.311739	.000356	.039130	109.813607	.009106	372
32	28.371501	3128.171655	.000319	.035246	110.257526	.009069	384
33	31.498139	3485.501648	.000286	.031747	110.657382	.009036	396
34	34.969343	3882.210635	.000257	.028596	111.017545	.009007	408
35	38.823085	4322.638321	.000231	.025757	111.341957	.008981	420
36	43.101523	4811.602659	.000207	.023201	111.634166	.008957	432
37	47.851459	5354.452558	.000186	.020898	111.897370	.008936	444
38	53.124855	5957.126384	.000167	.018823	112.134447	.008917	456
39	58.979398	6626.216945	.000150	.016955	112.347991	.008900	468
40	65.479131	7369.043594	.000135	.015272	112.540338	.008885	480
41	72.695157	8193.732303	.000122	.013756	112.713591	.008872	492
42	80.706414	9109.304562	.000109	.012390	112.869646	.008859	504
43	89.600540	10125.776030	.000098	.011160	113.010211	.008848	516
44	99.474828	11254.266170	.000088	.010052	113.136823	.008838	528
45	110.437298	12507.119810	.000079	.009054	113.250866	.008829	540
46	122.607869	13898.042240	.000071	.008156	113.353590	.008821	552
47	136.119680	15442.249150	.000064	.007346	113.446117	.008814	564
48	151.120538	17156.632960	.000058	.006617	113.529458	.008808	576
49	167.774543	19059.947790	.000052	.005960	113.604528	.008802	588
50	186.263876	21173.014470	.000047	.005368	113.672145	.008797	600

10½% QUARTERLY COMPOUND INTEREST TABLE 10½%

EFFECTIVE RATE = 2-5/8% BASE = 1.02625

QUARTERS	1 AMOUNT OF I AT COMPOUND INTEREST $S^n = (1+i)^n$	2 ACCUMULATION OF I PER PERIOD $S_{\overline{n}\rceil} = \frac{S^n - 1}{i}$	3 SINKING FUND FACTOR $1/S_{\overline{n}\rceil} = \frac{i}{S^n - 1}$	4 PRES. VALUE REVERSION OF I $V^n = \frac{1}{S^n}$	5 PRESENT VALUE ORD. ANNUITY 1 PER PERIOD $a_{\overline{n}\rceil} = \frac{1 - V^n}{i}$	6 INSTALMENT TO AMORTIZE I $1/a_{\overline{n}\rceil} = \frac{i}{1 - V^n}$	n QUARTERS
1	1.026250	1.000000	1.000000	.974421	.974421	1.026250	1
2	1.053189	2.026250	.493523	.949497	1.923919	.519773	2
3	1.080835	3.079439	.324734	.925210	2.849129	.350984	3
YEARS							
1	1.109207	4.160274	.240369	.901545	3.750674	.266619	4
2	1.230341	8.774881	.113962	.812783	7.132074	.140212	8
3	1.364703	13.893435	.071976	.732760	10.180558	.098226	12
4	1.513738	19.570973	.051096	.660616	12.928903	.077346	16
5	1.679049	25.868538	.038657	.595575	15.406659	.064907	20
6	1.862413	32.853843	.030438	.536938	17.640468	.056688	24
7	2.065802	40.601994	.024629	.484073	19.654346	.050879	28
8	2.291403	49.196298	.020327	.436414	21.469947	.046577	32
9	2.541641	58.729162	.017027	.393447	23.106793	.043277	36
10	2.819206	69.303084	.014429	.354710	24.582484	.040679	40
11	3.127084	81.031754	.012341	.319787	25.912884	.038591	44
12	3.468584	94.041280	.010634	.288302	27.112300	.036884	48
13	3.847378	108.471539	.009219	.259917	28.193627	.035469	52
14	4.267539	124.477687	.008034	.234327	29.168492	.034284	56
15	4.733585	142.231821	.007031	.211256	30.047377	.033281	60
16	5.250527	161.924834	.006176	.190457	30.839730	.032426	64
17	5.823922	183.768467	.005442	.171706	31.554073	.031692	68
18	6.459936	207.997581	.004808	.154800	32.198084	.031058	72
19	7.165408	234.872689	.004258	.139559	32.778690	.030508	76
20	7.947922	264.682752	.003778	.125819	33.302132	.030028	80
21	8.815893	297.748289	.003359	.113432	33.774038	.029609	84
22	9.778652	334.424821	.002990	.102264	34.199482	.029240	88
23	10.846551	375.106694	.002666	.092195	34.583040	.028916	92
24	12.031072	420.231321	.002380	.083118	34.928834	.028630	96
25	13.344952	470.283882	.002126	.074935	35.240583	.028376	100
26	14.802317	525.802543	.001902	.067557	35.521638	.028152	104
27	16.418836	587.384241	.001702	.060906	35.775023	.027952	108
28	18.211891	655.691104	.001525	.054909	36.003460	.027775	112
29	20.200761	731.457569	.001367	.049503	36.209406	.027617	116
30	22.406830	815.498277	.001226	.044629	36.395076	.027476	120
31	24.853817	908.716836	.001100	.040235	36.562466	.027350	124
32	27.568033	1012.115533	.000988	.036274	36.713375	.027238	128
33	30.578660	1126.806112	.000887	.032703	36.849427	.027137	132
34	33.918070	1254.021728	.000797	.029483	36.972083	.027047	136
35	37.622168	1395.130206	.000717	.026580	37.082664	.026967	140
36	41.730780	1551.648745	.000644	.023963	37.182357	.026894	144
37	46.288081	1725.260237	.000580	.021604	37.272235	.026830	148
38	51.343073	1917.831353	.000521	.019477	37.353264	.026771	152
39	56.950106	2131.432622	.000469	.017559	37.426315	.026719	156
40	63.169468	2368.360688	.000422	.015830	37.492174	.026672	160
41	70.068029	2631.163005	.000380	.014272	37.551549	.026630	164
42	77.719962	2922.665227	.000342	.012867	37.605078	.026592	168
43	86.207542	3246.001591	.000308	.011600	37.653337	.026558	172
44	95.622026	3604.648615	.000277	.010458	37.696844	.026527	176
45	106.064640	4002.462476	.000250	.009428	37.736068	.026500	180
46	117.647663	4443.720476	.000225	.008500	37.771430	.026475	184
47	130.495635	4933.167029	.000203	.007663	37.803311	.026453	188
48	144.746698	5476.064667	.000183	.006909	37.832053	.026433	192
49	160.554079	6078.250636	.000165	.006228	37.857965	.026415	196
50	178.087741	6746.199653	.000148	.005615	37.881325	.026398	200
51	197.536205	7487.093512	.000134	.005062	37.902386	.026384	204
52	219.108581	8308.898316	.000120	.004564	37.921373	.026370	208
53	243.036816	9220.450122	.000108	.004115	37.938491	.026358	212
54	269.578186	10231.549950	.000098	.003709	37.953924	.026348	216
55	299.018066	11353.069160	.000088	.003344	37.967837	.026338	220
56	331.672992	12597.066350	.000079	.003015	37.980380	.026329	224
57	367.894071	13976.916980	.000072	.002718	37.991689	.026322	228
58	408.070753	15507.457250	.000064	.002451	38.001884	.026314	232
59	452.635018	17205.143520	.000058	.002209	38.011075	.026308	236
60	502.066021	19088.229370	.000052	.001992	38.019361	.026302	240

10½% SEMI-ANNUAL COMPOUND INTEREST TABLE 10½%

EFFECTIVE RATE = 5¼% BASE = 1.0525

HALF YEARS	1 AMOUNT OF I AT COMPOUND INTEREST $S^n = (1+i)^n$	2 ACCUMULATION OF I PER PERIOD $S_{\overline{n\rvert}} = \frac{S^n - 1}{i}$	3 SINKING FUND FACTOR $1/S_{\overline{n\rvert}} = \frac{i}{S^n - 1}$	4 PRES. VALUE REVERSION OF I $V^n = \frac{1}{S^n}$	5 PRESENT VALUE ORD. ANNUITY 1 PER PERIOD $a_{\overline{n\rvert}} = \frac{1 - V^n}{i}$	6 INSTALMENT TO AMORTIZE I $1/a_{\overline{n\rvert}} = \frac{i}{1 - V^n}$	n HALF YEARS
1	1.052500	1.000000	1.000000	.950119	.950119	1.052500	1
YEARS							
1	1.107756	2.052500	.487211	.902726	1.852844	.539711	2
2	1.227124	4.326170	.231151	.814914	3.525455	.283651	4
3	1.359354	6.844842	.146095	.735643	5.035363	.198595	6
4	1.505833	9.634916	.103789	.664084	6.398396	.156289	8
5	1.668096	12.725638	.078582	.599486	7.628840	.131082	10
6	1.847844	16.149405	.061922	.541171	8.739595	.114422	12
7	2.046961	19.942105	.050145	.488529	9.742301	.102645	14
8	2.267533	24.143491	.041419	.441008	10.647469	.093919	16
9	2.511874	28.797603	.034725	.398109	11.464588	.087225	18
10	2.782544	33.953225	.029452	.359383	12.202223	.081952	20
11	3.082381	39.664397	.025212	.324425	12.868104	.077712	22
12	3.414527	45.990984	.021743	.292866	13.469212	.074243	24
13	3.782463	52.999300	.018868	.264378	14.011848	.071368	26
14	4.190047	60.762806	.016457	.238661	14.501699	.068957	28
15	4.641551	69.362878	.014417	.215445	14.943901	.066917	30
16	5.141707	78.889662	.012676	.194488	15.343087	.065176	32
17	5.695758	89.443016	.011180	.175569	15.703443	.063680	34
18	6.309512	101.133560	.009888	.158491	16.028745	.062388	36
19	6.989401	114.083833	.008765	.143074	16.322404	.061265	38
20	7.742553	128.429579	.007786	.129156	16.587498	.060286	40
21	8.576861	144.321169	.006929	.116593	16.826804	.059429	42
22	9.501072	161.925177	.006176	.105251	17.042833	.058676	44
23	10.524872	181.426126	.005512	.095013	17.237847	.058012	46
24	11.658992	203.028425	.004925	.085771	17.413891	.057425	48
25	12.915322	226.958507	.004406	.077427	17.572811	.056906	50
26	14.307028	253.467205	.003945	.069896	17.716272	.056445	52
27	15.848700	282.832380	.003536	.063097	17.845778	.056036	54
28	17.556496	315.361837	.003171	.056959	17.962686	.055671	56
29	19.448319	351.396546	.002846	.051418	18.068222	.055346	58
30	21.543997	391.314220	.002555	.046417	18.163493	.055055	60
31	23.865497	435.533273	.002296	.041901	18.249495	.054796	62
32	26.437153	484.517205	.002064	.037826	18.327132	.054564	64
33	29.285922	538.779462	.001856	.034146	18.397217	.054356	66
34	32.441663	598.888817	.001670	.030825	18.460485	.054170	68
35	35.937455	665.475330	.001503	.027826	18.517598	.054003	70
36	39.809940	739.236956	.001353	.025119	18.569155	.053853	72
37	44.099710	820.946858	.001218	.022676	18.615697	.053718	74
38	48.851729	911.461513	.001097	.020470	18.657712	.053597	76
39	54.115809	1011.729688	.000988	.018479	18.695640	.053488	78
40	59.947125	1122.802385	.000891	.016681	18.729879	.053391	80
41	66.406803	1245.843859	.000803	.015059	18.760787	.053303	82
42	73.562551	1382.143822	.000724	.013594	18.788688	.053224	84
43	81.489375	1533.130957	.000652	.012272	18.813875	.053152	86
44	90.270365	1700.387900	.000588	.011078	18.836613	.053088	88
45	99.997561	1885.667824	.000530	.010000	18.857138	.053030	90
46	110.772923	2090.912817	.000478	.009027	18.875667	.052978	92
47	122.709398	2318.274242	.000431	.008149	18.892394	.052931	94
48	135.932102	2570.135280	.000389	.007357	18.907493	.052889	96
49	150.579636	2849.135920	.000351	.006641	18.921124	.052851	98
50	166.805533	3158.200623	.000317	.005995	18.933428	.052817	100
51	184.779871	3500.568979	.000286	.005412	18.944536	.052786	102
52	204.691057	3879.829665	.000258	.004885	18.954564	.052758	104
53	226.747798	4299.958061	.000233	.004410	18.963616	.052733	106
54	251.181291	4765.357916	.000210	.003981	18.971787	.052710	108
55	278.247645	5280.907516	.000189	.003594	18.979163	.052689	110
56	308.230567	5852.010808	.000171	.003244	18.985822	.052671	112
57	341.444338	6484.654048	.000154	.002929	18.991834	.052654	114
58	378.237099	7185.468551	.000139	.002644	18.997260	.052639	116
59	418.994510	7961.800196	.000126	.002387	19.002159	.052626	118
60	464.143788	8821.786429	.000113	.002155	19.006581	.052613	120

10½% ANNUAL COMPOUND INTEREST TABLE 10½%

EFFECTIVE RATE = 10½%   BASE = 1.1050

YEARS	1 AMOUNT OF I AT COMPOUND INTEREST $S^n = (1+i)^n$	2 ACCUMULATION OF I PER PERIOD $S_{\overline{n}\vert} = \frac{S^n - 1}{i}$	3 SINKING FUND FACTOR $1/S_{\overline{n}\vert} = \frac{i}{S^n - 1}$	4 PRES. VALUE REVERSION OF I $V^n = \frac{1}{S^n}$	5 PRESENT VALUE ORD. ANNUITY 1 PER PERIOD $a_{\overline{n}\vert} = \frac{1 - V^n}{i}$	6 INSTALMENT TO AMORTIZE I $1/a_{\overline{n}\vert} = \frac{i}{1 - V^n}$	n YEARS
1	1.105000	1.000000	1.000000	.904977	.904977	1.105000	1
2	1.221025	2.105000	.475059	.818984	1.723961	.580059	2
3	1.349233	3.326025	.300659	.741162	2.465123	.405659	3
4	1.490902	4.675258	.213892	.670735	3.135858	.318892	4
5	1.647447	6.166160	.162175	.607000	3.742858	.267175	5
6	1.820429	7.813606	.127982	.549321	4.292179	.232982	6
7	2.011574	9.634035	.103799	.497123	4.789303	.208799	7
8	2.222789	11.645609	.085869	.449885	5.239188	.190869	8
9	2.456182	13.868398	.072106	.407136	5.646324	.177106	9
10	2.714081	16.324580	.061257	.368449	6.014773	.166257	10
11	2.999059	19.038660	.052525	.333438	6.348211	.157525	11
12	3.313961	22.037720	.045377	.301754	6.649964	.150377	12
13	3.661926	25.351680	.039445	.273080	6.923045	.144445	13
14	4.046429	29.013607	.034467	.247132	7.170176	.139467	14
15	4.471304	33.060035	.030248	.223648	7.393825	.135248	15
16	4.940791	37.531339	.026644	.202397	7.596221	.131644	16
17	5.459574	42.472130	.023545	.183164	7.779386	.128545	17
18	6.032829	47.931703	.020863	.165760	7.945146	.125863	18
19	6.666276	53.964532	.018531	.150009	8.095154	.123531	19
20	7.366235	60.630808	.016493	.135755	8.230909	.121493	20
21	8.139690	67.997043	.014707	.122855	8.353764	.119707	21
22	8.994357	76.136732	.013134	.111181	8.464945	.118134	22
23	9.938764	85.131089	.011747	.100616	8.565561	.116747	23
24	10.982335	95.069854	.010519	.091055	8.656616	.115519	24
25	12.135480	106.052188	.009429	.082403	8.739019	.114429	25
26	13.409705	118.187668	.008461	.074573	8.813592	.113461	26
27	14.817724	131.597373	.007599	.067487	8.881079	.112599	27
28	16.373585	146.415098	.006830	.061074	8.942153	.111830	28
29	18.092812	162.788683	.006143	.055271	8.997423	.111143	29
30	19.992557	180.881495	.005528	.050019	9.047442	.110528	30
31	22.091775	200.874051	.004978	.045266	9.092707	.109978	31
32	24.411412	222.965827	.004485	.040964	9.133672	.109485	32
33	26.974610	247.377239	.004042	.037072	9.170744	.109042	33
34	29.806944	274.351849	.003645	.033549	9.204293	.108645	34
35	32.936673	304.158793	.003288	.030361	9.234654	.108288	35
36	36.395024	337.095466	.002967	.027476	9.262131	.107967	36
37	40.216501	373.490490	.002677	.024865	9.286996	.107677	37
38	44.439234	413.706992	.002417	.022503	9.309499	.107417	38
39	49.105354	458.146226	.002183	.020364	9.329863	.107183	39
40	54.261416	507.251579	.001971	.018429	9.348292	.106971	40
41	59.958865	561.512995	.001781	.016678	9.364970	.106781	41
42	66.254545	621.471860	.001609	.015093	9.380064	.106609	42
43	73.211273	687.726405	.001454	.013659	9.393723	.106454	43
44	80.898456	760.937678	.001314	.012361	9.406084	.106314	44
45	89.392794	841.836134	.001188	.011187	9.417271	.106188	45
46	98.779037	931.228928	.001074	.010124	9.427394	.106074	46
47	109.150836	1030.007966	.000971	.009162	9.436556	.105971	47
48	120.611674	1139.158802	.000878	.008291	9.444847	.105878	48
49	133.275900	1259.770476	.000794	.007503	9.452350	.105794	49
50	147.269870	1393.046376	.000718	.006790	9.459140	.105718	50
51	162.733206	1540.316246	.000649	.006145	9.465285	.105649	51
52	179.820192	1703.049451	.000587	.005561	9.470847	.105587	52
53	198.701313	1882.869644	.000531	.005033	9.475879	.105531	53
54	219.564950	2081.570956	.000480	.004554	9.480434	.105480	54
55	242.619270	2301.135907	.000435	.004122	9.484555	.105435	55
56	268.094294	2543.755177	.000393	.003730	9.488285	.105393	56
57	296.244194	2811.849471	.000356	.003376	9.491661	.105356	57
58	327.349835	3108.093665	.000322	.003055	9.494716	.105322	58
59	361.721568	3435.443500	.000291	.002765	9.497480	.105291	59
60	399.702332	3797.165068	.000263	.002502	9.499982	.105263	60

10 3/4 % MONTHLY COMPOUND INTEREST TABLE 10 3/4 %

EFFECTIVE RATE = 43/48% BASE = 1.00895833

MONTHS	1 AMOUNT OF I AT COMPOUND INTEREST $S^n = (1+i)^n$	2 ACCUMULATION OF I PER PERIOD $S_{\overline{n}|} = \frac{S^n - 1}{i}$	3 SINKING FUND FACTOR $1/S_{\overline{n}|} = \frac{i}{S^n - 1}$	4 PRES. VALUE REVERSION OF I $V^n = \frac{1}{S^n}$	5 PRESENT VALUE ORD. ANNUITY 1 PER PERIOD $a_{\overline{n}|} = \frac{1 - V^n}{i}$	6 INSTALMENT TO AMORTIZE I $1/a_{\overline{n}|} = \frac{i}{1 - V^n}$	n MONTHS
1	1.008958	1.000000	1.000000	.991121	.991121	1.008958	1
2	1.017996	2.008958	.497770	.982321	1.973442	.506728	2
3	1.027116	3.026955	.330364	.973599	2.947041	.339323	3
4	1.036317	4.054071	.246665	.964955	3.911996	.255623	4
5	1.045601	5.090389	.196448	.956387	4.868384	.205406	5
6	1.054968	6.135990	.162972	.947895	5.816280	.171931	6
7	1.064419	7.190959	.139063	.939479	6.755759	.148021	7
8	1.073954	8.255378	.121133	.931138	7.686897	.130091	8
9	1.083575	9.329332	.107188	.922870	8.609768	.116147	9
10	1.093282	10.412907	.096034	.914676	9.524445	.104992	10
11	1.103076	11.506190	.086909	.906555	10.431001	.095868	11
YEARS							
1	1.112958	12.609266	.079306	.898506	11.329507	.088265	12
2	1.238675	26.642850	.037533	.807313	21.509144	.046491	24
3	1.378593	42.261640	.023662	.725376	30.655613	.032620	36
4	1.534317	59.644697	.016765	.651755	38.873775	.025724	48
5	1.707630	78.991310	.012659	.585606	46.257847	.021617	60
6	1.900521	100.523277	.009947	.526171	52.892483	.018906	72
7	2.115200	124.487453	.008032	.472768	58.853748	.016991	84
8	2.354128	151.158575	.006615	.424785	64.209982	.015573	96
9	2.620046	180.842413	.005529	.381672	69.022594	.014488	108
10	2.916001	213.879279	.004675	.342935	73.346756	.013633	120
11	3.245387	250.647924	.003989	.308129	77.232044	.012947	132
12	3.611980	291.569881	.003429	.276856	80.723001	.012388	144
13	4.019982	337.114301	.002966	.248757	83.859649	.011924	156
14	4.474071	387.803328	.002578	.223510	86.677946	.011536	168
15	4.979453	444.218087	.002251	.200825	89.210205	.011209	180
16	5.541922	507.005346	.001972	.180442	91.485456	.010930	192
17	6.167927	576.884927	.001733	.162129	93.529784	.010691	204
18	6.864644	654.657968	.001527	.145673	95.366626	.010485	216
19	7.640060	741.216096	.001349	.130889	97.017041	.010307	228
20	8.503066	837.551658	.001193	.117604	98.499949	.010152	240
21	9.463556	944.769095	.001058	.105668	99.832351	.010016	252
22	10.532540	1064.097599	.000939	.094943	101.029524	.009898	264
23	11.722275	1196.905214	.000835	.085307	102.105191	.009793	276
24	13.046400	1344.714512	.000743	.076649	103.071684	.009701	288
25	14.520096	1509.220055	.000662	.068870	103.940085	.009620	300
26	16.160257	1692.307818	.000590	.061880	104.720350	.009549	312
27	17.985688	1896.076808	.000527	.055599	105.421422	.009485	324
28	20.017315	2122.863140	.000471	.049956	106.051340	.009429	336
29	22.278431	2375.266803	.000421	.044886	106.617325	.009379	348
30	24.794959	2656.181484	.000376	.040330	107.125867	.009334	360
31	27.595748	2968.827729	.000336	.036237	107.582794	.009295	372
32	30.712909	3316.789869	.000301	.032559	107.993348	.009259	384
33	34.182178	3704.057123	.000269	.029255	108.362232	.009228	396
34	38.043329	4135.069312	.000241	.026285	108.693676	.009200	408
35	42.340627	4614.767785	.000216	.023617	108.991482	.009175	420
36	47.123341	5148.652038	.000194	.021220	109.259062	.009152	432
37	52.446299	5742.842801	.000174	.019067	109.499484	.009132	444
38	58.370529	6404.152170	.000156	.017131	109.715505	.009114	456
39	64.963948	7140.161723	.000140	.015393	109.909601	.009098	468
40	72.302146	7959.309459	.000125	.013830	110.083999	.009083	480
41	80.469253	8870.986494	.000112	.012427	110.240695	.009071	492
42	89.558900	9885.644744	.000101	.011165	110.381488	.009059	504
43	99.675295	11014.916780	.000090	.010032	110.507991	.0[illegible]49	516
44	110.934418	12271.749130	.000081	.009014	110.621655	.00[illegible]039	528
45	123.465350	13670.550780	.000073	.008099	110.723784	.009031	540
46	137.411750	15227.358270	.000065	.007277	110.815546	.009024	552
47	152.933508	16960.019630	.000058	.006538	110.897996	.009017	564
48	170.208573	18888.398990	.000052	.005875	110.972077	.009011	576
49	189.434995	21034.604230	.000047	.005278	111.038639	.009005	588
50	210.833195	23423.240560	.000042	.004743	111.098447	.009001	600

10¾% QUARTERLY COMPOUND INTEREST TABLE 10¾%

EFFECTIVE RATE = 2-11/16% BASE = 1.026875

QUARTERS	1 AMOUNT OF I AT COMPOUND INTEREST $S^n = (1+i)^n$	2 ACCUMULATION OF I PER PERIOD $S_{\overline{n}\vert} = \frac{S^n - 1}{i}$	3 SINKING FUND FACTOR $1/S_{\overline{n}\vert} = \frac{i}{S^n - 1}$	4 PRES. VALUE REVERSION OF I $V^n = \frac{1}{S^n}$	5 PRESENT VALUE ORD. ANNUITY 1 PER PERIOD $a_{\overline{n}\vert} = \frac{1 - V^n}{i}$	6 INSTALMENT TO AMORTIZE I $1/a_{\overline{n}\vert} = \frac{i}{1 - V^n}$	n QUARTERS
1	1.026875	1.000000	1.000000	.973828	.973828	1.026875	1
2	1.054472	2.026875	.493370	.948342	1.922170	.520245	2
3	1.082811	3.081347	.324533	.923522	2.845692	.351408	3
YEARS							
1	1.111912	4.164158	.240145	.899352	3.745044	.267020	4
2	1.236348	8.794335	.113710	.808834	7.113157	.140585	8
3	1.374710	13.942683	.071722	.727426	10.142275	.098597	12
4	1.528556	19.667192	.050846	.654212	12.866519	.077721	16
5	1.699619	26.032340	.038414	.588367	15.316573	.065289	20
6	1.889827	33.109824	.030203	.529149	17.520034	.057078	24
7	2.101320	40.979361	.024403	.475891	19.501720	.051278	28
8	2.336483	49.729592	.020109	.427994	21.283954	.046984	32
9	2.597963	59.459076	.016818	.384917	22.886809	.043693	36
10	2.888705	70.277405	.014229	.346176	24.328340	.041104	40
11	3.211985	82.306431	.012150	.311334	25.624784	.039025	44
12	3.571444	95.681647	.010451	.279999	26.790743	.037326	48
13	3.971131	110.553707	.009045	.251817	27.839351	.035920	52
14	4.415547	127.090125	.007868	.226473	28.782419	.034743	56
15	4.909699	145.477163	.006874	.203678	29.630568	.033749	60
16	5.459152	165.921927	.006027	.183179	30.393353	.032902	64
17	6.070095	188.654700	.005301	.164742	31.079365	.032176	68
18	6.749410	213.931538	.004674	.148161	31.696331	.031549	72
19	7.504748	242.037151	.004132	.133249	32.251201	.031007	76
20	8.344618	273.288113	.003659	.119838	32.750224	.030534	80
21	9.278479	308.036425	.003246	.107776	33.199022	.030121	84
22	10.316850	346.673481	.002885	.096929	33.602649	.029760	88
23	11.471427	389.634479	.002567	.087173	33.965652	.029442	92
24	12.755214	437.403317	.002286	.078399	34.292119	.029161	96
25	14.182673	490.518050	.002039	.070509	34.585728	.028914	100
26	15.769880	549.576947	.001820	.063412	34.849785	.028695	104
27	17.534716	615.245228	.001625	.057030	35.087266	.028500	108
28	19.497056	688.262562	.001453	.051290	35.300845	.028328	112
29	21.679006	769.451394	.001300	.046128	35.492927	.028175	116
30	24.105142	859.726212	.001163	.041485	35.665677	.028038	120
31	26.802791	960.103843	.001042	.037310	35.821040	.027917	124
32	29.802338	1071.714911	.000933	.033554	35.960766	.027808	128
33	33.137570	1195.816570	.000836	.030177	36.086429	.027711	132
34	36.846054	1333.806664	.000750	.027140	36.199444	.027625	136
35	40.969561	1487.239472	.000672	.024408	36.301084	.027547	140
36	45.554536	1657.843216	.000603	.021952	36.392494	.027478	144
37	50.652625	1847.539525	.000541	.019742	36.474705	.527416	148
38	56.321249	2058.465081	.000486	.017755	36.548640	.027361	152
39	62.624259	2292.995688	.000436	.015968	36.615135	.027311	156
40	69.632650	2553.773027	.000392	.014361	36.674937	.027267	160
41	77.425362	2843.734417	.000352	.012916	36.728719	.027227	164
42	86.090171	3166.145896	.000316	.011616	36.777089	.027191	168
43	95.724673	3524.639011	.000284	.010447	36.820591	.027159	172
44	106.437390	3923.251721	.000255	.009395	36.859714	.027130	176
45	118.348986	4366.473879	.000229	.008450	36.894899	.027104	180
46	131.593629	4859.297808	.000206	.007599	36.926543	.027081	184
47	146.320503	5407.274530	.000185	.006834	36.955002	.027060	188
48	162.695488	6016.576294	.000166	.006146	36.980597	.027041	192
49	180.903026	6694.066087	.000149	.005528	37.003616	.027024	196
50	201.148202	7447.374954	.000134	.004971	37.024318	.027009	200
51	22[illegible]659051	8284.987944	.000121	.004471	37.042936	.026996	204
52	2[illegible]689129	9216.339676	.000109	.004021	37.059681	.026984	208
53	27[illegible]520367	10251.920620	.000098	.003616	37.074740	.026973	212
54	30[illegible].466247	11403.395240	.000088	.003252	37.088283	.026963	216
55	341.875336	12683.733420	.000079	.002925	37.100464	.026954	220
56	380.135206	14107.356500	.000071	.002631	37.111418	.026946	224
57	422.676805	15690.299740	.000064	.002366	37.121270	.026939	228
58	469.979310	17450.392940	.000057	.002128	37.130130	.026932	232
59	522.575522	19407.461270	.000052	.001914	37.138099	.026927	236
60	581.057867	21583.548550	.000046	.001721	37.145265	.026921	240

10¾% SEMI-ANNUAL COMPOUND INTEREST TABLE 10¾%

EFFECTIVE RATE = 5-3/8%   BASE = 1.05375

HALF YEARS	1 AMOUNT OF I AT COMPOUND INTEREST $S^n = (1+i)^n$	2 ACCUMULATION OF I PER PERIOD $s_{\overline{n}\vert} = \frac{S^n - 1}{i}$	3 SINKING FUND FACTOR $1/s_{\overline{n}\vert} = \frac{i}{S^n - 1}$	4 PRES. VALUE REVERSION OF I $V^n = \frac{1}{S^n}$	5 PRESENT VALUE ORD. ANNUITY 1 PER PERIOD $a_{\overline{n}\vert} = \frac{1 - V^n}{i}$	6 INSTALMENT TO AMORTIZE I $1/a_{\overline{n}\vert} = \frac{i}{1 - V^n}$	n HALF YEARS
1	1.053750	1.000000	1.000000	.948992	.948992	1.053750	1
YEARS							
1	1.110389	2.053750	.486914	.900585	1.849577	.540664	2
2	1.232964	4.334212	.230722	.811054	3.515279	.284472	4
3	1.369070	6.866411	.145636	.730423	5.015385	.199386	6
4	1.520200	9.678138	.103326	.657808	6.366359	.157076	8
5	1.688013	12.800248	.078123	.592412	7.583026	.131873	10
6	1.874352	16.267006	.061474	.533518	8.678738	.115224	12
7	2.081259	20.116455	.049711	.480478	9.665520	.103461	14
8	2.311008	24.390842	.040999	.432712	10.554202	.094749	16
9	2.566118	29.137074	.034321	.389694	11.354535	.088071	18
10	2.849389	34.407238	.029064	.350952	12.075304	.082814	20
11	3.163930	40.259171	.024839	.316063	12.724417	.078589	22
12	3.513194	46.757093	.021387	.284641	13.308999	.075137	24
13	3.901012	53.972315	.018528	.256344	13.835465	.072278	26
14	4.331641	61.984018	.016133	.230859	14.309593	.069883	28
15	4.809807	70.880126	.014108	.207909	14.736585	.067858	30
16	5.340757	80.758267	.012383	.187239	15.121128	.066133	32
17	5.930318	91.726846	.010902	.168625	15.467441	.064652	34
18	6.584960	103.906236	.009624	.151861	15.779326	.063374	36
19	7.311868	117.430099	.008516	.136764	16.060205	.062266	38
20	8.119018	132.446847	.007550	.123168	16.313161	.061300	40
21	9.015269	149.121280	.006706	.110923	16.540969	.060456	42
22	10.010456	167.636389	.005965	.099896	16.746129	.059715	44
23	11.115501	188.195362	.005314	.089964	16.930894	.059064	46
24	12.342530	211.023822	.004739	.081021	17.097290	.058489	48
25	13.705011	236.372294	.004231	.072966	17.247144	.057981	50
26	15.217894	264.518959	.003780	.065712	17.382100	.057530	52
27	16.897783	295.772709	.003381	.059179	17.503640	.057131	54
28	18.763114	330.476532	.003026	.053296	17.613097	.056776	56
29	20.834356	369.011276	.002710	.047998	17.711672	.056460	58
30	23.134241	411.799835	.002428	.043226	17.800447	.056178	60
31	25.688008	459.311783	.002177	.038929	17.880397	.055927	62
32	28.523683	512.068530	.001953	.035059	17.952398	.055703	64
33	31.672386	570.649045	.001752	.031573	18.017242	.055502	66
34	35.168671	635.696208	.001573	.028434	18.075639	.055323	68
35	39.050908	707.923866	.001413	.025608	18.128231	.055163	70
36	43.361701	788.124669	.001269	.023062	18.175594	.055019	72
37	48.148358	877.178762	.001140	.020769	18.218249	.054890	74
38	53.463411	976.063453	.001025	.018704	18.256663	.054775	76
39	59.365186	1085.863933	.000921	.016845	18.291258	.054671	78
40	65.918454	1207.785184	.000828	.015170	18.322414	.054578	80
41	73.195130	1343.165208	.000745	.013662	18.350472	.054495	82
42	81.275072	1493.489707	.000670	.012304	18.375741	.054420	84
43	90.246951	1660.408385	.000602	.011081	18.398498	.054352	86
44	100.209227	1845.753060	.000542	.009979	18.418993	.054292	88
45	111.271230	2051.557760	.000487	.008987	18.437450	.054237	90
46	123.554356	2280.081047	.000439	.008094	18.454072	.054189	92
47	137.193406	2533.830807	.000395	.007289	18.469042	.054145	94
48	152.338057	2815.591766	.000355	.006564	18.482524	.054105	96
49	169.154513	3128.456050	.000320	.005912	18.494665	.054070	98
50	187.827321	3475.857131	.000288	.005324	18.505599	.054038	100
51	208.561403	3861.607492	.000259	.004795	18.515446	.054009	102
52	231.584300	4289.940473	.000233	.004318	18.524315	.053983	104
53	257.148674	4765.556729	.000210	.003889	18.532301	.053960	106
54	285.535075	5293.675820	.000189	.003502	18.539494	.053939	108
55	317.055025	5880.093481	.000170	.003154	18.545972	.053920	110
56	352.054432	6531.245237	.000153	.002840	18.551805	.053903	112
57	390.917390	7254.277027	.000138	.002558	18.557059	.053888	114
58	434.070394	8057.123617	.000124	.002304	18.561790	.053874	116
59	481.987018	8948.595689	.000112	.002075	18.566051	.053862	118
60	535.193113	9938.476528	.000101	.001868	18.569889	.053851	120

10¾% ANNUAL COMPOUND INTEREST TABLE 10¾%

EFFECTIVE RATE = 29/48%   BASE = 1.00604167

YEARS	1 AMOUNT OF I AT COMPOUND INTEREST $S^n = (1+i)^n$	2 ACCUMULATION OF I PER PERIOD $S_{\overline{n}\vert} = \frac{S^n - 1}{i}$	3 SINKING FUND FACTOR $1/S_{\overline{n}\vert} = \frac{i}{S^n - 1}$	4 PRES. VALUE REVERSION OF I $V^n = \frac{1}{S^n}$	5 PRESENT VALUE ORD. ANNUITY 1 PER PERIOD $a_{\overline{n}\vert} = \frac{1 - V^n}{i}$	6 INSTALMENT TO AMORTIZE I $1/a_{\overline{n}\vert} = \frac{i}{1 - V^n}$	n YEARS
1	1.107500	1.000000	1.000000	.902935	.902935	1.107500	1
2	1.226556	2.107500	.474496	.815291	1.718225	.581996	2
3	1.358411	3.334056	.299935	.736154	2.454380	.407435	3
4	1.504440	4.692467	.213108	.664699	3.119079	.320608	4
5	1.666168	6.196908	.161371	.600180	3.719258	.268871	5
6	1.845281	7.863075	.127177	.541923	4.261181	.234677	6
7	2.043648	9.708356	.103004	.489321	4.750502	.210504	7
8	2.263340	11.752004	.085092	.441825	5.192327	.192592	8
9	2.506650	14.015344	.071350	.398939	5.591266	.178850	9
10	2.776114	16.521994	.060525	.360216	5.951482	.168025	10
11	3.074547	19.298108	.051819	.325251	6.276733	.159319	11
12	3.405060	22.372655	.044697	.293681	6.570414	.152197	12
13	3.771104	25.777715	.038793	.265174	6.835588	.146293	13
14	4.176498	29.548820	.033842	.239435	7.075023	.141342	14
15	4.625472	33.725318	.029651	.216194	7.291217	.137151	15
16	5.122710	38.350789	.026075	.195209	7.486426	.133575	16
17	5.673401	43.473499	.023003	.176261	7.662687	.130503	17
18	6.283292	49.146900	.020347	.159152	7.821840	.127847	18
19	6.958746	55.430192	.018041	.143704	7.965544	.125541	19
20	7.706811	62.388938	.016028	.129755	8.095299	.123528	20
21	8.535293	70.095749	.014266	.117161	8.212460	.121766	21
22	9.452837	78.631042	.012718	.105788	8.318248	.120218	22
23	10.469017	88.083879	.011353	.095520	8.413768	.118853	23
24	11.594436	98.552895	.010147	.086248	8.500016	.117647	24
25	12.840838	110.147332	.009079	.077877	8.577893	.116579	25
26	14.221228	122.988170	.008131	.070317	8.648210	.115631	26
27	15.750010	137.209398	.007288	.063492	8.711702	.114788	27
28	17.443136	152.959409	.006538	.057329	8.769031	.114038	28
29	19.318274	170.402545	.005868	.051764	8.820796	.113368	29
30	21.394988	189.720818	.005271	.046740	8.867536	.112771	30
31	23.694949	211.115806	.004737	.042203	8.909739	.112237	31
32	26.242156	234.810756	.004259	.038107	8.947845	.111759	32
33	29.063188	261.052912	.003831	.034408	8.982253	.111331	33
34	32.187481	290.116100	.003447	.031068	9.013321	.110947	34
35	35.647635	322.303581	.003103	.028052	9.041373	.110603	35
36	39.479756	357.951215	.002794	.025329	9.066703	.110294	36
37	43.723829	397.430971	.002516	.022871	9.089574	.110016	37
38	48.424141	441.154801	.002267	.020651	9.110225	.109767	38
39	53.629736	489.578942	.002043	.018646	9.128871	.109543	39
40	59.394933	543.208678	.001841	.016836	9.145707	.109341	40
41	65.779888	602.603611	.001659	.015202	9.160910	.109159	41
42	72.851226	668.383499	.001496	.013727	9.174636	.108996	42
43	80.682733	741.234725	.001349	.012394	9.187030	.108849	43
44	89.356127	821.917458	.001217	.011191	9.198222	.108717	44
45	98.961910	911.273584	.001097	.010105	9.208327	.108597	45
46	109.600316	1010.235495	.000990	.009124	9.217451	.108490	46
47	121.382350	1119.835810	.000893	.008238	9.225689	.108393	47
48	134.430952	1241.218160	.000806	.007439	9.233128	.108306	48
49	148.882280	1375.649113	.000727	.006717	9.239845	.108227	49
50	164.887125	1524.531393	.000656	.006065	9.245909	.108156	50
51	182.612491	1689.418517	.000592	.005476	9.251385	.108092	51
52	202.243333	1872.031007	.000534	.004945	9.256330	.108034	52
53	223.984492	2074.274340	.000482	.004465	9.260794	.107982	53
54	248.062824	2298.258832	.000435	.004031	9.264826	.107935	54
55	274.729578	2546.321656	.000393	.003640	9.268466	.107893	55
56	304.263008	2821.051233	.000354	.003287	9.271752	.107854	56
57	336.971281	3125.314241	.000320	.002968	9.274720	.107820	57
58	373.195694	3462.285522	.000289	.002680	9.277399	.107789	58
59	413.314231	3835.481216	.000261	.002419	9.279819	.107761	59
60	457.745511	4248.795446	.000235	.002185	9.282004	.107735	60

11% MONTHLY COMPOUND INTEREST TABLE 11%

EFFECTIVE RATE = 11/12%   BASE = 1.00916667

MONTHS	1 AMOUNT OF 1 AT COMPOUND INTEREST $S^n = (1+i)^n$	2 ACCUMULATION OF 1 PER PERIOD $S_{\overline{n}\rvert} = \frac{S^n - 1}{i}$	3 SINKING FUND FACTOR $1/S_{\overline{n}\rvert} = \frac{i}{S^n - 1}$	4 PRES. VALUE REVERSION OF 1 $V^n = \frac{1}{S^n}$	5 PRESENT VALUE ORD. ANNUITY 1 PER PERIOD $a_{\overline{n}\rvert} = \frac{1 - V^n}{i}$	6 INSTALMENT TO AMORTIZE 1 $1/a_{\overline{n}\rvert} = \frac{i}{1 - V^n}$	n MONTHS
1	1.009166	1.000000	1.000000	.990916	.990916	1.009166	1
2	1.018417	2.009166	.497718	.981915	1.972832	.506885	2
3	1.027752	3.027584	.330296	.972996	2.945828	.339463	3
4	1.037173	4.055336	.246588	.964158	3.909987	.255755	4
5	1.046681	5.092510	.196366	.955400	4.865387	.205533	5
6	1.056275	6.139192	.162887	.946722	5.812110	.172054	6
7	1.065958	7.195468	.138976	.938122	6.750233	.148143	7
8	1.075729	8.261426	.121044	.929601	7.679834	.130211	8
9	1.085590	9.337156	.107098	.921157	8.600992	.116265	9
10	1.095541	10.422746	.095943	.912790	9.513782	.105110	10
11	1.105584	11.518288	.086818	.904499	10.418281	.095985	11
YEARS							
1	1.115718	12.623873	.079214	.896283	11.314564	.088381	12
2	1.244828	26.708565	.037441	.803323	21.455618	.046607	24
3	1.388878	42.423123	.023572	.720005	30.544874	.032738	36
4	1.549598	59.956150	.016678	.645328	38.691421	.025845	48
5	1.728915	79.518079	.012575	.578397	45.993033	.021742	60
6	1.928983	101.343692	.009867	.518407	52.537346	.019034	72
7	2.152203	125.694939	.007955	.464640	58.402903	.017122	84
8	2.401254	152.864084	.006541	.416449	63.660103	.015708	96
9	2.679124	183.177212	.005459	.373256	68.372043	.014625	108
10	2.989149	216.998138	.004608	.334543	72.595274	.013775	120
11	3.335050	254.732784	.003925	.299845	76.380486	.013092	132
12	3.720978	296.834038	.003368	.268746	79.773108	.012535	144
13	4.151566	343.807201	.002908	.240872	82.813858	.012075	156
14	4.631980	396.216043	.002523	.215890	85.539231	.011690	168
15	5.167987	454.689576	.002199	.193498	87.981936	.011365	180
16	5.766021	519.929598	.001923	.173429	90.171292	.011090	192
17	6.433258	592.719119	.001687	.155442	92.133575	.010853	204
18	7.177707	673.931759	.001483	.139320	93.892336	.010650	216
19	8.008303	764.542231	.001307	.124870	95.468684	.010474	228
20	8.935015	865.638042	.001155	.111919	96.881538	.010321	240
21	9.968965	978.432542	.001022	.100311	98.147855	.010188	252
22	11.122562	1104.279491	.000905	.089907	99.282835	.010072	264
23	12.409651	1244.689302	.000803	.080582	100.300097	.009970	276
24	13.845682	1401.347173	.000713	.072224	101.211853	.009880	288
25	15.447888	1576.133312	.000634	.064733	102.029043	.009801	300
26	17.235500	1771.145496	.000564	.058019	102.761477	.009731	312
27	19.229972	1988.724266	.000502	.052002	103.417946	.009669	324
28	21.455242	2231.480999	.000448	.046608	104.006327	.009614	336
29	23.938018	2502.329255	.000399	.041774	104.533684	.009566	348
30	26.708097	2804.519759	.000356	.037441	105.006345	.009523	360
31	29.798727	3141.679397	.000318	.033558	105.429983	.009484	372
32	33.247002	3517.854756	.000284	.030077	105.809682	.009450	384
33	37.094306	3937.560686	.000253	.026958	106.150002	.009420	396
34	41.386816	4405.834502	.000226	.024162	106.455022	.009393	408
35	46.176050	4928.296419	.000202	.021656	106.728408	.009369	420
36	51.519489	5511.217017	.000181	.019410	106.973440	.009348	432
37	57.481264	6161.592513	.000162	.017396	107.193057	.009328	444
38	64.132930	6887.228705	.000145	.015592	107.389896	.009311	456
39	71.554318	7696.834666	.000129	.013975	107.566320	.009296	468
40	79.834500	8600.127295	.000116	.012525	107.724446	.009282	480
41	89.072856	9607.947896	.000104	.011226	107.866170	.009270	492
42	99.380263	10732.392330	.000093	.010062	107.993196	.009259	504
43	110.880431	11986.956140	.000083	.009018	108.107048	.009250	516
44	123.711386	13386.696640	.000074	.008083	108.209091	.009241	528
45	138.027124	14948.413480	.000066	.007244	108.300550	.009233	540
46	153.999462	16690.850360	.000059	.006493	108.382523	.009226	552
47	171.820100	18634.920020	.000053	.005820	108.455995	.009220	564
48	191.702923	20803.955170	.000048	.005216	108.521846	.009214	576
49	213.886562	23223.988540	.000043	.004675	108.580868	.009209	588
50	238.637266	25924.065330	.000038	.004190	108.633767	.009205	600

11% QUARTERLY COMPOUND INTEREST TABLE 11%

EFFECTIVE RATE = 2¾% BASE = 1.0275

QUARTERS	1 AMOUNT OF I AT COMPOUND INTEREST $S^n = (1+i)^n$	2 ACCUMULATION OF I PER PERIOD $S_{\overline{n}\rvert} = \frac{S^n - 1}{i}$	3 SINKING FUND FACTOR $1/S_{\overline{n}\rvert} = \frac{i}{S^n - 1}$	4 PRES. VALUE REVERSION OF I $V^n = \frac{1}{S^n}$	5 PRESENT VALUE ORD. ANNUITY 1 PER PERIOD $a_{\overline{n}\rvert} = \frac{1 - V^n}{i}$	6 INSTALMENT TO AMORTIZE I $1/a_{\overline{n}\rvert} = \frac{i}{1 - V^n}$	n QUARTERS
1	1.027500	1.000000	1.000000	.973236	.973236	1.027500	1
2	1.055756	2.027500	.493218	.947188	1.920424	.520718	2
3	1.084790	3.083256	.324332	.921838	2.842262	.351832	3
YEARS							
1	1.114621	4.168046	.239921	.897166	3.739428	.267421	4
2	1.242381	8.813838	.113458	.804906	7.094314	.140958	8
3	1.384784	13.992137	.071469	.722134	10.104204	.098969	12
4	1.543509	19.763980	.050597	.647874	12.804573	.078097	16
5	1.720428	26.197398	.038172	.581251	15.227252	.065672	20
6	1.917626	33.368222	.029969	.521478	17.400797	.057469	24
7	2.137427	41.360975	.024177	.467852	19.350826	.051677	28
8	2.382421	50.269868	.019893	.419741	21.100326	.047393	32
9	2.655498	60.199910	.016611	.376577	22.669918	.044111	36
10	2.959874	71.268145	.014032	.337852	24.078101	.041532	40
11	3.299138	83.605035	.011961	.303109	25.341475	.039461	44
12	3.677290	97.355996	.010272	.271939	26.474931	.037772	48
13	4.098785	112.683108	.008874	.243975	27.491829	.036374	52
14	4.568593	129.767034	.007706	.218886	28.404155	.035206	56
15	5.092251	148.809141	.006720	.196377	29.222662	.034220	60
16	5.675932	170.033877	.005881	.176183	29.956999	.033381	64
17	6.326514	193.691420	.005163	.158065	30.615821	.032663	68
18	7.051667	220.060621	.004544	.141810	31.206893	.032044	72
19	7.859938	249.452292	.004009	.127227	31.737183	.031509	76
20	8.760854	282.212874	.003543	.114144	32.212941	.031043	80
21	9.765034	318.728514	.003137	.102406	32.639775	.030637	84
22	10.884315	359.429624	.002782	.091875	33.022715	.030282	88
23	12.131889	404.795946	.002470	.082427	33.366276	.029970	92
24	13.522461	455.362213	.002196	.073951	33.674508	.029696	96
25	15.072422	511.724449	.001954	.066346	33.951042	.029454	100
26	16.800042	574.546995	.001741	.059524	34.199140	.029241	104
27	18.725684	644.570341	.001551	.053403	34.421724	.029051	108
28	20.872046	722.619851	.001384	.047911	34.621419	.028884	112
29	23.264426	809.615495	.001235	.042984	34.800579	.028735	116
30	25.931024	906.582688	.001103	.038564	34.961315	.028603	120
31	28.903271	1014.664383	.000986	.034598	35.105521	.028486	124
32	32.216200	1135.134539	.000881	.031040	35.234899	.028381	128
33	35.908861	1269.413135	.000788	.027848	35.350972	.028288	132
34	40.024780	1419.082912	.000705	.024985	35.455108	.028205	136
35	44.612471	1585.908029	.000631	.022415	35.548536	.028131	140
36	49.726008	1771.854850	.000564	.020110	35.632356	.028064	144
37	55.425666	1979.115130	.000505	.018042	35.707557	.028005	148
38	61.778626	2210.131845	.000452	.016187	35.775024	.027952	152
39	68.859770	2467.627986	.000405	.014522	35.835554	.027905	156
40	76.752563	2754.638659	.000363	.013029	35.889859	.027863	160
41	85.550039	3074.546857	.000325	.011689	35.938579	.027825	164
42	95.355892	3431.123335	.000291	.010487	35.982290	.027791	168
43	106.285704	3828.571058	.000261	.009409	36.021505	.027761	172
44	118.468305	4271.574742	.000234	.008441	36.056688	.027734	176
45	132.047292	4765.356065	.000210	.007573	36.088253	.027710	180
46	147.182719	5315.735225	.000188	.006794	36.116572	.027688	184
47	164.052987	5929.199538	.000169	.006096	36.141978	.027669	188
48	182.856947	6612.979902	.000151	.005469	36.164773	.027651	192
49	203.816241	7375.136033	.000136	.004906	36.185223	.027636	196
50	227.177915	8224.651458	.000122	.004402	36.203570	.027622	200
51	253.217334	9171.539411	.000109	.003949	36.220030	.027609	204
52	282.241424	10226.960850	.000098	.003543	36.234798	.027598	208
53	314.592291	11403.356030	.000088	.003179	36.248047	.027588	212
54	350.651256	12714.591110	.000079	.002852	36.259933	.027579	216
55	390.843344	14176.121600	.000071	.002559	36.270597	.027571	220
56	435.642300	15805.174560	.000063	.002295	36.280165	.027563	224
57	485.576169	17620.951610	.000057	.002059	36.288749	.027557	228
58	541.233522	19644.855330	.000051	.001848	36.296450	.027551	232
59	603.270389	21900.741430	.000046	.001658	36.303359	.027546	236
60	672.418001	24415.200040	.000041	.001487	36.309557	.027541	240

11 % SEMI-ANNUAL COMPOUND INTEREST TABLE 11 %

EFFECTIVE RATE = 5½% BASE = 1.055

HALF YEARS	1 AMOUNT OF I AT COMPOUND INTEREST $S^n = (1+i)^n$	2 ACCUMULATION OF I PER PERIOD $S_{\overline{n}\vert} = \frac{S^n - 1}{i}$	3 SINKING FUND FACTOR $1/S_{\overline{n}\vert} = \frac{i}{S^n - 1}$	4 PRES. VALUE REVERSION OF I $V^n = \frac{1}{S^n}$	5 PRESENT VALUE ORD. ANNUITY 1 PER PERIOD $a_{\overline{n}\vert} = \frac{1 - V^n}{i}$	6 INSTALMENT TO AMORTIZE I $1/a_{\overline{n}\vert} = \frac{i}{1 - V^n}$	n HALF YEARS
1	1.055000	1.000000	1.000000	.947867	.947867	1.055000	1
YEARS							
1	1.113025	2.055000	.486618	.898452	1.846320	.541618	2
2	1.238825	4.342266	.230294	.807217	3.505150	.285294	4
3	1.378843	6.888051	.145179	.725246	4.995530	.200179	6
4	1.534687	9.721573	.102864	.651599	6.334566	.157864	8
5	1.708144	12.875354	.077668	.585431	7.537626	.132668	10
6	1.901207	16.385591	.061029	.525982	8.618518	.116029	12
7	2.116091	20.292572	.049279	.472569	9.589648	.104279	14
8	2.355263	24.641140	.040583	.424581	10.462162	.095583	16
9	2.621466	29.481205	.033920	.381466	11.246074	.088920	18
10	2.917757	34.868318	.028679	.342729	11.950382	.083679	20
11	3.247537	40.864310	.024471	.307926	12.583170	.079471	22
12	3.614590	47.537998	.021036	.276657	13.151699	.076036	24
13	4.023129	54.965980	.018193	.248563	13.662495	.073193	26
14	4.477843	63.233510	.015814	.223322	14.121422	.070814	28
15	4.983951	72.435478	.013805	.200644	14.533745	.068805	30
16	5.547262	82.677498	.012095	.180269	14.904198	.067095	32
17	6.174242	94.077122	.010630	.161963	15.237033	.065630	34
18	6.872085	106.765189	.009366	.145516	15.536068	.064366	36
19	7.648803	120.887324	.008272	.130739	15.804738	.063272	38
20	8.513309	136.605614	.007320	.117463	16.046125	.062320	40
21	9.475526	154.100464	.006489	.105535	16.262999	.061489	42
22	10.546497	173.572669	.005761	.094818	16.457851	.060761	44
23	11.738515	195.245720	.005122	.085190	16.632915	.060122	46
24	13.065260	219.368367	.004559	.076539	16.790203	.059559	48
25	14.541961	246.217477	.004061	.068767	16.931518	.059061	50
26	16.185566	276.101207	.003622	.061783	17.058483	.058622	52
27	18.014940	309.362546	.003232	.055509	17.172555	.058232	54
28	20.051079	346.383248	.002887	.049873	17.275043	.057887	56
29	22.317352	387.588214	.002580	.044808	17.367124	.057580	58
30	24.839770	433.450372	.002307	.040258	17.449854	.057307	60
31	27.647286	484.496101	.002064	.036170	17.524183	.057064	62
32	30.772120	541.311272	.001847	.032497	17.590965	.056847	64
33	34.250139	604.547979	.001654	.029197	17.650964	.056654	66
34	38.121261	674.932014	.001482	.026232	17.704871	.056482	68
35	42.429916	753.271205	.001328	.023568	17.753304	.056328	70
36	47.225558	840.464683	.001190	.021175	17.796819	.056190	72
37	52.563226	937.513204	.001067	.019025	17.835914	.056067	74
38	58.504185	1045.530634	.000956	.017093	17.871040	.055956	76
39	65.116620	1165.756734	.000858	.015357	17.902599	.055858	78
40	72.476426	1299.571389	.000769	.013798	17.930953	.055769	80
41	80.668074	1448.510445	.000690	.012396	17.956428	.055690	82
42	89.785584	1614.283338	.000619	.011138	17.979316	.055619	84
43	99.933599	1798.792713	.000556	.010007	17.999879	.055556	86
44	111.228594	2004.156260	.000499	.008990	18.018355	.055499	88
45	123.800206	2232.731022	.000448	.008078	18.034954	.055448	90
46	137.792725	2487.140445	.000402	.007257	18.049868	.055402	92
47	153.366747	2770.304495	.000361	.006520	18.063267	.055361	94
48	170.701024	3085.473160	.000324	.005858	18.075306	.055324	96
49	189.994507	3436.263764	.000291	.005263	18.086122	.055291	98
50	211.468636	3826.702476	.000261	.004729	18.095839	.055261	100
51	235.369879	4261.270524	.000235	.004249	18.104570	.055235	102
52	261.972559	4744.955625	.000211	.003817	18.112415	.055211	104
53	291.582008	5283.309235	.000189	.003430	18.119462	.055189	106
54	324.538064	5882.510262	.000170	.003081	18.125795	.055170	108
55	361.218979	6549.435984	.000153	.002768	18.131484	.055153	110
56	402.045754	7291.740985	.000137	.002487	18.136595	.055137	112
57	447.486976	8117.945011	.000123	.002235	18.141187	.055123	114
58	498.064191	9037.530746	.000111	.002008	18.145313	.055111	116
59	554.357896	10061.052660	.000099	.001804	18.149020	.055099	118
60	617.014197	11200.258130	.000089	.001621	18.152351	.055089	120

11% ANNUAL COMPOUND INTEREST TABLE 11%

EFFECTIVE RATE = 11% BASE = 1.11

YEARS	1 AMOUNT OF I AT COMPOUND INTEREST $S^n = (1+i)^n$	2 ACCUMULATION OF I PER PERIOD $S_{\overline{n}\rvert} = \frac{S^n - 1}{i}$	3 SINKING FUND FACTOR $1/S_{\overline{n}\rvert} = \frac{i}{S^n - 1}$	4 PRES. VALUE REVERSION OF I $V^n = \frac{1}{S^n}$	5 PRESENT VALUE ORD. ANNUITY 1 PER PERIOD $a_{\overline{n}\rvert} = \frac{1 - V^n}{i}$	6 INSTALMENT TO AMORTIZE I $1/a_{\overline{n}\rvert} = \frac{i}{1 - V^n}$	n YEARS
1	1.110000	1.000000	1.000000	.900901	.900901	1.110000	1
2	1.232100	2.110000	.473934	.811622	1.712523	.583934	2
3	1.367631	3.342100	.299213	.731191	2.443715	.409213	3
4	1.518070	4.709731	.212326	.658731	3.102446	.322326	4
5	1.685058	6.227801	.160570	.593451	3.695897	.270570	5
6	1.870415	7.912860	.126377	.534641	4.230538	.236377	6
7	2.076160	9.783274	.102215	.481658	4.712196	.212215	7
8	2.304538	11.859434	.084321	.433926	5.146123	.194321	8
9	2.558037	14.163972	.070602	.390925	5.537048	.180602	9
10	2.839421	16.722009	.059801	.352184	5.889232	.169801	10
11	3.151757	19.561430	.051121	.317283	6.206515	.161121	11
12	3.498451	22.713187	.044027	.285841	6.492356	.154027	12
13	3.883280	26.211638	.038151	.257514	6.749870	.148151	13
14	4.310441	30.094918	.033228	.231995	6.981865	.143228	14
15	4.784589	34.405359	.029065	.209004	7.190870	.139065	15
16	5.310894	39.189948	.025517	.188292	7.379162	.135517	16
17	5.895093	44.500843	.022471	.169633	7.548794	.132471	17
18	6.543553	50.395936	.019843	.152822	7.701617	.129843	18
19	7.263344	56.939488	.017563	.137678	7.839294	.127563	19
20	8.062312	64.202832	.015576	.124034	7.963328	.125576	20
21	8.949166	72.265144	.013838	.111742	8.075070	.123838	21
22	9.933574	81.214310	.012313	.100669	8.175739	.122313	22
23	11.026267	91.147884	.010971	.090693	8.266432	.120971	23
24	12.239157	102.174151	.009787	.081705	8.348137	.119787	24
25	13.585464	114.413307	.008740	.073608	8.421745	.118740	25
26	15.079865	127.998771	.007813	.066314	8.488058	.117813	26
27	16.738650	143.078636	.006989	.059742	8.547800	.116989	27
28	18.579901	159.817286	.006257	.053822	8.601622	.116257	28
29	20.623691	178.397187	.005605	.048488	8.650110	.115605	29
30	22.892297	199.020878	.005025	.043683	8.693793	.115025	30
31	25.410449	221.913175	.004506	.039354	8.733146	.114506	31
32	28.205599	247.323624	.004043	.035454	8.768600	.114043	32
33	31.308214	275.529222	.003629	.031940	8.800541	.113629	33
34	34.752118	306.837437	.003259	.028775	8.829316	.113259	34
35	38.574851	341.589555	.002927	.025924	8.855240	.112927	35
36	42.818085	380.164406	.002630	.023355	8.878594	.112630	36
37	47.528074	422.982490	.002364	.021040	8.899635	.112364	37
38	52.756162	470.510564	.002125	.018955	8.918590	.112125	38
39	58.559340	523.266726	.001911	.017077	8.935666	.111911	39
40	65.000867	581.826066	.001719	.015384	8.951051	.111719	40
41	72.150963	646.826934	.001546	.013860	8.964911	.111546	41
42	80.087569	718.977896	.001391	.012486	8.977397	.111391	42
43	88.897201	799.065465	.001251	.011249	8.988646	.111251	43
44	98.675893	887.962666	.001126	.010134	8.998780	.111126	44
45	109.530242	986.638559	.001014	.009130	9.007910	.111014	45
46	121.578568	1096.168801	.000912	.008225	9.016135	.110912	46
47	134.952211	1217.747369	.000821	.007410	9.023545	.110821	47
48	149.796954	1352.699580	.000739	.006676	9.030221	.110739	48
49	166.274619	1502.496534	.000666	.006014	9.036235	.110666	49
50	184.564827	1668.771153	.000599	.005418	9.041653	.110599	50
51	204.866958	1853.335979	.000540	.004881	9.046534	.110540	51
52	227.402323	2058.202936	.000486	.004397	9.050932	.110486	52
53	252.416579	2285.605259	.000438	.003962	9.054894	.110438	53
54	280.182402	2538.021837	.000394	.003569	9.058463	.110394	54
55	311.002466	2818.204239	.000355	.003215	9.061678	.110355	55
56	345.212738	3129.206705	.000320	.002897	9.064575	.110320	56
57	383.186139	3474.419443	.000288	.002610	9.067185	.110288	57
58	425.336614	3857.605581	.000259	.002351	9.069536	.110259	58
59	472.123641	4282.942195	.000233	.002118	9.071654	.110233	59
60	524.057242	4755.065835	.000210	.001908	9.073562	.110210	60

11¼ % MONTHLY COMPOUND INTEREST TABLE 11¼ %

EFFECTIVE RATE = 15/16% BASE = 1.009375

	1 AMOUNT OF I AT COMPOUND INTEREST $S^n = (1+i)^n$	2 ACCUMULATION OF I PER PERIOD $S_{\overline{n}\rvert} = \frac{S^n - 1}{i}$	3 SINKING FUND FACTOR $1/S_{\overline{n}\rvert} = \frac{i}{S^n - 1}$	4 PRES. VALUE REVERSION OF I $V^n = \frac{1}{S^n}$	5 PRESENT VALUE ORD. ANNUITY 1 PER PERIOD $a_{\overline{n}\rvert} = \frac{1 - V^n}{i}$	6 INSTALMENT TO AMORTIZE I $1/a_{\overline{n}\rvert} = \frac{i}{1 - V^n}$	n MONTHS
MONTHS							
1	1.009375	1.000000	1.000000	.990712	.990712	1.009375	1
2	1.018837	2.009375	.497667	.981510	1.972222	.507042	2
3	1.028389	3.028212	.330227	.972394	2.944616	.339602	3
4	11038030	4.056602	.246511	.963362	3.907979	.255886	4
5	1.047762	5.094633	.196284	.954415	4.862394	.205659	5
6	1.057584	6.142395	.162802	.945550	5.807944	.172177	6
7	1.067499	7.199980	.138889	.936768	6.744713	.148264	7
8	1.077507	8.267479	.120955	.928067	7.672780	.130330	8
9	1.087609	9.344987	.107009	.919447	8.592228	.116384	9
10	1.097805	10.432596	.095853	.910908	9.503136	.105228	10
11	1.108097	11.530402	.086727	.902447	10.405584	.096102	11
YEARS							
1	1.118485	12.638499	.079123	.894065	11.299650	.088498	12
2	1.251010	26.774484	.037348	.799353	21.402281	.046723	24
3	1.399237	42.585384	.023482	.714674	30.434697	.032857	36
4	1.565028	60.269653	.016592	.638966	38.510271	.025967	48
5	1.750461	80.049259	.012492	.571277	45.730366	.021867	60
6	1.957866	102.172471	.009787	.510759	52.185605	.019162	72
7	2.189846	126.916972	.007879	.456652	57.957014	.017254	84
8	2.449312	154.593349	.006468	.408277	63.117033	.015843	96
9	2.739521	185.548986	.005389	.365027	67.730430	.014764	108
10	3.064116	220.172432	.004541	.326358	71.855110	.013916	120
11	3.427171	258.898269	.003862	.291785	75.542845	.013237	132
12	3.833242	302.212573	.003308	.260875	78.839922	.012683	144
13	4.287428	350.659013	.002851	.233240	81.787727	.012226	156
14	4.795428	404.845675	.002470	.208531	84.423258	.011845	168
15	5.363619	465.452695	.002148	.186441	86.779597	.011523	180
16	5.999132	533.240794	.001875	.166690	88.886317	.011250	192
17	6.709945	609.060829	.001641	.149032	90.769865	.011016	204
18	7.504979	693.864472	.001441	.133244	92.453880	.010816	216
19	8.394213	788.716154	.001267	.119129	93.959501	.010642	228
20	9.388810	894.806427	.001117	.106509	95.305625	.010492	240
21	10.501252	1013.466906	.000986	.095226	96.509148	.010361	252
22	11.745502	1146.186982	.000872	.085138	971585176	.010247	264
23	13.137179	1294.632521	.000772	.076119	98.547216	.010147	276
24	14.693750	1460.666770	.000684	.068056	99.407345	.010059	288
25	16.434753	1646.373741	.000607	.060846	100.176355	.009982	300
26	18.382041	1854.084377	.000539	.054400	100.863901	.009914	312
27	20.560054	2086.405802	.000479	.048638	101.478613	.009854	324
28	22.996131	2346.254048	.000426	.043485	102.028205	.009801	336
29	25.720849	2636.890658	.000379	.038878	102.519577	.009754	348
30	28.768408	2961.963619	.000337	.034760	102.958895	.009712	360
31	32.177060	3325.553155	.000300	.031078	103.351675	.009675	372
32	35.989590	3732.222937	.000267	.027785	103.702847	.009642	384
33	40.253850	4187.077370	.000238	.024842	104.016816	.009613	396
34	45.023365	4695.825661	.000212	.022210	104.297526	.009587	408
35	50.358001	5264.853466	.000189	.019857	104.548499	.009564	420
36	56.324716	5901.303063	.000169	.017754	104.772885	.009544	432
37	62.998403	6613.162988	.000151	.015873	104.973501	.009526	444
38	70.462827	7409.368302	.000134	.014191	105.152865	.009509	456
39	78.811682	8299.912750	.000120	.012688	105.313229	.009495	468
40	88.149758	9295.974191	.000107	.011344	105.456605	.009482	480
41	98.594264	10410.054910	.000096	.010142	105.584791	.009471	492
42	110.276298	11656.138520	.000085	.009068	105.699399	.009460	504
43	123.342489	13049.865530	.000076	.008107	105.801866	.009451	516
44	137.956839	14608.729580	.000068	.007248	105.893478	.009443	528
45	154.302785	16352.297090	.000061	.006480	105.975385	.009436	540
46	172.585495	18302.452840	.000054	.005794	106.048615	.009429	552
47	193.034449	20483.674620	.000048	.005180	106.114087	.009423	564
48	215.906317	22923.340500	.000043	.004631	106.172624	.009418	576
49	241.488179	25652.072490	.000038	.004140	106.224961	.009413	588
50	270.101132	28704.120840	.000034	.003702	106.271752	.009409	600

11¼ % QUARTERLY COMPOUND INTEREST TABLE 11¼ %

EFFECTIVE RATE = 2-13/16%   BASE = 1.028125

QUARTERS	1 AMOUNT OF I AT COMPOUND INTEREST $S^n = (1+i)^n$	2 ACCUMULATION OF I PER PERIOD $S_{\overline{n}\rceil} = \frac{S^n - 1}{i}$	3 SINKING FUND FACTOR $1/S_{\overline{n}\rceil} = \frac{i}{S^n - 1}$	4 PRES. VALUE REVERSION OF I $V^n = \frac{1}{S^n}$	5 PRESENT VALUE ORD. ANNUITY 1 PER PERIOD $a_{\overline{n}\rceil} = \frac{1 - V^n}{i}$	6 INSTALMENT TO AMORTIZE I $1/a_{\overline{n}\rceil} = \frac{i}{1 - V^n}$	n QUARTERS
1	1.028125	1.000000	1.000000	.972644	.972644	1.028125	1
2	1.057041	2.028125	.493066	.946037	1.918681	.521191	2
3	1.086770	3.085166	.324132	.920158	2.838839	.352257	3
YEARS							
1	1.117336	4.171936	.239697	.894986	3.733825	.267822	4
2	1.248439	8.833390	.113207	.801000	7.075547	.141332	8
3	1.394926	14.041798	.071216	.716884	10.066342	.099341	12
4	1.558600	19.861339	.050349	.641601	12.743062	.078474	16
5	1.741480	26.363719	.037931	.574224	15.138690	.066056	20
6	1.945817	33.629061	.029736	.513923	17.282743	.057861	24
7	2.174131	41.746887	.023954	.459954	19.201641	.052079	28
8	2.429234	50.817224	.019678	.411652	20.919028	.047803	32
9	2.714270	60.951836	.016406	.368423	22.456066	.044531	36
10	3.032751	72.275599	.013836	.329734	23.831694	.041961	40
11	3.388601	84.928044	.011775	.295107	25.062862	.039900	44
12	3.786205	99.065072	.010094	.264117	26.164740	.038219	48
13	4.230462	114.860879	.008706	.236381	27.150905	.036831	52
14	4.726847	132.510098	.007547	.211558	28.033510	.035672	56
15	5.281474	152.230201	.006569	.189341	28.823429	.034694	60
16	5.901180	174.264175	.005738	.169458	29.530395	.033863	64
17	6.593599	198.883522	.005028	.151662	30.163120	.033153	68
18	7.367264	226.391598	.004417	.135736	30.729401	.032542	72
19	8.231707	257.127353	.003889	.121481	31.236214	.032014	76
20	9.197580	291.469509	.003431	.108724	31.689804	.031556	80
21	10.276785	329.841227	.003032	.097307	32.095762	.031157	84
22	11.482618	372.715317	.002683	.087088	32.459088	.030808	88
23	12.829939	420.620069	.002377	.077943	32.784260	.030502	92
24	14.335349	474.145760	.002109	.069758	33.075284	.030234	96
25	16.017398	533.951925	.001873	.062432	33.335747	.029998	100
26	17.896811	600.775488	.001665	.055876	33.568858	.029790	104
27	19.996746	675.439843	.001481	.050008	33.777488	.029606	108
28	22.343078	758.864991	.001318	.044757	33.964210	.029443	112
29	24.964719	852.078889	.001174	.040057	34.131323	.029299	116
30	27.893972	956.230106	.001046	.035850	34.280887	.029171	120
31	31.166931	1072.601979	.000932	.032085	34.414745	.029057	124
32	34.823925	1202.628429	.000832	.028716	34.534546	.028957	128
33	38.910014	1347.911625	.000742	.025700	34.641766	.028867	132
34	43.475549	1510.241727	.000662	.023001	34.737727	.028787	136
35	48.576783	1691.618946	.000591	.020586	34.823610	.028716	140
36	54.276574	1894.278191	.000528	.018424	34.900475	.028653	144
37	60.645154	2120.716601	.000472	.016489	34.969267	.028597	148
38	67.760997	2373.724322	.000421	.014758	35.030835	.028546	152
39	75.711781	2656.418885	.000376	.013208	35.085938	.028501	156
40	84.595477	2972.283614	.000336	.011821	35.135255	.028461	160
41	94.521547	3325.210554	.000301	.010580	35.179392	.028426	164
42	105.612300	3719.548427	.000269	.009469	35.218894	.028394	168
43	118.004394	4160.156213	.000240	.008474	35.254249	.028365	172
44	131.850523	4652.463026	.000215	.007584	35.285890	.028340	176
45	147.321297	5202.535008	.000192	.006788	35.314209	.028317	180
46	164.607346	5817.150076	.000172	.006075	35.339553	.028297	184
47	183.921666	6503.881440	.000154	.005437	35.362237	.028279	188
48	205.502245	7271.190916	.000138	.004866	35.382538	.028263	192
49	229.614996	8128.533191	.000123	.004355	35.400707	.028248	196
50	256.557034	9086.472331	.000110	.003898	35.416968	.028235	200
51	286.660336	10156.811940	.000098	.003488	35.431522	.028223	204
52	320.295830	11352.740600	.000088	.003122	35.444547	.028213	208
53	357.877968	12688.994410	.000079	.002794	35.456204	.028204	212
54	399.869833	14182.038500	.000071	.002501	35.466638	.028196	216
55	446.788843	15850.269970	.000063	.002238	35.475975	.028188	220
56	499.213128	17714.244570	.000056	.002003	35.484332	.028181	224
57	557.788655	19796.929940	.000051	.001793	35.491812	.028176	228
58	623.237182	22123.988680	.000045	.001605	35.498506	.028170	232
59	696.365158	24724.094510	.000040	.001436	35.504497	.028165	236
60	778.073658	27629.285600	.000036	.001285	35.509859	.028161	240

11¼ % SEMI-ANNUAL COMPOUND INTEREST TABLE 11¼ %

EFFECTIVE RATE = 5-5/8% BASE = 1.05625

	1 AMOUNT OF I AT COMPOUND INTEREST $S^n = (1+i)^n$	2 ACCUMULATION OF I PER PERIOD $S_{\overline{n}\rvert} = \frac{S^n - 1}{i}$	3 SINKING FUND FACTOR $1/S_{\overline{n}\rvert} = \frac{i}{S^n - 1}$	4 PRES. VALUE REVERSION OF I $V^n = \frac{1}{S^n}$	5 PRESENT VALUE ORD. ANNUITY 1 PER PERIOD $a_{\overline{n}\rvert} = \frac{1 - V^n}{i}$	6 INSTALMENT TO AMORTIZE I $1/a_{\overline{n}\rvert} = \frac{i}{1 - V^n}$	n HALF YEARS
HALF YEARS 1	1.056250	1.000000	1.000000	.946746	.946746	1.056250	1
YEARS							
1	1.115664	2.056250	.486322	.896327	1.843073	.542572	2
2	1.244706	4.350334	.229867	.803402	3.495069	.286117	4
3	1.388674	6.909762	.144723	.720111	4.975798	.200973	6
4	1.549294	9.765223	.102404	.645455	6.303015	.158654	8
5	1.728491	12.950958	.077214	.578539	7.492637	.133464	10
6	1.928416	16.505168	.060587	.518560	8.558926	.116837	12
7	2.151464	20.470473	.048851	.464800	9.514671	.105101	14
8	2.400311	24.894421	.040170	.416613	10.371331	.096420	16
9	2.677941	29.830061	.033523	.373421	11.139178	.089773	18
10	2.987682	35.336577	.028299	.334708	11.827421	.084549	20
11	3.333250	41.479999	.024108	.300008	12.444311	.080358	22
12	3.718787	48.333995	.020689	.268905	12.997247	.076939	24
13	4.148917	55.980751	.017863	.241027	13.492858	.074113	26
14	4.628798	64.511962	.015501	.216039	13.937088	.071751	28
15	5.164183	74.029928	.013508	.193641	14.335263	.069758	30
16	5.761494	84.648780	.011814	.173566	14.692158	.068064	32
17	6.427892	96.495851	.010363	.155572	15.012053	.066613	34
18	7.171368	109.713204	.009115	.139443	15.298784	.065365	36
19	8.000837	124.459329	.008035	.124987	15.555788	.064285	38
20	8.926247	140.911050	.007097	.112029	15.786148	.063347	40
21	9.958693	159.265645	.006279	.100415	15.992626	.062529	42
22	11.110555	179.743206	.005563	.090005	16.177698	.061813	44
23	12.395647	202.589286	.004936	.080673	16.343583	.061186	46
24	13.829378	228.077835	.004384	.072310	16.492270	.060634	48
25	15.428940	256.514494	.003898	.064813	16.625542	.060148	50
26	17.213514	288.240253	.003469	.058094	16.744998	.059719	52
27	19.204499	323.635542	.003090	.052071	16.852069	.059340	54
28	21.425770	363.124793	.002754	.046673	16.948040	.059004	56
29	23.903961	407.181532	.002456	.041834	17.034061	.058706	58
30	26.668790	456.334052	.002191	.037497	17.111164	.058441	60
31	29.753411	511.171753	.001956	.033610	17.180274	.058206	62
32	33.194811	572.352204	.001747	.030125	17.242219	.057997	64
33	37.034258	640.609035	.001561	.027002	17.297742	.057811	66
34	41.317791	716.760729	.001395	.024203	17.347508	.057645	68
35	46.096775	801.720437	.001247	.021693	17.392116	.057497	70
36	51.428515	896.506929	.001115	.019444	17.432098	.057365	72
37	57.376946	1002.256813	.000998	.017429	17.467936	.057248	74
38	64.013396	1120.238158	.000893	.015622	17.500058	.057143	76
39	71.417446	1251.865704	.000799	.014002	17.528850	.057049	78
40	79.677878	1398.717827	.000715	.012551	17.554657	.056965	80
41	88.893745	1562.555463	.000640	.011249	17.577789	.056890	82
42	99.175556	1745.343226	.000573	.010083	17.598522	.056823	84
43	110.646604	1949.272964	.000513	.009038	17.617106	.056763	86
44	123.444440	2176.790043	.000459	.008101	17.633763	.056709	88
45	137.722525	2430.622672	.000411	.007261	17.648694	.056661	90
46	153.652072	2713.814615	.000368	.006508	17.662076	.056618	92
47	171.424095	3029.761689	.000330	.005833	17.674071	.056580	94
48	191.251702	3382.252484	.000296	.005229	17.684823	.056546	96
49	213.372651	3775.513796	.000265	.004687	17.694460	.056515	98
50	238.052199	4214.261308	.000237	.004201	17.703098	.056487	100
51	265.586283	4703.756142	.000213	.003765	17.710840	.056463	102
52	296.305071	5249.867936	.000190	.003375	17.717780	.056440	104
53	330.576920	5859.145239	.000171	.003025	17.724000	.056421	106
54	368.812789	6538.894030	.000153	.002711	17.729575	.056403	108
55	411.471175	7297.265328	.000137	.002430	17.734572	.056387	110
56	459.063602	8143.352932	.000123	.002178	17.739052	.056373	112
57	512.160764	9087.302464	.000110	.001953	17.743066	.056360	114
58	571.399358	10140.433030	.000099	.001750	17.746665	.056349	116
59	637.489729	11315.372970	.000088	.001569	17.749891	.056338	118
60	711.224381	12626.211220	.000079	.001406	17.752782	.056329	120

11¼ % ANNUAL COMPOUND INTEREST TABLE 11¼ %

EFFECTIVE RATE = 11¼% BASE = 1.1125

YEARS	1 AMOUNT OF 1 AT COMPOUND INTEREST $S^n = (1+i)^n$	2 ACCUMULATION OF 1 PER PERIOD $S_{\overline{n}\rvert} = \frac{S^n - 1}{i}$	3 SINKING FUND FACTOR $1/S_{\overline{n}\rvert} = \frac{i}{S^n - 1}$	4 PRES. VALUE REVERSION OF 1 $V^n = \frac{1}{S^n}$	5 PRESENT VALUE ORD. ANNUITY 1 PER PERIOD $a_{\overline{n}\rvert} = \frac{1 - V^n}{i}$	6 INSTALMENT TO AMORTIZE 1 $1/a_{\overline{n}\rvert} = \frac{i}{1 - V^n}$	n YEARS
1	1.112500	1.000000	1.000000	.898876	.898876	1.112500	1
2	1.237656	2.112500	.473373	.807979	1.706855	.585873	2
3	1.376893	3.350156	.298494	.726273	2.433128	.410994	3
4	1.531793	4.727049	.211548	.652830	3.085958	.324048	4
5	1.704120	6.258842	.159774	.586813	3.672771	.272274	5
6	1.895833	7.962962	.125581	.527473	4.200244	.238081	6
7	2.109114	9.858795	.101432	.474133	4.674376	.213932	7
8	2.346390	11.967909	.083557	.426187	5.100563	.196057	8
9	2.610359	14.314299	.069860	.383089	5.483652	.182360	9
10	2.904024	16.924658	.059085	.344350	5.828002	.171585	10
11	3.230727	19.828681	.050432	.309528	6.137530	.162932	11
12	3.594183	23.059408	.043366	.278227	6.415757	.155866	12
13	3.998529	26.653592	.037518	.250092	6.665849	.150018	13
14	4.448364	30.652121	.032624	.224802	6.890651	.145124	14
15	4.948804	35.100484	.028490	.202069	7.092720	.140990	15
16	5.505545	40.049289	.024969	.181635	7.274355	.137469	16
17	6.124919	45.554834	.021952	.163267	7.437622	.134452	17
18	6.813972	51.679752	.019350	.146757	7.584380	.131850	18
19	7.580544	58.493725	.017096	.131917	7.716296	.129596	19
20	8.433355	66.074269	.015134	.118577	7.834873	.127634	20
21	9.382108	74.507624	.013421	.106586	7.941459	.125921	21
22	10.437595	83.889732	.011920	.095808	8.037267	.124420	22
23	11.611824	94.327326	.010601	.086119	8.123386	.123101	23
24	12.918154	105.939151	.009439	.077410	8.200796	.121939	24
25	14.371447	118.857305	.008413	.069582	8.270379	.120913	25
26	15.988235	133.228752	.007506	.062546	8.332925	.120006	26
27	17.786911	149.216987	.006702	.056221	8.389146	.119202	27
28	19.787938	167.003898	.005988	.050536	8.439681	.118488	28
29	22.014082	186.791836	.005354	.045425	8.485107	.117854	29
30	24.490666	208.805918	.004789	.040832	8.525939	.117289	30
31	27.245866	233.296584	.004286	.036703	8.562642	.116786	31
32	30.311026	260.542449	.003838	.032991	8.595633	.116338	32
33	33.721016	290.853475	.003438	.029655	8.625288	.115938	33
34	37.514630	324.574491	.003081	.026656	8.651944	.115581	34
35	41.735026	362.089121	.002762	.023961	8.675905	.115262	35
36	46.430217	403.824147	.002476	.021538	8.697443	.114976	36
37	51.653616	450.254364	.002221	.019360	8.716802	.114721	37
38	57.464648	501.907979	.001992	.017402	8.734204	.114492	38
39	63.929421	559.372627	.001788	.015642	8.749847	.114288	39
40	71.121480	623.302048	.001604	.014060	8.763907	.114104	40
41	79.122647	694.423528	.001440	.012639	8.776546	.113940	41
42	88.023945	773.546175	.001293	.011361	8.787906	.113793	42
43	97.926638	861.570120	.001161	.010212	8.798118	.113661	43
44	108.943385	959.496758	.001042	.009179	8.807297	.113542	44
45	121.199516	1068.440144	.000936	.008251	8.815548	.113436	45
46	134.834462	1189.639660	.000841	.007417	8.822964	.113341	46
47	150.003339	1324.474123	.000755	.006667	8.829631	.113255	47
48	166.878714	1474.477461	.000678	.005992	8.835623	.113178	48
49	185.652570	1641.356176	.000609	.005386	8.841010	.113109	49
50	206.538484	1827.008746	.000547	.004842	8.845851	.113047	50
51	229.774063	2033.547230	.000492	.004352	8.850204	.112992	51
52	255.623646	2263.321293	.000442	.003912	8.854116	.112942	52
53	284.381306	2518.944939	.000397	.003516	8.857632	.112897	53
54	316.374203	2803.326244	.000357	.003161	8.860793	.112857	54
55	351.966300	3119.700447	.000321	.002841	8.863634	.112821	55
56	391.562509	3471.666748	.000288	.002554	8.866188	.112788	56
57	435.613291	3863.229257	.000259	.002296	8.868483	.112759	57
58	484.619787	4298.842548	.000233	.002063	8.870547	.112733	58
59	539.139513	4783.462335	.000209	.001855	8.872402	.112709	59
60	599.792708	5322.601848	.000188	.001667	8.874069	.112688	60

11½ % MONTHLY COMPOUND INTEREST TABLE 11½ %

EFFECTIVE RATE = 23/24% BASE = 1.00958333

MONTHS	1 AMOUNT OF I AT COMPOUND INTEREST $S^n = (1+i)^n$	2 ACCUMULATION OF I PER PERIOD $S_{\overline{n}\vert} = \frac{S^n - 1}{i}$	3 SINKING FUND FACTOR $1/S_{\overline{n}\vert} = \frac{i}{S^n - 1}$	4 PRES. VALUE REVERSION OF I $V^n = \frac{1}{S^n}$	5 PRESENT VALUE ORD. ANNUITY 1 PER PERIOD $a_{\overline{n}\vert} = \frac{1 - V^n}{i}$	6 INSTALMENT TO AMORTIZE I $1/a_{\overline{n}\vert} = \frac{i}{1 - V^n}$	n MONTHS
1	1.009583	1.000000	1.000000	.990507	.990507	1.009583	1
2	1.019258	2.009583	.497615	.981105	1.971613	.507198	2
3	1.029026	3.028841	.330159	.971792	2.943405	.339742	3
4	1.038887	4.057868	.246434	.962567	3.905973	.256018	4
5	1.048843	5.096756	.196203	.953430	4.859403	.205786	5
6	1.058895	6.145600	.162718	.944380	5.803784	.172301	6
7	1.069043	7.204495	.138802	.935415	6.739200	.148385	7
8	1.079288	8.273538	.120867	.926536	7.665736	.130450	8
9	1.089631	9.352826	.106919	.917741	8.583478	.116502	9
10	1.100073	10.442457	.095762	.909030	9.492508	.105346	10
11	1.110615	11.542531	.086636	.900401	10.392910	.096219	11
YEARS							
1	1.121259	12.653147	.079031	.891854	11.284764	.088615	12
2	1.257222	26.840606	.037256	.795404	21.349130	.046840	24
3	1.409672	42.748427	.023392	.709384	30.325079	.032976	36
4	1.580608	60.585220	.016505	.632667	38.330317	.026089	48
5	1.772271	80.584891	.012409	.564247	45.469824	.021992	60
6	1.987176	103.009708	.009707	.503226	51.837225	.019291	72
7	2.228140	128.153743	.007803	.448804	57.516018	.017386	84
8	2.498322	156.346727	.006396	.400268	62.580675	.015979	96
9	2.801267	187.958374	.005320	.356981	67.097611	.014903	108
10	3.140947	223.403227	.004476	.318375	71.126060	.014059	120
11	3.521816	263.146099	.003800	.283944	74.718850	.013383	132
12	3.948869	307.708166	.003249	.253237	77.923095	.012833	144
13	4.427707	357.673798	.002795	.225850	80.780815	.012379	156
14	4.964608	413.698230	.002417	.201425	83.329484	.012000	168
15	5.566613	476.516147	.002098	.179642	85.602527	.011681	180
16	6.241616	546.951321	.001828	.160214	87.629749	.011411	192
17	6.998471	625.927419	.001597	.142888	89.437737	.011180	204
18	7.847100	714.480104	.001399	.127435	91.050198	.010982	216
19	8.798635	813.770629	.001228	.113653	92.488279	.010812	228
20	9.865551	925.101055	.001080	.101362	93.770837	.010664	240
21	11.061841	1049.931334	.000952	.090400	94.914693	.010535	252
22	12.403193	1189.898450	.000840	.080624	95.934845	.010423	264
23	13.907196	1346.837883	.000742	.071905	96.844672	.010325	276
24	15.593573	1522.807687	.000656	.064128	97.656106	.010240	288
25	17.484439	1720.115470	.000581	.057193	98.379787	.010164	300
26	19.604591	1941.348663	.000515	.051008	99.025204	.010098	312
27	21.981830	2189.408445	.000456	.045492	99.600822	.010040	324
28	24.647332	2467.547787	.000405	.040572	100.114191	.009988	336
29	27.636051	2779.414122	.000359	.036184	100.572039	.009943	348
30	30.987180	3129.097156	.000319	.032271	100.980375	.009902	360
31	34.744665	3521.182519	.000283	.028781	101.344550	.009867	372
32	38.957780	3960.811894	.000252	.025668	101.669341	.009835	384
33	43.681774	4453.750427	.000224	.022892	101.959007	.009807	396
34	48.978597	5006.462360	.000199	.020417	102.217348	.009783	408
35	54.917709	5626.195765	.000177	.018209	102.447750	.009761	420
36	61.576993	6321.077626	.000158	.016239	102.653235	.009741	432
37	69.043778	7100.220401	.000140	.014483	102.836498	.009724	444
38	77.415980	7973.841498	.000125	.012917	102.999941	.009708	456
39	86.803390	8953.397310	.000111	.011520	103.145710	.009695	468
40	97.329111	10051.733390	.000099	.010274	103.275713	.009682	480
41	109.131174	11283.252980	.000088	.009163	103.391657	.009671	492
42	122.364346	12664.105790	.000078	.008172	103.495063	.009662	504
43	137.202165	14212.399890	.000070	.007288	103.587285	.009653	516
44	153.839207	15948.439100	.000062	.006500	103.669534	.009646	528
45	172.493646	17894.989250	.000055	.005797	103.742888	.009639	540
46	193.410110	20077.576770	.000049	.005170	103.808310	.009633	552
47	216.862889	22524.823370	.000044	.004611	103.866656	.009627	564
48	243.159538	25268.821450	.000039	.004112	103.918692	.009622	576
49	272.644900	28345.554910	.000035	.003667	103.965102	.009618	588
50	305.705637	31795.370980	.000031	.003271	104.006492	.009614	600

11½ % QUARTERLY COMPOUND INTEREST TABLE 11½ %

EFFECTIVE RATE = 2-7/8% BASE = 1.02875

	1 AMOUNT OF I AT COMPOUND INTEREST $S^n = (1+i)^n$	2 ACCUMULATION OF I PER PERIOD $S_{\overline{n}\rvert} = \frac{S^n - 1}{i}$	3 SINKING FUND FACTOR $1/S_{\overline{n}\rvert} = \frac{i}{S^n - 1}$	4 PRES. VALUE REVERSION OF I $V^n = \frac{1}{S^n}$	5 PRESENT VALUE ORD. ANNUITY 1 PER PERIOD $a_{\overline{n}\rvert} = \frac{1 - V^n}{i}$	6 INSTALMENT TO AMORTIZE I $1/a_{\overline{n}\rvert} = \frac{i}{1 - V^n}$	n
QUARTERS							QUARTERS
1	1.028750	1.000000	1.000000	.972053	.972053	1.028750	1
2	1.058327	2.028750	.492914	.944888	1.916941	.521664	2
3	1.088753	3.087077	.323931	.918482	2.835423	.352681	3
YEARS							
1	1.120055	4.175830	.239473	.892813	3.728236	.268223	4
2	1.254523	8.852990	.112956	.797115	7.056855	.141706	8
3	1.405135	14.091666	.070964	.711675	10.028689	.099714	12
4	1.573829	19.959273	.050102	.635393	12.681982	.078852	16
5	1.762775	26.531316	.037691	.567287	15.050878	.066441	20
6	1.974406	33.892366	.029505	.506482	17.165859	.058255	24
7	2.211443	42.137148	.023732	.452193	19.054141	.052482	28
8	2.476938	51.371758	.019466	.403724	20.740025	.048216	32
9	2.774307	61.715030	.016204	.360450	22.245205	.044954	36
10	3.107377	73.300065	.013643	.321815	23.589049	.042393	40
11	3.480433	86.275943	.011591	.287321	24.788851	.040341	44
12	3.898277	100.809641	.009920	.256524	25.860050	.038670	48
13	4.366285	117.088183	.008541	.229028	26.816430	.037291	52
14	4.890480	135.321049	.007390	.204479	27.670299	.036140	56
15	5.477607	155.742862	.006421	.182561	28.432645	.035171	60
16	6.135222	178.616419	.005599	.162993	29.113277	.034349	64
17	6.871787	204.236064	.004896	.145523	29.720954	.033646	68
18	7.696780	232.931477	.004293	.129924	30.263497	.033043	72
19	8.620818	265.071922	.003773	.115998	30.747886	.032523	76
20	9.655791	301.070992	.003321	.103565	31.180355	.032071	80
21	10.815018	341.391934	.002929	.092464	31.566469	.031679	84
22	12.113416	386.553611	.002587	.082553	31.911197	.031337	88
23	13.567694	437.137178	.002288	.073704	32.218974	.031038	92
24	15.196565	493.793561	.002025	.065804	32.493762	.030775	96
25	17.020990	557.251833	.001795	.058751	32.739096	.030545	100
26	19.064447	628.328595	.001592	.052454	32.958134	.030342	104
27	21.353231	707.938485	.001413	.046831	33.153693	.030163	108
28	23.916796	797.105950	.001255	.041812	33.328291	.030005	112
29	26.788130	896.978425	.001115	.037330	33.484175	.029865	116
30	30.004182	1008.841101	.000991	.033329	33.623350	.029741	120
31	33.606337	1134.133463	.000882	.029756	33.747607	.029632	124
32	37.640950	1274.467814	.000785	.026567	33.858546	.029535	128
33	42.159938	1431.650021	.000698	.023719	33.957593	.029448	132
34	47.221454	1607.702756	.000622	.021177	34.046024	.029372	136
35	52.890631	1804.891522	.000554	.018907	34.124976	.029304	140
36	59.240422	2025.753807	.000494	.016880	34.195466	.029244	144
37	66.352538	2273.131739	.000440	.015071	34.258400	.029190	148
38	74.318499	2550.208657	.000392	.013456	34.314588	.029142	152
39	83.240815	2860.550075	.000350	.012013	34.364753	.029100	156
40	93.234300	3208.149567	.000312	.010726	34.409542	.029062	160
41	104.427555	3597.480157	.000278	.009576	34.449530	.029028	164
42	116.964616	4033.551871	.000248	.008550	34.485232	.028998	168
43	131.006817	4521.976226	.000221	.007633	34.517106	.028971	172
44	146.734855	5069.038421	.000197	.006815	34.545565	.028947	176
45	164.351124	5681.778230	.000176	.006085	34.570973	.028926	180
46	184.082317	6368.080588	.000157	.005432	34.593657	.028907	184
47	206.182340	7136.777050	.000140	.004850	34.613910	.028890	188
48	230.935584	7997.759454	.000125	.004330	34.631993	.028875	192
49	258.660582	8962.107196	.000112	.003866	34.648137	.028862	196
50	289.714107	10042.229820	.000100	.003452	34.662550	.028850	200
51	324.495767	11252.026680	.000089	.003082	34.675419	.028839	204
52	363.453143	12607.065840	.000079	.002751	34.686908	.028829	208
53	407.087551	14124.784390	.000071	.002456	34.697166	.028821	212
54	455.960493	15824.712800	.000063	.002193	34.706324	.028813	216
55	510.700881	17728.726310	.000056	.001958	34.714501	.028806	220
56	572.013133	19861.326380	.000050	.001748	34.721801	.028800	224
57	640.686235	22249.955990	.000045	.001561	34.728319	.028795	228
58	717.603893	24925.352800	.000040	.001394	34.734138	.028790	232
59	803.755909	27921.944670	.000036	.001244	34.739334	.028786	236
60	900.250916	31278.292720	.000032	.001111	34.743972	.028782	240

11½ % SEMI-ANNUAL COMPOUND INTEREST TABLE 11½ %

EFFECTIVE RATE = 5¾% BASE = 1.0575

HALF YEARS / YEARS	1 AMOUNT OF I AT COMPOUND INTEREST $S^n = (1+i)^n$	2 ACCUMULATION OF I PER PERIOD $s_{\overline{n}\rvert} = \frac{S^n - 1}{i}$	3 SINKING FUND FACTOR $1/s_{\overline{n}\rvert} = \frac{i}{S^n - 1}$	4 PRES. VALUE REVERSION OF I $V^n = \frac{1}{S^n}$	5 PRESENT VALUE ORD. ANNUITY 1 PER PERIOD $a_{\overline{n}\rvert} = \frac{1 - V^n}{i}$	6 INSTALMENT TO AMORTIZE I $1/a_{\overline{n}\rvert} = \frac{i}{1 - V^n}$	n HALF YEARS
1	1.057500	1.000000	1.000000	.945626	.945626	1.057500	1
YEARS							
1	1.118306	2.057500	.486027	.894209	1.839836	.543527	2
2	1.250609	4.358415	.229441	.799611	3.485035	.286941	4
3	1.398564	6.931543	.144268	.715019	4.956187	.201768	6
4	1.564023	9.809088	.101946	.639377	6.271705	.159446	8
5	1.749056	13.027064	.076763	.571737	7.448054	.134263	10
6	1.955980	16.625747	.060148	.511253	8.499956	.117648	12
7	2.187385	20.650177	.048426	.457167	9.440576	.105926	14
8	2.446167	25.150722	.039760	.408803	10.281688	.097260	16
9	2.735563	30.183710	.033130	.365555	11.033819	.090630	18
10	3.059198	35.812131	.027923	.326883	11.706381	.085423	20
11	3.421120	42.106430	.023749	.292302	12.307792	.081249	22
12	3.825860	49.145384	.020348	.261379	12.845580	.077848	24
13	4.278483	57.017090	.017539	.233728	13.326474	.075039	26
14	4.784654	65.820068	.015193	.209002	13.756495	.072693	28
15	5.350708	75.664494	.013216	.186891	14.141024	.070716	30
16	5.983731	86.673576	.011538	.167120	14.484873	.069038	32
17	6.691643	98.985102	.010103	.149440	14.792346	.067603	34
18	7.483307	112.753158	.008869	.133631	15.067291	.066369	36
19	8.368629	128.150061	.007803	.119494	15.313150	.065303	38
20	9.358690	145.368514	.006879	.106853	15.532999	.064379	40
21	10.465881	164.624018	.006074	.095549	15.729590	.063574	42
22	11.704060	186.157569	.005372	.085440	15.905384	.062872	44
23	13.088724	210.238672	.004756	.076402	16.062580	.062256	46
24	14.637201	237.168721	.004216	.068319	16.203147	.061716	48
25	16.368874	267.284763	.003741	.061092	16.328842	.061241	50
26	18.305414	300.963721	.003323	.054629	16.441241	.060823	52
27	20.471059	338.627111	.002953	.048849	16.541749	.060453	54
28	22.892913	380.746314	.002626	.043682	16.631624	.060126	56
29	25.601288	427.848483	.002337	.039061	16.711991	.059837	58
30	28.630080	480.523133	.002081	.034928	16.783856	.059581	60
31	32.017198	539.429522	.001854	.031233	16.848118	.059354	62
32	35.805032	605.304906	.001652	.027929	16.905582	.059152	64
33	40.040991	678.973760	.001473	.024974	16.956967	.058973	66
34	44.778091	761.358100	.001313	.022332	17.002916	.058813	68
35	50.075619	853.489021	.001172	.019970	17.044004	.058672	70
36	55.999877	956.519607	.001045	.017857	17.080745	.058545	72
37	62.625013	1071.739355	.000933	.015968	17.113599	.058433	74
38	70.033943	1200.590319	.000833	.014279	17.142978	.058333	76
39	78.319397	1344.685157	.000744	.012768	17.169248	.058244	78
40	87.585071	1505.827315	.000664	.011417	17.192740	.058164	80
41	97.946932	1686.033598	.000593	.010210	17.213746	.058093	82
42	109.534666	1887.559410	.000530	.009130	17.232530	.058030	84
43	122.493302	2112.926986	.000473	.008164	17.249327	.057973	86
44	136.985025	2364.956955	.000423	.007300	17.264347	.057923	88
45	153.191210	2646.803643	.000378	.006528	17.277778	.057878	90
46	171.314687	2961.994557	.000338	.005837	17.289788	.057838	92
47	191.582285	3314.474525	.000302	.005220	17.300527	.057802	94
48	214.247667	3708.655077	.000270	.004667	17.310131	.057770	96
49	239.594505	4149.469652	.000241	.004174	17.318718	.057741	98
50	267.940032	4642.435346	.000215	.003732	17.326397	.057715	100
51	299.639013	5193.721963	.000193	.003337	17.333263	.057693	102
52	335.088181	5810.229233	.000172	.002984	17.339404	.057672	104
53	374.731207	6499.673165	.000154	.002669	17.344894	.057654	106
54	419.064251	7270.682624	.000138	.002386	17.349804	.057638	108
55	468.642171	8132.907320	.000123	.002134	17.354194	.057623	110
56	524.085469	9097.138586	.000110	.001908	17.358120	.057610	112
57	586.088055	10175.444440	.000098	.001706	17.361631	.057598	114
58	655.425935	11381.320610	.000088	.001526	17.364770	.057588	116
59	732.966920	12729.859470	.000079	.001364	17.367577	.057579	118
60	819.681488	14237.938910	.000070	.001220	17.370087	.057570	120

11½ % ANNUAL COMPOUND INTEREST TABLE 11½ %

EFFECTIVE RATE = 11½% BASE = 1.1150

YEARS	1 AMOUNT OF I AT COMPOUND INTEREST $S^n = (1+i)^n$	2 ACCUMULATION OF I PER PERIOD $S_{\overline{n}|} = \frac{S^n - 1}{i}$	3 SINKING FUND FACTOR $1/S_{\overline{n}|} = \frac{i}{S^n - 1}$	4 PRES. VALUE REVERSION OF I $V^n = \frac{1}{S^n}$	5 PRESENT VALUE ORD. ANNUITY 1 PER PERIOD $a_{\overline{n}|} = \frac{1 - V^n}{i}$	6 INSTALMENT TO AMORTIZE I $1/a_{\overline{n}|} = \frac{i}{1 - V^n}$	n YEARS
1	1.115000	1.000000	1.000000	.896861	.896861	1.115000	1
2	1.243225	2.115000	.472813	.804360	1.701221	.587813	2
3	1.386196	3.358225	.297776	.721399	2.422619	.412776	3
4	1.545608	4.744421	.210774	.646994	3.069614	.325774	4
5	1.723353	6.290029	.158982	.580264	3.649878	.273982	5
6	1.921539	8.013383	.124791	.520416	4.170294	.239791	6
7	2.142516	9.934922	.100655	.466741	4.637035	.215655	7
8	2.388905	12.077438	.082799	.418602	5.055637	.197799	8
9	2.663629	14.466343	.069126	.375428	5.431064	.184126	9
10	2.969947	17.129972	.058377	.336706	5.767771	.173377	10
11	3.311491	20.099919	.049751	.301979	6.069750	.164751	11
12	3.692312	23.411410	.042714	.270833	6.340583	.157714	12
13	4.116928	27.103722	.036895	.242900	6.583482	.151895	13
14	4.590375	31.220650	.032030	.217847	6.801329	.147030	14
15	5.118268	35.811025	.027924	.195379	6.996708	.142924	15
16	5.706869	40.929293	.024432	.175227	7.171935	.139432	16
17	6.363159	46.636161	.021443	.157155	7.329090	.136443	17
18	7.094922	52.999320	.018868	.140946	7.470036	.133868	18
19	7.910838	60.094242	.016641	.126409	7.596445	.131641	19
20	8.820584	68.005080	.014705	.113371	7.709816	.129705	20
21	9.834951	76.825664	.013016	.101678	7.811494	.128016	21
22	10.965971	86.660615	.011539	.091191	7.902685	.126539	22
23	12.227057	97.626586	.010243	.081786	7.984471	.125243	23
24	13.633169	109.853643	.009103	.073351	8.057822	.124103	24
25	15.200983	123.486812	.008098	.065785	8.123607	.123098	25
26	16.949097	138.687796	.007210	.059000	8.182607	.122210	26
27	18.898243	155.636892	.006425	.052915	8.235522	.121425	27
28	21.071541	174.535135	.005730	.047457	8.282979	.120730	28
29	23.494768	195.606675	.005112	.042563	8.325542	.120112	29
30	26.196666	219.101443	.004564	.038173	8.363715	.119564	30
31	29.209283	245.298109	.004077	.034236	8.397951	.119077	31
32	32.568350	274.507391	.003643	.030705	8.428655	.118643	32
33	36.313710	307.075741	.003257	.027538	8.456193	.118257	33
34	40.489787	343.389452	.002912	.024698	8.480891	.117912	34
35	45.146112	383.879239	.002605	.022150	8.503041	.117605	35
36	50.337915	429.025351	.002331	.019866	8.522907	.117331	36
37	56.126776	479.363266	.002086	.017817	8.540723	.117086	37
38	62.581355	535.490042	.001867	.015979	8.556703	.116867	38
39	69.778211	598.071397	.001672	.014331	8.571034	.116672	39
40	77.802705	667.849608	.001497	.012853	8.583887	.116497	40
41	86.750016	745.652312	.001341	.011527	8.595414	.116341	41
42	96.726268	832.402328	.001201	.010338	8.605753	.116201	42
43	107.849789	929.128597	.001076	.009272	8.615025	.116076	43
44	120.252514	1036.978385	.000964	.008316	8.623341	.115964	44
45	134.081553	1157.230899	.000864	.007458	8.630799	.115864	45
46	149.500932	1291.312452	.000774	.006689	8.637488	.115774	46
47	166.693539	1440.813384	.000694	.005999	8.643487	.115694	47
48	185.863296	1607.506923	.000622	.005380	8.648867	.115622	48
49	207.237575	1793.370220	.000558	.004825	8.653692	.115558	49
50	231.069897	2000.607796	.000500	.004328	8.658020	.115500	50
51	257.642935	2231.677692	.000448	.003881	8.661901	.115448	51
52	287.271872	2489.320627	.000402	.003481	8.665382	.115402	52
53	320.308137	2776.592499	.000360	.003122	8.668504	.115360	53
54	357.143573	3096.900637	.000323	.002800	8.671304	.115323	54
55	398.215084	3454.044210	.000290	.002511	8.673816	.115290	55
56	444.009819	3852.259294	.000260	.002252	8.676068	.115260	56
57	495.070948	4296.269113	.000233	.002020	8.678088	.115233	57
58	552.004107	4791.340061	.000209	.001812	8.679899	.115209	58
59	615.484579	5343.344168	.000187	.001625	8.681524	.115187	59
60	686.265306	5958.828747	.000168	.001457	8.682981	.115168	60

11 3/4% MONTHLY COMPOUND INTEREST TABLE 11 3/4%

EFFECTIVE RATE = 47/48% BASE = 1.00979167

MONTHS	1 AMOUNT OF I AT COMPOUND INTEREST $s^n = (1+i)^n$	2 ACCUMULATION OF I PER PERIOD $s_{\overline{n}\|} = \frac{s^n - 1}{i}$	3 SINKING FUND FACTOR $1/s_{\overline{n}\|} = \frac{i}{s^n - 1}$	4 PRES. VALUE REVERSION OF I $v^n = \frac{1}{s^n}$	5 PRESENT VALUE ORD. ANNUITY 1 PER PERIOD $a_{\overline{n}\|} = \frac{1 - v^n}{i}$	6 INSTALMENT TO AMORTIZE I $1/a_{\overline{n}\|} = \frac{i}{1 - v^n}$	n MONTHS
1	1.009791	1.000000	1.000000	.990303	.990303	1.009791	1
2	1.019679	2.009791	.497564	.980700	1.971003	.507355	2
3	1.029663	3.029470	.330090	.971191	2.942194	.339882	3
4	1.039745	4.059134	.246357	.961773	3.903968	.256149	4
5	1.049926	5.098880	.196121	.952447	4.856416	.205913	5
6	1.060207	6.148806	.162633	.943211	5.799628	.172424	6
7	1.070588	7.209013	.138715	.934065	6.733694	.148506	7
8	1.081071	8.279601	.120778	.925008	7.658702	.130570	8
9	1.091656	9.360673	.106829	.916038	8.574741	.116621	9
10	1.102345	10.452329	.095672	.907156	9.481897	.105464	10
11	1.113139	11.554675	.086545	.898359	10.380257	.096336	11
YEARS							
1	1.124039	12.667814	.078940	.889648	11.269906	.088731	12
2	1.263463	26.906933	.037165	.791475	21.296166	.046956	24
3	1.420182	42.912257	.023303	.704134	30.216015	.033095	36
4	1.596340	60.902867	.016419	.626432	38.151549	.026211	48
5	1.794349	81.125014	.012326	.557305	45.211388	.022118	60
6	2.016918	103.855496	.009628	.495805	51.492165	.019420	72
7	2.267094	129.405446	.007727	.441093	57.079851	.017519	84
8	2.548303	158.124585	.006324	.392417	62.050930	.016115	96
9	2.864392	190.406019	.005251	.349114	66.473443	.015043	108
10	3.219688	226.691611	.004411	.310589	70.407928	.014202	120
11	3.619055	267.478031	.003738	.276315	73.908237	.013530	132
12	4.067959	313.323560	.003191	.245823	77.022283	.012983	144
13	4.572545	364.855722	.002740	.218696	79.792691	.012532	156
14	5.139719	422.779885	.002365	.194563	82.257381	.012156	168
15	5.777245	487.888903	.002049	.173092	84.450090	.011841	180
16	6.493849	561.073980	.001782	.153991	86.400829	.011573	192
17	7.299340	643.336863	.001554	.136998	88.136304	.011346	204
18	8.204743	735.803553	.001359	.121880	89.680266	.011150	216
19	9.222451	839.739721	.001190	.108431	91.053850	.010982	228
20	10.366395	956.568030	.001045	.096465	92.275858	.010837	240
21	11.652232	1087.887608	.000919	.085820	93.363016	.010710	252
22	13.097564	1235.495938	.000809	.076350	94.330204	.010601	264
23	14.722173	1401.413461	.000713	.067924	95.190663	.010505	276
24	16.548297	1587.911230	.000629	.060429	95.956169	.010421	288
25	18.600932	1797.542001	.000556	.053760	96.637200	.010347	300
26	20.908173	2033.175167	.000491	.047828	97.243078	.010283	312
27	23.501602	2298.036042	.000435	.042550	97.782097	.010226	324
28	26.416718	2595.750000	.000385	.037854	98.261635	.010176	336
29	29.693422	2930.392104	.000341	.033677	98.688255	.010132	348
30	33.376565	3306.542889	.000302	.029961	99.067797	.010094	360
31	37.516562	3729.351051	.000268	.026654	99.405456	.010059	372
32	42.170080	4204.603923	.000237	.023713	99.705855	.010029	384
33	47.400815	4738.806697	.000211	.021096	99.973104	.010002	396
34	53.280366	5339.271454	.000187	.018768	100.210861	.009978	408
35	59.889211	6014.217279	.000166	.016697	100.422382	.009957	420
36	67.317810	6772.882724	.000147	.014854	100.610562	.009939	432
37	75.667845	7625.652288	.000131	.013215	100.777975	.009922	444
38	85.053611	8584.198556	.000116	.011757	100.926914	.009908	456
39	95.603577	9661.641955	.000103	.010459	101.059418	.009895	468
40	107.462152	10872.730390	.000091	.009305	101.177300	.009883	480
41	120.791652	12234.041050	.000081	.008278	101.282173	.009873	492
42	135.774530	13764.207350	.000072	.007365	101.375473	.009864	504
43	152.615870	15484.173990	.000064	.006552	101.458477	.009856	516
44	171.546193	17417.483580	.000057	.005829	101.532322	.009849	528
45	192.824616	19590.599030	.000051	.005186	101.598019	.009842	540
46	216.742392	22033.265590	.000045	.004613	101.656465	.009837	552
47	243.626907	24778.918120	.000040	.004104	101.708462	.009832	564
48	273.846150	27865.138700	.000035	.003651	101.754721	.009827	576
49	307.813759	31334.171040	.000031	.003248	101.795875	.009823	588
50	345.994676	35233.498790	.000028	.002890	101.832487	.009820	600

11¾% QUARTERLY COMPOUND INTEREST TABLE 11¾%

EFFECTIVE RATE = 2-15/16% BASE = 1.029375

QUARTERS	1 AMOUNT OF I AT COMPOUND INTEREST $S^n = (1+i)^n$	2 ACCUMULATION OF I PER PERIOD $S_{\overline{n}\rvert} = \frac{S^n - 1}{i}$	3 SINKING FUND FACTOR $1/S_{\overline{n}\rvert} = \frac{i}{S^n - 1}$	4 PRES. VALUE REVERSION OF I $V^n = \frac{1}{S^n}$	5 PRESENT VALUE ORD. ANNUITY 1 PER PERIOD $a_{\overline{n}\rvert} = \frac{1 - V^n}{i}$	6 INSTALMENT TO AMORTIZE I $1/a_{\overline{n}\rvert} = \frac{i}{1 - V^n}$	n QUARTERS
1	1.029375	1.000000	1.000000	.971463	.971463	1.029375	1
2	1.059613	2.029375	.492763	.943741	1.915204	.522138	2
3	1.090739	3.088988	.323731	.916810	2.832014	.353106	3
YEARS							
1	1.122779	4.179727	.239250	.890647	3.722661	.268625	4
2	1.260634	8.872639	.112706	.793252	7.038237	.142081	8
3	1.415414	14.141743	.070713	.706507	9.991244	.100088	12
4	1.589197	20.057786	.049856	.629248	12.621330	.079231	16
5	1.784318	26.700198	.037453	.560438	14.963809	.066828	20
6	2.003396	34.158161	.029276	.499152	17.050130	.058651	24
7	2.249372	42.531809	.023512	.444569	18.908305	.052887	28
8	2.525549	51.933569	.019255	.395954	20.563282	.048630	32
9	2.835634	62.489673	.016003	.352655	22.037283	.045378	36
10	3.183792	74.341849	.013451	.314091	23.350097	.042826	40
11	3.574696	87.649229	.011409	.279744	24.519351	.040784	44
12	4.013595	102.590483	.009747	.249153	25.560743	.039122	48
13	4.506383	119.366215	.008378	.221907	26.488256	.037753	52
14	5.059674	138.201664	.007236	.197641	27.314342	.036611	56
15	5.680898	159.349719	.006276	.176029	28.050093	.035651	60
16	6.378396	183.094321	.005462	.156779	28.705388	.034837	64
17	7.161532	209.754273	.004767	.139635	29.289024	.034142	68
18	8.040821	239.687521	.004172	.124365	29.808837	.033547	72
19	9.028069	273.295956	.003659	.110766	30.271807	.033034	76
20	10.136530	311.030818	.003215	.098653	30.684150	.032590	80
21	11.381088	353.398746	.002830	.087865	31.051402	.032205	84
22	12.778452	400.968587	.002494	.078257	31.378494	.031869	88
23	14.347384	454.379027	.002201	.069699	31.669817	.031576	92
24	16.108948	514.347174	.001944	.062077	31.929283	.031319	96
25	18.086796	581.678178	.001719	.055289	32.160376	.031094	100
26	20.307484	657.276048	.001521	.049243	32.366198	.030896	104
27	22.800826	742.155785	.001347	.043858	32.549513	.030722	108
28	25.600300	837.457012	.001194	.039062	32.712782	.030569	112
29	28.743491	944.459274	.001059	.034790	32.858196	.030434	116
30	32.272602	1064.599217	.000939	.030986	32.987709	.030314	120
31	36.235015	1199.489880	.000834	.027598	33.103060	.030209	124
32	40.683931	1350.942348	.000740	.024580	33.205796	.030115	128
33	45.679083	1520.990071	.000657	.021892	33.297298	.030032	132
34	51.287537	1711.916165	.000584	.019498	33.378794	.029959	136
35	57.584594	1926.284065	.000519	.017366	33.451379	.029894	140
36	64.654801	2166.971944	.000461	.015467	33.516025	.029836	144
37	72.593084	2437.211355	.000410	.013775	33.573603	.029785	148
38	81.506024	2740.630620	.000365	.012269	33.624884	.029740	152
39	91.513292	3081.303544	.000325	.010927	33.670557	.029700	156
40	102.749246	3463.804112	.000289	.009732	33.711236	.029664	160
41	115.364745	3893.267901	.000257	.008668	33.747467	.029632	164
42	129.529168	4375.461028	.000229	.007720	33.779736	.029604	168
43	145.432691	4916.857576	.000203	.006876	33.808475	.029578	172
44	163.288841	5524.726509	.000181	.006124	33.834073	.029556	176
45	183.337360	6207.229273	.000161	.005454	33.856871	.029536	180
46	205.847425	6973.529369	.000143	.004858	33.877176	.029518	184
47	231.121265	7833.915391	.000128	.004327	33.895260	.029503	188
48	259.498213	8799.939159	.000114	.003854	33.911367	.029489	192
49	291.359268	9884.570822	.000101	.003432	33.925713	.029476	196
50	327.132207	11102.372990	.000090	.003057	33.938490	.029465	200
51	367.297328	12469.696280	.000080	.002723	33.949869	.029455	204
52	412.393903	14004.898810	.000071	.002425	33.960005	.029446	208
53	463.027411	15728.592700	.000064	.002160	33.969032	.029439	212
54	519.877674	17663.920830	.000057	.001924	33.977071	.029432	216
55	583.707984	19836.867540	.000050	.001713	33.984232	.029425	220
56	655.375346	22276.607510	.000045	.001526	33.990610	.029420	224
57	735.841988	25015.897470	.000040	.001359	33.996290	.029415	228
58	826.188284	28091.516030	.000036	.001210	34.001349	.029411	232
59	927.627250	31544.757440	.000032	.001078	34.005855	.029407	236
60	1041.520839	35421.986010	.000028	.000960	34.009868	.029403	240

11¾% SEMI-ANNUAL COMPOUND INTEREST TABLE 11¾%

EFFECTIVE RATE = 5-7/8% BASE = 1.05875

HALF YEARS	1 AMOUNT OF I AT COMPOUND INTEREST $S^n = (1+i)^n$	2 ACCUMULATION OF I PER PERIOD $S_{\overline{n}\vert} = \frac{S^n - 1}{i}$	3 SINKING FUND FACTOR $1/S_{\overline{n}\vert} = \frac{i}{S^n - 1}$	4 PRES. VALUE REVERSION OF I $V^n = \frac{1}{S^n}$	5 PRESENT VALUE ORD. ANNUITY 1 PER PERIOD $a_{\overline{n}\vert} = \frac{1 - V^n}{i}$	6 INSTALMENT TO AMORTIZE I $1/a_{\overline{n}\vert} = \frac{i}{1 - V^n}$	n HALF YEARS
1	1.058750	1.000000	1.000000	.944510	.944510	1.058750	1
YEARS							
1	1.120952	2.058750	.485732	.892099	1.836609	.544482	2
2	1.256532	4.366509	.229016	.795841	3.475047	.287766	4
3	1.408512	6.953395	.143815	.709969	4.936696	.202565	6
4	1.578874	9.853169	.101490	.633363	6.240632	.160240	8
5	1.769841	13.103675	.076314	.565023	7.403872	.135064	10
6	1.983906	16.747335	.059711	.504056	8.441597	.118461	12
7	2.223862	20.831702	.048004	.449668	9.367352	.106754	14
8	2.492842	25.410079	.039354	.401149	10.193216	.098104	16
9	2.794355	30.542217	.032742	.357864	10.929969	.091492	18
10	3.132337	36.295096	.027552	.319250	11.587226	.086302	20
11	3.511198	42.743795	.023395	.284803	12.173565	.082145	22
12	3.935883	49.972474	.020011	.254073	12.696637	.078761	24
13	4.411934	58.075472	.017219	.226658	13.163269	.075969	26
14	4.945564	67.158542	.014890	.202201	13.579551	.073640	28
15	5.543738	77.340222	.012930	.180384	13.950916	.071680	30
16	6.214262	88.753393	.011267	.160920	14.282210	.070017	32
17	6.965887	101.547004	.009848	.143557	14.577758	.068598	34
18	7.808421	115.888023	.008629	.128067	14.841415	.067379	36
19	8.752862	131.963611	.007578	.114248	15.076624	.066328	38
20	9.811534	149.983566	.006667	.101921	15.286454	.065417	40
21	10.998255	170.183062	.005876	.090924	15.473642	.064626	42
22	12.328511	192.825720	.005186	.081113	15.640633	.063936	44
23	13.819664	218.207042	.004583	.072361	15.789606	.063333	46
24	15.491174	246.658274	.004054	.064553	15.922504	.062804	48
25	17.364855	278.550728	.003590	.057588	16.041062	.062340	50
26	19.465162	314.300624	.003182	.051374	16.146828	.061932	52
27	21.819503	354.374525	.002822	.045831	16.241182	.061572	54
28	24.458606	399.295428	.002504	.040885	16.325355	.061254	56
29	27.416913	449.649584	.002224	.036474	16.400445	.060974	58
30	30.733032	506.094154	.001976	.032538	16.467434	.060726	60
31	34.450240	569.365783	.001756	.029027	16.527194	.060506	62
32	38.617050	640.290213	.001562	.025895	16.580506	.060312	64
33	43.287843	719.793065	.001389	.023101	16.628065	.060139	66
34	48.523575	808.911911	.001236	.020609	16.670493	.059986	68
35	54.392577	908.809821	.001100	.018385	16.708343	.059850	70
36	60.971444	1020.790539	.000980	.016401	16.742109	.059730	72
37	68.346036	1146.315499	.000872	.014631	16.772231	.059622	74
38	76.612595	1287.022900	.000777	.013053	16.799103	.059527	76
39	85.879009	1444.749081	.000692	.011644	16.823076	.059442	78
40	96.266209	1621.552490	.000617	.010388	16.844462	.059367	80
41	107.909757	1819.740548	.000550	.009267	16.863540	.059300	82
42	120.961611	2041.899760	.000490	.008267	16.880560	.059240	84
43	135.592107	2290.929476	.000437	.007375	16.895744	.059187	86
44	151.992184	2570.079726	.000389	.006579	16.909289	.059139	88
45	170.375876	2882.993634	.000347	.005869	16.921372	.059097	90
46	190.983104	3233.754969	.000309	.005236	16.932152	.059059	92
47	214.082809	3626.941435	.000276	.004671	16.941769	.059026	94
48	239.976460	4067.684419	.000246	.004167	16.950348	.058996	96
49	269.001987	4561.735956	.000219	.003717	16.958001	.058969	98
50	301.538198	5115.543797	.000195	.003316	16.964828	.058945	100
51	338.009714	5736.335563	.000174	.002958	16.970919	.058924	102
52	378.892517	6432.213062	.000155	.002639	16.976353	.058905	104
53	424.720159	7212.258032	.000139	.002354	16.981200	.058889	106
54	476.090726	8086.650660	.000124	.002100	16.985524	.058874	108
55	533.674644	9066.802444	.000110	.001874	16.989382	.058860	110
56	598.223426	10165.505120	.000098	.001672	16.992824	.058848	112
57	670.579484	11397.097590	.000088	.001491	16.995894	.058838	114
58	751.687120	12777.653110	.000078	.001330	16.998633	.058828	116
59	842.604852	14325.188970	.000070	.001187	17.001076	.058820	118
60	944.519225	16059.901710	.000062	.001059	17.003255	.058812	120

11¾% ANNUAL COMPOUND INTEREST TABLE 11¾%

EFFECTIVE RATE = 11¾% BASE = 1.1175

YEARS	1 AMOUNT OF I AT COMPOUND INTEREST $S^n = (1+i)^n$	2 ACCUMULATION OF I PER PERIOD $S_{\overline{n}\rvert} = \frac{S^n - 1}{i}$	3 SINKING FUND FACTOR $1/S_{\overline{n}\rvert} = \frac{i}{S^n - 1}$	4 PRES. VALUE REVERSION OF I $V^n = \frac{1}{S^n}$	5 PRESENT VALUE ORD. ANNUITY 1 PER PERIOD $a_{\overline{n}\rvert} = \frac{1 - V^n}{i}$	6 INSTALMENT TO AMORTIZE I $1/a_{\overline{n}\rvert} = \frac{i}{1 - V^n}$	n YEARS
1	1.117500	1.000000	1.000000	.894855	.894855	1.117500	1
2	1.248806	2.117500	.472255	.800765	1.695619	.589755	2
3	1.395541	3.366306	.297062	.716568	2.412187	.414562	3
4	1.559517	4.761847	.210003	.641224	3.053411	.327503	4
5	1.742760	6.321364	.158194	.573802	3.627214	.275694	5
6	1.947535	8.064125	.124006	.513470	4.140684	.241506	6
7	2.176370	10.011659	.099884	.459481	4.600164	.217384	7
8	2.432093	12.188029	.082048	.411168	5.011333	.199548	8
9	2.717864	14.620123	.068399	.367936	5.379269	.185899	9
10	3.037213	17.337987	.057677	.329249	5.708518	.175177	10
11	3.394086	20.375200	.049079	.294630	6.003148	.166579	11
12	3.792891	23.769287	.042071	.263651	6.266799	.159571	12
13	4.238556	27.562178	.036282	.235929	6.502728	.153782	13
14	4.736586	31.800734	.031446	.211123	6.713851	.148946	14
15	5.293135	36.537320	.027369	.188924	6.902775	.144869	15
16	5.915078	41.830455	.023906	.169059	7.071834	.141406	16
17	6.610100	47.745533	.020944	.151284	7.223118	.138444	17
18	7.386787	54.355633	.018397	.135377	7.358495	.135897	18
19	8.254734	61.742420	.016196	.121143	7.479637	.133696	19
20	9.224666	69.997155	.014286	.108405	7.588042	.131786	20
21	10.308564	79.221821	.012623	.097007	7.685049	.130123	21
22	11.519820	89.530384	.011169	.086807	7.771856	.128669	22
23	12.873399	101.050205	.009896	.077680	7.849536	.127396	23
24	14.386023	113.923604	.008778	.069512	7.919048	.126278	24
25	16.076381	128.309627	.007794	.062203	7.981251	.125294	25
26	17.965356	144.386008	.006926	.055663	8.036913	.124426	26
27	20.076285	162.351364	.006159	.049810	8.086723	.123659	27
28	22.435249	182.427650	.005482	.044573	8.131296	.122982	28
29	25.071391	204.862898	.004881	.039886	8.171182	.122381	29
30	28.517279	229.934289	.004349	.035692	8.206874	.121849	30
31	31.309309	257.951568	.003877	.031939	8.238814	.121377	31
32	34.988153	289.260877	.003457	.028581	8.267395	.120957	32
33	39.099261	324.249030	.003084	.025576	8.292971	.120584	33
34	43.693424	363.348291	.002752	.022887	8.315858	.120252	34
35	48.827402	407.041715	.002457	.020480	8.336338	.119957	35
36	54.564621	455.869117	.002194	.018327	8.354665	.119694	36
37	60.975964	510.433738	.001959	.016400	8.371065	.119459	37
38	68.140640	571.409703	.001750	.014676	8.385740	.119250	38
39	76.147165	639.550343	.001564	.013132	8.398873	.119064	39
40	85.094457	715.697508	.001397	.011752	8.410624	.118897	40
41	95.093056	800.791965	.001249	.010516	8.421140	.118749	41
42	106.266490	895.885020	.001116	.009410	8.430551	.118616	42
43	118.752803	1002.151511	.000998	.008421	8.438971	.118498	43
44	132.706257	1120.904313	.000892	.007535	8.446507	.118392	44
45	148.299242	1253.610570	.000798	.006743	8.453250	.118298	45
46	165.724403	1401.909812	.000713	.006034	8.459284	.118213	46
47	185.197020	1567.634214	.000638	.005400	8.464684	.118138	47
48	206.957670	1752.831235	.000571	.004832	8.469516	.118071	48
49	231.275196	1959.788905	.000510	.004324	8.473840	.118010	49
50	258.450032	2191.064101	.000456	.003869	8.477709	.117956	50
51	288.817911	2449.514134	.000408	.003462	8.481171	.117908	51
52	322.754015	2738.332044	.000365	.003098	8.484269	.117865	52
53	360.677612	3061.086060	.000327	.002773	8.487042	.117827	53
54	403.057231	3421.763672	.000292	.002481	8.489523	.117792	54
55	450.416456	3824.820903	.000261	.002220	8.491743	.117761	55
56	503.340390	4275.237359	.000234	.001987	8.493730	.117734	56
57	562.482886	4778.577749	.000209	.001778	8.495508	.117709	57
58	628.574625	5341.060634	.000187	.001591	8.497099	.117687	58
59	702.432143	5969.635259	.000168	.001424	8.498522	.117668	59
60	784.967920	6672.067402	.000150	.001274	8.499796	.117650	60

12% MONTHLY COMPOUND INTEREST TABLE 12%

EFFECTIVE RATE = 1% BASE = 1.0100

MONTHS	1 AMOUNT OF I AT COMPOUND INTEREST $S^n = (1+i)^n$	2 ACCUMULATION OF I PER PERIOD $S_{\overline{n}|} = \frac{S^n - 1}{i}$	3 SINKING FUND FACTOR $1/S_{\overline{n}|} = \frac{i}{S^n - 1}$	4 PRES. VALUE REVERSION OF I $V^n = \frac{1}{S^n}$	5 PRESENT VALUE ORD. ANNUITY 1 PER PERIOD $a_{\overline{n}|} = \frac{1 - V^n}{i}$	6 INSTALMENT TO AMORTIZE I $1/a_{\overline{n}|} = \frac{i}{1 - V^n}$	n MONTHS
1	1.010000	1.000000	1.000000	.990099	.990099	1.010000	1
2	1.020099	2.009999	.497512	.980296	1.970395	.507512	2
3	1.030300	3.030099	.330022	.970590	2.940985	.340022	3
4	1.040604	4.060400	.246281	.960980	3.901965	.256281	4
5	1.051010	5.101005	.196039	.951465	4.853431	.206039	5
6	1.061520	6.152015	.162548	.942045	5.795476	.172548	6
7	1.072135	7.213535	.138628	.932718	6.728194	.148628	7
8	1.082856	8.285670	.120690	.923483	7.651677	.130690	8
9	1.093685	9.368527	.106740	.914339	8.566017	.116740	9
10	1.104622	10.462212	.095582	.905286	9.471304	.105582	10
11	1.115668	11.566834	.086454	.896323	10.367628	.096454	11
YEARS							
1	1.126825	12.682503	.078848	.887449	11.255077	.088848	12
2	1.269734	26.973464	.037073	.787566	21.243387	.047073	24
3	1.430768	43.076878	.023214	.698924	30.107505	.033214	36
4	1.612226	61.222607	.016333	.620260	37.973959	.026333	48
5	1.816696	81.669669	.012244	.550449	44.955038	.022244	60
6	2.047099	104.709931	.009550	.488496	51.150391	.019550	72
7	2.306722	130.672274	.007652	.433515	56.648452	.017652	84
8	2.599272	159.927292	.006252	.384722	61.527703	.016252	96
9	2.928925	192.892579	.005184	.341422	65.857789	.015184	108
10	3.300386	230.038689	.004347	.302994	69.700522	.014347	120
11	3.718958	271.895856	.003677	.268892	73.110751	.013677	132
12	4.190615	319.061559	.003134	.238628	76.137157	.013134	144
13	4.722090	372.209054	.002686	.211770	78.822938	.012686	156
14	5.320969	432.096981	.002314	.187935	81.206433	.012314	168
15	5.995801	499.580197	.002001	.166783	83.321664	.012001	180
16	6.756219	575.621973	.001737	.148011	85.198823	.011787	192
17	7.613077	661.307750	.001512	.131352	86.864707	.011512	204
18	8.578606	757.860629	.001319	.116569	88.343095	.011319	216
19	9.666588	866.658829	.001153	.103449	89.655088	.011153	228
20	10.892553	989.255364	.001010	.091805	90.819416	.011010	240
21	12.274002	1127.400209	.000886	.081473	91.852697	.010886	252
22	13.830652	1283.065277	.000779	.072303	92.769683	.010779	264
23	15.584725	1458.472573	.000685	.064165	93.583461	.010685	276
24	17.561259	1656.125904	.000603	.056943	94.305647	.010603	288
25	19.788466	1878.846624	.000532	.050534	94.946551	.010532	300
26	22.298139	2129.813907	.000469	.044846	95.515320	.010469	312
27	25.126101	2412.610122	.000414	.039799	96.020074	.010414	324
28	28.312719	2731.271978	.000366	.035319	96.468018	.010366	336
29	31.903481	3090.348132	.000323	.031344	96.865546	.010323	348
30	35.949641	3494.964129	.000286	.027816	97.218330	.010286	360
31	40.508955	3950.895562	.000253	.024685	97.531409	.010253	372
32	45.646505	4464.650512	.000223	.021907	97.809251	.010223	384
33	51.435624	5043.562455	.000198	.019441	98.055821	.010198	396
34	57.958949	5695.894917	.000175	.017253	98.274641	.010175	408
35	65.309594	6430.959463	.000155	.015311	98.468831	.010155	420
36	73.592485	7259.248592	.000137	.013588	98.641165	.010137	432
37	82.925855	8192.585514	.000122	.012058	98.794103	.010122	444
38	93.442929	9244.292929	.000108	.010701	98.929827	.010108	456
39	105.293831	10429.383160	.000095	.009497	99.050277	.010095	468
40	118.647724	11764.772490	.000084	.008428	99.157169	.010084	480
41	133.695226	13269.522620	.000075	.007479	99.252029	.010075	492
42	150.651127	14965.112740	.000066	.006637	99.336214	.010066	504
43	169.757461	16875.746110	.000059	.005890	99.410924	.010059	516
44	191.286956	19028.695620	.000052	.005227	99.477225	.010052	528
45	215.546930	21454.693010	.000046	.004639	99.536064	.010046	540
46	242.883675	24188.367600	.000041	.004117	99.588280	.010041	552
47	273.687405	27268.740570	.000036	.003653	99.634619	.010036	564
48	308.397819	30739.781910	.000032	.003242	99.675743	.010032	576
49	347.510381	34651.038170	.000028	.002877	99.712238	.010028	588
50	391.583396	39058.339630	.000025	.002553	99.744626	.010025	600

12% QUARTERLY COMPOUND INTEREST TABLE 12%

EFFECTIVE RATE = 3% BASE = 1.0300

QUARTERS	1 AMOUNT OF I AT COMPOUND INTEREST $S^n = (1+i)^n$	2 ACCUMULATION OF I PER PERIOD $S_{\overline{n}\rceil} = \frac{S^n - 1}{i}$	3 SINKING FUND FACTOR $1/S_{\overline{n}\rceil} = \frac{i}{S^n - 1}$	4 PRES. VALUE REVERSION OF I $V^n = \frac{1}{S^n}$	5 PRESENT VALUE ORD. ANNUITY 1 PER PERIOD $a_{\overline{n}\rceil} = \frac{1 - V^n}{i}$	6 INSTALMENT TO AMORTIZE I $1/a_{\overline{n}\rceil} = \frac{i}{1 - V^n}$	n QUARTERS
1	1.030000	1.000000	1.000000	.970874	.970874	1.030000	1
2	1.060900	2.030000	.492611	.942596	1.913470	.522611	2
3	1.092727	3.090900	.323530	.915142	2.828611	.353530	3
YEARS							
1	1.125509	4.183627	.239027	.888487	3.717098	.269027	4
2	1.266770	8.892336	.112456	.789409	7.019692	.142456	8
3	1.425761	14.192030	.070462	.701380	9.954004	.100462	12
4	1.604706	20.156881	.049611	.623167	12.561102	.079611	16
5	1.806111	26.870374	.037216	.553676	14.877475	.067216	20
6	2.032794	34.426470	.029047	.491934	16.935542	.059047	24
7	2.287928	42.930923	.023293	.437077	18.764108	.053293	28
8	2.575083	52.502759	.019047	.388337	20.388766	.049047	32
9	2.898278	63.275944	.015804	.345032	21.832252	.045804	36
10	3.262038	75.401260	.013262	.306557	23.114772	.043262	40
11	3.671452	89.048409	.011230	.272372	24.254274	.041230	44
12	4.132252	104.408396	.009578	.241999	25.266707	.039578	48
13	4.650886	121.696197	.008217	.215013	26.166240	.038217	52
14	5.234613	141.153768	.007084	.191036	26.965464	.037084	56
15	5.891603	163.053437	.006133	.169733	27.675564	.036133	60
16	6.631051	187.701707	.005328	.150806	28.306478	.035328	64
17	7.463307	215.443551	.004642	.133989	28.867038	.034642	68
18	8.400017	246.667242	.004054	.119047	29.365088	.034054	72
19	9.454293	281.809781	.003548	.105772	29.807598	.033548	76
20	10.640891	321.363019	.003112	.093977	30.200763	.033112	80
21	11.976416	365.880536	.002733	.083497	30.550086	.032733	84
22	13.479562	415.985393	.002404	.074186	30.860454	.032404	88
23	15.171366	472.378852	.002117	.065914	31.136212	.032117	92
24	17.075506	535.850187	.001866	.058563	31.381219	.031866	96
25	19.218632	607.287733	.001647	.052033	31.598905	.031647	100
26	21.630740	687.691321	.001454	.046231	31.792317	.031454	104
27	24.345588	778.186267	.001285	.041075	31.964160	.031285	108
28	27.401174	880.039126	.001136	.036495	32.116840	.031136	112
29	30.840263	994.675417	.001005	.032425	32.252495	.031005	116
30	34.710987	1123.699572	.000890	.028809	32.373023	.030890	120
31	39.067522	1268.917395	.000788	.025597	32.480110	.030788	124
32	43.970840	1432.361334	.000698	.022742	32.575255	.030698	128
33	49.489568	1616.318928	.000619	.020206	32.659791	.030619	132
34	55.700945	1823.364820	.000548	.017953	32.734899	.030548	136
35	62.691904	2056.396796	.000486	.015951	32.801633	.030486	140
36	70.560290	2318.676338	.000431	.014172	32.860924	.030431	144
37	79.416228	2613.874273	.000383	.012592	32.913604	.030383	148
38	89.383665	2946.122150	.000339	.011188	32.960409	.030339	152
39	100.602102	3320.070063	.000301	.009940	33.001995	.030301	156
40	113.228552	3740.951733	.000267	.008832	33.038944	.030267	160
41	127.439733	4214.657760	.000237	.007847	33.071772	.030237	164
42	143.434542	4747.818067	.000211	.006972	33.100939	.030211	168
43	161.436841	5347.894690	.000187	.006194	33.126854	.030187	172
44	181.698587	6023.286217	.000166	.005504	33.149879	.030166	176
45	204.503360	6783.445330	.000147	.004890	33.170337	.030147	180
46	230.170333	7639.011110	.000131	.004345	33.188513	.030131	184
47	259.058738	8601.957930	.000116	.003860	33.204662	.030116	188
48	291.572892	9685.763060	.000103	.003430	33.219011	.030103	192
49	328.167859	10905.595280	.000092	.003047	33.231759	.030092	196
50	369.355816	12278.527200	.000081	.002707	33.243086	.030081	200
51	415.713225	13823.774160	.000072	.002406	33.253150	.030072	204
52	467.888897	15562.963230	.000064	.002137	33.262091	.030064	208
53	526.613076	17520.435860	.000057	.001899	33.270036	.030057	212
54	592.707656	19723.588540	.000051	.001687	33.277094	.030051	216
55	667.097689	22203.256290	.000045	.001499	33.283366	.030045	220
56	750.824326	24994.144200	.000040	.001332	33.288938	.030040	224
57	845.059394	28135.313120	.000036	.001183	33.293888	.030036	228
58	951.121793	31670.726420	.000032	.001051	33.298287	.030032	232
59	1070.495957	35649.865230	.000028	.000934	33.302195	.030028	236
60	1204.852631	40128.421030	.000025	.000830	33.305667	.030025	240

12% SEMI-ANNUAL COMPOUND INTEREST TABLE 12%

EFFECTIVE RATE = 6% BASE = 1.0600

HALF YEARS	1 AMOUNT OF I AT COMPOUND INTEREST $S^n = (1+i)^n$	2 ACCUMULATION OF I PER PERIOD $S_{\overline{n}\vert} = \frac{S^n - 1}{i}$	3 SINKING FUND FACTOR $1/S_{\overline{n}\vert} = \frac{i}{S^n - 1}$	4 PRES. VALUE REVERSION OF I $V^n = \frac{1}{S^n}$	5 PRESENT VALUE ORD.ANNUITY 1 PER PERIOD $a_{\overline{n}\vert} = \frac{1 - V^n}{i}$	6 INSTALMENT TO AMORTIZE I $1/a_{\overline{n}\vert} = \frac{i}{1 - V^n}$	n HALF YEARS
1	1.060000	1.000000	1.000000	.943396	.943396	1.060000	1
YEARS							
1	1.123600	2.060000	.485437	.889996	1.833393	.545437	2
2	1.262477	4.374616	.228591	.792094	3.465106	.288591	4
3	1.418519	6.975319	.143363	.704961	4.917324	.203363	6
4	1.593848	9.897468	.101036	.627412	6.209794	.161036	8
5	1.790848	13.180795	.075868	.558395	7.360087	.135868	10
6	2.012196	16.869941	.059277	.496969	8.383844	.119277	12
7	2.260904	21.015066	.047585	.442301	9.294984	.107585	14
8	2.540352	25.672528	.038952	.393646	10.105895	.098952	16
9	2.854339	30.905653	.032357	.350344	10.827603	.092357	18
10	3.207135	36.785591	.027185	.311805	11.469921	.087185	20
11	3.603537	43.392290	.023046	.277505	12.041582	.083046	22
12	4.048935	50.815577	.019679	.246979	12.550358	.079679	24
13	4.549383	59.156383	.016904	.219810	13.003166	.076904	26
14	5.111687	68.528112	.014593	.195630	13.406164	.074593	28
15	5.743491	79.058186	.012649	.174110	13.764831	.072649	30
16	6.453387	90.889778	.011002	.154957	14.084043	.071002	32
17	7.251025	104.183755	.009598	.137912	14.368141	.069598	34
18	8.147252	119.120867	.008395	.122741	14.620987	.068395	36
19	9.154252	135.904206	.007358	.109239	14.846019	.067358	38
20	10.285718	154.761966	.006462	.097222	15.046297	.066462	40
21	11.557033	175.950545	.005683	.086527	15.224543	.065683	42
22	12.985482	199.758032	.005006	.077009	15.383182	.065006	44
23	14.590487	226.508125	.004415	.068538	15.524370	.064415	46
24	16.393872	256.564529	.003898	.060998	15.650027	.063898	48
25	18.420154	290.335904	.003444	.054288	15.761861	.063444	50
26	20.696885	328.281422	.003046	.048316	15.861393	.063046	52
27	23.255020	370.917006	.002696	.043001	15.949976	.062696	54
28	26.129341	418.822348	.002388	.038271	16.028814	.062388	56
29	29.358927	472.648790	.002116	.034061	16.098980	.062116	58
30	32.987691	533.128181	.001876	.030314	16.161428	.061876	60
31	37.064969	601.082824	.001664	.026980	16.217006	.061664	62
32	41.646200	677.436661	.001476	.024012	16.266470	.061476	64
33	46.793670	763.227832	.001310	.021370	16.310493	.061310	66
34	52.577368	859.622792	.001163	.019020	16.349673	.061163	68
35	59.075930	967.932169	.001033	.016927	16.384544	.061033	70
36	66.377715	1089.628585	.000918	.015065	16.415578	.060918	72
37	74.582001	1226.366678	.000815	.013408	16.443199	.060815	74
38	83.800336	1380.005599	.000725	.011933	16.467781	.060725	76
39	94.158057	1552.634291	.000644	.010620	16.489659	.060644	78
40	105.795993	1746.599890	.000573	.009452	16.509131	.060573	80
41	118.872378	1964.539637	.000509	.008412	16.526460	.060509	82
42	133.565004	2209.416735	.000453	.007487	16.541883	.060453	84
43	150.073639	2484.560643	.000402	.006663	16.555610	.060402	86
44	168.622740	2793.712338	.000358	.005930	16.567827	.060358	88
45	189.464511	3141.075183	.000318	.005278	16.578699	.060318	90
46	212.882325	3531.372077	.000283	.004697	16.588376	.060283	92
47	239.194580	3969.909665	.000252	.004181	16.596988	.060252	94
48	268.759030	4462.650500	.000224	.003721	16.604653	.060224	96
49	301.977646	5016.294102	.000199	.003312	16.611475	.060199	98
50	339.302083	5638.368052	.000177	.002947	16.617546	.060177	100
51	381.239821	6337.330343	.000158	.002623	16.622950	.060158	102
52	428.361062	7122.684373	.000140	.002334	16.627759	.060140	104
53	481.306490	8005.108162	.000125	.002078	16.632039	.060125	106
54	540.795972	8996.599530	.000111	.001849	16.635848	.060111	108
55	607.638354	10110.639230	.000099	.001646	16.639238	.060099	110
56	682.742454	11362.374240	.000088	.001465	16.642255	.060088	112
57	767.129422	12768.823700	.000078	.001304	16.644941	.060078	114
58	861.946618	14349.110300	.000070	.001160	16.647331	.060070	116
59	968.483220	16124.720340	.000062	.001033	16.649458	.060062	118
60	1088.187746	18119.795770	.000055	.000919	16.651351	.060055	120

12% ANNUAL COMPOUND INTEREST TABLE 12%

EFFECTIVE RATE = 12% BASE = 1.1200

YEARS	1 AMOUNT OF I AT COMPOUND INTEREST $S^n = (1+i)^n$	2 ACCUMULATION OF I PER PERIOD $S_{\overline{n}\vert} = \frac{S^n - 1}{i}$	3 SINKING FUND FACTOR $1/S_{\overline{n}\vert} = \frac{i}{S^n - 1}$	4 PRES. VALUE REVERSION OF I $V^n = \frac{1}{S^n}$	5 PRESENT VALUE ORD. ANNUITY 1 PER PERIOD $a_{\overline{n}\vert} = \frac{1 - V^n}{i}$	6 INSTALMENT TO AMORTIZE I $1/a_{\overline{n}\vert} = \frac{i}{1 - V^n}$	n YEARS
1	1.120000	1.000000	1.000000	.892857	.892857	1.120000	1
2	1.254400	2.120000	.471698	.797194	1.690051	.591698	2
3	1.404928	3.374400	.296349	.711780	2.401831	.416349	3
4	1.573519	4.779328	.209234	.635518	3.037349	.329234	4
5	1.762342	6.352847	.157410	.567427	3.604776	.277410	5
6	1.973823	8.115189	.123226	.506631	4.111407	.243226	6
7	2.210681	10.089012	.099118	.452349	4.563757	.219118	7
8	2.475963	12.299693	.081303	.403883	4.967640	.201303	8
9	2.773079	14.775656	.067679	.360610	5.328250	.187679	9
10	3.105848	17.548735	.056984	.321973	5.650223	.176984	10
11	3.478550	20.654583	.048415	.287476	5.937699	.168415	11
12	3.895976	24.133133	.041437	.256675	6.194374	.161437	12
13	4.363493	28.029109	.035677	.229174	6.423548	.155677	13
14	4.887112	32.392602	.030871	.204620	6.628168	.150871	14
15	5.473566	37.279715	.026824	.182696	6.810864	.146824	15
16	6.130394	42.753280	.023390	.163122	6.973986	.143390	16
17	6.866041	48.883674	.020457	.145644	7.119630	.140457	17
18	7.689966	55.749715	.017937	.130040	7.249670	.137937	18
19	8.612762	63.439681	.015763	.116107	7.365777	.135763	19
20	9.646293	72.052442	.013879	.103667	7.469444	.133879	20
21	10.803848	81.698736	.012240	.092560	7.562003	.132240	21
22	12.100310	92.502584	.010811	.082643	7.644646	.130811	22
23	13.552347	104.602894	.009560	.073788	7.718434	.129560	23
24	15.178629	118.155241	.008463	.065882	7.784316	.128463	24
25	17.000064	133.333870	.007500	.058823	7.843139	.127500	25
26	19.040072	150.333934	.006652	.052521	7.895660	.126652	26
27	21.324881	169.374007	.005904	.046894	7.942554	.125904	27
28	23.883866	190.698887	.005244	.041869	7.984423	.125244	28
29	26.749930	214.582754	.004660	.037383	8.021806	.124660	29
30	29.959922	241.332684	.004144	.033378	8.055184	.124144	30
31	33.555113	271.292606	.003686	.029802	8.084986	.123686	31
32	37.581726	304.847719	.003280	.026609	8.111594	.123280	32
33	42.091533	342.429445	.002920	.023758	8.135352	.122920	33
34	47.142517	384.520979	.002601	.021212	8.156564	.122601	34
35	52.799620	431.663496	.002317	.018940	8.175504	.122317	35
36	59.135574	484.463116	.002064	.016910	8.192414	.122064	36
37	66.231843	543.598690	.001840	.015098	8.207513	.121840	37
38	74.179664	609.830532	.001640	.013481	8.220993	.121640	38
39	83.081224	684.010196	.001462	.012036	8.233030	.121462	39
40	93.050970	767.091420	.001304	.010747	8.243777	.121304	40
41	104.217087	860.142390	.001163	.009595	8.253372	.121163	41
42	116.723137	964.359477	.001037	.008567	8.261939	.121037	42
43	130.729914	1081.082614	.000925	.007649	8.269589	.120925	43
44	146.417503	1211.812527	.000825	.006830	8.276418	.120825	44
45	163.987604	1358.230031	.000736	.006098	8.282516	.120736	45
46	183.666116	1522.217634	.000657	.005445	8.287961	.120657	46
47	205.706050	1705.883750	.000586	.004861	8.292822	.120586	47
48	230.390776	1911.589800	.000523	.004340	8.297163	.120523	48
49	258.037669	2141.980576	.000467	.003875	8.301038	.120467	49
50	289.002189	2400.018245	.000417	.003460	8.304498	.120417	50
51	323.682452	2689.020434	.000372	.003089	8.307588	.120372	51
52	362.524346	3012.702886	.000332	.002758	8.310346	.120332	52
53	406.027268	3375.227233	.000296	.002463	8.312809	.120296	53
54	454.750540	3781.254500	.000264	.002199	8.315008	.120264	54
55	509.320605	4236.005040	.000236	.001963	8.316972	.120236	55
56	570.439077	4745.325645	.000211	.001753	8.318725	.120211	56
57	638.891767	5315.764723	.000188	.001565	8.320290	.120188	57
58	715.558779	5954.656489	.000168	.001398	8.321687	.120168	58
59	801.425832	6670.215267	.000150	.001248	8.322935	.120150	59
60	897.596932	7471.641099	.000134	.001114	8.324049	.120134	60

ANNUAL COMPOUND INTEREST TABLE

EFFECTIVE RATE = 13% BASE = 1.13

YEARS	1 AMOUNT OF I AT COMPOUND INTEREST $S^n = (1+i)^n$	2 ACCUMULATION OF I PER PERIOD $s_{\overline{n}\vert} = \frac{S^n - 1}{i}$	3 SINKING FUND FACTOR $1/s_{\overline{n}\vert} = \frac{i}{S^n - 1}$	4 PRES. VALUE REVERSION OF I $V^n = \frac{1}{S^n}$	5 PRESENT VALUE ORD. ANNUITY I PER PERIOD $a_{\overline{n}\vert} = \frac{1-V^n}{i}$	6 INSTALMENT TO AMORTIZE I $1/a_{\overline{n}\vert} = \frac{i}{1-V^n}$	n YEARS
1	1.130000	1.0000	1.000000	.884956	.884956	1.130000	1
2	1.276900	2.1300	.469483	.783147	1.668103	.599483	2
3	1.442897	3.4069	.293522	.693050	2.361153	.423522	3
4	1.630474	4.8498	.206194	.613319	2.974472	.336194	4
5	1.842436	6.4803	.154314	.542760	3.517232	.284314	5
6	2.081952	8.3227	.120153	.480318	3.997550	.250153	6
7	2.352607	10.4047	.096111	.425060	4.422610	.226111	7
8	2.658446	12.7573	.078387	.376160	4.798770	.208387	8
9	3.004044	15.4157	.064869	.332885	5.131655	.194869	9
10	3.394570	18.4198	.054290	.294588	5.426243	.184290	10
11	3.835864	21.8143	.045841	.260697	5.686940	.175841	11
12	4.334526	25.6502	.038986	.230706	5.917646	.168986	12
13	4.898014	29.9847	.033350	.204164	6.121810	.163350	13
14	5.534756	34.8827	.028668	.180676	6.302486	.158668	14
15	6.254274	40.4175	.024742	.159891	6.462377	.154742	15
16	7.067330	46.6718	.021426	.141496	6.603873	.151426	16
17	7.986083	53.7391	.018608	.125218	6.729091	.148608	17
18	9.024274	61.7252	.016201	.110812	6.839903	.146201	18
19	10.197430	70.7494	.014134	.098064	6.937967	.144134	19
20	11.523096	80.9469	.012354	.086782	7.024749	.142354	20
21	13.021098	92.4700	.010814	.076798	7.101547	.140814	21
22	14.713841	105.4911	.009480	.067963	7.169510	.139480	22
23	16.626640	120.2049	.008319	.060144	7.229654	.138319	23
24	18.788103	136.8316	.007308	.053225	7.282879	.137308	24
25	21.230556	155.6197	.006426	.047102	7.329984	.136426	25
26	23.990528	176.8502	.005655	.041683	7.371664	.135655	26
27	27.109297	200.8407	.004979	.036888	7.408552	.134979	27
28	30.633506	227.9500	.004387	.032644	7.441196	.134387	28
29	34.615862	258.5835	.003867	.028888	7.470084	.133867	29
30	39.115924	293.1994	.003411	.025565	7.495653	.133411	30

14% ANNUAL COMPOUND INTEREST TABLE 14%

EFFECTIVE RATE = 14% BASE = 1.14

YEARS	1 AMOUNT OF 1 AT COMPOUND INTEREST $S^n = (1+i)^n$	2 ACCUMULATION OF 1 PER PERIOD $s_{\overline{n}\rvert} = \frac{S^n - 1}{i}$	3 SINKING FUND FACTOR $1/s_{\overline{n}\rvert} = \frac{i}{S^n - 1}$	4 PRES. VALUE REVERSION OF 1 $V^n = \frac{1}{S^n}$	5 PRESENT VALUE ORD. ANNUITY 1 PER PERIOD $a_{\overline{n}\rvert} = \frac{1-V^n}{i}$	6 INSTALMENT TO AMORTIZE 1 $1/a_{\overline{n}\rvert} = \frac{i}{1-V^n}$	n YEARS
1	1.140000	1.0000	1.000000	.877193	.877193	1.140000	1
2	1.299600	2.1400	.467290	.769468	1.646661	.607290	2
3	1.481544	3.4396	.290731	.674971	2.321623	.430731	3
4	1.688960	4.9211	.203205	.592080	2.913712	.343205	4
5	1.925415	6.6101	.151284	.519368	3.433080	.291284	5
6	2.194973	8.5355	.117158	.455587	3.888667	.257158	6
7	2.502269	10.7305	.093192	.399637	4.288304	.233192	7
8	2.852586	13.2328	.075570	.350559	4.638863	.215570	8
9	3.251949	16.0853	.062168	.307508	4.946371	.202168	9
10	3.707221	19.3373	.051714	.269744	5.216115	.191714	10
11	4.226232	23.0445	.043394	.236617	5.452732	.183394	11
12	4.817905	27.2707	.036669	.207559	5.660291	.176669	12
13	5.492411	32.0887	.031164	.182069	5.842360	.171164	13
14	6.261349	37.5811	.026609	.159710	6.002070	.166609	14
15	7.137938	43.8424	.022809	.140096	6.142166	.162809	15
16	8.137249	50.9804	.019615	.122892	6.265058	.159615	16
17	9.276464	59.1176	.016915	.107800	6.372858	.156915	17
18	10.575169	68.3941	.014621	.094561	6.467419	.154621	18
19	12.055693	78.9692	.012663	.082948	6.550367	.152663	19
20	13.743490	91.0249	.010986	.072762	6.623129	.150986	20
21	15.667578	104.7684	.009545	.063826	6.686955	.149545	21
22	17.861039	120.4360	.008303	.055988	6.742943	.148303	22
23	20.361585	138.2970	.007231	.049112	6.792055	.147231	23
24	23.212207	158.6586	.006303	.043081	6.835136	.146303	24
25	26.461916	181.8708	.005498	.037790	6.872926	.145498	25
26	30.166584	208.3327	.004800	.033149	6.906075	.144800	26
27	34.389906	238.4993	.004193	.029078	6.935153	.144193	27
28	39.204492	272.8892	.003665	.025507	6.960660	.143665	28
29	44.693121	312.0937	.003204	.022375	6.983035	.143204	29
30	50.950158	356.7868	.002803	.019627	7.002662	.142803	30

15% ANNUAL COMPOUND INTEREST TABLE 15%

EFFECTIVE RATE = 15% BASE = 1.15

YEARS	1 AMOUNT OF I AT COMPOUND INTEREST $s^n = (1+i)^n$	2 ACCUMULATION OF I PER PERIOD $s_{\overline{n}\vert} = \frac{s^n - 1}{i}$	3 SINKING FUND FACTOR $1/s_{\overline{n}\vert} = \frac{i}{s^n - 1}$	4 PRES. VALUE REVERSION OF I $v^n = \frac{1}{s^n}$	5 PRESENT VALUE ORD. ANNUITY I PER PERIOD $a_{\overline{n}\vert} = \frac{1 - v^n}{i}$	6 INSTALMENT TO AMORTIZE I $1/a_{\overline{n}\vert} = \frac{i}{1 - v^n}$	n YEARS
1	1.150000	1.0000	1.000000	.869565	.869565	1.150000	1
2	1.322500	2.1500	.465116	.756144	1.625709	.615116	2
3	1.520875	3.4725	.287976	.657516	2.283225	.437976	3
4	1.749006	4.9934	.200265	.571753	2.854978	.350265	4
5	2.011357	6.7424	.148315	.497177	3.352155	.298315	5
6	2.313061	8.7537	.114236	.432328	3.784483	.264236	6
7	2.660020	11.0668	.090360	.375937	4.160420	.240360	7
8	3.059023	13.7268	.072850	.326902	4.487322	.222850	8
9	3.517876	16.7858	.059574	.284262	4.771584	.209574	9
10	4.045558	20.3037	.049252	.247185	5.018769	.199252	10
11	4.652391	24.3493	.041068	.214943	5.233712	.191068	11
12	5.350250	29.0017	.034480	.186907	5.420619	.184480	12
13	6.152788	34.3519	.029110	.162528	5.583147	.179110	13
14	7.075706	40.5047	.024688	.141329	5.724476	.174688	14
15	8.137062	47.5804	.021017	.122894	5.847370	.171017	15
16	9.357621	55.7175	.017947	.106865	5.954235	.167947	16
17	10.761264	65.0751	.015366	.092926	6.047161	.165366	17
18	12.375454	75.8364	.013186	.080805	6.127966	.163186	18
19	14.231772	88.2118	.011336	.070265	6.198231	.161336	19
20	16.366537	102.4436	.009761	.061100	6.259331	.159761	20
21	18.821518	118.8101	.008416	.053131	6.312462	.158416	21
22	21.644746	137.6316	.007265	.046201	6.358663	.157265	22
23	24.891458	159.2764	.006278	.040174	6.398837	.156278	23
24	28.625176	184.1678	.005429	.034934	6.433771	.155429	24
25	32.918953	212.7930	.004699	.030378	6.464149	.154699	25
26	37.856796	245.7120	.004069	.026415	6.490564	.154069	26
27	43.535315	283.5688	.003526	.022970	6.513534	.153526	27
28	50.065612	327.1041	.003010	.019974	6.535508	153010	28
29	57.575454	377.1697	.002651	.017369	6.550877	.152651	29
30	66.211772	434.7451	.002300	.015103	6.565980	.152300	30

ANNUAL COMPOUND INTEREST TABLE

EFFECTIVE RATE = 16% BASE = 1.16

YEARS	1 AMOUNT OF 1 AT COMPOUND INTEREST $S^n = (1+i)^n$	2 ACCUMULATION OF 1 PER PERIOD $S_{\overline{n}\vert} = \frac{S^n - 1}{i}$	3 SINKING FUND FACTOR $1/S_{\overline{n}\vert} = \frac{i}{S^n - 1}$	4 PRES. VALUE REVERSION OF 1 $V^n = \frac{1}{S^n}$	5 PRESENT VALUE ORD. ANNUITY 1 PER PERIOD $a_{\overline{n}\vert} = \frac{1-V^n}{i}$	6 INSTALMENT TO AMORTIZE 1 $1/a_{\overline{n}\vert} = \frac{i}{1-V^n}$	n YEARS
1	1.160000	1.0000	1.000000	.862068	.862068	1.160000	1
2	1.345600	2.1600	.462963	.743163	1.605231	.622963	2
3	1.560896	3.5056	.285257	.640658	2.245889	.445257	3
4	1.810639	5.0665	.197375	.552291	2.798180	.357375	4
5	2.100342	6.8771	.145409	.476113	3.274293	.305409	5
6	2.436396	8.9775	.111390	.410442	3.684735	.271390	6
7	2.826220	11.4139	.087613	.353829	4.038564	.247613	7
8	3.278415	14.2401	.070224	.305025	4.343589	.230224	8
9	3.802961	17.5185	.057083	.262953	4.606542	.217083	9
10	4.411435	21.3215	.046901	.226684	4.833226	.206901	10
11	5.117265	25.7329	.038861	.195417	5.028643	.198861	11
12	5.936027	30.8502	.032415	.168463	5.197106	.192415	12
13	6.885792	36.7862	.027184	.145227	5.342333	.187184	13
14	7.987518	43.6720	.022898	.125195	5.467528	.182898	14
15	9.265521	51.6595	.019358	.107927	5.575455	.179358	15
16	10.748005	60.9250	.016414	.093041	5.668496	.176414	16
17	12.467685	71.6730	.013952	.080207	5.748703	.173952	17
18	14.462515	84.1407	.011885	.069144	5.817847	.171885	18
19	16.776517	98.6032	.010142	.059607	5.877454	.170142	19
20	19.460760	115.3797	.008667	.051385	5.928839	.168667	20
21	22.574482	134.8405	.007416	.044298	5.973137	.167416	21
22	26.186399	157.4150	.006353	.038188	6.011325	.166353	22
23	30.376223	183.6014	.005447	.032920	6.044245	.165447	23
24	35.236418	213.9776	.004673	.028380	6.072625	.164673	24
25	40.874245	249.2140	.004013	.024465	6.097090	.164013	25
26	47.414124	290.0883	.003447	.021091	6.118181	.163447	26
27	55.000384	337.5024	.002963	.018182	6.136363	.162963	27
28	63.800446	392.5028	.002548	.015674	6.152037	.162548	28
29	74.008517	456.3032	.002192	.013512	6.165549	.162192	29
30	85.849880	530.3117	.001886	.011648	6.177197	.161886	30

17% ANNUAL COMPOUND INTEREST TABLE 17%

EFFECTIVE RATE = 17% BASE = 1.17

YEARS	1 AMOUNT OF I AT COMPOUND INTEREST $S^n = (1+i)^n$	2 ACCUMULATION OF I PER PERIOD $S_{\overline{n}\vert} = \frac{S^n - 1}{i}$	3 SINKING FUND FACTOR $1/S_{\overline{n}\vert} = \frac{i}{S^n - 1}$	4 PRES. VALUE REVERSION OF I $V^n = \frac{1}{S^n}$	5 PRESENT VALUE ORD. ANNUITY 1 PER PERIOD $a_{\overline{n}\vert} = \frac{1 - V^n}{i}$	6 INSTALMENT TO AMORTIZE I $1/a_{\overline{n}\vert} = \frac{i}{1 - V^n}$	n YEARS
1	1.170000	1.0000	1.000000	.854701	.854701	1.170000	1
2	1.368900	2.1700	.460829	730514	1.585215	.630829	2
3	1.601613	3.5389	.282573	.624371	2.209586	.452573	3
4	1.873887	5.1405	.194533	.533650	2.743236	.364533	4
5	2.192448	7.0144	.142564	.456111	3.199347	.312564	5
6	2.565164	9.2068	.108615	.389839	3.589186	.278615	6
7	3.001242	11.7720	.084947	.333195	3.922381	.254947	7
8	3.511453	14.7733	.067690	.284782	4.207163	.237690	8
9	4.108400	18.2847	.054690	.243404	4.450567	.224690	9
10	4.806828	22.3931	.044657	.208037	4.658604	.214657	10
11	5.623989	27.1999	.036765	.177810	4.836414	.206765	11
12	6.580067	32.8239	.030466	.151974	4.988388	.200466	12
13	7.698679	39.4040	.025378	.129892	5.118280	.195378	13
14	9.007454	47.1027	.021230	.111019	5.229299	.191230	14
15	10.538722	56.1101	.017822	.094888	5.324187	.187822	15
16	12.330304	66.6488	.015004	.081101	5.405288	.185004	16
17	14.426456	78.9792	.012662	.069317	5.474605	.182662	17
18	16.878954	93.4056	.010706	.059245	5.533850	.180706	18
19	19.748376	110.2846	.009067	.050637	5.584487	.179067	19
20	23.105599	130.0329	.007690	.043280	5.627767	.177690	20
21	27.033551	153.1385	.006530	.036991	5.664758	.176530	21
22	31.629255	180.1721	.005550	.031616	5.696374	.175550	22
23	37.006228	211.8013	.004721	.027022	5.723396	.174721	23
24	43.297287	248.8076	.004019	.023096	5.746492	.174019	24
25	50.657826	292.1049	.003423	.019740	5.766232	.173423	25
26	59.269657	342.7627	.002918	.016872	5.783104	.172918	26
27	69.345498	402.0323	.002487	.014421	5.797525	.172487	27
28	81.134233	471.3778	.002121	.012325	5.809850	.172121	28
29	94.927052	552.5121	.001810	.010534	5.820384	.171810	29
30	111.064651	647.4391	.001545	.009004	5.829388	.171545	30

ANNUAL COMPOUND INTEREST TABLE

EFFECTIVE RATE = 18% BASE = 1.18

YEARS	1 AMOUNT OF 1 AT COMPOUND INTEREST $S^n = (1+i)^n$	2 ACCUMULATION OF 1 PER PERIOD $S_{\overline{n}\rvert} = \frac{S^n - 1}{i}$	3 SINKING FUND FACTOR $1/S_{\overline{n}\rvert} = \frac{i}{S^n - 1}$	4 PRES. VALUE REVERSION OF 1 $V^n = \frac{1}{S^n}$	5 PRESENT VALUE ORD. ANNUITY 1 PER PERIOD $a_{\overline{n}\rvert} = \frac{1 - V^n}{i}$	6 INSTALMENT TO AMORTIZE 1 $1/a_{\overline{n}\rvert} = \frac{i}{1 - V^n}$	n YEARS
1	1.180000	1.0000	1.000000	.847458	.847458	1.180000	1
2	1.392400	2.1800	.458715	.718184	1.565642	.638715	2
3	1.643032	3.5724	.279923	.608631	2.174273	.459923	3
4	1.938778	5.2154	.191738	.515789	2.690062	.371738	4
5	2.287758	7.1542	.139778	.437109	3.127171	.319778	5
6	2.699554	9.4420	.105910	.370432	3.497603	.285910	6
7	3.185474	12.1415	.082362	.313925	3.811528	.262362	7
8	3.758859	15.3270	.065243	.266038	4.077566	.245243	8
9	4.435454	19.0859	.052395	.225456	4.303022	.232395	9
10	5.233836	23.5213	.042515	.191064	4.494086	.222515	10
11	6.175926	28.7551	.034776	.161919	4.656005	.214776	11
12	7.287593	34.9311	.028628	.137220	4.793225	.208628	12
13	8.599360	42.2187	.023686	.116288	4.909513	.203686	13
14	10.147244	50.8180	.019678	.098549	5.008062	.199678	14
15	11.973748	60.9653	.016403	.083516	5.091578	.196403	15
16	14.129023	72.9390	.013710	.070776	5.162354	.193710	16
17	16.672247	87.0680	.011485	.059980	5.222334	.191485	17
18	19.673251	103.7403	.009639	.050830	5.273164	.189639	18
19	23.214437	123.4135	.008103	.043077	5.316241	.188103	19
20	27.393035	146.6280	.006820	.036506	5.352747	,186820	20
21	32.323782	174.0210	.005746	.030937	5.383684	.185746	21
22	38.142063	206.3448	.004846	.026218	5.409902	.184846	22
23	45.007634	244.4869	.004090	.022218	5.432120	.184090	23
24	53.109008	289.4945	.003454	.018829	5.450949	.183454	24
25	62.668629	342.6035	.002919	.015957	5.466906	.182919	25
26	73.948983	405.2721	.002467	.013523	5.480429	.182467	26
27	87.259799	479.2211	.002087	.011460	5.491889	.182087	27
28	102.966563	566.4809	.001765	.009712	5.501601	.181765	28
29	121.500545	669.4475	.001494	.008230	5.509831	.181494	29
30	143.370643	790.9480	.001264	.006975	5.516806	.181264	30

19% ANNUAL COMPOUND INTEREST TABLE 19%

EFFECTIVE RATE = 19% BASE = 1.19

YEARS	1 AMOUNT OF I AT COMPOUND INTEREST $S^n = (1+i)^n$	2 ACCUMULATION OF I PER PERIOD $S_{\overline{n}\vert} = \frac{S^n - 1}{i}$	3 SINKING FUND FACTOR $1/S_{\overline{n}\vert} = \frac{i}{S^n - 1}$	4 PRES. VALUE REVERSION OF I $V^n = \frac{1}{S^n}$	5 PRESENT VALUE ORD. ANNUITY 1 PER PERIOD $a_{\overline{n}\vert} = \frac{1-V^n}{i}$	6 INSTALMENT TO AMORTIZE I $1/a_{\overline{n}\vert} = \frac{i}{1-V^n}$	n YEARS
1	1.190000	1.000000	1.000000	.840336	.840336	1.190000	1
2	1.416100	2.190000	.456621	.706165	1.546501	.646621	2
3	1.685159	3.606100	.277308	.593416	2.139917	.467308	3
4	2.005339	5.291259	.188991	.498669	2.638586	.378991	4
5	2.386354	7.296598	.137050	.419049	3.057635	.327050	5
6	2.839761	9.682952	.103274	.352142	3.409777	.293274	6
7	3.379315	12.522713	.079855	.295918	3.705695	.269855	7
8	4.021385	15.902028	.062885	.248671	3.954366	.252885	8
9	4.785449	19.923413	.050192	.208967	4.163333	.240192	9
10	5.694684	24.708862	.040471	.175602	4.338935	.230471	10
11	6.776674	30.403546	.032891	.147565	4.486500	.222891	11
12	8.064241	37.180220	.026896	.124004	4.610504	.216896	12
13	9.596447	45.244461	.022102	.104205	4.714709	.212102	13
14	11.419772	54.840908	.018235	.087567	4.802276	.208235	14
15	13.589528	66.260680	.015092	.073586	4.875862	.205092	15
16	16.171539	79.850208	.012523	.061837	4.937699	.202523	16
17	19.244131	96.021747	.010414	.051964	4.989663	.200414	17
18	22.900515	115.265878	.008676	.043667	5.033330	.198676	18
19	27.251613	138.166393	.007237	.036695	5.070025	.197238	19
20	32.429420	165.418006	.006045	.030836	5.100861	.196045	20
21	38.591009	197.847426	.005054	.025913	5.126774	.195054	21
22	45.923301	236.438435	.004229	.021775	5.148549	.194229	22
23	54.648728	282.361736	.003542	.018299	5.166848	.193542	23
24	65.031986	337.010464	.002967	.015377	5.182225	.192967	24
25	77.388063	402.042450	.002487	.012922	5.195147	.192487	25
26	92.092055	479.430513	.002086	.010859	5.206006	.192086	26
27	109.589251	571.522568	.001750	.009125	5.215131	.191750	27
28	130.411208	681.112114	.001468	.007668	5.222799	.191468	28
29	155.189337	811.523673	.001232	.006444	5.229243	.191232	29
30	184.675312	966.712169	.001034	.005415	5.234658	.191034	30

20% ANNUAL COMPOUND INTEREST TABLE 20%

EFFECTIVE RATE = 20% BASE = 1.20

YEARS	1 AMOUNT OF I AT COMPOUND INTEREST $S^n = (1+i)^n$	2 ACCUMULATION OF I PER PERIOD $S_{\overline{n}\rceil} = \frac{S^n - 1}{i}$	3 SINKING FUND FACTOR $1/S_{\overline{n}\rceil} = \frac{i}{S^n - 1}$	4 PRES. VALUE REVERSION OF I $V^n = \frac{1}{S^n}$	5 PRESENT VALUE ORD. ANNUITY 1 PER PERIOD $a_{\overline{n}\rceil} = \frac{1-V^n}{i}$	6 INSTALMENT TO AMORTIZE I $1/a_{\overline{n}\rceil} = \frac{i}{1-V^n}$	n YEARS
1	1.200000	1.000000	1.000000	.833333	.833333	1.200000	1
2	1.440000	2.200000	.454545	.694444	1.527777	.654545	2
3	1.728000	3.640000	.274725	.578704	2.106481	.474725	3
4	2.073600	5.368000	.186289	.482253	2.588734	.386289	4
5	2.488320	7.441600	.134380	.401878	2.990612	.334380	5
6	2.985984	9.929920	.100706	.334898	3.325510	.300706	6
7	3.583181	12.915904	.077424	.279082	3.604592	.277424	7
8	4.299817	16.499085	.060609	.232568	3.837160	.260609	8
9	5.159780	20.798902	.048079	.193807	4.030967	.248079	9
10	6.191736	25.958682	.038523	.161506	4.192473	.238523	10
11	7.430083	32.150418	.031104	.134588	4.327061	.231104	11
12	8.916100	39.580501	.025265	.112157	4.439218	.225265	12
13	10.699320	48.496601	.020620	.093464	4.532682	.220620	13
14	12.839184	59.195921	.016893	.077887	4.610569	.216893	14
15	15.407021	72.035105	.013882	.064905	4.675474	.213882	15
16	18.488514	87.442126	.011436	.054088	4.729562	.211436	16
17	22.186217	105.930640	.009440	.045073	4.774635	.209440	17
18	26.623460	128.116857	.007805	.037561	4.812196	.207805	18
19	31.948153	154.740317	.006462	.031301	4.843497	.206462	19
20	38.337783	186.688470	.005357	.026085	4.869582	.205357	20
21	46.005340	225.026253	.004444	.021737	4.891319	.204444	21
22	55.206408	271.031593	.003690	.018114	4.909433	.203690	22
23	66.247690	326.238001	.003065	.015095	4.924528	.203065	23
24	79.497228	392.485691	.002548	.012579	4.937107	.202548	24
25	95.396675	471.982919	.002119	.010483	4.947590	.202119	25
26	114.476010	567.379594	.001762	.008735	4.956325	.201762	26
27	137.371212	681.855604	.001467	.007280	4.963605	.201467	27
28	164.845454	819.226816	.001221	.006066	4.969671	.201221	28
29	197.814545	984.072270	.001016	.005055	4.974726	.201016	29
30	237.377454	1181.886815	.000846	.004213	4.978939	.200846	30

ANNUAL COMPOUND INTEREST TABLE

21%

EFFECTIVE RATE = 21% BASE = 1.21

YEARS	1 AMOUNT OF I AT COMPOUND INTEREST $S^n = (1+i)^n$	2 ACCUMULATION OF I PER PERIOD $S_{\overline{n}\rvert} = \frac{S^n - 1}{i}$	3 SINKING FUND FACTOR $1/S_{\overline{n}\rvert} = \frac{i}{S^n - 1}$	4 PRES. VALUE REVERSION OF I $V^n = \frac{1}{S^n}$	5 PRESENT VALUE ORD. ANNUITY 1 PER PERIOD $a_{\overline{n}\rvert} = \frac{1-V^n}{i}$	6 INSTALMENT TO AMORTIZE I $1/a_{\overline{n}\rvert} = \frac{i}{1-V^n}$	n YEARS
1	1.210000	1.000000	1.000000	.826446	.826446	1.210000	1
2	1.464100	2.210000	.452489	.683013	1.509459	.662489	2
3	1.771561	3.674100	.272175	.564474	2.073933	.482175	3
4	2.143589	5.445661	.183632	.466507	2.540440	.393632	4
5	2.593742	7.589250	.131765	.385543	2.925983	.341765	5
6	3.138428	10.182992	.098203	.318631	3.244614	.308203	6
7	3.797498	13.321420	.075067	.263331	3.507945	.285067	7
8	4.594973	17.118918	.058415	.217629	3.725574	.268415	8
9	5.559917	21.713891	.046053	.179859	3.905433	.256053	9
10	6.727500	27.273808	.036665	.148644	4.054077	.246665	10
11	8.140274	34.001308	.029411	.122846	4.176923	.239411	11
12	9.849732	42.141582	.023730	.101526	4.278449	.233730	12
13	11.918176	51.991314	.019234	.083905	4.362354	.229234	13
14	14.420992	63.909490	.015647	.069343	4.431697	.225647	14
15	17.449401	78.330482	.012766	.057309	4.489006	.222766	15
16	21.113775	95.779883	.010441	.047362	4.536368	.220441	16
17	25.547667	116.893658	.008555	.039143	4.575511	.218555	17
18	30.912677	142.441325	.007020	.032349	4.607860	.217020	18
19	37.404340	173.354002	.005769	.026735	4.634595	.215769	19
20	45.259251	210.758342	.004745	.022095	4.656690	.214745	20
21	54.763694	256.017593	.003906	.018260	4.674950	.213906	21
22	66.264069	310.781287	.003218	.015091	4.690041	.213218	22
23	80.179524	377.045356	.002652	.012472	4.702513	.212652	23
24	97.017224	457.224880	.002187	.010307	4.712820	.212187	24
25	117.390840	554.242104	.001804	.008519	4.721339	.211804	25

22% ANNUAL COMPOUND INTEREST TABLE 22%

EFFECTIVE RATE = 22% BASE = 1.22

YEARS	1 AMOUNT OF I AT COMPOUND INTEREST $S^n = (1+i)^n$	2 ACCUMULATION OF I PER PERIOD $S_{\overline{n}\rceil} = \frac{S^n - 1}{i}$	3 SINKING FUND FACTOR $1/S_{\overline{n}\rceil} = \frac{i}{S^n - 1}$	4 PRES. VALUE REVERSION OF I $V^n = \frac{1}{S^n}$	5 PRESENT VALUE ORD. ANNUITY 1 PER PERIOD $a_{\overline{n}\rceil} = \frac{1-V^n}{i}$	6 INSTALMENT TO AMORTIZE I $1/a_{\overline{n}\rceil} = \frac{i}{1-V^n}$	n YEARS
1	1.220000	1.000000	1.000000	.819672	.819672	1.220000	1
2	1.488400	2.220000	.450450	.671862	1.491534	.670450	2
3	1.815848	3.708400	.269658	.550707	2.042241	.489658	3
4	2.215335	5.524248	.181020	.451399	2.493640	.401020	4
5	2.702708	7.739583	.129206	.369999	2.863639	.349206	5
6	3.297304	10.442291	.095764	.303278	3.166917	.315764	6
7	4.022711	13.739595	.072782	.248589	3.415506	.292782	7
8	4.907707	17.762306	.056299	.203761	3.619267	.276299	8
9	5.987402	22.670013	.044111	.167017	3.786284	.264111	9
10	7.304631	28.657415	.034895	.136899	3.923183	.254895	10
11	8.911649	35.962046	.027807	.112213	4.035396	.247807	11
12	10.872213	44.873695	.022285	.091978	4.127374	.242285	12
13	13.264099	55.745908	.017939	.075391	4.202765	.237939	13
14	16.182201	69.010007	.014491	.061796	4.264561	.234491	14
15	19.742285	85.192208	.011738	.050653	4.315214	.231738	15
16	24.085588	104.934493	.009530	.041519	4.356733	.229530	16
17	29.384417	129.020081	.007751	.034032	4.390765	.227751	17
18	35.848989	158.404498	.006313	.027895	4.418660	.226313	18
19	43.735766	194.253487	.005148	.022865	4.441525	.225148	19
20	53.357635	237.989253	.004202	.018741	4.460266	.224202	20
21	65.096315	291.346888	.003432	.015362	4.475628	.223432	21
22	79.417504	356.443203	.002805	.012592	4.488220	.222805	22
23	96.889355	435.860707	.002294	.010321	4.498541	.222294	23
24	118.205016	532.750062	.001877	.008460	4.507001	.221877	24
25	144.210119	650.955078	.001536	.006934	4.513935	.221536	25

EFFECTIVE RATE = 23% **BASE = 1.23**

YEARS	1 AMOUNT OF I AT COMPOUND INTEREST $S^n = (1+i)^n$	2 ACCUMULATION OF I PER PERIOD $S_{\overline{n}\vert} = \frac{S^n - 1}{i}$	3 SINKING FUND FACTOR $1/S_{\overline{n}\vert} = \frac{i}{S^n - 1}$	4 PRES. VALUE REVERSION OF I $V^n = \frac{1}{S^n}$	5 PRESENT VALUE ORD. ANNUITY 1 PER PERIOD $a_{\overline{n}\vert} = \frac{1-V^n}{i}$	6 INSTALMENT TO AMORTIZE I $1/a_{\overline{n}\vert} = \frac{i}{1-V^n}$	n YEARS
1	1.230000	1.000000	1.000000	.813008	.813008	1.230000	1
2	1.512900	2.230000	.448430	.660982	1.473990	.678430	2
3	1.860867	3.742900	.267173	.537384	2.011374	.497173	3
4	2.288866	5.603767	.178451	.436897	2.448271	.408451	4
5	2.815306	7.892633	.126700	.355201	2.803472	.366700	5
6	3.462826	10.707939	.093389	.288782	3.092254	.323389	6
7	4.259276	14.170765	.070568	.234782	3.327036	.300568	7
8	5.238909	18.430041	.054259	.190879	3.517915	.284259	8
9	6.443858	23.668950	.042249	.155187	3.673102	.272249	9
10	7.925945	30.112808	.033208	.126168	3.799270	.263208	10
11	9.748913	38.038753	.026289	.102576	3.901846	.256289	11
12	11.991163	47.787666	.020926	.083395	3.985241	.250926	12
13	14.749130	59.778829	.016728	.067801	4.053042	.246728	13
14	18.141430	74.527959	.013418	.055122	4.108164	.243418	14
15	22.313959	92.669389	.010791	.044815	4.152979	.240791	15
16	27.446169	114.983348	.008697	.036435	4.189414	.238697	16
17	33.758788	142.429517	.007021	.029622	4.219036	.237021	17
18	41.523310	176.188305	.005676	.024083	4.243119	.235676	18
19	51.073671	217.711615	.004593	.019580	4.262699	.234593	19
20	62.820615	268.785286	.003720	.015918	4.278617	.233720	20
21	77.269357	331.605901	.003016	.012942	4.291559	.233016	21
22	95.041308	408.875258	.002446	.010522	4.302081	.232446	22
23	116.900809	503.916566	.001984	.008554	4.310635	.231984	23
24	143.787995	620.817375	.001611	.006955	4.317590	.231611	24
25	176.859234	764.605370	.001308	.005654	4.323243	.231308	25

24% ANNUAL COMPOUND INTEREST TABLE 24%

EFFECTIVE RATE = 24% BASE = 1.24

YEARS	1 AMOUNT OF I AT COMPOUND INTEREST $S^n = (1+i)^n$	2 ACCUMULATION OF I PER PERIOD $S_{\overline{n}\rvert} = \frac{S^n - 1}{i}$	3 SINKING FUND FACTOR $1/S_{\overline{n}\rvert} = \frac{i}{S^n - 1}$	4 PRES. VALUE REVERSION OF I $V^n = \frac{1}{S^n}$	5 PRESENT VALUE ORD. ANNUITY 1 PER PERIOD $a_{\overline{n}\rvert} = \frac{1-V^n}{i}$	6 INSTALMENT TO AMORTIZE I $1/a_{\overline{n}\rvert} = \frac{i}{1-V^n}$	n YEARS
1	1.240000	1.000000	1.000000	.806452	.806452	1.240000	1
2	1.537600	2.240000	.446429	.650364	1.456816	.686429	2
3	1.906624	3.777600	.264718	.524487	1.981303	.504718	3
4	2.364214	5.684224	.175926	.422974	2.404277	.415926	4
5	2,931625	8.048438	.124248	.341108	2.745385	.364248	5
6	3.635215	10.980063	.091074	.275087	3.020472	.331074	6
7	4.507666	14.615278	.068422	.221844	3.242316	.308422	7
8	5.589506	19.122944	.052293	.178907	3.421223	.292293	8
9	6.930988	24.712450	.040465	.144280	3.565503	.280465	9
10	8.594425	31.643438	.031602	.116354	3.681857	.271602	10
11	10.657087	40.237863	.024852	.093834	3.775691	.264852	11
12	13.214788	50.894950	.019648	.075673	3.851364	.259648	12
13	16.386337	64.109738	.015598	.061026	3.912390	.255598	13
14	20.319057	80.496075	.012423	.049215	3.961605	.252423	14
15	25.195631	100.815132	.009919	.039689	4.001294	.249919	15
16	31.242582	126.010763	.007936	.032008	4.033302	.247936	16
17	38.740802	157.253345	.006359	.025813	4.059115	.246359	17
18	48.038594	195.994147	.005102	.020817	4.079932	.245102	18
19	59.567857	244.032741	.004098	.016788	4.096720	.244098	19
20	73.864143	303.600598	.003294	.013538	4.110258	.243294	20
21	91.591537	377.464741	.002649	.010918	4.121176	.242649	21
22	113.573506	469.056278	.002132	.008805	4.129981	.242132	22
23	140.831147	582.629784	.001716	.007101	4.137082	.241716	23
24	174.630622	723.460931	.001382	.005726	4.142808	.241382	24
25	216.541971	898.091553	.001113	.004618	4.147426	.241113	25

ANNUAL COMPOUND INTEREST TABLE

EFFECTIVE RATE = 25% BASE = 1.25

n YEARS	1 AMOUNT OF I AT COMPOUND INTEREST $S^n = (1+i)^n$	2 ACCUMULATION OF I PER PERIOD $S_{\overline{n}\vert} = \frac{S^n - 1}{i}$	3 SINKING FUND FACTOR $1/S_{\overline{n}\vert} = \frac{i}{S^n - 1}$	4 PRES. VALUE REVERSION OF I $V^n = \frac{1}{S^n}$	5 PRESENT VALUE ORD. ANNUITY 1 PER PERIOD $a_{\overline{n}\vert} = \frac{1-V^n}{i}$	6 INSTALMENT TO AMORTIZE I $1/a_{\overline{n}\vert} = \frac{i}{1-V^n}$	n YEARS
1	1.250000	1.000000	1.000000	.800000	.800000	1.250000	1
2	1.562500	2.250000	.444444	.640000	1.440000	.694444	2
3	1.953125	3.812500	.262295	.512000	1.952000	.512295	3
4	2.441406	5.765625	.173442	.409600	2.361600	.423442	4
5	3.051758	8.207031	.121847	.327680	2.689280	.371847	5
6	3.814697	11.258789	.088819	.262144	2.951424	.338819	6
7	4.768372	15.073486	.066342	.209715	3.161139	.316342	7
8	5.960465	19.841858	.050399	.167772	3.328911	.300399	8
9	7.450581	25.802323	.038756	.134218	3.463129	.288756	9
10	9.313226	33.252904	.030073	.107374	3.570503	.280073	10
11	11.641532	42.566130	.023493	.085899	3.656402	.273493	11
12	14.551915	54.207662	.018448	.068719	3.725121	.268448	12
13	18.189893	68.759577	.014544	.054976	3.780097	.264544	13
14	22.737366	86.949470	.011501	.043980	3.824077	.261501	14
15	28.421708	109.686836	.009117	.035184	3.859261	.259117	15
16	35.527134	138.108544	.007241	.028147	3.887408	.257241	16
17	44.408918	173.635678	.005759	.022518	3.909926	.255759	17
18	55.511147	218.044596	.004586	.018014	3.927940	.254586	18
19	69.388934	273.555743	.003656	.014412	3.942352	.253656	19
20	86.736167	342.944677	.002916	.011529	3.953881	.252916	20
21	108.420208	429.680844	.002327	.009223	3.963104	.252327	21
22	135.525260	538.101052	.001858	.007379	3.970483	.251858	22
23	169.406575	673.626312	.001485	.005903	3.976386	.251485	23
24	211.758219	843.032887	.001186	.004722	3.981108	.251186	24
25	264.697727	1054.791106	.000948	.003778	3.984886	.250948	25

ANNUAL COMPOUND INTEREST TABLE

EFFECTIVE RATE = 26% BASE = 1.26

YEARS	1 AMOUNT OF I AT COMPOUND INTEREST $S^n = (1+i)^n$	2 ACCUMULATION OF I PER PERIOD $S_{\overline{n}\|} = \frac{S^n - 1}{i}$	3 SINKING FUND FACTOR $1/S_{\overline{n}\|} = \frac{i}{S^n - 1}$	4 PRES. VALUE REVERSION OF I $V^n = \frac{1}{S^n}$	5 PRESENT VALUE ORD. ANNUITY 1 PER PERIOD $a_{\overline{n}\|} = \frac{1-V^n}{i}$	6 INSTALMENT TO AMORTIZE I $1/a_{\overline{n}\|} = \frac{i}{1-V^n}$	n YEARS
1	1.260000	1.000000	1.000000	.793651	.793651	1.260000	1
2	1.587600	2.260000	.442478	.629882	1.423533	.702478	2
3	2.000376	3.847600	.259902	.499906	1.923439	.519902	3
4	2.520474	5.847976	.170999	.396751	2.320190	.430999	4
5	3.175797	8.368450	.119496	.314882	2.635072	.379496	5
6	4.001504	11.544247	.086623	.249906	2.884978	.346623	6
7	5.041895	15.545751	.064326	.198338	3.083316	.324326	7
8	6.352788	20.587646	.048573	.157411	3.240727	.308573	8
9	8.004513	26.940434	.037119	.124930	3.365657	.297119	9
10	10.085686	34.944947	.028616	.099150	3.464807	.288616	10
11	12.707964	45.030633	.022207	.078691	3.543498	.282207	11
12	16.012035	57.738591	.017319	.062453	3.605951	.277319	12
13	20.175164	73.750632	.013559	.049566	3.655517	.273559	13
14	25.420706	93.925796	.010647	.039338	3.694855	.270647	14
15	32.030090	119.346502	.008379	.031221	3.726076	.268379	15
16	40.357913	151.376592	.006606	.024778	3.750854	.266606	16
17	50.850971	191.734505	.005216	.019665	3.770519	.265216	17
18	64.072223	242.585476	.004122	.015607	3.786126	.264122	18
19	80.731001	306.657699	.003261	.012387	3.798513	.263261	19
20	101.721061	387.388700	.002581	.009831	3.808344	.262581	20
21	128.168537	489.109761	.002045	.007802	3.816146	.262045	21
22	161.492356	617.278298	.001620	.006192	3.822338	.261620	22
23	203.480369	778.770654	.001284	.004914	3.827252	.261284	23
24	256.385265	982.251023	.001018	.003900	3.831152	.261018	24
25	323.045434	1238.636288	.000807	.003096	3.834248	.260807	25

ANNUAL COMPOUND INTEREST TABLE

27%

EFFECTIVE RATE = 27% BASE = 1.27

YEARS	1 AMOUNT OF I AT COMPOUND INTEREST $S^n = (1+i)^n$	2 ACCUMULATION OF I PER PERIOD $S_{\overline{n}\rvert} = \frac{S^n - 1}{i}$	3 SINKING FUND FACTOR $1/S_{\overline{n}\rvert} = \frac{i}{S^n - 1}$	4 PRES. VALUE REVERSION OF I $V^n = \frac{1}{S^n}$	5 PRESENT VALUE ORD. ANNUITY 1 PER PERIOD $a_{\overline{n}\rvert} = \frac{1-V^n}{i}$	6 INSTALMENT TO AMORTIZE I $1/a_{\overline{n}\rvert} = \frac{i}{1-V^n}$	n YEARS
1	1.270000	1.000000	1.000000	.787402	.787402	1.270000	1
2	1.612900	2.270000	.440529	.620001	1.407403	.710529	2
3	2.048383	3.882900	.257539	.488190	1.895593	.527539	3
4	2.601446	5.931283	.168598	.384402	2.279995	.438598	4
5	3.303837	8.532729	.117196	.302678	2.582673	.387196	5
6	4.195873	11.836566	.084484	.238329	2.821002	.354484	6
7	5.328758	16.032439	.062374	.187661	3.008663	.332374	7
8	6.767523	21.361197	.046814	.147765	3.156428	.316814	8
9	8.594754	28.128720	.035551	.116350	3.272778	.305551	9
10	10.915338	36.723474	.027231	.091614	3.364392	.297231	10
11	13.862479	47.638812	.020991	.072137	3.436529	.290991	11
12	17.605349	61.501291	.016260	.056801	3.493330	.286260	12
13	22.358793	79.106640	.012641	.044725	3.538055	.282641	13
14	28.395667	101.465433	.009856	.035217	3.573272	.279856	14
15	36.062498	129.861100	.007701	.027730	3.601002	.277701	15
16	45.799372	165.923598	.006027	.021834	3.622836	.276027	16
17	58.165203	211.722970	.004723	.017192	3.640028	.274723	17
18	73.869808	269.888173	.003705	.013537	3.653565	.273705	18
19	93.814656	343.757981	.002909	.010659	3.664224	.272909	19
20	119.144613	437.572637	.002285	.008393	3.672617	.272285	20
21	151.313658	556.717250	.001796	.006609	3.679226	.271796	21
22	192.168346	708.030908	.001412	.005204	3.684430	.271412	22
23	244.053799	900.199254	.001111	.004097	3.688527	.271111	23
24	309.948331	1144.253053	.000874	.003226	3.691753	.270874	24
25	393.634380	1454.201384	.000688	.002540	3.694296	.270688	25

ANNUAL COMPOUND INTEREST TABLE

28%

EFFECTIVE RATE = 28% BASE = 1.28

YEARS	1 AMOUNT OF I AT COMPOUND INTEREST $S^n = (1+i)^n$	2 ACCUMULATION OF I PER PERIOD $S_{\overline{n}\|} = \frac{S^n - 1}{i}$	3 SINKING FUND FACTOR $1/S_{\overline{n}\|} = \frac{i}{S^n - 1}$	4 PRES. VALUE REVERSION OF I $V^n = \frac{1}{S^n}$	5 PRESENT VALUE ORD. ANNUITY 1 PER PERIOD $a_{\overline{n}\|} = \frac{1-V^n}{i}$	6 INSTALMENT TO AMORTIZE I $1/a_{\overline{n}\|} = \frac{i}{1-V^n}$	n YEARS
1	1.280000	1.000000	1.000000	.781250	.781250	1.280000	1
2	1.638400	2.280000	.438596	.610352	1.391602	.718596	2
3	2.097152	3.918400	.255206	.476837	1.868439	.535206	3
4	2.684355	6.015552	.166236	.372529	2.240968	.446236	4
5	3.435974	8.699907	.114944	.291038	2.532006	.394944	5
6	4.398047	12.135881	.082400	.227374	2.759380	.362400	6
7	5.629499	16.533928	.060482	.177636	2.937016	.340482	7
8	7.205759	22.163427	.045119	.138778	3.075794	.325119	8
9	9.223372	29.369186	.034049	.108420	3.184214	.314049	9
10	11.805916	38.592558	.025912	.084703	3.268917	.305912	10
11	15.111573	50.398474	.019842	.066174	3.335091	.299842	11
12	19.342813	65.510047	.015265	.051699	3.386790	.295265	12
13	24.758801	84.852860	.011785	.040390	3.427180	.291785	13
14	31.691265	109.611661	.009123	.031554	3.458734	.289123	14
15	40.564819	141.302926	.007077	.024652	3.483386	.287077	15
16	51.922968	181.867745	.005499	.019259	3.502645	.285499	16
17	66.461400	233.790713	.004277	.015046	3.517691	.284277	17
18	85.070592	300.252113	.003331	.011755	3.529446	.283331	18
19	108.890357	385.322705	.002595	.009184	3.538630	.282595	19
20	139.379657	494.213062	.002023	.007175	3.545805	.282023	20
21	178.405961	633.592719	.001578	.005605	3.551410	.281578	21
22	228.359631	811.998680	.001232	.004379	3.555789	.281232	22
23	292.300327	1040.358311	.000961	.003421	3.559210	.280961	23
24	374.144419	1332.658638	.000750	.002673	3.561883	.280750	24
25	478.904856	1706.803057	.000586	.002088	3.563971	.280586	25

EFFECTIVE RATE = 29% BASE = 1.29

YEARS	1 AMOUNT OF I AT COMPOUND INTEREST $S^n = (1+i)^n$	2 ACCUMULATION OF I PER PERIOD $S_{\overline{n}\vert} = \frac{S^n - 1}{i}$	3 SINKING FUND FACTOR $1/S_{\overline{n}\vert} = \frac{i}{S^n - 1}$	4 PRES. VALUE REVERSION OF I $V^n = \frac{1}{S^n}$	5 PRESENT VALUE ORD. ANNUITY 1 PER PERIOD $a_{\overline{n}\vert} = \frac{1-V^n}{i}$	6 INSTALMENT TO AMORTIZE I $1/a_{\overline{n}\vert} = \frac{i}{1-V^n}$	n YEARS
1	1.290000	1.000000	1.000000	.775194	.775194	1.290000	1
2	1.664100	2.290000	.436681	.600925	1.376119	.726681	2
3	2.146689	3.954100	.252902	.465834	1.841953	.542902	3
4	2.769229	6.100789	.163913	.361111	2.203064	.453913	4
5	3.572305	8.870018	.112739	.279931	2.482995	.402739	5
6	4.608274	12.442323	.080371	.217001	2.699996	.370371	6
7	5.944673	17.050597	.058649	.168218	2.868214	.348649	7
8	7.668628	22.995270	.043487	.130401	2.998615	.333487	8
9	9.892530	30.663898	.032612	.101086	3.099701	.322612	9
10	12.761364	40.556428	.024657	.078362	3.178063	.314657	10
11	16.462160	53.317792	.018755	.060745	3.238808	.308755	11
12	21.236186	69.779952	.014331	.047089	3.285897	.304331	12
13	27.394680	91.016138	.010987	.036503	3.322400	.300987	13
14	35.339137	118.410818	.008445	.028297	3.350697	.298445	14
15	45.587487	153.749955	.006405	.021936	3.372633	.296504	15
16	58.807858	199.337442	.005017	.017005	3.389638	.295017	16
17	75.862137	258.145300	.003874	.013182	3.402820	.293874	17
18	97.862157	334.007437	.002994	.010218	3.413038	.292994	18
19	126.242183	431.869594	.002316	.007921	3.420959	.292316	19
20	162.852416	558.111777	.001792	.006141	3.427100	.291792	20
21	210.079616	720.964193	.001387	.004760	3.431860	.291387	21
22	271.002705	931.043809	.001074	.003690	3.435550	.291074	22
23	349.593490	1202.046514	.000832	.002861	3.438411	.290832	23
24	450.975602	1551.640004	.000644	.002218	3.440629	.290644	24
25	581.758526	2002.615606	.000499	.001719	3.442348	.290499	25

ANNUAL COMPOUND INTEREST TABLE

EFFECTIVE RATE = 30% BASE = 1.30

YEARS	1 AMOUNT OF I AT COMPOUND INTEREST $S^n = (1+i)^n$	2 ACCUMULATION OF I PER PERIOD $S_{\overline{n}\rvert} = \frac{S^n - 1}{i}$	3 SINKING FUND FACTOR $1/S_{\overline{n}\rvert} = \frac{i}{S^n - 1}$	4 PRES. VALUE REVERSION OF I $V^n = \frac{1}{S^n}$	5 PRESENT VALUE ORD. ANNUITY 1 PER PERIOD $a_{\overline{n}\rvert} = \frac{1-V^n}{i}$	6 INSTALMENT TO AMORTIZE I $1/a_{\overline{n}\rvert} = \frac{i}{1-V^n}$	n YEARS
1	1.300000	1.000000	1.000000	.769231	.769231	1.300000	1
2	1.690000	2.300000	.434783	.591716	1.360941	.734783	2
3	2.197000	3.990000	.250627	.455166	1.816113	.550627	3
4	2.856100	6.187000	.161629	.350128	2.166241	.461629	4
5	3.712930	9.043100	.110582	.269329	2.435570	.410582	5
6	4.826809	12.756030	.078394	.207176	2.642746	.378394	6
7	6.274852	17.582839	.056874	.159366	2.802112	.356874	7
8	8.157307	23.857691	.041915	.122589	2.924701	.341915	8
9	10.604499	32.014998	.031235	.094300	3.019001	.331235	9
10	13.785849	42.619497	.023463	.072538	3.091539	.323463	10
11	17.921160	56.405346	.017729	.055799	3.147338	.317729	11
12	23.298085	74.326506	.013454	.042922	3.190260	.313454	12
13	30.287510	97.622591	.010244	.033017	3.223277	.310244	13
14	39.373763	127.910101	.007818	.025398	3.248675	.307818	14
15	51.185892	167.283864	.005978	.019537	3.268212	.305978	15
16	66.541660	218.469756	.004577	.015028	3.283240	.304577	16
17	86.504158	285.011416	.003509	.011560	3.294800	.303509	17
18	112.455405	371.515574	.002692	.008892	3.303692	.302692	18
19	146.192026	483.970979	.002066	.006840	3.310532	.302066	19
20	190.049634	630.163005	.001587	.005262	3.315794	.301587	20
21	247.064524	820.212639	.001219	.004048	3.319842	.301219	21
22	321.183882	1067.277163	.000937	.003113	3.322955	.300937	22
23	417.539046	1388.461054	.000720	.002395	3.325350	.300720	23
24	542.800760	1806.000091	.000554	.001842	3.327192	.300554	24
25	705.640988	2348.800851	.000426	.001417	3.328609	.300426	25

ANNUAL CONSTANT TABLES

Computed using interest rates 3% through 12¾% by ¼% increments. Monthly compounding – 2 through 40 years.

To find desired constant:

1. Find interest rate at top of table.
2. Find appropriate year in 1st column.
3. To convert to a monthly factor divide selected factor by 12.

Each of the table constants is the product of the computed monthly constant to 12-place accuracy, multiplied by 12, and then rounded up to six-place accuracy.

Example: 9¼% at 25 years (300 months)

1. Monthly Constant = .008563818519
2. Multiplied by 12 = .1027658222
3. Printed Annual Constant = .102766

ANNUAL CONSTANTS

Year	3%	3¼%	3½%	3¾%	4%	4¼%	4½%	4¾%
2	.515775	.517103	.518433	.519765	.521099	.522435	.523774	.525114
3	.348975	.350298	.351625	.352955	.354288	.355624	.356963	.358305
4	.265612	.266940	.268272	.269608	.270949	.272293	.273642	.274995
5	.215624	.216960	.218301	.219647	.220998	.222355	.223716	.225083
6	.182324	.183669	.185021	.186378	.187742	.189112	.190488	.191871
7	.158560	.159915	.161278	.162648	.164026	.165410	.166802	.168201
8	.140755	.142122	.143497	.144880	.146271	.147671	.149079	.150495
9	.126923	.128302	.129689	.131086	.132492	.133907	.135331	.136765
10	.115873	.117263	.118663	.120073	.121494	.122925	.124366	.125817
11	.106845	.108247	.109660	.111084	.112520	.113967	.115425	.116894
12	.099334	.100748	.102174	.103613	.105063	.106526	.108001	.109488
13	.092991	.094417	.095856	.097308	.098774	.100253	.101745	.103249
14	.087563	.089002	.090454	.091921	.093401	.094896	.096405	.097928
15	.082870	.084320	.085786	.087267	.088763	.090273	.091799	.093340
16	.078772	.080235	.081714	.083209	.084720	.086246	.087789	.089348
17	.075165	.076640	.078132	.079641	.081167	.082710	.084270	.085846
18	.071967	.073454	.074959	.076483	.078024	.079583	.081159	.082753
19	.069113	.070612	.072131	.073668	.075224	.076799	.078392	.080004
20	.066552	.068063	.069595	.071147	.072718	.074308	.075918	.077547
21	.064241	.065765	.067310	.068876	.070461	.072068	.073694	.075340
22	.062147	.063684	.065242	.066821	.068422	.070044	.071686	.073350
23	.060242	.061790	.063361	.064955	.066570	.068207	.069867	.071547
24	.058501	.060062	.061646	.063253	.064883	.066536	.068211	.069908
25	.056905	.058478	.060075	.061696	.063340	.065009	.066700	.068414
26	.055438	.057022	.058632	.060267	.061926	.063609	.065316	.067047
27	.054084	.055681	.057303	.058951	.060625	.062323	.064046	.065794
28	.052832	.054441	.056076	.057738	.059425	.061139	.062878	.064641
29	.051671	.053292	.054940	.056615	.058317	.060045	.061799	.063579
30	.050592	.052225	.053885	.055574	.057290	.059033	.060802	.062598
31	.049588	.051232	.052905	.054607	.056337	.058094	.059879	.061690
32	.048650	.050306	.051991	.053706	.055450	.057222	.059022	.060848
33	.047773	.049441	.051139	.052867	.054624	.056410	.058225	.060067
34	.046952	.048631	.050342	.052082	.053853	.055654	.057483	.059340
35	.046182	.047872	.049595	.051349	.053133	.054947	.056791	.058663
36	.045458	.047160	.048895	.050661	.052459	.054287	.056145	.058031
37	.044777	.046490	.048237	.050016	.051827	.053669	.055541	.057442
38	.044135	.045860	.047618	.049410	.051234	.053089	.054975	.056890
39	.043530	.045266	.047036	.048840	.050677	.052545	.054445	.056374
40	.042958	.044705	.046487	.048303	.050153	.052034	.053948	.055891

ANNUAL CONSTANTS

Year	5%	5¼%	5½%	5¾%	6%	6¼%	6½%	6¾%
2	.526457	.527801	.529148	.530497	.531847	.533200	.534555	.535912
3	.359651	.360999	.362351	.363705	.365063	.366424	.367788	.369155
4	.276352	.277713	.279078	.280447	.281820	.283198	.284579	.285965
5	.226455	.227832	.229214	.230601	.231994	.233391	.234794	.236202
6	.193259	.194654	.196055	.197462	.198875	.200294	.201719	.203151
7	.169607	.171020	.172441	.173868	.175303	.176744	.178193	.179649
8	.151919	.153351	.154792	.156240	.157697	.159162	.160635	.162116
9	.138207	.139659	.141120	.142590	.144069	.145557	.147054	.148560
10	.127279	.128750	.130232	.131723	.133225	.134736	.136258	.137789
11	.118374	.119865	.121367	.122880	.124404	.125939	.127485	.129042
12	.110987	.112498	.114021	.115555	.117102	.118660	.120231	.121812
13	.104767	.106298	.107841	.109398	.110967	.112549	.114143	.115750
14	.099464	.101015	.102579	.104157	.105748	.107353	.108972	.110603
15	.094895	.096465	.098050	.099649	.101263	.102891	.104533	.106189
16	.090922	.092511	.094116	.095737	.097373	.099023	.100689	.102370
17	.087439	.089048	.090673	.092315	.093972	.095645	.097335	.099039
18	.084364	.085992	.087638	.089300	.090979	.092675	.094387	.096116
19	.081633	.083281	.084946	.086629	.088330	.090048	.091783	.093535
20	.079195	.080861	.082546	.084250	.085972	.087711	.089469	.091244
21	.077006	.078692	.080396	.082120	.083863	.085624	.087404	.089201
22	.075034	.076738	.078462	.080206	.081969	.083751	.085553	.087373
23	.073249	.074971	.076715	.078478	.080262	.082065	.083888	.085730
24	.071628	.073369	.075131	.076914	.078717	.080541	.082385	.084249
25	.070151	.071910	.073690	.075493	.077316	.079160	.081025	.082909
26	.068801	.070578	.072377	.074198	.076041	.077905	.079790	.081695
27	.067565	.069359	.071176	.073016	.074878	.076762	.078667	.080592
28	.066429	.068241	.070076	.071934	.073815	.075718	.077642	.079587
29	.065383	.067212	.069065	.070941	.072841	.074762	.076706	.078670
30	.064419	.066264	.068135	.070029	.071946	.073886	.075848	.077832
31	.063527	.065389	.067277	.069188	.071123	.073081	.075062	.077064
32	.062701	.064580	.066484	.068413	.070366	.072341	.074340	.076360
33	.061936	.063831	.065751	.067697	.069666	.071659	.073675	.075713
34	.061224	.063135	.065072	.067034	.069020	.071030	.073063	.075118
35	.060563	.062489	.064442	.066420	.068423	.070449	.072499	.074570
36	.059946	.061888	.063857	.065851	.067869	.069912	.071977	.074065
37	.059371	.061328	.063312	.065322	.067356	.069414	.071496	.073599
38	.058835	.060807	.062805	.064830	.066880	.068953	.071050	.073169
39	.058333	.060320	.062333	.064373	.066437	.068526	.070637	.072771
40	.057864	.059864	.061892	.063947	.066026	.068129	.070255	.072403

ANNUAL CONSTANTS

Year	7%	7¼%	7½%	7¾%	8%	8¼%	8½%	8¾%
2	.537271	.538632	.539995	.541360	.542727	.544097	.545468	.546841
3	.370525	.371898	.373275	.374654	.376036	.377422	.378810	.380202
4	.287355	.288749	.290147	.291549	.292955	.294365	.295780	.297198
5	.237614	.239032	.240455	.241884	.243317	.244755	.246198	.247647
6	.204588	.206032	.207481	.208937	.210399	.211867	.213341	.214821
7	.181112	.182582	.184059	.185543	.187035	.188533	.190038	.191550
8	.163605	.165102	.166606	.168119	.169640	.171169	.172706	.174250
9	.150075	.151599	.153132	.154674	.156225	.157784	.159352	.160929
10	.139330	.140881	.142442	.144013	.145593	.147183	.148783	.150392
11	.130609	.132187	.133776	.135375	.136985	.138606	.140237	.141878
12	.123406	.125011	.126627	.128255	.129894	.131545	.133207	.134880
13	.117369	.119001	.120644	.122301	.123969	.125649	.127341	.129046
14	.112248	.113906	.115577	.117261	.118958	.120668	.122390	.124125
15	.107859	.109544	.111241	.112953	.114678	.116417	.118169	.119934
16	.104065	.105775	.107499	.109238	.110991	.112758	.114539	.116334
17	.100759	.102495	.104245	.106011	.107791	.109586	.111395	.113219
18	.097860	.099621	.101397	.103188	.104996	.106818	.108655	.110507
19	.095303	.097088	.098889	.100707	.102540	.104389	.106253	.108133
20	.093036	.094845	.096671	.098514	.100373	.102248	.104139	.106045
21	.091017	.092850	.094700	.096567	.098451	.100352	.102269	.104201
22	.089211	.091067	.092941	.094833	.096741	.098667	.100609	.102567
23	.087590	.089469	.091367	.093282	.095214	.097164	.099130	.101113
24	.086131	.088033	.089953	.091891	.093846	.095820	.097810	.099817
25	.084814	.086737	.088679	.090639	.092618	.094614	.096627	.098657
26	.083621	.085565	.087529	.089511	.091512	.093530	.095566	.097618
27	.082538	.084503	.086488	.088492	.090514	.092553	.094611	.096685
28	.081553	.083539	.085544	.087568	.089611	.091672	.093750	.095845
29	.080656	.082661	.084686	.086731	.088793	.090874	.092972	.095088
30	.079836	.081861	.083906	.085969	.088052	.090152	.092270	.094404
31	.079087	.081131	.083194	.085277	.087378	.089497	.091633	.093786
32	.078401	.080463	.082544	.084645	.086765	.088902	.091056	.093227
33	.077772	.079851	.081951	.084069	.086206	.088361	.090532	.092720
34	.077194	.079291	.081407	.083543	.085696	.087868	.090056	.092261
35	.076663	.078776	.080909	.083061	.085231	.087419	.089623	.091844
36	.076174	.078303	.080452	.082620	.084806	.087009	.089229	.091465
37	.075724	.077869	.080033	.082217	.084418	.086636	.088870	.091120
38	.075309	.077469	.079648	.081846	.084062	.086294	.088543	.090806
39	.074926	.077100	.079294	.081506	.083736	.085982	.088244	.090521
40	.074572	.076761	.078968	.081194	.083437	.085697	.087971	.090260

ANNUAL CONSTANTS

Year	9%	9¼%	9½%	9¾%	10%	10¼%	10½%	10¾%
2	.548217	.549594	.550974	.552355	.553739	.555125	.556512	.557902
3	.381597	.382995	.384395	.385799	.387206	.388616	.390029	.391445
4	.298621	.300047	.301478	.302912	.304351	.305794	.307241	.308691
5	.249100	.250559	.252022	.253491	.254965	.256443	.257927	.259415
6	.216306	.217798	.219296	.220800	.222310	.223826	.225348	.226875
7	.193069	.194595	.196128	.197668	.199214	.200768	.202328	.203895
8	.175802	.177363	.178931	.180506	.182090	.183681	.185280	.186887
9	.162515	.164109	.165712	.167324	.168944	.170573	.172210	.173856
10	.152011	.153639	.155277	.156924	.158581	.160247	.161922	.163606
11	.143530	.145192	.146864	.148546	.150239	.151941	.153654	.155376
12	.136564	.138259	.139965	.141682	.143409	.145148	.146897	.148657
13	.130762	.132489	.134229	.135980	.137742	.139515	.141300	.143096
14	.125873	.127632	.129404	.131188	.132984	.134792	.136612	.138444
15	.121712	.123503	.125307	.127124	.128953	.130794	.132648	.134514
16	.118142	.119964	.121799	.123647	.125508	.127382	.129269	.131168
17	.115056	.116908	.118774	.120653	.122545	.124451	.126370	.128301
18	.112373	.114254	.116149	.118058	.119981	.121918	.123867	.125830
19	.110028	.111937	.113861	.115799	.117751	.119717	.121697	.123690
20	.107967	.109904	.111856	.113822	.115803	.117797	.119806	.121827
21	.106150	.108113	.110092	.112086	.114094	.116116	.118152	.120202
22	.104541	.106531	.108535	.110555	.112590	.114638	.116701	.118777
23	.103112	.105127	.107157	.109202	.111262	.113336	.115424	.117526
24	.101840	.103879	.105933	.108002	.110087	.112185	.114298	.116424
25	.100704	.102766	.104844	.106936	.109044	.111166	.113302	.115451
26	.099687	.101772	.103872	.105987	.108117	.110261	.112420	.114591
27	.098775	.100881	.103003	.105140	.107292	.109457	.111636	.113829
28	.097956	.100083	.102226	.104383	.106555	.108741	.110940	.113153
29	.097219	.099366	.101529	.103706	.105897	.108102	.110321	.112552
30	.096555	.098721	.100903	.103099	.105309	.107532	.109769	.112018
31	.095955	.098140	.100340	.102554	.104781	.107022	.109276	.111542
32	.095414	.097616	.099833	.102064	.104309	.106566	.108836	.111118
33	.094924	.097143	.099377	.101624	.103884	.106158	.108443	.110740
34	.094481	.096716	.098965	.101228	.103503	.105791	.108091	.110402
35	.094079	.096329	.098593	.100871	.103161	.105463	.107776	.110100
36	.093715	.095980	.098258	.100549	.102853	.105168	.107494	.109831
37	.093384	.095663	.097955	.100259	.102575	.104903	.107241	.109590
38	.093084	.095376	.097680	.099997	.102325	.104665	.107014	.109374
39	.092811	.095115	.097432	.099761	.102100	.104451	.106811	.109181
40	.092563	.094879	.097207	.099547	.101898	.104258	.106628	.109008

ANNUAL CONSTANTS

Year	11%	11¼%	11½%	11¾%	12%	12¼%	12½%	12¾%
2	.559294	.560688	.562084	.563482	.564882	.566284	.567688	.569094
3	.392865	.394287	.395712	.397140	.398572	.400006	.401444	.402884
4	.310146	.311605	.313068	.314535	.316006	.317481	.318960	.320443
5	.260909	.262408	.263911	.265420	.266933	.268452	.269975	.271504
6	.228409	.229948	.231494	.233045	.234602	.236165	.237734	.239309
7	.205469	.207050	.208638	.210232	.211833	.213440	.215055	.216676
8	.188501	.190123	.191752	.193390	.195034	.196686	.198346	.200013
9	.175510	.177173	.178844	.180523	.182211	.183907	.185611	.187323
10	.165300	.167003	.168715	.170435	.172165	.173904	.175651	.177408
11	.157108	.158850	.160602	.162363	.164135	.165915	.167705	.169505
12	.150427	.152207	.153998	.155799	.157610	.159432	.161263	.163104
13	.144903	.146721	.148550	.150390	.152240	.154101	.155972	.157853
14	.140287	.142141	.144007	.145884	.147772	.149670	.151580	.153501
15	.136392	.138281	.140183	.142096	.144020	.145956	.147903	.149860
16	.133080	.135004	.136940	.138888	.140847	.142818	.144800	.146794
17	.130246	.132202	.134172	.136153	.138146	.140151	.142167	.144195
18	.127806	.129794	.131795	.133809	.135834	.137871	.139920	.141980
19	.125696	.127715	.129746	.131790	.133846	.135914	.137994	.140085
20	.123863	.125911	.127972	.130045	.132130	.134228	.136337	.138457
21	.122265	.124341	.126429	.128531	.130644	.132769	.134906	.137054
22	.120867	.122969	.125085	.127213	.129353	.131504	.133667	.135842
23	.119641	.121769	.123910	.126063	.128228	.130404	.132592	.134791
24	.118563	.120715	.122880	.125057	.127246	.129446	.131657	.133879
25	.117614	.119789	.121976	.124176	.126387	.128609	.130842	.133086
26	.116775	.118972	.121181	.123402	.125634	.127877	.130131	.132395
27	.116034	.118252	.120481	.122722	.124974	.127237	.129510	.131793
28	.115378	.117615	.119863	.122123	.124394	.126675	.128966	.131266
29	.114796	.117051	.119317	.121595	.123883	.126181	.128489	.130806
30	.114279	.116551	.118835	.121129	.123434	.125748	.128071	.130403
31	.113820	.116108	.118408	.120718	.123037	.125366	.127704	.130050
32	.113411	.115715	.118030	.120354	.122688	.125031	.127382	.129741
33	.113048	.115366	.117694	.120032	.122379	.124735	.127099	.129470
34	.112724	.115055	.117397	.119747	.122107	.124474	.126850	.129232
35	.112435	.114779	.117133	.119495	.121866	.124245	.126631	.129024
36	.112177	.114533	.116898	.119272	.121653	.124042	.126438	.128840
37	.111948	.114315	.116690	.119074	.121465	.123863	.126268	.128679
38	.111742	.114120	.116505	.118898	.121298	.123705	.126118	.128537
39	.111559	.113946	.116340	.118742	.121151	.123566	.125986	.128413
40	.111395	.113791	.116194	.118604	.121020	.123442	.125870	.128304

"C" TABLE "C"

MORTGAGE COEFFICIENTS FOR COMPUTING CAPITALIZATION RATES

Scope:—

Mortgage Amortization Terms; 10 years to 30 years by 5 year increments.

Mortgage Interest Rates:—3¼% to 12% by ¼% increments.

Income Projection Terms; 5 years to full amortization by 5 year increments.

Equity Yields; 4% to 30% by 1% increments.

To Find Desired Coefficient:—

1. Find Amortization Term in years.
2. Turn to page with desired mortgage interest rate and income projection term.
3. Find desired equity yield rate in *proper projection term bracket.* Move across on this line to column headed by desired mortgage interest rate.

$$Y - MC = r$$

Where:—

Y = Equity Yield

M = Ratio of Mortgage to Value

C = Coefficient from this table

r = Basic Capitalization Rate

Note:—Where coefficient is in italics or followed by a minus sign the formula is:

$$Y + MC = r$$

Mortgage Coefficients for Computing Capitalization Rates.

10 YEARS AMORTIZATION: 3¼% TO 4½%

	Interest Rate	3¼%	3½%	3¾%	4%	4¼%	4½%	$\frac{1}{s_{\overline{n}\rceil}}$
	Annual Requirement(f)	.11736	.11868	.12012	.12156	.12300	.12444	
	Installment f/12	.00978	.00989	.01001	.01013	.01025	.01037	
Projection	Balance (b)	.539955	.543483	.546411	.549388	.552417	.555497	+Dep.
	Equity Yield	Mortgage Coefficients						−App.
5 Years n = 5	4% .04	.0075	.0056	.0036	.0016	*.0004*	*.0024*	.1846
	5% .05	.0159	.0139	.0119	.0100	.0080	.0060	.1810
	6% .06	.0242	.0223	.0203	.0183	.0164	.0144	.1774
	7% .07	.0326	.0307	.0287	.0268	.0248	.0228	.1739
	8% .08	.0410	.0391	.0372	.0352	.0333	.0313	.1705
	9% .09	.0495	.0476	.0456	.0437	.0418	.0398	.1671
	10% .10	.0580	.0561	.0542	.0522	.0503	.0483	.1638
	11% .11	.0665	.0646	.0627	.0608	.0588	.0569	.1606
	12% .12	.0750	.0732	.0713	.0693	.0674	.0655	.1574
	13% .13	.0836	.0817	.0799	.0779	.0760	.0741	.1543
	14% .14	.0922	.0904	.0885	.0866	.0847	.0828	.1513
	15% .15	.1008	.0990	.0971	.0952	.0934	.0915	.1483
	16% .16	.1095	.1077	.1058	.1039	.1020	.1002	.1454
	17% .17	.1182	.1164	.1145	.1126	.1108	.1089	.1426
	18% .18	.1269	.1251	.1232	.1214	.1195	.1177	.1398
	19% .19	.1356	.1338	.1320	.1302	.1283	.1264	.1371
	20% .20	.1444	.1426	.1408	.1390	.1371	.1353	.1344
	21% .21	.1532	.1514	.1496	.1478	.1459	.1441	.1318
	22% .22	.1620	.1603	.1584	.1566	.1548	.1530	.1292
	23% .23	.1709	.1691	.1673	.1655	.1637	.1618	.1267
	24% .24	.1798	.1780	.1762	.1744	.1726	.1707	.1242
	25% .25	.1887	.1869	.1851	.1833	.1815	.1797	.1218
	26% .26	.1976	.1958	.1940	.1922	.1904	.1886	.1195
	27% .27	.2065	.2048	.2030	.2012	.1994	.1976	.1172
	28% .28	.2155	.2138	.2120	.2102	.2084	.2066	.1149
	29% .29	.2245	.2227	.2210	.2192	.2174	.2156	.1127
	30% .30	.2335	.2318	.2300	.2282	.2265	.2247	.1106
	Balance(b)	none	none	none	none	none	none	+Dep.
	Equity Yield	Mortgage Coefficients						−App.
10 Years n = 10	4% .04	.0059	.0046	.0031	.0017	.0003	*.0012*	.0833
	5% .05	.0121	.0108	.0094	.0079	.0065	.0050	.0795
	6% .06	.0185	.0172	.0157	.0143	.0128	.0114	.0759
	7% .07	.0250	.0237	.0222	.0208	.0194	.0179	.0724
	8% .08	.0316	.0303	.0289	.0274	.0260	.0246	.0690
	9% .09	.0384	.0371	.0357	.0342	.0328	.0314	.0658
	10% .10	.0454	.0440	.0426	.0412	.0397	.0383	.0628
	11% .11	.0524	.0511	.0497	.0482	.0468	.0453	.0598
	12% .12	.0596	.0583	.0568	.0554	.0540	.0525	.0570
	13% .13	.0669	.0656	.0641	.0627	.0613	.0598	.0543
	14% .14	.0743	.0730	.0716	.0701	.0687	.0672	.0517
	15% .15	.0819	.0805	.0791	.0777	.0762	.0748	.0493
	16% .16	.0895	.0882	.0867	.0853	.0839	.0824	.0469
	17% .17	.0972	.0959	.0945	.0930	.0916	.0902	.0447
	18% .18	.1051	.1038	.1023	.1009	.0995	.0980	.0425
	19% .19	.1131	.1117	.1103	.1089	.1074	.1060	.0405
	20% .20	.1211	.1198	.1184	.1169	.1155	.1140	.0385
	21% .21	.1293	.1279	.1265	.1251	.1236	.1222	.0367
	22% .22	.1375	.1362	.1347	.1333	.1318	.1304	.0349
	23% .23	.1458	.1445	.1430	.1416	.1402	.1387	.0332
	24% .24	.1542	.1529	.1514	.1500	.1486	.1471	.0316
	25% .25	.1627	.1613	.1599	.1585	.1570	.1556	.0301
	26% .26	.1712	.1699	.1684	.1670	.1656	.1641	.0286
	27% .27	.1798	.1785	.1771	.1756	.1742	.1727	.0272
	28% .28	.1885	.1872	.1857	.1843	.1829	.1814	.0259
	29% .29	.1972	.1959	.1945	.1930	.1916	.1902	.0247
	30% .30	.2061	.2047	.2033	.2019	.2004	.1990	.0235

TABLE C

Mortgage Coefficients for Computing Capitalization Rates

10 YEARS AMORTIZATION: 4¾% TO 6%

Interest Rate / Annual Requirement (f) / Installment f/12		4¾% .12588 .01049	5% .12732 .01061	5¼% .12876 .01073	5½% .13032 .01086	5¾% .13176 .01098	6% .13332 .01111	$\frac{1}{s_{\overline{n}|}}$
Projection	Balance (b)	.558629	.561814	.565053	.567658	.571003	.573705	+ Dep.
	Equity Yield	Mortgage Coefficients						− App.
	4% .04	*.0044*	*.0064*	*.0085*	*.0105*	*.0126*	*.0146*	.1846
	5% .05	.0041	.0020	.0000	*.0021*	*.0041*	*.0062*	.1810
	6% .06	.0124	.0104	.0084	.0064	.0043	.0023	.1774
	7% .07	.0208	.0188	.0168	.0148	.0128	.0108	.1739
	8% .08	.0293	.0273	.0254	.0233	.0213	.0193	.1705
5 Years n = 5	9% .09	.0378	.0359	.0339	.0319	.0299	.0279	.1671
	10% .10	.0464	.0444	.0425	.0405	.0385	.0365	.1638
	11% .11	.0550	.0530	.0511	.0491	.0471	.0451	.1606
	12% .12	.0636	.0616	.0597	.0577	.0557	.0538	.1574
	13% .13	.0722	.0703	.0683	.0664	.0644	.0624	.1543
	14% .14	.0809	.0789	.0770	.0751	.0731	.0711	.1513
	15% .15	.0896	.0876	.0857	.0838	.0818	.0799	.1483
	16% .16	.0983	.0964	.0944	.0925	.0906	.0886	.1454
	17% .17	.1070	.1051	.1032	.1013	.0994	.0974	.1426
	18% .18	.1158	.1139	.1120	.1101	.1082	.1062	.1398
	19% .19	.1246	.1227	.1208	.1189	.1170	.1151	.1371
	20% .20	.1334	.1315	.1296	.1277	.1258	.1239	.1344
	21% .21	.1422	.1404	.1385	.1366	.1347	.1328	.1318
	22% .22	.1511	.1493	.1474	.1455	.1436	.1417	.1292
	23% .23	.1600	.1582	.1563	.1544	.1526	.1507	.1267
	24% .24	.1689	.1671	.1652	.1634	.1615	.1596	.1242
	25% .25	.1779	.1760	.1742	.1723	.1705	.1686	.1218
	26% .26	.1868	.1850	.1832	.1813	.1795	.1776	.1195
	27% .27	.1958	.1940	.1922	.1903	.1885	.1866	.1172
	28% .28	.2048	.2030	.2012	.1993	.1975	.1956	.1149
	29% .29	.2138	.2120	.2102	.2084	.2066	.2047	.1127
	30% .30	.2229	.2211	.2193	.2174	.2156	.2138	.1106
	Balance (b)	none	none	none	none	none	none	+ Dep.
	Equity Yield	Mortgage Coefficients						− App.
	4% .04	*.0026*	*.0040*	*.0055*	*.0070*	*.0085*	*.0100*	.0833
	5% .05	.0036	.0022	.0007	*.0008*	*.0023*	*.0039*	.0795
	6% .06	.0100	.0085	.0071	.0055	.0041	.0025	.0759
	7% .07	.0165	.0150	.0136	.0120	.0106	.0090	.0724
	8% .08	.0231	.0217	.0202	.0187	.0172	.0157	.0690
10 Years n = 10	9% .09	.0299	.0285	.0270	.0255	.0240	.0225	.0658
	10% .10	.0368	.0354	.0340	.0324	.0310	.0294	.0628
	11% .11	.0439	.0425	.0410	.0395	.0380	.0365	.0598
	12% .12	.0511	.0496	.0482	.0466	.0452	.0436	.0570
	13% .13	.0584	.0569	.0555	.0539	.0525	.0509	.0543
	14% .14	.0658	.0644	.0629	.0614	.0599	.0584	.0517
	15% .15	.0733	.0719	.0705	.0689	.0675	.0659	.0493
	16% .16	.0810	.0795	.0781	.0765	.0751	.0735	.0469
	17% .17	.0887	.0873	.0858	.0843	.0828	.0813	.0447
	18% .18	.0966	.0951	.0937	.0921	.0907	.0891	.0425
	19% .19	.1045	.1031	.1017	.1001	.0987	.0971	.0405
	20% .20	.1126	.1112	.1097	.1082	.1067	.1052	.0385
	21% .21	.1207	.1193	.1179	.1163	.1149	.1133	.0367
	22% .22	.1290	.1275	.1261	.1245	.1231	.1215	.0349
	23% .23	.1373	.1358	.1344	.1328	.1314	.1298	.0332
	24% .24	.1457	.1442	.1428	.1412	.1398	.1382	.0316
	25% .25	.1541	.1527	.1513	.1497	.1483	.1467	.0301
	26% .26	.1627	.1612	.1598	.1582	.1568	.1552	.0286
	27% .27	.1713	.1699	.1684	.1669	.1654	.1639	.0272
	28% .28	.1800	.1785	.1771	.1755	.1741	.1725	.0259
	29% .29	.1887	.1873	.1859	.1843	.1828	.1813	.0247
	30% .30	.1975	.1961	.1947	.1931	.1917	.1901	.0235

Mortgage Coefficients for Computing Capitalization Rates.

10 YEARS AMORTIZATION: 6¼% TO 7½%

		Interest Rate	6¼%	6½%	6¾%	7%	7¼%	7½%	$\frac{1}{s_{\overline{n}\rceil}}$
		Annual Requirement (f)	.134760	.136320	.137880	.139440	.141000	.142560	
		Installment f/12	.011230	.011360	.011490	.011620	.011750	.011880	
Projection		Balance (b)	.577157	.579961	.582813	.585715	.588668	.591672	+ Dep. − App.
	Equity	Yield	Mortgage Coefficients						
5 Years n = 5	4 %	.04	.016691−	.018769−	.020856−	.022951−	.025057−	.027171−	.184627
	5 %	.05	.008236−	.010303−	.012379−	.014464−	.016559−	.018662−	.180974
	6 %	.06	.000250	.001806−	.003872−	.005947−	.008031−	.010124−	.177396
	7 %	.07	.008768	.006720	.004664	.002600	.000526	.001555−	.173890
	8 %	.08	.017316	.015278	.013232	.011177	.009114	.007042	.170456
	9 %	.09	.025893	.023865	.021828	.019783	.017730	.015668	.167092
	10 %	.10	.034500	.032481	.030454	.028418	.026375	.024323	.163797
	11 %	.11	.043135	.041125	.039107	.037081	.035047	.033005	.160570
	12 %	.12	.051799	.049798	.047789	.045772	.043747	.041714	.157409
	13 %	.13	.060490	.058498	.056497	.054490	.052474	.050450	.154314
	14 %	.14	.069209	.067224	.065233	.063234	.061227	.059213	.151283
	15 %	.15	.077954	.075978	.073995	.072004	.070006	.068001	.148315
	16 %	.16	.086725	.084757	.082782	.080800	.078811	.076814	.145409
	17 %	.17	.095522	.093562	.091595	.089621	.087641	.085652	.142563
	18 %	.18	.104343	.102392	.100433	.098467	.096495	.094515	.139777
	19 %	.19	.113190	.111246	.109295	.107337	.105373	.103401	.137050
	20 %	.20	.122061	.120124	.118181	.116231	.114274	.112310	.134379
	21 %	.21	.130955	.129026	.127090	.125148	.123199	.121243	.131765
	22 %	.22	.139873	.137951	.136022	.134087	.132146	.130198	.129205
	23 %	.23	.148814	.146899	.144977	.143049	.141115	.139175	.126700
	24 %	.24	.157777	.155868	.153954	.152033	.150107	.148173	.124247
	25 %	.25	.166761	.164860	.162952	.161039	.159119	.157193	.121846
	26 %	.26	.175768	.173873	.171972	.170065	.168152	.166233	.119496
	27 %	.27	.184795	.182906	.181012	.179112	.177206	.175294	.117195
	28 %	.28	.193843	.191960	.190072	.188179	.186279	.184374	.114943
	29 %	.29	.202910	.201034	.199153	.197266	.195373	.193474	.112739
	30 %	.30	.211998	.210128	.208253	.206372	.204485	.202593	.110581
		Balance (b)	none	none	none	none	none	none	+ Dep. − App.
	Equity	Yield	Mortgage Coefficients						
10 Years n = 10	4 %	.04	.011441−	.012956−	.014481−	.016017−	.017564−	.019123−	.083290
	5 %	.05	.005229−	.006745−	.008272−	.009809−	.011357−	.012916−	.079504
	6 %	.06	.001133	.000385−	.001913−	.003451−	.005000−	.006559−	.075867
	7 %	.07	.007641	.006120	.004591	.003052	.001503	.000055−	.072377
	8 %	.08	.014292	.012769	.011238	.009698	.008149	.006590	.069029
	9 %	.09	.021081	.019557	.018025	.016484	.014934	.013375	.065820
	10 %	.10	.028006	.026480	.024946	.023404	.021854	.020295	.062745
	11 %	.11	.035061	.033533	.031998	.030456	.028905	.027345	.059801
	12 %	.12	.042243	.040714	.039177	.037634	.036083	.034523	.056984
	13 %	.13	.049547	.048017	.046479	.044935	.043383	.041824	.054289
	14 %	.14	.056970	.055438	.053900	.052355	.050803	.049243	.051713
	15 %	.15	.064508	.062975	.061435	.059890	.058337	.056778	.049252
	16 %	.16	.072156	.070622	.069081	.067535	.065982	.064423	.046901
	17 %	.17	.079911	.078375	.076834	.075287	.073734	.072174	.044656
	18 %	.18	.087768	.086231	.084689	.083141	.081588	.080028	.042514
	19 %	.19	.095724	.094186	.092643	.091095	.089541	.087982	.040471
	20 %	.20	.103775	.102236	.100692	.099143	.097589	.096030	.038522
	21 %	.21	.111917	.110377	.108832	.107283	.105728	.104169	.036665
	22 %	.22	.120146	.118605	.117060	.115510	.113955	.112395	.034894
	23 %	.23	.128459	.126917	.125371	.123821	.122266	.120706	.033208
	24 %	.24	.136852	.135309	.133763	.132212	.130657	.129097	.031602
	25 %	.25	.145322	.143778	.142231	.140680	.139124	.137565	.030072
	26 %	.26	.153865	.152321	.150773	.149221	.147666	.146106	.028616
	27 %	.27	.162479	.160934	.159385	.157833	.156277	.154718	.027230
	28 %	.28	.171160	.169614	.168065	.166512	.164956	.163397	.025911
	29 %	.29	.179905	.178358	.176808	.175256	.173699	.172140	.024657
	30 %	.30	.188711	.187163	.185613	.184060	.182504	.180944	.023463

Mortgage Coefficients for Computing Capitalization Rates.

10 YEARS AMORTIZATION: 7¾% TO 9%

TABLE C

Interest Rate			7¾%	8%	8¼%	8½%	8¾%	9%	$\frac{1}{s_{\overline{n}\rvert}}$
Annual Requirement (f)			.144120	.145680	.147240	.148800	.150480	.152040	
Installment f/12			.012010	.012140	.012270	.012400	.012540	.012670	
Projection	Balance (b)		.594728	.597836	.600998	.604214	.606735	.610057	+ Dep.
	Equity	Yield	Mortgage Coefficients						– App.
	4 %	.04	.029295-	.031429-	.033573-	.035727-	.037872-	.040045-	.184627
	5 %	.05	.020776-	.022898-	.025030-	.027172-	.029309-	.031470-	.180974
	6 %	.06	.012226-	.014337-	.016458-	.018589-	.020716-	.022865-	.177396
	7 %	.07	.003647-	.005747-	.007857-	.009976-	.012095-	.014232-	.173890
	8 %	.08	.004961	.002871	.000772	.001335-	.003445-	.005571-	.170456
	9 %	.09	.013597	.011518	.009430	.007332	.005231	.003116	.167092
	10 %	.10	.022262	.020193	.018115	.016028	.013935	.011831	.163797
5 Years n = 5	11 %	.11	.030954	.028895	.026827	.024751	.022666	.020573	.160570
	12 %	.12	.039673	.037624	.035566	.033500	.031423	.029340	.157409
	13 %	.13	.048419	.046379	.044331	.042275	.040206	.038133	.154314
	14 %	.14	.057190	.055160	.053122	.051075	.049014	.046951	.151283
	15 %	.15	.065988	.063967	.061938	.059901	.057847	.055794	.148315
	16 %	.16	.074810	.072798	.070778	.068750	.066704	.064661	.145409
	17 %	.17	.083657	.081653	.079643	.077624	.075585	.073551	.142563
	18 %	.18	.092528	.090533	.088531	.086522	.084489	.082465	.139777
	19 %	.19	.101422	.099436	.097443	.095442	.093416	.091401	.137050
	20 %	.20	.110340	.108362	.106377	.104385	.102366	.100360	.134379
	21 %	.21	.119280	.117311	.115334	.113350	.111338	.109340	.131765
	22 %	.22	.128243	.126281	.124313	.122337	.120332	.118342	.129205
	23 %	.23	.137228	.135274	.133313	.131346	.129346	.127365	.126700
	24 %	.24	.146234	.144287	.142335	.140375	.138382	.136409	.124247
	25 %	.25	.155261	.153322	.151377	.149425	.147437	.145473	.121846
	26 %	.26	.164308	.162377	.160439	.158494	.156513	.154556	.119496
	27 %	.27	.173376	.171451	.169521	.167584	.165608	.163659	.117195
	28 %	.28	.182463	.180546	.178622	.176693	.174723	.172781	.114943
	29 %	.29	.191570	.189659	.187743	.185820	.183856	.181921	.112739
	30 %	.30	.200695	.198791	.196882	.194966	.193007	.191080	.110581
	Balance (b)		none	none	none	none	none	none	+ Dep.
	Equity	Yield	Mortgage Coefficients						– App.
	4 %	.04	.020694-	.022278-	.023875-	.025486-	.027072-	.028710-	.083290
	5 %	.05	.014487-	.016070-	.017665-	.019274-	.020864-	.022498-	.079504
	6 %	.06	.008129-	.009711-	.011305-	.012911-	.014506-	.016136-	.075867
	7 %	.07	.001625-	.003206-	.004798-	.006403-	.008001-	.009628-	.072377
	8 %	.08	.005020	.003440	.001850	.000248	.001354-	.002978-	.069029
	9 %	.09	.011806	.010227	.008637	.007037	.005432	.003810	.065820
	10 %	.10	.018726	.017148	.015560	.013962	.012353	.010734	.062745
	11 %	.11	.025777	.024200	.022613	.021017	.019405	.017789	.059801
	12 %	.12	.032956	.031379	.029794	.028199	.026583	.024970	.056984
	13 %	.13	.040257	.038681	.037097	.035504	.033885	.032275	.054289
	14 %	.14	.047676	.046102	.044518	.042927	.041305	.039697	.051713
	15 %	.15	.055211	.053637	.052055	.050465	.048840	.047235	.049252
10 Years n = 10	16 %	.16	.062856	.061283	.059702	.058113	.056486	.054883	.046901
	17 %	.17	.070608	.069035	.067455	.065868	.064239	.062637	.044656
	18 %	.18	.078463	.076890	.075312	.073726	.072094	.070494	.042514
	19 %	.19	.086416	.084844	.083266	.081682	.080047	.078450	.040471
	20 %	.20	.094464	.092893	.091316	.089733	.088096	.086500	.038522
	21 %	.21	.102604	.101033	.099457	.097875	.096236	.094642	.036665
	22 %	.22	.110831	.109261	.107685	.106104	.104463	.102871	.034894
	23 %	.23	.119142	.117572	.115997	.114417	.112774	.111184	.033208
	24 %	.24	.127533	.125963	.124389	.122810	.121166	.119576	.031602
	25 %	.25	.136001	.134432	.132858	.131280	.129634	.128046	.030072
	26 %	.26	.144542	.142974	.141401	.139824	.138176	.136589	.028616
	27 %	.27	.153154	.151586	.150014	.148437	.146788	.145203	.027230
	28 %	.28	.161833	.160266	.158694	.157118	.155467	.153883	.025911
	29 %	.29	.170576	.169009	.167438	.165863	.164211	.162628	.024657
	30 %	.30	.179381	.177814	.176244	.174669	.173016	.171434	.023463

Mortgage Coefficients for Computing Capitalization Rates.

10 YEARS AMORTIZATION: 9¼% TO 10½%

Interest Rate Annual Requirement (f) Installment f/12			9¼% .153720 .012810	9½% .155280 .012940	9¾% .156960 .013080	10% .158640 .013220	10¼% .160320 .013360	10½% .172000 .013500	$\frac{1}{s_{\overline{n}\rvert}}$
Projection	Balance (b)		.612675	.616105	.618823	.621590	.624406	.627272	+ Dep. – App.
	Equity	Yield	Mortgage Coefficients						
5 Years n = 5	4 %	.04	.042209-	.044402-	.046584-	.048775-	.050975-	.053184-	.184627
	5 %	.05	.033624-	.035804-	.037976-	.040157-	.042347-	.044545-	.180974
	6 %	.06	.025010-	.027178-	.029340-	.031511-	.033691-	.035879-	.177396
	7 %	.07	.016367-	.018524-	.020677-	.022838-	.025007-	.027186-	.173890
	8 %	.08	.007698-	.009842-	.011986-	.014137-	.016297-	.018466-	.170456
	9 %	.09	.000998	.001134-	.003268-	.005410-	.007561-	.009720-	.167092
	10 %	.10	.009722	.007600	.005475	.003342	.001201	.000948-	.163797
	11 %	.11	.018472	.016362	.014245	.012121	.009989	.007848	.160570
	12 %	.12	.027248	.025148	.023040	.020925	.018802	.016670	.157409
	13 %	.13	.036049	.033960	.031861	.029754	.027639	.025517	.154314
	14 %	.14	.044875	.042796	.040705	.038607	.036501	.034387	.151283
	15 %	.15	.053726	.051657	.049574	.047483	.045386	.043281	.148315
	16 %	.16	.062600	.060541	.058466	.056384	.054294	.052198	.145409
	17 %	.17	.071498	.069449	.067381	.065307	.063226	.061137	.142563
	18 %	.18	.080419	.078379	.076319	.074253	.072179	.070099	.139777
	19 %	.19	.089362	.087332	.085280	.083221	.081155	.079082	.137050
	20 %	.20	.098328	.096307	.094262	.092210	.090152	.088086	.134379
	21 %	.21	.107315	.105303	.103265	.101221	.099170	.097112	.131765
	22 %	.22	.116324	.114321	.112290	.110252	.108208	.106158	.129205
	23 %	.23	.125354	.123359	.121335	.119304	.117267	.115224	.126700
	24 %	.24	.134404	.132418	.130400	.128376	.126346	.124310	.124247
	25 %	.25	.143474	.141496	.139485	.137467	.135444	.133415	.121846
	26 %	.26	.152563	.150594	.148589	.146578	.144562	.142539	.119496
	27 %	.27	.161672	.159710	.157712	.155707	.153697	.151682	.117195
	28 %	.28	.170800	.168846	.166853	.164855	.162852	.160842	.114943
	29 %	.29	.179946	.178000	.176013	.174021	.172024	.170021	.112739
	30 %	.30	.189110	.187171	.185191	.183205	.181213	.179216	.110581
	Balance (b)		none	none	none	none	none	none	+ Dep. – App.
	Equity	Yield	Mortgage Coefficients						
10 Years n = 10	4 %	.04	.030319-	.031985-	.033619-	.035265-	.036923-	.038594-	.083290
	5 %	.05	.024110-	.025771-	.027407-	.029055-	.030714-	.032386-	.079504
	6 %	.06	.017751-	.019408-	.021046-	.022695-	.024355-	.026028-	.075867
	7 %	.07	.011246-	.012898-	.014539-	.016189-	.017850-	.019523-	.072377
	8 %	.08	.004599-	.006247-	.007889-	.009540-	.011203-	.012875-	.069029
	9 %	.09	.002187	.000543	.001100-	.002753-	.004416-	.006039-	.065820
	10 %	.10	.009108	.007468	.005823	.004168	.002504	.000831	.062745
	11 %	.11	.016160	.014524	.012877	.011221	.009557	.007883	.059801
	12 %	.12	.023339	.021706	.020058	.018401	.016736	.015062	.056984
	13 %	.13	.030641	.029012	.027362	.025704	.024038	.022363	.054289
	14 %	.14	.038061	.036436	.034784	.033125	.031459	.029784	.051713
	15 %	.15	.045597	.043974	.042321	.040661	.038994	.037319	.049252
	16 %	.16	.053243	.051623	.049969	.048308	.046640	.044965	.046901
	17 %	.17	.060995	.059378	.057723	.056061	.054393	.052717	.044656
	18 %	.18	.068850	.067236	.065580	.063917	.062248	.060572	.042514
	19 %	.19	.076804	.075193	.073535	.071872	.070202	.068526	.040471
	20 %	.20	.084853	.083244	.081585	.079921	.078251	.076575	.038522
	21 %	.21	.092993	.091386	.089727	.088062	.086391	.084715	.036665
	22 %	.22	.101221	.099616	.097955	.096290	.094619	.092942	.034894
	23 %	.23	.109532	.107930	.106268	.104601	.102930	.101253	.033208
	24 %	.24	.117923	.116323	.114661	.112994	.111322	.109645	.031602
	25 %	.25	.126392	.124794	.123130	.121462	.119790	.118113	.030072
	26 %	.26	.134934	.133337	.131673	.130005	.128332	.126655	.028616
	27 %	.27	.143546	.141951	.140286	.138618	.136945	.135267	.027230
	28 %	.28	.152225	.150632	.148967	.147297	.145624	.143947	.025911
	29 %	.29	.160969	.159378	.157711	.156041	.154368	.152690	.024657
	30 %	.30	.169774	.168184	.166517	.164847	.163173	.161495	.023463

Mortgage Coefficients for Computing Capitalization Rates.

10 YEARS AMORTIZATION: 10¾% TO 12%

Interest Rate Annual Requirement (f) Installment f/12		10¾% .163680 .013640	11% .165360 .013780	11¼% .167040 .013920	11½% .168720 .014060	11¾% .170520 .014210	12% .172200 .014350	$\frac{1}{s_{\overline{n}|}}$
Projection	**Balance (b)**	.630189	.633156	.636176	.639248	.641562	.644736	+ Dep.
	Equity Yield	**Mortgage Coefficients**						– App.
	4 % .04	.055402–	.057630–	.059868–	.062115–	.064342–	.066608–	.184627
	5 % .05	.046753–	.048970–	.051197–	.053433–	.055651–	.057906–	.180974
	6 % .06	.038076–	.040283–	.042498–	.044723–	.046934–	.049177–	.177396
	7 % .07	.029373–	.031569–	.033774–	.035988–	.038191–	.040423–	.173890
	8 % .08	.020643–	.022829–	.025023–	.027227–	.029422–	.031643–	.170456
	9 % .09	.011887–	.014063–	.016247–	.018441–	.020627–	.022838–	.167092
	10 % .10	.003105–	.005271–	.007446–	.009629–	.011808–	.014008–	.163797
	11 % .11	.005700	.003544	.001379	.000793–	.002965–	.005155–	.160570
	12 % .12	.014531	.012384	.010229	.008065	.005901	.003721	.157409
	13 % .13	.023387	.021249	.019103	.016949	.014792	.012622	.154314
	14 % .14	.032266	.030137	.028000	.025855	.023705	.021545	.151283
	15 % .15	.041168	.039048	.036920	.034785	.032641	.030491	.148315
5 Years	16 % .16	.050093	.047982	.045863	.043736	.041600	.039458	.145409
n = 5	17 % .17	.059041	.056938	.054828	.052710	.050580	.048447	.142563
	18 % .18	.068011	.065916	.063814	.061705	.059581	.057457	.139777
	19 % .19	.077002	.074915	.072822	.070721	.068603	.066488	.137050
	20 % .20	.086015	.083936	.081850	.079757	.077646	.075540	.134379
	21 % .21	.095048	.092977	.090899	.088814	.086709	.084611	.131765
	22 % .22	.104101	.102038	.099968	.097891	.095792	.093702	.129205
	23 % .23	.113175	.111119	.109056	.106987	.104894	.102811	.126700
	24 % .24	.122268	.120219	.118164	.116102	.114015	.111940	.124247
	25 % .25	.131380	.129338	.127290	.125236	.123154	.121087	.121846
	26 % .26	.140511	.138476	.136435	.134388	.132311	.130252	.119496
	27 % .27	.149660	.147632	.145598	.143558	.141487	.139435	.117195
	28 % .28	.158827	.156806	.154779	.152746	.150680	.148635	.114943
	29 % .29	.168012	.165997	.163977	.161950	.159889	.157852	.112739
	30 % .30	.177214	.175206	.173192	.171172	.169116	.167085	.110581
	Balance (b)	none	none	none	none	none	none	+ Dep.
	Equity Yield	**Mortgage Coefficients**						– App.
	4 % .04	.040279–	.041978–	.043692–	.045420–	.047095–	.048853–	.083290
	5 % .05	.034071–	.035769–	.037481–	.039207–	.040888–	.042642–	.079504
	6 % .06	.027712–	.029409–	.031120–	.032844–	.034530–	.036281–	.075867
	7 % .07	.021207–	.022903–	.024613–	.026335–	.028026–	.029774–	.072377
	8 % .08	.014559–	.016255–	.017963–	.019683–	.021380–	.023124–	.069029
	9 % .09	.007773–	.009468–	.011174–	.012893–	.014594–	.016335–	.065820
	10 % .10	.000852–	.002546–	.004251–	.005968–	.007674–	.009412–	.062745
	11 % .11	.006199	.004506	.002802	.001087	.000622–	.002358–	.059801
	12 % .12	.013378	.011685	.009983	.008269	.006555	.004822	.056984
	13 % .13	.020680	.018988	.017286	.015575	.013856	.012125	.054289
	14 % .14	.028101	.026409	.024708	.022998	.021276	.019548	.051713
	15 % .15	.035636	.033945	.032245	.030537	.028810	.027084	.049252
10 Years	16 % .16	.043282	.041591	.039893	.038185	.036456	.034732	.046901
n = 10	17 % .17	.051035	.049345	.047647	.045941	.044208	.042486	.044656
	18 % .18	.058890	.057200	.055503	.053798	.052062	.050343	.042514
	19 % .19	.066844	.065155	.063458	.061755	.060016	.058298	.040471
	20 % .20	.074893	.073204	.071509	.069806	.068064	.066348	.038522
	21 % .21	.083033	.081344	.079650	.077948	.076203	.074489	.036665
	22 % .22	.091260	.089572	.087878	.086178	.084430	.082718	.034894
	23 % .23	.099572	.097884	.096191	.094491	.092741	.091030	.033208
	24 % .24	.107963	.106276	.104583	.102885	.101132	.099423	.031602
	25 % .25	.116432	.114745	.113053	.111355	.109600	.107892	.030072
	26 % .26	.124973	.123287	.121596	.119899	.118142	.116435	.028616
	27 % .27	.133586	.131900	.130209	.128513	.126754	.125048	.027230
	28 % .28	.142265	.140579	.138889	.137194	.135433	.133729	.025911
	29 % .29	.151009	.149323	.147633	.145939	.144176	.142473	.024657
	30 % .30	.159814	.158128	.156439	.154745	.152980	.151279	.023463

Mortgage Coefficients for Computing Capitalization Rates

15 YEARS AMORTIZATION: 3¼% TO 4½%

Interest Rate Annual Requirement (f) Installment f/12		3¼% .08436 .00703	3½% .08580 .00715	3¾% .08736 .00728	4% .08880 .00740	4¼% .09036 .00753	4½% .09180 .00765	$\frac{1}{s_{\overline{n}\rceil}}$
Projection	Balance (b)	.718855	.722860	.726265	.730385	.733896	.738133	+ Dep.
	Equity Yield	Mortgage Coefficients						– App.
	4% .04	.0075	.0053	.0032	.0010	.0012	.0035	.1846
	5% .05	.0165	.0143	.0122	.0100	.0078	.0056	.1810
	6% .06	.0255	.0233	.0212	.0190	.0168	.0146	.1774
	7% .07	.0345	.0324	.0302	.0281	.0259	.0237	.1739
	8% .08	.0435	.0414	.0393	.0371	.0350	.0328	.1705
5 Years n = 5	9% .09	.0526	.0505	.0484	.0462	.0441	.0419	.1671
	10% .10	.0617	.0596	.0575	.0553	.0532	.0511	.1638
	11% .11	.0708	.0687	.0666	.0645	.0623	.0602	.1606
	12% .12	.0799	.0778	.0757	.0736	.0715	.0694	.1574
	13% .13	.0890	.0869	.0849	.0828	.0807	.0786	.1543
	14% .14	.0981	.0961	.0940	.0920	.0899	.0878	.1513
	15% .15	.1073	.1053	.1032	.1012	.0991	.0970	.1483
	16% .16	.1165	.1145	.1124	.1104	.1083	.1062	.1454
	17% .17	.1257	.1237	.1216	.1196	.1175	.1155	.1426
	18% .18	.1349	.1329	.1309	.1288	.1268	.1248	.1398
	19% .19	.1441	.1421	.1401	.1381	.1361	.1340	.1371
	20% .20	.1534	.1514	.1494	.1474	.1454	.1433	.1344
	21% .21	.1626	.1607	.1587	.1567	.1547	.1527	.1318
	22% .22	.1719	.1700	.1680	.1660	.1640	.1620	.1292
	23% .23	.1812	.1793	.1773	.1753	.1733	.1713	.1267
	24% .24	.1905	.1886	.1866	.1847	.1827	.1807	.1242
	25% .25	.1998	.1979	.1959	.1940	.1920	.1901	.1218
	26% .26	.2092	.2073	.2053	.2034	.2014	.1995	.1195
	27% .27	.2185	.2166	.2147	.2128	.2108	.2088	.1172
	28% .28	.2279	.2260	.2241	.2222	.2202	.2183	.1149
	29% .29	.2373	.2354	.2335	.2316	.2296	.2277	.1127
	30% .30	.2467	.2448	.2429	.2410	.2390	.2371	.1106
	Balance (b)	.388175	.392803	.396174	.401184	.404911	.410328	+ Dep.
	Equity Yield	Mortgage Coefficients						– App.
	4% .04	.0066	.0047	.0029	.0011	.0008	.0027	.0833
	5% .05	.0143	.0124	.0106	.0088	.0069	.0051	.0795
	6% .06	.0220	.0202	.0184	.0166	.0148	.0129	.0759
	7% .07	.0299	.0281	.0263	.0245	.0227	.0209	.0724
	8% .08	.0378	.0361	.0343	.0325	.0307	.0289	.0690
10 Years n = 10	9% .09	.0459	.0441	.0424	.0406	.0388	.0370	.0658
	10% .10	.0540	.0523	.0505	.0487	.0470	.0452	.0628
	11% .11	.0622	.0605	.0587	.0570	.0552	.0534	.0598
	12% .12	.0705	.0688	.0670	.0653	.0635	.0618	.0570
	13% .13	.0788	.0771	.0754	.0737	.0719	.0702	.0543
	14% .14	.0873	.0856	.0838	.0821	.0804	.0787	.0517
	15% .15	.0957	.0941	.0924	.0907	.0889	.0872	.0493
	16% .16	.1043	.1026	.1009	.0992	.0975	.0958	.0469
	17% .17	.1129	.1113	.1096	.1079	.1062	.1045	.0447
	18% .18	.1216	.1200	.1183	.1166	.1149	.1132	.0425
	19% .19	.1304	.1287	.1270	.1254	.1237	.1220	.0405
	20% .20	.1392	.1376	.1359	.1342	.1325	.1309	.0385
	21% .21	.1480	.1464	.1447	.1431	.1414	.1398	.0367
	22% .22	.1569	.1553	.1537	.1521	.1504	.1487	.0349
	23% .23	.1659	.1643	.1627	.1610	.1594	.1577	.0332
	24% .24	.1749	.1733	.1717	.1701	.1684	.1668	.0316
	25% .25	.1840	.1824	.1808	.1792	.1775	.1759	.0301
	26% .26	.1931	.1915	.1899	.1883	.1866	.1850	.0286
	27% .27	.2023	.2007	.1990	.1975	.1958	.1942	.0272
	28% .28	.2115	.2099	.2082	.2067	.2050	.2034	.0259
	29% .29	.2207	.2191	.2175	.2159	.2143	.2127	.0247
	30% .30	.2299	.2284	.2268	.2252	.2236	.2220	.0235

Mortgage Coefficients for Computing Capitalization Rates

15 YEARS AMORTIZATION: 3¼% TO 4½%

Interest Rate Annual Requirement (f) Installment f/12		3¼% .08436 .00703	3½% .08580 .00715	3¾% .08736 .00728	4% .08880 .00740	4¼% .09036 .00753	4½% .09180 .00765	$\frac{1}{s_{\overline{n}\rvert}}$
Projection	Balance (b)	none	none	none	none	none	none	+ Dep.
	Equity Yield	Mortgage Coefficients						− App.
	4% .04	.0056	.0041	.0026	.0011	.0004	.0019	.0500
	5% .05	.0120	.0105	.0090	.0075	.0060	.0045	.0464
	6% .06	.0186	.0171	.0156	.0141	.0126	.0111	.0430
	7% .07	.0254	.0240	.0224	.0210	.0194	.0180	.0398
	8% .08	.0324	.0310	.0294	.0280	.0264	.0250	.0368
15 Years	9% .09	.0397	.0382	.0368	.0352	.0337	.0322	.0341
n = 15	10% .10	.0471	.0456	.0441	.0426	.0411	.0396	.0315
	11% .11	.0547	.0532	.0517	.0502	.0487	.0472	.0291
	12% .12	.0624	.0610	.0594	.0580	.0564	.0550	.0268
	13% .13	.0704	.0689	.0674	.0659	.0644	.0629	.0248
	14% .14	.0784	.0770	.0754	.0740	.0724	.0710	.0228
	15% .15	.0866	.0852	.0836	.0822	.0806	.0792	.0210
	16% .16	.0950	.0935	.0920	.0905	.0890	.0875	.0194
	17% .17	.1034	.1020	.1004	.0990	.0974	.0960	.0178
	18% .18	.1120	.1106	.1090	.1076	.1060	.1046	.0164
	19% .19	.1207	.1193	.1177	.1163	.1147	.1133	.0151
	20% .20	.1295	.1280	.1265	.1250	.1235	.1220	.0139

TABLE C

Mortgage Coefficients for Computing Capitalization Rates

15 YEARS AMORTIZATION: 4¾% TO 6%

	Interest Rate	4¾%	5%	5¼%	5½%	5¾%	6%	$\frac{1}{s_{\overline{n}\vert}}$
	Annual Requirement(f)	.09336	.09492	.09648	.09816	.09972	.10128	
	Installment f/12	.00778	.00791	.00804	.00818	.00831	.00844	
Projection	Balance (b)	.741755	.745431	.749161	.752259	.756097	.759991	+ Dep.
	Equity Yield	Mortgage Coefficients						− App.
	4% .04	*.0057*	*.0079*	*.0102*	*.0124*	*.0147*	*.0170*	.1846
	5% .05	.0034	.0012	*.0011*	*.0033*	*.0056*	*.0079*	.1810
	6% .06	.0125	.0103	.0080	.0058	.0036	.0013	.1774
	7% .07	.0216	.0194	.0172	.0149	.0127	.0105	.1739
	8% .08	.0306	.0285	.0263	.0241	.0219	.0197	.1705
	9% .09	.0398	.0376	.0355	.0333	.0311	.0288	.1671
5 Years n = 5	10% .10	.0490	.0468	.0446	.0424	.0403	.0381	.1638
	11% .11	.0581	.0560	.0538	.0516	.0495	.0473	.1606
	12% .12	.0673	.0652	.0630	.0609	.0587	.0565	.1574
	13% .13	.0765	.0744	.0722	.0701	.0679	.0658	.1543
	14% .14	.0857	.0836	.0815	.0793	.0772	.0750	.1513
	15% .15	.0950	.0929	.0907	.0886	.0865	.0843	.1483
	16% .16	.1042	.1021	.1000	.0978	.0957	.0936	.1454
	17% .17	.1134	.1113	.1092	.1071	.1050	.1029	.1426
	18% .18	.1227	.1206	.1185	.1164	.1143	.1122	.1398
	19% .19	.1320	.1299	.1279	.1258	.1237	.1216	.1371
	20% .20	.1413	.1392	.1372	.1351	.1330	.1309	.1344
	21% .21	.1506	.1486	.1465	.1444	.1424	.1403	.1318
	22% .22	.1600	.1579	.1559	.1538	.1518	.1497	.1292
	23% .23	.1693	.1673	.1653	.1632	.1611	.1591	.1267
	24% .24	.1787	.1767	.1746	.1726	.1705	.1685	.1242
	25% .25	.1881	.1861	.1840	.1820	.1800	.1779	.1218
	26% .26	.1975	.1955	.1935	.1914	.1894	.1874	.1195
	27% .27	.2069	.2049	.2029	.2008	.1988	.1968	.1172
	28% .28	.2163	.2143	.2123	.2103	.2083	.2063	.1149
	29% .29	.2257	.2237	.2218	.2197	.2177	.2157	.1127
	30% .30	.2352	.2332	.2312	.2292	.2272	.2252	.1106
	Balance (b)	.414432	.418726	.423213	.426304	.431174	.436255	+ Dep.
	Equity Yield	Mortgage Coefficients						− App.
	4% .04	*.0046*	*.0065*	*.0084*	*.0104*	*.0123*	*.0143*	.0833
	5% .05	.0032	.0013	*.0006*	*.0026*	*.0045*	*.0065*	.0795
	6% .06	.0111	.0092	.0073	.0054	.0034	.0015	.0759
	7% .07	.0190	.0172	.0153	.0134	.0115	.0095	.0724
	8% .08	.0271	.0252	.0233	.0215	.0196	.0176	.0690
	9% .09	.0352	.0333	.0315	.0296	.0277	.0258	.0658
10 Years n = 10	10% .10	.0434	.0416	.0397	.0378	.0360	.0341	.0628
	11% .11	.0517	.0499	.0480	.0462	.0443	.0424	.0598
	12% .12	.0600	.0582	.0564	.0545	.0527	.0508	.0570
	13% .13	.0684	.0666	.0648	.0630	.0611	.0593	.0543
	14% .14	.0769	.0751	.0733	.0715	.0697	.0678	.0517
	15% .15	.0855	.0837	.0819	.0801	.0783	.0765	.0493
	16% .16	.0941	.0923	.0905	.0887	.0869	.0851	.0469
	17% .17	.1027	.1010	.0992	.0974	.0956	.0939	.0447
	18% .18	.1115	.1098	.1080	.1062	.1044	.1026	.0425
	19% .19	.1203	.1186	.1168	.1150	.1133	.1115	.0405
	20% .20	.1292	.1274	.1257	.1239	.1222	.1204	.0385
	21% .21	.1381	.1364	.1346	.1328	.1311	.1293	.0367
	22% .22	.1470	.1453	.1436	.1418	.1401	.1384	.0349
	23% .23	.1560	.1543	.1526	.1509	.1491	.1474	.0332
	24% .24	.1651	.1634	.1617	.1599	.1582	.1565	.0316
	25% .25	.1742	.1725	.1708	.1691	.1673	.1656	.0301
	26% .26	.1834	.1817	.1800	.1782	.1765	.1748	.0286
	27% .27	.1925	.1909	.1892	.1874	.1857	.1840	.0272
	28% .28	.2018	.2001	.1984	.1967	.1950	.1933	.0259
	29% .29	.2110	.2094	.2077	.2059	.2043	.2026	.0247
	30% .30	.2203	.2187	.2170	.2153	.2136	.2119	.0235

TABLE C

Mortgage Coefficients for Computing Capitalization Rates

15 YEARS AMORTIZATION: 4¾% TO 6%

	Interest Rate Annual Requirement(f) Installment f/12	4¾% .09336 .00778	5% .09492 .00791	5¼% .09648 .00804	5½% .09816 .00818	5¾% .09972 .00831	6% .10128 .00844	$\frac{1}{s_{\overline{n}\rvert}}$
Projection	Balance (b)	none	none	none	none	none	none	+ Dep.
	Equity Yield			Mortgage Coefficients				– App.
	4% .04	*.0034*	*.0049*	*.0065*	*.0082*	*.0098*	*.0113*	.0500
	5% .05	.0030	.0014	*.0001*	*.0018*	*.0034*	*.0049*	.0464
	6% .06	.0096	.0080	.0065	.0048	.0032	.0017	.0430
	7% .07	.0164	.0148	.0133	.0116	.0100	.0085	.0398
	8% .08	.0234	.0219	.0203	.0186	.0171	.0155	.0368
	9% .09	.0307	.0291	.0275	.0259	.0243	.0227	.0341
15 Years	10% .10	.0381	.0365	.0350	.0333	.0317	.0302	.0315
n = 15	11% .11	.0457	.0441	.0426	.0409	.0393	.0378	.0291
	12% .12	.0534	.0519	.0503	.0486	.0471	.0455	.0268
	13% .13	.0614	.0598	.0582	.0566	.0550	.0534	.0248
	14% .14	.0694	.0679	.0663	.0646	.0631	.0615	.0228
	15% .15	.0776	.0761	.0745	.0728	.0713	.0697	.0210
	16% .16	.0860	.0844	.0828	.0812	.0796	.0780	.0194
	17% .17	.0944	.0929	.0913	.0896	.0881	.0865	.0178
	18% .18	.1030	.1014	.0999	.0982	.0966	.0951	.0164
	19% .19	.1117	.1101	.1086	.1069	.1053	.1038	.0151
	20% .20	.1205	.1189	.1174	.1157	.1141	.1126	.0139

Mortgage Coefficients for Computing Capitalization Rates.

15 YEARS AMORTIZATION: 6¼% TO 7½%

Interest Rate Annual Requirement (f) Installment f/12		6¼% .102960 .008580	6½% .104640 .008720	6¾% .106200 .008850	7% .107880 .008990	7¼% .109560 .009130	7½% .111360 .009280	$\frac{1}{s_{\overline{n}\vert}}$
Projection	Balance (b)	.763241	.766540	.770600	.774005	.777460	.780242	+ Dep. − App.
	Equity Yield	Mortgage Coefficients						
5 Years n = 5	4 % .04	.019247−	.021537−	.023846−	.026155−	.028473−	.030786−	.184627
	5 % .05	.010112−	.012389−	.014684−	.016980−	.019285−	.021589−	.180974
	6 % .06	.000959−	.003225−	.005505−	.007789−	.010082−	.012375−	.177396
	7 % .07	.008210	.005956	.003690	.001418	.000862−	.003146−	.173890
	8 % .08	.017397	.015154	.012902	.010642	.008373	.006099	.170456
	9 % .09	.026600	.024369	.022130	.019882	.017624	.015359	.167092
	10 % .10	.035820	.033600	.031375	.029137	.026891	.024635	.163797
	11 % .11	.045056	.042846	.040634	.038408	.036173	.033926	.160570
	12 % .12	.054308	.052108	.049909	.047693	.045469	.043231	.157409
	13 % .13	.063575	.061386	.059199	.056994	.054781	.052551	.154314
	14 % .14	.072857	.070678	.068504	.066309	.064106	.061885	.151283
	15 % .15	.082155	.079985	.077823	.075638	.073446	.071233	.148315
	16 % .16	.091466	.089307	.087156	.084981	.082799	.080594	.145409
	17 % .17	.100793	.098642	.096504	.094338	.092166	.089969	.142563
	18 % .18	.110133	.107992	.105864	.103709	.101546	.099357	.139777
	19 % .19	.119487	.117355	.115239	.113092	.110939	.108757	.137050
	20 % .20	.128855	.126732	.124626	.122489	.120344	.118170	.134379
	21 % .21	.138236	.136121	.134026	.131898	.129762	.127596	.131765
	22 % .22	.147630	.145524	.143439	.141319	.139193	.137033	.129205
	23 % .23	.157037	.154939	.152864	.150753	.148635	.146483	.126700
	24 % .24	.166456	.164366	.162302	.160199	.158090	.155944	.124247
	25 % .25	.175888	.173806	.171751	.169656	.167555	.165416	.121846
	26 % .26	.185331	.183257	.181212	.179125	.177032	.174900	.119496
	27 % .27	.194787	.192720	.190684	.188605	.186520	.184394	.117195
	28 % .28	.204253	.202194	.200168	.198096	.196019	.193899	.114943
	29 % .29	.213732	.211680	.209662	.207598	.205528	.203415	.112739
	30 % .30	.223221	.221176	.219167	.217110	.215048	.212941	.110581
	Balance (b)	.439892	.443708	.449415	.453628	.458038	.460871	+ Dep. − App.
	Equity Yield	Mortgage Coefficients						
10 Years n = 10	4 % .04	.016308−	.018305−	.020341−	.022372−	.024419−	.026455−	.083290
	5 % .05	.008428−	.010412−	.012426−	.014441−	.016471−	.018496−	.079504
	6 % .06	.000465−	.002435−	.004428−	.006427−	.008442−	.010457−	.075867
	7 % .07	.007579	.005623	.003649	.001664	.000334−	.002339−	.072377
	8 % .08	.015703	.013760	.011806	.009835	.007851	.005855	.069029
	9 % .09	.023906	.021975	.020039	.018082	.016111	.014125	.065820
	10 % .10	.032184	.030264	.028346	.026402	.024445	.022467	.062745
	11 % .11	.040535	.038627	.036725	.034793	.032850	.030880	.059801
	12 % .12	.048957	.047059	.045174	.043254	.041323	.039361	.056984
	13 % .13	.057447	.055560	.053690	.051782	.049862	.047909	.054289
	14 % .14	.066005	.064127	.062272	.060374	.058466	.056520	.051713
	15 % .15	.074626	.072758	.070917	.069029	.067132	.065193	.049252
	16 % .16	.083309	.081450	.079623	.077745	.075858	.073925	.046901
	17 % .17	.092052	.090202	.038387	.086519	.084642	.082715	.044656
	18 % .18	.100852	.099010	.097207	.095348	.093481	.091560	.042514
	19 % .19	.109708	.107873	.106082	.104232	.102373	.100459	.040471
	20 % .20	.118616	.116789	.115010	.113167	.111317	.109408	.038522
	21 % .21	.127576	.125756	.123987	.122152	.120311	.118407	.036665
	22 % .22	.136584	.134771	.133012	.131185	.129351	.127452	.034894
	23 % .23	.145640	.143833	.142084	.140264	.138437	.136543	.033208
	24 % .24	.154740	.152940	.151199	.149386	.147567	.145677	.031602
	25 % .25	.163883	.162089	.160357	.158550	.156738	.154852	.030072
	26 % .26	.173068	.171279	.169555	.167755	.165949	.164067	.028616
	27 % .27	.182292	.180508	.178792	.176997	.175197	.173320	.027230
	28 % .28	.191553	.189774	.188066	.186277	.184483	.182609	.025911
	29 % .29	.200850	.199076	.197375	.195591	.193803	.191933	.024657
	30 % .30	.210182	.208412	.206718	.204939	.203156	.201289	.023463

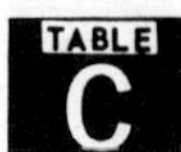

Mortgage Coefficients for Computing Capitalization Rates.

15 YEARS AMORTIZATION: 6¼% TO 7½%

Interest Rate Annual Requirement (f) Installment f/12			6¼% .102960 .008580	6½% .104640 .008720	6¾% .106200 .008850	7% .107880 .008990	7¼% .109560 .009130	7½% .111360 .009280	$\frac{1}{s_{\overline{n}|}}$
Projection	Balance (b)		none	none	none	none	none	none	+ Dep. – App.
	Equity	Yield	Mortgage Coefficients						
	4 %	.04	.012933-	.014563-	.016244-	.017911-	.019596-	.021255-	.049941
	5 %	.05	.006538-	.008172-	.009844-	.011512-	.013197-	.014866-	.046342
	6 %	.06	.000076	.001560-	.003225-	.004893-	.006578-	.008256-	.042962
	7 %	.07	.006902	.005262	.003605	.001936	.000252	.001435-	.039794
	8 %	.08	.013932	.012289	.010639	.008969	.007285	.005589	.036829
	9 %	.09	.021157	.019511	.017868	.016197	.014514	.012810	.034058
	10 %	.10	.028567	.026919	.025282	.023610	.021927	.020216	.031473
	11 %	.11	.036155	.034503	.032873	.031201	.029518	.027800	.029065
	12 %	.12	.043910	.042256	.040631	.038958	.037276	.035551	.026824
	13 %	.13	.051824	.050168	.048548	.046875	.045192	.043462	.024741
	14 %	.14	.059888	.058230	.056615	.054941	.053259	.051523	.022803
15 Years n = 15	15 %	.15	.068093	.066433	.064822	.063148	.061466	.059725	.021017
	16 %	.16	.076430	.074769	.073162	.071488	.069806	.068060	.019357
	17 %	.17	.084892	.083230	.081627	.079951	.078270	.076520	.017822
	18 %	.18	.093470	.091807	.090207	.088531	.086850	.085096	.016402
	19 %	.19	.102157	.100492	.098896	.097220	.095538	.093731	.015091
	20 %	.20	.110945	.109279	.107686	.106009	.104328	.102567	.013882
	21 %	.21	.119828	.118161	.116570	.114893	.113212	.111448	.012766
	22 %	.22	.128798	.127129	.125541	.123864	.122183	.120416	.011738
	23 %	.23	.137849	.136180	.134594	.132916	.131235	.129466	.010791
	24 %	.24	.146976	.145306	.143721	.142044	.140363	.138591	.009919
	25 %	.25	.156172	.154501	.152919	.151241	.149560	.147786	.009116
	26 %	.26	.165433	.163761	.162181	.160503	.158822	.157046	.008378
	27 %	.27	.174753	.173081	.171502	.169824	.168143	.166365	.007700
	28 %	.28	.184129	.182456	.180878	.179200	.177520	.175740	.007076
	29 %	.29	.193555	.191881	.190305	.188627	.186946	.185165	.006504
	30 %	.30	.203028	.201353	.199779	.198101	.196420	.194637	.005977

Mortgage Coefficients for Computing Capitalization Rates.

15 YEARS AMORTIZATION: 7¾% TO 9%

Interest Rate			7¾%	8%	8¼%	8½%	8¾%	9%	$\frac{1}{s_{\overline{n}\rvert}}$
Annual Requirement (f)			.113040	.114720	.116520	.118200	.120000	.121800	
Installment f/12			.009420	.009560	.009710	.009850	.010000	.010150	
Projection	Balance (b)		.783798	.787406	.790330	.794042	.797061	.800126	+ Dep. – App.
	Equity	Yield	Mortgage Coefficients						
5 Years n = 5	4 %	.04	.033123–	.035469–	.037809–	.040174–	.042531–	.044897–	.184627
	5 %	.05	.023912–	.026246–	.028575–	.030926–	.033273–	.035627–	.180974
	6 %	.06	.014686–	.017006–	.019325–	.021663–	.023999–	.026343–	.177396
	7 %	.07	.005444–	.007752–	.010060–	.012385–	.014710–	.017043–	.173890
	8 %	.08	.003812	.001517	.000780–	.003093–	.005407–	.007730–	.170456
	9 %	.09	.013085	.010802	.008514	.006213	.003909	.001597	.167092
	10 %	.10	.022373	.020102	.017823	.015535	.013240	.010938	.163797
	11 %	.11	.031675	.029416	.027146	.024870	.022585	.020293	.160570
	12 %	.12	.040992	.038744	.036484	.034219	.031944	.029662	.157409
	13 %	.13	.050323	.048086	.045835	.043582	.041316	.039043	.154314
	14 %	.14	.059667	.057441	.055199	.052957	.050701	.048437	.151283
	15 %	.15	.069026	.066810	.064577	.062346	.060098	.057844	.148315
	16 %	.16	.078397	.076193	.073967	.071748	.069509	.067263	.145409
	17 %	.17	.087782	.085588	.083371	.081162	.078931	.076694	.142563
	18 %	.18	.097180	.094995	.092787	.090588	.088366	.086137	.139777
	19 %	.19	.106590	.104415	.102215	.100026	.097812	.095592	137050
	20 %	.20	.116013	.113848	.111655	.109476	.107270	.105059	.134379
	21 %	.21	.125447	.123292	.121107	.118938	.116740	.114536	.131765
	22 %	.22	.134894	.132748	.130570	.128410	.126220	.124024	.129205
	23 %	.23	.144352	.142215	.140045	.137894	.135712	.133524	.126700
	24 %	.24	.153822	.151694	.149531	.147389	.145214	.143033	.124247
	25 %	.25	.163303	.161183	.159027	.156895	.154727	.152553	.121846
	26 %	.26	.172795	.170684	.168534	.166411	.164250	.162084	.119496
	27 %	.27	.182297	.180195	.178052	.175937	.173783	.171624	.117195
	28 %	.28	.191811	.189716	.187580	.185473	.183326	.181174	.114943
	29 %	.29	.201334	.199247	.197118	.195019	.192879	.190733	.112739
	30 %	.30	.210867	.208788	.206665	.204575	.202441	.200302	.110581
	Balance (b)		.465666	.470676	.474051	.479483	.483241	.487187	+ Dep. – App.
	Equity	Yield	Mortgage Coefficients						
10 Years n = 10	4 %	.04	.028534–	.030632–	.032713–	.034845–	.036958–	.039087–	.083290
	5 %	.05	.020558–	.022636–	.024704–	.026816–	.028915–	.031029–	.079504
	6 %	.06	.012501–	.014561–	.016617–	.018709–	.020794–	.022893–	.075867
	7 %	.07	.004366–	.006408–	.008453–	.010526–	.012598–	.014683–	.072377
	8 %	.08	.003844	.001818	.000214–	.002269–	.004328–	.006400–	.069029
	9 %	.09	.012129	.010120	.008097	.006060	.004013	.001953	.065820
	10 %	.10	.020486	.018492	.016480	.014459	.012424	.010376	.062745
	11 %	.11	.028913	.026934	.024932	.022927	.020902	.018866	.059801
	12 %	.12	.037408	.035443	.033450	.031461	.029447	.027422	.056984
	13 %	.13	.045968	.044016	.042033	.040058	.038054	.036040	.054289
	14 %	.14	.054592	.052653	.050678	.048717	.046723	.044719	.051713
	15 %	.15	.063277	.061350	.059384	.057436	.055451	.053457	.049252
	16 %	.16	.072020	.070105	.068147	.066212	.064236	.062251	.046901
	17 %	.17	.080821	.078917	.076967	.075044	.073076	.071100	.044656
	18 %	.18	.089677	.087784	.085840	.083929	.081969	.080002	.042514
	19 %	.19	.098585	.096702	.094765	.092865	.090913	.088954	.040471
	20 %	.20	.107544	.105671	.103740	.101851	.099906	.097954	.038522
	21 %	.21	.116551	.114687	.112764	.110884	.108947	.107002	.036665
	22 %	.22	.125605	.123750	.121832	.119963	.118032	.116094	.034894
	23 %	.23	.134704	.132858	.130945	.129085	.127160	.125229	.033208
	24 %	.24	.143846	.142007	.140101	.138249	.136330	.134405	.031602
	25 %	.25	.153028	.151198	.149296	.147453	.145540	.143621	.030072
	26 %	.26	.162250	.160427	.158530	.156695	.154787	.152874	.028616
	27 %	.27	.171510	.169693	.167801	.165973	.164071	.162164	.027230
	28 %	.28	.180805	.178995	.177103	.175287	.173390	.171487	.025911
	29 %	.29	.190135	.188331	.186448	.184634	.182741	.180844	.024657
	30 %	.30	.199497	.197699	.195820	.194013	.192124	.190232	.023463

Mortgage Coefficients for Computing Capitalization Rates.

15 YEARS AMORTIZATION: 7¾% TO 9%

TABLE C

Interest Rate / Annual Requirement (f) / Installment f/12			7¾% .113040 .009420	8% .114720 .009560	8¼% .116520 .009710	8½% .118200 .009850	8¾% .120000 .010000	9% .121800 .010150	$\frac{1}{s_{\overline{n}\rvert}}$
Projection	**Balance (b)**		. none	none	none	none	none	none	+ Dep. – App.
	Equity	**Yield**	**Mortgage Coefficients**						
	4 %	.04	.022976-	.024718-	.026427-	.028211-	.029957-	.031720-	.049941
	5 %	.05	.016584-	.018321-	.020036-	.021814-	.023563-	.025329-	.046342
	6 %	.06	.009971-	.011705-	.013426-	.015196-	.016949-	.018718-	.042962
	7 %	.07	.003147-	.004877-	.006604-	.008367-	.010124-	.011894-	.039794
	8 %	.08	.003879	.002153	.000421	.001335-	.003095-	.004868-	.036829
	9 %	.09	.011102	.009379	.007642	.005890	.004128	.002353	.034058
	10 %	.10	.018510	.016791	.015049	.013303	.011537	.009761	.031473
	11 %	.11	.026096	.024380	.022633	.020892	.019124	.017345	.029065
	12 %	.12	.033849	.032136	.030385	.028649	.026378	.025098	.026824
	13 %	.13	.041762	.040051	.038297	.036565	.034792	.033019	.024741
	14 %	.14	.049824	.048116	.046358	.044630	.042855	.041072	.022808
15 Years n = 15	15 %	.15	.058028	.056322	.054560	.052836	.051059	.049275	.021017
	16 %	.16	.066364	.064660	.062896	.061175	.059397	.057611	.019357
	17 %	.17	.074825	.073123	.071356	.069638	.067858	.066071	.017822
	18 %	.18	.083402	.081702	.079932	.078218	.076436	.074648	.016402
	19 %	.19	.092088	.090390	.088617	.086906	.085122	.083333	.015091
	20 %	.20	.100876	.099178	.097404	.095695	.093910	.092120	.013882
	21 %	.21	.109757	.108061	.106285	.104578	.102792	.101001	.012766
	22 %	.22	.118726	.117032	.115253	.113549	.111762	.109970	.011738
	23 %	.23	.127777	.126084	.124303	.122601	.120813	.119020	.010791
	24 %	.24	.136903	.135211	.133429	.131728	.129939	.128146	.009919
	25 %	.25	.146099	.144407	.142624	.140925	.139135	.137342	.009116
	26 %	.26	.155359	.153669	.151884	.150186	.148396	.146602	.008378
	27 %	.27	.164679	.162989	.161203	.159507	.157716	.155921	.007700
	28 %	.28	.174054	.172365	.170578	.168883	.167091	.165296	.007076
	29 %	.29	.183480	.181791	.180003	.178310	.176517	.174722	.006504
	30 %	.30	.192952	.191264	.189475	.187783	.185989	.184194	.005977

Mortgage Coefficients for Computing Capitalization Rates.

15 YEARS AMORTIZATION: 9¼% TO 10½%

Interest Rate Annual Requirement (f) Installment f/12			9¼% .123600 .010300	9½% .125400 .010450	9¾% .127200 .010600	10% .129000 .010750	10¼% .130800 .010900	10½% .132720 .011060	$\frac{1}{s_{\overline{n}\rvert}}$
Projection	Balance (b)		.803237	.806396	.809604	.812860	.816165	.818736	+ Dep. – App.
	Equity	Yield	Mortgage Coefficients						
	4 %	.04	.047272-	.049655-	.052047-	.054448-	.056859-	.059253-	.184627
	5 %	.05	.037990-	.040362-	.042743-	.045132-	.047530-	.049915-	.180974
	6 %	.06	.028695-	.031055-	.033424-	.035802-	.038188-	.040564-	.177396
	7 %	.07	.019384-	.021734-	.024091-	.026458-	.028832-	.031200-	.173890
	8 %	.08	.010060-	.012399-	.014745-	.017100-	.019464-	.021822-	.170456
	9 %	.09	.000722-	.003050-	.005386-	.007730-	.010082-	.012432-	.167092
	10 %	.10	.008629	.006311	.003986	.001652	.000688-	.003029-	.163797
	11 %	.11	.017994	.015686	.013371	.011049	.008718	.006385	.160570
	12 %	.12	.027372	.025075	.022770	.020457	.018137	.015812	.157409
	13 %	.13	.036763	.034475	.032180	.029878	.027568	.025251	.154314
	14 %	.14	.046166	.043888	.041603	.039311	.037011	.034702	.151283
	15 %	.15	.055582	.053314	.051038	.048755	.046465	.044164	.148315
5 Years n = 5	16 %	.16	.065011	.062751	.060485	.058211	.055931	.053637	.145409
	17 %	.17	.074451	.072200	.069943	.067679	.065408	.063121	.142563
	18 %	.18	.083903	.081661	.079413	.077157	.074895	.072616	.139777
	19 %	.19	.093366	.091133	.088893	.086647	.084394	.082122	.137050
	20 %	.20	.102840	.100616	.098385	.096147	.093903	.091638	.134379
	21 %	.21	.112326	.110110	.107887	.105658	.103422	.101164	.131765
	22 %	.22	.121822	.119614	.117400	.115179	.112952	.110700	.129205
	23 %	.23	.131329	.129129	.126923	.124710	.122491	.120246	.126700
	24 %	.24	.140847	.138654	.136456	.134251	.132040	.129801	.124247
	25 %	.25	.150374	.148189	.145999	.143802	.141599	.139366	.121846
	26 %	.26	.159912	.157734	.155551	.153362	.151167	.148940	.119496
	27 %	.27	.169459	.167289	.165113	.162931	.160744	.158523	.117195
	28 %	.28	.179016	.176853	.174684	.172510	.170330	.168115	.114943
	29 %	.29	.188582	.186426	.184265	.182097	.179925	.177715	.112739
	30 %	.30	.198158	.196008	.193854	.191694	.189528	.187324	.110581
	Balance (b)		.491325	.495662	.500204	.504957	.509929	.513017	+ Dep. – App.
	Equity	Yield	Mortgage Coefficients						
	4 %	.04	.041232-	.043393-	.045571-	.047767-	.049981-	.052158-	.083290
	5 %	.05	.033158-	.035302-	.037463-	.039641-	.041837-	.044002-	.079504
	6 %	.06	.025007-	.027136-	.029281-	.031442-	.033619-	.035773-	.075867
	7 %	.07	.016783-	.018897-	.021026-	.023170-	.025329-	.027473-	.072377
	8 %	.08	.008486-	.010585-	.012699-	.014827-	.016970-	.019103-	.069029
	9 %	.09	.000118-	.002204-	.004303-	.006416-	.008543-	.010666-	.065820
	10 %	.10	.008316	.006244	.004159	.002061	.000050-	.002164-	.062745
	11 %	.11	.016819	.014760	.012688	.010604	.008506	.006402	.059801
	12 %	.12	.025386	.023339	.021280	.019209	.017126	.015030	.056984
	13 %	.13	.034015	.031980	.029933	.027875	.025805	.023718	.054289
	14 %	.14	.042705	.040681	.038646	.036600	.034543	.032463	.051713
10 Years n = 10	15 %	.15	.051453	.049439	.047415	.045381	.043336	.041264	.049252
	16 %	.16	.060257	.058253	.056240	.054218	.052184	.050119	.046901
	17 %	.17	.069115	.067122	.065119	.063106	.061084	.059026	.044656
	18 %	.18	.078026	.076041	.074048	.072046	.070035	.067983	.042514
	19 %	.19	.086986	.085011	.083027	.081034	.079033	.076988	.040471
	20 %	.20	.095995	.094028	.092053	.090070	.088078	.086039	.038522
	21 %	.21	.105050	.103091	.101125	.099150	.097168	.095135	.036665
	22 %	.22	.114150	.112198	.110240	.108274	.106300	.104273	.034894
	23 %	.23	.123292	.121343	.119397	.117439	.115474	.113451	.033208
	24 %	.24	.132475	.130538	.128594	.126644	.124687	.122669	.031602
	25 %	.25	.141697	.139766	.137830	.135887	.133937	.131924	.030072
	26 %	.26	.150956	.149032	.147102	.145166	.143224	.141215	.028616
	27 %	.27	.160251	.158333	.156409	.154480	.152544	.150540	.027230
	28 %	.28	.169580	.167668	.165750	.163827	.161898	.159898	.025911
	29 %	.29	.178942	.177035	.175123	.173206	.171283	.169287	.024657
	30 %	.30	.188335	.186433	.184526	.182615	.180698	.178706	.023463

Mortgage Coefficients for Computing Capitalization Rates.

15 YEARS AMORTIZATION: 9¼% TO 10½%

Interest Rate Annual Requirement (f) Installment f/12			9¼% .123600 .010300	9½% .125400 .010450	9¾% .127200 .010600	10% .129000 .010750	10¼% .130800 .010900	10½% .132720 .011060	$\frac{1}{s_{\overline{n}\rvert}}$
Projection	**Balance (b)**		none	none	none	none	none	none	+ Dep. – App.
	Equity	Yield	Mortgage Coefficients						
	4 %	.04	.033502-	.035305-	.037129-	.038977-	.040848-	.042648-	.049941
	5 %	.05	.027112-	.028915-	.030738-	.032581-	.034448-	.036256-	.046342
	6 %	.06	.020502-	.022305-	.024126-	.025966-	.027828-	.029645-	.042962
	7 %	.07	.013680-	.015483-	.017302-	.019140-	.020997-	.022821-	.039794
	8 %	.08	.006655-	.008457-	.010275-	.012110-	.013962-	.015794-	.036829
	9 %	.09	.000565	.001236-	.003053-	.004885-	.006734-	.008572-	.034058
	10 %	.10	.007972	.006170	.004355	.002525	.000680	.001164-	.031473
	11 %	.11	.015556	.013754	.011940	.010112	.008271	.006421	.029065
	12 %	.12	.023308	.021506	.019693	.017868	.016029	.014174	.026824
	13 %	.13	.031219	.029417	.027605	.025782	.023946	.022086	.024741
15 Years	14 %	.14	.039280	.037478	.035667	.033846	.032013	.030148	.022808
n = 15	15 %	.15	.047482	.045681	.043871	.042051	.040221	.038351	.021017
	16 %	.16	.055818	.054016	.052207	.050389	.048561	.046688	.019357
	17 %	.17	.064277	.062476	.060668	.058851	.057025	.055148	.017822
	18 %	.18	.072854	.071053	.069245	.067429	.065606	.063725	.016402
	19 %	.19	.081539	.079738	.077930	.076116	.074295	.072411	.015091
	20 %	.20	.090325	.088524	.086717	.084904	.083085	.081198	.013882
	21 %	.21	.099206	.097405	.095599	.093787	.091969	.090079	.012766
	22 %	.22	.108174	.106374	.104568	.102757	.100940	.099048	.011738
	23 %	.23	.117224	.115424	.113618	.111808	.109993	.108099	.010791
	24 %	.24	.126350	.124549	.122744	.120935	.119121	.117225	.009919
	25 %	.25	.135545	.133744	.131940	.130131	.128318	.126420	.009116
	26 %	.26	.144805	.143004	.141200	.139392	.137580	.135680	.008378
	27 %	.27	.154124	.152324	.150520	.148713	.146902	.145000	.007700
	28 %	.28	.163499	.161698	.159895	.158088	.156278	.154375	.007076
	29 %	.29	.172924	.171124	.169320	.167514	.165705	.163801	.006504
	30 %	.30	.182396	.180596	.178793	.176987	.175179	.173273	.005977

TABLE C

Mortgage Coefficients for Computing Capitalization Rates.

15 YEARS AMORTIZATION: 10¾% TO 12%

Projection	Equity	Yield	10¾%	11%	11¼%	11½%	11¾%	12%	$\frac{1}{s_{\overline{n}\rvert}}$
Interest Rate			10¾%	11%	11¼%	11½%	11¾%	12%	
Annual Requirement (f)			.134520	.136440	.138360	.140280	.142200	.144120	
Installment f/12			.011210	.011370	.011530	.011690	.011850	.012010	
5 Years n = 5	Balance (b)		.822137	.824795	.827493	.830234	.833017	.835843	+ Dep. – App.
			Mortgage Coefficients						
	4 %	.04	.061681-	.064092-	.066510-	.068936-	.071370-	.073812-	.184627
	5 %	.05	.052331-	.054732-	.057140-	.059556-	.061980-	.064411-	.180974
	6 %	.06	.042967-	.045359-	.047758-	.050164-	.052577-	.054999-	.177396
	7 %	.07	.033591-	.035973-	.038362-	.040759-	.043163-	.045574-	.173890
	8 %	.08	.024202-	.026575-	.028955-	.031342-	.033736-	.036138-	.170456
	9 %	.09	.014800-	.017164-	.019535-	.021913-	.024298-	.026690-	.167092
	10 %	.10	.005386-	.007741-	.010103-	.012472-	.014848-	.017231-	.163797
	11 %	.11	.004039	.001692	.000660-	.003020-	.005337-	.007761-	.160570
	12 %	.12	.013477	.011138	.008794	.006442	.004084	.001719	.157409
	13 %	.13	.022926	.020596	.018260	.015917	.013567	.011211	.154314
	14 %	.14	.032387	.030065	.027737	.025402	.023061	.020714	.151283
	15 %	.15	.041859	.039545	.037225	.034898	.032566	.030226	.148315
	16 %	.16	.051342	.049036	.046724	.044405	.042080	.039749	.145409
	17 %	.17	.060836	.058537	.056233	.053922	.051605	.049282	.142563
	18 %	.18	.070341	.068049	.065752	.063449	.061140	.058825	.139777
	19 %	.19	.079856	.077571	.075281	.072986	.070684	.068377	.137050
	20 %	.20	.089381	.087103	.084821	.082533	.080239	.077939	.134379
	21 %	.21	.098916	.096645	.094370	.092089	.089802	.087510	.131765
	22 %	.22	.108460	.106197	.103928	.101654	.099375	.097089	.129205
	23 %	.23	.118015	.115758	.113496	.111229	.108956	.106678	.126709
	24 %	.24	.127573	.125328	.123073	.120812	.118547	.116276	.124247
	25 %	.25	.137151	.134908	.132659	.130405	.128146	.125881	.121846
	26 %	.26	.146733	.144496	.142253	.140006	.137753	.135496	.119496
	27 %	.27	.156324	.154093	.151856	.149615	.147369	.145118	.117195
	28 %	.28	.165924	.163698	.161468	.159233	.156993	.154748	.114943
	29 %	.29	.175532	.173312	.171088	.168859	.166625	.164386	.112739
	30 %	.30	.185148	.182934	.180715	.178492	.176265	.174032	.110581
10 Years n = 10	Balance (b)		.518415	.521880	.525528	.529363	.533393	.537622	+ Dep. – App.
			Mortgage Coefficients						
	4 %	.04	.054408-	.056616-	.058840-	.061080-	.063335-	.065608-	.083290
	5 %	.05	.046231-	.048427-	.050637-	.052862-	.055102-	.057358-	.079504
	6 %	.06	.037983-	.040166-	.042362-	.044573-	.046799-	.049040-	.075867
	7 %	.07	.029664-	.031834-	.034018-	.036216-	.038428-	.040654-	.072377
	8 %	.08	.021276-	.023435-	.025607-	.027792-	.029990-	.032202-	.069029
	9 %	.09	.012822-	.014970-	.017130-	.019302-	.021487-	.023686-	.065820
	10 %	.10	.004302-	.006440-	.008589-	.010749-	.012922-	.015107-	.062745
	11 %	.11	.004279	.002152	.000014	.002135-	.004296-	.006469-	.059801
	12 %	.12	.012922	.010805	.008677	.006538	.004389	.002228	.056984
	13 %	.13	.021625	.019516	.017398	.015270	.013131	.010982	.054289
	14 %	.14	.030384	.028285	.026176	.024058	.021929	.019791	.051713
	15 %	.15	.039199	.037108	.035008	.032899	.030781	.028653	.049252
	16 %	.16	.048066	.045984	.043893	.041793	.039684	.037566	.046901
	17 %	.17	.056985	.054911	.052828	.050737	.048637	.046528	.044656
	18 %	.18	.065954	.063887	.061811	.059728	.057637	.055537	.042514
	19 %	.19	.074970	.072910	.070842	.068767	.066684	.064593	.040471
	20 %	.20	.084031	.081978	.079917	.077850	.075774	.073692	.038522
	21 %	.21	.093137	.091090	.089036	.086975	.084908	.082833	.036665
	22 %	.22	.102284	.100243	.098196	.096142	.094082	.092014	.034894
	23 %	.23	.111472	.109437	.107396	.105349	.103295	.101234	.033208
	24 %	.24	.120699	.118669	.116634	.114593	.112545	.110492	.031602
	25 %	.25	.129962	.127938	.125908	.123873	.121832	.119784	.030072
	26 %	.26	.139261	.137242	.135217	.133187	.131152	.129111	.028616
	27 %	.27	.148593	.146579	.144560	.142535	.140505	.138470	.027230
	28 %	.28	.157958	.155948	.153934	.151914	.149890	.147861	.025911
	29 %	.29	.167354	.165348	.163339	.161324	.159305	.157280	.024657
	30 %	.30	.176779	.174778	.172772	.170762	.168748	.166728	.023463

Mortgage Coefficients for Computing Capitalization Rates.

15 YEARS AMORTIZATION: 10¾% TO 12%

TABLE C

Interest Rate Annual Requirement (f) Installment f/12			10¾% .134520 .011210	11% .136440 .011370	11¼% .138360 .011530	11½% .140280 .011690	11¾% .142200 .011850	12% .144120 .012010	$\frac{1}{s_{\overline{n}\rceil}}$
Projection	Balance (b)		none	none	none	none	none	none	+ Dep. – App.
	Equity	Yield	Mortgage Coefficients						
	4 %	.04	.044567–	.046407–	.048266–	.050146–	.052047–	.053971–	.049941
	5 %	.05	.038167–	.040012–	.041876–	.043758–	.045661–	.047585–	.046342
	6 %	.06	.031547–	.033398–	.035266–	.037151–	.039055–	.040978–	.042962
	7 %	.07	.024716–	.026572–	.028443–	.030331–	.032236–	.034159–	.039794
	8 %	.08	.017681–	.019542–	.021418–	.023308–	.025214–	.027137–	.036829
	9 %	.09	.010453–	.012318–	.014197–	.016089–	.017996–	.019919–	.034058
	10 %	.10	.003038–	.004908–	.006790–	.008684–	.010592–	.012515–	.031473
	11 %	.11	.004551	.002678	.000793	.001102–	.003011–	.004933–	.029065
	12 %	.12	.012310	.010433	.008546	.006647	.004737	.002815	.026824
	13 %	.13	.020227	.018347	.016457	.014557	.012646	.010724	.024741
	14 %	.14	.028294	.026410	.024518	.022617	.020705	.018783	.022808
15 Years	15 %	15	.036501	.034615	.032721	.030818	.028906	.026984	.021017
n = 15	16 %	.16	.044841	.042952	.041056	.039152	.037239	.035317	.019357
	17 %	.17	.053306	.051414	.049516	.047610	.045697	.043776	.017822
	18 %	.18	.061886	.059992	.058092	.056186	.054272	.052350	.016402
	19 %	.19	.070575	.068679	.066777	.064870	.062955	.061034	.015091
	20 %	.20	.079365	.077467	.075564	.073655	.071740	.069819	.013882
	21 %	.21	.088249	.086349	.084445	.082535	.080620	.078699	.012766
	22 %	.22	.097220	.095319	.093413	.091503	.089587	.087666	.011738
	23 %	.23	.106273	.104370	.102463	.100552	.098636	.096715	.010791
	24 %	.24	.115401	.113497	.111589	.109677	.107761	.105840	.009919
	25 %	.25	.124598	.122693	.120784	.118872	.116955	.115034	.009116
	26 %	.26	.133860	.131954	.130044	.128131	.126214	.124293	.008378
	27 %	.27	.143182	.141274	.139364	.137450	.135533	.133612	.007700
	28 %	.28	.152558	.150649	.148738	.146824	.144906	.142986	.007076
	29 %	.29	.161985	.160075	.158163	.156249	.154331	.152411	.006504
	30 %	.30	.171459	.169548	.167636	.165720	.163803	.161882	.005977

Mortgage Coefficients for Computing Capitalization Rates

20 YEARS AMORTIZATION: 3¼% TO 4½%

Interest Rate		3¼%	3½%	3¾%	4%	4¼%	4½%	$\frac{1}{s_{\overline{n}\rvert}}$
Annual Requirement(f)		.06816	.06960	.07116	.07272	.07440	.07596	
Installment f/12		.00568	.00580	.00593	.00606	.00620	.00633	
Projection	Balance(b)	.806679	.811240	.815205	.819225	.822635	.826765	+ Dep.
	Equity Yield	Mortgage Coefficients						− App.
	4% .04	.0075	.0052	.0029	.0006	*.0017*	*.0040*	.1846
	5% .05	.0168	.0145	.0123	.0099	.0077	.0054	.1810
	6% .06	.0261	.0239	.0216	.0193	.0170	.0147	.1774
	7% .07	.0354	.0332	.0309	.0287	.0264	.0241	.1739
	8% .08	.0448	.0426	.0403	.0381	.0358	.0335	.1705
	9% .09	.0541	.0519	.0497	.0475	.0452	.0430	.1671
5 Years n = 5	10% .10	.0635	.0613	.0591	.0569	.0546	.0524	.1638
	11% .11	.0729	.0707	.0685	.0663	.0641	.0618	.1606
	12% .12	.0822	.0801	.0779	.0757	.0735	.0713	.1574
	13% .13	.0916	.0895	.0873	.0851	.0829	.0807	.1543
	14% .14	.1011	.0989	.0968	.0946	.0924	.0902	.1513
	15% .15	.1105	.1084	.1062	.1041	.1019	.0997	.1483
	16% .16	.1199	.1178	.1157	.1135	.1114	.1092	.1454
	17% .17	.1294	.1273	.1251	.1230	.1208	.1187	.1426
	18% .18	.1388	.1367	.1346	.1325	.1304	.1282	.1398
	19% .19	.1483	.1462	.1441	.1420	.1399	.1377	.1371
	20% .20	.1578	.1557	.1536	.1515	.1494	.1473	.1344
	21% .21	.1673	.1652	.1631	.1611	.1589	.1568	.1318
	22% .22	.1768	.1747	.1727	.1706	.1685	.1664	.1292
	23% .23	.1863	.1843	.1822	.1801	.1780	.1759	.1267
	24% .24	.1958	.1938	.1918	.1897	.1876	.1855	.1242
	25% .25	.2054	.2034	.2013	.1993	.1972	.1951	.1218
	26% .26	.2149	.2129	.2109	.2088	.2068	.2047	.1195
	27% .27	.2245	.2225	.2205	.2184	.2163	.2143	.1172
	28% .28	.2340	.2321	.2300	.2280	.2259	.2239	.1149
	29% .29	.2436	.2416	.2396	.2376	.2356	.2335	.1127
	30% .30	.2532	.2512	.2492	.2472	.2452	.2432	.1106
	Balance(b)	.579297	.586436	.592363	.598499	.603357	.609909	+ Dep.
	Equity Yield	Mortgage Coefficients						− App.
	4% .04	.0069	.0048	.0028	.0007	*.0014*	*.0035*	.0833
	5% .05	.0153	.0133	.0112	.0092	.0071	.0050	.0795
	6% .06	.0237	.0218	.0197	.0177	.0157	.0136	.0759
	7% .07	.0323	.0303	.0283	.0263	.0243	.0222	.0724
	8% .08	.0409	.0389	.0370	.0350	.0330	.0309	.0690
	9% .09	.0495	.0476	.0456	.0437	.0417	.0397	.0658
10 Years n = 10	10% .10	.0582	.0563	.0544	.0524	.0505	.0485	.0628
	11% .11	.0670	.0651	.0632	.0613	.0593	.0573	.0598
	12% .12	.0758	.0739	.0720	.0701	.0682	.0662	.0570
	13% .13	.0847	.0828	.0809	.0790	.0771	.0752	.0543
	14% .14	.0936	.0918	.0899	.0880	.0861	.0842	.0517
	15% .15	.1025	.1007	.0989	.0970	.0951	.0932	.0493
	16% .16	.1115	.1098	.1079	.1061	.1042	.1024	.0469
	17% .17	.1206	.1188	.1170	.1152	.1133	.1116	.0447
	18% .18	.1297	.1279	.1261	.1243	.1224	.1207	.0425
	19% .19	.1388	.1371	.1353	.1335	.1316	.1299	.0405
	20% .20	.1480	.1463	.1445	.1427	.1408	.1391	.0385
	21% .21	.1572	.1555	.1537	.1520	.1501	.1484	.0367
	22% .22	.1665	.1648	.1630	.1613	.1594	.1577	.0349
	23% .23	.1758	.1741	.1723	.1706	.1687	.1671	.0332
	24% .24	.1851	.1834	.1817	.1799	.1781	.1764	.0316
	25% .25	.1945	.1928	.1911	.1893	.1875	.1858	.0301
	26% .26	.2038	.2022	.2005	.1987	.1969	.1952	.0286
	27% .27	.2133	.2116	.2099	.2082	.2064	.2047	.0272
	28% .28	.2227	.2211	.2194	.2176	.2158	.2142	.0259
	29% .29	.2322	.2306	.2289	.2271	.2253	.2237	.0247
	30% .30	.2417	.2401	.2384	.2367	.2349	.2332	.0235

Mortgage Coefficients for Computing Capitalization Rates

20 YEARS AMORTIZATION: 3¼% TO 4½%

Interest Rate		3¼%	3½%	3¾%	4%	4¼%	4½%	$\frac{1}{s_{\overline{n}\rceil}}$
Annual Requirement(f)		.06816	.06960	.07116	.07272	.07440	.07596	
Installment f/12		.00568	.00580	.00593	.00606	.00620	.00633	
Projection	Balance (b)	.311852	.318709	.323644	.328994	.332264	.338450	+ Dep.
	Equity Yield	Mortgage Coefficients						− App.
	4% .04	.0062	.0044	.0026	.0008	*.0011*	*.0029*	.0500
	5% .05	.0137	.0119	.0102	.0083	.0065	.0047	.0464
	6% .06	.0214	.0196	.0179	.0161	.0143	.0124	.0430
	7% .07	.0292	.0275	.0257	.0240	.0221	.0203	.0398
	8% .08	.0372	.0355	.0337	.0320	.0302	.0284	.0368
	9% .09	.0453	.0436	.0419	.0401	.0383	.0365	.0341
15 Years n = 15	10% .10	.0535	.0518	.0501	.0484	.0466	.0448	.0315
	11% .11	.0618	.0602	.0585	.0568	.0550	.0532	.0291
	12% .12	.0703	.0686	.0670	.0653	.0635	.0618	.0268
	13% .13	.0788	.0772	.0755	.0739	.0721	.0704	.0248
	14% .14	.0875	.0859	.0842	.0826	.0808	.0791	.0228
	15% .15	.0963	.0947	.0930	.0914	.0896	.0879	.0210
	16% .16	.1051	.1035	.1019	.1002	.0985	.0968	.0194
	17% .17	.1141	.1125	.1109	.1092	.1075	.1058	.0178
	18% .18	.1231	.1215	.1199	.1182	.1165	.1149	.0164
	19% .19	.1322	.1306	.1290	.1274	.1256	.1240	.0151
	20% .20	.1414	.1398	.1382	.1366	.1348	.1332	.0139
	Balance(b)	none	none	none	none	none	none	+ Dep.
	Equity Yield	Mortgage Coefficients						− App.
	4% .04	.0054	.0040	.0024	.0008	*.0008*	*.0024*	.0336
	5% .05	.0121	.0106	.0091	.0075	.0058	.0043	.0303
	6% .06	.0190	.0176	.0160	.0144	.0128	.0112	.0272
	7% .07	.0262	.0248	.0232	.0216	.0200	.0184	.0244
	8% .08	.0337	.0322	.0307	.0291	.0274	.0259	.0219
	9% .09	.0414	.0399	.0384	.0368	.0351	.0336	.0196
20 Years n = 20	10% .10	.0493	.0478	.0463	.0447	.0430	.0415	.0175
	11% .11	.0574	.0560	.0544	.0528	.0512	.0496	.0156
	12% .12	.0657	.0643	.0627	.0611	.0595	.0579	.0139
	13% .13	.0742	.0727	.0712	.0696	.0679	.0664	.0124
	14% .14	.0828	.0814	.0798	.0782	.0766	.0750	.0110
	15% .15	.0916	.0901	.0886	.0870	.0853	.0838	.0098
	16% .16	.1005	.0990	.0975	.0959	.0942	.0927	.0087
	17% .17	.1095	.1081	.1065	.1049	.1033	.1017	.0077
	18% .18	.1186	.1172	.1156	.1141	.1124	.1108	.0068
	19% .19	.1278	.1264	.1248	.1233	.1216	.1200	.0060
	20% .20	.1372	.1357	.1342	.1326	.1309	.1294	.0054

Mortgage Coefficients for Computing Capitalization Rates

20 YEARS AMORTIZATION: 4¾% TO 6%

Interest Rate		4¾%	5%	5¼%	5½%	5¾%	6%	$\frac{1}{s_{\overline{n}\vert}}$
Annual Requirement(f)		.07764	.07920	.08088	.08256	.08436	.08604	
Installment f/12		.00647	.00660	.00674	.00688	.00703	.00717	
Projection	Balance (b)	.830277	.834519	.838135	.841804	.844831	.848599	+ Dep. − App.
	Equity Yield	Mortgage Coefficients						
	4% .04	*.0063*	*.0086*	*.0110*	*.0134*	*.0157*	*.0181*	.1846
	5% .05	.0030	.0007	*.0016*	*.0039*	*.0063*	*.0087*	.1810
	6% .06	.0124	.0101	.0078	.0055	.0031	.0008	.1774
	7% .07	.0218	.0195	.0172	.0149	.0126	.0103	.1739
	8% .08	.0313	.0290	.0267	.0244	.0221	.0197	.1705
	9% .09	.0407	.0384	.0361	.0338	.0315	.0292	.1671
5 Years n = 5	10% .10	.0501	.0479	.0456	.0433	.0410	.0387	.1638
	11% .11	.0596	.0573	.0551	.0528	.0505	.0482	.1606
	12% .12	.0690	.0668	.0646	.0623	.0600	.0578	.1574
	13% .13	.0785	.0763	.0741	.0718	.0696	.0673	.1543
	14% .14	.0880	.0858	.0836	.0813	.0791	.0768	.1513
	15% .15	.0975	.0953	.0931	.0909	.0886	.0864	.1483
	16% .16	.1070	.1048	.1026	.1004	.0982	.0959	.1454
	17% .17	.1165	.1144	.1122	.1100	.1077	.1055	.1426
	18% .18	.1260	.1239	.1217	.1195	.1173	.1151	.1398
	19% .19	.1356	.1334	.1313	.1291	.1269	.1247	.1371
	20% .20	.1451	.1430	.1408	.1387	.1365	.1343	.1344
	21% .21	.1547	.1526	.1504	.1482	.1460	.1439	.1318
	22% .22	.1642	.1621	.1600	.1578	.1556	.1535	.1292
	23% .23	.1738	.1717	.1696	.1674	.1653	.1631	.1267
	24% .24	.1834	.1813	.1792	.1771	.1749	.1727	.1242
	25% .25	.1930	.1909	.1888	.1867	.1845	.1824	.1218
	26% .26	.2026	.2005	.1984	.1963	.1941	.1920	.1195
	27% .27	.2122	.2102	.2080	.2059	.2038	.2017	.1172
	28% .28	.2218	.2198	.2177	.2156	.2134	.2113	.1149
	29% .29	.2315	.2294	.2273	.2252	.2231	.2210	.1127
	30% .30	.2411	.2391	.2370	.2349	.2328	.2307	.1106
	Balance(b)	.615155	.622146	.627803	.633664	.638118	.644382	+ Dep. − App.
	Equity Yield	Mortgage Coefficients						
	4% .04	*.0056*	*.0077*	*.0099*	*.0121*	*.0142*	*.0164*	.0833
	5% .05	.0029	.0008	*.0013*	*.0034*	*.0056*	*.0078*	.0795
	6% .06	.0115	.0094	.0073	.0052	.0031	.0009	.0759
	7% .07	.0202	.0181	.0160	.0139	.0118	.0097	.0724
	8% .08	.0289	.0269	.0248	.0227	.0206	.0185	.0690
	9% .09	.0377	.0356	.0336	.0315	.0294	.0272	.0658
10 Years n = 10	10% .10	.0465	.0445	.0424	.0404	.0383	.0362	.0628
	11% .11	.0553	.0534	.0513	.0493	.0473	.0452	.0598
	12% .12	.0643	.0623	.0603	.0583	.0562	.0542	.0570
	13% .13	.0732	.0713	.0693	.0673	.0653	.0632	.0543
	14% .14	.0822	.0803	.0783	.0764	.0743	.0723	.0517
	15% .15	.0913	.0894	.0874	.0855	.0834	.0814	.0493
	16% .16	.1004	.0985	.0965	.0946	.0926	.0906	.0469
	17% .17	.1095	.1076	.1057	.1038	.1018	.0998	.0447
	18% .18	.1187	.1168	.1149	.1130	.1110	.1090	.0425
	19% .19	.1279	.1261	.1241	.1222	.1202	.1183	.0405
	20% .20	.1371	.1353	.1334	.1315	.1295	.1276	.0385
	21% .21	.1464	.1446	.1427	.1408	.1389	.1370	.0367
	22% .22	.1557	.1539	.1521	.1502	.1482	.1463	.0349
	23% .23	.1651	.1634	.1614	.1596	.1576	.1557	.0332
	24% .24	.1745	.1727	.1708	.1690	.1670	.1652	.0316
	25% .25	.1839	.1821	.1803	.1784	.1765	.1746	.0301
	26% .26	.1933	.1916	.1897	.1879	.1859	.1841	.0286
	27% .27	.2028	.2010	.1992	.1974	.1954	.1936	.0272
	28% .28	.2123	.2106	.2087	.2069	.2050	.2031	.0259
	29% .29	.2218	.2201	.2183	.2164	.2145	.2127	.0247
	30% .30	.2313	.2296	.2278	.2260	.2241	.2223	.0235

Mortgage Coefficients for Computing Capitalization Rates

20 YEARS AMORTIZATION: 4¾% TO 6%

TABLE C

Projection	Interest Rate	4¾%	5%	5¼%	5½%	5¾%	6%	$\frac{1}{s_{\overline{n}\rceil}}$
	Annual Requirement(f)	.07764	.07920	.08088	.08256	.08436	.08604	
	Installment f/12	.00647	.00660	.00674	.00688	.00703	.00717	
	Balance(b)	.342493	.349597	.354491	.359815	.362740	.368924	+ Dep.
	Equity Yield	Mortgage Coefficients						− App.
15 Years n = 15	4% .04	*.0048*	*.0067*	*.0086*	*.0106*	*.0125*	*.0145*	.0500
	5% .05	.0028	.0009	*.0010*	*.0029*	*.0048*	*.0068*	.0464
	6% .06	.0106	.0087	.0068	.0049	.0030	.0010	.0430
	7% .07	.0185	.0167	.0148	.0129	.0110	.0090	.0398
	8% .08	.0265	.0247	.0229	.0210	.0191	.0172	.0368
	9% .09	.0347	.0329	.0311	.0292	.0273	.0254	.0341
	10% .10	.0430	.0412	.0394	.0376	.0357	.0338	.0315
	11% .11	.0514	.0497	.0479	.0460	.0441	.0423	.0291
	12% .12	.0600	.0582	.0564	.0546	.0527	.0509	.0268
	13% .13	.0686	.0669	.0651	.0633	.0614	.0595	.0248
	14% .14	.0773	.0756	.0738	.0720	.0701	.0683	.0228
	15% .15	.0862	.0844	.0827	.0809	.0790	.0772	.0210
	16% .16	.0950	.0934	.0916	.0898	.0879	.0861	.0194
	17% .17	.1040	.1024	.1006	.0988	.0970	.0952	.0178
	18% .18	.1131	.1114	.1097	.1079	.1061	.1043	.0164
	19% .19	.1222	.1206	.1188	.1171	.1152	.1134	.0151
	20% .20	.1314	.1298	.1280	.1263	.1244	.1227	.0139
	Balance (b)	none	none	none	none	none	none	+ Dep.
	Equity Yield	Mortgage Coefficients						− App.
20 Years n = 20	4% .04	*.0041*	*.0056*	*.0073*	*.0090*	*.0108*	*.0125*	.0336
	5% .05	.0026	.0010	*.0006*	*.0023*	*.0041*	*.0058*	.0303
	6% .06	.0095	.0080	.0063	.0046	.0028	.0011	.0272
	7% .07	.0167	.0152	.0135	.0118	.0100	.0083	.0244
	8% .08	.0242	.0226	.0209	.0193	.0175	.0158	.0219
	9% .09	.0319	.0303	.0286	.0270	.0252	.0235	.0196
	10% .10	.0398	.0382	.0366	.0349	.0331	.0314	.0175
	11% .11	.0479	.0463	.0447	.0430	.0412	.0395	.0156
	12% .12	.0562	.0547	.0530	.0513	.0495	.0478	.0139
	13% .13	.0647	.0631	.0614	.0598	.0580	.0563	.0124
	14% .14	.0733	.0718	.0701	.0684	.0666	.0649	.0110
	15% .15	.0821	.0805	.0789	.0772	.0754	.0737	.0098
	16% .16	.0910	.0894	.0877	.0861	.0843	.0826	.0087
	17% .17	.1000	.0985	.0968	.0951	.0933	.0916	.0077
	18% .18	.1091	.1076	.1059	.1042	.1024	.1007	.0068
	19% .19	.1184	.1168	.1151	.1134	.1116	.1100	.0060
	20% .20	.1277	.1261	.1244	.1228	.1210	.1193	.0054

TABLE C

Mortgage Coefficients for Computing Capitalization Rates.

20 YEARS AMORTIZATION: 6¼% TO 7½%

Interest Rate / Annual Requirement (f) / Installment f/12	6¼% .087720 .007310	6½% .089520 .007460	6¾% .091320 .007610	7% .093120 .007760	7¼% .094920 .007910	7½% .096720 .008060	$\frac{1}{s_{\overline{n}\vert}}$

Projection: 5 Years, n = 5

Balance (b)	.852420	.855589	.858803	.862064	.865371	.868725	+ Dep. − App.
Equity Yield	Mortgage Coefficients						
4 % .04	.020472-	.022857-	.025251-	.027653-	.030063-	.032483-	.184627
5 % .05	.011011-	.013385-	.015767-	.018157-	.020555-	.022962-	.180974
6 % .06	.001539-	.003902-	.006272-	.008650-	.011037-	.013432-	.177396
7 % .07	.007942	.005591	.003232	.000865	.001509-	.003892-	.173890
8 % .08	.017435	.015095	.012747	.010392	.008028	.005656	.170456
9 % .09	.026939	.024609	.022272	.019928	.017575	.015214	.167092
10 % .10	.036453	.034134	.031807	.029473	.027131	.024782	.163797
11 % .11	.045976	.043668	.041351	.039028	.036697	.034358	.160570
12 % .12	.055510	.053211	.050905	.048592	.046271	.043943	.157409
13 % .13	.065053	.062764	.060468	.058165	.055855	.053537	.154314
14 % .14	.074606	.072326	.070040	.067747	.065447	.063139	.151283
15 % .15	.084168	.081898	.079621	.077338	.075047	.072749	.148315
16 % .16	.093739	.091478	.089211	.086937	.084656	.082368	.145409
17 % .17	.103319	.101067	.098809	.096544	.094273	.091994	.142563
18 % .18	.112908	.110665	.108416	.106160	.103898	.101629	.139777
19 % .19	.122505	.120271	.118030	.115784	.113530	.111271	.137050
20 % .20	.132111	.129885	.127653	.125415	.123171	.120920	.134379
21 % .21	.141725	.139508	.137284	.135055	.132819	.130577	.131765
22 % .22	.151348	.149138	.146923	.144702	.142474	.140241	.129205
23 % .23	.160978	.158776	.156569	.154356	.152137	.149912	.126700
24 % .24	.170616	.168422	.166223	.164018	.161807	.159590	.124247
25 % .25	.180262	.178075	.175884	.173687	.171484	.169275	.121846
26 % .26	.189915	.187736	.185552	.183362	.181167	.178966	.119496
27 % .27	.199575	.197404	.195227	.193045	.190857	.188664	.117195
28 % .28	.209243	.207079	.204909	.202734	.200554	.198369	.114943
29 % .29	.218917	.216760	.214598	.212430	.210257	.208079	.112739
30 % .30	.228599	.226449	.224293	.222133	.219967	.217796	.110581

Projection: 10 Years, n = 10

Balance (b)	.650867	.655896	.661113	.666523	.672132	.677946	+ Dep. − App.
Equity Yield	Mortgage Coefficients						
4 % .04	.018640-	.020859-	.023093-	.025344-	.027611-	.029895-	.083290
5 % .05	.009962-	.012162-	.014376-	.016607-	.018853-	.021115-	.079504
6 % .06	.001232-	.003413-	.005609-	.007819-	.010045-	.012286-	.075867
7 % .07	.007549	.005385	.003207	.001016	.001189-	.003410-	.072377
8 % .08	.016380	.014233	.012073	.009899	.007712	.005511	.069029
9 % .09	.025259	.023128	.020985	.018829	.016660	.014477	.065820
10 % .10	.034186	.032070	.029943	.027804	.025652	.023487	.062745
11 % .11	.043158	.041057	.038945	.036822	.034686	.032539	.059801
12 % .12	.052175	.050088	.047991	.045882	.043763	.041631	.056984
13 % .13	.061234	.059161	.057078	.054984	.052879	.050764	.054289
14 % .14	.070334	.068274	.066205	.064125	.062035	.059934	.051713
15 % .15	.079475	.077427	.075370	.073304	.071228	.069141	.049252
16 % .16	.088654	.086618	.084574	.082520	.080457	.078384	.046901
17 % .17	.097871	.095846	.093813	.091771	.089721	.087661	.044656
18 % .18	.107123	.105109	.103087	.101057	.099019	.096972	.042514
19 % .19	.116409	.114406	.112395	.110376	.108349	.106313	.040471
20 % .20	.125729	.123735	.121734	.119726	.117710	.115686	.038522
21 % .21	.135081	.133096	.131105	.129106	.127101	.125088	.036665
22 % .22	.144462	.142487	.140505	.138516	.136520	.134518	.034894
23 % .23	.153874	.151907	.149933	.147954	.145967	.143974	.033208
24 % .24	.163313	.161354	.159389	.157418	.155441	.153457	.031602
25 % .25	.172779	.170828	.168871	.166908	.164939	.162964	.030072
26 % .26	.182270	.180327	.178377	.176422	.174462	.172496	.028616
27 % .27	.191787	.189850	.187908	.185960	.184008	.182049	.027230
28 % .28	.201326	.199396	.197461	.195520	.193575	.191624	.025911
29 % .29	.210888	.208964	.207035	.205102	.203164	.201220	.024657
30 % .30	.220471	.218553	.216631	.214704	.212772	.210836	.023463

Mortgage Coefficients for Computing Capitalization Rates.

20 YEARS AMORTIZATION: 6¼% TO 7½%

Interest Rate / Annual Requirement (f) / Installment f/12			6¼% .087720 .007310	6½% .089520 .007460	6½% .091320 .007610	7% .093120 .007760	7¼% .094920 .007910	7½% .096720 .008060	$\frac{1}{s_{\overline{n}\rvert}}$
Projection	Balance (b)		.375599	.379756	.384323	.389319	.394766	.400686	+ Dep. – App.
	Equity	Yield	Mortgage Coefficients						
	4 %	.04	.016536–	.018544–	.020572–	.022621–	.024693–	.026789–	.049941
	5 %	.05	.008783–	.010776–	.012788–	.014819–	.016872–	.018946–	.046342
	6 %	.06	.000894–	.002872–	.004868–	.006883–	.008917–	.010971–	.042962
	7 %	.07	.007127	.005162	.003180	.001181	.000834–	.002870–	.039794
	8 %	.08	.015276	.013323	.011355	.009371	.007370	.005352	.036829
	9 %	.09	.023546	.021604	.019649	.017679	.015693	.013691	.034058
	10 %	.10	.031932	.030001	.028057	.026100	.024128	.022142	.031473
	11 %	.11	.040428	.038507	.036574	.034629	.032671	.030699	.029065
	12 %	.12	.049029	.047117	.045195	.043261	.041314	.039356	.026824
	13 %	.13	.057728	.055825	.053912	.051989	.050054	.048108	.024741
	14 %	.14	.066521	.064627	.062722	.060808	.058884	.056949	.022808
	15 %	.15	.075403	.073515	.071619	.069714	.067800	.065875	.021017
	16 %	.16	.084366	.082486	.080597	.078701	.076795	.074881	.019357
	17 %	.17	.093408	.091534	.089652	.087763	.085866	.083961	.017822
	18 %	.18	.102521	.100653	.098778	.096896	.095007	.093110	.016402
15 Years n = 15	19 %	.19	.111703	.109840	.107971	.106096	.104214	.102324	.015091
	20 %	.20	.120948	.119090	.117226	.115357	.113481	.111599	.013882
	21 %	.21	.130251	.128398	.126539	.124676	.122806	.120931	.012766
	22 %	.22	.139609	.137760	.135906	.134048	.132184	.130314	.011738
	23 %	.23	.149017	.147173	.145323	.143469	.141611	.139747	.010791
	24 %	.24	.158473	.156632	.154786	.152937	.151083	.149224	.009919
	25 %	.25	.167972	.166134	.164293	.162447	.160597	.158743	.009116
	26 %	.26	.177511	.175676	.173838	.171996	.170151	.168301	.008378
	27 %	.27	.187088	.185256	.183421	.181582	.179740	.177895	.007700
	28 %	.28	.196698	.194869	.193037	.191201	.189363	.187521	.007076
	29 %	.29	.206341	.204514	.202684	.200851	.199016	.197177	.006504
	30 %	.30	.216012	.214187	.212360	.210530	.208697	.206862	.005977
	Balance (b)		none	none	none	none	none	none	+ Dep. – App.
	Equity	Yield	Mortgage Coefficients						
	4 %	.04	.014126–	.015867–	.017630–	.019415–	.021225–	.023062–	.033581
	5 %	.05	.007467–	.009214–	.010980–	.012766–	.014576–	.016409–	.030242
	6 %	.06	.000526–	.002278–	.004048–	.005836–	.007644–	.009474–	.027184
	7 %	.07	.006681	.004923	.003151	.001362	.000445–	.002272–	.024392
	8 %	.08	.014139	.012377	.010602	.008812	.007005	.005181	.021852
	9 %	.09	.021833	.020067	.018289	.016497	.014691	.012870	.019546
	10 %	.10	.029745	.027976	.026195	.024403	.022598	.020778	.017459
	11 %	.11	.037860	.036088	.034305	.032512	.030707	.028890	.015575
	12 %	.12	.046163	.044387	.042603	.040809	.039005	.037190	.013878
	13 %	.13	.054638	.052859	.051073	.049278	.047475	.045661	.012353
	14 %	.14	.063269	.061489	.059701	.057906	.056102	.054290	.010986
20 Years n = 20	15 %	.15	.072044	.070261	.068472	.066677	.064874	.063063	.009761
	16 %	.16	.080949	.079165	.077374	.075578	.073776	.071966	.008667
	17 %	.17	.089972	.088186	.086395	.084598	.082796	.080987	.007690
	18 %	.18	.099102	.097314	.095521	.093724	.091922	.090115	.006819
	19 %	.19	.108327	.106537	.104744	.102947	.101145	.099338	.006045
	20 %	.20	.117638	.115847	.114053	.112256	.110454	.108648	.005356
	21 %	.21	.127026	.125234	.123440	.121642	.119840	.118035	.004744
	22 %	.22	.136483	.134690	.132895	.131097	.129295	.127491	.004201
	23 %	.23	.146001	.144208	.142412	.140614	.138812	.137008	.003720
	24 %	.24	.155574	.153780	.151984	.150185	.148384	.146581	.003293
	25 %	.25	.165196	.163402	.161605	.159806	.158005	.156202	.002915
	26 %	.26	.174862	.173066	.171269	.169470	.167670	.165867	.002581
	27 %	.27	.184566	.182770	.180972	.179173	.177372	.175570	.002285
	28 %	.28	.194304	.192507	.190709	.188910	.187110	.185307	.002023
	29 %	.29	.204072	.202275	.200477	.198678	.196877	.195075	.001791
	30 %	.30	.213867	.212070	.210271	.208472	.206672	.204870	.001586

Mortgage Coefficients for Computing Capitalization Rates.

20 YEARS AMORTIZATION: 7¾% TO 9%

Projection	Equity	Yield	7¾%	8%	8¼%	8½%	8¾%	9%	$\frac{1}{s_{\overline{n}\vert}}$
Interest Rate			7¾%	8%	8¼%	8½%	8¾%	9%	
Annual Requirement (f)			.098520	.100440	.102360	.104160	.106080	.108000	
Installment f/12			.008210	.008370	.008530	.008680	.008840	.009000	
5 Years n = 5	Balance (b)		.872128	.874844	.877600	.881140	.883981	.886863	+ Dep. – App.
			Mortgage Coefficients						
	4 %	.04	.034911-	.037332-	.039761-	.042215-	.044659-	.047111-	.184627
	5 %	.05	.025378-	.027739-	.030208-	.032649-	.035083-	.037525-	.180974
	6 %	.06	.015836-	.018237-	.020646-	.023074-	.025498-	.027930-	.177396
	7 %	.07	.006284-	.008676-	.011075-	.013491-	.015905-	.018326-	.173890
	8 %	.08	.003276	.000893	.001496-	.003899-	.006303-	.008715-	.170456
	9 %	.09	.012846	.010472	.008092	.005700	.003305	.000904	.167092
	10 %	.10	.022425	.020060	.017688	.015308	.012923	.010531	.163797
	11 %	.11	.032012	.029656	.027293	.024925	.022549	.020166	.160570
	12 %	.12	.041608	.039260	.036906	.034549	.032182	.029808	.157409
	13 %	.13	.051212	.048873	.046528	.044181	.041823	.039458	.154314
	14 %	.14	.060824	.058493	.056157	.053821	.051471	.049115	.151283
	15 %	.15	.070445	.068122	.065793	.063468	.061127	.058779	.148315
	16 %	.16	.080073	.077758	.075438	.073123	.070790	.068451	.145409
	17 %	.17	.089709	.087402	.085089	.082785	.080460	.078129	.142563
	18 %	.18	.099353	.097053	.094748	.092453	.090136	.087813	.139777
	19 %	.19	.109004	.106712	.104414	.102129	.099820	.097505	.137050
	20 %	.20	.118663	.116378	.114088	.111812	.109510	.107203	.134379
	21 %	.21	.128329	.126051	.123768	.121501	.119207	.116907	.131765
	22 %	.22	.138001	.135730	.133454	.131197	.128910	.126617	.129205
	23 %	.23	.147681	.145417	.143148	.140899	.138619	.136334	.126700
	24 %	.24	.157367	.155110	.152847	.150608	.148335	.146056	.124247
	25 %	.25	.167060	.164809	.162554	.160322	.158056	.155785	.121846
	26 %	.26	.176760	.174515	.172266	.170043	.167783	.165519	.119496
	27 %	.27	.186466	.184227	.181984	.179769	.177516	.175259	.117195
	28 %	.28	.196178	.193945	.191709	.189502	.187255	.185004	.114943
	29 %	.29	.205896	.203669	.201439	.199240	.196999	.194754	.112739
	30 %	.30	.215620	.213399	.211175	.208983	.206749	.204510	.110581
10 Years n = 10	Balance (b)		.683970	.688381	.692964	.699605	.704573	.709728	+ Dep. – App.
			Mortgage Coefficients						
	4 %	.04	.032197-	.034485-	.036786-	.039139-	.041473-	.043823-	.083290
	5 %	.05	.023394-	.025664-	.027949-	.030277-	.032592-	.034922-	.079504
	6 %	.06	.014543-	.016798-	.019065-	.021369-	.023666-	.025977-	.075867
	7 %	.07	.005646-	.007885-	.010137-	.012418-	.014697-	.016990-	.072377
	8 %	.08	.003295	.001070	.001165-	.003423-	.005686-	.007962-	.069029
	9 %	.09	.012281	.010070	.007849	.005611	.003365	.001105	.065820
	10 %	.10	.021309	.019112	.016905	.014688	.012456	.010213	.062745
	11 %	.11	.030379	.028195	.026001	.023804	.021586	.019358	.059801
	12 %	.12	.039488	.037317	.035136	.032957	.030754	.028540	.056984
	13 %	.13	.048637	.046477	.044308	.042148	.039958	.037758	.054289
	14 %	.14	.057823	.055674	.053517	.051374	.049197	.047010	.051713
	15 %	.15	.067045	.064907	.062762	.060635	.058470	.056296	.049252
	16 %	.16	.076302	.074175	.072040	.069928	.067775	.065614	.046901
	17 %	.17	.085592	.083475	.081351	.079254	.077112	.074962	.044656
	18 %	.18	.094915	.092808	.090693	.088611	.086479	.084340	.042514
	19 %	.19	.104270	.102171	.100066	.097997	.095876	.093747	.040471
	20 %	.20	.113654	.111564	.109467	.107412	.105300	.103182	.038522
	21 %	.21	.123067	.120985	.118897	.116854	.114751	.112642	.036665
	22 %	.22	.132507	.130433	.128353	.126322	.124228	.122129	.034894
	23 %	.23	.141974	.139908	.137836	.135815	.133730	.131639	.033208
	24 %	.24	.151467	.149407	.147342	.145333	.143256	.141173	.031602
	25 %	.25	.160983	.158931	.156873	.154873	.152804	.150729	.030072
	26 %	.26	.170523	.168477	.166426	.164436	.162374	.160306	.028616
	27 %	.27	.180085	.178045	.176000	.174019	.171964	.169904	.027230
	28 %	.28	.189668	.187634	.185595	.183623	.181575	.179521	.025911
	29 %	.29	.199272	.197243	.195210	.193246	.191204	.189157	.024657
	30 %	.30	.208895	.206871	.204844	.202888	.200851	.198810	.023463

Mortgage Coefficients for Computing Capitalization Rates.

20 YEARS AMORTIZATION: 7¾% TO 9%

TABLE C

Interest Rate / Annual Requirement (f) / Installment f/12			7¾% .098520 .008210	8% .100440 .008370	8¼% .102360 .008530	8½% .104160 .008680	8¾% .106080 .008840	9% .108000 .009000	$\frac{1}{s_{\overline{n|}}}$
Projection	Balance (b)		.407103	.410581	.414450	.422347	.427141	.432391	+ Dep. – App.
	Equity	Yield	Mortgage Coefficients						
	4 %	.04	.028910-	.031003-	.033116-	.035311-	.037470-	.039652-	.049941
	5 %	.05	.021043-	.023125-	.025224-	.027390-	.029532-	.031695-	.046342
	6 %	.06	.013047-	.015116-	.017203-	.019342-	.021468-	.023613-	.042962
	7 %	.07	.004925-	.006984-	.009058-	.011172-	.013283-	.015412-	.039794
	8 %	.08	.003316	.001268	.000794-	.002885-	.004981-	.007095-	.036829
	9 %	.09	.011673	.009634	.007583	.005514	.003430	.001332	.034058
	10 %	.10	.020140	.018111	.016069	.014020	.011950	.009864	.031473
	11 %	.11	.028712	.026691	.024659	.022629	.020570	.018497	.029065
	12 %	.12	.037383	.035370	.033346	.031335	.029286	.027225	.026824
	13 %	.13	.046149	.044143	.042127	.040132	.038093	.036043	.024741
	14 %	.14	.055003	.053004	.050995	.049015	.046986	.044946	.022808
15 Years n = 15	15 %	.15	.063940	.061947	.059946	.057980	.055959	.053929	.021017
	16 %	.16	.072956	.070969	.068974	.067021	.065009	.062987	.019357
	17 %	.17	.082046	.080064	.078075	.076134	.074129	.072115	.017822
	18 %	.18	.091205	.089228	.087244	.085315	.083316	.081310	.016402
	19 %	.19	.100427	.098455	.096477	.094557	.092565	.090566	.015091
	20 %	.20	.109710	.107742	.105768	.103859	.101872	.099879	.013882
	21 %	.21	.119049	.117084	.115115	.113214	.111233	.109246	.012766
	22 %	.22	.128439	.126478	.124513	.122620	.120644	.118662	.011738
	23 %	.23	.137877	.135920	.133958	.132073	.130101	.128125	.010791
	24 %	.24	.147361	.145406	.143448	.141569	.139602	.137630	.009919
	25 %	.25	.156885	.154933	.152978	.151106	.149142	.147174	.009116
	26 %	.26	.166447	.164498	.162546	.160680	.158719	.156755	.008378
	27 %	.27	.176045	.174098	.172149	.170288	.168331	.166370	.007700
	28 %	.28	.185675	.183731	.181783	.179928	.177974	.176016	.007076
	29 %	.29	.195336	.193393	.191448	.189597	.187645	.185691	.006504
	30 %	.30	.205024	.203083	.201140	.199293	.197344	.195393	.005977
	Balance (b)		none	none	none	none	none	none	+ Dep. – App.
	Equity	Yield	Mortgage Coefficients						
	4 %	.04	.024928-	.026747-	.028587-	.030541-	.032435-	.034356-	.033581
	5 %	.05	.018268-	.020097-	.021945-	.023883-	.025780-	.027702-	.030242
	6 %	.06	.011327-	.013165-	.015021-	.016945-	.018844-	.020765-	.027184
	7 %	.07	.004119-	.005966-	.007828-	.009740-	.011641-	.013562-	.024392
	8 %	.08	.003338	.001484	.000383-	.002283-	.004186-	.006107-	.021852
	9 %	.09	.011032	.009170	.007297	.005408	.003503	.001582	.019546
	10 %	.10	.018944	.017077	.015198	.013318	.011412	.009491	.017459
	11 %	.11	.027060	.025187	.023304	.021432	.019524	.017604	.015575
	12 %	.12	.035362	.033484	.031597	.029734	.027824	.025904	.013878
	13 %	.13	.043837	.041954	.040063	.038207	.036296	.034376	.012353
	14 %	.14	.052469	.050582	.048688	.046838	.044926	.043006	.010986
20 Years n = 20	15 %	.15	.061244	.059353	.057456	.055612	.053699	.051779	.009761
	16 %	.16	.070149	.068255	.066356	.064516	.062603	.060682	.008667
	17 %	.17	.079172	.077275	.075374	.073538	.071624	.069704	.007690
	18 %	.18	.088301	.086402	.084498	.082667	.080752	.078832	.006819
	19 %	.19	.097527	.095625	.093719	.091891	.089976	.088056	.006045
	20 %	.20	.106338	.104934	.103026	.101202	.099286	.097366	.005356
	21 %	.21	.116226	.114320	.112411	.110590	.108673	.106753	.004744
	22 %	.22	.125683	.123775	.121865	.120046	.118129	.116209	.004201
	23 %	.23	.135201	.133292	.131381	.129564	.127647	.125727	.003720
	24 %	.24	.144774	.142864	.140952	.139137	.137219	.135299	.003293
	25 %	.25	.154396	.152485	.150572	.148759	.146841	.144921	.002915
	26 %	.26	.164062	.162149	.160236	.158424	.156506	.154586	.002581
	27 %	.27	.173766	.171852	.169938	.168127	.166209	.164289	.002285
	28 %	.28	.183504	.181590	.179674	.177865	.175947	.174027	.002023
	29 %	.29	.193272	.191357	.189441	.187633	.185715	.183795	.001791
	30 %	.30	.203067	.201152	.199235	.197428	.195509	.193589	.001586

Mortgage Coefficients for Computing Capitalization Rates.

20 YEARS AMORTIZATION: 9¼% TO 10½%

Interest Rate Annual Requirement (f) Installment f/12		9¼% .109920 .009160	9½% .111960 .009330	9¾% .113880 .009490	10% .115920 .009660	10¼% .117840 .009820	10½% .119880 .009990	$\frac{1}{s_{\overline{n}\vert}}$
Projection	**Balance (b)**	.889787	.891989	.894993	.897266	.900352	.902698	+ Dep. – App.
	Equity Yield	**Mortgage Coefficients**						
	4 % .04	.049571-	.052018-	.054493-	.056952-	.059442-	.061915-	.184627
	5 % .05	.039974-	.042412-	.044876-	.047327-	.049806-	.052270-	.180974
	6 % .06	.030368-	.032799-	.035252-	.037695-	.040162-	.042619-	.177396
	7 % .07	.020755-	.023178-	.025620-	.028055-	.030512-	.032660-	.173890
	8 % .08	.011133-	.013548-	.015981-	.018408-	.020854-	.023294-	.170456
	9 % .09	.001504-	.003912-	.006334-	.008754-	.011189-	.013621-	.167092
	10 % .10	.008132	.005731	.003319	.000907	.001518-	.003942-	.163797
	11 % .11	.017776	.015383	.012980	.010575	.008160	.005743	.160570
	12 % .12	.027428	.025041	.022648	.020251	.017845	.015436	.157409
	13 % .13	.037087	.034707	.032323	.029933	.027537	.025135	.154314
	14 % .14	.046753	.044380	.042005	.039621	.037234	.034840	.151283
	15 % .15	.056426	.054059	.051694	.049316	.046939	.044551	.148315
5 Years n = 5	16 % .16	.066105	.063745	.061388	.059018	.056649	.054268	.145409
	17 % .17	.075792	.073438	.071090	.068726	.066366	.063991	.142563
	18 % .18	.085485	.083137	.080797	.078439	.076088	.073720	.139777
	19 % .19	.095184	.092842	.090511	.088159	.085816	.083455	.137050
	20 % .20	.104890	.102554	.100230	.097885	.095550	.093195	.134379
	21 % .21	.114602	.112271	.109956	.107616	.105290	.102940	.131765
	22 % .22	.124320	.121995	.119687	.117353	.115035	.112691	.129205
	23 % .23	.134043	.131724	.129424	.127096	.124785	.122448	.126700
	24 % .24	.143773	.141460	.139166	.136844	.134540	.132209	.124247
	25 % .25	.153508	.151200	.148914	.146597	.144301	.141975	.121846
	26 % .26	.163249	.160946	.158667	.156356	.154067	.151747	.119496
	27 % .27	.172996	.170698	.168426	.166119	.163838	.161523	.117195
	28 % .28	.182748	.180455	.178189	.175888	.173613	.171304	.114943
	29 % .29	.192505	.190216	.187958	.185662	.183394	.181089	.112739
	30 % .30	.202267	.199983	.197731	.195440	.193179	.190879	.110581
	Balance (b)	.715076	.718632	.724355	.728238	.734357	.738589	+ Dep. – App.
	Equity Yield	**Mortgage Coefficients**						
	4 % .04	.046188-	.048524-	.050921-	.053284-	.055714-	.058106-	.083290
	5 % .05	.037267-	.039590-	.041964-	.044313-	.046720-	.049096-	.079504
	6 % .06	.028303-	.030613-	.032667-	.035302-	.037686-	.040047-	.075867
	7 % .07	.019297-	.021595-	.023929-	.026250-	.028613-	.030959-	.072377
	8 % .08	.010251-	.012537-	.014852-	.017160-	.019502-	.021834-	.069029
	9 % .09	.001166-	.003440-	.005737-	.008032-	.010355-	.012673-	.065820
	10 % .10	.007957	.005694	.003415	.001131	.001172-	.003477-	.062745
	11 % .11	.017118	.014866	.012603	.010331	.008045	.005752	.059801
	12 % .12	.026316	.024073	.021827	.019566	.017297	.015016	.056984
	13 % .13	.035548	.033315	.031084	.028833	.026581	.024311	.054289
	14 % .14	.044814	.042590	.040374	.038133	.035897	.033638	.051713
10 Years n = 10	15 % .15	.054113	.051897	.049696	.047464	.045243	.042994	.049252
	16 % .16	.063443	.061236	.059048	.056825	.054618	.052380	.046901
	17 % .17	.072803	.070604	.068429	.066215	.064022	.061793	.044656
	18 % .18	.082193	.080002	.077838	.075633	.073453	.071233	.042514
	19 % .19	.091611	.089427	.087275	.085078	.082910	.080699	.040471
	20 % .20	.101056	.098879	.096738	.094548	.092393	.090190	.038522
	21 % .21	.110526	.108356	.106226	.104044	.101899	.099704	.036665
	22 % .22	.120022	.117858	.115738	.113563	.111429	.109241	.034894
	23 % .23	.129541	.127383	.125273	.123104	.120981	.118801	.033208
	24 % .24	.139084	.136931	.134830	.132668	.130554	.128381	.031602
	25 % .25	.148648	.146501	.144409	.142252	.140148	.137981	.030072
	26 % .26	.158233	.156091	.154007	.151856	.149761	.147600	.028616
	27 % .27	.167838	.165701	.163625	.161480	.159393	.157238	.027230
	28 % .28	.177762	.175330	.173262	.171121	.169043	.166893	.025611
	29 % .29	.187105	.184977	.182916	.180780	.178709	.176565	.024657
	30 % .30	.196765	.194641	.192587	.190456	.188392	.186253	.023463

TABLE C

Mortgage Coefficients for Computing Capitalization Rates.

20 YEARS AMORTIZATION: 9¼% TO 10½%

Interest Rate			9¼%	9½%	9¾%	10%	10¼%	10½%	$\frac{1}{s_{\overline{n}\rfloor}}$
Annual Requirement (f)			.109920	.111960	.113880	.115920	.117840	.119880	
Installment f/12			.009160	.009330	.009490	.009660	.009820	.009990	
Projection	Balance (b)		.438120	.440392	.447060	.450136	.457837	.461803	+ Dep. – App.
	Equity	Yield	Mortgage Coefficients						
15 Years n = 15	4 %	.04	.041859–	.044012–	.046265–	.048459–	.050763–	.053001–	.049941
	5 %	.05	.033881–	.036026–	.038255–	.040438–	.042714–	.044938–	.046342
	6 %	.06	.025780–	.027617–	.030124–	.032296–	.034547–	.036757–	.042962
	7 %	.07	.017560–	.019690–	.021875–	.024038–	.026264–	.028462–	.039794
	8 %	.08	.009226–	.011349–	.013515–	.015668–	.017872–	.020058–	.036829
	9 %	.09	.000783–	.002600–	.005547–	.007[illegible]92–	.009374–	.011549–	.034058
	10 %	.10	.007764	.005652	.003523	.001386	.000776–	.002940–	.031473
	11 %	.11	.016411	.014305	.012191	.010061	.007918	.005762	.029065
	12 %	.12	.025151	.023051	.020952	.018829	.016703	.014556	.026824
	13 %	.13	.033981	.031885	.029800	.027684	.025574	.023435	.024741
	14 %	.14	.042895	.040804	.038731	.036621	.034526	.032395	.022808
	15 %	.15	.051889	.049801	.047741	.045636	.043554	.041431	.021017
	16 %	.16	.060956	.058872	.056823	.054724	.052654	.050538	.019357
	17 %	.17	.070093	.068013	.065974	.063879	.061822	.059711	.017822
	18 %	.18	.079296	.077219	.075189	.073099	.071052	.068947	.016402
	19 %	.19	.088559	.086485	.084464	.082378	.080342	.078242	.015091
	20 %	.20	.097880	.095808	.093795	.091713	.089686	.087591	.013882
	21 %	.21	.107253	.105184	.103179	.101099	.099081	.096990	.012766
	22 %	.22	.116675	.114608	.112610	.110534	.108523	.106437	.011738
	23 %	.23	.126143	.124078	.122086	.120013	.118010	.115927	.010791
	24 %	.24	.135653	.133590	.131604	.129534	.127537	.125458	.009919
	25 %	.25	.145202	.143141	.141161	.139093	.137102	.135026	.009116
	26 %	.26	.154787	.152728	.150753	.148687	.146702	.144629	.008378
	27 %	.27	.164406	.162349	.160377	.158314	.156334	.154264	.007700
	28 %	.28	.174056	.172000	.170033	.167971	.165996	.163928	.007076
	29 %	.29	.183734	.181679	.179716	.177656	.175686	.173620	.006504
	30 %	.30	.193438	.191385	.189425	.187366	.185400	.183337	.005977
	Balance (b)		none	none	none	none	none	none	+ Dep. – App.
	Equity	Yield	Mortgage Coefficients						
20 Years n = 20	4 %	.04	.036307–	.038170–	.040178–	.042088–	.044164–	.046129–	.033581
	5 %	.05	.029649–	.031530–	.033529–	.035452–	.037512–	.039485–	.030242
	6 %	.06	.022710–	.024607–	.026598–	.028533–	.030579–	.032558–	.027184
	7 %	.07	.015504–	.017416–	.019400–	.021345–	.023378–	.025364–	.024392
	8 %	.08	.008047–	.009972–	.011950–	.013905–	.015926–	.017917–	.021852
	9 %	.09	.000355–	.002292–	.004264–	.006228–	.008238–	.010235–	.019546
	10 %	.10	.007555	.005607	.003641	.001669	.000331–	.002332–	.017459
	11 %	.11	.015669	.013711	.011750	.009771	.007779	.005773	.015575
	12 %	.12	.023971	.022004	.020048	.018061	.016077	.014068	.013878
	13 %	.13	.032445	.030470	.028517	.026525	.024548	.022535	.012353
	14 %	.14	.041076	.039093	.037145	.035147	.033176	.031161	.010986
	15 %	.15	.049850	.047861	.045916	.043913	.041948	.039930	.009761
	16 %	.16	.058754	.056760	.054817	.052811	.050851	.048830	.008667
	17 %	.17	.067777	.065777	.063837	.061827	.059871	.057849	.007690
	18 %	.18	.076906	.074902	.072964	.070950	.068999	.066974	.006819
	19 %	.19	.086130	.084122	.082186	.080170	.078222	.076195	.006045
	20 %	.20	.095441	.093429	.091495	.089476	.087531	.085503	.005356
	21 %	.21	.104829	.102814	.100881	.098860	.096918	.094888	.004744
	22 %	.22	.114285	.112267	.110336	.108313	.106373	.104342	.004201
	23 %	.23	.123803	.121783	.119853	.117828	.115890	.113859	.003720
	24 %	.24	.133376	.131354	.129425	.127398	.125463	.123430	.003293
	25 %	.25	.142998	.140973	.139046	.137017	.135084	.133050	.002915
	26 %	.26	.152663	.150637	.148710	.146680	.144748	.142714	.002581
	27 %	.27	.162367	.160339	.158413	.156382	.154451	.152416	.002285
	28 %	.28	.172105	.170075	.168150	.166118	.164189	.162153	.002023
	29 %	.29	.181873	.179842	.177918	.175885	.173956	.171920	.001791
	30 %	.30	.191668	.189636	.187712	.185678	.183751	.181714	.001586

Mortgage Coefficients for Computing Capitalization Rates.

20 YEARS AMORTIZATION: 10¾% TO 12%

Projection	Equity	Yield	10¾%	11%	11¼%	11½%	11¾%	12%	$\frac{1}{s_{\overline{n}|}}$
Interest Rate			10¾%	11%	11¼%	11½%	11¾%	12%	
Annual Requirement (f)			.121920	.123960	.126000	.128040	.130080	.132240	
Installment f/12			.010160	.010330	.010500	.010670	.010840	.011020	
5 Years n = 5	Balance (b)		.905078	.907493	.909944	.912431	.914953	.916696	+ Dep. − App.
	Equity	Yield	Mortgage Coefficients						
	4 %	.04	.064394−	.066880−	.069373−	.071872−	.074378−	.076859−	.184627
	5 %	.05	.054741−	.057218−	.059702−	.062192−	.064688−	.067164−	.180974
	6 %	.06	.045081−	.047549−	.050024−	.052505−	.054993−	.057462−	.177396
	7 %	.07	.035414−	.037874−	.040340−	.042812−	.045291−	.047754−	.173890
	8 %	.08	.025740−	.028191−	.030649−	.033113−	.035583−	.038040−	.170456
	9 %	.09	.016059−	.018502−	.020952−	.023407−	.025869−	.028320−	.167092
	10 %	.10	.006372−	.008807−	.011249−	.013696−	.016149−	.018595−	.163797
	11 %	.11	.003321	.000893	.001539−	.003979−	.006424−	.008864−	.160570
	12 %	.12	.013021	.010601	.008175	.005744	.003307	.000872	.157409
	13 %	.13	.022727	.020315	.017896	.015473	.013043	.010614	.154314
	14 %	.14	.032440	.030034	.027623	.025207	.022786	.020362	.151283
	15 %	.15	.042158	.039760	.037356	.034947	.032533	.030115	.148315
	16 %	.16	.051882	.049491	.047094	.044693	.042286	.039873	.145409
	17 %	.17	.061612	.059223	.056838	.054444	.052044	.049636	.142563
	18 %	.18	.071347	.068970	.066587	.064200	.061807	.059403	.139777
	19 %	.19	.081083	.078717	.076342	.073961	.071575	.069176	.137050
	20 %	.20	.090835	.088470	.086101	.083727	.081348	.078954	.134379
	21 %	.21	.100587	.098229	.095866	.093498	.091126	.088736	.131765
	22 %	.22	.110344	.107992	.105635	.103274	.100908	.098523	.129205
	23 %	.23	.120106	.117760	.115410	.113055	.110695	.108314	.126700
	24 %	.24	.129873	.127533	.125189	.122840	.120486	.118110	.124247
	25 %	.25	.139645	.137311	.134972	.132629	.130282	.127910	.121846
	26 %	.26	.149422	.147094	.144761	.142424	.140082	.137714	.119496
	27 %	.27	.159204	.156881	.154554	.152222	.149887	.147522	.117195
	28 %	.28	.168990	.166672	.164351	.162025	.159695	.157335	.114943
	29 %	.29	.178781	.176469	.174152	.171832	.169508	.167151	.112739
	30 %	.30	.188576	.186269	.183958	.181643	.179324	.176971	.110581
10 Years n = 10	Balance (b)		.742938	.747558	.752306	.757235	.762351	.765360	+ Dep. − App.
	Equity	Yield	Mortgage Coefficients						
	4 %	.04	.060513−	.062933−	.065369−	.067819−	.070286−	.072696−	.083290
	5 %	.05	.051486−	.053889−	.056307−	.058739−	.061185−	.063585−	.079504
	6 %	.06	.042421−	.044807−	.047207−	.049621−	.052050−	.054438−	.075867
	7 %	.07	.033318−	.035688−	.038072−	.040469−	.042879−	.045257−	.072377
	8 %	.08	.024178−	.026534−	.028901−	.031282−	.033675−	.036042−	.069029
	9 %	.09	.015003−	.017344−	.019696−	.022061−	.024437−	.026796−	.065820
	10 %	.10	.005793−	.008120−	.010458−	.012807−	.015168−	.017517−	.062745
	11 %	.11	.003449	.001136	.001187−	.003522−	.005868−	.008208−	.059801
	12 %	.12	.012725	.010425	.008114	.005793	.003462	.001130	.056984
	13 %	.13	.022033	.019744	.017447	.015139	.012821	.010498	.054289
	14 %	.14	.031370	.029094	.026809	.024514	.022209	.019894	.051713
	15 %	.15	.040738	.038473	.036199	.033916	.031624	.029316	.049252
	16 %	.16	.050134	.047879	.045617	.043345	.041065	.038764	.046901
	17 %	.17	.059557	.057313	.055061	.052801	.050532	.048238	.044656
	18 %	.18	.069006	.066772	.064530	.062281	.060023	.057735	.042514
	19 %	.19	.078481	.076256	.074024	.071785	.069537	.067256	.040471
	20 %	.20	.087980	.085764	.083541	.081311	.079074	.076798	.038522
	21 %	.21	.097503	.095295	.093081	.090861	.088633	.086363	.036665
	22 %	.22	.107048	.104848	.102643	.100431	.098212	.095947	.034894
	23 %	.23	.116614	.114423	.112225	.110021	.107811	.105552	.033208
	24 %	.24	.126202	.124017	.121827	.119631	.117430	.115175	.031602
	25 %	.25	.135808	.133631	.131448	.129260	.127066	.124816	.030072
	26 %	.26	.145434	.143263	.141088	.138907	.136720	.134474	.028616
	27 %	.27	.155078	.152914	.150744	.148570	.146391	.144149	.027230
	28 %	.28	.164739	.162581	.160418	.158250	.156077	.153839	.025911
	29 %	.29	.174417	.172264	.170107	.167945	.165779	.163545	.024657
	30 %	.30	.184110	.181963	.179811	.177656	.175496	.173265	.023463

Mortgage Coefficients for Computing Capitalization Rates.

20 YEARS AMORTIZATION: 10¾% TO 12%

Interest Rate		10¾%	11%	11¼%	11½%	11¾%	12%	$\frac{1}{s_{\overline{n}\rvert}}$
Annual Requirement (f)		.121920	.123960	.126000	.128040	.130080	.132240	
Installment f/12		.010160	.010330	.010500	.010670	.010840	.011020	
Projection	**Balance (b)**	.466197	.471044	.476365	.482185	.488529	.490428	+ Dep. – App.
	Equity Yield	**Mortgage Coefficients**						
15 Years n = 15	4 % .04	.055261-	.057543-	.059849-	.062179-	.064536-	.066791-	.049941
	5 % .05	.047182-	.049446-	.051733-	.054043-	.056377-	.058625-	.046342
	6 % .06	.038986-	.041234-	.043503-	.045793-	.048105-	.050347-	.042962
	7 % .07	.030677-	.032910-	.035162-	.037433-	.039726-	.041961-	.039794
	8 % .08	.022260-	.024478-	.026714-	.028969-	.031242-	.033472-	.036829
	9 % .09	.013739-	.015944-	.018165-	.020403-	.022659-	.024884-	.034058
	10 % .10	.005119-	.007311-	.009519-	.011742-	.013982-	.016201-	.031473
	11 % .11	.003595	.001414	.000780-	.002989-	.005213-	.007429-	.029065
	12 % .12	.012398	.010228	.008046	.005849	.003639	.001428	.026824
	13 % .13	.021287	.019127	.016955	.014771	.012574	.010367	.024741
	14 % .14	.030255	.028104	.025943	.023770	.021586	.019382	.022808
	15 % .15	.039298	.037157	.035005	.032842	.030669	.028469	.021017
	16 % .16	.048413	.046279	.044136	.041983	.039820	.037624	.019357
	17 % .17	.057593	.055467	.053332	.051188	.049035	.046841	.017822
	18 % .18	.066835	.064716	.062589	.060453	.058309	.056118	.016402
	19 % .19	.076136	.074022	.071902	.069774	.067639	.065450	.015091
	20 % .20	.085490	.083383	.081269	.079148	.077020	.074833	.013882
	21 % .21	.094894	.092792	.090684	.088570	.086449	.084265	.012766
	22 % .22	.104345	.102248	.100146	.098038	.095923	.093741	.011738
	23 % .23	.113840	.111747	.109650	.107547	.105439	.103258	.010791
	24 % .24	.123374	.121286	.119194	.117096	.114993	.112814	.009919
	25 % .25	.132946	.130862	.128773	.126680	.124583	.122405	.009116
	26 % .26	.142552	.140472	.138387	.136298	.134205	.132029	.008378
	27 % .27	.152190	.150113	.148032	.145947	.143858	.141683	.007700
	28 % .28	.161857	.159783	.157705	.155624	.153539	.151366	.007076
	29 % .29	.171551	.169480	.167405	.165327	.163246	.161074	.006504
	30 % .30	.181270	.179201	.177130	.175055	.172977	.170806	.005977
	Balance (b)	none	none	none	none	none	none	+ Dep. – App.
	Equity Yield	**Mortgage Coefficients**						
20 Years n = 20	4 % .04	.048121-	.050142-	.052194-	.054281-	.056404-	.058354-	.033581
	5 % .05	.041482-	.043504-	.045556-	.047637-	.049752-	.051724-	.030242
	6 % .06	.034559-	.036584-	.038634-	.040712-	.042819-	.044809-	.027184
	7 % .07	.027369-	.029395-	.031444-	.033518-	.035618-	.037626-	.024392
	8 % .08	.019926-	.021954-	.024002-	.026072-	.028166-	.030190-	.021852
	9 % .09	.012247-	.014276-	.016323-	.018390-	.020478-	.022516-	.019546
	10 % .10	.004347-	.006377-	.008424-	.010488-	.012571-	.014622-	.017459
	11 % .11	.003756	.001725	.000320-	.002382-	.004460-	.006523-	.015575
	12 % .12	.012048	.010016	.007971	.005912	.003837	.001764	.013878
	13 % .13	.020513	.018480	.016436	.014378	.012308	.010225	.012353
	14 % .14	.029136	.027103	.025059	.023003	.020936	.018845	.010986
	15 % .15	.037904	.035870	.033826	.031772	.029708	.027609	.009761
	16 % .16	.046803	.044767	.042724	.040672	.038611	.036505	.008667
	17 % .17	.055820	.053784	.051741	.049690	.047631	.045519	.007690
	18 % .18	.064944	.062907	.060865	.058815	.056759	.054641	.006819
	19 % .19	.074164	.072127	.070085	.068037	.065982	.063859	.006045
	20 % .20	.083471	.081434	.079392	.077344	.075291	.073164	.005356
	21 % .21	.092855	.090818	.088776	.086729	.084678	.082547	.004744
	22 % .22	.102309	.100271	.098229	.096184	.094133	.091999	.004201
	23 % .23	.111824	.109786	.107745	.105700	.103650	.101514	.003720
	24 % .24	.121395	.119356	.117315	.115271	.113223	.111083	.003293
	25 % .25	.131014	.128976	.126935	.124891	.122844	.120702	.002915
	26 % .26	.140678	.138639	.136598	.134555	.132508	.130364	.002581
	27 % .27	.150380	.148341	.146300	.144257	.142211	.140065	.002285
	28 % .28	.160116	.158077	.156036	.153994	.151949	.149801	.002023
	29 % .29	.169883	.167844	.165803	.163761	.161716	.159567	.001791
	30 % .30	.179677	.177638	.175597	.173555	.171511	.169361	.001586

Mortgage Coefficients for Computing Capitalization Rates

25 YEARS AMORTIZATION: 3¼% TO 4½%

Interest Rate		3¼%	3½%	3¾%	4%	4¼%	4½%	$\frac{1}{s_{\overline{n}|}}$
Annual Requirement(f)		.05856	.06012	.06180	.06336	.06504	.06672	
Installment f/12		.00488	.00501	.00515	.00528	.00542	.00556	
Projection	Balance(b)	.858723	.862958	.866592	.870938	.874677	.878467	+ Dep.
	Equity Yield	Mortgage Coefficients						− App.
5 Years n = 5	4% .04	.0075	.0052	.0028	.0004	*.0019*	*.0043*	.1846
	5% .05	.0170	.0147	.0123	.0100	.0076	.0052	.1810
	6% .06	.0265	.0242	.0218	.0195	.0172	.0148	.1774
	7% .07	.0360	.0337	.0314	.0291	.0267	.0244	.1739
	8% .08	.0455	.0432	.0409	.0386	.0363	.0340	.1705
	9% .09	.0550	.0528	.0505	.0482	.0459	.0436	.1671
	10% .10	.0646	.0623	.0600	.0578	.0555	.0532	.1638
	11% .11	.0741	.0719	.0696	.0673	.0651	.0628	.1606
	12% .12	.0837	.0814	.0792	.0769	.0747	.0724	.1574
	13% .13	.0932	.0910	.0888	.0865	.0843	.0820	.1543
	14% .14	.1028	.1006	.0984	.0961	.0939	.0916	.1513
	15% .15	.1124	.1102	.1080	.1058	.1035	.1013	.1483
	16% .16	.1219	.1198	.1176	.1154	.1131	.1109	.1454
	17% .17	.1315	.1294	.1272	.1250	.1228	.1206	.1426
	18% .18	.1411	.1390	.1368	.1346	.1324	.1302	.1398
	19% .19	.1508	.1486	.1464	.1443	.1421	.1399	.1371
	20% .20	.1604	.1583	.1561	.1539	.1518	.1496	.1344
	21% .21	.1700	.1679	.1657	.1636	.1614	.1593	.1318
	22% .22	.1797	.1775	.1754	.1733	.1711	.1689	.1292
	23% .23	.1893	.1872	.1851	.1830	.1808	.1786	.1267
	24% .24	.1990	.1969	.1947	.1926	.1905	.1883	.1242
	25% .25	.2086	.2065	.2044	.2023	.2002	.1980	.1218
	26% .26	.2183	.2162	.2141	.2120	.2099	.2078	.1195
	27% .27	.2280	.2259	.2238	.2217	.2196	.2175	.1172
	28% .28	.2376	.2356	.2335	.2314	.2293	.2272	.1149
	29% .29	.2473	.2453	.2432	.2412	.2390	.2369	.1127
	30% .30	.2570	.2550	.2529	.2509	.2488	.2467	.1106
	Balance (b)	.692554	.699748	.705717	.713354	.719739	.726332	+ Dep.
	Equity Yield	Mortgage Coefficients						− App.
10 Years n = 10	4% .04	.0070	.0049	.0027	.0005	*.0017*	*.0039*	.0833
	5% .05	.0159	.0137	.0116	.0094	.0072	.0050	.0795
	6% .06	.0247	.0226	.0205	.0184	.0162	.0140	.0759
	7% .07	.0337	.0316	.0295	.0274	.0252	.0231	.0724
	8% .08	.0426	.0406	.0385	.0364	.0343	.0321	.0690
	9% .09	.0517	.0496	.0475	.0455	.0434	.0413	.0658
	10% .10	.0607	.0587	.0566	.0546	.0525	.0504	.0628
	11% .11	.0698	.0678	.0658	.0638	.0617	.0596	.0598
	12% .12	.0789	.0770	.0749	.0730	.0709	.0688	.0570
	13% .13	.0881	.0862	.0842	.0822	.0802	.0781	.0543
	14% .14	.0973	.0954	.0934	.0914	.0894	.0874	.0517
	15% .15	.1066	.1046	.1027	.1007	.0987	.0967	.0493
	16% .16	.1158	.1139	.1120	.1100	.1081	.1061	.0469
	17% .17	.1251	.1232	.1213	.1194	.1174	.1155	.0447
	18% .18	.1345	.1326	.1307	.1288	.1268	.1249	.0425
	29% .19	.1438	.1420	.1401	.1382	.1363	.1343	.0405
	20% .20	.1532	.1514	.1495	.1476	.1457	.1438	.0385
	21% .21	.1627	.1608	.1489	.1571	.1552	.1533	.0367
	22% .22	.1721	.1703	.1684	.1666	.1647	.1628	.0349
	23% .23	.1816	.1798	.1779	.1761	.1742	.1723	.0332
	24% .24	.1911	.1893	.1875	.1857	.1838	.1819	.0316
	25% .25	.2006	.1989	.1970	.1952	.1933	.1915	.0301
	26% .26	.2102	.2084	.2066	.2048	.2029	.2011	.0286
	27% .27	.2198	.2180	.2162	.2144	.2126	.2107	.0272
	28% .28	.2294	.2276	.2258	.2240	.2222	.2203	.0259
	29% .29	.2390	.2372	.2354	.2337	.2318	.2300	.0247
	30% .30	.2486	.2469	.2451	.2433	.2415	.2397	.0235

Mortgage Coefficients for Computing Capitalization Rates

25 YEARS AMORTIZATION: 3¼% TO 4½%

Interest Rate		3¼%	3½%	3¾%	4%	4¼%	4½%	$\frac{1}{s_{\overline{n}\rceil}}$
Annual Requirement(f)		.05856	.06012	.06180	.06336	.06504	.06672	
Installment f/12		.00488	.00501	.00515	.00528	.00542	.00556	
Projection	Balance(b)	.497108	.505375	.511722	.520944	.528189	.535889	+ Dep.
	Equity Yield	Mortgage Coefficients						− App.
	4% .04	.0065	.0046	.0026	.0005	*.0015*	*.0036*	.0500
	5% .05	.0147	.0128	.0108	.0088	.0068	.0048	.0464
	6% .06	.0230	.0211	.0192	.0172	.0152	.0132	.0430
	7% .07	.0314	.0295	.0276	.0257	.0237	.0217	.0398
	8% .08	.0399	.0381	.0362	.0343	.0323	.0303	.0368
	9% .09	.0485	.0467	.0448	.0429	.0410	.0391	.0341
15 Years n = 15	10% .10	.0572	.0554	.0535	.0517	.0498	.0479	.0315
	11% .11	.0660	.0642	.0624	.0605	.0586	.0567	.0291
	12% .12	.0749	.0731	.0713	.0695	.0676	.0657	.0268
	13% .13	.0839	.0821	.0803	.0785	.0766	.0747	.0248
	14% .14	.0929	.0911	.0893	.0875	.0857	.0838	.0228
	15% .15	.1020	.1003	.0984	.0967	.0949	.0930	.0210
	16% .16	.1111	.1094	.1076	.1059	.1041	.1022	.0194
	17% .17	.1204	.1187	.1169	.1151	.1133	.1115	.0178
	18% .18	.1296	.1280	.1262	.1245	.1227	.1209	.0164
	19% .19	.1390	.1373	.1355	.1338	.1320	.1302	.0151
	20% .20	.1484	.1467	.1449	.1432	.1415	.1397	.0139
	Balance(b)	.267227	.273887	.277788	.286012	.291376	.297495	+ Dep.
	Equity Yield	Mortgage Coefficients						− App.
	4% .04	.0060	.0042	.0024	.0006	*.0013*	*.0031*	.0336
	5% .05	.0136	.0118	.0100	.0082	.0064	.0045	.0303
	6% .06	.0213	.0196	.0178	.0160	.0142	.0124	.0272
	7% .07	.0293	.0276	.0258	.0240	.0222	.0204	.0244
	8% .08	.0374	.0357	.0340	.0322	.0304	.0286	.0219
	9% .09	.0457	.0440	.0423	.0406	.0388	.0370	.0196
20 Years n = 20	10% .10	.0542	.0525	.0508	.0491	.0473	.0455	.0175
	11% .11	.0628	.0612	.0594	.0577	.0560	.0542	.0156
	12% .12	.0716	.0699	.0682	.0665	.0648	.0630	.0139
	13% .13	.0805	.0788	.0771	.0754	.0737	.0719	.0124
	14% .14	.0895	.0878	.0861	.0845	.0827	.0810	.0110
	15% .15	.0986	.0969	.0952	.0936	.0919	.0901	.0098
	16% .16	.1078	.1061	.1044	.1028	.1011	.0993	.0087
	17% .17	.1170	.1154	.1137	.1121	.1104	.1086	.0077
	18% .18	.1264	.1248	.1231	.1215	.1198	.1180	.0068
	19% .19	.1358	.1342	.1325	.1309	.1292	.1275	.0060
	20% .20	.1453	.1437	.1420	.1404	.1387	.1370	.0054
	Balance(b)	none	none	none	none	none	none	+ Dep.
	Equity Yield	Mortgage Coefficients						− App.
	4% .04	.0054	.0039	.0022	.0006	*.0010*	*.0027*	.0240
	5% .05	.0124	.0108	.0091	.0076	.0059	.0042	.0210
	6% .06	.0196	.0181	.0164	.0148	.0132	.0115	.0182
	7% .07	.0272	.0257	.0240	.0224	.0207	.0191	.0158
	8% .08	.0351	.0335	.0319	.0303	.0286	.0269	.0137
	9% .09	.0432	.0417	.0400	.0384	.0367	.0351	.0118
25 Years n = 25	10% .10	.0516	.0500	.0483	.0468	.0451	.0434	.0102
	11% .11	.0602	.0586	.0569	.0554	.0537	.0520	.0088
	12% .12	.0689	.0674	.0657	.0641	.0624	.0608	.0075
	13% .13	.0778	.0763	.0746	.0730	.0714	.0697	.0064
	14% .14	.0869	.0854	.0837	.0821	.0804	.0788	.0055
	15% .15	.0961	.0946	.0929	.0913	.0896	.0880	.0047
	16% .16	.1054	.1039	.1022	.1006	.0989	.0973	.0040
	17% .17	.1148	.1133	.1116	.1100	.1083	.1067	.0034
	18% .18	.1243	.1228	.1211	.1195	.1178	.1162	.0029
	19% .19	.1339	.1323	.1306	.1291	.1274	.1257	.0025
	20% .20	.1435	.1420	.1403	.1387	.1370	.1354	.0021

Mortgage Coefficients for Computing Capitalization Rates

25 YEARS AMORTIZATION: 4¾% TO 6%

Projection	Equity Yield	4¾%	5%	5¼%	5½%	5¾%	6%	$\frac{1}{s_{\overline{n}\rvert}}$
	Interest Rate	4¾%	5%	5¼%	5½%	5¾%	6%	
	Annual Requirement(f)	.06852	.07020	.07200	.07380	.07560	.07740	
	Installment f/12	.00571	.00585	.00600	.00615	.00630	.00645	
5 Years n = 5	Balance(b)	.881633	.885523	.888782	.892087	.895437	.898833	+ Dep. − App.
	Equity Yield	Mortgage Coefficients						
	4% .04	*.0067*	*.0091*	*.0115*	*.0139*	*.0163*	*.0187*	.1846
	5% .05	.0029	.0005	*.0019*	*.0043*	*.0067*	*.0091*	.1810
	6% .06	.0125	.0101	.0077	.0053	.0029	.0005	.1774
	7% .07	.0220	.0197	.0173	.0149	.0126	.0102	.1739
	8% .08	.0316	.0293	.0269	.0246	.0222	.0198	.1705
	9% .09	.0412	.0389	.0366	.0342	.0318	.0295	.1671
	10% .10	.0508	.0485	.0462	.0439	.0415	.0391	.1638
	11% .11	.0605	.0582	.0557	.0535	.0512	.0488	.1606
	12% .12	.0701	.0678	.0654	.0632	.0608	.0585	.1574
	13% .13	.0797	.0774	.0750	.0728	.0705	.0682	.1543
	14% .14	.0894	.0871	.0847	.0825	.0802	.0779	.1513
	15% .15	.0990	.0968	.0944	.0922	.0899	.0876	.1483
	16% .16	.1087	.1064	.1041	.1019	.0996	.0973	.1454
	17% .17	.1183	.1161	.1138	.1115	.1093	.1070	.1426
	18% .18	.1280	.1258	.1235	.1212	.1190	.1167	.1398
	19% .19	.1377	.1354	.1332	.1309	.1287	.1264	.1371
	20% .20	.1473	.1451	.1429	.1407	.1384	.1362	.1344
	21% .21	.1570	.1548	.1526	.1504	.1481	.1459	.1318
	22% .22	.1667	.1646	.1623	.1601	.1579	.1556	.1292
	23% .23	.1764	.1743	.1721	.1698	.1676	.1654	.1267
	24% .24	.1861	.1840	.1818	.1796	.1774	.1751	.1242
	25% .25	.1959	.1937	.1915	.1893	.1871	.1849	.1218
	26% .26	.2056	.2034	.2013	.1991	.1969	.1946	.1195
	27% .27	.2153	.2132	.2110	.2088	.2066	.2044	.1172
	28% .28	.2250	.2229	.2207	.2186	.2164	.2142	.1149
	29% .29	.2348	.2327	.2305	.2283	.2261	.2240	.1127
	30% .30	.2445	.2424	.2403	.2381	.2359	.2337	.1106
10 Years n = 10	Balance (b)	.731604	.738608	.744262	.750104	.756141	.762375	+ Dep. − App.
	Equity Yield	Mortgage Coefficients						
	4% .04	*.0062*	*.0084*	*.0107*	*.0130*	*.0153*	*.0176*	.0833
	5% .05	.0028	.0006	*.0017*	*.0039*	*.0062*	*.0085*	.0795
	6% .06	.0118	.0096	.0074	.0051	.0029	.0006	.0759
	7% .07	.0209	.0187	.0165	.0143	.0120	.0098	.0724
	8% .08	.0300	.0278	.0256	.0234	.0212	.0190	.0690
	9% .09	.0391	.0370	.0348	.0326	.0304	.0282	.0658
	10% .10	.0483	.0462	.0440	.0419	.0397	.0375	.0628
	11% .11	.0575	.0554	.0533	.0511	.0490	.0468	.0598
	12% .12	.0667	.0647	.0625	.0604	.0583	.0561	.0570
	13% .13	.0760	.0740	.0719	.0697	.0676	.0655	.0543
	14% .14	.0853	.0833	.0812	.0791	.0770	.0749	.0517
	15% .15	.0947	.0926	.0906	.0885	.0864	.0843	.0493
	16% .16	.1040	.1020	.1000	.0979	.0958	.0937	.0469
	17% .17	.1134	.1114	.1094	.1073	.1053	.1032	.0447
	18% .18	.1229	.1209	.1188	.1168	.1147	.1127	.0425
	19% .19	.1323	.1303	.1283	.1263	.1242	.1222	.0405
	20% .20	.1418	.1398	.1378	.1358	.1338	.1317	.0385
	21% .21	.1513	.1493	.1473	.1453	.1433	.1413	.0367
	22% .22	.1608	.1589	.1569	.1549	.1529	.1509	.0349
	23% .23	.1704	.1684	.1665	.1645	.1625	.1605	.0332
	24% .24	.1799	.1780	.1760	.1741	.1721	.1701	.0316
	25% .25	.1895	.1876	.1857	.1837	.1817	.1797	.0301
	26% .26	.1991	.1972	.1953	.1933	.1913	.1894	.0286
	27% .27	.2087	.2069	.2049	.2030	.2010	.1990	.0272
	28% .28	.2184	.2165	.2146	.2126	.2107	.2087	.0259
	29% .29	.2281	.2262	.2243	.2223	.2204	.2184	.0247
	30% .30	.2377	.2359	.2340	.2320	.2301	.2281	.0235

Mortgage Coefficients for Computing Capitalization Rates

25 YEARS AMORTIZATION: 4¾% TO 6%

Projection	Equity Yield	4¾%	5%	5¼%	5½%	5¾%	6%	$\frac{1}{s_{\overline{n}\rceil}}$
	Interest Rate	4¾%	5%	5¼%	5½%	5¾%	6%	
	Annual Requirement(f)	.06852	.07020	.07200	.07380	.07560	.07740	
	Installment f/12	.00571	.00585	.00600	.00615	.00630	.00645	
15 Years n = 15	Balance(b)	.541447	.550064	.556469	.563299	.570573	.578313	+ Dep. − App.
	Equity Yield	Mortgage Coefficients						
	4% .04	*.0056*	*.0077*	*.0099*	*.0120*	*.0142*	*.0163*	.0500
	5% .05	.0027	.0006	*.0015*	*.0036*	*.0057*	*.0079*	.0464
	6% .06	.0112	.0091	.0070	.0049	.0028	.0007	.0430
	7% .07	.0197	.0177	.0156	.0135	.0114	.0094	.0398
	8% .08	.0283	.0263	.0243	.0223	.0203	.0181	.0368
	9% .09	.0371	.0351	.0331	.0311	.0291	.0269	.0341
	10% .10	.0459	.0439	.0419	.0399	.0379	.0359	.0315
	11% .11	.0548	.0529	.0509	.0489	.0469	.0448	.0291
	12% .12	.0638	.0618	.0599	.0579	.0559	.0539	.0268
	13% .13	.0728	.0709	.0689	.0670	.0651	.0630	.0248
	14% .14	.0819	.0800	.0781	.0761	.0741	.0722	.0228
	15% .15	.0911	.0892	.0873	.0854	.0835	.0814	.0210
	16% .16	.1003	.0985	.0965	.0946	.0927	.0907	.0194
	17% .17	.1096	.1078	.1059	.1039	.1020	.1001	.0178
	18% .18	.1190	.1171	.1152	.1133	.1114	.1095	.0164
	19% .19	.1284	.1266	.1247	.1228	.1208	.1189	.0151
	20% .20	.1378	.1360	.1341	.1322	.1303	.1284	.0139
20 Years n = 20	Balance(b)	.300425	.308093	.312443	.317518	.323365	.330040	+ Dep. − App.
	Equity Yield	Mortgage Coefficients						
	4% .04	*.0050*	*.0070*	*.0089*	*.0109*	*.0129*	*.0149*	.0336
	5% .05	.0026	.0007	*.0012*	*.0032*	*.0051*	*.0071*	.0303
	6% .06	.0105	.0086	.0067	.0047	.0028	.0008	.0272
	7% .07	.0185	.0167	.0147	.0128	.0109	.0089	.0244
	8% .08	.0267	.0249	.0230	.0211	.0192	.0172	.0219
	9% .09	.0351	.0333	.0314	.0295	.0276	.0257	.0196
	10% .10	.0437	.0419	.0400	.0381	.0362	.0343	.0175
	11% .11	.0524	.0506	.0487	.0468	.0449	.0430	.0156
	12% .12	.0612	.0594	.0575	.0556	.0538	.0519	.0139
	13% .13	.0701	.0683	.0665	.0646	.0627	.0609	.0124
	14% .14	.0791	.0774	.0755	.0737	.0718	.0699	.0110
	15% .15	.0883	.0865	.0847	.0828	.0810	.0791	.0098
	16% .16	.0975	.0958	.0939	.0921	.0902	.0884	.0087
	17% .17	.1068	.1051	.1032	.1014	.0996	.0977	.0077
	18% .18	.1162	.1145	.1126	.1108	.1090	.1071	.0068
	19% .19	.1257	.1239	.1221	.1203	.1185	.1166	.0060
	20% .20	.1352	.1335	.1316	.1298	.1280	.1261	.0054
25 Years n = 25	Balance(b)	none	none	none	none	none	none	+ Dep. − App.
	Equity Yield	Mortgage Coefficients						
	4% .04	*.0045*	*.0062*	*.0080*	*.0098*	*.0116*	*.0134*	.0240
	5% .05	.0024	.0007	*.0010*	*.0028*	*.0046*	*.0064*	.0210
	6% .06	.0097	.0080	.0062	.0044	.0026	.0008	.0182
	7% .07	.0173	.0156	.0138	.0120	.0102	.0084	.0158
	8% .08	.0251	.0235	.0217	.0199	.0181	.0163	.0137
	9% .09	.0333	.0316	.0298	.0280	.0262	.0244	.0118
	10% .10	.0416	.0399	.0381	.0363	.0345	.0327	.0102
	11% .11	.0502	.0485	.0467	.0449	.0431	.0413	.0088
	12% .12	.0590	.0573	.0555	.0537	.0519	.0501	.0075
	13% .13	.0679	.0662	.0644	.0626	.0608	.0590	.0064
	14% .14	.0770	.0753	.0735	.0717	.0699	.0681	.0055
	15% .15	.0862	.0845	.0827	.0809	.0791	.0773	.0047
	16% .16	.0955	.0938	.0920	.0902	.0884	.0866	.0040
	17% .17	.1049	.1032	.1014	.0996	.0978	.0960	.0034
	18% .18	.1144	.1127	.1109	.1091	.1073	.1055	.0029
	19% .19	.1239	.1222	.1204	.1186	.1168	.1150	.0025
	20% .20	.1336	.1319	.1301	.1283	.1265	.1247	.0021

TABLE C

Mortgage Coefficients for Computing Capitalization Rates.

25 YEARS AMORTIZATION: 6¼% TO 7½%

Projection	Equity	Yield	6¼%	6½%	6¾%	7%	7¼%	7½%	$\frac{1}{s_{\overline{n}\vert}}$
Interest Rate			6¼%	6½%	6¾%	7%	7¼%	7½%	
Annual Requirement (f)			.079200	.081120	.082920	.084840	.086760	.088680	
Installment f/12			.006600	.006760	.006910	.007070	.007230	.007390	
5 Years n = 5	Balance (b)		.902276	.905061	.908595	.911463	.914370	.917319	+ Dep. – App.
	Equity	Yield	Mortgage Coefficients						
	4 %	.04	.021157-	.023591-	.026044-	.028493-	.030950-	.033414-	.184627
	5 %	.05	.011514-	.013938-	.016378-	.018817-	.021263-	.023716-	.180974
	6 %	.06	.001864-	.004278-	.006705-	.009133-	.011569-	.014012-	.177396
	7 %	.07	.007793	.005388	.002974	.000555	.001869-	.004302-	.173890
	8 %	.08	.017457	.015062	.012660	.010251	.007836	.005413	.170456
	9 %	.09	.027128	.024743	.022352	.019953	.017547	.015135	.167092
	10 %	.10	.036806	.034430	.032051	.029662	.027265	.024862	.163797
	11 %	.11	.046491	.044124	.041756	.039376	.036989	.034596	.160570
	12 %	.12	.056182	.053824	.051467	.049096	.046718	.044334	.157409
	13 %	.13	.065880	.063530	.061184	.058822	.056453	.054078	.154314
	14 %	.14	.075583	.073242	.070907	.068554	.066194	.063828	.151283
	15 %	.15	.085293	.082960	.080636	.078291	.075940	.073582	.148315
	16 %	.16	.095009	.092684	.090371	.088034	.085691	.083342	.145409
	17 %	.17	.104731	.102414	.100110	.097782	.095447	.093107	.142563
	18 %	.18	.114459	.112150	.109856	.107535	.105209	.102876	.139777
	19 %	.19	.124192	.121891	.119606	.117293	.114975	.112651	.137050
	20 %	.20	.133931	.131637	.129362	.127057	.124746	.122430	.134379
	21 %	.21	.143676	.141389	.139123	.136826	.134522	.132214	.131765
	22 %	.22	.153426	.151146	.148889	.146599	.144303	.142002	.129205
	23 %	.23	.163181	.160908	.158660	.156377	.154089	.151795	.126700
	24 %	.24	.172941	.170675	.168436	.166160	.163879	.161592	.124247
	25 %	.25	.182707	.180447	.178217	.175947	.173673	.171394	.121846
	26 %	.26	.192477	.190224	.188002	.185739	.183472	.181200	.119496
	27 %	.27	.202252	.200006	.197792	.195536	.193275	.191009	.117195
	28 %	.28	.212032	.209792	.207586	.205336	.203082	.200823	.114943
	29 %	.29	.221817	.219583	.217384	.215141	.212893	.210641	.112739
	30 %	.30	.231606	.229378	.227187	.224950	.222708	.220462	.110581
10 Years n = 10	Balance (b)		.768813	.773773	.780619	.785951	.791463	.797159	+ Dep. – App.
	Equity	Yield	Mortgage Coefficients						
	4 %	.04	.019944-	.022277-	.024647-	.027011-	.029390-	.031785-	.083290
	5 %	.05	.010819-	.013134-	.015478-	.017822-	.020180-	.022553-	.079504
	6 %	.06	.001660-	.003957-	.006276-	.008600-	.010938-	.013290-	.075867
	7 %	.07	.007532	.005253	.002958	.000652	.001666-	.003998-	.072377
	8 %	.08	.016758	.014495	.012223	.009935	.007635	.005321	.069029
	9 %	.09	.026016	.023769	.021519	.019248	.016965	.014670	.065820
	10 %	.10	.035305	.033074	.030845	.028590	.026324	.024047	.062745
	11 %	.11	.044625	.042408	.040199	.037960	.035710	.033450	.059801
	12 %	.12	.053973	.051771	.049581	.047357	.045123	.042878	.056984
	13 %	.13	.063351	.061161	.058990	.056780	.054561	.052332	.054289
	14 %	.14	.072755	.070578	.068424	.066229	.064024	.061809	.051713
	15 %	.15	.082186	.080021	.077884	.075702	.073510	.071310	.049252
	16 %	.16	.091642	.089490	.087369	.085199	.083020	.080833	.046901
	17 %	.17	.101123	.098982	.096876	.094718	.092552	.090378	.044656
	18 %	.18	.110628	.108497	.106406	.104260	.102105	.099943	.042514
	19 %	.19	.120156	.118035	.115958	.113822	.111679	.109529	.040471
	20 %	.20	.129705	.127594	.125531	.123405	.121273	.119133	.038522
	21 %	.21	.139276	.137174	.135123	.133008	.130886	.128757	.036665
	22 %	.22	.148867	.146773	.144735	.142629	.140516	.138398	.034894
	23 %	.23	.158477	.156392	.154365	.152268	.150165	.148056	.033208
	24 %	.24	.168105	.166029	.164012	.161924	.159830	.157730	.031602
	25 %	.25	.177752	.175683	.173677	.171596	.169511	.167419	.030072
	26 %	.26	.187415	.185353	.183357	.181285	.179207	.177124	.028616
	27 %	.27	.197095	.195040	.193053	.190988	.188918	.186843	.027230
	28 %	.28	.206790	.204741	.202764	.200706	.198643	.196575	.025911
	29 %	.29	.216500	.214457	.212489	.210437	.208381	.206321	.024657
	30 %	.30	.226224	.224187	.222227	.220182	.218132	.216079	.023463

TABLE C

Mortgage Coefficients for Computing Capitalization Rates.

25 YEARS AMORTIZATION: 6¼% TO 7½%

Interest Rate / Annual Requirement (f) / Installment f/12			6¼% .079200 .006600	6½% .081120 .006760	6¾% .082920 .006910	7% .084840 .007070	7¼% .086760 .007230	7½% .088680 .007390	$\frac{1}{s_{\overline{n}|}}$
Projection	Balance (b)		.586538	.592238	.601438	.608023	.615047	.622532	+ Dep. − App.
	Equity	Yield	Mortgage Coefficients						
15 Years n = 15	4 %	.04	.018551−	.020755−	.023015−	.025264−	.027535−	.029828−	.049941
	5 %	.05	.010039−	.012223−	.014449−	.016674−	.018920−	.021187−	.046342
	6 %	.06	.001436−	.003601−	.005796−	.007999−	.010221−	.012462−	.042962
	7 %	.07	.007253	.005106	.002940	.000758	.001440−	.003658−	.039794
	8 %	.08	.016027	.013897	.011758	.009596	.007417	.005221	.036829
	9 %	.09	.024882	.022767	.020654	.018510	.016351	.014176	.034058
	10 %	.10	.033813	.031713	.029624	.027496	.025355	.023200	.031473
	11 %	.11	.042817	.040731	.038664	.036552	.034428	.032291	.029065
	12 %	.12	.051890	.049817	.047771	.045674	.043566	.041445	.026824
	13 %	.13	.061029	.058968	.056941	.054858	.052764	.050659	.024741
	14 %	.14	.070230	.068180	.066170	.064100	.062020	.059929	.022808
	15 %	.15	.079489	.077449	.075456	.073398	.071330	.069253	.021017
	16 %	.16	.088803	.086773	.084795	.082747	.080691	.078626	.019357
	17 %	.17	.098168	.096147	.094183	.092145	.090100	.088047	.017822
	18 %	.18	.107581	.105568	.103617	.101599	.099554	.097511	.016402
	19 %	.19	.117039	.115033	.113095	.111075	.109049	.107016	.015091
	20 %	.20	.126539	.124540	.122612	.120601	.118583	.116560	.013882
	21 %	.21	.136078	.134085	.132168	.130164	.128154	.126138	.012766
	22 %	.22	.145653	.143666	.141758	.139761	.137758	.135750	.011738
	23 %	.23	.155261	.153280	.151380	.149389	.147394	.145393	.010791
	24 %	.24	.164901	.162924	.161033	.159048	.157058	.155064	.009919
	25 %	.25	.174569	.172597	.170713	.168733	.166749	.164761	.009116
	26 %	.26	.184264	.182296	.180419	.178444	.176465	.174482	.008378
	27 %	.27	.193983	.192019	.190149	.188178	.186204	.184226	.007700
	28 %	.28	.203726	.201765	.199900	.197934	.195964	.193991	.007076
	29 %	.29	.213489	.211532	.209672	.207709	.205743	.203775	.006504
	30 %	.30	.223271	.221317	.219462	.217503	.215541	.213576	.005977
	Balance (b)		.337600	.341201	.350564	.355787	.361829	.368746	+ Dep. − App.
	Equity	Yield	Mortgage Coefficients						
20 Years n = 20	4 %	.04	.016955−	.018996−	.021110−	.023206−	.025329−	.027481−	.033581
	5 %	.05	.009167−	.011196−	.013279−	.015357−	.017460−	.019589−	.030242
	6 %	.06	.001192−	.003210−	.005265−	.007327−	.009411−	.011519−	.027184
	7 %	.07	.006957	.004950	.002921	.000874	.001193−	.003281−	.024392
	8 %	.08	.015274	.013276	.011271	.009237	.007185	.005114	.021852
	9 %	.09	.023747	.021757	.019774	.017752	.015713	.013658	.019546
	10 %	.10	.032365	.030382	.028418	.026407	.024382	.022341	.017459
	11 %	.11	.041117	.039141	.037195	.035194	.033179	.031152	.015575
	12 %	.12	.049993	.048023	.046093	.044100	.042097	.040081	.013878
	13 %	.13	.058983	.057018	.055102	.053118	.051123	.049118	.012353
	14 %	.14	.068077	.066117	.064214	.062237	.060250	.058254	.010986
	15 %	.15	.077265	.075310	.073419	.071448	.069469	.067481	.009761
	16 %	.16	.086541	.084589	.082708	.080743	.078771	.076791	.008667
	17 %	.17	.095894	.093946	.092074	.090114	.088147	.086174	.007690
	18 %	.18	.105317	.103372	.101509	.099553	.097592	.095625	.006819
	19 %	.19	.114804	.112862	.111006	.109054	.107097	.105136	.006045
	20 %	.20	.124348	.122408	.120558	.118610	.116658	.114701	.005356
	21 %	.21	.133942	.132005	.130161	.128216	.126267	.124315	.004744
	22 %	.22	.143583	.141648	.139808	.137866	.135921	.133972	.004201
	23 %	.23	.153264	.151331	.149496	.147556	.145614	.143668	.003720
	24 %	.24	.162981	.161049	.159219	.157281	.155342	.153399	.003293
	25 %	.25	.172731	.170801	.168973	.167038	.165100	.163160	.002915
	26 %	.26	.182509	.180580	.178756	.176822	.174887	.172949	.002581
	27 %	.27	.192313	.190385	.188564	.186632	.184698	.182762	.002285
	28 %	.28	.202140	.200213	.198394	.196463	.194531	.192597	.002023
	29 %	.29	.211986	.210060	.208243	.206314	.204383	.202451	.001791
	30 %	.30	.221851	.219925	.218110	.216182	.214252	.212321	.001586

Mortgage Coefficients for Computing Capitalization Rates.

25 YEARS AMORTIZATION: 6¼% TO 7½%

TABLE C

Interest Rate / Annual Requirement (f) / Installment f/12		6¼% .079200 .006600	6½% .081120 .006760	6¾% .082920 .006910	7% .084840 .007070	7¼% .086760 .007230	7½% .088680 .007390	$\frac{1}{s_{\overline{n}\vert}}$
Projection	Balance (b)	none	none	none	none	none	none	+ Dep. – App.
	Equity / Yield	Mortgage Coefficients						
	4 % / .04	.015130-	.016965-	.018891-	.020785-	.022708-	.024666-	.024011
	5 % / .05	.008197-	.010043-	.011953-	.013850-	.015773-	.017725-	.020952
	6 % / .06	.000929-	.002785-	.004680-	.006580-	.008503-	.010451-	.018226
	7 % / .07	.006648	.004784	.002901	.000998	.000923-	.002868-	.015810
	8 % / .08	.014511	.012639	.010768	.008863	.006941	.004999	.013678
	9 % / .09	.022634	.020756	.018894	.016987	.015065	.013127	.011806
	10 % / .10	.030992	.029108	.027255	.025346	.023424	.021488	.010168
	11 % / .11	.039561	.037672	.035826	.033915	.031994	.030060	.008740
	12 % / .12	.048317	.046424	.044585	.042673	.040752	.038820	.007499
	13 % / .13	.057241	.055344	.053510	.051597	.049676	.047746	.006425
	14 % / .14	.066311	.064411	.062582	.060668	.058747	.056818	.005498
25 Years n = 25	15 % / .15	.075510	.073607	.071782	.069867	.067947	.066019	.004699
	16 % / .16	.084822	.082916	.081095	.079179	.077259	.075332	.004012
	17 % / .17	.094231	.092323	.090505	.088589	.086669	.084743	.003423
	18 % / .18	.103725	.101816	.100000	.098084	.096163	.094239	.002918
	19 % / .19	.113293	.111382	.109569	.107651	.105731	.103807	.002487
	20 % / .20	.122923	.121011	.119200	.117282	.115362	.113438	.002118
	21 % / .21	.132608	.130694	.128885	.126967	.125047	.123124	.001804
	22 % / .22	.142339	.140425	.138617	.136698	.134778	.132856	.001536
	23 % / .23	.152110	.150195	.148388	.146470	.144549	.142627	.001307
	24 % / .24	.161916	.160000	.158194	.156275	.154355	.152433	.001113
	25 % / .25	.171750	.169833	.168028	.166109	.164189	.162268	.000948
	26 % / .26	.181609	.179692	.177887	.175968	.174048	.172127	.000807
	27 % / .27	.191489	.189571	.187768	.185848	.183928	.182007	.000687
	28 % / .28	.201387	.199469	.197666	.195746	.193826	.191905	.000585
	29 % / .29	.211300	.209382	.207579	.205660	.203740	.201819	.000499
	30 % / .30	.221226	.219308	.217506	.215586	.213666	.211745	.000425

TABLE C

Mortgage Coefficients for Computing Capitalization Rates.

25 YEARS AMORTIZATION: 7¾% TO 9%

Interest Rate Annual Requirement (f) Installment f/12			7¾% .090720 .007560	8% .092640 .007720	8¼% .094680 .007890	8½% .096720 .008060	8¾% .098760 .008230	9% .100800 .008400	$\frac{1}{s_{\overline{n}|}}$
Projection	Balance (b)		.919578	.922604	.924932	.927294	.926689	.932118	+ Dep. − App.
	Equity	Yield	Mortgage Coefficients						
5 Years n = 5	4 %	.04	.035871−	.038350−	.040820−	.043296−	.045778−	.048267−	.184627
	5 %	.05	.026165−	.028633−	.031094−	.033562−	.036035−	.038515−	.180974
	6 %	.06	.016453−	.018910−	.021363−	.023822−	.026287−	.028758−	.177396
	7 %	.07	.006735−	.009181−	.011626−	.014077−	.016533−	.018996−	.173860
	8 %	.08	.002988	.000552	.001884−	.004326−	.006775−	.009229−	.170456
	9 %	.09	.012717	.010292	.007863	.005428	.002988	.000542	.167092
	10 %	.10	.022452	.020037	.017615	.015188	.012756	.010318	.163797
	11 %	.11	.032193	.029787	.027373	.024954	.022529	.020099	.160570
	12 %	.12	.041939	.039542	.037136	.034724	.032307	.029885	.157409
	13 %	.13	.051690	.049303	.046903	.044499	.042089	.039675	.157314
	14 %	.14	.061446	.059068	.056676	.054279	.051876	.049469	.151283
	15 %	.15	.071207	.068838	.066453	.064063	.061668	.059267	.148315
	16 %	.16	.080974	.078614	.076235	.073852	.071463	.069070	.145409
	17 %	.17	.090745	.088393	.086021	.083645	.081263	.078877	.142563
	18 %	.18	.100521	.098178	.095812	.093442	.091067	.088688	.139777
	19 %	.19	.110301	.107967	.105607	.103244	.100876	.098503	.137050
	20 %	.20	.120087	.117760	.115407	.113050	.110688	.108321	.134379
	21 %	.21	.129876	.127558	.125211	.122860	.120504	.118144	.131765
	22 %	.22	.139670	.137359	.135019	.132673	.130324	.127970	.129205
	23 %	.23	.149469	.147166	.144831	.142491	.140148	.137800	.126700
	24 %	.24	.159272	.156976	.154646	.152313	.149975	.147634	.124247
	25 %	.25	.169079	.166790	.164466	.162138	.159807	.157471	.121846
	26 %	.26	.178890	.176608	.174290	.171968	.169641	.167311	.119496
	27 %	.27	.188705	.186430	.184117	.181800	.179480	.177155	.117195
	28 %	.28	.198523	.196256	.193948	.191637	.189321	.187002	.114943
	29 %	.29	.208346	.206085	.203783	.201476	.199166	.196852	.112739
	30 %	.30	.218173	.215918	.213621	.211319	.209015	.206706	.110581
	Balance (b)		.801241	.807296	.811697	.816251	.820963	.825837	+ Dep. − App.
	Equity	Yield	Mortgage Coefficients						
10 Years n = 10	4 %	.04	.034165−	.036589−	.038996−	.041415−	.043847−	.046293−	.083290
	5 %	.05	.024917−	.027319−	.029709−	.032111−	.034525−	.036953−	.079504
	6 %	.06	.015640−	.018020−	.020393−	.022779−	.025176−	.027586−	.075867
	7 %	.07	.006334−	.008692−	.011051−	.013420−	.015801−	.018194−	.072377
	8 %	.08	.003000	.000662	.001681−	.004035−	.006401−	.008777−	.069029
	9 %	.09	.012362	.010043	.007714	.005374	.003024	.000663	.065820
	10 %	.10	.021751	.019451	.017135	.014809	.012473	.010127	.062745
	11 %	.11	.031166	.028883	.026580	.024268	.021946	.019615	.059801
	12 %	.12	.040606	.038341	.036050	.033750	.031442	.029124	.056984
	13 %	.13	.050070	.047821	.045542	.043255	.040959	.038655	.054289
	14 %	.14	.059558	.057325	.055057	.052782	.050498	.048206	.051713
	15 %	.15	.069069	.066851	.064594	.062329	.060057	.057777	.049252
	16 %	.16	.078602	.076397	.074151	.071898	.069637	.067368	.046901
	17 %	.17	.088155	.085965	.083728	.081485	.079235	.076977	.044656
	18 %	.18	.097730	.095552	.093325	.091092	.088851	.086604	.042514
	19 %	.19	.107324	.105158	.102940	.100716	.098485	.096248	.040471
	20 %	.20	.116936	.114783	.112573	.110358	.108136	.105909	.038522
	21 %	.21	.126567	.124425	.122224	.120017	.117804	.115585	.036665
	22 %	.22	.136215	.134084	.131890	.129691	.127487	.125277	.034894
	23 %	.23	.145880	.143759	.141573	.139382	.137185	.134983	.033208
	24 %	.24	.155561	.153449	.151270	.149086	.146897	.144703	.031602
	25 %	.25	.165257	.163155	.160982	.158805	.156624	.154437	.030072
	26 %	.26	.174967	.172874	.170708	.168538	.166363	.164183	.028616
	27 %	.27	.184692	.182607	.180447	.178283	.176115	.173942	.027230
	28 %	.28	.194430	.192353	.190199	.188041	.185879	.183712	.025911
	29 %	.29	.204180	.202111	.199962	.197810	.195654	.193494	.024657
	30 %	.30	.213943	.211881	.209738	.207591	.205440	.203286	.023463

Mortgage Coefficients for Computing Capitalization Rates.

25 YEARS AMORTIZATION: 7¾% TO 9%

Interest Rate Annual Requirement (f) Installment f/12			7¾% .090720 .007560	8% .092640 .007720	8¼% .094680 .007890	8½% .096720 .008060	8¾% .098760 .008230	9% .100800 .008400	$\frac{1}{s_{\overline{n}|}}$
Projection	Balance (b)		.627112	.635506	.640886	.646655	.652831	.659434	+ Dep. – App.
	Equity	Yield	Mortgage Coefficients						
	4 %	.04	.032097-	.034436-	.036745-	.039073-	.041422-	.043791-	.049941
	5 %	.05	.023439-	.025748-	.028037-	.030345-	.032671-	.035017-	.046342
	6 %	.06	.014699-	.016980-	.019251-	.021539-	.023844-	.026168-	.042962
	7 %	.07	.005881-	.008135-	.010389-	.012658-	.014944-	.017247-	.039794
	8 %	.08	.003013	.000784	.001454-	.003706-	.005973-	.008257-	.036829
	9 %	.09	.011980	.009774	.007551	.005314	.003064	.000799	.034058
	10 %	.10	.021016	.018831	.016622	.014401	.012166	.009918	.031473
	11 %	.11	.030118	.027954	.025757	.023550	.021330	.019098	.029065
	12 %	.12	.039282	.037137	.034952	.032758	.030552	.028335	.026824
	13 %	.13	.048505	.046378	.044205	.042022	.039829	.037626	.024741
	14 %	.14	.057785	.055673	.053511	.051339	.049158	.046967	.022808
	15 %	.15	.067116	.065020	.062867	.060706	.058536	.056357	.021017
	16 %	.16	.076498	.074415	.072271	.070119	.067960	.065792	.019357
15 Years n = 15	17 %	.17	.085925	.083856	.081720	.079577	.077427	.075269	.017822
	18 %	.18	.095396	.093338	.091210	.089075	.086934	.084786	.016402
	19 %	.19	.104907	.102860	.100739	.098612	.096479	.094339	.015091
	20 %	.20	.114456	.112419	.110305	.108185	.106059	.103927	.013882
	21 %	.21	.124040	.122013	.119904	.117790	.115672	.113547	.012766
	22 %	.22	.133657	.131638	.129535	.127427	.125315	.123197	.011738
	23 %	.23	.143303	.141293	.139195	.137092	.134986	.132875	.010791
	24 %	.24	.152978	.150975	.148882	.146784	.144683	.142578	.009919
	25 %	.25	.162679	.160683	.158593	.156501	.154405	.152304	.009116
	26 %	.26	.172404	.170414	.168328	.166240	.164148	.162053	.008378
	27 %	.27	.182151	.180166	.178085	.176000	.173913	.171822	.007700
	28 %	.28	.191918	.189939	.187861	.185780	.183696	.181610	.007076
	29 %	.29	.201705	.199730	.197655	.195578	.193498	.191415	.006504
	30 %	.30	.211509	.209538	.207466	.205392	.203315	.201235	.005977
	Balance (b)		.370890	.379565	.383224	.387631	.392837	.398901	+ Dep. – App.
	Equity	Yield	Mortgage Coefficients						
	4 %	.04	.029593-	.031804-	.033967-	.036155-	.038370-	.040614-	.033581
	5 %	.05	.021694-	.023876-	.026027-	.028200-	.030397-	.032621-	.030242
	6 %	.06	.013617-	.015773-	.017913-	.020073-	.022254-	.024459-	.027184
	7 %	.07	.005374-	.007505-	.009635-	.011782-	.013949-	.016137-	.024392
	8 %	.08	.003027	.000917	.001202-	.003338-	.005492-	.007664-	.021852
	9 %	.09	.011576	.009487	.007375	.005249	.003107	.000949	.019546
	10 %	.10	.020264	.018192	.016088	.013971	.011840	.009694	.017459
	11 %	.11	.029078	.027023	.024926	.022818	.020696	.018562	.015575
	12 %	.12	.038011	.035970	.033880	.031778	.029666	.027542	.013878
	13 %	.13	.047051	.045024	.042939	.040845	.038740	.036625	.012353
	14 %	.14	.056191	.054176	.052095	.050007	.047910	.045803	.010986
	15 %	.15	.065421	.063416	.061340	.059257	.057166	.055067	.009761
	16 %	.16	.074732	.072737	.070665	.068587	.066502	.064409	.008667
20 Years n = 20	17 %	.17	.084118	.082131	.080063	.077989	.075909	.073822	.007690
	18 %	.18	.093570	.091591	.089526	.087456	.085380	.083299	.006819
	19 %	.19	.103083	.101110	.099048	.096981	.094910	.092833	.006045
	20 %	.20	.112649	.110683	.108623	.106560	.104492	.102419	.005356
	21 %	.21	.122264	.120303	.118246	.116185	.114120	.112052	.004744
	22 %	.22	.131923	.129966	.127911	.125853	.123791	.121725	.004201
	23 %	.23	.141620	.139668	.137614	.135558	.133498	.131436	.003720
	24 %	.24	.151352	.149403	.147351	.145297	.143239	.141179	.003293
	25 %	.25	.161114	.159169	.157118	.155065	.153010	.150952	.002915
	26 %	.26	.170903	.168961	.166912	.164860	.162807	.160751	.002581
	27 %	.27	.180717	.178777	.176729	.174679	.172627	.170573	.002285
	28 %	.28	.190552	.188615	.186567	.184519	.182468	.180416	.002023
	29 %	.29	.200407	.198471	.196425	.194377	.192327	.190277	.001791
	30 %	.30	.210278	.208344	.206298	.204251	.202203	.200153	.001586

Mortgage Coefficients for Computing Capitalization Rates.

25 YEARS AMORTIZATION: 7¾% TO 9%

Interest Rate / Annual Requirement (f) / Installment f/12		7¾% .090720 .007560	8% .092640 .007720	8¼% .094680 .007890	8½% .096720 .008060	8¾% .098760 .008230	9% .100800 .008400	$\frac{1}{s_{\overline{n}\rvert}}$
Projection	Balance (b)	none	none	none	none	none	none	+ Dep. – App.
	Equity Yield	Mortgage Coefficients						
	4 % .04	.026560–	.028586–	.030537–	.032516–	.034526–	.036571–	.024011
	5 % .05	.019639–	.021650–	.023613–	.025600–	.027614–	.029658–	.020952
	6 % .06	.012381–	.014381–	.016354–	.018347–	.020365–	.022409–	.018226
	7 % .07	.004812–	.006801–	.008783–	.010783–	.012803–	.014847–	.015810
	8 % .08	.003042	.001062	.000926–	.002932–	.004955–	.006997–	.013678
	9 % .09	.011158	.009186	.007190	.005180	.003154	.001112	.011806
	10 % .10	.019510	.017545	.015543	.013529	.011501	.009459	.010168
	11 % .11	.028073	.026115	.024107	.022089	.020060	.018018	.008740
	12 % .12	.036825	.034873	.032860	.030839	.028809	.026767	.007499
	13 % .13	.045745	.043797	.041780	.039757	.037725	.035683	.006425
	14 % .14	.054812	.052868	.050848	.048822	.046789	.044747	.005498
	15 % .15	.064008	.062067	.060044	.058016	.055982	.053941	.004699
25 Years	16 % .16	.073317	.071379	.069354	.067324	.065289	.063248	.004012
n = 25	17 % .17	.082724	.080789	.078762	.076730	.074694	.072654	.003423
	18 % .18	.092216	.090283	.088254	.086222	.084185	.082145	.002918
	19 % .19	.101782	.099851	.097820	.095787	.093750	.091709	.002487
	20 % .20	.111411	.109482	.107450	.105415	.103378	.101337	.002118
	21 % .21	.121095	.119167	.117134	.115098	.113060	.111020	.001804
	22 % .22	.130825	.128898	.126864	.124828	.122790	.120750	.001536
	23 % .23	.140595	.138670	.136634	.134598	.132559	.130519	.001307
	24 % .24	.150400	.148475	.146439	.144402	.142363	.140323	.001113
	25 % .25	.160233	.158309	.156273	.154235	.152196	.150156	.000948
	26 % .26	.170092	.168168	.166131	.164093	.162054	.160014	.000807
	27 % .27	.179971	.178048	.176011	.173973	.171933	.169893	.000687
	28 % .28	.189869	.187946	.185909	.183870	.181831	.179791	.000585
	29 % .29	.199782	.197860	.195822	.193783	.191743	.189703	.000499
	30 % .30	.209708	.207786	.205748	.203709	.201669	.199629	.000425

Mortgage Coefficients for Computing Capitalization Rates.

25 YEARS AMORTIZATION: 9¼% TO 10½%

Interest Rate / Annual Requirement (f) / Installment f/12			9¼%	9½%	9¾%	10%	10¼%	10½%	$\frac{1}{s_{\overline{n}\rceil}}$
Annual Requirement (f)			.102840	.104880	.107040	.109080	.111240	.113400	
Installment f/12			.008570	.008740	.008920	.009090	.009270	.009450	
Projection	Balance (b)		.934581	.937079	.938842	.941405	.943225	.945071	+ Dep. – App.
	Equity	Yield	Mortgage Coefficients						
	4 %	.04	.050761–	.053263–	.055748–	.058261–	.060757–	.063258–	.184627
	5 %	.05	.041000–	.043492–	.045972–	.048475–	.050965–	.053459–	.180974
	6 %	.06	.031234–	.033718–	.036190–	.038685–	.041168–	.043655–	.177396
	7 %	.07	.021464–	.023938–	.026405–	.028891–	.031367–	.033848–	.173890
	8 %	.08	.011688–	.014154–	.016615–	.019092–	.021562–	.024037–	.170456
	9 %	.09	.001909–	.004366–	.006821–	.009289–	.011753–	.014221–	.167092
	10 %	.10	.007875	.005426	.002977	.000517	.001940–	.004402–	.163797
	11 %	.11	.017664	.015223	.012780	.010328	.007876	.005419	.160570
	12 %	.12	.027457	.025024	.022586	.020143	.017696	.015246	.157409
	13 %	.13	.037255	.034829	.032397	.029961	.027521	.025076	.154314
	14 %	.14	.047056	.044638	.042212	.039784	.037349	.034909	.151283
5 Years n = 5	15 %	.15	.056862	.054452	.052030	.049610	.047180	.044746	.148315
	16 %	.16	.066672	.064269	.061852	.059440	.057015	.054587	.145409
	17 %	.17	.076486	.074090	.071678	.069273	.066853	.064430	.142563
	18 %	.18	.086304	.083914	.081508	.079110	.076695	.074277	.139777
	19 %	.19	.096125	.093743	.091341	.088950	.086540	.084127	.137050
	20 %	.20	.105950	.103575	.101178	.098793	.096389	.093981	.134379
	21 %	.21	.115779	.113410	.111018	.108640	.106240	.103837	.131765
	22 %	.22	.125612	.123249	.120861	.118490	.116095	.113697	.129205
	23 %	.23	.135448	.133092	.130708	.128343	.125953	.123559	.126700
	24 %	.24	.145288	.142937	.140558	.138200	.135814	.133424	.124247
	25 %	.25	.155131	.152786	.150411	.148059	.145677	.143292	.121846
	26 %	.26	.164977	.162638	.160268	.157921	.155544	.153163	.119496
	27 %	.27	.174826	.172494	.170127	.167786	.165413	.163037	.117195
	28 %	.28	.184679	.182352	.179989	.177655	.175285	.172913	.114943
	29 %	.29	.194535	.192213	.189854	.187525	.185160	.182792	.112739
	30 %	.30	.204394	.202077	.199722	.197399	.195038	.192674	.110581
	Balance (b)		.830877	.836090	.839459	.845000	.848649	.852429	+ Dep. – App.
	Equity	Yield	Mortgage Coefficients						
	4 %	.04	.048753–	.051227–	.053668–	.056169–	.058633–	.061108–	.083290
	5 %	.05	.039394–	.041848–	.044276–	.046756–	.049206–	.051667–	.079504
	6 %	.06	.030009–	.032444–	.034860–	.037320–	.039757–	.042204–	.075867
	7 %	.07	.020599–	.023016–	.025420–	.027861–	.030285–	.032719–	.072377
	8 %	.08	.011165–	.013565–	.015957–	.018380–	.020792–	.023213–	.069029
	9 %	.09	.001708–	.004091–	.006473–	.008877–	.011278–	.013686–	.065820
	10 %	.10	.007771	.005404	.003033	.000645	.001743–	.004140–	.062745
	11 %	.11	.017273	.014922	.012560	.010189	.007810	.005424	.059801
	12 %	.12	.026797	.024460	.022108	.019752	.017384	.015009	.056984
	13 %	.13	.036341	.034018	.031675	.029334	.026976	.024611	.054289
	14 %	.14	.045905	.043596	.041262	.038935	.036586	.034231	.051713
10 Years n = 10	15 %	.15	.055489	.053192	.050866	.048554	.046214	.043868	.049252
	16 %	.16	.065092	.062807	.060489	.058189	.055858	.053521	.046901
	17 %	.17	.074712	.072439	.070129	.067841	.065518	.063189	.044656
	18 %	.18	.084350	.082088	.079785	.077509	.075194	.072873	.042514
	19 %	.19	.094004	.091753	.089457	.087193	.084885	.082572	.040471
	20 %	.20	.103675	.101434	.099144	.096891	.094590	.092284	.038522
	21 %	.21	.113360	.111129	.108846	.106603	.104309	.102010	.036665
	22 %	.22	.123061	.120839	.118562	.116328	.114041	.111749	.034894
	23 %	.23	.132776	.130563	.128291	.126067	.123786	.121500	.033208
	24 %	.24	.142504	.140299	.138033	.135818	.133542	.131263	.031602
	25 %	.25	.152245	.150049	.147787	.145581	.143311	.141037	.030072
	26 %	.26	.161999	.159810	.157554	.155355	.153091	.150822	.028616
	27 %	.27	.171765	.169583	.167331	.165140	.162881	.160618	.027230
	28 %	.28	.181542	.179367	.177119	.174936	.172681	.170423	.025911
	29 %	.29	.191330	.189161	.186918	.184741	.182491	.180238	.024657
	30 %	.30	.201128	.198965	.196726	.194556	.192311	.190062	.023463

Mortgage Coefficients for Computing Capitalization Rates.

25 YEARS AMORTIZATION: 9¼% TO 10½%

Interest Rate Annual Requirement (f) Installment f/12			9¼% .102840 .008570	9½% .104880 .008740	9¾% .107040 .008920	10% .109080 .009090	10¼% .111240 .009270	10½% .113400 .009450	$\frac{1}{s_{\overline{n}\rvert}}$
Projection	**Balance (b)**		.666484	.674002	.677958	.686384	.691101	.696179	+ Dep. – App.
	Equity	**Yield**	**Mortgage Coefficients**						
	4 %	.04	.046183–	.048599–	.050956–	.053417–	.055813–	.058226–	.049941
	5 %	.05	.037384–	.039772–	.042115–	.044546–	.046924–	.049320–	.046342
	6 %	.06	.028511–	.030874–	.033204–	.035606–	.037968–	.040347–	.042962
	7 %	.07	.019567–	.021907–	.024224–	.026599–	.028947–	.031309–	.039794
	8 %	.08	.010556–	.012873–	.015179–	.017529–	.019863–	.022210–	.036829
	9 %	.09	.001480–	.003776–	.006071–	.008398–	.010719–	.013052–	.034058
	10 %	.10	.007656	.005380	.003095	.000790	.001517–	.003837–	.031473
	11 %	.11	.016853	.014595	.012320	.010035	.007738	.005430	.029065
	12 %	.12	.026106	.023864	.021598	.019332	.017045	.014749	.026824
	13 %	.13	.035411	.033185	.030927	.028679	.026402	.024117	.024741
	14 %	.14	.044767	.042555	.040305	.038073	.035805	.033529	.022808
	15 %	.15	.054169	.051971	.049728	.047511	.045252	.042985	.021017
	16 %	.16	.063616	.061430	.059193	.056990	.054739	.052481	.019357
15 Years **n = 15**	17 %	.17	.073103	.070929	.068699	.066509	.064265	.062014	.017822
	18 %	.18	.082630	.080467	.078242	.076064	.073826	.071583	.016402
	19 %	.19	.092193	.090039	.087820	.085653	.083421	.081185	.015091
	20 %	.20	.101789	.099645	.097430	.095273	.093048	.090817	.013882
	21 %	.21	.111417	.109281	.107071	.104923	.102703	.100478	.012766
	22 %	.22	.121074	.118946	.116740	.114601	.112385	.110166	.011738
	23 %	.23	.130758	.128637	.126435	.124304	.122093	.119878	.010791
	24 %	.24	.140468	.138353	.136154	.134030	.131824	.129613	.009919
	25 %	.25	.150200	.148092	.145896	.143779	.141576	.139369	.009116
	26 %	.26	.159954	.157851	.155658	.153547	.151348	.149145	.008378
	27 %	.27	.169728	.167630	.165439	.163335	.161138	.158939	.007700
	28 %	.28	.179520	.177427	.175239	.173139	.170946	.168750	.007076
	29 %	.29	.189329	.187240	.185054	.182959	.180769	.178576	.006504
	30 %	.30	.199153	.197068	.194885	.192794	.190606	.188416	.005977
	Balance (b)		.405884	.413849	.415513	.425410	.428653	.432646	+ Dep. – App.
	Equity	**Yield**	**Mortgage Coefficients**						
	4 %	.04	.042888–	.045196–	.047411–	.049784–	.052053–	.054347–	.033581
	5 %	.05	.034872–	.037153–	.039363–	.041702–	.043961–	.046241–	.030242
	6 %	.06	.026689–	.028945–	.031150–	.033460–	.035708–	.037976–	.027184
	7 %	.07	.018347–	.020582–	.022782–	.025064–	.027303–	.029560–	.024392
	8 %	.08	.009857–	.012071–	.014267–	.016523–	.018754–	.021002–	.021852
	9 %	.09	.001227–	.003422–	.005615–	.007848–	.010072–	.012310–	.019546
	10 %	.10	.007533	.005353	.003164	.000952	.001264–	.003494–	.017459
	11 %	.11	.016413	.014249	.012063	.009869	.007659	.005436	.015575
	12 %	.12	.025405	.023255	.021071	.018894	.016689	.014474	.013878
	13 %	.13	.034499	.032361	.030180	.028018	.025818	.023608	.012353
20 Years **n = 20**	14 %	.14	.043686	.041559	.039381	.037232	.035036	.032832	.010986
	15 %	.15	.052959	.050841	.048665	.046528	.044337	.042138	.009761
	16 %	.16	.062309	.060200	.058025	.055899	.053711	.051517	.008667
	17 %	.17	.071728	.069627	.067454	.065338	.063153	.060963	.007690
	18 %	.18	.081211	.079117	.076946	.074838	.072656	.070469	.006819
	19 %	.19	.090751	.088663	.086493	.084393	.082213	.080029	.006045
	20 %	.20	.100342	.098259	.096090	.093997	.091820	.089639	.005356
	21 %	.21	.109978	.107901	.105733	.103646	.101470	.099291	.004744
	22 %	.22	.119656	.117582	.115415	.113334	.111160	.108983	.004201
	23 %	.23	.129370	.127300	.125134	.123057	.120885	.118710	.003720
	24 %	.24	.139116	.137050	.134885	.132812	.130641	.128468	.003293
	25 %	.25	.148892	.146829	.144664	.142595	.140426	.138254	.002915
	26 %	.26	.158693	.156633	.154468	.152403	.150234	.148064	.002581
	27 %	.27	.168517	.166459	.164295	.162233	.160065	.157896	.002285
	28 %	.28	.178362	.176306	.174142	.172082	.169916	.167747	.002023
	29 %	.29	.188224	.186170	.184007	.181949	.179783	.177616	.001791
	30 %	.30	.198102	.196050	.193887	.191831	.189666	.187500	.001586

Mortgage Coefficients for Computing Capitalization Rates.

25 YEARS AMORTIZATION: 9¼% TO 10½%

Interest Rate Annual Requirement (f) Installment f/12			9¼% .102840 .008570	9½% .104880 .008740	9¾% .107040 .008920	10% .109080 .009090	10¼% .111240 .009270	10½% .113400 .009450	$\frac{1}{s_{\overline{n}\rvert}}$
Projection	Balance (b)		none	none	none	none	none	none	+ Dep. – App.
	Equity	Yield	Mortgage Coefficients						
	4 %	.04	.038654–	.040779–	.042764–	.044972–	.047022–	.049104–	.024011
	5 %	.05	.031736–	.033850–	.035857–	.038044–	.040108–	.042199–	.020952
	6 %	.06	.024481–	.026585–	.028613–	.030780–	.032857–	.034957–	.018226
	7 %	.07	.016915–	.019011–	.021056–	.023206–	.025294–	.027402–	.015810
	8 %	.08	.009062–	.011150–	.013211–	.015346–	.017444–	.019559–	.013678
	9 %	.09	.000948–	.003030–	.005104–	.007226–	.009332–	.011454–	.011806
	10 %	.10	.007401	.005325	.003239	.001128	.000985–	.003111–	.010168
	11 %	.11	.015963	.013892	.011796	.009694	.007574	.005443	.008740
	12 %	.12	.024714	.022647	.020542	.018449	.016324	.014188	.007499
	13 %	.13	.033632	.031569	.029456	.027371	.025240	.023101	.006425
	14 %	.14	.042698	.040638	.038518	.036440	.034305	.032163	.005498
25 Years n = 25	15 %	.15	.051893	.049836	.047710	.045638	.043499	.041354	.004699
	16 %	.16	.061201	.059147	.057016	.054948	.052806	.050660	.004012
	17 %	.17	.070608	.068556	.066420	.064357	.062212	.060063	.003423
	18 %	.18	.080099	.078049	.075910	.073850	.071703	.069553	.002918
	19 %	.19	.089665	.087616	.085474	.083417	.081268	.079116	.002487
	20 %	.20	.099294	.097246	.095101	.093047	.090896	.088743	.002118
	21 %	.21	.108977	.106930	.104784	.102731	.100579	.098425	.001804
	22 %	.22	.118707	.116661	.114513	.112462	.110309	.108154	.001536
	23 %	.23	.128477	.126432	.124282	.122233	.120079	.117923	.001307
	24 %	.24	.138281	.136237	.134085	.132037	.129882	.127726	.001113
	25 %	.25	.148114	.146071	.143918	.141871	.139716	.137559	.000948
	26 %	.26	.157973	.155930	.153776	.151730	.149574	.147416	.000807
	27 %	.27	.167852	.165810	.163655	.161610	.159453	.157295	.000687
	28 %	.28	.177750	.175708	.173552	.171508	.169350	.167192	.000585
	29 %	.29	.187662	.185621	.183464	.181421	.179263	.177105	.000499
	30 %	.30	.197588	.195547	.193390	.191347	.189189	.187030	.000425

Mortgage Coefficients for Computing Capitalization Rates.

25 YEARS AMORTIZATION: 10¾% TO 12%

									$\frac{1}{s_{\overline{n}\rvert}}$
Interest Rate			10¾%	11%	11¼%	11½%	11¾%	12%	
Annual Requirement (f)			.115560	.117720	.119880	.122040	.124200	.126480	
Installment f/12			.009630	.009810	.009990	.010170	.010350	.010540	
Projection	Balance (b)		.946944	.948843	.950769	.952723	.954705	.955898	+ Dep. – App.
	Equity	Yield	Mortgage Coefficients						
	4 %	.04	.065764–	.068275–	.070790–	.073311–	.075837–	.078337–	.184627
	5 %	.05	.055958–	.058461–	.060970–	.063484–	.066002–	.068498–	.180974
	6 %	.06	.046148–	.048644–	.051146–	.053653–	.056164–	.058656–	.177396
	7 %	.07	.036334–	.038824–	.041319–	.043819–	.046323–	.048811–	.173890
	8 %	.08	.026516–	.029000–	.031488–	.033981–	.036479–	.038962–	.170456
	9 %	.09	.016694–	.019172–	.021653–	.024140–	.026631–	.029110–	.167092
	10 %	.10	.006869–	.009340–	.011816–	.014296–	.016780–	.019256–	.163797
	11 %	.11	.002959	.000494	.001975–	.004448–	.006926–	.009398–	.160570
	12 %	.12	.012791	.010332	.007869	.005401	.002929	.000462	.157409
	13 %	.13	.022627	.020174	.017716	.015255	.012789	.010325	.154314
	14 %	.14	.032466	.030019	.027567	.025112	.022652	.020191	.151283
5 Years n = 5	15 %	.15	.042309	.039867	.037421	.034971	.032517	.030060	.148315
	16 %	.16	.052154	.049718	.047278	.044834	.042386	.039932	.145409
	17 %	.17	.062003	.059573	.057138	.054699	.052257	.049807	.142563
	18 %	.18	.071856	.069430	.067001	.064568	.062131	.059684	.139777
	19 %	.19	.081711	.079291	.076867	.074439	.072007	.069564	.137050
	20 %	.20	.091569	.089154	.086735	.084312	.081886	.079446	.134379
	21 %	.21	.101430	.099020	.096606	.094189	.091768	.089331	.131765
	22 %	.22	.111295	.108889	.106480	.104068	.101652	.099218	.129205
	23 %	.23	.121162	.118761	.116357	.113949	.111538	.109107	.126700
	24 %	.24	.131032	.128636	.126236	.123833	.121427	.118999	.124247
	25 %	.25	.140904	.138513	.136118	.133720	.131319	.128893	.121846
	26 %	.26	.150779	.148393	.146002	.143609	.141212	.138789	.119496
	27 %	.27	.160657	.158275	.155889	.153500	.151108	.148688	.117195
	28 %	.28	.170538	.168160	.165778	.163394	.161006	.158589	.114943
	29 %	.29	.180421	.178047	.175670	.173289	.170906	.168491	.112739
	30 %	.30	.190306	.187936	.185563	.183187	.180808	.178396	.110581
	Balance (b)		.856344	.860397	.864593	.868936	.873430	.875779	+ Dep. – App.
	Equity	Yield	Mortgage Coefficients						
	4 %	.04	.063594–	.066092–	.068601–	.071123–	.073657–	.076133–	.083290
	5 %	.05	.054138–	.056620–	.059114–	.061619–	.064137–	.066603–	.079504
	6 %	.06	.044661–	.047128–	.049607–	.052096–	.054597–	.057055–	.075867
	7 %	.07	.035162–	.037615–	.040079–	.042553–	.045039–	.047489–	.072377
	8 %	.08	.025643–	.028083–	.030532–	.032992–	.035462–	.037905–	.069029
	9 %	.09	.016104–	.018531–	.020967–	.023413–	.025869–	.028303–	.065820
	10 %	.10	.006546–	.008960–	.011383–	.013816–	.016258–	.018685–	.062745
	11 %	.11	.003030	.000628	.001782–	.004202–	.006630–	.009051–	.059801
	12 %	.12	.012626	.010235	.007836	.005428	.003012	.000598	.056984
	13 %	.13	.022238	.019858	.017471	.015075	.012671	.010263	.054289
	14 %	.14	.031868	.029499	.027122	.024737	.022345	.019943	.051713
10 Years n = 10	15 %	.15	.041515	.039155	.036789	.034415	.032033	.029638	.049252
	16 %	.16	.051177	.048827	.046470	.044107	.041736	.039346	.046901
	17 %	.17	.060855	.058514	.056166	.053812	.051452	.049067	.044656
	18 %	.18	.070547	.068215	.065876	.063532	.061181	.058801	.042514
	19 %	.19	.080253	.077929	.075600	.073264	.070922	.068547	.040471
	20 %	.20	.089974	.087657	.085336	.083008	.080675	.078305	.038522
	21 %	.21	.099707	.097398	.095084	.092765	.090440	.088074	.036665
	22 %	.22	.109452	.107151	.104844	.102533	.100216	.097854	.034894
	23 %	.23	.119210	.116915	.114616	.112312	.110003	.107645	.033208
	24 %	.24	.128979	.126691	.124399	.122101	.119799	.117445	.031602
	25 %	.25	.138760	.136478	.134192	.131901	.129606	.127255	.030072
	26 %	.26	.148550	.146274	.143994	.141710	.139421	.137074	.028616
	27 %	.27	.158351	.156081	.153807	.151528	.149246	.146902	.027230
	28 %	.28	.168162	.165897	.163628	.161356	.159079	.156738	.025911
	29 %	.29	.177982	.175722	.173458	.171191	.168920	.166582	.024657
	30 %	.30	.187810	.185555	.183297	.181035	.178769	.176434	.023463

Mortgage Coefficients for Computing Capitalization Rates.

25 YEARS AMORTIZATION: 10¾% TO 12%

Interest Rate / Annual Requirement (f) / Installment f/12			10¾% .115560 .009630	11% .117720 .009810	11¼% .119880 .009990	11½% .122040 .010170	11¾% .124200 .010350	12% .126480 .010540	$\frac{1}{s_{\overline{n}\rvert}}$
Projection	Balance (b)		.701633	.707483	.713746	.720443	.727595	.730226	+ Dep.
	Equity	Yield	Mortgage Coefficients						– App.
	4 %	.04	.060659–	.063111–	.065584–	.068078–	.070595–	.073007–	.049941
	5 %	.05	.051733–	.054164–	.056614–	.059084–	.061576–	.063978–	.046342
	6 %	.06	.042741–	.045152–	.047581–	.050029–	.052496–	.054889–	.042962
	7 %	.07	.033686–	.036079–	.038488–	.040915–	.043359–	.045744–	.039794
	8 %	.08	.024571–	.026946–	.029337–	.031744–	.034167–	.036544–	.036829
	9 %	.09	.015397–	.017757–	.020130–	.022518–	.024922–	.027291–	.034058
	10 %	.10	.006169–	.008513–	.010870–	.013241–	.015626–	.017989–	.031473
	11 %	.11	.003112	.000782	.001559–	.003914–	.006282–	.008638–	.029065
	12 %	.12	.012443	.010126	.007798	.005458	.003107	.000756	.026824
	13 %	.13	.021822	.019517	.017202	.014876	.012539	.010194	.024741
	14 %	.14	.031245	.028952	.026649	.024336	.022013	.019673	.022808
	15 %	.15	.040710	.038427	.036136	.033835	.031525	.029189	.021017
15 Years n = 15	16 %	.16	.050215	.047942	.045661	.043371	.041073	.038742	.019357
	17 %	.17	.059757	.057493	.055221	.052942	.050654	.048327	.017822
	18 %	.18	.069334	.067078	.064815	.062545	.060268	.057945	.016402
	19 %	.19	.078942	.076694	.074440	.072179	.069911	.067591	.015091
	20 %	.20	.088581	.086340	.084093	.081840	.079581	.077265	.013882
	21 %	.21	.098249	.096014	.093774	.091528	.089277	.086964	.012766
	22 %	.22	.107942	.105713	.103480	.101241	.098997	.096686	.011738
	23 %	.23	.117659	.115436	.113208	.110976	.108739	.106431	.010791
	24 %	.24	.127399	.125181	.122959	.120732	.118502	.116195	.009919
	25 %	.25	.137160	.134946	.132729	.130508	.128283	.125979	.009116
	26 %	.26	.146940	.144730	.142518	.140302	.138082	.135780	.008378
	27 %	.27	.156737	.154532	.152324	.150112	.147897	.145597	.007700
	28 %	.28	.166551	.164350	.162145	.159938	.157727	.155429	.007076
	29 %	.29	.176380	.174182	.171981	.169778	.167571	.165274	.006504
	30 %	.30	.186223	.184028	.181831	.179631	.177428	.175132	.005977
	Balance (b)		.437444	.443106	.449694	.457274	.465916	.465802	+ Dep.
	Equity	Yield	Mortgage Coefficients						– App.
	4 %	.04	.056668–	.059018–	.061399–	.063814–	.066264–	.068540–	.033581
	5 %	.05	.048546–	.050878–	.053237–	.055626–	.058047–	.060324–	.030242
	6 %	.06	.040267–	.042581–	.044920–	.047286–	.049681–	.051958–	.027184
	7 %	.07	.031837–	.034135–	.036456–	.038801–	.041172–	.043449–	.024392
	8 %	.08	.023266–	.025550–	.027854–	.030180–	.032529–	.034806–	.021852
	9 %	.09	.014564–	.016834–	.019123–	.021431–	.023760–	.026038–	.019546
	10 %	.10	.005737–	.007996–	.010271–	.012564–	.014875–	.017153–	.017459
	11 %	.11	.003202	.000953	.001308–	.003586–	.005881–	.008159–	.015575
	12 %	.12	.012247	.010009	.007757	.005492	.003212	.000934	.013878
	13 %	.13	.021389	.019159	.016918	.014664	.012397	.010119	.012353
	14 %	.14	.030620	.028398	.026165	.023922	.021667	.019388	.010986
20 Years n = 20	15 %	.15	.039931	.037716	.035491	.033257	.031013	.028734	.009761
	16 %	.16	.049315	.047106	.044889	.042665	.040428	.038149	.008667
	17 %	.17	.058766	.056562	.054352	.052133	.049907	.047628	.007690
	18 %	.18	.068276	.066078	.063873	.061661	.059442	.057163	.006819
	19 %	.19	.077840	.075646	.073446	.071240	.069028	.066749	.006045
	20 %	.20	.087453	.085263	.083067	.080867	.078660	.076381	.005356
	21 %	.21	.097109	.094922	.092731	.090535	.088334	.086054	.004744
	22 %	.22	.106803	.104619	.102432	.100240	.098044	.095764	.004201
	23 %	.23	.116532	.114351	.112167	.109979	.107787	.105507	.003720
	24 %	.24	.126292	.124114	.121932	.119747	.117559	.115279	.003293
	25 %	.25	.136080	.133903	.131724	.129542	.127357	.125077	.002915
	26 %	.26	.145892	.143717	.141540	.139360	.137178	.134898	.002581
	27 %	.27	.155725	.153552	.151377	.149200	.147020	.144740	.002285
	28 %	.28	.165578	.163406	.161233	.159058	.156880	.154600	.002023
	29 %	.29	.175447	.173277	.171106	.168932	.166756	.164477	.001791
	30 %	.30	.185332	.183163	.180993	.178821	.176647	.174367	.001586

Mortgage Coefficients for Computing Capitalization Rates.

25 YEARS AMORTIZATION: 10¾% TO 12%

Interest Rate / Annual Requirement (f) / Installment f/12		10¾% .115560 .009630	11% .117720 .009810	11¼% .119880 .009990	11½% .122040 .010170	11¾% .124200 .010350	12% .126480 .010540	$\frac{1}{s_{\overline{n}|}}$
Projection	Balance (b)	none	none	none	none	none	none	+ Dep. – App.
	Equity Yield	Mortgage Coefficients						
	4 % .04	.051219-	.053372-	.055567-	.057808-	.060100-	.062118-	.024011
	5 % .05	.044320-	.046474-	.048665-	.050896-	.053171-	.055222-	.020952
	6 % .06	.037083-	.039238-	.041425-	.043646-	.045907-	.047987-	.018226
	7 % .07	.029532-	.031688-	.033871-	.036085-	.038332-	.040439-	.015810
	8 % .08	.021693-	.023850-	.026029-	.028236-	.030471-	.032601-	.013678
	9 % .09	.013592-	.015748-	.017925-	.020125-	.022350-	.024501-	.011806
	10 % .10	.005252-	.007409-	.009584-	.011779-	.013995-	.016163-	.010168
	11 % .11	.003299	.001142	.001030-	.003219-	.005428-	.007612-	.008740
	12 % .12	.012042	.009884	.007713	.005528	.003327	.001129	.007499
	13 % .13	.020953	.018795	.016626	.014444	.012249	.010039	.006425
	14 % .14	.030013	.027855	.025687	.023508	.021318	.019098	.005498
25 Years n = 25	15 % .15	.039203	.037045	.034878	.032702	.030516	.028287	.004699
	16 % .16	.048507	.046348	.044182	.042009	.039827	.037591	.004012
	17 % .17	.057910	.055751	.053586	.051414	.049235	.046993	.003423
	18 % .18	.067398	.065239	.063075	.060905	.058729	.056481	.002918
	19 % .19	.076961	.074802	.072638	.070470	.068296	.066043	.002487
	20 % .20	.086587	.084428	.082265	.080098	.077926	.075669	.002118
	21 % .21	.096268	.094109	.091946	.089780	.087610	.085350	.001804
	22 % .22	.105997	.103837	.101675	.099510	.097341	.095078	.001536
	23 % .23	.115765	.113606	.111444	.109279	.107112	.104846	.001307
	24 % .24	.125568	.123409	.121247	.119083	.116917	.114649	.001113
	25 % .25	.135401	.133241	.131079	.128916	.126751	.124481	.000948
	26 % .26	.145258	.143098	.140937	.138774	.136610	.134339	.000807
	27 % .27	.155137	.152977	.150816	.148653	.146490	.144217	.000687
	28 % .28	.165033	.162874	.160713	.158551	.156388	.154114	.000585
	29 % .29	.174946	.172786	.170625	.168463	.166301	.164026	.000499
	30 % .30	.184871	.182711	.180551	.178389	.176227	.173951	.000425

Mortgage Coefficients for Computing Capitalization Rates

30 YEARS AMORTIZATION: 3¼% TO 4½%

Projection	Interest Rate Annual Requirement(f) Installment f/12	3¼% .05232 .00436	3½% .05400 .00450	3¾% .05568 .00464	4% .05736 .00478	4¼% .05904 .00492	4½% .06084 .00507	$\frac{1}{s_{\overline{n}\rceil}}$
	Balance (b)	.892551	.896345	.900191	.904088	.908037	.911368	+ Dep.
	Equity Yield	Mortgage Coefficients						− App.
	4% .04	.0075	.0051	.0027	.0003	.0021	.0045	.1846
	5% .05	.0171	.0147	.0124	.0100	.0076	.0052	.1810
	6% .06	.0267	.0244	.0220	.0196	.0173	.0149	.1774
	7% .07	.0363	.0340	.0317	.0293	.0269	.0246	.1739
	8% .08	.0460	.0436	.0413	.0390	.0366	.0342	.1705
	9% .09	.0556	.0533	.0510	.0487	.0463	.0439	.1671
5 Years n = 5	10% .10	.0653	.0630	.0607	.0583	.0560	.0537	.1638
	11% .11	.0749	.0726	.0703	.0680	.0657	.0634	.1606
	12% .12	.0846	.0823	.0800	.0777	.0754	.0731	.1574
	13% .13	.0942	.0920	.0897	.0874	.0851	.0828	.1543
	14% .14	.1039	.1017	.0994	.0971	.0949	.0925	.1513
	15% .15	.1136	.1114	.1091	.1068	.1046	.1023	.1483
	16% .16	.1233	.1210	.1188	.1165	.1143	.1120	.1454
	17% .17	.1330	.1307	.1285	.1263	.1240	.1218	.1426
	18% .18	.1427	.1404	.1382	.1360	.1338	.1315	.1398
	19% .19	.1524	.1502	.1480	.1457	.1435	.1413	.1371
	20% .20	.1621	.1599	.1577	.1555	.1533	.1510	.1344
	21% .21	.1718	.1696	.1674	.1652	.1630	.1608	.1318
	22% .22	.1815	.1794	.1772	.1750	.1728	.1706	.1292
	23% .23	.1913	.1891	.1869	.1847	.1826	.1803	.1267
	24% .24	.2010	.1988	.1967	.1945	.1923	.1901	.1242
	25% .25	.2107	.2086	.2064	.2043	.2021	.1999	.1218
	26% .26	.2205	.2183	.2162	.2141	.2119	.2097	.1195
	27% .27	.2302	.2281	.2260	.2238	.2217	.2195	.1172
	28% .28	.2400	.2379	.2358	.2336	.2315	.2293	.1149
	29% .29	.2498	.2476	.2455	.2434	.2413	.2391	.1127
	30% .30	.2595	.2574	.2553	.2532	.2511	.2489	.1106
	Balance(b)	.766171	.772899	.779833	.786979	.794342	.800419	+ Dep.
	Equity Yield	Mortgage Coefficients						− App.
	4% .04	.0071	.0049	.0026	.0004	.0019	.0042	.0833
	5% .05	.0163	.0140	.0118	.0096	.0073	.0050	.0795
	6% .06	.0254	.0232	.0210	.0188	.0165	.0143	.0759
	7% .07	.0346	.0324	.0302	.0280	.0258	.0236	.0724
	8% .08	.0438	.0417	.0395	.0373	.0351	.0329	.0690
	9% .09	.0531	.0509	.0488	.0466	.0445	.0423	.0658
10 Years n − 10	10% .10	.0623	.0602	.0581	.0560	.0538	.0517	.0628
	11% .11	.0716	.0696	.0675	.0654	.0632	.0611	.0598
	12% .12	.0810	.0789	.0768	.0748	.0727	.0705	.0570
	13% .13	.0904	.0883	.0863	.0842	.0821	.0800	.0543
	14% .14	.0998	.0977	.0957	.0936	.0916	.0895	.0517
	15% .15	.1092	.1072	.1051	.1031	.1011	.0990	.0493
	16% .16	.1186	.1166	.1146	.1126	.1106	.1085	.0469
	17% .17	.1281	.1261	.1241	.1221	.1201	.1180	.0447
	18% .18	.1376	.1356	.1336	.1317	.1297	.1276	.0425
	19% .19	.1471	.1452	.1432	.1412	.1392	.1372	.0405
	20% .20	.1566	.1547	.1528	.1508	.1488	.1468	.0385
	21% .21	.1662	.1643	.1624	.1604	.1585	.1564	.0367
	22% .22	.1758	.1739	.1720	.1700	.1681	.1661	.0349
	23% .23	.1854	.1835	.1816	.1797	.1777	.1757	.0332
	24% .24	.1950	.1931	.1912	.1893	.1874	.1854	.0316
	25% .25	.2047	.2028	.2009	.1990	.1971	.1951	.0301
	26% .26	.2143	.2125	.2106	.2087	.2068	.2048	.0286
	27% .27	.2240	.2221	.2203	.2184	.2165	.2146	.0272
	28% .28	.2337	.2318	.2300	.2281	.2262	.2243	.0259
	29% .29	.2434	.2416	.2397	.2379	.2360	.2340	.0247
	30% .30	.2531	.2513	.2494	.2476	.2457	.2438	.0235

Mortgage Coefficients for Computing Capitalization Rates

30 YEARS AMORTIZATION: 3¼% TO 4½%

								$\frac{1}{s_{\overline{n}\mid}}$
Interest Rate		3¼%	3½%	3¾%	4%	4¼%	4½%	
Annual Requirement(f)		.05232	.05400	.05568	.05736	.05904	.06084	
Installment f/12		.00436	.00450	.00464	.00478	.00492	.00507	
Projection	Balance(b)	.617524	.625881	.634695	.643989	.653782	.661533	+ Dep.
	Equity Yield	Mortgage Coefficients						− App.
	4% .04	.0068	.0047	.0025	.0004	.0017	.0039	.0500
	5% .05	.0154	.0133	.0112	.0091	.0070	.0048	.0464
	6% .06	.0241	.0221	.0200	.0179	.0158	.0137	.0430
	7% .07	.0329	.0309	.0288	.0268	.0247	.0226	.0398
	8% .08	.0417	.0398	.0378	.0357	.0337	.0316	.0368
	9% .09	.0507	.0487	.0467	.0447	.0427	.0407	.0341
15 Years n = 15	10% .10	.0597	.0578	.0558	.0538	.0518	.0498	.0315
	11% .11	.0688	.0669	.0649	.0630	.0610	.0590	.0291
	12% .12	.0779	.0760	.0741	.0722	.0702	.0682	.0268
	13% .13	.0871	.0852	.0833	.0814	.0795	.0775	.0248
	14% .14	.0964	.0945	.0926	.0907	.0888	.0869	.0228
	15% .15	.1057	.1038	.1020	.1001	.0982	.0963	.0210
	16% .16	.1150	.1132	.1114	.1095	.1076	.1057	.0194
	17% .17	.1245	.1226	.1208	.1189	.1171	.1152	.0178
	18% .18	.1339	.1321	.1303	.1284	.1266	.1247	.0164
	19% .19	.1434	.1416	.1398	.1380	.1361	.1342	.0151
	20% .20	.1529	.1512	.1494	.1475	.1457	.1438	.0139
	Balance(b)	.442686	.450790	.459678	.469399	.480007	.487675	+ Dep.
	Equity Yield	Mortgage Coefficients						− App.
	4% .04	.0064	.0044	.0024	.0004	.0016	.0036	.0336
	5% .05	.0145	.0126	.0106	.0087	.0067	.0046	.0303
	6% .06	.0228	.0209	.0190	.0170	.0151	.0131	.0272
	7% .07	.0313	.0294	.0275	.0256	.0236	.0216	.0244
	8% .08	.0398	.0380	.0361	.0342	.0323	.0303	.0219
	9% .09	.0486	.0467	.0449	.0430	.0411	.0392	.0196
20 Years n = 20	10% .10	.0574	.0556	.0537	.0519	.0500	.0481	.0175
	11% .11	.0663	.0645	.0627	.0609	.0590	.0571	.0156
	12% .12	.0754	.0736	.0718	.0700	.0682	.0662	.0139
	13% .13	.0845	.0828	.0810	.0792	.0774	.0755	.0124
	14% .14	.0938	.0920	.0902	.0884	.0867	.0848	.0110
	15% .15	.1031	.1013	.0996	.0978	.0960	.0941	.0098
	16% .16	.1125	.1107	.1090	.1072	.1054	.1036	.0087
	17% .17	.1219	.1202	.1184	.1167	.1149	.1131	.0077
	18% .18	.1314	.1297	.1280	.1262	.1245	.1226	.0068
	19% .19	.1410	.1393	.1375	.1358	.1341	.1322	.0060
	20% .20	.1506	.1489	.1472	.1454	.1437	.1419	.0054

Mortgage Coefficients for Computing Capitalization Rates

30 YEARS AMORTIZATION: 3¾% TO 4½%

Interest Rate		3¼%	3½%	3¾%	4%	4¼%	4½%	$\frac{1}{s_{\overline{n}\rceil}}$
Annual Requirement(f)		.05232	.05400	.05568	.05736	.05904	.06084	
Installment f/12		.00436	.00450	.00464	.00478	.00492	.00507	
Projection	Balance(b)	.237045	.242268	.248628	.256226	.265169	.270043	+ Dep.
	Equity Yield	Mortgage Coefficients						− App.
25 Years n = 25	4% .04	.0060	.0042	.0023	.0005	.0014	.0033	.0240
	5% .05	.0136	.0119	.0100	.0082	.0063	.0044	.0210
	6% .06	.0216	.0198	.0180	.0162	.0143	.0124	.0182
	7% .07	.0297	.0280	.0262	.0244	.0226	.0207	.0158
	8% .08	.0381	.0363	.0346	.0328	.0310	.0291	.0137
	9% .09	.0467	.0449	.0432	.0414	.0396	.0378	.0118
	10% .10	.0554	.0537	.0519	.0502	.0484	.0466	.0102
	11% .11	.0643	.0626	.0609	.0591	.0574	.0555	.0088
	12% .12	.0734	.0717	.0699	.0682	.0665	.0646	.0075
	13% .13	.0826	.0808	.0791	.0774	.0757	.0738	.0064
	14% .14	.0919	.0901	.0884	.0867	.0850	.0832	.0055
	15% .15	.1012	.0995	.0978	.0961	.0944	.0926	.0047
	16% .16	.1107	.1090	.1073	.1056	.1039	.1020	.0040
	17% .17	.1203	.1186	.1169	.1151	.1134	.1116	.0034
	18% .18	.1299	.1282	.1265	.1248	.1231	.1213	.0029
	19% .19	.1395	.1378	.1361	.1344	.1327	.1309	.0025
	20% .20	.1493	.1476	.1459	.1442	.1425	.1407	.0021
	Balance(b)	none	none	none	none	none	none	+ Dep.
	Equity Yield	Mortgage Coefficients						− App.
30 Years n = 30	4% .04	.0055	.0038	.0021	.0005	.0012	.0030	.0179
	5% .05	.0127	.0110	.0094	.0077	.0060	.0042	.0151
	6% .06	.0203	.0186	.0169	.0153	.0136	.0118	.0127
	7% .07	.0282	.0266	.0249	.0232	.0215	.0197	.0106
	8% .08	.0365	.0348	.0331	.0314	.0298	.0280	.0089
	9% .09	.0450	.0433	.0416	.0400	.0383	.0365	.0074
	10% .10	.0537	.0521	.0504	.0487	.0470	.0452	.0061
	11% .11	.0627	.0610	.0593	.0576	.0560	.0542	.0050
	12% .12	.0718	.0701	.0684	.0668	.0651	.0633	.0042
	13% .13	.0811	.0794	.0777	.0760	.0744	.0726	.0034
	14% .14	.0905	.0888	.0871	.0854	.0837	.0819	.0028
	15% .15	.1000	.0983	.0966	.0949	.0932	.0914	.0023
	16% .16	.1095	.1078	.1062	.1045	.1028	.1010	.0019
	17% .17	.1192	.1175	.1158	.1141	.1125	.1107	.0015
	18% .18	.1289	.1272	.1255	.1239	.1222	.1204	.0013
	19% .19	.1387	.1370	.1353	.1336	.1320	.1302	.0010
	20% .20	.1485	.1468	.1451	.1434	.1418	.1400	.0008

Mortgage Coefficients for Computing Capitalization Rates

30 YEARS AMORTIZATION: 4¾% TO 6%

TABLE C

Projection	Equity Yield	4¾%	5%	5¼%	5½%	5¾%	6%	$\frac{1}{s_{\overline{n}\rceil}}$
	Annual Requirement (f)	.06264	.06444	.06636	.06816	.07008	.07200	
	Installment f/12	.00522	.00537	.00553	.00568	.00584	.00600	
5 Years n = 5	Balance (b)	.914744	.918166	.920950	.924461	.927326	.930230	+ Dep. − App.
	Equity Yield	Mortgage Coefficients						
	4% .04	*.0069*	*.0093*	*.0118*	*.0142*	*.0167*	*.0191*	.1846
	5% .05	.0028	.0003	*.0021*	*.0045*	*.0069*	*.0094*	.1810
	6% .06	.0125	.0101	.0076	.0052	.0028	.0004	.1774
	7% .07	.0222	.0198	.0174	.0150	.0125	.0101	.1739
	8% .08	.0319	.0295	.0271	.0247	.0223	.0199	.1705
	9% .09	.0416	.0392	.0368	.0344	.0320	.0296	.1671
	10% .10	.0513	.0489	.0466	.0442	.0418	.0394	.1638
	11% .11	.0610	.0587	.0563	.0539	.0516	.0492	.1606
	12% .12	.0708	.0684	.0661	.0637	.0613	.0590	.1574
	13% .13	.0805	.0782	.0758	.0735	.0711	.0687	.1543
	14% .14	.0902	.0879	.0856	.0832	.0809	.0785	.1513
	15% .15	.1000	.0977	.0953	.0930	.0907	.0883	.1483
	16% .16	.1097	.1074	.1051	.1028	.1004	.0981	.1454
	17% .17	.1195	.1172	.1149	.1126	.1102	.1079	.1426
	18% .18	.1292	.1270	.1246	.1224	.1200	.1177	.1398
	19% .19	.1390	.1367	.1344	.1322	.1298	.1275	.1371
	20% .20	.1488	.1465	.1442	.1420	.1396	.1373	.1344
	21% .21	.1586	.1563	.1540	.1518	.1495	.1472	.1318
	22% .22	.1683	.1661	.1638	.1616	.1593	.1570	.1292
	23% .23	.1781	.1759	.1736	.1714	.1691	.1668	.1267
	24% .24	.1879	.1857	.1834	.1812	.1789	.1766	.1242
	25% .25	.1977	.1955	.1932	.1910	.1887	.1865	.1218
	26% .26	.2075	.2053	.2030	.2008	.1986	.1963	.1195
	27% .27	.2173	.2151	.2129	.2107	.2084	.2061	.1172
	28% .28	.2271	.2249	.2227	.2205	.2182	.2160	.1149
	29% .29	.2369	.2347	.2325	.2303	.2281	.2258	.1127
	30% .30	.2467	.2446	.2423	.2402	.2379	.2357	.1106
10 Years n = 10	Balance (b)	.806684	.813143	.818229	.825073	.830511	.836121	+ Dep. − App.
	Equity Yield	Mortgage Coefficients						
	4% .04	*.0065*	*.0089*	*.0112*	*.0136*	*.0160*	*.0184*	.0833
	5% .05	.0027	.0004	*.0019*	*.0043*	*.0066*	*.0090*	.0795
	6% .06	.0120	.0097	.0074	.0051	.0028	.0004	.0759
	7% .07	.0213	.0191	.0168	.0145	.0122	.0098	.0724
	8% .08	.0307	.0284	.0262	.0239	.0216	.0193	.0690
	9% .09	.0401	.0378	.0356	.0333	.0311	.0288	.0658
	10% .10	.0495	.0473	.0450	.0428	.0405	.0383	.0628
	11% .11	.0589	.0567	.0545	.0523	.0500	.0478	.0598
	12% .12	.0684	.0662	.0640	.0618	.0596	.0573	.0570
	13% .13	.0778	.0757	.0735	.0713	.0691	.0669	.0543
	14% .14	.0873	.0852	.0830	.0809	.0787	.0765	.0517
	15% .15	.0969	.0947	.0926	.0904	.0882	.0861	.0493
	16% .16	.1064	.1043	.1021	.1000	.0978	.0956	.0469
	17% .17	.1160	.1139	.1117	.1096	.1074	.1053	.0447
	18% .18	.1255	.1235	.1213	.1192	.1171	.1149	.0425
	19% .19	.1351	.1331	.1310	.1289	.1267	.1246	.0405
	20% .20	.1449	.1427	.1406	.1385	.1364	.1343	.0385
	21% .21	.1546	.1524	.1503	.1482	.1461	.1440	.0367
	22% .22	.1642	.1620	.1599	.1579	.1558	.1537	.0349
	23% .23	.1739	.1717	.1696	.1676	.1655	.1634	.0332
	24% .24	.1836	.1814	.1793	.1773	.1752	.1731	.0316
	25% .25	.1933	.1911	.1891	.1871	.1850	.1829	.0301
	26% .26	.2030	.2009	.1988	.1968	.1947	.1926	.0286
	27% .27	.2127	.2106	.2085	.2066	.2045	.2024	.0272
	28% .28	.2225	.2204	.2183	.2163	.2143	.2122	.0259
	29% .29	.2322	.2301	.2281	.2261	.2241	.2220	.0247
	30% .30	.2420	.2399	.2379	.2359	.2339	.2318	.0235

Mortgage Coefficients for Computing Capitalization Rates

30 YEARS AMORTIZATION: 4¾% TO 6%

								$\frac{1}{s_{\overline{n}\rvert}}$
Interest Rate		4¾%	5%	5¼%	5½%	5¾%	6%	
Annual Requirement(f)		.06264	.06444	.06636	.06816	.07008	.07200	
Installment f/12		.00522	.00537	.00553	.00568	.00584	.00600	
Projection	Balance (b)	.669720	.678362	.684752	.694309	.701536	.709182	+ Dep.
	Equity Yield	Mortgage Coefficients						− App.
	4% .04	*.0062*	*.0084*	*.0106*	*.0129*	*.0152*	*.0175*	.0500
	5% .05	.0026	.0004	*.0018*	*.0040*	*.0063*	*.0085*	.0464
	6% .06	.0115	.0094	.0072	.0050	.0027	.0005	.0430
	7% .07	.0205	.0183	.0162	.0140	.0118	.0096	.0398
	8% .08	.0295	.0274	.0252	.0231	.0209	.0187	.0368
	9% .09	.0386	.0365	.0344	.0322	.0201	.0279	.0341
15 Years n = 15	10% .10	.0477	.0457	.0435	.0414	.0393	.0371	.0315
	11% .11	.0569	.0549	.0528	.0507	.0486	.0464	.0291
	12% .12	.0662	.0642	.0621	.0600	.0579	.0558	.0268
	13% .13	.0755	.0735	.0714	.0694	.0673	.0652	.0248
	14% .14	.0849	.0829	.0808	.0788	.0767	.0746	.0228
	15% .15	.0943	.0923	.0902	.0882	.0862	.0841	.0210
	16% .16	.1037	.1017	.0997	.0977	.0957	.0936	.0194
	17% .17	.1132	.1113	.1092	.1072	.1052	.1031	.0178
	18% .18	.1227	.1208	.1188	.1168	.1148	.1127	.0164
	19% .19	.1323	.1304	.1284	.1264	.1244	.1223	.0151
	20% .20	.1419	.1400	.1380	.1360	.1340	.1320	.0139
	Balance(b)	.496120	.505389	.511306	.522262	.529720	.537957	+ Dep.
	Equity Yield	Mortgage Coefficients						− App.
	4% .04	*.0057*	*.0078*	*.0100*	*.0121*	*.0143*	*.0165*	.0336
	5% .05	.0026	.0005	*.0016*	*.0037*	*.0059*	*.0080*	.0303
	6% .06	.0110	.0090	.0069	.0048	.0027	.0005	.0272
	7% .07	.0196	.0176	.0155	.0135	.0114	.0092	.0244
	8% .08	.0283	.0263	.0243	.0223	.0202	.0181	.0219
	9% .09	.0372	.0352	.0332	.0312	.0291	.0270	.0196
20 Years n − 20	10% .10	.0461	.0442	.0422	.0402	.0381	.0360	.0175
	11% .11	.0552	.0532	.0512	.0493	.0472	.0452	.0156
	12% .12	.0643	.0624	.0604	.0584	.0564	.0544	.0139
	13% .13	.0736	.0716	.0697	.0677	.0657	.0637	.0124
	14% .14	.0829	.0810	.0790	.0771	.0751	.0731	.0110
	15% .15	.0923	.0904	.0884	.0865	.0845	.0825	.0098
	16% .16	.1017	.0998	.0978	.0959	.0940	.0920	.0087
	17% .17	.1112	.1093	.1074	.1055	.1035	.1015	.0077
	18% .18	.1208	.1189	.1169	.1151	.1131	.1111	.0068
	19% .19	.1304	.1285	.1266	.1247	.1227	.1208	.0060
	20% .20	.1400	.1382	.1362	.1344	.1324	.1304	.0054

Mortgage Coefficients for Computing Capitalization Rates

30 YEARS AMORTIZATION: 4¾% TO 6%

Interest Rate		4¾%	5%	5¼%	5½%	5¾%	6%	$\frac{1}{s_{\overline{n}|}}$
Annual Requirement(f)		.06264	.06444	.06636	.06816	.07008	.07200	
Installment f/12		.00522	.00537	.00553	.00568	.00584	.00600	
Projection	Balance(b)	.276086	.283403	.285925	.295899	.300830	.307006	+ Dep. – App.
	Equity Yield	Mortgage Coefficients						
	4% .04	*.0053*	*.0072*	*.0092*	*.0113*	*.0133*	*.0154*	.0240
	5% .05	.0025	.0006	*.0014*	*.0034*	*.0054*	*.0075*	.0210
	6% .06	.0105	.0086	.0066	.0047	.0026	.0006	.0182
	7% .07	.0188	.0169	.0149	.0130	.0110	.0089	.0158
	8% .08	.0272	.0253	.0234	.0215	.0195	.0175	.0137
	9% .09	.0359	.0340	.0320	.0301	.0282	.0262	.0118
25 Years n = 25	10% .10	.0447	.0428	.0409	.0390	.0370	.0350	.0102
	11% .11	.0537	.0518	.0499	.0480	.0460	.0440	.0088
	12% .12	.0628	.0609	.0590	.0571	.0551	.0532	.0075
	13% .13	.0720	.0701	.0682	.0663	.0644	.0624	.0064
	14% .14	.0813	.0795	.0775	.0757	.0737	.0718	.0055
	15% .15	.0907	.0889	.0870	.0851	.0832	.0812	.0047
	16% .16	.1002	.0984	.0965	.0946	.0927	.0907	.0040
	17% .17	.1098	.1080	.1060	.1042	.1023	.1003	.0034
	18% .18	.1194	.1176	.1157	.1139	.1119	.1100	.0029
	19% .19	.1291	.1273	.1254	.1236	.1216	.1197	.0025
	20% .20	.1389	.1370	.1351	.1333	.1314	.1294	.0021
	Balance(b)	none	none	none	none	none	none	+ Dep. – App.
	Equity Yield	Mortgage Coefficients						
	4% .04	*.0048*	*.0066*	*.0085*	*.0103*	*.0122*	*.0142*	.0179
	5% .05	.0024	.0006	*.0013*	*.0031*	*.0050*	*.0070*	.0151
	6% .06	.0100	.0082	.0063	.0045	.0025	.0006	.0127
	7% .07	.0179	.0161	.0142	.0124	.0105	.0086	.0106
	8% .08	.0262	.0244	.0224	.0206	.0187	.0168	.0089
	9% .09	.0347	.0329	.0310	.0292	.0272	.0253	.0074
30 Years n - 30	10% .10	.0434	.0416	.0397	.0379	.0360	.0341	.0061
	11% .11	.0524	.0506	.0486	.0468	.0449	.0430	.0050
	12% .12	.0615	.0597	.0578	.0560	.0540	.0521	.0042
	13% .13	.0707	.0690	.0670	.0652	.0633	.0614	.0034
	14% .14	.0801	.0783	.0764	0746	.0727	.0708	.0028
	15% .15	.0896	.0878	.0859	.0841	.0822	.0803	.0023
	16% .16	.0992	.0974	.0955	.0937	.0918	.0898	.0019
	17% .17	.1089	.1071	.1051	.1033	.1014	.0995	.0015
	18% .18	.1186	.1168	.1149	.1131	.1111	.1092	.0013
	19% .19	.1284	.1266	.1246	.1228	.1209	.1190	.0010
	20% .20	.1382	.1364	.1344	.1326	.1307	.1288	.0008

Mortgage Coefficients for Computing Capitalization Rates.

30 YEARS AMORTIZATION: 6¼% TO 7½%

Interest Rate Annual Requirement (f) Installment f/12			6¼% .073920 .006160	6½% .075960 .006330	6¾% .077880 .006490	7% .079920 .006660	7¼% .081960 .006830	7½% .084000 .007000	$\frac{1}{s_{\overline{n}\rceil}}$
Projection	Balance (b)		.933173	.935451	.938471	.940816	.943194	.945604	+ Dep. – App.
	Equity	Yield	Mortgage Coefficients						
	4 %	.04	.021582–	.024042–	.026520–	.028993–	.031472–	.033957–	.184627
	5 %	.05	.011826–	.014278–	.016744–	.019209–	.021679–	.024155–	.180974
	6 %	.06	.002065–	.004509–	.006965–	.009421–	.011882–	.014350–	.177396
	7 %	.07	.007700	.005264	.002819	.000371	.002082–	.004541–	.173890
	8 %	.08	.017470	.015042	.012607	.010168	.007722	.005272	.170456
	9 %	.09	.027246	.024825	.022400	.019969	.017531	.015089	.167092
	10 %	.10	.037025	.034612	.032198	.029774	.027344	.024909	.163797
	11 %	.11	.046810	.044404	.041999	.039583	.037161	.034734	.160570
	12 %	.12	.056599	.054200	.051805	.049396	.046981	.044562	.157409
	13 %	.13	.066392	.064000	.061614	.059212	.056805	.054393	.154314
	14 %	.14	.076189	.073805	.071428	.069033	.066633	.064229	.151283
5 Years n = 5	15 %	.15	.085991	.083613	.081245	.078857	.076465	.074067	.148315
	16 %	.16	.095797	.093426	.091066	.088685	.086300	.083909	.145409
	17 %	.17	.105606	.103242	.100891	.098517	.096138	.093754	.142563
	18 %	.18	.115420	.113062	.110720	.108352	.105980	.103603	.139777
	19 %	.19	.125238	.122886	.120552	.118191	.115825	.113454	.137050
	20 %	.20	.135060	.132714	.130388	.128033	.125673	.123309	.134379
	21 %	.21	.144885	.142545	.140227	.137878	.135525	.133167	.131765
	22 %	.22	.154714	.152380	.150069	.147726	.145379	.143028	.129205
	23 %	.23	.164546	.162218	.159915	.157578	.155237	.152891	.126700
	24 %	.24	.174382	.172060	.169764	.167433	.165097	.162758	.124247
	25 %	.25	.184222	.181905	.179617	.177291	.174961	.172627	.121846
	26 %	.26	.194065	.191753	.189472	.187152	.184828	.182500	.119496
	27 %	.27	.203911	.201604	.199330	.197016	.194697	.192374	.117195
	28 %	.28	.213761	.211459	.209192	.206882	.204569	.202252	.114943
	29 %	.29	.223613	.221317	.219056	.216752	.214444	.212132	.112739
	30 %	.30	.233469	.231177	.228923	.226624	.224321	.222015	.110581
	Balance (b)		.841907	.846191	.852323	.856916	.861657	.866552	+ Dep. – App.
	Equity	Yield	Mortgage Coefficients						
	4 %	.04	.020752–	.023149–	.025579–	.028002–	.030437–	.032885–	.083290
	5 %	.05	.011350–	.013731–	.016139–	.018544–	.020961–	.023390–	.079504
	6 %	.06	.001925–	.004290–	.006676–	.009064–	.011464–	.013875–	.075867
	7 %	.07	.007522	.005172	.002808	.000436	.001947–	.004341–	.072377
	8 %	.08	.016993	.014657	.012314	.009956	.007589	.005211	.069029
	9 %	.09	.026485	.024163	.021840	.019497	.017145	.014783	.065820
	10 %	.10	.035999	.033690	.031385	.029057	.026720	.024373	.062745
	11 %	.11	.045534	.043237	.040951	.038636	.036313	.033980	.059801
	12 %	.12	.055088	.052804	.050535	.048233	.045923	.043604	.056984
	13 %	.13	.064662	.062390	.060137	.057847	.055550	.053244	.054289
10 Years n = 10	14 %	.14	.074255	.071993	.069756	.067479	.065194	.062901	.051713
	15 %	.15	.083866	.081615	.079393	.077127	.074853	.072572	.049252
	16 %	.16	.093494	.091253	.089046	.086790	.084528	.082258	.046901
	17 %	.17	.103139	.100908	.098714	.096469	.094217	.091959	.044656
	18 %	.18	.112801	.110579	.108398	.106163	.103921	.101673	.042514
	19 %	.19	.122478	.120264	.118096	.115870	.113638	.111400	.040471
	20 %	.20	.132170	.129965	.127808	.125591	.123369	.121140	.038522
	21 %	.21	.141876	.139679	.137534	.135326	.133112	.130892	.036665
	22 %	.22	.151596	.149407	.147273	.145072	.142867	.140656	.034894
	23 %	.23	.161330	.159147	.157024	.154831	.152634	.150431	.033208
	24 %	.24	.171076	.168900	.166786	.164601	.162411	.160217	.031602
	25 %	.25	.180834	.178665	.176561	.174382	.172200	.170013	.030072
	26 %	.26	.190604	.188441	.186345	.184174	.181998	.179818	.028616
	27 %	.27	.200384	.198228	.196141	.193976	.191807	.189633	.027230
	28 %	.28	.210176	.208025	.205946	.203787	.201624	.199457	.025911
	29 %	.29	.219978	.217832	.215761	.213608	.211451	.209290	.024657
	30 %	.30	.229789	.227648	.225584	.223437	.221285	.219131	.023463

TABLE C

Mortgage Coefficients for Computing Capitalization Rates.

30 YEARS AMORTIZATION: 6¼% TO 7½%

TABLE C

Interest Rate / Annual Requirement (f) / Installment f/12		6¼% / .073920 / .006160	6½% / .075960 / .006330	6¾% / .077880 / .006490	7% / .979920 / .006660	7¼% / .081960 / .006830	7½% / .084000 / .007000	$\frac{1}{s_{\overline{n}|}}$
Projection	Balance (b)	.717261	.722762	.731707	.737977	.744624	.751665	+ Dep. – App.
	Equity Yield	Mortgage Coefficients						
	4 % .04	.019799–	.022114–	.024481–	.026834–	.029206–	.031597–	.049941
	5 % .05	.010817–	.013112–	.015446–	.017777–	.020125–	.022491–	.046342
	6 % .06	.001772–	.004049–	.006353–	.008662–	.010988–	.013330–	.042962
	7 % .07	.007331	.005072	.002796	.000507	.001797–	.004117–	.039794
	8 % .08	.016493	.014250	.012001	.009730	.007445	.005146	.036829
	9 % .09	.025709	.023482	.021257	.019004	.016737	.014457	.034058
	10 % .10	.034978	.032765	.030564	.028326	.026077	.023816	.031473
	11 % .11	.044297	.042097	.039917	.037695	.035462	.033217	.029065
	12 % .12	.053664	.051476	.049316	.047108	.044890	.042661	.026824
	13 % .13	.063075	.060899	.058758	.056562	.054358	.052144	.024741
	14 % .14	.072528	.070363	.068239	.066056	.063864	.061664	.022808
15 Years n = 15	15 % .15	.082022	.079866	.077758	.075586	.073407	.071219	.021017
	16 % .16	.091553	.089406	.087313	.085152	.082983	.080807	.019357
	17 % .17	.101118	.098980	.096901	.094749	.092591	.090425	.017822
	18 % .18	.110717	.108587	.106520	.104377	.102228	.100073	.016402
	19 % .19	.120347	.118224	.116169	.114034	.111894	.109747	.015091
	20 % .20	.130005	.127888	.125844	.123717	.121585	.119447	.013882
	21 % .21	.139689	.137579	.135545	.133425	.131300	.129170	.012766
	22 % .22	.149398	.147294	.145269	.143155	.141037	.138914	.011738
	23 % .23	.159131	.157031	.155015	.152907	.150795	.148679	.010791
	24 % .24	.168884	.166789	.164781	.162679	.160573	.158463	.009919
	25 % .25	.178657	.176567	.174565	.172468	.170368	.168264	.009116
	26 % .26	.188449	.186362	.184368	.182275	.180179	.178080	.008378
	27 % .27	.198257	.196174	.194185	.192097	.190006	.187912	.007700
	28 % .28	.208080	.206002	.204018	.201934	.199847	.197757	.007076
	29 % .29	.217918	.215843	.213864	.211784	.209700	.207615	.006504
	30 % .30	.227770	.225697	.223723	.221646	.219566	.217484	.005977
	Balance (b)	.547030	.552082	.562831	.569367	.576641	.584701	+ Dep. – App.
	Equity Yield	Mortgage Coefficients						
	4 % .04	.018708–	.020918–	.023199–	.025458–	.027742–	.030053–	.033581
	5 % .05	.002928–	.005202–	.007620–	.009963–	.012340–	.014754–	.046342
	6 % .06	.001606–	.003783–	.005995–	.008213–	.010451–	.012710–	.027184
	7 % .07	.007129	.004966	.002783	.000584	.001633–	.003869–	.024392
	8 % .08	.015978	.013827	.011673	.009490	.007291	.005075	.021852
	9 % .09	.024933	.022795	.020665	.018497	.016315	.014117	.019546
	10 % .10	.033988	.031860	.029752	.027598	.025431	.023250	.017459
	11 % .11	.043135	.041016	.038929	.036787	.034634	.032468	.015575
	12 % .12	.052366	.050256	.048187	.046056	.043915	.041763	.013878
	13 % .13	.061675	.059573	.057520	.055399	.053270	.051130	.012353
	14 % .14	.071056	.068960	.066922	.064810	.062691	.060562	.010986
20 Years n = 20	15 % .15	.080501	.078412	.076387	.074283	.072172	.070053	.009761
	16 % .16	.090005	.087922	.085908	.083812	.081709	.079599	.008667
	17 % .17	.099563	.097484	.095481	.093391	.091295	.089193	.007690
	18 % .18	.109169	.107094	.105101	.103016	.100927	.098832	.006819
	19 % .19	.118818	.116747	.114762	.112683	.110599	.108510	.006045
	20 % .20	.128506	.126439	.124461	.122386	.120307	.118224	.005356
	21 % .21	.138229	.136165	.134194	.132123	.130048	.127970	.004744
	22 % .22	.147983	.145922	.143956	.141889	.139818	.137745	.004201
	23 % .23	.157765	.155706	.153746	.151682	.149615	.147545	.003720
	24 % .24	.167571	.165515	.163559	.161498	.159434	.157367	.003293
	25 % .25	.177400	.175346	.173394	.171335	.169274	.167210	.002915
	26 % .26	.187249	.185196	.183248	.181191	.179132	.177072	.002581
	27 % .27	.197115	.195063	.193119	.191064	.189007	.186949	.002285
	28 % .28	.206996	.204946	.203004	.200951	.198896	.196840	.002023
	29 % .29	.216891	.214842	.212903	.210851	.208798	.206744	.001791
	30 % .30	.226798	.224750	.222813	.220763	.218711	.216659	.001586

Mortgage Coefficients for Computing Capitalization Rates.

30 YEARS AMORTIZATION: 6¼% TO 7½%

Interest Rate Annual Requirement (f) Installment f/12		6¼% .073920 .006160	6½% .075960 .006330	6¾% .077880 .006490	7% .079920 .006660	7¼% .081960 .006830	7½% .084000 .007000	$\frac{1}{s_{\overline{n}\rvert}}$
Projection: 25 Years, n = 25	Balance (b)	.314539	.316062	.326384	.330340	.335525	.342054	+ Dep. – App.
Equity	Yield	Mortgage Coefficients						
4 %	.04	.017460–	.019537–	.021705–	.023840–	.026004–	.028201–	.024011
5 %	.05	.009557–	.011629–	.013766–	.015888–	.018037–	.020214–	.020952
6 %	.06	.001426–	.003494–	.005602–	.007714–	.009848–	.012007–	.018226
7 %	.07	.006917	.004853	.002770	.000667	.001454–	.003597–	.015810
8 %	.08	.015456	.013395	.011334	.009240	.007129	.004999	.013678
9 %	.09	.024172	.022114	.020072	.017986	.015884	.013767	.011806
10 %	.10	.033049	.030994	.028969	.026889	.024796	.022690	.010168
11 %	.11	.042071	.040017	.038007	.035932	.033847	.031750	.008740
12 %	.12	.051220	.049169	.047172	.045102	.043023	.040934	.007499
13 %	.13	.060484	.058434	.056448	.054383	.052309	.050227	.006425
14 %	.14	.069848	.067800	.065823	.063762	.061693	.059617	.005498
15 %	.15	.079301	.077254	.075285	.073226	.071162	.069091	.004699
16 %	.16	.088830	.086784	.084822	.082767	.080706	.078640	.004012
17 %	.17	.098426	.096381	.094426	.092372	.090314	.088252	.003423
18 %	.18	.108080	.106036	.104086	.102034	.099979	.097920	.002918
19 %	.19	.117784	.115741	.113795	.111745	.109692	.107636	.002487
20 %	.20	.127532	.125489	.123547	.121498	.119447	.117394	.002118
21 %	.21	.137316	.135274	.133335	.131288	.129238	.127187	.001804
22 %	.22	.147133	.145090	.143154	.141108	.139060	.137010	.001536
23 %	.23	.156976	.154934	.153000	.150955	.148909	.146860	.001307
24 %	.24	.166843	.164801	.162870	.160825	.158779	.156732	.001113
25 %	.25	.176729	.174688	.172758	.170714	.168669	.166623	.000948
26 %	.26	.186633	.184592	.182663	.180620	.178576	.176531	.000807
27 %	.27	.196551	.194510	.192583	.190540	.188496	.186452	.000687
28 %	.28	.206481	.204440	.202514	.200472	.198429	.196385	.000585
29 %	.29	.216422	.214381	.212456	.210414	.208371	.206328	.000499
30 %	.30	.226371	.224331	.222406	.220365	.218322	.216280	.000425

Projection: 30 Years, n = 30	Balance (b)	none	none	none	none	none	none	+ Dep. – App.
Equity	Yield	Mortgage Coefficients						
4 %	.04	.016036–	.017946–	.019966–	.021938–	.023941–	.025981–	.017830
5 %	.05	.008823–	.010753–	.012758–	.014740–	.016749–	.018789–	.015051
6 %	.06	.001233–	.003180–	.005172–	.007163–	.009177–	.011217–	.012648
7 %	.07	.006697	.004735	.002755	.000756	.001261–	.003301–	.010586
8 %	.08	.014933	.012958	.010988	.008982	.006960	.004920	.008827
9 %	.09	.023438	.021451	.019490	.017478	.015453	.013413	.007336
10 %	.10	.032177	.030181	.028227	.026210	.024183	.022143	.006079
11 %	.11	.041119	.039116	.037168	.035147	.033117	.031077	.005024
12 %	.12	.050236	.048226	.046283	.044258	.042227	.040187	.004143
13 %	.13	.059500	.057485	.055546	.053519	.051486	.049446	.003410
14 %	.14	.068891	.066871	.064935	.062906	.060872	.058832	.002802
15 %	.15	.078387	.076363	.074430	.072399	.070364	.068324	.002300
16 %	.16	.087971	.085945	.084014	.081981	.079945	.077905	.001885
17 %	.17	.097629	.095600	.093671	.091637	.089600	.087560	.001544
18 %	.18	.107348	.105317	.103390	.101355	.099317	.097277	.001264
19 %	.19	.117117	.115085	.113159	.111123	.109085	.107045	.001034
20 %	.20	.126928	.124894	.122970	.120933	.118895	.116855	.000846
21 %	.21	.136774	.134739	.132815	.130777	.128739	.126699	.000691
22 %	.22	.146647	.144611	.142688	.140650	.138611	.136571	.000565
23 %	.23	.156544	.154507	.152585	.150546	.148507	.146467	.000462
24 %	.24	.166459	.164422	.162500	.160461	.158422	.156382	.000378
25 %	.25	.176390	.174353	.172431	.170392	.168353	.166313	.000309
26 %	.26	.186334	.184296	.182374	.180335	.178296	.176256	.000253
27 %	.27	.196288	.194249	.192328	.190289	.188249	.186209	.000207
28 %	.28	.206250	.204212	.202291	.200251	.198212	.196172	.000170
29 %	.29	.216220	.214181	.212260	.210220	.208181	.206141	.000139
30 %	.30	.226194	.224155	.222235	.220195	.218155	.216115	.000114

Mortgage Coefficients for Computing Capitalization Rates.

30 YEARS AMORTIZATION: 7¾% TO 9%

Interest Rate / Annual Requirement (f) / Installment f/12			7¾% .086040 .007170	8% .088080 .007340	8½% .090240 .007520	8½% .092280 .007690	8¾% .094440 .007870	9% .096600 .008050	$\frac{1}{s_{\overline{n}\rvert}}$
Projection	Balance (b)		.948048	.950525	.952297	.954838	.956664	.958516	+ Dep. – App.
	Equity	Yield	Mortgage Coefficients						
5 Years n = 5	4 %	.04	.036448–	.038945–	.041432–	.043941–	.046439–	.048941–	.184627
	5 %	.05	.026638–	.029126–	.031607–	.034106–	.036597–	.039092–	.180974
	6 %	.06	.016823–	.019303–	.021777–	.024268–	.026752–	.029241–	.177396
	7 %	.07	.007006–	.009476–	.011944–	.014426–	.016904–	.019386–	.173890
	8 %	.08	.002815	.000353	.002108–	.004581–	.007053–	.009528–	.170456
	9 %	.09	.012640	.010186	.007730	.005266	.002800	.000331	.167092
	10 %	.10	.022469	.020023	.017573	.015117	.012658	.010194	.163797
	11 %	.11	.032301	.029864	.027419	.024971	.022518	.020060	.160570
	12 %	.12	.042137	.039707	.037268	.034828	.032381	.029929	.157409
	13 %	.13	.051976	.049554	.047121	.044689	.042247	.039801	.154314
	14 %	.14	.061819	.059404	.056976	.054552	.052115	.049675	.151283
	15 %	.15	.071665	.069257	.066835	.064418	.061987	.059552	.148315
	16 %	.16	.081514	.079114	.076696	.074286	.071861	.069432	.145409
	17 %	.17	.091366	.088973	.086560	.084158	.081738	.079314	.142563
	18 %	.18	.101221	.098835	.096427	.094032	.091617	.089198	.139777
	19 %	.19	.111079	.108700	.106297	.103909	.101499	.099085	.137050
	20 %	.20	.120941	.118568	.116170	.113788	.111383	.108974	.134379
	21 %	.21	.130805	.128439	.126045	.123670	.121270	.118866	.131765
	22 %	.22	.140672	.138312	.135923	.133555	.131159	.128759	.129205
	23 %	.23	.150542	.148188	.145803	.143442	.141050	.138655	.126700
	24 %	.24	.160414	.158067	.155686	.153331	.150944	.148554	.124247
	25 %	.25	.170290	.167948	.165572	.163222	.160840	.158454	.121846
	26 %	.26	.180168	.177832	.175460	.173116	.170738	.168357	.119496
	27 %	.27	.190048	.187718	.185350	.183012	.180638	.178261	.117195
	28 %	.28	.199931	.197606	.195243	.192911	.190541	.188168	.114943
	29 %	.29	.209816	.207497	.205137	.202811	.200445	.198076	.112739
	30 %	.30	.219704	.217390	.215035	.212714	.210352	.207987	.110581
	Balance (b)		.871603	.876816	.880339	.885862	.889652	.893567	+ Dep. – App.
	Equity	Yield	Mortgage Coefficients						
10 Years n = 10	4 %	.04	.035345–	.037819–	.040273–	.042773–	.045249–	.047735–	.083290
	5 %	.05	.025831–	.028286–	.030726–	.033205–	.035666–	.038138–	.079504
	6 %	.06	.016298–	.018734–	.021161–	.023620–	.026068–	.028525–	.075867
	7 %	.07	.006746–	.009164–	.011579–	.014019–	.016453–	.018896–	.072377
	8 %	.08	.002823	.000423	.001979–	.004401–	.006822–	.009252–	.069029
	9 %	.09	.012411	.010027	.007636	.005232	.002823	.000405	.065820
	10 %	.10	.022016	.019649	.017268	.014881	.012483	.010078	.062745
	11 %	.11	.031638	.029286	.026915	.024545	.022158	.019764	.059801
	12 %	.12	.041276	.038939	.036578	.034224	.031848	.029464	.056984
	13 %	.13	.050930	.048607	.046256	.043916	.041550	.039178	.054289
	14 %	.14	.060599	.058290	.055948	.053622	.051266	.048904	.051713
	15 %	.15	.070283	.067987	.065653	.063341	.060994	.058642	.049252
	16 %	.16	.079981	.077697	.075372	.073073	.070735	.068391	.046901
	17 %	.17	.089693	.087420	.085103	.082816	.080487	.078152	.044656
	18 %	.18	.099418	.097157	.094847	.092572	.090251	.087924	.042514
	19 %	.19	.109156	.106905	.104602	.102339	.100025	.097707	.040471
	20 %	.20	.118906	.116665	.114369	.112116	.109810	.107500	.038522
	21 %	.21	.128667	.126436	.124147	.121904	.119605	.117302	.036665
	22 %	.22	.138440	.136218	.133935	.131702	.129410	.127113	.034894
	23 %	.23	.148223	.146010	.143733	.141510	.139224	.136934	.033208
	24 %	.24	.158017	.155812	.153541	.151326	.149047	.146763	.031602
	25 %	.25	.167821	.165624	.163358	.161152	.158878	.156600	.030072
	26 %	.26	.177634	.175445	.173184	.170986	.168717	.166445	.028616
	27 %	.27	.187456	.185274	.183018	.180828	.178564	.176298	.027230
	28 %	.28	.197286	.195111	.192860	.190677	.188419	.186157	.025911
	29 %	.29	.207125	.204957	.202710	.200534	.198280	.196024	.024657
	30 %	.30	.216972	.214810	.212567	.210398	.208149	.205897	.023463

Mortgage Coefficients for Computing Capitalization Rates.
30 YEARS AMORTIZATION: 7¾% TO 9%

Projection	Equity	Yield	7¾%	8%	8¼%	8½%	8¾%	9%	$\frac{1}{s_{\overline{n}|}}$
Interest Rate			7¾%	8%	8¼%	8½%	8¾%	9%	
Annual Requirement (f)			.086040	.088080	.090240	.092280	.094440	.096600	
Installment f/12			.007170	.007340	.007520	.007690	.007870	.008050	
Projection	Balance (b)		.759118	.767000	.771794	.780516	.786025	.791876	+ Dep. − App.
	Equity	Yield	Mortgage Coefficients						
	4 %	.04	.034010−	.036443−	.038843−	.041318−	.043753−	.046206−	.049941
	5 %	.05	.024876−	.027282−	.029664−	.032108−	.034523−	.036955−	.046342
	6 %	.06	.015691−	.018069−	.020435−	.022850−	.025247−	.027658−	.042962
	7 %	.07	.006454−	.008807−	.011158−	.013545−	.015924−	.018317−	.039794
	8 %	.08	.002831	.000501	.001835−	.004196−	.006559−	.008934−	.036829
	9 %	.09	.012164	.009855	.007532	.005195	.002847	.000488	.034058
	10 %	.10	.021541	.019253	.016942	.014627	.012294	.009950	.031473
	11 %	.11	.030961	.028692	.026392	.024099	.021779	.019449	.029065
	12 %	.12	.040421	.038170	.035881	.033607	.031299	.028982	.026824
	13 %	.13	.049919	.047684	.045406	.043150	.040854	.038549	.024741
	14 %	.14	.059454	.057234	.054965	.052726	.050440	.048147	.022808
15 Years	15 %	.15	.069022	.066816	.064556	.062332	.060057	.057774	.021017
n = 15	16 %	.16	.078622	.076430	.074177	.071968	.069702	.067428	.019357
	17 %	.17	.088253	.086072	.083827	.081631	.079373	.077109	.017822
	18 %	.18	.097911	.095741	.093503	.091320	.089069	.086813	.016402
	19 %	.19	.107595	.105436	.103204	.101032	.098789	.096540	.015091
	20 %	.20	.117303	.115154	.112927	.110766	.108530	.106289	.013882
	21 %	.21	.127035	.124894	.122673	.120522	.118291	.116056	.012766
	22 %	.22	.136787	.134654	.132438	.130296	.128071	.125842	.011738
	23 %	.23	.146559	.144434	.142222	.140088	.137869	.135645	.010791
	24 %	.24	.156349	.154231	.152023	.149897	.147682	.145464	.009919
	25 %	.25	.166156	.164044	.161840	.159721	.157510	.155297	.009116
	26 %	.26	.175978	.173872	.171672	.169559	.167352	.165143	.008378
	27 %	.27	.185814	.183714	.181517	.179410	.177207	.175002	.007700
	28 %	.28	.195664	.193568	.191375	.189273	.187074	.184872	.007076
	29 %	.29	.205526	.203435	.201244	.199147	.196951	.194753	.006504
	30 %	.30	.215399	.213312	.211124	.209032	.206839	.204644	.005977
	Balance (b)		.593600	.603392	.608059	.619620	.625780	.632662	+ Dep. − App.
	Equity	Yield	Mortgage Coefficients						
	4 %	.04	.032392−	.034761−	.037077−	.039506−	.041873−	.044264−	.033581
	5 %	.05	.023749−	.026085−	.028386−	.030776−	.033122−	.035490−	.030242
	6 %	.06	.014992−	.017298−	.019585−	.021939−	.024267−	.026614−	.027184
	7 %	.07	.006126−	.008405−	.010679−	.013001−	.015311−	.017639−	.024392
	8 %	.08	.002840	.000586	.001675−	.003967−	.006262−	.008572−	.021852
	9 %	.09	.011903	.009672	.007421	.005155	.002874	.000580	.019546
	10 %	.10	.021055	.018844	.016603	.014361	.012093	.009813	.017459
	11 %	.11	.030289	.028097	.025864	.023644	.021388	.019121	.015575
	12 %	.12	.039600	.037424	.035199	.032999	.030753	.028498	.013878
	13 %	.13	.048980	.046819	.044601	.042419	.040183	.037938	.012353
	14 %	.14	.058424	.056277	.054065	.051898	.049671	.047435	.010986
20 Years	15 %	.15	.067927	.065791	.063585	.061433	.059212	.056985	.009761
n = 20	16 %	.16	.077482	.075357	.073156	.071016	.068803	.066583	.008667
	17 %	.17	.087085	.084970	.082774	.080645	.078437	.076224	.007690
	18 %	.18	.096731	.094624	.092433	.090314	.088112	.085905	.006819
	19 %	.19	.106416	.104317	.102129	.100019	.097822	.095620	.006045
	20 %	.20	.116136	.114044	.111859	.109757	.107564	.105367	.005356
	21 %	.21	.125888	.123801	.121619	.119524	.117335	.115142	.004744
	22 %	.22	.135667	.133586	.131406	.129318	.127132	.124943	.004201
	23 %	.23	.145471	.143395	.141218	.139135	.136952	.134766	.003720
	24 %	.24	.155298	.153226	.151050	.148972	.146792	.144609	.003293
	25 %	.25	.165145	.163076	.160902	.158829	.156651	.154471	.002915
	26 %	.26	.175009	.172943	.170771	.168701	.166526	.164348	.002581
	27 %	.27	.184888	.182826	.180655	.178589	.176415	.174239	.002285
	28 %	.28	.194782	.192722	.190553	.188489	.186317	.184143	.002023
	29 %	.29	.204688	.202630	.200462	.198401	.196230	.194058	.001791
	30 %	.30	.214604	.212549	.210381	.208323	.206153	.203982	.001586

Mortgage Coefficients for Computing Capitalization Rates.

30 YEARS AMORTIZATION: 7¾% TO 9%

Interest Rate Annual Requirement (f) Installment f/12			7¾% .086040 .007170	8% .088080 .007340	8¼% .090240 .007520	8½% .092280 .007690	8¾% .094440 .007870	9% .096600 .008050	$\frac{1}{s_{\overline{n}\rvert}}$
Projection	**Balance (b)**		.350048	.359642	.361070	.373884	.377982	.383382	+ Dep. – App.
	Equity	**Yield**	**Mortgage Coefficients**						
	4 %	.04	.030433–	.032703–	.034898–	.037245–	.039504–	.041793–	.024011
	5 %	.05	.022421–	.024662–	.026852–	.029161–	.031407–	.033680–	.020952
	6 %	.06	.014193–	.016408–	.018594–	.020867–	.023102–	.025361–	.018226
	7 %	.07	.005763–	.007955–	.010138–	.012380–	.014605–	.016850–	.015810
	8 %	.08	.002850	.000679	.001500–	.003715–	.005931–	.008165–	.013678
	9 %	.09	.011633	.009480	.007303	.005112	.002903	.000679	.011806
	10 %	.10	.020568	.018431	.016256	.014086	.011884	.009669	.010168
	11 %	.11	.029640	.027516	.025344	.023192	.020996	.018789	.008740
	12 %	.12	.038834	.036722	.034551	.032415	.030225	.028024	.007499
	13 %	.13	.048136	.046034	.043865	.041743	.039557	.037362	.006425
	14 %	.14	.057533	.055440	.053273	.051162	.048980	.046790	.005498
25 Years n = 25	15 %	.15	.067014	.064929	.062762	.065662	.058483	.056297	.004699
	16 %	.16	.076568	.074489	.072323	.070232	.068055	.065874	.004012
	17 %	.17	.086185	.084112	.081947	.079863	.077689	.075510	.003423
	18 %	.18	.095857	.093789	.091624	.089547	.087375	.085199	.002918
	19 %	.19	.105576	.103512	.101349	.099277	.097107	.094933	.002487
	20 %	.20	.115337	.113276	.111113	.109046	.106877	.104706	.002118
	21 %	.21	.125132	.123075	.120912	.118849	.116682	.114512	.001804
	22 %	.22	.134958	.132903	.130741	.128681	.126515	.124347	.001536
	23 %	.23	.144810	.142757	.140595	.138538	.136373	.134206	.001307
	24 %	.24	.154683	.152633	.150471	.148417	.146252	.144086	.001113
	25 %	.25	.164576	.162527	.160365	.158213	.156149	.153984	.000948
	26 %	.26	.174484	.172436	.170275	.168225	.166062	.163897	.000807
	27 %	.27	.184406	.182360	.180199	.178150	.175987	.173824	.000687
	28 %	.28	.194340	.192295	.190134	.188086	.185924	.183761	.000585
	29 %	.29	.204284	.202239	.200079	.198032	.195870	.193707	.000499
	30 %	.30	.214236	.212192	.210032	.207986	.205824	.203662	.000425
	Balance (b)		none	none	none	none	none	none	+ Dep. – App.
	Equity	**Yield**	**Mortgage Coefficients**						
	4 %	.04	.028061–	.030187–	.032204–	.034424–	.036517–	.038646–	.017830
	5 %	.05	.020863–	.022975–	.025015–	.027207–	.029310–	.031444–	.015051
	6 %	.06	.013285–	.015386–	.017445–	.019613–	.021725–	.023863–	.012648
	7 %	.07	.005365–	.007456–	.009531–	.011678–	.013798–	.015940–	.010586
	8 %	.08	.002860	.000778	.001311–	.003439–	.005566–	.007711–	.008827
	9 %	.09	.011357	.009282	.007180	.005066	.002934	.000787	.007336
	10 %	.10	.020089	.018020	.015909	.013807	.011670	.009521	.006079
	11 %	.11	.029026	.026962	.024842	.022751	.020610	.018459	.005024
	12 %	.12	.038138	.036078	.033951	.031869	.029725	.027572	.004143
	13 %	.13	.047399	.045342	.043209	.041135	.038988	.036834	.003410
	14 %	.14	.056786	.054732	.052595	.050526	.048377	.046222	.002802
30 Years n = 30	15 %	.15	.066279	.064228	.062086	.060023	.057872	.055716	.002300
	16 %	.16	.075861	.073812	.071667	.069608	.067455	.065298	.001885
	17 %	.17	.085517	.083469	.081322	.079266	.077112	.074955	.001544
	18 %	.18	.095234	.093188	.091038	.088986	.086830	.084673	.001264
	19 %	.19	.105003	.102958	.100806	.098755	.096599	.094441	.001034
	20 %	.20	.114813	.112769	.110615	.108567	.106410	.104251	.000846
	21 %	.21	.124657	.122614	.120459	.118412	.116255	.114096	.000691
	22 %	.22	.134530	.132487	.130332	.128286	.126128	.123969	.000565
	23 %	.23	.144426	.142384	.140228	.138183	.136025	.133866	.000462
	24 %	.24	.154341	.152299	.150143	.148099	.145940	.143781	.000378
	25 %	.25	.164272	.162230	.160073	.158030	.155871	.153712	.000309
	26 %	.26	.174215	.172174	.170016	.167974	.165814	.163655	.000253
	27 %	.27	.184169	.182128	.179970	.177928	.175768	.173609	.000207
	28 %	.28	.194131	.192090	.189932	.187890	.185731	.183571	.000170
	29 %	.29	.204100	.202060	.199901	.197859	.195700	.193540	.000139
	30 %	.30	.214075	.212034	.209875	.207834	.205675	.203515	.000114

Mortgage Coefficients for Computing Capitalization Rates.

30 YEARS AMORTIZATION: 9¼% TO 10½%

Interest Rate Annual Requirement (f) Installment f/12			9¼% .098760 .008230	9½% .100920 .008410	9¾% .103200 .008600	10% .105360 .008780	10¼% .107640 .008970	10½% .109800 .009150	$\frac{1}{s_{\overline{n}\|}}$
Projection	**Balance (b)**		.960394	.962298	.963459	.965411	.966611	.968612	+ Dep. – App.
	Equity	**Yield**	**Mortgage Coefficients**						
	4 %	.04	.051447–	.053959–	.056453–	.058974–	.061475–	.064005–	.184627
	5 %	.05	.041592–	.044096–	.046587–	.049100–	.051597–	.054119–	.180974
	6 %	.06	.031734–	.034231–	.036717–	.039224–	.041716–	.044231–	.177396
	7 %	.07	.021872–	.024364–	.026845–	.029345–	.031833–	.034341–	.173890
	8 %	.08	.012008–	.014493–	.016971–	.019464–	.021948–	.024449–	.170456
	9 %	.09	.002142–	.004620–	.007094–	.009580–	.012060–	.014555–	.167092
	10 %	.10	.007727	.005255	.002785	.000305	.002170–	.004658–	.163797
	11 %	.11	.017599	.015133	.012667	.010193	.007721	.005239	.160570
	12 %	.12	.027474	.025014	.022551	.020084	.017615	.015140	.157409
	13 %	.13	.037351	.034897	.032438	.029977	.027512	.025043	.154314
	14 %	.14	.047231	.044783	.042327	.039872	.037411	.034948	.151283
5 Years **n = 5**	15 %	.15	.057114	.054671	.052219	.049770	.047312	.044855	.148315
	16 %	.16	.066999	.064562	.062113	.059669	.057215	.054764	.145409
	17 %	.17	.076886	.074454	.072009	.069571	.067120	.064674	.142563
	18 %	.18	.086775	.084349	.081907	.079474	.077027	.074587	.139777
	19 %	.19	.096667	.094247	.091807	.089380	.086935	.084501	.137050
	20 %	.20	.106562	.104146	.101710	.099288	.096846	.094417	.134379
	21 %	.21	.116458	.114047	.111614	.109197	.106759	.104335	.131765
	22 %	.22	.126357	.123951	.121521	.119109	.116674	.114255	.129205
	23 %	.23	.136258	.133856	.131429	.129022	.126590	.124176	.126700
	24 %	.24	.146160	.143764	.141340	.138937	.136508	.134099	.124247
	25 %	.25	.156065	.153673	.151252	.148854	.146428	.144024	.121846
	26 %	.26	.165972	.163585	.161166	.158773	.156349	.153950	.119496
	27 %	.27	.175881	.173498	.171082	.168693	.166273	.163878	.117195
	28 %	.28	.185792	.183413	.181000	.178615	.176197	.173807	.114943
	29 %	.29	.195705	.193330	.190919	.188539	.186124	.183738	.112739
	30 %	.30	.205619	.203249	.200840	.198464	.196052	.193670	.110581
	Balance (b)		.897610	.901786	.904079	.908502	.910990	.915674	+ Dep. – App.
	Equity	**Yield**	**Mortgage Coefficients**						
	4 %	.04	.050231–	.052739–	.055210–	.057739–	.060226–	.062776–	.083290
	5 %	.05	.040619–	.043111–	.045573–	.048085–	.050563–	.053095–	.079504
	6 %	.06	.030991–	.033468–	.035922–	.038418–	.040887–	.043402–	.075867
	7 %	.07	.021349–	.023811–	.026257–	.028737–	.031197–	.033696–	.072377
	8 %	.08	.011692–	.014140–	.016578–	.019043–	.021495–	.023979–	.069029
	9 %	.09	.002020–	.004455–	.006886–	.009337–	.011781–	.014249–	.065820
	10 %	.10	.007664	.005242	.002818	.000381	.002055–	.004508–	.062745
	11 %	.11	.017363	.014953	.012536	.010111	.007682	.005242	.059801
	12 %	.12	.027074	.024676	.022265	.019853	.017432	.015005	.056984
	13 %	.13	.036798	.034411	.032007	.029607	.027192	.024778	.054289
10 Years **n = 10**	14 %	.14	.046534	.044158	.041760	.039371	.036962	.034560	.051713
	15 %	.15	.056282	.053917	.051524	.049146	.046743	.044353	.049252
	16 %	.16	.066042	.063686	.061298	.058931	.056534	.054154	.046901
	17 %	.17	.075812	.073465	.071083	.068725	.066334	.063965	.044656
	18 %	.18	.085593	.083255	.080878	.078529	.076144	.073785	.042514
	19 %	.19	.095383	.093054	.090682	.088343	.085962	.083612	.040471
	20 %	.20	.105184	.102863	.100495	.098164	.095788	.093448	.038522
	21 %	.21	.114994	.112681	.110316	.107994	.105623	.103291	.036665
	22 %	.22	.124812	.122507	.120147	.117832	.115465	.113142	.034894
	23 %	.23	.134640	.132341	.129985	.127678	.125315	.123000	.033208
	24 %	.24	.144475	.142183	.139831	.137531	.135172	.132864	.031602
	25 %	.25	.154319	.152033	.149684	.147391	.145036	.142735	.030072
	26 %	.26	.164170	.161890	.159544	.157258	.154907	.152613	.028616
	27 %	.27	.174028	.171754	.169411	.167131	.164783	.162496	.027230
	28 %	.28	.183893	.181624	.179285	.177010	.174666	.172385	.025911
	29 %	.29	.193764	.191501	.189165	.186896	.184554	.182279	.024657
	30 %	.30	.203642	.201384	.199050	.196786	.194448	.192178	.023463

30 YEARS AMORTIZATION: 9¼% TO 10½%

TABLE C

Interest Rate Annual Requirement (f) Installment f/12		9¼% .098760 .008230	9½% .100920 .008410	9¾% .103200 .008600	10% .105360 .008780	10¼% .107640 .008970	10½% .109800 .009150	$\frac{1}{s_{\overline{n}\vert}}$
Projection: 15 Years, n = 15	Balance (b)	.798084	.804665	.807585	.814869	.818336	.826388	+ Dep. − App.
Equity	Yield	Mortgage Coefficients						
4 %	.04	.048676−	.051164−	.053590−	.056114−	.058567−	.061129−	.049941
5 %	.05	.039402−	.041867−	.044283−	.046780−	.049221−	.051754−	.046342
6 %	.06	.030085−	.032527−	.034933−	.037406−	.039835−	.042341−	.042962
7 %	.07	.020724−	.023146−	.025542−	.027992−	.030410−	.032891−	.039794
8 %	.08	.011323−	.013725−	.016113−	.018541−	.020949−	.023405−	.036829
9 %	.09	.001882−	.004267−	.006646−	.009054−	.011452−	.013886−	.034058
10 %	.10	.007595	.005227	.002856	.000466	.001922−	.004335−	.031473
11 %	.11	.017108	.014757	.012392	.010020	.007640	.005246	.029065
12 %	.12	.026656	.024319	.021961	.019605	.017232	.014857	.026824
13 %	.13	.036235	.033912	.031560	.029220	.026854	.024495	.024741
14 %	.14	.045845	.043535	.041188	.038862	.036503	.034159	.022808
15 %	.15	.055483	.053185	.050843	.048530	.046178	.043848	.021017
16 %	.16	.065148	.062861	.060524	.058223	.055876	.053560	.019357
17 %	.17	.074838	.072561	.070229	.067939	.065597	.063294	.017822
18 %	.18	.084551	.082284	.079956	.077676	.075339	.073047	.016402
19 %	.19	.094287	.092027	.089703	.087433	.085101	.082820	.015091
20 %	.20	.104043	.101791	.099471	.097209	.094881	.092610	.013882
21 %	.21	.113817	.111573	.109256	.107003	.104679	.102416	.012766
22 %	.22	.123610	.121372	.119058	.116813	.114492	.112237	.011738
23 %	.23	.133418	.131187	.128876	.126637	.124320	.122073	.010791
24 %	.24	.143242	.141017	.138708	.136476	.134161	.131922	.009919
25 %	.25	.153080	.150860	.148554	.146327	.144016	.141782	.009116
26 %	.26	.162931	.160716	.158412	.156191	.153882	.151654	.008378
27 %	.27	.172794	.170584	.168281	.166065	.163758	.161536	.007700
28 %	.28	.182668	.180462	.178161	.175950	.173645	.171428	.007076
29 %	.29	.192553	.190350	.188051	.185844	.183541	.181329	.006504
30 %	.30	.202447	.200247	.197950	.195746	.193445	.191237	.005977
Projection: 20 Years, n = 20	Balance (b)	.640312	.648784	.650778	.660815	.663990	.675798	+ Dep. − App.
Equity	Yield	Mortgage Coefficients						
4 %	.04	.046681−	.049125−	.051472−	.053969−	.056356−	.058912−	.033581
5 %	.05	.037882−	.040298−	.042638−	.045102−	.047478−	.049995−	.030242
6 %	.06	.028982−	.031372−	.033706−	.036139−	.038505−	.040986−	.027184
7 %	.07	.019986−	.022352−	.024681−	.027086−	.029443−	.031891−	.024392
8 %	.08	.010900−	.013245−	.015568−	.017948−	.020297−	.022715−	.021852
9 %	.09	.001729−	.004054−	.006373−	.008730−	.011072−	.013462−	.019546
10 %	.10	.007520	.005212	.002897	.000562	.001773−	.004139−	.017459
11 %	.11	.016842	.014550	.012239	.009923	.007593	.005249	.015575
12 %	.12	.026232	.023954	.021646	.019347	.017023	.014699	.013878
13 %	.13	.035683	.033418	.031114	.028830	.026510	.024205	.012353
14 %	.14	.045191	.042938	.040636	.038366	.036051	.033761	.010986
15 %	.15	.054751	.052508	.050208	.047950	.045639	.043364	.009761
16 %	.16	.064357	.062123	.059826	.057579	.055272	.053009	.008667
17 %	.17	.074006	.071780	.069485	.067248	.064944	.062693	.007690
18 %	.18	.083693	.081475	.079181	.076953	.074651	.072411	.006819
19 %	.19	.093414	.091203	.088911	.086690	.084391	.082159	.006045
20 %	.20	.103166	.100961	.098670	.096456	.094159	.091936	.005356
21 %	.21	.112946	.110746	.108456	.106249	.103954	.101738	.004744
22 %	.22	.122751	.120555	.118267	.116065	.113771	.111562	.004201
23 %	.23	.132578	.130386	.128099	.125901	.123610	.121406	.003720
24 %	.24	.142424	.140236	.137950	.135757	.133466	.131267	.003293
25 %	.25	.152288	.150104	.147818	.145629	.143339	.141145	.002915
26 %	.26	.162168	.159986	.157701	.155515	.153227	.151036	.002581
27 %	.27	.172062	.169882	.167598	.165415	.163127	.160940	.002285
28 %	.28	.181967	.179790	.177506	.175326	.173039	.170855	.002023
29 %	.29	.191884	.189709	.187425	.185247	.182962	.180780	.001791
30 %	.30	.201810	.199637	.197354	.195178	.192893	.190714	.001586

Mortgage Coefficients for Computing Capitalization Rates.

30 YEARS AMORTIZATION: 9¼% TO 10½%

Interest Rate / Annual Requirement (f) / Installment f/12			9¼% .098760 .008230	9½% .100920 .008410	9¾% .103200 .008600	10% .105360 .008780	10¼% .107640 .008970	10½% .109800 .009150	$\frac{1}{s_{\overline{n}|}}$
Projection	Balance (b)		.390209	.398593	.395961	.407347	.406877	.421812	+ Dep. − App.
	Equity	Yield	Mortgage Coefficients						
	4 %	.04	.044117−	.046479−	.048695−	.051129−	.053397−	.055916−	.024011
	5 %	.05	.035983−	.038319−	.040543−	.042942−	.045212−	.047685−	.020952
	6 %	.06	.027645−	.029958−	.032190−	.034557−	.036829−	.039261−	.018226
	7 %	.07	.019118−	.021411−	.023649−	.025989−	.028262−	.030658−	.015810
	8 %	.08	.010418−	.012693−	.014937−	.017253−	.019526−	.021891−	.013678
	9 %	.09	.001560−	.003819−	.006068−	.008362−	.010637−	.012973−	.011806
	10 %	.10	.007440	.005195	.002941	.000666	.001609−	.003920−	.010168
	11 %	.11	.016569	.014336	.012079	.009819	.007544	.005253	.008740
	12 %	.12	.025813	.023590	.021330	.019084	.016808	.014536	.007499
	13 %	.13	.035158	.032944	.030681	.028448	.026171	.023915	.006425
	14 %	.14	.044592	.042386	.040121	.037898	.035621	.033379	.005498
	15 %	.15	.054105	.051906	.049638	.047425	.045147	.042917	.004699
25 Years n = 25	16 %	.16	.063686	.061493	.059223	.057018	.054739	.052520	.004012
	17 %	.17	.073327	.071138	.068867	.066668	.064390	.062179	.003423
	18 %	.18	.083019	.080835	.078563	.076369	.074091	.071887	.002918
	19 %	.19	.092756	.090575	.088302	.086114	.083835	.081638	.002487
	20 %	.20	.102531	.100354	.098079	.095895	.093616	.091425	.002118
	21 %	.21	.112340	.110165	.107889	.105709	.103430	.101243	.001804
	22 %	.22	.122176	.120003	.117727	.115550	.113271	.111088	.001536
	23 %	.23	.132037	.129866	.127589	.125415	.123135	.120956	.001307
	24 %	.24	.141918	.139749	.137472	.135299	.133020	.130843	.001113
	25 %	.25	.151818	.149650	.147372	.145201	.142922	.140748	.000948
	26 %	.26	.161732	.159565	.157287	.155118	.152838	.150666	.000807
	27 %	.27	.171659	.169493	.167215	.165047	.162767	.160597	.000687
	28 %	.28	.181597	.179432	.177153	.174987	.172707	.170538	.000585
	29 %	.29	.191544	.189380	.187101	.184935	.182656	.180488	.000499
	30 %	.30	.201499	.199336	.197057	.194892	.192612	.190446	.000425
	Balance (b)		none	none	none	none	none	none	+ Dep. − App.
	Equity	Yield	Mortgage Coefficients						
	4 %	.04	.040818−	.043037−	.045046−	.047357−	.049427−	.051852−	.017830
	5 %	.05	.033614−	.035823−	.037875−	.040162−	.042265−	.044649−	.015051
	6 %	.06	.026031−	.028233−	.030321−	.032588−	.034720−	.037068−	.012648
	7 %	.07	.018107−	.020302−	.022421−	.024671−	.026826−	.029144−	.010586
	8 %	.08	.009877−	.012066−	.014212−	.016447−	.018623−	.020914−	.008827
	9 %	.09	.001377−	.003561−	.005730−	.007952−	.010146−	.012415−	.007336
	10 %	.10	.007357	.005177	.002989	.000778	.001430−	.003680−	.006079
	11 %	.11	.016296	.014119	.011915	.009713	.007492	.005257	.005024
	12 %	.12	.025409	.023235	.021018	.018823	.016592	.014370	.004143
	13 %	.13	.034672	.032500	.030272	.028083	.025843	.023633	.003410
	14 %	.14	.044060	.041891	.039653	.037469	.035222	.033021	.002802
	15 %	.15	.053554	.051387	.049141	.046962	.044709	.042515	.002300
30 Years n = 30	16 %	.16	.063137	.060971	.058719	.056543	.054286	.052098	.001885
	17 %	.17	.072794	.070629	.068372	.066199	.063937	.061754	.001544
	18 %	.18	.082512	.080348	.078087	.075916	.073651	.071472	.001264
	19 %	.19	.092280	.090117	.087853	.085684	.083416	.081241	.001034
	20 %	.20	.102091	.099928	.097661	.095494	.093224	.091051	.000846
	21 %	.21	.111936	.109774	.107504	.105338	.103066	.100896	.000691
	22 %	.22	.121809	.119647	.117376	.115211	.112938	.110769	.000565
	23 %	.23	.131705	.129544	.127271	.125107	.122832	.120665	.000462
	24 %	.24	.141621	.139459	.137185	.135022	.132746	.130581	.000378
	25 %	.25	.151551	.149390	.147115	.144952	.142676	.140511	.000309
	26 %	.26	.161495	.159334	.157058	.154896	.152619	.150455	.000253
	27 %	.27	.171449	.169288	.167011	.164849	.162572	.160409	.000207
	28 %	.28	.181411	.179250	.176973	.174811	.172533	.170371	.000170
	29 %	.29	.191380	.189220	.186942	.184780	.182502	.180340	.000139
	30 %	.30	.201355	.199194	.196916	.194755	.192477	.190315	.000114

Mortgage Coefficients for Computing Capitalization Rates.

30 YEARS AMORTIZATION: 10¾% TO 12%

Interest Rate / Annual Requirement (f) / Installment f/12			10¾% .112080 .009340	11% .114360 .009530	11¼% .116640 .009720	11½% .118920 .009910	11¾% .121200 .010100	12% .123480 .010290	$\frac{1}{s_{\overline{n}|}}$
Projection	**Balance (b)**		.969851	.971108	.972383	.973675	.974986	.976315	**+ Dep. – App.**
	Equity	**Yield**	**Mortgage Coefficients**						
	4 %	.04	.066513-	.069025-	.071541-	.074059-	.076581-	.079107-	.184627
	5 %	.05	.056623-	.059131-	.061642-	.064155-	.066673-	.069193-	.180974
	6 %	.06	.046731-	.049234-	.051740-	.054250-	.056762-	.059278-	.177396
	7 %	.07	.036837-	.039336-	.041837-	.044342-	.046850-	.049361-	.173890
	8 %	.08	.026941-	.029435-	.031932-	.034432-	.036936-	.039442-	.170456
	9 %	.09	.017042-	.019532-	.022025-	.024521-	.027020-	.029522-	.167092
	10 %	.10	.007141-	.009627-	.012116-	.014608-	.017102-	.019600-	.163797
	11 %	.11	.002760	.000279	.002205-	.004693-	.007183-	.009677-	.160570
	12 %	.12	.012665	.010187	.007707	.005223	.002737	.000248	.157409
	13 %	.13	.022572	.020098	.017621	.015142	.012659	.010174	.154314
	14 %	.14	.032480	.030010	.027537	.025062	.022584	.020103	.151283
5 Years n = 5	15 %	.15	.042391	.039925	.037456	.034984	.032509	.030032	.148315
	16 %	.16	.052303	.049841	.047375	.044907	.042437	.039963	.145409
	17 %	.17	.062218	.059758	.057297	.054832	.052366	.049896	.142563
	18 %	.18	.072134	.069678	.067220	.064759	.062296	.059830	.139777
	19 %	.19	.082051	.079599	.077144	.074687	.072228	.069765	.137050
	20 %	.20	.091971	.089522	.087071	.084617	.082161	.079702	.134379
	21 %	.21	.101892	.099446	.096998	.094548	.092095	.089640	.131765
	22 %	.22	.111815	.109372	.106928	.104481	.102031	.099580	.129205
	23 %	.23	.121739	.119300	.116859	.114415	.111969	.109520	.126700
	24 %	.24	.131665	.129229	.126791	.124350	.121907	.119462	.124247
	25 %	.25	.141593	.139160	.136725	.134287	.131847	.129405	.121846
	26 %	.26	.151522	.149092	.146660	.144225	.141789	.139350	.119496
	27 %	.27	.161453	.159025	.156596	.154165	.151731	.149295	.117195
	28 %	.28	.171385	.168960	.166534	.164105	.161675	.159242	.114943
	29 %	.29	.181318	.178897	.176473	.174047	.171620	.169190	.112739
	30 %	.30	.191253	.188834	.186413	.183990	.181566	.179139	.110581
	Balance (b)		.918369	.921157	.924040	.927021	.930103	.933288	**+ Dep. – App.**
	Equity	**Yield**	**Mortgage Coefficients**						
	4 %	.04	.065280-	.067793-	.070313-	.072841-	.075378-	.077923-	.083290
	5 %	.05	.055589-	.058091-	.060600-	.063117-	.065642-	.068176-	.079504
	6 %	.06	.045886-	.048378-	.050877-	.053383-	.055897-	.058418-	.075867
	7 %	.07	.036171-	.038653-	.041142-	.043638-	.046141-	.048651-	.072377
	8 %	.08	.026445-	.028917-	.031396-	.033882-	.036375-	.038874-	.069029
	9 %	.09	.016707-	.019170-	.021640-	.024116-	.026599-	.029089-	.065820
	10 %	.10	.006958-	.009412-	.011873-	.014340-	.016814-	.019294-	.062745
	11 %	.11	.002801	.000354	.002097-	.004555-	.007020-	.009490-	.059801
	12 %	.12	.012571	.010132	.007688	.005238	.002782	.000321	.056984
	13 %	.13	.022351	.019920	.017483	.015041	.012594	.010141	.054289
10 Years n = 10	14 %	.14	.032141	.029717	.027288	.024853	.022414	.019969	.051713
	15 %	.15	.041940	.039523	.037101	.034674	.032242	.029805	.049252
	16 %	.16	.051748	.049337	.046922	.044502	.042078	.039648	.046901
	17 %	.17	.061565	.059160	.056752	.054338	.051921	.049499	.044656
	18 %	.18	.071390	.068991	.066589	.064182	.061771	.059356	.042514
	19 %	.19	.081223	.078830	.076434	.074033	.071628	.069219	.040471
	20 %	.20	.091064	.088677	.086286	.083891	.081492	.079089	.038522
	21 %	.21	.100913	.098530	.096145	.093755	.091362	.088965	.036665
	22 %	.22	.110768	.108391	.106010	.103626	.101239	.098847	.034894
	23 %	.23	.120630	.118258	.115882	.113503	.111121	.108735	.033208
	24 %	.24	.130499	.128131	.125760	.123386	.121008	.118628	.031602
	25 %	.25	.140374	.138011	.135644	.133274	.130901	.128526	.030072
	26 %	.26	.150255	.147896	.145533	.143168	.140800	.138429	.028616
	27 %	.27	.160142	.157786	.155428	.153067	.150703	.148336	.027230
	28 %	.28	.170035	.167682	.165328	.162970	.160611	.158248	.025911
	29 %	.29	.179932	.177584	.175232	.172879	.170523	.168164	.024657
	30 %	.30	.189835	.187489	.185142	.182792	.180440	.178085	.023463

Mortgage Coefficients for Computing Capitalization Rates.

30 YEARS AMORTIZATION: 10¾% TO 12%

Projection	Equity	Yield	10¾%	11%	11¼%	11½%	11¾%	12%	$\frac{1}{s_{\overline{n}\rceil}}$
Interest Rate			10¾%	11%	11¼%	11½%	11¾%	12%	
Annual Requirement (f)			.112080	.114360	.116640	.118920	.121200	.123480	
Installment f/12			.009340	.009530	.009720	.009910	.010100	.010290	
	Balance (b)		.830456	.834796	.839418	.844338	.849567	.855121	+ Dep. − App.
	Equity	Yield	Mortgage Coefficients						
	4 %	.04	.063612−	.066109−	.068620−	.071146−	.073687−	.076244−	.049941
	5 %	.05	.054222−	.056704−	.059198−	.061706−	.064228−	.066766−	.046342
	6 %	.06	.044795−	.047262−	.049740−	.052232−	.054737−	.057255−	.042962
	7 %	.07	.035333−	.037785−	.040249−	.042725−	.045213−	.047714−	.039794
	8 %	.08	.025835−	.028275−	.030725−	.033187−	.035659−	.038144−	.036829
	9 %	.09	.016305−	.018733−	.021170−	.023618−	.026076−	.028545−	.034058
	10 %	.10	.006743−	.009160−	.011585−	.014020−	.016465−	.018920−	.031473
	11 %	.11	.002847	.000441	.001972−	.004395−	.006827−	.009269−	.029065
	12 %	.12	.012467	.010071	.007667	.005255	.002835	.000406	.026824
	13 %	.13	.022114	.019727	.017333	.014931	.012521	.010104	.024741
	14 %	.14	.031787	.029408	.027022	.024630	.022231	.019824	.022858
15 Years n = 15	15 %	.15	.041483	.039112	.036734	.034351	.031961	.029564	.021017
	16 %	.16	.051201	.048837	.046468	.044093	.041711	.039324	.019357
	17 %	.17	.060941	.058584	.056221	.053854	.051481	.049102	.017822
	18 %	.18	.070700	.068349	.065993	.063633	.061267	.058896	.016402
	19 %	.19	.080478	.078133	.075783	.073429	.071070	.068706	.015091
	20 %	.20	.090273	.087933	.085589	.083240	.080888	.078531	.013882
	21 %	.21	.100084	.097749	.095410	.093067	.090720	.088369	.012766
	22 %	.22	.109910	.107579	.105244	.102907	.100565	.098220	.011738
	23 %	.23	.119749	.117422	.115092	.112759	.110423	.108083	.010791
	24 %	.24	.129601	.127278	.124952	.122624	.120292	.117957	.009919
	25 %	.25	.139465	.137146	.134823	.132499	.130171	.127840	.009116
	26 %	.26	.149340	.147024	.144705	.142384	.140060	.137733	.008378
	27 %	.27	.159225	.156912	.154596	.152278	.149958	.147635	.007700
	28 %	.28	.169119	.166809	.164496	.162181	.159864	.157545	.007076
	29 %	.29	.179022	.176714	.174404	.172092	.169778	.167462	.006504
	30 %	.30	.188933	.186627	.184319	.182010	.179699	.177386	.005977
	Balance (b)		.680334	.685484	.691291	.697800	.705058	.713115	+ Dep. − App.
	Equity	Yield	Mortgage Coefficients						
	4 %	.04	.061345−	.063798−	.066273−	.068771−	.071295−	.073845−	.033581
	5 %	.05	.052412−	.054843−	.057303−	.059780−	.062280−	.064803−	.030242
	6 %	.06	.043390−	.045810−	.048247−	.050704−	.053182−	.055681−	.027184
	7 %	.07	.034282−	.036688−	.039109−	.041548−	.044005−	.046482−	.024392
	8 %	.08	.025094−	.027487−	.029894−	.032316−	.034754−	.037210−	.021852
	9 %	.09	.015831−	.018212−	.020605−	.023013−	.025434−	.027872−	.019546
	10 %	.10	.006498−	.008868−	.011250−	.013643−	.016050−	.018471−	.017459
	11 %	.11	.002898	.000538	.001831−	.004213−	.006606−	.009011−	.015575
	12 %	.12	.012356	.010005	.007644	.005274	.002893	.000501	.013878
	13 %	.13	.021869	.019525	.017173	.014813	.012443	.010064	.012353
	14 %	.14	.031431	.029095	.026751	.024399	.022040	.019671	.010986
20 Years n = 20	15 %	.15	.041040	.038710	.036373	.034029	.031679	.029320	.009761
	16 %	.16	.050690	.048365	.046035	.043699	.041356	.039006	.008667
	17 %	.17	.060378	.058058	.055734	.053404	.051068	.048726	.007690
	18 %	.18	.070100	.067784	.065465	.063140	.060811	.058476	.006819
	19 %	.19	.079852	.077541	.075226	.072906	.070583	.068254	.006045
	20 %	.20	.089632	.087324	.085013	.082698	.080379	.078056	.005356
	21 %	.21	.099436	.097132	.094824	.092513	.090199	.087881	.004744
	22 %	.22	.109263	.106961	.104657	.102349	.100039	.097725	.004201
	23 %	.23	.119109	.116810	.114508	.112204	.109897	.107587	.003720
	24 %	.24	.128972	.126675	.124376	.122075	.119771	.117464	.003293
	25 %	.25	.138852	.136557	.134260	.131961	.129660	.127356	.002915
	26 %	.26	.148745	.146451	.144156	.141860	.139561	.137260	.002581
	27 %	.27	.158650	.156358	.154065	.151770	.149474	.147175	.002285
	28 %	.28	.168566	.166276	.163984	.161691	.159396	.157100	.002023
	29 %	.29	.178492	.176203	.173913	.171621	.169328	.167034	.001791
	30 %	.30	.188427	.186139	.183849	.181559	.179268	.176975	.001586

Mortgage Coefficients for Computing Capitalization Rates.

30 YEARS AMORTIZATION: 10¾% TO 12%

Interest Rate Annual Requirement (f) Installment f/12			10¾% .112080 .009340	11% .114360 .009530	11¼% .116640 .009720	11½% .118920 .009910	11¾% .121200 .010100	12% .123480 .010290	$\frac{1}{s_{\overline{n}\vert}}$
Projection	Balance (b)		.423981	.427338	.432001	.4389095	.445757	.455134	+ Dep. – App.
	Equity	Yield	Mortgage Coefficients						
	4 %	.04	.058248–	.060609–	.063001–	.065427–	.067891–	.070396–	.024011
	5 %	.05	.050010–	.052361–	.054739–	.057146–	.059587–	.062063–	.020952
	6 %	.06	.041581–	.043922–	.046287–	.048678–	.051097–	.053548–	.018226
	7 %	.07	.032972–	.035305–	.037659–	.040036–	.042437–	.044865–	.015810
	8 %	.08	.024200–	.026526–	.028870–	.031233–	.033618–	.036026–	.013678
	9 %	.09	.015279–	.017599–	.019934–	.022286–	.024656–	.027047–	.011806
	10 %	.10	.006222–	.008537–	.010864–	.013206–	.015564–	.017939–	.010168
	11 %	.11	.002954	.000645	.001675–	.004008–	.006355–	.008717–	.008740
	12 %	.12	.012240	.009934	.007619	.005294	.002956	.000606	.007499
	13 %	.13	.021621	.019319	.017009	.014690	.012361	.010021	.006425
	14 %	.14	.031087	.028788	.026483	.024169	.021847	.019515	.005498
25 Years n = 25	15 %	.15	.040626	.038331	.036029	.033720	.031404	.029080	.004699
	16 %	.16	.050231	.047937	.045639	.043334	.041023	.038706	.004012
	17 %	.17	.059891	.057600	.055304	.053003	.050697	.048385	.003423
	18 %	.18	.069601	.067311	.065017	.062720	.060417	.058110	.002918
	19 %	.19	.079352	.077064	.074772	.072477	.070178	.067875	.002487
	20 %	.20	.089140	.086853	.084563	.082270	.079974	.077674	.002118
	21 %	.21	.098959	.096673	.094384	.092093	.089799	.087503	.001804
	22 %	.22	.108804	.106519	.104232	.101943	.099651	.097357	.001536
	23 %	.23	.118673	.116388	.114102	.111814	.109524	.107232	.001307
	24 %	.24	.128561	.126277	.123992	.121705	.119417	.117126	.001113
	25 %	.25	.138466	.136182	.133898	.131612	.129325	.127036	.000948
	26 %	.26	.148385	.146102	.143818	.141533	.139247	.136959	.000807
	27 %	.27	.158316	.156033	.153750	.151466	.149181	.146894	.000687
	28 %	.28	.168257	.165975	.163692	.161409	.159124	.156839	.000585
	29 %	.29	.178207	.175925	.173643	.171360	.169076	.166792	.000499
	30 %	.30	.188165	.185883	.183601	.181319	.179035	.176751	.000425
	Balance (b)		none	none	none	none	none	none	+ Dep. – App.
	Equity	Yield	Mortgage Coefficients						
	4 %	.04	.054004–	.056191–	.058419–	.060694–	.063021–	.065408–	.017830
	5 %	.05	.046821–	.049022–	.051259–	.053534–	.055854–	.058224–	.015051
	6 %	.06	.039256–	.041471–	.043714–	.045990–	.048304–	.050659–	.012648
	7 %	.07	.031347–	.033572–	.035821–	.038098–	.040406–	.042750–	.010585
	8 %	.08	.023130–	.025365–	.027619–	.029896–	.032200–	.034533–	.008827
	9 %	.09	.014642–	.016884–	.019143–	.021420–	.023720–	.026044–	.007336
	10 %	.10	.005917–	.008165–	.010427–	.012705–	.015002–	.017318–	.006079
	11 %	.11	.003013	.000759	.001505–	.003783–	.006077–	.008387–	.005024
	12 %	.12	.012120	.009862	.007594	.005315	.003024	.000719	.004143
30 Years n = 25	13 %	.13	.021377	.019115	.016845	.014566	.012277	.009976	.003410
	14 %	.14	.030761	.028495	.026224	.023944	.021657	.019360	.002802
	15 %	.15	.040251	.037983	.035710	.033431	.031145	.028851	.002300
	16 %	.16	.049831	.047561	.045286	.043007	.040722	.038431	.001885
	17 %	.17	.059485	.057213	.054938	.052658	.050374	.048085	.001544
	18 %	.18	.069201	.066928	.064651	.062372	.060088	.057801	.001264
	19 %	.19	.078968	.076694	.074417	.072137	.069854	.067568	.001034
	20 %	.20	.088777	.086502	.084224	.081944	.079662	.077377	.000846
	21 %	.21	.098621	.096345	.094067	.091787	.089505	.087221	.000691
	22 %	.22	.108493	.106216	.103938	.101658	.099376	.097093	.000565
	23 %	.23	.118389	.116111	.113832	.111553	.109271	.106989	.000462
	24 %	.24	.128303	.126025	.123746	.121467	.119186	.116903	.000378
	25 %	.25	.138234	.135955	.133676	.131396	.129115	.126834	.000309
	26 %	.26	.148177	.145898	.143619	.141339	.139058	.136777	.000253
	27 %	.27	.158130	.155851	.153572	.151292	.149011	.146730	.000207
	28 %	.28	.168092	.165813	.163533	.161254	.158973	.156692	.000170
	29 %	.29	.178061	.175782	.173502	.171222	.168942	.166661	.000139
	30 %	.30	.188036	.185756	.183477	.181197	.178916	.176636	.000114

AUXILIARY TABLE Ca

ANNUAL CONSTANT MORTGAGE FACTORS

Each page presents factors pertaining to mortgage interest rate at top of page.

Column No.

1. "f"; Annual mortgage requirement per dollar for interest and amortization.
2. Full amortization term in years and months; monthly installment basis.

3, 4, 5, 6, "P"; Fraction amortized in 5, 10, 15 and 20 years.

7. Constant multiplier of (Sp — 1) to find "P" for any other projection term.

Sinking fund factors for equity yields 5% to 30% for 5 and 10 years, and 5% to 20% for 15 and 20 years repeated on each page.

Use:

For calculating mortgage coefficients and capitalization rates.

Example:

Interest rate 5¾%; Annual Constant 7½%; (i.e. .0750). Mortgage ratio "M," 75%. Income projected 10 years at $32,760 per year. Allow for 10% value decline in 10 years and appraise to yield 12% on equity.

Solution: (All factors from Ca at I = 5¾%)

	Y;	.1200
Plus; P $1/s_{\overline{n}|}$; .235776 × .057,		.0134
Adjusted Y,		.1334
Less "f"		.0750
	C;	.0584
Y — MC; = .12 — (.75 × .0584)	=	.0762
Plus; dep. $1/s_{\overline{n}|}$, .10 × .057,		.0057
	R;	.0819
Valuation: $32,760/.0819	=	$400,000

"Ca" Auxiliary Table "Ca"

ANNUAL CONSTANT LOANS WITH INTEREST AT 4%

"f" Annual Constant	F.A.T. * Yrs.&Mos.	"P" 5 Years	Fraction Amortized 10 Years	15 Years	"P" 20 Years	$\frac{f}{I} - 1$
.0500	40 – 4	.055249	.122708	.205076	.305646	.250000
.0525	36 – 0	.069062	.153385	.256344	.382057	.312500
.0550	32 – 7	.082874	.184862	.307613	.458468	.375000
.0575	29 – 10	.096686	.214739	.358882	.534880	.437500
.0600	27 – 7	.110498	.245416	.410151	.611291	.500000
.0625	25 – 8	.124311	.276094	.461420	.687702	.562500
.0650	24 – 0	.138123	.306771	.512689	.764114	.625000
.0675	22 – 6	.151935	.337448	.563958	.840525	.687500
.0700	21 – 3	.165748	.368125	.615227	.916937	.750000
.0725	20 – 2	.179560	.398802	.666495	.993348	.812500
.0750	19 – 2	.193372	.429479	.717764		.875000
.0775	18 – 3	.207185	.460156	.769033		.937500
.0800	17 – 5	.220997	.490833	.820302		1.000000
.0825	16 – 8	.234809	.521510	.871571		1.062500
.0850	16 – 0	.248622	.552187	.922840		1.125000
.0875	15 – 4	.262434	.582864	.974109		1.187500
.0900	14 – 9	.276246	.613541			1.250000
.0925	14 – 3	.290059	.644218			1.312500
.0950	13 – 9	.303871	.674895			1.375000
.0975	13 – 3	.317683	.705572			1.437500
.1000	12 – 10	.331495	.736249			1.500000
.1025	12 – 4	.345308	.766927			1.562500
.1050	12 – 1	.359120	.797604			1.625000
.1075	11 – 8	.372932	.828281			1.687500
.1100	11 – 4	.386745	.858958			1.750000
.1125	11 – 0	.400557	.889635			1.812500
.1150	10 – 9	.414369	.920312			1.875000
.1175	10 – 6	.428182	.950989			1.937500
.1200	10 – 2	.441994	.981666			2.000000

Sinking Fund Factors

Y	5 Yrs.	10 Yrs.	15 Yrs.	20 Yrs.
5%	.1810	.0795	.0464	.0303
6%	.1774	.0759	.0430	.0272
7%	.1739	.0724	.0398	.0244
8%	.1705	.0690	.0368	.0219
9%	.1671	.0658	.0341	.0196
10%	.1638	.0628	.0315	.0175
11%	.1606	.0598	.0291	.0156
12%	.1574	.0570	.0268	.0139
13%	.1543	.0543	.0248	.0124
14%	.1513	.0517	.0228	.0110
15%	.1483	.0493	.0210	.0098
16%	.1454	.0469	.0194	.0087
17%	.1426	.0447	.0178	.0077
18%	.1398	.0425	.0164	.0068
19%	.1370	.0405	.0151	.0060
20%	.1344	.0385	.0139	.0054
21%	.1318	.0367		
22%	.1292	.0349		
23%	.1267	.0332		
24%	.1242	.0316		
25%	.1218	.0301		
26%	.1195	.0286		
27%	.1172	.0272		
28%	.1149	.0259		
29%	.1127	.0247		
30%	.1106	.0235		

"Ca" Auxiliary Table "Ca"

ANNUAL CONSTANT LOANS WITH INTEREST AT 4¼%

"f" Annual Constant	F.A.T. Yrs.&Mos.	"P" 5 Years	Fraction Amortized 10 Years	Fraction Amortized 15 Years	"P" 20 Years	$\frac{f}{I} - 1$
.0525	39 – 2	.055600	.124339	.209321	.314385	.235294
.0550	35 – 0	.069501	.155424	.261652	.392981	.294118
.0575	31 – 9	.083401	.186509	.313982	.471577	.352941
.0600	29 – 1	.097301	.217594	.366312	.550174	.411765
.0625	26 – 11	.111201	.248679	.418643	.628770	.470588
.0650	25 – 1	.125101	.279763	.470973	.707366	.529412
.0675	23 – 5	.139001	.310848	.523303	.785962	.588235
.0700	22 – 1	.152901	.341933	.575634	.864559	.647059
.0725	20 – 10	.166801	.373018	.627964	.943155	.705882
.0750	19 – 9	.180702	.404103	.680295		.764706
.0775	18 – 9	.194602	.435187	.732625		.823529
.0800	17 – 11	.208502	.466272	.784955		.882353
.0825	17 – 1	.222402	.497357	.837286		.941176
.0850	16 – 5	.236302	.528442	.889616		1.000000
.0875	15 – 9	.250202	.559527	.941946		1.058824
.0900	15 – 1	.264102	.590612	.994277		1.117647
.0925	14 – 7	.278002	.621696			1.176471
.0950	14 – 0	.291902	.652781			1.235294
.0975	13 – 6	.305803	.683866			1.294118
.1000	13 – 1	.319703	.714951			1.352941
.1025	12 – 8	.333603	.746036			1.411765
.1050	12 – 3	.347503	.777120			1.470588
.1075	11 – 11	.361403	.808205			1.529412
.1100	11 – 7	.375303	.839290			1.588235
.1125	11 – 3	.389203	.870375			1.647059
.1150	10 – 10	.403103	.901460			1.705882
.1175	10 – 7	.417003	.932545			1.764706
.1200	10 – 4	.430904	.963629			1.823529
.1225	10 – 1	.444804	.994714			1.882353

Sinking Fund Factors

Y	5 Yrs.	10 Yrs.	15 Yrs.	20 Yrs.
5%	.1810	.0795	.0464	.0303
6%	.1774	.0759	.0430	.0272
7%	.1739	.0724	.0398	.0244
8%	.1705	.0690	.0368	.0219
9%	.1671	.0658	.0341	.0196
10%	.1638	.0628	.0315	.0175
11%	.1606	.0598	.0291	.0156
12%	.1574	.0570	.0268	.0139
13%	.1543	.0543	.0248	.0124
14%	.1513	.0517	.0228	.0110
15%	.1483	.0493	.0210	.0098
16%	.1454	.0469	.0194	.0087
17%	.1426	.0447	.0178	.0077
18%	.1398	.0425	.0164	.0068
19%	.1370	.0405	.0151	.0060
20%	.1344	.0385	.0139	.0054
21%	.1318	.0367		
22%	.1292	.0349		
23%	.1267	.0332		
24%	.1242	.0316		
25%	.1218	.0301		
26%	.1195	.0286		
27%	.1172	.0272		
28%	.1149	.0259		
29%	.1127	.0247		
30%	.1106	.0235		

"Ca" Auxiliary Table "Ca"

ANNUAL CONSTANT LOANS WITH INTEREST AT 4½%

"f" Annual Constant	F.A.T. Yrs.&Mos.	"P" 5 Years	Fraction Amortized 10 Years	Fraction Amortized 15 Years	"P" 20 Years	$\frac{f}{I} - 1$
.0550	38 – 0	.055955	.125998	.213679	.323437	.222222
.0575	34 – 0	.069943	.157498	.267099	.404296	.277777
.0600	30 – 11	.083932	.188998	.320518	.485155	.333333
.0625	28 – 5	.097921	.220497	.373938	.566015	.388889
.0650	26 – 3	.111909	.251997	.427358	.646874	.444444
.0675	24 – 6	.125898	.283496	.480777	.727733	.500000
.0700	23 – 0	.139887	.314996	.534197	.808592	.555555
.0725	21 – 7	.153875	.346496	.587617	.889451	.611111
.0750	20 – 5	.167864	.377995	.641037	.970311	.666667
.0775	19 – 5	.181853	.409495	.694456		.722222
.0800	18 – 5	.195841	.440995	.747876		.777778
.0825	17 – 7	.209830	.472494	.801296		.833333
.0850	16 – 10	.223819	.503994	.854716		.888889
.0875	16 – 1	.237807	.535493	.908135		.944444
.0900	15 – 6	.251796	.566993	.961555		1.000000
.0925	14 – 11	.265785	.598493			1.055555
.0950	14 – 4	.279773	.629992			1.111111
.0975	13 – 10	.293762	.661492			1.166667
.1000	13 – 4	.307751	.692991			1.222222
.1025	12 – 11	.321739	.724491			1.277778
.1050	12 – 6	.335728	.755991			1.333333
.1075	12 – 1	.349717	.787490			1.388889
.1100	11 – 9	.363705	.818990			1.444444
.1125	11 – 5	.377694	.850489			1.500000
.1150	11 – 1	.391683	.881989			1.555555
.1175	10 – 9	.405671	.913489			1.611111
.1200	10 – 6	.419660	.944988			1.666667
.1225	10 – 3	.433649	.976488			1.722222

Sinking Fund Factors

Y	5 Yrs.	10 Yrs.	15 Yrs.	20 Yrs.
5%	.1810	.0795	.0464	.0303
6%	.1774	.0759	.0430	.0272
7%	.1739	.0724	.0398	.0244
8%	.1705	.0690	.0368	.0219
9%	.1671	.0658	.0341	.0196
10%	.1638	.0628	.0315	.0175
11%	.1606	.0598	.0291	.0156
12%	.1574	.0570	.0268	.0139
13%	.1543	.0543	.0248	.0124
14%	.1513	.0517	.0228	.0110
15%	.1483	.0493	.0210	.0098
16%	.1454	.0469	.0194	.0087
17%	.1426	.0447	.0178	.0077
18%	.1398	.0425	.0164	.0068
19%	.1370	.0405	.0151	.0060
20%	.1344	.0385	.0139	.0054
21%	.1318	.0367		
22%	.1292	.0349		
23%	.1267	.0332		
24%	.1242	.0316		
25%	.1218	.0301		
26%	.1195	.0286		
27%	.1172	.0272		
28%	.1149	.0259		
29%	.1127	.0247		
30%	.1106	.0235		

"Ca" Auxiliary Table "Ca"

ANNUAL CONSTANT LOANS WITH INTEREST AT 4¾%

"f" Annual Constant	F.A.T. Yrs.&Mos.	5 Years	Fraction Amortized 10 Years	15 Years	"P" 20 Years	f/I − 1
.0575	36 – 11	.056312	.127686	.218151	.332814	.210526
.0600	33 – 2	.070390	.159607	.272689	.416017	.263158
.0625	30 – 2	.084468	.191529	.327226	.499221	.315789
.0650	27 – 9	.098546	.223450	.381764	.582424	.368421
.0675	25 – 8	.112624	.255371	.436302	.665627	.421053
.0700	24 – 0	.126702	.287293	.490840	.748831	.473684
.0725	22 – 6	.140779	.319214	.545377	.832034	.526316
.0750	21 – 2	.154857	.351136	.599915	.915238	.578947
.0775	20 – 1	.168935	.383057	.654453	.998441	.631579
.0800	19 – 0	.183013	.414978	.708991		.684211
.0825	18 – 2	.197091	.446900	.763528		.736842
.0850	17 – 4	.211169	.478821	.818066		.789474
.0875	16 – 7	.225247	.510743	.872604		.842105
.0900	15 – 10	.239325	.542664	.927142		.894737
.0925	15 – 3	.253403	.574586	.981679		.947368
.0950	14 – 8	.267481	.606507			1.000000
.0975	14 – 2	.281559	.638428			1.052632
.1000	13 – 8	.295637	.670350			1.105263
.1025	13 – 2	.309715	.702271			1.157895
.1050	12 – 9	.323793	.734193			1.210526
.1075	12 – 4	.337871	.766114			1.263158
.1100	12 – 0	.351949	.798036			1.315789
.1125	11 – 7	.366027	.829957			1.368421
.1150	11 – 3	.380105	.861878			1.421053
.1175	11 – 0	.394183	.893800			1.473684
.1200	10 – 8	.408260	.925721			1.526316
.1225	10 – 5	.422338	.957643			1.578947
.1250	10 – 1	.436416	.989564			1.631579

Sinking Fund Factors

Y	5 Yrs.	10 Yrs.	15 Yrs.	20 Yrs.
5%	.1810	.0795	.0464	.0303
6%	.1774	.0759	.0430	.0272
7%	.1739	.0724	.0398	.0244
8%	.1705	.0690	.0368	.0219
9%	.1671	.0658	.0341	.0196
10%	.1638	.0628	.0315	.0175
11%	.1606	.0598	.0291	.0156
12%	.1574	.0570	.0268	.0139
13%	.1543	.0543	.0248	.0124
14%	.1513	.0517	.0228	.0110
15%	.1483	.0493	.0210	.0098
16%	.1454	.0469	.0194	.0087
17%	.1426	.0447	.0178	.0077
18%	.1398	.0425	.0164	.0068
19%	.1370	.0405	.0151	.0060
20%	.1344	.0385	.0139	.0054
21%	.1318	.0367		
22%	.1292	.0349		
23%	.1267	.0332		
24%	.1242	.0316		
25%	.1218	.0301		
26%	.1195	.0286		
27%	.1172	.0272		
28%	.1149	.0259		
29%	.1127	.0247		
30%	.1106	.0235		

"Ca" Auxiliary Table "Ca"

ANNUAL CONSTANT LOANS WITH INTEREST AT 5%

"f" Annual Constant	F.A.T. Yrs.&Mos.	"P" 5 Years	Fraction Amprtized 10 Years	15 Years	"P" 20 Years	$\frac{f}{I} - 1$
.0600	35 – 11	.056672	.129402	.222741	.342528	.200000
.0625	32 – 4	.070840	.161753	.278426	.428160	.250000
.0650	29 – 5	.085008	.194103	.334111	.513792	.300000
.0675	27 – 1	.099176	.226454	.389796	.599424	.350000
.0700	25 – 2	.113344	.258804	.445482	.685056	.400000
.0725	23 – 6	.127512	.291155	.501167	.770688	.450000
.0750	22 – 1	.141680	.323505	.556852	.856320	.500000
.0775	20 – 10	.155847	.355856	.612537	.941952	.550000
.0800	19 – 8	.170015	.388206	.668222		.600000
.0825	18 – 9	.184183	.420557	.723908		.650000
.0850	17 – 10	.198351	.452907	.779593		.700000
.0875	17 – 0	.212519	.485258	.835278		.750000
.0900	16 – 4	.226687	.517608	.890963		.800000
.0925	15 – 8	.240855	.549959	.946648		.850000
.0950	15 – 0	.255023	.582309	1.		.900000
.0975	14 – 5	.269191	.614660			.950000
.1000	13 – 11	.283359	.647010			1.000000
.1025	13 – 5	.297527	.679361			1.050000
.1050	13 – 0	.311695	.711711			1.100000
.1075	12 – 7	.325863	.744062			1.150000
.1100	12 – 2	.340031	.776412			1.200000
.1125	11 – 10	.354199	.808763			1.250000
.1150	11 – 6	.368367	.841113			1.300000
.1175	11 – 2	.382535	.873464			1.350000
.1200	10 – 10	.396703	.905814			1.400000
.1225	10 – 7	.410871	.938165			1.450000
.1250	10 – 3	.425039	.970515			1.500000
.1275	10 – 0	.439206	1. +			1.550000

Sinking Fund Factors	Y	5 Yrs.	10 Yrs.	15 Yrs.	20 Yrs.
	5%	.1810	.0795	.0464	.0303
	6%	.1774	.0759	.0430	.0272
	7%	.1739	.0724	.0398	.0244
	8%	.1705	.0690	.0368	.0219
	9%	.1671	.0658	.0341	.0196
	10%	.1638	.0628	.0315	.0175
	11%	.1606	.0598	.0291	.0156
	12%	.1574	.0570	.0268	.0139
	13%	.1543	.0543	.0248	.0124
	14%	.1513	.0517	.0228	.0110
	15%	.1483	.0493	.0210	.0098
	16%	.1454	.0469	.0194	.0087
	17%	.1426	.0447	.0178	.0077
	18%	.1398	.0425	.0164	.0068
	19%	.1370	.0405	.0151	.0060
	20%	.1344	.0385	.0139	.0054
	21%	.1318	.0367		
	22%	.1292	.0349		
	23%	.1267	.0332		
	24%	.1242	.0316		
	25%	.1218	.0301		
	26%	.1195	.0286		
	27%	.1172	.0272		
	28%	.1149	.0259		
	29%	.1127	.0247		
	30%	.1106	.0235		

"Ca" Auxiliary Table "Ca"

ANNUAL CONSTANT LOANS WITH INTEREST AT 5¼%

"f" Annual Constant	F.A.T. Yrs. & Mos.	"P" 5 Years	Fraction Amortized 10 Years	15 Years	"P" 20 Years	$\frac{f}{I} - 1$
.0625	35 – 0	.057035	.131147	.227452	.352593	.190476
.0650	31 – 6	.071293	.163934	.284315	.440741	.238095
.0675	28 – 9	.085552	.196721	.341178	.528890	.285714
.0700	26 – 6	.099811	.229508	.398041	.617038	.333333
.0725	24 – 8	.114069	.262295	.454904	.705186	.380952
.0750	23 – 0	.128328	.295082	.511767	.793335	.428571
.0775	21 – 8	.142587	.327869	.568630	.881483	.476190
.0800	20 – 5	.156845	.360656	.625493	.969631	.532810
.0825	19 – 4	.171104	.393442	.682356		.571429
.0850	18 – 5	.185363	.426229	.739219		.619048
.0875	17 – 6	.199621	.459016	.796082		.666667
.0900	16 – 9	.213880	.491803	.852945		.714286
.0925	16 – 1	.228139	.524590	.909808		.761905
.0950	15 – 5	.242397	.557377	.966671		.809524
.0975	14 – 10	.256656	.590163			.857143
.1000	14 – 3	.270915	.622950			.904762
.1025	13 – 9	.285173	.655737			.952381
.1050	13 – 3	.299432	.688524			1.000000
.1075	12 – 10	.313691	.721311			1.047619
.1100	12 – 5	.327949	.754098			1.095238
.1125	12 – 0	.342208	.786885			1.142857
.1150	11 – 8	.356467	.819671			1.190476
.1175	11 – 4	.370725	.852458			1.238095
.1200	11 – 0	.384984	.885245			1.285714
.1225	10 – 9	.399243	.918032			1.333333
.1250	10 – 5	.413501	.950819			1.380952
.1275	10 – 2	.427760	.983606			1.428571
.1300	9 – 11	.442019				1.476190

Sinking Fund Factors

Y	5 Yrs.	10 Yrs.	15 Yrs.	20 Yrs.
5%	.1810	.0795	.0464	.0303
6%	.1774	.0759	.0430	.0272
7%	.1739	.0724	.0398	.0244
8%	.1705	.0690	.0368	.0219
9%	.1671	.0658	.0341	.0196
10%	.1638	.0628	.0315	.0175
11%	.1606	.0598	.0291	.0156
12%	.1574	.0570	.0268	.0139
13%	.1543	.0543	.0248	.0124
14%	.1513	.0517	.0228	.0110
15%	.1483	.0493	.0210	.0098
16%	.1454	.0469	.0194	.0087
17%	.1426	.0447	.0178	.0077
18%	.1398	.0425	.0164	.0068
19%	.1370	.0405	.0151	.0060
20%	.1344	.0385	.0139	.0054
21%	.1318	.0367		
22%	.1292	.0349		
23%	.1267	.0332		
24%	.1242	.0316		
25%	.1218	.0301		
26%	.1195	.0286		
27%	.1172	.0272		
28%	.1149	.0259		
29%	.1127	.0247		
30%	.1106	.0235		

"Ca" Auxiliary Table "Ca"

ANNUAL CONSTANT LOANS WITH INTEREST At 5½%

"f" Annual Constant	F.A.T. Yrs. & Mos.	"P" 5 Years	Fraction Amortized 10 Years	Fraction Amortized 15 Years	"P" 20 Years	$\frac{f}{I} - 1$
.0650	34 – 2	.057401	.132923	.232288	.363023	.181818
.0675	30 – 9	.071751	.166154	.290360	.453779	.227273
.0700	28 – 1	.086101	.199384	.348432	.544534	.272727
.0725	25 – 11	.100451	.232615	.406504	.635290	.318182
.0750	24 – 2	.114801	.265846	.464576	.726046	.363636
.0775	22 – 7	.129152	.299077	.522648	.816802	.409091
.0800	21 – 3	.143502	.332307	.580720	.907557	.454545
.0825	20 – 1	.157852	.365538	.638792	.998313	.500000
.0850	19 – 1	.172202	.398769	.696864		.545455
.0875	18 – 1	.186552	.431999	.754936		.590909
.0900	17 – 3	.200903	.465230	.813008		.636364
.0925	16 – 6	.215253	.498461	.871080		.681818
.0950	15 – 10	.229603	.531692	.929152		.727273
.0975	15 – 2	.243953	.564922	.987224		.772727
.1000	14 – 7	.258303	.598153			.818182
.1025	14 – 1	.272653	.631384			.863636
.1050	13 – 7	.287004	.664615			.909091
.1075	13 – 1	.301354	.697845			.954545
.1100	12 – 8	.315704	.731076			1.000000
.1125	12 – 3	.330054	.764307			1.045455
.1150	11 – 11	.344404	.797537			1.090900
.1175	11 – 7	.358755	.830768			1.136364
.1200	11 – 3	.373105	.863999			1.181818
.1225	10 – 11	.387455	.897230			1.227273
.1250	10 – 7	.401805	.930460			1.272727
.1275	10 – 4	.416155	.963691			1.318182
.1300	10 – 1	.430505	.996922			1.363636
.1325	9 – 10	.444856				1.409091

Sinking Fund Factors

Y	5 Yrs.	10 Yrs.	15 Yrs.	20 Yrs.
5%	.1810	.0795	.0464	.0303
6%	.1774	.0759	.0430	.0272
7%	.1739	.0724	.0398	.0244
8%	.1705	.0690	.0368	.0219
9%	.1671	.0658	.0341	.0196
10%	.1638	.0628	.0315	.0175
11%	.1606	.0598	.0291	.0156
12%	.1574	.0570	.0268	.0139
13%	.1543	.0543	.0248	.0124
14%	.1513	.0517	.0228	.0110
15%	.1483	.0493	.0210	.0098
16%	.1454	.0469	.0194	.0087
17%	.1426	.0447	.0178	.0077
18%	.1398	.0425	.0164	.0068
19%	.1370	.0405	.0151	.0060
20%	.1344	.0385	.0139	.0054
21%	.1318	.0367		
22%	.1292	.0349		
23%	.1267	.0332		
24%	.1242	.0316		
25%	.1218	.0301		
26%	.1195	.0286		
27%	.1172	.0272		
28%	.1149	.0259		
29%	.1127	.0247		
30%	.1106	.0235		

"Ca" Auxiliary Table "Ca"

ANNUAL CONSTANT LOANS WITH INTEREST AT 5¾%

"f" Annual Constant	F.A.T. Yrs.&Mos.	"P" 5 Years	Fraction Amortized 10 Years	15 Years	"P" 20 Years	$\frac{f}{I}-1$
.0675	33 – 4	.057770	.134729	.237252	.373831	.173913
.0700	30 – 1	.072212	.168411	.296565	.467289	.217391
.0725	27 – 6	.086655	.202094	.355879	.560879	.260870
.0750	25 – 5	.101097	.235776	.415192	.654205	.304348
.0775	23 – 8	.115539	.269458	.474505	.747663	.347826
.0800	22 – 2	.129982	.303140	.533818	.841121	.391304
.0825	20 – 10	.144424	.336823	.593131	.934579	.434783
.0850	19 – 9	.158867	.370505	.652444		.478261
.0875	18 – 8	.173309	.404187	.711757		.521739
.0900	17 – 10	.187752	.437869	.771070		.565217
.0925	17 – 0	.202194	.471552	.830383		.608696
.0950	16 – 3	.216637	.505234	.889696		.652174
.0975	15 – 7	.231079	.538916	.949009		.695652
.1000	14 – 11	.245521	.572598			.739130
.1025	14 – 5	.259964	.606281			.782609
.1050	13 – 10	.274406	.639963			.826087
.1075	13 – 5	.288849	.673645			.869565
.1100	12 – 11	.303291	.707327			.913043
.1125	12 – 6	.317734	.741010			.956522
.1150	12 – 2	.332176	.774692			1.000000
.1175	11 – 9	.346618	.808374			1.043478
.1200	11 – 5	.361061	.842057			1.086957
.1225	11 – 1	.375503	.875739			1.130435
.1250	10 – 9	.389946	.909421			1.173913
.1275	10 – 6	.404388	.943103			1.217391
.1300	10 – 3	.418831	.976786			1.260870
.1325	10 – 0	.433273	1.			1.304348

Sinking Fund Factors

Y	5 Yrs.	10 Yrs.	15 Yrs.	20 Yrs.
5%	.1810	.0795	.0464	.0303
6%	.1774	.0759	.0430	.0272
7%	.1739	.0724	.0398	.0244
8%	.1705	.0690	.0368	.0219
9%	.1671	.0658	.0341	.0196
10%	.1638	.0628	.0315	.0175
11%	.1606	.0598	.0291	.0156
12%	.1574	.0570	.0268	.0139
13%	.1543	.0543	.0248	.0124
14%	.1513	.0517	.0228	.0110
15%	.1483	.0493	.0210	.0098
16%	.1454	.0469	.0194	.0087
17%	.1426	.0447	.0178	.0077
18%	.1398	.0425	.0164	.0068
19%	.1370	.0405	.0151	.0060
20%	.1344	.0385	.0139	.0054
21%	.1318	.0367		
22%	.1292	.0349		
23%	.1267	.0332		
24%	.1242	.0316		
25%	.1218	.0301		
26%	.1195	.0286		
27%	.1172	.0272		
28%	.1149	.0259		
29%	.1127	.0247		
30%	.1106	.0235		

"Ca" Auxiliary Table "Ca"

ANNUAL CONSTANT LOANS WITH INTEREST AT 6%

"f" Annual Constant	F.A.T. Yrs.&Mos.	"P" 5 Years	Fraction Amortized 10 Years	Fraction Amortized 15 Years	"P" 20 Years	$\frac{f}{I} - 1$
.0700	32 – 7	.058142	.136566	.242349	.385034	.166667
.0725	29 – 5	.072677	.170708	.302936	.481293	.208333
.0750	26 – 11	.087213	.204849	.363524	.577551	.250000
.0775	25 – 0	.101748	.238991	.424111	.673810	.291667
.0800	23 – 2	.116283	.273132	.484698	.770068	.333333
.0825	21 – 9	.130819	.307274	.545285	.866327	.375000
.0850	20 – 6	.145354	.341415	.605873	.962585	.416667
.0875	19 – 5	.159890	.375557	.666460		.458333
.0900	18 – 5	.174425	.409699	.727047		.500000
.0925	17 – 6	.188960	.443840	.787634		.541667
.0950	16 – 9	.203496	.477982	.848222		.583333
.0975	16 – 0	.218031	.512123	.908809		.625000
.1000	15 – 4	.232567	.546265	.969396		.666667
.1025	14 – 9	.247102	.580406			.708333
.1050	14 – 2	.261638	.614548			.750000
.1075	13 – 8	.276173	.648689			.791667
.1100	13 – 3	.290708	.682831			.833333
.1125	12 – 10	.305244	.716972			.875000
.1150	12 – 4	.319779	.751114			.916667
.1175	12 – 0	.334315	.785255			.958333
.1200	11 – 7	.348850	.819397			1.000000
.1225	11 – 3	.363385	.853539			1.041667
.1250	11 – 0	.377921	.887680			1.083333
.1275	10 – 8	.392456	.921822			1.1250000
.1300	10 – 5	.406992	.955963			1.166667
.1325	10 – 1	.421527	.990105			1.208333

Sinking Fund Factors	Y	5 Yrs.	10 Yrs.	15 Yrs.	20 Yrs.
	5%	.1810	.0795	.0464	.0303
	6%	.1774	.0759	.0430	.0272
	7%	.1739	.0724	.0398	.0244
	8%	.1705	.0690	.0368	.0219
	9%	.1671	.0658	.0341	.0196
	10%	.1638	.0628	.0315	.0175
	11%	.1606	.0598	.0291	.0156
	12%	.1574	.0570	.0268	.0139
	13%	.1543	.0543	.0248	.0124
	14%	.1513	.0517	.0228	.0110
	15%	.1483	.0493	.0210	.0098
	16%	.1454	.0469	.0194	.0087
	17%	.1426	.0447	.0178	.0077
	18%	.1398	.0425	.0164	.0068
	19%	.1370	.0405	.0151	.0060
	20%	.1344	.0385	.0139	.0054
	21%	.1318	.0367		
	22%	.1292	.0349		
	23%	.1267	.0332		
	24%	.1242	.0316		
	25%	.1218	.0301		
	26%	.1195	.0286		
	27%	.1172	.0272		
	28%	.1149	.0259		
	29%	.1127	.0247		
	30%	.1106	.0235		

"Ca" Auxiliary Table "Ca"

ANNUAL CONSTANT LOANS WITH INTEREST AT 6¼%

"f" Annual Constant	F.A.T. Yrs.&Mos.	"P" 5 Years	Fraction Amortized 10 Years	15 Years	"P" 20 Years	$\frac{f}{I} - 1$
.0725	31 – 10	.058517	.138435	.247581	.396646	.160000
.0750	28 – 9	.073146	.173044	.309477	.495808	.200000
.0775	26 – 5	.087775	.207652	.371372	.594969	.240000
.0800	24 – 5	.102404	.242261	.433268	.694131	.280000
.0825	22 – 9	.117034	.276870	.495163	.793292	.320000
.0850	21 – 4	.131663	.311478	.557058	.892454	.360000
.0875	20 – 2	.146292	.346087	.618954	.991616	.400000
.0900	19 – 1	.160921	.380696	.680849		.440000
.0925	18 – 2	.175550	.415305	.742744		.480000
.0950	17 – 3	.190180	.449913	.804640		.520000
.0975	16 – 6	.204809	.484522	.866535		.560000
.1000	15 – 9	.219438	.519131	.928430		.600000
.1025	15 – 2	.234067	.553740	.990326		.640000
.1050	14 – 7	.248696	.588348			.680000
.1075	14 – 0	.263326	.622957			.720000
.1100	13 – 6	.277955	.657566			.760000
.1125	13 – 1	.292584	.692174			.800000
.1150	12 – 7	.307213	.726783			.840000
.1175	12 – 3	.321842	.761392			.880000
.1200	11 – 10	.336472	.796001			.920000
.1225	11 – 6	.351101	.830609			.960000
.1250	11 – 2	.365730	.865218			1.000000
.1275	10 – 10	.380359	.899827			1.040000
.1300	10 – 7	.394988	.934435			1.080000
.1325	10 – 3	.409618	.969044			1.120000
.1350	10 – 0	.424247	1.			1.160000

Sinking Fund Factors	Y	5 Yrs.	10 Yrs.	15 Yrs.	20 Yrs.
	5%	.1810	.0795	.0464	.0303
	6%	.1774	.0759	.0430	.0272
	7%	.1739	.0724	.0398	.0244
	8%	.1705	.0690	.0368	.0219
	9%	.1671	.0658	.0341	.0196
	10%	.1638	.0628	.0315	.0175
	11%	.1606	.0598	.0291	.0156
	12%	.1574	.0570	.0268	.0139
	13%	.1543	.0543	.0248	.0124
	14%	.1513	.0517	.0228	.0110
	15%	.1483	.0493	.0210	.0098
	16%	.1454	.0469	.0194	.0087
	17%	.1426	.0447	.0178	.0077
	18%	.1398	.0425	.0164	.0068
	19%	.1370	.0405	.0151	.0060
	20%	.1344	.0385	.0139	.0054
	21%	.1318	.0367		
	22%	.1292	.0349		
	23%	.1267	.0332		
	24%	.1242	.0316		
	25%	.1218	.0301		
	26%	.1195	.0286		
	27%	.1172	.0272		
	28%	.1149	.0259		
	29%	.1127	.0247		
	30%	.1106	.0235		

"Ca" Auxiliary Table "Ca"

ANNUAL CONSTANT LOANS WITH INTEREST AT 6½%

"f" Annual Constant	F.A.T. Yrs.&Mos.	"P" 5 Years	Fraction Amortized 10 Years	15 Years	"P" 20 Years	$\frac{f}{I} - 1$
.0750	31 – 1	.058895	.140336	.252954	.408684	.153846
.0775	28 – 2	.073619	.175420	.316193	.510855	.192308
.0800	25 – 10	.088342	.210504	.379431	.613026	.230769
.0825	24 – 0	.103066	.245588	.442670	.715197	.269231
.0850	22 – 4	.117790	.280672	.505908	.817368	.307692
.0875	21 – 0	.132514	.315756	.569147	.919540	.346154
.0900	19 – 10	.147237	.350840	.632385		.384615
.0925	18 – 9	.161961	.385924	.695624		.423077
.0950	17 – 10	.176685	.421008	.758862		.461538
.0975	17 – 0	.191409	.456092	.822101		.500000
.1000	16 – 3	.206132	.491176	.885339		.538462
.1025	15 – 7	.220856	.526260	.948578		.576923
.1050	14 – 11	.235580	.561344			.615385
.1075	14 – 4	.250303	.596428			.653846
.1100	13 – 10	.265027	.631512			.692308
.1125	13 – 4	.279751	.666596			.730769
.1150	12 – 11	.294475	.701680			.769231
.1175	12 – 6	.309198	.736764			.807692
.1200	12 – 1	.323922	.771848			.846154
.1225	11 – 8	.338646	.806932			.884615
.1250	11 – 4	.353370	.842016			.923077
.1275	11 – 0	.368093	.877100			.961538
.1300	10 – 9	.382817	.912184			1.000000
.1325	10 – 5	.397541	.947268			1.038462
.1350	10 – 2	.412264	.982352			1.076923

Sinking Fund Factors

Y	5 Yrs.	10 Yrs.	15 Yrs.	20 Yrs.
5%	.1810	.0795	.0464	.0303
6%	.1774	.0759	.0430	.0272
7%	.1739	.0724	.0398	.0244
8%	.1705	.0690	.0368	.0219
9%	.1671	.0658	.0341	.0196
10%	.1638	.0628	.0315	.0175
11%	.1606	.0598	.0291	.0156
12%	.1574	.0570	.0268	.0139
13%	.1543	.0543	.0248	.0124
14%	.1513	.0517	.0228	.0110
15%	.1483	.0493	.0210	.0098
16%	.1454	.0469	.0194	.0087
17%	.1426	.0447	.0178	.0077
18%	.1398	.0425	.0164	.0068
19%	.1370	.0405	.0151	.0060
20%	.1344	.0385	.0139	.0054
21%	.1318	.0367		
22%	.1292	.0349		
23%	.1267	.0332		
24%	.1242	.0316		
25%	.1218	.0301		
26%	.1195	.0286		
27%	.1172	.0272		
28%	.1149	.0259		
29%	.1127	.0247		
30%	.1106	.0235		

"Ca" Auxiliary Table "Ca"

ANNUAL CONSTANT LOANS WITH INTEREST AT 6¾%

"f" Annual Constant	F.A.T. Yrs. & Mos.	5 Years	10 Years	15 Years	20 Years	$\frac{f}{I} - 1$
.0775	30 – 6	.059276	.142270	.258470	.421165	.148148
.0800	27 – 7	.074095	.177837	.323088	.526456	.185185
.0825	25 – 4	.088914	.213405	.387705	.631747	.222222
.0850	23 – 6	.103733	.248972	.452323	.737038	.259259
.0875	22 – 0	.118552	.284539	.516941	.842329	.296296
.0900	20 – 8	.133371	.320107	.581558	.947620	.333333
.0925	19 – 5	.148191	.355674	.646176		.370370
.0950	18 – 5	.163010	.391242	.710794		.407407
.0975	17 – 7	.177829	.426809	.775412		.444444
.1000	16 – 9	.192648	.462376	.840029		.481481
.1025	16 –	.207467	.497944	.904647		.518518
.1050	15 – 4	.222286	.533512	.969264		.555555
.1075	14 – 9	.237105	.569079			.592592
.1100	14 – 2	.251924	.604647			.629629
.1125	13 – 8	.266743	.640214			.666667
.1150	13 – 2	.281562	.675782			.703704
.1175	12 – 9	.296381	.711349			.740741
.1200	12 – 4	.311200	.746916			.777778
.1225	11 – 11	.326019	.782484			.814815
.1250	11 – 7	.340839	.818051			.851852
.1275	11 – 3	.355658	.853619			.888889
.1300	10 – 11	.370477	.889186			.925926
.1325	10 – 7	.385296	.924753			.962963
.1350	10 – 4	.400115	.960321			1.000000
.1375	10 – 1	.414934	.995889			1.037037
.1400	9 – 10	.429753				1.074074

Sinking Fund Factors	Y	5 Yrs.	10 Yrs.	15 Yrs.	20 Yrs.
	5%	.1810	.0795	.0464	.0303
	6%	.1774	.0759	.0430	.0272
	7%	.1739	.0724	.0398	.0244
	8%	.1705	.0690	.0368	.0219
	9%	.1671	.0658	.0341	.0196
	10%	.1638	.0628	.0315	.0175
	11%	.1606	.0598	.0291	.0156
	12%	.1574	.0570	.0268	.0139
	13%	.1543	.0543	.0248	.0124
	14%	.1513	.0517	.0228	.0110
	15%	.1483	.0493	.0210	.0098
	16%	.1454	.0469	.0194	.0087
	17%	.1426	.0447	.0178	.0077
	18%	.1398	.0425	.0164	.0068
	19%	.1370	.0405	.0151	.0060
	20%	.1344	.0385	.0139	.0054
	21%	.1318	.0367		
	22%	.1292	.0349		
	23%	.1267	.0332		
	24%	.1242	.0316		
	25%	.1218	.0301		
	26%	.1195	.0286		
	27%	.1172	.0272		
	28%	.1149	.0259		
	29%	.1127	.0247		
	30%	.1106	.0235		

"Ca" Auxiliary Table "Ca"

ANNUAL CONSTANT LOANS WITH INTEREST AT 7%

"f" Annual Constant	F.A.T. Yrs. & Mos.	"P" Fraction Amortized "P" 5 Years	10 Years	15 Years	20 Years	$\frac{f}{I} - 1$
.0800	29 – 10	.059661	.144237	.264135	.434105	.142857
.0825	27 – 1	.074576	.180297	.330170	.542632	.178571
.0850	24 – 11	.089491	.216356	.396203	.651158	.214286
.0875	23 – 1	.104406	.252415	.462237	.759685	.250000
.0900	21 – 7	.119322	.288474	.528270	.868211	.285714
.0925	20 – 4	.134237	.324534	.594304	.976737	.321429
.0950	19 – 2	.149152	.360593	.660338		.357143
.0975	18 – 2	.164067	.396652	.726372		.392857
.1000	17 – 3	.178982	.432712	.792406		.428572
.1025	16 – 6	.193898	.468771	.858439		.464286
.1050	15 – 9	.208813	.504830	.924473		.500000
.1075	15 – 2	.223728	.540890	.990507		.535714
.1100	14 – 6	.238643	.576949			.571429
.1125	14 – 0	.253558	.613008			.607143
.1150	13 – 6	.268474	.649067			.642857
.1175	13 – 0	.283389	.685127			.678572
.1200	12 – 7	.298304	.721186			.714286
.1225	12 – 2	.313219	.757245			.750000
.1250	11 – 10	.328134	.793305			.785715
.1275	11 – 5	.343050	.829364			.821429
.1300	11 – 1	.357965	.865423			.857143
.1325	10 – 10	.372880	.901483			.892857
.1350	10 – 6	.387795	.937542			.928572
.1375	10 – 3	.402710	.973601			.964286
.1400	10 – 0	.417626				1.000000

Sinking Fund Factors	Y	5 Yrs.	10 Yrs.	15 Yrs.	20 Yrs.
	5%	.1810	.0795	.0464	.0303
	6%	.1774	.0759	.0430	.0272
	7%	.1739	.0724	.0398	.0244
	8%	.1705	.0690	.0368	.0219
	9%	.1671	.0658	.0341	.0196
	10%	.1638	.0628	.0315	.0175
	11%	.1606	.0598	.0291	.0156
	12%	.1574	.0570	.0268	.0139
	13%	.1543	.0543	.0248	.0124
	14%	.1513	.0517	.0228	.0110
	15%	.1483	.0493	.0210	.0098
	16%	.1454	.0469	.0194	.0087
	17%	.1426	.0447	.0178	.0077
	18%	.1398	.0425	.0164	.0068
	19%	.1370	.0405	.0151	.0060
	20%	.1344	.0385	.0139	.0054
	21%	.1318	.0367		
	22%	.1292	.0349		
	23%	.1267	.0332		
	24%	.1242	.0316		
	25%	.1218	.0301		
	26%	.1195	.0286		
	27%	.1172	.0272		
	28%	.1149	.0259		
	29%	.1127	.0247		
	30%	.1106	.0235		

"Ca" Auxiliary Table "Ca"

ANNUAL CONSTANT LOANS WITH INTEREST AT 7¼%

"f" Annual Constant	F.A.T. Yrs. & Mos.	"P" Fraction Amortized "P" 5 Years	10 Years	15 Years	20 Years	$\frac{f}{I} - 1$
.0800	32-9	.045036	.109677	.202463	.335642	.103448
.0825	29-3	.060048	.146237	.269951	.447523	.137931
.0850	26-7	.075060	.182796	.337439	.559404	.172413
.0875	24-5	.090072	.219355	.404927	.671285	.206896
.0900	22-8	.105084	.255915	.472415	.783166	.241379
.0925	21-3	.120096	.292474	.539903	.895047	.275862
.0950	19-11	.135108	.329033	.607391		.310344
.0975	18-10	.150120	.365593	.674879		.344827
.1000	17-11	.165132	.402152	.742367		.379310
.1025	17-0	.180144	.438711	.809855		.413793
.1050	16-3	.195156	.475271	.877343		.448275
.1075	15-6	.210169	.511830	.944831		.482758
.1100	14-11	.225181	.548389			.517241
.1125	14-4	.240193	.584948			.551724
.1150	1310	.255205	.621508			.586206
.1175	13-4	.270217	.658067			.620689
.1200	12-10	.285229	.694626			.655172
.1225	12-5	.300241	.731186			.689655
.1250	12-0	.315253	.767745			.724137
.1275	11-8	.330265	.804304			.758620
.1300	11-4	.345277	.840864			.793103
.1325	11-0	.360289	.877423			.827586
.1350	10-8	.375301	.913982			.862068
.1375	10-5	.390313	.950542			.896551
.1400	10-1	.405325	.987101			.931034
.1425	9-10					.965517

Sinking Fund Factors

Y	5 Yrs.	10 Yrs.	15 Yrs.	20 Yrs.
5%	.1810	.0795	.0464	.0303
6%	.1774	.0759	.0430	.0272
7%	.1739	.0724	.0398	.0244
8%	.1705	.0690	.0368	.0219
9%	.1671	.0658	.0341	.0196
10%	.1638	.0628	.0315	.0175
11%	.1606	.0598	.0291	.0156
12%	.1574	.0570	.0268	.0139
13%	.1543	.0543	.0248	.0124
14%	.1513	.0517	.0228	.0110
15%	.1483	.0493	.0210	.0098
16%	.1454	.0469	.0194	.0087
17%	.1426	.0447	.0178	.0077
18%	.1398	.0425	.0164	.0068
19%	.1370	.0405	.0151	.0060
20%	.1344	.0385	.0139	.0054
21%	.1318	.0367		
22%	.1292	.0349		
23%	.1267	.0332		
24%	.1242	.0316		
25%	.1218	.0301		
26%	.1195	.0286		
27%	.1172	.0272		
28%	.1149	.0259		
29%	.1127	.0247		
30%	.1106	.0235		

"Ca" Auxiliary Table "Ca"

ANNUAL CONSTANT LOANS WITH INTEREST AT 7½%

"f" Annual Constant	F.A.T. Yrs.&Mos.	"P" Fraction Amortized "P" 5 Years	10 Years	15 Years	20 Years	$\frac{f}{I} - 1$
.0850	28 – 8	.060439	.148275	.275927	.461442	.133333
.0875	26 – 1	.075549	.185344	.344908	.576803	.166667
.0900	24 – 0	.090659	.222413	.413890	.692163	.200000
.0925	22 – 4	.105768	.259481	.482872	.807523	.233333
.0950	20 – 11	.120878	.296550	.551853	.922884	.266667
.0975	19 – 8	.135988	.333619	.620835		.300000
.1000	18 – 7	.151097	.370688	.689816		.333331
.1025	17 – 8	.166207	.407756	.758798		.366667
.1050	16 – 10	.181317	.444825	.827780		.400000
.1075	16 – 0	.196427	.481894	.896761		.433333
.1100	15 – 4	.211536	.518962	.965743		.466667
.1125	14 – 9	.226646	.556031			.500000
.1150	14 – 2	.241756	.593010			.533333
.1175	13 – 8	.256865	.630168			.566667
.1200	13 – 2	.271975	.667237			.600000
.1225	12 – 9	.287085	.704306			.633333
.1250	12 – 4	.302194	.741375			.666667
.1275	11 – 11	.317304	.778443			.700000
.1300	11 – 7	.332414	.815512			.733333
.1325	11 – 2	.347524	.852581			.766667
.1350	10 – 11	.362633	.889649			.800000
.1375	10 – 7	.377743	.926718			.833333
.1400	10 – 4	.392853	.963787			.866667
.1425	10 – 0	.407962				.900000
.1450	9 – 9	.423072				.933333

Sinking Fund Factors

Y	5 Yrs.	10 Yrs.	15 Yrs.	20 Yrs.
5%	.1810	.0795	.0464	.0303
6%	.1774	.0759	.0430	.0272
7%	.1739	.0724	.0398	.0244
8%	.1705	.0690	.0368	.0219
9%	.1671	.0658	.0341	.0196
10%	.1638	.0628	.0315	.0175
11%	.1606	.0598	.0291	.0156
12%	.1574	.0570	.0268	.0139
13%	.1543	.0543	.0248	.0124
14%	.1513	.0517	.0228	.0110
15%	.1483	.0493	.0210	.0098
16%	.1454	.0469	.0194	.0087
17%	.1426	.0447	.0178	.0077
18%	.1398	.0425	.0164	.0068
19%	.1370	.0405	.0151	.0060
20%	.1344	.0385	.0139	.0054
21%	.1318	.0367		
22%	.1292	.0349		
23%	.1267	.0332		
24%	.1242	.0316		
25%	.1218	.0301		
26%	.1195	.0286		
27%	.1172	.0272		
28%	.1149	.0259		
29%	.1127	.0247		
30%	.1106	.0235		

"Ca" Auxiliary Table "Ca"

ANNUAL CONSTANT LOANS WITH INTEREST AT 8%

"f" Annual Constant	F.A.T. Yrs.&Mos.	"P" Fraction Amortized "P" 5 Years	10 Years	15 Years	20 Years	$\frac{f}{I} - 1$
.0900	27 – 7	.061231	.152455	.288365	.490850	.125000
.0925	25 – 2	.076538	.190569	.360456	.613563	.156250
.0950	23 – 2	.091846	.228682	.432548	.736275	.187500
.0975	21 – 7	.107154	.266796	.504639	.858988	.218750
.1000	20 – 3	.122462	.304910	.576730	.981700	.250000
.1025	19 – 1	.137769	.343024	.648821		.281250
.1050	18 – 0	.153077	.381137	.720912		.312500
.1075	17 – 2	.168385	.419251	.793004		.343750
.1100	16 – 4	.183692	.457365	.865095		.375000
.1125	15 – 7	.190000	.495478	.937186		.406250
.1150	15 – 0	.214308	.533592			.437500
.1175	14 – 4	.229615	.571706			.468750
.1200	13 – 10	.244923	.609819			.500000
.1225	13 – 4	.260231	.647933			.531250
.1250	12 – 10	.275539	.686047			.562500
.1275	12 – 5	.290846	.724161			.593750
.1300	12 – 0	.306154	.762274			.625000
.1325	11 – 8	.321462	.800388			.656250
.1350	11 – 4	.336769	.838502			.687500
.1375	11 – 0	.352077	.876615			.718750
.1400	10 – 8	.367385	.914729			.750000
.1425	10 – 5	.382692	.952843			.781250
.1450	10 – 1	.398000	.990956			.812500
.1475	9 – 10	.413308				.843750
.1500	9 – 7	.428616				.875000

Sinking Fund Factors

Y	5 Yrs.	10 Yrs.	15 Yrs.	20 Yrs.
5%	.1810	.0795	.0464	.0303
6%	.1774	.0759	.0430	.0272
7%	.1739	.0724	.0398	.0244
8%	.1705	.0690	.0368	.0219
9%	.1671	.0658	.0341	.0196
10%	.1638	.0628	.0315	.0175
11%	.1606	.0598	.0291	.0156
12%	.1574	.0570	.0268	.0139
13%	.1543	.0543	.0248	.0124
14%	.1513	.0517	.0228	.0110
15%	.1483	.0493	.0210	.0098
16%	.1454	.0469	.0194	.0087
17%	.1426	.0447	.0178	.0077
18%	.1398	.0425	.0164	.0068
19%	.1370	.0405	.0151	.0060
20%	.1344	.0385	.0139	.0054
21%	.1318	.0367		
22%	.1292	.0349		
23%	.1267	.0332		
24%	.1242	.0316		
25%	.1218	.0301		
26%	.1195	.0286		
27%	.1172	.0272		
28%	.1149	.0259		
29%	.1127	.0247		
30%	.1106	.0235		

"Ca" Auxiliary Table "Ca"

ANNUAL CONSTANT LOANS WITH INTEREST AT 7¾%

"f" Annual Constant	F.A.T. Yrs. & Mos.	"P" Fraction Amortized "P" 5 Years	10 Years	15 Years	20 Years	f/I −1
.0850	31-5	.045624	.112759	.211546	.356907	.096774
.0875	28-1	.060833	.150345	.282061	.475876	.129032
.0900	25-7	.076041	.187932	.352577	.594845	.161290
.0925	23-7	.091249	.225518	.423092	.713814	.193548
.0950	21-11	.106458	.263105	.493608	.832783	.225806
.0975	20-6	.121666	.300691	.564123	.951752	.258064
.1000	19-4	.136874	.338278	.634639		.290322
.1025	18-3	.152083	.375864	.705154		.322580
.1050	17-4	.167291	.413450	.775670		.354838
.1075	16-6	.182499	.451037	.846185		.387096
.1100	15-10	.197708	.488623	.916701		.419354
.1125	15-2	.212916	.526210	.987216		.451612
.1150	14-6	.228124	.563796			.483870
.1175	14-0	.243333	.601383			.516129
.1200	13-6	.258541	.638969			.548387
.1225	13-0	.273749	.676556			.580645
.1250	12-6	.288957	.714142			.612903
.1275	12-2	.304166	.751729			.645161
.1300	11-9	.319374	.789315			.677419
.1325	11-5	.334582	.826901			.709677
.1350	11-1	.349791	.864488			.741935
.1375	10-9	.364999	.902074			.774193
.1400	10-6	.380207	.939661			.806451
.1425	10-2	.395416	.977247			.838709
.1450	9-11					.870968

Sinking Fund Factors

Y	5 Yrs.	10 Yrs.	15 Yrs.	20 Yrs.
5%	.1810	.0795	.0464	.0303
6%	.1774	.0759	.0430	.0272
7%	.1739	.0724	.0398	.0244
8%	.1705	.0690	.0368	.0219
9%	.1671	.0658	.0341	.0196
10%	.1638	.0628	.0315	.0175
11%	.1606	.0598	.0291	.0156
12%	.1574	.0570	.0268	.0139
13%	.1543	.0543	.0248	.0124
14%	.1513	.0517	.0228	.0110
15%	.1483	.0493	.0210	.0098
16%	.1454	.0469	.0194	.0087
17%	.1426	.0447	.0178	.0077
18%	.1398	.0425	.0164	.0068
19%	.1370	.0405	.0151	.0060
20%	.1344	.0385	.0139	.0054
21%	.1318	.0367		
22%	.1292	.0349		
23%	.1267	.0332		
24%	.1242	.0316		
25%	.1218	.0301		
26%	.1195	.0286		
27%	.1172	.0272		
28%	.1149	.0259		
29%	.1127	.0247		
30%	.1106	.0235		

"Ca" Auxiliary Table "Ca"

ANNUAL CONSTANT LOANS WITH INTEREST AT 8¼%

"f" Annual Constant	F.A.T. Yrs. & Mos.	"P" Fraction Amortized "P" 5 Years	10 Years	15 Years	20 Years	$\frac{f}{I}$ −1
.0900	30-3	.046223	.115949	.221128	.379787	.090909
.0925	27-1	.061631	.154598	.294837	.506382	.121212
.0950	24-8	.077039	.193248	.368546	.632978	.151515
.0975	22-9	.092446	.231898	.442256	.759574	.181818
.1000	21-3	.107854	.270547	.515965	.886169	.212121
.1025	19-11	.123262	.309197	.589675		.242424
.1050	18-9	.138670	.347847	.663384		.272727
.1075	17-9	.154078	.386496	.737093		.303030
.1100	16-11	.169486	.425146	.810803		.333333
.1125	16-1	.184893	.463796	.884512		.363636
.1150	15-5	.200301	.502446	.958222		.393939
.1175	14-9	.215709	.541095			.424242
.1200	14-2	.231117	.579745			.454545
.1225	13.8	.246525	.618395			.484848
.1250	13-2	.261933	.657044			.515151
.1275	12-8	.277340	.695694			.545454
.1300	12-3	.292748	.734344			.575757
.1325	11-11	.308156	.772993			.606060
.1350	11-6	.323564	.811643			.636363
.1375	11-2	.338972	.850293			.666666
.1400	10-10	.354380	.888943			.696969
.1425	10-7	.369787	.927592			.727272
.1450	10-3	.385195	.966242			.757575
.1475	10-0					.787879

Sinking Fund Factors

Y	5 Yrs.	10 Yrs.	15 Yrs.	20 Yrs.
5%	.1810	.0795	.0464	.0303
6%	.1774	.0759	.0430	.0272
7%	.1739	.0724	.0398	.0244
8%	.1705	.0690	.0368	.0219
9%	.1671	.0658	.0341	.0196
10%	.1638	.0628	.0315	.0175
11%	.1606	.0598	.0291	.0156
12%	.1574	.0570	.0268	.0139
13%	.1543	.0543	.0248	.0124
14%	.1513	.0517	.0228	.0110
15%	.1483	.0493	.0210	.0098
16%	.1454	.0469	.0194	.0087
17%	.1426	.0447	.0178	.0077
18%	.1398	.0425	.0164	.0068
19%	.1370	.0405	.0151	.0060
20%	.1344	.0385	.0139	.0054
21%	.1318	.0367		
22%	.1292	.0349		
23%	.1267	.0332		
24%	.1242	.0316		
25%	.1218	.0301		
26%	.1195	.0286		
27%	.1172	.0272		
28%	.1149	.0259		
29%	.1127	.0247		
30%	.1106	.0235		

"Ca" Auxiliary Table "Ca"

ANNUAL CONSTANT LOANS WITH INTEREST AT 8½%

"f" Annual Constant	F.A.T. Yrs. & Mos.	"P" Fraction Amortized "P" 5 Years	10 Years	15 Years	20 Years	$\frac{f}{I}$ −1
.0925	29–8	.046526	.117585	.226116	.391873	.088235
.0950	26–7	.062035	.156781	.301488	.522498	.117647
.0975	24–3	.077544	.195976	.376860	.653123	.147058
.1000	22–5	.093052	.235171	.452232	.783747	.176470
.1025	20–11	.108561	.274367	.527604	.914372	.205882
.1050	19–7	.124070	.313562	.602976		.235294
.1075	18–6	.139579	.352757	.678348		.264705
.1100	17–6	.155088	.391952	.753720		.294117
.1125	16–8	.170597	.431148	.829092		.323529
.1150	15–11	.186105	.470343	.904464		.352941
.1175	15–2	.201614	.509538	.979836		.382352
.1200	14–7	.217123	.548734			.411764
.1225	14–0	.232632	.587929			.441176
.1250	13–6	.248141	.627124			.470588
.1275	13–0	.263650	.666320			.500000
.1300	12–6	.279158	.705515			.529411
.1325	12–2	.294667	.744710			.558823
.1350	11–9	.310176	.783905			.588235
.1375	11–5	.325685	.823101			.617647
.1400	11–1	.341194	.862296			.647058
.1425	10–9	.356703	.901491			.676470
.1450	10–5	.372211	.940687			.705882
.1475	10–2	.387720	.979882			.735294
.1500	9–11					.764706

Sinking Fund Factors

Y	5 Yrs.	10 Yrs.	15 Yrs.	20 Yrs.
5%	.1810	.0795	.0464	.0303
6%	.1774	.0759	.0430	.0272
7%	.1739	.0724	.0398	.0244
8%	.1705	.0690	.0368	.0219
9%	.1671	.0658	.0341	.0196
10%	.1638	.0628	.0315	.0175
11%	.1606	.0598	.0291	.0156
12%	.1574	.0570	.0268	.0139
13%	.1543	.0543	.0248	.0124
14%	.1513	.0517	.0228	.0110
15%	.1483	.0493	.0210	.0098
16%	.1454	.0469	.0194	.0087
17%	.1426	.0447	.0178	.0077
18%	.1398	.0425	.0164	.0068
19%	.1370	.0405	.0151	.0060
20%	.1344	.0385	.0139	.0054
21%	.1318	.0367		
22%	.1292	.0349		
23%	.1267	.0332		
24%	.1242	.0316		
25%	.1218	.0301		
26%	.1195	.0286		
27%	.1172	.0272		
28%	.1149	.0259		
29%	.1127	.0247		
30%	.1106	.0235		

"Ca" Auxiliary Table "Ca"

ANNUAL CONSTANT LOANS WITH INTEREST AT 8¾%

"f" Annual Constant	F.A.T. Yrs. & Mos.	"P" Fraction Amortized "P" 5 Years	10 Years	15 Years	20 Years	$\frac{f}{I} - 1$
.0925	33-6	.031221	.079501	.154159	.269610	.057142
.0950	29-2	.046832	.119251	.231239	.404415	.085714
.0975	26-2	.062442	.159002	.308318	.539220	.114285
.1000	23-11	.078053	.198752	.385398	.674025	.142857
.1025	22-1	.093664	.238503	.462478	.808830	.171428
.1050	20-7	.109274	.278254	.539558	.943635	.200000
.1075	19-4	.124885	.318004	.616637		.228571
.1100	18-3	.140496	.357755	.693717		.257142
.1125	17-3	.156106	.397505	.770797		.285714
.1150	16-5	.171717	.437256	.847876		.314285
.1175	15-8	.187328	.477006	.924956		.342857
.1200	15-0	.202938	.516757			.371428
.1225	14-5	.218549	.556508			.400000
.1250	13-10	.234160	.596258			.428571
.1275	13-4	.249770	.636009			.457142
.1300	12-10	.265381	.675759			.485714
.1325	12-5	.280992	.715510			.514285
.1350	12-0	.296602	.755260			.542857
.1375	11-8	.312213	.795011			.571428
.1400	11-3	.327824	.834762			.600000
.1425	10-11	.343434	.874512			.628571
.1450	10-8	.359045	.914263			.657142
.1475	10-4	.374656	.954013			.685714
.1500	10-1	.390266	.993764			.714285
.1525	9-10					.745827

Sinking Fund Factors

Y	5 Yrs.	10 Yrs.	15 Yrs.	20 Yrs.
5%	.1810	.0795	.0464	.0303
6%	.1774	.0759	.0430	.0272
7%	.1739	.0724	.0398	.0244
8%	.1705	.0690	.0368	.0219
9%	.1671	.0658	.0341	.0196
10%	.1638	.0628	.0315	.0175
11%	.1606	.0598	.0291	.0156
12%	.1574	.0570	.0268	.0139
13%	.1543	.0543	.0248	.0124
14%	.1513	.0517	.0228	.0110
15%	.1483	.0493	.0210	.0098
16%	.1454	.0469	.0194	.0087
17%	.1426	.0447	.0178	.0077
18%	.1398	.0425	.0164	.0068
19%	.1370	.0405	.0151	.0060
20%	.1344	.0385	.0139	.0054
21%	.1318	.0367		
22%	.1292	.0349		
23%	.1267	.0332		
24%	.1242	.0316		
25%	.1218	.0301		
26%	.1195	.0286		
27%	.1172	.0272		
28%	.1149	.0259		
29%	.1127	.0247		
30%	.1106	.0235		

"Ca" Auxiliary Table "Ca"

ANNUAL CONSTANT LOANS WITH INTEREST AT 9%

"f" Annual Constant	F.A.T. Yrs. & Mos.	"P" Fraction Amortized "P" 5 Years	10 Years	15 Years	20 Years	$\frac{f}{I}$ −1
.0950	32-10	.031426	.080630	.157668	.278285	.055555
.0975	28-8	.047140	.120945	.236502	.417428	.083333
.1000	25-8	.062853	.161261	.315336	.556571	.111111
.1025	23-6	.078566	.201576	.394170	.695714	.138888
.1050	21-9	.094280	.241891	.473005	.834857	.166666
.1075	20-3	.109993	.282206	.551839	.974000	.194444
.1100	19-0	.125706	.322522	.630673		.222222
.1125	18-0	.141420	.362837	.709507		.250000
.1150	17-1	.157133	.403152	.788341		.277777
.1175	16-3	.172846	.443468	.867175		.305555
.1200	15-6	.188560	.483783	.946009		.333333
.1225	14-10	.204273	.524098			.361111
.1250	14-3	.219986	.564413			.388888
.1275	13-8	.235700	.604729			.416666
.1300	13-2	.251413	.645044			.444444
.1325	12-8	.267126	.685359			.472222
.1350	12-3	.282840	.725675			.500000
.1375	11-10	.298553	.765990			.527777
.1400	11-6	.314266	.806305			.555555
.1425	11-2	.329980	.846620			.583333
.1450	10-10	.345693	.886936			.611111
.1475	10-6	.361407	.927251			.638888
.1500	10-3	.377120	.967566			.666666
.1525	10-0					.694444

Sinking Fund Factors

Y	5 Yrs.	10 Yrs.	15 Yrs.	20 Yrs.
5%	.1810	.0795	.0464	.0303
6%	.1774	.0759	.0430	.0272
7%	.1739	.0724	.0398	.0244
8%	.1705	.0690	.0368	.0219
9%	.1671	.0658	.0341	.0196
10%	.1638	.0628	.0315	.0175
11%	.1606	.0598	.0291	.0156
12%	.1574	.0570	.0268	.0139
13%	.1543	.0543	.0248	.0124
14%	.1513	.0517	.0228	.0110
15%	.1483	.0493	.0210	.0098
16%	.1454	.0469	.0194	.0087
17%	.1426	.0447	.0178	.0077
18%	.1398	.0425	.0164	.0068
19%	.1370	.0405	.0151	.0060
20%	.1344	.0385	.0139	.0054
21%	.1318	.0367		
22%	.1292	.0349		
23%	.1267	.0332		
24%	.1242	.0316		
25%	.1218	.0301		
26%	.1195	.0286		
27%	.1172	.0272		
28%	.1149	.0259		
29%	.1127	.0247		
30%	.1106	.0235		

"Ca" Auxiliary Table "Ca"

ANNUAL CONSTANT LOANS WITH INTEREST AT 9¼%

"f" Annual Constant	F.A.T. Yrs. & Mos.	"P" Fraction Amortized "P" 5 Years	10 Years	15 Years	20 Years	$\frac{f}{I} - 1$
.0975	32-3	.031633	.081779	.161274	.287289	.054054
.1000	28-2	.047450	.122669	.241911	.430934	.081081
.1025	25-3	.063267	.163559	.322548	.574578	.108108
.1050	23-2	.079084	.204449	.403185	.718223	.135135
.1075	21-5	.094901	.245339	.483822	.861868	.162162
.1100	20-0	.110718	.286229	.564459		.189189
.1125	18-9	.126535	.327119	.645096		.216216
.1150	17-9	.142351	.368009	.725733		.243243
.1175	16-10	.158168	.408899	.806370		.270270
.1200	16-0	.173985	.449789	.887007		.297297
.1225	15-4	.189802	.490679	.967644		.324324
.1250	14-8	.205619	.531569			.351351
.1275	14-1	.221436	.572459			.378378
.1300	13-6	.237253	.613349			.405405
.1325	13-0	.253070	.654239			.432432
.1350	12-7	.268887	.695129			.459459
.1375	12-2	.284703	.736019			.486486
.1400	11-9	.300520	.776910			.513513
.1425	11-5	.316337	.817800			.540540
.1450	11-1	.332154	.858690			.567567
.1475	10-9	.347971	.899580			.594594
.1500	10-5	.363788	.940470			.621621
.1525	10-2	.379605	.981360			.648648
.1550	9-11					.675676

Sinking Fund Factors

Y	5 Yrs.	10 Yrs.	15 Yrs.	20 Yrs.
5%	.1810	.0795	.0464	.0303
6%	.1774	.0759	.0430	.0272
7%	.1739	.0724	.0398	.0244
8%	.1705	.0690	.0368	.0219
9%	.1671	.0658	.0341	.0196
10%	.1638	.0628	.0315	.0175
11%	.1606	.0598	.0291	.0156
12%	.1574	.0570	.0268	.0139
13%	.1543	.0543	.0248	.0124
14%	.1513	.0517	.0228	.0110
15%	.1483	.0493	.0210	.0098
16%	.1454	.0469	.0194	.0087
17%	.1426	.0447	.0178	.0077
18%	.1398	.0425	.0164	.0068
19%	.1370	.0405	.0151	.0060
20%	.1344	.0385	.0139	.0054
21%	.1318	.0367		
22%	.1292	.0349		
23%	.1267	.0332		
24%	.1242	.0316		
25%	.1218	.0301		
26%	.1195	.0286		
27%	.1172	.0272		
28%	.1149	.0259		
29%	.1127	.0247		
30%	.1106	.0235		

"Ca" Auxiliary Table "Ca"

ANNUAL CONSTANT LOANS WITH INTEREST AT 9½%

"f" Annual Constant	F.A.T. Yrs. & Mos.	"P" Fraction Amortized "P" 5 Years	10 Years	15 Years	20 Years	f/I −1
.1000	31-8	.031842	.082950	.164978	.296634	.052631
.1025	27-8	.047763	.124424	.247467	.444951	.078947
.1050	24-11	.063685	.165900	.329956	.593268	.105263
.1075	22-9	.079606	.207374	.412446	.741586	.131578
.1100	21-1	.095527	.248850	.494935	.889903	.157894
.1125	19-8	.111449	.290324	.577424		.184210
.1150	18-6	.127370	.331800	.659913		.210526
.1175	17-6	.143291	.373274	.742402		.236842
.1200	16-7	.159212	.414750	.824892		.263157
.1225	15-10	.175134	.456224	.907381		.289473
.1250	15-1	.191055	.497700	.989870		.315789
.1275	14-6	.206976	.539174			.342105
.1300	13-11	.222898	.580650			.368421
.1325	13-4	.238819	.622124			.394736
.1350	12-11	.254740	.663600			.421052
.1375	12-5	.270661	.705074			.447368
.1400	12-0	.286583	.746550			.473684
.1425	11-8	.302504	.788025			.500000
.1450	11-3	.318425	.829499			.526315
.1475	11-0	.334347	.870975			.552631
.1500	10-8	.350268	.912449			.578947
.1525	10-4	.366189	.953925			.605263
.1550	10-1	.382110	.995399			.631578
.1575	9-10					.697895

Sinking Fund Factors

Y	5 Yrs.	10 Yrs.	15 Yrs.	20 Yrs.
5%	.1810	.0795	.0464	.0303
6%	.1774	.0759	.0430	.0272
7%	.1739	.0724	.0398	.0244
8%	.1705	.0690	.0368	.0219
9%	.1671	.0658	.0341	.0196
10%	.1638	.0628	.0315	.0175
11%	.1606	.0598	.0291	.0156
12%	.1574	.0570	.0268	.0139
13%	.1543	.0543	.0248	.0124
14%	.1513	.0517	.0228	.0110
15%	.1483	.0493	.0210	.0098
16%	.1454	.0469	.0194	.0087
17%	.1426	.0447	.0178	.0077
18%	.1398	.0425	.0164	.0068
19%	.1370	.0405	.0151	.0060
20%	.1344	.0385	.0139	.0054
21%	.1318	.0367		
22%	.1292	.0349		
23%	.1267	.0332		
24%	.1242	.0316		
25%	.1218	.0301		
26%	.1195	.0286		
27%	.1172	.0272		
28%	.1149	.0259		
29%	.1127	.0247		
30%	.1106	.0235		

"Ca" Auxiliary Table "Ca"

ANNUAL CONSTANT LOANS WITH INTEREST AT 9¾%

"f" Annual Constant	F.A.T. Yrs. & Mos.	"P" Fraction Amortized "P" 5 Years	10 Years	15 Years	20 Years	f/I −1
.1025	31-2	.032053	.084140	.168784	.306333	.051282
.1050	27-3	.048079	.126210	.253176	.459500	.076923
.1075	24-6	.064106	.168281	.337568	.612667	.102564
.1100	22-5	.080132	.210351	.421960	.765834	.128205
.1125	20-9	.096159	.252421	.506352	.919001	.153846
.1150	19-5	.112185	.294491	.590744		.179487
.1175	18-3	.128212	.336562	.675136		.205128
.1200	17-3	.144238	.378632	.759528		.230769
.1225	16-5	.160265	.420702	.843920		.256410
.1250	15-7	.176292	.462772	.928312		.282051
.1275	14-11	.192318	.504843			.307692
.1300	14-4	.208345	.546913			.333333
.1325	13-9	.224371	.588983			.358974
.1350	13-3	.240398	.631053			.384615
.1375	12-9	.256424	.673124			.410256
.1400	12-4	.272451	.715194			.435897
.1425	11-11	.288477	.757264			.461538
.1450	11-6	.304504	.799334			.487179
.1475	11-2	.320530	.841405			.512820
.1500	10-10	.336557	.883475			.538461
.1525	10-6	.352584	.925545			.564102
.1550	10-3	.368610	.967615			.589743
.1575	10-0					.615385

Sinking Fund Factors

Y	5 Yrs.	10 Yrs.	15 Yrs.	20 Yrs.
5%	.1810	.0795	.0464	.0303
6%	.1774	.0759	.0430	.0272
7%	.1739	.0724	.0398	.0244
8%	.1705	.0690	.0368	.0219
9%	.1671	.0658	.0341	.0196
10%	.1638	.0628	.0315	.0175
11%	.1606	.0598	.0291	.0156
12%	.1574	.0570	.0268	.0139
13%	.1543	.0543	.0248	.0124
14%	.1513	.0517	.0228	.0110
15%	.1483	.0493	.0210	.0098
16%	.1454	.0469	.0194	.0087
17%	.1426	.0447	.0178	.0077
18%	.1398	.0425	.0164	.0068
19%	.1370	.0405	.0151	.0060
20%	.1344	.0385	.0139	.0054
21%	.1318	.0367		
22%	.1292	.0349		
23%	.1267	.0332		
24%	.1242	.0316		
25%	.1218	.0301		
26%	.1195	.0286		
27%	.1172	.0272		
28%	.1149	.0259		
29%	.1127	.0247		
30%	.1106	.0235		

"Ca" Auxiliary Table "Ca"

ANNUAL CONSTANT LOANS WITH INTEREST AT 10%

"f" Annual Constant	F.A.T. Yrs. & Mos.	"P" Fraction Amortized "P" 5 Years	10 Years	15 Years	20 Years	f/I −1
.1050	30-7	.032265	.085352	.172695	.316403	.050000
.1075	26-9	.048398	.128028	.259043	.474605	.075000
.1100	24-1	.064530	.170704	.345391	.632806	.100000
.1125	22-1	.080663	.213380	.431738	.791008	.125000
.1150	20-6	.096796	.256056	.518086	.949210	.150000
.1175	19-2	.112929	.298732	.604434		.175000
.1200	18-0	.129061	.341408	.690782		.200000
.1225	17-1	.145194	.384084	.777129		.225000
.1250	16-2	.161327	.426760	.863477		.250000
.1275	15-5	.177459	.469436	.949825		.275000
.1300	14-9	.193592	.512112			.300000
.1325	14-2	.209725	.554788			.325000
.1350	13-7	.225858	.597464			.350000
.1375	13-1	.241990	.640140			.375000
.1400	12-7	.258123	.682816			.400000
.1425	12-2	.274256	.725492			.425000
.1450	11-9	.290388	.768168			.450000
.1475	11-5	.306521	.810844			.475000
.1500	11-1	.322654	.853520			.500000
.1525	10-9	.338787	.896196			.525000
.1550	10-5	.354919	.938872			.550000
.1575	10-2	.371052	.981548			.575000
.1600	9-11					.600000

Sinking Fund Factors

Y	5 Yrs.	10 Yrs.	15 Yrs.	20 Yrs.
5%	.1810	.0795	.0464	.0303
6%	.1774	.0759	.0430	.0272
7%	.1739	.0724	.0398	.0244
8%	.1705	.0690	.0368	.0219
9%	.1671	.0658	.0341	.0196
10%	.1638	.0628	.0315	.0175
11%	.1606	.0598	.0291	.0156
12%	.1574	.0570	.0268	.0139
13%	.1543	.0543	.0248	.0124
14%	.1513	.0517	.0228	.0110
15%	.1483	.0493	.0210	.0098
16%	.1454	.0469	.0194	.0087
17%	.1426	.0447	.0178	.0077
18%	.1398	.0425	.0164	.0068
19%	.1370	.0405	.0151	.0060
20%	.1344	.0385	.0139	.0054
21%	.1318	.0367		
22%	.1292	.0349		
23%	.1267	.0332		
24%	.1242	.0316		
25%	.1218	.0301		
26%	.1195	.0286		
27%	.1172	.0272		
28%	.1149	.0259		
29%	.1127	.0247		
30%	.1106	.0235		

"Ca" Auxiliary Table "Ca"

ANNUAL CONSTANT LOANS WITH INTEREST AT 10¼%

"f" Annual Constant	F.A.T. Yrs. & Mos.	"P" Fraction Amortized "P" 5 Years	10 Years	15 Years	20 Years	$\frac{f}{I} - 1$
.1075	30-1	.032479	.086584	.176714	.326856	.048780
.1100	26-4	.048719	.129876	.265071	.490285	.073170
.1125	23-9	.064959	.173168	.353429	.653713	.097560
.1150	21-9	.081198	.216460	.441786	.817141	.121951
.1175	20-2	.097438	.259753	.530143	.980570	.146341
.1200	18-11	.113678	.303045	.618501		.170731
.1225	17-9	.129918	.346337	.706858		.195121
.1250	16-10	.146157	.389629	.795215		.219512
.1275	16-0	.162397	.432921	.883573		.243902
.1300	15-3	.178637	.476214	.971930		.268292
.1325	14-7	.194877	.519506			.292682
.1350	14-0	.211116	.562798			.317073
.1375	13-5	.227356	.606090			.341463
.1400	12-11	.243596	.649382			.365853
.1425	12-6	.259836	.692675			.390243
.1450	12-1	.276075	.735967			.414634
.1475	11-8	.292315	.779259			.439024
.1500	11-4	.308555	.822551			.463414
.1525	11-0	.324795	.865843			.487804
.1550	10-8	.341034	.909136			.512195
.1575	10-4	.357274	.952428			.536585
.1600	10-1	.373514	.995720			.560975
.1625	9-10					.585366

Sinking Fund Factors

Y	5 Yrs.	10 Yrs.	15 Yrs.	20 Yrs.
5%	.1810	.0795	.0464	.0303
6%	.1774	.0759	.0430	.0272
7%	.1739	.0724	.0398	.0244
8%	.1705	.0690	.0368	.0219
9%	.1671	.0658	.0341	.0196
10%	.1638	.0628	.0315	.0175
11%	.1606	.0598	.0291	.0156
12%	.1574	.0570	.0268	.0139
13%	.1543	.0543	.0248	.0124
14%	.1513	.0517	.0228	.0110
15%	.1483	.0493	.0210	.0098
16%	.1454	.0469	.0194	.0087
17%	.1426	.0447	.0178	.0077
18%	.1398	.0425	.0164	.0068
19%	.1370	.0405	.0151	.0060
20%	.1344	.0385	.0139	.0054
21%	.1318	.0367		
22%	.1292	.0349		
23%	.1267	.0332		
24%	.1242	.0316		
25%	.1218	.0301		
26%	.1195	.0286		
27%	.1172	.0272		
28%	.1149	.0259		
29%	.1127	.0247		
30%	.1106	.0235		

ANNUAL CONSTANT LOANS WITH INTEREST AT 10½%

"f" Annual Constant	F.A.T. Yrs. & Mos.	"P" Fraction Amortized "P" 5 Years	10 Years	15 Years	20 Years	f / I −1
.1100	29-7	.032695	.087839	.180845	.337710	.047619
.1125	25-11	.049043	.131758	.271268	.506565	.071428
.1150	23-5	.065390	.175678	.361691	.675420	.095238
.1175	21-6	.081738	.219597	.452114	.844275	.119047
.1200	19-11	.098086	.263517	.542537		.142857
.1225	18-8	.114433	.307436	.632960		.166666
.1250	17-7	.130781	.351356	.723382		.190476
.1275	16-7	.147129	.395275	.813805		.214285
.1300	15-10	.163476	.439195	.904228		.238095
.1325	15-1	.179824	.483114	.994651		.261904
.1350	14-5	.196172	.527034			.285714
.1375	13-10	.212519	.570953			.309523
.1400	13-4	.228867	.614873			.333333
.1425	12-10	.245215	.658792			.357142
.1450	12-4	.261563	.702712			.380952
.1475	11-11	.277910	.746631			.404761
.1500	11-7	.294258	.790551			.428571
.1525	11-2	.310606	.834470			.452380
.1550	10-10	.326953	.878390			.476190
.1575	10-6	.343301	.922310			.500000
.1600	10-3	.359649	.966229			.523809
.1625	10-0					.547619

Sinking Fund Factors

Y	5 Yrs.	10 Yrs.	15 Yrs.	20 Yrs.
5%	.1810	.0795	.0464	.0303
6%	.1774	.0759	.0430	.0272
7%	.1739	.0724	.0398	.0244
8%	.1705	.0690	.0368	.0219
9%	.1671	.0658	.0341	.0196
10%	.1638	.0628	.0315	.0175
11%	.1606	.0598	.0291	.0156
12%	.1574	.0570	.0268	.0139
13%	.1543	.0543	.0248	.0124
14%	.1513	.0517	.0228	.0110
15%	.1483	.0493	.0210	.0098
16%	.1454	.0469	.0194	.0087
17%	.1426	.0447	.0178	.0077
18%	.1398	.0425	.0164	.0068
19%	.1370	.0405	.0151	.0060
20%	.1344	.0385	.0139	.0054
21%	.1318	.0367		
22%	.1292	.0349		
23%	.1267	.0332		
24%	.1242	.0316		
25%	.1218	.0301		
26%	.1195	.0286		
27%	.1172	.0272		
28%	.1149	.0259		
29%	.1127	.0247		
30%	.1106	.0235		

"Ca" Auxiliary Table "Ca"

ANNUAL CONSTANT LOANS WITH INTEREST AT 10¾%

"f" Annual Constant	F.A.T. Yrs. & Mos.	"P" Fraction Amortized "P" 5 Years	10 Years	15 Years	20 Years	f/I −1
.1125	29-1	.032913	.089115	.185090	.348979	.046511
.1150	25-6	.049369	.133673	.277635	.523469	.069767
.1175	23-1	.065826	.178231	.370180	.697958	.093023
.1200	21-2	.082282	.222789	.462725	.872448	.116279
.1225	19-8	.098739	.267347	.555270		.139534
.1250	18-5	.115195	.311905	.647815		.162790
.1275	17-4	.131652	.356463	.740360		.186046
.1300	16-5	.148108	.401021	.832906		.209302
.1325	15-7	.164565	.445579	.925451		.232558
.1350	14-11	.181021	.490136			.255813
.1375	14-3	.197478	.534694			.279069
.1400	13-8	.213934	.579252			.302325
.1425	13-2	.230391	.623810			.325581
.1450	12-8	.246847	.668368			.348837
.1475	12-3	.263304	.712926			.372093
.1500	11-10	.279760	.757484			.395348
.1525	11-5	.296217	.802042			.418604
.1550	11-1	.312673	.846600			.441860
.1575	10-9	.329130	.891158			.465116
.1600	10-5	.345586	.935716			.488372
.1625	10-2	.362043	.980273			.511627
.1650	9-11					.534884

Sinking Fund Factors

Y	5 Yrs.	10 Yrs.	15 Yrs.	20 Yrs.
5%	.1810	.0795	.0464	.0303
6%	.1774	.0759	.0430	.0272
7%	.1739	.0724	.0398	.0244
8%	.1705	.0690	.0368	.0219
9%	.1671	.0658	.0341	.0196
10%	.1638	.0628	.0315	.0175
11%	.1606	.0598	.0291	.0156
12%	.1574	.0570	.0268	.0139
13%	.1543	.0543	.0248	.0124
14%	.1513	.0517	.0228	.0110
15%	.1483	.0493	.0210	.0098
16%	.1454	.0469	.0194	.0087
17%	.1426	.0447	.0178	.0077
18%	.1398	.0425	.0164	.0068
19%	.1370	.0405	.0151	.0060
20%	.1344	.0385	.0139	.0054
21%	.1318	.0367		
22%	.1292	.0349		
23%	.1267	.0332		
24%	.1242	.0316		
25%	.1218	.0301		
26%	.1195	.0286		
27%	.1172	.0272		
28%	.1149	.0259		
29%	.1127	.0247		
30%	.1106	.0235		

ANNUAL CONSTANT LOANS WITH INTEREST AT 11%

"f" Annual Constant	F.A.T. Yrs. & Mos.	"P" Fraction Amortized "P" 5 Years	10 Years	15 Years	20 Years	f/I −1
.1150	28-8	.033132	.090415	.189453	.360681	.045454
.1175	25-2	.049698	.135623	.284180	.541022	.068181
.1200	22-9	.066264	.180830	.378907	.721363	.090909
.1225	20-11	.082831	.226038	.473634	.901704	.113636
.1250	19-5	.099397	.271246	.568360		.136363
.1275	18-2	.115963	.316454	.663087		.159090
.1300	17-2	.132529	.361661	.757814		.181818
.1325	16-3	.149096	.406869	.852541		.204545
.1350	15-5	.165662	.452077	.947268		.227272
.1375	14-9	.182228	.497285			.250000
.1400	14-1	.198794	.542492			.272727
.1425	13-6	.215361	.587700			.295454
.1450	13-0	.231927	.632908			.318181
.1475	12-6	.248493	.678115			.340909
.1500	12-1	.265059	.723323			.363636
.1525	11-8	.281626	.768531			.386363
.1550	11-4	.298192	.813739			.409090
.1575	11-0	.314758	.858946			.431818
.1600	10-8	.331324	.904154			.454545
.1625	10-4	.347891	.949362			.477272
.1650	10-1	.364457	.994570			.500000
.1675	9-10					.522727

Sinking Fund Factors

Y	5 Yrs.	10 Yrs.	15 Yrs.	20 Yrs.
5%	.1810	.0795	.0464	.0303
6%	.1774	.0759	.0430	.0272
7%	.1739	.0724	.0398	.0244
8%	.1705	.0690	.0368	.0219
9%	.1671	.0658	.0341	.0196
10%	.1638	.0628	.0315	.0175
11%	.1606	.0598	.0291	.0156
12%	.1574	.0570	.0268	.0139
13%	.1543	.0543	.0248	.0124
14%	.1513	.0517	.0228	.0110
15%	.1483	.0493	.0210	.0098
16%	.1454	.0469	.0194	.0087
17%	.1426	.0447	.0178	.0077
18%	.1398	.0425	.0164	.0068
19%	.1370	.0405	.0151	.0060
20%	.1344	.0385	.0139	.0054
21%	.1318	.0367		
22%	.1292	.0349		
23%	.1267	.0332		
24%	.1242	.0316		
25%	.1218	.0301		
26%	.1195	.0286		
27%	.1172	.0272		
28%	.1149	.0259		
29%	.1127	.0247		
30%	.1106	.0235		

"Ca" Auxiliary Table "Ca"

ANNUAL CONSTANT LOANS WITH INTEREST AT 11¼%

"f" Annual Constant	F.A.T. Yrs. & Mos.	"P" Fraction Amortized "P" 5 Years	10 Years	15 Years	20 Years	$\frac{f}{I}$ −1
.1175	28-3	.033353	.091738	.193938	.372835	.044444
.1200	24-10	.050030	.137607	.290907	.559252	.066666
.1225	22-5	.066707	.183476	.387876	.745670	.088888
.1250	20-7	.083384	.229345	.484845	.932088	.111111
.1275	19-2	.100061	.275214	.581814		.133333
.1300	17-11	.116738	.321083	.678783		.155555
.1325	16-11	.133415	.366952	.775752		.177777
.1350	16-0	.150092	.412822	.872722		.200000
.1375	15-3	.166769	.458691	.969691		.222222
.1400	14-7	.183446	.504560			.244444
.1425	13-11	.200122	.550429			.266666
.1450	13-5	.216799	.596298			.288888
.1475	12-11	.233476	.642167			.311111
.1500	12-5	.250153	.688036			.333333
.1525	12-0	.266830	.733905			.355555
.1550	11-7	.283507	.779774			.377777
.1575	11-3	.300184	.825644			.400000
.1600	10-11	.316861	.871513			.422222
.1625	10-7	.333538	.917382			.444444
.1650	10-3	.350215	.963251			.466666
.1675	10-0					.488889

Sinking Fund Factors

Y	5 Yrs.	10 Yrs.	15 Yrs.	20 Yrs.
5%	.1810	.0795	.0464	.0303
6%	.1774	.0759	.0430	.0272
7%	.1739	.0724	.0398	.0244
8%	.1705	.0690	.0368	.0219
9%	.1671	.0658	.0341	.0196
10%	.1638	.0628	.0315	.0175
11%	.1606	.0598	.0291	.0156
12%	.1574	.0570	.0268	.0139
13%	.1543	.0543	.0248	.0124
14%	.1513	.0517	.0228	.0110
15%	.1483	.0493	.0210	.0098
16%	.1454	.0469	.0194	.0087
17%	.1426	.0447	.0178	.0077
18%	.1398	.0425	.0164	.0068
19%	.1370	.0405	.0151	.0060
20%	.1344	.0385	.0139	.0054
21%	.1318	.0367		
22%	.1292	.0349		
23%	.1267	.0332		
24%	.1242	.0316		
25%	.1218	.0301		
26%	.1195	.0286		
27%	.1172	.0272		
28%	.1149	.0259		
29%	.1127	.0247		
30%	.1106	.0235		

"Ca" Auxiliary Table "Ca"

ANNUAL CONSTANT LOANS WITH INTEREST AT 11½%

"f" Annual Constant	F.A.T. Yrs. & Mos.	"P" Fraction Amortized "P" 5 Years	10 Years	15 Years	20 Years	$\frac{f}{I} - 1$
.1200	27-10	.033577	.093084	.198547	.385458	.043478
.1225	24-5	.050365	.139626	.297821	.578187	.065217
.1250	22-1	.067154	.186168	.397095	.770916	.086956
.1275	20-4	.083942	.232710	.496369	.963645	.108695
.1300	18-11	.100731	.279253	.595643		.130434
.1325	17-9	.117519	.325795	.694917		.152173
.1350	16-9	.134308	.372337	.794191		.173913
.1375	15-10	.151096	.418879	.893465		.195652
.1400	15-1	.167885	.465421	.992739		.217391
.1425	14-5	.184673	.511963			.239130
.1450	13-10	.201462	.558506			.260869
.1475	13-3	.218250	.605048			.282608
.1500	12-9	.235039	.651590			.304347
.1525	12-3	.251827	.698132			.326086
.1550	11-10	.268616	.744674			.347826
.1575	11-6	.285404	.791216			.369565
.1600	11-1	.302193	.837759			.391304
.1625	10-9	.318981	.884301			.413043
.1650	10-6	.335770	.930843			.434782
.1675	10-2	.352558	.977385			.456521
.1700	9-11					.478261

Sinking Fund Factors

Y	5 Yrs.	10 Yrs.	15 Yrs.	20 Yrs.
5%	.1810	.0795	.0464	.0303
6%	.1774	.0759	.0430	.0272
7%	.1739	.0724	.0398	.0244
8%	.1705	.0690	.0368	.0219
9%	.1671	.0658	.0341	.0196
10%	.1638	.0628	.0315	.0175
11%	.1606	.0598	.0291	.0156
12%	.1574	.0570	.0268	.0139
13%	.1543	.0543	.0248	.0124
14%	.1513	.0517	.0228	.0110
15%	.1483	.0493	.0210	.0098
16%	.1454	.0469	.0194	.0087
17%	.1426	.0447	.0178	.0077
18%	.1398	.0425	.0164	.0068
19%	.1370	.0405	.0151	.0060
20%	.1344	.0385	.0139	.0054
21%	.1318	.0367		
22%	.1292	.0349		
23%	.1267	.0332		
24%	.1242	.0316		
25%	.1218	.0301		
26%	.1195	.0286		
27%	.1172	.0272		
28%	.1149	.0259		
29%	.1127	.0247		
30%	.1106	.0235		

"Ca" Auxiliary Table "Ca"

ANNUAL CONSTANT LOANS WITH INTEREST AT 11¾%

"f" Annual Constant	F.A.T. Yrs. & Mos.	"P" Fraction Amortized "P" 5 Years	10 Years	15 Years	20 Years	f/I −1
.1225	27-5	.033802	.094454	.203286	.398569	.042553
.1250	24-1	.050703	.141681	.304929	.597853	.063829
.1275	21-10	.067604	.188908	.406572	.797138	.085106
.1300	20-1	.084505	.236136	.508215	.996422	.106382
.1325	18-8	.101406	.283363	.609859		.127659
.1350	17-6	.118307	.330590	.711502		.148936
.1375	16-6	.135208	.377817	.813145		.170212
.1400	15-8	.152109	.425045	.914788		.191489
.1425	14-11	.169010	.472272			.212765
.1450	14-3	.185911	.519499			.234042
.1475	13-8	.202812	.566726			.255319
.1500	13-1	.219713	.613954			.276595
.1525	12-7	.236614	.661181			.297872
.1550	12-2	.253515	.708408			.319148
.1575	11-9	.270416	.755635			.340425
.1600	11-4	.287317	.802862			.361702
.1625	11-0	.304218	.850090			.382978
.1650	10-8	.321119	.897317			.404255
.1675	10-4	.338020	.944544			.425531
.1700	10-1	.354921	.991771			.446808
.1725	9-10					.468085

Sinking Fund Factors

Y	5 Yrs.	10 Yrs.	15 Yrs.	20 Yrs.
5%	.1810	.0795	.0464	.0303
6%	.1774	.0759	.0430	.0272
7%	.1739	.0724	.0398	.0244
8%	.1705	.0690	.0368	.0219
9%	.1671	.0658	.0341	.0196
10%	.1638	.0628	.0315	.0175
11%	.1606	.0598	.0291	.0156
12%	.1574	.0570	.0268	.0139
13%	.1543	.0543	.0248	.0124
14%	.1513	.0517	.0228	.0110
15%	.1483	.0493	.0210	.0098
16%	.1454	.0469	.0194	.0087
17%	.1426	.0447	.0178	.0077
18%	.1398	.0425	.0164	.0068
19%	.1370	.0405	.0151	.0060
20%	.1344	.0385	.0139	.0054
21%	.1318	.0367		
22%	.1292	.0349		
23%	.1267	.0332		
24%	.1242	.0316		
25%	.1218	.0301		
26%	.1195	.0286		
27%	.1172	.0272		
28%	.1149	.0259		
29%	.1127	.0247		
30%	.1106	.0235		

ANNUAL CONSTANT LOANS WITH INTEREST AT 12%

"f" Annual Constant	F.A.T. Yrs. & Mos.	"P" Fraction Amortized "P" 5 Years	10 Years	15 Years	20 Years	$\frac{f}{I}-1$
.1250	27-0	.034029	.095849	.208158	.412189	.041666
.1275	23-9	.051043	.143773	.312237	.618284	.062500
.1300	21-6	.068058	.191698	.416316	.824379	.083333
.1325	19-10	.085072	.239622	.520395		.104166
.1350	18-5	.102087	.287547	.624475		.125000
.1375	17-4	.119101	.335472	.728554		.145833
.1400	16-4	.136116	.383396	.832633		.166666
.1425	15-6	.153130	.431321	.936712		.187500
.1450	14-9	.170145	.479245			.208333
.1475	14-1	.187159	.527170			.229166
.1500	13-6	.204174	.575095			.250000
.1525	13-0	.221188	.623019			.270833
.1550	12-6	.238203	.670944			.291666
.1575	12-1	.255217	.718868			.312500
.1600	11-8	.272232	.766793			.333333
.1625	11-3	.289246	.814717			.354166
.1650	10-11	.306261	.862642			.375000
.1675	10-7	.323275	.910567			.395833
.1700	10-3	.340290	.958491			.416666
.1725	10-0					.437500

Sinking Fund Factors

Y	5 Yrs.	10 Yrs.	15 Yrs.	20 Yrs.
5%	.1810	.0795	.0464	.0303
6%	.1774	.0759	.0430	.0272
7%	.1739	.0724	.0398	.0244
8%	.1705	.0690	.0368	.0219
9%	.1671	.0658	.0341	.0196
10%	.1638	.0628	.0315	.0175
11%	.1606	.0598	.0291	.0156
12%	.1574	.0570	.0268	.0139
13%	.1543	.0543	.0248	.0124
14%	.1513	.0517	.0228	.0110
15%	.1483	.0493	.0210	.0098
16%	.1454	.0469	.0194	.0087
17%	.1426	.0447	.0178	.0077
18%	.1398	.0425	.0164	.0068
19%	.1370	.0405	.0151	.0060
20%	.1344	.0385	.0139	.0054
21%	.1318	.0367		
22%	.1292	.0349		
23%	.1267	.0332		
24%	.1242	.0316		
25%	.1218	.0301		
26%	.1195	.0286		
27%	.1172	.0272		
28%	.1149	.0259		
29%	.1127	.0247		
30%	.1106	.0235		

AUXILIARY TABLE Cp

Scope:—

Presents (Sp — 1) factors and annual constant requirement "f" for terms of from 1 to 40 years with mortgage interest rates from 3% to 12%.

Use:—

For calculating fraction of mortgage amortized "P" where projection and amortization terms are outside the scope of Table C.

Example:—

Interest rate 7%. Amortization 27 years. Projection 12 years.

$$\left(\frac{f}{I} - 1\right) \quad (Sp - 1) = \left[\left(\frac{.08256}{.07}\right) - 1\right] 1.3107 = .235177$$

"f" factors from this table may be used in conjunction with Table "Cy" for calculating mortgage coefficients and basic cap. rate.

Auxiliary Factors for Computing Capitalization Rates

MORTGAGE COMPONENTS

Interest Rates

Term Years	3%		3¼%		3½%		3¾%	
	Sp – 1	Ann. Req. (f)	Sp – 1	Ann. Req. (f)	Sp – 1	Ann. Req. (f)	Sp – 1	Ann. Req. (f)
1	.0304	1.01633	.0330	1.01772	.0356	1.01916	.0382	1.02048
2	.0618	.51579	.0671	.51720	.0724	.51852	.0778	.51984
3	.0941	.34898	.1023	.35040	.1105	.35172	.1189	.35304
4	.1273	.26568	.1386	.26700	.1500	.26832	.1616	.26964
5	.1616	.21564	.1762	.21696	.1909	.21840	.2059	.21972
6	.1969	.18240	.2150	.18372	.2333	.18504	.2519	.18648
7	.2334	.15864	.2551	.15996	.2772	.16128	.2996	.16272
8	.2709	.14076	.2965	.14220	.3226	.14352	.3492	.14496
9	.3095	.12696	.3392	.12840	.3696	.12972	.4007	.13116
10	.3494	.11592	.3834	.11736	.4183	.11868	.4541	.12012
11	.3904	.10692	.4291	.10824	.4688	.10968	.5096	.11112
12	.4327	.09936	.4762	.10080	.5210	.10224	.5672	.10368
13	.4763	.09300	.5249	.09444	.5751	.09588	.6270	.09732
14	.5217	.08760	.5752	.08904	.6312	.09048	.6891	.09204
15	.5674	.08292	.6272	.08436	.6892	.08580	.7535	.08736
16	.6151	.07884	.6808	.08028	.7492	.08172	.8204	.08328
17	.6642	.07524	.7363	.07668	.8115	.07824	.8899	.07968
18	.7149	.07200	.7936	.07356	.8759	.07500	.9620	.07656
19	.7670	.06912	.8527	.07068	.9426	.07220	1.0368	.07368
20	.8208	.06660	.9139	.06816	1.0117	.06960	1.1145	.07116
21	.8761	.06432	.9770	.06588	1.0833	.06732	1.1952	.06888
22	.9332	.06216	1.0422	.06372	1.1573	.06528	1.2789	.06684
23	.9920	.06036	1.1096	.06180	1.2341	.06340	1.3659	.06504
24	1.0526	.05856	1.1792	.06012	1.3135	.06168	1.4562	.06336
25	1.1150	.05700	1.2511	.05856	1.3958	.06012	1.5499	.06180
26	1.1793	.05544	1.3253	.05712	1.4810	.05868	1.6471	.06036
27	1.2456	.05412	1.4020	.05580	1.5693	.05736	1.7481	.05904
28	1.3139	.05292	1.4813	.05448	1.6607	.05616	1.8530	.05784
29	1.3843	.05172	1.5631	.05340	1.7553	.05496	1.9618	.05664
30	1.4568	.05064	1.6477	.05232	1.8533	.05400	2.0748	.05568
31	1.5316	.04968	1.7350	.05124	1.9548	.05292	2.1921	.05460
32	1.6086	.04872	1.8252	.05040	2.0599	.05208	2.3139	.05376
33	1.6879	.04788	1.9184	.04945	2.1687	.05124	2.4403	.05292
34	1.7697	.04704	2.0147	.04872	2.2814	.05040	2.5716	.05210
35	1.8539	.04620	2.1142	.04788	2.3981	.04968	2.7079	.05136
36	1.9407	.04548	2.2170	.04716	2.5190	.04896	2.8493	.05076
37	2.0302	.04488	2.3231	.04656	2.6441	.04824	2.9962	.05004
38	2.1223	.04416	2.4328	.04596	2.7737	.04764	3.1486	.04944
39	2.2173	.04356	2.5460	.04536	2.9080	.04704	3.3069	.04884
40	2.3151	.04296	2.6630	.04476	3.0469	.04656	3.4712	.04836

Auxiliary Factors for Computing Capitalization Rates

MORTGAGE COMPONENTS

Interest Rates

Term Years	4%		4¼%		4½%		4¾%	
	Sp – 1	Ann. Req. (f)	Sp – 1	Ann. Req. (f)	Sp – 1	Ann. Req. (f)	Sp – 1	Ann. Req. (f)
1	.0407	1.02180	.0433	1.02324	.0459	1.02456	.0486	1.02600
2	.0832	.52116	.0886	.52248	.0904	.52384	.0995	.52512
3	.1273	.35436	.1357	.35568	.1443	.35700	.1528	.35832
4	.1732	.27096	.1850	.27240	.1968	.27372	.2088	.27504
5	.2210	.22104	.2363	.22236	.2518	.22380	.2675	.22512
6	.2708	.18780	.2899	.18912	.3093	.19056	.3290	.19188
7	.3225	.16404	.3458	.16548	.3695	.16680	.3935	.16824
8	.3764	.14628	.4041	.14772	.4324	.14916	.4612	.15060
9	.4325	.13260	.4650	.13392	.4982	.13536	.5321	.13680
10	.4908	.12156	.5285	.12300	.5670	.12444	.6065	.12588
11	.5516	.11256	.5947	.11400	.6390	.11544	.6845	.11700
12	.6148	.10512	.6638	.10656	.7143	.10800	.7663	.10956
13	.6806	.09888	.7359	.10032	.7930	.10176	.8520	.10332
14	.7491	.09348	.8111	.09492	.8754	.09648	.9419	.09804
15	.8203	.08880	.8896	.09036	.9616	.09180	1.0362	.09336
16	.8945	.08472	.9715	.08628	1.0517	.08784	1.1351	.08940
17	.9717	.08124	1.0569	.08280	1.1459	.08436	1.2387	.08592
18	1.0520	.07812	1.1461	.07968	1.2445	.08124	1.3474	.08280
19	1.1356	.07524	1.2391	.07680	1.3476	.07848	1.4614	.08004
20	1.2226	.07272	1.3361	.07440	1.4555	.07596	1.5809	.07764
21	1.3131	.07056	1.4374	.07212	1.5683	.07380	1.7062	.07536
22	1.4074	.06852	1.5430	.07008	1.6863	.07176	1.8375	.07344
23	1.5055	.06660	1.6532	.06828	1.8097	.06996	1.9753	.07164
24	1.6075	.06492	1.7682	.06660	1.9387	.06828	2.1197	.06996
25	1.7138	.06336	1.8882	.06504	2.0737	.06672	2.2712	.06852
26	1.8243	.06204	2.0133	.06360	2.2149	.06540	2.4300	.06708
27	1.9394	.06072	2.1439	.06240	2.3626	.06408	2.5965	.06588
28	2.0592	.05952	2.2802	.06120	2.5171	.06288	2.7711	.06468
29	2.1838	.05832	2.4223	.06012	2.6787	.06180	2.9542	.06360
30	2.3135	.05736	2.5706	.05904	2.8477	.06084	3.1462	.06264
31	2.4485	.05640	2.7254	.05820	3.0245	.05988	3.3475	.06180
32	2.5890	.05556	2.8868	.05724	3.2093	.05904	3.5585	.06096
33	2.7352	.05472	3.0553	.05650	3.4027	.05832	3.7798	.06012
34	2.8874	.05388	3.2310	.05568	3.6050	.05760	4.0119	.05940
35	3.0458	.05316	3.4144	.05496	3.8165	.05688	4.2552	.05868
36	3.2106	.05256	3.6057	.05436	4.0378	.05616	4.5103	.05808
37	3.3822	.05184	3.8053	.05376	4.2692	.05556	4.7778	.05748
38	3.5607	.05124	4.0136	.05316	4.5113	.05508	5.0583	.05700
39	3.7465	.05076	4.2309	.05256	4.7645	.05448	5.3525	.05640
40	3.9399	.05016	4.4575	.05208	5.0293	.05400	5.6609	.05592

Auxiliary Factors for Computing Capitalization Rates

MORTGAGE COMPONENTS

Interest Rates

Term Years	5% Sp − 1	5% Ann. Req. (f)	5¼% Sp − 1	5¼% Ann. Req. (f)	5½% Sp − 1	5½% Ann. Req. (f)	5¾% Sp − 1	5¾% Ann. Req. (f)
1	.0512	1.02732	.0538	1.02876	.0564	1.03008	.0590	1.03152
2	.1049	.52656	.1105	.52776	.1160	.52920	.1216	.53052
3	.1615	.35965	.1702	.36108	.1789	.36240	.1878	.36372
4	.2209	.27636	.2331	.27780	.2455	.27912	.2579	.28056
5	.2834	.22656	.2994	.22788	.3157	.22932	.3322	.23064
6	.3490	.19332	.3693	.19476	.3899	.19608	.4108	.19752
7	.4180	.16968	.4430	.17112	.4683	.17244	.4941	.17388
8	.4906	.15192	.5206	.15336	.5511	.15480	.5823	.15624
9	.5668	.13824	.6023	.13968	.6386	.13112	.6758	.14268
10	.6470	.12732	.6885	.12876	.7311	.13032	.7747	.13176
11	.7313	.11844	.7793	.11988	.8287	.12144	.8795	.12288
12	.8198	.11100	.8750	.11256	.9319	.11412	.9904	.11556
13	.9130	.10478	.9759	.10632	1.0409	.10788	1.1079	.10944
14	1.0108	.09948	1.0821	.10104	1.1560	.10260	1.2324	.10416
15	1.1137	.09492	1.1941	.09648	1.2776	.09816	1.3642	.09972
16	1.2218	.09096	1.3121	.09252	1.4061	.09420	1.5038	.09576
17	1.3355	.08748	1.4365	.08906	1.5418	.09072	1.6516	.09240
18	1.4550	.08448	1.5675	.08604	1.6852	.08772	1.8082	.08940
19	1.5806	.08172	1.7056	.08330	1.8366	.08496	1.9739	.08664
20	1.7126	.07920	1.8511	.08088	1.9966	.08256	2.1495	.08436
21	1.8514	.07704	2.0045	.07872	2.1657	.08040	2.3355	.08220
22	1.9973	.07512	2.1660	.07680	2.3442	.07848	2.5324	.08028
23	2.1507	.07332	2.3363	.07500	2.5329	.07680	2.7410	.07848
24	2.3118	.07164	2.5157	.07344	2.7321	.07524	2.9618	.07692
25	2.4813	.07020	2.7048	.07200	2.9427	.07380	3.1957	.07560
26	2.6594	.06888	2.9041	.07068	3.1651	.07248	3.4434	.07428
27	2.8466	.06768	3.1141	.06936	3.4000	.07128	3.7058	.07308
28	3.0434	.06648	3.3353	.06828	3.6482	.07008	3.9836	.07200
29	3.2503	.06540	3.5685	.06732	3.9104	.06912	4.2778	.07104
30	3.4677	.06444	3.8142	.06636	4.1874	.06816	4.5894	.07008
31	3.6963	.06360	4.0731	.06540	4.4800	.06732	4.9194	.06924
32	3.9366	.06276	4.3459	.06468	4.7891	.06660	5.2689	.06852
33	4.1892	.06204	4.6334	.06384	5.1157	.06576	5.6390	.06780
34	4.4546	.06132	4.9364	.06324	5.4606	.06516	6.0310	.06708
35	4.7337	.06060	5.2557	.06252	5.8251	.06456	6.4461	.06648
36	5.0271	.06000	5.5921	.06192	6.2101	.06396	6.8857	.06588
37	5.3354	.05940	5.9467	.06140	6.6168	.06336	7.3513	.06540
38	5.6596	.05892	6.3203	.06084	7.0464	.06288	7.8444	.06492
39	6.0003	.05844	6.7140	.06036	7.5003	.06240	8.3665	.06444
40	6.3584	.05796	7.1289	.05988	7.9798	.06192	8.9195	.06396

Auxiliary Factors for Computing Capitalization Rates

MORTGAGE COMPONENTS

Interest Rates

Term Years	6% Sp − 1	6% Ann. Req. (f)	6¼% Sp − 1	6¼% Ann. Req. (f)	6½% Sp − 1	6½% Ann. Req. (f)	6¾% Sp − 1	6¾% Ann. Req. (f)
1	.0617	1.03284	.0643	1.03428	.0670	1.03560	.0696	1.03704
2	.1272	.53190	.1328	.53328	.1384	.54360	.1441	.53592
3	.1967	.36516	.2056	.36648	.2147	.36780	.2238	.36924
4	.2705	.28188	.2832	.28320	.2960	.28464	.3090	.28600
5	.3488	.23208	.3657	.23340	.3828	.23484	.4001	.23628
6	.4320	.19896	.4536	.20040	.4754	.20172	.4976	.20316
7	.5204	.17532	.5471	.17676	.5742	.17820	.6019	.17970
8	.6141	.15780	.6466	.15924	.6797	.16068	.7134	.16212
9	.7137	.14412	.7525	.14556	.7922	.14712	.8327	.14860
10	.8194	.13332	.8652	.13476	.9122	.13632	.9603	.13788
11	.9316	.12444	.9852	.12600	1.0402	.12756	1.0968	.12912
12	1.0508	.11712	1.1129	.11868	1.1769	.12024	1.2428	.12192
13	1.1772	.11100	1.2488	.11256	1.3227	.11424	1.3990	.11580
14	1.3115	.10584	1.3934	.10740	1.4782	.10908	1.5660	.11064
15	1.4541	.10128	1.5474	.10296	1.6442	.10464	1.7447	.10620
16	1.6055	.09744	1.7112	.09912	1.8213	.10070	1.9358	.10240
17	1.7662	.09408	1.8856	.09564	2.0102	.09744	2.1402	.09912
18	1.9368	.09108	2.0712	.09276	2.2118	.09444	2.3588	.09612
19	2.1179	.08844	2.2688	.09012	2.4269	.09180	2.5927	.09360
20	2.3102	.08604	2.4790	.08772	2.6564	.08952	2.8429	.09132
21	2.5144	.08388	2.7028	.08568	2.9013	.08748	3.1104	.08928
22	2.7311	.08208	2.9410	.08376	3.1626	.08556	3.3966	.08748
23	2.9613	.08028	3.1945	.08208	3.4414	.08390	3.7028	.08580
24	3.2056	.07872	3.4643	.08064	3.7388	.08244	4.0302	.08430
25	3.4650	.07740	3.7514	.07920	4.0562	.08112	4.3804	.08292
26	3.7404	.07608	4.0570	.07800	4.3948	.07980	4.7551	.08172
27	4.0327	.07488	4.3823	.07680	4.7561	.07872	5.1558	.08064
28	4.3431	.07392	4.7285	.07572	5.1416	.07770	5.5844	.07968
29	4.6727	.07284	5.0970	.07480	5.5529	.07680	6.0429	.07872
30	5.0226	.07200	5.4892	.07392	5.9918	.07596	6.5332	.07788
31	5.3940	.07116	5.9066	.07310	6.4601	.07512	7.0578	.07716
32	5.7884	.07044	6.3508	.07236	6.9597	.07440	7.6188	.07644
33	6.2071	.06972	6.8236	.07176	7.4927	.07368	8.2189	.07572
34	6.6516	.06912	7.3269	.07104	8.0615	.07308	8.8608	.07512
35	7.1236	.06852	7.8625	.07050	8.6684	.07260	9.5474	.07464
36	7.6246	.06792	8.4325	.06996	9.3159	.07200	10.2818	.07416
37	8.1565	.06744	9.0392	.06948	10.0068	.07152	11.0673	.07368
38	8.7213	.06696	9.6850	.06900	10.7439	.07110	11.9076	.07320
39	9.3209	.06648	10.3722	.06860	11.5304	.07068	12.8063	.07284
40	9.9575	.06612	11.1037	.06816	12.3696	.07032	13.7676	.07248

Auxiliary Factors for Computing Capitalization Rates

MORTGAGE COMPONENTS

Interest Rates

Term Years	7% Sp−1	7% Ann. Req. (f)	7¼% Sp−1	7¼% Ann. Req. (f)	7½% Sp−1	7½% Ann. Req. (f)	7¾% Sp−1	7¾% Ann. Req. (f)
1	.0722	1.038360	.0749	1.039800	.0776	1.041120	.0803	1.042560
2	.1498	.537360	.1555	.538680	.1612	.540000	.1670	.541440
3	.2329	.370560	.2421	.372000	.2514	.373320	.2608	.374760
4	.3220	.287400	.3352	.288840	.3485	.290160	.3620	.291600
5	.4176	.237720	.4353	.239040	.4532	.240480	.4714	.241920
6	.5201	.204600	.5429	.206040	.5661	.207600	.5896	.209040
7	.6299	.181200	.6585	.182640	.6876	.184080	.7173	.185640
8	.7478	.163680	.7829	.165120	.8187	.166680	.8552	.168120
9	.8741	.150120	.9165	.151680	.9599	.153240	1.0042	.154680
10	1.0096	.139440	1.0602	.141000	1.1120	.142560	1.1651	.144120
11	1.1549	.130680	1.2146	.132240	1.2760	.133800	1.3390	.135480
12	1.3107	.123480	1.3806	.125040	1.4527	.126720	1.5269	.128280
13	1.4777	.117480	1.5591	.119040	1.6431	.120720	1.7298	.122400
14	1.6568	.112320	1.7509	.114000	1.8483	.115680	1.9491	.117360
15	1.8489	.107880	1.9571	.109560	2.0694	.111360	2.1859	.113040
16	2.0548	.104160	2.1788	.105840	2.3077	.107520	2.4418	.109320
17	2.2757	.100800	2.4170	.102600	2.5645	.104280	2.7182	.106080
18	2.5125	.097920	2.6732	.099720	2.8412	.101400	3.0169	.103200
19	2.7664	.095400	2.9485	.097200	3.1394	.099000	3.3395	.100800
20	3.0387	.093120	3.2445	.094920	3.4608	.096720	3.6880	.098520
21	3.3306	.091080	3.5627	.092880	3.8071	.094800	4.0645	.096600
22	3.6437	.089280	3.9047	.091080	4.1803	.093000	4.4713	.094920
23	3.9794	.087600	4.2723	.089520	4.5824	.091440	4.9107	.093360
24	4.3394	.086160	4.6675	.088080	5.0158	.090000	5.3854	.091920
25	4.7254	.084840	5.0924	.086760	5.4828	.088680	5.8982	.090720
26	5.1393	.083640	5.5491	.085680	5.9861	.087600	6.4522	.089520
27	5.5831	.082560	6.0400	.084600	6.5285	.086520	7.0508	.088560
28	6.0590	.081600	6.5677	.083640	7.1129	.085560	7.6973	.087600
29	6.5693	.080760	7.1349	.082680	7.7428	.084720	8.3959	.086760
30	7.1164	.079920	7.7447	.081960	8.4215	.084000	9.1505	.086040
31	7.7032	.079200	8.4002	.081240	9.1529	.083280	9.9657	.085320
32	8.3323	.078480	9.1048	.080520	9.9411	.082560	10.8464	.084720
33	9.0070	.077880	9.8623	.079920	10.7905	.081960	11.7978	.084120
34	9.7304	.077280	10.6765	.079320	11.7058	.081480	12.8256	.083640
35	10.5061	.076680	11.5518	.078840	12.6922	.081000	13.9360	.083160
36	11.3379	.076200	12.4926	.078360	13.7552	.080520	15.1356	.082680
37	12.2298	.075840	13.5040	.077880	14.9007	.080040	16.4315	.082320
38	13.1862	.075360	14.5912	.077520	16.1351	.079680	17.8314	.081960
39	14.2117	.075000	15.7599	.077160	17.4653	.079320	19.3439	.081600
40	15.3114	.074640	17.0162	.076800	18.8988	.079080	20.9777	.081240

Auxiliary Factors for Computing Capitalization Rates

MORTGAGE COMPONENTS

Interest Rates

Term Years	8% Sp−1	8% Ann. Req. (f)	8¼% Sp−1	8¼% Ann. Req. (f)	8½% Sp−1	8½% Ann. Req. (f)	8¾% Sp−1	8¾% Ann. Req. (f)
1	.0829	1.043880	.0856	1.045320	.0883	1.046640	.0910	1.048080
2	.1728	.542760	.1787	.544200	.1845	.545520	.1904	.546960
3	.2702	.376080	.2797	.377520	.2893	.378840	.2989	.380280
4	.3756	.293040	.3893	.294480	.4032	.295800	.4172	.297240
5	.4898	.243360	.5084	.244800	.5273	.246240	.5463	.247680
6	.6135	.210480	.6377	.211920	.6623	.213360	.6872	.214920
7	.7474	.187080	.7780	.188640	.8092	.190080	.8409	.191640
8	.8924	.169680	.9304	.171240	.9691	.172800	1.0086	.174360
9	1.0495	.156240	1.0958	.157800	1.1432	.159360	1.1916	.161040
10	1.2196	.145680	1.2754	.147240	1.3326	.148800	1.3912	.150480
11	1.4038	.137040	1.4704	.138720	1.5388	.140280	1.6091	.141960
12	1.6033	.129960	1.6821	.131640	1.7632	.133320	1.8467	.134880
13	1.8194	.124080	1.9119	.125760	2.0074	.127440	2.1061	.129120
14	2.0534	.119040	2.1615	.120720	2.2733	.122400	2.3890	.124200
15	2.3069	.114720	2.4324	.116520	2.5626	.118200	2.6977	.120000
16	2.5813	.111000	2.7265	.112800	2.8775	.114600	3.0346	.116400
17	2.8786	.107880	3.0458	.109680	3.2203	.111480	3.4021	.113280
18	3.2005	.105000	3.3925	.106920	3.5933	.108720	3.8032	.110520
19	3.5492	.102600	3.7689	.104400	3.9993	.106320	4.2407	.108240
20	3.9268	.100440	4.1776	.102360	4.4412	.104160	4.7181	.106080
21	4.3357	.098520	4.6213	.100440	4.9221	.102360	5.2390	.104280
22	4.7785	.096840	5.1030	.098760	5.4456	.100680	5.8074	.102600
23	5.2582	.095280	5.6260	.097200	6.0154	.099240	6.4275	.101160
24	5.7776	.093960	6.1938	.095880	6.6355	.097920	7.1041	.099840
25	6.3401	.092640	6.8102	.094680	7.3104	.096720	7.8424	.098760
26	6.9494	.091560	7.4795	.093600	8.0449	.095640	8.6479	.097680
27	7.6092	.090600	8.2062	.092640	8.8444	.094680	9.5268	.096720
28	8.3237	.089640	8.9951	.091680	9.7146	.093840	10.4857	.095880
29	9.0976	.088800	9.8516	.090960	10.6617	.093000	11.5321	.095160
30	9.9357	.088080	10.7815	.090240	11.6924	.092280	12.6737	.094440
31	10.8433	.087480	11.7910	.089520	12.8144	.091680	13.9193	.093840
32	11.8263	.086880	12.8871	.088920	14.0354	.091080	15.2784	.093240
33	12.8909	.086280	14.0772	.088440	15.3644	.090600	16.7613	.092760
34	14.0439	.085800	15.3692	.087960	16.8109	.090120	18.3793	.092280
35	15.2925	.085320	16.7719	.087480	18.3852	.089640	20.1446	.091920
36	16.6448	.084840	18.2948	.087120	20.0987	.089280	22.0708	.091560
37	18.1093	.084480	19.9482	.086640	21.9636	.088920	24.1725	.091200
38	19.6954	.084120	21.7433	.086400	23.9934	.088560	26.4656	.090840
39	21.4131	.083760	23.6922	.086040	26.2026	.088320	28.9676	.090600
40	23.2733	.083520	25.8082	.085800	28.6071	.088080	31.6975	.090360

Auxiliary Factors for Computing Capitalization Rates

TABLE Cp

MORTGAGE COMPONENTS

Interest Rates

Term Years	9% Sp−1	9% Ann. Req. (f)	9¼% Sp−1	9¼% Ann. Req. (f)	9½% Sp−1	9½% Ann. Req. (f)	9¾% Sp−1	9¾% Ann. Req. (f)
1	.0938	1.049520	.0965	1.050840	.0992	1.052280	.1019	1.053600
2	.1964	.548280	.2023	.549600	.2083	.551040	.2143	.552360
3	.3086	.381600	.3184	.383040	.3282	.384480	.3381	.385800
4	.4314	.298680	.4456	.300120	.4600	.301560	.4746	.303000
5	.5656	.249120	.5852	.250560	.6050	.252120	.6250	.253560
6	.7125	.216360	.7382	.217800	.7643	.219360	.7907	.220920
7	.8732	.193080	.9060	.194640	.9394	.196200	.9733	.197760
8	1.0489	.175920	1.0899	.177480	1.1318	.179040	1.1746	.180600
9	1.2411	.162600	1.2917	.164160	1.3434	.165720	1.3963	.167400
10	1.4513	.152040	1.5129	.153720	1.5760	.155280	1.6407	.156960
11	1.6813	.143640	1.7554	.145200	1.8317	.146880	1.9100	.148560
12	1.9328	.136680	2.0214	.138360	2.1127	.140040	2.2067	.141720
13	2.2079	.130800	2.3131	.132600	2.4216	.134280	2.5338	.136080
14	2.5088	.125880	2.6329	.127680	2.7612	.129480	2.8941	.131280
15	2.8380	.121800	2.9835	.123600	3.1345	.125400	3.2913	.127200
16	3.1980	.118200	3.3680	.120000	3.5449	.121800	3.7289	.123720
17	3.5918	.115080	3.7897	.117000	3.9960	.118800	4.2111	.120720
18	4.0226	.112440	4.2520	.114360	4.4918	.116160	4.7425	.118080
19	4.4937	.110040	4.7589	.111960	5.0369	.113880	5.3281	.115800
20	5.0091	.108000	5.3148	.109920	5.6360	.111960	5.9735	.113880
21	5.5728	.106200	5.9244	.108120	6.2946	.110160	6.6846	.112200
22	6.1894	.104640	6.5927	.106560	7.0186	.108600	7.4683	.110640
23	6.8638	.103200	7.3256	.105240	7.8144	.107160	8.3319	.109320
24	7.6015	.101880	8.1292	.103920	8.6893	.105960	9.2835	.108120
25	8.4084	.100800	9.0104	.102840	9.6509	.104880	10.3322	.107040
26	9.2909	.099720	9.9767	.101880	10.7080	.103920	11.4878	.106080
27	10.2563	.098880	11.0362	.100920	11.8700	.103080	12.7613	.105240
28	11.3122	.098040	12.1980	.100200	13.1473	.102240	14.1646	.104400
29	12.4672	.097320	13.4719	.099480	14.5514	.101640	15.7111	.103800
30	13.7305	.096600	14.8688	.098760	16.0948	.100920	17.4152	.103200
31	15.1124	.096000	16.4005	.098160	17.7914	.100440	19.2932	.102600
32	16.6238	.095520	18.0801	.097680	19.6564	.099840	21.3626	.102120
33	18.2771	.095040	19.9218	.097200	21.7066	.099480	23.6431	.101640
34	20.0854	.094560	21.9413	.096720	23.9601	.099000	26.1561	.101280
35	22.0633	.094080	24.1557	.096360	26.4374	.098640	28.9255	.100920
36	24.2268	.093720	26.5838	.096000	29.1605	.098280	31.9772	.100560
37	26.5933	.093480	29.2463	.095760	32.1538	.098040	35.3401	.100320
38	29.1817	.093120	32.1658	.095400	35.4443	.097800	39.0460	.100080
39	32.0130	.092880	35.3671	.095160	39.0613	.097440	43.1298	.099840
40	35.1099	.092640	38.8775	.094920	43.0373	.097320	47.6300	.099600

Auxiliary Factors for Computing Capitalization Rates

MORTGAGE COMPONENTS

Interest Rates

Term Years	10%		10¼%		10½%		10¾%	
	Sp−1	Ann. Req. (f)	Sp−1	Ann. Req. (f)	Sp−1	Ann. Req. (f)	Sp−1	Ann. Req. (f)
1	.1047	1.055040	.1074	1.056480	.1102	1.057800	.1129	1.059240
2	.2203	.553800	.2264	.555240	.2325	.556560	.2386	.558000
3	.3481	.387240	.3582	.388680	.3683	.390120	.3785	.391560
4	.4893	.304440	.5041	.305880	.5191	.307320	.5343	.308760
5	.6453	.255000	.6658	.256560	.6866	.258000	.7076	.259440
6	.8175	.222360	.8448	.223920	.8724	.225360	.9005	.226920
7	1.0079	.199320	1.0430	.200880	1.0788	.202440	1.1152	.204000
8	1.2181	.182160	1.2626	.183720	1.3079	.185400	1.3541	.186960
9	1.4504	.168960	1.5057	.170640	1.5622	.172320	1.6200	.173880
10	1.7070	.158640	1.7749	.160320	1.8446	.162000	1.9160	.163680
11	1.9905	.150240	2.0731	.152040	2.1581	.153720	2.2453	.155400
12	2.3036	.143520	2.4034	.145200	2.5061	.147000	2.6119	.148680
13	2.6495	.137760	2.7691	.139560	2.8925	.141360	3.0199	.143160
14	3.0317	.133080	3.1741	.134880	3.3215	.136680	3.4740	.138480
15	3.4539	.129000	3.6226	.130800	3.7977	.132720	3.9794	.134520
16	3.9203	.125520	4.1193	.127440	4.3264	.129360	4.5419	.131280
17	4.4355	.122640	4.6694	.124560	4.9134	.126480	5.1679	.128400
18	5.0046	.120000	5.2787	.121920	5.5651	.123960	5.8646	.125880
19	5.6334	.117840	5.9533	.119760	6.2886	.121800	6.6400	.123720
20	6.3280	.115920	6.7005	.117840	7.0919	.119880	7.5030	.121920
21	7.0954	.114120	7.5280	.116160	7.9836	.118200	8.4635	.120240
22	7.9431	.112680	8.4444	.114720	8.9737	.116760	9.5325	.118800
23	8.8795	.111360	9.4592	.113400	10.0728	.115440	10.7222	.117600
24	9.9140	.110160	10.5831	.112200	11.2931	.114360	12.0464	.116520
25	11.0569	.109080	11.8278	.111240	12.6478	.113400	13.5200	.115560
26	12.3194	.108120	13.2062	.110280	14.1518	.112440	15.1602	.114600
27	13.7141	.107400	14.7327	.109560	15.8216	.111720	16.9856	.113880
28	15.2549	.106560	16.4233	.108840	17.6754	.111000	19.0173	.113160
29	16.9570	.105960	18.2955	.108120	19.7335	.110400	21.2784	.112560
30	18.8373	.105360	20.3690	.107640	22.0185	.109800	23.7949	.112080
31	20.9146	.104880	22.6652	.107040	24.5552	.109320	26.5957	.111600
32	23.2093	.104400	25.2081	.106680	27.3715	.108840	29.7129	.111120
33	25.7444	.103920	28.0243	.106200	30.4981	.108480	33.1821	.110760
34	28.5449	.103560	31.1431	.105840	33.9693	.108120	37.0433	.110520
35	31.6386	.103200	34.5971	.105480	37.8230	.107880	41.3406	.110160
36	35.0563	.102960	38.4222	.105240	42.1015	.107520	46.1233	.109920
37	38.8319	.102600	42.6583	.105000	46.8514	.107280	51.4462	.109680
38	43.0028	.102360	47.3496	.104760	52.1248	.107040	57.3705	.109440
39	47.6105	.102120	52.5450	.104520	57.9793	.106920	63.9639	.109200
40	52.7006	.102000	58.2987	.104280	64.4791	.106680	71.3021	.109080

Auxiliary Factors for Computing Capitalization Rates

MORTGAGE COMPONENTS

Interest Rates

Term Years	11% Sp−1	11% Ann. Req. (f)	11¼% Sp−1	11¼% Ann. Req. (f)	11½% Sp−1	11½% Ann. Req. (f)	11¾% Sp−1	11¾% Ann. Req. (f)
1	.1157	1.060680	.1184	1.062000	.1212	1.063440	.1240	1.064880
2	.2448	.559320	.2510	.560760	.2572	.562200	.2634	.563520
3	.3888	.392880	.3992	.394320	.4096	.395760	.4201	.397200
4	.5495	.310200	.5650	.311640	.5806	.313080	.5963	.314640
5	.7289	.261000	.7504	.262440	.7722	.264000	.7943	.265440
6	.9289	.228480	.9578	.230040	.9871	.231600	1.0169	.233160
7	1.1522	.205560	1.1898	.207120	1.2281	.208680	1.2670	.210240
8	1.4012	.188520	1.4493	.190200	1.4983	.191760	1.5483	.193440
9	1.6791	.175560	1.7395	.177240	1.8012	.178920	1.8643	.180600
10	1.9891	.165360	2.0641	.167040	2.1409	.168720	2.2196	.170520
11	2.3350	.157200	2.4271	.158880	2.5218	.160680	2.6190	.162480
12	2.7209	.150480	2.8332	.152280	2.9488	.154080	3.0679	.155880
13	3.1515	.144960	3.2874	.146760	3.4277	.148560	3.5725	.150480
14	3.6319	.140400	3.7954	.142200	3.9646	.144120	4.1397	.145920
15	4.1679	.136440	4.3636	.138360	4.5666	.140280	4.7772	.142200
16	4.7660	.133200	4.9991	.135120	5.2416	.137040	5.4938	.138960
17	5.4332	.130320	5.7099	.132240	5.9984	.134280	6.2993	.136200
18	6.1777	.127920	6.5049	.129840	6.8471	.131880	7.2047	.133920
19	7.0083	.125760	7.3942	.127800	7.7986	.129840	8.2224	.131880
20	7.9350	.123960	8.3888	.126000	8.8655	.128040	9.3663	.130080
21	8.9689	.122280	9.5012	.124440	10.0618	.126480	10.6522	.128640
22	10.1225	.120960	10.7455	.123000	11.4031	.125160	12.0975	.127320
23	11.4096	.119760	12.1371	.121800	12.9071	.123960	13.7221	.126120
24	12.8456	.118680	13.6937	.120720	14.5935	.123000	15.5482	.125160
25	14.4478	.117720	15.4347	.119880	16.4844	.122040	17.6009	.124200
26	16.2355	.116880	17.3820	.119040	18.6045	.121200	19.9081	.123480
27	18.2299	.116040	19.5600	.118320	20.9818	.120600	22.5016	.122760
28	20.4552	.115440	21.9961	.117720	23.6473	.119880	25.4167	.122160
29	22.9380	.114840	24.7208	.117120	26.6360	.119400	28.6934	.121680
30	25.7080	.114360	27.7684	.116640	29.9871	.118920	32.3765	.121200
31	28.7987	.113880	31.1770	.116160	33.7446	.118440	36.5165	.120720
32	32.2470	.113520	34.9895	.115800	37.9577	.118080	41.1700	.120360
33	36.0943	.113160	39.2538	.115440	42.6817	.117720	46.4008	.120120
34	40.3868	.112800	44.0233	.115080	47.9785	.117480	52.2803	.119760
35	45.1760	.112440	49.3580	.114840	53.9177	.117240	58.8892	.119520
36	50.5194	.112200	55.3247	.114600	60.5769	.117000	66.3178	.119280
37	56.4812	.111960	61.9984	.114360	68.0437	.116760	74.6678	.119160
38	63.1329	.111840	69.4628	.114120	76.4159	.116520	84.0536	.118920
39	70.5543	.111600	77.8116	.114000	85.8033	.116400	94.6035	.118800
40	78.8345	.111480	87.1497	.113880	96.3291	.116280	106.4621	.118680

Auxiliary Factors for Computing Capitalization Rates

MORTGAGE COMPONENTS

Interest Rates

Term Years	12% Sp−1	12% Ann. Req. (f)	12¼% Sp−1	12¼% Ann. Req. (f)	12½% Sp−1	12½% Ann. Req. (f)	12¾% Sp−1	12¾% Ann. Req. (f)
1	.1268	1.066200	.1296	1.067640	.1324	1.069080	.1352	1.070520
2	.2697	.564960	.2760	.566400	.2823	.567720	.2887	.569160
3	.4307	.398640	.4414	.400080	.4521	.401520	.4629	.402960
4	.6122	.316080	.6282	.317520	.6444	.318960	.6608	.320520
5	.8166	.267000	.8393	.268560	.8622	.270000	.8853	.271560
6	1.0470	.234720	1.0777	.236280	1.1088	.237840	1.1403	.239400
7	1.3067	.211920	1.3470	.213480	1.3880	.215160	1.4297	.216720
8	1.5992	.195120	1.6512	.196800	1.7042	.198360	1.7583	.200040
9	1.9289	.182280	1.9948	.183960	2.0623	.185640	2.1312	.187440
10	2.3003	.172200	2.3830	.174000	2.4678	.175680	2.5547	.177480
11	2.7189	.164160	2.8215	.165960	2.9270	.167760	3.0353	.169560
12	3.1906	.157680	3.3169	.159480	3.4470	.161280	3.5810	.163200
13	3.7220	.152280	3.8764	.154200	4.0359	.156000	4.2005	.157920
14	4.3209	.147840	4.5085	.149760	4.7027	.151680	4.9037	.153600
15	4.9958	.144120	5.2225	.146040	5.4578	.147960	5.7020	.149880
16	5.7562	.140880	6.0291	.142920	6.3130	.144840	6.6082	.146880
17	6.6130	.138240	6.9402	.140160	7.2813	.142200	7.6370	.144240
18	7.5786	.135840	7.9694	.137880	8.3779	.140040	8.8050	.142080
19	8.6665	.133920	9.1320	.135960	9.6197	.138000	10.1308	.140160
20	9.8925	.132240	10.4453	.134280	11.0259	.136440	11.6359	.138480
21	11.2740	.130680	11.9288	.132840	12.6184	.135000	13.3446	.137160
22	12.8306	.129360	13.6046	.131520	14.4217	.133680	15.2843	.135960
23	14.5847	.128280	15.4976	.130440	16.4637	.132600	17.4863	.134880
24	16.5612	.127320	17.6359	.129480	18.7762	.131760	19.9860	.133920
25	18.7884	.126480	20.0515	.128640	21.3949	.130920	22.8238	.133200
26	21.2981	.125640	22.7801	.127920	24.3604	.130200	26.0452	.132480
27	24.1261	.125040	25.8625	.127320	27.7185	.129600	29.7023	.131880
28	27.3127	.124440	29.3443	.126720	31.5213	.129000	33.8539	.131280
29	30.9034	.123960	33.2775	.126240	35.8276	.128520	38.5669	.130920
30	34.9496	.123480	37.7204	.125760	40.7042	.128160	43.9172	.130440
31	39.5089	.123120	42.7393	.125400	46.2265	.127800	49.9910	.130080
32	44.6465	.122760	48.4087	.125040	52.4801	.127440	56.8861	.129840
33	50.4356	.122400	54.8129	.124800	59.5617	.127200	64.7135	.129480
34	56.9589	.122160	62.0472	.124560	67.5811	.126960	73.5993	.129240
35	64.3095	.121920	70.2192	.124320	76.6623	.126720	83.6867	.129120
36	72.5924	.121680	79.4505	.124080	86.9460	.126480	95.1382	.128880
37	81.9258	.121560	89.8783	.123960	98.5915	.126360	108.1381	.128760
38	92.4429	.121320	101.6577	.123720	111.7790	.126120	122.8959	.128640
39	104.2938	.121200	114.9639	.123600	126.7128	.126000	139.6492	.128520
40	117.6477	.121080	129.9949	.123480	143.6240	.125880	158.6679	.128400

"Cy" TABLE "Cy"

Sinking fund factors and income analysis factors for equity yield rates "Y" from 3% to 30% for terms from 1 to 40 years. Income adjustment factor is represented by symbol "J." It is used as follows to find changes in both income and property value during any selected projection term which would result in a selected yield to equity.

$$\frac{r - R}{RJ + 1/s_{\overline{n|}}} = \text{dep. or app.}$$

If quotient is negative, it will indicate the decline in both income and property value for the yield on which "r" is based. If it is positive, it will indicate the increase in both income and property value. See text for demonstration.

To compute overall cap. rate for any given change in income and value, i.e., (depreciation or appreciation) with any equity yield.

$$\frac{r + \text{dep. } 1/s_{\overline{n|}}}{1 - \text{dep. } J} = R$$

$$\frac{r - \text{app. } 1/s_{\overline{n|}}}{1 + \text{app. } J} = R$$

Auxiliary Factors for Computing & Analyzing Capitalization Rates

SINKING FUND & INCOME ADJUSTMENT FACTORS

Equity Yield

Projection Years	3%		4%		5%		6%	
	$1/s_{\overline{n}\rvert}$	J	$1/s_{\overline{n}\rvert}$	J	$1/s_{\overline{n}\rvert}$	J	$1/s_{\overline{n}\rvert}$	J
1	1.000000	.9999	1.000000	1.0000	.999999	1.0000	1.000000	.9999
2	.492610	.7425	.490196	.7400	.487804	.7376	.485436	.7352
3	.323530	.6534	.320348	.6490	.317208	.6447	.314109	.6404
4	.239027	.6063	.235490	.6002	.232011	.5941	.228591	.5881
5	.188354	.5761	.184627	.5683	.180974	.5605	.177396	.5528
6	.154597	.5544	.150761	.5448	.147017	.5354	.143362	.5260
7	.130506	.5374	.126609	.5262	.122819	.5152	.119135	.5042
8	.112456	.5234	.108527	.5106	.104721	.4980	.101035	.4854
9	.098433	.5115	.094492	.4971	.090690	.4828	.087022	.4687
10	.087230	.5010	.083290	.4849	.079504	.4691	.075867	.4535
11	.078077	.4915	.074149	.4738	.070388	.4565	.066792	.4394
12	.070462	.4827	.066552	.4635	.062825	.4446	.059277	.4261
13	.064029	.4746	.060143	.4538	.056455	.4334	.052960	.4135
14	.058526	.4669	.054668	.4446	.051023	.4228	.047584	.4014
15	.053766	.4597	.049941	.4358	.046342	.4125	.042962	.3898
16	.049610	.4527	.045819	.4274	.042269	.4026	.038952	.3786
17	.045952	.4460	.042198	.4192	.038699	.3930	.035444	.3677
18	.042708	.4395	.038993	.4112	.035546	.3837	.032356	.3572
19	.039813	.4332	.036138	.4035	.032745	.3747	.029620	.3469
20	.037215	.4271	.033581	.3959	.030242	.3658	.027184	.3369
21	.034871	.4211	.031280	.3885	.027996	.3571	.025004	.3271
22	.032747	.4152	.029198	.3813	.025970	.3487	.023045	.3176
23	.030813	.4095	.027309	.3742	.024136	.3404	.021278	.3083
24	.029047	.4038	.025586	.3672	.022470	.3322	.019679	.2992
25	.027427	.3983	.024011	.3603	.020952	.3242	.018226	.2903
26	.025938	.3928	.022567	.3536	.019564	.3164	.016904	.2816
27	.024564	.3874	.021238	.3469	.018291	.3087	.015697	.2730
28	.023293	.3821	.020012	.3404	.017122	.3011	.014592	.2647
29	.022114	.3769	.018879	.3339	.016045	.2937	.013579	.2566
30	.021019	.3717	.017830	.3275	.015051	.2864	.012648	.2486
31	.019998	.3666	.016855	.3213	.014132	.2792	.011792	.2408
32	.019046	.3615	.015948	.3151	.013280	.2722	.011002	.2332
33	.018156	.3565	.015103	.3090	.012490	.2653	.010272	.2258
34	.017321	.3516	.014314	3030	.011755	.2585	.009598	.2185
35	.016539	.3467	.013577	.2970	.011071	.2518	.008973	.2114
36	.015803	.3418	.012886	.2912	.010434	.2453	.008394	.2045
37	.015111	.3370	.012239	.2854	.009839	.2389	.007857	.1978
38	.014459	.3323	.011631	.2797	.009284	.2326	.007358	.1912
39	.013843	.3275	.011060	.2741	.008764	.2264	.006893	.1848
40	.013262	.3229	.010523	.2685	.008278	.2203	.006461	.1786

Auxiliary Factors for Computing & Analyzing Capitalization Rates

SINKING FUND & INCOME ADJUSTMENT FACTORS

Equity Yield

Projection Years	7%		8%		9%		10%	
	$1/s_{\overline{n}\rceil}$	J	$1/s_{\overline{n}\rceil}$	J	$1/s_{\overline{n}\rceil}$	J	$1/s_{\overline{n}\rceil}$	J
1	.999999	.9999	1.000000	1.0000	1.000000	1.0000	1.000000	1.0000
2	.483091	.7328	.480769	.7303	.478468	.7280	.476190	.7256
3	.311051	.6361	.308033	.6318	.305054	.6276	.302114	.6233
4	.225228	.5820	.221920	.5761	.218668	.5701	.215470	.5642
5	.173890	.5451	.170456	.5375	.167092	.5299	.163797	.5224
6	.139795	.5167	.136315	.5075	.132919	.4984	.129607	.4894
7	.115553	.4933	.112072	.4826	.108690	.4719	.105405	.4615
8	.097467	.4730	.094014	.4608	.090674	.4487	.087444	.4368
9	.083486	.4548	.080079	.4411	.076798	.4276	.073640	.4144
10	.072377	.4381	.069029	.4230	.065820	.4082	.062745	.3936
11	.063356	.4226	.060076	.4061	.056946	.3900	.053963	.3742
12	.055901	.4079	.052695	.3901	.049650	.3728	.046763	.3559
13	.049650	.3939	.046521	.3749	.043566	.3564	.040778	.3385
14	.044344	.3806	.041296	.3603	.038433	.3408	.035746	.3218
15	.039794	.3677	.036829	.3464	.034058	.3257	.031473	.3059
16	.035857	.3553	.032976	.3329	.030299	.3113	.027816	.2907
17	.032425	.3433	.029629	.3198	.027046	.2974	.024664	.2760
18	.029412	.3317	.026702	.3072	.024212	.2840	.021930	.2620
19	.026753	.3203	.024127	.2950	.021730	.2711	.019546	.2485
20	.024392	.3093	.021852	.2832	.019546	.2586	.017459	.2355
21	.022289	.2986	.019832	.2718	.017616	.2466	.015624	.2231
22	.020405	.2882	.018032	.2607	.015904	.2350	.014005	.2112
23	.018713	.2781	.016422	.2499	.014381	.2238	.012571	.1997
24	.017189	.2682	.014977	.2395	.013022	.2130	.011299	.1888
25	.015810	.2586	.013678	.2294	.011806	.2026	.010168	.1783
26	.014561	.2493	.012507	.2196	.010715	.1927	.009159	.1683
27	.013425	.2402	.011448	.2102	.009734	.1831	.008257	.1587
28	.012391	.2313	.010488	.2010	.008852	.1738	.007451	.1496
29	.011448	.2227	.009618	.1922	.008055	.1650	.006728	.1409
30	.010586	.2143	.008827	.1837	.007336	.1565	.006079	.1326
31	.009796	.2062	.008107	.1754	.006685	.1483	.005496	.1247
32	.009072	.1983	.007450	.1674	.006096	.1405	.004971	.1172
33	.008408	.1906	.006851	.1598	.005561	.1330	.004499	.1101
34	.007796	.1832	.006304	.1524	.005076	.1259	.004073	.1034
35	.007233	.1760	.005803	.1453	.004635	.1191	.003689	.0970
36	.006715	.1690	.005344	.1384	.004235	.1125	.003343	.0909
37	.006236	.1622	.004924	.1318	.003870	.1063	.003029	.0852
38	.005795	.1556	.004538	.1255	.003538	.1004	.002746	.0797
39	.005386	.1492	.004185	.1194	.003235	.0947	.002490	.0746
40	.005009	.1431	.003860	.1136	.002959	.0893	.002259	.0698

Auxiliary Factors for Computing & Analyzing
Capitalization Rates

SINKING FUND & INCOME ADJUSTMENT FACTORS

Equity Yield

Projection Years	11%		12%		13%		14%	
	$1/s_{\overline{n}\vert}$	J	$1/s_{\overline{n}\vert}$	J	$1/s_{\overline{n}\vert}$	J	$1/s_{\overline{n}\vert}$	J
1	1.000000	.9999	1.000000	1.0000	1.000000	.9999	1.000000	1.0000
2	.473933	.7232	.471698	.7208	.469483	.7185	.467289	.7162
3	.299213	.6192	.296348	.6150	.293521	.6109	.290731	.6067
4	.212326	.5584	.209234	.5526	.206194	.5468	.203204	.5411
5	.160570	.5150	.157409	.5077	.154314	.5004	.151283	.4932
6	.126376	.4805	.123225	.4717	.120153	.4629	.117157	.4543
7	.102215	.4511	.099117	.4409	.096110	.4308	.093192	.4209
8	.084321	.4251	.081302	.4135	.078386	.4022	.075570	.3911
9	.070601	.4014	.067678	.3886	.064868	.3761	.062168	.3639
10	.059801	.3794	.056984	.3655	.054289	.3520	.051713	.3387
11	.051121	.3589	.048415	.3439	.045841	.3294	.043394	.3153
12	.044027	.3395	.041436	.3236	.038986	.3082	.036669	.2933
13	.038150	.3211	.035677	.3043	.033350	.2882	.031163	.2727
14	.033228	.3036	.030871	.2861	.028667	.2693	.026609	.2532
15	.029065	.2869	.026824	.2687	.024741	.2514	.022808	.2349
16	.025516	.2710	.023390	.2522	.021426	.2345	.019615	.2177
17	.022471	.2557	.020456	.2365	.018608	.2184	.016915	.2014
18	.019842	.2412	.017937	.2216	.016200	.2033	.014621	.1862
19	.017562	.2273	.015763	.2074	.014134	.1890	.012663	.1719
20	.015575	.2140	.013878	.1940	.012353	.1755	.010986	.1584
21	.013837	.2013	.012240	.1812	.010814	.1628	.009544	.1459
22	.012313	.1892	.010810	.1691	.009479	.1508	.008303	.1341
23	.010971	.1777	.009559	.1577	.008319	.1395	.007230	.1232
24	.009787	.1668	.008463	.1469	.007308	.1290	.006302	.1130
25	.008740	.1564	.007499	.1367	.006425	.1191	.005498	.1035
26	.007812	.1465	.006651	.1271	.005654	.1099	.004800	.0947
27	.006989	.1371	.005904	.1180	.004979	.1012	.004192	.0866
28	.006257	.1282	.005243	.1095	.004386	.0932	.003664	.0791
29	.005605	.1198	.004660	.1015	.003867	.0857	.003204	.0721
30	.005024	.1119	.004143	.0940	.003410	.0787	.002802	.0657
31	.004506	.1044	.003686	.0870	.003009	.0722	.002452	.0598
32	.004043	.0973	.003280	.0805	.002655	.0662	.002146	.0544
33	.003629	.0907	.002920	.0743	.002344	.0607	.001879	.0494
34	.003259	.0844	.002600	.0686	.002070	.0555	.001646	.0448
35	.002927	.0785	.002316	.0633	.001829	.0508	.001441	.0406
36	.002630	.0730	.002064	.0583	.001616	.0464	.001263	.0368
37	.002364	.0678	.001839	.0537	.001428	.0424	.001106	.0333
38	.002125	.0630	.001639	.0494	.001262	.0387	.000969	.0301
39	.001911	.0584	.001461	.0455	.001115	.0353	.000850	.0272
40	.001718	.0541	.001303	.0418	.000986	.0321	.000745	.0246

Auxiliary Factors for Computing & Analyzing Capitalization Rates

SINKING FUND & INCOME ADJUSTMENT FACTORS

TABLE Cy

Equity Yield

Projection Years	15%		16%		17%		18%	
	$1/s_{\overline{n}\rvert}$	J	$1/s_{\overline{n}\rvert}$	J	$1/s_{\overline{n}\rvert}$	J	$1/s_{\overline{n}\rvert}$	J
1	.999999	.9999	1.000000	.9999	1.000000	1.0000	.999999	.9999
2	.465116	.7138	.462962	.7115	.460829	.7092	.458715	.7070
3	.287976	.6026	.285257	.5986	.282573	.5946	.279923	.5905
4	.200265	.5354	.197375	.5298	.194533	.5242	.191738	.5187
5	.148315	.4860	.145409	.4789	.142563	.4719	.139777	.4650
6	.114236	.4458	.111389	.4374	.108614	.4291	.105910	.4209
7	.090360	.4111	.087612	.4015	.084947	.3920	.082361	.3827
8	.072850	.3801	.070224	.3694	.067689	.3589	.065244	.3486
9	.059574	.3519	.057082	.3402	.054690	.3288	.052394	.3177
10	.049252	.3258	.046901	.3133	.044656	.3011	.042514	.2893
11	.041068	.3016	.038860	.2884	.036764	.2756	.034776	.2632
12	.034480	.2790	.032414	.2651	.030465	.2518	.028627	.2391
13	.029110	.2578	.027184	.2435	.025378	.2298	.023686	.2168
14	.024688	.2379	.022897	.2233	.021230	.2094	.019678	.1962
15	.021017	.2193	.019357	.2045	.017822	.1905	.016402	.1773
16	.017947	.2018	.016413	.1869	.015004	.1729	.013710	.1599
17	.015366	.1855	.013952	.170[illegible]	.012661	.1567	.011485	.1439
18	.013186	.1703	.011884	.1555	010705	.1418	.009639	.1292
19	.011336	.1560	.010141	.1415	.009067	.1281	.008102	.1158
20	.009761	.1428	.008667	.1285	.007690	.1155	.006819	.1036
21	.008416	.1305	.007416	.1166	.006530	.1039	.005746	.0926
22	.007265	.1191	.006352	.1056	.005550	.0934	.004846	.0825
23	.006278	.1085	.005446	.0954	.004721	.0838	.004090	.0734
24	.005429	.0988	.004673	.0862	.004019	.0750	.003454	.0653
25	.004699	.0898	.004012	.0777	.003423	.0671	.002918	.0579
26	.004069	.0815	.003447	.0700	.002917	.0599	.002467	.0513
27	.003526	.0739	.002962	.0629	.002487	.0535	.002086	.0454
28	.003057	.0669	.002547	.0565	.002121	.0476	.001765	.0401
29	.002651	.0605	.002191	.0507	.001809	.0423	.001493	.0353
30	.002300	.0547	.001885	.0454	.001544	.0376	.001264	.0311
31	.001996	.0493	.001622	.0406	.001318	.0334	.001070	.0274
32	.001732	.0445	.001397	.0363	.001125	.0296	.000906	.0241
33	.001504	.0401	.001202	.0324	.000961	.0262	.000767	.0211
34	.001306	.0360	.001035	.0289	.000820	.0232	.000649	.0185
35	.001134	.0324	.000892	.0258	.000701	.0205	.000550	.0162
36	.000985	.0291	.000768	.0229	.000598	.0181	.000466	.0142
37	.000856	.0261	.000662	.0204	.000511	.0159	.000394	.0124
38	.000744	.0234	.000570	.0181	.000437	.0140	.000334	.0108
39	.000646	.0210	.000491	.0161	.000373	.0123	.000283	.0094
40	.000562	.0188	.000423	.0143	.000319	.0109	.000240	.0082

Auxiliary Factors for Computing & Analyzing Capitalization Rates

SINKING FUND & INCOME ADJUSTMENT FACTORS

Equity Yield

Projection Years	19%		20%		21%		22%	
	$1/s_{\overline{n}\rceil}$	J	$1/s_{\overline{n}\rceil}$	J	$1/s_{\overline{n}\rceil}$	J	$1/s_{\overline{n}\rceil}$	J
1	1.000000	1.0000	1.000000	.9999	1.000000	1.0000	1.000000	1.0000
2	.456621	.7047	.454545	.7024	.452488	.7002	.450450	.6979
3	.277307	.5866	.274725	.5826	.272175	.5787	.269658	.5748
4	.188990	.5132	.186289	.5077	.183632	.5023	.181020	.4970
5	.137050	.4582	.134379	.4514	.131765	.4447	.129205	.4381
6	.103274	.4129	.100705	.4049	.098202	.3971	.095764	.3894
7	.079854	.3736	.077423	.3646	.075067	.3558	.072782	.3471
8	.062885	.3386	.060609	.3287	.058414	.3191	.056298	.3097
9	.050192	.3068	.048079	.2963	.046053	.2860	.044111	.2760
10	.040471	.2779	.038522	.2668	.036665	.2560	.034894	.2456
11	.032890	.2513	.031103	.2398	.029410	.2287	.027807	.2181
12	.026896	.2268	.025264	.2151	.023729	.2039	.022284	.1932
13	.022102	.2044	.020620	.1925	.019233	.1813	.017938	.1706
14	.018234	.1838	.016893	.1720	.015647	.1608	.014490	.1503
15	.015091	.1649	.013882	.1532	.012766	.1423	.011738	.1321
16	.012523	.1476	.011436	.1362	.010440	.1256	.009529	.1157
17	.010414	.1319	.009440	.1208	.008554	.1106	.007750	.1011
18	.008675	.1176	.007805	.1069	.007020	.0971	.006312	.0881
19	.007237	.1046	.006462	.0944	.005768	.0851	.005147	.0766
20	.006045	.0929	.005356	.0832	.004744	.0744	.004201	.0665
21	.005054	.0823	.004443	.0731	.003905	.0649	.003432	.0576
22	.004229	.0728	.003689	.0642	.003217	.0565	.002805	.0497
23	.003541	.0643	.003065	.0562	.002652	.0491	.002294	.0428
24	.002967	.0567	.002547	.0491	.002187	.0426	.001877	.0369
25	.002487	.0499	.002118	.0429	.001804	.0369	.001536	.0316
26	.002085	.0438	.001762	.0374	.001488	.0318	.001257	.0271
27	.001749	.0384	.001466	.0325	.001228	.0275	.001029	.0232
28	.001468	.0336	.001220	.0282	.001014	.0237	.000843	.0198
29	.001232	.0294	.001016	.0245	.000837	.0204	.000690	.0169
30	.001034	.0257	.000846	.0212	.000691	.0175	.000565	.0144
31	.000868	.0224	.000704	.0183	.000571	.0150	.000463	.0122
32	.000729	.0195	.000586	.0158	.000472	.0128	.000379	.0104
33	.000612	.0170	.000488	.0137	.000390	.0110	.000311	.0088
34	.000514	.0148	.000407	.0118	.000322	.0094	.000255	.0075
35	.000432	.0128	.000339	.0101	.000266	.0080	.000209	.0063
36	.000362	.0111	.000282	.0087	.000219	.0068	.000171	.0053
37	.000304	.0096	.000235	.0075	.000181	.0058	.000140	.0045
38	.000256	.0083	.000196	.0064	.000150	.0049	.000115	.0038
39	.000215	.0072	.000163	.0055	.000124	.0042	.000094	.0032
40	.000180	.0062	.000136	.0047	.000102	.0036	.000077	.0027

Auxiliary Factors for Computing & Analyzing Capitalization Rates

SINKING FUND & INCOME ADJUSTMENT FACTORS

Equity Yield

Projection Years	23%		24%		25%		26%	
	$1/s_{\overline{n}\vert}$	J	$1/s_{\overline{n}\vert}$	J	$1/s_{\overline{n}\vert}$	J	$1/s_{\overline{n}\vert}$	J
1	.999999	.9999	1.000000	1.0000	1.000000	1.0000	.999999	.9999
2	.448430	.6957	.446428	.6935	.444444	.6913	.442477	.6891
3	.267172	.5709	.264718	.5671	.262295	.5632	.259902	.5594
4	.178451	.4917	.175925	.4865	.173441	.4813	.170999	.4761
5	.126700	.4316	.124247	.4251	.121846	.4187	.119496	.4124
6	.093388	.3818	.091074	.3743	.088819	.3669	.086623	.3597
7	.070567	.3387	.068421	.3304	.066341	.3222	.064326	.3142
8	.054259	.3005	.052293	.2916	.050398	.2828	.048572	.2743
9	.042249	.2664	.040465	.2569	.038756	.2478	.037118	.2389
10	.033208	.2356	.031602	.2259	.030072	.2166	.028616	.2075
11	.026288	.2079	.024852	.1981	.023492	.1887	.022207	.1797
12	.020925	.1829	.019648	.1732	.018447	.1639	.017319	.1550
13	.016728	.1605	.015598	.1509	.014543	.1418	.013559	.1333
14	.013417	.1404	.012422	.1311	.011500	.1224	.010646	.1142
15	.010791	.1225	.009919	.1136	.009116	.1052	.008378	.0975
16	.008696	.1065	.007935	.0981	.007240	.0902	.006606	.0829
17	.007021	.0924	.006359	.0844	.005759	.0771	.005215	.0703
18	.005675	.0800	.005102	.0725	.004586	.0657	.004122	.0595
19	.004593	.0690	.004097	.0621	.003655	.0558	.003260	.0501
20	.003720	.0594	.003293	.0530	.002915	.0473	.002581	.0422
21	.003015	.0510	.002649	.0452	.002327	.0400	.002044	.0354
22	.002445	.0437	.002131	.0384	.001858	.0337	.001620	.0296
23	.001984	.0374	.001716	.0326	.001484	.0284	.001284	.0247
24	.001610	.0319	.001382	.0276	.001186	.0238	.001018	.0206
25	.001307	.0271	.001113	.0233	.000948	.0199	.000807	.0171
26	.001062	.0231	.000897	.0196	.000757	.0167	.000640	.0142
27	.000862	.0196	.000722	.0165	.000605	.0139	.000507	.0117
28	.000700	.0166	.000582	.0139	.000484	.0116	.000402	.0097
29	.000569	.0140	.000469	.0116	.000387	.0097	.000319	.0080
30	.000462	.0119	.000378	.0097	.000309	.0080	.000253	.0066
31	.000376	.0100	.000305	.0082	.000247	.0066	.000201	.0054
32	.000305	.0084	.000246	.0068	.000198	.0055	.000159	.0045
33	.000248	.0071	.000198	.0057	.000158	.0046	.000126	.0036
34	.000201	.0059	.000160	.0047	.000126	.0038	.000100	.0030
35	.000164	.0050	.000129	.0039	.000101	.0031	.000079	.0024
36	.000133	.0042	.000104	.0033	.000081	.0025	.000063	.0020
37	.000108	.0035	.000083	.0027	.000064	.0021	.000050	.0016
38	.000088	.0029	.000067	.0022	.000051	.0017	.000039	.0013
39	.000071	.0024	.000054	.0019	.000041	.0014	.000031	.0011
40	.000058	.0020	.000043	.0015	.000033	.0011	.000025	.0009

Auxiliary Factors for Computing & Analyzing
Capitalization Rates

SINKING FUND & INCOME ADJUSTMENT FACTORS

Equity Yield

Projection Years	27%		28%		29%		30%	
	$1/s_{\overline{n}\rceil}$	J	$1/s_{\overline{n}\rceil}$	J	$1/s_{\overline{n}\rceil}$	J	$1/s_{\overline{n}\rceil}$	J
1	999999	.9999	1.000000	1.0000	.999999	.9999	.999999	.9999
2	.440528	.6869	.438596	.6848	.436681	.6826	.434782	.6805
3	.257539	.5557	.255206	.5519	.252902	.5482	.250626	.5445
4	.168597	.4710	.166235	.4660	.163913	.4610	.161629	.4560
5	.117195	.4062	.114943	.4001	.112739	.3940	.110581	.3881
6	.084483	.3526	.082400	.3456	.080370	.3387	.078394	.3319
7	.062373	.3064	.060481	.2988	.058648	.2913	.056873	.2840
8	.046813	.2660	.045119	.2579	.043487	.2501	.041915	.2424
9	.035550	.2304	.034049	.2221	.032611	.2140	.031235	.2062
10	.027230	.1989	.025911	.1905	.024657	.1825	.023463	.1747
11	.020991	.1711	.019841	.1628	.018755	.1549	.017728	.1474
12	.016259	.1466	.015264	.1386	.014330	.1310	.013454	.1238
13	.012641	.1252	.011785	.1175	.010987	.1103	.010243	.1035
14	.009855	.1065	.009123	.0993	.008445	.0925	.007817	.0862
15	.007700	.0902	.007076	.0835	.006504	.0773	.005977	.0715
16	.006026	.0762	.005498	.0700	.005016	.0643	.004577	.0590
17	.004723	.0642	.004277	.0585	.003873	.0533	.003508	.0486
18	.003705	.0538	.003330	.0487	.002993	.0441	.002691	.0399
19	.002909	.0450	.002595	.0404	.002315	.0363	.002066	.0326
20	.002285	.0376	.002023	.0335	.001791	.0298	.001586	.0266
21	.001796	.0313	.001578	.0276	.001387	.0244	.001219	.0216
22	.001412	.0260	.001231	.0228	.001074	.0200	.000936	.0175
23	.001110	.0215	.000961	.0187	.000831	.0163	.000720	.0142
24	.000873	.0178	.000750	.0153	.000644	.0132	.000553	.0114
25	.000687	.0146	.000585	.0125	.000499	.0107	.000425	.0092
26	.000541	.0120	.000457	.0102	.000386	.0087	.000327	.0074
27	.000425	.0099	.000357	.0083	.000299	.0070	.000251	.0059
28	.000335	.0081	.000279	.0068	.000232	.0057	.000193	.0047
29	.000263	.0066	.000217	.0055	.000180	.0046	.000148	.0038
30	.000207	.0054	.000170	.0045	.000139	.0037	.000114	.0030
31	.000163	.0044	.000133	.0036	.000108	.0029	.000088	.0024
32	.000128	.0036	.000103	.0029	.000083	.0023	.000067	.0019
33	.000101	.0029	.000081	.0023	.000065	.0019	.000052	.0015
34	.000079	.0024	.000063	.0019	.000050	.0015	.000040	.0012
35	.000062	.0019	.000049	.0015	.000039	.0012	.000030	.0009
36	.000049	.0015	.000038	.0012	.000030	.0009	.000023	.0007
37	.000038	.0012	.000030	.0010	.000023	.0007	.000018	.0006
38	.000030	.0010	.000023	.0008	.000018	.0006	.000014	.0004
39	.000024	.0008	.000018	.0006	.000014	.0005	.000010	.0003
40	.000019	.0006	.000014	.0005	.000010	.0003	.000008	.0003

BASIC CAPITALIZATION RATE TABLES WITH 75% MORTGAGE FINANCING

Computed by use of Table C coefficients.

75% Table computed as, $r = Y - .75C$

Except where positive coefficients are involved.

To Find Desired Rate "r":

1. Find amortization term at top of table.
2. Find pages on which mortgage interest rate appears.
3. Find desired income projection term bracket.
4. Read across on Equity Yield line to basic capitalization Rate in mortgage interest rate column.

Applicable sinking fund factor for depreciation or appreciation adjustment is on equity yield line in column at far right.

Each table is supplemented by tabulated analyses of selected Overall Capitalization Rates showing rounded percentage of depreciation and appreciation applicable to various equity yields. Minus sign indicates depreciation. Plus sign indicates appreciation.

CAPITALIZATION RATES

Assuming 75% of Purchase Price Financed by Mortgage.

10 YEARS AMORTIZATION: 3¼% TO 4½%

Interest Rate		3¼%	3½%	3¾%	4%	4¼%	4½%	$\frac{1}{s_{\overline{n}\rceil}}$
Annual Requirement(f)		.11736	.11868	.12012	.12156	.12300	.12444	
Coverage Min. Rate		.08802	.08901	.09009	.09117	.09225	.09333	
Projection	Balance(b)	.539955	.543483	.546411	.549388	.552417	.555497	+ Dep
	Equity Yield	Basic Rate before Depreciation or Appreciation						− App
5 Years n=5	5% .05	.0381	.0396	.0411	.0424	.0440	.0455	.1810
	6% .06	.0419	.0433	.0448	.0463	.0477	.0492	.1774
	7% .07	.0456	.0470	.0485	.0499	.0514	.0529	.1739
	8% .08	.0493	.0507	.0521	.0536	.0550	.0565	.1705
	9% .09	.0529	.0543	.0558	.0572	.0587	.0602	.1671
	10% .10	.0565	.0579	.0594	.0609	.0623	.0638	.1638
	11% .11	.0601	.0616	.0630	.0644	.0659	.0673	.1606
	12% .12	.0638	.0651	.0665	.0680	.0695	.0709	.1574
	13% .13	.0673	.0687	.0701	.0716	.0730	.0744	.1543
	14% .14	.0709	.0722	.0736	.0751	.0765	.0779	.1513
	15% .15	.0744	.0758	.0772	.0786	.0800	.0814	.1483
	16% .16	.0779	.0792	.0807	.0821	.0835	.0849	.1454
	17% .17	.0814	.0827	.0841	.0856	.0869	.0883	.1426
	18% .18	.0848	.0862	.0876	.0890	.0904	.0917	.1398
	19% .19	.0883	.0897	.0910	.0924	.0938	.0952	.1371
	20% .20	.0917	.0931	.0944	.0958	.0972	.0985	.1344
	Balance(b)		none	none	none	none	none	+ Dep
	Equity Yield	Basic Rate before Depreciation or Appreciation						− App
10 Years n = 10	5% .05	.0409	.0419	.0430	.0441	.0451	.0463	.0795
	6% .06	.0461	.0471	.0482	.0493	.0504	.0515	.0759
	7% .07	.0513	.0522	.0534	.0544	.0555	.0566	.0724
	8% .08	.0563	.0573	.0583	.0595	.0605	.0616	.0690
	9% .09	.0612	.0622	.0632	.0644	.0654	.0665	.0658
	10% .10	.0660	.0670	.0681	.0691	.0702	.0713	.0628
	11% .11	.0707	.0717	.0727	.0739	.0749	.0760	.0598
	12% .12	.0753	.0763	.0774	.0785	.0795	.0806	.0570
	13% .13	.0798	.0808	.0819	.0830	.0840	.0852	.0543
	14% .14	.0843	.0853	.0863	.0874	.0885	.0896	.0517
	15% .15	.0886	.0896	.0907	.0917	.0929	.0939	.0493
	16% .16	.0929	0939	.0950	.0960	.0971	.0982	.0469
	17% .17	.0971	.0981	.0991	.1003	.1013	.1024	.0447
	18% .18	.1012	.1022	.1033	.1043	.1054	.1064	.0425
	19% .19	.1052	.1062	.1073	.1083	.1095	.1105	.0405
	20% .20	.1092	.1102	.1112	.1123	.1134	.1145	.0385

CAPITALIZATION RATES

Assuming 75% of Purchase Price Financed by Mortgage.

10 YEARS AMORTIZATION: 4¾% TO 6%

Interest Rate / Annual Requirement (f) / Coverage Min. Rate		4¾% .12588 .09441	5% .12732 .09549	5¼% .12876 .09657	5½% .13032 .09774	5¾% .13176 .09882	6% .13332 .09999	$\frac{1}{s_{\overline{n}\rvert}}$
Projection	Balance(b)	.558629	.561814	.565053	.567658	.571003	.573705	+ Dep − App
	Equity Yield	Basic Rate Before Depreciation or Appreciation						
	5% .05	.0470	.0485	.0500	.0516	.0531	.0547	.1810
	6% .06	.0507	.0522	.0537	.0552	.0568	.0583	.1774
	7% .07	.0544	.0559	.0574	.0589	.0604	.0619	.1739
	8% .08	.0581	.0596	.0610	.0626	.0641	.0656	.1705
	9% .09	.0617	.0631	.0646	.0661	.0676	.0691	.1671
5 Years n=5	10% .10	.0652	.0667	.0682	.0697	.0712	.0727	.1638
	11% .11	.0688	.0703	.0717	.0732	.0747	.0762	.1606
	12% .12	.0723	.0738	.0753	.0768	.0783	.0797	.1574
	13% .13	.0759	.0773	.0788	.0802	.0817	.0832	.1543
	14% .14	.0794	.0809	.0823	.0837	.0852	.0867	.1513
	15% .15	.0828	.0843	.0858	.0872	.0887	.0901	.1483
	16% .16	.0863	.0877	.0892	.0907	.0921	.0936	.1454
	17% .17	.0898	.0912	.0926	.0941	.0955	.0970	.1426
	18% .18	.0932	.0946	.0960	.0975	.0989	.1004	.1398
	19% .19	.0966	.0980	.0994	.1009	.1023	.1037	.1371
	20% .20	.1000	.1014	.1028	.1043	.1057	.1071	.1344
	Balance(b)		none	none	none	none	none	+ Dep − App
	Equity Yield	Basic Rate Before Depreciation or Appreciation						
	5% .05	.0473	.0484	.0495	.0506	.0518	.0530	.0795
	6% .06	.0525	.0537	.0547	.0559	.0569	.0582	.0759
	7% .07	.0577	.0588	.0598	.0610	.0621	.0633	.0724
	8% .08	.0627	.0638	.0649	.0660	.0671	.0683	.0690
	9% .09	.0676	.0687	.0698	.0709	.0720	.0732	.0658
10 Years n= 10	10% .10	.0724	.0735	.0745	.0757	.0768	.0780	.0628
	11% .11	.0771	.0782	.0793	.0804	.0815	.0827	.0598
	12% .12	.0817	.0828	.0839	.0851	.0861	.0873	.0570
	13% .13	.0862	.0873	.0884	.0896	.0907	.0919	.0543
	14% .14	.0907	.0917	.0929	.0940	.0951	.0962	.0517
	15% .15	.0951	.0961	.0972	.0984	.0994	.1006	.0493
	16% .16	.0993	.1004	.1015	.1027	.1037	.1049	.0469
	17% .17	.1035	.1046	.1057	.1068	.1079	.1091	.0447
	18% .18	.1076	.1087	.1098	.1110	.1120	.1132	.0425
	19% .19	.1117	.1127	.1138	.1150	.1160	.1172	.0405
	20% .20	.1156	.1166	.1178	.1189	.1200	.1211	.0385

CAPITALIZATION RATES

Assuming 75% of Purchase Price Financed by Mortgage

10 YEARS AMORTIZATION: 6¼ TO 7½%

Interest Rate / Annual Requirement (f) / Coverage Min. Rate			6¼%	6½%	6¾%	7%	7¼%	7½%	$\frac{1}{s_{\overline{n}\rceil}}$
Annual Requirement (f)			.134760	.136320	.137880	.139440	.141000	.142560	
Coverage Min. Rate			.101070	.102240	.103410	.104580	.105750	.106920	
Projection	Balance (b)		.577157	.579961	.582813	.585715	.588668	.591672	+ Dep – App
	Equity	Yield	Basic Rate before Depreciation or Appreciation						
5 Years n = 5	6 %	.06	.059811	.061354	.062904	.064460	.066023	.067593	.177396
	7 %	.07	.063423	.064959	.066501	.068049	.069604	.071166	.173890
	8 %	.08	.067012	.068541	.070075	.071616	.073164	.074718	.170456
	9 %	.09	.070579	.072100	.073628	.075162	.076702	.078248	.167092
	10 %	.10	.074124	.075639	.077159	.078685	.080218	.081757	.163797
	11 %	.11	.077648	.079155	.080669	.082188	.083714	.085246	.160570
	12 %	.12	.081150	.082651	.084158	.085670	.087189	.088713	.157409
	13 %	.13	.084631	.086126	.087626	.089132	.090644	.092161	.154314
	14 %	.14	.088093	.089581	.091074	.092574	.094079	.095590	.151283
	15 %	.15	.091534	.093016	.094503	.095996	.097494	.098998	.148315
	16 %	.16	.094956	.096431	.097912	.099399	.100891	.102389	.145409
	17 %	.17	.098358	.099828	.101303	.102783	.104269	.105760	.142563
	18 %	.18	.101742	.103205	.104674	.106149	.107628	.109113	.139777
	19 %	.19	.105107	.106565	.108028	.109496	.110970	.112448	.137050
	20 %	.20	.108453	.109906	.111363	.112826	.114294	.115766	.134379
	21 %	.21	.111783	.113230	.114681	.116138	.117600	.119067	.131765
	22 %	.22	.115094	.116536	.117982	.119434	.120890	.122351	.129205
	23 %	.23	.118389	.119825	.121266	.122712	.124163	.125618	.126700
	24 %	.24	.121667	.123098	.124534	.125974	.127419	.128869	.124247
	25 %	.25	.124928	.126354	.127785	.129220	.130660	.132104	.121846
	26 %	.26	.128173	.129595	.131020	.132450	.133885	.135324	.119496
	27 %	.27	.131403	.132819	.134240	.135665	.137095	.138529	.117195
	28 %	.28	.134617	.136029	.137445	.138865	.140290	.141718	.114943
	29 %	.29	.137816	.139223	.140635	.142050	.143470	.144894	.112739
	30 %	.30	.141001	.142403	.143810	.145220	.146635	.148054	.110581
	Balance (b)		none	none	none	none	none	none	+ Dep – App
	Equity	Yield	Basic Rate before Depreciation or Appreciation						
10 Years n = 10	6 %	.06	.059150	.060289	.061435	.062588	.063750	.064919	.075867
	7 %	.07	.064268	.065409	.066556	.067710	.068872	.070041	.072377
	8 %	.08	.069280	.070422	.071570	.072725	.073887	.075057	.069029
	9 %	.09	.074188	.075331	.076480	.077636	.078799	.079968	.065820
	10 %	.10	.078995	.080139	.081289	.082446	.083609	.084778	.062745
	11 %	.11	.083704	.084849	.086000	.087157	.088321	.089490	.059801
	12 %	.12	.088317	.089464	.090616	.091774	.092937	.094107	.056984
	13 %	.13	.092839	.093987	.095140	.096298	.097462	.098631	.054289
	14 %	.14	.097272	.098420	.099574	.100733	.101897	.103067	.051713
	15 %	.15	.101618	.102768	.103923	.105082	.106246	.107416	.049252
	16 %	.16	.105882	.107033	.108188	.109348	.110513	.111682	.046901
	17 %	.17	.110066	.111218	.112374	.113534	.114699	.115869	.044656
	18 %	.18	.114173	.115326	.116482	.117643	.118808	.119978	.042514
	19 %	.19	.118206	.119359	.120517	.121678	.122843	.124013	.040471
	20 %	.20	.122168	.123322	.124480	.125642	.126807	.127977	.038522
	21 %	.21	.126061	.127216	.128375	.129537	.130703	.131873	.036665
	22 %	.22	.129890	.131045	.132204	.133367	.134533	.135703	.034894
	23 %	.23	.133655	.134811	.135971	.137134	.138300	.139470	.033208
	24 %	.24	.137360	.138517	.139677	.140840	.142007	.143176	.031602
	25 %	.25	.141008	.142165	.143326	.144489	.145656	.146826	.030072
	26 %	.26	.144600	.145758	.146919	.148083	.149250	.150420	.028616
	27 %	.27	.148140	.149299	.150460	.151624	.152791	.153961	.027230
	28 %	.28	.151629	.152789	.153951	.155115	.156282	.157452	.025911
	29 %	.29	.155071	.156231	.157393	.158557	.159725	.160894	.024657
	30 %	.30	.158466	.159627	.160789	.161954	.163121	.164291	.023463

CAPITALIZATION RATES

Assuming 75% of Purchase Price Financed by Mortgage

10 YEARS AMORTIZATION: 7¼ TO 9%

			7¼%	8%	8¼%	8½%	8¾%	9%	$\frac{1}{s_{\overline{n}\vert}}$
Interest Rate			7¼%	8%	8¼%	8½%	8¾%	9%	
Annual Requirement (f)			.144120	.145680	.147240	.148800	.150480	.152040	
Coverage Min. Rate			.108090	.109260	.110430	.111600	.112860	.114030	
Projection	Balance (b)		.594728	.597836	.600998	.604214	.606735	.610057	Dep
	Equity	Yield	Basic Rate before Depreciation or Appreciation						– App
	6 %	.06	.069169	.070753	.072343	.073941	.075537	.077149	.177396
	7 %	.07	.072735	.074310	.075893	.077482	.079071	.080674	.173890
	8 %	.08	.076279	.077846	.079420	.081001	.082584	.084178	.170456
	9 %	.09	.079801	.081361	.082927	.084500	.086076	.087662	.167092
	10 %	.10	.083303	.084854	.086413	.087978	.089548	.091126	.163797
	11 %	.11	.086784	.088328	.089879	.091436	.093000	.094570	.160570
	12 %	.12	.090244	.091781	.093324	.094874	.096432	.097994	.157409
	13 %	.13	.093685	.095215	.096751	.098293	.099845	.101399	.154314
	14 %	.14	.097106	.098629	.100158	.101693	.103239	.104786	.151283
	15 %	.15	.100508	.102024	.103546	.105074	.106614	.108154	.148315
	16 %	.16	.103892	.105401	.106916	.108436	.109971	.111503	.145409
	17 %	.17	.107257	.108759	.110267	.111781	.113311	.114836	.142563
5 Years	18 %	.18	.110603	.112099	.113601	.115108	.116632	.118150	.139777
n = 5	19 %	.19	.113933	.115422	.116917	.118418	.119937	.121448	.137050
	20 %	.20	.117244	.118728	.120216	.121710	.123224	.124729	.134379
	21 %	.21	.120539	.122016	.123499	.124986	.126496	.127994	.131765
	22 %	.22	.123817	.125288	.126764	.128246	.129750	.131242	.129205
	23 %	.23	.127078	.128544	.130014	.131490	.132989	.134475	.126700
	24 %	.24	.130324	.131784	.133248	.134718	.136213	.137692	.124247
	25 %	.25	.133554	.135008	.136467	.137931	.139421	.140895	.121846
	26 %	.26	.136768	.138217	.139670	.141128	.142614	.144082	.119496
	27 %	.27	.139967	.141411	.142859	.144311	.145793	.147255	.117195
	28 %	.28	.143152	.144590	.146032	.147480	.148957	.150413	.114943
	29 %	.29	.146322	.147755	.149192	.150634	.152107	.153558	.112739
	30 %	.30	.149478	.150906	.152338	.153775	.155244	.156689	.110581
	Balance (b)		none	none	none	none	none	none	+ Dep
	Equity	Yield	Basic Rate before Depreciation or Appreciation						– App
	6 %	.06	.066097	.067283	.068479	.069683	.070879	.072102	.075867
	7 %	.07	.071219	.072404	.073599	.074802	.076001	.077221	.072377
	8 %	.08	.076234	.077419	.078612	.079813	.081015	.082233	.069029
	9 %	.09	.081145	.082329	.083521	.084721	.085925	.087141	.065820
	10 %	.10	.085955	.087138	.088329	.089528	.090735	.091948	.062745
	11 %	.11	.090666	.091849	.093039	.094236	.095446	.096657	.059801
	12 %	.12	.095282	.096465	.097654	.098850	.100062	.101271	.056984
	13 %	.13	.099807	.100988	.102177	.103371	.104585	.105793	.054289
	14 %	.14	.104242	.105423	.106610	.107804	.109020	.110226	.051713
	15 %	.15	.108591	.109772	.110958	.112151	.113369	.114573	.049252
10 Years	16 %	.16	.112857	.114037	.115223	.116414	.117635	.118837	.046901
n = 10	17 %	.17	.117043	.118223	.119408	.120598	.121820	.123021	.044656
	18 %	.18	.121152	.122331	.123515	.124705	.125929	.127129	.042514
	19 %	.19	.125187	.126366	.127549	.128738	.129964	.131162	.040471
	20 %	.20	.129151	.130329	.131512	.132700	.133927	.135124	.038522
	21 %	.21	.133046	.134224	.135406	.136593	.137822	.139018	.036665
	22 %	.22	.136876	.138054	.139235	.140421	.141652	.142846	.034894
	23 %	.23	.140643	.141820	.143001	.144186	.145418	.146611	.033208
	24 %	.24	.144350	.145527	.146707	.147892	.149125	.150317	.031602
	25 %	.25	.147999	.149175	.150355	.151539	.152774	.153965	.030072
	26 %	.26	.151593	.152769	.153948	.155131	.156367	.157557	.028616
	27 %	.27	.155134	.156310	.157489	.158671	.159908	.161097	.027230
	28 %	.28	.158624	.159800	.160979	.162160	.163399	.164587	.025911
	29 %	.29	.162067	.163242	.164420	.165602	.166841	.168028	.024657
	30 %	.30	.165464	.166639	.167816	.168997	.170237	.171424	.023463

CAPITALIZATION RATES

Assuming 75% of Purchase Price Financed by Mortgage

10 YEARS AMORTIZATION: 9¼% TO 10½%

			9¼%	9½%	9¾%	10%	10¼%	10½%	$\frac{1}{s_{\overline{n}\rceil}}$
Interest Rate			9¼%	9½%	9¾%	10%	10¼%	10½%	
Annual Requirement (f)			.153720	.155280	.156960	.158640	.160320	.162000	
Coverage Min. Rate			.115290	.116460	.117720	.118980	.120240	.121500	
Projection	Balance (b)		.612675	.616105	.618823	.621590	.624406	.627272	+ Dep − App
	Equity	Yield	Basic Rate before Depreciation or Appreciation						
	6 %	.06	.078757	.080383	.082005	.083633	.085268	.086909	.177396
	7 %	.07	.082275	.083893	.085507	.087128	.088755	.090389	.173890
	8 %	.08	.085773	.087382	.088989	.090603	.092223	.093849	.170456
	9 %	.09	.089250	.090850	.092451	.094058	.095670	.097290	.167092
	10 %	.10	.092707	.094299	.095893	.097493	.099099	.100711	.163797
	11 %	.11	.096145	.097728	.099315	.100909	.102508	.104113	.160570
	12 %	.12	.099563	.101138	.102719	.104306	.105898	.107496	.157409
	13 %	.13	.102962	.104529	.106104	.107684	.109270	.110862	.154314
	14 %	.14	.106343	.107902	.109470	.111044	.112624	.114209	.151283
	15 %	.15	.109705	.111256	.112819	.114387	.115960	.117539	.148315
	16 %	.16	.113049	.114593	.116150	.117711	.119278	.120851	.145409
5 Years	17 %	.17	.116376	.117912	.119463	.121019	.122580	.124146	.142563
n = 5	18 %	.18	.119685	.121215	.122760	.124310	.125865	.127425	.139777
	19 %	.19	.122977	.124500	.126039	.127584	.129133	.130688	.137050
	20 %	.20	.126253	.127769	.129303	.130842	.132385	.133934	.134379
	21 %	.21	.129513	.131022	.132550	.134084	.135622	.137165	.131765
	22 %	.22	.132756	.134258	.135782	.137310	.138843	.140381	.129205
	23 %	.23	.135984	.137480	.138998	.140521	.142049	.143581	.126700
	24 %	.24	.139196	.140686	.142199	.143717	.145240	.146767	.124247
	25 %	.25	.142394	.143877	.145386	.146899	.148416	.149938	.121846
	26 %	.26	.145577	.147054	.148558	.150066	.151578	.153095	.119496
	27 %	.27	.148745	.150216	.151715	.153219	.154726	.156238	.117195
	28 %	.28	.151899	.153365	.154859	.156358	.157860	.159367	.114943
	29 %	.29	.155039	.156499	.157989	.159483	.160981	.162484	.112739
	30 %	.30	.158166	.159621	.161106	.162596	.164089	.165587	.110581
	Balance (b)		none	none	none	none	none	none	+ Dep − App
	Equity	Yield	Basic Rate before Depreciation or Appreciation						
	6 %	.06	.073313	.074556	.075784	.077021	.078266	.079521	.075867
	7 %	.07	.078435	.079674	.080904	.082142	.083388	.084642	.072377
	8 %	.08	.083449	.084685	.085916	.087155	.088402	.089656	.069029
	9 %	.09	.088359	.089592	.090825	.092065	.093312	.094567	.065820
	10 %	.10	.093168	.094398	.095632	.096873	.098121	.099376	.062745
	11 %	.11	.097879	.099106	.100341	.101583	.102832	.104087	.059801
	12 %	.12	.102495	.103719	.104956	.106198	.107447	.108703	.056984
	13 %	.13	.107019	.108240	.109478	.110721	.111971	.113227	.054289
	14 %	.14	.111453	.112672	.113911	.115155	.116405	.117661	.051713
	15 %	.15	.115802	.117019	.118258	.119503	.120754	.122010	.049252
	16 %	.16	.120067	.121282	.122523	.123768	.125019	.126275	.046901
10 Years	17 %	.17	.124253	.125465	.126707	.127953	.129205	.130461	.044656
n = 10	18 %	.18	.128361	.129572	.130814	.132061	.133313	.134570	.042514
	19 %	.19	.132396	.133605	.134848	.136095	.137348	.138604	.040471
	20 %	.20	.136359	.137566	.138810	.140058	.141311	.142568	.038522
	21 %	.21	.140254	.141459	.142704	.143953	.145206	.146463	.036665
	22 %	.22	.144084	.145287	.146533	.147782	.149035	.150292	.034894
	23 %	.23	.147850	.149052	.150298	.151548	.152802	.154059	.033208
	24 %	.24	.151557	.152757	.154004	.155254	.156508	.157765	.031602
	25 %	.25	.155205	.156404	.157652	.158902	.160156	.161414	.030072
	26 %	.26	.158799	.159996	.161244	.162496	.163750	.165008	.028616
	27 %	.27	.162340	.163536	.164784	.166036	.167291	.168549	.027230
	28 %	.28	.165830	.167025	.168274	.169526	.170781	.172039	.025911
	29 %	.29	.169272	.170466	.171716	.172968	.174223	.175481	.024657
	30 %	.30	.172669	.173861	.175111	.176364	.177620	.178878	.023463

CAPITALIZATION RATES

Assuming 75% of Purchase Price Financed by Mortgage

10 YEARS AMORTIZATION: 10¾% TO 12%

Projection	Equity	Yield	10¾%	11%	11¼%	11½%	11¾%	12%	$\frac{1}{s_{\overline{n}\rceil}}$
Interest Rate			10¾%	11%	11¼%	11½%	11¾%	12%	
Annual Requirement (f)			.163680	.165360	.167040	.168720	.170520	.172200	
Coverage Min. Rate			.122760	.124020	.125280	.126540	.127890	.129150	
Projection	Balance (b)		.630189	.633156	.636176	.639248	.641562	.644736	+ Dep − App
	Equity	Yield	Basic Rate before Depreciation or Appreciation						
	6 %	.06	.088557	.090212	.091874	.093542	.095200	.096883	.177396
	7 %	.07	.092029	.093677	.095330	.096991	.098643	.100317	.173890
	8 %	.08	.095482	.097121	.098767	.100420	.102066	.103732	.170456
	9 %	.09	.098915	.100547	.102185	.103830	.105470	.107128	.167092
	10 %	.10	.102329	.103953	.105584	.107222	.108856	.110506	.163797
	11 %	.11	.105724	.107341	.108965	.110595	.112224	.113866	.160570
	12 %	.12	.109101	.110711	.112327	.113950	.115573	.117208	.157409
	13 %	.13	.112459	.114063	.115672	.117288	.118905	.120533	.154314
	14 %	.14	.115800	.117396	.118999	.120608	.122220	.123840	.151283
	15 %	.15	.119123	.120713	.122309	.123911	.125518	.127131	.148315
5 Years n = 5	16 %	.16	.122429	.124013	.125602	.127197	.128799	.130406	.145409
	17 %	.17	.125718	.127296	.128878	.130467	.132064	.133664	.142563
	18 %	.18	.128991	.130562	.132139	.133721	.135313	.136906	.139777
	19 %	.19	.132248	.133813	.135383	.136959	.138547	.140133	.137050
	20 %	.20	.135488	.137047	.138612	.140181	.141764	.143344	.134379
	21 %	.21	.138713	.140267	.141825	.143389	.144967	.146541	.131765
	22 %	.22	.141923	.143471	.145023	.146581	.148155	.149723	.129205
	23 %	.23	.145118	.146660	.148207	.149759	.151329	.152891	.126700
	24 %	.24	.148298	.149835	.151376	.152923	.154488	.156044	.124247
	25 %	.25	.151464	.152995	.154531	.156072	.157634	.159184	.121846
	26 %	.26	.154616	.156142	.157673	.159208	.160766	.162310	.119496
	27 %	.27	.157754	.159275	.160801	.162331	.163884	.165423	.117195
	28 %	.28	.160879	.162395	.163915	.165440	.166989	.168523	.114943
	29 %	.29	.163990	.165501	.167017	.168536	.170082	.171610	.112739
	30 %	.30	.167089	.168595	.170105	.171620	.173162	.174685	.110581
	Balance (b)		none	none	none	none	none	none	+ Dep − App
	Equity	Yield	Basic Rate before Depreciation or Appreciation						
	6 %	.06	.080784	.082057	.083340	.084633	.085898	.087211	.075867
	7 %	.07	.085905	.087177	.088459	.089751	.091020	.092330	.072377
	8 %	.08	.090919	.092191	.093472	.094762	.096035	.097343	.069029
	9 %	.09	.095830	.097101	.098381	.099669	.100945	.102251	.065820
	10 %	.10	.100639	.101909	.103188	.104476	.105755	.107059	.062745
	11 %	.11	.105350	.106620	.107898	.109184	.110467	.111768	.059801
	12 %	.12	.109965	.111235	.112512	.113797	.115083	.116383	.056984
	13 %	.13	.114489	.115758	.117034	.118318	.119607	.120905	.054289
	14 %	.14	.118923	.120192	.121468	.122750	.124042	.125338	.051713
	15 %	.15	.123272	.124540	.125815	.127097	.128391	.129686	.049252
10 Years n = 10	16 %	.16	.127538	.128806	.130080	.131360	.132657	.133950	.046901
	17 %	.17	.131723	.132991	.134264	.135544	.136843	.138135	.044656
	18 %	.18	.135832	.137099	.138372	.139650	.140953	.142242	.042514
	19 %	.19	.139866	.141133	.142405	.143683	.144987	.146276	.040471
	20 %	.20	.143830	.145096	.146368	.147644	.148951	.150238	.038522
	21 %	.21	.147725	.148991	.150262	.151538	.152847	.154132	.036665
	22 %	.22	.151554	.152820	.154090	.155366	.156676	.157961	.034894
	23 %	.23	.155320	.156586	.157856	.159131	.160443	.161727	.033208
	24 %	.24	.159027	.160292	.161562	.162835	.164150	.165432	.031602
	25 %	.25	.162675	.163941	.165210	.166483	.167799	.169080	.030072
	26 %	.26	.166269	.167534	.168802	.170075	.171393	.172673	.028616
	27 %	.27	.169810	.171074	.172343	.173615	.174934	.176213	.027230
	28 %	.28	.173300	.174565	.175832	.177104	.178425	.179703	.025911
	29 %	.29	.176742	.178007	.179274	.180545	.181867	.183144	.024657
	30 %	.30	.180139	.181403	.182670	.183940	.185264	.186540	.023463

CAPITALIZATION RATES

Assuming 75% of Purchase Price Financed by Mortgage.

15 YEARS AMORTIZATION: 3¼% TO 4½%

Interest Rate / Annual Requirement (f) / Coverage Min. Rate		3¼% .08436 .06327	3½% .08580 .06435	3¾% .08736 .06552	4% .08880 .06660	4¼% .09036 .06777	4½ .09180 .06885	$\frac{1}{s_{\overline{n}\rceil}}$
Projection	Balance (b)	.718855	.722860	.726265	.730385	.733896	.738133	+ Dep − App
	Equity Yield	Basic Rate before Depreciation or Appreciation						
	5% .05	.0377	.0393	.0409	.0425	.0442	.0458	.1810
	6% .06	.0409	.0426	.0441	.0458	.0474	.0491	.1774
	7% .07	.0442	.0457	.0474	.0490	.0506	.0523	.1739
	8% .08	.0474	.0490	.0506	.0522	.0538	.0554	.1705
	9% .09	.0506	.0522	.0537	.0554	.0570	.0586	.1671
5 Years n = 5	10% .10	.0538	.0553	.0569	.0586	.0601	.0617	.1638
	11% .11	.0569	.0585	.0601	.0617	.0633	.0649	.1606
	12% .12	.0601	.0617	.0633	.0648	.0664	.0680	.1574
	13% .13	.0633	.0649	.0664	.0679	.0695	.0711	.1543
	14% .14	.0665	.0680	.0695	.0710	.0726	.0742	.1513
	15% .15	.0696	.0711	.0726	.0741	.0757	.0773	.1483
	16% .16	.0727	.0742	.0757	.0772	.0788	.0804	.1454
	17% .17	.0758	.0773	.0788	.0803	.0819	.0834	.1426
	18% .18	.0789	.0804	.0819	.0834	.0849	.0864	.1398
	19% .19	.0820	.0835	.0850	.0865	.0880	.0895	.1371
	20% .20	.0850	.0865	.0880	.0895	.0910	.0926	.1344
	Balance (b)	.388175	.392803	.396174	.401184	.404911	.410328	+ Dep − App
	Equity Yield	Basic Rate before Depreciation or Appreciation						
	5% .05	.0393	.0407	.0421	.0434	.0449	.0462	.0795
	6% .06	.0435	.0449	.0462	.0476	.0489	.0504	.0759
	7% .07	.0476	.0490	.0503	.0517	.0530	.0544	.0724
	8% .08	.0517	.0530	.0543	.0557	.0570	.0584	.0690
	9% .09	.0556	.0570	.0582	.0596	.0609	.0623	.0658
10 Years n = 10	10% .10	.0595	.0608	.0622	.0635	.0648	.0661	.0628
	11% .11	.0634	.0647	.0660	.0673	.0686	.0700	.0598
	12% .12	.0672	.0684	.0698	.0711	.0724	.0737	.0570
	13% .13	.0709	.0722	.0735	.0748	.0761	.0774	.0543
	14% .14	.0746	.0758	.0772	.0785	.0797	.0810	.0517
	15% .15	.0783	.0795	.0807	.0820	.0834	.0846	.0493
	16% .16	.0818	.0831	.0844	.0856	.0869	.0882	.0469
	17% .17	.0854	.0866	.0878	.0891	.0904	.0917	.0447
	18% .18	.0888	.0900	.0913	.0926	.0939	.0951	.0425
	19% .19	.0922	.0935	.0948	.0960	.0973	.0985	.0405
	20% .20	.0956	.0968	.0981	.0994	.1007	.1019	.0385

CAPITALIZATION RATES

Assuming 75% of Purchase Price Financed by Mortgage.

15 YEARS AMORTIZATION: 3¼% TO 4½%

Interest Rate Annual Requirement (f) Coverage Min. Rate		3¼% .08436 .06327	3½% .08580 .06435	3¾% .08736 .06552	4% .08880 .06660	4¼% .09036 .06777	4½% .09180 .06885	$\frac{1}{s_{\overline{n}|}}$
Projection	Balance (b)	none	none	none	none	none	none	+ Dep − App
	Equity Yield	Basic Rate before Depreciation or Appreciation						
15 Years n = 15	5% .05	.0410	.0422	.0433	.0444	.0455	.0467	.0464
	6% .06	.0461	.0472	.0483	.0495	.0506	.0517	.0430
	7% .07	.0510	.0520	.0532	.0543	.0555	.0565	.0398
	8% .08	.0557	.0568	.0580	.0590	.0602	.0613	.0368
	9% .09	.0603	.0614	.0624	.0636	.0648	.0659	.0341
	10% .10	.0647	.0658	.0670	.0681	.0692	.0703	.0315
	11% .11	.0690	.0701	.0713	.0724	.0735	.0746	.0291
	12% .12	.0732	.0743	.0755	.0765	.0777	.0788	.0268
	13% .13	.0772	.0784	.0795	.0806	.0817	.0829	.0248
	14% .14	.0812	.0823	.0835	.0845	.0857	.0868	.0228
	15% .15	.0851	.0861	.0873	.0884	.0896	.0906	.0210
	16% .16	.0888	.0899	.0910	.0922	.0933	.0944	.0194
	17% .17	.0925	.0935	.0947	.0958	.0970	.0980	.0178
	18% .18	.0960	.0971	.0983	.0993	.1005	.1016	.0164
	19% .19	.0995	.1006	.1018	.1028	.1040	.1051	.0151
	20% .20	.1029	.1040	.1052	.1063	.1074	.1085	.0139

CAPITALIZATION RATES

Assuming 75% of Purchase Price Financed by Mortgage.

15 YEARS AMORTIZATION: 4¾% TO 6%

		4¾%	5%	5¼%	5½%	5¾%	6%	$\frac{1}{s_{\overline{n}|}}$
Interest Rate		4¾%	5%	5¼%	5½%	5¾%	6%	
Annual Requirement (f)		.09336	.09492	.09648	.09816	.09972	.10128	
Coverage Min. Rate		.07002	.07119	.07236	.07362	.07479	.07596	
Projection	Balance (b)	.741755	.745431	.749161	.752259	.756097	.759991	+ Dep – App
	Equity Yield	Basic Rate before Depreciation or Appreciation						
5 Years n= 5	5% .05	.0475	.0491	.0509	.0525	.0542	.0560	.1810
	6% .06	.0507	.0523	.0540	.0557	.0573	.0591	.1774
	7% .07	.0538	.0555	.0571	.0589	.0605	.0622	.1739
	8% .08	.0571	.0587	.0603	.0620	.0636	.0653	.1705
	9% .09	.0602	.0618	.0634	.0651	.0667	.0684	.1671
	10% .10	.0633	.0649	.0666	.0682	.0698	.0715	.1638
	11% .11	.0665	.0680	.0697	.0713	.0729	.0746	.1606
	12% .12	.0696	.0711	.0728	.0744	.0760	.0777	.1574
	13% .13	.0727	.0742	.0759	.0775	.0791	.0807	.1543
	14% .14	.0758	.0773	.0789	.0806	.0821	.0838	.1513
	15% .15	.0788	.0804	.0820	.0836	.0852	.0868	.1483
	16% .16	.0819	.0835	.0850	.0867	.0883	.0898	.1454
	17% .17	.0850	.0866	.0881	.0897	.0913	.0929	.1426
	18% .18	.0880	.0896	.0911	.0927	.0943	.0959	.1398
	19% .19	.0910	.0926	.0941	.0957	.0973	.0988	.1371
	20% .20	.0941	.0956	.0971	.0987	.1003	.1019	.1344
	Balance (b)	.414432	.418726	.423213	.426304	.431174	.436255	+ Dep – App
	Equity Yield	Basic Rate before Depreciation or Appreciation						
10 Years n = 10	5% .05	.0476	.0491	.0505	.0520	.0534	.0549	.0795
	6% .06	.0517	.0531	.0546	.0560	.0575	.0589	.0759
	7% .07	.0558	.0571	.0586	.0600	.0614	.0629	.0724
	8% .08	.0597	.0611	.0626	.0639	.0653	.0668	.0690
	9% .09	.0636	.0651	.0664	.0678	.0693	.0707	.0658
	10% .10	.0675	.0688	.0703	.0717	.0730	.0745	.0628
	11% .11	.0713	.0726	.0740	.0754	.0768	.0782	.0598
	12% .12	.0750	.0764	.0777	.0792	.0805	.0819	.0570
	13% .13	.0787	.0801	.0814	.0828	.0842	.0856	.0543
	14% .14	.0824	.0837	.0851	.0864	.0878	.0892	.0517
	15% .15	.0859	.0873	.0886	.0900	.0913	.0927	.0493
	16% .16	.0895	.0908	.0922	.0935	.0949	.0962	.0469
	17% .17	.0930	.0943	.0956	.0970	.0983	.0996	.0447
	18% .18	.0964	.0977	.0990	.1004	.1017	.1031	.0425
	19% .19	.0998	.1011	.1024	.1038	.1051	.1064	.0405
	20% .20	.1031	.1045	.1058	.1071	.1084	.1097	.0385

CAPITALIZATION RATES

Assuming 75% of Purchase Price Financed by Mortgage.

15 YEARS AMORTIZATION: 4¾% TO 6%

Interest Rate Annual Requirement (f) Coverage Min. Rate		4¾% .09336 .07002	5% .09492 .07119	5¼% .09648 .07236	5½% .09816 .07362	5¾% .09972 .07479	6% .10128 .07596	$\frac{1}{s_{\overline{n}|}}$
Projection	Balance (b)	none	none	none	none	none	none	+ Dep − App
	Equity Yield	Basic Rate before Depreciation or Appreciation						
	5% .05	.0478	.0490	.0501	.0514	.0526	.0537	.0464
	6% .06	.0528	.0540	.0552	.0564	.0576	.0588	.0430
	7% .07	.0577	.0589	.0601	.0613	.0625	.0637	.0398
	8% .08	.0625	.0636	.0648	.0661	.0672	.0684	.0368
	9% .09	.0670	.0682	.0694	.0706	.0718	.0730	.0341
15 Years	10% .10	.0715	.0727	.0738	.0751	.0763	.0774	.0315
n = 15	11% .11	.0758	.0770	.0781	.0794	.0806	.0817	.0291
	12% .12	.0800	.0811	.0823	.0836	.0847	.0859	.0268
	13% .13	.0840	.0852	.0864	.0876	.0888	.0900	.0248
	14% .14	.0880	.0891	.0903	.0916	.0927	.0939	.0228
	15% .15	.0918	.0930	.0942	.0954	.0966	.0978	.0210
	16% .16	.0955	.0967	.0979	.0991	.1003	.1015	.0194
	17% .17	.0992	.1004	.1016	.1028	.1040	.1052	.0178
	18% .18	.1028	.1040	.1051	.1064	.1076	.1087	.0164
	19% .19	.1063	.1075	.1086	.1099	.1111	.1122	.0151
	20% .20	.1097	.1109	.1120	.1133	.1145	.1156	.0139

CAPITALIZATION RATES

Assuming 75% of Purchase Price Financed by Mortgage

15 YEARS AMORTIZATION: 6½% TO 7½%

Interest Rate			6¼%	6½%	6¾%	7%	7¼%	7½%	$\frac{1}{s_{\overline{n}\|}}$
Annual Requirement (f)			.102960	.104640	.106200	.107880	.109560	.111360	
Coverage Min. Rate			.077220	.078480	.079650	.080910	.082170	.083520	
Projection	Balance (b)		.763241	.766540	.770600	.774005	.777460	.780242	+ Dep – App
	Equity	Yield	Basic Rate before Depreciation or Appreciation						
	6 %	.06	.060719	.062418	.064129	.065841	.067561	.069281	.177396
	7 %	.07	.063842	.065532	.067232	.068936	.070646	.072359	.173890
	8 %	.08	.066952	.068633	.070323	.072018	.073720	.075425	.170456
	9 %	.09	.070049	.071722	.073401	.075088	.076781	.078480	.167092
	10 %	.10	.073134	.074799	.076468	.078146	.079831	.081523	.163797
	11 %	.11	.076207	.077864	.079523	.081193	.082870	.084555	.160570
	12 %	.12	.079268	.080918	.082567	.084229	.085897	.087576	.157409
	13 %	.13	.082318	.083960	.085600	.087254	.088914	.090586	.154314
	14 %	.14	.085356	.086991	.088621	.090268	.091920	.093585	.151283
	15 %	.15	.088383	.090010	.091632	.093271	.094915	.096574	.148315
	16 %	.16	.091399	.093019	.094632	.096263	.097900	.099553	.145409
5 Years	17 %	.17	.094405	.096017	.097621	.099245	.100875	.102522	.142563
n = 5	18 %	.18	.097399	.099005	.100601	.102218	.103840	.105482	.139777
	19 %	.19	.100384	.101983	.103570	.105180	.106795	.108431	.137050
	20 %	.20	.103358	.104950	.106530	.108133	.109741	.111371	.134379
	21 %	.21	.106322	.107908	.109479	.111076	.112677	.114302	.131765
	22 %	.22	.109277	.110856	.112420	.114010	.115604	.117224	.129205
	23 %	.23	.112221	.113795	.115351	.116934	.118523	.120137	.126700
	24 %	.24	.115157	.116724	.118273	.119850	.121432	.123041	.124247
	25 %	.25	.118083	.119645	.121186	.122757	.124333	.125937	.121846
	26 %	.26	.121001	.122556	.124090	.125655	.127225	.128824	.119496
	27 %	.27	.123909	.125459	.126986	.128545	.130109	.131704	.117195
	28 %	.28	.126809	.128353	.129873	.131427	.132985	.134575	.114943
	29 %	.29	.129700	.131239	.132753	.134301	.135853	.137438	.112739
	30 %	.30	.132584	.134117	.135624	.137166	.138713	.140294	.110581
	Balance (b)		.439892	.443708	.449415	.453628	.458038	.460871	+ Dep – App
	Equity	Yield	Basic Rate before Depreciation or Appreciation						
	6 %	.06	.060349	.061826	.063321	.064820	.066331	.067843	.075867
	7 %	.07	.064315	.065782	.067262	.068751	.070250	.071754	.072377
	8 %	.08	.068222	.069679	.071145	.072623	.074111	.075608	.069029
	9 %	.09	.072070	.073518	.074970	.076438	.077916	.079405	.065820
	10 %	.10	.075861	.077301	.078740	.080198	.081665	.083149	.062745
	11 %	.11	.079598	.081029	.082455	.083904	.085362	.086839	.059801
	12 %	.12	.083282	.084705	.086119	.087559	.089007	.090478	.056984
	13 %	.13	.086914	.088329	.089731	.091163	.092602	.094068	.054289
	14 %	.14	.090496	.091904	.093295	.094718	.096149	.097609	.051713
	15 %	.15	.094030	.095431	.096811	.098227	.099650	.101105	.049252
10 Years	16 %	.16	.097517	.098911	.100282	.101690	.103106	.104555	.046901
n = 10	17 %	.17	.100960	.102348	.103709	.105110	.106518	.107963	.044656
	18 %	.18	.104360	.105742	.107094	.108488	.109889	.111329	.042514
	19 %	.19	.107718	.109094	.110437	.111825	.113219	.114655	.040471
	20 %	.20	.111037	.112407	.113742	.115124	.116511	.117943	.038522
	21 %	.21	.114317	.115682	.117009	.118385	.119766	.121194	.036665
	22 %	.22	.117561	.118921	.120240	.121610	.122986	.124410	.034894
	23 %	.23	.120769	.122124	.123436	.124801	.126171	.127592	.033208
	24 %	.24	.123944	.125294	.126600	.127960	.129324	.130741	.031602
	25 %	.25	.127087	.128433	.129731	.131086	.132446	.133860	.030072
	26 %	.26	.130198	.131540	.132833	.134183	.135538	.136949	.028616
	27 %	.27	.133280	.134618	.135905	.137251	.138601	.140009	.027230
	28 %	.28	.136334	.137669	.138950	.140291	.141637	.143042	.025911
	29 %	.29	.139362	.140692	.141968	.143306	.144647	.146050	.024657
	30 %	.30	.142363	.143690	.144961	.146295	.147632	.149032	.023463

CAPITALIZATION RATES

Assuming 75% of Purchase Price Financed by Mortgage

15 YEARS AMORTIZATION: 7¾% TO 9%

									$\frac{1}{s_{\overline{n}\rvert}}$
Interest Rate			6¼%	6½%	6¾%	7%	7¼%	7½%	
Annual Requirement (f)			.102960	.104640	.106200	.107880	.109560	.111360	
Coverage Min. Rate			.077220	.078480	.079650	.080910	.082170	.083520	
Projection	Balance (b)		none	none	none	none	none	none	+ Dep
	Equity	Yield	Basic Rate before Depreciation or Appreciation						– App
	6 %	.06	.059942	.061170	.062418	.063670	.064933	.066192	.042962
	7 %	.07	.064822	.066053	.067295	.068547	.069810	.071076	.039794
	8 %	.08	.069550	.070782	.072020	.073272	.074535	.075807	.036829
	9 %	.09	.074132	.075366	.076598	.077851	.079114	.080392	.034058
	10 %	.10	.078574	.079810	.081038	.082291	.083554	.084837	.031473
	11 %	.11	.082883	.084122	.085344	.086599	.087861	.089149	.029065
	12 %	.12	.087067	.088307	.089526	.090780	.092042	.093336	.026824
	13 %	.13	.091131	.092373	.093588	.094843	.096105	.097402	.024741
	14 %	.14	.095083	.096326	.097538	.098793	.100055	.101357	.022808
	15 %	.15	.098930	.100174	.101382	.102638	.103900	.105205	.021017
15 Years	16 %	.16	.102676	.103922	.105127	.106383	.107645	.108954	.019357
n = 15	17 %	.17	.106330	.107577	.108779	.110036	.111297	.112609	.017822
	18 %	.18	.109896	.111144	.112344	.113601	.114862	.116177	.016402
	19 %	.19	.113381	.114630	.115827	.117084	.118346	.119664	.015091
	20 %	.20	.116790	.118040	.119235	.120492	.121753	.123074	.013882
	21 %	.21	.120128	.121379	.122572	.123829	.125090	.126413	.012766
	22 %	.22	.123401	.124652	.125843	.127101	.128362	.129687	.011738
	23 %	.23	.126612	.127864	.129054	.130312	.131573	.132900	.010791
	24 %	.24	.129767	.131020	.132208	.133466	.134727	.136056	.009919
	25 %	.25	.132870	.134123	.135310	.136568	.137829	.139159	.009116
	26 %	.26	.135925	.137178	.138364	.139622	.140882	.142215	.008378
	27 %	.27	.138934	.140188	.141372	.142631	.143892	.145225	.007700
	28 %	.28	.141903	.143157	.144340	.145599	.146859	.148194	.007076
	29 %	.29	.144833	.146088	.147270	.148529	.149789	.151125	.006504
	30 %	.30	.147728	.148984	.150165	.151424	.152684	.154022	.005977

CAPITALIZATION RATES

Assuming 75% of Purchase Price Financed by Mortgage

15 YEARS AMORTIZATION: 7¼% TO 9%

Interest Rate			7¼%	8%	8¼%	8½%	8¾%	9%	$\frac{1}{s_{\overline{n}\rvert}}$
Annual Requirement (f)			.113040	.114720	.116520	.118200	.120000	.121800	
Coverage Min. Rate			.084780	.086040	.087390	.088650	.090000	.091350	
Projection	Balance (b)		.783798	.787406	.790330	.794042	.797061	.800126	+ Dep − App
	Equity	Yield	Basic Rate before Depreciation or Appreciation						
	6 %	.06	.071014	.072755	.074493	.076247	.077999	.079757	.177396
	7 %	.07	.074083	.075814	.077545	.079289	.081033	.082782	.173890
	8 %	.08	.077140	.078861	.080585	.082319	.084055	.085797	.170456
	9 %	.09	.080185	.081897	.083614	.085339	.087067	.088801	.167092
	10 %	.10	.083220	.084923	.086632	.088348	.090069	.091795	.163797
	11 %	.11	.086243	.087937	.089639	.091347	.093060	.094779	.160570
	12 %	.12	.089255	.090941	.092636	.094335	.096041	.097753	.157409
	13 %	.13	.092257	.093935	.095623	.097313	.099012	.100717	.154314
	14 %	.14	.095249	.096918	.098600	.100281	.101974	.103671	.151283
	15 %	.15	.098230	.099891	.101567	.103239	.104925	.106616	.148315
5 Years n = 5	16 %	.16	.101201	.102855	.104524	.106188	.107868	.109552	.145409
	17 %	.17	.104163	.105808	.107471	.109128	.110801	.112478	.142563
	18 %	.18	.107114	.108753	.110409	.112058	.113725	.115396	.139777
	19 %	.19	.110057	.111688	.113338	.114980	.116640	.118305	.137050
	20 %	.20	.112990	.114613	.116258	.117892	.119546	.121205	.134379
	21 %	.21	.115914	.117530	.119169	.120796	.122444	.124097	.131765
	22 %	.22	.118829	.120438	.122072	.123691	.125334	.126981	.129205
	23 %	.23	.121735	.123338	.124966	.126578	.128215	.129856	.126700
	24 %	.24	.124633	.126229	.127851	.129457	.131088	.132724	.124247
	25 %	.25	.127522	.129112	.130729	.132328	.133954	.135584	.121846
	26 %	.26	.130403	.131986	.133598	.135191	.136812	.138436	.119496
	27 %	.27	.133276	.134853	.136460	.138046	.139662	.141281	.117195
	28 %	.28	.136141	.137712	.139314	.140894	.142505	.144119	.114943
	29 %	.29	.138999	.140564	.142161	.143735	.145340	.146949	.112739
	30 %	.30	.141849	.143408	.145000	.146568	.148169	.149773	.110581
	Balance (b)		.465666	.470676	.474051	.479483	.483241	.487187	+ Dep − App
	Equity	Yield	Basic Rate before Depreciation or Appreciation						
	6 %	.06	.069375	.070920	.072463	.074032	.075595	.077170	.075867
	7 %	.07	.073274	.074806	.076339	.077894	.079448	.081012	.072377
	8 %	.08	.077116	.078635	.080160	.081701	.083246	.084800	.069029
	9 %	.09	.080902	.082409	.083926	.085454	.086990	.088534	.065820
	10 %	.10	.084634	.086130	.087639	.089155	.090681	.092217	.062745
	11 %	.11	.088314	.089799	.091300	.092804	.094322	.095849	.059801
	12 %	.12	.091943	.093417	.094911	.096404	.097914	.099433	.056984
	13 %	.13	.095523	.096987	.098474	.099956	.101459	.102969	.054289
	14 %	.14	.099055	.100510	.101991	.103461	.104957	.106460	.051713
	15 %	.15	.102542	.103987	.105461	.106922	.108411	.109907	.049252
10 Years n = 10	16 %	.16	.105984	.107420	.108889	.110340	.111822	.113311	.046901
	17 %	.17	.109383	.110811	.112274	.113716	.115192	.116674	.044656
	18 %	.18	.112742	.114161	.115619	.117052	.118522	.119998	.042514
	19 %	.19	.116061	.117473	.118925	.120350	.121814	.123284	.040471
	20 %	.20	.119341	.120746	.122194	.123611	.125069	.126533	.038522
	21 %	.21	.122586	.123984	.125426	.126836	.128289	.129748	.036665
	22 %	.22	.125795	.127186	.128625	.130027	.131475	.132929	.034894
	23 %	.23	.128971	.130356	.131790	.133185	.134629	.136077	.033208
	24 %	.24	.132115	.133494	.134924	.136312	.137752	.139195	.031602
	25 %	.25	.135228	.136601	.138027	.139410	.140844	.142283	.030072
	26 %	.26	.138311	.139679	.141101	.142478	.143909	.145343	.028616
	27 %	.27	.141367	.142729	.144148	.145519	.146946	.148376	.027230
	28 %	.28	.144395	.145753	.147168	.148534	.149957	.151384	.025911
	29 %	.29	.147398	.148751	.150163	.151524	.152943	.154366	.024657
	30 %	.30	.150377	.151725	.153134	.154490	.155906	.157325	.023463

CAPITALIZATION RATES

Assuming 75% of Purchase Price Financed by Mortgage

15 YEARS AMORTIZATION: 7¾% TO 9%

Interest Rate Annual Requirement (f) Coverage Min. Rate			7¾% .113040 .084780	8% .114720 .086040	8¼% .116520 .087390	8½% .118200 .088650	8¾% .120000 .090000	9% .121800 .091350	$\frac{1}{s_{\overline{n}\rvert}}$
	Balance (b)		none	none	none	none	none	none	+ Dep
Projection	Equity	Yield	Basic Rate before Depreciation or Appreciation						– App
	6 %	.06	.067478	.068779	.070069	.071397	.072712	.074038	.042962
	7 %	.07	.072360	.073658	.074953	.076275	.077593	.078921	.039794
	8 %	.08	.077090	.078384	.079683	.081001	.082321	.083651	.036829
	9 %	.09	.081673	.082965	.084268	.085581	.086903	.088234	.034058
	10 %	.10	.086116	.087406	.088712	.090022	.091346	.092679	.031473
	11 %	.11	.090427	.091714	.093024	.094330	.095656	.096990	.029065
	12 %	.12	.094612	.095897	.097210	.098512	.099840	.101175	.026824
	13 %	.13	.098678	.099961	.101277	.102576	.103905	.105242	.024741
	14 %	.14	.102631	.103912	.105231	.106527	.107858	.109195	.022808
	15 %	.15	.106478	.107758	.109079	.110372	.111705	.113043	.021017
	16 %	.16	.110226	.111504	.112827	.114118	.115452	.116791	.019357
15 Years	17 %	.17	.113880	.115157	.116482	.117770	.119106	.120446	.017822
n = 15	18 %	.18	.117447	.118723	.120050	.121336	.122672	.124013	.016402
	19 %	.19	.120933	.122207	.123536	.124820	.126157	.127499	.015091
	20 %	.20	.124342	.125615	.126946	.128228	.129567	.130909	.013882
	21 %	.21	.127681	.128953	.130286	.131566	.132905	.134248	.012766
	22 %	.22	.130954	.132225	.133559	.134838	.136178	.137521	.011738
	23 %	.23	.134166	.135436	.136772	.138049	.139390	.140734	.010791
	24 %	.24	.137322	.138591	.139928	.141203	.142545	.143889	.009919
	25 %	.25	.140425	.141694	.143031	.144305	.145648	.146993	.009116
	26 %	.26	.143480	.144748	.146086	.147359	.148702	.150048	.008378
	27 %	.27	.146490	.147757	.149097	.150369	.151712	.153058	.007700
	28 %	.28	.149459	.150725	.152066	.153337	.154681	.156027	.007076
	29 %	.29	.152389	.153656	.154997	.156267	.157611	.158958	.006504
	30 %	.30	.155285	.156551	.157893	.159162	.160507	.161854	.005977

CAPITALIZATION RATES

Assuming 75% of Purchase Price Financed by Mortgage

15 YEARS AMORTIZATION: 9¼% TO 10½%

nterest Rate			9¼%	9½%	9¾%	10%	10½%	10½%	$\frac{1}{s_{\overline{n}\rceil}}$
ınnual Requirement (f)			.123600	.125400	.127200	.129000	.130800	.132720	
Coverage Min. Rate			.092700	.094050	.095400	.096750	.098100	.099540	
Projection	Balance (b)		.803237	.806396	.809604	.812860	.816165	.818736	+ Dep – App
	Equity	Yield	Basic Rate before Depreciation or Appreciation						
	6 %	.06	.081521	.083291	.085068	.086851	.088641	.090423	.177396
	7 %	.07	.084538	.086300	.088068	.089843	.091624	.093400	.173890
	8 %	.08	.087545	.089299	.091059	.092825	.094598	.096366	.170456
	9 %	.09	.090541	.092287	.094039	.095797	.097562	.099324	.167092
	10 %	.10	.093528	.095266	.097010	.098760	.100516	.102272	.163797
	11 %	.11	.096504	.098234	.099971	.101713	.103461	.105210	.160570
	12 %	.12	.099470	.101193	.102922	.104656	.106397	.108140	.157409
	13 %	.13	.102427	.104143	.105864	.107591	.109323	.111061	.154314
	14 %	.14	.105374	.107083	.108797	.110516	.112241	.113973	.151283
	15 %	.15	.108312	.110014	.111721	.113433	.115150	.116876	.148315
5 Years n = 5	16 %	.16	.111241	.112936	.114636	.116341	.118051	.119771	.145409
	17 %	.17	.114161	.115849	.117542	.119240	.120943	.122658	.142563
	18 %	.18	.117072	.118753	.120440	.122131	.123828	.125537	.139777
	19 %	.19	.119975	.121650	.123329	.125014	.126704	.128408	.137050
	20 %	.20	.122869	.124537	.126211	.127889	.129572	.131271	.134379
	21 %	.21	.125755	.127417	.129084	.130756	.132432	.134126	.131765
	22 %	.22	.128632	.130289	.131949	.133615	.135285	.136974	.129205
	23 %	.23	.131502	.133152	.134807	.136467	.138131	.139815	.126700
	24 %	.24	.134364	.136008	.137657	.139311	.140969	.142648	.124247
	25 %	.25	.137218	.138857	.140500	.142148	.143800	.145475	.121846
	26 %	.26	.140065	.141698	.143336	.144978	.146624	.148294	.119496
	27 %	.27	.142905	.144532	.146164	.147801	.149441	.151107	.117195
	28 %	.28	.145737	.147359	.148986	.150617	.152252	.153913	.114943
	29 %	.29	.148562	.150179	.151801	.153426	.155055	.156713	.112739
	30 %	.30	.151381	.152993	.154609	.156229	.157853	.159506	.110581
	Balance (b)		.491325	.495662	.500204	.504957	.509929	.513017	+ Dep – App
	Equity	Yield	Basic Rate before Depreciation or Appreciation						
	6 %	.06	.078755	.080352	.081961	.083581	.085214	.086830	.075867
	7 %	.07	.082587	.084172	.085769	.087377	.088997	.090605	.072377
	8 %	.08	.086364	.087939	.089524	.091120	.092728	.094327	.069029
	9 %	.09	.090089	.091653	.093227	.094812	.096407	.098000	.065820
	10 %	.10	.093762	.095316	.096880	.098453	.100037	.101623	.062745
	11 %	.11	.097385	.098929	.100483	.102046	.103619	.105198	.059801
	12 %	.12	.100960	.102495	.104039	.105592	.107155	.108727	.056984
	13 %	.13	.104488	.106014	.107549	.109093	.110645	.112211	.054289
	14 %	.14	.107970	.109489	.111015	.112549	.114092	.115652	.051713
10 Years n = 10	15 %	.15	.111410	.112920	.114438	.115963	.117497	.119051	.049252
	16 %	.16	.114806	.116309	.117819	.119336	.120861	.122410	.046901
	17 %	.17	.118163	.119658	.121160	.122669	.124186	.125729	.044656
	18 %	.18	.121480	.122968	.124463	.125965	.127473	.129012	.042514
	19 %	.19	.124759	.126241	.127729	.129223	.130724	.132258	.040471
	20 %	.20	.128003	.129478	.130959	.132447	.133940	.135470	.038522
	21 %	.21	.131211	.132681	.134156	.135636	.137123	.138648	.036665
	22 %	.22	.134387	.135850	.137319	.138794	.140274	.141795	.034894
	23 %	.23	.137530	.138988	.140451	.141920	.143394	.144911	.033208
	24 %	.24	.140643	.142096	.143554	.145016	.146484	.147997	.031602
	25 %	.25	.143727	.145174	.146627	.148084	.149546	.151056	.030072
	26 %	.26	.146782	.148225	.149673	.151125	.152581	.154088	.028616
	27 %	.27	.149811	.151249	.152692	.154139	.155591	.157094	.027230
	28 %	.28	.152814	.154248	.155687	.157129	.158576	.160076	.025911
	29 %	.29	.155793	.157223	.158657	.160095	.161537	.163034	.024657
	30 %	.30	.158748	.160174	.161604	.163038	.164475	.165970	.023463

CAPITALIZATION RATES

Assuming 75% of Purchase Price Financed by Mortgage

15 YEARS AMORTIZATION: 9¼% TO 10½%

Interest Rate			9¼%	9½%	9¾%	10%	10¼%	10½%	$\frac{1}{s_{\overline{n}\mid}}$
Annual Requirement (f)			.123600	.125400	.127200	.129000	.130800	.132720	
Coverage Min. Rate			.092700	.094050	.095400	.096750	.098100	.099540	
Projection	Balance (b)		none	none	none	none	none	none	+ Dep
	Equity	Yield	Basic Rate before Depreciation or Appreciation						– App
	6 %	.06	.075377	.076729	.078094	.079475	.080871	.082233	.042962
	7 %	.07	.080260	.081612	.082976	.084355	.085747	.087116	.039794
	8 %	.08	.084991	.086343	.087706	.089082	.090472	.091845	.036829
	9 %	.09	.089575	.090927	.092289	.093664	.095050	.096429	.034058
	10 %	.10	.094020	.095372	.096733	.098106	.099489	.100873	.031473
	11 %	.11	.098332	.099684	.101044	.102415	.103796	.105184	.029065
	12 %	.12	.102518	.103870	.105229	.106598	.107977	.109369	.026824
	13 %	.13	.106585	.107936	.109295	.110663	.112039	.113435	.024741
	14 %	.14	.110539	.111890	.113249	.114615	.115989	.117388	.022808
	15 %	.15	.114387	.115738	.117096	.118461	.119833	.121236	.021017
15 Years	16 %	.16	.118136	.119487	.120844	.122208	.123578	.124983	.019357
n = 15	17 %	.17	.121791	.123142	.124498	.125861	.127230	.128638	.017822
	18 %	.18	.125359	.126710	.128066	.129427	.130795	.132205	.016402
	19 %	.19	.128845	.130196	.131551	.132912	.134278	.135691	.015091
	20 %	.20	.132255	.133606	.134961	.136321	.137686	.139101	.013882
	21 %	.21	.135595	.136945	.138300	.139659	.141023	.142440	.012766
	22 %	.22	.138868	.140219	.141573	.142931	.144294	.145713	.011738
	23 %	.23	.142081	.143431	.144785	.146143	.147505	.148925	.010791
	24 %	.24	.145237	.146587	.147941	.149298	.150659	.152081	.009919
	25 %	.25	.148340	.149691	.151044	.152401	.153760	.155184	.009116
	26 %	.26	.151396	.152746	.154099	.155455	.156814	.158239	.008378
	27 %	.27	.154406	.155756	.157109	.158465	.159823	.161249	.007700
	28 %	.28	.157375	.158725	.160078	.161433	.162791	.164218	.007076
	29 %	.29	.160306	.161656	.163009	.164363	.165720	.167149	.006504
	30 %	.30	.163202	.164552	.165905	.167259	.168615	.170044	.005977

CAPITALIZATION RATES

Assuming 75% of Purchase Price Financed by Mortgage

15 YEARS AMORTIZATION: 10¾% TO 12%

Interest Rate	10¾%	11%	11¼%	11½%	11¾%	12%	$\frac{1}{s_{\overline{n}\rvert}}$
Annual Requirement (f)	.134520	.136440	.138360	.140280	.142200	.144120	
Coverage Min. Rate	.100890	.102330	.103770	.105210	.106650	.108090	

Projection: 5 Years, n = 5

Equity Yield	10¾%	11%	11¼%	11½%	11¾%	12%	+ Dep − App
Balance (b)	.822137	.824795	.827493	.830234	.833017	.835843	
Basic Rate before Depreciation or Appreciation							
6 % .06	.092225	.094019	.095818	.097623	.099433	.101249	.177396
7 % .07	.095193	.096980	.098772	.100569	.102372	.104181	.173890
8 % .08	.098151	.099931	.101716	.103506	.105302	.107103	.170456
9 % .09	.101100	.102873	.104651	.106435	.108223	.110018	.167092
10 % .10	.104039	.105806	.107577	.109354	.111136	.112923	.163797
11 % .11	.106970	.108730	.110495	.112265	.114040	.115821	.160570
12 % .12	.109892	.111645	.113404	.115167	.116936	.118710	.157409
13 % .13	.112804	.114552	.116304	.118062	.119824	.121591	.154314
14 % .14	.115709	.117450	.119196	.120947	.122703	.124464	.151283
15 % .15	.118605	.120340	.122080	.123825	.125575	.127329	.148315
16 % .16	.121492	.123222	.124956	.126695	.128439	.130187	.145409
17 % .17	.124372	.126096	.127825	.129558	.131295	.133037	.142563
18 % .18	.127244	.128962	.130685	.132412	.134144	.135880	.139777
19 % .19	.130107	.131821	.133538	.135260	.136986	.138716	.137050
20 % .20	.132964	.134672	.136384	.138100	.139820	.141545	.134379
21 % .21	.135812	.137515	.139222	.140933	.142648	.144367	.131765
22 % .22	.138654	.140351	.142053	.143758	.145468	.147182	.129205
23 % .23	.141488	.143181	.144877	.146577	.148282	.149991	.126700
24 % .24	.144315	.146003	.147694	.149390	.151089	.152792	.124247
25 % .25	.147136	.148818	.150505	.152195	.153890	.155588	.121846
26 % .26	.149949	.151627	.153309	.154995	.156684	.158377	.119496
27 % .27	.152756	.154430	.156107	.157788	.159472	.161161	.117195
28 % .28	.155556	.157225	.158898	.160574	.162254	.163938	.114943
29 % .29	.158350	.160015	.161683	.163355	.165030	.166709	.112739
30 % .30	.161138	.162799	.164463	.166130	.167801	.169475	.110581

Projection: 10 Years, n = 10

Equity Yield	10¾%	11%	11¼%	11½%	11¾%	12%	+ Dep − App
Balance (b)	.518415	.521880	.525528	.529363	.533393	.537622	
Basic Rate before Depreciation or Appreciation							
6 % .06	.088487	.090124	.091772	.093430	.095099	.096780	.075867
7 % .07	.092248	.093876	.095514	.097162	.098821	.100490	.072377
8 % .08	.095957	.097576	.099205	.100844	.102492	.104151	.069029
9 % .09	.099616	.101227	.102847	.104477	.106115	.107764	.065820
10 % .10	.103227	.104830	.106441	.108062	.109691	.111330	.062745
11 % .11	.106790	.108385	.109989	.111601	.113222	.114851	.059801
12 % .12	.110307	.111896	.113491	.115095	.116703	.118328	.056984
13 % .13	.113781	.115362	.116950	.118547	.120151	.121763	.054289
14 % .14	.117211	.118786	.120367	.121956	.123552	.125156	.051713
15 % .15	.120600	.122168	.123743	.125325	.126913	.128510	.049252
16 % .16	.123949	.125511	.127080	.128654	.130236	.131825	.046901
17 % .17	.127260	.128816	.130378	.131947	.133522	.135103	.044656
18 % .18	.130534	.132084	.133641	.135203	.136771	.138346	.042514
19 % .19	.133772	.135317	.136868	.138424	.139986	.141555	.040471
20 % .20	.136976	.138516	.140061	.141612	.143168	.144730	.038522
21 % .21	.140146	.141682	.143222	.144768	.146318	.147875	.036665
22 % .22	.143286	.144817	.146352	.147892	.149438	.150989	.034894
23 % .23	.146395	.147921	.149452	.150988	.152528	.154073	.033208
24 % .24	.149475	.150997	.152524	.154055	.155590	.157130	.031602
25 % .25	.152528	.154046	.155568	.157095	.158625	.160161	.030072
26 % .26	.155554	.157068	.158586	.160109	.161635	.163166	.028616
27 % .27	.158554	.160065	.161579	.163098	.164620	.166146	.027230
28 % .28	.161530	.163038	.164549	.166063	.167582	.169104	.025911
29 % .29	.164484	.165988	.167495	.169006	.170521	.172039	.024657
30 % .30	.167415	.168916	.170420	.171927	.173438	.174953	.023463

CAPITALIZATION RATES

Assuming 75% of Purchase Price Financed by Mortgage

15 YEARS AMORTIZATION: 10¾% TO 12%

Interest Rate Annual Requirement (f) Coverage Min. Rate			10¾% .134520 .100890	11% .136440 .102330	11¼% .138360 .103770	11½% .140280 .105210	11¾% .142200 .106650	12% .144120 .108090	$\frac{1}{s_{\overline{n}\rceil}}$
Projection	Balance (b)		none	none	none	none	none	none	+ Dep
	Equity	Yield	Basic Rate before Depreciation or Appreciation						− App
	6 %	.06	.083660	.085048	.086449	.087863	.089291	.090734	.042962
	7 %	.07	.088537	.089929	.091332	.092748	.094177	.095619	.039794
	8 %	.08	.093261	.094657	.096063	.097481	.098910	.100353	.036829
	9 %	.09	.097839	.099239	.100647	.102067	.103497	.104939	.034058
	10 %	.10	.102279	.103681	.105092	.106513	.107944	.109386	.031473
	11 %	.11	.106586	.107991	.109404	.110826	.112258	.113700	.029065
	12 %	.12	.110767	.112174	.113590	.115014	.116446	.117888	.026824
	13 %	.13	.114829	.116239	.117657	.119082	.120515	.121956	.024741
	14 %	.14	.118779	.120191	.121611	.123037	.124470	.125912	.022808
	15 %	.15	.122623	.124038	.125459	.126886	.128320	.129761	.021017
15 Years n = 15	16 %	.16	.126368	.127785	.129207	.130635	.132070	.133511	.019357
	17 %	.17	.130020	.131438	.132862	.134291	.135726	.137167	.017822
	18 %	.18	.133585	.135005	.136430	.137860	.139295	.140736	.016402
	19 %	.19	.137068	.138490	.139916	.141347	.142783	.144224	.015091
	20 %	.20	.140476	.141899	.143326	.144758	.146194	.147635	.013882
	21 %	.21	.143812	.145237	.146665	.148098	.149534	.150975	.012766
	22 %	.22	.147084	.148510	.149939	.151372	.152809	.154249	.011738
	23 %	.23	.150294	.151721	.153152	.154585	.156022	.157463	.010791
	24 %	.24	.153448	.154877	.156307	.157741	.159179	.160619	.009919
	25 %	.25	.156550	.157979	.159411	.160845	.162283	.163723	.009116
	26 %	.26	.159604	.161034	.162466	.163901	.165339	.166779	.008378
	27 %	.27	.162613	.164044	.165476	.166912	.168350	.169790	.007700
	28 %	.28	.165581	.167012	.168446	.169881	.171319	.172760	.007076
	29 %	.29	.168510	.169943	.171377	.172813	.174251	.175691	.006504
	30 %	.30	.171405	.172838	.174272	.175709	.177147	.178588	.005977

CAPITALIZATION RATES

Assuming 75% of Purchase Price Financed by Mortgage.

20 YEARS AMORTIZATION: 3¼% TO 4½%

Interest Rate Annual Requirement (f) Coverage Min. Rate		3¼% .06816 .05112	3½% .06960 .05220	3¾% .07116 .05337	4% .07272 .05454	4¼% .07440 .05580	4½% .07596 .05697	$\frac{1}{s_{\overline{n}\rvert}}$
Projection	Balance (b)	.806679	.811240	.815205	.819225	.822635	.826765	+ Dep − App
	Equity Yield	Basic Rate before Depreciation or Appreciation						
	5% .05	.0374	.0392	.0408	.0426	.0443	.0460	.1810
	6% .06	.0405	.0421	.0438	.0456	.0473	.0490	.1774
	7% .07	.0435	.0451	.0469	.0485	.0502	.0520	.1739
	8% .08	.0464	.0481	.0498	.0515	.0532	.0549	.1705
	9% .09	.0495	.0511	.0528	.0544	.0561	.0578	.1671
5 Years n = 5	10% .10	.0524	.0541	.0557	.0574	.0591	.0607	.1638
	11% .11	.0554	.0570	.0587	.0603	.0620	.0637	.1606
	12% .12	.0584	.0600	.0616	.0633	.0649	.0666	.1574
	13% .13	.0613	.0629	.0646	.0662	.0679	.0695	.1543
	14% .14	.0642	.0659	.0674	.0691	.0707	.0724	.1513
	15% .15	.0672	.0687	.0704	.0720	.0736	.0753	.1483
	16% .16	.0701	.0717	.0733	.0749	.0765	.0781	.1454
	17% .17	.0730	.0746	.0762	.0778	.0794	.0810	.1426
	18% .18	.0759	.0775	.0791	.0807	.0822	.0839	.1398
	19% .19	.0788	.0804	.0820	.0835	.0851	.0868	.1371
	20% .20	.0817	.0833	.0848	.0864	.0880	.0896	.1344
	Balance (b)	.579297	.586436	.592363	.598499	.603357	.609909	+ Dep − App
	Equity Yield	Basic Rate before Depreciation or Appreciation						
	5% .05	.0386	.0401	.0416	.0431	.0447	.0463	.0795
	6% .06	.0423	.0437	.0453	.0468	.0483	.0498	.0759
	7% .07	.0458	.0473	.0488	.0503	.0518	.0534	.0724
	8% .08	.0494	.0509	.0523	.0538	.0553	.0569	.0690
	9% .09	.0529	.0543	.0558	.0573	.0588	.0603	.0658
10 Years n = 10	10% .10	.0564	.0578	.0592	.0607	.0622	.0637	.0628
	11% .11	.0598	.0612	.0626	.0641	.0656	.0671	.0598
	12% .12	.0632	.0646	.0660	.0675	.0689	.0704	.0570
	13% .13	.0665	.0679	.0694	.0708	.0722	.0736	.0543
	14% .14	.0698	.0712	.0726	.0740	.0755	.0769	.0517
	15% .15	.0732	.0744	.0759	.0773	.0787	.0801	.0493
	16% .16	.0764	.0777	.0791	.0805	.0819	.0832	.0469
	17% .17	.0796	.0809	.0823	.0836	.0851	.0863	.0447
	18% .18	.0828	.0841	.0855	.0868	.0882	.0895	.0425
	19% .19	.0859	.0872	.0886	.0899	.0913	.0926	.0405
	20% .20	.0890	.0903	.0917	.0930	.0944	.0957	.0385

CAPITALIZATION RATES

Assuming 75% of Purchase Price Financed by Mortgage.

20 YEARS AMORTIZATION: 3¼% TO 4½%

Interest Rate Annual Requirement (f) Coverage Min. Rate		3¼% .06816 .05112	3½% .06960 .05220	3¾% .07116 .05337	4% .07272 .05454	4¼% .07440 .05580	4½% .07596 .05697	$\frac{1}{s_{\overline{n}|}}$
Projection	Balance (b)	.311852	.318709	.323644	.328994	.332264	.338450	+ Dep − App
	Equity Yield	Basic Rate before Depreciation or Appreciation						
	5% .05	.0398	.0411	.0424	.0438	.0452	.0465	.0464
	6% .06	.0440	.0453	.0466	.0480	.0493	.0507	.0430
	7% .07	.0481	.0494	.0508	.0520	.0535	.0548	.0398
	8% .08	.0521	.0534	.0548	.0560	.0574	.0587	.0368
	9% .09	.0561	.0573	.0586	.0600	.0613	.0627	.0341
15 Years	10% .10	.0599	.0612	.0625	.0637	.0651	.0664	.0315
n = 15	11% .11	.0637	.0649	.0662	.0674	.0688	.0701	.0291
	12% .12	.0673	.0686	.0698	.0711	.0724	.0737	.0268
	13% .13	.0709	.0721	.0734	.0746	.0760	.0772	.0248
	14% .14	.0744	.0756	.0769	.0781	.0794	.0807	.0228
	15% .15	.0778	.0790	.0803	.0815	.0828	.0841	.0210
	16% .16	.0812	.0824	.0836	.0849	.0862	.0874	.0194
	17% .17	.0845	.0857	.0869	.0881	.0894	.0907	.0178
	18% .18	.0877	.0889	.0901	.0914	.0927	.0939	.0164
	19% .19	.0909	.0921	.0933	.0945	.0958	.0970	.0151
	20% .20	.0940	.0952	.0964	.0976	.0989	.1001	.0139
	Balance (b)	none	none	none	none	none	none	+ Dep − App
	Equity Yield	Basic Rate before Depreciation or Appreciation						
	5% .05	.0410	.0421	.0432	.0444	.0457	.0468	.0303
	6% .06	.0458	.0468	.0480	.0492	.0504	.0516	.0272
	7% .07	.0504	.0514	.0526	.0538	.0550	.0562	.0244
	8% .08	.0548	.0559	.0570	.0582	.0595	.0606	.0219
	9% .09	.0590	.0601	.0612	.0624	.0637	.0648	.0196
20 Years	10% .10	.0631	.0642	.0653	.0665	.0678	.0689	.0175
n = 20	11% .11	.0670	.0680	.0692	.0704	.0716	.0728	.0156
	12% .12	.0708	.0718	.0730	.0742	.0754	.0766	.0139
	13% .13	.0744	.0755	.0766	.0778	.0791	.0802	.0124
	14% .14	.0779	.0790	.0802	.0814	.0826	.0838	.0110
	15% .15	.0813	.0825	.0836	.0848	.0861	.0872	.0098
	16% .16	.0847	.0858	.0869	.0881	.0894	.0905	.0087
	17% .17	.0879	.0890	.0902	.0914	.0926	.0938	.0077
	18% .18	.0911	.0921	.0933	.0945	.0957	.0969	.0068
	19% .19	.0942	.0952	.0964	.0976	.0988	.1000	.0060
	20% .20	.0971	.0983	.0994	.1006	.1019	.1030	.0054

CAPITALIZATION RATES

Assuming 75% of Purchase Price Financed by Mortgage.

20 YEARS AMORTIZATION: 4¾% TO 6%

Interest Rate		4¾%	5%	5¼%	5½%	5¾%	6%	$\frac{1}{s_{\overline{n}\rceil}}$
Annual Requirement (f)		.07764	.07920	.08088	.08256	.08436	.08604	
Coverage Min. Rate		.05823	.05940	.06066	.06192	.06327	.06453	
Projection	Balance(b)	.830277	.834519	.838135	.841804	.844831	.848599	+ Dep
	Equity Yield	Basic Rate before Depreciation or Appreciation						− App
	5% .05	.0478	.0495	.0512	.0530	.0548	.0566	.1810
	6% .06	.0507	.0525	.0542	.0559	.0577	:0594	.1774
	7% .07	.0537	.0554	.0571	.0589	.0606	.0623	.1739
	8% .08	.0566	.0583	.0600	.0617	.0635	.0653	.1705
	9% .09	.0595	.0612	.0630	.0647	.0664	.0681	.1671
5 Years	10% .10	.0625	.0641	.0658	.0676	.0693	.0710	.1638
n = 5	11% .11	.0653	.0671	.0687	.0704	.0722	.0739	.1606
	12% .12	.0683	.0699	.0716	.0733	.0750	.0767	.1574
	13% .13	.0712	.0728	.0745	.0762	.0778	.0796	.1543
	14% .14	.0740	.0757	.0774	.0791	.0807	.0824	.1513
	15% .15	.0769	.0786	.0802	.0819	.0836	.0852	.1483
	16% .16	.0798	.0814	.0831	.0847	.0864	.0881	.1454
	17% .17	.0827	.0842	.0859	.0875	.0893	.0909	.1426
	18% .18	.0855	.0871	.0888	.0904	.0921	.0937	.1398
	19% .19	.0883	.0900	.0916	.0932	.0949	.0965	.1371
	20% .20	.0912	.0928	.0944	.0960	.0977	.0993	.1344
	Balance (b)	.615155	.622146	.627803	.633664	.638118	.644382	+ Dep
	Equity Yield	Basic Rate before Depreciation or Appreciation						− App
	5% .05	.0479	.0494	.0510	.0526	.0542	.0559	.0795
	6% .06	.0514	.0530	.0546	.0561	.0577	.0594	.0759
	7% :07	.0549	.0565	.0580	.0596	.0612	.0628	.0724
	8% .08	.0584	.0599	.0614	.0630	.0646	.0662	.0690
	9% .09	.0618	.0633	.0648	.0664	.0680	.0696	.0658
10 Years	10% .10	.0652	.0667	.0682	.0697	.0713	.0728	.0628
n = 10	11% .11	.0686	.0700	.0716	.0731	.0746	.0761	.0598
	12% .12	.0718	.0733	.0748	.0763	.0779	.0794	.0570
	13% .13	.0751	.0766	.0781	.0796	.0811	.0826	.0543
	14% .14	.0784	.0798	.0813	.0827	.0843	.0858	.0517
	15% .15	.0816	.0830	.0845	.0859	.0875	.0890	.0493
	16% .16	.0847	.0862	.0877	.0891	.0906	.0921	.0469
	17% .17	.0879	.0893	.0908	.0922	.0937	.0952	.0447
	18% .18	.0910	.0924	.0939	.0953	.0968	.0983	.0425
	19% .19	.0941	.0955	.0970	.0984	.0999	.1013	.0405
	20% .20	.0972	.0986	.1000	.1014	.1029	.1043	.0385

CAPITALIZATION RATES

Assuming 75% of Purchase Price Financed by Mortgage.

20 YEARS AMORTIZATION: 4¾% TO 6%

Interest Rate		4¾%	5%	5¼%	5½%	5¾%	6%	$\frac{1}{s_{\overline{n}\rceil}}$
Annual Requirement (f)		.07764	.07920	.08088	.08256	.08436	.08604	
Coverage Min. Rate		.05823	.05940	.06066	.06192	.06327	.06453	
Projection	Balance (b)	.342493	.349597	.354491	.359815	.362740	.368924	+ Dep
	Equity Yield	Basic Rate before Depreciation or Appreciation						− App
	5% .05	.0479	.0494	.0508	.0522	.0536	.0551	.0464
	6% .06	.0521	.0535	.0549	.0564	.0578	.0593	.0430
	7% .07	.0562	.0575	.0589	.0604	.0618	.0633	.0398
	8% .08	.0602	.0615	.0629	.0643	.0657	.0671	.0368
	9% .09	.0640	.0654	.0667	.0681	.0696	.0710	.0341
15 Years n = 15	10% .10	.0678	.0691	.0705	.0718	.0733	.0747	.0315
	11% .11	.0715	.0728	.0741	.0755	.0770	.0783	.0291
	12% .12	.0750	.0764	.0777	.0791	.0805	.0819	.0268
	13% .13	.0786	.0799	.0812	.0826	.0840	.0854	.0248
	14% .14	.0821	.0833	.0847	.0860	.0875	.0888	.0228
	15% .15	.0854	.0867	.0880	.0894	.0908	.0921	.0210
	16% .16	.0888	.0900	.0913	.0927	.0941	.0955	.0194
	17% .17	.0920	.0932	.0946	.0959	.0973	.0986	.0178
	18% .18	.0952	.0965	.0978	.0991	.1005	.1018	.0164
	19% .19	.0984	.0996	.1009	.1022	.1036	.1050	.0151
	20% .20	.1015	.1027	.1040	.1053	.1067	.1080	.0139
	Balance (b)	none	none	none	none	none	none	+ Dep
	Equity Yield	Basic Rate before Depreciation or Appreciation						− App
	5% .05	.0481	.0493	.0505	.0518	.0531	.0544	.0303
	6% .06	.0529	.0540	.0553	.0566	.0579	.0592	.0272
	7% .07	.0575	.0586	.0599	.0612	.0625	.0638	.0244
	8% .08	.0619	.0631	.0644	.0656	.0669	.0682	.0219
	9% .09	.0661	.0673	.0686	.0698	.0711	.0724	.0196
20 Years n = 20	10% .10	.0702	.0714	.0726	.0739	.0752	.0765	.0175
	11% .11	.0741	.0753	.0765	.0778	.0791	.0804	.0156
	12% .12	.0779	.0790	.0803	.0816	.0829	.0842	.0139
	13% .13	.0815	.0827	.0840	.0852	.0865	.0878	.0124
	14% .14	.0851	.0862	.0875	.0887	.0901	.0914	.0110
	15% .15	.0885	.0897	.0909	.0921	.0935	.0948	.0098
	16% .16	.0918	.0930	.0943	.0955	.0968	.0981	.0087
	17% .17	.0950	.0962	.0974	.0987	.1001	.1013	.0077
	18% .18	.0982	.0993	.1006	.1019	.1032	.1045	.0068
	19% .19	.1012	.1024	.1037	.1050	.1063	.1075	.0060
	20% .20	.1043	.1055	.1067	.1079	.1093	.1106	.0054

CAPITALIZATION RATES

Assuming 75% of Purchase Price Financed by Mortgage

20 YEARS AMORTIZATION: 6¼% TO 7½%

Interest Rate / Annual Requirement (f) / Coverage Min. Rate			6¼%	6½%	6¾%	7%	7¼%	7½%	$\frac{1}{s_{\overline{n}\rvert}}$
Annual Requirement (f)			.087720	.089520	.091320	.093120	.094920	.096720	
Coverage Min. Rate			.065790	.067140	.068490	.069840	.071190	.072540	
Projection	Balance (b)		.852420	.855589	.858803	.862064	.865371	.868725	+ Dep − App
	Equity	Yield	Basic Rate before Depreciation or Appreciation						
	6 %	.06	.061154	.062926	.064704	.066488	.068278	.070074	.177396
	7 %	.07	.064042	.065806	.067575	.069350	.071132	.072919	.173890
	8 %	.08	.066923	.068678	.070439	.072205	.073978	.075757	.170456
	9 %	.09	.069795	.071542	.073295	.075053	.076818	.078588	.167092
	10 %	.10	.072660	.074399	.076144	.077894	.079651	.081413	.163797
	11 %	.11	.075517	.077248	.078986	.080728	.082476	.084230	.160570
	12 %	.12	.078367	.080091	.081820	.083555	.085296	.087042	.157409
	13 %	.13	.081209	.082926	.084648	.086375	.088108	.089846	.154314
	14 %	.14	.084045	.085754	.087469	.089189	.090914	.092645	.151283
	15 %	.15	.086873	.088576	.090283	.091996	.093714	.095437	.148315
	16 %	.16	.089695	.091391	.093091	.094797	.096507	.098223	.145409
5 Years	17 %	.17	.092510	.094199	.095892	.097591	.099295	.101003	.142563
n = 5	18 %	.18	.095318	.097000	.098687	.100379	.102076	.103778	.139777
	19 %	.19	.098120	.099796	.101476	.103161	.104851	.106546	.137050
	20 %	.20	.100916	.102585	.104259	.105938	.107621	.109309	.134379
	21 %	.21	.103705	.105368	.107036	.108708	.110385	.112066	.131765
	22 %	.22	.106488	.108145	.109807	.111473	.113143	.114818	.129205
	23 %	.23	.109266	.110917	.112572	.114232	.115896	.117565	.126700
	24 %	.24	.112037	.113682	.115332	.116986	.118644	.120307	.124247
	25 %	.25	.114803	.116443	.118086	.119734	.121386	.123043	.121846
	26 %	.26	.117563	.119197	.120835	.122477	.124124	.125774	.119496
	27 %	.27	.120318	.121946	.123579	.125215	.126856	.128501	.117195
	28 %	.28	.123067	.124690	.126317	.127948	.129583	.131223	.114943
	29 %	.29	.125811	.127429	.129051	.130676	.132306	.133940	.112739
	30 %	.30	.128550	.130163	.131779	.133400	.135024	.136652	.110581
	Balance (b)		.650867	.655896	.661113	.666523	.672132	.677946	+ Dep − App
	Equity	Yield	Basic Rate before Depreciation or Appreciation						
	6 %	.06	.060924	.062560	.064207	.065864	.067534	.069214	.075867
	7 %	.07	.064337	.065960	.067594	.069237	.070892	.072557	.072377
	8 %	.08	.067714	.069325	.070945	.072575	.074215	.075866	.069029
	9 %	.09	.071055	.072653	.074260	.075877	.077504	.079141	.065820
	10 %	.10	.074360	.075946	.077542	.079146	.080760	.082384	.062745
	11 %	.11	.077631	.079206	.080790	.082383	.083984	.085595	.059801
	12 %	.12	.080868	.082433	.084006	.085587	.087177	.088776	.056984
	13 %	.13	.084074	.085629	.087191	.088761	.090340	.091926	.054289
	14 %	.14	.087248	.088793	.090346	.091906	.093473	.095049	.051713
	15 %	.15	.090393	.091929	.093471	.095021	.096578	.098143	.049252
	16 %	.16	.093508	.095035	.096569	.098109	.099656	.101211	.046901
10 Years	17 %	.17	.096596	.098115	.099639	.101171	.102708	.104253	.044656
n = 10	18 %	.18	.099657	.101167	.102684	.104206	.105735	.107270	.042514
	19 %	.19	.102692	.104195	.105703	.107217	.108738	.110264	.040471
	20 %	.20	.105702	.107198	.108698	.110205	.111717	.113235	.038522
	21 %	.21	.108689	.110177	.111670	.113169	.114673	.116183	.036665
	22 %	.22	.111652	.113134	.114620	.116112	.117609	.119111	.034894
	23 %	.23	.114594	.116069	.117549	.119034	.120524	.122018	.033208
	24 %	.24	.117514	.118984	.120457	.121936	.123419	.124906	.031602
	25 %	.25	.120415	.121878	.123346	.124818	.126295	.127776	.030072
	26 %	.26	.123296	.124754	.126216	.127682	.129153	.130627	.028616
	27 %	.27	.126159	.127612	.129068	.130529	.131993	.133462	.027230
	28 %	.28	.129005	.130452	.131904	.133359	.134818	.136281	.025911
	29 %	.29	.131833	.133276	.134723	.136173	.137626	.139084	.024657
	30 %	.30	.134646	.136084	.137526	.138971	.140420	.141872	.023463

CAPITALIZATION RATES

Assuming 75% of Purchase Price Financed by Mortgage

20 YEARS AMORTIZATION: 6¼% TO 7½%

Interest Rate			6¼%	6½%	6¾%	7%	7¼%	7½%	$\frac{1}{s_{\overline{n}\rceil}}$
Annual Requirement (f)			.087720	.089520	.091320	.093120	.094920	.096720	
Coverage Min. Rate			.065790	.067140	.068490	.069840	.071190	.072540	
Projection	Balance (b)		.375599	.379756	.384323	.389319	.394766	.400686	+ Dep – App
	Equity	Yield	Basic Rate before Depreciation or Appreciation						
	6 %	.06	.060670	.062154	.063651	.065162	.066688	.068228	.042962
	7 %	.07	.064654	.066128	.067614	.069113	.070626	.072152	.039794
	8 %	.08	.068542	.070007	.071483	.072971	.074472	.075985	.036829
	9 %	.09	.072340	.073796	.075263	.076740	.078229	.079731	.034058
	10 %	.10	.076050	.077498	.078956	.080424	.081903	.083393	.031473
	11 %	.11	.079678	.081119	.082568	.084027	.085496	.086975	.029065
	12 %	.12	.083228	.084661	.086103	.087554	.089013	.090482	.026824
	13 %	.13	.086703	.088130	.089565	.091008	.092459	.093918	.024741
	14 %	.14	.090108	.091529	.092957	.094393	.095836	.097287	.022808
	15 %	.15	.093447	.094863	.096285	.097713	.099149	.100593	.021017
15 Years	16 %	.16	.096724	.098135	.099551	.100974	.102403	.103839	.019357
n = 15	17 %	.17	.099943	.101349	.102760	.104177	.105600	.107029	.017822
	18 %	.18	.103108	.104509	.105915	.107327	.108744	.110167	.016402
	19 %	.19	.106222	.107619	.109021	.110427	.111839	.113256	.015091
	20 %	.20	.109288	.110682	.112079	.113481	.114888	.116300	.013882
	21 %	.21	.112311	.113701	.115095	.116492	.117894	.119301	.012766
	22 %	.22	.115293	.116679	.118069	.119463	.120861	.122263	.011738
	23 %	.23	.118236	.119620	.121007	.122397	.123791	.125189	.010791
	24 %	.24	.121144	.122525	.123909	.125296	.126687	.128081	.009919
	25 %	.25	.124020	.125398	.126780	.128164	.129551	.130942	.009116
	26 %	.26	.126866	.128242	.129620	.131002	.132386	.133773	.008378
	27 %	.27	.129683	.131057	.132434	.133813	.135194	.136578	.007700
	28 %	.28	.132475	.133847	.135222	.136598	.137977	.139358	.007076
	29 %	.29	.135244	.136614	.137986	.139361	.140737	.142116	.006504
	30 %	.30	.137990	.139359	.140729	.142102	.143476	.144853	.005977
	Balance (b)		none	none	none	none	none	none	+ Dep – App
	Equity	Yield	Basic Rate before Depreciation or Appreciation						
	6 %	.06	.060394	.061708	.063036	.064377	.065733	.067105	.027184
	7 %	.07	.064989	.066307	.067636	.068978	.070333	.071704	.024392
	8 %	.08	.069395	.070716	.072048	.073390	.074745	.076113	.021852
	9 %	.09	.073625	.074949	.076283	.077626	.078981	.080347	.019546
	10 %	.10	.077690	.079017	.080353	.081697	.083051	.084415	.017459
	11 %	.11	.081604	.082933	.084270	.085615	.086969	.088331	.015575
	12 %	.12	.085377	.086709	.088047	.089392	.090746	.092107	.013878
	13 %	.13	.089021	.090355	.091694	.093040	.094393	.095753	.012353
	14 %	.14	.092547	.093883	.095224	.096570	.097922	.099281	.010986
	15 %	.15	.095966	.097303	.098645	.099992	.101344	.102702	.009761
	16 %	.16	.099287	.100626	.101968	.103315	.104667	.106025	.008667
	17 %	.17	.102520	.103860	.105203	.106551	.107902	.109259	.007690
20 Years	18 %	.18	.105673	.107014	.108358	.109706	.111057	.112413	.006819
n = 20	19 %	.19	.108754	.110096	.111441	.112789	.114140	.115495	.006045
	20 %	.20	.111771	.113114	.114459	.115807	.117159	.118513	.005356
	21 %	.21	.114730	.116073	.117419	.118768	.120119	.121473	.004744
	22 %	.22	.117637	.118982	.120328	.121677	.123028	.124381	.004201
	23 %	.23	.120498	.121843	.123190	.124539	.125890	.127243	.003720
	24 %	.24	.123318	.124664	.126011	.127360	.128711	.130064	.003293
	25 %	.25	.126102	.127448	.128796	.130145	.131495	.132848	.002915
	26 %	.26	.128853	.130199	.131547	.132896	.134247	.135599	.002581
	27 %	.27	.131575	.132922	.134270	.135619	.136970	.138322	.002285
	28 %	.28	.134271	.135619	.136967	.138316	.139667	.141019	.002023
	29 %	.29	.136945	.138293	.139641	.140991	.142341	.143693	.001791
	30 %	.30	.139599	.140947	.142296	.143645	.144995	.146347	.001586

CAPITALIZATION RATES

Assuming 75% of Purchase Price Financed by Mortgage

20 YEARS AMORTIZATION: 7¼% TO 9%

			7¼%	8%	8¼%	8½%	8¾%	9%	$\frac{1}{s_{\overline{n}\rvert}}$
:rest Rate									
nnual Requirement (f)			.098520	.100440	.102360	.104160	.106080	.108000	
overage Min. Rate			.073890	.075330	.076770	.078120	.079560	.081000	
rojection	Balance (b)		.872128	.874844	.877600	.881140	.883981	.886863	+ Dep − App
	Equity	Yield	Basic Rate before Depreciation or Appreciation						
	6 %	.06	.071877	.073678	.075485	.077306	.079124	.080947	.177396
	7 %	.07	.074713	.076507	.078306	.080118	.081929	.083745	.173890
	8 %	.08	.077542	.079329	.081122	.082924	.084727	.086536	.170456
	9 %	.09	.080365	.082145	.083930	.085724	.087520	.089321	.167092
	10 %	.10	.083181	.084954	.086733	.088518	.090307	.092101	.163797
	11 %	.11	.085990	.087757	.089529	.091305	.093088	.094875	.160570
	12 %	.12	.088793	.090554	.092319	.094087	.095863	.097643	.157409
5 Years n = 5	13 %	.13	.091590	.093345	.095103	.096863	.098632	.100406	.154314
	14 %	.14	.094381	.096129	.097882	.099633	.101396	.103163	.151283
	15 %	.15	.097165	.098908	.100654	.102398	.104154	.105915	.148315
	16 %	.16	.099944	.101680	.103421	.105157	.106907	.108661	.145409
	17 %	.17	.102717	.104448	.106182	.107911	.109654	.111403	.142563
	18 %	.18	.105484	.107209	.108938	.110659	.112397	.114139	.139777
	19 %	.19	.108246	.109965	.111688	.113402	.115134	.116870	.137050
	20 %	.20	.111002	.112716	.114433	.116140	.117867	.119597	.134379
	21 %	.21	.113753	.115461	.117173	.118873	.120594	.122319	.131765
	22 %	.22	.116498	.118201	.119908	.121601	.123317	.125036	.129205
	23 %	.23	.119238	.120937	.122638	.124325	.126035	.127749	.126700
	24 %	.24	.121974	.123667	.125364	.127043	.128748	.130457	.124247
	25 %	.25	.124704	.126392	.128084	.129757	.131457	.133161	.121846
	26 %	.26	.127429	.129113	.130800	.132467	.134162	.135860	.119496
	27 %	.27	.130150	.131829	.133511	.135172	.136862	.138555	.117195
	28 %	.28	.132866	.134540	.136218	.137873	.139558	.141246	.114943
	29 %	.29	.135577	.137247	.138920	.140569	.142250	.143933	.112739
	30 %	.30	.138284	.139950	.141618	.143262	.144937	.146616	.110581
	Balance (b)		.683970	.688381	.692964	.699605	.704573	.709728	+ Dep − App
	Equity	Yield	Basic Rate before Depreciation or Appreciation						
	6 %	.06	.070907	.072598	.074299	.076027	.077749	.079483	.075867
	7 %	.07	.074234	.075914	.077603	.079313	.081023	.082743	.072377
	8 %	.08	.077528	.079196	.080874	.082567	.084265	.085972	.069029
	9 %	.09	.080789	.082446	.084113	.085791	.087476	.089170	.065820
	10 %	.10	.084017	.085665	.087321	.088983	.090657	.092340	.062745
	11 %	.11	.087215	.088853	.090499	.092146	.093809	.095481	.059801
	12 %	.12	.090383	.092012	.093647	.095281	.096934	.098594	.056984
	13 %	.13	.093522	.095141	.096768	.098388	.100031	.101680	.054289
	14 %	.14	.096632	.098243	.099861	.101469	.103101	.104741	.051713
	15 %	.15	.099716	.101319	.102928	.104523	.106147	.107777	.049252
10 Years n = 10	16 %	.16	.102773	.104368	.105969	.107553	.109168	.110789	.046901
	17 %	.17	.105805	.107393	.108986	.110559	.112165	.113778	.044656
	18 %	.18	.108813	.110393	.111979	.113541	.115140	.116744	.042514
	19 %	.19	.111797	.113371	.114950	.116501	.118092	.119689	.040471
	20 %	.20	.114759	.116326	.117899	.119440	.121024	.122613	.038522
	21 %	.21	.117699	.119260	.120826	.122359	.123936	.125517	.036665
	22 %	.22	.120619	.122174	.123734	.125258	.126828	.128403	.034894
	23 %	.23	.123518	.125068	.126622	.128138	.129702	.131270	.033208
	24 %	.24	.126399	.127944	.129492	.131000	.132557	.134120	.031602
	25 %	.25	.129262	.130801	.132345	.133844	.135396	.136953	.030072
	26 %	.26	.132107	.133641	.135180	.136672	.138219	.139770	.028616
	27 %	.27	.134935	.136465	.137999	.139485	.141026	.142571	.027230
	28 %	.28	.137748	.139274	.140803	.142282	.143818	.145358	.025911
	29 %	.29	.140545	.142067	.143592	.145064	.146596	.148132	.024657
	30 %	.30	.143328	.144846	.146366	.147833	.149361	.150891	.023463

CAPITALIZATION RATES

Assuming 75% of Purchase Price Financed by Mortgage

20 YEARS AMORTIZATION: 7¾% TO 9%

			7¾%	8%	8¼%	8½%	8¾%	9%	$\frac{1}{s_{\overline{n}\rvert}}$
Interest Rate			7¾%	8%	8¼%	8½%	8¾%	9%	
Annual Requirement (f)			.098520	.100440	.102360	.104160	.106080	.108000	
Coverage Min. Rate			.073890	.075330	.076770	.078120	.079560	.081000	
Projection	Balance (b)		.407103	.410581	.414450	.422347	.427141	.432391	+ Dep – App
	Equity	Yield	Basic Rate before Depreciation or Appreciation						
	6 %	.06	.069785	.071337	.072902	.074506	.076101	.077710	.042962
	7 %	.07	.073694	.075238	.076793	.078379	.079962	.081559	.039794
	8 %	.08	.077512	.079048	.080595	.082163	.083736	.085321	.036829
	9 %	.09	.081244	.082773	.084312	.085864	.087426	.089000	.034058
	10 %	.10	.084894	.086416	.087947	.089484	.091037	.092601	.031473
	11 %	.11	.088465	.089981	.091505	.093027	.094572	.096126	.029065
	12 %	.12	.091962	.093471	.094989	.096498	.098035	.099580	.026824
	13 %	.13	.095388	.096892	.098404	.099900	.101429	.102967	.024741
	14 %	.14	.098747	.100246	.101753	.103238	.104760	.106290	.022808
	15 %	.15	.102044	.103539	.105040	.106514	.108030	.109552	.021017
15 Years	16 %	.16	.105282	.106772	.108268	.109733	.111243	.112759	.019357
n = 15	17 %	.17	.108465	.109951	.111443	.112898	.114402	.115913	.017822
	18 %	.18	.111596	.113078	.114566	.116013	.117512	.119017	.016402
	19 %	.19	.114679	.116158	.117642	.119081	.120575	.122075	.015091
	20 %	.20	.117717	.119193	.120673	.122105	.123595	.125090	.013882
	21 %	.21	.120713	.122186	.123663	.125089	.126574	.128065	.012766
	22 %	.22	.123670	.125140	.126615	.128034	.129516	.131002	.011738
	23 %	.23	.126591	.128059	.129530	.130944	.132423	.133906	.010791
	24 %	.24	.129479	.130945	.132413	.133822	.135298	.136777	.009919
	25 %	.25	.132335	.133799	.135266	.136670	.138142	.139618	.009116
	26 %	.26	.135164	.136625	.138090	.139489	.140960	.142433	.008378
	27 %	.27	.137965	.139425	.140888	.142283	.143751	.145221	.007700
	28 %	.28	.140743	.142201	.143662	.145053	.146519	.147987	.007076
	29 %	.29	.143497	.144954	.146413	.147802	.149265	.150731	.006504
	30 %	.30	.146231	.147687	.149144	.150530	.151991	.153455	.005977
	Balance (b)		none	none	none	none	none	none	+ Dep – App
	Equity	Yield	Basic Rate before Depreciation or Appreciation						
	6 %	.06	.068495	.069874	.071265	.072708	.074133	.075574	.027184
	7 %	.07	.073089	.074474	.075871	.077305	.078731	.080171	.024392
	8 %	.08	.077496	.078886	.080287	.081712	.083140	.084580	.021852
	9 %	.09	.081725	.083121	.084526	.085943	.087372	.088813	.019546
	10 %	.10	.085791	.087192	.088600	.090010	.091440	.092881	.017459
	11 %	.11	.089704	.091109	.092521	.093925	.095356	.096796	.015575
	12 %	.12	.093477	.094886	.096301	.097699	.099131	.100571	.013878
	13 %	.13	.097121	.098534	.099952	.101344	.102777	.104217	.012353
	14 %	.14	.100648	.102063	.103483	.104871	.106305	.107745	.010986
	15 %	.15	.104066	.105484	.106907	.108290	.109725	.111165	.009761
	16 %	.16	.107387	.108808	.110232	.111612	.113047	.114487	.008667
	17 %	.17	.110620	.112043	.113469	.114845	.116281	.117721	.007690
20 Years	18 %	.18	.113773	.115198	.116625	.117999	.119435	.120875	.006819
n = 20	19 %	.19	.116854	.118281	.119710	.121081	.122517	.123957	.006045
	20 %	.20	.119871	.121299	.122729	.124098	.125535	.126975	.005356
	21 %	.21	.122830	.124259	.125691	.127057	.128494	.129934	.004744
	22 %	.22	.125737	.127168	.128600	.129965	.131402	.132842	.004201
	23 %	.23	.128598	.130030	.131463	.132826	.134264	.135704	.003720
	24 %	.24	.131418	.132851	.134285	.135646	.137085	.138525	.003293
	25 %	.25	.134202	.135635	.137070	.138430	.139868	.141309	.002915
	26 %	.26	.136953	.138387	.139822	.141181	.142620	.144060	.002581
	27 %	.27	.139675	.141110	.142546	.143904	.145342	.146782	.002285
	28 %	.28	.142371	.143807	.145243	.146600	.148039	.149479	.002023
	29 %	.29	.145045	.146481	.147918	.149274	.150713	.152153	.001791
	30 %	.30	.147699	.149135	.150573	.151928	.153367	.154807	.001586

CAPITALIZATION RATES

Assuming 75% of Purchase Price Financed by Mortgage

20 YEARS AMORTIZATION: 9¼% TO 10½%

			9¼%	9½%	9¾%	10%	10¼%	10½%	$\frac{1}{s_{\overline{n}\vert}}$
Interest Rate			9¼%	9½%	9¾%	10%	10¼%	10½%	
Annual Requirement (f)			.109920	.111960	.113880	.115920	.117840	.119880	
Coverage Min. Rate			.082440	.083970	.085410	.086940	.088380	.089910	
Projection	Balance (b)		.889787	.891989	.894993	.897266	.900352	.902698	+ Dep − App
	Equity	Yield	Basic Rate before Depreciation or Appreciation						
5 Years n = 5	6 %	.06	.082776	.084599	.086439	.088271	.090122	.091964	.177396
	7 %	.07	.085566	.087383	.089215	.091041	.092884	.094720	.173890
	8 %	.08	.088350	.090161	.091985	.093806	.095640	.097470	.170456
	9 %	.09	.091128	.092934	.094750	.096565	.098392	.100216	.167092
	10 %	.10	.093900	.095701	.097510	.099319	.101138	.102956	.163797
	11 %	.11	.096667	.098462	.100264	.102068	.103879	.105692	.160570
	12 %	.12	.099428	.101218	.103013	.104811	.106615	.108422	.157409
	13 %	.13	.102184	.103969	.105757	.107550	.109347	.111148	.154314
	14 %	.14	.104935	.106714	.108495	.110283	.112073	.113869	.151283
	15 %	.15	.107680	.109455	.111229	.113012	.114795	.116586	.148315
	16 %	.16	.110420	.112190	.113958	.115736	.117512	.119298	.145409
	17 %	.17	.113155	.114921	.116682	.118455	.120225	.122006	.142563
	18 %	.18	.115886	.117646	.119401	.121170	.122933	.124709	.139777
	19 %	.19	.118611	.120367	.122116	.123880	.125637	.127408	.137050
	20 %	.20	.121332	.123084	.124826	.126586	.128337	.130103	.134379
	21 %	.21	.124048	.125796	.127532	.129287	.131032	.132794	.131765
	22 %	.22	.126759	.128503	.130234	.131984	.133723	.135481	.129205
	23 %	.23	.129467	.131206	.132931	.134677	.136410	.138163	.126700
	24 %	.24	.132169	.133904	.135624	.137366	.139094	.140842	.124247
	25 %	.25	.134868	.136599	.138314	.140051	.141773	.143518	.121846
	26 %	.26	.137562	.139289	.140999	.142732	.144449	.146189	.119496
	27 %	.27	.140252	.141976	.143680	.145410	.147121	.148857	.117195
	28 %	.28	.142938	.144658	.146357	.148083	.149789	.151521	.114943
	29 %	.29	.145621	.147337	.149031	.150753	.152454	.154182	.112739
	30 %	.30	.148299	.150012	.151701	.153419	.155115	.156840	.110581
	Balance (b)		.715076	.718632	.724355	.728238	.734357	.738589	+ Dep − App
	Equity	Yield	Basic Rate before Depreciation or Appreciation						
10 Years n = 10	6 %	.06	.081227	.082959	.084725	.086476	.088264	.090035	.075867
	7 %	.07	.084473	.086196	.087947	.089687	.091460	.093219	.072377
	8 %	.08	.087688	.089403	.091139	.092870	.094627	.096376	.069029
	9 %	.09	.090874	.092580	.094302	.096024	.097766	.099505	.065820
	10 %	.10	.094031	.095729	.097438	.099151	.100879	.102608	.062745
	11 %	.11	.097160	.098850	.100547	.102251	.103965	.105685	.059801
	12 %	.12	.100262	.101944	.103629	.105325	.107026	.108737	.056984
	13 %	.13	.103338	.105013	.106686	.108374	.110063	.111766	.054289
	14 %	.14	.106389	.108057	.109719	.111399	.113077	.114771	.051713
	15 %	.15	.109415	.111076	.112727	.114401	.116067	.117753	.049252
	16 %	.16	.112417	.114072	.115713	.117380	.119035	.120714	.046901
	17 %	.17	.115397	.117046	.118677	.120338	.121982	.123654	.044656
	18 %	.18	.118354	.119998	.121620	.123274	.124909	.126574	.042514
	19 %	.19	.121291	.122929	.124543	.126191	.127816	.129475	.040471
	20 %	.20	.124207	.125840	.127446	.129088	.130705	.132357	.038522
	21 %	.21	.127104	.128732	.130330	.131966	.133575	.135221	.036665
	22 %	.22	.129983	.131606	.133196	.134827	.136427	.138068	.034894
	23 %	.23	.132843	.134462	.136044	.137671	.139263	.140899	.033208
	24 %	.24	.135686	.137301	.138876	.140498	.142083	.143714	.031602
	25 %	.25	.138513	.140123	.141692	.143310	.144888	.146514	.030072
	26 %	.26	.141324	.142931	.144494	.146107	.147678	.149299	.028616
	27 %	.27	.144121	.145723	.147280	.148889	.150454	.152071	.027230
	28 %	.28	.146902	.148501	.150053	.151658	.153217	.154829	.025911
	29 %	.29	.149670	.151266	.152812	.154414	.155967	.157575	.024657
	30 %	.30	.152426	.154018	.155559	.157157	.158705	.160309	.023463

CAPITALIZATION RATES

Assuming 75% of Purchase Price Financed by Mortgage

20 YEARS AMORTIZATION: 9¼% TO 10½%

Projection	Equity	Yield	9¼%	9½%	9¾%	10%	10¼%	10½%	$\frac{1}{s_{\overline{n}\rceil}}$
Interest Rate			9¼%	9½%	9¾%	10%	10¼%	10½%	
Annual Requirement (f)			.109920	.111960	.113880	.115920	.117840	.119880	
Coverage Min. Rate			.082440	.083970	.085410	.086940	.088380	.089910	
	Balance (b)		.438120	.440392	.447060	.450136	.457837	.461803	+ Dep – App
	Equity	Yield	Basic Rate before Depreciation or Appreciation						
	6 %	.06	.079335	.080938	.082593	.084222	.085910	.087568	.042962
	7 %	.07	.083170	.084767	.086406	.088028	.089698	.091346	.039794
	8 %	.08	.086919	.088512	.090136	.091751	.093404	.095043	.036829
	9 %	.09	.090587	.092175	.093785	.095394	.097030	.098662	.034058
	10 %	.10	.094176	.095760	.097357	.098960	.100582	.102205	.031473
	11 %	.11	.097691	.099271	.100856	.102453	.104061	.105677	.029065
	12 %	.12	.101136	.102711	.104285	.105877	.107472	.109082	.026824
	13 %	.13	.104513	.106085	.107649	.109236	.110819	.112423	.024741
	14 %	.14	.107828	.109396	.110951	.112533	.114105	.115703	.022808
	15 %	.15	.111083	.112649	.114194	.115772	.117334	.118926	.021017
	16 %	.16	.114282	.115845	.117382	.118956	.120508	.122096	.019357
15 Years	17 %	.17	.117429	.118989	.120519	.122090	.123633	.125216	.017822
n = 15	18 %	.18	.120527	.122085	.123607	.125175	.126710	.128289	.016402
	19 %	.19	.123580	.125135	.126651	.128216	.129743	.131318	.015091
	20 %	.20	.126589	.128143	.129653	.131215	.132735	.134306	.013882
	21 %	.21	.129560	.131111	.132615	.134175	.135688	.137256	.012766
	22 %	.22	.132493	.134043	.135542	.137099	.138607	.140171	.011738
	23 %	.23	.135392	.136940	.138434	.139989	.141492	.143054	.010791
	24 %	.24	.138259	.139806	.141296	.142849	.144346	.145906	.009919
	25 %	.25	.141098	.142643	.144129	.145680	.147172	.148729	.009116
	26 %	.26	.143909	.145453	.146935	.148484	.149972	.151527	.008378
	27 %	.27	.146694	.148238	.149716	.151264	.152748	.154301	.007700
	28 %	.28	.149457	.150999	.152475	.154021	.155502	.157053	.007076
	29 %	.29	.152199	.153740	.155212	.156757	.158235	.159784	.006504
	30 %	.30	.154920	.156461	.157930	.159474	.160949	.162497	.005977
	Balance (b)		none	none	none	none	none	none	+ Dep – App
	Equity	Yield	Basic Rate before Depreciation or Appreciation						
	6 %	.06	.077032	.078455	.079949	.081400	.082934	.084419	.027184
	7 %	.07	.081628	.083062	.084550	.086009	.087534	.089023	.024392
	8 %	.08	.086035	.087479	.088962	.090429	.091944	.093438	.021852
	9 %	.09	.090266	.091719	.093198	.094671	.096179	.097676	.019546
	10 %	.10	.094333	.095794	.097268	.098747	.100248	.101749	.017459
	11 %	.11	.098247	.099716	.101186	.102671	.104165	.105669	.015575
	12 %	.12	.102021	.103496	.104963	.106453	.107941	.109448	.013878
	13 %	.13	.105666	.107147	.108611	.110105	.111588	.113098	.012353
	14 %	.14	.109192	.110679	.112141	.113639	.115117	.116629	.010986
20 Years	15 %	.15	.112612	.114103	.115562	.117064	.118538	.120052	.009761
n = 20	16 %	.16	.115933	.117429	.118886	.120391	.121861	.123377	.008667
	17 %	.17	.119166	.120666	.122121	.123629	.125096	.126613	.007690
	18 %	.18	.122320	.123823	.125276	.126787	.128250	.129769	.006819
	19 %	.19	.125401	.126907	.128359	.129872	.131333	.132853	.006045
	20 %	.20	.128418	.129927	.131378	.132892	.134351	.135872	.005356
	21 %	.21	.131378	.132889	.134338	.135854	.137311	.138833	.004744
	22 %	.22	.134285	.135799	.137247	.138765	.140219	.141742	.004201
	23 %	.23	.137147	.138662	.140109	.141628	.143081	.144605	.003720
	24 %	.24	.139967	.141484	.142930	.144451	.145902	.147427	.003293
	25 %	.25	.142751	.144269	.145715	.147236	.148686	.150212	.002915
	26 %	.26	.145502	.147021	.148467	.149989	.151438	.152964	.002581
	27 %	.27	.148224	.149745	.151189	.152713	.154161	.155687	.002285
	28 %	.28	.150921	.152443	.153887	.155411	.156858	.158384	.002023
	29 %	.29	.153594	.155117	.156561	.158086	.159532	.161059	.001791
	30 %	.30	.156248	.157772	.159215	.160740	.162186	.163713	.001586

CAPITALIZATION RATES

Assuming 75% of Purchase Price Financed by Mortgage

20 YEARS AMORTIZATION: 10¾% TO 12%

Interest Rate			10¾%	11%	11¼%	11½%	11¾%	12%	$\frac{1}{s_{\overline{n}\|}}$
Annual Requirement (f)			.121920	.123960	.126000	.128040	.130080	.132240	
Coverage Min. Rate			.091440	.092970	.094500	.096030	.097560	.099180	
Projection	Balance		.905078	.907493	.909944	.912431	.914953	.916696	+ Dep − App
	Equity	Yield	Basic Rate before Depreciation or Appreciation						
	6 %	.06	.093810	.095662	.097518	.099379	.101244	.103096	.177396
	7 %	.07	.096560	.098405	.100255	.102109	.103968	.105815	.173890
	8 %	.08	.099305	.101143	.102987	.104834	.106687	.108530	.170456
	9 %	.09	.102044	.103877	.105714	.107555	.109402	.111240	.167092
	10 %	.10	.104779	.106605	.108436	.110272	.112112	.113946	.163797
	11 %	.11	.107508	.109329	.111154	.112984	.114818	.116648	.160570
	12 %	.12	.110233	.112048	.113868	.115691	.117519	.119345	.157409
	13 %	.13	.112954	.114763	.116577	.118395	.120217	.122038	.154314
	14 %	.14	.115669	.117474	.119282	.121094	.122910	.124728	.151283
	15 %	.15	.118381	.120179	.121982	.123789	.125599	.127413	.148315
5 Years n = 5	16 %	.16	.121088	.122881	.124678	.126479	.128285	.130095	.145409
	17 %	.17	.123790	.125578	.127371	.129166	.130966	.132772	.142563
	18 %	.18	.126489	.128272	.130059	.131849	.133644	.135447	.139777
	19 %	.19	.129183	.130961	.132743	.134528	.136318	.138117	.137050
	20 %	.20	.131873	.133646	.135423	.137204	.138988	.140784	.134379
	21 %	.21	.134559	.136328	.138100	.139876	.141655	.143447	.131765
	22 %	.22	.137241	.139005	.140773	.142544	.144318	.146107	.129205
	23 %	.23	.139920	.141679	.143442	.145208	.146978	.148764	.126700
	24 %	.24	.142594	.144349	.146108	.147869	.149634	.151417	.124247
	25 %	.25	.145265	.147016	.148770	.150527	.152288	.154067	.121846
	26 %	.26	.147932	.149679	.151429	.153181	.154937	.156714	.119496
	27 %	.27	.150596	.152339	.154084	.155832	.157584	.159357	.117195
	28 %	.28	.153257	.154995	.156736	.158480	.160228	.161998	.114943
	29 %	.29	.155913	.157648	.159385	.161125	.162868	.164636	.112739
	30 %	.30	.158567	.160297	.162031	.163767	.165506	.167271	.110581
	Balance (b)		.742988	.747558	.752306	.757235	.762351	.765360	+ Dep − App
	Equity	Yield	Basic Rate before Depreciation or Appreciation						
	6 %	.06	.091815	.093605	.095405	.097216	.099037	.100828	.075867
	7 %	.07	.094988	.096766	.098554	.100351	.102159	.103943	.072377
	8 %	.08	.098133	.099900	.101676	.103461	.105256	.107032	.069029
	9 %	.09	.101252	.103008	.104772	.106545	.108328	.110097	.065820
	10 %	.10	.104345	.106090	.107843	.109605	.111376	.113138	.062745
	11 %	.11	.107412	.109147	.110890	.112641	.114401	.116156	.059801
	12 %	.12	.110455	.112181	.113914	.115654	.117403	.119151	.056984
	13 %	.13	.113475	.115191	.116914	.118645	.120383	.122126	.054289
	14 %	.14	.116471	.118179	.119893	.121614	.123342	.125079	.051713
	15 %	.15	.119446	.121145	.122850	.124562	.126281	.128012	.049252
10 Years n = 10	16 %	.16	.122399	.124090	.125787	.127490	.129200	.130926	.046901
	17 %	.17	.125332	.127015	.128704	.130399	.132100	.133821	.044656
	18 %	.18	.128244	.129920	.131602	.133289	.134982	.136698	.042514
	19 %	.19	.131138	.132807	.134481	.136161	.137846	.139557	.040471
	20 %	.20	.134014	.135676	.137343	.139016	.140693	.142400	.038522
	21 %	.21	.136872	.138528	.140188	.141854	.143524	.145227	.036665
	22 %	.22	.139713	.141363	.143017	.144676	.146340	.148039	.034894
	23 %	.23	.142538	.144182	.145830	.147483	.149141	.150835	.033208
	24 %	.24	.145348	.146986	.148629	.150276	.151927	.153618	.031602
	25 %	.25	.148143	.149776	.151413	.153054	.154699	.156387	.030072
	26 %	.26	.150923	.152552	.154183	.155819	.157459	.159144	.028616
	27 %	.27	.153691	.155314	.156941	.158572	.160206	.161887	.027230
	28 %	.28	.156445	.158064	.159686	.161312	.162941	.164620	.025911
	29 %	.29	.159187	.160801	.162419	.164040	.165665	.167340	.024657
	30 %	.30	.161917	.163527	.165141	.166757	.168377	.170050	.023463

CAPITALIZATION RATES

Assuming 75% of Purchase Price Financed by Mortgage

20 YEARS AMORTIZATION: 10¾% TO 12%

Interest Rate Annual Requirement (f) Coverage Min. Rate			10¾% .121920 .091440	11% .123960 .092970	11¼% .126000 .094500	11½% .128040 .096030	11¾% .130080 .097560	12% .132240 .099180	$\frac{1}{s_{\overline{n}\rvert}}$
Projection	Balance (b)		.466197	.471044	.476365	.482185	.488529	.490428	+ Dep − App
	Equity	Yield	Basic Rate before Depreciation or Appreciation						
	6 %	.06	.089239	.090925	.092627	.094344	.096079	.097760	.042962
	7 %	.07	.093008	.094682	.096371	.098075	.099794	.101471	.039794
	8 %	.08	.096695	.098359	.100036	.101726	.103432	.105104	.036829
	9 %	.09	.100304	.101958	.103624	.105302	.106994	.108663	.034058
	10 %	.10	.103839	.105483	.107139	.108806	.110486	.112151	.031473
	11 %	.11	.107303	.108939	.110585	.112242	.113910	.115571	.029065
	12 %	.12	.110700	.112328	.113965	.115612	.117270	.118928	.026824
	13 %	.13	.114034	.115654	.117283	.118921	.120568	.122224	.024741
	14 %	.14	.117308	.118921	.120542	.122171	.123810	.125462	.022808
	15 %	.15	.120525	.122132	.123746	.125367	.126997	.128647	.021017
	16 %	.16	.123690	.125290	.126897	.128512	.130134	.131781	.019357
	17 %	.17	.126804	.128399	.130000	.131608	.133223	.134868	.017822
15 Years	18 %	.18	.129873	.131462	.133058	.134659	.136267	.137911	.016402
n = 15	19 %	.19	.132897	.134482	.136073	.137668	.139270	.140912	.015091
	20 %	.20	.135882	.137462	.139048	.140638	.142234	.143874	.013882
	21 %	.21	.138828	.140405	.141986	.143572	.145162	.146800	.012766
	22 %	.22	.141740	.143313	.144890	.146471	.148057	.149693	.011738
	23 %	.23	.144619	.146189	.147762	.149339	.150920	.152555	.010791
	24 %	.24	.147468	.149034	.150604	.152177	.153754	.155389	.009919
	25 %	.25	.150290	.151853	.153419	.154989	.156562	.158195	.009116
	26 %	.26	.153085	.154645	.156209	.157775	.159345	.160977	.008378
	27 %	.27	.155857	.157415	.158975	.160539	.162106	.163737	.007700
	28 %	.28	.158606	.160162	.161720	.163281	.164845	.166475	.007076
	29 %	.29	.161336	.162889	.164445	.166004	.167565	.169194	.006504
	30 %	.30	.164046	.165598	.167152	.168708	.170266	.171895	.005977
	Balance (b)		none	none	none	none	none	none	+ Dep − App
	Equity	Yield	Basic Rate before Depreciation or Appreciation						
	6 %	.06	.085919	.087438	.088975	.090534	.092114	.093607	.027184
	7 %	.07	.090527	.092046	.093583	.095138	.096714	.098219	.024392
	8 %	.08	.094945	.096465	.098001	.099554	.101124	.102642	.021852
	9 %	.09	.099185	.100707	.102242	.103792	.105359	.106887	.019546
	10 %	.10	.103260	.104783	.106318	.107866	.109428	.110966	.017459
	11 %	.11	.107182	.108706	.110240	.111786	.113345	.114892	.015575
	12 %	.12	.110963	.112487	.114021	.115565	.117121	.118676	.013878
	13 %	.13	.114614	.116139	.117672	.119215	.120768	.122330	.012353
	14 %	.14	.118147	.119672	.121205	.122747	.124297	.125866	.010986
	15 %	.15	.121571	.123097	.124630	.126170	.127718	.129292	.009761
20 Years n = 20	16 %	.16	.124897	.126424	.127956	.129495	.131041	.132620	.008667
	17 %	.17	.128134	.129661	.131193	.132731	.134276	.135860	.007690
	18 %	.18	.131291	.132819	.134350	.135888	.137430	.139018	.006819
	19 %	.19	.134376	.135904	.137435	.138972	.140513	.142105	.006045
	20 %	.20	.137396	.138924	.140455	.141991	.143531	.145126	.005356
	21 %	.21	.140358	.141886	.143417	.144952	.146491	.148089	.004744
	22 %	.22	.143268	.144796	.146327	.147861	.149399	.151000	.004201
	23 %	.23	.146131	.147660	.149191	.150724	.152261	.153864	.003720
	24 %	.24	.148953	.150482	.152013	.153546	.155082	.156687	.003293
	25 %	.25	.151738	.153267	.154798	.156331	.157866	.159473	.002915
	26 %	.26	.154491	.156020	.157551	.159083	.160618	.162226	.002581
	27 %	.27	.157214	.158743	.160274	.161806	.163341	.164950	.002285
	28 %	.28	.159912	.161441	.162972	.164504	.166038	.167648	.002023
	29 %	.29	.162587	.164116	.165647	.167179	.168712	.170324	.001791
	30 %	.30	.165242	.166771	.168301	.169833	.171366	.172979	.001586

CAPITALIZATION RATES

Assuming 75% of Purchase Price Financed by Mortgage

25 YEARS AMORTIZATION: 3¼% TO 4½%

Interest Rate Annual Requirement(f) Coverage Min. Rate		3¼% .05856 .04392	3½% .06012 .04509	3¾% .06180 .04635	4% .06336 .04752	4¼% .06504 .04878	4½% .06672 .05004	$\frac{1}{s_{\overline{n}\rceil}}$
Projection	Balance(b)	.858723	.862958	.866592	.870938	.874677	.878467	+ Dep − App
	Equity Yield	Basic Rate before Depreciation or Appreciation						
	5% .05	.0373	.0390	.0408	.0425	.0443	.0461	.1810
	6% .06	.0402	.0419	.0437	.0454	.0471	.0489	.1774
	7% .07	.0430	.0448	.0465	.0482	.0500	.0517	.1739
	8% .08	.0459	.0476	.0494	.0511	.0528	.0545	.1705
	9% .09	.0488	.0504	.0522	.0539	.0556	.0573	.1671
5 Years	10% .10	.0516	.0533	.0550	.0567	.0584	.0601	.1638
n = 5	11% .11	.0545	.0561	.0578	.0596	.0612	.0629	.1606
	12% .12	.0573	.0590	.0606	.0624	.0640	.0657	.1574
	13% .13	.0601	.0618	.0634	.0652	.0668	.0685	.1543
	14% .14	.0629	.0646	.0662	.0680	.0696	.0713	.1513
	15% .15	.0657	.0674	.0690	.0707	.0724	.0741	.1483
	16% .16	.0686	.0702	.0718	.0735	.0752	.0769	.1454
	17% .17	.0714	.0730	.0746	.0763	.0779	.0796	.1426
	18% .18	.0742	.0758	.0774	.0791	.0807	.0824	.1398
	19% .19	.0769	.0786	.0802	.0818	.0835	.0851	.1371
	20% .20	.0797	.0813	.0830	.0846	.0862	.0878	.1344
	Balance (b)	.692554	.699748	.705717	.713354	.719739	.726332	+ Dep − App
	Equity Yield	Basic Rate before Depreciation or Appreciation						
	5% .05	.0381	.0398	.0413	.0430	.0446	.0463	.0795
	6% .06	.0415	.0431	.0447	.0462	.0479	.0495	.0759
	7% .07	.0448	.0463	.0479	.0495	.0511	.0527	.0724
	8% .08	.0481	.0496	.0512	.0527	.0543	.0560	.0690
	9% .09	.0513	.0528	.0544	.0559	.0575	.0591	.0658
10 Years	10% .10	.0545	.0560	.0576	.0591	.0607	.0622	.0628
n = 10	11% .11	.0577	.0592	.0607	.0622	.0638	.0653	.0598
	12% .12	.0609	.0623	.0639	.0653	.0669	.0684	.0570
	13% .13	.0640	.0654	.0669	.0684	.0699	.0715	.0543
	14% .14	.0671	.0685	.0700	.0715	.0730	.0745	.0517
	15% .15	.0701	.0716	.0730	.0745	.0760	.0775	.0493
	16% .16	.0732	.0746	.0760	.0775	.0790	.0805	.0469
	17% .17	.0762	.0776	.0791	.0805	.0820	.0834	.0447
	18% .18	.0792	.0806	.0820	.0834	.0849	.0864	.0425
	19% .19	.0822	.0835	.0850	.0864	.0878	.0893	.0405
	20% .20	.0851	.0865	.0879	.0893	.0908	.0922	.0385

CAPITALIZATION RATES

Assuming 75% of Purchase Price Financed by Mortgage.

25 YEARS AMORTIZATION: 3¼% TO 4½%

Interest Rate		3¼%	3½%	3¾%	4%	4¼%	4½%	$\frac{1}{s_{\overline{n}\rceil}}$
Annual Requirement (f)		.05856	.06012	.06180	.06336	.06504	.06672	
Coverage Min. Rate		.04392	.04509	.04635	.04752	.04878	.05004	
Projection	Balance (b)	.497108	.505375	.511722	.520944	.528189	.535889	+ Dep
	Equity Yield	Basic Rate before Depreciation or Appreciation						− App
	5% .05	.0390	.0404	.0419	.0434	.0449	.0464	.0464
	6% .06	.0428	.0442	.0456	.0471	.0486	.0501	.0430
	7% .07	.0465	.0479	.0493	.0507	.0522	.0537	.0398
	8% .08	.0501	.0514	.0529	.0543	.0558	.0573	.0368
	9% .09	.0536	.0550	.0564	.0578	.0593	.0607	.0341
15 Years	10% .10	.0571	.0585	.0599	.0612	.0627	.0641	.0315
n = 15	11% .11	.0605	.0619	.0632	.0646	.0661	.0675	.0291
	12% .12	.0638	.0652	.0665	.0679	.0693	.0707	.0268
	13% .13	.0671	.0684	.0698	.0711	.0726	.0740	.0248
	14% .14	.0703	.0717	.0730	.0744	.0757	.0772	.0228
	15% .15	.0735	.0748	.0762	.0775	.0788	.0803	.0210
	16% .16	.0767	.0780	.0793	.0806	.0819	.0834	.0194
	17% .17	.0797	.0810	.0823	.0837	.0850	.0864	.0178
	18% .18	.0828	.0840	.0854	.0866	.0880	.0893	.0164
	19% .19	.0858	.0870	.0884	.0897	.0910	.0924	.0151
	20% .20	.0887	.0900	.0913	.0926	.0939	.0952	.0139
	Balance (b)	.267227	.273887	.277788	.286012	.291376	.297495	+ Dep
	Equity Yield	Basic Rate before Depreciation or Appreciation						− App
	5% .05	.0398	.0412	.0425	.0439	.0452	.0466	.0303
	6% .06	.0440	.0453	.0467	.0480	.0494	.0507	.0272
	7% .07	.0480	.0493	.0507	.0520	.0534	.0547	.0244
	8% .08	.0520	.0532	.0545	.0559	.0572	.0586	.0219
	9% .09	.0557	.0570	.0583	.0596	.0609	.0623	.0196
20 Years	10% .10	.0594	.0606	.0619	.0632	.0645	.0659	.0175
n = 20	11% .11	.0629	.0641	.0655	.0667	.0680	.0694	.0156
	12% .12	.0663	.0676	.0689	.0701	.0714	.0728	.0139
	13% .13	.0696	.0709	.0722	.0735	.0747	.0761	.0124
	14% .14	.0729	.0742	.0754	.0766	.0780	.0793	.0110
	15% .15	.0761	.0773	.0786	.0798	.0811	.0824	.0098
	16% .16	.0792	.0804	.0817	.0829	.0842	.0855	.0087
	17% .17	.0823	.0835	.0847	.0859	.0872	.0886	.0077
	18% .18	.0852	.0864	.0877	.0889	.0902	.0915	.0068
	19% .19	.0882	.0894	.0906	.0918	.0931	.0944	.0061
	20% .20	.0910	.0922	.0935	.0947	.0960	.0973	.0054

CAPITALIZATION RATES

Assuming 75% of Purchase Price Financed by Mortgage

25 YEARS AMORTIZATION: 3¼% TO 4½%

Interest Rate Annual Requirement (f) Coverage Min. Rate		3¼% .05856 .04392	3½% .06012 .04509	3¾% .06180 .04635	4% .06336 .04752	4¼% .06504 .04878	4½% .06672 .05004	$\frac{1}{s_{\overline{n}\rceil}}$
Projection	Balance(b)	none	none	none	none	none	none	+ Dep − App
	Equity Yield	Basic Rate before Depreciation or Appreciation						
	5% .05	.0407	.0419	.0432	.0443	.0456	.0469	.0210
	6% .06	.0453	.0464	.0477	.0489	.0501	.0514	.0182
	7% .07	.0496	.0507	.0520	.0532	.0545	.0557	.0158
	8% .08	.0537	.0549	.0561	.0573	.0586	.0598	.0137
	9% .09	.0576	.0587	.0600	.0612	.0625	.0637	.0118
25 Years	10% .10	.0613	.0625	.0638	.0649	.0662	.0675	.0102
n = 25	11% .11	.0649	.0661	.0673	.0685	.0697	.0710	.0088
	12% .12	.0683	.0695	.0707	.0719	.0732	.0744	.0075
	13% .13	.0717	.0728	.0741	.0753	.0765	.0777	.0064
	14% .14	.0748	.0760	.0772	.0784	.0797	.0809	.0055
	15% .15	.0779	.0791	.0803	.0815	.0828	.0840	.0047
	16% .16	.0810	.0821	.0834	.0846	.0858	.0870	.0040
	17% .17	.0839	.0850	.0863	.0875	.0888	.0900	.0035
	18% .18	.0868	.0879	.0892	.0904	.0917	.0929	.0029
	19% .19	.0896	.0908	.0921	.0932	.0945	.0957	.0025
	20% .20	.0924	.0935	.0948	.0960	.0973	.0985	.0021

CAPITALIZATION RATES

Assuming 75% of Purchase Price Financed by Mortgage

25 YEARS AMORTIZATION: 4¾% TO 6%

Interest Rate / Annual Requirement(f) / Coverage Min. Rate		4¾%	5%	5¼%	5½%	5¾%	6%	$\frac{1}{s_{\overline{n}\rvert}}$
Annual Requirement(f)		.06852	.07020	.07200	.07380	.07560	.07740	
Coverage Min. Rate		.05139	.05265	.05400	.05535	.05670	.05805	
Projection	Balance (b)	.881633	.885523	.888782	.892087	.895437	.898833	+ Dep
	Equity Yield	Basic Rate before Depreciation or Appreciation						− App
5 Years n = 5	5% .05	.0479	.0497	.0515	.0533	.0551	.0569	.1810
	6% .06	.0507	.0525	.0543	.0561	.0579	.0597	.1774
	7% .07	.0535	.0553	.0571	.0589	.0606	.0624	.1739
	8% .08	.0563	.0581	.0599	.0616	.0634	.0652	.1705
	9% .09	.0591	.0609	.0626	.0644	.0662	.0679	.1671
	10% .10	.0619	.0637	.0654	.0671	.0689	.0707	.1638
	11% .11	.0647	.0664	.0683	.0699	.0716	.0734	.1606
	12% .12	.0675	.0692	.0710	.0726	.0744	.0762	.1574
	13% .13	.0703	.0720	.0738	.0754	.0772	.0789	.1543
	14% .14	.0730	.0747	.0765	.0782	.0799	.0816	.1513
	15% .15	.0758	.0774	.0792	.0809	.0826	.0843	.1483
	16% .16	.0785	.0802	.0820	.0836	.0853	.0871	.1454
	17% .17	.0813	.0830	.0847	.0864	.0881	.0898	.1426
	18% .18	.0840	.0857	.0874	.0891	.0908	.0925	.1398
	19% .19	.0868	.0885	.0901	.0919	.0935	.0952	.1371
	20% .20	.0896	.0912	.0929	.0945	.0962	.0979	.1344
	Balance (b)	.731604	.738608	.744262	.750105	.756141	.762375	+ Dep
	Equity Yield	Basic Rate before Depreciation or Appreciation						− App
10 Years n = 10	5% .05	.0479	.0496	.0513	.0530	.0547	.0564	.0795
	6% .06	.0512	.0528	.0545	.0562	.0579	.0596	.0759
	7% .07	.0544	.0560	.0577	.0593	.0610	.0627	.0724
	8% .08	.0575	.0592	.0608	.0625	.0641	.0658	.0690
	9% .09	.0607	.0623	.0639	.0656	.0672	.0689	.0658
	10% .10	.0638	.0654	.0670	.0686	.0703	.0719	.0628
	11% .11	.0669	.0685	.0701	.0717	.0733	.0749	.0598
	12% .12	.0700	.0715	.0732	.0747	.0763	.0780	.0570
	13% .13	.0730	.0745	.0761	.0778	.0793	.0809	.0543
	14% .14	.0761	.0776	.0791	.0807	.0823	.0839	.0517
	15% .15	.0790	.0806	.0821	.0837	.0852	.0868	.0493
	16% .16	.0820	.0835	.0850	.0866	.0882	.0898	.0469
	17% .17	.0850	.0865	.0880	.0896	.0911	.0926	.0447
	18% .18	.0879	.0894	.0909	.0924	.0940	.0955	.0425
	19% .19	.0908	.0923	.0938	.0953	.0969	.0984	.0405
	20% .20	.0937	.0952	.0967	.0982	.0997	.1013	.0385

CAPITALIZATION RATES

Assuming 75% of Purchase Price Financed by Mortgage

25 YEARS AMORTIZATION: 4¾% TO 6%

Interest Rate		4¾%	5%	5¼%	5½%	5¾%	6%	$\frac{1}{s_{\overline{n}\rceil}}$
Annual Requirement (f)		.06852	.07020	.07200	.07380	.07560	.07740	
Coverage Min. Rate		.05139	.05265	.05400	.05535	.05670	.05805	
Projection	Balance (b)	.541447	.550064	.556469	.563299	.570573	.578313	+ Dep − App
	Equity Yield	Basic Rate before Depreciation or Appreciation						
	5% .05	.0480	.0496	.0511	.0527	.0543	.0559	.0464
	6% .06	.0516	.0532	.0548	.0563	.0579	.0595	.0430
	7% .07	.0552	.0567	.0583	.0599	.0615	.0630	.0398
	8% .08	.0588	.0603	.0618	.0633	.0648	.0664	.0368
	9% .09	.0622	.0637	.0652	.0667	.0682	.0698	.0341
15 Years n = 15	10% .10	.0656	.0671	.0686	.0701	.0716	.0731	.0315
	11% .11	.0689	.0703	.0718	.0733	.0748	.0764	.0291
	12% .12	.0722	.0737	.0751	.0766	.0781	.0796	.0268
	13% .13	.0754	.0768	.0783	.0798	.0812	.0828	.0248
	14% .14	.0786	.0800	.0814	.0829	.0844	.0859	.0228
	15% .15	.0817	.0831	.0845	.0860	.0874	.0890	.0210
	16% .16	.0848	.0861	.0876	.0891	.0905	.0920	.0194
	17% .17	.0878	.0892	.0906	.0921	.0935	.0949	.0178
	18% .18	.0908	.0922	.0936	.0950	.0965	.0979	.0164
	19% .19	.0937	.0951	.0965	.0979	.0994	.1008	.0151
	20% .20	.0967	.0980	.0994	.1009	.1023	.1037	.0139
	Balance(b)	.300425	.308093	.312443	.317518	.323365	.330040	+ Dep − App
	Equity Yield	Basic Rate before Depreciation or Appreciation						
	5% .05	.0481	.0495	.0509	.0524	.0538	.0553	.0303
	6% .06	.0521	.0536	.0550	.0565	.0579	.0594	.0272
	7% .07	.0561	.0575	.0590	.0604	.0618	.0633	.0244
	8% .08	.0600	.0613	.0628	.0642	.0656	.0671	.0219
	9% .09	.0637	.0650	.0665	.0679	.0693	.0707	.0196
20 Years n = 20	10% .10	.0672	.0686	.0700	.0714	.0729	.0743	.0175
	11% .11	.0707	.0721	.0735	.0749	.0763	.0778	.0156
	12% .12	.0741	.0755	.0769	.0783	.0797	.0811	.0139
	13% .13	.0774	.0788	.0801	.0816	.0830	.0843	.0124
	14% .14	.0807	.0820	.0834	.0847	.0862	.0876	.0110
	15% .15	.0838	.0851	.0865	.0879	.0893	.0907	.0098
	16% .16	.0869	.0882	.0896	.0909	.0924	.0937	.0087
	17% .17	.0899	.0912	.0926	.0940	.0953	.0967	.0077
	18% .18	.0929	.0941	.0965	.0969	.0983	.0997	.0068
	19% .19	.0957	.0971	.0984	.0998	.1011	.1026	.0061
	20% .20	.0986	.0999	.1013	.1027	.1040	.1054	.0054

CAPITALIZATION RATES

Assuming 75% of Purchase Price Financed by Mortgage

25 YEARS AMORTIZATION: 4¾% TO 6%

Interest Rate Annual Requirement(f) Coverage Min. Rate		4¾% .06852 .05139	5% .07020 .05265	5¼% .07200 .05400	5½% .07380 .05535	5¾% .07560 .05670	6% .07740 .05805	$\frac{1}{s_{\overline{n}\rceil}}$
Projection	Balance (b)	None	None	None	None	None	None	+ Dep − App
	Equity Yield	Basic Rate before Depreciation or Appreciation						
	5% .05	.0482	.0495	.0508	.0521	.0535	.0548	.0210
	6% .06	.0527	.0540	.0554	.0567	.0581	.0594	.0182
	7% .07	.0570	.0583	.0597	.0610	.0624	.0637	.0158
	8% .08	.0612	.0624	.0637	.0651	.0664	.0678	.0137
	9% .09	.0650	.0663	.0677	.0690	.0704	.0717	.0118
25 Years n = 25	10% .10	.0688	.0701	.0714	.0728	.0741	.0755	.0102
	11% .11	.0724	.0736	.0750	.0763	.0777	.0790	.0088
	12% .12	.0758	.0770	.0784	.0797	.0811	.0824	.0075
	13% .13	.0791	.0804	.0817	.0831	.0844	.0858	.0064
	14% .14	.0823	.0835	.0849	.0862	.0876	.0889	.0055
	15% .15	.0854	.0866	.0880	.0893	.0907	.0920	.0047
	16% .16	.0884	.0897	.0910	.0924	.0937	.0951	.0040
	17% .17	.0913	.0926	.0940	.0953	.0967	.0980	.0034
	18% .18	.0942	.0955	.0968	.0982	.0995	.1009	.0029
	19% .19	.0971	.0984	.0997	.1011	.1024	.1038	.0025
	20% .20	.0998	.1011	.1024	.1038	.1051	.1065	.0021

CAPITALIZATION RATES

Assuming 75% of Purchase Price Financed by Mortgage

25 YEARS AMORTIZATION: 6¼% TO 7½%

Interest Rate			6¼%	6½%	6¾%	7%	7¼%	7½%	$\frac{1}{s_{\overline{n}|}}$
Annual Requirement (f)			.079200	.081120	.082920	.084840	.086760	.088680	
Coverage Min. Rate			.059400	.060840	.062190	.063630	.065070	.066510	
Projection	Balance (b)		.902276	.905061	.908595	.911463	.914370	.917319	+ Dep − App
	Equity	Yield	Basic Rate before Depreciation or Appreciation						
5 Years n = 5	6 %	.06	.061398	.063208	.065028	.066850	.068677	.070509	.177396
	7 %	.07	.064155	.065958	.067769	.069583	.071402	.073226	.173890
	8 %	.08	.066906	.068702	.070504	.072311	.074122	.075939	.170456
	9 %	.09	.069653	.071442	.073235	.075034	.076839	.078648	.167092
	10 %	.10	.072394	.074176	.075961	.077753	.079550	.081352	.163797
	11 %	.11	.075131	.076906	.078682	.080467	.082257	.084052	.160570
	12 %	.12	.077863	.079631	.081399	.083177	.084960	.086748	.157409
	13 %	.13	.080589	.082352	.084111	.085883	.087659	.089440	.154314
	14 %	.14	.083312	.085068	.086819	.088584	.090354	.092128	.151283
	15 %	.15	.086029	.087779	.089522	.091281	.093044	.094812	.148315
	16 %	.16	.088742	.090486	.092221	.093974	.095731	.097493	.145409
	17 %	.17	.091451	.093188	.094916	.096663	.098414	.100169	.142563
	18 %	.18	.094155	.095887	.097607	.099348	.101093	.102842	.139777
	19 %	.19	.096855	.098581	.100294	.102029	.103768	.105511	.137050
	20 %	.20	.099551	.101271	.102977	.104706	.106439	.108177	.134379
	21 %	.21	.102242	.103957	.105657	.107380	.109107	.110839	.131765
	22 %	.22	.104930	.106640	.108332	.110050	.111772	.113497	.129205
	23 %	.23	.107613	.109318	.111004	.112716	.114433	.116153	.126700
	24 %	.24	.110293	.111993	.113672	.115379	.117090	.118805	.124247
	25 %	.25	.112969	.114664	.116337	.118039	.119744	.121454	.121846
	26 %	.26	.115641	.117331	.118998	.120695	.122395	.124099	.119496
	27 %	.27	.118310	.119995	.121655	.123347	.125043	.126742	.117195
	28 %	.28	.120975	.122655	.124310	.125997	.127688	.129382	.114943
	29 %	.29	.123637	.125312	.126961	.128643	.130329	.132018	.112739
	30 %	.30	.126295	.127966	.129609	.131287	.132968	.134652	.110581
	Balance (b)		.768813	.773778	.780619	.785951	.791463	.797159	+ Dep − App
	Equity	Yield	Basic Rate before Depreciation or Appreciation						
10 Years n = 10	6 %	.06	.061245	.062967	.064707	.066450	.068204	.069968	.075867
	7 %	.07	.064350	.066059	.067781	.069510	.071249	.072999	.072377
	8 %	.08	.067430	.069128	.070832	.072548	.074273	.076008	.069029
	9 %	.09	.070487	.072172	.073860	.075563	.077275	.078996	.065820
	10 %	.10	.073520	.075194	.076866	.078557	.080256	.081964	.062745
	11 %	.11	.076531	.078193	.079850	.081529	.083216	.084912	.059801
	12 %	.12	.079519	.081171	.082814	.084481	.086157	.087840	.056984
	13 %	.13	.082486	.084128	.085757	.087414	.089078	.090750	.054289
	14 %	.14	.085433	.087065	.088681	.090328	.091981	.093642	.051713
	15 %	.15	.088360	.089983	.091586	.093223	.094866	.096517	.049252
	16 %	.16	.091267	.092882	.094473	.096100	.097734	.099374	.046901
	17 %	.17	.094157	.095763	.097342	.098961	.100585	.102216	.044656
	18 %	.18	.097028	.098626	.100194	.101804	.103420	.105042	.042514
	19 %	.19	.099882	.101473	.103031	.104632	.106240	.107853	.040471
	20 %	.20	.102720	.104303	.105851	.107445	.109044	.110649	.038522
	21 %	.21	.105542	.107119	.108657	.110243	.111835	.113432	.036665
	22 %	.22	.108349	.109919	.111448	.113028	.114612	.116201	.034894
	23 %	.23	.111141	.112705	.114226	.115798	.117376	.118957	.033208
	24 %	.24	.113920	.115478	.116990	.118556	.120127	.121702	.031602
	25 %	.25	.116685	.118237	.119742	.121302	.122866	.124435	.030072
	26 %	.26	.119438	.120984	.122481	.124036	.125594	.127156	.028616
	27 %	.27	.122178	.123719	.125209	.126758	.128311	.129867	.027230
	28 %	.28	.124907	.126443	.127926	.129470	.131017	.132568	.025911
	29 %	.29	.127624	.129156	.130633	.132171	.133713	.135258	.024657
	30 %	.30	.130331	.131859	.133329	.134863	.136400	.137940	.023463

CAPITALIZATION RATES

Assuming 75% of Purchase Price Financed by Mortgage

25 YEARS AMORTIZATION: 6¼% TO 7½%

			6¼%	6½%	6¾%	7%	7½%	7½%	$\frac{1}{s_{\overline{n}\rceil}}$
Interest Rate			6¼%	6½%	6¾%	7%	7½%	7½%	
Annual Requirement (f)			.079200	.081120	.082920	.084840	.086760	.088680	
Coverage Min. Rate			.059400	.060840	.062190	.063630	.065070	.066510	
Projection	Balance (b)		.586538	.592238	.601438	.608023	.615047	.622532	+ Dep − App
	Equity	Yield	Basic Rate before Depreciation or Appreciation						
	6 %	.06	.061077	.062701	.064347	.065999	.067666	.069347	.042962
	7 %	.07	.064559	.066169	.067794	.069431	.071080	.072744	.039794
	8 %	.08	.067979	.069576	.071180	.072802	.074436	.076083	.036829
	9 %	.09	.071338	.072924	.074509	.076117	.077736	.079367	.034058
	10 %	.10	.074640	.076214	.077781	.079377	.080983	.082599	.031473
	11 %	.11	.077886	.079451	.081001	.082585	.084178	.085781	.029065
	12 %	.12	.081081	.082636	.084171	.085744	.087325	.088916	.026824
	13 %	.13	.084227	.085773	.087294	.088856	.090426	.092005	.024741
	14 %	.14	.087327	.088864	.090371	.091924	.093484	.095052	.022808
	15 %	.15	.090382	.091912	.093407	.094951	.096502	.098060	.021017
15 Years n = 15	16 %	.16	.093397	.094920	.096403	.097939	.099481	.101029	.019357
	17 %	.17	.096373	.097889	.099362	.100890	.102424	.103964	.017822
	18 %	.18	.099313	.100823	.102286	.103807	.105334	.106866	.016402
	19 %	.19	.102220	.103724	.105178	.106693	.108212	.109737	.015091
	20 %	.20	.105095	.106594	.108040	.109548	.111062	.112579	.013882
	21 %	.21	.107941	.109435	.110873	.112376	.113884	.115395	.012766
	22 %	.22	.110760	.112250	.113681	.115179	.116681	.118186	.011738
	23 %	.23	.113553	.115039	.116464	.117957	.119454	.120955	.010791
	24 %	.24	.116324	.117806	.119224	.120713	.122206	.123701	.009919
	25 %	.25	.119072	.120551	.121964	.123449	.124937	.126429	.009116
	26 %	.26	.121801	.123277	.124685	.126166	.127650	.129137	.008378
	27 %	.27	.124512	.125985	.127388	.128866	.130346	.131829	.007700
	28 %	.28	.127205	.128675	.130074	.131549	.133026	.134506	.007076
	29 %	.29	.129883	.131350	.132745	.134217	.135692	.137168	.006504
	30 %	.30	.132546	.134011	.135403	.136872	.138344	.139817	.005977
	Balance (b)		.337600	.341201	.350564	.355787	.361829	.368746	+ Dep − App
	Equity	Yield	Basic Rate before Depreciation or Appreciation						
	6 %	.06	.060894	.062408	.063949	.065495	.067058	.068639	.027184
	7 %	.07	.064781	.066287	.067808	.069344	.070894	.072461	.024392
	8 %	.08	.068543	.070042	.071546	.073071	.074610	.076164	.021852
	9 %	.09	.072189	.073682	.075169	.076685	.078214	.079755	.019546
	10 %	.10	.075726	.077213	.078685	.080194	.081713	.083243	.017459
	11 %	.11	.079162	.080644	.082103	.083604	.085115	.086635	.015575
	12 %	.12	.082505	.083982	.085429	.086924	.088427	.089939	.013878
	13 %	.13	.085762	.087236	.088672	.090161	.091657	.093161	.012353
	14 %	.14	.088942	.090411	.091838	.093322	.094811	.096308	.010986
20 Years n = 20	15 %	.15	.092050	.093516	.094935	.096413	.097897	.099388	.009761
	16 %	.16	.095094	.096557	.097968	.099442	.100921	.102406	.008667
	17 %	.17	.098079	.099540	.100944	.102414	.103889	.105369	.007690
	18 %	.18	.101011	.102470	.103868	.105334	.106805	.108281	.006819
	19 %	.19	.103896	.105353	.106745	.108209	.109676	.111147	.006045
	20 %	.20	.106738	.108193	.109580	.111041	.112506	.113974	.005356
	21 %	.21	.109542	.110995	.112378	.113837	.115299	.116763	.004744
	22 %	.22	.112312	.113763	.115143	.116599	.118058	.119520	.004201
	23 %	.23	.115051	.116501	.117877	.119332	.120789	.122248	.003720
	24 %	.24	.117763	.119212	.120585	.122038	.123493	.124950	.003293
	25 %	.25	.120451	.121899	.123269	.124721	.126174	.127629	.002915
	26 %	.26	.123117	.124564	.125932	.127382	.128834	.130287	.002581
	27 %	.27	.125764	.127210	.128576	.130025	.131476	.132928	.002285
	28 %	.28	.128394	.129840	.131204	.132652	.134101	.135552	.002023
	29 %	.29	.131009	.132454	.133817	.135264	.136712	.138161	.001791
	30 %	.30	.133611	.135055	.136417	.137863	.139310	.140758	.001586

CAPITALIZATION RATES

Assuming 75% of Purchase Price Financed by Mortgage

25 YEARS AMORTIZATION: 6¼% TO 7½%

Interest Rate			6¼%	6½%	6¾%	7%	7¼%	7½%	$\frac{1}{s_{\overline{n}|}}$
Annual Requirement (f)			.079200	.081120	.082920	.084840	.086760	.088680	
Coverage Min. Rate			.059400	.060840	.062190	.063630	.065070	.066510	
Projection	Balance (b)		none	none	none	none	none	none	+ Dep – App
	Equity	Yield	Basic Rate before Depreciation or Appreciation						
	6 %	.06	.060697	.062088	.063510	.064935	.066377	.067838	.018226
	7 %	.07	.065013	.066411	.067823	.069250	.070692	.072151	.015810
	8 %	.08	.069116	.070520	.071923	.073352	.074794	.076250	.013678
	9 %	.09	.073024	.074432	.075829	.077259	.078700	.080154	.011806
	10 %	.10	.076755	.078168	.079558	.080990	.082431	.083883	.010168
	11 %	.11	.080329	.081745	.083130	.084563	.086004	.087454	.008740
	12 %	.12	.083761	.085181	.086561	.087994	.089435	.090884	.007499
	13 %	.13	.087069	.088491	.089867	.091301	.092742	.094190	.006425
	14 %	.14	.090266	.091691	.093063	.094498	.095939	.097385	.005498
	15 %	.15	.093367	.094794	.096163	.097599	.099039	.100485	.004699
	16 %	.16	.096383	.097812	.099178	.100615	.102055	.103500	.004012
25 Years	17 %	.17	.099326	.100757	.102120	.103557	.104998	.106442	.003423
n = 25	18 %	.18	.102205	.103637	.104999	.106436	.107877	.109320	.002918
	19 %	.19	.105030	.106463	.107823	.109261	.110701	.112144	.002487
	20 %	.20	.107807	.109241	.110599	.112038	.113478	.114920	.002118
	21 %	.21	.110543	.111978	.113335	.114774	.116214	.117656	.001804
	22 %	.22	.113245	.114681	.116037	.117475	.118915	.120357	.001536
	23 %	.23	.115916	.117353	.118708	.120147	.121587	.123029	.001307
	24 %	.24	.118562	.119999	.121354	.122793	.124233	.125674	.001113
	25 %	.25	.121187	.122624	.123978	.125417	.126857	.128298	.000948
	26 %	.26	.123793	.125230	.126584	.128023	.129463	.130904	.000807
	27 %	.27	.126383	.127821	.129173	.130613	.132053	.133494	.000687
	28 %	.28	.128959	.130397	.131750	.133189	.134629	.136070	.000585
	29 %	.29	.131524	.132963	.134315	.135754	.137194	.138635	.000499
	30 %	.30	.134079	.135518	.136870	.138310	.139750	.141190	.000425

CAPITALIZATION RATES

Assuming 75% of Purchase Price Financed by Mortgage

25 YEARS AMORTIZATION: 7¾% TO 9%

			7¾%	8%	8¼%	8½%	8¾%	9%	$\frac{1}{s_{\overline{n}\rvert}}$
Interest Rate			7¾%	8%	8¼%	8½%	8¾%	9%	
Annual Requirement (f)			.090720	.092640	.094680	.096720	.098760	.100800	
Coverage Min. Rate			.068040	.069480	.071010	.072540	.074070	.075600	
Projection	Balance (b)		.919578	.922604	.924932	.927294	.929689	.932118	+ Dep – App
	Equity	Yield	Basic Rate before Depreciation or Appreciation						
	6 %	.06	.072340	.074182	.076022	.077866	.079715	.081568	.177396
	7 %	.07	.075051	.076886	.078719	.080557	.082400	.084247	.173890
	8 %	.08	.077758	.079585	.081413	.083245	.085081	.086921	.170456
	9 %	.09	.080461	.082280	.084102	.085928	.087758	.089593	.167092
	10 %	.10	.083160	.084972	.086788	.088608	.090432	.092260	.163797
	11 %	.11	.085854	.087659	.089469	.091284	.093102	.094925	.160570
	12 %	.12	.088545	.090342	.092147	.093956	.095769	.097586	.157409
	13 %	.13	.091232	.093022	.094822	.096625	.098432	.100243	.154314
	14 %	.14	.093915	.095698	.097492	.099290	.101092	.102897	.151283
	15 %	.15	.096594	.098370	.100159	.101952	.103748	.105549	.148315
5 Years	16 %	.16	.099269	.101039	.102823	.104610	.106402	.108197	.145409
n = 5	17 %	.17	.101941	.103704	.105483	.107266	.109052	.110841	.142563
	18 %	.18	.104609	.106366	.108140	.109918	.111699	.113483	.139777
	19 %	.19	.107273	.109024	.110794	.112566	.114342	.116122	.137050
	20 %	.20	.109934	.111679	.113444	.115212	.116983	.118758	.134379
	21 %	.21	.112592	.114331	.116091	.117854	.119621	.121391	.131765
	22 %	.22	.115246	.116980	.118735	.120494	.122256	.124021	.129205
	23 %	.23	.117897	.119625	.121376	.123131	.124888	.126649	.126700
	24 %	.24	.120545	.122267	.124014	.125764	.127518	.129274	.124247
	25 %	.25	.123190	.124907	.126649	.128395	.130144	.131896	.121846
	26 %	.26	.125832	.127543	.129282	.131023	.132768	.134516	.119496
	27 %	.27	.128471	.130177	.131911	.133649	.135389	.137133	.117195
	28 %	.28	.131107	.132807	.134538	.136272	.138008	.139748	.114943
	29 %	.29	.133739	.135435	.137162	.138892	.140624	.142360	.112739
	30 %	.30	.136370	.138061	.139784	.141510	.143238	.144970	.110581
	Balance (b)		.801241	.807296	.811697	.816251	.820963	.825837	+ Dep – App
	Equity	Yield	Basic Rate before Depreciation or Appreciation						
	6 %	.06	.071730	.073515	.075295	.077084	.078882	.080689	.075867
	7 %	.07	.074750	.076519	.078288	.080065	.081851	.083645	.072377
	8 %	.08	.077749	.079503	.081261	.083026	.084800	.086583	.069029
	9 %	.09	.080728	.082467	.084214	.085969	.087731	.089502	.065820
	10 %	.10	.083686	.085411	.087148	.088892	.090644	.092404	.062745
	11 %	.11	.086625	.088337	.090064	.091798	.093540	.095288	.059801
	12 %	.12	.089545	.091244	.092962	.094686	.096418	.098156	.056984
	13 %	.13	.092447	.094133	.095842	.097558	.099280	.101008	.054289
	14 %	.14	.095331	.097005	.098706	.100413	.102126	.103845	.051713
	15 %	.15	.098198	.099861	.101554	.103252	.104956	.106666	.049252
	16 %	.16	.101048	.102701	.104386	.106076	.107772	.109473	.046901
10 Years	17 %	.17	.103883	.105525	.107203	.108885	.110573	.112266	.044656
n = 10	18 %	.18	.106702	.108335	.110005	.111680	.113361	.115046	.042514
	19 %	.19	.109506	.111130	.112794	.114462	.116135	.117813	.040471
	20 %	.20	.112297	.113912	.115569	.117231	.118897	.120568	.038522
	21 %	.21	.115074	.116680	.118331	.119987	.121646	.123310	.036665
	22 %	.22	.117838	.119436	.121081	.122731	.124384	.126041	.034894
	23 %	.23	.120589	.122180	.123820	.125463	.127110	.128762	.033208
	24 %	.24	.123329	.124912	.126546	.128184	.129826	.131472	.031602
	25 %	.25	.126057	.127633	.129262	.130895	.132531	.134171	.030072
	26 %	.26	.128774	.130344	.131968	.133596	.135227	.136862	.028616
	27 %	.27	.131480	.133044	.134664	.136287	.137913	.139543	.027230
	28 %	.28	.134177	.135735	.137350	.138969	.140590	.142215	.025911
	29 %	.29	.136864	.138416	.140027	.141641	.143259	.144879	.024657
	30 %	.30	.139542	.141088	.142696	.144306	.145919	.147535	.023463

CAPITALIZATION RATES

Assuming 75% of Purchase Price Financed by Mortgage

25 YEARS AMORTIZATION: 7¾% TO 9%

			7¾%	8%	8¼%	8½%	8¾%	9%	$\frac{1}{s_{\overline{n}\vert}}$
Interest Rate			7¾%	8%	8¼%	8½%	8¾%	9%	
Annual Requirement (f)			.090720	.092640	.094680	.096720	.098760	.100800	
Coverage Min. Rate			.068040	.069480	.071010	.072540	.074070	.075600	
Projection	Balance (b)		.627112	.635506	.640886	.646655	.652831	.659434	+ Dep – App
	Equity	Yield	Basic Rate before Depreciation or Appreciation						
	6 %	.06	.071024	.072735	.074438	.076154	.077883	.079626	.042962
	7 %	.07	.074410	.076101	.077791	.079494	.081208	.082935	.039794
	8 %	.08	.077740	.079411	.081090	.082779	.084480	.086192	.036829
	9 %	.09	.081014	.082669	.084336	.086014	.087701	.089400	.034058
	10 %	.10	.084237	.085876	.087533	.089199	.090874	.092560	.031473
	11 %	.11	.087411	.089034	.090681	.092337	.094002	.095676	.029065
	12 %	.12	.090538	.092147	.093785	.095431	.097085	.098748	.026824
	13 %	.13	.093620	.095216	.096846	.098483	.100127	.101780	.024741
	14 %	.14	.096661	.098244	.099866	.101495	.103131	.104774	.022808
	15 %	.15	.099662	.101234	.102849	.104470	.106097	.107731	.021017
15 Years n = 15	16 %	.16	.102626	.104188	.105796	.107410	.109029	.110655	.019357
	17 %	.17	.105555	.107107	.108709	.110316	.111929	.113547	.017822
	18 %	.18	.108452	.109995	.111592	.113193	.114799	.116410	.016402
	19 %	.19	.111319	.112854	.114445	.116040	.117640	.119245	.015091
	20 %	.20	.114157	.115685	.117271	.118861	.120455	.122054	.013882
	21 %	.21	.116969	.118490	.120071	.121656	.123245	.124839	.012766
	22 %	.22	.119757	.121271	.122848	.124429	.126013	.127601	.011738
	23 %	.23	.122522	.124030	.125603	.127180	.128760	.130343	.010791
	24 %	.24	.125265	.126768	.128338	.129911	.131487	.133066	.009919
	25 %	.25	.127990	.129487	.131054	.132623	.134196	.135771	.009116
	26 %	.26	.130696	.132189	.133753	.135319	.136888	.138459	.008378
	27 %	.27	.133386	.134874	.136435	.137999	.139564	.141133	.007700
	28 %	.28	.136060	.137545	.139103	.140664	.142227	.143792	.007076
	29 %	.29	.138721	.140201	.141758	.143316	.144876	.146438	.006504
	30 %	.30	.141368	.142845	.144399	.145955	.147513	.149073	.005977
	Balance (b)		.370890	.379565	.383224	.387631	.392837	.398901	+ Dep – App
	Equity	Yield	Basic Rate before Depreciation or Appreciation						
	6 %	.06	.070213	.071830	.073434	.075054	.076690	.078344	.027184
	7 %	.07	.074030	.075629	.077226	.078836	.080462	.082103	.024392
	8 %	.08	.077729	.079311	.080901	.082503	.084119	.085748	.021852
	9 %	.09	.081317	.082884	.084468	.086062	.087669	.089287	.019546
	10 %	.10	.084801	.086355	.087933	.089521	.091119	.092728	.017459
	11 %	.11	.088190	.089732	.091305	.092886	.094477	.096078	.015575
	12 %	.12	.091491	.093021	.094589	.096165	.097749	.099343	.013878
	13 %	.13	.094711	.096231	.097795	.099366	.100944	.102530	.012353
	14 %	.14	.097856	.099367	.100928	.102494	.104067	.105647	.010986
20 Years n = 20	15 %	.15	.100934	.102437	.103994	.105556	.107124	.108699	.009761
	16 %	.16	.103950	.105447	.107000	.108559	.110123	.111692	.008667
	17 %	.17	.106911	.108401	.109952	.111507	.113068	.114633	.007690
	18 %	.18	.109822	.111306	.112855	.114407	.115964	.117525	.006819
	19 %	.19	.112687	.114166	.115713	.117263	.118817	.120374	.006045
	20 %	.20	.115512	.116987	.118532	.120079	.121630	.123185	.005356
	21 %	.21	.118301	.119772	.121315	.122860	.124409	.125960	.004744
	22 %	.22	.121057	.122524	.124066	.125610	.127156	.128705	.004201
	23 %	.23	.123784	.125248	.126788	.128331	.129875	.131422	.003720
	24 %	.24	.126485	.127947	.129486	.131027	.132570	.134115	.003293
	25 %	.25	.129164	.130623	.132161	.133700	.135242	.136785	.002915
	26 %	.26	.131822	.133278	.134815	.136354	.137894	.139436	.002581
	27 %	.27	.134461	.135916	.137452	.138990	.140529	.142069	.002285
	28 %	.28	.137085	.138538	.140074	.141610	.143148	.144687	.002023
	29 %	.29	.139694	.141146	.142681	.144217	.145754	.147292	.001791
	30 %	.30	.142291	.143741	.145275	.146811	.148347	.149884	.001586

CAPITALIZATION RATES

Assuming 75% of Purchase Price Financed by Mortgage

25 YEARS AMORTIZATION: 7¼% TO 9%

			7¼%	8%	8¼%	8½%	8¾%	9%	$\frac{1}{s_{\overline{n}\rceil}}$
Interest Rate			7¼%	8%	8¼%	8½%	8¾%	9%	
Annual Requirement (f)			.090720	.092640	.094680	.096720	.098760	.100800	
Coverage Min. Rate			.068040	.069480	.071010	.072540	.074070	.075600	
Projection	Balance (b)		none	none	none	none	none	none	+ Dep
	Equity	Yield	Basic Rate before Depreciation or Appreciation						– App
	6 %	.06	.069286	.070786	.072265	.073760	.075274	.076806	.018226
	7 %	.07	.073609	.075101	.076587	.078087	.079602	.081135	.015810
	8 %	.08	.077718	.079202	.080695	.082199	.083716	.085248	.013678
	9 %	.09	.081631	.083109	.084607	.086114	.087633	.089165	.011806
	10 %	.10	.085367	.086840	.088342	.089853	.091373	.092905	.010168
	11 %	.11	.088944	.090413	.091919	.093432	.094954	.096485	.008740
	12 %	.12	.092380	.093845	.095354	.096870	.098393	.099924	.007499
	13 %	.13	.095691	.097152	.098664	.100182	.101706	.103237	.006425
	14 %	.14	.098890	.100348	.101863	.103383	.104908	.106439	.005498
25 Years	15 %	.15	.101993	.103449	.104966	.106487	.108012	.109543	.004699
n = 25	16 %	.16	.105012	.106465	.107984	.109506	.111032	.112563	.004012
	17 %	.17	.107956	.109407	.110928	.112451	.113978	.115509	.003423
	18 %	.18	.110837	.112287	.113808	.115333	.116860	.118391	.002918
	19 %	.19	.113663	.115111	.116634	.118159	.119687	.121217	.002487
	20 %	.20	.116441	.117888	.119412	.120938	.122466	.123996	.002118
	21 %	.21	.119178	.120624	.122149	.123676	.125204	.126734	.001804
	22 %	.22	.121880	.123325	.124851	.126378	.127907	.129437	.001536
	23 %	.23	.124553	.125997	.127523	.129051	.130580	.132110	.001307
	24 %	.24	.127199	.128643	.130170	.131698	.133227	.134757	.001113
	25 %	.25	.129824	.131267	.132795	.134323	.135852	.137382	.000948
	26 %	.26	.132430	.133873	.135401	.136929	.138458	.139989	.000807
	27 %	.27	.135021	.136463	.137991	.139520	.141049	.142579	.000687
	28 %	.28	.137597	.139039	.140568	.142097	.143626	.145156	.000585
	29 %	.29	.140163	.141604	.143133	.144662	.146192	.147722	.000499
	30 %	.30	.142718	.144160	.145688	.147218	.148747	.150277	.000425

CAPITALIZATION RATES

Assuming 75% of Purchase Price Financed by Mortgage

25 YEARS AMORTIZATION: 9¼% TO 10½%

Projection	Equity	Yield	9¼%	9½%	9¾%	10%	10¼%	10½%	$\frac{1}{s_{\overline{n}\rceil}}$
Interest Rate			9¼%	9½%	9¾%	10%	10¼%	10½%	
Annual Requirement (f)			.102840	.104880	.107040	.109080	.111240	.113400	
Coverage Min. Rate			.077130	.078660	.080280	.081810	.083430	.085050	
Projection	Balance (b)		.934581	.937079	.938842	.941405	.943225	.945071	+ Dep − App
	Equity	Yield	Basic Rate before Depreciation or Appreciation						
5 Years n = 5	6 %	.06	.083426	.085288	.087143	.089014	.090876	.092741	.177396
	7 %	.07	.086098	.087953	.089803	.091668	.093525	.095386	.173890
	8 %	.08	.088766	.090616	.092461	.094319	.096171	.098027	.170456
	9 %	.09	.091431	.093274	.095115	.096967	.098815	.100666	.167092
	10 %	.10	.094093	.095930	.097766	.099611	.101455	.103302	.163797
	11 %	.11	.096751	.098582	.100414	.102253	.104092	.105935	.160570
	12 %	.12	.099406	.101231	.103059	.104892	.106727	.108565	.157409
	13 %	.13	.102058	.103877	.105701	.107528	.109359	.111192	.154314
	14 %	.14	.104707	.106520	.108340	.110161	.111988	.113817	.151283
	15 %	.15	.107353	.109160	.110977	.112792	.114614	.116439	.148315
	16 %	.16	.109995	.111798	.113610	.115419	.117238	.119059	.145409
	17 %	.17	.112635	.114432	.116240	.118044	.119859	.121676	.142563
	18 %	.18	.115271	.117063	.118868	.120667	.122478	.124291	.139777
	19 %	.19	.117905	.119692	.121493	.123287	.125094	.126904	.137050
	20 %	.20	.120536	.122318	.124116	.125904	.127708	.129514	.134379
	21 %	.21	.123165	.124941	.126736	.128519	.130319	.132121	.131765
	22 %	.22	.125790	.127562	.129353	.131131	.132928	.134727	.129205
	23 %	.23	.128413	.130180	.131968	.133742	.135535	.137330	.126700
	24 %	.24	.131033	.132796	.134580	.136349	.138139	.139931	.124247
	25 %	.25	.133651	.135409	.137191	.138955	.140741	.142530	.121846
	26 %	.26	.136267	.138020	.139798	.141558	.143341	.145127	.119496
	27 %	.27	.138879	.140629	.142404	.144159	.145939	.147721	.117195
	28 %	.28	.141490	.143235	.145007	.146758	.148535	.150314	.114943
	29 %	.29	.144098	.145839	.147608	.149355	.151129	.152905	.112739
	30 %	.30	.146704	.148441	.150207	.151950	.153721	.155494	.110581
	Balance (b)		.830877	.836090	.839459	.845000	.848649	.852429	+ Dep − App
	Equity	Yield	Basic Rate before Depreciation or Appreciation						
10 Years n = 10	6 %	.06	.082506	.084333	.086145	.087990	.089818	.091653	.075867
	7 %	.07	.085449	.087262	.089065	.090896	.092714	.094539	.072377
	8 %	.08	.088374	.090174	.091968	.093785	.095594	.097409	.069029
	9 %	.09	.091281	.093068	.094854	.096658	.098458	.100265	.065820
	10 %	.10	.094171	.095946	.097725	.099515	.101307	.103105	.062745
	11 %	.11	.097044	.098808	.100579	.102358	.104141	.105931	.059801
	12 %	.12	.099902	.101654	.103418	.105185	.106961	.108743	.056984
	13 %	.13	.102743	.104486	.106243	.107998	.109767	.111541	.054289
	14 %	.14	.105570	.107302	.109053	.110798	.112559	.114326	.051713
	15 %	.15	.108382	.110105	.111849	.113584	.115339	.117098	.049252
	16 %	.16	.111180	.112894	.114632	.116357	.118106	.119859	.046901
	17 %	.17	.113965	.115670	.117403	.119118	.120860	.122607	.044656
	18 %	.18	.116737	.118433	.120161	.121867	.123604	.125344	.042514
	19 %	.19	.119496	.121184	.122907	.124605	.126335	.128070	.040471
	20 %	.20	.122243	.123924	.125641	.127331	.129057	.130786	.038522
	21 %	.21	.124979	.126652	.128365	.130047	.131768	.133491	.036665
	22 %	.22	.127703	.129370	.131078	.132753	.134468	.136187	.034894
	23 %	.23	.130417	.132077	.133781	.135449	.137160	.138874	.033208
	24 %	.24	.133121	.134775	.136474	.138136	.139842	.141552	.031602
	25 %	.25	.135815	.137463	.139159	.140814	.142516	.144221	.030072
	26 %	.26	.138500	.140142	.141834	.143483	.145181	.146882	.028616
	27 %	.27	.141176	.142812	.144501	.146144	.147838	.149536	.027230
	28 %	.28	.143843	.145474	.147160	.148797	.150488	.152182	.025911
	29 %	.29	.146502	.148128	.149811	.151443	.153131	.154821	.024657
	30 %	.30	.149153	.150775	.152454	.154082	.155766	.157453	.023463

CAPITALIZATION RATES

Assuming 75% of Purchase Price Financed by Mortgage

25 YEARS AMORTIZATION: 9¼% TO 10½%

									$\frac{1}{s_{\overline{n}\vert}}$
Interest Rate			9¼%	9½%	9¾%	10%	10¼%	10½%	
Annual Requirement (f)			.102840	.104880	.107040	.109080	.111240	.113400	
Coverage Min. Rate			.077130	.078660	.080280	.081810	.083430	.085050	
Projection	Balance (b)		.666484	.674002	.677958	.686384	.691101	.696179	+ Dep − App
	Equity	Yield	Basic Rate before Depreciation or Appreciation						
	6 %	.06	.081383	.083155	.084903	.086704	.088476	.090260	.042962
	7 %	.07	.084675	.086430	.088168	.089949	.091710	.093482	.039794
	8 %	.08	.087917	.089655	.091384	.093147	.094897	.096657	.036829
	9 %	.09	.091110	.092832	.094553	.096298	.098039	.099789	.034058
	10 %	.10	.094257	.095964	.097678	.099406	.101138	.102878	.031473
	11 %	.11	.097359	.099053	.100759	.102473	.104196	.105927	.029065
	12 %	.12	.100420	.102101	.103801	.105500	.107215	.108937	.026824
	13 %	.13	.103441	.105110	.106804	.108490	.110197	.111912	.024741
	14 %	.14	.106424	.108083	.109770	.111445	.113145	.114852	.022808
	15 %	.15	.109372	.111021	.112703	.114366	.116060	.117760	.021017
	16 %	.16	.112287	.113927	.115604	.117256	.118945	.120639	.019357
15 Years	17 %	.17	.115172	.116802	.118475	.120118	.121801	.123488	.017822
n = 15	18 %	.18	.118027	.119649	.121318	.122951	.124629	.126312	.016402
	19 %	.19	.120854	.122470	.124134	.125760	.127433	.129111	.015091
	20 %	.20	.123657	.125265	.126927	.128544	.130213	.131886	.013882
	21 %	.21	.126436	.128038	.129696	.131307	.132972	.134640	.012766
	22 %	.22	.129193	.130790	.132444	.134049	.135710	.137375	.011738
	23 %	.23	.131930	.133521	.135173	.136771	.138429	.140091	.010791
	24 %	.24	.134648	.136234	.137884	.139476	.141131	.142789	.009919
	25 %	.25	.137349	.138930	.140577	.142165	.143817	.145472	.009116
	26 %	.26	.140034	.141611	.143256	.144839	.146488	.148140	.008378
	27 %	.27	.142703	.144277	.145920	.147498	.149145	.150795	.007700
	28 %	.28	.145359	.146929	.148570	.150145	.151790	.153437	.007076
	29 %	.29	.148003	.149569	.151209	.152780	.154423	.156067	.006504
	30 %	.30	.150634	.152198	.153836	.155403	.157045	.158687	.005977
	Balance (b)		.405884	.413849	.415513	.425410	.428653	.432646	+ Dep − App
	Equity	Yield	Basic Rate before Depreciation or Appreciation						
	6 %	.06	.080016	.081709	.083363	.085095	.086781	.088482	.027184
	7 %	.07	.083760	.085436	.087086	.088798	.090477	.092170	.024392
	8 %	.08	.087392	.089053	.090700	.092392	.094066	.095751	.021852
	9 %	.09	.090920	.092567	.094211	.095886	.097554	.099232	.019546
	10 %	.10	.094350	.095984	.097626	.099285	.100948	.102620	.017459
	11 %	.11	.097689	.099312	.100952	.102597	.104255	.105922	.015575
	12 %	.12	.100945	.102558	.104196	.105829	.107482	.109144	.013878
	13 %	.13	.104125	.105729	.107364	.108986	.110636	.112293	.012353
	14 %	.14	.107234	.108830	.110464	.112075	.113722	.115375	.010986
20 Years	15 %	.15	.110280	.111868	.113500	.115103	.116747	.118396	.009761
n = 20	16 %	.16	.113268	.114849	.116480	.118075	.119716	.121362	.008667
	17 %	.17	.116203	.117779	.119408	.120995	.122634	.124277	.007690
	18 %	.18	.119091	.120661	.122290	.123870	.125507	.127147	.006819
	19 %	.19	.121936	.123502	.125129	.126704	.128339	.129977	.006045
	20 %	.20	.124743	.126305	.127931	.129501	.131134	.132770	.005356
	21 %	.21	.127515	.129074	.130700	.132265	.133896	.135531	.004744
	22 %	.22	.130257	.131812	.133438	.134999	.136629	.138262	.004201
	23 %	.23	.132972	.134524	.136149	.137706	.139335	.140966	.003720
	24 %	.24	.135662	.137212	.138836	.140390	.142018	.143648	.003293
	25 %	.25	.138330	.139878	.141501	.143053	.144680	.146309	.002915
	26 %	.26	.140979	.142525	.144148	.145697	.147323	.148951	.002581
	27 %	.27	.143611	.145155	.146778	.148325	.149950	.151577	.002285
	28 %	.28	.146228	.147770	.149393	.150938	.152562	.154189	.002023
	29 %	.29	.148831	.150372	.151994	.153537	.155162	.156787	.001791
	30 %	.30	.151422	.152962	.154584	.156126	.157750	.159374	.001586

CAPITALIZATION RATES

Assuming 75% of Purchase Price Financed by Mortgage

25 YEARS AMORTIZATION: 9¼% TO 10½%

Interest Rate			9¼%	9½%	9¾%	10%	10¼%	10½%	$\frac{1}{s_{\overline{n}\rceil}}$
Annual Requirement (f)			.102840	.104880	.107040	.109080	.111240	.113400	
Coverage Min. Rate			.077130	.078660	.080280	.081810	.083430	.085050	
Projection	Balance (b)		none	none	none	none	none	none	
	Equity	Yield	Basic Rate before Depreciation or Appreciation						
	6 %	.06	.078361	.079939	.081460	.083085	.084643	.086218	.018226
	7 %	.07	.082686	.084258	.085792	.087405	.088970	.090551	.015810
	8 %	.08	.086796	.088362	.089908	.091510	.093083	.094669	.013678
	9 %	.09	.090711	.092272	.093828	.095420	.096999	.098590	.011806
	10 %	.10	.094448	.096005	.097570	.099153	.100738	.102333	.010168
	11 %	.11	.098027	.099580	.101152	.102728	.104318	.105917	.008740
	12 %	.12	.101464	.103014	.104593	.106162	.107756	.109358	.007499
	13 %	.13	.104775	.106322	.107907	.109471	.111069	.112673	.006425
	14 %	.14	.107976	.109520	.111110	.112669	.114270	.115877	.005498
	15 %	.15	.111079	.112622	.114216	.115771	.117375	.118983	.004699
25 Years	16 %	.16	.114098	.115639	.117237	.118788	.120394	.122004	.004012
n = 25	17 %	.17	.117043	.118582	.120184	.121732	.123340	.124952	.003423
	18 %	.18	.119925	.121462	.123066	.124612	.126222	.127834	.002918
	19 %	.19	.122751	.124287	.125894	.127437	.129048	.130662	.002487
	20 %	.20	.125529	.127065	.128673	.130214	.131827	.133442	.002118
	21 %	.21	.128267	.129801	.131411	.132951	.134565	.136180	.001804
	22 %	.22	.130969	.132503	.134115	.135653	.137268	.138884	.001536
	23 %	.23	.133642	.135175	.136788	.138325	.139940	.141557	.001307
	24 %	.24	.136288	.137821	.139435	.140971	.142587	.144205	.001113
	25 %	.25	.138913	.140446	.142061	.143596	.145212	.146830	.000948
	26 %	.26	.141520	.143052	.144667	.146202	.147819	.149437	.000807
	27 %	.27	.144110	.145642	.147258	.148792	.150409	.152028	.000687
	28 %	.28	.146687	.148218	.149835	.151368	.152986	.154605	.000585
	29 %	.29	.149252	.150784	.152401	.153934	.155552	.157171	.000499
	30 %	.30	.151808	.153339	.154957	.156489	.158107	.159726	.000425

CAPITALIZATION RATES

Assuming 75% of Purchase Price Financed by Mortgage

25 YEARS AMORTIZATION: 10¾% TO 12%

	Interest Rate	10¾%	11%	11¼%	11½%	11¾%	12%	$\frac{1}{s_{\overline{n}\rceil}}$
	Annual Requirement (f)	.115560	.117720	.119880	.122040	.124200	.126480	
	Coverage Min. Rate	.086670	.088290	.089910	.091530	.093150	.094860	
Projection	Balance (b)	.946944	.948843	.950769	.952723	.954705	.955898	+ Dep – App
	Equity Yield	Basic Rate before Depreciation or Appreciation						
	6 % .06	.094611	.096483	.098360	.100239	.102123	.103992	.177396
	7 % .07	.097250	.099118	.100989	.102864	.104742	.106608	.173890
	8 % .08	.099887	.101750	.103616	.105486	.107359	.109221	.170456
	9 % .09	.102521	.104379	.106240	.108105	.109973	.111833	.167092
	10 % .10	.105152	.107005	.108862	.110722	.112585	.114442	.163797
	11 % .11	.107780	.109629	.111481	.113336	.115195	.117048	.160570
	12 % .12	.110406	.112250	.114098	.115948	.117802	.119653	.157409
	13 % .13	.113029	.114869	.116712	.118558	.120407	.122255	.154314
	14 % .14	.115650	.117485	.119324	.121165	.123010	.124856	.151283
	15 % .15	.118268	.120099	.121933	.123771	.125611	.127454	.148315
5 Years n = 5	16 % .16	.120883	.122711	.124541	.126374	.128210	.130050	.145409
	17 % .17	.123497	.125320	.127146	.128975	.130806	.132644	.142563
	18 % .18	.126107	.127927	.129749	.131573	.133401	.135236	.139777
	19 % .19	.128716	.130531	.132349	.134170	.135994	.137826	.137050
	20 % .20	.131322	.133134	.134948	.136765	.138584	.140415	.134379
	21 % .21	.133926	.135734	.137544	.139357	.141173	.143001	.131765
	22 % .22	.136528	.138332	.140139	.141948	.143760	.145586	.129205
	23 % .23	.139128	.140928	.142731	.144537	.146345	.148169	.126700
	24 % .24	.141725	.143522	.145322	.147124	.148929	.150750	.124247
	25 % .25	.144321	.146115	.147911	.149709	.151510	.153329	.121846
	26 % .26	.146915	.148705	.150497	.152292	.154090	.155907	.119496
	27 % .27	.149506	.151293	.153082	.154874	.156668	.158483	.117195
	28 % .28	.152096	.153879	.155665	.157454	.159245	.161058	.114943
	29 % .29	.154683	.156464	.158247	.160032	.161820	.163631	.112739
	30 % .30	.157269	.159047	.160827	.162609	.164393	.166202	.110581
	Balance (b)	.856344	.860397	.864593	.868936	.873430	.875779	+ Dep – App
	Equity Yield	Basic Rate before Depreciation or Appreciation						
	6 % .06	.093495	.095346	.097205	.099072	.100948	.102791	.075867
	7 % .07	.096371	.098211	.100059	.101915	.103779	.105616	.072377
	8 % .08	.099232	.101062	.102899	.104744	.106597	.108428	.069029
	9 % .09	.102078	.103898	.105725	.107560	.109401	.111227	.065820
	10 % .10	.104909	.106720	.108537	.110362	.112193	.114014	.062745
	11 % .11	.107726	.109528	.111336	.113151	.114973	.116788	.059801
	12 % .12	.110530	.112323	.114122	.115928	.117740	.119551	.056984
	13 % .13	.113320	.115105	.116896	.118693	.120496	.122302	.054289
	14 % .14	.116098	.117875	.119658	.121446	.123240	.125042	.051713
10 Years n = 10	15 % .15	.118863	.120633	.122408	.124188	.125974	.127771	.049252
	16 % .16	.121616	.123379	.125146	.126919	.128697	.130490	.046901
	17 % .17	.124358	.126114	.127874	.129640	.131410	.133199	.044656
	18 % .18	.127089	.128838	.130592	.132350	.134114	.135899	.042514
	19 % .19	.129809	.131552	.133299	.135051	.136808	.138589	.040471
	20 % .20	.132519	.134256	.135997	.137743	.139493	.141271	.038522
	21 % .21	.135219	.136951	.138686	.140425	.142169	.143944	.036665
	22 % .22	.137910	.139636	.141366	.143099	.144837	.146608	.034894
	23 % .23	.140592	.142313	.144037	.145765	.147497	.149266	.033208
	24 % .24	.143265	.144981	.146700	.148423	.150150	.151915	.031602
	25 % .25	.145929	.147641	.149355	.151073	.152795	.154558	.030072
	26 % .26	.148586	.150293	.152003	.153717	.155433	.157193	.028616
	27 % .27	.151236	.152938	.154644	.156353	.158065	.159823	.027230
	28 % .28	.153878	.155577	.157278	.158982	.160690	.162445	.025911
	29 % .29	.156513	.158208	.159905	.161606	.163309	.165062	.024657
	30 % .30	.159142	.160833	.162527	.164223	.165922	.167674	.023463

CAPITALIZATION RATES

Assuming 75% of Purchase Price Financed by Mortgage

25 YEARS AMORTIZATION: 10¾% TO 12%

Interest Rate / Annual Requirement (f) / Coverage Min. Rate			10¾% / .115560 / .086670	11% / .117720 / .088290	11¼% / .119880 / .089910	11½% / .122040 / .091530	11¾% / .124200 / .093150	12% / .126480 / .094860	$\frac{1}{s_{\overline{n}\vert}}$
Projection	Balance (b)		.701633	.707483	.713746	.720443	.727595	.730226	+ Dep – App
15 Years n = 15	Equity	Yield	Basic Rate before Depreciation or Appreciation						
	6 %	.06	.092056	.093864	.095686	.097522	.099372	.101167	.042962
	7 %	.07	.095264	.097059	.098866	.100686	.102519	.104308	.039794
	8 %	.08	.098428	.100210	.102003	.103808	.105625	.107408	.036829
	9 %	.09	.101548	.103317	.105097	.106888	.108691	.110468	.034058
	10 %	.10	.104626	.106385	.108152	.109930	.111719	.113491	.031473
	11 %	.11	.107665	.109413	.111169	.112935	.114711	.116479	.029065
	12 %	.12	.110667	.112405	.114151	.115905	.117669	.119432	.026824
	13 %	.13	.113633	.115361	.117098	.118842	.120595	.122353	.024741
	14 %	.14	.116565	.118285	.120013	.121747	.123490	.125245	.022808
	15 %	.15	.119466	.121179	.122897	.124623	.126356	.128107	.021017
	16 %	.16	.122338	.124043	.125754	.127471	.129195	.130943	.019357
	17 %	.17	.125181	.126880	.128583	.130293	.132008	.133754	.017822
	18 %	.18	.127999	.129691	.131388	.133090	.134798	.136541	.016402
	19 %	.19	.130792	.132479	.134169	.135865	.137566	.139306	.015091
	20 %	.20	.133563	.135244	.136929	.138619	.140313	.142051	.013882
	21 %	.21	.136313	.137989	.139669	.141353	.143041	.144776	.012766
	22 %	.22	.139043	.140714	.142389	.144068	.145751	.147485	.011738
	23 %	.23	.141755	.143422	.145093	.146767	.148445	.150176	.010791
	24 %	.24	.144450	.146113	.147780	.149450	.151123	.152853	.009919
	25 %	.25	.147129	.148789	.150452	.152118	.153787	.155515	.009116
	26 %	.26	.149794	.151451	.153111	.154773	.156438	.158164	.008378
	27 %	.27	.152446	.154100	.155756	.157415	.159076	.160801	.007700
	28 %	.28	.155086	.156737	.158390	.160046	.161704	.163428	.007076
	29 %	.29	.157714	.159363	.161013	.162666	.164321	.166044	.006504
	30 %	.30	.160332	.161978	.163626	.165276	.166928	.168650	.005977
	Balance (b)		.437444	.443106	.449694	.457274	.465916	.465802	+ Dep – App
20 Years n = 20	Equity	Yield	Basic Rate before Depreciation or Appreciation						
	6 %	.06	.090200	.091935	.093690	.095464	.097260	.098968	.027184
	7 %	.07	.093878	.095601	.097342	.099100	.100879	.102587	.024392
	8 %	.08	.097450	.099162	.100890	.102635	.104396	.106104	.021852
	9 %	.09	.100923	.102626	.104342	.106073	.107820	.109528	.019546
	10 %	.10	.104303	.105997	.107703	.109423	.111156	.112864	.017459
	11 %	.11	.107598	.109284	.110981	.112690	.114410	.116119	.015575
	12 %	.12	.110814	.112493	.114181	.115880	.117590	.119299	.013878
	13 %	.13	.113957	.115630	.117311	.119001	.120701	.122410	.012353
	14 %	.14	.117034	.118701	.120375	.122058	.123749	.125458	.010986
	15 %	.15	.120051	.121712	.123381	.125056	.126739	.128449	.009761
	16 %	.16	.123013	.124670	.126332	.128002	.129678	.131387	.008667
	17 %	.17	.125925	.127577	.129235	.130899	.132569	.134278	.007690
	18 %	.18	.128792	.130441	.132095	.133753	.135418	.137127	.006819
	19 %	.19	.131619	.133265	.134914	.136569	.138228	.139937	.006045
	20 %	.20	.134409	.136052	.137699	.139349	.141004	.142713	.005356
	21 %	.21	.137168	.138808	.140451	.142098	.143749	.145459	.004744
	22 %	.22	.139897	.141535	.143175	.144819	.146466	.148176	.004201
	23 %	.23	.142600	.144236	.145874	.147515	.149159	.150869	.003720
	24 %	.24	.145280	.146914	.148550	.150189	.151830	.153540	.003293
	25 %	.25	.147939	.149572	.151206	.152843	.154481	.156191	.002915
	26 %	.26	.150580	.152211	.153844	.155479	.157115	.158825	.002581
	27 %	.27	.153205	.154835	.156466	.158099	.159734	.161444	.002285
	28 %	.28	.155816	.157444	.159074	.160706	.162339	.164049	.002023
	29 %	.29	.158414	.160041	.161670	.163300	.164932	.166642	.001791
	30 %	.30	.161000	.162627	.164255	.165884	.167514	.169224	.001586

CAPITALIZATION RATES

Assuming 75% of Purchase Price Financed by Mortgage

25 YEARS AMORTIZATION: 10¾% TO 12%

Interest Rate			10¾%	11%	11¼%	11½%	11¾%	12%	$\frac{1}{s_{\overline{n}\rvert}}$
Annual Requirement (f)			.115560	.117720	.119880	.122040	.124200	.126480	
Coverage Min. Rate			.086670	.088290	.089910	.091530	.093150	.094860	
Projection	Balance (b)		none	none	none	none	none	none	+ Dep
	Equity	Yield	Basic Rate before Depreciation or Appreciation						– App
	6 %	.06	.087812	.089428	.091068	.092735	.094430	.095990	.018226
	7 %	.07	.092149	.093766	.095403	.097063	.098749	.100329	.015810
	8 %	.08	.096270	.097887	.099522	.101177	.102853	.104451	.013678
	9 %	.09	.100194	.101811	.103444	.105094	.106763	.108376	.011806
	10 %	.10	.103939	.105557	.107188	.108834	.110496	.112122	.010168
	11 %	.11	.107525	.109143	.110772	.112414	.114071	.115709	.008740
	12 %	.12	.110968	.112586	.114214	.115853	.117504	.119153	.007499
	13 %	.13	.114284	.115903	.117530	.119166	.120813	.122470	.006425
	14 %	.14	.117489	.119108	.120734	.122368	.124011	.125676	.005498
	15 %	.15	.120597	.122216	.123841	.125473	.127112	.128784	.004699
25 Years	16 %	.16	.123619	.125238	.126862	.128493	.130129	.131806	.004012
n = 25	17 %	.17	.126567	.128186	.129810	.131438	.133073	.134755	.003423
	18 %	.18	.129450	.131070	.132693	.134320	.135952	.137638	.002918
	19 %	.19	.132278	.133898	.135521	.137147	.138777	.140467	.002487
	20 %	.20	.135059	.136678	.138301	.139926	.141555	.143247	.002118
	21 %	.21	.137798	.139417	.141039	.142664	.144291	.145987	.001804
	22 %	.22	.140502	.142121	.143743	.145367	.146993	.148691	.001536
	23 %	.23	.143175	.144795	.146416	.148040	.149665	.151364	.001307
	24 %	.24	.145823	.147443	.149064	.150687	.152311	.154012	.001113
	25 %	.25	.148449	.150069	.151690	.153312	.154936	.156638	.000948
	26 %	.26	.151056	.152676	.154296	.155918	.157542	.159245	.000807
	27 %	.27	.153647	.155267	.156887	.158509	.160132	.161836	.000687
	28 %	.28	.156224	.157844	.159465	.161086	.162708	.164414	.000585
	29 %	.29	.158790	.160410	.162030	.163652	.165274	.166980	.000499
	30 %	.30	.161346	.162966	.164586	.166207	.167829	.169536	.000425

CAPITALIZATION RATES

Assuming 75% of Purchase Price Financed by Mortgage

30 YEARS AMORTIZATION: 3¼% TO 4½%

	Interest Rate Annual Requirement (f) Coverage Min. Rate	3¼% .05232 .03924	3½% .05400 .04050	3¾% .05568 .04176	4% .05736 .04302	4¼% .05904 .04428	4½% .06084 .04563	$\frac{1}{s_{\overline{n}\rceil}}$
Projection	Balance (b)	.892551	.896345	.900191	.904088	.908037	.911368	+ Dep − App
	Equity Yield	Basic Rate before Depreciation or Appreciation						
	5% .05	.0372	.0390	.0407	.0425	.0443	.0461	.1810
	6% .06	.0400	.0417	.0435	.0453	.0471	.0489	.1774
	7% .07	.0428	.0445	.0463	.0481	.0499	.0516	.1739
	8% .08	.0455	.0473	.0491	.0508	.0526	.0544	.1705
	9% .09	.0483	.0501	.0518	.0535	.0553	.0571	.1671
5 Years n = 5	10% .10	.0511	.0528	.0545	.0563	.0580	.0598	.1638
	11% .11	.0539	.0556	.0573	.0590	.0608	.0625	.1606
	12% .12	.0566	.0583	.0600	.0618	.0635	.0652	.1574
	13% .13	.0594	.0610	.0628	.0645	.0662	.0679	.1543
	14% .14	.0621	.0638	.0655	.0672	.0689	.0707	.1513
	15% .15	.0648	.0665	.0682	.0699	.0716	.0733	.1483
	16% .16	.0676	.0693	.0709	.0727	.0743	.0760	.1454
	17% .17	.0703	.0720	.0737	.0753	.0770	.0787	.1426
	18% .18	.0730	.0747	.0764	.0780	.0797	.0814	.1398
	19% .19	.0757	.0774	.0790	.0808	.0824	.0841	.1371
	20% .20	.0785	.0801	.0818	.0834	.0851	.0868	.1344
	Balance (b)	.766171	.772899	.779833	.786979	.794342	.800419	+ Dep − App
	Equity Yield	Basic Rate before Depreciation or Appreciation						
	5% .05	.0378	.0395	.0412	.0428	.0446	.0463	.0795
	6% .06	.0410	.0426	.0443	.0459	.0477	.0493	.0759
	7% .07	.0441	.0457	.0474	.0490	.0507	.0523	.0724
	8% .08	.0472	.0489	.0506	.0522	.0539	.0555	.0690
	9% .09	.0502	.0519	.0534	.0551	.0567	.0583	.0658
10 Years n = 10	10% .10	.0533	.0549	.0565	.0580	.0597	.0613	.0628
	11% .11	.0563	.0578	.0594	.0610	.0626	.0642	.0598
	12% .12	.0593	.0609	.0624	.0639	.0655	.0672	.0570
	13% .13	.0622	.0638	.0653	.0669	.0685	.0700	.0543
	14% .14	.0652	.0668	.0683	.0698	.0713	.0729	.0517
	15% .15	.0681	.0696	.0712	.0727	.0742	.0758	.0493
	16% .16	.0711	.0726	.0741	.0756	.0771	.0787	.0469
	17% .17	.0740	.0755	.0770	.0785	.0800	.0815	.0447
	18% .18	.0768	.0783	.0798	.0813	.0828	.0843	.0425
	19% .19	.0797	.0811	.0826	.0841	.0856	.0871	.0405
	20% .20	.0826	.0840	.0854	.0869	.0884	.0899	.0385

CAPITALIZATION RATES

Assuming 75% of Purchase Price Financed by Mortgage

30 YEARS AMORTIZATION: 3¼% TO 4½%

Interest Rate Annual Requirement(f) Coverage Min. Rate		3¼% .05232 .03924	3½% .05400 .04050	3¾% .05568 .04176	4% .05736 .04302	4¼% .05904 .04428	4½% .06084 .04563	$\frac{1}{s_{\overline{n}\rceil}}$
Projection	Balance (b)	.617524	.625881	.634695	.643989	.653782	.661533	+ Dep – App
	Equity Yield	Basic Rate before Depreciation or Appreciation						
	5% .05	.0385	.0400	.0416	.0431	.0448	.0464	.0464
	6% .06	.0419	.0434	.0450	.0466	.0482	.0497	.0430
	7% .07	.0453	.0468	.0484	.0499	.0515	.0531	.0398
	8% .08	.0487	.0502	.0517	.0532	.0547	.0563	.0368
	9% .09	.0520	.0535	.0550	.0565	.0580	.0595	.0341
15 Years n = 15	10% .10	.0552	.0567	.0582	.0597	.0612	.0627	.0315
	11% .11	.0584	.0598	.0613	.0628	.0643	.0658	.0291
	12% .12	.0616	.0630	.0644	.0659	.0674	.0689	.0268
	13% .13	.0647	.0661	.0675	.0690	.0704	.0719	.0248
	14% .14	.0677	.0691	.0706	.0720	.0734	.0748	.0228
	15% .15	.0707	.0722	.0735	.0749	.0764	.0778	.0210
	16% .16	.0738	.0751	.0765	.0779	.0793	.0807	.0194
	17% .17	.0766	.0781	.0794	.0808	.0822	.0836	.0178
	18% .18	.0796	.0809	.0823	.0837	.0851	.0865	.0164
	19% .19	.0825	.0838	.0852	.0865	.0879	.0894	.0151
	20% .20	.0853	.0866	.0880	.0894	.0907	.0922	.0139
	Balance (b)	.442686	.450790	.459678	.469399	.480007	.487675	+ Dep – App
	Equity Yield	Basic Rate before Depreciation or Appreciation						
	5% .05	.0391	.0406	.0421	.0435	.0450	.0466	.0303
	6% .06	.0429	.0443	.0458	.0473	.0487	.0502	.0272
	7% .07	.0465	.0480	.0494	.0508	.0523	.0538	.0244
	8% .08	.0502	.0515	.0529	.0544	.0558	.0573	.0219
	9% .09	.0536	.0550	.0563	.0578	.0592	.0606	.0196
20 Years n = 20	10% .10	.0570	.0583	.0597	.0611	.0625	.0639	.0175
	11% .11	.0603	.0616	.0630	.0643	.0658	.0672	.0156
	12% .12	.0635	.0648	.0662	.0675	.0689	.0704	.0139
	13% .13	.0666	.0679	.0693	.0706	.0720	.0734	.0124
	14% .14	.0697	.0710	.0724	.0737	.0750	.0764	.0110
	15% .15	.0727	.0740	.0753	.0767	.0780	.0794	.0098
	16% .16	.0756	.0770	.0783	.0796	.0810	.0823	.0087
	17% .17	.0786	.0799	.0812	.0825	.0838	.0852	.0077
	18% .18	.0815	.0827	.0840	.0854	.0866	.0881	.0068
	19% .19	.0843	.0855	.0869	.0882	.0894	.0909	.0061
	20% .20	.0871	.0883	.0896	.0910	.0922	.0936	.0054

CAPITALIZATION RATES

Assuming 75% of Purchase Price Financed by Mortgage

30 YEARS AMORTIZATION: 3¼% TO 4½%

Interest Rate Annual Requirement (f) Coverage Min. Rate		3¼% .05232 .03924	3½% .05400 .04050	3¾% .05568 .04176	4% .05736 .04302	4¼% .05904 .04428	4½% .06084 .04563	$\frac{1}{s_{\overline{n}\|}}$
Projection	Balance (b)	.237045	.242268	.248628	.256226	.265169	.270043	+ Dep − App
	Equity Yield	Basic Rate before Depreciation or Appreciation						
	5% .05	.0398	.0411	.0425	.0439	.0453	.0467	.0210
	6% .06	.0438	.0452	.0465	.0479	.0493	.0507	.0182
	7% .07	.0477	.0490	.0504	.0517	.0531	.0545	.0158
	8% .08	.0514	.0528	.0541	.0554	.0568	.0582	.0137
	9% .09	.0550	.0563	.0576	.0590	.0603	.0617	.0118
25 Years n = 25	10% .10	.0585	.0597	.0611	.0624	.0637	.0651	.0102
	11% .11	.0618	.0631	.0643	.0657	.0670	.0684	.0088
	12% .12	.0650	.0662	.0676	.0689	.0701	.0716	.0075
	13% .13	.0681	.0694	.0707	.0720	.0732	.0747	.0064
	14% .14	.0711	.0724	.0737	.0750	.0763	.0776	.0055
	15% .15	.0741	.0754	.0767	.0779	.0792	.0806	.0047
	16% .16	.0770	.0783	.0795	.0808	.0821	.0835	.0040
	17% .17	.0798	.0811	.0824	.0837	.0850	.0863	.0034
	18% .18	.0826	.0839	.0851	.0864	.0877	.0890	.0029
	19% .19	.0854	.0867	.0879	.0892	.0905	.0918	.0025
	20% .20	.0880	.0893	.0906	.0919	.0931	.0945	.0021
	Balance (b)	None	None	None	None	None	None	+ Dep − App
	Equity Yield	Basic Rate before Depreciation or Appreciation						
	5% .05	.0405	.0418	.0430	.0442	.0455	.0469	.0151
	6% .06	.0448	.0461	.0473	.0485	.0498	.0512	.0127
	7% .07	.0489	.0501	.0513	.0526	.0539	.0552	.0106
	8% .08	.0526	.0539	.0552	.0565	.0577	.0590	.0089
	9% .09	.0563	.0575	.0588	.0600	.0613	.0626	.0074
30 Years n = 30	10% .10	.0597	.0609	.0622	.0635	.0648	.0661	.0061
	11% .11	.0630	.0643	.0655	.0668	.0680	.0694	.0050
	12% .12	.0662	.0674	.0687	.0699	.0712	.0725	.0042
	13% .13	.0692	.0705	.0717	.0730	.0742	.0756	.0034
	14% .14	.0721	.0734	.0747	.0760	.0772	.0786	.0028
	15% .15	.0750	.0763	.0776	.0788	.0801	.0815	.0023
	16% .16	.0779	.0792	.0804	.0816	.0829	.0843	.0019
	17% .17	.0806	.0819	.0832	.0844	.0856	.0870	.0015
	18% .18	.0833	.0846	.0859	.0871	.0884	.0897	.0013
	19% .19	.0860	.0873	.0885	.0898	.0910	.0924	.0010
	20% .20	.0886	.0899	.0912	.0925	.0937	.0950	.0008

CAPITALIZATION RATES

Assuming 75% of Purchase Price Financed by Mortgage

30 YEARS AMORTIZATION: 4¾% TO 6%

Interest Rate Annual Requirement (f) Coverage Min. Rate		4¾% .06264 .04698	5% .06444 .04833	5¼% .06636 .04977	5½% .06816 .05112	5¾% .07008 .05256	6% .07200 .05400	$\frac{1}{s_{\overline{n}|}}$
Projection	Balance (b)	.914744	.918166	.920950	.924461	.927326	.930230	+ Dep − App
	Equity Yield	Basic Rate before Depreciation or Appreciation						
	5% .05	.0479	.0498	.0516	.0534	.0552	.0571	.1810
	6% .06	.0507	.0525	.0543	.0561	.0579	.0597	.1774
	7% .07	.0534	.0552	.0570	.0588	.0607	.0625	.1739
	8% .08	.0561	.0579	.0597	.0615	.0633	.0651	.1705
	9% .09	.0588	.0606	.0624	.0642	.0660	.0678	.1671
5 Years n = 5	10% .10	.0616	.0634	.0651	.0669	.0687	.0705	.1638
	11% .11	.0643	.0660	.0678	.0696	.0713	.0731	.1606
	12% .12	.0669	.0687	.0705	.0723	.0741	.0758	.1574
	13% .13	.0697	.0714	.0732	.0749	.0767	.0785	.1543
	14% .14	.0724	.0741	.0758	.0776	.0794	.0812	.1513
	15% .15	.0750	.0768	.0786	.0803	.0820	.0838	.1483
	16% .16	.0778	.0795	.0812	.0829	.0847	.0865	.1454
	17% .17	.0804	.0821	.0839	.0856	.0874	.0891	.1426
	18% .18	.0831	.0848	.0866	.0882	.0900	.0918	.1398
	19% .19	.0858	.0875	.0892	.0909	.0927	.0944	.1371
	20% .20	.0884	.0902	.0919	.0935	.0953	.0971	.1344
	Balance (b)	.806684	.813143	.818229	.825073	.830511	.836121	+ Dep − App
	Equity Yield	Basic Rate before Depreciation or Appreciation						
	5% .05	.0480	.0497	.0515	.0533	.0550	.0568	.0795
	6% .06	.0510	.0528	.0545	.0562	.0579	.0597	.0759
	7% .07	.0541	.0557	.0574	.0592	.0609	.0627	.0724
	8% .08	.0570	.0587	.0604	.0621	.0638	.0656	.0690
	9% .09	.0600	.0617	.0633	.0651	.0667	.0684	.0658
10 Years n = 10	10% .10	.0629	.0646	.0663	.0679	.0697	.0713	.0628
	11% .11	.0659	.0675	.0692	.0708	.0725	.0742	.0598
	12% .12	.0687	.0704	.0720	.0737	.0753	.0771	.0570
	13% .13	.0717	.0733	.0749	.0766	.0782	.0799	.0543
	14% .14	.0746	.0761	.0778	.0794	.0810	.0827	.0517
	15% .15	.0774	.0790	.0806	.0822	.0839	.0855	.0493
	16% .16	.0802	.0818	.0835	.0850	.0867	.0883	.0469
	17% .17	.0830	.0846	.0863	.0878	.0895	.0911	.0447
	18% .18	.0859	.0874	.0891	.0906	.0922	.0939	.0425
	19% .19	.0887	.0902	.0918	.0934	.0950	.0966	.0405
	20% .20	.0914	.0930	.0946	.0962	.0977	.0993	.0385

CAPITALIZATION RATES

Assuming 75% of Purchase Price Financed by Mortgage

30 YEARS AMORTIZATION: 4¾% TO 6%

Interest Rate / Annual Requirement (f) / Coverage Min. Rate		4¾% .06264 .04698	5% .06444 .04833	5¼% .06636 .04977	5½% .06816 .05112	5¾% .07008 .05256	6% .07200 .05400	$\frac{1}{s_{\overline{n}\mid}}$
Projection	Balance (b)	.669720	.678362	.684752	.694309	.701536	.709182	+ Dep − App
	Equity Yield	Basic Rate before Depreciation or Appreciation						
	5% .05	.0481	.0497	.0514	.0530	.0547	.0564	.0464
	6% .06	.0514	.0530	.0546	.0563	.0580	.0596	.0430
	7% .07	.0546	.0563	.0579	.0595	.0612	.0628	.0398
	8% .08	.0579	.0595	.0611	.0627	.0643	.0660	.0368
	9% .09	.0611	.0626	.0642	.0659	.0674	.0691	.0341
15 Years	10% .10	.0642	.0657	.0674	.0690	.0705	.0722	.0315
n = 15	11% .11	.0673	.0688	.0704	.0720	.0736	.0752	.0291
	12% .12	.0704	.0719	.0734	.0750	.0766	.0782	.0268
	13% .13	.0734	.0749	.0765	.0780	.0795	.0811	.0248
	14% .14	.0763	.0778	.0794	.0809	.0825	.0841	.0228
	15% .15	.0793	.0808	.0824	.0839	.0854	.0869	.0210
	16% .16	.0822	.0837	.0852	.0867	.0882	.0898	.0194
	17% .17	.0851	.0865	.0881	.0896	.0911	.0927	.0178
	18% .18	.0880	.0894	.0909	.0924	.0939	.0955	.0164
	19% .19	.0908	.0922	.0937	.0952	.0967	.0983	.0151
	20% .20	.0936	.0950	.0965	.0980	.0995	.1010	.0139
	Balance (b)	.496120	.505389	.511306	.522262	.529720	.537957	+ Dep − App
	Equity Yield	Basic Rate before Depreciation or Appreciation						
	5% .05	.0481	.0496	.0512	.0528	.0544	.0560	.0303
	6% .06	.0518	.0533	.0548	.0564	.0580	.0596	.0272
	7% .07	.0553	.0568	.0584	.0599	.0615	.0631	.0244
	8% .08	.0588	.0603	.0618	.0633	.0649	.0664	.0219
	9% .09	.0621	.0636	.0651	.0666	.0682	.0698	.0196
20 Years	10% .10	.0654	.0669	.0684	.0699	.0714	.0730	.0175
n = 20	11% .11	.0686	.0701	.0716	.0730	.0746	.0761	.0156
	12% .12	.0718	.0732	.0747	.0762	.0777	.0792	.0139
	13% .13	.0748	.0763	.0777	.0792	.0807	.0822	.0124
	14% .14	.0778	.0793	.0808	.0822	.0837	.0852	.0110
	15% .15	.0808	.0822	.0837	.0851	.0866	.0881	.0098
	16% .16	.0837	.0852	.0867	.0881	.0895	.0910	.0087
	17% .17	.0866	.0880	.0895	.0909	.0924	.0939	.0077
	18% .18	.0894	.0908	.0923	.0937	.0952	.0967	.0068
	19% .19	.0922	.0936	.0951	.0965	.0980	.0994	.0061
	20% .20	.0950	.0964	.0979	.0992	.1007	.1022	.0054

CAPITALIZATION RATES

Assuming 75% of Purchase Price Financed by Mortgage

30 YEARS AMORTIZATION: 4¾% TO 6%

Interest Rate / Annual Requirement(f) / Coverage Min. Rate		4¾% / .06264 / .04698	5% / .06444 / .04833	5¼% / .06636 / .04977	5½% / .06816 / .05112	5¾% / .07008 / .05256	6% / .07200 / .05400	$\frac{1}{s_{\overline{n}|}}$
Projection	Balance(b)	.276086	.283403	.285925	.295899	.300830	.307006	+ Dep − App
	Equity Yield	Basic Rate before Depreciation or Appreciation						
	5% .05	.0481	.0496	.0511	.0526	.0541	.0556	.0210
	6% .06	.0521	.0536	.0551	.0565	.0581	.0596	.0182
	7% .07	.0559	.0573	.0588	.0603	.0618	.0633	.0158
	8% .08	.0596	.0610	.0625	.0639	.0654	.0669	.0137
	9% .09	.0631	.0645	.0660	.0674	.0689	.0704	.0118
25 Years n = 25	10% .10	.0665	.0679	.0693	.0708	.0723	.0738	.0102
	11% .11	.0697	.0712	.0726	.0740	.0755	.0770	.0088
	12% .12	.0729	.0743	.0758	.0772	.0787	.0801	.0075
	13% .13	.0760	.0774	.0789	.0803	.0817	.0832	.0064
	14% .14	.0790	.0804	.0819	.0832	.0847	.0862	.0055
	15% .15	.0820	.0833	.0848	.0862	.0876	.0891	.0047
	16% .16	.0849	.0862	.0876	.0891	.0905	.0920	.0040
	17% .17	.0877	.0890	.0905	.0919	.0933	.0948	.0034
	18% .18	.0905	.0918	.0932	.0946	.0961	.0975	.0029
	19% .19	.0932	.0945	.0960	.0973	.0988	.1002	.0025
	20% .20	.0958	.0973	.0987	.1000	.1015	.1030	.0021
	Balance (b)	None	None	None	None	None	None	+ Dep − App
	Equity Yield	Basic Rate before Depreciation or Appreciation						
	5% .05	.0482	.0496	.0510	.0523	.0538	.0553	.0151
	6% .06	.0525	.0539	.0553	.0566	.0581	.0596	.0127
	7% .07	.0566	.0579	.0594	.0607	.0621	.0636	.0106
	8% .08	.0604	.0617	.0632	.0646	.0660	.0674	.0089
	9% .09	.0640	.0653	.0668	.0681	.0696	.0710	.0074
30 Years n = 30	10% .10	.0675	.0688	.0702	.0716	.0730	.0744	.0061
	11% .11	.0707	.0721	.0736	.0749	.0763	.0778	.0050
	12% .12	.0739	.0752	.0767	.0780	.0795	.0809	.0042
	13% .13	.0770	.0783	.0798	.0811	.0825	.0840	.0034
	14% .14	.0799	.0813	.0827	.0841	.0855	.0869	.0028
	15% .15	.0828	.0842	.0856	.0869	.0884	.0898	.0023
	16% .16	.0856	.0870	.0884	.0897	.0912	.0927	.0019
	17% .17	.0883	.0897	.0912	.0925	.0940	.0954	.0015
	18% .18	.0911	.0924	.0938	.0952	.0967	.0981	.0013
	19% .19	.0937	.0951	.0966	.0979	.0993	.1008	.0010
	20% .20	.0964	.0977	.0992	.1006	.1020	.1034	.0008

CAPITALIZATION RATES

Assuming 75% of Purchase Price Financed by Mortgage

30 YEARS AMORTIZATION: 6¼% TO 7½%

Projection	Equity	Yield	6¼%	6½%	6¾%	7%	7¼%	7½%	$\frac{1}{s_{\overline{n}\rvert}}$
Interest Rate			6¼%	6½%	6¾%	7%	7¼%	7½%	
Annual Requirement (f)			.073920	.075960	.077880	.079920	.081960	.084000	
Coverage Min. Rate			.055440	.056970	.058410	.059940	.061470	.063000	
Projection	Balance (b)		.933173	.935451	.938471	.940816	.943194	.945604	+ Dep − App
	Equity	Yield	Basic Rate before Depreciation or Appreciation						
	6 %	.06	.061548	.063381	.065223	.067065	.068912	.070762	.177396
	7 %	.07	.064224	.066051	.067885	.069721	.071561	.073405	.173890
	8 %	.08	.066896	.068717	.070544	.072373	.074207	.076045	.170456
	9 %	.09	.069565	.071380	.073199	.075023	.076851	.078683	.167092
	10 %	.10	.072230	.074040	.075851	.077669	.079491	.081317	.163797
	11 %	.11	.074892	.076696	.078500	.080312	.082129	.083949	.160570
	12 %	.12	.077550	.079349	.081146	.082952	.084763	.086578	.157409
	13 %	.13	.080205	.081999	.083788	.085590	.087395	.089204	.154314
	14 %	.14	.082857	.084646	.086428	.088224	.090024	.091828	.151283
	15 %	.15	.085506	.087289	.089065	.090856	.092651	.094449	.148315
5 Years n = 5	16 %	.16	.088152	.089930	.091699	.093485	.095274	.097067	.145409
	17 %	.17	.090794	.092568	.094331	.096111	.097896	.099683	.142563
	18 %	.18	.093434	.095203	.096959	.098735	.100514	.102297	.139777
	19 %	.19	.096071	.097835	.099585	.101356	.103131	.104908	.137050
	20 %	.20	.098704	.100464	.102208	.103975	.105744	.107517	.134379
	21 %	.21	.101335	.103091	.104829	.106591	.108356	.110124	.131765
	22 %	.22	.103964	.105714	.107447	.109204	.110965	.112728	.129205
	23 %	.23	.106589	.108336	.110063	.111816	.113572	.115331	.126700
	24 %	.24	.109212	.110954	.112676	.114424	.116176	.117931	.124247
	25 %	.25	.111833	.113571	.115287	.117031	.118778	.120529	.121846
	26 %	.26	.114450	.116184	.117895	.119635	.121378	.123124	.119496
	27 %	.27	.117066	.118796	.120501	.122237	.123976	.125718	.117195
	28 %	.28	.119679	.121405	.123105	.124837	.126572	.128310	.114943
	29 %	.29	.122289	.124012	.125707	.127435	.129166	.130900	.112739
	30 %	.30	.124897	.126616	.128307	.130031	.131758	.133488	.110581
	Balance (b)		.841907	.846191	.852323	.856916	.861657	.866552	+ Dep − App
	Equity	Yield	Basic Rate before Depreciation or Appreciation						
	6 %	.06	.061444	.063218	.065007	.066798	.068598	.070406	.075867
	7 %	.07	.064358	.066120	.067893	.069672	.071460	.073256	.072377
	8 %	.08	.067255	.069007	.070764	.072532	.074307	.076091	.069029
	9 %	.09	.070135	.071877	.073619	.075376	.077140	.078912	.065820
	10 %	.10	.073000	.074731	.076460	.078206	.079959	.081720	.062745
	11 %	.11	.075849	.077571	.079286	.081022	.082765	.084514	.059801
	12 %	.12	.078683	.080396	.082098	.083824	.085557	.087296	.056984
	13 %	.13	.081502	.083207	.084897	.086614	.088337	.090066	.054289
	14 %	.14	.084308	.086004	.087682	.089390	.091104	.092824	.051713
10 Years n = 10	15 %	.15	.087100	.088788	.090454	.092154	.093859	.095570	.049252
	16 %	.16	.089878	.091559	.093215	.094906	.096603	.098305	.046901
	17 %	.17	.092645	.094318	.095963	.097647	.099336	.101030	.044656
	18 %	.18	.095399	.097065	.098701	.100377	.102058	.103744	.042514
	19 %	.19	.098141	.099801	.101427	.103096	.104770	.106449	.040471
	20 %	.20	.100872	.102526	.104143	.105806	.107473	.109144	.038522
	21 %	.21	.103592	.105240	.106849	.108505	.110165	.111830	.036665
	22 %	.22	.106302	.107944	.109545	.111195	.112849	.114507	.034894
	23 %	.23	.109002	.110639	.112231	.113876	.115524	.117176	.033208
	24 %	.24	.111692	.113324	.114909	.116548	.118191	.119837	.031602
	25 %	.25	.114374	.116000	.117579	.119212	.120849	.122490	.030072
	26 %	.26	.117046	.118668	.120240	.121869	.123500	.125135	.028616
	27 %	.27	.119711	.121328	.122894	.124517	.126144	.127774	.027230
	28 %	.28	.122367	.123980	.125540	.127159	.128781	.130406	.025911
	29 %	.29	.125016	.126625	.128179	.129793	.131411	.133032	.024657
	30 %	.30	.127657	.129263	.130811	.132422	.134035	.135651	.023463

CAPITALIZATION RATES

Assuming 75% of Purchase Price Financed by Mortgage

30 YEARS AMORTIZATION: 6¼% TO 7½%

Interest Rate Annual Requirement (f) Coverage Min. Rate			6¼% .073920 .055440	6½% .075960 .056970	6¾% .077880 .058410	7% .079920 .059940	7¼% .081960 .061470	7½% .084000 .063000	$\frac{1}{s_{\overline{n}\rceil}}$
Projection	Balance (b)		.717261	.722762	.731707	.737977	.744624	.751665	+ Dep – App
	Equity	Yield	Basic Rate before Depreciation or Appreciation						
	6 %	.06	.061329	.063036	.064765	.066497	.068241	.069998	.042962
	7 %	.07	.064501	.066195	.067902	.069619	.071348	.073088	.039794
	8 %	.08	.067630	.069312	.070999	.072702	.074415	.076140	.036829
	9 %	.09	.070717	.072388	.074056	.075746	.077446	.079156	.034058
	10 %	.10	.073765	.075425	.077076	.078754	.080441	.082137	.031473
	11 %	.11	.076776	.078426	.080061	.081728	.083403	.085086	.029065
	12 %	.12	.079751	.081392	.083012	.084668	.086332	.088003	.026824
	13 %	.13	.082693	.084325	.085931	.087577	.089231	.090891	.024741
	14 %	.14	.085603	.087227	.088820	.090457	.092101	.093751	.022808
	15 %	.15	.088483	.090099	.091680	.093309	.094944	.096585	.021017
15 Years n = 15	16 %	.16	.091335	.092945	.094514	.096135	.097762	.099394	.019357
	17 %	.17	.094160	.095764	.097323	.098937	.100556	.102180	.017822
	18 %	.18	.096961	.098559	.100109	.101716	.103328	.104944	.016402
	19 %	.19	.099739	.101331	.102873	.104474	.106079	.107689	.015091
	20 %	.20	.102496	.104083	.105616	.107211	.108811	.110414	.013882
	21 %	.21	.105232	.106815	.108341	.109931	.111524	.113122	.012766
	22 %	.22	.107950	.109529	.111048	.112633	.114221	.115813	.011738
	23 %	.23	.110651	.112226	.113738	.115319	.116903	.118490	.010791
	24 %	.24	.113336	.114907	.116414	.117990	.119570	.121152	.009919
	25 %	.25	.116006	.117574	.119075	.120648	.122223	.123801	.009116
	26 %	.26	.118663	.120227	.121723	.123293	.124865	.126439	.008378
	27 %	.27	.121307	.122868	.124360	.125926	.127495	.129065	.007700
	28 %	.28	.123939	.125498	.126985	.128549	.130114	.131681	.007076
	29 %	.29	.126560	.128117	.129601	.131161	.132724	.134288	.006504
	30 %	.30	.129172	.130727	.132207	.133765	.135325	.136886	.005977

Projection	Balance (b)		.547030	.552082	.562831	.569367	.576641	.584701	+ Dep – App
	Equity	Yield	Basic Rate before Depreciation or Appreciation						
	6 %	.06	.061204	.062837	.064496	.066160	.067838	.069532	.027184
	7 %	.07	.064653	.066275	.067912	.069561	.071224	.072902	.024392
	8 %	.08	.068016	.069629	.071245	.072882	.074531	.076193	.021852
	9 %	.09	.071299	.072903	.074501	.076126	.077763	.079411	.019546
	10 %	.10	.074508	.076104	.077685	.079300	.080926	.082561	.017459
	11 %	.11	.077648	.079237	.080803	.082409	.084024	.085648	.015575
	12 %	.12	.080724	.082307	.083859	.085457	.087063	.088677	.013878
	13 %	.13	.083743	.085319	.086859	.088450	.090047	.091652	.012353
	14 %	.14	.086707	.088279	.089807	.091391	.092981	.094578	.010986
	15 %	.15	.089623	.091190	.092709	.094287	.095870	.097459	.009761
20 Years n = 20	16 %	.16	.092495	.094058	.095568	.097140	.098718	.100300	.008667
	17 %	.17	.095327	.096886	.098388	.099956	.101528	.103104	.007690
	18 %	.18	.098123	.099678	.101173	.102737	.104304	.105875	.006819
	19 %	.19	.100886	.102439	.103927	.105487	.107050	.108617	.006045
	20 %	.20	.103620	.105170	.106653	.108209	.109769	.111331	.005356
	21 %	.21	.106328	.107876	.109354	.110907	.112463	.114022	.004744
	22 %	.22	.109012	.110558	.112032	.113582	.115135	.116691	.004201
	23 %	.23	.111676	.113220	.114690	.116238	.117788	.119341	.003720
	24 %	.24	.114321	.115863	.117330	.118876	.120424	.121974	.003293
	25 %	.25	.116949	.118490	.119953	.121498	.123044	.124591	.002915
	26 %	.26	.119563	.121102	.122563	.124106	.125650	.127195	.002581
	27 %	.27	.122163	.123702	.125160	.126701	.128244	.129788	.002285
	28 %	.28	.124752	.126290	.127746	.129286	.130827	.132369	.002023
	29 %	.29	.127331	.128868	.130322	.131861	.133401	.134941	.001791
	30 %	.30	.129900	.131436	.132889	.134427	.135966	.137505	.001586

CAPITALIZATION RATES

Assuming 75% of Purchase Price Financed by Mortgage

30 YEARS AMORTIZATION: 6¼% TO 7½%

Interest Rate			6¼%	6½%	6¾%	7%	7¼%	7½%	$\frac{1}{s_{\overline{n}\rceil}}$
Annual Requirement (f)			.073920	.075960	.077880	.079920	.081960	.084000	
Coverage Min. Rate			.055440	.056970	.058410	.059940	.061470	.063000	
Projection	Balance (b)		.314539	.316062	.326384	.330340	.335525	.342054	+ Dep − App
	Equity	Yield	Basic Rate before Depreciation or Appreciation						
	6 %	.06	.061069	.062620	.064201	.065785	.067386	.069005	.018226
	7 %	.07	.064811	.066359	.067922	.069499	.071090	.072698	.015810
	8 %	.08	.068407	.069953	.071499	.073069	.074653	.076250	.013678
	9 %	.09	.071870	.073413	.074945	.076510	.078086	.079674	.011806
	10 %	.10	.075212	.076754	.078272	.079833	.081402	.082982	.010168
	11 %	.11	.078446	.079986	.081494	.083050	.084614	.086187	.008740
	12 %	.12	.081584	.083122	.084620	.086173	.087732	.089299	.007499
	13 %	.13	.084636	.086173	.087663	.089212	.090767	.092329	.006425
	14 %	.14	.087613	.089149	.090632	.092178	.093729	.095286	.005498
	15 %	.15	.090524	.092059	.093535	.095079	.096628	.098181	.004699
25 Years n = 25	16 %	.16	.093377	.094911	.096382	.097924	.099470	.101019	.004012
	17 %	.17	.096180	.097713	.099180	.100720	.102263	.103810	.003423
	18 %	.18	.098939	.100472	.101935	.103474	.105015	.106559	.002918
	19 %	.19	.101661	.103194	.104653	.106190	.107730	.109272	.002487
	20 %	.20	.104350	.105883	.107339	.108875	.110414	.111954	.002118
	21 %	.21	.107012	.108544	.109998	.111533	.113070	.114609	.001804
	22 %	.22	.109650	.111181	.112633	.114168	.115704	.117241	.001536
	23 %	.23	.112267	.113799	.115249	.116783	.118318	.119854	.001307
	24 %	.24	.114867	.116398	.117847	.119380	.120915	.122450	.001113
	25 %	.25	.117452	.118983	.120431	.121963	.123497	.125032	.000948
	26 %	.26	.120024	.121555	.123002	.124534	.126067	.127601	.000807
	27 %	.27	.122586	.124117	.125562	.127094	.128627	.130160	.000687
	28 %	.28	.125138	.126669	.128114	.129645	.131178	.132710	.000585
	29 %	.29	.127683	.129213	.130657	.132189	.133721	.135253	.000499
	30 %	.30	.130221	.131751	.133194	.134726	.136257	.137789	.000425
	Balance (b)		none	none	none	none	none	none	+ Dep App
	Equity	Yield	Basic Rate before Depreciation or Appreciation						
	6 %	.06	.060925	.062385	.063879	.065372	.066883	.068412	.012648
	7 %	.07	.064976	.066448	.067933	.069432	.070946	.072476	.010586
	8 %	.08	.068799	.070281	.071758	.073263	.074779	.076309	.008827
	9 %	.09	.072421	.073911	.075382	.076890	.078409	.079939	.007336
	10 %	.10	.075866	.077363	.078829	.080341	.081862	.083392	.006079
	11 %	.11	.079160	.080662	.082123	.083639	.085161	.086691	.005024
	12 %	.12	.082322	.083830	.085287	.086805	.088329	.089859	.004143
	13 %	.13	.085374	.086885	.088340	.089860	.091385	.092914	.003410
	14 %	.14	.088331	.089846	.091298	.092820	.094345	.095875	.002802
	15 %	.15	.091209	.092727	.094176	.095700	.097226	.098756	.002300
30 Years n = 30	16 %	.16	.094021	.095541	.096989	.098513	.100040	.101570	.001885
	17 %	.17	.096778	.098299	.099746	.101271	.102799	.104329	.001544
	18 %	.18	.099488	.101011	.102457	.103983	.105511	.107041	.001264
	19 %	.19	.102161	.103686	.105130	.106657	.108185	.109715	.001034
	20 %	.20	.104803	.106328	.107772	.109300	.110828	.112358	.000846
	21 %	.21	.107419	.108945	.110388	.111916	.113445	.114975	.000691
	22 %	.22	.110014	.111541	.112983	.114511	.116041	.117571	.000565
	23 %	.23	.112591	.114119	.115561	.117089	.118619	.120149	.000462
	24 %	.24	.115155	.116683	.118124	.119653	.121183	.122713	.000378
	25 %	.25	.117706	.119235	.120676	.122205	.123735	.125265	.000309
	26 %	.26	.120249	.121777	.123218	.124748	.126277	.127807	.000253
	27 %	.27	.122783	.124312	.125753	.127282	.128812	.130342	.000207
	28 %	.28	.125311	.126840	.128281	.129811	.131340	.132870	.000170
	29 %	.29	.127834	.129364	.130804	.132334	.133864	.135394	.000139
	30 %	.30	.130353	.131883	.133323	.134853	.136383	.137913	.000114

CAPITALIZATION RATES

Assuming 75% of Purchase Price Financed by Mortgage

30 YEARS AMORTIZATION: 7¼% TO 9%

Projection	Equity	Yield	7¼%	8%	8¼%	8½%	8¾%	9%	$\frac{1}{s_{\overline{n}\rceil}}$
Interest Rate			7¼%	8%	8¼%	8½%	8¾%	9%	
Annual Requirement (f)			.086040	.088080	.090240	.092280	.094440	.096600	
Coverage Min. Rate			.064530	.066060	.067680	.069210	.070830	.072450	
5 Years n = 5	Balance (b)		.948048	.950525	.952297	.954838	.956664	.958516	+ Dep − App
	Equity	Yield	Basic Rate before Depreciation or Appreciation						
	6 %	.06	.072617	.074477	.076333	.078201	.080064	.081930	.177396
	7 %	.07	.075254	.077107	.078958	.080820	.082678	.084539	.173890
	8 %	.08	.077888	.079735	.081581	.083436	.085289	.087146	.170456
	9 %	.09	.080519	.082359	.084201	.086050	.087899	.089751	.167092
	10 %	.10	.083147	.084982	.086819	.088661	.090506	.092353	.163797
	11 %	.11	.085773	.087601	.089435	.091271	.093111	.094954	.160570
	12 %	.12	.088396	.090219	.092048	.093878	.095713	.097552	.157409
	13 %	.13	.091017	.092834	.094659	.096483	.098314	.100148	.154314
	14 %	.14	.093635	.095446	.097267	.099085	.100913	.102743	.151283
	15 %	.15	.096251	.098056	.099873	.101686	.103509	.105335	.148315
	16 %	.16	.098864	.100664	.102477	.104284	.106103	.107925	.145409
	17 %	.17	.101475	.103270	.105079	.106881	.108696	.110514	.142563
	18 %	.18	.104083	.105873	.107679	.109475	.111287	.113101	.139777
	19 %	.19	.106690	.108474	.110276	.112067	.113875	.115686	.137050
	20 %	.20	.109294	.111073	.112872	.114658	.116462	.118269	.134379
	21 %	.21	.111895	.113670	.115465	.117246	.119047	.120850	.131765
	22 %	.22	.114495	.116265	.118057	.119833	.121630	.123430	.129205
	23 %	.23	.117093	.118858	.120647	.122418	.124212	.126008	.126700
	24 %	.24	.119688	.121449	.123234	.125001	.126791	.128584	.124247
	25 %	.25	.122282	.124038	.125820	.127582	.129369	.131159	.121846
	26 %	.26	.124873	.126625	.128404	.130162	.131946	.133732	.119496
	27 %	.27	.127463	.129211	.130987	.132740	.134520	.136303	.117195
	28 %	.28	.130051	.131794	.133567	.135316	.137094	.138873	.114943
	29 %	.29	.132637	.134376	.136146	.137891	.139665	.141442	.112739
	30 %	.30	.135221	.136956	.138723	.140464	.142235	.144009	.110581
10 Years n = 10	Balance (b)		.871603	.876816	.880339	.885862	.889652	.893567	+ Dep − App
	Equity	Yield	Basic Rate before Depreciation or Appreciation						
	6 %	.06	.072224	.074050	.075871	.077715	.079551	.081393	.075867
	7 %	.07	.075060	.076873	.078684	.080514	.082339	.084172	.072377
	8 %	.08	.077882	.079682	.081484	.083300	.085117	.086939	.069029
	9 %	.09	.080691	.082479	.084272	.086075	.087882	.089695	.065820
	10 %	.10	.083487	.085263	.087048	.088838	.090637	.092441	.062745
	11 %	.11	.086271	.088035	.089813	.091590	.093380	.095176	.059801
	12 %	.12	.089042	.090795	.092565	.094331	.096113	.097901	.056984
	13 %	.13	.091802	.093544	.095307	.097062	.098836	.100616	.054289
	14 %	.14	.094550	.096282	.098038	.099783	.101550	.103321	.051713
	15 %	.15	.097287	.099009	.100759	.102493	.104253	.106018	.049252
	16 %	.16	.100013	.101726	.103470	.105195	.106948	.108706	.046901
	17 %	.17	.102729	.104434	.106172	.107887	.109634	.111385	.044656
	18 %	.18	.105435	.107132	.108864	.110570	.112311	.114056	.042514
	19 %	.19	.108132	.109820	.111547	.113245	.114980	.116719	.040471
	20 %	.20	.110820	.112500	.114222	.115912	.117641	.119374	.038522
	21 %	.21	.113499	.115172	.116889	.118571	.120295	.122023	.036665
	22 %	.22	.116169	.117836	.119548	.121222	.122942	.124664	.034894
	23 %	.23	.118832	.120491	.122199	.123867	.125581	.127299	.033208
	24 %	.24	.121486	.123140	.124843	.126504	.128214	.129927	.031602
	25 %	.25	.124134	.125781	.127481	.129135	.130841	.132549	.030072
	26 %	.26	.126774	.128416	.130111	.131760	.133461	.135165	.028616
	27 %	.27	.129407	.131044	.132736	.134378	.136076	.137776	.027230
	28 %	.28	.132034	.133666	.135354	.136991	.138685	.140381	.025911
	29 %	.29	.134655	.136281	.137967	.139599	.141289	.142981	.024657
	30 %	.30	.137270	.138892	.140574	.142201	.143888	.145577	.023463

CAPITALIZATION RATES

Assuming 75% of Purchase Price Financed by Mortgage

30 YEARS AMORTIZATION: 7¾% TO 9%

Interest Rate			7¾%	8%	8¼%	8½%	8¾%	9%	$\frac{1}{s_{\overline{n}\rvert}}$
Annual Requirement (f)			.086040	.088080	.090240	.092280	.094440	.096600	
Coverage Min. Rate			.064530	.066060	.067680	.069210	.070830	.072450	
Projection	Balance (b)		.759118	.767000	.771794	.780516	.786025	.791876	+ Dep − App
	Equity	Yield	Basic Rate before Depreciation or Appreciation						
	6 %	.06	.071768	.073552	.075326	.077137	.078935	.080743	.042962
	7 %	.07	.074840	.076605	.078368	.080159	.081943	.083738	.039794
	8 %	.08	.077876	.079624	.081376	.083147	.084919	.086701	.036829
	9 %	.09	.080876	.082608	.084350	.086103	.087864	.089633	.034058
	10 %	.10	.083843	.085559	.087293	.089029	.090779	.092537	.031473
	11 %	.11	.086779	.088480	.090205	.091925	.093665	.095413	.029065
	12 %	.12	.089683	.091372	.093088	.094794	.096525	.098262	.026824
	13 %	.13	.092560	.094236	.095945	.097637	.099359	.101087	.024741
	14 %	.14	.095409	.097074	.098776	.100455	.102169	.103889	.022808
	15 %	.15	.098233	.099887	.101582	.103250	.104957	.106669	.021017
15 Years n = 15	16 %	.16	.101032	.102677	.104366	.106023	.107723	.109428	.019357
	17 %	.17	.103810	.105445	.107129	.108776	.110469	.112168	.017822
	18 %	.18	.106566	.108193	.109872	.111509	.113197	.114889	.016402
	19 %	.19	.109303	.110922	.112596	.114225	.115908	.117594	.015091
	20 %	.20	.112022	.113634	.115304	.116924	.118602	.120283	.013882
	21 %	.21	.114723	.116329	.117994	.119608	.121281	.122957	.012766
	22 %	.22	.117409	.119008	.120670	.122277	.123946	.125617	.011738
	23 %	.23	.120080	.121674	.123333	.124933	.126598	.128265	.010791
	24 %	.24	.122737	.124326	.125982	.127577	.129238	.130901	.009919
	25 %	.25	.125382	.126966	.128619	.130209	.131866	.133526	.009116
	26 %	.26	.128016	.129595	.131245	.132830	.134485	.136142	.008378
	27 %	.27	.130638	.132214	.133862	.135442	.137094	.138748	.007700
	28 %	.28	.133251	.134823	.136468	.138045	.139694	.141345	.007076
	29 %	.29	.135854	.137423	.139066	.140639	.142286	.143934	.006504
	30 %	.30	.138450	.140015	.141656	.143225	.144870	.146516	.005977
	Balance (b)		.593600	.603392	.608059	.619620	.625780	.632662	+ Dep − App
	Equity	Yield	Basic Rate before Depreciation or Appreciation						
	6 %	.06	.071244	.072973	.074688	.076454	.078200	.079960	.027184
	7 %	.07	.074595	.076304	.078009	.079751	.081483	.083229	.024392
	8 %	.08	.077869	.079559	.081256	.082975	.084696	.086429	.021852
	9 %	.09	.081072	.082745	.084434	.086133	.087844	.089564	.019546
	10 %	.10	.084208	.085866	.087547	.089229	.090929	.092639	.017459
	11 %	.11	.087282	.088926	.090601	.092266	.093958	.095658	.015575
	12 %	.12	.090299	.091931	.093600	.095250	.096934	.098626	.013878
	13 %	.13	.093264	.094885	.096548	.098185	.099862	.101546	.012353
	14 %	.14	.096181	.097792	.099450	.101075	.102746	.104423	.010986
	15 %	.15	.099054	.100656	.102310	.103925	.105590	.107260	.009761
20 Years n = 20	16 %	.16	.101888	.103481	.105132	.106737	.108397	.110062	.008667
	17 %	.17	.104685	.106272	.107919	.109516	.111171	.112831	.007690
	18 %	.18	.107451	.109031	.110675	.112264	.113915	.115571	.006819
	19 %	.19	.110187	.111761	.113402	.114985	.116633	.118284	.006045
	20 %	.20	.112897	.114466	.116105	.117681	.119326	.120974	.005356
	21 %	.21	.115583	.117148	.118785	.120356	.121998	.123642	.004744
	22 %	.22	.118249	.119810	.121444	.123011	.124650	.126292	.004201
	23 %	.23	.120896	.122453	.124086	.125648	.127285	.128925	.003720
	24 %	.24	.123526	.125080	.126711	.128270	.129905	.131542	.003293
	25 %	.25	.126141	.127692	.129322	.130878	.132511	.134146	.002915
	26 %	.26	.128743	.130292	.131921	.133473	.135105	.136738	.002581
	27 %	.27	.131333	.132880	.134508	.136058	.137688	.139320	.002285
	28 %	.28	.133913	.135458	.137085	.138632	.140262	.141892	.002023
	29 %	.29	.136483	.138027	.139653	.141198	.142827	.144456	.001791
	30 %	.30	.139046	.140587	.142213	.143757	.145384	.147012	.001586

CAPITALIZATION RATES

Assuming 75% of Purchase Price Financed by Mortgage

30 YEARS AMORTIZATION: 7¾% TO 9%

Interest Rate			7¾%	8%	8¼%	8½%	8¾%	9%	$\frac{1}{s_{\overline{n}\rceil}}$
Annual Requirement (f)			.086040	.088080	.090240	.092280	.094440	.096600	
Coverage Min. Rate			.064530	.066060	.067680	.069210	.070830	.072450	
Projection	Balance (b)		.350048	.359642	.361070	.373884	.377982	.383382	+ Dep − App
	Equity	Yield	Basic Rate before Depreciation or Appreciation						
	6 %	.06	.070645	.072306	.073945	.075650	.077326	.079020	.018226
	7 %	.07	.074322	.075966	.077603	.079285	.080954	.082638	.015810
	8 %	.08	.077862	.079490	.081125	.082786	.084448	.086124	.013678
	9 %	.09	.081274	.082889	.084522	.086165	.087822	.089490	.011806
	10 %	.10	.084573	.086176	.087807	.089435	.091086	.092747	.010168
	11 %	.11	.087769	.089362	.090991	.092605	.094252	.095907	.008740
	12 %	.12	.090874	.092458	.094086	.095688	.097331	.098981	.007499
	13 %	.13	.093897	.095473	.097100	.098692	.100332	.101978	.006425
	14 %	.14	.096849	.098419	.100045	.101628	.103264	.104907	.005498
	15 %	.15	.099739	.101303	.102928	.104503	.106137	.107776	.004699
25 Years	16 %	.16	.102573	.104132	.105757	.107325	.108958	.110594	.004012
n = 25	17 %	.17	.105361	.106915	.108539	.110102	.111732	.113366	.003423
	18 %	.18	.108107	.109658	.111281	.112839	.114468	.116100	.002918
	19 %	.19	.110817	.112365	.113988	.115541	.117169	.118799	.002487
	20 %	.20	.113497	.115042	.116664	.118215	.119841	.121470	.002118
	21 %	.21	.116150	.117693	.119315	.120862	.122488	.124115	.001804
	22 %	.22	.118781	.120322	.121943	.123488	.125113	.126739	.001536
	23 %	.23	.121392	.122931	.124553	.126095	.127719	.129345	.001307
	24 %	.24	.123987	.125525	.127146	.128687	.130310	.131935	.001113
	25 %	.25	.126567	.128104	.129725	.131264	.132887	.134511	.000948
	26 %	.26	.129136	.130672	.132293	.133830	.135453	.137076	.000807
	27 %	.27	.131694	.133229	.134850	.136387	.138009	.139631	.000687
	28 %	.28	.134244	.135778	.137399	.138934	.140556	.142179	.000585
	29 %	.29	.136786	.138320	.139940	.141475	.143097	.144719	.000499
	30 %	.30	.139322	.140855	.142475	.144010	.145631	.147253	.000425
	Balance (b)		none	none	none	none	none	none	+ Dep − App
	Equity	Yield	Basic Rate before Depreciation or Appreciation						
	6 %	.06	.069964	.071540	.073084	.074709	.076293	.077897	.012648
	7 %	.07	.074024	.075592	.077148	.078758	.080348	.081955	.010586
	8 %	.08	.077854	.079416	.080983	.082579	.084174	.085783	.008827
	9 %	.09	.081481	.083038	.084614	.086199	.087799	.089409	.007336
	10 %	.10	.084932	.086484	.088068	.089644	.091246	.092859	.006079
	11 %	.11	.088230	.089778	.091368	.092936	.094541	.096155	.005024
	12 %	.12	.091396	.092941	.094536	.096097	.097706	.099320	.004143
	13 %	.13	.094450	.095993	.097592	.099148	.100758	.102374	.003410
	14 %	.14	.097410	.098950	.100553	.102104	.103716	.105333	.002802
	15 %	.15	.100290	.101828	.103435	.104982	.106595	.108212	.002300
	16 %	.16	.103103	.104640	.106249	.107793	.109408	.111025	.001885
30 Years	17 %	.17	.105861	.107397	.109008	.110549	.112165	.113783	.001544
n = 30	18 %	.18	.108573	.110108	.111720	.113260	.114876	.116495	.001264
	19 %	.19	.111247	.112781	.114395	.115933	.117550	.119168	.001034
	20 %	.20	.113890	.115423	.117038	.118574	.120192	.121811	.000846
	21 %	.21	.116506	.118039	.119655	.121190	.122808	.124427	.000691
	22 %	.22	.119102	.120634	.122250	.123784	.125403	.127022	.000565
	23 %	.23	.121679	.123211	.124828	.126362	.127981	.129600	.000462
	24 %	.24	.124243	.125775	.127392	.128925	.130544	.132164	.000378
	25 %	.25	.126795	.128326	.129944	.131477	.133096	.134715	.000309
	26 %	.26	.129338	.130869	.132487	.134019	.135638	.137258	.000253
	27 %	.27	.131872	.133403	.135022	.136553	.138173	.139793	.000207
	28 %	.28	.134401	.135931	.137550	.139082	.140701	.142321	.000170
	29 %	.29	.136924	.138454	.140074	.141605	.143224	.144844	.000139
	30 %	.30	.139443	.140973	.142593	.144123	.145743	.147363	.000114

CAPITALIZATION RATES

Assuming 75% of Purchase Price Financed by Mortgage

30 YEARS AMORTIZATION: 9¼% TO 10½%

			9¼%	9½%	9¾%	10%	10¼%	10½%	$\frac{1}{s_{\overline{n}\rceil}}$
Interest Rate			9¼%	9½%	9¾%	10%	10¼%	10½%	
Annual Requirement (f)			.098760	.100920	.103200	.105360	.107640	.109800	
Coverage Min. Rate			.074070	.075690	.077400	.079020	.080730	.082350	
Projection	Balance (b)		.960394	.962298	.963459	.965411	.966611	.968612	+ Dep – App
	Equity	Yield							
	6 %	.06	.083800	.085673	.087538	.089418	.091287	.093173	.177396
	7 %	.07	.086404	.088273	.090134	.092009	.093875	.095756	.173890
	8 %	.08	.089006	.090870	.092728	.094598	.096461	.098337	.170456
	9 %	.09	.091606	.093465	.095320	.097185	.099045	.100916	.167092
	10 %	.10	.094204	.096058	.097911	.099770	.101628	.103494	.163797
	11 %	.11	.096800	.098649	.100499	.102354	.104209	.106070	.160570
	12 %	.12	.099394	.101239	.103086	.104936	.106788	.108644	.157409
	13 %	.13	.101986	.103826	.105670	.107516	.109365	.111217	.154314
	14 %	.14	.104576	.106412	.108254	.110095	.111941	.113788	.151283
	15 %	.15	.107164	.108996	.110835	.112672	.114515	.116358	.148315
	16 %	.16	.109750	.111578	.113414	.115247	.117088	.118926	.145409
5 Years	17 %	.17	.112335	.114158	.115992	.117821	.119659	.121493	.142563
n = 5	18 %	.18	.114918	.116737	.118569	.120393	.122229	.124059	.139777
	19 %	.19	.117499	.119314	.121144	.122964	.124798	.126623	.137050
	20 %	.20	.120078	.121890	.123717	.125533	.127364	.129186	.134379
	21 %	.21	.122656	.124464	.126288	.128101	.129930	.131748	.131765
	22 %	.22	.125232	.127036	.128859	.130668	.132494	.134308	.129205
	23 %	.23	.127806	.129607	.131427	.133233	.135057	.136867	.126700
	24 %	.24	.130379	.132176	.133994	.135796	.137618	.139425	.124247
	25 %	.25	.132950	.134744	.136560	.138359	.140178	.141981	.121846
	26 %	.26	.135520	.137311	.139125	.140920	.142737	.144536	.119496
	27 %	.27	.138088	.139876	.141688	.143479	.145295	.147091	.117195
	28 %	.28	.140655	.142439	.144249	.146038	.147851	.149644	.114943
	29 %	.29	.143221	.145002	.146810	.148595	.150406	.152196	.112739
	30 %	.30	.145785	.147563	.149369	.151151	.152960	.154746	.110581
	Balance (b)		.897610	.901786	.904079	.908502	.910990	.915674	+ Dep – App
	Equity	Yield							
	6 %	.06	.083243	.085101	.086942	.088813	.090665	.092551	.075867
	7 %	.07	.086011	.087858	.089693	.091553	.093398	.095272	.072377
	8 %	.08	.088769	.090605	.092433	.094282	.096121	.097984	.069029
	9 %	.09	.091515	.093341	.095164	.097003	.098836	.100687	.065820
	10 %	.10	.094251	.096068	.097886	.099714	.101541	.103381	.062745
	11 %	.11	.096977	.098785	.100597	.102416	.104237	.106067	.059801
	12 %	.12	.099694	.101492	.103300	.105109	.106925	.108746	.056984
	13 %	.13	.102401	.104191	.105994	.107794	.109605	.111416	.054289
	14 %	.14	.105098	.106880	.108679	.110471	.112277	.114079	.051713
	15 %	.15	.107787	.109562	.111356	.113140	.114942	.116735	.049252
10 Yrs.	16 %	.16	.110468	.112235	.114025	.115801	.117599	.119383	.046901
n = 10	17 %	.17	.113140	.114900	.116687	.118455	.120248	.122025	.044656
	18 %	.18	.115805	.117558	.119341	.121102	.122891	.124661	.042514
	19 %	.19	.118462	.120208	.121988	.123742	.125528	.127290	.040471
	20 %	.20	.121111	.122852	.124628	.126376	.128158	.129913	.038522
	21 %	.21	.123754	.125489	.127262	.129003	.130782	.132531	.036665
	22 %	.22	.126390	.128119	.129889	.131625	.133400	.135143	.034894
	23 %	.23	.129019	.130743	.132510	.134241	.136013	.137749	.033208
	24 %	.24	.131643	.133362	.135126	.136851	.138620	.140351	.031602
	25 %	.25	.134260	.135974	.137736	.139456	.141222	.142948	.030072
	26 %	.26	.136872	.138582	.140341	.142056	.143819	.145540	.028616
	27 %	.27	.139478	.141184	.142941	.144651	.146412	.148127	.027230
	28 %	.28	.142080	.143781	.145535	.147241	.149000	.150711	.025911
	29 %	.29	.144676	.146373	.148126	.149827	.151583	.153290	.024657
	30 %	.30	.147268	.148961	.150712	.152409	.154163	.155866	.023463

CAPITALIZATION RATES

Assuming 75% of Purchase Price Financed by Mortgage

30 YEARS AMORTIZATION: 9¼% TO 10½%

Projection	Equity	Yield	9¼%	9½%	9¾%	10%	10¼%	10½%	$\frac{1}{s_{\overline{n}\rvert}}$
Interest Rate			9¼%	9½%	9¾%	10%	10¼%	10½%	
Annual Requirement (f)			.098760	.100920	.103200	.105360	.107640	.109800	
Coverage Min. Rate			.074070	.075690	.077400	.079020	.080730	.082350	
15 Years n = 15	Balance (b)		.798084	.804665	.807585	.814869	.818336	.826388	+ Dep − App
	Equity	Yield	Basic Rate before Depreciation or Appreciation						
	6 %	.06	.082563	.084395	.086200	.088054	.089876	.091755	.042962
	7 %	.07	.085543	.087360	.089157	.090994	.092808	.094668	.039794
	8 %	.08	.088492	.090294	.092085	.093906	.095712	.097554	.036829
	9 %	.09	.091412	.093200	.094984	.096791	.098589	.100415	.034058
	10 %	.10	.094303	.096079	.097857	.099649	.101441	.103251	.031473
	11 %	.11	.097168	.098931	.100705	.102484	.104269	.106065	.029065
	12 %	.12	.100007	.101760	.103528	.105295	.107075	.108857	.026824
	13 %	.13	.102823	.104565	.106329	.108084	.109858	.111628	.024741
	14 %	.14	.105615	.107348	.109108	.110853	.112622	.114380	.022808
	15 %	.15	.108387	.110110	.111867	.113601	.115366	.117113	.021017
	16 %	.16	.111138	.112854	.114606	.116332	.118092	.119829	.019357
	17 %	.17	.113871	.115579	.117328	.119045	.120801	.122529	.017822
	18 %	.18	.116586	.118286	.120032	.121742	.123495	.125214	.016402
	19 %	.19	.119284	.120979	.122722	.124424	.126173	.127884	.015091
	20 %	.20	.121967	.123656	.125396	.127092	.128838	.130542	.013882
	21 %	.21	.124636	.126319	.128057	.129747	.131490	.133187	.012766
	22 %	.22	.127292	.128970	.130706	.132390	.134130	.135821	.011738
	23 %	.23	.129935	.131609	.133342	.135021	.136759	.138444	.010791
	24 %	.24	.132567	.134236	.135968	.137642	.139378	.141058	.009919
	25 %	.25	.135189	.136854	.138584	.140254	.141987	.143662	.009116
	26 %	.26	.137801	.139462	.141190	.142856	.144588	.146258	.008378
	27 %	.27	.140403	.142061	.143788	.145450	.147180	.148847	.007700
	28 %	.28	.142998	.144653	.146378	.148037	.149765	.151428	.007076
	29 %	.29	.145585	.147237	.148961	.150616	.152343	.154003	.006504
	30 %	.30	.148164	.149814	.151537	.153190	.154915	.156571	.005977
20 Years n = 20	Balance (b)		.640312	.648784	.650778	.660815	.663990	.675798	+ Dep − App
	Equity	Yield	Basic Rate before Depreciation or Appreciation						
	6 %	.06	.081736	.083529	.085279	.087104	.088879	.090740	.027184
	7 %	.07	.084989	.086764	.088511	.090314	.092082	.093918	.024392
	8 %	.08	.088175	.089933	.091676	.093461	.095223	.097036	.021852
	9 %	.09	.091297	.093041	.094780	.096547	.098304	.100097	.019546
	10 %	.10	.094359	.096090	.097827	.099578	.101330	.103104	.017459
	11 %	.11	.097368	.099087	.100820	.102557	.104304	.106062	.015575
	12 %	.12	.100325	.102034	.103764	.105489	.107232	.108975	.013878
	13 %	.13	.103237	.104935	.106664	.108377	.110116	.111846	.012353
	14 %	.14	.106106	.107796	.109522	.111225	.112961	.114678	.010986
	15 %	.15	.108936	.110618	.112343	.114036	.115770	.117476	.009761
	16 %	.16	.111731	.113407	.115129	.116815	.118545	.120242	.008667
	17 %	.17	.114495	.116164	.117885	.119563	.121291	.122980	.007690
	18 %	.18	.117230	.118893	.120613	.122285	.124011	.125691	.006819
	19 %	.19	.119939	.121597	.123316	.124982	.126706	.128380	.006045
	20 %	.20	.122624	.124279	.125997	.127657	.129380	.131047	.005356
	21 %	.21	.125290	.126940	.128657	.130312	.132034	.133696	.004744
	22 %	.22	.127936	.129583	.131299	.132951	.134671	.136328	.004201
	23 %	.23	.130566	.132209	.133925	.135573	.137292	.138945	.003720
	24 %	.24	.133181	.134822	.136537	.138182	.139899	.141549	.003293
	25 %	.25	.135783	.137421	.139136	.140778	.142495	.144140	.002915
	26 %	.26	.138373	.140010	.141723	.143363	.145079	.146722	.002581
	27 %	.27	.140953	.142588	.144301	.145938	.147654	.149294	.002285
	28 %	.28	.143524	.145157	.146870	.148505	.150220	.151858	.002023
	29 %	.29	.146086	.147718	.149430	.151064	.152778	.154414	.001791
	30 %	.30	.148641	.150271	.151984	.153616	.155330	.156964	.001586

CAPITALIZATION RATES

Assuming 75% of Purchase Price Financed by Mortgage

30 YEARS AMORTIZATION: 9¼% TO 10½%

Interest Rate			9¼%	9½%	9¾%	10%	10¼%	10½%	$\frac{1}{s_{\overline{n}\vert}}$
Annual Requirement (f)			.098760	.100920	.103200	.105360	.107640	.109800	
Coverage Min. Rate			.074070	.075690	.077400	.079020	.080730	.082350	
Projection	Balance (b)		.390209	.398593	.395961	.407347	.406877	.421812	+ Dep – App
	Equity	Yield	Basic Rate before Depreciation or Appreciation						
	6 %	.06	.080734	.082468	.084142	.085918	.087621	.089446	.018226
	7 %	.07	.084339	.086058	.087737	.089492	.091196	.092993	.015810
	8 %	.08	.087814	.089520	.091203	.092939	.094645	.096418	.013678
	9 %	.09	.091170	.092864	.094551	.096272	.097978	.099730	.011806
	10 %	.10	.094419	.096103	.097793	.099500	.101206	.102940	.010168
	11 %	.11	.097572	.099247	.100940	.102635	.104341	.106059	.008740
	12 %	.12	.100639	.102307	.104002	.105686	.107393	.109097	.007499
	13 %	.13	.103631	.105291	.106988	.108663	.110371	.112063	.006425
	14 %	.14	.106555	.108209	.109909	.111576	.113284	.114965	.005498
	15 %	.15	.109420	.111070	.112771	.114431	.116139	.117812	.004699
25 Years n = 25	16 %	.16	.112234	.113880	.115582	.117236	.118945	.120609	.004012
	17 %	.17	.115004	.116645	.118349	.119998	.121707	.123365	.003423
	18 %	.18	.117735	.119373	.121077	.122722	.124431	.126084	.002918
	19 %	.19	.120432	.122068	.123773	.125414	.127123	.128771	.002487
	20 %	.20	.123101	.124734	.126440	.128078	.129787	.131431	.002118
	21 %	.21	.125744	.127376	.129082	.130718	.132427	.134067	.001804
	22 %	.22	.128367	.129997	.131704	.133337	.135046	.136683	.001536
	23 %	.23	.130971	.132600	.134307	.135938	.137648	.139282	.001307
	24 %	.24	.133560	.135187	.136895	.138525	.140234	.141867	.001113
	25 %	.25	.136136	.137762	.139470	.141098	.142808	.144438	.000948
	26 %	.26	.138700	.140325	.142034	.143661	.145370	.146999	.000807
	27 %	.27	.141255	.142879	.144588	.146214	.147924	.149551	.000687
	28 %	.28	.143802	.145425	.147134	.148759	.150469	.152095	.000585
	29 %	.29	.146341	.147964	.149673	.151298	.153007	.154633	.000499
	30 %	.30	.148875	.150497	.152207	.153830	.155540	.157165	.000425
	Balance (b)		none	none	none	none	none	none	+ Dep – App
	Equity	Yield	Basic Rate before Depreciation or Appreciation						
	6 %	.06	.079523	.081175	.082741	.084441	.086040	.087801	.012648
	7 %	.07	.083580	.085226	.086816	.088503	.090120	.091858	.010586
	8 %	.08	.087407	.089049	.090659	.092335	.093967	.095685	.008827
	9 %	.09	.091033	.092671	.094298	.095964	.097609	.099311	.007336
	10 %	.10	.094482	.096117	.097757	.099416	.101072	.102760	.006079
	11 %	.11	.097777	.099410	.101063	.102715	.104380	.106056	.005024
	12 %	.12	.100942	.102573	.104235	.105882	.107555	.109221	.004143
	13 %	.13	.103995	.105624	.107295	.108937	.110617	.112275	.003410
	14 %	.14	.106954	.108581	.110259	.111897	.113582	.115234	.002802
	15 %	.15	.109834	.111459	.113143	.114778	.116467	.118113	.002300
30 Years n = 30	16 %	.16	.112646	.114271	.115960	.117592	.119285	.120926	.001885
	17 %	.17	.115404	.117028	.118720	.120350	.122046	.123683	.001544
	18 %	.18	.118115	.119738	.121434	.123062	.124761	.126395	.001264
	19 %	.19	.120789	.122411	.124110	.125736	.127437	.129069	.001034
	20 %	.20	.123431	.125053	.126753	.128379	.130081	.131711	.000846
	21 %	.21	.126047	.127669	.129371	.130995	.132699	.134327	.000691
	22 %	.22	.128642	.130264	.131967	.133591	.135296	.136922	.000565
	23 %	.23	.131220	.132841	.134546	.136169	.137875	.139500	.000462
	24 %	.24	.133784	.135405	.137110	.138733	.140439	.142064	.000378
	25 %	.25	.136336	.137956	.139663	.141285	.142992	.144616	.000309
	26 %	.26	.138878	.140499	.142206	.143827	.145535	.147158	.000253
	27 %	.27	.141413	.143033	.144741	.146362	.148070	.149693	.000207
	28 %	.28	.143941	.145561	.147269	.148891	.150599	.152221	.000170
	29 %	.29	.146464	.148084	.149793	.151414	.153123	.154744	.000139
	30 %	.30	.148983	.150603	.152312	.153933	.155642	.157263	.000114

CAPITALIZATION RATES

Assuming 75% of Purchase Price Financed by Mortgage

30 YEARS AMORTIZATION: 10¾% TO 12%

			10¾%	11%	11¼%	11½%	11¾%	12%	$\frac{1}{s_{\overline{n}\rceil}}$
Interest Rate			10¾%	11%	11¼%	11½%	11¾%	12%	
Annual Requirement (f)			.112080	.114360	.116640	.118920	.121200	.123480	
Coverage Min. Rate			.084060	.085770	.087480	.089190	.090900	.092610	
Projection	Balance (b)		.969851	.971108	.972383	.973675	.974986	.976315	+ Dep – App
	Equity	Yield	Basic Rate before Depreciation or Appreciation						
	6 %	.06	.095048	.096926	.098805	.100687	.102572	.104458	.177396
	7 %	.07	.097628	.099502	.101378	.103256	.105137	.107021	.173890
	8 %	.08	.100205	.102076	.103949	.105824	.107702	.109582	.170456
	9 %	.09	.102781	.104649	.106519	.108391	.110265	.112141	.167092
	10 %	.10	.105356	.107220	.109087	.110956	.112827	.114700	.163797
	11 %	.11	.107929	.109790	.111654	.113519	.115387	.117257	.160570
	12 %	.12	.110500	.112359	.114219	.116082	.117946	.119813	.157409
	13 %	.13	.113070	.114926	.116783	.118643	.120505	.122368	.154314
	14 %	.14	.115639	.117491	.119346	.121203	.123061	.124922	.151283
	15 %	.15	.118206	.120056	.121907	.123761	.125617	.127475	.148315
	16 %	.16	.120772	.122619	.124468	.126319	.128172	.130027	.145409
	17 %	.17	.123336	.125180	.127027	.128875	.130725	.132577	.142563
5 Years n = 5	18 %	.18	.125899	.127741	.129584	.131430	.133277	.135127	.139777
	19 %	.19	.128461	.130300	.132141	.133984	.135828	.137675	.137050
	20 %	.20	.131021	.132858	.134696	.136536	.138379	.140222	.134379
	21 %	.21	.133580	.135414	.137250	.139088	.140928	.142769	.131765
	22 %	.22	.136138	.137970	.139803	.141639	.143476	.145314	.129205
	23 %	.23	.138695	.140524	.142355	.144188	.146023	.147859	.126700
	24 %	.24	.141250	.143077	.144906	.146736	.148569	.150402	.124247
	25 %	.25	.143804	.145629	.147456	.149284	.151114	.152945	.121846
	26 %	.26	.146358	.148180	.150004	.151830	.153658	.155487	.119496
	27 %	.27	.148910	.150730	.152552	.154376	.156201	.158028	.117195
	28 %	.28	.151460	.153279	.155099	.156920	.158743	.160568	.114943
	29 %	.29	.154010	.155827	.157644	.159464	.161284	.163107	.112739
	30 %	.30	.156559	.158373	.160189	.162006	.163825	.165645	.110581
	Balance (b)		.918369	.921157	.924040	.927021	.930103	.933288	+ Dep – App
	Equity	Yield	Basic Rate before Depreciation or Appreciation						
	6 %	.06	.094415	.096283	.098157	.100037	.101922	.103814	.075867
	7 %	.07	.097128	.098990	.100856	.102728	.104605	.106488	.072377
	8 %	.08	.099833	.101688	.103547	.105411	.107281	.109156	.069029
	9 %	.09	.102530	.104377	.106230	.108087	.109949	.111816	.065820
	10 %	.10	.105218	.107059	.108905	.110755	.112610	.114470	.062745
	11 %	.11	.107898	.109733	.111573	.113416	.115265	.117117	.059801
	12 %	.12	.110571	.112400	.114233	.116071	.117912	.119758	.056984
	13 %	.13	.113236	.115059	.116887	.118718	.120554	.122393	.054289
	14 %	.14	.115893	.117712	.119533	.121359	.123189	.125022	.051713
	15 %	.15	.118544	.120357	.122174	.123994	.125818	.127645	.049252
10 Years n = 10	16 %	.16	.121188	.122996	.124808	.126622	.128441	.130263	.046901
	17 %	.17	.123825	.125629	.127435	.129245	.131058	.132875	.044656
	18 %	.18	.126457	.128256	.130057	.131863	.133671	.135482	.042514
	19 %	.19	.129082	.130876	.132674	.134474	.136278	.138085	.040471
	20 %	.20	.131701	.133492	.135285	.137081	.138880	.140682	.038522
	21 %	.21	.134315	.136101	.137891	.139683	.141477	.143275	.036665
	22 %	.22	.136923	.138706	.140492	.142280	.144070	.145864	.034894
	23 %	.23	.139526	.141306	.143088	.144872	.146659	.148448	.033208
	24 %	.24	.142125	.143901	.145679	.147460	.149243	.151028	.031602
	25 %	.25	.144718	.146491	.148266	.150044	.151823	.153605	.030072
	26 %	.26	.147308	.149077	.150849	.152623	.154399	.156178	.028616
	27 %	.27	.149892	.151659	.153428	.155199	.156972	.158747	.027230
	28 %	.28	.152473	.154237	.156003	.157771	.159541	.161313	.025911
	29 %	.29	.155050	.156811	.158575	.160340	.162107	.163876	.024657
	30 %	.30	.157623	.159382	.161143	.162905	.164669	.166436	.023463

CAPITALIZATION RATES

Assuming 75% of Purchase Price Financed by Mortgage

30 YEARS AMORTIZATION: 10¾% TO 12%

		10¾%	11%	11¼%	11½%	11¾%	12%	$\frac{1}{s_{\overline{n}\rvert}}$
terest Rate		10¾%	11%	11¼%	11½%	11¾%	12%	
.nnual Requirement (f)		.112080	.114360	.116640	.118920	.121200	.123480	
Coverage Min. Rate		.084060	.085770	.087480	.089190	.090900	.092610	
Projection	Balance (b)	.830456	.834796	.839418	.844338	.849567	.855121	+ Dep – App
	Equity Yield	Basic Rate before Depreciation or Appreciation						
	6 % .06	.093596	.095446	.097305	.099174	.101052	.102941	.042962
	7 % .07	.096499	.098339	.100187	.102044	.103910	.105785	.039794
	8 % .08	.099376	.101206	.103044	.104890	.106744	.108608	.036829
	9 % .09	.102229	.104050	.105878	.107713	.109557	.111409	.034058
	10 % .10	.105057	.106870	.108689	.110515	.112348	.114190	.031473
	11 % .11	.107864	.109668	.111479	.113296	.115120	.116951	.029065
	12 % .12	.110649	.112446	.114249	.116058	.117873	.119695	.026824
	13 % .13	.113413	.115204	.117000	.118801	.120608	.122421	.024741
	14 % .14	.116159	.117943	.119732	.121527	.123326	.125131	.022808
	15 % .15	.118887	.120665	.122448	.124236	.126028	.127826	.021017
	16 % .16	.121598	.123371	.125148	.126930	.128716	.130506	.019357
	17 % .17	.124293	.126061	.127833	.129609	.131389	.133173	.017822
15 Years n = 15	18 % .18	.126974	.128737	.130504	.132275	.134049	.135827	.016402
	19 % .19	.129640	.131400	.133162	.134928	.136697	.138470	.015091
	20 % .20	.132294	.134049	.135808	.137569	.139333	.141101	.013882
	21 % .21	.134936	.136688	.138442	.140199	.141959	.143722	.012766
	22 % .22	.137567	.139315	.141066	.142819	.144575	.146334	.011738
	23 % .23	.140187	.141932	.143680	.145430	.147182	.148937	.010791
	24 % .24	.142798	.144540	.146285	.148031	.149780	.151532	.009919
	25 % .25	.145400	.147140	.148882	.150625	.152371	.154119	.009116
	26 % .26	.147994	.149731	.151470	.153211	.154954	.156699	.008378
	27 % .27	.150580	.152315	.154052	.155790	.157531	.159273	.007700
	28 % .28	.153160	.154893	.156627	.158363	.160101	.161841	.007076
	29 % .29	.155732	.157464	.159196	.160930	.162666	.164403	.006504
	30 % .30	.158299	.160029	.161760	.163492	.165225	.166960	.005977
	Balance (b)	.680334	.685484	.691291	.697800	.705058	.713115	+ Dep – App
	Equity Yield	Basic Rate before Depreciation or Appreciation						
	6 % .06	.092542	.094357	.096185	.098028	.099886	.101760	.027184
	7 % .07	.095711	.097516	.099332	.101161	.103004	.104861	.024392
	8 % .08	.098820	.100615	.102420	.104237	.106066	.107908	.021852
	9 % .09	.101873	.103659	.105454	.107259	.109076	.110904	.019546
	10 % .10	.104874	.106651	.108437	.110232	.112037	.113853	.017459
	11 % .11	.107825	.109595	.111373	.113159	.114954	.116758	.015575
	12 % .12	.110732	.112496	.114266	.116044	.117829	.119623	.013878
	13 % .13	.113598	.115355	.117119	.118890	.120667	.122451	.012353
	14 % .14	.116426	.118178	.119936	.121700	.123469	.125246	.010986
	15 % .15	.119219	.120967	.122719	.124477	.126240	.128009	.009761
20 Years n = 20	16 % .16	.121982	.123725	.125473	.127225	.128982	.130745	.008667
	17 % .17	.124716	.126455	.128199	.129946	.131698	.133455	.007690
	18 % .18	.127424	.129161	.130900	.132644	.134391	.136142	.006819
	19 % .19	.130110	.131843	.133580	.135319	.137062	.138809	.006045
	20 % .20	.132775	.134506	.136239	.137975	.139715	.141457	.005356
	21 % .21	.135422	.137150	.138881	.140614	.142350	.144089	.004744
	22 % .22	.138052	.139778	.141507	.143237	.144970	.146705	.004201
	23 % .23	.140668	.142392	.144118	.145846	.147577	.149309	.003720
	24 % .24	.143270	.144993	.146717	.148443	.150171	.151901	.003293
	25 % .25	.145860	.147582	.149304	.151029	.152754	.154482	.002915
	26 % .26	.148441	.150161	.151882	.153604	.155328	.157054	.002581
	27 % .27	.151012	.152730	.154450	.156172	.157894	.159618	.002285
	28 % .28	.153574	.155292	.157011	.158731	.160452	.162174	.002023
	29 % .29	.156130	.157847	.159565	.161283	.163003	.164724	.001791
	30 % .30	.158679	.160395	.162112	.163830	.165548	.167268	.001586

CAPITALIZATION RATES

Assuming 75% of Purchase Price Financed by Mortgage

30 YEARS AMORTIZATION: 10¾% TO 12%

			10¾%	11%	11¼%	11½%	11¾%	12%	$\frac{1}{s_{\overline{n}\rceil}}$
Interest Rate			10¾%	11%	11¼%	11½%	11¾%	12%	
Annual Requirement (f)			.112080	.114360	.116640	.118920	.121200	.123480	
Coverage Min. Rate			.084060	.085770	.087480	.089190	.090900	.092610	
Projection	Balance (b)		.423981	.427338	.432001	.438095	.445757	.455134	+ Dep − App
	Equity	Yield	Basic Rate before Depreciation or Appreciation						
	6 %	.06	.091185	.092941	.094715	.096508	.098323	.100161	.018226
	7 %	.07	.094729	.096479	.098244	.100027	.101827	.103649	.015810
	8 %	.08	.098150	.099895	.101652	.103425	.105213	.107020	.013678
	9 %	.09	.101459	.103199	.104950	.106714	.108492	.110285	.011806
	10 %	.10	.104667	.106402	.108148	.109904	.111673	.113454	.010168
	11 %	.11	.107784	.109516	.111256	.113006	.114766	.116538	.008740
	12 %	.12	.110819	.112548	.114285	.116029	.117782	.119545	.007499
	13 %	.13	.113783	.115510	.117242	.118981	.120728	.122484	.006425
	14 %	.14	.116684	.118408	.120137	.121872	.123614	.125363	.005498
	15 %	.15	.119529	.121251	.122978	.124709	.126446	.128189	.004699
	16 %	.16	.122326	.124046	.125770	.127498	.129232	.130970	.004012
25 Years	17 %	.17	.125081	.126799	.128521	.130247	.131976	.133711	.003423
n = 25	18 %	.18	.127799	.129516	.131236	.132959	.134686	.136417	.002918
	19 %	.19	.130485	.132201	.133920	.135641	.137366	.139093	.002487
	20 %	.20	.133144	.134860	.136577	.138297	.140019	.141744	.002118
	21 %	.21	.135780	.137495	.139211	.140929	.142650	.144372	.001804
	22 %	.22	.138396	.140110	.141825	.143542	.145261	.146982	.001536
	23 %	.23	.140994	.142708	.144422	.146138	.147856	.149575	.001307
	24 %	.24	.143578	.145291	.147005	.148720	.150437	.152154	.001113
	25 %	.25	.146150	.147862	.149576	.151290	.153005	.154722	.000948
	26 %	.26	.148711	.150423	.152136	.153849	.155564	.157280	.000807
	27 %	.27	.151262	.152974	.154687	.156400	.158114	.159828	.000687
	28 %	.28	.153806	.155518	.157230	.158943	.160656	.162370	.000585
	29 %	.29	.156344	.158055	.159767	.161479	.163192	.164905	.000499
	30 %	.30	.158876	.160587	.162298	.164010	.165723	.167436	.000425
	Balance (b)		none	none	none	none	none	none	+ Dep − App
	Equity	Yield	Basic Rate before Depreciation or Appreciation						
	6 %	.06	.089442	.091103	.092785	.094492	.096228	.097994	.012648
	7 %	.07	.093510	.095179	.096866	.098574	.100305	.102062	.010586
	8 %	.08	.097348	.099023	.100714	.102422	.104150	.105899	.008827
	9 %	.09	.100981	.102663	.104357	.106065	.107790	.109533	.007336
	10 %	.10	.104437	.106124	.107820	.109529	.111251	.112988	.006079
	11 %	.11	.107739	.109430	.111129	.112837	.114558	.116290	.005024
	12 %	.12	.110909	.112603	.114304	.116013	.117731	.119460	.004143
	13 %	.13	.113966	.115663	.117366	.119075	.120792	.122517	.003410
	14 %	.14	.116928	.118628	.120331	.122041	.123756	.125479	.002802
30 Years	15 %	.15	.119811	.121512	.123217	.124926	.126641	.128361	.002300
n = 30	16 %	.16	.122626	.124328	.126034	.127744	.129458	.131176	.001885
	17 %	.17	.125385	.127089	.128796	.130505	.132218	.133935	.001544
	18 %	.18	.128098	.129803	.131511	.133220	.134933	.136648	.001264
	19 %	.19	.130773	.132479	.134187	.135896	.137609	.139323	.001034
	20 %	.20	.133416	.135123	.136831	.138541	.140253	.141966	.000846
	21 %	.21	.136033	.137741	.139449	.141159	.142870	.144583	.000691
	22 %	.22	.138629	.140337	.142046	.143756	.145467	.147179	.000565
	23 %	.23	.141208	.142916	.144625	.146335	.148046	.149758	.000462
	24 %	.24	.143772	.145480	.147189	.148899	.150610	.152322	.000378
	25 %	.25	.146324	.148033	.149742	.151452	.153163	.154874	.000309
	26 %	.26	.148867	.150576	.152285	.153995	.155706	.157417	.000253
	27 %	.27	.151402	.153111	.154820	.156530	.158241	.159952	.000207
	28 %	.28	.153930	.155639	.157349	.159059	.160769	.162480	.000170
	29 %	.29	.156453	.158163	.159873	.161582	.163293	.165003	.000139
	30 %	.30	.158972	.160682	.162392	.164102	.165812	.167522	.000114

75% Mortgage

ANALYSIS OF SELECTED CAPITALIZATION RATES

Depreciation or Appreciation in 5 years and 10 years for yields of 6%, 9%, 12% and 15% on 25% equity.

MORTGAGE INTEREST RATE 4¼%

Projection & Yield	CAPITALIZATION RATES .0650	.0675	.0700	.0725	.0750	.0775	.0800	.0825	.0850	.0875	.0900	.0925
	Amortization 15 Years.											
6%	− 10	− 11	− 13	− 14	− 16	− 17	− 18	− 20	− 21	− 23	− 24	− 25
5 9%	− 5	− 6	− 8	− 9	− 11	− 12	− 14	− 15	− 17	− 18	− 20	− 21
Yr. 12%	+ 1	− 1	− 2	− 4	− 5	− 7	− 9	− 10	− 12	− 13	− 15	− 17
15%	+ 7	+ 6	+ 4	+ 2	0	− 1	− 3	− 5	− 6	− 8	− 10	− 11
6%	− 21	− 25	− 28	− 31	− 34	− 38	− 41	− 44	− 48	− 51	− 54	− 57
10 9%	− 6	− 10	− 14	− 18	− 21	− 25	− 29	− 33	− 37	− 40	− 44	− 48
Yr. 12%	+ 13	+ 9	+ 4	0	− 5	− 9	− 13	− 18	− 22	− 26	− 31	− 35
15%	+ 37	+ 32	+ 27	+ 22	+ 17	+ 12	+ 7	+ 2	− 3	− 8	− 13	− 18
	Amortization 20 Years.											
6%	− 10	− 11	− 13	− 14	− 15	− 17	− 18	− 20	− 21	− 22	− 24	− 25
5 9%	− 5	− 7	− 8	− 10	− 11	− 13	− 14	− 16	− 17	− 19	− 20	− 22
Yr. 12%	0	− 2	− 3	− 5	− 6	− 8	− 9	− 11	− 13	− 14	− 16	− 17
15%	+ 6	+ 4	+ 3	+ 1	− 1	− 2	− 4	− 6	− 8	− 9	− 11	− 13
6%	− 22	− 25	− 28	− 32	− 35	− 38	− 42	− 45	− 48	− 51	− 55	− 58
10 9%	− 9	− 13	− 17	− 21	− 24	− 28	− 32	− 36	− 40	− 43	− 47	− 51
Yr. 12%	+ 7	+ 3	− 2	− 6	− 11	− 15	− 19	− 24	− 28	− 32	− 37	− 41
15%	+ 28	+ 23	+ 18	+ 13	+ 8	+ 3	− 2	− 8	− 13	− 18	− 23	− 28
	Amortization 25 Years.											
6%	− 10	− 11	− 13	− 14	− 16	− 17	− 18	− 20	− 21	− 23	− 24	− 25
5 9%	− 6	− 7	− 9	− 10	− 12	− 13	− 15	− 16	− 17	− 19	− 20	− 22
Yr. 12%	− 1	− 2	− 4	− 5	− 7	− 8	− 10	− 12	− 13	− 15	− 16	− 18
15%	+ 5	+ 3	+ 2	0	− 2	− 3	− 5	− 7	− 8	− 10	− 12	− 13
6%	− 22	− 26	− 29	− 32	− 36	− 39	− 42	− 45	− 49	− 52	− 55	− 59
10 9%	− 11	− 15	− 19	− 23	− 26	− 30	− 34	− 38	− 42	− 45	− 49	− 53
Yr. 12%	+ 3	− 1	− 5	− 10	− 14	− 19	− 23	− 27	− 32	− 36	− 40	− 45
15%	+ 22	+ 17	+ 12	+ 7	+ 2	− 3	− 8	− 13	− 18	− 23	− 28	− 33
	Amortization 30 Years.											
6%	− 10	− 11	− 13	− 14	− 16	− 17	− 18	− 20	− 21	− 23	− 24	− 25
5 9%	− 6	− 7	− 9	− 10	− 12	− 13	− 15	− 16	− 18	− 19	− 21	− 22
Yr. 12%	− 1	− 2	− 4	− 6	− 7	− 9	− 10	− 12	− 14	− 15	− 17	− 18
15%	+ 5	+ 3	+ 1	− 1	− 2	− 4	− 6	− 7	− 9	− 11	− 12	− 14
6%	− 23	− 26	− 29	− 33	− 36	− 39	− 42	− 46	− 49	− 52	− 56	− 59
10 9%	− 13	− 16	− 20	− 24	− 28	− 32	− 35	− 39	− 43	− 47	− 50	− 54
Yr. 12%	+ 1	− 3	− 8	− 12	− 17	− 21	− 25	− 30	− 34	− 39	− 43	− 47
15%	+ 19	+ 14	+ 9	+ 4	− 2	− 7	− 12	− 17	− 22	− 27	− 32	− 37

75% Mortgage

ANALYSIS OF SELECTED CAPITALIZATION RATES

Depreciation or Appreciation in 5 years and 10 years for yields of 6%, 9%, 12% and 15% on 25% equity.

MORTGAGE INTEREST RATE 4½%

Projection & Yield	CAPITALIZATION RATES											
	.0650	.0675	.0700	.0725	.0750	.0775	.0800	.0825	.0850	.0875	.0900	.0925
	Amortization 15 Years.											
6%	− 9	− 10	− 12	− 13	− 15	− 16	− 17	− 19	− 20	− 22	− 23	− 24
5 9%	− 4	− 5	− 7	− 8	− 10	− 11	− 13	− 14	− 16	− 17	− 19	− 20
Yr. 12%	+ 2	0	− 1	− 3	− 4	− 6	− 8	− 9	− 11	− 12	− 14	− 16
15%	+ 8	+ 7	+ 5	+ 3	+ 2	0	− 2	− 4	− 5	− 7	− 9	− 10
6%	− 19	− 23	− 26	− 29	− 32	− 36	− 39	− 42	− 46	− 49	− 52	− 55
10 9%	− 4	− 8	− 12	− 16	− 19	− 23	− 27	− 31	− 34	− 38	− 42	− 46
Yr. 12%	+ 15	+ 11	+ 6	+ 2	− 2	− 7	− 11	− 15	− 20	− 24	− 29	− 33
15%	+ 40	+ 35	+ 30	+ 25	+ 19	+ 14	+ 9	+ 4	− 1	− 6	− 11	− 16
	Amortization 20 Years.											
6%	− 9	− 11	− 12	− 13	− 14	− 16	− 17	− 19	− 20	− 22	− 23	− 24
5 9%	− 4	− 6	− 7	− 9	− 10	− 12	− 13	− 15	− 16	− 18	− 19	− 21
Yr. 12%	+ 1	0	− 2	− 3	− 5	− 7	− 8	− 10	− 11	− 13	− 15	− 16
15%	+ 7	+ 5	+ 4	+ 2	0	− 1	− 3	− 5	− 6	− 8	− 10	− 11
6%	− 20	− 23	− 27	− 30	− 33	− 36	− 40	− 43	− 46	− 50	− 53	− 56
10 9%	− 7	− 11	− 15	− 18	− 22	− 26	− 30	− 34	− 37	− 41	− 45	− 49
Yr. 12%	+ 9	+ 5	+ 1	− 4	− 8	− 12	− 17	− 21	− 26	− 30	− 34	− 39
15%	+ 31	+ 26	+ 20	+ 15	+ 10	+ 5	0	− 5	− 10	− 15	− 20	− 25
	Amortization 25 Years.											
6%	− 9	− 10	− 12	− 13	− 15	− 16	− 17	− 19	− 20	− 22	− 23	− 24
5 9%	− 5	− 6	− 8	− 9	− 10	− 12	− 13	− 15	− 16	− 18	− 19	− 21
Yr. 12%	+ 1	− 1	− 3	− 4	− 6	− 7	− 9	− 11	− 12	− 14	− 15	− 17
15%	+ 6	+ 4	+ 3	+ 1	− 1	− 2	− 4	− 6	− 7	− 9	− 11	− 12
6%	− 20	− 24	− 27	− 30	− 34	− 37	− 40	− 43	− 47	− 50	− 53	− 57
10 9%	− 9	− 13	− 16	− 20	− 24	− 28	− 32	− 35	− 39	− 43	− 47	− 51
Yr. 12%	+ 6	+ 2	− 3	− 7	− 11	− 16	− 20	− 25	− 29	− 33	− 38	− 42
15%	+ 25	+ 20	+ 15	+ 10	+ 5	0	− 5	− 10	− 15	− 20	− 25	− 30
	Amortization 30 Years.											
6%	− 9	− 10	− 12	− 13	− 15	− 16	− 17	− 19	− 20	− 22	− 23	− 24
5 9%	− 5	− 6	− 8	− 9	− 11	− 12	− 14	− 15	− 17	− 18	− 20	− 21
Yr. 12%	0	− 1	− 3	− 5	− 6	− 8	− 9	− 11	− 12	− 14	− 16	− 17
15%	+ 6	+ 4	+ 2	+ 1	− 1	− 3	− 4	− 6	− 8	− 9	− 11	− 13
6%	− 21	− 24	− 27	− 30	− 34	− 37	− 40	− 44	− 47	− 50	− 54	− 57
10 9%	− 10	− 14	− 18	− 21	− 25	− 29	− 33	− 37	− 40	− 44	− 48	− 52
Yr. 12%	+ 4	− 1	− 5	− 9	− 14	− 18	− 22	− 27	− 31	− 36	− 40	− 44
15%	+ 22	+ 17	+ 12	+ 7	+ 2	− 3	− 8	− 14	− 19	− 24	− 29	− 34

75% Mortgage

ANALYSIS OF SELECTED CAPITALIZATION RATES

Depreciation or Appreciation in 5 years and 10 years for yields of 6%, 9%, 12% and 15% on 25% equity.

MORTGAGE INTEREST RATE 4¾%

Projection & Yield	CAPITALIZATION RATES											
	.0650	.0675	.0700	.0725	.0750	.0775	.0800	.0825	.0850	.0875	.0900	.0925
	Amortization 15 Years.											
6%	– 8	– 9	– 11	– 12	– 14	– 15	– 17	– 18	– 19	– 21	– 22	– 24
5 9%	– 3	– 4	– 6	– 7	– 9	– 10	– 12	– 13	– 15	– 16	– 18	– 19
Yr. 12%	+ 3	+ 1	0	– 2	– 3	– 5	– 7	– 8	– 10	– 11	– 13	– 15
15%	+ 9	+ 8	+ 6	+ 4	+ 3	+ 1	– 1	– 2	– 4	– 6	– 8	– 9
6%	– 18	– 21	– 24	– 27	– 31	– 34	– 37	– 41	– 44	– 47	– 50	– 54
10 9%	– 2	– 6	– 10	– 14	– 17	– 21	– 25	– 29	– 33	– 36	– 40	– 44
Yr. 12%	+ 17	+ 13	+ 9	– 4	0	– 4	– 9	– 13	– 18	– 22	– 26	– 31
15%	+ 42	+ 37	+ 32	+ 27	+ 22	+ 17	+ 12	+ 7	+ 2	– 3	– 8	– 13
	Amortization 20 Years.											
6%	– 8	– 9	– 11	– 12	– 13	– 15	– 16	– 18	– 19	– 21	– 22	– 23
5 9%	– 3	– 5	– 6	– 8	– 9	– 11	– 12	– 14	– 15	– 17	– 18	– 20
Yr. 12%	+ 2	0	– 1	– 2	– 4	– 6	– 7	– 9	– 10	– 12	– 14	– 15
15%	+ 8	+ 6	+ 5	+ 3	+ 1	0	– 2	– 4	– 5	– 7	– 9	– 11
6%	– 18	– 21	– 24	– 28	– 31	– 34	– 38	– 41	– 44	– 47	– 51	– 54
10 9%	– 5	– 8	– 12	– 16	– 20	– 24	– 27	– 31	– 35	– 39	– 43	– 46
Yr. 12%	+ 12	+ 8	+ 3	– 1	– 5	– 10	– 14	– 19	– 23	– 27	– 32	– 36
15%	+ 34	+ 29	+ 24	+ 18	+ 13	+ 8	+ 3	– 2	– 7	– 12	– 17	– 22
	Amortization 25 Years.											
6%	– 8	– 9	– 11	– 12	– 14	– 15	– 16	– 18	– 19	– 21	– 22	– 23
5 9%	– 3	– 5	– 6	– 8	– 9	– 11	– 12	– 14	– 15	– 17	– 18	– 20
Yr. 12%	+ 2	0	– 1	– 3	– 5	– 6	– 8	– 9	– 11	– 13	– 14	– 16
15%	+ 7	+ 6	+ 4	+ 2	+ 1	– 1	– 3	– 4	– 6	– 8	– 9	– 11
6%	– 18	– 21	– 25	– 28	– 31	– 35	– 38	– 41	– 44	– 48	– 51	– 54
10 9%	– 6	– 10	– 14	– 18	– 22	– 25	– 29	– 33	– 37	– 41	– 44	– 48
Yr. 12%	+ 9	+ 4	0	– 4	– 9	– 13	– 17	– 22	– 26	– 31	– 35	– 39
15%	+ 28	+ 23	+ 18	+ 13	+ 8	+ 3	– 2	– 7	– 12	– 17	– 22	– 27
	Amortization 30 Years.											
6%	– 8	– 9	– 11	– 12	– 14	– 15	– 16	– 18	– 19	– 21	– 22	– 23
5 9%	– 4	– 5	– 7	– 8	– 10	– 11	– 13	– 14	– 16	– 17	– 19	– 20
Yr. 12%	+ 1	– 1	– 2	– 3	– 5	– 7	– 8	– 10	– 11	– 13	– 15	– 16
15%	+ 7	+ 5	+ 3	+ 2	0	– 2	– 3	– 5	– 7	– 8	– 10	– 12
6%	– 18	– 22	– 25	– 28	– 32	– 35	– 38	– 41	– 45	– 48	– 51	– 55
10 9%	– 8	– 11	– 15	– 19	– 23	– 27	– 30	– 34	– 38	– 42	– 46	– 49
Yr. 12%	+ 7	+ 2	– 2	– 7	– 11	– 15	– 20	– 24	– 29	– 33	– 37	– 42
15%	+ 25	+ 20	+ 15	+ 10	+ 5	0	– 5	– 10	– 15	– 20	– 26	– 31

75% Mortgage

ANALYSIS OF SELECTED CAPITALIZATION RATES

Depreciation or Appreciation in 5 years and 10 years for yields of 6%, 9%, 12% and 15% on 25% equity.

MORTGAGE INTEREST RATE 5%

Projection & Yield	CAPITALIZATION RATES											
	.0650	.0675	.0700	.0725	.0750	.0775	0.800	.0825	.0850	.0875	.0900	.0925
	Amortization 15 Years.											
6%	- 7	- 9	- 10	- 11	- 13	- 14	- 16	- 17	- 18	- 20	- 21	- 23
5 9%	- 2	- 3	- 5	- 6	- 8	- 9	- 11	- 12	- 14	- 15	- 17	- 18
Yr. 12%	+ 4	+ 2	+ 1	- 1	- 2	- 4	- 6	- 7	- 9	- 10	- 12	- 14
15%	+ 10	+ 9	+ 7	+ 5	+ 4	+ 2	0	- 1	- 3	- 5	- 6	- 8
6%	- 16	- 19	- 22	- 26	- 29	- 32	- 35	- 39	- 42	- 45	- 49	- 52
10 9%	0	- 4	- 7	- 11	- 15	- 19	- 23	- 26	- 30	- 34	- 38	- 42
Yr. 12%	+ 20	+ 16	+ 11	+ 7	+ 2	- 2	- 6	- 11	- 15	- 19	- 24	- 28
15%	+ 45	+ 40	+ 35	+ 30	+ 25	+ 20	+ 15	+ 10	+ 5	0	- 5	- 11
	Amortization 20 Years.											
6%	- 7	- 8	- 10	- 11	- 13	- 14	- 15	- 17	- 18	- 20	- 21	- 22
5 9%	- 2	- 4	- 5	- 7	- 8	- 10	- 11	- 13	- 14	- 16	- 17	- 19
Yr. 12%	+ 3	+ 2	0	- 1	- 3	- 5	- 6	- 8	- 9	- 11	- 13	- 14
15%	+ 9	+ 7	+ 6	+ 4	+ 2	+ 1	- 1	- 3	- 4	- 6	- 8	- 9
6%	- 16	- 19	- 22	- 26	- 29	- 32	- 35	- 39	- 42	- 45	- 49	- 52
10 9%	- 2	- 6	- 10	- 14	- 18	- 21	- 25	- 29	- 33	- 37	- 40	- 44
Yr. 12%	+ 15	+ 10	+ 6	+ 1	- 3	- 7	- 12	- 16	- 20	- 25	- 29	- 34
15%	+ 37	+ 31	+ 26	+ 21	+ 16	+ 11	+ 6	+ 1	- 4	- 9	- 14	- 19
	Amortization 25 Years.											
6%	- 7	- 8	- 10	- 11	- 13	- 14	- 15	- 17	- 18	- 20	- 21	- 22
5 9%	- 2	- 4	- 5	- 7	- 8	- 10	- 11	- 13	- 14	- 16	- 17	- 19
Yr. 12%	+ 3	+ 1	- 1	- 2	- 4	- 5	- 7	- 8	- 10	- 12	- 13	- 15
15%	+ 8	+ 7	+ 5	+ 3	+ 2	0	- 2	- 3	- 5	- 7	- 8	- 10
6%	- 16	- 19	- 23	- 26	- 29	- 32	- 36	- 39	- 42	- 46	- 49	- 52
10 9%	- 4	- 8	- 12	- 15	- 19	- 23	- 27	- 31	- 34	- 38	- 42	- 46
Yr. 12%	+ 12	+ 7	+ 3	- 2	- 6	- 10	- 15	- 19	- 24	- 28	- 32	- 37
15%	+ 32	+ 27	+ 22	+ 17	+ 11	+ 6	+ 1	- 4	- 9	- 14	- 19	- 24
	Amortization 30 Years.											
6%	- 7	- 8	- 10	- 11	- 13	- 14	- 15	- 17	- 18	- 20	- 21	- 22
5 9%	- 3	- 4	- 6	- 7	- 9	- 10	- 12	- 13	- 15	- 16	- 17	- 19
Yr. 12%	+ 2	+ 1	- 1	- 2	- 4	- 5	- 7	- 9	- 10	- 12	- 13	- 15
15%	+ 8	+ 6	+ 5	+ 3	+ 1	- 1	- 2	- 4	- 5	- 7	- 9	- 10
6%	- 16	- 19	- 23	- 26	- 29	- 32	- 36	- 39	- 42	- 46	- 49	- 52
10 9%	- 5	- 9	- 13	- 16	- 20	- 24	- 28	- 32	- 35	- 39	- 43	- 47
Yr. 12%	+ 10	+ 5	+ 1	- 4	- 8	- 12	- 17	- 21	- 26	- 30	- 34	- 39
15%	+ 28	+ 23	+ 18	+ 13	+ 8	+ 3	- 2	- 7	- 12	- 17	- 22	- 27

75% Mortgage

ANALYSIS OF SELECTED CAPITALIZATION RATES

Depreciation or Appreciation in 5 years and 10 years for yields of 6%, 9%, 12% and 15% on 25% equity.

MORTGAGE INTEREST RATE 5¼%

Projection & Yield	CAPITALIZATION RATES											
	.0675	.0700	.0725	.0750	.0775	.0800	.0825	.0850	.0875	.0900	.0925	.0950
	Amortization 15 Years.											
6%	- 8	- 9	- 10	- 12	- 13	- 15	- 16	- 17	- 19	- 20	- 22	- 23
5 9%	- 2	- 4	- 5	- 7	- 8	- 10	- 11	- 13	- 14	- 16	- 17	- 19
Yr. 12%	+ 3	+ 2	0	- 1	- 3	- 5	- 6	- 8	- 9	- 11	- 13	- 14
15%	+ 10	+ 8	+ 6	+ 5	+ 3	+ 1	0	- 2	- 4	- 5	- 7	- 9
6%	- 17	- 20	- 24	- 27	- 30	- 33	- 37	- 40	- 43	- 47	- 50	- 53
10 9%	- 2	- 5	- 9	- 13	- 17	- 21	- 24	- 28	- 32	- 36	- 40	- 43
Yr. 12%	+ 18	+ 14	+ 9	+ 5	0	- 4	- 8	- 13	- 17	- 22	- 26	- 30
15%	+ 43	+ 38	+ 33	+ 28	+ 22	+ 17	+ 12	+ 7	+ 2	- 3	- 8	- 13
	Amortization 20 Years.											
6%	- 7	- 9	- 10	- 12	- 13	- 14	- 16	- 17	- 19	- 20	- 21	- 23
5 9%	- 3	- 4	- 6	- 7	- 9	- 10	- 12	- 13	- 15	- 16	- 18	- 19
Yr. 12%	+ 3	+ 1	- 1	- 2	- 4	- 5	- 7	- 8	- 10	- 12	- 13	- 15
15%	+ 9	+ 7	+ 5	+ 4	+ 2	0	- 2	- 3	- 5	- 7	- 8	- 10
6%	- 17	- 20	- 23	- 27	- 30	- 33	- 37	- 40	- 43	- 47	- 50	- 53
10 9%	- 4	- 8	- 12	- 15	- 19	- 23	- 27	- 31	- 34	- 38	- 42	- 46
Yr. 12%	+ 13	+ 8	+ 4	0	- 5	- 9	- 13	- 18	- 22	- 27	- 31	- 35
15%	+ 35	+ 29	+ 24	+ 19	+ 14	+ 9	+ 4	- 1	- 6	- 11	- 16	- 21
	Amortization 25 Years.											
6%	- 7	- 9	- 10	- 12	- 13	- 14	- 16	- 17	- 19	- 20	- 21	- 23
5 9%	- 3	- 4	- 6	- 7	- 9	- 10	- 12	- 13	- 15	- 16	- 18	- 19
Yr. 12%	+ 2	+ 1	- 1	- 2	- 4	- 6	- 7	- 9	- 10	- 12	- 14	- 15
15%	+ 8	+ 6	+ 5	+ 3	+ 1	- 1	- 2	- 4	- 5	- 7	- 9	- 11
6%	- 17	- 20	- 24	- 27	- 30	- 34	- 37	- 40	- 43	- 47	- 50	- 53
10 9%	- 5	- 9	- 13	- 17	- 21	- 24	- 28	- 32	- 36	- 40	- 43	- 47
Yr. 12%	+ 10	+ 6	+ 1	- 3	- 7	- 12	- 16	- 21	- 25	- 29	- 34	- 38
15%	+ 30	+ 25	+ 20	+ 14	+ 9	+ 4	- 1	- 6	- 11	- 16	- 21	- 26
	Amortization 30 Years.											
6%	- 7	- 9	- 10	- 12	- 13	- 14	- 16	- 17	- 19	- 20	- 21	- 23
5 9%	- 3	- 4	- 6	- 7	- 9	- 10	- 12	- 13	- 15	- 16	- 18	- 19
Yr. 12%	+ 2	+ 1	- 1	- 3	- 4	- 6	- 8	- 9	- 11	- 12	- 14	- 15
15%	+ 8	+ 6	+ 4	+ 2	+ 1	- 1	- 3	- 4	- 6	- 8	- 9	- 11
6%	- 17	- 20	- 24	- 27	- 30	- 34	- 37	- 40	- 43	- 47	- 50	- 53
10 9%	- 6	- 10	- 14	- 18	- 21	- 25	- 29	- 33	- 37	- 40	- 44	- 48
Yr. 12%	+ 8	+ 4	- 1	- 5	- 10	- 14	- 18	- 23	- 27	- 31	- 36	- 40
15%	+ 27	+ 22	+ 17	+ 11	+ 6	+ 1	- 4	- 9	- 14	- 19	- 24	- 29

75% Mortgage

ANALYSIS OF SELECTED CAPITALIZATION RATES

Depreciation or Appreciation in 5 years and 10 years for yields of 6%, 9%, 12% and 15% on 25% equity.

MORTGAGE INTEREST RATE 5½%

Projection & Yield	CAPITALIZATION RATES											
	.0675	.0700	.0725	.0750	.0775	.0800	.0825	.0850	.0875	.0900	.0925	.0950
	Amortization 15 Years.											
6%	− 7	− 8	− 9	− 11	− 12	− 14	− 15	− 17	− 18	− 19	− 21	− 22
5 9%	− 1	− 3	− 4	− 6	− 7	− 9	− 10	− 12	− 13	− 15	− 16	− 18
Yr. 12%	+ 4	+ 3	+ 1	0	− 2	− 4	− 5	− 7	− 8	− 10	− 11	− 13
15%	+ 11	+ 9	+ 7	+ 6	+ 4	+ 2	+ 1	− 1	− 3	− 4	− 6	− 8
6%	− 15	− 18	− 22	− 25	− 28	− 32	− 35	− 38	− 42	− 45	− 48	− 51
10 9%	0	− 3	− 7	− 11	− 15	− 19	− 22	− 26	− 30	− 34	− 38	− 41
Yr. 12%	+ 21	+ 16	+ 12	+ 7	+ 3	− 1	− 6	− 10	− 15	− 19	− 23	− 28
15%	+ 46	+ 41	+ 35	+ 30	+ 25	+ 20	+ 15	+ 10	+ 5	0	− 5	− 10
	Amortization 20 Years.											
6%	− 7	− 8	− 9	− 11	− 12	− 13	− 15	− 16	− 18	− 19	− 21	− 22
5 9%	− 2	− 3	− 5	− 6	− 8	− 9	− 11	− 12	− 14	− 15	− 17	− 18
Yr. 12%	+ 4	+ 2	+ 1	− 1	− 3	− 4	− 6	− 7	− 9	− 11	− 12	− 14
15%	+ 10	+ 8	+ 6	+ 5	+ 3	+ 1	0	− 2	− 4	− 5	− 7	− 9
6%	− 15	− 18	− 22	− 25	− 28	− 31	− 35	− 38	− 41	− 45	− 48	− 51
10 9%	− 2	− 5	− 9	− 13	− 17	− 21	− 24	− 28	− 32	− 36	− 40	− 43
Yr. 12%	+ 15	+ 11	+ 7	+ 2	− 2	− 6	− 11	− 15	− 20	− 24	− 28	− 33
15%	+ 37	+ 32	+ 27	+ 22	+ 17	+ 12	+ 7	+ 2	− 3	− 8	− 13	− 19
	Amortization 25 Years.											
6%	− 6	− 8	− 9	− 11	− 12	− 13	− 15	− 16	− 18	− 19	− 20	− 22
5 9%	− 2	− 3	− 5	− 6	− 8	− 9	− 11	− 12	− 14	− 15	− 17	− 18
Yr. 12%	+ 3	+ 2	0	− 1	− 3	− 5	− 6	− 8	− 9	− 11	− 13	− 14
15%	+ 9	+ 7	+ 6	+ 4	+ 2	+ 1	− 1	− 3	− 4	− 6	− 8	− 9
6%	− 15	− 18	− 21	− 25	− 28	− 31	− 35	− 38	− 41	− 44	− 48	− 51
10 9%	− 3	− 7	− 10	− 14	− 18	− 22	− 26	− 29	− 33	− 37	− 41	− 45
Yr. 12%	+ 13	+ 8	+ 4	− 1	− 5	− 9	− 14	− 18	− 22	− 27	− 31	− 36
15%	+ 33	+ 28	+ 23	+ 18	+ 13	+ 8	+ 2	− 3	− 8	− 13	− 18	− 23
	Amortization 30 Years.											
6%	− 6	− 8	− 9	− 11	− 12	− 13	− 15	− 16	− 18	− 19	− 20	− 22
5 9%	− 2	− 3	− 5	− 6	− 8	− 9	− 11	− 12	− 14	− 15	− 17	− 18
Yr. 12%	+ 3	+ 2	0	− 2	− 3	− 5	− 6	− 8	− 10	− 11	− 13	− 14
15%	+ 9	+ 7	+ 5	+ 4	+ 2	0	− 1	− 3	− 5	− 6	− 8	− 10
6%	− 15	− 18	− 21	− 25	− 28	− 31	− 35	− 38	− 41	− 44	− 48	− 51
10 9%	− 4	− 7	− 11	− 15	− 19	− 23	− 26	− 30	− 34	− 38	− 42	− 45
Yr. 12%	+ 11	+ 7	+ 2	− 2	− 7	− 11	− 15	− 20	− 24	− 29	− 33	− 37
15%	+ 30	+ 25	+ 20	+ 15	+ 10	+ 5	− 1	− 6	− 11	− 16	− 21	− 26

75% Mortgage

ANALYSIS OF SELECTED CAPITALIZATION RATES

Depreciation or Appreciation in 5 years and 10 years for yields of 6%, 9%, 12% and 15% on 25% equity.

MORTGAGE INTEREST RATE 5¾%

Projection & Yield	CAPITALIZATION RATES											
	.0675	.0700	.0725	.0750	.0775	.0800	.0825	.0850	.0875	.0900	.0925	.0950
	Amortization 15 Years.											
6%	– 6	– 7	– 9	– 10	– 11	– 13	– 14	– 16	– 17	– 18	– 20	– 21
5 9%	– 1	– 2	– 3	– 5	– 6	– 8	– 9	– 11	– 12	– 14	– 15	– 17
Yr. 12%	+ 5	+ 4	+ 2	+ 1	– 1	– 3	– 4	– 6	– 7	– 9	– 10	– 12
15%	+ 12	+ 10	+ 9	+ 7	+ 5	+ 4	+ 2	0	– 2	– 3	– 5	– 7
6%	– 13	– 16	– 20	– 23	– 26	– 30	– 33	– 36	– 40	– 43	– 46	– 49
10 9%	+ 3	– 1	– 5	– 9	– 12	– 16	– 20	– 24	– 28	– 31	– 35	– 39
Yr. 12%	+ 23	+ 18	+ 14	+ 10	+ 5	+ 1	– 4	– 8	– 12	– 17	– 21	– 25
15%	+ 48	+ 43	+ 38	+ 33	+ 28	+ 23	+ 18	+ 13	+ 8	+ 3	– 2	– 8
	Amortization 20 Years.											
6%	– 5	– 7	– 8	– 10	– 11	– 12	– 14	– 15	– 17	– 18	– 20	– 21
5 9%	– 1	– 2	– 4	– 5	– 7	– 8	– 10	– 11	– 13	– 14	– 16	– 17
Yr. 12%	+ 5	+ 3	+ 2	0	– 2	– 3	– 5	– 6	– 8	– 9	– 11	– 13
15%	+ 11	+ 9	+ 7	+ 6	+ 4	+ 2	+ 1	– 1	– 3	– 4	– 6	– 8
6%	– 13	– 16	– 19	– 23	– 26	– 29	– 33	– 36	– 39	– 42	– 46	– 49
10 9%	+ 1	– 3	– 7	– 11	– 14	– 18	– 22	– 26	– 30	– 33	– 37	– 41
Yr. 12%	+ 18	+ 14	+ 9	+ 5	+ 1	– 4	– 8	– 12	– 17	– 21	– 26	– 30
15%	+ 41	+ 35	+ 30	+ 25	+ 20	+ 15	+ 10	+ 5	0	– 5	– 10	– 15
	Amortization 25 Years.											
6%	– 5	– 7	– 8	– 10	– 11	– 12	– 14	– 15	– 17	– 18	– 19	– 21
5 9%	– 1	– 2	– 4	– 5	– 7	– 8	– 10	– 11	– 13	– 14	– 16	– 17
Yr. 12%	+ 4	+ 3	+ 1	0	– 2	– 3	– 5	– 7	– 8	– 10	– 11	– 13
15%	+ 10	+ 9	+ 7	+ 5	+ 4	+ 2	0	– 2	– 3	– 5	– 7	– 8
6%	– 13	– 16	– 19	– 22	– 26	– 29	– 32	– 36	– 39	– 42	– 46	– 49
10 9%	– 1	– 4	– 8	– 12	– 16	– 19	– 23	– 27	– 31	– 35	– 38	– 42
Yr. 12%	+ 16	+ 11	+ 7	+ 2	– 2	– 6	– 11	– 15	– 20	– 24	– 28	– 33
15%	+ 36	+ 31	+ 26	+ 21	+ 16	+ 11	+ 6	0	– 5	– 10	– 15	– 20
	Amortization 30 Years.											
6%	– 5	– 7	– 8	– 10	– 11	– 12	– 14	– 15	– 17	– 18	– 19	– 21
5 9%	– 1	– 2	– 4	– 5	– 7	– 8	– 10	– 11	– 13	– 14	– 16	– 17
Yr. 12%	+ 4	+ 3	+ 1	– 1	– 2	– 4	– 5	– 7	– 8	– 10	– 12	– 13
15%	+ 10	+ 8	+ 7	+ 5	+ 3	+ 1	0	– 2	– 4	– 5	– 7	– 9
6%	– 13	– 16	– 19	– 22	– 26	– 29	– 32	– 36	– 39	– 42	– 46	– 49
10 9%	– 1	– 5	– 9	– 13	– 16	– 20	– 24	– 28	– 32	– 35	– 39	– 43
Yr. 12%	+ 14	+ 9	+ 5	+ 1	– 4	– 8	– 13	– 17	– 21	– 26	– 30	– 34
15%	+ 33	+ 28	+ 23	+ 18	+ 13	+ 8	+ 3	– 2	– 7	– 12	– 17	– 22

75% Mortgage

ANALYSIS OF SELECTED CAPITALIZATION RATES

Depreciation or Appreciation in 5 years and 10 years for yields of 6%, 9%, 12% and 15% on 25% equity.

MORTGAGE INTEREST RATE 6%

Projection & Yield	CAPITALIZATION RATES											
	.0675	.0700	.0725	.0750	.0775	.0800	.0825	.0850	.0875	.0900	.0925	.0950
	Amortization 15 Years.											
6%	– 5	– 6	– 8	– 9	– 10	– 12	– 13	– 15	– 16	– 17	– 19	– 20
5 9%	+ 1	– 1	– 2	– 4	– 5	– 7	– 8	– 10	– 11	– 13	– 14	– 16
Yr. 12%	+ 7	+ 5	+ 3	+ 2	0	– 1	– 3	– 5	– 6	– 8	– 9	– 11
15%	+ 13	+ 11	+ 10	+ 8	+ 6	+ 5	+ 3	+ 1	0	– 2	– 4	– 6
6%	– 11	– 15	– 18	– 21	– 25	– 28	– 31	– 34	– 38	– 41	– 44	– 48
10 9%	+ 5	+ 1	– 3	– 7	– 10	– 14	– 18	– 22	– 26	– 29	– 33	– 37
Yr. 12%	+ 25	+ 21	+ 17	+ 12	+ 8	+ 3	– 1	– 6	– 10	– 14	– 19	– 23
15%	+ 51	+ 46	+ 41	+ 36	+ 31	+ 26	+ 21	+ 16	+ 11	+ 5	0	– 5
	Amortization 20 Years.											
6%	– 5	– 6	– 7	– 9	– 10	– 12	– 13	– 14	– 16	– 17	– 19	– 20
5 9%	+ 1	– 1	– 3	– 4	– 6	– 7	– 9	– 10	– 12	– 13	– 15	– 16
Yr. 12%	+ 6	+ 4	+ 3	+ 1	– 1	– 2	– 4	– 5	– 7	– 8	– 10	– 12
15%	+ 12	+ 10	+ 9	+ 7	+ 5	+ 4	+ 2	0	– 2	– 3	– 5	– 7
6%	– 11	– 14	– 17	– 21	– 24	– 27	– 30	– 34	– 37	– 40	– 44	– 47
10 9%	+ 3	– 1	– 4	– 8	– 12	– 16	– 19	– 23	– 27	– 31	– 35	– 38
Yr. 12%	+ 21	+ 16	+ 12	+ 8	+ 3	– 1	– 5	– 10	– 14	– 19	– 23	– 27
15%	+ 44	+ 39	+ 34	+ 28	+ 23	+ 18	+ 13	+ 8	+ 3	– 2	– 7	– 12
	Amortization 25 Years.											
6%	– 4	– 6	– 7	– 9	– 10	– 11	– 13	– 14	– 16	– 17	– 18	– 20
5 9%	+ 1	– 1	– 3	– 4	– 6	– 7	– 9	– 10	– 12	– 13	– 15	– 16
Yr. 12%	+ 6	+ 4	+ 2	+ 1	– 1	– 2	– 4	– 6	– 7	– 9	– 10	– 12
15%	+ 11	+ 10	+ 8	+ 6	+ 5	+ 3	+ 1	– 1	– 2	– 4	– 5	– 7
6%	– 10	– 14	– 17	– 20	– 24	– 27	– 30	– 33	– 37	– 40	– 43	– 47
10 9%	+ 2	– 2	– 5	– 9	– 13	– 17	– 21	– 24	– 28	– 32	– 36	– 40
Yr. 12%	+ 18	+ 14	+ 10	+ 5	+ 1	– 4	– 8	– 12	– 17	– 21	– 25	– 30
15%	+ 39	+ 34	+ 29	+ 24	+ 19	+ 14	+ 9	+ 4	– 1	– 7	– 12	– 17
	Amortization 30 Years.											
6%	– 4	– 6	– 7	– 9	– 10	– 11	– 13	– 14	– 16	– 17	– 18	– 20
5 9%	0	– 1	– 3	– 4	– 6	– 7	– 9	– 10	– 12	– 13	– 15	– 16
Yr. 12%	+ 5	+ 4	+ 2	+ 1	– 1	– 3	– 4	– 6	– 7	– 9	– 11	– 12
15%	+ 11	+ 9	+ 8	+ 6	+ 4	+ 3	+ 1	– 1	– 2	– 4	– 6	– 7
6%	– 10	– 13	– 17	– 20	– 23	– 27	– 30	– 33	– 37	– 40	– 43	– 46
10 9%	+ 1	– 2	– 6	– 10	– 14	– 18	– 21	– 25	– 29	– 33	– 37	– 40
Yr. 12%	+ 17	+ 13	+ 8	+ 4	– 1	– 5	– 9	– 14	– 18	– 23	– 27	– 31
15%	+ 37	+ 32	+ 26	+ 21	+ 16	+ 11	+ 6	+ 1	– 4	– 9	– 14	– 19

75% Mortgage

ANALYSIS OF SELECTED CAPITALIZATION RATES

Depreciation or Appreciation in 5 years and 10 years for yields of 6%, 9%, 12% and 15% on 25% equity.

MORTGAGE INTEREST RATE 6¼%

Projection & Yield	CAPITALIZATION RATES											
	.0700	.0725	.0750	.0775	.0800	.0825	.0850	.0875	.0900	.0925	.0950	.0975
	Amortization 15 Years.											
6%	− 5	− 7	− 8	− 9	− 11	− 12	− 14	− 15	− 16	− 18	− 19	− 21
5 9%	0	− 1	− 3	− 4	− 6	− 7	− 9	− 10	− 12	− 13	− 15	− 16
Yr. 12%	+ 6	+ 4	+ 3	+ 1	0	− 2	− 4	− 5	− 7	− 8	− 10	− 12
15%	+ 13	+ 11	+ 9	+ 8	+ 6	+ 4	+ 2	+ 1	− 1	− 3	− 4	− 6
6%	− 13	− 16	− 19	− 23	− 26	− 29	− 32	− 36	− 39	− 42	− 46	− 49
10 9%	+ 3	− 1	− 4	− 8	− 12	− 16	− 19	− 23	− 27	− 31	− 35	− 38
Yr. 12%	+ 24	+ 19	+ 15	+ 10	+ 6	+ 2	− 3	− 7	− 11	− 16	− 20	− 25
15%	+ 49	+ 44	+ 39	+ 34	+ 29	+ 24	+ 18	+ 13	+ 8	+ 3	− 2	− 7
	Amortization 20 Years.											
6%	− 5	− 6	− 8	− 9	− 10	− 12	− 13	− 15	− 16	− 18	− 19	− 20
5 9%	0	− 2	− 3	− 5	− 6	− 8	− 9	− 11	− 12	− 14	− 15	− 17
Yr. 12%	+ 5	+ 4	+ 2	+ 1	− 1	− 3	− 4	− 6	− 7	− 9	− 10	− 12
15%	+ 12	+ 10	+ 8	+ 6	+ 5	+ 3	+ 1	0	− 2	− 4	− 5	− 7
6%	− 12	− 15	− 18	− 22	− 25	− 28	− 32	− 35	− 38	− 42	− 45	− 48
10 9%	+ 2	− 2	− 6	− 10	− 14	− 17	− 21	− 25	− 29	− 32	− 36	− 40
Yr. 12%	+ 19	+ 15	+ 11	+ 6	+ 2	− 3	− 7	− 11	− 16	− 20	− 25	− 29
15%	+ 41	+ 36	+ 31	+ 26	+ 21	+ 16	+ 11	+ 6	+ 1	− 4	− 9	− 14
	Amortization 25 Years.											
6%	− 5	− 6	− 8	− 9	− 10	− 12	− 13	− 15	− 16	− 17	− 19	− 20
5 9%	0	− 2	− 3	− 5	− 6	− 8	− 9	− 11	− 12	− 14	− 15	− 17
Yr. 12%	+ 5	+ 4	+ 2	+ 1	− 1	− 3	− 4	− 6	− 8	− 9	− 11	− 12
15%	+ 11	+ 9	+ 8	+ 6	+ 4	+ 3	+ 1	− 1	− 3	− 4	− 6	− 8
6%	− 11	− 15	− 18	− 21	− 25	− 28	− 31	− 34	− 38	− 41	− 44	− 48
10 9%	+ 1	− 3	− 7	− 11	− 14	− 18	− 22	− 26	− 30	− 33	− 37	− 41
Yr. 12%	+ 17	+ 13	+ 8	+ 4	− 1	− 5	− 9	− 14	− 18	− 23	− 27	− 31
15%	+ 37	+ 32	+ 27	+ 22	+ 17	+ 12	+ 7	+ 2	− 3	− 8	− 13	− 18
	Amortization 30 Years.											
6%	− 5	− 6	− 7	− 9	− 10	− 12	− 13	− 15	− 16	− 17	− 19	− 20
5 9%	0	− 2	− 3	− 5	− 6	− 8	− 9	− 11	− 12	− 14	− 15	− 17
Yr. 12%	+ 5	+ 3	+ 2	0	− 1	− 3	− 5	− 6	− 8	− 9	− 11	− 13
15%	+ 11	+ 9	+ 7	+ 5	+ 4	+ 2	+ 1	− 1	− 3	− 5	− 6	− 8
6%	− 11	− 14	− 18	− 21	− 24	− 28	− 31	− 34	− 37	− 41	− 44	− 47
10 9%	+ 1	− 3	− 7	− 11	− 15	− 19	− 22	− 26	− 30	− 34	− 38	− 41
Yr. 12%	+ 15	+ 11	+ 7	+ 2	− 2	− 7	− 11	− 15	− 20	− 24	− 29	− 33
15%	+ 35	+ 30	+ 25	+ 20	+ 15	+ 10	+ 5	− 1	− 6	− 11	− 16	− 21

75% Mortgage

ANALYSIS OF SELECTED CAPITALIZATION RATES

Depreciation or Appreciation in 5 years and 10 years for yields of 6%, 9%, 12% and 15% on 25% equity.

MORTGAGE INTEREST RATE 6½%

Projection & Yield	CAPITALIZATION RATES											
	.0700	.0725	.0750	.0775	.0800	.0825	.0850	.0875	.0900	.0925	.0950	.0975
	Amortization 15 Years.											
6%	– 4	– 6	– 7	– 9	– 10	– 11	– 13	– 14	– 16	– 17	– 18	– 20
5 9%	+ 1	0	– 2	– 3	– 5	– 6	– 8	– 9	– 11	– 12	– 14	– 15
Yr. 12%	+ 7	+ 5	+ 4	+ 2	+ 1	– 1	– 2	– 4	– 6	– 7	– 9	– 10
15%	+ 14	+ 12	+ 10	+ 8	+ 7	+ 5	+ 3	+ 2	0	– 2	– 3	– 5
6%	– 11	– 14	– 17	– 21	– 24	– 27	– 31	– 34	– 37	– 40	– 44	– 47
10 9%	+ 5	+ 2	– 2	– 6	– 10	– 14	– 17	– 21	– 25	– 29	– 33	– 36
Yr. 12%	+ 26	+ 22	+ 17	+ 13	+ 8	+ 4	0	– 5	– 9	– 14	– 18	– 22
15%	+ 52	+ 47	+ 42	+ 37	+ 31	+ 26	+ 21	+ 16	+ 11	+ 6	+ 1	– 4
	Amortization 20 Years.											
6%	– 4	– 5	– 7	– 8	– 10	– 11	– 12	– 14	– 15	– 17	– 18	– 19
5 9%	+ 1	– 1	– 2	– 4	– 5	– 7	– 8	– 10	– 11	– 12	– 14	– 15
Yr. 12%	+ 6	+ 5	+ 3	+ 2	0	– 2	– 3	– 5	– 6	– 8	– 9	– 11
15%	+ 13	+ 11	+ 9	+ 7	+ 6	+ 4	+ 2	+ 1	– 1	– 3	– 4	– 6
6%	– 10	– 13	– 16	– 20	– 23	– 26	– 29	– 33	– 36	– 39	– 43	– 46
10 9%	+ 4	0	– 3	– 7	– 11	– 15	– 19	– 22	– 26	– 30	– 34	– 38
Yr. 12%	+ 22	+ 18	+ 13	+ 9	+ 4	0	– 4	– 9	– 13	– 18	– 22	– 26
15%	+ 45	+ 40	+ 34	+ 29	+ 24	+ 19	+ 14	+ 9	+ 4	– 1	– 6	– 11
	Amortization 25 Years.											
6%	– 4	– 5	– 7	– 8	– 9	– 11	– 12	– 14	– 15	– 16	– 18	– 19
5 9%	+ 1	– 1	– 2	– 4	– 5	– 7	– 8	– 10	– 11	– 13	– 14	– 16
Yr. 12%	+ 6	+ 5	+ 3	+ 1	0	– 2	– 3	– 5	– 6	– 8	– 10	– 11
15%	+ 12	+ 10	+ 9	+ 7	+ 5	+ 4	+ 2	+ 1	– 1	– 3	– 5	– 6
6%	– 9	– 12	– 16	– 19	– 22	– 26	– 29	– 32	– 35	– 39	– 42	– 45
10 9%	+ 4	0	– 4	– 8	– 12	– 15	– 19	– 23	– 27	– 31	– 34	– 38
Yr. 12%	+ 20	+ 16	+ 11	+ 7	+ 2	– 2	– 6	– 11	– 15	– 20	– 24	– 28
15%	+ 41	+ 36	+ 31	+ 25	+ 20	+ 15	+ 10	+ 5	0	– 5	– 10	– 15
	Amortization 30 Years.											
6%	– 4	– 5	– 6	– 8	– 9	– 11	– 12	– 13	– 15	– 16	– 18	– 19
5 9%	+ 1	– 1	– 2	– 4	– 5	– 7	– 8	– 10	– 11	– 13	– 14	– 16
Yr. 12%	+ 6	+ 4	+ 3	+ 1	0	– 2	– 3	– 5	– 7	– 8	– 10	– 11
15%	+ 12	+ 10	+ 8	+ 7	+ 5	+ 3	+ 2	0	– 2	– 3	– 5	– 7
6%	– 9	– 12	– 15	– 19	– 22	– 25	– 28	– 32	– 35	– 38	– 42	– 45
10 9%	+ 3	– 1	– 4	– 8	– 12	– 16	– 20	– 23	– 27	– 31	– 35	– 39
Yr. 12%	+ 18	+ 14	+ 10	+ 5	+ 1	– 4	– 8	– 12	– 17	– 21	– 26	– 30
15%	+ 38	+ 33	+ 28	+ 23	+ 18	+ 13	+ 8	+ 3	– 2	– 7	– 13	– 18

ANALYSIS OF SELECTED CAPITALIZATION RATES

Depreciation or Appreciation in 5 years and 10 years for yields of 6%, 9%, 12% and 15% on 25% equity.

MORTGAGE INTEREST RATE 6¾%

Projection & Yield	CAPITALIZATION RATES											
	.0750	.0775	.0800	.0825	.0850	.0875	.0900	.0925	.0950	.0975	.1000	.1025
	Amortization 15 Years.											
5 Yr. 6%	- 6	- 8	- 9	- 10	- 12	- 13	- 15	- 16	- 17	- 19	- 20	- 22
9%	- 1	- 2	- 4	- 5	- 7	- 8	- 9	- 11	- 12	- 14	- 15	- 16
12%	+ 5	+ 3	+ 2	0	- 2	- 3	- 5	- 6	- 8	- 10	- 11	- 13
15%	+ 11	+ 10	+ 8	+ 6	+ 5	+ 3	+ 1	- 1	- 2	- 4	- 6	- 7
10 Yr. 6%	- 15	- 19	- 22	- 25	- 28	- 32	- 35	- 38	- 42	- 45	- 48	- 52
9%	0	- 4	- 7	- 11	- 15	- 19	- 23	- 27	- 30	- 34	- 38	- 42
12%	+ 20	+ 15	+ 11	+ 7	+ 2	- 2	- 7	- 11	- 15	- 20	- 24	- 29
15%	+ 44	+ 39	+ 34	+ 29	+ 24	+ 19	+ 14	+ 9	+ 4	- 1	- 6	- 11
	Amortization 20 Years.											
5 Yr. 6%	- 6	- 7	- 8	- 10	- 11	- 13	- 14	- 16	- 17	- 18	- 20	- 21
9%	- 1	- 2	- 4	- 5	- 7	- 8	- 10	- 11	- 13	- 14	- 16	- 17
12%	+ 4	+ 3	+ 1	0	- 2	- 4	- 5	- 7	- 8	- 10	- 11	- 13
15%	+ 10	+ 9	+ 7	+ 5	+ 4	+ 2	0	- 1	- 3	- 5	- 6	- 8
10 Yr. 6%	- 14	- 17	- 21	- 24	- 27	- 31	- 34	- 37	- 40	- 44	- 47	- 50
9%	- 1	- 5	- 9	- 12	- 16	- 20	- 24	- 28	- 31	- 35	- 39	- 43
12%	+ 16	+ 11	+ 7	+ 3	- 2	- 6	- 10	- 15	- 19	- 24	- 28	- 32
15%	+ 38	+ 33	+ 28	+ 23	+ 17	+ 12	+ 7	+ 2	- 3	- 8	- 13	- 18
	Amortization 25 Years.											
5 Yr. 6%	- 5	- 7	- 8	- 10	- 11	- 13	- 14	- 15	- 17	- 18	- 20	- 21
9%	- 1	- 2	- 4	- 5	- 7	- 8	- 10	- 11	- 13	- 14	- 16	- 17
12%	+ 4	+ 3	+ 1	- 1	- 2	- 4	- 5	- 7	- 8	- 10	- 12	- 13
15%	+ 10	+ 8	+ 7	+ 5	+ 3	+ 2	0	- 2	- 4	- 5	- 7	- 9
10 Yr. 6%	- 13	- 17	- 20	- 23	- 27	- 30	- 33	- 36	- 40	- 43	- 46	- 50
9%	- 2	- 5	- 9	- 13	- 17	- 21	- 24	- 28	- 32	- 36	- 40	- 43
12%	+ 14	+ 9	+ 5	+ 1	- 4	- 8	- 13	- 17	- 21	- 26	- 30	- 34
15%	+ 34	+ 29	+ 24	+ 18	+ 13	+ 8	+ 3	- 2	- 7	- 12	- 17	- 22
	Amortization 30 Years.											
5 Yr. 6%	- 5	- 7	- 8	- 10	- 11	- 12	- 14	- 15	- 17	- 18	- 19	- 21
9%	- 1	- 2	- 4	- 5	- 7	- 8	- 10	- 11	- 13	- 14	- 16	- 17
12%	+ 4	+ 2	+ 1	- 1	- 2	- 4	- 6	- 7	- 9	- 10	- 12	- 13
15%	+ 10	+ 8	+ 6	+ 5	+ 3	+ 1	- 1	- 2	- 4	- 6	- 7	- 9
10 Yr. 6%	- 13	- 16	- 20	- 23	- 26	- 29	- 33	- 36	- 39	- 43	- 46	- 49
9%	- 2	- 6	- 9	- 13	- 17	- 21	- 25	- 28	- 32	- 36	- 40	- 44
12%	+ 13	+ 8	+ 4	- 1	- 5	- 9	- 14	- 18	- 22	- 27	- 31	- 36
15%	+ 32	+ 26	+ 21	+ 16	+ 11	+ 6	+ 1	- 4	- 9	- 14	- 19	- 24

ANALYSIS OF SELECTED CAPITALIZATION RATES

Depreciation or Appreciation in 5 years and 10 years for yields of 6%, 9%, 12% and 15% on 25% equity.

MORTGAGE INTEREST RATE 7%

Projection & Yield	CAPITALIZATION RATES											
	.0750	.0775	.0800	.0825	.0850	.0875	.0900	.0925	.0950	.0975	.1000	.1025
	Amortization 15 Years.											
6%	− 5	− 7	− 8	− 9	− 11	− 12	− 14	− 15	− 16	− 18	− 19	− 21
5 9%	0	− 2	− 3	− 5	− 6	− 8	− 9	− 11	− 12	− 14	− 15	− 16
Yr. 12%	+ 6	+ 4	+ 3	+ 1	− 1	− 2	− 4	− 5	− 7	− 8	− 10	− 12
15%	+ 12	+ 11	+ 9	+ 7	+ 6	+ 4	+ 2	+ 1	− 1	− 3	− 4	− 6
6%	− 13	− 17	− 20	− 23	− 26	− 30	− 33	− 36	− 40	− 43	− 46	− 50
10 9%	+ 2	− 1	− 5	− 9	− 13	− 17	− 21	− 24	− 28	− 32	− 36	− 40
Yr. 12%	+ 22	+ 18	+ 13	+ 9	+ 5	0	− 4	− 8	− 13	− 17	− 22	− 26
15%	+ 47	+ 42	+ 37	+ 32	+ 27	+ 22	+ 17	+ 12	+ 7	+ 2	− 3	− 8
	Amortization 20 Years.											
6%	− 5	− 6	− 8	− 9	− 10	− 12	− 13	− 15	− 16	− 17	− 19	− 20
5 9%	0	− 1	− 3	− 4	− 6	− 7	− 9	− 10	− 12	− 13	− 15	− 16
Yr. 12%	+ 5	+ 4	+ 2	+ 1	− 1	− 2	− 4	− 6	− 7	− 9	− 10	− 12
15%	+ 12	+ 10	+ 8	+ 6	+ 5	+ 3	+ 1	0	− 2	− 4	− 5	− 7
6%	− 12	− 15	− 18	− 22	− 25	− 28	− 32	− 35	− 38	− 42	− 45	− 48
10 9%	+ 1	− 2	− 6	− 10	− 14	− 18	− 21	− 25	− 29	− 33	− 37	− 40
Yr. 12%	+ 19	+ 14	+ 10	+ 5	+ 1	− 3	− 8	− 12	− 16	− 21	− 25	− 30
15%	+ 41	+ 36	+ 31	+ 26	+ 20	+ 15	+ 10	+ 5	0	− 5	− 10	− 15
	Amortization 25 Years.											
6%	− 4	− 6	− 7	− 9	− 10	− 12	− 13	− 14	− 16	− 17	− 19	− 20
5 9%	0	− 1	− 3	− 4	− 6	− 7	− 9	− 10	− 12	− 13	− 15	− 16
Yr. 12%	+ 5	+ 4	+ 2	+ 1	− 1	− 3	− 4	− 6	− 7	− 9	− 11	− 12
15%	+ 11	+ 9	+ 8	+ 6	+ 4	+ 3	+ 1	− 1	− 2	− 4	− 6	− 7
6%	− 11	− 14	− 18	− 21	− 24	− 28	− 31	− 34	− 37	− 41	− 44	− 47
10 9%	+ 1	− 3	− 7	− 10	− 14	− 18	− 22	− 26	− 29	− 33	− 37	− 41
Yr. 12%	+ 17	+ 13	+ 8	+ 4	− 1	− 5	− 9	− 14	− 18	− 23	− 27	− 31
15%	+ 37	+ 32	+ 27	+ 22	+ 17	+ 12	+ 7	+ 2	− 3	− 8	− 14	− 19
	Amortization 30 Years.											
6%	− 4	− 6	− 7	− 9	− 10	− 11	− 13	− 14	− 16	− 17	− 18	− 20
5 9%	0	− 1	− 3	− 4	− 6	− 7	− 9	− 10	− 12	− 13	− 15	− 16
Yr. 12%	+ 5	+ 4	+ 2	+ 1	− 1	− 3	− 4	− 6	− 8	− 9	− 11	− 12
15%	+ 11	+ 9	+ 7	+ 6	+ 4	+ 2	+ 1	− 1	− 3	− 4	− 6	− 8
6%	− 11	− 14	− 17	− 20	− 24	− 27	− 30	− 34	− 37	− 40	− 44	− 47
10 9%	+ 1	− 3	− 7	− 11	− 14	− 18	− 22	− 26	− 30	− 33	− 37	− 41
Yr. 12%	+ 16	+ 11	+ 7	+ 3	− 2	− 6	− 11	− 15	− 19	− 24	− 28	− 33
15%	+ 35	+ 30	+ 25	+ 20	+ 15	+ 10	+ 5	− 1	− 6	− 11	− 16	− 21

75% Mortgage

ANALYSIS OF SELECTED CAPITALIZATION RATES
Depreciation or appreciation in 5 years, 10 years and amortization term
for yields of 6%, 9%, 12% and 15% on 1/3rd equity

MORTGAGE INTEREST RATE 7¼ %

Projection & Yield		CAPITALIZATION RATES											
		.080	.0825	.0850	.0875	.090	.0925	.0950	.0975	.1000	.1025	.1050	.1075
		Amortization 15 years.											
5 Yr.	6%	-7	-8	-10	-11	-13	-14	-15	-17	-18	-20	-21	-23
	9%	-2	-3	-5	-6	-8	-9	-11	-12	-14	-15	-17	-18
	12%	4	2	1	-1	-3	-4	-6	-7	-9	-11	-12	-14
	15%	10	8	7	5	3	2	-0	-2	-3	-5	-7	-8
10 Yr.	6%	-18	-21	-25	-28	-31	-34	-38	-41	-44	-48	-51	-54
	9%	-3	-7	-11	-15	-18	-22	-26	-30	-34	-37	-41	-45
	12%	16	11	7	3	-2	-6	-11	-15	-19	-24	-28	-32
	15%	40	35	30	25	20	15	9	4	-1	-6	-11	-16
		Amortization 20 years.											
5 Yr.	6%	-7	-8	-9	-11	-12	-14	-15	-16	-18	-19	-21	-22
	9%	-2	-3	-5	-6	-8	-9	-11	-12	-14	-15	-17	-18
	12%	3	2	0	-1	-3	-5	-6	-8	-9	-11	-13	-14
	15%	9	8	6	4	3	1	-1	-3	-4	-6	-8	-9
10 Yr.	6%	-16	-20	-23	-26	-30	-33	-36	-39	-43	-46	-49	-53
	9%	-4	-8	-11	-15	-19	-23	-27	-30	-34	-38	-42	-46
	12%	13	8	4	-1	-5	-9	-14	-18	-23	-27	-31	-36
	15%	34	29	23	18	13	8	3	-2	-7	-12	-17	-22
		Amortization 25 years.											
5 Yr.	6%	-6	-8	-9	-11	-12	-13	-15	-16	-18	-19	-20	-22
	9%	-2	-3	-5	-6	-8	-9	-11	-12	-14	-15	-17	-18
	12%	3	2	-0	-2	-3	-5	-6	-8	-10	-11	-13	-14
	15%	9	7	5	4	2	0	-1	-3	-5	-6	-8	-10
10 Yr.	6%	-16	-19	-22	-25	-29	-32	-35	-39	-42	-45	-48	-52
	9%	-4	-8	-12	-16	-19	-23	-27	-31	-35	-38	-42	-46
	12%	11	6	2	-2	-7	-11	-16	-20	-24	-29	-33	-37
	15%	30	25	20	15	10	5	-0	-5	-10	-16	-21	-26
		Amortization 30 years.											
5 Yr.	6%	-6	-8	-9	-10	-12	-13	-15	-16	-18	-19	-20	-22
	9%	-2	-3	-5	-6	-8	-9	-11	-12	-14	-15	-17	-18
	12%	3	1	-0	-2	-3	-5	-7	-8	-10	-11	-13	-14
	15%	9	7	5	3	2	0	-2	-3	-5	-7	-8	-10
10 Yr.	6%	-15	-18	-22	-25	-28	-31	-35	-38	-41	-45	-48	-51
	9%	-4	-8	-12	-16	-20	-23	-27	-31	-35	-39	-42	-46
	12%	10	5	1	-3	-8	-12	-17	-21	-25	-30	-34	-39
	15%	28	23	18	13	8	3	-2	-7	-13	-18	-23	-28

75% Mortgage

ANALYSIS OF SELECTED CAPITALIZATION RATES

Depreciation or appreciation in 5 years, 10 years and amortization term for yields of 6%, 9%, 12% and 15% on 1/3rd equity

MORTGAGE INTEREST RATE 7½ %

Projection & Yield	CAPITALIZATION RATES											
	.080	.0825	.0850	.0875	.090	.0925	.0950	.0975	.1000	.1025	.1050	.1075
	Amortization 15 years.											
5 Yr. 6%	-6	-7	-9	-10	-12	-13	-14	-16	-17	-19	-20	-22
9%	-1	-2	-4	-5	-7	-8	-10	-11	-13	-14	-16	-17
12%	5	3	2	0	-2	-3	-5	-6	-8	-9	-11	-13
15%	11	9	8	6	4	3	1	-1	-2	-4	-6	-7
10 Yr. 6%	-16	-19	-23	-26	-29	-32	-36	-39	-42	-46	-49	-52
9%	-1	-5	-9	-12	-16	-20	-24	-27	-31	-35	-39	-43
12%	18	14	10	5	1	-4	-8	-12	-17	-21	-26	-30
15%	43	38	33	28	22	17	12	7	2	-3	-8	-13
	Amortization 20 years.											
5 Yr. 6%	-6	-7	-8	-10	-11	-13	-14	-15	-17	-18	-20	-21
9%	-1	-2	-4	-5	-7	-8	-10	-11	-13	-14	-16	-17
12%	4	3	1	-0	-2	-3	-5	-7	-8	-10	-11	-13
15%	10	9	7	5	4	2	0	-1	-3	-5	-6	-8
10 Yr. 6%	-14	-18	-21	-24	-27	-31	-34	-37	-41	-44	-47	-50
9%	-1	-5	-9	-13	-16	-20	-24	-28	-32	-35	-39	-43
12%	15	11	7	2	-2	-7	-11	-15	-20	-24	-28	-33
15%	37	32	27	22	17	11	6	1	-4	-9	-14	-19
	Amortization 25 years.											
5 Yr. 6%	-5	-7	-8	-10	-11	-12	-14	-15	-17	-18	-19	-21
9%	-1	-2	-4	-5	-7	-8	-10	-11	-13	-14	-16	-17
12%	4	3	1	-0	-2	-4	-5	-7	-8	-10	-12	-13
15%	10	8	7	5	3	2	-0	-2	-3	-5	-7	-9
10 Yr. 6%	-13	-17	-20	-23	-26	-30	-33	-36	-40	-43	-46	-49
9%	-2	-5	-9	-13	-17	-21	-24	-28	-32	-36	-40	-43
12%	14	9	5	1	-4	-8	-13	-17	-21	-26	-30	-34
15%	34	28	23	18	13	8	3	-2	-7	-12	-17	-22
	Amortization 30 years.											
5 Yr. 6%	-5	-7	-8	-9	-11	-12	-14	-15	-16	-18	-19	-21
9%	-1	-2	-4	-5	-7	-8	-10	-11	-13	-14	-16	-17
12%	4	3	1	-1	-2	-4	-5	-7	-9	-10	-12	-13
15%	10	8	6	5	3	1	-0	-2	-4	-5	-7	-9
10 Yr. 6%	-13	-16	-19	-23	-26	-29	-32	-36	-39	-42	-46	-49
9%	-2	-5	-9	-13	-17	-21	-24	-28	-32	-36	-40	-43
12%	13	8	4	-0	-5	-9	-14	-18	-22	-27	-31	-35
15%	32	26	21	16	11	6	1	-4	-9	-14	-19	-24

75% Mortgage

ANALYSIS OF SELECTED CAPITALIZATION RATES

Depreciation or appreciation in 5 years, 10 years and amortization term

for yields of 6%, 9%, 12% and 15% on 1/3rd equity

MORTGAGE INTEREST RATE 7¾%

CAPITALIZATION RATES

Projection &	Yield	.080	.0825	.0850	.0875	.090	.0925	.0950	.0975	.1000	.1025	.1050	.1075
		Amortization 15 years.											
5 Yr.	6%	-5	-6	-8	-9	-11	-12	-14	-15	-16	-18	-19	-21
	9%	0	-1	-3	-4	-6	-7	-9	-10	-12	-13	-15	-16
	12%	6	4	3	1	-0	-2	-4	-5	-7	-8	-10	-12
	15%	12	11	9	7	6	4	2	0	-1	-3	-5	-6
10 Yr.	6%	-14	-17	-21	-24	-27	-30	-34	-37	-40	-44	-47	-50
	9%	1	-2	-6	-10	-14	-18	-21	-25	-29	-33	-37	-40
	12%	21	17	12	8	3	-1	-5	-10	-14	-19	-23	-27
	15%	46	41	36	31	25	20	15	10	5	0	-5	-10
		Amortization 20 years.											
5 Yr.	6%	-5	-6	-7	-9	-10	-12	-13	-14	-16	-17	-19	-20
	9%	0	-1	-3	-4	-6	-7	-9	-10	-12	-13	-15	-16
	12%	6	4	2	1	-1	-2	-4	-6	-7	-9	-10	-12
	15%	12	10	8	7	5	3	1	-0	-2	-4	-5	-7
10 Yr.	6%	-12	-15	-19	-22	-25	-28	-32	-35	-38	-42	-45	-48
	9%	1	-3	-6	-10	-14	-18	-22	-25	-29	-33	-37	-41
	12%	18	14	9	5	1	-4	-8	-12	-17	-21	-26	-30
	15%	40	35	30	25	20	15	10	4	-1	-6	-11	-16
		Amortization 25 years.											
5 Yr.	6%	-4	-6	-7	-9	-10	-11	-13	-14	-16	-17	-18	-20
	9%	0	-1	-3	-4	-6	-7	-9	-10	-12	-13	-15	-16
	12%	5	4	2	1	-1	-3	-4	-6	-7	-9	-10	-12
	15%	11	9	8	6	4	3	1	-1	-2	-4	-6	-7
10 Yr.	6%	-11	-14	-17	-21	-24	-27	-31	-34	-37	-41	-44	-47
	9%	1	-3	-6	-10	-14	-18	-22	-25	-29	-33	-37	-41
	12%	17	12	8	4	-1	-5	-10	-14	-18	-23	-27	-32
	15%	37	32	27	22	17	12	6	1	-4	-9	-14	-19
		Amortization 30 years.											
5 Yr.	6%	-4	-6	-7	-8	-10	-11	-13	-14	-15	-17	-18	-20
	9%	0	-1	-3	-4	-6	-7	-9	-10	-12	-13	-15	-16
	12%	5	4	2	1	-1	-3	-4	-6	-7	-9	-11	-12
	15%	11	9	8	6	4	3	1	-1	-3	-4	-6	-8
10 Yr.	6%	-10	-14	-17	-20	-23	-27	-30	-33	-37	-40	-43	-46
	9%	1	-3	-7	-10	-14	-18	-22	-26	-29	-33	-37	-41
	12%	16	11	7	3	-2	-6	-10	-15	-19	-24	-28	-32
	15%	35	30	25	20	15	10	5	-0	-6	-11	-16	-21

75% Mortgage

ANALYSIS OF SELECTED CAPITALIZATION RATES

Depreciation or appreciation in 5 years, 10 years and amortization term for yields of 6%, 9%, 12% and 15% on 1/3rd equity

MORTGAGE INTEREST RATE 8%

CAPITALIZATION RATES

Projection & Yield		.0850	.0875	.090	.0925	.0950	.0975	.1000	.1025	.1050	.1075	.1100	.1125
		Amortization 15 years.											
	6%	-7	-8	-10	-11	-13	-14	-15	-17	-18	-20	-21	-22
5	9%	-2	-3	-5	-6	-8	-9	-11	-12	-14	-15	-17	-18
Yr.	12%	4	2	1	-1	-3	-4	-6	-7	-9	-11	-12	-14
	15%	10	8	7	5	3	2	-0	-2	-3	-5	-7	-9
	6%	-19	-22	-25	-28	-32	-35	-38	-42	-45	-48	-52	-55
10	9%	-4	-8	-12	-15	-19	-23	-27	-31	-34	-38	-42	-46
Yr.	12%	15	10	6	2	-3	-7	-12	-16	-20	-25	-29	-33
	15%	39	33	28	23	18	13	8	3	-2	-7	-12	-17
		Amortization 20 years.											
	6%	-6	-8	-9	-11	-12	-13	-15	-16	-18	-19	-20	-22
5	9%	-2	-3	-5	-6	-8	-9	-11	-12	-14	-15	-17	-18
Yr.	12%	4	2	0	-1	-3	-4	-6	-8	-9	-11	-12	-14
	15%	9	8	6	4	3	1	-1	-2	-4	-6	-7	-9
	6%	-16	-20	-23	-26	-30	-33	-36	-39	-43	-46	-49	-53
10	9%	-4	-8	-11	-15	-19	-23	-27	-30	-34	-38	-42	-46
Yr.	12%	12	8	4	-1	-5	-10	-14	-18	-23	-27	-32	-36
	15%	33	28	23	18	13	8	3	-2	-7	-13	-18	-23
		Amortization 25 years.											
	6%	-6	-8	-9	-10	-12	-13	-15	-16	-17	-19	-20	-22
5	9%	-2	-3	-5	-6	-8	-9	-11	-12	-14	-15	-17	-18
Yr.	12%	3	2	0	-1	-3	-5	-6	-8	-9	-11	-12	-14
	15%	9	7	6	4	2	1	-1	-3	-4	-6	-8	-10
	6%	-15	-18	-22	-25	-28	-32	-35	-38	-41	-45	-48	-51
10	9%	-4	-8	-11	-15	-19	-23	-27	-30	-34	-38	-42	-46
Yr.	12%	11	7	2	-2	-7	-11	-15	-20	-24	-29	-33	-37
	15%	30	25	20	15	10	5	-0	-5	-10	-16	-21	-26
		Amortization 30 years.											
	6%	-6	-7	-9	-10	-12	-13	-14	-16	-17	-19	-20	-21
5	9%	-2	-3	-5	-6	-8	-9	-11	-12	-14	-15	-17	-18
Yr.	12%	3	2	0	-1	-3	-5	-6	-8	-9	-11	-13	-14
	15%	9	7	5	4	2	0	-1	-3	-5	-6	-8	-10
	6%	-14	-18	-21	-24	-28	-31	-34	-37	-41	-44	-47	-51
10	9%	-4	-8	-11	-15	-19	-23	-27	-30	-34	-38	-42	-46
Yr.	12%	10	6	1	-3	-7	-12	-16	-21	-25	-29	-34	-38
	15%	28	23	18	13	8	3	-2	-7	-12	-17	-22	-27

75% Mortgage

ANALYSIS OF SELECTED CAPITALIZATION RATES

Depreciation or appreciation in 5 years, 10 years and amortization term for yields of 6%, 9%, 12% and 15% on 1/3rd equity

MORTGAGE INTEREST RATE 8¼%

Projection & Yield		CAPITALIZATION RATES											
		.090	.0925	.0950	.0975	.1000	.1025	.1050	.1075	.1100	.1125	.1150	.1175
		Amortization 15 years.											
5 Yr.	6%	-9	-10	-12	-13	-14	-16	-17	-19	-20	-21	-23	-24
	9%	-4	-5	-7	-8	-10	-11	-13	-14	-16	-17	-19	-20
	12%	2	0	-2	-3	-5	-6	-8	-9	-11	-13	-14	-16
	15%	8	6	4	3	1	-1	-2	-4	-6	-7	-9	-11
10 Yr.	6%	-23	-26	-30	-33	-36	-40	-43	-46	-49	-53	-56	-59
	9%	-9	-13	-17	-21	-24	-28	-32	-36	-40	-43	-47	-51
	12%	9	4	-0	-5	-9	-13	-18	-22	-26	-31	-35	-40
	15%	31	26	21	16	11	6	1	-4	-9	-14	-19	-24
		Amortization 20 years.											
5 Yr.	6%	-8	-10	-11	-12	-14	-15	-17	-18	-19	-21	-22	-24
	9%	-4	-5	-7	-8	-10	-11	-13	-14	-16	-17	-19	-20
	12%	1	-0	-2	-3	-5	-6	-8	-10	-11	-13	-14	-16
	15%	7	5	4	2	0	-1	-3	-5	-6	-8	-10	-11
10 Yr.	6%	-21	-24	-27	-31	-34	-37	-40	-44	-47	-50	-54	-57
	9%	-9	-13	-17	-20	-24	-28	-32	-36	-39	-43	-47	-51
	12%	6	2	-2	-7	-11	-16	-20	-24	-29	-33	-37	-42
	15%	26	21	16	11	6	1	-4	-9	-14	-19	-25	-30
		Amortization 25 years.											
5 Yr.	6%	-8	-9	-11	-12	-14	-15	-16	-18	-19	-21	-22	-23
	9%	-4	-5	-7	-8	-10	-11	-13	-14	-15	-17	-18	-20
	12%	1	-0	-2	-3	-5	-7	-8	-10	-11	-13	-15	-16
	15%	7	5	3	2	0	-2	-3	-5	-7	-8	-10	-12
10 Yr.	6%	-19	-23	-26	-29	-33	-36	-39	-42	-46	-49	-52	-56
	9%	-9	-13	-16	-20	-24	-28	-32	-35	-39	-43	-47	-51
	12%	5	1	-4	-8	-12	-17	-21	-26	-30	-34	-39	-43
	15%	23	18	13	8	3	-2	-7	-12	-17	-22	-27	-32
		Amortization 30 years.											
5 Yr.	6%	-8	-9	-11	-12	-13	-15	-16	-18	-19	-20	-22	-23
	9%	-3	-5	-6	-8	-9	-11	-12	-14	-15	-17	-18	-20
	12%	1	-0	-2	-3	-5	-7	-8	-10	-11	-13	-15	-16
	15%	7	5	3	2	-0	-2	-3	-5	-7	-9	-10	-12
10 Yr.	6%	-19	-22	-25	-28	-32	-35	-38	-42	-45	-48	-52	-55
	9%	-9	-12	-16	-20	-24	-28	-31	-35	-39	-43	-47	-50
	12%	4	0	-4	-9	-13	-17	-22	-26	-31	-35	-39	-44
	15%	22	17	12	7	2	-4	-9	-14	-19	-24	-29	-34

75% Mortgage

ANALYSIS OF SELECTED CAPITALIZATION RATES

Depreciation or appreciation in 5 years, 10 years and amortization term for yields of 6%, 9%, 12% and 15% on 1/3rd equity

MORTGAGE INTEREST RATE 8½ %

CAPITALIZATION RATES

Projection & Yield		.090	.0925	.0950	.0975	.1000	.1025	.1050	.1075	.1100	.1125	.1150	.1175
		Amortization 15 years.											
	6%	-8	-9	-11	-12	-13	-15	-16	-18	-19	-20	-22	-23
5	9%	-3	-4	-6	-7	-9	-10	-12	-13	-15	-16	-18	-19
Yr.	12%	3	1	-0	-2	-4	-5	-7	-8	-10	-12	-13	-15
	15%	9	7	6	4	2	0	-1	-3	-5	-6	-8	-10
	6%	-21	-24	-28	-31	-34	-38	-41	-44	-47	-51	-54	-57
10	9%	-7	-11	-15	-18	-22	-26	-30	-33	-37	-41	-45	-49
Yr.	12%	11	7	2	-2	-6	-11	-15	-19	-24	-28	-33	-37
	15%	34	29	24	19	14	9	4	-1	-6	-11	-16	-21
		Amortization 20 years.											
	6%	-7	-9	-10	-11	-13	-14	-16	-17	-18	-20	-21	-23
5	9%	-3	-4	-6	-7	-9	-10	-12	-13	-15	-16	-18	-19
Yr.	12%	3	1	-1	-2	-4	-5	-7	-9	-10	-12	-13	-15
	15%	8	7	5	3	2	-0	-2	-3	-5	-7	-8	-10
	6%	-18	-22	-25	-28	-32	-35	-38	-41	-45	-48	-51	-55
10	9%	-6	-10	-14	-18	-22	-25	-29	-33	-37	-41	-44	-48
Yr.	12%	9	5	0	-4	-8	-13	-17	-21	-26	-30	-35	-39
	15%	29	24	19	14	9	4	-1	-6	-11	-16	-21	-26
		Amortization 25 years.											
	6%	-7	-8	-10	-11	-12	-14	-15	-17	-18	-20	-21	-22
5	9%	-2	-4	-5	-7	-8	-10	-11	-13	-14	-16	-17	-19
Yr.	12%	3	1	-1	-2	-4	-5	-7	-9	-10	-12	-13	-15
	15%	8	6	5	3	1	-0	-2	-4	-5	-7	-9	-10
	6%	-17	-20	-24	-27	-30	-33	-37	-40	-43	-47	-50	-53
10	9%	-6	-10	-14	-18	-21	-25	-29	-33	-37	-40	-44	-48
Yr.	12%	8	4	-1	-5	-9	-14	-18	-22	-27	-31	-36	-40
	15%	27	22	17	12	7	1	-4	-9	-14	-19	-24	-29
		Amortization 30 years.											
	6%	-7	-8	-9	-11	-12	-14	-15	-17	-18	-19	-21	-22
5	9%	-2	-4	-5	-7	-8	-10	-11	-13	-14	-16	-17	-19
Yr.	12%	2	1	-1	-2	-4	-5	-7	-9	-10	-12	-13	-15
	15%	8	6	5	3	1	-1	-2	-4	-6	-7	-9	-11
	6%	-16	-19	-23	-26	-29	-33	-36	-39	-43	-46	-49	-52
10	9%	-6	-10	-14	-17	-21	-25	-29	-33	-36	-40	-44	-48
Yr.	12%	8	3	-1	-6	-10	-14	-19	-23	-27	-32	-36	-41
	15%	25	20	15	10	5	-0	-5	-10	-15	-20	-25	-30

75% Mortgage

ANALYSIS OF SELECTED CAPITALIZATION RATES

Depreciation or appreciation in 5 years, 10 years and amortization term for yields of 6%, 9%, 12% and 15% on 1/3rd equity

MORTGAGE INTEREST RATE 8¾%

CAPITALIZATION RATES

Projection & Yield		.090	.0925	.0950	.0975	.1000	.1025	.1050	.1075	.1100	.1125	.1150	.1175
		Amortization 15 years.											
5 Yr.	6%	-7	-8	-10	-11	-12	-14	-15	-17	-18	-19	-21	-22
	9%	-2	-3	-5	-6	-8	-9	-11	-12	-14	-15	-17	-18
	12%	4	2	1	-1	-3	-4	-6	-7	-9	-10	-12	-14
	15%	10	8	7	5	3	2	-0	-2	-3	-5	-7	-8
10 Yr.	6%	-19	-22	-26	-29	-32	-35	-39	-42	-45	-49	-52	-55
	9%	-5	-8	-12	-16	-20	-24	-27	-31	-35	-39	-43	-46
	12%	14	9	5	1	-4	-8	-12	-17	-21	-26	-30	-34
	15%	37	32	27	22	17	12	7	2	-3	-8	-13	-18
		Amortization 20 years.											
5 Yr.	6%	-6	-8	-9	-10	-12	-13	-15	-16	-17	-19	-20	-22
	9%	-1	-3	-4	-6	-7	-9	-10	-12	-13	-15	-16	-18
	12%	4	2	1	-1	-3	-4	-6	-7	-9	-11	-12	-14
	15%	10	8	6	4	3	1	-1	-2	-4	-6	-7	-9
10 Yr.	6%	-16	-19	-23	-26	-29	-33	-36	-39	-43	-46	-49	-52
	9%	-4	-8	-11	-15	-19	-23	-27	-30	-34	-38	-42	-46
	12%	12	8	3	-1	-5	-10	-14	-19	-23	-27	-32	-36
	15%	33	28	23	18	12	7	2	-3	-8	-13	-18	-23
		Amortization 25 years.											
5 Yr.	6%	-6	-7	-9	-10	-11	-13	-14	-16	-17	-18	-20	-21
	9%	-1	-3	-4	-6	-7	-9	-10	-12	-13	-15	-16	-18
	12%	4	2	0	-1	-3	-4	-6	-7	-9	-11	-12	-14
	15%	9	8	6	4	3	1	-1	-3	-4	-6	-8	-9
10 Yr.	6%	-15	-18	-21	-25	-28	-31	-34	-38	-41	-44	-48	-51
	9%	-3	-7	-11	-15	-19	-22	-26	-30	-34	-38	-41	-45
	12%	11	7	2	-2	-6	-11	-15	-19	-24	-28	-33	-37
	15%	30	25	20	15	10	5	-0	-5	-10	-15	-20	-26
		Amortization 30 years.											
5 Yr.	6%	-6	-7	-8	-10	-11	-13	-14	-15	-17	-18	-20	-21
	9%	-1	-3	-4	-6	-7	-9	-10	-12	-13	-15	-16	-18
	12%	4	2	0	-1	-3	-4	-6	-7	-9	-11	-12	-14
	15%	9	7	6	4	2	1	-1	-3	-4	-6	-8	-9
10 Yr.	6%	-14	-17	-20	-24	-27	-30	-34	-37	-40	-43	-47	-50
	9%	-3	-7	-11	-15	-18	-22	-26	-30	-34	-37	-41	-45
	12%	11	6	2	-2	-7	-11	-16	-20	-24	-29	-33	-38
	15%	29	24	19	14	9	4	-2	-7	-12	-17	-22	-27

75% Mortgage

ANALYSIS OF SELECTED CAPITALIZATION RATES

Depreciation or appreciation in 5 years, 10 years and amortization term for yields of 9%, 12%, 15% and 18% on 1/3rd equity

MORTGAGE INTEREST RATE 9%

Projection & Yield		CAPITALIZATION RATES											
		.0925	.0950	.0975	.1000	.1025	.1050	.1075	.1100	.1125	.1150	.1175	.1200
		Amortization 15 years.											
5 Yr.	9%	-2	-4	-5	-7	-8	-10	-11	-13	-14	-16	-17	-19
	12%	3	2	0	-1	-3	-5	-6	-8	-9	-11	-13	-14
	15%	10	8	6	4	3	1	-1	-2	-4	-6	-7	-9
	18%	16	15	13	11	9	7	6	4	2	0	-2	-3
10 Yr.	9%	-6	-10	-14	-17	-21	-25	-29	-33	-36	-40	-44	-48
	12%	12	8	3	-1	-5	-10	-14	-19	-23	-27	-32	-36
	15%	35	30	25	20	15	10	5	-0	-5	-10	-15	-21
	18%	65	59	53	47	41	35	29	23	18	12	6	-0
		Amortization 20 years.											
5 Yr.	9%	-2	-3	-5	-6	-8	-9	-11	-12	-14	-15	-17	-18
	12%	3	2	0	-1	-3	-5	-6	-8	-9	-11	-13	-14
	15%	9	7	6	4	2	1	-1	-3	-4	-6	-8	-9
	18%	15	14	12	10	8	7	5	3	1	-1	-2	-4
10 Yr.	9%	-5	-9	-13	-16	-20	-24	-28	-32	-35	-39	-43	-47
	12%	11	6	2	-2	-7	-11	-16	-20	-24	-29	-33	-38
	15%	31	26	21	16	11	6	1	-5	-10	-15	-20	-25
	18%	57	51	45	39	33	28	22	16	10	4	-2	-8
		Amortization 25 years.											
5 Yr.	9%	-2	-3	-5	-6	-8	-9	-11	-12	-14	-15	-17	-18
	12%	3	2	0	-2	-3	-5	-6	-8	-9	-11	-13	-14
	15%	9	7	5	4	2	0	-1	-3	-5	-6	-8	-10
	18%	15	13	11	10	8	6	4	2	1	-1	-3	-5
10 Yr.	9%	-5	-8	-12	-16	-20	-24	-27	-31	-35	-39	-43	-46
	12%	10	6	1	-3	-8	-12	-16	-21	-25	-30	-34	-38
	15%	29	24	19	14	8	3	-2	-7	-12	-17	-22	-27
	18%	53	47	41	35	29	24	18	12	6	0	-6	-12
		Amortization 30 years.											
5 Yr.	9%	-2	-3	-5	-6	-8	-9	-11	-12	-14	-15	-17	-18
	12%	3	2	0	-2	-3	-5	-6	-8	-9	-11	-13	-14
	15%	9	7	5	4	2	0	-1	-3	-5	-7	-8	-10
	18%	15	13	11	9	8	6	4	2	0	-1	-3	-5
10 Yr.	9%	-4	-8	-12	-16	-19	-23	-27	-31	-35	-38	-42	-46
	12%	9	5	1	-4	-8	-12	-17	-21	-26	-30	-34	-39
	15%	27	22	17	12	7	2	-3	-8	-13	-18	-23	-28
	18%	51	45	39	33	27	21	15	10	4	-2	-8	-14

75% Mortgage

ANALYSIS OF SELECTED CAPITALIZATION RATES

Depreciation or appreciation in 5 years, 10 years and amortization term for yields of 9%, 12%, 15% and 18% on 1/3rd equity

MORTGAGE INTEREST RATE 9¼%

CAPITALIZATION RATES

Projection & Yield		.0925	.0950	.0975	.1000	.1025	.1050	.1075	.1100	.1125	.1150	.1175	.1200
Amortization 15 years.													
5 Yr.	9%	-1	-3	-4	-6	-7	-9	-10	-12	-13	-15	-16	-18
	12%	4	3	1	-0	-2	-4	-5	-7	-8	-10	-11	-13
	15%	11	9	7	6	4	2	1	-1	-3	-5	-6	-8
	18%	18	16	14	12	10	9	7	5	3	1	-0	-2
10 Yr.	9%	-4	-7	-11	-15	-19	-23	-26	-30	-34	-38	-42	-45
	12%	15	10	6	2	-3	-7	-11	-16	-20	-25	-29	-33
	15%	38	33	28	23	18	13	8	3	-2	-7	-12	-17
	18%	68	62	56	50	45	39	33	27	21	15	9	3
Amortization 20 years.													
5 Yr.	9%	-1	-2	-4	-5	-7	-8	-10	-11	-13	-14	-16	-17
	12%	4	3	1	-0	-2	-4	-5	-7	-8	-10	-11	-13
	15%	10	9	7	5	3	2	0	-2	-3	-5	-7	-8
	18%	17	15	13	11	10	8	6	4	2	1	-1	-3
10 Yr.	9%	-2	-6	-10	-14	-18	-21	-25	-29	-33	-37	-40	-44
	12%	14	9	5	0	-4	-8	-13	-17	-21	-26	-30	-35
	15%	34	29	24	19	14	9	4	-1	-6	-11	-16	-21
	18%	61	55	49	43	37	31	26	20	14	8	2	-4
Amortization 25 years.													
5 Yr.	9%	-1	-2	-4	-5	-7	-8	-10	-11	-13	-14	-16	-17
	12%	4	3	1	-0	-2	-4	-5	-7	-8	-10	-11	-13
	15%	10	8	7	5	3	2	-0	-2	-3	-5	-7	-9
	18%	16	14	13	11	9	7	6	4	2	0	-2	-3
10 Yr.	9%	-2	-6	-9	-13	-17	-21	-25	-28	-32	-36	-40	-44
	12%	13	9	4	-0	-5	-9	-13	-18	-22	-27	-31	-35
	15%	32	27	22	17	12	7	2	-3	-8	-13	-19	-24
	18%	57	51	45	39	33	28	22	16	10	4	-2	-8
Amortization 30 years.													
5 Yr.	9%	-1	-2	-4	-5	-7	-8	-10	-11	-13	-14	-15	-17
	12%	4	3	1	-0	-2	-4	-5	-7	-8	-10	-12	-13
	15%	10	8	7	5	3	1	-0	-2	-4	-5	-7	-9
	18%	16	14	12	11	9	7	5	4	2	-0	-2	-4
10 Yr.	9%	-1	-5	-9	-13	-17	-20	-24	-28	-32	-36	-39	-43
	12%	13	8	4	-1	-5	-9	-14	-18	-22	-27	-31	-36
	15%	31	26	21	16	11	6	1	-5	-10	-15	-20	-25
	18%	55	49	43	37	31	25	20	14	8	2	-4	-10

75% Mortgage

ANALYSIS OF SELECTED CAPITALIZATION RATES
Depreciation or appreciation in 5 years, 10 years and amortization term
for yields of 9%, 12%, 15% and 18% on 1/3rd equity

MORTGAGE INTEREST RATE 9½ %

Projection & Yield		CAPITALIZATION RATES											
		.0925	.0950	.0975	.1000	.1025	.1050	.1075	.1100	.1125	.1150	.1175	.1200
		Amortization 15 years.											
5 Yr.	9%	-0	-2	-3	-5	-6	-8	-9	-11	-12	-14	-15	-17
	12%	6	4	2	1	-1	-2	-4	-6	-7	-9	-10	-12
	15%	12	10	8	7	5	3	2	0	-2	-3	-5	-7
	18%	19	17	15	13	12	10	8	6	4	3	1	-1
10 Yr.	9%	-1	-5	-9	-13	-16	-20	-24	-28	-32	-35	-39	-43
	12%	18	13	9	4	-0	-4	-9	-13	-18	-22	-26	-31
	15%	41	36	31	26	21	16	11	6	1	-4	-9	-14
	18%	72	66	60	54	48	42	36	30	25	19	13	7
		Amortization 20 years.											
5 Yr.	9%	0	-1	-3	-4	-6	-7	-9	-10	-12	-13	-15	-16
	12%	6	4	2	1	-1	-2	-4	-6	-7	-9	-10	-12
	15%	11	10	8	6	5	3	1	-0	-2	-4	-5	-7
	18%	18	16	14	13	11	9	7	5	4	2	0	-2
10 Yr.	9%	0	-4	-7	-11	-15	-19	-23	-26	-30	-34	-38	-42
	12%	17	12	8	3	-1	-5	-10	-14	-19	-23	-27	-32
	15%	38	33	28	22	17	12	7	2	-3	-8	-13	-18
	18%	65	59	53	47	41	35	29	23	18	12	6	-0
		Amortization 25 years.											
5 Yr.	9%	0	-1	-3	-4	-6	-7	-9	-10	-12	-13	-14	-16
	12%	6	4	2	1	-1	-2	-4	-6	-7	-9	-10	-12
	15%	11	10	8	6	4	3	1	-1	-2	-4	-6	-7
	18%	18	16	14	12	10	9	7	5	3	1	-0	-2
10 Yr.	9%	1	-3	-7	-11	-14	-18	-22	-26	-30	-33	-37	-41
	12%	16	12	7	3	-1	-6	-10	-15	-19	-23	-28	-32
	15%	36	31	26	21	15	10	5	0	-5	-10	-15	-20
	18%	61	55	49	43	37	32	26	20	14	8	2	-4
		Amortization 30 years.											
5 Yr.	9%	1	-1	-2	-4	-5	-7	-8	-10	-11	-13	-14	-16
	12%	6	4	2	1	-1	-2	-4	-6	-7	-9	-10	-12
	15%	11	9	8	6	4	3	1	-1	-2	-4	-6	-7
	18%	17	16	14	12	10	8	7	5	3	1	-1	-2
10 Yr.	9%	1	-3	-6	-10	-14	-18	-22	-25	-29	-33	-37	-40
	12%	16	11	7	3	-2	-6	-11	-15	-19	-24	-28	-32
	15%	35	30	24	19	14	9	4	-1	-6	-11	-16	-21
	18%	59	53	47	41	35	30	24	18	12	6	0	-6

75% Mortgage

ANALYSIS OF SELECTED CAPITALIZATION RATES

Depreciation or appreciation in 5 years, 10 years and amortization term for yields of 9%, 12%, 15% and 18% on 1/3rd equity

MORTGAGE INTEREST RATE 9¾%

CAPITALIZATION RATES

Projection & Yield		.0950	.0975	.1000	.1025	.1050	.1075	.1100	.1125	.1150	.1175	.1200	.1225
		Amortization 15 years.											
5 Yr.	9%	-1	-2	-4	-5	-7	-8	-10	-11	-13	-14	-16	-17
	12%	5	3	2	0	-1	-3	-4	-6	-8	-9	-11	-12
	15%	11	10	8	6	5	3	1	-1	-2	-4	-6	-7
	18%	18	16	15	13	11	9	7	6	4	2	0	-1
10 Yr.	9%	-3	-6	-10	-14	-18	-22	-25	-29	-33	-37	-41	-44
	12%	16	11	7	3	-2	-6	-10	-15	-19	-24	-28	-32
	15%	39	34	29	24	19	14	9	4	-1	-6	-11	-16
	18%	69	63	58	52	46	40	34	28	22	16	10	5
		Amortization 20 years.											
5 Yr.	9%	-0	-2	-3	-5	-6	-8	-9	-11	-12	-14	-15	-17
	12%	5	4	2	0	-1	-3	-4	-6	-8	-9	-11	-12
	15%	11	9	8	6	4	3	1	-1	-3	-4	-6	-8
	18%	17	16	14	12	10	9	7	5	3	1	-0	-2
10 Yr.	9%	-1	-5	-9	-12	-16	-20	-24	-28	-31	-35	-39	-43
	12%	15	11	6	2	-2	-7	-11	-16	-20	-24	-29	-33
	15%	36	31	26	21	16	11	6	0	-5	-10	-15	-20
	18%	63	57	51	45	39	33	27	21	16	10	4	-2
		Amortization 25 years.											
5 Yr.	9%	0	-1	-3	-4	-6	-7	-9	-10	-12	-13	-15	-16
	12%	5	4	2	0	-1	-3	-4	-6	-8	-9	-11	-12
	15%	11	9	7	6	4	2	1	-1	-3	-4	-6	-8
	18%	17	15	13	12	10	8	6	5	3	1	-1	-3
10 Yr.	9%	-0	-4	-8	-12	-15	-19	-23	-27	-31	-34	-38	-42
	12%	15	10	6	2	-3	-7	-12	-16	-20	-25	-29	-33
	15%	34	29	24	19	14	9	4	-1	-6	-11	-17	-22
	18%	59	53	47	41	36	30	24	18	12	6	0	-6
		Amortization 30 years.											
5 Yr.	9%	0	-1	-3	-4	-6	-7	-9	-10	-12	-13	-15	-16
	12%	5	4	2	0	-1	-3	-4	-6	-8	-9	-11	-12
	15%	11	9	7	6	4	2	1	-1	-3	-4	-6	-8
	18%	17	15	13	11	10	8	6	4	3	1	-1	-3
10 Yr.	9%	0	-4	-7	-11	-15	-19	-23	-26	-30	-34	-38	-42
	12%	15	10	6	1	-3	-7	-12	-16	-21	-25	-29	-34
	15%	33	28	23	18	13	8	3	-2	-7	-12	-18	-23
	18%	57	51	45	40	34	28	22	16	10	4	-2	-7

75% Mortgage

ANALYSIS OF SELECTED CAPITALIZATION RATES
Depreciation or appreciation in 5 years, 10 years and amortization term
for yields of 9%, 12%, 15% and 18% on 1/3rd equity

MORTGAGE INTEREST RATE 10%

Projection &	Yield	CAPITALIZATION RATES											
		.0950	.0975	.1000	.1025	.1050	.1075	.1100	.1125	.1150	.1175	.1200	.1225
		Amortization 15 years.											
5 Yr.	9%	0	-1	-3	-4	-6	-7	-8	-10	-11	-13	-14	-16
	12%	6	5	3	1	-0	-2	-3	-5	-7	-8	-10	-11
	15%	12	11	9	7	6	4	2	1	-1	-3	-4	-6
	18%	19	18	16	14	12	10	9	7	5	3	2	-0
10 Yr.	9%	-0	-4	-8	-12	-15	-19	-23	-27	-31	-34	-38	-42
	12%	19	14	10	5	1	-3	-8	-12	-17	-21	-25	-30
	15%	43	37	32	27	22	17	12	7	2	-3	-8	-13
	18%	73	67	61	55	49	43	38	32	26	20	14	8
		Amortization 20 years.											
5 Yr.	9%	1	-1	-2	-4	-5	-7	-8	-10	-11	-13	-14	-16
	12%	6	5	3	1	-0	-2	-3	-5	-6	-8	-10	-11
	15%	12	10	9	7	5	4	2	0	-1	-3	-5	-6
	18%	19	17	15	13	12	10	8	6	4	3	1	-1
10 Yr.	9%	2	-2	-6	-10	-14	-17	-21	-25	-29	-33	-36	-40
	12%	18	14	9	5	1	-4	-8	-13	-17	-21	-26	-30
	15%	39	34	29	24	19	14	9	4	-1	-6	-11	-16
	18%	66	61	55	49	43	37	31	25	19	14	8	2
		Amortization 25 years.											
5 Yr.	9%	1	-0	-2	-3	-5	-6	-8	-9	-11	-12	-14	-15
	12%	6	5	3	2	-0	-2	-3	-5	-6	-8	-10	-11
	15%	12	10	9	7	5	4	2	0	-1	-3	-5	-7
	18%	18	17	15	13	11	9	8	6	4	2	0	-1
10 Yr.	9%	3	-1	-5	-9	-13	-16	-20	-24	-28	-32	-35	-39
	12%	18	13	9	5	0	-4	-8	-13	-17	-22	-26	-30
	15%	38	33	28	22	17	12	7	2	-3	-8	-13	-18
	18%	63	57	51	46	40	34	28	22	16	10	4	-2
		Amortization 30 years.											
5 Yr.	9%	1	-0	-2	-3	-5	-6	-8	-9	-11	-12	-14	-15
	12%	6	5	3	2	-0	-2	-3	-5	-6	-8	-10	-11
	15%	12	10	9	7	5	3	2	0	-2	-3	-5	-7
	18%	18	16	15	13	11	9	7	6	4	2	0	-2
10 Yr.	9%	3	-1	-5	-8	-12	-16	-20	-24	-27	-31	-35	-39
	12%	18	13	9	5	0	-4	-9	-13	-17	-22	-26	-31
	15%	37	32	27	22	17	11	6	1	-4	-9	-14	-19
	18%	61	55	50	44	38	32	26	20	14	8	3	-3

BASIC CAPITALIZATION RATE TABLES WITH 66⅔% MORTGAGE FINANCING

Computed by use of Table C coefficients.

66⅔% Table computed as, $r = Y - .66\,⅔C$

Except where positive coefficients are involved.

To Find Desired Rate "r":

1. Find amortization term at top of table.
2. Find pages on which mortgage interest rate appears.
3. Find desired income projection term bracket.
4. Read across on Equity Yield line to basic capitalization Rate in mortgage interest rate column.

Applicable sinking fund factor for depreciation or appreciation adjustment is on equity yield line in column at far right.

Table is supplemented by tabulated analyses of selected Overall Capitalization Rates showing rounded percentage of depreciation and appreciation applicable to various equity yields. Minus sign indicates depreciation. Plus sign indicates appreciation.

CAPITALIZATION RATES

Assuming 2/3rds of Purchase Price Financed by Mortgage

10 YEARS AMORTIZATION: 3¼% TO 4½%

Interest Rate Annual Requirement (f) Coverage, Min. Rate		3¼% .11736 .07824	3½% .11868 .07912	3¾% .12012 .08008	4% .12156 .08104	4¼% .12300 .08200	4½% .12444 .08296	$\frac{1}{s_{\overline{n}|}}$
Projection	Balance (b)	.539955	.543483	.546411	.549388	.552417	.555497	+ Dep.
	Equity Yield	Basic Rate before Depreciation or Appreciation						− App.
	4% .04	.0350	.0363	.0376	.0389	.0403	.0416	.1846
	5% .05	.0394	.0407	.0421	.0433	.0447	.0460	.1810
	6% .06	.0439	.0451	.0465	.0478	.0491	.0504	.1774
	7% .07	.0483	.0495	.0509	.0521	.0535	.0548	.1739
	8% .08	.0527	.0539	.0552	.0565	.0578	.0591	.1705
5 Years n = 5	9% .09	.0570	.0583	.0596	.0609	.0621	.0635	.1671
	10% .10	.0613	.0626	.0639	.0652	.0665	.0678	.1638
	11% .11	.0657	.0669	.0682	.0695	.0708	.0721	.1606
	12% .12	.0700	.0712	.0725	.0738	.0751	.0763	.1574
	13% .13	.0743	.0755	.0767	.0781	.0793	.0806	.1543
	14% .14	.0785	.0797	.0810	.0823	.0835	.0848	.1513
	15% .15	.0828	.0840	.0853	.0865	.0877	.0890	.1483
	Balance (b)	none	none	none	none	none	none	+ Dep.
	Equity Yield	Basic Rate before Depreciation or Appreciation						− App.
	4% .04	.0361	.0369	.0379	.0389	.0398	.0408	.0833
	5% .05	.0419	.0428	.0437	.0447	.0457	.0467	.0795
	6% .06	.0477	.0485	.0495	.0505	.0515	.0524	.0759
	7% .07	.0533	.0542	.0552	.0561	.0571	.0581	.0724
	8% .08	.0589	.0598	.0607	.0617	.0627	.0636	.0690
10 Years n = 10	9% .09	.0644	.0653	.0662	.0672	.0681	.0691	.0658
	10% .10	.0697	.0707	.0716	.0725	.0735	.0745	.0628
	11% .11	.0751	.0759	.0769	.0779	.0788	.0798	.0598
	12% .12	.0803	.0811	.0821	.0831	.0840	.0850	.0570
	13% .13	.0854	.0863	.0873	.0882	.0891	.0901	.0543
	14% .14	.0905	.0913	.0923	.0933	.0942	.0952	.0517
	15% .15	.0954	.0963	.0973	.0982	.0992	.1001	.0493

CAPITALIZATION RATES

Assuming 2/3rds of Purchase Price Financed by Mortgage

10 YEARS AMORTIZATION: 4¾% TO 6%

Interest Rate / Annual Requirement (f) / Coverage, Min. Rate		4¾% .12588 .08392	5% .12732 .08488	5¼% .12876 .08584	5½% .13032 .08688	5¾% .13176 .08784	6% .13332 .08888	$\frac{1}{s_{\overline{n}|}}$
Projection	Balance(b)	.558629	.561814	.565053	.567658	.571003	.573705	+ Dep. − App.
	Equity Yield	Basic Rate before Depreciation or Appreciation						
	4% .04	.0429	.0443	.0457	.0470	.0484	.0497	.1846
	5% .05	.0473	.0487	.0500	.0514	.0527	.0541	.1810
	6% .06	.0517	.0531	.0544	.0557	.0571	.0585	.1774
	7% .07	.0561	.0575	.0588	.0601	.0615	.0628	.1739
	8% .08	.0605	.0618	.0631	.0645	.0658	.0671	.1705
5 Years n = 5	9% .09	.0648	.0661	.0674	.0687	.0701	.0714	.1671
	10% .10	.0691	.0704	.0717	.0730	.0743	.0757	.1638
	11% .11	.0733	.0747	.0759	.0773	.0786	.0799	.1606
	12% .12	.0776	.0789	.0802	.0815	.0829	.0841	.1574
	13% .13	.0819	.0831	.0845	.0857	.0871	.0884	.1543
	14% .14	.0861	.0874	.0887	.0899	.0913	.0926	.1513
	15% .15	.0903	.0916	.0929	.0941	.0955	.0967	.1483
	Balance(b)	none	none	none	none	none	none	+ Dep. − App.
	Equity Yield	Basic Rate before Depreciation or Appreciation						
	4% .04	.0417	.0427	.0437	.0447	.0457	.0467	.0833
	5% .05	.0476	.0485	.0495	.0505	.0515	.0526	.0795
	6% .06	.0533	.0543	.0553	.0563	.0573	.0583	.0759
	7% .07	.0590	.0600	.0609	.0620	.0629	.0640	.0724
	8% .08	.0646	.0655	.0665	.0675	.0685	.0695	.0690
10 Years n = 10	9% .09	.0701	.0710	.0720	.0730	.0740	.0750	.0658
	10% .10	.0755	.0764	.0773	.0784	.0793	.0804	.0628
	11% .11	.0807	.0817	.0827	.0837	.0847	.0857	.0598
	12% .12	.0859	.0869	.0879	.0889	.0899	.0909	.0570
	13% .13	.0911	.0921	.0930	.0941	.0950	.0961	.0543
	14% .14	.0961	.0971	.0981	.0991	.1001	.1011	.0517
	15% .15	.1011	.1021	.1030	.1041	.1050	.1061	.0493

CAPITALIZATION RATES

Assuming 2/3rds of Purchase Price Financed by Mortgage

10 YEARS AMORTIZATION: 6¼% TO 8%

Interest Rate		6¼%	6½%	6¾%	7%	7½%	8%	$\frac{1}{s_{\overline{n}\rceil}}$
Annual Requirement (f)		.13476	.13632	.13788	.13944	.14256	.14568	
Coverage, Min. Rate		.08984	.09088	.09192	.09296	.09504	.09712	
Projection	Balance (b)	.577158	.579961	.582814	.585715	.591672	.597837	+ Dep.
	Equity Yield	Basic Rate before Depreciation or Appreciation						− App.
	4% .04	.0511	.0525	.0539	.0553	.0581	.0609	.1846
	5% .05	.0555	.0569	.0583	.0597	.0625	.0653	.1810
	6% .06	.0599	.0612	.0626	.0639	.0667	.0695	.1774
	7% .07	.0642	.0655	.0669	.0683	.0711	.0738	.1739
	8% .08	.0685	.0698	.0712	.0725	.0753	.0781	.1705
5 Years n = 5	9% .09	.0727	.0741	.0755	.0768	.0796	.0823	.1671
	10% .10	.0770	.0783	.0797	.0811	.0838	.0865	.1638
	11% .11	.0813	.0826	.0839	.0853	.0880	.0907	.1606
	12% .12	.0855	.0868	.0881	.0895	.0922	.0949	.1574
	13% .13	.0897	.0910	.0923	.0937	.0964	.0991	.1543
	14% .14	.0939	.0952	.0965	.0979	.1005	.1033	.1513
	15% .15	.0981	.0993	.1007	.1020	.1047	.1074	.1483
	Balance (b)	none	none	none	none	none	none	+ Dep.
	Equity Yield	Basic Rate before Depreciation or Appreciation						− App.
	4% .04	.0477	.0487	.0497	.0508	.0529	.0549	.0833
	5% .05	.0535	.0545	.0556	.0566	.0587	.0608	.0795
	6% .06	.0593	.0603	.0613	.0624	.0645	.0665	.0759
	7% .07	.0649	.0659	.0670	.0681	.0701	.0722	.0724
	8% .08	.0705	.0715	.0726	.0736	.0757	.0778	.0690
10 Years n = 10	9% .09	.0760	.0770	.0781	.0791	.0812	.0833	.0658
	10% .10	.0813	.0824	.0835	.0845	.0865	.0887	.0628
	11% .11	.0867	.0877	.0887	.0898	.0919	.0939	.0598
	12% .12	.0919	.0929	.0939	.0950	.0971	.0991	.0570
	13% .13	.0970	.0981	.0991	.1001	.1022	.1043	.0543
	14% .14	.1021	.1031	.1041	.1052	.1073	.1093	.0517
	15% .15	.1070	.1081	.1091	.1101	.1122	.1143	.0493

CAPITALIZATION RATES
Assuming 2/3rds of Purchase Price Financed by Mortgage

10 YEARS AMORTIZATION: 8¼ % TO 9½ %

Interest Rate / Annual Requirement (f) / Coverage, Min. Rate		8¼ % / .147183 / .098122	8½ % / .148782 / .099188	8¾ % / .150392 / .100261	9% / .152010 / .101340	9¼ % / .153639 / .102426	9½ % / .155277 / .103518	$\frac{1}{s_{\overline{n}\rvert}}$
Projection	Balance (b)	.601348	.604320	.607284	.610239	.613186	.616124	+ Dep.
	Equity Yield	Basic Rate before Depreciation or Appreciation						– App.
	4% .04	.0624	.0638	.0653	.0667	.0681	.0696	.1846
	5% .05	.0667	.0681	.0695	.0710	.0724	.0739	.1810
	6% .06	.0710	.0724	.0738	.0752	.0767	.0781	.1774
	7% .07	.0752	.0767	.0781	.0795	.0809	.0823	.1739
	8% .08	.0795	.0809	.0823	.0837	.0851	.0866	.1705
5 Years	9% .09	.0837	.0851	.0865	.0879	.0893	.0908	.1671
n = 5	10% .10	.0879	.0893	.0907	.0921	.0935	.0949	.1638
	11% .11	.0921	.0935	.0949	.0963	.0977	.0991	.1606
	12% .12	.0963	.0977	.0990	.1004	.1018	.1032	.1574
	13% .13	.1004	.1018	.1032	.1046	.1060	.1074	.1543
	14% .14	.1046	.1059	.1073	.1087	.1101	.1115	.1513
	15% .15	.1087	.1101	.1114	.1128	.1142	.1156	.1483
	Balance (b)	none	none	none	none	none	none	+ Dep.
	Equity Yield	Basic Rate before Depreciation or Appreciation						– App.
	4% .04	.0559	.0570	.0581	.0591	.0602	.0613	.0833
	5% .05	.0618	.0629	.0639	.0650	.0661	.0672	.0795
	6% .06	.0675	.0686	.0697	.0708	.0718	.0729	.0759
	7% .07	.0732	.0743	.0753	.0764	.0775	.0786	.0724
	8% .08	.0788	.0798	.0809	.0820	.0831	.0842	.0690
10 Years	9% .09	.0842	.0853	.0864	.0875	.0885	.0896	.0658
n = 10	10% .10	.0896	.0907	.0918	.0928	.0939	.0950	.0627
	11% .11	.0949	.0960	.0971	.0981	.0992	.1003	.0598
	12% .12	.1001	.1012	.1023	.1034	.1044	.1055	.0570
	13% .13	.1053	.1063	.1074	.1085	.1096	.1107	.0543
	14% .14	.1103	.1114	.1125	.1135	.1146	.1157	.0517
	15% .15	.1153	.1164	.1174	.1185	.1196	.1207	.0493

CAPITALIZATION RATES
Assuming 2/3rds of Purchase Price Financed by Mortgage

10 YEARS AMORTIZATION: 9¾% TO 11%

Interest Rate / Annual Requirement (f) / Coverage, Min. Rate			9¾%	10%	10¼%	10½%	10¾%	11%	$\frac{1}{s_{\overline{n}\rvert}}$
			.156924	.158580	.160246	.161921	.163606	.165300	
			.104616	.105720	.106831	.107947	.109070	.110200	
Projection	Balance (b)		.619052	.621972	.624882	.627782	.630673	.633554	+ Dep.
	Equity	Yield	Basic Rate before Depreciation or Appreciation						− App.
5 Years n = 5	4%	.04	.0711	.0725	.0740	.0755	.0769	.0784	.1846
	5%	.05	.0753	.0768	.0782	.0797	.0812	.0827	.1810
	6%	.06	.0796	.0810	.0825	.0839	.0854	.0869	.1774
	7%	.07	.0838	.0852	.0867	.0881	.0896	.0911	.1739
	8%	.08	.0880	.0894	.0909	.0923	.0938	.0952	.1705
	9%	.09	.0922	.0936	.0950	.0965	.0979	.0994	.1671
	10%	.10	.0964	.0978	.0992	.1006	.1021	.1035	.1638
	11%	.11	.1005	.1019	.1033	.1048	.1062	.1076	.1606
	12%	.12	.1046	.1061	.1075	.1089	.1103	.1117	.1574
	13%	.13	.1088	.1102	.1116	.1130	.1144	.1158	.1543
	14%	.14	.1129	.1143	.1157	.1171	.1185	.1199	.1513
	15%	.15	.1169	.1183	.1197	.1211	.1226	.1240	.1483
	Balance (b)		none	none	none	none	none	none	+ Dep.
	Equity	Yield	Basic Rate before Depreciation or Appreciation						− App.
10 Years n = 10	4%	.04	.0624	.0635	.0646	.0658	.0669	.0680	.0833
	5%	.05	.0683	.0694	.0705	.0716	.0727	.0739	.0795
	6%	.06	.0740	.0751	.0763	.0774	.0785	.0796	.0759
	7%	.07	.0797	.0808	.0819	.0830	.0842	.0853	.0724
	8%	.08	.0853	.0864	.0875	.0886	.0897	.0908	.0690
	9%	.09	.0907	.0918	.0930	.0941	.0952	.0963	.0658
	10%	.10	.0961	.0972	.0983	.0995	.1006	.1017	.0627
	11%	.11	.1014	.1025	.1036	.1047	.1059	.1070	.0598
	12%	.12	.1066	.1077	.1088	.1100	.1111	.1122	.0570
	13%	.13	.1118	.1129	.1140	.1151	.1162	.1173	.0543
	14%	.14	.1168	.1179	.1190	.1201	.1213	.1224	.0517
	15%	.15	.1218	.1229	.1240	.1251	.1262	.1274	.0493

CAPITALIZATION RATES

Assuming 2/3rds of Purchase Price Financed by Mortgage

15 YEARS AMORTIZATION: 3¼% TO 4½%

Interest Rate		3¼%	3½%	3¾%	4%	4¼%	4½%	$\frac{1}{s_{\overline{n\|}}}$
Annual Requirement (f)		.08436	.08580	.08736	.08880	.09036	.09180	
Coverage, Min. Rate		.05624	.05720	.05824	.05920	.06024	.06120	
Projection	Balance(b)	.718855	.722860	.726265	.730385	.733896	.738133	+ Dep.
	Equity Yield	Basic Rate before Depreciation or Appreciation						− App.
	4% .04	.0350	.0365	.0379	.0393	.0408	.0423	.1846
	5% .05	.0390	.0405	.0419	.0433	.0448	.0463	.1810
	6% .06	.0430	.0445	.0459	.0473	.0488	.0503	.1774
	7% .07	.0470	.0484	.0499	.0513	.0527	.0542	.1739
	8% .08	.0510	.0524	.0538	.0553	.0567	.0581	.1705
5 Years n = 5	9% .09	.0549	.0563	.0577	.0592	.0606	.0621	.1671
	10% .10	.0589	.0603	.0617	.0631	.0645	.0659	.1638
	11% .11	.0628	.0642	.0656	.0670	.0685	.0699	.1606
	12% .12	.0667	.0681	.0695	.0709	.0723	.0737	.1574
	13% .13	.0707	.0721	.0734	.0748	.0762	.0776	.1543
	14% .14	.0746	.0759	.0773	.0787	.0801	.0815	.1513
	15% .15	.0785	.0798	.0812	.0825	.0839	.0853	.1483
	Balance(b)	.388175	.392803	.396174	.401184	.404911	.410328	+ Dep.
	Equity Yield	Basic Rate before Depreciation or Appreciation						− App.
	4% .04	.0356	.0369	.0381	.0393	.0405	.0418	.0833
	5% .05	.0405	.0417	.0429	.0441	.0453	.0466	.0795
	6% .06	.0453	.0465	.0477	.0489	.0501	.0514	.0759
	7% .07	.0501	.0513	.0525	.0537	.0549	.0561	.0724
	8% .08	.0548	.0559	.0571	.0583	.0595	.0607	.0690
10 Years n = 10	9% .09	.0594	.0606	.0617	.0629	.0641	.0653	.0658
	10% .10	.0640	.0651	.0663	.0675	.0687	.0699	.0628
	11% .11	.0685	.0697	.0709	.0720	.0732	.0744	.0598
	12% .12	.0730	.0741	.0753	.0765	.0777	.0788	.0570
	13% .13	.0775	.0786	.0797	.0809	.0820	.0832	.0543
	14% .14	.0818	.0829	.0841	.0853	.0864	.0875	.0517
	15% .15	.0862	.0873	.0884	.0895	.0907	.0919	.0493
	Balance(b)	none	none	none	none	none	none	+ Dep.
	Equity Yield	Basic Rate before Depreciation or Appreciation						− App.
	4% .04	.0363	.0373	.0383	.0393	.0403	.0413	.0500
	5% .05	.0420	.0430	.0440	.0450	.0460	.0470	.0464
	6% .06	.0476	.0486	.0496	.0506	.0516	.0526	.0430
	7% .07	.0531	.0540	.0551	.0560	.0571	.0580	.0398
	8% .08	.0584	.0593	.0604	.0613	.0624	.0633	.0368
15 Years n = 15	9% .09	.0635	.0645	.0655	.0665	.0675	.0685	.0341
	10% .10	.0686	.0696	.0706	.0716	.0726	.0736	.0315
	11% .11	.0735	.0745	.0755	.0765	.0775	.0785	.0291
	12% .12	.0784	.0793	.0804	.0813	.0824	.0833	.0268
	13% .13	.0831	.0841	.0851	.0861	.0871	.0881	.0248
	14% .14	.0877	.0887	.0897	.0907	.0917	.0927	.0228
	15% .15	.0923	.0932	.0943	.0952	.0963	.0972	.0210

CAPITALIZATION RATES

Assuming 2/3rds of Purchase Price Financed by Mortgage

15 YEARS AMORTIZATION: 4¾% TO 6%

Interest Rate / Annual Requirement (f) / Coverage, Min. Rate		4¾% / .09336 / .06224	5% / .09492 / .06328	5¼% / .09648 / .06432	5½% / .09816 / .06544	5¾% / .09972 / .06648	6% / .10128 / .06752	$\frac{1}{s_{\overline{n}|}}$
Projection	Balance(b)	.741755	.745431	.749161	.752259	.756097	.759991	+ Dep. − App.
	Equity Yield	Basic Rate before Depreciation or Appreciation						
	4% .04	.0438	.0453	.0468	.0483	.0498	.0514	.1846
	5% .05	.0478	.0492	.0508	.0522	.0538	.0553	.1810
	6% .06	.0517	.0532	.0547	.0562	.0576	.0592	.1774
	7% .07	.0556	.0571	.0586	.0601	.0616	.0630	.1739
	8% .08	.0596	.0610	.0625	.0640	.0654	.0669	.1705
5 Years n = 5	9% .09	.0635	.0650	.0664	.0678	.0693	.0708	.1671
	10% .10	.0674	.0688	.0703	.0718	.0732	.0746	.1638
	11% .11	.0713	.0727	.0742	.0756	.0770	.0785	.1606
	12% .12	.0752	.0766	.0780	.0794	.0809	.0824	.1574
	13% .13	.0790	.0804	.0819	.0833	.0848	.0862	.1543
	14% .14	.0829	.0843	.0857	.0872	.0886	.0900	.1513
	15% .15	.0867	.0881	.0896	.0909	.0924	.0938	.1483
	Balance(b)	.414433	.418726	.423213	.426304	.431174	.436255	+ Dep. − App.
	Equity Yield	Basic Rate before Depreciation or Appreciation						
	4% .04	.0431	.0444	.0456	.0470	.0482	.0496	.0833
	5% .05	.0479	.0492	.0504	.0518	.0530	.0544	.0795
	6% .06	.0526	.0539	.0552	.0564	.0578	.0590	.0759
	7% .07	.0574	.0585	.0598	.0611	.0624	.0637	.0724
	8% .08	.0620	.0632	.0645	.0657	.0670	.0682	.0690
10 Years n = 10	9% .09	.0666	.0678	.0690	.0703	.0716	.0728	.0658
	10% .10	.0711	.0723	.0736	.0748	.0760	.0773	.0628
	11% .11	.0756	.0768	.0780	.0792	.0805	.0818	.0598
	12% .12	.0800	.0812	.0824	.0837	.0849	.0862	.0570
	13% .13	.0844	.0856	.0868	.0880	.0893	.0905	.0543
	14% .14	.0888	.0899	.0912	.0924	.0936	.0948	.0517
	15% .15	.0930	.0942	.0954	.0966	.0978	.0990	.0493
	Balance(b)	none	none	none	none	none	none	+ Dep. − App.
	Equity Yield	Basic Rate before Depreciation or Appreciation						
	4% .04	.0423	.0433	.0444	.0455	.0466	.0476	.0500
	5% .05	.0480	.0491	.0501	.0512	.0523	.0533	.0464
	6% .06	.0536	.0547	.0557	.0568	.0579	.0589	.0430
	7% .07	.0591	.0602	.0612	.0623	.0634	.0644	.0398
	8% .08	.0644	.0654	.0665	.0676	.0686	.0697	.0368
15 Years n = 15	9% .09	.0696	.0706	.0717	.0728	.0738	.0749	.0341
	10% .10	.0746	.0757	.0767	.0778	.0789	.0799	.0315
	11% .11	.0796	.0806	.0816	.0828	.0838	.0848	.0291
	12% .12	.0844	.0854	.0865	.0876	.0886	.0897	.0268
	13% .13	.0891	.0902	.0912	.0923	.0934	.0944	.0248
	14% .14	.0938	.0948	.0958	.0970	.0980	.0990	.0228
	15% .15	.0983	.0993	.1004	.1015	.1025	.1036	.0210

CAPITALIZATION RATES

Assuming 2/3rds of Purchase Price Financed by Mortgage

15 YEARS AMORTIZATION: 6¼% TO 8%

Projection		6¼%	6½%	6¾%	7%	7½%	8%	$\frac{1}{s_{\overline{n}\rceil}}$
Interest Rate		6¼%	6½%	6¾%	7%	7½%	8%	
Annual Requirement (f)		.10296	.10464	.10620	.10788	.11124	.11472	
Coverage, Min. Rate		.06864	.06976	.07080	.07192	.07416	.07648	
Projection	Balance(b)	.763241	.766540	.770601	.774005	.780968	.787407	+ Dep. – App.
	Equity Yield	Basic Rate before Depreciation or Appreciation						
	4% .04	.0528	.0543	.0559	.0575	.0605	.0637	.1846
	5% .05	.0567	.0582	.0598	.0613	.0644	.0675	.1810
	6% .06	.0606	.0621	.0637	.0652	.0683	.0713	.1774
	7% .07	.0645	.0661	.0675	.0691	.0721	.0751	.1739
	8% .08	.0684	.0699	.0714	.0729	.0759	.0790	.1705
5 Years n = 5	9% .09	.0723	.0738	.0753	.0767	.0798	.0828	.1671
	10% .10	.0761	.0776	.0791	.0806	.0836	.0866	.1638
	11% .11	.0800	.0815	.0829	.0844	.0874	.0904	.1606
	12% .12	.0838	.0853	.0867	.0882	.0912	.0942	.1574
	13% .13	.0877	.0891	.0905	.0920	.0950	.0979	.1543
	14% .14	.0915	.0929	.0943	.0958	.0987	.1017	.1513
	15% .15	.0953	.0967	.0981	.0996	.1025	.1055	.1483
	Balance(b)	.439892	.443708	.449416	.453629	.462651	.470676	+ Dep. – App.
	Equity Yield	Basic Rate before Depreciation or Appreciation						
	4% .04	.0509	.0522	.0535	.0549	.0577	.0604	.0833
	5% .05	.0555	.0568	.0582	.0595	.0623	.0650	.0795
	6% .06	.0602	.0615	.0629	.0642	.0669	.0696	.0759
	7% .07	.0649	.0663	.0676	.0689	.0714	.0741	.0724
	8% .08	.0695	.0709	.0721	.0735	.0761	.0788	.0690
10 Years n = 10	9% .09	.0741	.0753	.0767	.0779	.0806	.0833	.0658
	10% .10	.0785	.0799	.0811	.0824	.0850	.0877	.0628
	11% .11	.0830	.0843	.0855	.0868	.0894	.0921	.0598
	12% .12	.0874	.0887	.0899	.0912	.0937	.0964	.0570
	13% .13	.0917	.0930	.0942	.0955	.0981	.1007	.0543
	14% .14	.0960	.0973	.0985	.0997	.1023	.1049	.0517
	15% .15	.1003	.1015	.1027	.1040	.1065	.1091	.0493
	Balance(b)	none	none	none	none	none	none	+ Dep. – App.
	Equity Yield	Basic Rate before Depreciation or Appreciation						
	4% .04	.0487	.0498	.0508	.0519	.0542	.0565	.0500
	5% .05	.0544	.0555	.0565	.0577	.0599	.0623	.0464
	6% .06	.0600	.0611	.0621	.0633	.0655	.0679	.0430
	7% .07	.0655	.0666	.0676	.0687	.0709	.0733	.0398
	8% .08	.0707	.0719	.0729	.0741	.0763	.0786	.0368
15 Years n = 15	9% .09	.0759	.0771	.0781	.0792	.0815	.0838	.0341
	10% .10	.0810	.0821	.0832	.0843	.0865	.0889	.0315
	11% .11	.0859	.0871	.0881	.0892	.0915	.0938	.0291
	12% .12	.0908	.0919	.0929	.0941	.0963	.0986	.0268
	13% .13	.0955	.0966	.0977	.0988	.1010	.1033	.0248
	14% .14	.1001	.1013	.1023	.1034	.1057	.1079	.0228
	15% .15	.1047	.1057	.1068	.1079	.1101	.1125	.0210

CAPITALIZATION RATES
Assuming 2/3rds of Purchase Price Financed by Mortgage
15 YEARS AMORTIZATION: 8¼ % TO 9½ %

Interest Rate			8¼ %	8½ %	8¾ %	9%	9¼ %	9½ %	$\frac{1}{s_{\overline{n}\rceil}}$
Annual Requirement (f)			.116416	.118168	.119933	.121711	.123503	.125306	
Coverage, Min. Rate			.077611	.078779	.079955	.081141	.082335	.083537	
Projection	Balance (b)		.790965	.794236	.797474	.800679	.803850	.806989	+ Dep.
	Equity	Yield	Basic Rate before Depreciation or Appreciation						– App.
	4%	.04	.0652	.0668	.0684	.0699	.0715	.0731	.1846
	5%	.05	.0691	.0706	.0722	.0738	.0753	.0769	.1810
	6%	.06	.0729	.0744	.0760	.0776	.0791	.0807	.1774
	7%	.07	.0767	.0783	.0798	.0814	.0829	.0845	.1739
	8%	.08	.0805	.0821	.0836	.0852	.0867	.0883	.1705
5 Years	9%	.09	.0843	.0859	.0874	.0889	.0905	.0920	.1671
n = 5	10%	.10	.0881	.0896	.0912	.0927	.0942	.0958	.1638
	11%	.11	.0919	.0934	.0949	.0965	.0980	.0995	.1606
	12%	.12	.0957	.0972	.0987	.1002	.1018	.1033	.1574
	13%	.13	.0994	.1009	.1025	.1040	.1055	.1070	.1543
	14%	.14	.1032	.1047	.1062	.1077	.1092	.1107	.1513
	15%	.15	.1069	.1084	.1099	.1114	.1129	.1145	.1483
	Balance (b)		.475646	.479973	.484293	.488606	.492910	.497205	+ Dep.
	Equity	Yield	Basic Rate before Depreciation or Appreciation						– App.
	4%	.04	.0618	.0632	.0647	.0661	.0675	.0690	.0833
	5%	.05	.0665	.0679	.0693	.0707	.0721	.0736	.0795
	6%	.06	.0711	.0725	.0739	.0753	.0767	.0781	.0759
	7%	.07	.0756	.0770	.0784	.0798	.0812	.0826	.0724
	8%	.08	.0801	.0815	.0829	.0843	.0857	.0871	.0690
10 Years	9%	.09	.0846	.0860	.0873	.0887	.0901	.0915	.0658
n = 10	10%	.10	.0890	.0904	.0917	.0931	.0945	.0958	.0627
	11%	.11	.0934	.0947	.0961	.0974	.0988	.1002	.0598
	12%	.12	.0977	.0990	.1004	.1017	.1031	.1044	.0570
	13%	.13	.1020	.1033	.1046	.1060	.1073	.1087	.0543
	14%	.14	.1062	.1075	.1088	.1102	.1115	.1129	.0517
	15%	.15	.1104	.1117	.1130	.1143	.1157	.1170	.0493
	Balance (b)		none	none	none	none	none	none	+ Dep.
	Equity	Yield	Basic Rate before Depreciation or Appreciation						– App.
	4%	.04	.0577	.0588	.0600	.0612	.0624	.0636	.0499
	5%	.05	.0634	.0646	.0657	.0669	.0681	.0693	.0463
	6%	.06	.0690	.0701	.0713	.0725	.0737	.0749	.0430
	7%	.07	.0744	.0756	.0768	.0779	.0791	.0803	.0398
	8%	.08	.0797	.0809	.0821	.0833	.0844	.0857	.0368
15 Years	9%	.09	.0849	.0861	.0872	.0884	.0896	.0908	.0341
n = 15	10%	.10	.0900	.0911	.0923	.0935	.0947	.0959	.0315
	11%	.11	.0949	.0961	.0972	.0984	.0996	.1008	.0291
	12%	.12	.0997	.1009	.1021	.1033	.1045	.1057	.0268
	13%	.13	.1045	.1056	.1068	.1080	.1092	.1104	.0247
	14%	.14	.1091	.1102	.1114	.1126	.1138	.1150	.0228
	15%	.15	.1136	.1148	.1159	.1171	.1183	.1195	.0210

CAPITALIZATION RATES
Assuming 2/3rds of Purchase Price Financed by Mortgage
15 YEARS AMORTIZATION: 9¾% TO 11%

Interest Rate / Annual Requirement (f) / Coverage, Min. Rate			9¾% / .127123 / .084749	10% / .128952 / .085968	10¼% / .130794 / .087196	10½% / .132647 / .088431	10¾% / .134513 / .089675	11% / .136391 / .090927	$\frac{1}{s_{\overline{n}|}}$
Projection	Balance (b)		.810094	.813166	.816204	.819208	.822178	.825115	+ Dep.
	Equity	Yield	Basic Rate before Depreciation or Appreciation						− App.
	4%	.04	.0747	.0763	.0779	.0795	.0811	.0827	.1846
	5%	.05	.0785	.0801	.0817	.0833	.0849	.0865	.1810
	6%	.06	.0823	.0839	.0855	.0871	.0886	.0902	.1774
	7%	.07	.0861	.0876	.0892	.0908	.0924	.0940	.1739
	8%	.08	.0898	.0914	.0930	.0946	.0961	.0977	.1705
5 Years	9%	.09	.0936	.0952	.0967	.0983	.0999	.1014	.1671
n = 5	10%	.10	.0973	.0989	.1005	.1020	.1036	.1052	.1638
	11%	.11	.1011	.1026	.1042	.1057	.1073	.1089	.1606
	12%	.12	.1048	.1064	.1079	.1095	.1110	.1126	.1574
	13%	.13	.1085	.1101	.1116	.1132	.1147	.1163	.1543
	14%	.14	.1123	.1138	.1153	.1169	.1184	.1200	.1513
	15%	.15	.1160	.1175	.1190	.1206	.1221	.1236	.1483
	Balance (b)		.501491	.505766	.510031	.514284	.518526	.522755	+ Dep.
	Equity	Yield	Basic Rate before Depreciation or Appreciation						− App.
	4%	.04	.0704	.0719	.0733	.0748	.0763	.0778	.0833
	5%	.05	.0750	.0764	.0779	.0794	.0808	.0823	.0795
	6%	.06	.0795	.0810	.0824	.0839	.0853	.0868	.0759
	7%	.07	.0840	.0855	.0869	.0883	.0898	.0912	.0724
	8%	.08	.0885	.0899	.0913	.0927	.0942	.0956	.0690
10 Years	9%	.09	.0929	.0943	.0957	.0971	.0985	.1000	.0658
n = 10	10%	.10	.0972	.0986	.1000	.1014	.1029	.1043	.0627
	11%	.11	.1015	.1029	.1043	.1057	.1071	.1086	.0598
	12%	.12	.1058	.1072	.1086	.1100	.1114	.1128	.0570
	13%	.13	.1100	.1114	.1128	.1142	.1156	.1170	.0543
	14%	.14	.1142	.1156	.1170	.1184	.1197	.1211	.0517
	15%	.15	.1184	.1197	.1211	.1225	.1239	.1253	.0493
	Balance (b)		none	none	none	none	none	none	+ Dep.
	Equity	Yield	Basic Rate before Depreciation or Appreciation						− App.
	4%	.04	.0648	.0660	.0672	.0685	.0697	.0710	.0499
	5%	.05	.0705	.0717	.0730	.0742	.0754	.0767	.0463
	6%	.06	.0761	.0773	.0786	.0798	.0810	.0823	.0430
	7%	.07	.0816	.0828	.0840	.0852	.0865	.0877	.0398
	8%	.08	.0869	.0881	.0893	.0905	.0918	.0930	.0368
15 Years	9%	.09	.0920	.0933	.0945	.0957	.0970	.0982	.0341
n = 15	10%	.10	.0971	.0983	.0995	.1008	.1020	.1033	.0315
	11%	.11	.1020	.1033	.1045	.1057	.1070	.1082	.0291
	12%	.12	.1069	.1081	.1093	.1105	.1118	.1130	.0268
	13%	.13	.1116	.1128	.1140	.1153	.1165	.1178	.0247
	14%	.14	.1162	.1174	.1187	.1199	.1211	.1224	.0228
	15%	.15	.1207	.1220	.1232	.1244	.1257	.1269	.0210

CAPITALIZATION RATES

Assuming 2/3rds of Purchase Price Financed by Mortgage

20 YEARS AMORTIZATION: 3¼% TO 4½%

Interest Rate Annual Requirement (f) Coverage, Min. Rate		3¼% .06816 .04544	3½% .06960 .04640	3¾% .07116 .04744	4% .07272 .04848	4¼% .07440 .04960	4½% .07596 .05064	$\frac{1}{s_{\overline{n}\vert}}$
Projection	Balance(b)	.806679	.811240	.815205	.819225	.822635	.826765	+ Dep. – App.
	Equity Yield	Basic Rate before Depreciation or Appreciation						
	4% .04	.0350	.0365	.0381	.0396	.0411	.0427	.1846
	5% .05	.0388	.0403	.0418	.0434	.0449	.0464	.1810
	6% .06	.0426	.0441	.0456	.0471	.0487	.0502	.1774
	7% .07	.0464	.0479	.0494	.0509	.0524	.0539	.1739
	8% .08	.0501	.0516	.0531	.0546	.0561	.0577	.1705
5 Years n = 5	9% .09	.0539	.0554	.0569	.0583	.0599	.0613	.1671
	10% .10	.0577	.0591	.0606	.0621	.0636	.0651	.1638
	11% .11	.0614	.0629	.0643	.0658	.0673	.0688	.1606
	12% .12	.0652	.0665	.0681	.0695	.0710	.0725	.1574
	13% .13	.0689	.0703	.0718	.0733	.0747	.0762	.1543
	14% .14	.0726	.0741	.0755	.0769	.0784	.0799	.1513
	15% .15	.0763	.0777	.0792	.0806	.0821	.0835	.1483
	Balance(b)	.579297	.586436	.592363	.589499	.603357	.609909	+ Dep. – App.
	Equity Yield	Basic Rate before Depreciation or Appreciation						
	4% .04	.0354	.0368	.0381	.0395	.0411	.0425	0833
	5% .05	.0398	.0411	.0425	.0439	.0453	.0467	.0795
	6% .06	.0442	.0455	.0469	.0482	.0495	.0509	.0759
	7% .07	.0485	.0498	.0511	.0525	.0538	.0552	.0724
	8% .08	.0527	.0541	.0553	.0567	.0580	.0594	.0690
10 Years n = 10	9% .09	.0570	.0583	.0596	.0609	.0622	.0635	.0658
	10% .10	.0612	.0625	.0637	.0651	.0663	.0677	.0628
	11% .11	.0653	.0666	.0679	.0691	.0705	.0718	.0598
	12% .12	.0695	.0707	.0720	.0733	.0745	.0759	.0570
	13% .13	.0735	.0748	.0761	.0773	.0786	.0799	.0543
	14% .14	.0776	.0788	.0801	.0813	.0826	.0839	.0517
	15% .15	.0817	.0829	.0841	.0853	.0866	.0879	.0493

CAPITALIZATION RATES

Assuming 2/3rds of Purchase Price Financed by Mortgage

20 YEARS AMORTIZATION: 3¼% TO 4½%

Interest Rate Annual Requirement (f) Coverage, Min. Rate		3¼% .06816 .04544	3½% .06960 .04640	3¾% .07116 .04744	4% .07272 .04848	4¼% .07440 .04960	4½% .07596 .05064	$\frac{1}{s_{\overline{n}\vert}}$
Projection	Balance(b)	.311852	.318709	.323644	.328994	.332264	.338450	+ Dep. – App.
	Equity Yield	Basic Rate before Depreciation or Appreciation						
	4% .04	.0359	.0371	.0383	.0395	.0407	.0419	.0500
	5% .05	.0409	.0421	.0432	.0445	.0457	.0469	.0464
	6% .06	.0457	.0469	.0481	.0493	.0505	.0517	.0430
	7% .07	.0505	.0517	.0529	.0540	.0553	.0565	.0398
	8% .08	.0552	.0563	.0575	.0587	.0599	.0611	.0368
15 Years	9% .09	.0598	.0609	.0621	.0633	.0645	.0657	.0341
n = 15	10% .10	.0643	.0655	.0666	.0677	.0689	.0701	.0315
	11% .11	.0688	.0699	.0710	.0721	.0733	.0745	.0291
	12% .12	.0731	.0743	.0753	.0765	.0777	.0788	.0268
	13% .13	.0775	.0785	.0797	.0807	.0819	.0831	.0248
	14% .14	.0817	.0827	.0838	.0849	.0861	.0873	.0228
	15% .15	.0858	.0869	.0880	.0891	.0903	.0914	.0210
	Balance(b)	none	none	none	none	none	none	+ Dep. – App.
	Equity Yield	Basic Rate before Depreciation or Appreciation						
	4% .04	.0364	.0373	.0384	.0395	.0405	.0416	.0336
	5% .05	.0419	.0429	.0439	.0450	.0461	.0471	.0303
	6% .06	.0473	.0483	.0493	.0504	.0515	.0525	.0272
	7% .07	.0525	.0535	.0545	.0556	.0567	.0577	.0244
	8% .08	.0575	.0585	.0595	.0606	.0617	.0627	.0219
20 Years	9% .09	.0624	.0634	.0644	.0655	.0666	.0676	.0196
n = 20	10% .10	.0671	.0681	.0691	.0702	.0713	.0723	.0175
	11% .11	.0717	.0727	.0737	.0748	.0759	.0769	.0156
	12% .12	.0762	.0771	.0782	.0793	.0803	.0814	.0139
	13% .13	.0805	.0815	.0825	.0836	.0847	.0857	.0124
	14% .14	.0848	.0857	.0868	.0879	.0889	.0900	.0110
	15% .15	.0889	.0899	.0909	.0920	.0931	.0941	.0098

CAPITALIZATION RATES

Assuming 2/3rds of Purchase Price Financed by Mortgage

20 YEARS AMORTIZATION: 4¾% TO 6%

Interest Rate / Annual Requirement (f) / Coverage, Min. Rate		4¾% .07764 .05176	5% .07920 .05280	5¼% .08088 .05392	5½% .08256 .05504	5¾% .08436 .05624	6% .08604 .05736	$\frac{1}{s_{\overline{n}\rceil}}$
Projection	Balance(b)	.830277	.834519	.838135	.841804	.844831	.848599	+ Dep. − App.
	Equity Yield	Basic Rate before Depreciation or Appreciation						
	4% .04	.0442	.0458	.0474	.0490	.0505	.0521	.1846
	5% .05	.0480	.0496	.0511	.0526	.0542	.0558	.1810
	6% .06	.0518	.0533	.0548	.0564	.0580	.0595	.1774
	7% .07	.0555	.0570	.0586	.0601	.0616	.0632	.1739
	8% .08	.0592	.0607	.0622	.0638	.0653	.0669	.1705
5 Years	9% .09	.0629	.0644	.0660	.0675	.0690	.0706	.1671
n = 5	10% .10	.0666	.0681	.0696	.0712	.0727	.0742	.1638
	11% .11	.0703	.0718	.0733	.0748	.0764	.0779	.1606
	12% .12	.0740	.0755	.0770	.0785	.0800	.0815	.1574
	13% .13	.0777	.0792	.0806	.0822	.0836	.0852	.1543
	14% .14	.0817	.0828	.0843	.0858	.0873	.0888	.1513
	15% .15	.0850	.0865	.0880	.0894	.0910	.0924	.1483
	Balance(b)	.615155	.622146	.627803	.633664	.638118	.644382	+ Dep. − App.
	Equity Yield	Basic Rate before Depreciation or Appreciation						
	4% .04	.0438	.0452	.0466	.0481	.0495	.0510	.0833
	5% .05	.0481	.0495	.0509	.0523	.0538	.0552	.0795
	6% .06	.0524	.0538	.0552	.0566	.0580	.0594	.0759
	7% .07	.0566	.0580	.0594	.0608	.0622	.0636	.0724
	8% .08	.0608	.0621	.0635	.0649	.0663	.0677	.0690
10 Years	9% .09	.0649	.0663	.0676	.0690	.0704	.0719	.0658
n = 10	10% .10	.0690	.0704	.0718	.0731	.0745	.0759	.0628
	11% .11	.0732	.0744	.0758	.0772	.0785	.0799	.0598
	12% .12	.0772	.0785	.0798	.0812	.0826	.0839	.0570
	13% .13	.0812	.0825	.0838	.0852	.0865	.0879	.0543
	14% .14	.0852	.0865	.0878	.0891	.0905	.0918	.0517
	15% .15	.0892	.0904	.0918	.0930	.0944	.0958	.0493

CAPITALIZATION RATES

Assuming 2/3rds of Purchase Price Financed by Mortgage

20 YEARS AMORTIZATION: 4¾% TO 6%

Interest Rate Annual Requirement (f) Coverage, Min. Rate		4¾% .07764 .05176	5% .07920 .05280	5¼% .08088 .05392	5½% .08256 .05504	5¾% .08436 .05624	6% .08604 .05736	$\frac{1}{s_{\overline{n}\vert}}$
Projection	Balance(b)	.342493	.349597	.354491	.359815	.362740	.368924	+ Dep. – App.
	Equity Yield	Basic Rate before Depreciation or Appreciation						
	4% .04	.0432	.0445	.0458	.0471	.0484	.0497	.0500
	5% .05	.0482	.0494	.0507	.0520	.0532	.0546	.0464
	6% .06	.0530	.0542	.0555	.0568	.0580	.0594	.0430
	7% .07	.0577	.0590	.0602	.0615	.0627	.0640	.0398
	8% .08	.0624	.0636	.0648	.0660	.0673	.0686	.0368
15 Years n = 15	9% .09	.0669	.0681	.0693	.0706	.0718	.0731	.0341
	10% .10	.0714	.0726	.0738	.0750	.0762	.0775	.0315
	11% .11	.0758	.0769	.0781	.0794	.0806	.0818	.0291
	12% .12	.0800	.0812	.0824	.0836	.0849	.0861	.0268
	13% .13	.0843	.0854	.0866	.0878	.0891	.0904	.0248
	14% .14	.0885	.0896	.0908	.0920	.0933	.0945	.0228
	15% .15	.0925	.0938	.0949	.0961	.0974	.0986	.0210
	Balance(b)	none	none	none	none	none	none	+ Dep. – App.
	Equity Yield	Basic Rate before Depreciation or Appreciation						
	4% .04	.0428	.0438	.0449	.0460	.0472	.0484	.0336
	5% .05	.0483	.0494	.0504	.0516	.0528	.0539	.0303
	6% .06	.0537	.0547	.0558	.0570	.0582	.0593	.0272
	7% .07	.0589	.0599	.0610	.0622	.0634	.0645	.0244
	8% .08	.0639	.0650	.0661	.0672	.0684	.0695	.0219
20 Years n = 20	9% .09	.0688	.0698	.0710	.0720	.0732	.0744	.0196
	10% .10	.0735	.0746	.0756	.0768	.0780	.0791	.0175
	11% .11	.0781	.0792	.0802	.0814	.0826	.0837	.0156
	12% .12	.0826	.0836	.0847	.0858	.0870	.0882	.0139
	13% .13	.0869	.0880	.0891	.0902	.0914	.0925	.0124
	14% .14	.0912	.0922	.0933	.0944	.0956	.0968	.0110
	15% .15	.0953	.0964	.0974	.0986	.0998	.1009	.0098

CAPITALIZATION RATES

Assuming 2/3rds of Purchase Price Financed by Mortgage

20 YEARS AMORTIZATION: 6¼% TO 8%

Interest Rate Annual Requirement (f) Coverage, Min. Rate		6¼% .08772 .05848	6½% .08952 .05968	6¾% .09132 .06088	7% .09312 .06208	7½% .09672 .06448	8% .10044 .06696	$\frac{1}{s_{\overline{n}\rceil}}$
Projection	Balance (b)	.852421	.855589	.858804	.862064	.868726	.874845	+ Dep. – App.
	Equity Yield	Basic Rate before Depreciation or Appreciation						
	4% .04	.0536	.0552	.0568	.0585	.0617	.0649	.1846
	5% .05	.0573	.0589	.0605	.0621	.0653	.0685	.1810
	6% .06	.0610	.0626	.0642	.0657	.0689	.0721	.1774
	7% .07	.0647	.0663	.0679	.0695	.0726	.0758	.1739
	8% .08	.0684	.0699	.0715	.0731	.0763	.0794	.1705
5 Years n = 5	9% .09	.0721	.0736	.0752	.0767	.0799	.0831	.1671
	10% .10	.0757	.0773	.0788	.0804	.0835	.0867	.1638
	11% .11	.0793	.0809	.0825	.0840	.0871	.0903	.1606
	12% .12	.0830	.0845	.0861	.0876	.0907	.0939	.1574
	13% .13	.0867	.0882	.0897	.0912	.0943	.0975	.1543
	14% .14	.0903	.0918	.0933	.0949	.0979	.1010	.1513
	15% .15	.0939	.0954	.0969	.0985	.1015	.1046	.1483
	Balance (b)	.650867	.655896	.661113	.666523	.677946	.688382	+ Dep. – App.
	Equity Yield	Basic Rate before Depreciation or Appreciation						
	4% .04	.0524	.0539	.0554	.0569	.0599	.0630	.0833
	5% .05	.0567	.0581	.0596	.0611	.0641	.0671	.0795
	6% .06	.0608	.0623	.0637	.0652	.0682	.0712	.0759
	7% .07	.0650	.0664	.0679	.0693	.0723	.0753	.0724
	8% .08	.0691	.0705	.0720	.0734	.0763	.0793	.0690
10 Years n = 10	9% .09	.0732	.0746	.0760	.0775	.0803	.0833	.0658
	10% .10	.0772	.0787	.0801	.0815	.0843	.0873	.0628
	11% .11	.0813	.0827	.0841	.0855	.0883	.0912	.0598
	12% .12	.0853	.0866	.0880	.0894	.0923	.0951	.0570
	13% .13	.0892	.0906	.0919	.0933	.0962	.0990	.0543
	14% .14	.0931	.0945	.0959	.0973	.1001	.1029	.0517
	15% .15	.0970	.0984	.0998	.1011	.1039	.1067	.0493

CAPITALIZATION RATES

Assuming 2/3rds of Purchase Price Financed by Mortgage

20 YEARS AMORTIZATION: 6¼% TO 8%

Interest Rate / Annual Requirement (f) / Coverage, Min. Rate		6¼% / .08772 / .05848	6½% / .08952 / .05968	6¾% / .09132 / .06088	7% / .09312 / .06208	7½% / .09672 / .06448	8% / .10044 / .06696	$\frac{1}{s_{\overline{n}\rvert}}$
Projection	Balance (b)	.375599	.379757	.384323	.389320	.400687	.410581	+ Dep. − App.
	Equity Yield	Basic Rate before Depreciation or Appreciation						
	4% .04	.0510	.0523	.0537	.0551	.0579	.0607	.0500
	5% .05	.0559	.0572	.0585	.0599	.0626	.0654	.0464
	6% .06	.0606	.0619	.0633	.0646	.0673	.0701	.0430
	7% .07	.0653	.0666	.0679	.0692	.0719	.0747	.0398
	8% .08	.0698	.0711	.0725	.0738	.0765	.0792	.0368
15 Years n = 15	9% .09	.0743	.0756	.0769	.0782	.0809	.0836	.0341
	10% .10	.0787	.0800	.0813	.0826	.0853	.0879	.0315
	11% .11	.0831	.0843	.0857	.0869	.0895	.0922	.0291
	12% .12	.0873	.0886	.0899	.0912	.0938	.0965	.0268
	13% .13	.0915	.0928	.0941	.0953	.0979	.1007	.0248
	14% .14	.0957	.0969	.0982	.0995	.1021	.1047	.0228
	15% .15	.0997	.1010	.1023	.1035	.1061	.1087	.0210
	Balance (b)	none	none	none	none	none	none	+ Dep. − App.
	Equity Yield	Basic Rate before Depreciation or Appreciation						
	4% .04	.0494	.0506	.0518	.0530	.0554	.0579	.0336
	5% .05	.0550	.0562	.0574	.0586	.0610	.0635	.0303
	6% .06	.0603	.0615	.0627	.0639	.0663	.0689	.0272
	7% .07	.0656	.0668	.0680	.0692	.0715	.0740	.0244
	8% .08	.0706	.0718	.0730	.0742	.0766	.0791	.0219
20 Years n = 20	9% .09	.0755	.0767	.0779	.0791	.0815	.0839	.0196
	10% .10	.0802	.0814	.0826	.0838	.0862	.0887	.0175
	11% .11	.0848	.0860	.0872	.0884	.0908	.0933	.0156
	12% .12	.0893	.0905	.0917	.0929	.0953	.0977	.0139
	13% .13	.0936	.0948	.0960	.0972	.0966	.1021	.0124
	14% .14	.0979	.0991	.1003	.1015	.1039	.1063	.0110
	15% .15	.1020	.1032	.1044	.1056	.1080	.1105	.0098

CAPITALIZATION RATES
Assuming 2/3rds of Purchase Price Financed by Mortgage

20 YEARS AMORTIZATION: 8¼% TO 9½%

Interest Rate			8¼%	8½%	8¾%	9%	9¼%	9½%	$\frac{1}{s_{\overline{n}\rceil}}$
Annual Requirement (f)			.102247	.104138	.106045	.107967	.109904	.111855	
Coverage, Min. Rate			.068165	.069425	.070696	.071978	.073269	.074570	
Projection	Balance (b)		.878291	.881271	.884198	.887070	.889888	.892653	+ Dep.
	Equity	Yield	Basic Rate before Depreciation or Appreciation						− App.
	4%	.04	.0665	.0681	.0698	.0714	.0730	.0747	.1846
	5%	.05	.0701	.0718	.0734	.0750	.0767	.0783	.1810
	6%	.06	.0738	.0754	.0770	.0786	.0802	.0819	.1774
	7%	.07	.0774	.0790	.0806	.0822	.0838	.0855	.1739
	8%	.08	.0810	.0826	.0842	.0858	.0874	.0890	.1705
5 Years	9%	.09	.0846	.0862	.0878	.0894	.0910	.0926	.1671
n = 5	10%	.10	.0882	.0898	.0914	.0930	.0946	.0962	.1638
	11%	.11	.0918	.0934	.0950	.0966	.0981	.0997	.1606
	12%	.12	.0954	.0970	.0985	.1001	.1017	.1033	.1574
	13%	.13	.0990	.1005	.1021	.1037	.1053	.1069	.1543
	14%	.14	.1026	.1041	.1057	.1073	.1088	.1104	.1513
	15%	.15	.1061	.1077	.1092	.1108	.1124	.1140	.1483
	Balance (b)		.694698	.699938	.705125	.710258	.715338	.720362	+ Dep.
	Equity	Yield	Basic Rate before Depreciation or Appreciation						− App.
	4%	.04	.0645	.0661	.0677	.0692	.0708	.0724	.0833
	5%	.05	.0686	.0702	.0717	.0733	.0748	.0764	.0795
	6%	.06	.0727	.0742	.0758	.0773	.0789	.0804	.0759
	7%	.07	.0768	.0783	.0798	.0813	.0829	.0844	.0724
	8%	.08	.0808	.0823	.0838	.0853	.0868	.0884	.0690
10 Years	9%	.09	.0848	.0863	.0878	.0893	.0908	.0923	.0658
n = 10	10%	.10	.0887	.0902	.0917	.0932	.0947	.0962	.0627
	11%	.11	.0927	.0941	.0956	.0971	.0986	.1001	.0598
	12%	.12	.0966	.0980	.0995	.1010	.1025	.1039	.0570
	13%	.13	.1004	.1019	.1034	.1048	.1063	.1078	.0543
	14%	.14	.1043	.1057	.1072	.1087	.1101	.1116	.0517
	15%	.15	.1081	.1096	.1110	.1125	.1139	.1154	.0493
	Balance (b)		.417756	.422987	.428211	.433428	.438635	.443832	+ Dep.
	Equity	Yield	Basic Rate before Depreciation or Appreciation						− App.
	4%	.04	.0621	.0635	.0650	.0664	.0679	.0694	.0499
	5%	.05	.0668	.0683	.0697	.0711	.0726	.0741	.0463
	6%	.06	.0715	.0729	.0743	.0758	.0772	.0786	.0430
	7%	.07	.0761	.0775	.0789	.0803	.0817	.0831	.0398
	8%	.08	.0805	.0819	.0833	.0847	.0862	.0876	.0368
15 Years	9%	.09	.0849	.0863	.0877	.0891	.0905	.0919	.0341
n = 15	10%	.10	.0893	.0907	.0920	.0934	.0948	.0962	.0315
	11%	.11	.0935	.0949	.0963	.0977	.0991	.1005	.0291
	12%	.12	.0978	.0991	.1005	.1018	.1032	.1046	.0268
	13%	.13	.1019	.1032	.1046	.1060	.1073	.1087	.0247
	14%	.14	.1060	.1073	.1087	.1100	.1114	.1128	.0228
	15%	.15	.1100	.1113	.1127	.1140	.1154	.1168	.0210

CAPITALIZATION RATES
Assuming 2/3rds of Purchase Price Financed by Mortgage

20 YEARS AMORTIZATION: 9¾% TO 11%

Interest Rate			9¾%	10%	10¼%	10½%	10¾%	11%	$\frac{1}{s_{\overline{n}\rceil}}$
Annual Requirement (f)			.113822	.115802	.117797	.119805	.121827	.123862	
Coverage, Min. Rate			.075881	.077201	.078531	.079870	.081218	.082575	
Projection	Balance (b)		.895365	.898024	.900630	.903185	.905687	.908139	+ Dep.
	Equity	Yield	Basic Rate before Depreciation or Appreciation						– App.
	4%	.04	.0763	.0780	.0796	.0813	.0829	.0846	.1846
	5%	.05	.0799	.0816	.0832	.0849	.0865	.0882	.1810
	6%	.06	.0835	.0851	.0868	.0884	.0901	.0917	.1774
	7%	.07	.0871	.0887	.0903	.0920	.0936	.0953	.1739
	8%	.08	.0907	.0923	.0939	.0955	.0972	.0988	.1705
5 Years	9%	.09	.0942	.0958	.0975	.0991	.1007	.1023	.1671
n = 5	10%	.10	.0978	.0994	.1010	.1026	.1043	.1059	.1638
	11%	.11	.1013	.1030	.1046	.1062	.1078	.1094	.1606
	12%	.12	.1049	.1065	.1081	.1097	.1113	.1129	.1574
	13%	.13	.1085	.1100	.1116	.1132	.1148	.1165	.1543
	14%	.14	.1120	.1136	.1152	.1168	.1184	.1200	.1513
	15%	.15	.1155	.1171	.1187	.1203	.1219	.1235	.1483
	Balance (b)		.725330	.730243	.735098	.739896	.744637	.749320	+ Dep.
	Equity	Yield	Basic Rate before Depreciation or Appreciation						– App.
	4%	.04	.0740	.0756	.0772	.0788	.0804	.0820	.0833
	5%	.05	.0780	.0796	.0812	.0828	.0843	.0860	.0795
	6%	.06	.0820	.0836	.0851	.0867	.0883	.0899	.0759
	7%	.07	.0860	.0875	.0891	.0907	.0922	.0938	.0724
	8%	.08	.0899	.0915	.0930	.0946	.0961	.0977	.0690
10 Years	9%	.09	.0938	.0954	.0969	.0985	.1000	.1016	.0658
n = 10	10%	.10	.0977	.0993	.1008	.1023	.1039	.1054	.0627
	11%	.11	.1016	.1031	.1046	.1062	.1077	.1092	.0598
	12%	.12	.1054	.1070	.1085	.1100	.1115	.1131	.0570
	13%	.13	.1093	.1108	.1123	.1138	.1153	.1168	.0543
	14%	.14	.1131	.1146	.1161	.1176	.1191	.1206	.0517
	15%	.15	.1169	.1183	.1198	.1213	.1228	.1243	.0493
	Balance (b)		.449018	.454190	.459350	.464494	.469623	.474734	+ Dep.
	Equity	Yield	Basic Rate before Depreciation or Appreciation						– App.
	4%	.04	.0709	.0724	.0739	.0754	.0769	.0784	.0499
	5%	.05	.0755	.0770	.0785	.0800	.0815	.0830	.0463
	6%	.06	.0801	.0816	.0830	.0845	.0860	.0875	.0430
	7%	.07	.0846	.0861	.0875	.0890	.0905	.0920	.0398
	8%	.08	.0890	.0905	.0919	.0934	.0949	.0963	.0368
15 Years	9%	.09	.0934	.0948	.0963	.0977	.0992	.1006	.0341
n = 15	10%	.10	.0977	.0991	.1005	.1020	.1034	.1049	.0315
	11%	.11	.1019	.1033	.1047	.1062	.1076	.1091	.0291
	12%	.12	.1060	.1074	.1089	.1103	.1117	.1132	.0268
	13%	.13	.1101	.1115	.1129	.1144	.1158	.1172	.0247
	14%	.14	.1142	.1156	.1170	.1184	.1198	.1213	.0228
	15%	.15	.1182	.1196	.1210	.1224	.1238	.1252	.0210

CAPITALIZATION RATES

Assuming 2/3rds of Purchase Price Financed by Mortgage

25 YEARS AMORTIZATION: 3¼% TO 4½%

Interest Rate Annual Requirement (f) Coverage, Min. Rate		3¼% .05856 .03904	3½% .06012 .04008	3¾% .06180 .04120	4% .06336 .04224	4¼% .06504 .04336	4½% .06672 .04448	$\frac{1}{s_{\overline{n}\rvert}}$
Projection	Balance(b)	.858723	.862958	.866592	.870938	.874677	.878467	+ Dep. – App.
	Equity Yield	Basic Rate before Depreciation or Appreciation						
	4% .04	.0350	.0365	.0381	.0397	.0413	.0429	.1846
	5% .05	.0387	.0402	.0418	.0433	.0449	.0465	.1810
	6% .06	.0423	.0439	.0455	.0470	.0485	.0501	.1774
	7% .07	.0460	.0475	.0491	.0506	.0522	.0537	.1739
	8% .08	.0497	.0512	.0527	.0543	.0558	.0573	.1705
5 Years n = 5	9% .09	.0533	.0548	.0563	.0579	.0594	.0609	.1671
	10% .10	.0569	.0585	.0600	.0615	.0630	.0645	.1638
	11% .11	.0606	.0621	.0636	.0651	.0666	.0681	.1606
	12% .12	.0642	.0657	.0672	.0687	.0702	.0717	.1574
	13% .13	.0679	.0693	.0708	.0723	.0738	.0753	.1543
	14% .14	.0715	.0729	.0744	.0759	.0774	.0789	.1513
	15% .15	.0751	.0765	.0780	.0795	.0810	.0825	.1483
	Balance(b)	.692554	.699748	.705717	.713354	.719739	.726332	+ Dep. – App.
	Equity Yield	Basic Rate before Depreciation or Appreciation						
	4% .04	.0353	.0367	.0382	.0397	.0411	.0426	.0833
	5% .05	.0394	.0409	.0423	.0437	.0452	.0467	.0795
	6% .06	.0435	.0449	.0463	.0477	.0492	.0507	.0759
	7% .07	.0475	.0489	.0503	.0517	.0532	.0546	.0724
	8% .08	.0516	.0529	.0543	.0557	.0571	.0586	.0690
10 Years n = 10	9% .09	.0555	.0569	.0583	.0597	.0611	.0625	.0658
	10% .10	.0595	.0609	.0623	.0636	.0650	.0664	.0628
	11% .11	.0635	.0648	.0661	.0675	.0689	.0703	.0598
	12% .12	.0674	.0687	.0701	.0713	.0727	.0741	.0570
	13% .13	.0713	.0725	.0739	.0752	.0765	.0779	.0543
	14% .14	.0751	.0764	.0777	.0791	.0804	.0817	.0517
	15% .15	.0789	.0803	.0815	.0829	.0842	.0855	.0493

CAPITALIZATION RATES

Assuming 2/3rds of Purchase Price Financed by Mortgage

25 YEARS AMORTIZATION: 3¼% TO 4½%

	Interest Rate	3¼%	3½%	3¾%	4%	4¼%	4½%	$\frac{1}{s_{\overline{n}\rvert}}$
	Annual Requirement (f)	.05856	.06012	.06180	.06336	.06504	.06672	
	Coverage, Min. Rate	.03904	.04008	.04120	.04224	.04336	.04448	
Projection	Balance(b)	.497108	.505375	.511722	.520944	.528189	.535889	+ Dep. – App.
	Equity Yield	Basic Rate before Depreciation or Appreciation						
	4% .04	.0357	.0369	.0383	.0397	.0410	.0424	.0500
	5% .05	.0402	.0415	.0428	.0441	.0455	.0468	.0464
	6% .06	.0447	.0459	.0472	.0485	.0499	.0512	.0430
	7% .07	.0491	.0503	.0516	.0529	.0542	.0555	.0398
	8% .08	.0534	.0546	.0559	.0571	.0585	.0598	.0368
15 Years n = 15	9% .09	.0577	.0589	.0601	.0614	.0627	.0639	.0341
	10% .10	.0619	.0631	.0643	.0655	.0668	.0681	.0315
	11% .11	.0660	.0672	.0684	.0697	.0709	.0722	.0291
	12% .12	.0701	.0713	.0725	.0737	.0749	.0762	.0268
	13% .13	.0741	.0753	.0765	.0777	.0789	.0802	.0248
	14% .14	.0781	.0793	.0805	.0817	.0829	.0841	.0228
	15% .15	.0820	.0831	.0844	.0855	.0867	.0880	.0210
	Balance(b)	.267227	.273887	.277788	.286012	.291376	.297495	+ Dep. – App.
	Equity Yield	Basic Rate before Depreciation or Appreciation						
	4% .04	.0360	.0372	.0384	.0396	.0409	.0421	.0336
	5% .05	.0409	.0421	.0433	.0445	.0457	.0470	.0303
	6% .06	.0458	.0469	.0481	.0493	.0505	.0517	.0272
	7% .07	.0505	.0516	.0528	.0540	.0552	.0564	.0244
	8% .08	.0551	.0562	.0573	.0585	.0597	.0609	.0219
20 Years n = 20	9% .09	.0595	.0607	.0618	.0629	.0641	.0653	.0196
	10% .10	.0639	.0650	.0661	.0673	.0685	.0697	.0175
	11% .11	.0681	.0692	.0704	.0715	.0727	.0739	.0156
	12% .12	.0723	.0734	.0745	.0757	.0768	.0780	.0139
	13% .13	.0763	.0775	.0786	.0797	.0809	.0821	.0124
	14% .14	.0803	.0815	.0826	.0837	.0849	.0860	.0110
	15% .15	.0843	.0854	.0865	.0876	.0887	.0899	.0098
	Balance(b)	none	none	none	none	none	none	+ Dep. – App.
	Equity Yield	Basic Rate before Depreciation or Appreciation						
	4% .04	.0364	.0374	.0385	.0396	.0407	.0418	.0240
	5% .05	.0417	.0428	.0439	.0449	.0461	.0472	.0210
	6% .06	.0469	.0479	.0491	.0501	.0512	.0523	.0182
	7% .07	.0519	.0529	.0540	.0551	.0562	.0573	.0158
	8% .08	.0566	.0577	.0587	.0598	.0609	.0621	.0137
25 Years n = 25	9% .09	.0612	.0622	.0633	.0644	.0655	.0666	.0118
	10% .10	.0656	.0667	.0678	.0688	.0699	.0711	.0102
	11% .11	.0699	.0709	.0721	.0731	.0742	.0753	.0088
	12% .12	.0741	.0751	.0762	.0773	.0784	.0795	.0075
	13% .13	.0781	.0791	.0803	.0813	.0824	.0835	.0064
	14% .14	.0821	.0831	.0842	.0853	.0864	.0875	.0055
	15% .15	.0859	.0869	.0881	.0891	.0903	.0913	.0047

CAPITALIZATION RATES

Assuming 2/3rds of Purchase Price Financed by Mortgage

25 YEARS AMORTIZATION: 4¾% TO 6%

Projection		Interest Rate	4¾%	5%	5¼%	5½%	5¾%	6%	$\frac{1}{s_{\overline{n}\rceil}}$
		Annual Requirement (f)	.06852	.07020	.07200	.07380	.07560	.07740	
		Coverage, Min. Rate	.04568	.04680	.04800	.04920	.05040	.05160	
Projection	Balance(b)		.881633	.885523	.888782	.892087	.895437	.898833	+ Dep. − App.
	Equity Yield		Basic Rate before Depreciation or Appreciation						
	4%	.04	.0445	.0461	.0477	.0493	.0509	.0525	.1846
	5%	.05	.0481	.0497	.0513	.0529	.0545	.0561	.1810
	6%	.06	.0517	.0533	.0549	.0565	.0581	.0597	.1774
	7%	.07	.0553	.0569	.0585	.0601	.0616	.0632	.1739
	8%	.08	.0589	.0605	.0621	.0636	.0652	.0668	.1705
5 Years	9%	.09	.0625	.0641	.0656	.0672	.0688	.0703	.1671
n = 5	10%	.10	.0661	.0677	.0692	.0707	.0723	.0739	.1638
	11%	.11	.0697	.0712	.0729	.0743	.0759	.0775	.1606
	12%	.12	.0733	.0748	.0764	.0779	.0795	.0810	.1574
	13%	.13	.0769	.0784	.0800	.0815	.0830	.0845	.1543
	14%	.14	.0804	.0819	.0835	.0850	.0865	.0881	.1513
	15%	.15	.0840	.0855	.0871	.0885	.0901	.0916	.1483
	Balance(b)		.731604	.738608	.744262	.750104	.756141	.762375	+ Dep. − App.
	Equity Yield		Basic Rate before Depreciation or Appreciation						
	4%	.04	.0441	.0456	.0471	.0487	.0502	.0517	.0833
	5%	.05	.0481	.0496	.0511	.0526	.0541	.0557	.0795
	6%	.06	.0521	.0536	.0551	.0566	.0581	.0596	.0759
	7%	.07	.0561	.0575	.0590	.0605	.0620	.0635	.0724
	8%	.08	.0600	.0615	.0629	.0644	.0659	.0673	.0690
10 Years	9%	.09	.0639	.0653	.0668	.0683	.0697	.0712	.0658
n = 10	10%	.10	.0678	.0692	.0707	.0721	.0735	.0750	.0628
	11%	.11	.0717	.0731	.0745	.0759	.0773	.0788	.0598
	12%	.12	.0755	.0769	.0783	.0797	.0811	.0826	.0570
	13%	.13	.0793	.0807	.0821	.0835	.0849	.0863	.0543
	14%	.14	.0831	.0845	.0859	.0873	.0887	.0901	.0517
	15%	.15	.0869	.0883	.0896	.0910	.0924	.0938	.0493

CAPITALIZATION RATES

Assuming 2/3rds of Purchase Price Financed by Mortgage

25 YEARS AMORTIZATION: 4¾% TO 6%

Interest Rate		4¾%	5%	5¼%	5½%	5¾%	6%	$\frac{1}{s_{\overline{n}\vert}}$
Annual Requirement (f)		.06852	.07020	.07200	.07380	.07560	.07740	
Coverage, Min. Rate		.04568	.04680	.04800	.04920	.05040	.05160	
Projection	Balance (b)	.541447	.550064	.556469	.563299	.570573	.578313	+ Dep. – App.
	Equity Yield	Basic Rate before Depreciation or Appreciation						
	4% .04	.0437	.0451	.0466	.0480	.0495	.0509	.0500
	5% .05	.0482	.0496	.0510	.0524	.0538	.0553	.0464
	6% .06	.0525	.0539	.0553	.0567	.0581	.0595	.0430
	7% .07	.0569	.0582	.0596	.0610	.0624	.0637	.0398
	8% .08	.0611	.0625	.0638	.0651	.0665	.0679	.0368
15 Years n = 15	9% .09	.0653	.0666	.0679	.0693	.0706	.0721	.0341
	10% .10	.0694	.0707	.0721	.0734	.0747	.0761	.0315
	11% .11	.0735	.0747	.0761	.0774	.0787	.0801	.0291
	12% .12	.0775	.0788	.0801	.0814	.0827	.0841	.0268
	13% .13	.0815	.0827	.0841	.0853	.0866	.0880	.0248
	14% .14	.0854	.0867	.0879	.0893	.0906	.0919	.0228
	15% .15	.0893	.0905	.0918	.0931	.0943	.0957	.0210
	Balance (b)	.300425	.308093	.312443	.317518	.323365	.330040	+ Dep. – App.
	Equity Yield	Basic Rate before Depreciation or Appreciation						
	4% .04	.0433	.0447	.0459	.0473	.0486	.0499	.0336
	5% .05	.0483	.0495	.0508	.0521	.0534	.0547	.0303
	6% .06	.0530	.0543	.0555	.0569	.0581	.0595	.0272
	7% .07	.0577	.0589	.0602	.0615	.0627	.0641	.0244
	8% .08	.0623	.0634	.0647	.0659	.0672	.0685	.0219
20 Years n = 20	9% .09	.0666	.0678	.0691	.0703	.0716	.0729	.0196
	10% .10	.0709	.0721	.0734	.0747	.0759	.0772	.0175
	11% .11	.0751	.0763	.0775	.0788	.0801	.0813	.0156
	12% .12	.0792	.0804	.0817	.0829	.0841	.0854	.0139
	13% .13	.0833	.0845	.0857	.0869	.0882	.0894	.0124
	14% .14	.0873	.0884	.0897	.0909	.0921	.0934	.0110
	15% .15	.0911	.0923	.0935	.0948	.0960	.0973	.0098
	Balance (b)	none	none	none	none	none	none	+ Dep. – App.
	Equity Yield	Basic Rate before Depreciation or Appreciation						
	4% .04	.0430	.0441	.0453	.0465	.0477	.0489	.0240
	5% .05	.0484	.0495	.0507	.0519	.0531	.0543	.0210
	6% .06	.0535	.0547	.0559	.0571	.0583	.0595	.0182
	7% .07	.0585	.0596	.0608	.0620	.0632	.0644	.0158
	8% .08	.0633	.0643	.0655	.0667	.0679	.0691	.0137
25 Years n = 25	9% .09	.0678	.0689	.0701	.0713	.0725	.0737	.0118
	10% .10	.0723	.0734	.0746	.0758	.0770	.0782	.0102
	11% .11	.0765	.0777	.0789	.0801	.0813	.0825	.0088
	12% .12	.0807	.0818	.0830	.0842	.0854	.0866	.0075
	13% .13	.0847	.0859	.0871	.0883	.0895	.0907	.0064
	14% .14	.0887	.0898	.0910	.0922	.0934	.0946	.0055
	15% .15	.0925	.0937	.0949	.0961	.0973	.0985	.0047

CAPITALIZATION RATES

Assuming 2/3rds of Purchase Price Financed by Mortgage

25 YEARS AMORTIZATION: 6¼% TO 8%

Interest Rate Annual Requirement (f) Coverage, Min. Rate		6¼% .07920 .05280	6½% .08112 .05408	6¾% .08292 .05528	7% .08484 .05656	7½% .08868 .05912	8% .09264 .06176	$\frac{1}{s_{\overline{n}\vert}}$
Projection	Balance (b)	.902277	.905061	.908596	.911463	.917319	.922605	+ Dep. - App.
	Equity Yield	Basic Rate before Depreciation or Appreciation						
	4% .04	.0541	.0557	.0573	.0590	.0623	.0656	.1846
	5% .05	.0577	.0593	.0609	.0625	.0658	.0693	.1810
	6% .06	.0613	.0629	.0645	.0661	.0693	.0731	.1774
	7% .07	.0648	.0664	.0681	.0697	.0729	.0769	.1739
	8% .08	.0684	.0700	.0716	.0732	.0764	.0797	.1705
5 Years n = 5	9% .09	.0719	.0735	.0751	.0767	.0799	.0831	.1671
	10% .10	.0755	.0771	.0787	.0803	.0835	.0867	.1638
	11% .11	.0790	.0806	.0822	.0837	.0869	.0901	.1606
	12% .12	.0825	.0841	.0857	.0873	.0905	.0937	.1574
	13% .13	.0861	.0877	.0892	.0908	.0939	.0971	.1543
	14% .14	.0896	.0912	.0927	.0943	.0975	.1007	.1513
	15% .15	.0931	.0947	.0963	.0978	.1009	.1041	.1483
	Balance (b)	.768814	.773779	.780620	.785951	.797160	.807297	+ Dep. – App.
	Equity Yield	Basic Rate before Depreciation or Appreciation						
	4% .04	.0533	.0549	.0565	.0580	.0612	.0644	.0833
	5% .05	.0572	.0587	.0603	.0619	.0651	.0682	.0795
	6% .06	.0611	.0627	.0642	.0657	.0689	.0720	.0759
	7% .07	.0650	.0665	.0681	.0696	.0727	.0758	.0724
	8% .08	.0689	.0703	.0719	.0734	.0765	.0796	.0690
10 Years n = 10	9% .09	.0727	.0742	.0757	.0772	.0803	.0833	.0658
	10% .10	.0756	.0780	.0795	.0809	.0840	.0871	.0628
	11% .11	.0803	.0817	.0832	.0847	.0877	.0907	.0598
	12% .12	.0841	.0855	.0869	.0885	.0914	.0945	.0570
	13% .13	.0878	.0893	.0907	.0921	.0951	.0981	.0543
	14% .14	.0915	.0929	.0944	.0959	.0988	.1018	.0517
	15% .15	.0952	.0967	.0981	.0995	.1025	.1055	.0493

CAPITALIZATION RATES

Assuming 2/3rds of Purchase Price Financed by Mortgage

25 YEARS AMORTIZATION: 6¼% TO 8%

Interest Rate		6¼%	6½%	6¾%	7%	7½%	8%	$\frac{1}{s_{\overline{n}\vert}}$
Annual Requirement (f)		.07920	.08112	.08292	.08484	.08868	.09264	
Coverage, Min. Rate		.05280	.05408	.05528	.05656	.05912	.06176	
Projection	Balance (b)	.586539	.592238	.601439	.608024	.622532	.635506	+ Dep. – App.
	Equity Yield	Basic Rate before Depreciation or Appreciation						
	4% .04	.0524	.0539	.0553	.0569	.0599	.0629	.0500
	5% .05	.0567	.0581	.0597	.0611	.0641	.0672	.0464
	6% .06	.0609	.0624	.0639	.0653	.0683	.0713	.0430
	7% .07	.0652	.0666	.0681	.0695	.0725	.0754	.0398
	8% .08	.0693	.0707	.0722	.0736	.0765	.0795	.0368
15 Years n = 15	9% .09	.0734	.0749	.0763	.0777	.0805	.0835	.0341
	10% .10	.0775	.0789	.0803	.0817	.0845	.0875	.0315
	11% .11	.0815	.0829	.0843	.0857	.0885	.0914	.0291
	12% .12	.0854	.0868	.0882	.0896	.0924	.0953	.0268
	13% .13	.0893	.0907	.0921	.0935	.0963	.0991	.0248
	14% .14	.0932	.0945	.0959	.0973	.1001	.1029	.0228
	15% .15	.0970	.0984	.0997	.1011	.1039	.1067	.0210
	Balance (b)	.337601	.341202	.350564	.355788	.368747	.379565	+ Dep. – App.
	Equity Yield	Basic Rate before Depreciation or Appreciation						
	4% .04	.0513	.0527	.0541	.0555	.0583	.0612	.0336
	5% .05	.0561	.0575	.0589	.0603	.0631	.0659	.0303
	6% .06	.0608	.0621	.0635	.0649	.0677	.0705	.0272
	7% .07	.0654	.0667	.0681	.0695	.0722	.0750	.0244
	8% .08	.0699	.0711	.0725	.0739	.0766	.0794	.0219
20 Years n = 20	9% .09	.0742	.0755	.0769	.0782	.0809	.0837	.0196
	10% .10	.0785	.0797	.0811	.0824	.0851	.0879	.0175
	11% .11	.0826	.0839	.0851	.0865	.0893	.0920	.0156
	12% .12	.0867	.0880	.0893	.0906	.0933	.0961	.0139
	13% .13	.0907	.0920	.0933	.0946	.0973	.1000	.0124
	14% .14	.0946	.0959	.0972	.0985	.1012	.1039	.0110
	15% .15	.0985	.0998	.1011	.1024	.1050	.1077	.0098
	Balance (b)	none	none	none	none	none	none	+ Dep. – App.
	Equity Yield	Basic Rate before Depreciation or Appreciation						
	4% .04	.0501	.0514	.0526	.0539	.0565	.0591	.0240
	5% .05	.0555	.0568	.0580	.0593	.0618	.0645	.0210
	6% .06	.0607	.0619	.0631	.0644	.0669	.0696	.0182
	7% .07	.0656	.0669	.0681	.0694	.0719	.0745	.0158
	8% .08	.0703	.0717	.0729	.0741	.0767	.0793	.0137
25 Years n = 25	9% .09	.0749	.0762	.0774	.0787	.0813	.0839	.0118
	10% .10	.0794	.0807	.0819	.0831	.0857	.0883	.0102
	11% .11	.0837	.0849	.0861	.0874	.0900	.0926	.0088
	12% .12	.0878	.0891	.0903	.0916	.0941	.0968	.0075
	13% .13	.0919	.0931	.0943	.0956	.0982	.1008	.0064
	14% .14	.0958	.0971	.0983	.0996	.1021	.1048	.0055
	15% .15	.0997	.1009	.1021	.1035	.1060	.1087	.0047

CAPITALIZATION RATES
Assuming 2/3rds of Purchase Price Financed by Mortgage
25 YEARS AMORTIZATION: 8¼ % TO 9½ %

Interest Rate			8¼ %	8½ %	8¾ %	9%	9¼ %	9½ %	$\frac{1}{s_{\overline{n}\vert}}$
Annual Requirement (f)			.094614	.096627	.098657	.100703	.102765	.104843	
Coverage, Min. Rate			.063076	.064418	.065771	.067135	.068510	.069895	
Projection	Balance (b)		.925339	.927869	.930331	.932724	.935050	.937310	+ Dep.
	Equity	Yield	Basic Rate before Depreciation or Appreciation						– App.
5 Years n = 5	4%	.04	.0672	.0689	.0705	.0722	.0738	.0755	.1846
	5%	.05	.0707	.0724	.0740	.0757	.0773	.0790	.1810
	6%	.06	.0742	.0759	.0775	.0792	.0808	.0825	.1774
	7%	.07	.0778	.0794	.0810	.0827	.0843	.0860	.1739
	8%	.08	.0813	.0829	.0845	.0862	.0878	.0894	.1705
	9%	.09	.0848	.0864	.0880	.0896	.0913	.0929	.1671
	10%	.10	.0883	.0899	.0915	.0931	.0948	.0964	.1638
	11%	.11	.0918	.0934	.0950	.0966	.0982	.0999	.1606
	12%	.12	.0952	.0968	.0985	.1001	.1017	.1033	.1574
	13%	.13	.0987	.1003	.1019	.1035	.1052	.1068	.1543
	14%	.14	.1022	.1038	.1054	.1070	.1086	.1102	.1513
	15%	.15	.1057	.1073	.1089	.1105	.1121	.1137	.1483
	Balance (b)		.812717	.817705	.822597	.827392	.832091	.836694	+ Dep.
	Equity	Yield	Basic Rate before Depreciation or Appreciation						– App.
10 Years n = 10	4%	.04	.0660	.0676	.0693	.0709	.0725	.0742	.0833
	5%	.05	.0698	.0714	.0730	.0747	.0763	.0779	.0795
	6%	.06	.0736	.0752	.0768	.0784	.0800	.0816	.0759
	7%	.07	.0774	.0790	.0805	.0821	.0837	.0853	.0724
	8%	.08	.0811	.0827	.0843	.0859	.0875	.0890	.0690
	9%	.09	.0849	.0864	.0880	.0896	.0911	.0927	.0658
	10%	.10	.0886	.0901	.0917	.0932	.0948	.0964	.0627
	11%	.11	.0923	.0938	.0954	.0969	.0985	.1001	.0598
	12%	.12	.0960	.0975	.0990	.1006	.1021	.1037	.0570
	13%	.13	.0996	.1012	.1027	.1042	.1058	.1073	.0543
	14%	.14	.1033	.1048	.1063	.1079	.1094	.1109	.0517
	15%	.15	.1069	.1084	.1099	.1115	.1130	.1145	.0493
	Balance (b)		.642831	.649451	.656000	.662475	.668877	.675203	+ Dep.
	Equity	Yield	Basic Rate before Depreciation or Appreciation						– App.
15 Years n = 15	4%	.04	.0645	.0661	.0677	.0692	.0708	.0724	.0499
	5%	.05	.0687	.0703	.0718	.0734	.0749	.0765	.0463
	6%	.06	.0728	.0744	.0759	.0775	.0790	.0806	.0430
	7%	.07	.0769	.0785	.0800	.0815	.0831	.0846	.0398
	8%	.08	.0810	.0825	.0840	.0855	.0870	.0886	.0368
	9%	.09	.0850	.0865	.0880	.0895	.0910	.0925	.0341
	10%	.10	.0889	.0904	.0919	.0934	.0949	.0964	.0315
	11%	.11	.0928	.0943	.0958	.0973	.0988	.1003	.0291
	12%	.12	.0967	.0981	.0996	.1011	.1026	.1041	.0268
	13%	.13	.1005	.1020	.1034	.1049	.1064	.1079	.0247
	14%	.14	.1043	.1058	.1072	.1087	.1101	.1116	.0228
	15%	.15	.1081	.1095	.1110	.1124	.1139	.1153	.0210

CAPITALIZATION RATES
Assuming 2/3rds of Purchase Price Financed by Mortgage
25 YEARS AMORTIZATION: 9¾% TO 11%

Interest Rate			9¾%	10%	10¼%	10½%	10¾%	11%	$\frac{1}{s_{\overline{n}\rceil}}$
Annual Requirement (f)			.106936	.109044	.111165	.113301	.115451	.117613	
Coverage, Min. Rate			.071290	.072696	.074110	.075534	.076967	.078409	
Projection	Balance (b)		.939506	.941637	.943706	.945713	.947660	.949548	+ Dep.
	Equity	Yield	Basic Rate before Depreciation or Appreciation						– App.
	4%	.04	.0772	.0788	.0805	.0822	.0839	.0855	.1846
	5%	.05	.0807	.0823	.0840	.0857	.0873	.0890	.1810
	6%	.06	.0841	.0858	.0875	.0891	.0908	.0924	.1774
	7%	.07	.0876	.0893	.0909	.0926	.0942	.0959	.1739
	8%	.08	.0911	.0927	.0944	.0960	.0977	.0993	.1705
5 Years	9%	.09	.0946	.0962	.0978	.0995	.1011	.1028	.1671
n = 5	10%	.10	.0980	.0997	.1013	.1029	.1046	.1062	.1638
	11%	.11	.1015	.1031	.1048	.1064	.1080	.1097	.1606
	12%	.12	.1049	.1066	.1082	.1098	.1115	.1131	.1574
	13%	.13	.1084	.1100	.1117	.1133	.1149	.1166	.1543
	14%	.14	.1119	.1135	.1151	.1167	.1184	.1200	.1513
	15%	.15	.1153	.1169	.1185	.1202	.1218	.1234	.1483
	Balance (b)		.841201	.845613	.849931	.854154	.858284	.862322	+ Dep.
	Equity	Yield	Basic Rate before Depreciation or Appreciation						– App.
	4%	.04	.0758	.0775	.0791	.0808	.0824	.0841	.0833
	5%	.05	.0795	.0812	.0828	.0845	.0861	.0878	.0795
	6%	.06	.0833	.0849	.0865	.0882	.0898	.0914	.0759
	7%	.07	.0870	.0886	.0902	.0918	.0935	.0951	.0724
	8%	.08	.0906	.0923	.0939	.0955	.0971	.0987	.0690
10 Years	9%	.09	.0943	.0959	.0975	.0991	.1007	.1024	.0658
n = 10	10%	.10	.0980	.0996	.1012	.1028	.1044	.1060	.0627
	11%	.11	.1016	.1032	.1048	.1064	.1080	.1096	.0598
	12%	.12	.1053	.1068	.1084	.1100	.1116	.1132	.0570
	13%	.13	.1089	.1104	.1120	.1136	.1152	.1168	.0543
	14%	.14	.1125	.1140	.1156	.1172	.1187	.1203	.0517
	15%	.15	.1161	.1176	.1192	.1207	.1223	.1239	.0493
	Balance (b)		.681452	.687624	.693717	.699730	.705663	.711515	+ Dep.
	Equity	Yield	Basic Rate before Depreciation or Appreciation						– App.
	4%	.04	.0740	.0756	.0772	.0789	.0805	.0821	.0499
	5%	.05	.0781	.0797	.0813	.0829	.0845	.0862	.0463
	6%	.06	.0822	.0837	.0853	.0869	.0885	.0901	.0430
	7%	.07	.0862	.0877	.0893	.0909	.0925	.0941	.0398
	8%	.08	.0901	.0917	.0933	.0948	.0964	.0980	.0368
15 Years	9%	.09	.0941	.0956	.0972	.0987	.1003	.1019	.0341
n = 15	10%	.10	.0979	.0995	.1010	.1026	.1041	.1057	.0315
	11%	.11	.1018	.1033	.1048	.1064	.1079	.1095	.0291
	12%	.12	.1056	.1071	.1086	.1102	.1117	.1133	.0268
	13%	.13	.1094	.1109	.1124	.1139	.1154	.1170	.0247
	14%	.14	.1131	.1146	.1161	.1176	.1192	.1207	.0228
	15%	.15	.1168	.1183	.1198	.1213	.1228	.1244	.0210

CAPITALIZATION RATES

Assuming 2/3rds of Purchase Price Financed by Mortgage

30 YEARS AMORTIZATION: 3¼% TO 4½%

Interest Rate Annual Requirement (f) Coverage, Min. Rate		3¼% .05232 .03488	3½% .05400 .03600	3¾% .05568 .03712	4% .05736 .03824	4¼% .05904 .03936	4½% .06084 .04056	$\frac{1}{s_{\overline{n}\rceil}}$
Projection	Balance (b)	.892551	.896345	.900191	.904088	.908037	.911368	+ Dep. – App.
	Equity Yield	Basic Rate before Depreciation or Appreciation						
	4% .04	.0350	.0366	.0382	.0398	.0414	.0430	.1846
	5% .05	.0386	.0402	.0417	.0433	.0449	.0465	.1810
	6% .06	.0422	.0437	.0453	.0469	.0485	.0501	.1774
	7% .07	.0458	.0473	.0489	.0505	.0521	.0536	.1739
	8% .08	.0493	.0509	.0525	.0540	.0556	.0572	.1705
5 Years	9% .09	.0529	.0545	.0560	.0575	.0591	.0607	.1671
n = 5	10% .10	.0565	.0580	.0595	.0611	.0627	.0642	.1638
	11% .11	.0601	.0616	.0631	.0647	.0662	.0677	.1606
	12% .12	.0636	.0651	.0667	.0682	.0697	.0713	.1574
	13% .13	.0672	.0687	.0702	.0717	.0733	.0748	.1543
	14% .14	.0707	.0722	.0737	.0753	.0767	.0783	.1513
	15% .15	.0743	.0757	.0773	.0788	.0803	.0818	.1483
	Balance (b)	.766171	.772899	.779833	.786979	.794342	.800419	+ Dep. – App.
	Equity Yield	Basic Rate before Depreciation or Appreciation						
	4% .04	.0353	.0367	.0383	.0397	.0413	.0428	.0833
	5% .05	.0391	.0407	.0421	.0436	.0451	.0467	.0795
	6% .06	.0431	.0445	.0460	.0475	.0490	.0505	.0759
	7% .07	.0469	.0484	.0499	.0513	.0528	.0543	.0724
	8% .08	.0508	.0522	.0537	.0551	.0566	.0581	.0690
10 Years	9% .09	.0546	.0561	.0575	.0589	.0603	.0618	.0658
n = 10	10% .10	.0585	.0599	.0613	.0627	.0641	.0655	.0628
	11% .11	.0623	.0636	.0650	.0664	.0679	.0693	.0598
	12% .12	.0660	.0674	.0688	.0701	.0715	.0730	.0570
	13% .13	.0697	.0711	.0725	.0739	.0753	.0767	.0543
	14% .14	.0735	.0749	.0762	.0776	.0789	.0803	.0517
	15% .15	.0772	.0785	.0799	.0813	.0826	.0840	.0493

CAPITALIZATION RATES

Assuming 2/3rds of Purchase Price Financed by Mortgage

30 YEARS AMORTIZATION: 3¼% TO 4½%

Projection		3¼%	3½%	3¾%	4%	4¼%	4½%	$\frac{1}{s_{\overline{n}|}}$
Interest Rate		3¼%	3½%	3¾%	4%	4¼%	4½%	
Annual Requirement (f)		.05232	.05400	.05568	.05736	.05904	.06084	
Coverage, Min. Rate		.03488	.03600	.03712	.03824	.03936	.04056	
Projection	Balance (b)	.617524	.625881	.634695	.643989	.653782	.661533	+ Dep. – App.
	Equity Yield	Basic Rate before Depreciation or Appreciation						
	4% .04	.0355	.0369	.0383	.0397	.0411	.0426	.0500
	5% .05	.0397	.0411	.0425	.0439	.0453	.0468	.0464
	6% .06	.0439	.0453	.0467	.0481	.0495	.0509	.0430
	7% .07	.0481	.0494	.0508	.0521	.0535	.0549	.0398
	8% .08	.0522	.0535	.0548	.0562	.0575	.0589	.0368
15 Years	9% .09	.0562	.0575	.0589	.0602	.0615	.0629	.0341
n = 15	10% .10	.0602	.0615	.0628	.0641	.0655	.0668	.0315
	11% .11	.0641	.0654	.0667	.0680	.0693	.0707	.0291
	12% .12	.0681	.0693	.0706	.0719	.0732	.0745	.0268
	13% .13	.0719	.0732	.0745	.0757	.0770	.0783	.0248
	14% .14	.0757	.0770	.0783	.0795	.0808	.0821	.0228
	15% .15	.0795	.0808	.0820	.0833	.0845	.0858	.0210
	Balance (b)	.442686	.450790	.459678	.469399	.480007	.487675	+ Dep. – App.
	Equity Yield	Basic Rate before Depreciation or Appreciation						
	4% .04	.0357	.0371	.0384	.0397	.0411	.0424	.0336
	5% .05	.0403	.0416	.0429	.0442	.0455	.0469	.0303
	6% .06	.0448	.0461	.0473	.0487	.0499	.0513	.0272
	7% .07	.0491	.0504	.0517	.0529	.0543	.0556	.0244
	8% .08	.0535	.0547	.0559	.0572	.0585	.0598	.0219
20 Years	9% .09	.0576	.0589	.0601	.0613	.0626	.0639	.0196
n = 20	10% .10	.0617	.0629	.0642	.0654	.0667	.0679	.0175
	11% .11	.0658	.0670	.0682	.0694	.0707	.0719	.0156
	12% .12	.0697	.0709	.0721	.0733	.0745	.0759	.0139
	13% .13	.0737	.0748	.0760	.0772	.0784	.0797	.0124
	14% .14	.0775	.0787	.0799	.0811	.0822	.0835	.0110
	15% .15	.0813	.0825	.0836	.0848	.0860	.0873	.0098

CAPITALIZATION RATES

Assuming 2/3rds of Purchase Price Financed by Mortgage

30 YEARS AMORTIZATION: 3¼% TO 4½%

Interest Rate Annual Requirement (f) Coverage, Min. Rate		3¼% .05232 .03488	3½% .05400 .03600	3¾% .05568 .03712	4% .05736 .03824	4¼% .05904 .03936	4½% .06084 .04056	$\frac{1}{s_{\overline{n}|}}$
Projection	Balance (b)	.237045	.242268	.248628	.256226	.265169	.270043	+ Dep. – App.
	Equity Yield	Basic Rate before Depreciation or Appreciation						
	4% .04	.0360	.0372	.0385	.0397	.0409	.0422	.0240
	5% .05	.0409	.0421	.0433	.0445	.0458	.0471	.0210
	6% .06	.0456	.0468	.0480	.0492	.0505	.0517	.0182
	7% .07	.0502	.0513	.0525	.0537	.0549	.0562	.0158
	8% .08	.0546	.0558	.0569	.0581	.0593	.0606	.0137
25 Years	9% .09	.0589	.0601	.0612	.0624	.0636	.0648	.0118
n = 25	10% .10	.0631	.0642	.0654	.0665	.0677	.0689	.0102
	11% .11	.0671	.0683	.0694	.0706	.0717	.0730	.0088
	12% .12	.0711	.0722	.0734	.0745	.0757	.0769	.0075
	13% .13	.0749	.0761	.0773	.0784	.0795	.0808	.0064
	14% .14	.0787	.0799	.0811	.0822	.0833	.0845	.0055
	15% .15	.0825	.0836	.0848	.0859	.0871	.0883	.0047
	Balance (b)	none	none	none	none	none	none	+ Dep. – App.
	Equity Yield	Basic Rate before Depreciation or Appreciation						
	4% .04	.0363	.0375	.0386	.0397	.0408	.0420	.0179
	5% .05	.0415	.0427	.0437	.0449	.0460	.0472	.0151
	6% .06	.0465	.0476	.0487	.0498	.0509	.0521	.0127
	7% .07	.0512	.0523	.0534	.0545	.0557	.0569	.0106
	8% .08	.0557	.0568	.0579	.0591	.0601	.0613	.0089
30 Years	9% .09	.0600	.0611	.0623	.0633	.0645	.0657	.0074
n = 30	10% .10	.0642	.0653	.0664	.0675	.0687	.0699	.0061
	11% .11	.0682	.0693	.0705	.0716	.0727	.0739	.0050
	12% .12	.0721	.0733	.0744	.0755	.0766	.0778	.0042
	13% .13	.0759	.0771	.0782	.0793	.0804	.0816	.0034
	14% .14	.0797	.0808	.0819	.0831	.0842	.0854	.0028
	15% .15	.0833	.0845	.0856	.0867	.0879	.0891	.0023

CAPITALIZATION RATES

Assuming 2/3rds of Purchase Price Financed by Mortgage

30 YEARS AMORTIZATION: 4¾% TO 6%

Interest Rate Annual Requirement (f) Coverage, Min. Rate		4¾% .06264 .04176	5% .06444 .04296	5¼% .06636 .04424	5½% .06816 .04544	5¾% .07008 .04672	6% .07200 .04800	$\frac{1}{s_{\overline{n}\rceil}}$
Projection	Balance (b)	.914744	.918166	.920950	.924461	.927326	.930230	+ Dep. − App.
	Equity Yield	Basic Rate before Depreciation or Appreciation						
	4% .04	.0446	.0462	.0479	.0495	.0511	.0527	.1846
	5% .05	.0481	.0498	.0514	.0530	.0546	.0563	.1810
	6% .06	.0517	.0533	.0549	.0565	.0581	.0597	.1774
	7% .07	.0552	.0568	.0584	.0600	.0617	.0633	.1739
	8% .08	.0587	.0603	.0619	.0635	.0651	.0667	.1705
5 Years	9% .09	.0623	.0639	.0655	.0671	.0687	.0703	.1671
n = 5	10% .10	.0658	.0674	.0689	.0705	.0721	.0737	.1638
	11% .11	.0693	.0709	.0725	.0741	.0756	.0772	.1606
	12% .12	.0728	.0744	.0759	.0775	.0791	.0807	.1574
	13% .13	.0763	.0779	.0795	.0810	.0826	.0842	.1543
	14% .14	.0799	.0814	.0829	.0845	.0861	.0877	.1513
	15% .15	.0833	.0849	.0865	.0880	.0895	.0911	.1483
	Balance (b)	.806684	.813143	.818229	.825073	.830511	.836121	+ Dep. − App.
	Equity Yield	Basic Rate before Depreciation or Appreciation						
	4% .04	.0443	.0459	.0475	.0491	.0507	.0523	.0833
	5% .05	.0482	.0497	.0513	.0529	.0544	.0560	.0795
	6% .06	.0520	.0535	.0551	.0566	.0581	.0597	.0759
	7% .07	.0558	.0573	.0588	.0603	.0619	.0635	.0724
	8% .08	.0595	.0611	.0625	.0641	.0656	.0671	.0690
10 Years	9% .09	.0632	.0648	.0663	.0678	.0693	.0708	.0658
n = 10	10% .10	.0670	.0685	.0700	.0715	.0730	.0745	.0628
	11% .11	.0707	.0722	.0737	.0751	.0767	.0781	.0598
	12% .12	.0744	.0759	.0773	.0788	.0803	.0818	.0570
	13% .13	.0781	.0795	.0810	.0825	.0839	.0854	.0543
	14% .14	.0818	.0832	.0847	.0861	.0875	.0890	.0517
	15% .15	.0854	.0869	.0883	.0897	.0912	.0926	.0493

CAPITALIZATION RATES

Assuming 2/3rds of Purchase Price Financed by Mortgage

30 YEARS AMORTIZATION: 4¾% TO 6%

Interest Rate Annual Requirement (f) Coverage, Min. Rate		4¾% .06264 .04176	5% .06444 .04296	5¼% .06636 .04424	5½% .06816 .04544	5¾% .07008 .04672	6% .07200 .04800	$\frac{1}{s_{\overline{n}\mid}}$
Projection	Balance (b)	.669720	.678362	.684752	.694309	.701536	.709182	+ Dep. – App.
	Equity Yield	Basic Rate before Depreciation or Appreciation						
	4% .04	.0441	.0456	.0471	.0486	.0501	.0517	.0500
	5% .05	.0483	.0497	.0512	.0527	.0542	.0557	.0464
	6% .06	.0523	.0537	.0552	.0567	.0582	.0597	.0430
	7% .07	.0563	.0578	.0592	.0607	.0621	.0636	.0398
	8% .08	.0603	.0617	.0632	.0646	.0661	.0675	.0368
15 Years n = 15	9% .09	.0642	.0656	.0671	.0686	.0699	.0714	.0341
	10% .10	.0682	.0695	.0710	.0724	.0738	.0753	.0315
	11% .11	.0721	.0734	.0748	.0762	.0776	.0791	.0291
	12% .12	.0758	.0772	.0786	.0800	.0814	.0828	.0268
	13% .13	.0797	.0810	.0824	.0837	.0851	.0865	.0248
	14% .14	.0834	.0847	.0861	.0875	.0889	.0903	.0228
	15% .15	.0871	.0885	.0899	.0912	.0925	.0939	.0210
	Balance (b)	.496120	.505389	.511306	.522262	.529720	.537959	+ Dep. – App.
	Equity Yield	Basic Rate before Depreciation or Appreciation						
	4% .04	.0438	.0452	.0467	.0481	.0495	.0510	.0336
	5% .05	.0483	.0497	.0511	.0525	.0539	.0553	.0303
	6% .06	.0527	.0540	.0554	.0568	.0582	.0597	.0272
	7% .07	.0569	.0583	.0597	.0610	.0624	.0639	.0244
	8% .08	.0611	.0625	.0638	.0651	.0665	.0679	.0219
20 Years n = 20	9% .09	.0652	.0665	.0679	.0692	.0706	.0720	.0196
	10% .10	.0693	.0705	.0719	.0732	.0746	.0760	.0175
	11% .11	.0732	.0745	.0759	.0771	.0785	.0799	.0156
	12% .12	.0771	.0784	.0797	.0811	.0824	.0837	.0139
	13% .13	.0809	.0823	.0835	.0849	.0862	.0875	.0124
	14% .14	.0847	.0860	.0873	.0886	.0899	.0913	.0110
	15% .15	.0885	.0897	.0911	.0923	.0937	.0950	.0098

CAPITALIZATION RATES

Assuming 2/3rds of Purchase Price Financed by Mortgage

30 YEARS AMORTIZATION: 4¾% TO 6%

Interest Rate Annual Requirement (f) Coverage, Min. Rate		4¾% .06264 .04176	5% .06444 .04296	5¼% .06636 .04424	5½% .06816 .04544	5¾% .07008 .04672	6% .07200 .04800	$\frac{1}{s_{\overline{n}\rceil}}$
Projection	Balance (b)	.276086	.283403	.285925	.295899	.300830	.307006	+ Dep. – App.
	Equity Yield	Basic Rate before Depreciation or Appreciation						
	4% .04	.0435	.0448	.0461	.0475	.0489	.0503	.0240
	5% .05	.0483	.0496	.0509	.0523	.0536	.0550	.0210
	6% .06	.0530	.0543	.0556	.0569	.0583	.0596	.0182
	7% .07	.0575	.0587	.0601	.0613	.0627	.0641	.0158
	8% .08	.0619	.0631	.0644	.0657	.0670	.0683	.0137
25 Years n = 25	9% .09	.0661	.0673	.0687	.0699	.0712	.0725	.0118
	10% .10	.0702	.0715	.0727	.0740	.0753	.0767	.0102
	11% .11	.0742	.0755	.0767	.0780	.0793	.0807	.0088
	12% .12	.0781	.0794	.0807	.0819	.0833	.0845	.0075
	13% .13	.0820	.0833	.0845	.0858	.0871	.0884	.0064
	14% .14	.0858	.0870	.0883	.0895	.0909	.0921	.0055
	15% .15	.0895	.0907	.0920	.0933	.0945	.0959	.0047
	Balance (b)	none	none	none	none	none	none	+ Dep. – App.
	Equity Yield	Basic Rate before Depreciation or Appreciation						
	4% .04	.0432	.0444	.0457	.0469	.0481	.0495	.0179
	5% .05	.0484	.0496	.0509	.0521	.0533	.0547	.0151
	6% .06	.0533	.0545	.0558	.0570	.0583	.0596	.0127
	7% .07	.0581	.0593	.0605	.0617	.0630	.0643	.0106
	8% .08	.0625	.0637	.0651	.0663	.0675	.0688	.0089
30 Years n = 30	9% .09	.0669	.0681	.0693	.0705	.0719	.0731	.0074
	10% .10	.0711	.0723	.0735	.0747	.0760	.0773	.0061
	11% .11	.0751	.0763	.0776	.0788	.0801	.0813	.0050
	12% .12	.0790	.0802	.0815	.0827	.0840	.0853	.0042
	13% .13	.0829	.0840	.0853	.0865	.0878	.0891	.0034
	14% .14	.0866	.0878	.0891	.0903	.0915	.0928	.0028
	15% .15	.0903	.0915	.0927	.0939	.0952	.0965	.0023

CAPITALIZATION RATES

Assuming 2/3rd of Purchase Price Financed by Mortgage

30 YEARS AMORTIZATION: 6¼% TO 8%

Interest Rate Annual Requirement (f) Coverage, Min. Rate		6¼% .07392 .04928	6½% .07596 .05064	6¾% .07788 .05192	7% .07992 .05328	7½% .08400 .05600	8% .08808 .05872	$\frac{1}{s_{\overline{n}\rceil}}$
Projection	Balance (b)	.933174	.935451	.938471	.940816	.945604	.950526	+ Dep. – App.
	Equity Yield	Basic Rate before Depreciation or Appreciation						
	4% .04	.0544	.0561	.0577	.0593	.0627	.0660	.1846
	5% .05	.0579	.0595	.0611	.0628	.0661	.0694	.1810
	6% .06	.0614	.0630	.0647	.0663	.0696	.0729	.1774
	7% .07	.0649	.0665	.0681	.0697	.0731	.0763	.1739
	8% .08	.0683	.0700	.0716	.0733	.0765	.0798	.1705
5 Years n = 5	9% .09	.0719	.0735	.0751	.0767	.0799	.0832	.1671
	10% .10	.0753	.0769	.0785	.0801	.0834	.0867	.1638
	11% .11	.0788	.0804	.0820	.0836	.0869	.0901	.1606
	12% .12	.0823	.0839	.0855	.0871	.0903	.0935	.1574
	13% .13	.0857	.0873	.0889	.0905	.0937	.0970	.1543
	14% .14	.0892	.0908	.0924	.0940	.0972	.1004	.1513
	15% .15	.0927	.0943	.0959	.0975	.1007	.1039	.1483
	Balance (b)	.841907	.846192	.852324	.856916	.866553	.876816	+ Dep. - App.
	Equity Yield	Basic Rate before Depreciation or Appreciation						
	4% .04	.0539	.0554	.0571	.0587	.0619	.0652	.0833
	5% .05	.0576	.0591	.0607	.0623	.0656	.0689	.0795
	6% .06	.0613	.0629	.0645	.0661	.0693	.0725	.0759
	7% .07	.0650	.0665	.0681	.0697	.0729	.0761	.0724
	8% .08	.0687	.0703	.0718	.0734	.0765	.0797	.0690
10 Years n = 10	9% .09	.0723	.0739	.0755	.0770	.0801	.0833	.0658
	10% .10	.0760	.0775	.0791	.0807	.0837	.0869	.0628
	11% .11	.0797	.0812	.0827	.0843	.0873	.0905	.0598
	12% .12	.0833	.0848	.0863	.0879	.0909	.0941	.0570
	13% .13	.0869	.0884	.0899	.0915	.0945	.0976	.0543
	14% .14	.0905	.0920	.0935	.0950	.0981	.1011	.0517
	15% .15	.0941	.0956	.0971	.0986	.1016	.1047	.0493

CAPITALIZATION RATES

Assuming 2/3rds of Purchase Price Financed by Mortgage

30 YEARS AMORTIZATION: 6¼% TO 8%

Interest Rate		6¼%	6½%	6¾%	7%	7½%	8%	$\frac{1}{s_{\overline{n}\rceil}}$
Annual Requirement (f)		.07392	.07596	.07788	.07992	.08400	.08808	
Coverage, Min. Rate		.04928	.05064	.05192	.05328	.05600	.05872	
Projection	Balance (b)	.717262	.722763	.731708	.737978	.751666	.767000	+ Dep. – App.
	Equity Yield	Basic Rate before Depreciation or Appreciation						
	4% .04	.0532	.0547	.0563	.0579	.0611	.0643	.0500
	5% .05	.0572	.0587	.0603	.0619	.0650	.0682	.0464
	6% .06	.0612	.0627	.0643	.0658	.0689	.0721	.0430
	7% .07	.0651	.0666	.0681	.0697	.0727	.0759	.0398
	8% .08	.0690	.0705	.0720	.0735	.0766	.0797	.0368
15 Years n = 15	9% .09	.0729	.0743	.0759	.0773	.0804	.0835	.0341
	10% .10	.0767	.0782	.0797	.0811	.0841	.0872	.0315
	11% .11	.0805	.0819	.0834	.0849	.0879	.0909	.0291
	12% .12	.0843	.0857	.0871	.0886	.0916	.0946	.0268
	13% .13	.0879	.0894	.0909	.0923	.0953	.0982	.0248
	14% .14	.0917	.0931	.0945	.0960	.0989	.1019	.0228
	15% .15	.0953	.0968	.0982	.0996	.1025	.1055	.0210
	Balance (b)	.547030	.552083	.562831	.569367	.584702	.603393	+ Dep. – App.
	Equity Yield	Basic Rate before Depreciation or Appreciation						
	4% .04	.0525	.0539	.0555	.0570	.0601	.0632	.0336
	5% .05	.0568	.0583	.0598	.0613	.0643	.0674	.0303
	6% .06	.0611	.0625	.0640	.0655	.0685	.0715	.0272
	7% .07	.0653	.0667	.0681	.0696	.0726	.0756	.0244
	8% .08	.0693	.0708	.0722	.0737	.0766	.0796	.0219
20 Years n = 20	9% .09	.0734	.0748	.0763	.0777	.0806	.0835	.0196
	10% .10	.0773	.0788	.0802	.0816	.0845	.0875	.0175
	11% .11	.0813	.0827	.0841	.0855	.0884	.0913	.0156
	12% .12	.0851	.0865	.0879	.0893	.0922	.0951	.0139
	13% .13	.0889	.0903	.0917	.0931	.0959	.0988	.0124
	14% .14	.0927	.0941	.0954	.0968	.0997	.1025	.0110
	15% .15	.0963	.0977	.0991	.1005	.1033	.1061	.0098

CAPITALIZATION RATES

Assuming 2/3rds of Purchase Price Financed by Mortgage

30 YEARS AMORTIZATION: 6¼% TO 8%

Interest Rate Annual Requirement (f) Coverage, Min. Rate		6¼% .07392 .04928	6½% .07596 .05064	6¾% .07788 .05192	7% .07992 .05328	7½% .08400 .05600	8% .08808 .05872	$\frac{1}{s_{\overline{n}\rceil}}$
Projection	Balance (b)	.314539	.316063	.326385	.330341	.342054	.359642	+ Dep. – App.
	Equity Yield	Basic Rate before Depreciation or Appreciation						
	4% .04	.0517	.0530	.0545	.0559	.0588	.0618	.0240
	5% .05	.0564	.0577	.0592	.0606	.0635	.0665	.0210
	6% .06	.0609	.0623	.0637	.0651	.0680	.0709	.0182
	7% .07	.0654	.0668	.0682	.0696	.0724	.0753	.0158
	8% .08	.0697	.0711	.0725	.0739	.0767	.0795	.0137
25 Years n = 25	9% .09	.0739	.0753	.0766	.0780	.0809	.0837	.0118
	10% .10	.0780	.0793	.0807	.0821	.0849	.0877	.0102
	11% .11	.0820	.0833	.0847	.0861	.0889	.0917	.0088
	12% .12	.0859	.0873	.0885	.0899	.0927	.0955	.0075
	13% .13	.0897	.0911	.0924	.0937	.0965	.0993	.0064
	14% .14	.0935	.0948	.0961	.0975	.1003	.1031	.0055
	15% .15	.0971	.0985	.0998	.1012	.1039	.1067	.0047
	Balance (b)	none	none	none	none	none	none	+ Dep. – App.
	Equity Yield	Basic Rate before Depreciation or Appreciation						
	4% .04	.0507	.0521	.0534	.0547	.0575	.0602	.0179
	5% .05	.0559	.0573	.0585	.0599	.0627	.0653	.0151
	6% .06	.0609	.0622	.0635	.0649	.0676	.0703	.0127
	7% .07	.0656	.0669	.0682	.0696	.0723	.0750	.0106
	8% .08	.0701	.0715	.0727	.0741	.0768	.0795	.0089
30 Years n = 30	9% .09	.0744	.0757	.0771	.0784	.0811	.0839	.0074
	10% .10	.0786	.0799	.0812	.0826	.0853	.0880	.0061
	11% .11	.0826	.0840	.0853	.0866	.0893	.0921	.0050
	12% .12	.0865	.0879	.0892	.0905	.0833	.0960	.0042
	13% .13	.0903	.0917	.0930	.0943	.0971	.0998	.0034
	14% .14	.0941	.0955	.0967	.0981	.1008	.1035	.0028
	15% .15	.0977	.0991	.1004	.1017	.1045	.1072	.0023

CAPITALIZATION RATES
Assuming 2/3rds of Purchase Price Financed by Mortgage

30 YEARS AMORTIZATION: 8¼ % TO 9½ %

Interest Rate			8¼ %	8½ %	8¾ %	9%	9¼ %	9½ %	$\frac{1}{s_{\overline{n}\mid}}$
Annual Requirement (f)			.090151	.092269	.094404	.096554	.098721	.100902	
Coverage, Min. Rate			.060101	.061513	.062936	.064369	.065814	.067268	
Projection	Balance (b)		.952839	.954902	.956889	.958801	.960640	.962409	+ Dep.
	Equity	Yield	Basic Rate before Depreciation or Appreciation						– App.
	4%	.04	.0676	.0693	.0710	.0726	.0743	.0760	.1846
	5%	.05	.0711	.0727	.0744	.0761	.0777	.0794	.1810
	6%	.06	.0745	.0762	.0778	.0795	.0812	.0828	.1774
	7%	.07	.0780	.0796	.0813	.0829	.0846	.0862	.1739
	8%	.08	.0814	.0831	.0847	.0864	.0880	.0897	.1705
5 Years	9%	.09	.0848	.0865	.0881	.0898	.0914	.0931	.1671
n = 5	10%	.10	.0883	.0899	.0916	.0932	.0948	.0965	.1638
	11%	.11	.0917	.0934	.0950	.0966	.0983	.0999	.1606
	12%	.12	.0952	.0968	.0984	.1000	.1017	.1033	.1574
	13%	.13	.0986	.1002	.1018	.1035	.1051	.1067	.1543
	14%	.14	.1020	.1036	.1053	.1069	.1085	.1101	.1513
	15%	.15	.1054	.1071	.1087	.1103	.1119	.1136	.1483
	Balance (b)		.881700	.886025	.890223	.894297	.898247	.902077	+ Dep.
	Equity	Yield	Basic Rate before Depreciation or Appreciation						– App.
	4%	.04	.0669	.0685	.0702	.0718	.0735	.0752	.0833
	5%	.05	.0705	.0721	.0738	.0754	.0771	.0787	.0795
	6%	.06	.0741	.0757	.0774	.0790	.0807	.0823	.0759
	7%	.07	.0777	.0793	.0810	.0826	.0842	.0859	.0724
	8%	.08	.0813	.0829	.0846	.0862	.0878	.0894	.0690
10 Years	9%	.09	.0849	.0865	.0881	.0897	.0913	.0930	.0658
n = 10	10%	.10	.0885	.0901	.0917	.0933	.0949	.0965	.0627
	11%	.11	.0921	.0936	.0952	.0968	.0984	.1000	.0598
	12%	.12	.0956	.0972	.0988	.1004	.1019	.1035	.0570
	13%	.13	.0992	.1007	.1023	.1039	.1055	.1071	.0543
	14%	.14	.1027	.1043	.1058	.1074	.1090	.1106	.0517
	15%	.15	.1062	.1078	.1093	.1109	.1125	.1141	.0493
	Balance (b)		.774389	.780829	.787134	.793304	.799340	.805242	+ Dep.
	Equity	Yield	Basic Rate before Depreciation or Appreciation						– App.
	4%	.04	.0659	.0675	.0692	.0708	.0725	.0741	.0499
	5%	.05	.0698	.0714	.0730	.0747	.0763	.0779	.0463
	6%	.06	.0736	.0752	.0768	.0784	.0801	.0817	.0430
	7%	.07	.0774	.0790	.0806	.0822	.0838	.0854	.0398
	8%	.08	.0812	.0828	.0844	.0860	.0876	.0892	.0368
15 Years	9%	.09	.0850	.0865	.0881	.0897	.0913	.0928	.0341
n = 15	10%	.10	.0887	.0902	.0918	.0934	.0949	.0965	.0315
	11%	.11	.0924	.0939	.0955	.0970	.0986	.1002	.0291
	12%	.12	.0961	.0976	.0991	.1007	.1022	.1038	.0268
	13%	.13	.0997	.1012	.1028	.1043	.1058	.1074	.0247
	14%	.14	.1033	.1048	.1064	.1079	.1094	.1110	.0228
	15%	.15	.1069	.1084	.1100	.1115	.1130	.1145	.0210

CAPITALIZATION RATES
Assuming 2/3rds of Purchase Price Financed by Mortgage

30 YEARS AMORTIZATION: 9¾% TO 11%

			9¾%	10%	10¼%	10½%	10¾%	11%	$\frac{1}{s_{\overline{n}\rceil}}$
Interest Rate			9¾%	10%	10¼%	10½%	10¾%	11%	
Annual Requirement (f)			.103098	.105308	.107532	.109768	.112017	.114278	
Coverage, Min. Rate			.068732	.070205	.071688	.073179	.074678	.076185	
Projection	Balance (b)		.964109	.965743	.967311	.968817	.970261	.971646	+ Dep.
	Equity	Yield	Basic Rate before Depreciation or Appreciation						– App.
	4%	.04	.0776	.0793	.0810	.0827	.0844	.0860	.1846
	5%	.05	.0811	.0827	.0844	.0861	.0878	.0894	.1810
	6%	.06	.0845	.0862	.0878	.0895	.0912	.0928	.1774
	7%	.07	.0879	.0896	.0912	.0929	.0946	.0962	.1739
	8%	.08	.0913	.0930	.0946	.0963	.0980	.0996	.1705
5 Years	9%	.09	.0947	.0964	.0980	.0997	.1014	.1030	.1671
n = 5	10%	.10	.0981	.0998	.1015	.1031	.1048	.1064	.1638
	11%	.11	.1016	.1032	.1049	.1065	.1082	.1098	.1606
	12%	.12	.1050	.1066	.1083	.1099	.1116	.1132	.1574
	13%	.13	.1084	.1100	.1117	.1133	.1150	.1166	.1543
	14%	.14	.1118	.1134	.1151	.1167	.1183	.1200	.1513
	15%	.15	.1152	.1168	.1185	.1201	.1217	.1234	.1483
	Balance (b)		.905787	.909380	.912858	.916223	.919478	.922625	+ Dep.
	Equity	Yield	Basic Rate before Depreciation or Appreciation						– App.
	4%	.04	.0768	.0785	.0802	.0819	.0835	.0852	.0833
	5%	.05	.0804	.0821	.0837	.0854	.0871	.0888	.0795
	6%	.06	.0840	.0856	.0873	.0889	.0906	.0923	.0759
	7%	.07	.0875	.0892	.0908	.0925	.0941	.0958	.0724
	8%	.08	.0911	.0927	.0943	.0960	.0976	.0993	.0690
10 Years	9%	.09	.0946	.0962	.0979	.0995	.1011	.1028	.0658
n = 10	10%	.10	.0981	.0997	.1014	.1030	.1046	.1063	.0627
	11%	.11	.1016	.1033	.1049	.1065	.1081	.1098	.0598
	12%	.12	.1052	.1068	.1084	.1100	.1116	.1132	.0570
	13%	.13	.1087	.1103	.1119	.1135	.1151	.1167	.0543
	14%	.14	.1122	.1137	.1154	.1170	.1186	.1202	.0517
	15%	.15	.1156	.1172	.1188	.1204	.1220	.1236	.0493
	Balance (b)		.811010	.816645	.822148	.827519	.832760	.837872	+ Dep.
	Equity	Yield	Basic Rate before Depreciation or Appreciation						– App.
	4%	.04	.0758	.0774	.0791	.0808	.0824	.0841	.0499
	5%	.05	.0796	.0812	.0829	.0845	.0862	.0878	.0463
	6%	.06	.0833	.0850	.0866	.0882	.0899	.0915	.0430
	7%	.07	.0871	.0887	.0903	.0919	.0936	.0952	.0398
	8%	.08	.0908	.0924	.0940	.0956	.0972	.0989	.0368
15 Years	9%	.09	.0944	.0960	.0976	.0993	.1009	.1025	.0341
n = 15	10%	.10	.0981	.0997	.1013	.1029	.1045	.1061	.0315
	11%	.11	.1017	.1033	.1049	.1065	.1081	.1097	.0291
	12%	.12	.1054	.1069	.1085	.1101	.1117	.1133	.0268
	13%	.13	.1089	.1105	.1121	.1137	.1153	.1168	.0247
	14%	.14	.1125	.1141	.1157	.1172	.1188	.1204	.0228
	15%	.15	.1161	.1176	.1192	.1208	.1223	.1239	.0210

66-2/3% Mortgage

ANALYSIS OF SELECTED CAPITALIZATION RATES

Depreciation or appreciation in 5 years, 10 years and amortization term
for yields of 5%, 10% and 15% on 1/3rd equity

MORTGAGE INTEREST RATE 3¾%

Projection & Yield	CAPITALIZATION RATES											
	.0650	.0675	.0700	.0725	.0750	.0775	.0800	.0825	.0850	.0875	.0900	.0925
	Amortization 15 years.											
5 5%	– 13	– 14	– 16	– 17	– 18	– 20	– 21	– 22	– 24	– 25	– 27	– 28
Yr. 10%	– 2	– 4	– 5	– 7	– 8	– 10	– 11	– 13	– 14	– 16	– 17	– 19
15%	+ 11	+ 9	+ 8	+ 6	+ 4	+ 2	+ 1	– 1	– 3	– 4	– 6	– 8
10 5%	– 28	– 31	– 34	– 37	– 40	– 44	– 47	– 50	– 53	– 56	– 59	– 62
Yr. 10%	+ 2	– 2	– 6	– 10	– 14	– 18	– 22	– 26	– 30	– 34	– 38	– 42
15%	+ 47	+ 42	+ 37	+ 32	+ 27	+ 22	+ 17	+ 12	+ 7	+ 2	– 3	– 8
15 5%	– 45	– 51	– 56	– 61	– 67	– 72	– 78	– 83	– 88	– 94	– 99	
Yr. 10%	+ 18	+ 10	+ 2	– 6	– 14	– 22	– 30	– 38	– 46	– 54	– 62	– 70
15%	+ 140	+ 128	+ 116	+ 104	+ 92	+ 80	+ 68	+ 56	+ 44	+ 32	+ 20	+ 9
	Amortization 20 years.											
5 5%	– 13	– 14	– 16	– 17	– 18	– 20	– 21	– 22	– 24	– 25	– 27	– 28
Yr. 10%	– 3	– 4	– 6	– 7	– 9	– 10	– 12	– 13	– 15	– 16	– 18	– 19
15%	+ 10	+ 8	+ 6	+ 5	+ 3	+ 1	– 1	– 2	– 4	– 6	– 7	– 9
10 5%	– 28	– 31	– 35	– 38	– 41	– 44	– 47	– 50	– 53	– 57	– 60	– 63
Yr. 10%	– 2	– 6	– 10	– 14	– 18	– 22	– 26	– 30	– 34	– 38	– 42	– 46
15%	+ 39	+ 34	+ 29	+ 24	+ 18	+ 13	+ 8	+ 3	– 2	– 7	– 12	– 17
20 5%	– 70	– 78	– 86	– 94								
Yr. 10%	+ 23	+ 9	– 5	– 19	– 34	– 48	– 62	– 77	– 91			
15%	+ 264	+ 239	+ 213	+ 188	+ 162	+ 137	+ 111	+ 86	+ 60	+ 35	+ 9	– 16
	Amortization 25 years.											
5 5%	– 13	– 14	– 16	– 17	– 18	– 20	– 21	– 22	– 24	– 25	– 27	– 28
Yr. 10%	– 3	– 5	– 6	– 8	– 9	– 11	– 12	– 14	– 15	– 17	– 18	– 20
15%	+ 9	+ 7	+ 5	+ 4	+ 2	0	– 1	– 3	– 5	– 6	– 8	– 10
10 5%	– 29	– 32	– 35	– 38	– 41	– 44	– 47	– 51	– 54	– 57	– 60	– 63
Yr. 10%	– 4	– 8	– 12	– 16	– 20	– 24	– 28	– 32	– 36	– 40	– 44	– 48
15%	+ 33	+ 28	+ 23	+ 18	+ 13	+ 8	+ 3	– 2	– 7	– 12	– 17	– 22
25 5%	Entire line over 100% depreciation											
Yr. 10%	+ 27	+ 3	– 22	– 46	– 71	– 95						
15%	+ 491	+ 438	+ 385	+ 332	+ 279	+ 226	+ 172	+ 119	+ 66	+ 13	– 40	– 94
	Amortization 30 years.											
5 5%	– 13	– 14	– 16	– 17	– 18	– 20	– 21	– 23	– 24	– 25	– 27	– 28
Yr. 10%	– 3	– 5	– 6	– 8	– 9	– 11	– 13	– 14	– 16	– 17	– 19	– 20
15%	+ 8	+ 7	+ 5	+ 3	+ 2	0	– 2	– 4	– 5	– 7	– 9	– 10
10 5%	– 29	– 32	– 35	– 38	– 41	– 45	– 48	– 51	– 54	– 57	– 60	– 63
Yr. 10%	– 6	– 10	– 14	– 18	– 22	– 26	– 30	– 34	– 38	– 42	– 46	– 50
15%	+ 30	+ 25	+ 20	+ 15	+ 10	+ 5	0	– 5	– 10	– 15	– 20	– 26
30 5%	Entire line over 100% depreciation											
Yr. 10%	+ 23	– 18	– 59									
15%	+ 896	+ 787	+ 678	+ 570	+ 461	+ 352	+ 243	+ 135	+ 26	– 83		

66-2/3 % Mortgage

ANALYSIS OF SELECTED CAPITALIZATION RATES

Depreciation or appreciation in 5 years, 10 years and amortization term for yields of 5%, 10% and 15% on 1/3rd equity

MORTGAGE INTEREST RATE 4%

Projection & Yield	CAPITALIZATION RATES											
	.0650	.0675	.0700	.0725	.0750	.0775	.0800	.0825	.0850	.0875	.0900	.0925
	Amortization 15 years.											
5 5%	− 12	− 13	− 15	− 16	− 18	− 19	− 20	− 22	− 23	− 24	− 26	− 27
Yr. 10%	− 1	− 3	− 4	− 6	− 7	− 9	− 10	− 12	− 13	− 15	− 16	− 18
15%	+ 12	+ 10	+ 8	+ 7	+ 5	+ 3	+ 2	0	− 2	− 3	− 5	− 7
10 5%	− 26	− 29	− 33	− 36	− 39	− 42	− 45	− 48	− 51	− 55	− 58	− 61
Yr. 10%	+ 4	0	− 4	− 8	− 12	− 16	− 20	− 24	− 28	− 32	− 36	− 40
15%	+ 50	+ 45	+ 40	+ 34	+ 29	+ 24	+ 19	+ 14	+ 9	+ 4	0	− 6
15 5%	− 43	− 48	− 54	− 59	− 65	− 70	− 75	− 81	− 86	− 92	− 97	
Yr. 10%	+ 21	+ 13	+ 5	− 3	− 11	− 19	− 27	− 35	− 43	− 50	− 58	− 66
15%	+ 144	+ 132	+ 120	+ 108	+ 96	+ 84	+ 72	+ 60	+ 49	+ 37	+ 25	+ 13
	Amortization 20 years.											
5 5%	− 12	− 13	− 15	− 16	− 17	− 19	− 20	− 22	− 23	− 24	− 26	− 27
Yr. 10%	− 2	− 3	− 5	− 6	− 8	− 9	− 11	− 12	− 14	− 16	− 17	− 19
15%	+ 11	+ 9	+ 7	+ 5	+ 4	+ 2	0	− 1	− 3	− 5	− 6	− 8
10 5%	− 27	− 30	− 33	− 36	− 39	− 42	− 45	− 49	− 52	− 55	− 58	− 61
Yr. 10%	0	− 4	− 8	− 12	− 16	− 20	− 24	− 28	− 32	− 36	− 40	− 44
15%	+ 41	+ 36	+ 31	+ 26	+ 21	+ 16	+ 11	+ 6	+ 1	− 5	− 10	− 15
20 5%	− 66	− 74	− 83	− 91	− 99							
Yr. 10%	+ 30	+ 15	+ 1	− 13	− 27	− 42	− 56	− 70	− 85	− 99		
15%	+ 276	+ 250	+ 224	+ 199	+ 173	+ 148	+ 122	+ 97	+ 71	+ 46	+ 20	− 5
	Amortization 25 years.											
5 5%	− 12	− 13	− 15	− 16	− 18	− 19	− 20	− 22	− 23	− 24	− 26	− 27
Yr. 10%	− 2	− 4	− 5	− 7	− 8	− 10	− 11	− 13	− 14	− 16	− 17	− 19
15%	+ 10	+ 8	+ 6	+ 5	+ 3	+ 1	0	− 2	− 4	− 5	− 7	− 9
10 5%	− 27	− 30	− 33	− 36	− 39	− 43	− 46	− 49	− 52	− 55	− 58	− 61
Yr. 10%	− 2	− 6	− 10	− 14	− 18	− 22	− 26	− 30	− 34	− 38	− 42	− 46
15%	+ 36	+ 31	+ 26	+ 21	+ 16	+ 11	+ 6	+ 1	− 4	− 9	− 14	− 19
25 5%	− 96											
Yr. 10%	+ 37	+ 13	− 12	− 36	− 61	− 85						
15%	+ 513	+ 460	+ 406	+ 353	+ 300	+ 247	+ 194	+ 104	+ 87	+ 34	− 19	− 72
	Amortization 30 years.											
5 5%	− 12	− 13	− 15	− 16	− 18	− 19	− 20	− 22	− 23	− 24	− 26	− 27
Yr. 10%	− 2	− 4	− 5	− 7	− 8	− 10	− 12	− 13	− 15	− 16	− 18	− 19
15%	+ 9	+ 8	+ 6	+ 4	+ 3	+ 1	− 1	− 2	− 4	− 6	− 8	− 9
10 5%	− 27	− 30	− 33	− 36	− 39	− 43	− 46	− 49	− 52	− 55	− 58	− 62
Yr. 10%	− 4	− 8	− 12	− 16	− 20	− 24	− 28	− 32	− 36	− 39	− 43	− 47
15%	+ 33	+ 28	+ 23	+ 18	+ 13	+ 8	+ 3	− 2	− 8	− 13	− 18	− 23
30 5%	Entire line over 100% depreciation											
Yr. 10%	+ 41	0	− 41	− 82								
15%	+ 943	+ 835	+ 726	+ 617	+ 509	+ 400	+ 291	+ 183	+ 74	− 35		

66-2/3% Mortgage

ANALYSIS OF SELECTED CAPITALIZATION RATES

Depreciation or appreciation in 5 years, 10 years and amortization term for yields of 5%, 10% and 15% on 1/3rd equity

MORTGAGE INTEREST RATE 4¼%

CAPITALIZATION RATES

Projection & Yield	.0650	.0675	.0700	.0725	.0750	.0775	.0800	.0825	.0850	.0875	.0900	.0925
	Amortization 15 years.											
5 Yr. 5%	− 11	− 13	− 14	− 15	− 17	− 18	− 19	− 21	− 22	− 24	− 25	− 26
10%	0	− 2	− 3	− 5	− 6	− 8	− 9	− 11	− 13	− 14	− 16	− 17
15%	+ 13	+ 11	+ 9	+ 8	+ 6	+ 4	+ 3	+ 1	− 1	− 2	− 4	− 6
10 Yr. 5%	− 25	− 28	− 31	− 34	− 37	− 41	− 44	− 47	− 50	− 53	− 56	− 59
10%	+ 6	+ 2	− 2	− 6	− 10	− 14	− 18	− 22	− 26	− 30	− 34	− 38
15%	+ 52	+ 47	+ 42	+ 37	+ 32	+ 27	+ 22	+ 17	+ 12	+ 6	+ 1	− 4
15 Yr. 5%	− 41	− 46	− 52	− 57	− 62	− 68	− 73	− 79	− 84	− 89	− 95	
10%	+ 24	+ 16	+ 8	0	− 8	− 16	− 23	− 31	− 39	− 47	− 55	− 63
15%	+ 149	+ 137	+ 125	+ 113	+ 101	+ 90	+ 78	+ 66	+ 54	+ 42	+ 30	+ 18
	Amortization 20 years.											
5 Yr. 5%	− 11	− 12	− 14	− 15	− 17	− 18	− 19	− 21	− 22	− 24	− 25	− 26
10%	− 1	− 2	− 4	− 5	− 7	− 8	− 10	− 12	− 13	− 15	− 16	− 18
15%	+ 12	+ 10	+ 8	+ 6	+ 5	+ 3	+ 1	0	− 2	− 4	− 5	− 7
10 Yr. 5%	− 25	− 28	− 31	− 34	− 37	− 41	− 44	− 47	− 50	− 53	− 56	− 59
10%	+ 2	− 2	− 6	− 10	− 14	− 18	− 22	− 26	− 30	− 34	− 38	− 42
15%	+ 44	+ 39	+ 34	+ 29	+ 24	+ 18	+ 13	+ 8	+ 3	− 2	− 7	− 12
20 Yr. 5%	− 62	− 71	− 79	− 87	− 95							
10%	+ 36	+ 22	+ 7	− 7	− 21	− 35	− 50	− 64	− 78	− 93		
15%	+ 287	+ 261	+ 236	+ 210	+ 185	+ 159	+ 134	+ 108	+ 83	+ 57	+ 32	+ 6
	Amortization 25 years.											
5 Yr. 5%	− 11	− 12	− 14	− 15	− 17	− 18	− 19	− 21	− 22	− 24	− 25	− 26
10%	− 1	− 3	− 4	− 6	− 7	− 9	− 10	− 12	− 13	− 15	− 16	− 18
15%	+ 11	+ 9	+ 7	+ 6	+ 4	+ 2	+ 1	− 1	− 3	− 4	− 6	− 8
10 Yr. 5%	− 25	− 28	− 31	− 34	− 37	− 41	− 44	− 47	− 50	− 53	− 56	− 59
10%	0	− 4	− 8	− 12	− 16	− 20	− 24	− 28	− 32	− 36	− 40	− 44
15%	+ 39	+ 34	+ 29	+ 24	+ 19	+ 14	+ 9	+ 3	− 2	− 7	− 12	− 17
25 Yr. 5%	− 90											
10%	+ 45	+ 24	− 1	− 25	− 50	− 75	− 99					
15%	+ 538	+ 485	+ 432	+ 379	+ 326	+ 272	+ 219	+ 166	+ 113	+ 60	+ 6	− 47
	Amortization 30 years.											
5 Yr. 5%	− 11	− 12	− 14	− 15	− 17	− 18	− 19	− 21	− 22	− 24	− 25	− 26
10%	− 1	− 3	− 4	− 6	− 8	− 9	− 11	− 12	− 14	− 15	− 17	− 18
15%	+ 10	+ 9	+ 7	+ 5	+ 4	+ 2	0	− 1	− 3	− 5	− 7	− 8
10 Yr. 5%	− 25	− 28	− 31	− 34	− 38	− 41	− 44	− 47	− 50	− 53	− 56	− 60
10%	− 1	− 5	− 9	− 13	− 17	− 21	− 25	− 29	− 33	− 37	− 41	− 45
15%	+ 36	+ 31	+ 26	+ 20	+ 15	+ 10	+ 5	0	− 5	− 10	− 15	− 20
30 Yr. 5%	Entire line over 100% depreciation.											
10%	+ 61	+ 20	− 21	− 62								
15%	+ 996	+ 887	+ 778	+ 670	+ 561	+ 452	+ 343	+ 235	+ 126	+ 17	− 91	

66-2/3 % Mortgage

ANALYSIS OF SELECTED CAPITALIZATION RATES

Depreciation or appreciation in 5 years, 10 years and amortization term
for yields of 5%, 10% and 15% on 1/3rd equity

MORTGAGE INTEREST RATE 4½%

Projection & Yield		CAPITALIZATION RATES											
		.0650	.0675	.0700	.0725	.0750	.0775	.0800	.0825	.0850	.0875	.0900	.0925
		Amortization 15 years.											
5 Yr.	5%	- 10	- 12	- 13	- 14	- 16	- 17	- 19	- 20	- 21	- 23	- 24	- 26
	10%	+ 1	- 1	- 3	- 4	- 6	- 7	- 9	- 10	- 12	- 13	- 15	- 16
	15%	+ 14	+ 12	+ 10	+ 9	+ 7	+ 5	+ 4	+ 2	0	- 1	- 3	- 5
10 Yr.	5%	- 23	- 26	- 29	- 33	- 36	- 39	- 42	- 45	- 48	- 51	- 55	- 58
	10%	+ 8	+ 4	0	- 4	- 8	- 12	- 16	- 20	- 24	- 28	- 32	- 36
	15%	+ 55	+ 49	+ 44	+ 39	+ 34	+ 29	+ 24	+ 19	+ 14	+ 9	+ 4	- 1
15 Yr.	5%	- 39	- 44	- 50	- 55	- 60	- 66	- 71	- 77	- 82	- 87	- 93	- 98
	10%	+ 27	+ 19	+ 11	+ 3	- 4	- 12	- 20	- 28	- 36	- 44	- 52	- 60
	15%	+ 153	+ 141	+ 130	+ 118	+ 106	+ 94	+ 82	+ 70	+ 58	+ 46	+ 34	+ 22
		Amortization 20 years.											
5 Yr.	5%	- 10	- 12	- 13	- 14	- 16	- 17	- 19	- 20	- 21	- 23	- 24	- 25
	10%	0	- 1	- 3	- 5	- 6	- 8	- 9	- 11	- 12	- 14	- 15	- 17
	15%	+ 12	+ 11	+ 9	+ 7	+ 6	+ 4	+ 2	+ 1	- 1	- 3	- 4	- 6
10 Yr.	5%	- 23	- 26	- 29	- 32	- 36	- 39	- 42	- 45	- 48	- 51	- 54	- 58
	10%	+ 4	0	- 4	- 8	- 12	- 16	- 20	- 24	- 28	- 32	- 36	- 39
	15%	+ 46	+ 41	+ 36	+ 31	+ 26	+ 21	+ 16	+ 11	+ 6	+ 1	- 4	- 9
20 Yr.	5%	- 59	- 67	- 76	- 84	- 92							
	10%	+ 47	+ 27	+ 13	0	- 15	- 30	- 44	- 58	- 73	- 87		
	15%	+ 297	+ 271	+ 246	+ 220	+ 195	+ 169	+ 144	+ 118	+ 93	+ 67	+ 42	+ 16
		Amortization 25 years.											
5 Yr.	5%	- 10	- 12	- 13	- 14	- 16	- 17	- 19	- 20	- 21	- 23	- 24	- 25
	10%	0	- 2	- 3	- 5	- 6	- 8	- 9	- 11	- 13	- 14	- 16	- 17
	15%	+ 12	+ 10	+ 8	+ 7	+ 5	+ 3	+ 2	0	- 2	- 3	- 5	- 7
10 Yr.	5%	- 23	- 26	- 29	- 32	- 36	- 39	- 42	- 45	- 48	- 51	- 54	- 58
	10%	+ 2	- 2	- 6	- 10	- 14	- 18	- 22	- 26	- 30	- 34	- 38	- 42
	15%	+ 42	+ 37	+ 31	+ 26	+ 21	+ 16	+ 11	+ 6	+ 1	- 4	- 9	- 14
25 Yr.	5%	- 85	- 97										
	10%	+ 60	+ 35	+ 11	- 14	- 38	- 63	- 87					
	15%	+ 560	+ 506	+ 453	+ 400	+ 347	+ 294	+ 240	+ 187	+ 134	+ 81	+ 28	- 26
		Amortization 30 years											
5 Yr.	5%	- 10	- 12	- 13	- 14	- 16	- 17	- 19	- 20	- 21	- 23	- 24	- 25
	10%	0	- 2	- 4	- 5	- 7	- 8	- 10	- 11	- 13	- 14	- 16	- 17
	15%	+ 11	+ 10	+ 8	+ 6	+ 5	+ 3	+ 1	0	- 2	- 4	- 6	- 7
10 Yr.	5%	- 23	- 26	- 29	- 32	- 36	- 39	- 42	- 45	- 48	- 51	- 54	- 58
	10%	+ 1	- 3	- 7	- 11	- 15	- 19	- 23	- 27	- 31	- 35	- 39	- 43
	15%	+ 39	+ 33	+ 28	+ 23	+ 18	+ 13	+ 8	+ 3	- 2	- 7	- 12	- 17
30 Yr.	5%	Entire line over 100% depreciation.											
	10%	+ 80	+ 39	- 2	- 43	- 84							
	15%	m	+ 939	+ 830	+ 722	+ 613	+ 504	+ 396	+ 287	+ 178	+ 70	- 39	

66-2/3% Mortgage

ANALYSIS OF SELECTED CAPITALIZATION RATES

Depreciation or appreciation in 5 years, 10 years and amortization term for yields of 5%, 10% and 15% on 1/3rd equity

MORTGAGE INTEREST RATE 4¾%

Projection & Yield	CAPITALIZATION RATES											
	.0650	.0675	.0700	.0725	.0750	.0775	.0800	.0825	.0850	.0875	.0900	.0925
	Amortization 15 years.											
5 Yr. 5%	- 10	- 11	- 12	- 14	- 15	- 16	- 18	- 19	- 21	- 22	- 23	- 25
10%	+ 1	0	- 2	- 3	- 5	- 6	- 8	- 9	- 11	- 12	- 14	- 15
15%	+ 15	+ 13	+ 11	+ 10	+ 8	+ 6	+ 5	+ 3	+ 1	- 1	- 2	- 4
10 Yr. 5%	- 22	- 25	- 28	- 31	- 34	- 37	- 40	- 44	- 47	- 50	- 53	- 56
10%	+ 10	+ 6	+ 2	- 2	- 6	- 10	- 14	- 18	- 22	- 26	- 30	- 34
15%	+ 57	+ 52	+ 47	+ 42	+ 37	+ 31	+ 26	+ 21	+ 16	+ 11	+ 6	+ 1
15 Yr. 5%	- 37	- 42	- 47	- 53	- 58	- 64	- 69	- 74	- 80	- 85	- 91	- 96
10%	+ 30	+ 23	+ 15	+ 7	- 1	- 9	- 17	- 25	- 33	- 41	- 49	- 57
15%	+ 159	+ 147	+ 135	+ 123	+ 111	+ 99	+ 87	+ 75	+ 63	+ 51	+ 40	+ 28
	Amortization 20 years.											
5 Yr. 5%	- 9	- 11	- 12	- 14	- 15	- 16	- 18	- 19	- 20	- 22	- 23	- 25
10%	+ 1	- 1	- 2	- 4	- 5	- 7	- 8	- 10	- 11	- 13	- 14	- 16
15%	+ 13	+ 12	+ 10	+ 8	+ 7	+ 5	+ 3	+ 2	0	- 2	- 3	- 5
10 Yr. 5%	- 21	- 24	- 28	- 31	- 34	- 37	- 40	- 43	- 46	- 50	- 53	- 56
10%	+ 6	+ 2	- 2	- 6	- 10	- 14	- 18	- 21	- 25	- 29	- 33	- 37
15%	+ 49	+ 44	+ 39	+ 34	+ 29	+ 24	+ 19	+ 14	+ 9	+ 3	- 2	- 7
20 Yr. 5%	- 55	- 63	- 72	- 80	- 88	- 96						
10%	+ 49	+ 34	+ 20	+ 6	- 9	- 23	- 37	- 51	- 66	- 80	- 94	
15%	+ 309	+ 284	+ 258	+ 233	+ 207	+ 182	+ 156	+ 131	+ 105	+ 80	+ 54	+ 29
	Amortization 25 years.											
5 Yr. 5%	- 9	- 11	- 12	- 13	- 15	- 16	- 18	- 19	- 20	- 22	- 23	- 25
10%	+ 1	- 1	- 2	- 4	- 5	- 7	- 8	- 10	- 12	- 13	- 15	- 16
15%	+ 13	+ 12	+ 10	+ 8	+ 6	+ 5	+ 3	+ 1	- 1	- 2	- 4	- 6
10 Yr. 5%	- 21	- 24	- 28	- 31	- 34	- 37	- 40	- 43	- 46	- 50	- 53	- 56
10%	+ 4	0	- 4	- 7	- 11	- 15	- 19	- 23	- 27	- 31	- 35	- 39
15%	+ 44	+ 39	+ 34	+ 29	+ 24	+ 19	+ 14	+ 9	+ 4	- 1	- 6	- 11
25 Yr. 5%	- 79	- 91										
10%	+ 72	+ 47	+ 23	- 2	- 26	- 51	- 75					
15%	+ 585	+ 532	+ 479	+ 426	+ 372	+ 319	+ 266	+ 213	+ 160	+ 106	+ 53	0
	Amortization 30 years.											
5 Yr. 5%	- 9	- 11	- 12	- 13	- 15	- 16	- 18	- 19	- 20	- 22	- 23	- 25
10%	0	- 1	- 3	- 4	- 6	- 7	- 9	- 10	- 12	- 13	- 15	- 16
15%	+ 12	+ 11	+ 9	+ 7	+ 6	+ 4	+ 2	+ 1	- 1	- 3	- 5	- 6
10 Yr. 5%	- 21	- 24	- 27	- 31	- 34	- 37	- 40	- 43	- 46	- 49	- 53	- 56
10%	+ 3	- 1	- 5	- 9	- 13	- 17	- 21	- 25	- 29	- 33	- 37	- 41
15%	+ 41	+ 36	+ 31	+ 26	+ 21	+ 16	+ 11	+ 6	+ 1	- 4	- 9	- 14
30 Yr. 5%	Entire line over 100% depreciation											
10%	+ 100	+ 59	+ 18	- 23	- 64							
15%	m	+ 991	+ 883	+ 774	+ 665	+ 556	+ 448	+ 339	+ 230	+ 121	+ 13	- 96

66-2/3% Mortgage

ANALYSIS OF SELECTED CAPITALIZATION RATES

Depreciation or appreciation in 5 years, 10 years and amortization term for yields of 5%, 10% and 15% on 1/3rd equity

MORTGAGE INTEREST RATE 5%

Projection & Yield	CAPITALIZATION RATES											
	.0675	.0700	.0725	.0750	.0775	.0800	.0825	.0850	.0875	.0900	.0925	.0950
	Amortization 15 years.											
5 Yr. 5%	– 10	– 11	– 13	– 14	– 16	– 17	– 18	– 20	– 21	– 23	– 24	– 25
10%	+ 1	– 1	– 2	– 4	– 5	– 7	– 8	– 10	– 11	– 13	– 14	– 16
15%	+ 14	+ 12	+ 11	+ 9	+ 7	+ 5	+ 4	+ 2	0	– 1	– 3	– 5
10 Yr. 5%	– 23	– 26	– 29	– 32	– 36	– 39	– 42	– 45	– 48	– 51	– 54	– 58
10%	+ 8	+ 4	0	– 4	– 8	– 12	– 16	– 20	– 24	– 28	– 32	– 36
15%	+ 54	+ 49	+ 44	+ 39	+ 34	+ 29	+ 24	+ 19	+ 14	+ 9	+ 3	– 2
15 Yr. 5%	– 40	– 45	– 50	– 56	– 61	– 67	– 72	– 77	– 83	– 88	– 94	– 99
10%	+ 26	+ 18	+ 10	+ 2	– 6	– 14	– 22	– 30	– 37	– 45	– 53	– 61
15%	+ 151	+ 140	+ 128	+ 116	+ 104	+ 92	+ 80	+ 68	+ 56	+ 44	+ 32	+ 20
	Amortization 20 years.											
5 Yr. 5%	– 10	– 11	– 13	– 14	– 15	– 17	– 18	– 20	– 21	– 22	– 24	– 25
10%	0	– 1	– 3	– 4	– 6	– 7	– 9	– 10	– 12	– 13	– 15	– 16
15%	+ 13	+ 11	+ 9	+ 8	+ 6	+ 4	+ 3	+ 1	– 1	– 2	– 4	– 6
10 Yr. 5%	– 23	– 26	– 29	– 32	– 35	– 38	– 42	– 45	– 48	– 51	– 54	– 57
10%	+ 5	+ 1	– 3	– 7	– 11	– 15	– 19	– 23	– 27	– 31	– 35	– 39
15%	+ 46	+ 41	+ 36	+ 31	+ 26	+ 21	+ 16	+ 11	+ 6	+ 1	– 4	– 9
20 Yr. 5%	– 60	– 68	– 76	– 84	– 93							
10%	+ 41	+ 26	+ 12	– 2	– 17	– 31	– 45	– 59	– 74	– 88		
15%	+ 295	+ 269	+ 244	+ 218	+ 193	+ 167	+ 142	+ 116	+ 91	+ 65	+ 40	+ 14
	Amortization 25 years.											
5 Yr. 5%	– 10	– 11	– 13	– 14	– 15	– 17	– 18	– 20	– 21	– 22	– 24	– 25
10%	0	– 1	– 3	– 4	– 6	– 8	– 9	– 11	– 12	– 14	– 15	– 17
15%	+ 12	+ 10	+ 9	+ 7	+ 5	+ 4	+ 2	0	– 1	– 3	– 5	– 6
10 Yr. 5%	– 23	– 26	– 29	– 32	– 35	– 38	– 41	– 45	– 48	– 51	– 54	– 57
10%	+ 3	– 1	– 5	– 9	– 13	– 17	– 21	– 25	– 29	– 33	– 37	– 41
15%	+ 42	+ 37	+ 32	+ 27	+ 22	+ 17	+ 12	+ 7	+ 2	– 3	– 9	– 14
25 Yr. 5%	– 86	– 98										
10%	+ 58	+ 33	+ 9	– 16	– 40	– 65	– 89					
15%	+ 557	+ 504	+ 451	+ 398	+ 345	+ 291	+ 238	+ 185	+ 132	+ 79	+ 26	– 28
	Amortization 30 years.											
5 Yr. 5%	– 10	– 11	– 13	– 14	– 15	– 17	– 18	– 19	– 21	– 22	– 24	– 25
10%	0	– 1	– 3	– 5	– 6	– 8	– 9	– 11	– 12	– 14	– 15	– 17
15%	+ 12	+ 10	+ 8	+ 7	+ 5	+ 3	+ 2	0	– 2	– 3	– 5	– 7
10 Yr. 5%	– 22	– 26	– 29	– 32	– 35	– 38	– 41	– 44	– 48	– 51	– 54	– 57
10%	+ 2	– 2	– 6	– 10	– 14	– 18	– 22	– 26	– 30	– 34	– 38	– 42
15%	+ 39	+ 34	+ 29	+ 24	+ 19	+ 14	+ 9	+ 4	– 1	– 6	– 11	– 16
30 Yr. 5%	Entire line over 100% depreciation.											
10%	+ 79	+ 38	– 3	– 44	– 85							
15%	m	+ 935	+ 826	+ 717	+ 609	+ 500	+ 391	+ 283	+ 174	+ 65	– 43	

66-2/3% Mortgage

ANALYSIS OF SELECTED CAPITALIZATION RATES

Depreciation or appreciation in 5 years, 10 years and amortization term for yields of 5%, 10% and 15% on 1/3rd equity

MORTGAGE INTEREST RATE 5¼%

Projection & Yield	CAPITALIZATION RATES											
	.0675	.0700	.0725	.0750	.0775	.0800	.0825	.0850	.0875	.0900	.0925	.0950
	Amortization 15 years.											
5 5%	- 9	- 11	- 12	- 13	- 15	- 16	- 18	- 19	- 20	- 22	- 23	- 24
Yr. 10%	+ 2	0	- 1	- 3	- 4	- 6	- 7	- 9	- 11	- 12	- 14	- 15
15%	+ 15	+ 13	+ 12	+ 10	+ 8	+ 6	+ 5	+ 3	+ 1	0	- 2	- 4
10 5%	- 22	- 25	- 28	- 31	- 34	- 37	- 40	- 44	- 47	- 50	- 53	- 56
Yr. 10%	+ 10	+ 6	+ 2	- 2	- 6	- 10	- 14	- 18	- 22	- 26	- 30	- 34
15%	+ 57	+ 52	+ 46	+ 41	+ 36	+ 31	+ 26	+ 21	+ 16	+ 11	+ 6	+ 1
15 5%	- 38	- 43	- 48	- 54	- 59	- 64	- 70	- 75	- 81	- 86	- 91	- 97
Yr. 10%	+ 29	+ 21	+ 13	+ 5	- 3	- 10	- 18	- 26	- 34	- 42	- 50	- 58
15%	+ 157	+ 145	+ 133	+ 121	+ 109	+ 97	+ 85	+ 73	+ 61	+ 50	+ 38	+ 26
	Amortization 20 years.											
5 5%	- 9	- 10	- 12	- 13	- 15	- 16	- 17	- 19	- 20	- 21	- 23	- 24
Yr. 10%	+ 1	0	- 2	- 3	- 5	- 6	- 8	- 9	- 11	- 12	- 14	- 16
15%	+ 14	+ 12	+ 10	+ 9	+ 7	+ 5	+ 4	+ 2	0	- 1	- 3	- 5
10 5%	- 21	- 24	- 27	- 30	- 33	- 37	- 40	- 43	- 46	- 49	- 52	- 55
Yr. 10%	+ 7	+ 3	- 1	- 5	- 9	- 13	- 17	- 21	- 25	- 29	- 33	- 37
15%	+ 49	+ 44	+ 39	+ 34	+ 29	+ 24	+ 19	+ 14	+ 9	+ 4	- 1	- 6
20 5%	- 56	- 65	- 73	- 81	- 89	- 98						
Yr. 10%	+ 46	+ 32	+ 18	+ 3	- 11	- 25	- 39	- 54	- 68	- 82	- 97	
15%	+ 305	+ 280	+ 254	+ 229	+ 203	+ 178	+ 152	+ 127	+ 101	+ 76	+ 50	+ 24
	Amortization 25 years.											
5 5%	- 9	- 10	- 12	- 13	- 14	- 16	- 17	- 19	- 20	- 21	- 23	- 24
Yr. 10%	+ 1	0	- 2	- 4	- 5	- 7	- 8	- 10	- 11	- 13	- 14	- 16
15%	+ 13	+ 12	+ 10	+ 8	+ 6	+ 5	+ 3	+ 1	0	- 2	- 4	- 5
10 5%	- 21	- 24	- 27	- 30	- 33	- 36	- 39	- 43	- 46	- 49	- 52	- 55
Yr. 10%	+ 5	+ 1	- 3	- 7	- 11	- 15	- 19	- 23	- 27	- 31	- 35	- 39
15%	+ 45	+ 40	+ 35	+ 30	+ 25	+ 19	+ 14	+ 9	+ 4	- 1	- 6	- 11
25 5%	- 80	- 92										
Yr. 10%	+ 70	+ 45	+ 21	- 4	- 28	- 53	- 77					
15%	+ 583	+ 530	+ 477	+ 423	+ 370	+ 317	+ 264	+ 211	+ 157	+ 104	+ 51	- 2
	Amortization 30 years.											
5 5%	- 9	- 10	- 12	- 13	- 14	- 16	- 17	- 19	- 20	- 21	- 23	- 24
Yr. 10%	+ 1	- 1	- 2	- 4	- 5	- 7	- 8	- 10	- 11	- 13	- 14	- 16
15%	+ 13	+ 11	+ 9	+ 8	+ 6	+ 4	+ 3	+ 1	- 1	- 2	- 4	- 6
10 5%	- 20	- 24	- 27	- 30	- 33	- 36	- 39	- 42	- 46	- 49	- 52	- 55
Yr. 10%	+ 4	0	- 4	- 8	- 12	- 16	- 20	- 24	- 28	- 32	- 36	- 40
15%	+ 42	+ 37	+ 32	+ 27	+ 22	+ 17	+ 12	+ 7	+ 2	- 3	- 9	- 14
30 5%	Entire line over 100% depreciation											
Yr. 10%	+ 98	+ 57	+ 16	- 25	- 66							
15%	+ m	+ 987	+ 878	+ 770	+ 661	+ 552	+ 443	+ 335	+ 226	+ 117	+ 9	

66-2/3% Mortgage

ANALYSIS OF SELECTED CAPITALIZATION RATES

Depreciation or appreciation in 5 years, 10 years and amortization term
for yields of 5%, 10% and 15% on 1/3rd equity

MORTGAGE INTEREST RATE 5½%

Projection & Yield	CAPITALIZATION RATES											
	.0700	.0725	.0750	.0775	.0800	.0825	.0850	.0875	.0900	.0925	.0950	.0975
	Amortization 15 years.											
5 5%	- 10	- 11	- 13	- 14	- 15	- 17	- 18	- 20	- 21	- 22	- 24	- 25
Yr. 10%	+ 1	0	- 2	- 3	- 5	- 7	- 8	- 10	- 11	- 13	- 14	- 16
15%	+ 14	+ 12	+ 11	+ 9	+ 7	+ 6	+ 4	+ 2	+ 1	- 1	- 1	- 4
10 5%	- 23	- 26	- 29	- 32	- 35	- 39	- 42	- 45	- 48	- 51	- 54	- 57
Yr. 10%	+ 8	+ 4	+ 0	- 4	- 8	- 12	- 16	- 20	- 24	- 28	- 32	- 36
15%	+ 54	+ 49	+ 44	+ 39	+ 34	+ 29	+ 24	+ 18	+ 13	+ 8	+ 3	- 2
15 5%	- 41	- 46	- 51	- 57	- 62	- 67	- 73	- 78	- 84	- 89	- 94	- 100
Yr. 10%	+ 25	+ 17	+ 9	0	- 7	- 15	- 23	- 31	- 39	- 47	- 55	- 63
15%	+ 150	+ 138	+ 126	+ 114	+ 102	+ 90	+ 79	+ 67	+ 55	+ 43	+ 31	+ 19
	Amortization 20 years.											
5 5%	- 10	- 11	- 12	- 14	- 15	- 17	- 18	- 19	- 21	- 22	- 23	- 25
Yr. 10%	+ 1	- 1	- 2	- 4	- 5	- 7	- 8	- 10	- 11	- 13	- 15	- 16
15%	+ 13	+ 11	+ 10	+ 8	+ 6	+ 5	+ 3	+ 1	0	- 2	- 4	- 5
10 5%	- 22	- 25	- 29	- 32	- 35	- 38	- 41	- 44	- 47	- 51	- 54	- 57
Yr. 10%	+ 5	+ 1	- 3	- 7	- 11	- 15	- 19	- 23	- 27	- 31	- 35	- 39
15%	+ 47	+ 42	+ 37	+ 31	+ 26	+ 21	+ 16	+ 11	+ 6	+ 1	- 4	- 9
20 5%	- 61	- 69	- 77	- 85	- 94							
Yr. 10%	+ 39	+ 25	+ 10	- 4	- 18	- 33	- 47	- 61	- 75	- 90		
15%	+ 292	+ 266	+ 241	+ 215	+ 190	+ 164	+ 139	+ 113	+ 88	+ 62	+ 37	+ 11
	Amortization 25 years.											
5 5%	- 9	- 11	- 12	- 14	- 15	- 16	- 18	- 19	- 20	- 22	- 23	- 25
Yr. 10%	0	- 1	- 3	- 4	- 6	- 7	- 9	- 10	- 12	- 13	- 15	- 16
15%	+ 12	+ 11	+ 9	+ 7	+ 6	+ 4	+ 2	+ 1	- 1	- 3	- 4	- 6
10 5%	- 22	- 25	- 28	- 31	- 34	- 38	- 41	- 44	- 47	- 50	- 53	- 56
Yr. 10%	+ 3	- 1	- 5	- 9	- 13	- 17	- 21	- 25	- 29	- 32	- 36	- 40
15%	+ 43	+ 38	+ 32	+ 27	+ 22	+ 17	+ 12	+ 7	+ 2	- 3	- 8	- 13
25 5%	- 86	- 98										
Yr. 10%	+ 57	+ 32	+ 8	- 17	- 41	- 66	- 90					
15%	+ 555	+ 502	+ 449	+ 396	+ 343	+ 289	+ 236	+ 183	+ 130	+ 77	+ 23	- 30
	Amortization 30 years.											
5 5%	- 9	- 11	- 12	- 14	- 15	- 16	- 18	- 19	- 20	- 22	- 23	- 25
Yr. 10%	0	- 1	- 3	- 4	- 6	- 7	- 9	- 10	- 12	- 13	- 15	- 16
15%	+ 12	+ 10	+ 9	+ 7	+ 5	+ 4	+ 2	0	- 1	- 3	- 5	- 6
10 5%	- 22	- 25	- 28	- 31	- 34	- 37	- 40	- 44	- 47	- 50	- 53	- 56
Yr. 10%	+ 2	- 2	- 6	- 10	- 14	- 18	- 21	- 25	- 29	- 33	- 37	- 41
15%	+ 40	+ 35	+ 30	+ 25	+ 20	+ 15	+ 10	+ 4	- 1	- 6	- 11	- 16
30 5%	Entire line over 100% depreciation.											
Yr. 10%	+ 77	+ 36	- 5	- 46	- 87							
15%	m	+ 930	+ 822	+ 713	+ 604	+ 496	+ 387	+ 278	+ 170	+ 61	- 48	

66-2/3% Mortgage

ANALYSIS OF SELECTED CAPITALIZATION RATES

Depreciation or appreciation in 5 years, 10 years and amortization term
for yields of 5%, 10% and 15% on 1/3rd equity

MORTGAGE INTEREST RATE 5¾%

Projection & Yield	CAPITALIZATION RATES											
	.0700	.0725	.0750	.0775	.0800	.0825	.0850	.0875	.0900	.0925	.0950	.0975
	Amortization 15 years.											
5 5%	- 9	- 10	- 12	- 13	- 14	- 16	- 17	- 10	- 20	- 21	- 23	- 24
yr. 10%	+ 2	0	- 1	- 3	- 4	- 6	- 7	- 9	- 10	- 12	- 13	- 15
15%	+ 15	+ 13	+ 12	+ 10	+ 8	+ 7	+ 5	+ 3	+ 2	0	- 2	- 3
10 5%	- 21	- 25	- 28	- 31	- 34	- 37	- 40	- 43	- 47	- 50	- 53	- 56
Yr. 10%	+ 10	+ 6	+ 2	- 2	- 6	- 10	- 14	- 18	- 22	- 26	- 30	- 34
15%	+ 56	+ 51	+ 46	+ 41	+ 36	+ 31	+ 26	+ 21	+ 16	+ 11	+ 6	+ 1
15 5%	- 38	- 44	- 49	- 54	- 60	- 65	- 70	- 76	- 81	- 87	- 92	- 97
Yr. 10%	+ 28	+ 20	+ 12	+ 4	- 3	- 11	- 19	- 27	- 35	- 43	- 51	- 59
15%	+ 155	+ 143	+ 131	+ 119	+ 107	+ 95	+ 83	+ 71	+ 60	+ 48	+ 36	+ 24
	Amortization 20 years.											
5 5%	- 9	- 10	- 11	- 13	- 14	- 16	- 17	- 18	- 20	- 21	- 23	- 24
Yr. 10%	+ 2	0	- 1	- 3	- 4	- 6	- 8	- 9	- 11	- 12	- 14	- 15
15%	+ 14	+ 12	+ 11	+ 9	+ 7	+ 6	+ 4	+ 2	+ 1	- 1	- 3	- 4
10 5%	- 20	- 24	- 27	- 30	- 33	- 36	- 39	- 42	- 46	- 49	- 52	- 55
Yr. 10%	+ 7	+ 3	- 1	- 5	- 9	- 13	- 17	- 21	- 25	- 29	- 33	- 37
15%	+ 49	+ 44	+ 39	+ 34	+ 29	+ 24	+ 19	+ 14	+ 9	+ 4	- 1	- 6
20 5%	- 57	- 65	- 73	- 82	- 90	- 98						
Yr. 10%	+ 46	+ 31	+ 17	+ 3	- 11	- 26	- 40	- 54	- 69	- 83	- 97	
15%	+ 304	+ 279	+ 253	+ 228	+ 202	+ 177	+ 151	+ 126	+ 100	+ 74	+ 49	+ 23
	Amortization 25 years.											
5 5%	- 9	- 10	- 11	- 13	- 14	- 15	- 17	- 18	- 20	- 21	- 22	- 24
Yr. 10%	+ 1	0	- 2	- 3	- 5	- 6	- 8	- 9	- 11	- 12	- 14	- 15
15%	+ 14	+ 12	+ 10	+ 8	+ 7	+ 5	+ 3	+ 2	+ 0	- 2	- 3	- 5
10 5%	- 20	- 23	- 26	- 29	- 33	- 36	- 39	- 42	- 45	- 48	- 51	- 55
Yr. 10%	+ 6	+ 1	- 2	- 6	- 10	- 14	- 18	- 22	- 26	- 30	- 34	- 38
15%	+ 45	+ 40	+ 35	+ 30	+ 25	+ 20	+ 15	+ 10	+ 5	0	- 5	- 10
25 5%	- 80	- 92										
Yr. 10%	+ 69	+ 44	+ 19	- 5	- 29	- 54	- 78					
15%	+ 581	+ 528	+ 474	+ 421	+ 368	+ 315	+ 262	+ 209	+ 155	+ 102	+ 49	- 4
	Amortization 30 years.											
5 5%	- 9	- 10	- 11	- 13	- 14	- 15	- 17	- 18	- 20	- 21	- 22	- 24
Yr. 10%	+ 1	0	- 2	- 3	- 5	- 6	- 8	- 9	- 11	- 12	- 14	- 16
15%	+ 13	+ 11	+ 10	+ 8	+ 6	+ 5	+ 3	+ 1	0	- 2	- 4	- 5
10 5%	- 20	- 23	- 26	- 29	- 32	- 35	- 38	- 42	- 45	- 48	- 51	- 54
Yr. 10%	+ 5	+ 1	- 3	- 7	- 11	- 15	- 19	- 23	- 27	- 31	- 35	- 39
15%	+ 43	+ 38	+ 33	+ 28	+ 23	+ 18	+ 13	+ 8	+ 2	- 3	- 8	- 13
30 5%	Entire line over 100% depreciation											
Yr. 10%	+ 98	+ 57	+ 16	- 25	- 66							
15%	m	+ 987	+ 878	+ 770	+ 661	+ 552	+ 443	+ 335	+ 226	+ 117	+ 9	

66-2/3% Mortgage

ANALYSIS OF SELECTED CAPITALIZATION RATES

Depreciation or appreciation in 5 years, 10 years and amortization term for yields of 5%, 10% and 15% on 1/3rd equity

MORTGAGE INTEREST RATE 6%

Projection & Yield	CAPITALIZATION RATES											
	.0725	.0750	.0775	.0800	.0825	.0850	.0875	.0900	.0925	.0950	.0975	.1000
	Amortization 15 years.											
5 Yr. 5%	- 10	- 11	- 12	- 14	- 15	- 16	- 18	- 19	- 21	- 22	- 23	- 25
10%	+ 1	0	- 2	- 3	- 5	- 6	- 8	- 9	- 11	- 12	- 14	- 16
15%	+ 15	+ 13	+ 11	+ 10	+ 8	+ 6	+ 5	+ 3	+ 1	- 1	- 2	- 4
10 Yr. 5%	- 23	- 26	- 29	- 32	- 35	- 38	- 42	- 45	- 48	- 51	- 54	- 57
10%	+ 8	+ 4	0	- 4	- 8	- 12	- 16	- 20	- 24	- 28	- 32	- 36
15%	+ 54	+ 49	+ 44	+ 39	+ 33	+ 28	+ 23	+ 18	+ 13	+ 8	+ 3	- 2
15 Yr. 5%	- 41	- 47	- 52	- 58	- 63	- 68	- 74	- 79	- 84	- 90	- 95	- 100
10%	+ 23	+ 16	+ 8	0	- 8	- 16	- 24	- 32	- 40	- 48	- 56	- 64
15%	+ 148	+ 136	+ 124	+ 112	+ 100	+ 89	+ 77	+ 65	+ 53	+ 41	+ 29	+ 17
	Amortization 20 years.											
5 Yr. 5%	- 9	- 11	- 12	- 13	- 15	- 16	- 18	- 19	- 20	- 22	- 23	- 24
10%	+ 1	0	- 2	- 4	- 5	- 7	- 8	- 10	- 11	- 13	- 14	- 16
15%	+ 13	+ 12	+ 10	+ 8	+ 7	+ 5	+ 3	+ 2	0	- 2	- 3	- 5
10 Yr. 5%	- 22	- 25	- 28	- 31	- 34	- 37	- 41	- 44	- 47	- 50	- 53	- 56
10%	+ 5	+ 1	- 3	- 7	- 11	- 14	- 18	- 22	- 26	- 30	- 34	- 38
15%	+ 47	+ 42	+ 37	+ 32	+ 27	+ 22	+ 17	+ 12	+ 7	+ 2	- 3	- 9
20 Yr. 5%	- 61	- 70	- 78	- 86	- 94							
10%	+ 38	+ 23	+ 9	- 5	- 19	- 34	- 48	- 62	- 77	- 91		
15%	+ 290	+ 264	+ 239	+ 213	+ 188	+ 162	+ 137	+ 111	+ 86	+ 60	+ 35	+ 9
	Amortization 25 years.											
5 Yr. 5%	- 9	- 10	- 12	- 13	- 15	- 16	- 17	- 19	- 20	- 21	- 23	- 24
10%	+ 1	- 1	- 2	- 4	- 5	- 7	- 8	- 10	- 11	- 13	- 14	- 16
15%	+ 13	+ 11	+ 10	+ 8	+ 6	+ 4	+ 3	+ 1	- 1	- 2	- 4	- 6
10 Yr. 5%	- 21	- 24	- 27	- 31	- 34	- 37	- 40	- 43	- 46	- 49	- 53	- 56
10%	+ 4	0	- 4	- 8	- 12	- 16	- 20	- 24	- 28	- 32	- 36	- 40
15%	+ 43	+ 38	+ 33	+ 28	+ 23	+ 18	+ 13	+ 8	+ 3	- 2	- 8	- 13
25 Yr. 5%	- 87	- 99										
10%	+ 56	+ 31	+ 7	- 18	- 42	- 67	- 91					
15%	+ 553	+ 500	+ 447	+ 394	+ 340	+ 287	+ 234	+ 181	+ 128	+ 74	+ 21	- 32
	Amortization 30 years.											
5 Yr. 5%	- 9	- 10	- 12	- 13	- 14	- 16	- 17	- 19	- 20	- 21	- 23	- 24
10%	+ 1	- 1	- 2	- 4	- 5	- 7	- 8	- 10	- 11	- 13	- 15	- 16
15%	+ 13	+ 11	+ 9	+ 7	+ 6	+ 4	+ 2	+ 1	- 1	- 3	- 4	- 6
10 Yr. 5%	- 21	- 24	- 27	- 30	- 33	- 36	- 40	- 43	- 46	- 49	- 52	- 55
10%	+ 3	- 1	- 5	- 9	- 13	- 17	- 21	- 25	- 29	- 33	- 37	- 41
15%	+ 41	+ 36	+ 31	+ 26	+ 20	+ 15	+ 10	+ 5	0	- 5	- 10	- 15
30 Yr. 5%	Entire line over 100% depreciation											
10%	+ 79	+ 38	- 3	- 44	- 85							
15%	m	+ 935	+ 826	+ 717	+ 609	+ 500	+ 391	+ 283	+ 174	+ 65	- 43	

ANALYSIS OF SELECTED CAPITALIZATION RATES

Depreciation or appreciation in 5 years, 10 years and amortization term for yields of 5%, 10% and 15% on 1/3rd equity

MORTGAGE INTEREST RATE 6¼%

Projection & Yield	CAPITALIZATION RATES											
	.0725	.0750	.0775	.0800	.0825	.0850	.0875	.0900	.0925	.0950	.0975	.1000
	Amortization 15 years.											
5 Yr. 5%	- 9	- 10	- 11	- 13	- 14	- 16	- 17	- 18	- 20	- 21	- 23	- 24
10%	+ 2	+ 1	- 1	- 2	- 4	- 5	- 7	- 8	- 10	- 12	- 13	- 15
15%	+ 15	+ 14	+ 12	+ 10	+ 9	+ 7	+ 5	+ 4	+ 2	0	- 1	- 3
10 Yr. 5%	- 21	- 25	- 28	- 31	- 34	- 37	- 40	- 43	- 47	- 50	- 53	- 56
10%	+ 10	+ 6	+ 2	- 2	- 6	- 10	- 14	- 18	- 22	- 26	- 30	- 34
15%	+ 56	+ 51	+ 46	+ 41	+ 36	+ 31	+ 26	+ 31	+ 16	+ 11	+ 6	+ 1
15 Yr. 5%	- 39	- 44	- 50	- 55	- 60	- 66	- 71	- 77	- 82	- 87	- 93	- 98
10%	+ 27	+ 19	+ 11	+ 3	- 4	- 13	- 21	- 29	- 37	- 44	- 52	- 60
15%	+ 153	+ 141	+ 130	+ 118	+ 106	+ 94	+ 82	+ 70	+ 58	+ 46	+ 34	+ 22
	Amortization 20 years.											
5 Yr. 5%	- 8	- 10	- 11	- 13	- 14	- 15	- 17	- 18	- 19	- 21	- 22	- 24
10%	+ 2	0	- 1	- 3	- 4	- 6	- 7	- 9	- 10	- 12	- 13	- 15
15%	+ 14	+ 13	+ 11	+ 9	+ 8	+ 6	+ 4	+ 3	+ 1	- 1	- 2	- 4
10 Yr. 5%	- 20	- 23	- 26	- 29	- 32	- 36	- 39	- 42	- 45	- 48	- 51	- 54
10%	+ 7	+ 4	0	- 4	- 8	- 12	- 16	- 20	- 24	- 28	- 32	- 36
15%	+ 50	+ 45	+ 40	+ 34	+ 29	+ 24	+ 19	+ 14	+ 9	+ 4	- 1	- 6
20 Yr. 5%	- 58	- 66	- 74	- 83	- 91	- 99						
10%	+ 44	+ 30	+ 15	+ 1	- 13	- 27	- 42	- 56	- 70	- 85	- 99	
15%	+ 301	+ 276	+ 250	+ 224	+ 199	+ 173	+ 148	+ 122	+ 97	+ 71	+ 46	+ 20
	Amortization 25 years.											
5 Yr. 5%	- 8	- 10	- 11	- 12	- 14	- 15	- 16	- 18	- 19	- 21	- 22	- 23
10%	0	- 2	- 3	- 5	- 6	- 8	- 10	- 11	- 13	- 14	- 16	- 17
15%	+ 14	+ 12	+ 11	+ 9	+ 7	+ 5	+ 4	+ 2	0	- 1	- 3	- 5
10 Yr. 5%	- 19	- 22	- 26	- 29	- 32	- 35	- 38	- 41	- 44	- 48	- 51	- 54
10%	+ 6	+ 2	- 2	- 6	- 10	- 14	- 18	- 21	- 25	- 29	- 33	- 37
15%	+ 46	+ 41	+ 36	+ 31	+ 26	+ 21	+ 16	+ 11	+ 5	0	- 5	- 10
25 Yr. 5%	- 81	- 93										
10%	+ 68	+ 43	+ 19	- 6	- 30	- 55	- 79					
15%	+ 579	+ 526	+ 472	+ 419	+ 366	+ 313	+ 260	+ 206	+ 153	+ 100	+ 47	- 6
	Amortization 30 years.											
5 Yr. 5%	- 8	- 9	- 11	- 12	- 14	- 15	- 16	- 18	- 19	- 20	- 22	- 23
10%	+ 2	0	- 1	- 3	- 4	- 6	- 7	- 9	- 11	- 12	- 14	- 15
15%	+ 14	+ 12	+ 10	+ 9	+ 7	+ 5	+ 4	+ 2	0	- 2	- 3	- 5
10 Yr. 5%	- 19	- 22	- 25	- 28	- 31	- 34	- 38	- 41	- 44	- 47	- 50	- 53
10%	+ 6	+ 2	- 2	- 6	- 10	- 14	- 18	- 22	- 26	- 30	- 34	- 38
15%	+ 44	+ 39	+ 34	+ 29	+ 24	+ 18	+ 13	+ 8	+ 3	- 2	- 7	- 12
30 Yr. 5%	Entire line over 100% depreciation.											
10%	+ 100	+ 59	+ 18	- 23	- 64							
15%	m	+ 987	+ 878	+ 770	+ 661	+ 552	+ 443	+ 335	+ 226	+ 117	+ 9	- 100

ANALYSIS OF SELECTED CAPITALIZATION RATES

Depreciation or appreciation in 5 years, 10 years and amortization term for yields of 5%, 10% and 15% on 1/3rd equity

MORTGAGE INTEREST RATE 6½%

Projection & Yield	.0725	.0750	.0775	.0800	.0825	.0850	.0875	.0900	.0925	.0950	.0975	.1000
	Amortization 15 years.											
5 Yr. 5%	– 8	– 9	– 11	– 12	– 13	– 15	– 16	– 18	– 19	– 20	– 22	– 23
10%	+ 3	+ 2	0	– 1	– 3	– 5	– 6	– 8	– 9	– 11	– 12	– 14
15%	+ 16	+ 15	+ 13	+ 11	+ 10	+ 8	+ 6	+ 5	+ 3	+ 1	– 1	– 2
10 Yr. 5%	– 20	– 23	– 26	– 29	– 32	– 35	– 39	– 42	– 45	– 48	– 51	– 54
10%	+ 12	+ 8	+ 4	0	– 4	– 8	– 12	– 16	– 20	– 24	– 28	– 32
15%	+ 59	+ 54	+ 49	+ 44	+ 39	+ 33	+ 28	+ 23	+ 18	+ 13	+ 8	+ 3
15 Yr. 5%	– 37	– 42	– 47	– 53	– 58	– 64	– 69	– 74	– 80	– 85	– 91	– 96
10%	+ 30	+ 23	+ 15	+ 7	– 1	– 9	– 17	– 25	– 33	– 41	– 49	– 57
15%	+ 158	+ 146	+ 134	+ 122	+ 110	+ 99	+ 87	+ 75	+ 63	+ 51	+ 39	+ 27
	Amortization 20 years.											
5 Yr. 5%	– 8	– 9	– 10	– 12	– 13	– 14	– 16	– 17	– 19	– 20	– 21	– 23
10%	+ 3	+ 1	0	– 2	– 3	– 5	– 6	– 8	– 9	– 11	– 12	– 14
15%	+ 15	+ 14	+ 12	+ 10	+ 9	+ 7	+ 5	+ 3	+ 2	+ 0	– 1	– 3
10 Yr. 5%	– 18	– 21	– 24	– 28	– 31	– 34	– 37	– 40	– 43	– 46	– 50	– 53
10%	+ 10	+ 6	+ 2	– 2	– 6	– 10	– 14	– 18	– 22	– 26	– 30	– 34
15%	+ 53	+ 47	+ 42	+ 37	+ 32	+ 27	+ 22	+ 17	+ 12	+ 7	+ 2	– 3
20 Yr. 5%	– 54	– 62	– 70	– 79	– 87	– 95						
10%	+ 51	+ 37	+ 22	+ 8	– 6	– 21	– 35	– 49	– 63	– 78	– 92	
15%	+ 313	+ 288	+ 262	+ 237	+ 211	+ 186	+ 160	+ 135	+ 109	+ 84	+ 58	+ 33
	Amortization 25 years.											
5 Yr. 5%	– 7	– 9	– 10	– 11	– 13	– 14	– 16	– 17	– 18	– 20	– 21	– 22
10%	+ 3	+ 1	0	– 2	– 3	– 5	– 6	– 8	– 9	– 11	– 12	– 14
15%	+ 15	+ 13	+ 12	+ 10	+ 8	+ 7	+ 5	+ 3	+ 1	0	– 2	– 4
10 Yr. 5%	– 17	– 21	– 24	– 27	– 30	– 33	– 36	– 39	– 43	– 46	– 49	– 52
10%	+ 9	+ 5	+ 1	– 3	– 7	– 11	– 15	– 19	– 23	– 27	– 31	– 35
15%	+ 49	+ 44	+ 39	+ 34	+ 29	+ 24	+ 19	+ 14	+ 9	+ 3	– 2	– 7
25 Yr. 5%	– 75	– 87	– 99									
10%	+ 80	+ 56	+ 31	+ 7	– 18	– 42	– 67	– 91				
15%	+ 604	+ 551	+ 498	+ 445	+ 391	+ 338	+ 285	+ 232	+ 179	+ 126	+ 72	+ 19
	Amortization 30 years.											
5 Yr. 5%	– 7	– 9	– 10	– 11	– 13	– 14	– 15	– 17	– 18	– 20	– 21	– 22
10%	+ 3	+ 1	0	– 2	– 3	– 5	– 6	– 8	– 10	– 11	– 13	– 14
15%	+ 15	+ 13	+ 11	+ 10	+ 8	+ 6	+ 5	+ 3	+ 1	0	– 2	– 4
10 Yr. 5%	– 17	– 20	– 23	– 26	– 29	– 33	– 36	– 39	– 42	– 45	– 48	– 51
10%	+ 8	+ 4	0	– 4	– 8	– 12	– 16	– 20	– 24	– 28	– 32	– 36
15%	+ 47	+ 42	+ 37	+ 32	+ 27	+ 22	+ 16	+ 11	+ 6	+ 1	– 4	– 9
30 Yr. 5%	Entire line over 100% depreciation.											
10%	+ 121	+ 80	+ 39	– 2	– 43	– 84						
15%	m	m	+ 939	+ 830	+ 722	+ 613	+ 504	+ 396	+ 287	+ 178	+ 70	– 39

66-2/3% Mortgage

ANALYSIS OF SELECTED CAPITALIZATION RATES

Depreciation or appreciation in 5 years, 10 years and amortization term
for yields of 6%, 9%, 12% and 15% on 1/3rd equity

MORTGAGE INTEREST RATE 6¾%

Projection & Yield		CAPITALIZATION RATES											
		.075	.0775	.080	.0825	.0850	.0875	.090	.0925	.0950	.0975	.1000	.1025
		Amortization 15 years.											
5 Yr.	6%	-6	-8	-9	-11	-12	-13	-15	-16	-18	-19	-20	-22
	9%	0	-1	-3	-4	-6	-7	-9	-10	-12	-13	-15	-16
	12%	7	6	4	3	1	-0	-2	-4	-5	-7	-8	-10
	15%	16	14	12	11	9	7	5	4	2	0	-1	-3
10 Yr.	6%	-16	-19	-22	-26	-29	-32	-36	-39	-42	-46	-49	-52
	9%	2	-1	-5	-9	-13	-16	-20	-24	-28	-32	-35	-39
	12%	26	22	17	13	9	4	-0	-5	-9	-13	-18	-22
	15%	56	51	46	41	36	31	26	21	16	11	6	0
		Amortization 20 years.											
5 Yr.	6%	-6	-8	-9	-10	-12	-13	-15	-16	-17	-19	-20	-22
	9%	0	-1	-3	-4	-6	-7	-9	-10	-12	-13	-15	-16
	12%	7	5	4	2	1	-1	-3	-4	-6	-7	-9	-10
	15%	15	13	11	10	8	6	5	3	1	-0	-2	-4
10 Yr.	6%	-15	-18	-21	-25	-28	-31	-35	-38	-41	-44	-48	-51
	9%	2	-2	-6	-10	-14	-17	-21	-25	-29	-33	-36	-40
	12%	23	18	14	10	5	1	-4	-8	-12	-17	-21	-25
	15%	50	45	40	35	30	25	20	15	10	5	-1	-6
		Amortization 25 years.											
5 Yr.	6%	-6	-7	-9	-10	-12	-13	-14	-16	-17	-19	-20	-21
	9%	0	-1	-3	-4	-6	-7	-9	-10	-12	-13	-15	-16
	12%	7	5	4	2	0	-1	-3	-4	-6	-8	-9	-11
	15%	14	13	11	9	8	6	4	3	1	-1	-3	-4
10 Yr.	6%	-14	-18	-21	-24	-27	-31	-34	-37	-41	-44	-47	-51
	9%	1	-3	-7	-10	-14	-18	-22	-26	-29	-33	-37	-41
	12%	21	17	12	8	3	-1	-5	-10	-14	-19	-23	-27
	15%	47	42	37	32	27	21	16	11	6	1	-4	-9
		Amortization 30 years.											
5 Yr.	6%	-6	-7	-9	-10	-11	-13	-14	-16	-17	-19	-20	-21
	9%	0	-1	-3	-4	-6	-7	-9	-10	-12	-13	-15	-16
	12%	7	5	3	2	0	-1	-3	-4	-6	-8	-9	-11
	15%	14	12	11	9	7	6	4	2	1	-1	-3	-4
10 Yr.	6%	-14	-17	-20	-24	-27	-30	-34	-37	-40	-44	-47	-50
	9%	1	-3	-7	-11	-15	-18	-22	-26	-30	-34	-37	-41
	12%	20	15	11	7	2	-2	-6	-11	-15	-20	-24	-28
	15%	45	40	35	30	24	19	14	9	4	-1	-6	-11

66-2/3% Mortgage

ANALYSIS OF SELECTED CAPITALIZATION RATES

Depreciation or appreciation in 5 years, 10 years and amortization term for yields of 6%, 9%, 12% and 15% on 1/3rd equity

MORTGAGE INTEREST RATE 7%

Projection & Yield		CAPITALIZATION RATES											
		.075	.0775	.080	.0825	.0850	.0875	.090	.0925	.0950	.0975	.1000	.1025
		Amortization 15 years.											
	6%	-6	-7	-8	-10	-11	-13	-14	-15	-17	-18	-20	-21
5	9%	1	-0	-2	-3	-5	-6	-8	-9	-11	-12	-14	-15
Yr.	12%	8	7	5	4	2	0	-1	-3	-4	-6	-7	-9
	15%	17	15	13	12	10	8	6	5	3	1	-0	-2
	6%	-14	-17	-21	-24	-27	-31	-34	-37	-40	-44	-47	-50
10	9%	4	1	-3	-7	-11	-15	-18	-22	-26	-30	-34	-37
Yr.	12%	28	24	20	15	11	6	2	-2	-7	-11	-16	-20
	15%	59	54	49	44	39	33	28	23	18	13	8	3
		Amortization 20 years.											
	6%	-5	-7	-8	-9	-11	-12	-14	-15	-16	-18	-19	-21
5	9%	1	-0	-2	-3	-5	-6	-8	-9	-11	-12	-14	-15
Yr.	12%	8	6	5	3	2	0	-2	-3	-5	-6	-8	-9
	15%	16	14	12	11	9	7	6	4	2	1	-1	-3
	6%	-13	-16	-19	-23	-26	-29	-33	-36	-39	-43	-46	-49
10	9%	4	-0	-4	-8	-11	-15	-19	-23	-27	-30	-34	-38
Yr.	12%	25	21	16	12	8	3	-1	-5	-10	-14	-19	-23
	15%	53	48	43	38	33	28	23	17	12	7	2	-3
		Amortization 25 years.											
	6%	-5	-6	-8	-9	-11	-12	-13	-15	-16	-18	-19	-21
5	9%	1	-0	-2	-3	-5	-6	-8	-9	-11	-12	-14	-15
Yr.	12%	8	6	5	3	1	-0	-2	-3	-5	-7	-8	-10
	15%	15	14	12	10	9	7	5	4	2	0	-1	-3
	6%	-12	-16	-19	-22	-25	-29	-32	-35	-39	-42	-45	-48
10	9%	3	-1	-4	-8	-12	-16	-19	-23	-27	-31	-35	-38
Yr.	12%	24	19	15	10	6	2	-3	-7	-12	-16	-20	-25
	15%	50	45	40	35	29	24	19	14	9	4	-1	-6
		Amortization 30 years.											
	6%	-5	-6	-8	-9	-11	-12	-13	-15	-16	-18	-19	-20
5	9%	1	-0	-2	-3	-5	-6	-8	-9	-11	-12	-14	-15
Yr.	12%	8	6	4	3	1	-0	-2	-3	-5	-7	-8	-10
	15%	15	13	12	10	8	7	5	3	2	-0	-2	-3
	6%	-12	-15	-18	-22	-25	-28	-32	-35	-38	-41	-45	-48
10	9%	3	-1	-5	-8	-12	-16	-20	-24	-27	-31	-35	-39
Yr.	12%	23	18	14	9	5	1	-4	-8	-13	-17	-21	-26
	15%	48	43	38	33	28	22	17	12	7	2	-3	-8

66-2/3% Mortgage

ANALYSIS OF SELECTED CAPITALIZATION RATES
Depreciation or appreciation in 5 years, 10 years and amortization term
for yields of 6%, 9%, 12% and 15% on 1/3rd equity

MORTGAGE INTEREST RATE 7¼ %

Projection	Yield	.080	.0825	.0850	.0875	.090	.0925	.0950	.0975	.1000	.1025	.1050	.1075
							CAPITALIZATION RATES						
							Amortization 15 years.						
5 Yr.	6%	-7	-9	-10	-12	-13	-15	-16	-17	-19	-20	-22	-23
	9%	-1	-3	-4	-6	-7	-9	-10	-12	-13	-15	-16	-18
	12%	6	5	3	1	-0	-2	-3	-5	-7	-8	-10	-11
	15%	14	12	11	9	7	6	4	2	1	-1	-3	-4
10 Yr.	6%	-19	-22	-26	-29	-32	-35	-39	-42	-45	-49	-52	-55
	9%	-1	-5	-9	-13	-16	-20	-24	-28	-32	-35	-39	-43
	12%	22	17	13	9	4	-0	-4	-9	-13	-18	-22	-26
	15%	51	46	41	36	31	26	21	16	11	6	0	-5
							Amortization 20 years.						
5 Yr.	6%	-7	-9	-10	-11	-13	-14	-16	-17	-18	-20	-21	-23
	9%	-1	-3	-4	-6	-7	-9	-10	-12	-13	-14	-16	-17
	12%	6	4	3	1	-1	-2	-4	-5	-7	-8	-10	-12
	15%	13	12	10	8	7	5	3	2	-0	-2	-3	-5
10 Yr.	6%	-18	-21	-24	-27	-31	-34	-37	-41	-44	-47	-50	-54
	9%	-2	-5	-9	-13	-17	-21	-24	-28	-32	-36	-40	-43
	12%	19	15	10	6	1	-3	-7	-12	-16	-21	-25	-29
	15%	46	41	36	30	25	20	15	10	5	0	-5	-10
							Amortization 25 years.						
5 Yr.	6%	-7	-8	-10	-11	-13	-14	-15	-17	-18	-20	-21	-22
	9%	-1	-3	-4	-6	-7	-8	-10	-11	-13	-14	-16	-17
	12%	6	4	2	1	-1	-2	-4	-5	-7	-9	-10	-12
	15%	13	11	10	8	6	5	3	1	-0	-2	-4	-5
10 Yr.	6%	-17	-20	-23	-27	-30	-33	-37	-40	-43	-46	-50	-53
	9%	-2	-6	-10	-13	-17	-21	-25	-29	-32	-36	-40	-44
	12%	17	13	9	4	-0	-5	-9	-13	-18	-22	-26	-31
	15%	43	38	32	27	22	17	12	7	2	-3	-8	-13
							Amortization 30 years.						
5 Yr.	6%	-7	-8	-10	-11	-12	-14	-15	-17	-18	-19	-21	-22
	9%	-1	-3	-4	-5	-7	-8	-10	-11	-13	-14	-16	-17
	12%	6	4	2	1	-1	-2	-4	-6	-7	-9	-10	-12
	15%	13	11	9	8	6	4	3	1	-1	-2	-4	-6
10 Yr.	6%	-16	-20	-23	-26	-29	-33	-36	-39	-43	-46	-49	-53
	9%	-2	-6	-10	-14	-17	-21	-25	-29	-33	-36	-40	-44
	12%	16	12	8	3	-1	-5	-10	-14	-19	-23	-27	-32
	15%	41	36	31	26	20	15	10	5	0	-5	-10	-15

66-2/3% Mortgage

ANALYSIS OF SELECTED CAPITALIZATION RATES

Depreciation or appreciation in 5 years, 10 years and amortization term for yields of 6%, 9%, 12% and 15% on 1/3rd equity

MORTGAGE INTEREST RATE 7½ %

Projection & Yield		CAPITALIZATION RATES											
		.080	.0825	.0850	.0875	.090	.0925	.0950	.0975	.1000	.1025	.1050	.1075
		Amortization 15 years.											
5 Yr.	6%	-7	-8	-9	-11	-12	-14	-15	-16	-18	-19	-21	-22
	9%	-0	-2	-3	-5	-6	-8	-9	-11	-12	-14	-15	-17
	12%	7	6	4	2	1	-1	-2	-4	-6	-7	-9	-10
	15%	15	13	12	10	8	7	5	3	2	0	-2	-3
10 Yr.	6%	-17	-20	-24	-27	-30	-34	-37	-40	-44	-47	-50	-53
	9%	1	-3	-7	-11	-14	-18	-22	-26	-30	-33	-37	-41
	12%	24	20	15	11	7	2	-2	-7	-11	-15	-20	-24
	15%	54	49	44	39	34	28	23	18	13	8	3	-2
		Amortization 20 years.											
5 Yr.	6%	-6	-8	-9	-10	-12	-13	-15	-16	-17	-19	-20	-22
	9%	-0	-2	-3	-5	-6	-8	-9	-11	-12	-14	-15	-17
	12%	7	5	4	2	0	-1	-3	-4	-6	-7	-9	-11
	15%	14	13	11	9	8	6	4	3	1	-1	-2	-4
10 Yr.	6%	-16	-19	-22	-25	-29	-32	-35	-39	-42	-45	-49	-52
	9%	1	-3	-7	-11	-15	-18	-22	-26	-30	-34	-37	-41
	12%	21	17	13	8	4	-0	-5	-9	-14	-18	-22	-27
	15%	49	43	38	33	28	23	18	13	8	3	-2	-7
		Amortization 25 years.											
5 Yr.	6%	-6	-7	-9	-10	-12	-13	-14	-16	-17	-19	-20	-22
	9%	-0	-2	-3	-5	-6	-8	-9	-11	-12	-14	-15	-17
	12%	7	5	3	2	0	-1	-3	-4	-6	-8	-9	-11
	15%	14	12	11	9	7	6	4	2	1	-1	-3	-4
10 Yr.	6%	-15	-18	-21	-25	-28	-31	-34	-38	-41	-44	-48	-51
	9%	0	-3	-7	-11	-15	-19	-22	-26	-30	-34	-38	-41
	12%	20	16	11	7	2	-2	-6	-11	-15	-19	-24	-28
	15%	46	41	35	30	25	20	15	10	5	-0	-5	-10
		Amortization 30 years.											
5 Yr.	6%	-6	-7	-9	-10	-12	-13	-14	-16	-17	-19	-20	-21
	9%	-0	-2	-3	-5	-6	-8	-9	-11	-12	-14	-15	-16
	12%	7	5	3	2	0	-1	-3	-5	-6	-8	-9	-11
	15%	14	12	11	9	7	5	4	2	0	-1	-3	-5
10 Yr.	6%	-14	-17	-21	-24	-27	-31	-34	-37	-41	-44	-47	-50
	9%	0	-4	-7	-11	-15	-19	-23	-26	-30	-34	-38	-42
	12%	19	15	10	6	2	-3	-7	-12	-16	-20	-25	-29
	15%	44	39	34	29	24	18	13	8	3	-2	-7	-12

66-2/3% Mortgage

ANALYSIS OF SELECTED CAPITALIZATION RATES

Depreciation or appreciation in 5 years, 10 years and amortization term for yields of 6%, 9%, 12% and 15% on 1/3rd equity

MORTGAGE INTEREST RATE 7¾%

Projection & Yield		CAPITALIZATION RATES											
		.080	.0825	.0850	.0875	.090	.0925	.0950	.0975	.1000	.1025	.1050	.1075
		Amortization 15 years.											
	6%	-6	-7	-9	-10	-11	-13	-14	-16	-17	-18	-20	-21
5	9%	1	-1	-2	-4	-5	-7	-8	-10	-11	-13	-14	-16
Yr.	12%	8	6	5	3	2	0	-1	-3	-5	-6	-8	-9
	15%	16	14	13	11	9	8	6	4	3	1	-1	-2
	6%	-15	-19	-22	-25	-29	-32	-35	-38	-42	-45	-48	-52
10	9%	3	-1	-5	-8	-12	-16	-20	-24	-27	-31	-35	-39
Yr.	12%	26	22	18	13	9	4	0	-4	-9	-13	-17	-22
	15%	56	51	46	41	36	31	26	21	16	11	6	1
		Amortization 20 years.											
	6%	-5	-7	-8	-10	-11	-12	-14	-15	-17	-18	-19	-21
5	9%	1	-1	-2	-4	-5	-7	-8	-10	-11	-13	-14	-16
Yr.	12%	8	6	5	3	1	-0	-2	-3	-5	-7	-8	-10
	15%	16	14	12	10	9	7	5	4	2	0	-1	-3
	6%	-14	-17	-20	-23	-27	-30	-33	-37	-40	-43	-47	-50
10	9%	3	-1	-5	-9	-12	-16	-20	-24	-28	-31	-35	-39
Yr.	12%	24	20	15	11	6	2	-2	-7	-11	-15	-20	-24
	15%	51	46	41	36	31	26	21	16	11	6	1	-4
		Amortization 25 years.											
	6%	-5	-6	-8	-9	-11	-12	-14	-15	-16	-18	-19	-21
5	9%	1	-1	-2	-4	-5	-7	-8	-10	-11	-13	-14	-16
Yr.	12%	8	6	4	3	1	-0	-2	-3	-5	-7	-8	-10
	15%	15	14	12	10	8	7	5	3	2	0	-2	-3
	6%	-13	-16	-19	-22	-26	-29	-32	-36	-39	-42	-46	-49
10	9%	3	-1	-5	-9	-13	-16	-20	-24	-28	-32	-35	-39
Yr.	12%	23	18	14	10	5	1	-4	-8	-12	-17	-21	-26
	15%	49	44	38	33	28	23	18	13	8	3	-2	-7
		Amortization 30 years.											
	6%	-5	-6	-8	-9	-11	-12	-13	-15	-16	-18	-19	-20
5	9%	1	-1	-2	-4	-5	-7	-8	-10	-11	-13	-14	-16
Yr.	12%	8	6	4	3	1	-0	-2	-4	-5	-7	-8	-10
	15%	15	13	12	10	8	7	5	3	1	-0	-2	-4
	6%	-12	-15	-19	-22	-25	-29	-32	-35	-38	-42	-45	-48
10	9%	3	-1	-5	-9	-13	-16	-20	-24	-28	-32	-35	-39
Yr.	12%	22	18	13	9	4	-0	-4	-9	-13	-18	-22	-26
	15%	47	42	37	32	27	22	17	11	6	1	-4	-9

66-2/3% Mortgage

ANALYSIS OF SELECTED CAPITALIZATION RATES

Depreciation or appreciation in 5 years, 10 years and amortization term

for yields of 9%, 12%, 15% and 18% on 1/3rd equity

MORTGAGE INTEREST RATE 8%

Projection & Yield		CAPITALIZATION RATES											
		.0850	.0875	.090	.0925	.0950	.0975	.1000	.1025	.1050	.1075	.1100	.1125
		Amortization 15 years.											
	9%	-1	-3	-4	-6	-7	-9	-10	-12	-13	-15	-16	-18
5	12%	6	4	3	1	-1	-2	-4	-5	-7	-8	-10	-12
Yr.	15%	14	12	10	9	7	5	4	2	0	-1	-3	-5
	18%	23	21	19	17	15	14	12	10	8	7	5	3
	9%	-3	-6	-10	-14	-18	-22	-25	-29	-33	-37	-41	-44
10	12%	20	16	11	7	2	-2	-6	-11	-15	-20	-24	-28
Yr.	15%	49	44	39	34	29	24	18	13	8	3	-2	-7
	18%	86	80	74	68	62	56	50	45	39	33	27	21
		Amortization 20 years.											
	9%	-1	-3	-4	-6	-7	-9	-10	-12	-13	-15	-16	-18
5	12%	6	4	2	1	-1	-2	-4	-6	-7	-9	-10	-12
Yr.	15%	13	12	10	8	6	5	3	1	-0	-2	-4	-5
	18%	22	20	18	16	15	13	11	9	7	6	4	2
	9%	-3	-6	-10	-14	-18	-22	-25	-29	-33	-37	-41	-44
10	12%	18	13	9	5	0	-4	-9	-13	-17	-22	-26	-31
Yr.	15%	44	39	34	29	24	19	14	9	3	-2	-7	-12
	18%	78	72	66	60	54	48	43	37	31	25	19	13
		Amortization 25 years.											
	9%	-1	-3	-4	-6	-7	-9	-10	-12	-13	-15	-16	-18
5	12%	5	4	2	1	-1	-2	-4	-6	-7	-9	-10	-12
Yr.	15%	13	11	10	8	6	4	3	1	-1	-2	-4	-6
	18%	21	19	18	16	14	12	10	9	7	5	3	1
	9%	-3	-6	-10	-14	-18	-22	-25	-29	-33	-37	-41	-44
10	12%	17	12	8	3	-1	-5	-10	-14	-19	-23	-27	-32
Yr.	15%	41	36	31	26	21	16	11	6	1	-4	-9	-14
	18%	74	68	62	56	50	44	38	32	27	21	15	9
		Amortization 30 years.											
	9%	-1	-3	-4	-6	-7	-9	-10	-12	-13	-15	-16	-18
5	12%	5	4	2	1	-1	-3	-4	-6	-7	-9	-10	-12
Yr.	15%	13	11	9	8	6	4	3	1	-1	-2	-4	-6
	18%	21	19	17	15	14	12	10	8	7	5	3	1
	9%	-3	-6	-10	-14	-18	-22	-25	-29	-33	-37	-41	-44
10	12%	16	11	7	3	-2	-6	-10	-15	-19	-24	-28	-32
Yr.	15%	40	35	30	25	20	15	9	4	-1	-6	-11	-16
	18%	71	65	59	53	48	42	36	30	24	18	12	6

66-2/3% Mortgage

ANALYSIS OF SELECTED CAPITALIZATION RATES

Depreciation or appreciation in 5 years, 10 years and amortization term

for yields of 9%, 12%, 15% and 18% on 1/3rd equity

MORTGAGE INTEREST RATE 8¼%

Projection &	Yield	CAPITALIZATION RATES											
		.090	.0925	.0950	.0975	.1000	.1025	.1050	.1075	.1100	.1125	.1150	.1175
		Amortization 15 years.											
	9%	-3	-5	-6	-8	-9	-11	-12	-14	-15	-17	-18	-20
5	12%	4	2	0	-1	-3	-4	-6	-8	-9	-11	-12	-14
Yr.	15%	11	10	8	6	5	3	1	-0	-2	-4	-5	-7
	18%	20	18	17	15	13	11	9	8	6	4	2	0
	9%	-8	-12	-16	-20	-23	-27	-31	-35	-39	-42	-46	-50
10	12%	13	9	5	0	-4	-8	-13	-17	-22	-26	-30	-35
Yr.	15%	41	36	31	26	21	16	11	6	1	-4	-9	-14
	18%	77	71	65	59	54	48	42	36	30	24	18	12
		Amortization 20 years.											
	9%	-3	-5	-6	-8	-9	-11	-12	-14	-15	-17	-18	-20
5	12%	3	2	0	-1	-3	-5	-6	-8	-9	-11	-12	-14
Yr.	15%	11	9	8	6	4	2	1	-1	-3	-4	-6	-8
	18%	19	17	16	14	12	10	8	7	5	3	1	-0
	9%	-8	-12	-16	-19	-23	-27	-31	-35	-38	-42	-46	-50
10	12%	12	7	3	-2	-6	-10	-15	-19	-24	-28	-32	-37
Yr.	15%	37	32	27	22	17	11	6	1	-4	-9	-14	-19
	18%	69	64	58	52	46	40	34	28	22	16	11	5
		Amortization 25 years.											
	9%	-3	-5	-6	-8	-9	-11	-12	-14	-15	-17	-18	-20
5	12%	3	2	0	-1	-3	-5	-6	-8	-9	-11	-13	-14
Yr.	15%	11	9	7	6	4	2	0	-1	-3	-5	-6	-8
	18%	19	17	15	13	12	10	8	6	4	3	1	-1
	9%	-8	-12	-15	-19	-23	-27	-31	-34	-38	-42	-46	-50
10	12%	10	6	2	-3	-7	-11	-16	-20	-25	-29	-33	-38
Yr.	15%	34	29	24	19	14	9	4	-1	-6	-11	-16	-21
	18%	65	59	54	48	42	36	30	24	18	12	7	1
		Amortization 30 years.											
	9%	-3	-5	-6	-8	-9	-11	-12	-14	-15	-17	-18	-20
5	12%	3	2	0	-1	-3	-5	-6	-8	-9	-11	-13	-14
Yr.	15%	10	9	7	5	4	2	0	-1	-3	-5	-6	-8
	18%	18	17	15	13	11	9	8	6	4	2	1	-1
	9%	-8	-12	-15	-19	-23	-27	-31	-34	-38	-42	-46	-50
10	12%	10	5	1	-3	-8	-12	-16	-21	-25	-30	-34	-38
Yr.	15%	33	28	23	18	13	8	2	-3	-8	-13	-18	-23
	18%	63	57	51	45	39	34	28	22	16	10	4	-2

66-2/3% Mortgage

ANALYSIS OF SELECTED CAPITALIZATION RATES

Depreciation or appreciation in 5 years, 10 years and amortization term

for yields of 9%, 12%, 15% and 18% on 1/3rd equity

MORTGAGE INTEREST RATE 8½ %

CAPITALIZATION RATES

Projection & Yield		.090	.0925	.0950	.0975	.1000	.1025	.1050	.1075	.1100	.1125	.1150	.1175
		Amortization 15 years.											
5 Yr.	9%	-2	-4	-5	-7	-8	-10	-11	-13	-14	-16	-17	-19
	12%	5	3	1	-0	-2	-3	-5	-7	-8	-10	-11	-13
	15%	12	11	9	7	6	4	2	1	-1	-3	-4	-6
	18%	21	19	18	16	14	12	10	9	7	5	3	2
10 Yr.	9%	-6	-10	-14	-18	-21	-25	-29	-33	-37	-40	-44	-48
	12%	16	11	7	3	-2	-6	-10	-15	-19	-24	-28	-32
	15%	44	39	34	29	24	19	14	9	3	-2	-7	-12
	18%	80	74	68	62	57	51	45	39	33	27	21	15
		Amortization 20 years.											
5 Yr.	9%	-2	-4	-5	-7	-8	-10	-11	-13	-14	-16	-17	-19
	12%	4	3	1	-0	-2	-4	-5	-7	-8	-10	-11	-13
	15%	12	10	9	7	5	3	2	0	-2	-3	-5	-7
	18%	20	19	17	15	13	11	10	8	6	4	2	1
10 Yr.	9%	-6	-9	-13	-17	-21	-25	-28	-32	-36	-40	-44	-47
	12%	14	10	5	1	-3	-8	-12	-17	-21	-25	-30	-34
	15%	40	35	30	25	19	14	9	4	-1	-6	-11	-16
	18%	73	67	61	55	49	43	37	32	26	20	14	8
		Amortization 25 years.											
5 Yr.	9%	-2	-4	-5	-7	-8	-10	-11	-13	-14	-16	-17	-19
	12%	4	3	1	-0	-2	-4	-5	-7	-8	-10	-12	-13
	15%	12	10	8	7	5	3	2	-0	-2	-4	-5	-7
	18%	20	18	16	14	13	11	9	7	6	4	2	0
10 Yr.	9%	-5	-9	-13	-17	-21	-24	-28	-32	-36	-40	-43	-47
	12%	13	9	4	-0	-4	-9	-13	-18	-22	-26	-31	-35
	15%	37	32	27	22	17	12	7	2	-3	-8	-13	-18
	18%	69	63	57	51	45	39	34	28	22	16	10	4
		Amortization 30 years.											
5 Yr.	9%	-2	-4	-5	-7	-8	-10	-11	-13	-14	-16	-17	-19
	12%	4	3	1	-0	-2	-4	-5	-7	-8	-10	-12	-13
	15%	11	10	8	6	5	3	1	-0	-2	-4	-5	-7
	18%	20	18	16	14	12	11	9	7	5	3	2	-0
10 Yr.	9%	-5	-9	-13	-17	-20	-24	-28	-32	-36	-39	-43	-47
	12%	13	8	4	-1	-5	-9	-14	-18	-22	-27	-31	-36
	15%	36	31	26	21	16	11	6	1	-5	-10	-15	-20
	18%	67	61	55	49	43	37	31	25	19	14	8	2

66-2/3% Mortgage

ANALYSIS OF SELECTED CAPITALIZATION RATES

Depreciation or appreciation in 5 years, 10 years and amortization term

for yields of 9%, 12%, 15% and 18% on 1/3rd equity

MORTGAGE INTEREST RATE 8¾%

CAPITALIZATION RATES

Projection &	Yield	.090	.0925	.0950	.0975	.1000	.1025	.1050	.1075	.1100	.1125	.1150	.1175
		Amortization 15 years.											
	9%	-2	-3	-5	-6	-8	-9	-11	-12	-14	-15	-17	-18
5	12%	6	4	2	1	-1	-2	-4	-6	-7	-9	-10	-12
Yr.	15%	13	12	10	8	7	5	3	2	-0	-2	-3	-5
	18%	22	20	19	17	15	13	12	10	8	6	4	3
	9%	-4	-8	-12	-15	-19	-23	-27	-31	-34	-38	-42	-46
10	12%	18	14	9	5	1	-4	-8	-13	-17	-21	-26	-30
Yr.	15%	47	42	37	32	26	21	16	11	6	1	-4	-9
	18%	83	77	71	65	60	54	48	42	36	30	24	18
		Amortization 20 years.											
	9%	-1	-3	-4	-6	-7	-9	-10	-12	-13	-15	-16	-18
5	12%	5	4	2	1	-1	-3	-4	-6	-7	-9	-10	-12
Yr.	15%	13	11	10	8	6	5	3	1	-1	-2	-4	-6
	18%	21	20	18	16	14	12	11	9	7	5	4	2
	9%	-3	-7	-11	-15	-19	-22	-26	-30	-34	-38	-41	-45
10	12%	17	12	8	4	-1	-5	-10	-14	-18	-23	-27	-32
Yr.	15%	43	38	33	27	22	17	12	7	2	-3	-8	-13
	18%	76	70	64	58	53	47	41	35	29	23	17	11
		Amortization 25 years.											
	9%	-1	-3	-4	-6	-7	-9	-10	-12	-13	-15	-16	-18
5	12%	5	4	2	1	-1	-3	-4	-6	-7	-9	-11	-12
Yr.	15%	13	11	9	8	6	4	3	1	-1	-2	-4	-6
	18%	21	19	17	16	14	12	10	8	7	5	3	1
	9%	-3	-7	-11	-14	-18	-22	-26	-30	-33	-37	-41	-45
10	12%	16	11	7	3	-2	-6	-10	-15	-19	-24	-28	-32
Yr.	15%	40	35	30	25	20	15	10	5	-0	-5	-10	-15
	18%	72	66	61	55	49	43	37	31	25	19	14	8
		Amortization 30 years.											
	9%	-1	-3	-4	-6	-7	-9	-10	-12	-13	-15	-16	-18
5	12%	5	4	2	1	-1	-3	-4	-6	-7	-9	-11	-12
Yr.	15%	13	11	9	8	6	4	2	1	-1	-3	-4	-6
	18%	21	19	17	15	14	12	10	8	6	5	3	1
	9%	-3	-7	-10	-14	-18	-22	-26	-29	-33	-37	-41	-45
10	12%	15	11	7	2	-2	-7	-11	-15	-20	-24	-28	-33
Yr.	15%	39	34	29	24	19	14	9	4	-1	-6	-12	-17
	18%	70	64	58	53	47	41	35	29	23	17	11	5

66-2/3% Mortgage

ANALYSIS OF SELECTED CAPITALIZATION RATES

Depreciation or appreciation in 5 years, 10 years and amortization term for yields of 9%, 12%, 15% and 18% on 1/3rd equity

MORTGAGE INTEREST RATE 9%

Projection & Yield	CAPITALIZATION RATES											
	.0925	.0950	.0975	.1000	.1025	.1050	.1075	.1100	.1125	.1150	.1175	.1200
	Amortization 15 years.											
5 Yr. 9%	-2	-4	-5	-7	-8	-10	-11	-13	-14	-16	-17	-19
12%	5	3	2	0	-1	-3	-5	-6	-8	-9	-11	-13
15%	13	11	9	8	6	4	3	1	-1	-2	-4	-6
18%	22	20	18	16	14	13	11	9	7	5	4	2
10 Yr. 9%	-6	-10	-13	-17	-21	-25	-29	-32	-36	-40	-44	-48
12%	16	12	7	3	-1	-6	-10	-15	-19	-23	-28	-32
15%	44	39	34	29	24	19	14	9	4	-1	-6	-11
18%	80	74	69	63	57	51	45	39	33	27	22	16
	Amortization 20 years.											
5 Yr. 9%	-2	-3	-5	-6	-8	-9	-11	-12	-14	-15	-17	-18
12%	5	3	2	0	-2	-3	-5	-6	-8	-9	-11	-13
15%	12	11	9	7	6	4	2	1	-1	-3	-5	-6
18%	21	19	17	15	14	12	10	8	6	5	3	1
10 Yr. 9%	-5	-9	-13	-16	-20	-24	-28	-32	-35	-39	-43	-47
12%	15	10	6	2	-3	-7	-11	-16	-20	-25	-29	-33
15%	41	35	30	25	20	15	10	5	-0	-5	-10	-15
18%	74	68	62	56	50	44	38	32	26	21	15	9
	Amortization 25 years.											
5 Yr. 9%	-2	-3	-5	-6	-8	-9	-11	-12	-14	-15	-17	-18
12%	5	3	2	0	-2	-3	-5	-6	-8	-9	-11	-13
15%	12	10	9	7	5	4	2	0	-1	-3	-5	-6
18%	20	19	17	15	13	11	10	8	6	4	2	1
10 Yr. 9%	-4	-8	-12	-16	-20	-23	-27	-31	-35	-39	-42	-46
12%	14	10	5	1	-3	-8	-12	-17	-21	-25	-30	-34
15%	39	33	28	23	18	13	8	3	-2	-7	-12	-17
18%	70	64	58	52	46	41	35	29	23	17	11	5
	Amortization 30 years.											
5 Yr. 9%	-2	-3	-5	-6	-8	-9	-11	-12	-14	-15	-17	-18
12%	5	3	2	0	-2	-3	-5	-6	-8	-9	-11	-13
15%	12	10	9	7	5	4	2	0	-1	-3	-5	-7
18%	20	18	16	15	13	11	9	8	6	4	2	0
10 Yr. 9%	-4	-8	-12	-16	-19	-23	-27	-31	-35	-38	-42	-46
12%	14	9	5	1	-4	-8	-13	-17	-21	-26	-30	-34
15%	37	32	27	22	17	12	7	2	-3	-8	-13	-18
18%	68	62	56	50	44	39	33	27	21	15	9	3

66-2/3% Mortgage

ANALYSIS OF SELECTED CAPITALIZATION RATES

Depreciation or appreciation in 5 years, 10 years and amortization term for yields of 9%, 12%, 15% and 18% on 1/3rd equity

MORTGAGE INTEREST RATE 9¼ %

Projection & Yield		CAPITALIZATION RATES											
		.0925	.0950	.0975	.1000	.1025	.1050	.1075	.1100	.1125	.1150	.1175	.1200
		Amortization 15 years.											
	9%	-1	-3	-4	-6	-7	-9	-10	-12	-13	-15	-16	-18
5	12%	6	4	3	1	-0	-2	-4	-5	-7	-8	-10	-12
Yr.	15%	14	12	10	9	7	5	4	2	0	-1	-3	-5
	18%	23	21	19	17	15	14	12	10	8	6	5	3
	9%	-4	-7	-11	-15	-19	-23	-26	-30	-34	-38	-42	-45
10	12%	19	14	10	5	1	-3	-8	-12	-17	-21	-25	-30
Yr.	15%	47	42	37	32	27	22	17	12	6	1	-4	-9
	18%	83	78	72	66	60	54	48	42	36	30	25	19
		Amortization 20 years.											
	9%	-1	-2	-4	-5	-7	-8	-10	-11	-13	-14	-16	-17
5	12%	6	4	3	1	-0	-2	-4	-5	-7	-8	-10	-12
Yr.	15%	13	12	10	8	7	5	3	2	-0	-2	-3	-5
	18%	22	20	18	16	15	13	11	9	8	6	4	2
	9%	-3	-6	-10	-14	-18	-22	-25	-29	-33	-37	-41	-44
10	12%	17	13	9	4	-0	-4	-9	-13	-18	-22	-26	-31
Yr.	15%	43	38	33	28	23	18	13	8	3	-2	-7	-12
	18%	77	71	65	59	53	48	42	36	30	24	18	12
		Amortization 25 years.											
	9%	-1	-2	-4	-5	-7	-8	-10	-11	-13	-14	-16	-17
5	12%	6	4	3	1	-1	-2	-4	-5	-7	-8	-10	-12
Yr.	15%	13	12	10	8	6	5	3	1	-0	-2	-4	-5
	18%	21	20	18	16	14	12	11	9	7	5	4	2
	9%	-2	-6	-10	-13	-17	-21	-25	-29	-32	-36	-40	-44
10	12%	17	13	8	4	-1	-5	-9	-14	-18	-23	-27	-31
Yr.	15%	42	37	31	26	21	16	11	6	1	-4	-9	-14
	18%	74	68	62	56	50	44	38	32	26	21	15	9
		Amortization 30 years.											
	9%	-1	-2	-4	-5	-7	-8	-10	-11	-13	-14	-16	-17
5	12%	6	4	3	1	-1	-2	-4	-5	-7	-8	-10	-12
Yr.	15%	13	11	10	8	6	5	3	1	-0	-2	-4	-5
	18%	21	19	18	16	14	12	10	9	7	5	3	2
	9%	-2	-6	-9	-13	-17	-21	-25	-28	-32	-36	-40	-44
10	12%	17	12	8	3	-1	-5	-10	-14	-19	-23	-27	-32
Yr.	15%	41	35	30	25	20	15	10	5	-0	-5	-10	-15
	18%	72	66	60	54	48	42	36	30	25	19	13	7

66-2/3% Mortgage

ANALYSIS OF SELECTED CAPITALIZATION RATES

Depreciation or appreciation in 5 years, 10 years and amortization term for yields of 9%, 12%, 15% and 18% on 1/3rd equity

MORTGAGE INTEREST RATE 9½%

Projection &	Yield	.0925	.0950	.0975	.1000	.1025	.1050	.1075	.1100	.1125	.1150	.1175	.1200
		CAPITALIZATION RATES											
		Amortization 15 years.											
5 Yr.	9%	−0	−2	−3	−5	−6	−8	−9	−11	−12	−14	−15	−17
	12%	7	5	4	2	0	−1	−3	−4	−6	−7	−9	−11
	15%	15	13	11	10	8	6	5	3	1	−0	−2	−4
	18%	24	22	20	18	16	15	13	11	9	8	6	4
10 Yr.	9%	−2	−5	−9	−13	−17	−21	−24	−28	−32	−36	−40	−43
	12%	21	17	12	8	3	−1	−5	−10	−14	−19	−23	−27
	15%	50	45	40	35	29	24	19	14	9	4	−1	−6
	18%	87	81	75	69	63	57	51	45	39	34	28	22
		Amortization 20 years.											
5 Yr.	9%	0	−1	−3	−4	−6	−7	−9	−10	−12	−13	−15	−16
	12%	7	5	4	2	1	−1	−3	−4	−6	−7	−9	−11
	15%	14	13	11	9	8	6	4	3	1	−1	−2	−4
	18%	23	21	19	18	16	14	12	10	9	7	5	3
10 Yr.	9%	−0	−4	−8	−12	−15	−19	−23	−27	−31	−34	−38	−42
	12%	20	16	11	7	3	−2	−6	−11	−15	−19	−24	−28
	15%	46	41	36	31	26	21	16	11	6	1	−4	−9
	18%	80	74	69	63	57	51	45	39	33	27	22	16
		Amortization 25 years.											
5 Yr.	9%	0	−1	−3	−4	−6	−7	−9	−10	−12	−13	−15	−16
	12%	7	5	4	2	1	−1	−3	−4	−6	−7	−9	−11
	15%	14	13	11	9	8	6	4	2	1	−1	−3	−4
	18%	23	21	19	17	15	14	12	10	8	6	5	3
10 Yr.	9%	0	−3	−7	−11	−15	−19	−22	−26	−30	−34	−38	−41
	12%	20	15	11	6	2	−2	−7	−11	−15	−20	−24	−29
	15%	45	40	35	30	24	19	14	9	4	−1	−6	−11
	18%	77	71	65	59	54	48	42	36	30	24	18	12
		Amortization 30 years.											
5 Yr.	9%	0	−1	−3	−4	−6	−7	−9	−10	−12	−13	−15	−16
	12%	7	5	4	2	1	−1	−3	−4	−6	−7	−9	−11
	15%	14	13	11	9	7	6	4	2	1	−1	−3	−4
	18%	22	21	19	17	15	13	12	10	8	6	4	3
10 Yr.	9%	1	−3	−7	−11	−14	−18	−22	−26	−30	−33	−37	−41
	12%	19	15	11	6	2	−3	−7	−11	−16	−20	−24	−29
	15%	44	39	34	29	23	18	13	8	3	−2	−7	−12
	18%	75	69	63	58	52	46	40	34	28	22	16	11

66-2/3% Mortgage

ANALYSIS OF SELECTED CAPITALIZATION RATES

Depreciation or appreciation in 5 years, 10 years and amortization term for yields of 9%, 12%, 15% and 18% on 1/3rd equity

MORTGAGE INTEREST RATE 9¾%

Projection & Yield		CAPITALIZATION RATES											
		.0950	.0975	.1000	.1025	.1050	.1075	.1100	.1125	.1150	.1175	.1200	.1225
		Amortization 15 years.											
5 Yr.	9%	-1	-2	-4	-5	-7	-8	-10	-11	-13	-14	-16	-17
	12%	6	5	3	1	-0	-2	-3	-5	-6	-8	-10	-11
	15%	14	12	11	9	7	6	4	2	1	-1	-3	-4
	18%	23	21	19	18	16	14	12	10	9	7	5	3
10 Yr.	9%	-3	-7	-11	-15	-18	-22	-26	-30	-34	-37	-41	-45
	12%	19	15	10	6	1	-3	-7	-12	-16	-21	-25	-29
	15%	47	42	37	32	27	22	17	12	7	2	-3	-8
	18%	84	78	72	66	60	54	49	43	37	31	25	19
		Amortization 20 years.											
5 Yr.	9%	-0	-2	-3	-5	-6	-8	-9	-11	-12	-14	-15	-17
	12%	6	5	3	2	-0	-2	-3	-5	-6	-8	-10	-11
	15%	14	12	10	9	7	5	4	2	0	-1	-3	-5
	18%	22	20	19	17	15	13	12	10	8	6	4	3
10 Yr.	9%	-2	-6	-9	-13	-17	-21	-25	-28	-32	-36	-40	-44
	12%	18	14	10	5	1	-4	-8	-12	-17	-21	-26	-30
	15%	44	39	34	29	24	19	14	9	4	-1	-6	-11
	18%	78	72	66	60	54	48	43	37	31	25	19	13
		Amortization 25 years.											
5 Yr.	9%	-0	-2	-3	-5	-6	-8	-9	-11	-12	-14	-15	-17
	12%	6	5	3	2	-0	-2	-3	-5	-6	-8	-10	-11
	15%	14	12	10	9	7	5	4	2	0	-1	-3	-5
	18%	22	20	18	17	15	13	11	9	8	6	4	2
10 Yr.	9%	-1	-5	-9	-12	-16	-20	-24	-28	-31	-35	-39	-43
	12%	18	14	9	5	0	-4	-8	-13	-17	-21	-26	-30
	15%	43	38	33	28	22	17	12	7	2	-3	-8	-13
	18%	75	69	63	57	51	45	39	34	28	22	16	10
		Amortization 30 years.											
5 Yr.	9%	-0	-2	-3	-5	-6	-8	-9	-11	-12	-14	-15	-17
	12%	6	5	3	2	-0	-2	-3	-5	-6	-8	-10	-11
	15%	14	12	10	9	7	5	3	2	0	-2	-3	-5
	18%	22	20	18	16	15	13	11	9	7	6	4	2
10 Yr.	9%	-1	-4	-8	-12	-16	-20	-23	-27	-31	-35	-39	-42
	12%	18	13	9	5	0	-4	-9	-13	-17	-22	-26	-30
	15%	42	37	32	27	22	17	11	6	1	-4	-9	-14
	18%	73	67	61	55	50	44	38	32	26	20	14	8

66-2/3% Mortgage

ANALYSIS OF SELECTED CAPITALIZATION RATES

Depreciation or appreciation in 5 years, 10 years and amortization term for yields of 9%, 12%, 15% and 18% on 1/3rd equity

MORTGAGE INTEREST RATE 10%

Projection & Yield		CAPITALIZATION RATES											
		.0950	.0975	.1000	.1025	.1050	.1075	.1100	.1125	.1150	.1175	.1200	.1225
		Amortization 15 years.											
5 Yr.	9%	0	-1	-3	-4	-6	-7	-9	-10	-12	-13	-15	-16
	12%	7	6	4	2	1	-1	-2	-4	-5	-7	-9	-10
	15%	15	13	12	10	8	7	5	3	2	-0	-2	-3
	18%	24	22	20	19	17	15	13	11	10	8	6	4
10 Yr.	9%	-1	-5	-9	-12	-16	-20	-24	-28	-31	-35	-39	-43
	12%	21	17	13	8	4	-1	-5	-9	-14	-18	-22	-27
	15%	50	45	40	35	30	25	20	15	10	5	-1	-6
	18%	87	81	75	69	63	58	52	46	40	34	28	22
		Amortization 20 years.											
5 Yr.	9%	1	-1	-2	-4	-5	-7	-8	-10	-11	-13	-14	-16
	12%	7	6	4	3	1	-1	-2	-4	-5	-7	-9	-10
	15%	15	13	12	10	8	6	5	3	1	-0	-2	-4
	18%	23	22	20	18	16	14	13	11	9	7	6	4
10 Yr.	9%	1	-3	-7	-11	-15	-18	-22	-26	-30	-34	-37	-41
	12%	21	17	12	8	3	-1	-5	-10	-14	-19	-23	-27
	15%	47	42	37	32	27	22	17	12	7	2	-3	-8
	18%	81	75	70	64	58	52	46	40	34	28	22	17
		Amortization 25 years.											
5 Yr.	9%	1	-1	-2	-4	-5	-7	-8	-10	-11	-13	-14	-16
	12%	7	6	4	3	1	-1	-2	-4	-5	-7	-9	-10
	15%	15	13	11	10	8	6	5	3	1	-0	-2	-4
	18%	23	21	20	18	16	14	12	11	9	7	5	3
10 Yr.	9%	1	-2	-6	-10	-14	-18	-21	-25	-29	-33	-37	-40
	12%	21	16	12	8	3	-1	-6	-10	-14	-19	-23	-27
	15%	46	41	36	31	26	21	15	10	5	0	-5	-10
	18%	78	72	67	61	55	49	43	37	31	25	20	14
		Amortization 30 years.											
5 Yr.	9%	1	-1	-2	-4	-5	-7	-8	-10	-11	-13	-14	-16
	12%	7	6	4	3	1	-1	-2	-4	-5	-7	-9	-10
	15%	15	13	11	10	8	6	5	3	1	-0	-2	-4
	18%	23	21	19	18	16	14	12	10	9	7	5	3
10 Yr.	9%	2	-2	-6	-10	-13	-17	-21	-25	-29	-32	-36	-40
	12%	21	16	12	7	3	-1	-6	-10	-14	-19	-23	-28
	15%	45	40	35	30	25	20	15	10	5	-1	-6	-11
	18%	77	71	65	59	53	47	41	36	30	24	18	12

PURCHASE-LEASEBACK TABLES, IV

Table IV:

Monthly and quarterly rent requirements for full recapture of investment during lease term at indicated yield rates. (Compound Interest Column No. 6 factors adjusted for payment in advance.)

Annual Requirement captioned "Cap. Rate" is 12 times monthly factor and 4 times quarterly factor.

Scope: Full recapture rates 3% to 12¼%.
Lease terms 10 to 50 years.

TABLE IV

PURCHASE–LEASEBACK RENT FACTORS and CAPITALIZATION RATES

Rate	3%				3¼%			
Payable	Monthly		Quarterly		Monthly		Quarterly	
Term Years	Rent	Cap Rate	Rent	Cap Rate	Rent	Cap Rate	Rent	Cap Rate
10	.009632	.115584	.028814	.115256	.009746	.116952	.029146	.116584
11	.008882	.106584	.026568	.106272	.008996	.107952	.026904	.107616
12	.008257	.099084	.024700	.098800	.008373	.100476	.025039	.100156
13	.007730	.092760	.023122	.092488	.007847	.094164	.023465	.093860
14	.007279	.087348	.021772	.087088	.007397	.088764	.022118	.088472
15	.006889	.082668	.020604	.082416	.007008	.084096	.020954	.083816
16	.006548	.078576	.019584	.078336	.006668	.080016	.019938	.079752
17	.006248	.074976	.018687	.074748	.006369	.076428	.019044	.076176
18	.005982	.071784	.017891	.071564	.006105	.073260	.018252	.073008
19	.005745	.068940	.017181	.068724	.005869	.070428	.017545	.070180
20	.005532	.066384	.016544	.066176	.005657	.067884	.016911	.067644
21	.005340	.064080	.015969	.063876	.005466	.065592	.016340	.065360
22	.005166	.061092	.015448	.061792	.005293	.063516	.015822	.063288
23	.005008	.060196	.014974	.059896	.005135	.061620	.015351	.061404
24	.004863	.058356	.014541	.058164	.004992	.059904	.014921	.059684
25	.004730	.056760	.014144	.056576	.004860	.058320	.014527	.058108
26	.004608	.055296	.013779	.055116	.004739	.056868	.014165	.056660
27	.004496	.053952	.013442	.053768	.004628	.055536	.013831	.055324
28	.004392	.052704	.013131	.052524	.004524	.054288	.013523	.054092
29	.004295	.051540	.012842	.051368	.004429	.053148	.013237	.052948
30	.004205	.050460	.012573	.050292	.004340	.052080	.012972	.051888
31	.004122	.049464	.012323	.049292	.004258	.051096	.012725	.050900
32	.004044	.048528	.012090	.048360	.004181	.050172	.012494	.049976
33	.003971	.047652	.011872	.047488	.004109	.049308	.012279	.049116
34	.003903	.046836	.011667	.046668	.004042	.048504	.012078	.048312
35	.003839	.046068	.011476	.045904	.003979	.047748	.011889	.047556
36	.003779	.045348	.011296	.045184	.003919	.047028	.011712	.046848
37	.003722	.044664	.011126	.044504	.003864	.046368	.011545	.046180
38	.003669	.044028	.010966	.043864	.003811	.045732	.011388	.045552
39	.003618	.043416	.010816	.043264	.003762	.045144	.011240	.044960
40	.003571	.042852	.010673	.042692	.003715	.044580	.011101	.044404
41	.003526	.042312	.010539	.042156	.003671	.044052	.010969	.043876
42	.003483	.041796	.010411	.041644	.003630	.043560	.010844	.043376
43	.003443	.041316	.010291	.041164	.003590	.043080	.010726	.042904
44	.003405	.040860	.010176	.040704	.003553	.042636	.010614	.042456
45	.003368	.040416	.010067	.040268	.003517	.042204	.010508	.042032
46	.003334	.040008	.009964	.039856	.003484	.041808	.010408	.041632
47	.003301	.039612	.009866	.039464	.003452	.041424	.010312	.041248
48	.003270	.039240	.009772	.039088	.003422	.041064	.010221	.040884
49	.003240	.038880	.009683	.038732	.003393	.040716	.010134	.040536
50	.003212	.038544	.009598	.038792	.003365	.040380	.010052	.040208

Factors in this table are computed for payment of rent monthly and quarterly in advance. Cap. Rates are 12 times the monthly factors and 4 times the quarterly factors. These may be used as divisors of net annual rent to compute value or as multipliers of investment cost to compute net annual rent.

TABLE IV

PURCHASE–LEASEBACK RENT FACTORS and CAPITALIZATION RATES.

RATE	3½%				3¾%			
Payable	Monthly		Quarterly		Monthly		Quarterly	
Term Years	Rent	Cap Rate	Rent	Cap Rate	Rent	Cap Rate	Rent	Cap Rate
10	.009860	.118320	.029480	.117920	.009975	.119700	.029816	.119264
11	.009112	.109344	.027242	.108968	.009229	.110748	.027583	.110332
12	.008490	.101880	.025382	.101528	.008608	.103396	.025726	.102904
13	.007965	.095580	.024802	.099208	.008084	.097008	.024160	.096640
14	.007516	.090192	.022468	.089872	.007637	.091644	.022821	.091284
15	.007128	.085536	.021308	.085232	.007250	.087000	.021665	.086660
16	.006790	.081480	.020296	.081184	.006913	.082956	.020656	.082624
17	.006493	.077916	.019405	.077620	.006616	.079492	.019770	.079080
18	.006229	.074748	.018617	.074468	.006354	.076248	.018985	.075940
19	.005994	.071928	.017913	.071652	.006120	.073440	.018285	.073140
20	.005783	.069396	.017283	.069132	.005911	.070932	.017659	.070636
21	.005593	.067116	.016715	.066860	.005722	.068664	.017094	.068376
22	.005421	.065052	.016201	.064804	.005551	.066612	.016584	.066336
23	.005265	.063180	.015733	.062932	.005396	.064752	.016120	.064480
24	.005123	.061476	.015307	.061228	.005225	.063060	.015697	.062788
25	.004992	.059904	.014916	.059664	.005126	.061512	.015310	.061240
26	.004872	.058464	.014557	.058228	.005007	.060084	.014955	.059820
27	.004762	.057144	.014227	.056908	.004898	.058776	.014628	.058512
28	.004660	.055920	.013922	.055688	.004797	.057564	.014326	.057304
29	.004565	.054780	.013639	.054556	.004704	.056448	.014047	.056188
30	.004478	.053736	.013377	.053508	.004617	.055404	.013788	.055152
31	.004396	.052752	.013133	.052532	.004537	.054444	.013548	.054192
32	.004320	.051840	.012906	.051624	.004462	.053544	.013324	.053296
33	.004250	.051000	.012694	.050776	.004392	.052704	.013115	.052460
34	.004183	.050196	.012496	.049984	.004327	.051924	.012920	.051680
35	.004121	.049452	.012310	.049240	.004266	.051292	.012737	.050948
36	.004063	.048756	.012136	.048544	.004209	.050508	.012566	.050264
37	.004008	.048096	.011972	.047888	.004155	.049860	.012406	.049624
38	.003957	.047484	.011818	.047272	.004105	.049260	.012255	.049020
39	.003909	.046908	.011673	.046692	.004058	.048696	.012114	.048456
40	.003863	.046356	.011537	.046148	.004013	.048156	.011980	.047920
41	.003820	.045840	.011408	.045632	.003971	.047652	.011854	.047416
42	.003779	.045348	.011286	.045144	.003931	.047172	.011735	.046940
43	.003741	.044892	.011171	.044684	.003894	.046728	.011623	.046492
44	.003704	.044448	.011062	.044248	.003859	.046308	.011517	.046068
45	.003670	.044040	.010959	.043836	.003825	.045900	.011417	.045668
46	.003637	.043644	.010861	.043444	.003793	.045516	.011322	.045288
47	.003606	.043272	.010768	.043072	.003763	.045156	.011232	.044928
48	.003577	.042924	.010679	.042716	.003735	.044820	.011146	.044584
49	.003549	.042588	.010595	.042380	.003708	.044496	.011065	.044260
50	.003522	.042264	.010516	.042064	.003672	.044064	.010988	.043952

Factors in this table are computed for payment of rent monthly and quarterly in advance. Cap. Rates are 12 times the monthly factors and 4 times the quarterly factors. These may be used as divisors of net annual rent to compute value or as multipliers of investment cost to compute net annual rent.

TABLE IV

PURCHASE–LEASEBACK RENT FACTORS and CAPITALIZATION RATES.

RATE	4%				4¼%			
Payable	Monthly		Quarterly		Monthly		Quarterly	
Term Years	Rent	Cap Rate	Rent	Cap Rate	Rent	Cap Rate	Rent	Cap Rate
10	.010091	.121092	.030154	.120616	.010208	.122596	.030495	.121980
11	.009346	.112152	.027926	.111704	.009464	.113568	.028271	.113084
12	.008727	.104724	.026073	.104292	.008846	.106152	.026423	.105692
13	.008204	.098448	.024511	.098044	.008325	.099900	.024866	.099464
14	.007758	.093096	.023177	.092708	.007880	.094560	.023536	.094144
15	.007373	.088476	.022025	.088100	.007497	.089964	.022388	.089552
16	.007037	.084444	.021020	.084080	.007162	.085944	.021388	.085552
17	.006742	.080904	.020138	.080552	.006869	.082428	.020510	.082040
18	.006481	.077772	.019357	.077428	.006609	.079308	.019733	.078932
19	.006248	.074976	.018662	.074648	.006378	.076536	.019042	.076168
20	.006040	.072480	.018039	.072156	.006171	.074052	.018423	.073692
21	.005853	.070236	.017478	.069912	.005985	.071820	.017867	.071468
22	.005683	.068196	.016972	.067888	.005817	.069804	.017364	.069456
23	.005529	.066348	.016512	.066048	.005664	.067968	.016908	.067632
24	.005389	.064668	.016092	.064368	.005525	.066300	.016493	.065972
25	.005261	.063132	.015709	.062836	.005399	.064788	.016114	.064456
26	.005144	.061728	.015358	.061432	.005282	.063384	.015766	.063064
27	.005036	.060432	.015034	.060136	.005176	.062112	.015446	.061784
28	.004936	.059232	.014736	.058944	.005077	.060924	.015221	.060884
29	.004844	.058128	.014461	.057844	.004987	.059844	.014881	.059524
30	.004759	.057108	.014205	.056820	.004902	.058824	.014629	.058516
31	.004680	.056160	.013969	.055876	.004825	.057900	.014396	.057584
32	.004606	.055272	.013748	.054992	.004752	.057024	.014179	.056716
33	.004537	.054444	.013543	.054172	.004685	.056220	.013977	.055908
34	.004473	.053676	.013351	.053404	.004622	.055464	.013789	.055156
35	.004413	.052956	.013172	.052688	.004563	.054756	.013614	.054456
36	.004357	.052284	.013005	.052020	.004508	.054096	.013450	.053800
37	.004305	.051660	.012847	.051388	.004457	.053484	.013296	.053184
38	.004256	.051072	.012700	.050800	.004409	.052908	.013152	.052608
39	.004209	.050508	.012561	.050244	.004364	.052368	.013017	.052068
40	.004166	.049992	.012431	.049724	.004321	.051852	.012890	.051560
41	.004125	.049500	.012308	.049232	.004281	.051372	.012770	.051080
42	.004086	.049032	.012193	.048772	.004244	.050928	.012658	.050632
43	.004050	.048600	.012084	.048336	.004208	.050496	.012552	.050208
44	.004015	.048180	.011981	.047924	.004175	.050100	.012452	.049808
45	.003983	.047796	.011883	.047532	.004144	.049728	.012358	.049432
46	.003952	.047424	.011791	.047164	.004114	.049368	.012268	.049072
47	.003923	.047076	.011704	.046816	.004086	.049032	.012184	.048736
48	.003896	.046752	.011621	.046484	.004059	.048708	.012105	.048420
49	.003869	.046428	.011543	.046172	.004034	.048408	.012029	.048116
50	.003845	.046140	.011469	.045876	.004010	.048120	.011958	.047832

Factors in this table are computed for payment of rent monthly and quarterly in advance. Cap. Rates are 12 times the monthly factors and 4 times the quarterly factors. These may be used as divisors of net annual rent to compute value or as multipliers of investment cost to compute net annual rent.

TABLE IV

PURCHASE-LEASEBACK RENT FACTORS and CAPITALIZATION RATES

RATE	4½%				4¾%			
Payable	Monthly		Quarterly		Monthly		Quarterly	
Term Years	Rent	Cap Rate	Rent	Cap Rate	Rent	Cap Rate	Rent	Cap Rate
10	.010325	.123900	.030837	.123348	.010444	.125328	.031181	.124724
11	.009583	.114996	.028986	.115944	.009703	.116436	.028968	.115872
12	.008967	.107604	.026775	.107100	.009088	.109056	.027130	.108520
13	.008447	.101364	.025223	.100892	.008571	.102852	.025583	.102332
14	.008004	.096048	.023897	.095588	.008129	.097548	.024262	.097048
15	.007622	.091464	.022754	.091016	.007748	.092976	.023124	.092496
16	.007289	.087468	.021759	.087036	.007417	.089004	.022133	.088532
17	.006997	.083964	.020885	.083540	.007126	.085512	.021264	.085056
18	.006738	.080856	.020113	.080452	.006869	.082428	.020497	.081988
19	.006509	.078108	.019426	.077704	.006641	.079692	.019815	.079260
20	.006303	.075636	.018812	.075248	.006437	.077244	.019205	.076820
21	.006119	.073428	.018260	.073040	.006254	.075048	.018657	.074628
22	.005952	.071424	.017761	.071044	.006089	.073068	.018163	.072652
23	.005801	.069612	.017310	.069240	.005939	.071268	.017716	.070864
24	.005663	.067956	.016898	.067592	.005803	.069636	.017309	.069236
25	.005538	.066456	.016523	.066092	.005679	.068148	.016938	.067752
26	.005423	.065076	.016180	.064720	.005566	.066792	.016599	.066396
27	.005318	.063816	.015864	.063456	.005462	.065544	.016287	.065148
28	.005221	.062652	.015574	.062296	.005366	.064392	.016001	.064004
29	.005131	.061572	.015306	.061224	.005278	.063336	.015737	.062948
30	.005048	.060576	.015058	.060232	.005196	.062352	.015494	.061976
31	.004972	.059664	.014829	.059316	.005121	.061452	.015268	.061072
32	.004901	.058812	.014616	.058464	.005051	.060612	.015059	.060236
33	.004834	.058008	.014418	.057672	.004986	.059832	.014865	.059460
34	.004773	.057276	.014234	.056936	.004926	.059112	.014685	.058740
35	.004715	.056580	.014062	.056248	.004870	.058440	.014516	.058064
36	.004662	.055944	.013901	.055604	.004817	.057804	.014359	.057436
37	.004612	.055344	.013751	.055004	.004768	.057216	.014213	.056852
38	.004564	.054768	.013610	.054440	.004723	.056676	.014076	.056304
39	.004521	.054252	.013479	.053916	.004680	.056160	.013948	.055792
40	.004479	.053748	.013355	.053420	.004640	.055680	.013827	.055308
41	.004440	.053280	.013239	.052956	.004602	.055224	.013714	.054856
42	.004404	.052848	.013130	.052520	.004567	.054804	.013609	.054436
43	.004370	.052440	.013027	.052108	.004533	.054396	.013509	.054036
44	.004337	.052044	.012930	.051720	.004502	.054024	.013416	.053664
45	.004307	.051684	.012839	.051356	.004473	.053676	.013328	.053312
46	.004278	.051336	.012753	.051012	.004445	.053340	.013245	.052980
47	.004251	.051012	.012672	.050688	.004419	.053028	.013167	.052668
48	.004226	.050712	.012595	.050380	.004395	.052740	.013093	.052372
49	.004201	.050412	.012523	.050092	.004371	.052452	.013024	.052096
50	.004179	.050148	.012454	.049816	.004350	.052200	.012958	.051832

Factors in this table are computed for payment of rent monthly and quarterly in advance. Cap. Rates are 12 times the monthly factors and 4 times the quarterly factors. These may be used as divisors of net annual rent to compute value or as multipliers of investment cost to compute net annual rent.

TABLE IV

PURCHASE-LEASEBACK RENT FACTORS and CAPITALIZATION RATES

RATE	5%				5¼%			
Payable	Monthly		Quarterly		Monthly		Quarterly	
Term Years	Rent	Cap Rate	Rent	Cap Rate	Rent	Cap Rate	Rent	Cap Rate
10	.010563	.126756	.031528	.126112	.010682	.128184	.031876	.127504
11	.009824	.117888	.029320	.117280	.009946	.119352	.029674	.118696
12	.009211	.110532	.027488	.109952	.009334	.112008	.027847	.111388
13	.008695	.104340	.025945	.103780	.008820	.105840	.026310	.105240
14	.008255	.099060	.024630	.098520	.008382	.100584	.025000	.100000
15	.007875	.094500	.023497	.093988	.008004	.096048	.023872	.095488
16	.007546	.090552	.022511	.090044	.007676	.092112	.022892	.091568
17	.007257	.087084	.021647	.086588	.007389	.088668	.022033	.088132
18	.007002	.084024	.020884	.083536	.007135	.085620	.021276	.085104
19	.006775	.081300	.020207	.080828	.006910	.082920	.020603	.082412
20	.006573	.078876	.019602	.078408	.006709	.080508	.020003	.080012
21	.006391	.076692	.019059	.076236	.006529	.078348	.019465	.077860
22	.006227	.074724	.018569	.074276	.006367	.076404	.018980	.075920
23	.006079	.072948	.018127	.072508	.006221	.074652	.018542	.074168
24	.005945	.071340	.017724	.070896	.006088	.073056	.018144	.072576
25	.005822	.069864	.017358	.069432	.005967	.071604	.017782	.071128
26	.005710	.068520	.017023	.068092	.005856	.070272	.017452	.070168
27	.005607	.067284	.016715	.066860	.005755	.069060	.017149	.068596
28	.005513	.066156	.016434	.065736	.005662	.067944	.016872	.067488
29	.005426	.065112	.016174	.064696	.005577	.066924	.016617	.066468
30	.005346	.064152	.015934	.063736	.005498	.065976	.016381	.065524
31	.005272	.063264	.015713	.062852	.005426	.065112	.016164	.064656
32	.005204	.062448	.015508	.062032	.005359	.064308	.015963	.063852
33	.005140	.061680	.015318	.061272	.005296	.063552	.015777	.063108
34	.005081	.060972	.015141	.060564	.005239	.062868	.015604	.062416
35	.005026	.060312	.014977	.059908	.005185	.062220	.015444	.061776
36	.004975	.059700	.014824	.059296	.005135	.061620	.015294	.061176
37	.004927	.059124	.014681	.058724	.005089	.061068	.015155	.060620
38	.004883	.058596	.014548	.058192	.005046	.060552	.015026	.060104
39	.004841	.058092	.014423	.057692	.005005	.060060	.014905	.059620
40	.004802	.057624	.014306	.057224	.004967	.059604	.014792	.059168
41	.004766	.057292	.014197	.056788	.004932	.059184	.014686	.058744
42	.004732	.056784	.014095	.056380	.004899	.058788	.014587	.058348
43	.004700	.056400	.013999	.055996	.004868	.058416	.014494	.057976
44	.004670	.056040	.013908	.055632	.004839	.058068	.014407	.057628
45	.004641	.055692	.013824	.055296	.004812	.057744	.014325	.057300
46	.004615	.055380	.013744	.054976	.004786	.057432	.014249	.056996
47	.004590	.055080	.013669	.054676	.004762	.057144	.014177	.056708
48	.004566	.054792	.013598	.054392	.004740	.056880	.014109	.056436
49	.004544	.054528	.013532	.054128	.004719	.056628	.014046	.056184
50	.004523	.054276	.013469	.053876	.004699	.056388	.013986	.055944

Factors in this table are computed for payment of rent monthly and quarterly in advance. Cap. Rates are 12 times the monthly factors and 4 times the quarterly factors. These may be used as divisors of net annual rent to compute value or as multipliers of investment cost to compute net annual rent.

TABLE IV

PURCHASE–LEASEBACK RENT FACTORS and CAPITALIZATION RATES

RATE	5½%				5¾%			
Payable	Monthly		Quarterly		Monthly		Quarterly	
Term Years	Rent	Cap Rate	Rent	Cap Rate	Rent	Cap Rate	Rent	Cap Rate
10	.010803	.129636	.032226	.128904	.010925	.131100	.032579	.130316
11	.010068	.120816	.030030	.120120	.010192	.122304	.030389	.121556
12	.009459	.113508	.028210	.112840	.009584	.115008	.028574	.114296
13	.008946	.107352	.026678	.108712	.009073	.108876	.027049	.108196
14	.008510	.102120	.025374	.101496	.008639	.103668	.025750	.103000
15	.008134	.097608	.024251	.097004	.008265	.099180	.024634	.098536
16	.007808	.093796	.023276	.093104	.007940	.095280	.023664	.094656
17	.007522	.090264	.022423	.089692	.007657	.091884	.022816	.091264
18	.007270	.087240	.021671	.086684	.007407	.088884	.022069	.088276
19	.007047	.084564	.021003	.084012	.007185	.086220	.021407	.085628
20	.006848	.082176	.020408	.081632	.006988	.083856	.020817	.083268
21	.006670	.080040	.019875	.079500	.006811	.081732	.020289	.081156
22	.006509	.078108	.019395	.077580	.006652	.079824	.019814	.079256
23	.006364	.076368	.018962	.075848	.006509	.078108	.019386	.077544
24	.006233	.074706	.018569	.074276	.006379	.076548	.018998	.075992
25	.006113	.073356	.018212	.072848	.006261	.075132	.018646	.074584
26	.006004	.072048	.017886	.071544	.006154	.073848	.018325	.073300
27	.005905	.070860	.017588	.070352	.006056	.072672	.018032	.072128
28	.005813	.069756	.017315	.069260	.005966	.071592	.017763	.071052
29	.005730	.068760	.017064	.068256	.005884	.070608	.017517	.070068
30	.005652	.067824	.016833	.067332	.005808	.069696	.017290	.069160
31	.005581	.066972	.016620	.066480	.005739	.068868	.017082	.068328
32	.005516	.066192	.016423	.065692	.005674	.068088	.016889	.067556
33	.005455	.065460	.016241	.064964	.005615	.067380	.016711	.066844
34	.005398	.064776	.016073	.064292	.005560	.066720	.016547	.066188
35	.005346	.064152	.015916	.063664	.005509	.066108	.016394	.065576
36	.005298	.063576	.015771	.063084	.005462	.065544	.016253	.065012
37	.005252	.063024	.015636	.062544	.005418	.065016	.016122	.064488
38	.005210	.062520	.015510	.062040	.005377	.064524	.015999	.063996
39	.005171	.062052	.015392	.061568	.005339	.064068	.015886	.063544
40	.005135	.061620	.015283	.061132	.005305	.063660	.015780	.063120
41	.005100	.061200	.015181	.060724	.005271	.063252	.015681	.062724
42	.005069	.060828	.015085	.060340	.005240	.062880	.015589	.062356
43	.005039	.060468	.014996	.059984	.005212	.062544	.015503	.062012
44	.005011	.060132	.014912	.059648	.005185	.062220	.015423	.061692
45	.004985	.059820	.014834	.059336	.005160	.061920	.015347	.061388
46	.004960	.059520	.014760	.059040	.005136	.061632	.015277	.061108
47	.004937	.059244	.014691	.058764	.005114	.061368	.015211	.060844
48	.004916	.058992	.014627	.058508	.005094	.061128	.015150	.060600
49	.004895	.058740	.014566	.058264	.005074	.060888	.015092	.060368
50	.004877	.058524	.014509	.058036	.005056	.060672	.015038	.060152

Factors in this table are computed for payment of rent monthly and quarterly in advance. Cap. Rates are 12 times the monthly factors and 4 times the quarterly factors. These may be used as divisors of net annual rent to compute value or as multipliers of investment cost to compute net annual rent.

TABLE IV

PURCHASE–LEASEBACK RENT FACTORS and CAPITALIZATION RATES

RATE	6%				6¼%			
Payable	Monthly		Quarterly		Monthly		Quarterly	
Term Years.	Rent	Cap Rate	Rent	Cap Rate	Rent	Cap Rate	Rent	Cap Rate
10	.011047	.132564	.032934	.131736	.011170	.134040	.033290	.133160
11	.010316	.123892	.030750	.123000	.010441	.125292	.031113	.124452
12	.009710	.116520	.028941	.115764	.009838	.118056	.029311	.117244
13	.009202	.110424	.027422	.109688	.009331	.111972	.027798	.111192
14	.008769	.105228	.026130	.104520	.008900	.106800	.026512	.106048
15	.008397	.100764	.025019	.100076	.008530	.102360	.025407	.101628
16	.008074	.096888	.024055	.096220	.008210	.098520	.024449	.097796
17	.007792	.093504	.023213	.092852	.007930	.095160	.023612	.094448
18	.007544	.090528	.022471	.089884	.007683	.092196	.022877	.091508
19	.007325	.087900	.021815	.087260	.007466	.089692	.022226	.088904
20	.007129	.085548	.021230	.084920	.007272	.087264	.021647	.086588
21	.006954	.083448	.020708	.082832	.007099	.085188	.021130	.084520
22	.006797	.081564	.020238	.080952	.006944	.083328	.020666	.082664
23	.006656	.079872	.019815	.079260	.006804	.081648	.020248	.080992
24	.006528	.078336	.019432	.077728	.006677	.080124	.019870	.079480
25	.006411	.076932	.019085	.076340	.006563	.078756	.019528	.078112
26	.006306	.075672	.018769	.075076	.006459	.077508	.019217	.076868
27	.006209	.074508	.018480	.073920	.006364	.076368	.018933	.075732
28	.006121	.073452	.018216	.072864	.006278	.075336	.018674	.074696
29	.006040	.072480	.017975	.071900	.006198	.074376	.018437	.073748
30	.005966	.071592	.017753	.071012	.006126	.073512	.018220	.072880
31	.005898	.070776	.017548	.070192	.006059	.072708	.018020	.072080
32	.005835	.070020	.017360	.069440	.005998	.071976	.017837	.071348
33	.005777	.069324	.017187	.068748	.005941	.071292	.017667	.070668
34	.005723	.068676	.017026	.068104	.005889	.070668	.017511	.070044
35	.005674	.068088	.016878	.067512	.005841	.070092	.017367	.069468
36	.005628	.067536	.016741	.066964	.005796	.069552	.017233	.068932
37	.005585	.067020	.016613	.066452	.005755	.069060	.017110	.068440
38	.005546	.066552	.016495	.065980	.005717	.068604	.016995	.067980
39	.005509	.066108	.016385	.065540	.005681	.068172	.016889	.067556
40	.005475	.065700	.016282	.065128	.005648	.067776	.016790	.067160
41	.005443	.065316	.016187	.064748	.005618	.067416	.016698	.066792
42	.005414	.064968	.016098	.064392	.005589	.067068	.016613	.066452
43	.005386	.064632	.016016	.064064	.005563	.066756	.016534	.066136
44	.005361	.064332	.015939	.063756	.005538	.066456	.016460	.065840
45	.005336	.064032	.015867	.063468	.005515	.066180	.016391	.065564
46	.005314	.063768	.015799	.063196	.005494	.065928	.016327	.065308
47	.005293	.063516	.015737	.062948	.005474	.065688	.016267	.065068
48	.005274	.063288	.015678	.062712	.005455	.065460	.016211	.064844
49	.005255	.063060	.015623	.062492	.005438	.065256	.016159	.064636
50	.005238	.062856	.015571	.062284	.005422	.065064	.016110	.064440

Factors in this table are computed for payment of rent monthly and quarterly in advance. Cap. Rates are 12 times the monthly factors and 4 times the quarterly factors. These may be used as divisors of net annual rent to compute value or as multipliers of investment cost to compute net annual rent.

TABLE IV

PURCHASE–LEASEBACK RENT FACTORS and CAPITALIZATION RATES

RATE	6½%				6¾%			
Payable	Monthly		Quarterly		Monthly		Quarterly	
Term Years	Rent	Cap Rate	Rent	Cap Rate	Rent	Cap Rate	Rent	Cap Rate
10	.011294	.135528	.033648	.134592	.011419	.137028	.034009	.136036
11	.010577	.126924	.031478	.125912	.010694	.128328	.031845	.127380
12	.009966	.119592	.029683	.118732	.010095	.121140	.030057	.120228
13	.009461	.113532	.028176	.112704	.009592	.115104	.028557	.114228
14	.009032	.108384	.026896	.107584	.009166	.109992	.027284	.109136
15	.008665	.103980	.025798	.103192	.008800	.105600	.026192	.104768
16	.008346	.100152	.024846	.099384	.008483	.101796	.025246	.100984
17	.008068	.096816	.024016	.096064	.008208	.098596	.024422	.097688
18	.007824	.093888	.023286	.093144	.007965	.095580	.023698	.094792
19	.007608	.091296	.022641	.090564	.007751	.093012	.023059	.092236
20	.007416	.088992	.022068	.088272	.007561	.090732	.022492	.089968
21	.007245	.086940	.021556	.086224	.007392	.088704	.021986	.087944
22	.007091	.085092	.021098	.084392	.007241	.086892	.021533	.086132
23	.006953	.083436	.020685	.082740	.007105	.085260	.021126	.084504
24	.006829	.081948	.020313	.081252	.006982	.083784	.020759	.083036
25	.006716	.080592	.019976	.079904	.006871	.082452	.020428	.081712
26	.006614	.079368	.019670	.078780	.006770	.081240	.020127	.080508
27	.006521	.078252	.019391	.077564	.006679	.080148	.019853	.079412
28	.006436	.077232	.019137	.076548	.006596	.079152	.019604	.078416
29	.006356	.076272	.018905	.075620	.006520	.078240	.019377	.077508
30	.006287	.075444	.018692	.074768	.006450	.077400	.019169	.076676
31	.006222	.074664	.018497	.073988	.006386	.076632	.018978	.075912
32	.006162	.073944	.018318	.073272	.006328	.075936	.018803	.075212
33	.006107	.073284	.018153	.072612	.006275	.075300	.018643	.074572
34	.006056	.072672	.018001	.072004	.006225	.074700	.018495	.073980
35	.006009	.072108	.017860	.071440	.006180	.074160	.018359	.073436
36	.005966	.071592	.017731	.070924	.006138	.073656	.018233	.072932
37	.005926	.071112	.017611	.070444	.006099	.073188	.018118	.072472
38	.005889	.070668	.017501	.070004	.006064	.072768	.018011	.072044
39	.005855	.070260	.017398	.069592	.006031	.072372	.017912	.071655
40	.005823	.069876	.017303	.069212	.006000	.072000	.017820	.071280
41	.005794	.069528	.017215	.068860	.005972	.071664	.017736	.070944
42	.005767	.069204	.017133	.068532	.005946	.071352	.017657	.070628
43	.005741	.068892	.017057	.068228	.005922	.071064	.017584	.070336
44	.005718	.068616	.016986	.067944	.005899	.070788	.017517	.070068
45	.005696	.068352	.016920	.067680	.005878	.070536	.017454	.069816
46	.005676	.068112	.016859	.067436	.005859	.070308	.017396	.069584
47	.005657	.067884	.016802	.067208	.005841	.070092	.017341	.069364
48	.005639	.067668	.016749	.066996	.005824	.069888	.017291	.069164
49	.005623	.067476	.016699	.066796	.005809	.069708	.017244	.068976
50	.005607	.067284	.016653	.066612	.005794	.069528	.017201	.068804

Factors in this table are computed for payment of rent monthly and quarterly in advance. Cap. Rates are 12 times the monthly factors and 4 times the quarterly factors. These may be used as divisors of net annual rent to compute value or as multipliers of investment cost to compute net annual rent.

TABLE IV

PURCHASE-LEASEBACK RENT FACTORS and CAPITALIZATION RATES

RATE	7%				7¼%			
Payable	Monthly		Quarterly		Monthly		Quarterly	
Term Years	Rent	Cap Rate	Rent	Cap Rate	Rent	Cap Rate	Rent	Cap Rate
10	.011543	.138522	.034370	.137482	.011669	.140035	.034734	.138939
11	.010820	.129851	.032214	.128857	.010949	.131393	.032586	.130344
12	.010224	.122690	.030433	.121732	.010354	.124259	.030812	.123248
13	.009724	.116688	.028940	.115760	.009857	.118285	.029326	.117304
14	.009299	.111597	.027673	.110694	.009435	.113222	.028066	.112266
15	.008936	.107233	.026588	.106352	.009073	.108885	.026987	.107951
16	.008621	.103461	.025649	.102597	.008761	.105139	.026055	.104222
17	.008347	.100174	.024831	.099325	.008489	.101879	.025244	.100977
18	.008107	.097292	.024114	.096456	.008251	.099022	.024533	.098133
19	.007895	.094750	.023481	.093924	.008042	.096505	.023906	.095626
20	.007708	.092496	.022919	.091679	.007856	.094275	.023351	.093405
21	.007540	.090488	.022419	.089679	.007691	.092292	.022857	.091430
22	.007391	.088693	.021972	.087890	.007543	.090520	.022416	.089664
23	.007256	.087082	.021571	.086285	.007411	.088932	.022020	.088082
24	.007135	.085631	.021209	.084839	.007291	.087503	.021664	.086658
25	.007026	.084321	.020883	.083533	.007184	.086215	.021343	.085374
26	.006927	.083135	.020587	.082350	.007087	.085051	.021053	.084212
27	.006838	.082059	.020319	.081277	.006999	.083995	.020790	.083160
28	.006756	.081080	.020075	.080300	.006919	.083037	.020550	.082203
29	.006682	.080187	.019852	.079410	.006847	.082164	.020333	.081333
30	.006614	.079373	.019649	.078597	.006780	.081369	.020134	.080539
31	.006552	.078628	.019463	.077853	.006720	.080643	.019953	.079814
32	.006495	.077946	.019293	.077172	.006664	.079979	.019787	.079151
33	.006443	.077320	.019136	.076547	.006614	.079371	.019635	.078543
34	.006395	.076746	.018993	.075973	.006567	.078814	.019496	.077986
35	.006351	.076218	.018861	.075446	.006525	.078302	.019368	.077475
36	.006311	.075732	.018740	.074960	.006486	.077833	.019251	.077005
37	.006273	.075284	.018628	.074512	.006450	.077401	.019143	.076573
38	.006239	.074871	.018524	.074099	.006416	.077003	.019043	.076175
39	.006207	.074490	.018429	.073718	.006386	.076637	.018952	.075809
40	.006178	.074139	.018341	.073366	.006358	.076299	.018867	.075471
41	.006151	.073814	.018260	.073041	.006332	.075988	.018789	.075159
42	.006126	.073513	.018185	.072740	.006308	.075700	.018717	.074871
43	.006102	.073235	.018115	.072462	.006286	.075435	.018651	.074605
44	.006081	.072978	.018051	.072204	.006265	.075190	.018589	.074359
45	.006061	.072739	.017991	.071965	.006246	.074963	.018533	.074132
46	.006043	.072518	.017935	.071743	.006229	.074753	.018480	.073921
47	.006026	.072313	.017884	.071538	.006213	.074559	.018431	.073727
48	.006010	.072123	.017836	.071347	.006198	.074380	.018386	.073546
49	.005995	.071947	.017792	.071170	.006184	.074213	.018344	.073379
50	.005981	.071783	.017751	.071006	.006171	.074059	.018306	.073225

Factors in this table are computed for payment of rent monthly and quarterly in advance. Cap. Rates are 12 times the monthly factors and 4 times the quarterly factors. These may be used as divisors of net annual rent to compute value or as multipliers of investment cost to compute net annual rent.

TABLE IV

PURCHASE-LEASEBACK RENT FACTORS and CAPITALIZATION RATES

RATE	7½%				7¾%			
Payable	Monthly		Quarterly		Monthly		Quarterly	
Term Years	Rent	Cap Rate	Rent	Cap Rate	Rent	Cap Rate	Rent	Cap Rate
10	.011796	.141557	.035100	.140403	.011924	.143088	.035469	.141876
11	.011078	.132945	.032959	.131839	.011208	.134506	.033335	.133342
12	.010486	.125840	.031193	.124773	.010619	.127432	.031576	.126307
13	.009991	.119895	.029714	.118858	.010126	.121515	.030105	.120422
14	.009571	.114859	.028462	.113848	.009709	.116508	.028860	.115441
15	.009212	.110550	.027390	.109561	.009352	.112228	.027795	.111182
16	.008902	.106831	.026465	.105860	.009044	.108537	.026877	.107509
17	.008633	.103597	.025660	.102641	.008777	.105330	.026079	.104318
18	.008397	.100767	.024955	.099823	.008543	.102526	.025381	.101526
19	.008189	.098275	.024335	.097342	.008338	.100060	.024767	.099071
20	.008005	.096070	.023786	.095146	.008156	.097881	.024225	.096901
21	.007842	.094111	.023298	.093195	.007995	.095947	.023743	.094974
22	.007696	.092363	.022863	.091453	.007852	.094224	.023314	.093257
23	.007566	.090799	.022473	.089894	.007723	.092683	.022930	.091721
24	.007449	.089393	.022123	.088493	.007608	.091301	.022585	.090343
25	.007344	.088128	.021807	.087231	.007504	.090057	.022275	.089103
26	.007248	.086985	.021522	.086091	.007411	.088936	.021996	.087985
27	.007162	.085950	.021264	.085059	.007326	.087923	.021743	.086974
28	.007084	.085012	.021030	.084123	.007250	.087006	.021514	.086059
29	.007013	.084160	.020818	.083272	.007181	.086174	.021307	.085228
30	.006948	.083384	.020624	.082497	.007118	.085417	.021118	.084472
31	.006889	.082677	.020447	.081791	.007060	.084729	.020946	.083785
32	.006835	.082031	.020286	.081146	.007008	.084102	.020789	.083158
33	.006786	.081441	.020139	.080556	.006960	.083529	.020646	.082585
34	.006741	.080901	.020004	.080016	.006917	.083006	.020515	.082062
35	.006700	.080406	.019880	.079521	.006877	.082528	.020396	.081584
36	.006662	.079952	.019766	.079067	.006840	.082090	.020286	.081145
37	.006628	.079536	.019662	.078651	.006807	.081688	.020186	.080744
38	.006596	.079153	.019567	.078268	.006776	.081321	.020093	.080375
39	.006566	.078801	.019478	.077915	.006748	.080983	.020009	.080037
40	.006539	.078477	.019397	.077591	.006722	.080673	.019931	.079726
41	.006514	.078179	.019323	.077292	.006699	.080388	.019860	.079441
42	.006492	.077905	.019254	.077017	.006677	.080126	.019794	.079178
43	.006471	.077652	.019190	.076763	.006657	.079885	.019734	.078936
44	.006451	.077419	.019132	.076529	.006638	.079663	.019678	.078714
45	.006433	.077203	.019078	.076313	.006621	.079459	.019627	.078508
46	.006417	.077005	.019028	.076114	.006605	.079271	.019580	.078320
47	.006401	.076821	.018982	.075930	.006591	.079098	.019536	.078145
48	.006387	.076652	.018939	.075759	.006578	.078938	.019496	.077985
49	.006374	.076495	.018900	.075602	.006565	.078791	.019459	.077837
50	.006362	.076350	.018864	.075456	.006554	.078655	.019425	.077700

Factors in this table are computed for payment of rent monthly and quarterly in advance. Cap. Rates are 12 times the monthly factors and 4 times the quarterly factors. These may be used as divisors of net annual rent to compute value or as multipliers of investment cost to compute net annual rent.

TABLE IV

PURCHASE-LEASEBACK RENT FACTORS and CAPITALIZATION RATES

RATE	8%				8¼%			
Payable	Monthly		Quarterly		Monthly		Quarterly	
Term Years	Rent	Cap Rate	Rent	Cap Rate	Rent	Cap Rate	Rent	Cap Rate
10	.012052	.144628	.035838	.143355	.012181	.146178	.036210	.144843
11	.011339	.136078	.033713	.134854	.011471	.137659	.034093	.136374
12	.010752	.129034	.031962	.127850	.010887	.130646	.032350	.129402
13	.010262	.123147	.030499	.121996	.010399	.124791	.030894	.123579
14	.009847	.118170	.029261	.117045	.009986	.119843	.029664	.118659
15	.009493	.113918	.028203	.112815	.009635	.115621	.028614	.114459
16	.009187	.110255	.027292	.109170	.009332	.111988	.027710	.110843
17	.008923	.107076	.026501	.106006	.009069	.108837	.026926	.107707
18	.008691	.104300	.025810	.103242	.008840	.106088	.026242	.104970
19	.008488	.101861	.025203	.100813	.008639	.103676	.025642	.102569
20	.008309	.099708	.024667	.098669	.008462	.101549	.025112	.100450
21	.008149	.097799	.024191	.096767	.008305	.099666	.024643	.098574
22	.008008	.096100	.023768	.095075	.008166	.097993	.024226	.096907
23	.007881	.094583	.023390	.093563	.008041	.096500	.023854	.095419
24	.007768	.093224	.023052	.092208	.007930	.095165	.023521	.094087
25	.007667	.092004	.022747	.090991	.007830	.093967	.023223	.092893
26	.007575	.090905	.022473	.089894	.007740	.092891	.022954	.091819
27	.007492	.089914	.022226	.088905	.007660	.091921	.022712	.090850
28	.007418	.089017	.022002	.088010	.007587	.091045	.022494	.089976
29	.007350	.088205	.021799	.087199	.007521	.090253	.022296	.089185
30	.007289	.087468	.021615	.086463	.007461	.089536	.022117	.088468
31	.007233	.086799	.021448	.085794	.007407	.088885	.021954	.087817
32	.007182	.086189	.021296	.085185	.007357	.088294	.021806	.087226
33	.007136	.085634	.021157	.084630	.007313	.087757	.021672	.086689
34	.007094	.085128	.021030	.084123	.007272	.087267	.021549	.086199
35	.007055	.084666	.020915	.083661	.007235	.086822	.021438	.085753
36	.007020	.084244	.020809	.083238	.007201	.086415	.021336	.085345
37	.006988	.083858	.020712	.082851	.007170	.086044	.021243	.084973
38	.006958	.083505	.020624	.082497	.007142	.085705	.021158	.084633
39	.006931	.083181	.020543	.082173	.007116	.085395	.021080	.084322
40	.006907	.082884	.020468	.081875	.007092	.085111	.021009	.084038
41	.006884	.082612	.020400	.081602	.007071	.084852	.020944	.083777
42	.006863	.082363	.020338	.081352	.007051	.084614	.020884	.083539
43	.006844	.082134	.020280	.081122	.007033	.084396	.020830	.083320
44	.006826	.081923	.020227	.080910	.007016	.084197	.020779	.083119
45	.006810	.081730	.020179	.080716	.007001	.084014	.020733	.082935
46	.006796	.081552	.020134	.080537	.006987	.083846	.020691	.082766
47	.006782	.081389	.020093	.080373	.006974	.083692	.020652	.082611
48	.006769	.081238	.020055	.080222	.006962	.083551	.020617	.082469
49	.006758	.081100	.020020	.080082	.006951	.083421	.020584	.082338
50	.006747	.080973	.019988	.079954	.006941	.083302	.020554	.082218

Factors in this table are computed for payment of rent monthly and quarterly in advance. Cap. Rates are 12 times the monthly factors and 4 times the quarterly factors. These may be used as divisors of net annual rent to compute value or as multipliers of investment cost to compute net annual rent.

TABLE IV

PURCHASE-LEASEBACK RENT FACTORS and CAPITALIZATION RATES

RATE	8½%				8¾%			
Payable	Monthly		Quarterly		Monthly		Quarterly	
Term Years	Rent	Cap Rate	Rent	Cap Rate	Rent	Cap Rate	Rent	Cap Rate
10	.012311	.147736	.036584	.146337	.012441	.149303	.036959	.147839
11	.011604	.139250	.034475	.137903	.011737	.140850	.034859	.139439
12	.011022	.132269	.032740	.130963	.011158	.133903	.033133	.132533
13	.010537	.126445	.031293	.125172	.010675	.128111	.031693	.126774
14	.010127	.121529	.030070	.120283	.010268	.123226	.030479	.121917
15	.009778	.117337	.029028	.116113	.009922	.119065	.029444	.117778
16	.009477	.113733	.028131	.112527	.009624	.115491	.028555	.114222
17	.009217	.110611	.027355	.109420	.009366	.112399	.027786	.111144
18	.008990	.107890	.026677	.106711	.009142	.109706	.027116	.108464
19	.008792	.105506	.026084	.104337	.008945	.107350	.026529	.106117
20	.008617	.103406	.025561	.102245	.008773	.105277	.026013	.104052
21	.008462	.101549	.025098	.100395	.008620	.103447	.025557	.102228
22	.008325	.099901	.024688	.098752	.008485	.101824	.025152	.100611
23	.008202	.098433	.024322	.097289	.008365	.100381	.024793	.099172
24	.008093	.097121	.023995	.095981	.008257	.099094	.024472	.097888
25	.007995	.095947	.023702	.094809	.008161	.097943	.024184	.096739
26	.007907	.094893	.023439	.093757	.008075	.096911	.023927	.095709
27	.007828	.093945	.023202	.092810	.007998	.095984	.023696	.094784
28	.007757	.093090	.022989	.091956	.007929	.095150	.023487	.093951
29	.007693	.092318	.022796	.091185	.007866	.094399	.023300	.093200
30	.007635	.091620	.022622	.090488	.007810	.093720	.023130	.092521
31	.007582	.090988	.022464	.089856	.007758	.093107	.022976	.091907
32	.007534	.090415	.022320	.089282	.007712	.092552	.022838	.091352
33	.007491	.089895	.022190	.088762	.007670	.092049	.022712	.090848
34	.007451	.089422	.022072	.088288	.007632	.091592	.022597	.090391
35	.007416	.088992	.021964	.087858	.007598	.091178	.022494	.089976
36	.007383	.088601	.021866	.087466	.007566	.090802	.022399	.089599
37	.007353	.088244	.021777	.087108	.007538	.090460	.022313	.089255
38	.007326	.087919	.021695	.086782	.007512	.090148	.022235	.088943
39	.007301	.087623	.021621	.086484	.007488	.089865	.022164	.088658
40	.007279	.087352	.021553	.086212	.007467	.089607	.022099	.088398
41	.007258	.087105	.021491	.085964	.007447	.089371	.022040	.088162
42	.007239	.086879	.021434	.085737	.007429	.089157	.021986	.087946
43	.007222	.086672	.021382	.085529	.007413	.088961	.021937	.087749
44	.007206	.086483	.021334	.085339	.007398	.088782	.021892	.087569
45	.007192	.086310	.021291	.085165	.007384	.088619	.021851	.087404
46	.007179	.086152	.021251	.085006	.007372	.088470	.021813	.087254
47	.007167	.086007	.021215	.084860	.007361	.088334	.021779	.087117
48	.007156	.085875	.021181	.084726	.007350	.088209	.021747	.086991
49	.007146	.085753	.021150	.084603	.007341	.088095	.021719	.086877
50	.007136	.085642	.021122	.084491	.007332	.087991	.021692	.086771

Factors in this table are computed for payment of rent monthly and quarterly in advance. Cap. Rates are 12 times the monthly factors and 4 times the quarterly factors. These may be used as divisors of net annual rent to compute value or as multipliers of investment cost to compute net annual rent.

TABLE IV

PURCHASE-LEASEBACK RENT FACTORS and CAPITALIZATION RATES

RATE	9%				9¼%			
Payable	Monthly		Quarterly		Monthly		Quarterly	
Term Years	Rent	Cap Rate	Rent	Cap Rate	Rent	Cap Rate	Rent	Cap Rate
10	.012573	.150879	.037337	.149349	.012705	.152464	.037716	.150865
11	.011871	.142461	.035245	.140983	.012006	.144080	.035634	.142536
12	.011295	.135547	.033527	.134111	.011433	.137201	.033924	.135698
13	.010815	.129788	.032096	.128386	.010956	.131475	.032501	.130007
14	.010411	.124935	.030890	.123561	.010554	.126655	.031303	.125214
15	.010067	.120805	.029863	.119453	.010213	.122558	.030284	.121139
16	.009771	.117262	.028982	.115928	.009920	.119046	.029411	.117644
17	.009516	.114199	.028220	.112880	.009667	.116013	.028656	.114627
18	.009294	.111536	.027557	.110228	.009448	.113380	.028001	.112005
19	.009100	.109208	.026977	.107910	.009256	.111080	.027428	.109714
20	.008930	.107163	.026468	.105872	.009088	.109063	.026926	.107705
21	.008779	.105359	.026018	.104075	.008940	.107286	.026483	.105934
22	.008646	.103762	.025620	.102483	.008809	.105715	.026091	.104367
23	.008528	.102344	.025267	.101069	.008693	.104322	.025744	.102978
24	.008423	.101081	.024952	.099808	.008590	.103084	.025435	.101742
25	.008329	.099953	.024670	.098683	.008498	.101979	.025159	.100639
26	.008245	.098944	.024418	.097675	.008416	.100993	.024913	.099654
27	.008169	.098039	.024192	.096771	.008342	.100109	.024692	.098771
28	.008102	.097226	.023989	.095959	.008276	.099317	.024494	.097979
29	.008041	.096495	.023806	.095227	.008217	.098606	.024316	.097267
30	.007986	.095835	.023642	.094568	.008163	.097965	.024156	.096627
31	.007936	.095241	.023493	.093972	.008115	.097389	.024012	.096050
32	.007891	.094703	.023358	.093434	.008072	.096869	.023882	.095529
33	.007851	.094217	.023236	.092947	.008033	.096400	.023764	.095058
34	.007814	.093777	.023126	.092506	.007997	.095975	.023658	.094633
35	.007781	.093378	.023026	.092106	.007966	.095592	.023562	.094248
36	.007751	.093017	.022935	.091743	.007937	.095245	.023475	.093900
37	.007724	.092689	.022853	.091414	.007910	.094931	.023396	.093584
38	.007699	.092391	.022778	.091115	.007887	.094646	.023324	.093298
39	.007676	.092120	.022710	.090843	.007865	.094387	.023259	.093038
40	.007656	.091874	.022648	.090595	.007846	.094153	.023200	.092802
41	.007637	.091650	.022592	.090370	.007828	.093940	.023147	.092588
42	.007620	.091446	.022541	.090165	.007812	.093747	.023098	.092393
43	.007605	.091261	.022494	.089978	.007797	.093572	.023054	.092216
44	.007591	.091092	.022452	.089808	.007784	.093412	.023013	.092055
45	.007578	.090938	.022413	.089653	.007772	.093267	.022977	.091909
46	.007566	.090798	.022377	.089511	.007761	.093136	.022944	.091776
47	.007555	.090670	.022345	.089382	.007751	.093016	.022913	.091655
48	.007546	.090553	.022316	.089265	.007742	.092907	.022886	.091545
49	.007537	.090447	.022289	.089157	.007733	.092807	.022861	.091444
50	.007529	.090350	.022264	.089059	.007726	.092717	.022838	.091353

Factors in this table are computed for payment of rent monthly and quarterly in advance. Cap. Rates are 12 times the monthly factors and 4 times the quarterly factors. These may be used as divisors of net annual rent to compute value or as multipliers of investment cost to compute net annual rent.

TABLE IV

PURCHASE-LEASEBACK RENT FACTORS and CAPITALIZATION RATES

RATE	9½%				9¾%			
Payable	Monthly		Quarterly		Monthly		Quarterly	
Term Years	Rent	Cap Rate	Rent	Cap Rate	Rent	Cap Rate	Rent	Cap Rate
10	.012838	.154057	.038097	.152389	.012971	.155659	.038480	.153920
11	.012142	.145710	.036024	.144096	.012279	.147348	.036416	.145664
12	.011572	.138865	.034323	.137294	.011711	.140539	.034724	.138898
13	.011097	.133174	.032909	.131637	.011240	.134883	.033319	.133276
14	.010698	.128387	.031719	.126878	.010844	.130130	.032137	.128551
15	.010360	.124322	.030708	.122835	.010508	.126098	.031135	.124541
16	.010070	.120842	.029843	.119372	.010220	.122650	.030277	.121110
17	.009820	.117840	.029096	.116385	.009973	.119680	.029538	.118154
18	.009603	.115237	.028448	.113792	.009758	.117106	.028897	.115591
19	.009413	.112966	.027882	.111531	.009572	.114865	.028339	.113359
20	.009248	.110977	.027387	.109549	.009408	.112904	.027851	.111405
21	.009102	.109227	.026951	.107805	.009265	.111182	.027421	.109687
22	.008973	.107682	.026566	.106264	.009138	.109664	.027043	.108173
23	.008859	.106315	.026225	.104900	.009026	.108321	.026708	.106834
24	.008758	.105100	.025922	.103688	.008927	.107132	.026411	.105646
25	.008668	.104020	.025652	.102608	.008839	.106074	.026147	.104590
26	.008587	.103055	.025411	.101645	.008761	.105133	.025912	.103648
27	.008516	.102194	.025196	.100784	.008691	.104292	.025702	.102808
28	.008451	.101422	.025003	.100012	.008628	.103542	.025514	.102057
29	.008394	.100731	.024830	.099320	.008572	.102869	.025346	.101384
30	.008342	.100109	.024674	.098698	.008522	.102267	.025195	.100781
31	.008295	.099551	.024534	.098139	.008477	.101727	.025059	.100239
32	.008254	.099048	.024408	.097635	.008436	.101241	.024938	.099752
33	.008216	.098595	.024295	.097181	.008400	.100804	.024828	.099314
34	.008182	.098187	.024192	.096771	.008367	.100411	.024729	.098919
35	.008151	.097818	.024100	.096401	.008338	.100057	.024641	.098564
36	.008123	.097486	.024016	.096066	.008311	.099738	.024560	.098243
37	.008098	.097185	.023941	.095764	.008287	.099450	.024488	.097953
38	.008076	.096913	.023872	.095490	.008265	.099191	.024423	.097692
39	.008055	.096666	.023810	.095242	.008246	.098956	.024364	.097456
40	.008036	.096443	.023754	.095018	.008228	.098744	.024310	.097242
41	.008020	.096241	.023703	.094814	.008212	.098553	.024262	.097049
42	.008004	.096059	.023657	.094630	.008198	.098380	.024218	.096874
43	.007991	.095893	.023615	.094462	.008185	.098223	.024179	.096716
44	.007978	.095742	.023577	.094311	.008173	.098081	.024143	.096573
45	.007967	.095606	.023543	.094173	.008162	.097953	.024110	.096443
46	.007956	.095482	.023512	.094048	.008153	.097837	.024081	.096326
47	.007947	.095370	.023483	.093934	.008144	.097732	.024054	.096219
48	.007939	.095268	.023457	.093831	.008136	.097637	.024030	.096123
49	.007931	.095176	.023434	.093737	.008129	.097551	.024008	.096035
50	.007924	.095092	.023413	.093652	.008122	.097473	.023989	.095956

Factors in this table are computed for payment of rent monthly and quarterly in advance. Cap. Rates are 12 times the monthly factors and 4 times the quarterly factors. These may be used as divisors of net annual rent to compute value or as multipliers of investment cost to compute net annual rent.

TABLE IV

PURCHASE-LEASEBACK RENT FACTORS and CAPITALIZATION RATES

RATE	10%				10¼%			
Payable	Monthly		Quarterly		Monthly		Quarterly	
Term Years	Rent	Cap Rate	Rent	Cap Rate	Rent	Cap Rate	Rent	Cap Rate
10	.013105	.157270	.038864	.155458	.013240	.158889	.039250	.157003
11	.012416	.148996	.036810	.147240	.012554	.150654	.037205	.148823
12	.011852	.142224	.035127	.140511	.011993	.143918	.035532	.142131
13	.011383	.136603	.033731	.134924	.011527	.138333	.034145	.136581
14	.010990	.131885	.032558	.130233	.011137	.133650	.032981	.131925
15	.010657	.127886	.031564	.126257	.010807	.129686	.031995	.127982
16	.010372	.124470	.030714	.122858	.010525	.126303	.031154	.124616
17	.010127	.121532	.029983	.119933	.010283	.123396	.030430	.121723
18	.009915	.118989	.029350	.117401	.010073	.120885	.029805	.119222
19	.009731	.116777	.028799	.115198	.009891	.118703	.029262	.117048
20	.009570	.114845	.028318	.113272	.009733	.116799	.028787	.115150
21	.009429	.113150	.027895	.111582	.009594	.115132	.028372	.113488
22	.009304	.111659	.027523	.110094	.009472	.113667	.028006	.112026
23	.009195	.110342	.027194	.108779	.009364	.112376	.027684	.110737
24	.009098	.109176	.026904	.107616	.009269	.111235	.027399	.109597
25	.009011	.108142	.026645	.106582	.009185	.110224	.027146	.108587
26	.008935	.107223	.026415	.105663	.009110	.109327	.026922	.107690
27	.008867	.106405	.026211	.104844	.009044	.108530	.026723	.106892
28	.008806	.105674	.026028	.104113	.008985	.107820	.026545	.106181
29	.008751	.105022	.025865	.103460	.008932	.107186	.026386	.105546
30	.008703	.104438	.025718	.102875	.008885	.106621	.026244	.104979
31	.008659	.103915	.025587	.102350	.008842	.106115	.026118	.104472
32	.008620	.103446	.025470	.101880	.008805	.105663	.026004	.104018
33	.008585	.103025	.025364	.101458	.008771	.105258	.025902	.103611
34	.008553	.102647	.025269	.101078	.008741	.104895	.025811	.103245
35	.008525	.102308	.025184	.100736	.008714	.104569	.025729	.102918
36	.008500	.102002	.025107	.100429	.008689	.104277	.025655	.102623
37	.008477	.101727	.025038	.100152	.008667	.104014	.025589	.102359
38	.008456	.101479	.024975	.099902	.008648	.103778	.025530	.102121
39	.008438	.101256	.024919	.099677	.008630	.103566	.025476	.101906
40	.008421	.101055	.024868	.099474	.008614	.103375	.025428	.101714
41	.008406	.100873	.024822	.099291	.008600	.103203	.025385	.101540
42	.008392	.100710	.024781	.099126	.008587	.103048	.025346	.101384
43	.008380	.100562	.024744	.098976	.008575	.102909	.025310	.101243
44	.008369	.100429	.024710	.098841	.008565	.102784	.025279	.101116
45	.008359	.100308	.024680	.098720	.008555	.102671	.025250	.101001
46	.008350	.100200	.024652	.098609	.008547	.102569	.025224	.100898
47	.008341	.100101	.024627	.098510	.008539	.102477	.025201	.100805
48	.008334	.100013	.024605	.098420	.008532	.102395	.025180	.100721
49	.008327	.099932	.024584	.098338	.008526	.102320	.025161	.100645
50	.008321	.099860	.024566	.098265	.008521	.102253	.025144	.100577

Factors in this table are computed for payment of rent monthly and quarterly in advance. Cap. Rates are 12 times the monthly factors and 4 times the quarterly factors. These may be used as divisors of net annual rent to compute value or as multipliers of investment cost to compute net annual rent.

TABLE IV

PURCHASE-LEASEBACK RENT FACTORS and CAPITALIZATION RATES

RATE	10½%				10¾%			
Payable	Monthly		Quarterly		Monthly		Quarterly	
Term Years	Rent	Cap Rate	Rent	Cap Rate	Rent	Cap Rate	Rent	Cap Rate
10	.013376	.160517	.039638	.158555	.013512	.162153	.040028	.160114
11	.012693	.152320	.037603	.150414	.012833	.153996	.038003	.152013
12	.012135	.145622	.035940	.143760	.012278	.147336	.036349	.145397
13	.011672	.140074	.034561	.138247	.011818	.141825	.034980	.139921
14	.011285	.135427	.033406	.133626	.011434	.137214	.033834	.135336
15	.010958	.131497	.032429	.129718	.011109	.133319	.032865	.131462
16	.010678	.128147	.031596	.126385	.010833	.130003	.032040	.128163
17	.010439	.125273	.030881	.123524	.010596	.127162	.031333	.125334
18	.010232	.122792	.030263	.121053	.010392	.124712	.030723	.122894
19	.010053	.120641	.029727	.118909	.010215	.122591	.030195	.120780
20	.009897	.118766	.029260	.117040	.010062	.120745	.029735	.118940
21	.009760	.117126	.028851	.115404	.009927	.119134	.029333	.117332
22	.009640	.115688	.028492	.113969	.009810	.117722	.028980	.115922
23	.009535	.114422	.028176	.112705	.009706	.116482	.028670	.114683
24	.009442	.113306	.027897	.111589	.009615	.115390	.028398	.113592
25	.009359	.112319	.027650	.110602	.009535	.114426	.028156	.112627
26	.009287	.111444	.027431	.109727	.009464	.113573	.027943	.111774
27	.009222	.110668	.027237	.108949	.009401	.112818	.027754	.111017
28	.009164	.109978	.027064	.108258	.009345	.112148	.027586	.110346
29	.009113	.109363	.026910	.107642	.009296	.111552	.027437	.109749
30	.009068	.108816	.026773	.107093	.009251	.111023	.027304	.109217
31	.009027	.108328	.026650	.106603	.009212	.110551	.027185	.108743
32	.008991	.107892	.026541	.106165	.009177	.110131	.027080	.108321
33	.008958	.107502	.026443	.105773	.009146	.109756	.026986	.107944
34	.008929	.107153	.026355	.105422	.009118	.109421	.026901	.107606
35	.008903	.106841	.026277	.105108	.009093	.109122	.026826	.107305
36	.008880	.106561	.026206	.104826	.009071	.108855	.026759	.107036
37	.008859	.106310	.026143	.104573	.009051	.108616	.026698	.106794
38	.008840	.106086	.026086	.104346	.009033	.108402	.026644	.106578
39	.008823	.105884	.026035	.104142	.009017	.108211	.026596	.106385
40	.008808	.105703	.025989	.103959	.009003	.108039	.026552	.106211
41	.008795	.105541	.025948	.103795	.008990	.107886	.026514	.106056
42	.008782	.105395	.025911	.103647	.008979	.107748	.026479	.105916
43	.008772	.105264	.025878	.103515	.008968	.107625	.026447	.105791
44	.008762	.105146	.025848	.103395	.008959	.107514	.026419	.105679
45	.008753	.105040	.025822	.103288	.008951	.107415	.026394	.105578
46	.008745	.104945	.025797	.103191	.008943	.107326	.026372	.105488
47	.008738	.104859	.025776	.103104	.008937	.107246	.026351	.105406
48	.008731	.104782	.025756	.103026	.008931	.107175	.026333	.105333
49	.008726	.104713	.025738	.102955	.008925	.107110	.026317	.105268
50	.008720	.104651	.025723	.102892	.008921	.107053	.026302	.105209

Factors in this table are computed for payment of rent monthly and quarterly in advance. Cap. Rates are 12 times the monthly factors and 4 times the quarterly factors. These may be used as divisors of net annual rent to compute value or as multipliers of investment cost to compute net annual rent.

TABLE IV

PURCHASE-LEASEBACK RENT FACTORS and CAPITALIZATION RATES

RATE	11%				11¼%			
Payable	Monthly		Quarterly		Monthly		Quarterly	
Term Years	Rent	Cap Rate	Rent	Cap Rate	Rent	Cap Rate	Rent	Cap Rate
10	.013649	.163798	.040419	.161679	.013787	.165451	.040813	.163252
11	.012973	.155681	.038404	.153619	.013114	.157374	.038808	.155232
12	.012421	.149060	.036760	.147042	.012566	.150793	.037173	.148695
13	.011965	.143587	.035400	.141603	.012113	.145358	.035823	.143294
14	.011584	.139012	.034263	.137055	.011735	.140820	.034695	.138783
15	.011262	.135152	.033304	.133216	.011416	.136997	.033744	.134979
16	.010989	.131871	.032487	.129951	.011145	.133749	.032937	.131748
17	.010755	.129062	.031788	.127154	.010914	.130974	.032246	.128984
18	.010553	.126645	.031186	.124746	.010715	.128588	.031651	.126607
19	.010379	.124553	.030665	.122661	.010544	.126528	.031138	.124553
20	.010228	.122737	.030212	.120850	.010395	.124741	.030692	.122770
21	.010096	.121153	.029817	.119269	.010265	.123185	.030304	.121217
22	.009980	.119768	.029471	.117886	.010152	.121827	.029965	.119860
23	.009879	.118554	.029168	.116673	.010053	.120638	.029668	.118672
24	.009790	.117486	.028901	.115605	.009966	.119594	.029406	.117627
25	.009712	.116545	.028665	.114663	.009889	.118676	.029177	.116708
26	.009642	.115714	.028457	.113831	.009822	.117867	.028974	.115898
27	.009581	.114980	.028273	.113095	.009762	.117153	.028795	.115182
28	.009527	.114329	.028110	.112443	.009710	.116522	.028637	.114549
29	.009479	.113752	.027966	.111864	.009663	.115963	.028497	.113988
30	.009436	.113240	.027837	.111350	.009622	.115468	.028372	.113491
31	.009398	.112785	.027723	.110892	.009585	.115030	.028262	.113049
32	.009365	.112381	.027621	.110485	.009553	.114640	.028164	.112657
33	.009335	.112020	.027530	.110122	.009524	.114294	.028077	.112308
34	.009308	.111699	.027449	.109799	.009498	.113986	.027999	.111998
35	.009284	.111413	.027377	.109510	.009476	.113713	.027930	.111722
36	.009263	.111158	.027313	.109253	.009455	.113469	.027869	.111476
37	.009244	.110930	.027255	.109022	.009437	.113252	.027814	.111257
38	.009227	.110727	.027204	.108817	.009421	.113059	.027765	.111061
39	.009212	.110545	.027158	.108633	.009407	.112887	.027721	.110887
40	.009198	.110383	.027117	.108469	.009394	.112734	.027682	.110731
41	.009186	.110238	.027080	.108322	.009383	.112597	.027648	.110592
42	.009175	.110108	.027047	.108190	.009372	.112475	.027617	.110468
43	.009166	.109992	.027018	.108072	.009363	.112366	.027589	.110357
44	.009157	.109889	.026991	.107967	.009355	.112268	.027564	.110258
45	.009149	.109796	.026968	.107872	.009348	.112182	.027542	.110170
46	.009142	.109713	.026947	.107788	.009342	.112104	.027522	.110091
47	.009136	.109638	.026928	.107712	.009336	.112035	.027505	.110020
48	.009131	.109572	.026911	.107644	.009331	.111973	.027489	.109957
49	.009126	.109512	.026895	.107583	.009326	.111918	.027475	.109901
50	.009121	.109459	.026882	.107529	.009322	.111869	.027462	.109850

Factors in this table are computed for payment of rent monthly and quarterly in advance. Cap. Rates are 12 times the monthly factors and 4 times the quarterly factors. These may be used as divisors of net annual rent to compute value or as multipliers of investment cost to compute net annual rent.

TABLE IV

PURCHASE-LEASEBACK RENT FACTORS and CAPITALIZATION RATES

RATE	11½%				11¾%			
Payable	Monthly		Quarterly		Monthly		Quarterly	
Term Years	Rent	Cap Rate	Rent	Cap Rate	Rent	Cap Rate	Rent	Cap Rate
10	.013926	.167113	.041207	.164831	.014065	.168782	.041604	.166416
11	.013256	.159077	.039213	.156853	.013399	.160789	.039620	.158481
12	.012711	.152536	.037589	.150356	.012857	.154288	.038006	.152024
13	.012261	.147140	.036248	.144993	.012410	.148931	.036675	.146700
14	.011886	.142639	.035129	.140519	.012039	.144468	.035566	.142264
15	.011571	.138852	.034187	.136751	.011726	.140717	.034633	.138532
16	.011303	.135639	.033388	.133554	.011461	.137540	.033842	.135370
17	.011074	.132897	.032705	.130823	.011236	.134832	.033168	.132672
18	.010878	.130544	.032119	.128478	.011042	.132511	.032589	.130359
19	.010709	.128514	.031613	.126454	.010876	.130512	.032091	.128365
20	.010563	.126756	.031175	.124700	.010731	.128783	.031660	.126640
21	.010435	.125229	.030793	.123175	.010607	.127284	.031285	.125142
22	.010324	.123897	.030461	.121844	.010498	.125979	.030959	.123838
23	.010227	.122733	.030170	.120680	.010403	.124840	.030674	.122698
24	.010142	.121713	.029915	.119660	.010320	.123844	.030425	.121701
25	.010068	.120818	.029690	.118763	.010247	.122971	.030206	.120827
26	.010002	.120030	.029493	.117974	.010183	.122205	.030014	.120058
27	.009944	.119337	.029319	.117278	.010127	.121531	.029845	.119382
28	.009893	.118725	.029166	.116664	.010078	.120938	.029696	.118786
29	.009848	.118184	.029030	.116120	.010034	.120415	.029565	.118261
30	.009808	.117706	.028910	.115640	.009996	.119954	.029449	.117796
31	.009773	.117283	.028803	.115214	.009962	.119547	.029346	.117386
32	.009742	.116909	.028709	.114837	.009932	.119186	.029255	.117023
33	.009714	.116577	.028625	.114502	.009905	.118868	.029175	.116701
34	.009690	.116282	.028551	.114204	.009882	.118586	.029104	.116416
35	.009668	.116021	.028485	.113940	.009861	.118336	.029041	.116164
36	.009649	.115788	.028426	.113705	.009842	.118115	.028985	.115940
37	.009631	.115582	.028374	.113496	.009826	.117919	.028935	.115741
38	.009616	.115399	.028327	.113310	.009812	.117744	.028891	.115564
39	.009602	.115235	.028286	.113145	.009799	.117590	.028852	.115408
40	.009590	.115090	.028249	.112998	.009787	.117453	.028817	.115268
41	.009580	.114961	.028216	.112866	.009777	.117331	.028786	.115145
42	.009570	.114846	.028187	.112750	.009768	.117224	.028758	.115035
43	.009562	.114744	.028161	.112645	.009760	.117128	.028734	.114937
44	.009554	.114653	.028138	.112553	.009753	.117042	.028712	.114850
45	.009547	.114572	.028117	.112470	.009747	.116967	.028693	.114772
46	.009541	.114500	.028099	.112396	.009741	.116899	.028676	.114704
47	.009536	.114436	.028082	.112330	.009736	.116840	.028660	.114642
48	.009531	.114378	.028068	.112272	.009732	.116787	.028647	.114588
49	.009527	.114327	.028054	.112219	.009728	.116739	.028635	.114540
50	.009523	.114282	.028043	.112173	.009724	.116697	.028624	.114496

Factors in this table are computed for payment of rent monthly and quarterly in advance. Cap. Rates are 12 times the monthly factors and 4 times the quarterly factors. These may be used as divisors of net annual rent to compute value or as multipliers of investment cost to compute net annual rent.

TABLE IV

PURCHASE-LEASEBACK RENT FACTORS and CAPITALIZATION RATES

RATE	12%				12¼%			
Payable	Monthly		Quarterly		Monthly		Quarterly	
Term Years	Rent	Cap Rate	Rent	Cap Rate	Rent	Cap Rate	Rent	Cap Rate
10	.014205	.170460	.042002	.168009	.014345	.172146	.042401	.169607
11	.013542	.162509	.040028	.160115	.013686	.164238	.040439	.161757
12	.013004	.156049	.038425	.153700	.013151	.157820	.038845	.155383
13	.012561	.150732	.037104	.148416	.012711	.152543	.037534	.150139
14	.012192	.146308	.036004	.144017	.012346	.148158	.036444	.145778
15	.011882	.142594	.035080	.140322	.012040	.144480	.035530	.142120
16	.011621	.139452	.034298	.137194	.011781	.141374	.034756	.139027
17	.011398	.136778	.033632	.134530	.011561	.138734	.034099	.136397
18	.011207	.134489	.033062	.132248	.011373	.136478	.033536	.134147
19	.011043	.132521	.032571	.130285	.011211	.134540	.033053	.132214
20	.010901	.130822	.032147	.128589	.011072	.132871	.032636	.130547
21	.010779	.129350	.031779	.127118	.010952	.131427	.032276	.129104
22	.010672	.128071	.031460	.125840	.010847	.130175	.031962	.127851
23	.010579	.126958	.031181	.124725	.010757	.129086	.031690	.126761
24	.010498	.125985	.030938	.123752	.010678	.128137	.031452	.125811
25	.010427	.125135	.030724	.122899	.010609	.127309	.031245	.124980
26	.010365	.124390	.030538	.122152	.010548	.126585	.031063	.124252
27	.010311	.123736	.030373	.121495	.010495	.125950	.030903	.123615
28	.010263	.123161	.030229	.120917	.010449	.125394	.030763	.123055
29	.010221	.122656	.030102	.120409	.010408	.124906	.030641	.122564
30	.010184	.122211	.029990	.119960	.010373	.124476	.030532	.122131
31	.010151	.121819	.029891	.119565	.010341	.124099	.030437	.121750
32	.010122	.121473	.029804	.119216	.010313	.123767	.030353	.121414
33	.010097	.121167	.029726	.118907	.010289	.123474	.030279	.121118
34	.010074	.120897	.029658	.118634	.010268	.123216	.030214	.120857
35	.010054	.120659	.029598	.118393	.010249	.122989	.030156	.120627
36	.010037	.120448	.029544	.118179	.010232	.122788	.030105	.120423
37	.010021	.120262	.029497	.117990	.010217	.122611	.030061	.120244
38	.010008	.120097	.029455	.117823	.010204	.122454	.030021	.120085
39	.009995	.119951	.029418	.117674	.010193	.122316	.029986	.119944
40	.009985	.119821	.029385	.117542	.010182	.122194	.029955	.119820
41	.009975	.119707	.029356	.117426	.010173	.122087	.029927	.119710
42	.009967	.119605	.029330	.117322	.010165	.121991	.029903	.119613
43	.009959	.119515	.029307	.117231	.010158	.121907	.029881	.119526
44	.009953	.119436	.029287	.117149	.010152	.121833	.029862	.119450
45	.009947	.119365	.029269	.117077	.010147	.121767	.029845	.119383
46	.009941	.119303	.029253	.117013	.010142	.121709	.029830	.119323
47	.009937	.119247	.029239	.116956	.010138	.121657	.029817	.119270
48	.009933	.119198	.029226	.116905	.010134	.121612	.029805	.119223
49	.009929	.119154	.029215	.116860	.010130	.121571	.029795	.119182
50	.009926	.119116	.029205	.116821	.010128	.121536	.029786	.119145

Factors in this table are computed for payment of rent monthly and quarterly in advance. Cap. Rates are 12 times the monthly factors and 4 times the quarterly factors. These may be used as divisors of net annual rent to compute value or as multipliers of investment cost to compute net annual rent.

PURCHASE-LEASEBACK TABLES, V

Table V:

Investment yield characteristics including the effect of reversion at various percentages of the original investment. May be used in negotiating repurchase or renewal options for realization of selected overall yields.

Expansion of this table is in revised form showing:

1. Interest rate. 2. Annual rent (payable monthly in advance) to fully amortize investment during lease term. 3. Investment yield rates in excess of interest rate. 4. Reversionary multiplier of original investment to find price at which property must sell at end of lease term to produce indicated yield.

Example:—

Investment \$1,200,000. Lease Term 20 yrs. Interest 8%. Annual rent \$1,200,000 × .0997 = \$119,640 (payable \$9,970 monthly in advance). Sale price at end of 20 years for investment yield of 10%:

$$\$1,200,000 \times .9658 = \$1,158,960$$

TABLE V

PURCHASE – LEASEBACK INVESTMENT YIELD CHARACTERISTICS

with allowance for reversion at end of term at 0% to 100% of original investment.

LEASE TERM 10 YEARS

Ann. Rent %	10.633	10.762	10.892	11.024	11.156	11.289	11.424
Reversion %	YIELDS %						
0	1.25	1.50	1.75	2.00	2.25	2.50	2.75
5	2.10	2.35	2.55	2.78	3.02	3.24	3.49
10	2.88	3.08	3.26	3.51	3.76	3.98	4.20
15	3.59	3.80	4.00	4.24	4.44	4.62	4.81
20	4.23	4.45	4.63	4.85	5.05	5.22	5.42
25	4.83	5.02	5.17	5.41	5.61	5.78	5.99
30	5.40	5.56	5.74	5.94	6.13	6.30	6.49
35	5.90	6.10	6.28	6.45	6.63	6.80	6.98
40	6.37	6.59	6.77	6.93	7.09	7.27	7.44
45	6.83	7.05	7.23	7.36	7.55	7.70	7.88
50	7.29	7.49	7.66	7.80	7.98	8.11	8.28
55	7.68	7.89	8.01	8.18	8.32	8.49	8.66
60	8.07	8.27	8.40	8.57	8.70	8.88	9.04
65	8.46	8.63	8.77	8.94	9.06	9.24	9.40
70	8.84	8.99	9.12	9.29	9.41	9.58	9.73
75	9.17	9.34	9.48	9.64	9.75	9.90	10.04
80	9.50	9.67	9.80	9.98	10.08	10.22	10.37
85	9.82	9.99	10.11	10.30	10.40	10.53	10.68
90	10.13	10.29	10.41	10.58	10.69	10.82	10.97
95	10.40	10.56	10.67	10.83	10.95	11.09	11.24
100	10.64	10.78	10.91	11.04	11.18	11.31	11.45

Ann. Rent %	11.558	11.695	11.832	11.971	12.110	12.249	12.390
Reversion %	YIELDS %						
0	3.00	3.25	3.50	3.75	4.00	4.25	4.50
5	3.72	3.97	4.21	4.46	4.70	4.92	5.16
10	4.41	4.66	4.88	5.10	5.34	5.53	5.77
15	5.03	5.28	5.52	5.71	5.90	6.14	6.35
20	5.61	5.83	6.05	6.23	6.45	6.69	6.88
25	6.15	6.35	6.58	6.76	6.96	7.18	7.36
30	6.67	6.87	7.04	7.26	7.44	7.65	7.84
35	7.17	7.36	7.52	7.71	7.90	8.09	8.25
40	7.62	7.79	7.98	8.15	8.34	8.50	8.68
45	8.05	8.20	8.38	8.56	8.76	8.91	9.10
50	8.46	8.60	8.78	8.98	9.13	9.30	9.49
55	8.83	8.99	9.13	9.31	9.49	9.65	9.85
60	9.22	9.36	9.51	9.69	9.84	10.01	10.20
65	9.56	9.71	9.86	10.02	10.17	10.35	10.51
70	9.90	10.03	10.20	10.35	10.50	10.67	10.82
75	10.22	10.37	10.52	10.68	10.81	10.98	11.12
80	10.53	10.68	10.83	10.98	11.11	11.27	11.41
85	10.83	10.99	11.13	11.28	11.40	11.56	11.70
90	11.11	11.28	11.41	11.55	11.68	11.83	11.99
95	11.38	11.51	11.65	11.79	11.92	12.07	12.22
100	11.59	11.73	11.87	12.01	12.15	12.29	12.44

TABLE V

PURCHASE – LEASEBACK INVESTMENT YIELD CHARACTERISTICS

with allowance for reversion at end of term at 0% to 100% of original investment

LEASE TERM 15 YEARS

Ann. Rent %	8.410	8.554	8.700	8.847	8.996	9.146	9.298
Reversion %			YIELDS %				
0	3.25	3.50	3.75	4.00	4.25	4.50	4.75
5	3.69	3.92	4.16	4.39	4.65	4.88	5.10
10	4.06	4.30	4.53	4.76	4.99	5.23	5.45
15	4.42	4.66	4.89	5.10	5.30	5.55	5.76
20	4.76	5.00	5.20	5.40	5.61	5.86	6.05
25	5.10	5.32	5.50	5.70	5.91	6.13	6.33
30	5.41	5.61	5.80	6.00	6.20	6.40	6.60
35	5.70	5.90	6.09	6.28	6.46	6.67	6.86
40	5.98	6.16	6.35	6.54	6.71	6.92	7.11
45	6.24	6.40	6.60	6.80	6.95	7.15	7.34
50	6.48	6.65	6.84	7.01	7.18	7.36	7.56
55	6.71	6.89	7.06	7.22	7.40	7.57	7.77
60	6.94	7.10	7.28	7.43	7.61	7.78	7.98
65	7.16	7.31	7.49	7.64	7.81	7.99	8.18
70	7.36	7.51	7.68	7.85	8.01	8.19	8.37
75	7.56	7.71	7.87	8.05	8.21	8.38	8.56
80	7.76	7.90	8.06	8.24	8.40	8.56	8.74
85	7.96	8.09	8.25	8.42	8.58	8.75	8.90
90	8.12	8.27	8.43	8.59	8.75	8.91	9.06
95	8.29	8.43	8.59	8.74	8.90	9.05	9.20
100	8.43	8.58	8.73	8.88	9.03	9.18	9.33

Ann. Rent %	9.450	9.605	9.760	9.918	10.076	10.237	10.397
Reversion %			YIELDS %				
0	5.00	5.25	5.50	5.75	6.00	6.25	6.50
5	5.32	5.53	5.84	6.07	6.32	6.55	6.80
10	5.65	5.91	6.13	6.37	6.61	6.85	7.09
15	5.99	6.21	6.42	6.66	6.89	7.12	7.35
20	6.27	6.48	6.71	6.93	7.16	7.37	7.60
25	6.54	6.74	6.98	7.18	7.40	7.60	7.83
30	6.81	7.01	7.21	7.42	7.64	7.83	8.06
35	7.06	7.22	7.46	7.66	7.86	8.06	8.28
40	7.29	7.46	7.69	7.88	8.08	8.28	8.48
45	7.51	7.69	7.91	8.10	8.28	8.49	8.68
50	7.74	7.91	8.10	8.30	8.49	8.70	8.87
55	7.95	8.12	8.31	8.49	8.67	8.88	9.05
60	8.15	8.32	8.50	8.68	8.86	9.06	9.24
65	8.34	8.51	8.69	8.86	9.04	9.25	9.41
70	8.53	8.70	8.87	9.04	9.23	9.42	9.59
75	8.71	8.88	9.05	9.21	9.40	9.59	9.75
80	8.88	9.05	9.22	9.38	9.57	9.74	9.91
85	9.05	9.21	9.38	9.54	9.73	9.89	10.06
90	9.21	9.37	9.53	9.70	9.88	10.03	10.20
95	9.35	9.52	9.67	9.84	10.01	10.16	10.33
100	9.49	9.65	9.80	9.98	10.13	10.29	10.45

TABLE V

PURCHASE – LEASEBACK INVESTMENT YIELD CHARACTERISTICS

with allowance for reversion at end of term at 0% to 100% of original investment

LEASE TERM 20 YEARS

Ann. Rent %	6.788	6.940	7.093	7.248	7.405	7.564	7.725
Reversion %			YIELDS %				
0	3.25	3.50	3.75	4.00	4.25	4.50	4.75
5	3.49	3.75	4.01	4.26	4.48	4.71	4.98
10	3.82	4.03	4.27	4.49	4.70	4.94	5.18
15	4.04	4.27	4.49	4.74	4.92	5.17	5.38
20	4.26	4.48	4.70	4.94	5.13	5.38	5.57
25	4.47	4.69	4.90	5.12	5.34	5.58	5.76
30	4.68	4.90	5.09	5.30	5.53	5.73	5.92
35	4.89	5.09	5.26	5.48	5.70	5.90	6.09
40	5.07	5.26	5.43	5.65	5.87	6.05	6.25
45	5.24	5.43	5.60	5.81	6.02	6.20	6.40
50	5.41	5.60	5.78	5.98	6.17	6.35	6.55
55	5.58	5.76	5.94	6.14	6.31	6.49	6.69
60	5.74	5.92	6.10	6.28	6.45	6.62	6.82
65	5.90	6.08	6.25	6.42	6.60	6.76	6.96
70	6.05	6.23	6.41	6.56	6.74	6.90	7.10
75	6.20	6.37	6.54	6.70	6.86	7.03	7.22
80	6.34	6.49	6.67	6.83	6.99	7.16	7.34
85	6.48	6.63	6.79	6.95	7.11	7.27	7.45
90	6.60	6.75	6.90	7.06	7.22	7.39	7.56
95	6.71	6.86	7.01	7.17	7.32	7.50	7.66
100	6.81	6.96	7.11	7.27	7.43	7.59	7.76

Ann. Rent %	7.887	8.052	8.217	8.385	8.555	8.726	8.899
Reversion %			YIELDS %				
0	5.00	5.25	5.50	5.75	6.00	6.25	6.50
5	5.20	5.45	5.70	5.95	6.18	6.42	6.66
10	5.41	5.65	5.89	6.12	6.36	6.59	6.82
15	5.61	5.84	6.08	6.30	6.52	6.75	6.99
20	5.80	6.01	6.24	6.46	6.68	6.90	7.13
25	5.98	6.18	6.40	6.61	6.84	7.05	7.27
30	6.13	6.35	6.56	6.76	6.99	7.20	7.41
35	6.29	6.51	6.71	6.91	7.14	7.34	7.55
40	6.45	6.65	6.86	7.06	7.28	7.47	7.69
45	6.60	6.79	7.00	7.20	7.41	7.60	7.81
50	6.74	6.93	7.13	7.33	7.53	7.73	7.94
55	6.88	7.07	7.26	7.46	7.65	7.84	8.04
60	7.01	7.20	7.39	7.58	7.77	7.96	8.15
65	7.13	7.32	7.51	7.69	7.89	8.08	8.26
70	7.26	7.45	7.62	7.80	8.00	8.20	8.37
75	7.39	7.56	7.74	7.91	8.11	8.31	8.48
80	7.51	7.68	7.85	8.02	8.22	8.41	8.58
85	7.62	7.79	7.96	8.13	8.32	8.51	8.68
90	7.73	7.90	8.08	8.23	8.42	8.60	8.77
95	7.82	8.00	8.17	8.33	8.51	8.69	8.86
100	7.92	8.09	8.26	8.43	8.60	8.77	8.95

TABLE V

PURCHASE – LEASEBACK INVESTMENT YIELD CHARACTERISTICS

with allowance for reversion at end of term at 0% to 100% of original investment.

LEASE TERM 25 YEARS

Ann. Rent %	5.833	5.991	6.151	6.314	6.479	6.646	6.815
Reversion %			YIELDS %				
0	3.25	3.50	3.75	4.00	4.25	4.50	4.75
5	3.46	3.69	3.93	4.16	4.42	4.68	4.90
10	3.63	3.86	4.10	4.33	4.57	4.82	5.05
15	3.80	4.02	4.26	4.49	4.72	4.98	5.19
20 20	3.97	4.18	4.42	4.63	4.86	5.11	5.32
25	4.13	4.33	4.57	4.76	4.99	5.22	5.44
30	4.28	4.49	4.71	4.90	5.13	5.35	5.55
35	4.42	4.62	4.84	5.03	5.24	5.46	5.66
40	4.55	4.76	4.96	5.16	5.36	5.58	5.78
45	4.69	4.89	5.08	5.28	5.48	5.69	5.89
50	4.81	5.01	5.20	5.40	5.59	5.80	5.99
55	4.93	5.12	5.31	5.50	5.69	5.90	6.08
60	5.05	5.23	5.42	5.60	5.79	5.99	6.13
65	5.16	5.35	5.52	5.70	5.89	6.08	6.25
70	5.27	5.46	5.63	5.80	5.99	6.17	6.34
75	5.38	5.56	5.73	5.90	6.08	6.25	6.43
80	5.48	5.66	5.83	5.99	6.17	6.34	6.52
85	5.58	5.75	5.92	6.08	6.26	6.42	6.60
90	5.68	5.84	6.01	6.17	6.35	6.51	6.68
95	5.76	5.93	6.09	6.26	6.43	6.59	6.76
100	5.85	6.01	6.17	6.33	6.50	6.67	6.84

Ann. Rent %	6.986	7.160	7.336	7.514	7.694	7.875	8.059
Reversion %			YIELDS %				
0	5.00	5.25	5.50	5.75	6.00	6.25	6.50
5	5.16	5.39	5.62	5.86	6.12	6.37	6.61
10	5.30	5.53	5.76	5.99	6.24	6.48	6.71
15	5.42	5.66	5.88	6.10	6.35	6.58	6.80
20	5.54	5.78	5.99	6.20	6.45	6.68	6.90
25	5.66	5.88	6.10	6.31	6.55	6.78	6.99
30	5.77	5.99	6.20	6.42	6.64	6.87	7.08
35	5.88	6.10	6.30	6.51	6.73	6.96	7.17
40	5.98	6.20	6.40	6.61	6.82	7.04	7.25
45	6.08	6.29	6.49	6.70	6.91	7.12	7.33
50	6.17	6.39	6.57	6.79	7.00	7.20	7.41
55	6.27	6.48	6.66	6.87	7.08	7.28	7.49
60	6.37	6.57	6.75	6.96	7.16	7.36	7.57
65	6.46	6.66	6.83	7.04	7.24	7.44	7.65
70	6.55	6.74	6.92	7.13	7.32	7.52	7.73
75	6.64	6.82	7.01	7.21	7.40	7.60	7.80
80	6.72	6.90	7.08	7.28	7.47	7.67	7.86
85	6.79	6.98	7.15	7.35	7.54	7.73	7.93
90	6.86	7.06	7.21	7.42	7.60	7.80	7.99
95	6.93	7.14	7.29	7.49	7.67	7.86	8.05
100	7.01	7.20	7.37	7.55	7.73	7.92	8.10

TABLE V

PURCHASE – LEASEBACK INVESTMENT YIELD CHARACTERISTICS

with allowance for reversion at end of term at 0% to 100% of original investment

LEASE TERM 30 YEARS

Ann. Rent %	5.209	5.374	5.541	5.710	5.883	6.058	6.236
Reversion %			YIELDS %				
0	3.25	3.50	3.75	4.00	4.25	4.50	4.75
5	3.42	3.66	3.89	4.12	4.36	4.61	4.85
10	3.53	3.79	4.01	4.23	4.47	4.71	4.95
15	3.66	3.91	4.13	4.34	4.58	4.81	5.04
20	3.79	4.01	4.24	4.45	4.68	4.91	5.13
25	3.91	4.12	4.34	4.56	4.78	5.01	5.22
30	4.02	4.22	4.45	4.66	4.87	5.09	5.30
35	4.13	4.32	4.54	4.74	4.96	5.17	5.38
40	4.23	4.42	4.63	4.83	5.05	5.26	5.46
45	4.33	4.52	4.72	4.92	5.13	5.34	5.54
50	4.42	4.61	4.81	5.01	5.21	5.42	5.62
55	4.51	4.70	4.90	5.08	5.29	5.49	5.69
60	4.60	4.79	4.98	5.16	5.36	5.56	5.77
65	4.69	4.88	5.06	5.24	5.44	5.63	5.83
70	4.78	4.96	5.15	5.32	5.52	5.70	5.89
75	4.86	5.04	5.23	5.40	5.59	5.77	5.96
80	4.94	5.11	5.31	5.47	5.65	5.83	6.02
85	5.02	5.19	5.37	5.54	5.71	5.90	6.08
90	5.09	5.26	5.44	5.60	5.78	5.97	6.14
95	5.16	5.32	5.51	5.66	5.84	6.02	6.20
100	5.22	5.39	5.56	5.73	5.90	6.08	6.26

Ann. Rent %	6.416	6.598	6.783	6.970	7.160	7.351	7.544
Reversion %			YIELDS %				
0	5.00	5.25	5.50	5.75	6.00	6.25	6.50
5	5.10	5.34	5.58	5.83	6.07	6.32	6.57
10	5.19	5.42	5.67	5.91	6.14	6.39	6.63
15	5.28	5.51	5.75	5.99	6.22	6.46	6.70
20	5.37	5.60	5.82	6.06	6.28	6.53	6.76
25	5.45	5.68	5.90	6.13	6.35	6.59	6.82
30	5.53	5.76	5.98	6.20	6.42	6.66	6.88
35	5.60	5.82	6.05	6.27	6.49	6.71	6.94
40	5.67	5.89	6.11	6.33	6.55	6.77	6.99
45	5.76	5.97	6.18	6.39	6.61	6.83	7.06
50	5.82	6.03	6.24	6.46	6.67	6.89	7.11
55	5.89	6.10	6.30	6.52	6.73	6.95	7.17
60	5.96	6.16	6.36	6.57	6.78	7.00	7.22
65	6.03	6.22	6.43	6.63	6.84	7.06	7.27
70	6.10	6.29	6.49	6.69	6.90	7.11	7.32
75	6.16	6.35	6.54	6.75	6.96	7.16	7.38
80	6.22	6.41	6.60	6.80	7.01	7.21	7.42
85	6.29	6.47	6.66	6.85	7.06	7.26	7.46
90	6.34	6.52	6.71	6.90	7.10	7.31	7.51
95	6.39	6.57	6.76	6.95	7.14	7.35	7.55
100	6.44	6.62	6.81	7.00	7.19	7.39	7.58

TABLE V

PURCHASE – LEASEBACK INVESTMENT YIELD CHARACTERISTICS

with allowance for reversion at end of term at 0% to 100% of original investment

LEASE TERM 35 YEARS

Ann. Rent %	4.775	4.945	5.129	5.296	5.475	5.658	5.844
Reversion %			YIELDS %				
0	3.25	3.50	3.75	4.00	4.25	4.50	4.75
5	3.36	3.60	3.84	4.08	4.33	4.58	4.82
10	3.47	3.70	3.93	4.17	4.41	4.65	4.89
15	3.57	3.80	4.02	4.26	4.49	4.72	4.96
20	3.67	3.89	4.11	4.33	4.56	4.78	5.03
25	3.76	3.97	4.19	4.41	4.63	4.86	5.09
30	3.84	4.05	4.27	4.48	4.71	4.93	5.15
35	3.93	4.13	4.34	4.56	4.77	4.99	5.21
40	4.01	4.21	4.42	4.62	4.83	5.05	5.27
45	4.08	4.28	4.49	4.69	4.90	5.11	5.33
50	4.15	4.35	4.56	4.76	4.97	5.17	5.38
55	4.22	4.42	4.62	4.82	5.02	5.23	5.43
60	4.29	4.49	4.68	4.88	5.08	5.28	5.49
65	4.36	4.55	4.75	4.94	5.13	5.33	5.54
70	4.42	4.61	4.81	5.01	5.19	5.39	5.59
75	4.49	4.67	4.87	5.06	5.25	5.44	5.64
80	4.56	4.73	4.93	5.11	5.30	5.49	5.69
85	4.62	4.80	4.98	5.17	5.35	5.54	5.74
90	4.67	4.85	5.04	5.22	5.40	5.59	5.78
95	4.73	4.90	5.09	5.27	5.45	5.64	5.83
100	4.79	4.96	5.14	5.32	5.50	5.68	5.87

Ann. Rent %	6.031	6.222	6.416	6.610	6.808	7.009	7.211
Reversion %			YIELDS %				
0	5.00	5.25	5.50	5.75	6.00	6.25	6.50
5	5.07	5.31	5.56	5.80	6.05	6.30	6.54
10	5.13	5.37	5.61	5.86	6.10	6.34	6.58
15	5.20	5.43	5.67	5.91	6.15	6.38	6.63
20	5.26	5.49	5.73	5.96	6.20	6.43	6.67
25	5.32	5.55	5.78	6.01	6.24	6.48	6.72
30	5.38	5.61	5.83	6.06	6.28	6.52	6.76
35	5.44	5.66	5.88	6.11	6.33	6.57	6.80
40	5.49	5.71	5.93	6.15	6.38	6.61	6.84
45	5.54	5.76	5.98	6.20	6.42	6.65	6.88
50	5.59	5.81	6.03	6.24	6.46	6.68	6.92
55	5.64	5.86	6.07	6.29	6.51	6.72	6.95
60	5.69	5.91	6.12	6.33	6.55	6.76	6.98
65	5.74	5.95	6.16	6.37	6.58	6.80	7.02
70	5.79	6.00	6.20	6.41	6.62	6.84	7.05
75	5.84	6.04	6.25	6.45	6.66	6.87	7.09
80	5.88	6.08	6.29	6.49	6.70	6.91	7.12
85	5.93	6.12	6.33	6.53	6.74	6.94	7.16
90	5.98	6.17	6.37	6.57	6.78	6.98	7.19
95	6.02	6.21	6.41	6.61	6.82	7.02	7.22
100	6.06	6.25	6.45	6.65	6.85	7.05	7.25

TABLE V

PURCHASE-LEASEBACK INVESTMENT YIELD CHARACTERISTICS

LEASE TERM 10 YEARS

Interest Rate	.0600		.0625		.0650		.0675	
Annual Rent	.1326		.1340		.1355		.1370	
	Yield	Reversion	Yield	Reversion	Yield	Reversion	Yield	Reversion
	.0675	.0637	.0700	.0650	.0725	.0663	.0750	.0677
	.0750	.1342	.0775	.1369	.0800	.1397	.0825	.1425
	.0825	.2119	.0850	.2162	.0875	.2207	.0900	.2252
	.0900	.2976	.0925	.3037	.0950	.3099	.0975	.3162
	.0975	.3918	.1000	.3998	.1025	.4080	.1050	.4164
	.1050	.4954	.1075	.5056	.1100	.5159	.1125	.5265
	.1125	.6091	.1150	.6216	.1175	.6344	.1200	.6474
	.1200	.7337	.1225	.7489	.1250	.7643	.1275	.7801
	.1275	.8703	.1300	.8883	.1325	.9067	.1350	.9254
	.1350	1.0198	.1375	1.0409	.1400	1.0625	.1425	1.0844

Interest Rate	.0700		.0725		.0750		.0775	
Annual Rent	.1385		.1400		.1416		.1431	
	Yield	Reversion	Yield	Reversion	Yield	Reversion	Yield	Reversion
	.0775	.0690	.0800	.0705	.0825	.0719	.0850	.0733
	.0850	.1454	.0875	.1484	.0900	.1514	.0925	.1545
	.0925	.2297	.0950	.2344	.0975	.2392	.1000	.2441
	.1000	.3227	.1025	.3292	.1050	.3360	.1075	.3428
	.1075	.4249	.1100	.4336	.1125	.4425	.1150	.4515
	.1150	.5373	.1175	.5483	.1200	.5596	.1225	.5710
	.1225	.6607	.1250	.6743	.1275	.6881	.1300	.7022
	.1300	.7961	.1325	.8125	.1350	.8292	.1375	.8462
	.1375	.9445	.1400	.9639	.1425	.9838	.1450	1.0040
	.1450	1.1068	.1475	1.1297	.1500	1.1530	.1525	1.1768

Interest Rate	.0800		.0825		.0850		.0875	
Annual Rent	.1446		.1462		.1477		.1493	
	Yield	Reversion	Yield	Reversion	Yield	Reversion	Yield	Reversion
	.0875	.0748	.0900	.0763	.0925	.0779	.0950	.0794
	.0950	.1576	.0975	.1608	.1000	.1641	.1025	.1674
	.1025	.2490	.1050	.2541	.1075	.2592	.1100	.2645
	.1100	.3498	.1125	.3569	.1150	.3641	.1175	.3715
	.1175	.4607	.1200	.4701	.1225	.4797	.1250	.4894
	.1250	.5827	.1275	.5946	.1300	.6067	.1325	.6191
	.1325	.7166	.1350	.7313	.1375	.7462	.1400	.7615
	.1400	.8636	.1425	.8813	.1450	.8993	.1475	.9178
	.1475	1.0246	.1500	1.0457	.1525	1.0672	.1550	1.0890
	.1550	1.2010	.1575	1.2257	.1600	1.2509	.1625	1.2766

Interest Rate	.0900		.0925		.0950		.0975	
Annual Rent	.1509		.1525		.1541		.1557	
	Yield	Reversion	Yield	Reversion	Yield	Reversion	Yield	Reversion
	.0975	.0810	.1000	.0827	.1025	.0843	.1050	.0860
	.1050	.1708	.1075	.1742	.1100	.1777	.1125	.1813
	.1125	.2698	.1150	.2753	.1175	.2808	.1200	.2865
	.1200	.3791	.1225	.3868	.1250	.3946	.1275	.4026
	.1275	.4994	.1300	.5095	.1325	.5199	.1350	.5304
	.1350	.6317	.1375	.6445	.1400	.6577	.1425	.6710
	.1425	.7770	.1450	.7929	.1475	.8090	.1500	.8255
	.1500	.9365	.1525	.9557	.1550	.9752	.1575	.9951
	.1575	1.1114	.1600	1.1341	.1625	1.1573	.1650	1.1810
	.1650	1.3028	.1675	1.3296	.1700	1.3568	.1725	1.3846

TABLE V

PURCHASE-LEASEBACK INVESTMENT YIELD CHARACTERISTICS

LEASE TERM 15 YEARS

Interest Rate	.0700		.0725		.0750		.0775	
Annual Rent	.1072		.1089		.1106		.1122	
	Yield	Reversion	Yield	Reversion	Yield	Reversion	Yield	Reversion
	.0750	.0920	.0775	.0948	.0800	.0977	.0825	.1007
	.0800	.1940	.0825	.1999	.0850	.2060	.0875	.2123
	.0850	.3067	.0875	.3161	.0900	.3258	.0925	.3357
	.0900	.4311	.0925	.4444	.0950	.4580	.0975	.4720
	.0950	.5683	.0975	.5857	.1000	.6037	.1025	.6222
	.1000	.7192	.1025	.7414	.1050	.7642	.1075	.7877
	.1050	.8852	.1075	.9125	.1100	.9407	.1125	.9697
	.1100	1.0675	.1125	1.1005	.1150	1.1346	.1175	1.1696
	.1150	1.2675	.1175	1.3068	.1200	1.3473	.1225	1.3890
	.1200	1.4868	.1225	1.5330	.1250	1.5806	.1275	1.6296

Interest Rate	.0800		.0825		.0850		.0875	
Annual Rent	.1139		.1156		.1173		.1191	
	Yield	Reversion	Yield	Reversion	Yield	Reversion	Yield	Reversion
	.0850	.1038	.0875	.1069	.0900	.1101	.0925	.1135
	.0900	.2188	.0925	.2254	.0950	.2323	.0975	.2393
	.0950	.3460	.0975	.3565	.1000	.3674	.1025	.3785
	.1000	.4864	.1025	.5013	.1050	.5166	.1075	.5323
	.1050	.6413	.1075	.6609	.1100	.6812	.1125	.7020
	.1100	.8119	.1125	.8368	.1150	.8625	.1175	.8889
	.1150	.9995	.1175	1.0303	.1200	1.0619	.1225	1.0945
	.1200	1.2057	.1225	1.2429	.1250	1.2811	.1275	1.3206
	.1250	1.4320	.1275	1.4762	.1300	1.5218	.1325	1.5687
	.1300	1.6801	.1325	1.7321	.1350	1.7857	.1375	1.8409

Interest Rate	.0900		.0925		.0950		.0975	
Annual Rent	.1208		.1226		.1243		.1261	
	Yield	Reversion	Yield	Reversion	Yield	Reversion	Yield	Reversion
	.0950	.1169	.0975	.1204	.1000	.1241	.1025	.1278
	.1000	.2466	.1025	.2540	.1050	.2617	.1075	.2696
	.1050	.3900	.1075	.4019	.1100	.4141	.1125	.4266
	.1100	.5485	.1125	.5652	.1150	.5824	.1175	.6001
	.1150	.7234	.1175	.7455	.1200	.7682	.1225	.7916
	.1200	.9161	.1225	.9441	.1250	.9730	.1275	1.0027
	.1250	1.1281	.1275	1.1627	.1300	1.1983	.1325	1.2350
	.1300	1.3612	.1325	1.4030	.1350	1.4461	.1375	1.4904
	.1350	1.6171	.1375	1.6669	.1400	1.7182	.1425	1.7710
	.1400	1.8978	.1425	1.9563	.1450	2.0166	.1475	2.0788

Interest Rate	.1000		.1025		.1050		.1075	
Annual Rent	.1279		.1297		.1315		.1333	
	Yield	Reversion	Yield	Reversion	Yield	Reversion	Yield	Reversion
	.1050	.1317	.1075	.1356	.1100	.1397	.1125	.1439
	.1100	.2778	.1125	.2862	.1150	.2948	.1175	.3037
	.1150	.4395	.1175	.4529	.1200	.4666	.1225	.4807
	.1200	.6184	.1225	.6371	.1250	.6565	.1275	.6763
	.1250	.8157	.1275	.8405	.1300	.8661	.1325	.8924
	.1300	1.0333	.1325	1.0648	.1350	1.0972	.1375	1.1306
	.1350	1.2728	.1375	1.3117	.1400	1.3517	.1425	1.3930
	.1400	1.5361	.1425	1.5832	.1450	1.6316	.1475	1.6816
	.1450	1.8254	.1475	1.8814	.1500	1.9391	.1525	1.9986
	.1500	2.1428	.1525	2.2087	.1550	2.2766	.1575	2.3466

TABLE V

PURCHASE-LEASEBACK INVESTMENT YIELD CHARACTERISTICS

LEASE TERM 20 YEARS

Interest Rate	.0700		.0725		.0750		.0775	
Annual Rent	.0925		.0943		.0961		.0979	
	Yield	Reversion	Yield	Reversion	Yield	Reversion	Yield	Reversion
	.0740	.1309	.0765	.1362	.0790	.1417	.0815	.1475
	.0780	.2770	.0805	.2883	.0830	.3001	.0855	.3123
	.0820	.4399	.0845	.4579	.0870	.4766	.0895	.4960
	.0860	.6211	.0885	.6466	.0910	.6730	.0935	.7006
	.0900	.8224	.0925	.8562	.0950	.8913	.0975	.9278
	.0940	1.0456	.0965	1.0886	.0990	1.1334	.1015	1.1800
	.0980	1.2927	.1005	1.3461	.1030	1.4016	.1055	1.4594
	.1020	1.5661	.1045	1.6309	.1070	1.6984	.1095	1.7685
	.1060	1.8681	.1085	1.9456	.1110	2.0263	.1135	2.1102
	.1100	2.2014	.1125	2.2930	.1150	2.3883	.1175	2.4874

Interest Rate	.0800		.0825		.0850		.0875	
Annual Rent	.0997		.1015		.1034		.1053	
	Yield	Reversion	Yield	Reversion	Yield	Reversion	Yield	Reversion
	.0840	.1534	.0865	.1596	.0890	.1661	.0915	.1728
	.0880	.3249	.0905	.3381	.0930	.3518	.0955	.3661
	.0920	.5162	.0945	.5372	.0970	.5591	.0995	.5818
	.0960	.7292	.0985	.7589	.1010	.7899	.1035	.8221
	.1000	.9658	.1025	1.0054	.1050	1.0465	.1075	1.0892
	.1040	1.2285	.1065	1.2789	.1090	1.3313	.1115	1.3858
	.1080	1.5195	.1105	1.5820	.1130	1.6470	.1155	1.7146
	.1120	1.8415	.1145	1.9175	.1170	1.9965	.1195	2.0787
	.1160	2.1975	.1185	2.2884	.1210	2.3829	.1235	2.4813
	.1200	2.5906	.1225	2.6979	.1250	2.8097	.1275	2.9259

Interest Rate	.0900		.0925		.0950		.0975	
Annual Rent	.1072		.1091		.1110		.1129	
	Yield	Reversion	Yield	Reversion	Yield	Reversion	Yield	Reversion
	.0940	.1798	.0965	.1870	.0990	.1946	.1015	.2024
	.0980	.3809	.1005	.3964	.1030	.4124	.1055	.4291
	.1020	.6054	.1045	.6300	.1070	.6556	.1095	.6821
	.1060	.8556	.1085	.8904	.1110	.9266	.1135	.9642
	.1100	1.1337	.1125	1.1800	.1150	1.2281	.1175	1.2781
	.1140	1.4426	.1165	1.5016	.1190	1.5630	.1215	1.6268
	.1180	1.7850	.1205	1.8582	.1230	1.9344	.1255	2.0137
	.1220	2.1642	.1245	2.2532	.1270	2.3458	.1295	2.4422
	.1260	2.5836	.1285	2.6901	.1310	2.8010	.1335	2.9163
	.1300	3.0469	.1325	3.1728	.1350	3.3039	.1375	3.4403

Interest Rate	.1000		.1025		.1050		.1075	
Annual Rent	.1148		.1168		.1188		.1207	
	Yield	Reversion	Yield	Reversion	Yield	Reversion	Yield	Reversion
	.1040	.2106	.1065	.2191	.1090	.2279	.1115	.2371
	.1080	.4464	.1105	.4644	.1130	.4831	.1155	.5026
	.1120	.7098	.1145	.7385	.1170	.7684	.1195	.7995
	.1160	1.0034	.1185	1.0441	.1210	1.0865	.1235	1.1306
	.1200	1.3302	.1225	1.3843	.1250	1.4407	.1275	1.4993
	.1240	1.6933	.1265	1.7624	.1290	1.8343	.1315	1.9091
	.1280	2.0961	.1305	2.1819	.1330	2.2711	.1355	2.3640
	.1320	2.5424	.1345	2.6467	.1370	2.7553	.1395	2.8682
	.1360	3.0363	.1385	3.1612	.1410	3.2912	.1435	3.4264
	.1400	3.5822	.1425	3.7299	.1450	3.8836	.1475	4.0436

TABLE V
PURCHASE-LEASEBACK INVESTMENT YIELD CHARACTERISTICS

LEASE TERM 25 YEARS

Interest Rate	.0700		.0725		.0750		.0775	
Annual Rent	.0843		.0862		.0881		.0901	
	Yield	Reversion	Yield	Reversion	Yield	Reversion	Yield	Reversion
	.0730	.1620	.0755	.1703	.0780	.1789	.0805	.1880
	.0760	.3421	.0785	.3595	.0810	.3778	.0835	.3971
	.0790	.5417	.0815	.5694	.0840	.5985	.0865	.6291
	.0820	.7627	.0845	.8018	.0870	.8429	.0895	.8860
	.0850	1.0069	.0875	1.0587	.0900	1.1131	.0925	1.1702
	.0880	1.2765	.0905	1.3423	.0930	1.4114	.0955	1.4841
	.0910	1.5736	.0935	1.6550	.0960	1.7404	.0985	1.8302
	.0940	1.9008	.0965	1.9992	.0990	2.1027	.1015	2.2115
	.0970	2.2605	.0995	2.3779	.1020	2.5013	.1045	2.6310
	.1000	2.6558	.1025	2.7940	.1050	2.9394	.1075	3.0922

Interest Rate	.0800		.0825		.0850		.0875	
Annual Rent	.0920		.0940		.0959		.0979	
	Yield	Reversion	Yield	Reversion	Yield	Reversion	Yield	Reversion
	.0830	.1976	.0855	.2076	.0880	.2181	.0905	.2292
	.0860	.4173	.0885	.4385	.0910	.4608	.0935	.4842
	.0890	.6612	.0915	.6949	.0940	.7303	.0965	.7675
	.0920	.9314	.0945	.9790	.0970	1.0290	.0995	1.0816
	.0950	1.2303	.0975	1.2933	.1000	1.3596	.1025	1.4293
	.0980	1.5604	.1005	1.6406	.1030	1.7249	.1055	1.8135
	.1010	1.9246	.1035	2.0238	.1060	2.1280	.1085	2.2376
	.1040	2.3258	.1065	2.4460	.1090	2.5723	.1115	2.7050
	.1070	2.7674	.1095	2.9107	.1120	3.0613	.1145	3.2197
	.1100	3.2528	.1125	3.4216	.1150	3.5992	.1175	3.7858

Interest Rate	.0900		.0925		.0950		.0975	
Annual Rent	.1000		.1020		.1040		.1061	
	Yield	Reversion	Yield	Reversion	Yield	Reversion	Yield	Reversion
	.0930	.2408	.0955	.2530	.0980	.2658	.1005	.2792
	.0960	.5088	.0985	.5347	.1010	.5618	.1035	.5903
	.0990	.8066	.1015	.8477	.1040	.8908	.1065	.9362
	.1020	1.1368	.1045	1.1949	.1070	1.2559	.1095	1.3199
	.1050	1.5024	.1075	1.5793	.1100	1.6601	.1125	1.7451
	.1080	1.9066	.1105	2.0044	.1130	2.1072	.1155	2.2153
	.1110	2.3527	.1135	2.4737	.1160	2.6010	.1185	2.7347
	.1140	2.8446	.1165	2.9913	.1190	3.1455	.1215	3.3076
	.1170	3.3862	.1195	3.5613	.1220	3.7453	.1245	3.9389
	.1200	3.9821	.1225	4.1884	.1250	4.4054	.1275	4.6336

Interest Rate	.1000		.1025		.1050		.1075	
Annual Rent	.1081		.1102		.1123		.1144	
	Yield	Reversion	Yield	Reversion	Yield	Reversion	Yield	Reversion
	.1030	.2934	.1055	.3082	.1080	.3238	.1105	.3402
	.1060	.6203	.1085	.6517	.1110	.6848	.1135	.7195
	.1090	.9838	.1115	1.0338	.1140	1.0864	.1165	1.1417
	.1120	1.3873	.1145	1.4580	.1170	1.5324	.1195	1.6105
	.1150	1.8343	.1175	1.9281	.1200	2.0267	.1225	2.1303
	.1180	2.3289	.1205	2.4483	.1230	2.5738	.1255	2.7057
	.1210	2.8753	.1235	3.0230	.1260	3.1784	.1285	3.3417
	.1240	3.4781	.1265	3.6573	.1290	3.8457	.1315	4.0438
	.1270	4.1423	.1295	4.3563	.1320	4.5812	.1345	4.8178
	.1300	4.8735	.1325	5.1258	.1350	5.3911	.1375	5.6702

TABLE V

PURCHASE-LEASEBACK INVESTMENT YIELD CHARACTERISTICS

LEASE TERM 30 YEARS

Interest Rate	.0700		.0725		.0750		.0775	
Annual Rent	.0794		.0814		.0834		.0854	
	Yield	Reversion	Yield	Reversion	Yield	Reversion	Yield	Reversion
	.0720	.1697	.0745	.1801	.0770	.1911	.0795	.2028
	.0740	.3547	.0765	.3764	.0790	.3995	.0815	.4240
	.0760	.5559	.0785	.5901	.0810	.6264	.0835	.6649
	.0780	.7746	.0805	.8224	.0830	.8730	.0855	.9268
	.0800	1.0121	.0825	1.0746	.0850	1.1409	.0875	1.2113
	.0820	1.2696	.0845	1.3482	.0870	1.4316	.0895	1.5201
	.0840	1.5486	.0865	1.6446	.0890	1.7466	.0915	1.8548
	.0860	1.8506	.0885	1.9656	.0910	2.0878	.0935	2.2174
	.0880	2.1773	.0905	2.3129	.0930	2.4569	.0955	2.6098
	.0900	2.5304	.0925	2.6883	.0950	2.8560	.0975	3.0341

Interest Rate	.0800		.0825		.0850		.0875	
Annual Rent	.0875		.0895		.0916		.0937	
	Yield	Reversion	Yield	Reversion	Yield	Reversion	Yield	Reversion
	.0820	.2152	.0845	.2284	.0870	.2424	.0895	.2572
	.0840	.4500	.0865	.4776	.0890	.5068	.0915	.5379
	.0860	.7057	.0885	.7490	.0910	.7950	.0935	.8439
	.0880	.9838	.0905	1.0444	.0930	1.1087	.0955	1.1769
	.0900	1.2861	.0925	1.3654	.0950	1.4496	.0975	1.5390
	.0920	1.6141	.0945	1.7139	.0970	1.8198	.0995	1.9322
	.0940	1.9698	.0965	2.0918	.0990	2.2213	.1015	2.3589
	.0960	2.3551	.0985	2.5013	.1010	2.6565	.1035	2.8214
	.0980	2.7722	.1005	2.9446	.1030	3.1277	.1055	3.3222
	.1000	3.2232	.1025	3.4241	.1050	3.6375	.1075	3.8641

Interest Rate	.0900		.0925		.0950		.0975	
Annual Rent	.0958		.0980		.1001		.1023	
	Yield	Reversion	Yield	Reversion	Yield	Reversion	Yield	Reversion
	.0920	.2729	.0945	.2896	.0970	.3073	.0995	.3261
	.0940	.5709	.0965	.6058	.0990	.6430	.1015	.6824
	.0960	.8957	.0985	.9507	.1010	1.0091	.1035	1.0711
	.0980	1.2493	.1005	1.3262	.1030	1.4079	.1055	1.4945
	.1000	1.6339	.1025	1.7347	.1050	1.8417	.1075	1.9553
	.1020	2.0517	.1045	2.1785	.1070	2.3132	.1095	2.4562
	.1040	2.5050	.1065	2.6602	.1090	2.8250	.1115	3.0000
	.1060	2.9965	.1085	3.1825	.1110	3.3800	.1135	3.5899
	.1080	3.5288	.1105	3.7483	.1130	3.9814	.1155	4.2291
	.1100	4.1049	.1125	4.3607	.1150	4.6325	.1175	4.9212

Interest Rate	.1000		.1025		.1050		.1075	
Annual Rent	.1044		.1066		.1088		.1110	
	Yield	Reversion	Yield	Reversion	Yield	Reversion	Yield	Reversion
	.1020	.3460	.1045	.3672	.1070	.3897	.1095	.4136
	.1040	.7242	.1065	.7687	.1090	.8159	.1115	.8660
	.1060	1.1369	.1085	1.2068	.1110	1.2811	.1135	1.3599
	.1080	1.5866	.1105	1.6844	.1130	1.7882	.1155	1.8985
	.1100	2.0760	.1125	2.2042	.1150	2.3404	.1175	2.4851
	.1120	2.6081	.1145	2.7695	.1170	2.9409	.1195	3.1231
	.1140	3.1859	.1165	3.3835	.1190	3.5933	.1215	3.8163
	.1160	3.8128	.1185	4.0497	.1210	4.3014	.1235	4.5689
	.1180	4.4923	.1205	4.7719	.1230	5.0691	.1255	5.3849
	.1200	5.2281	.1225	5.5542	.1250	5.9007	.1275	6.2691

TABLE V

PURCHASE-LEASEBACK INVESTMENT YIELD CHARACTERISTICS

LEASE TERM 35 YEARS

Interest Rate	.0700		.0725		.0750		.0775	
Annual Rent	.0762		.0783		.0804		.0825	
	Yield	Reversion	Yield	Reversion	Yield	Reversion	Yield	Reversion
	.0715	.1953	.0740	.2094	.0765	.2244	.0790	.2405
	.0730	.4062	.0755	.4354	.0780	.4668	.0805	.5003
	.0745	.6336	.0770	.6792	.0795	.7282	.0820	.7807
	.0760	.8784	.0785	.9419	.0810	1.0099	.0835	1.0828
	.0775	1.1419	.0800	1.2246	.0825	1.3132	.0850	1.4082
	.0790	1.4252	.0815	1.5286	.0840	1.6394	.0865	1.7582
	.0805	1.7296	.0830	1.8552	.0855	1.9900	.0880	2.1345
	.0820	2.0564	.0845	2.2060	.0870	2.3665	.0895	2.5387
	.0835	2.4069	.0860	2.5823	.0885	2.7706	.0910	2.9726
	.0850	2.7827	.0875	2.9859	.0900	3.2039	.0925	3.4379

Interest Rate	.0800		.0825		.0850		.0875	
Annual Rent	.0847		.0868		.0890		.0912	
	Yield	Reversion	Yield	Reversion	Yield	Reversion	Yield	Reversion
	.0815	.2578	.0840	.2763	.0865	.2962	.0890	.3175
	.0830	.5363	.0855	.5749	.0880	.6163	.0905	.6607
	.0845	.8369	.0870	.8973	.0895	.9620	.0920	1.0315
	.0860	1.1610	.0885	1.2449	.0910	1.3349	.0935	1.4314
	.0875	1.5101	.0900	1.6194	.0925	1.7367	.0950	1.8625
	.0890	1.8857	.0915	2.0225	.0940	2.1692	.0965	2.3266
	.0905	2.2896	.0930	2.4559	.0955	2.6344	.0980	2.8260
	.0920	2.7235	.0945	2.9217	.0970	3.1345	.0995	3.3628
	.0935	3.1893	.0960	3.4219	.0985	3.6715	.1010	3.9394
	.0950	3.6890	.0975	3.9585	.1000	4.2478	.1025	4.5584

Interest Rate	.0900		.0925		.0950		.0975	
Annual Rent	.0934		.0956		.0978		.1001	
	Yield	Reversion	Yield	Reversion	Yield	Reversion	Yield	Reversion
	.0915	.3403	.0940	.3648	.0965	.3911	.0990	.4193
	.0930	.7084	.0955	.7595	.0980	.8143	.1005	.8731
	.0945	1.1060	.0970	1.1859	.0995	1.2717	.1020	1.3637
	.0960	1.5350	.0985	1.6461	.1010	1.7654	.1035	1.8934
	.0975	1.9975	.1000	2.1424	.1025	2.2979	.1050	2.4649
	.0990	2.4956	.1015	2.6770	.1040	2.8717	.1065	3.0807
	.1005	3.0316	.1030	3.2523	.1055	3.4893	.1080	3.7437
	.1020	3.6079	.1045	3.8711	.1070	4.1536	.1095	4.4570
	.1035	4.2271	.1060	4.5359	.1085	4.8676	.1110	5.2237
	.1050	4.8918	.1075	5.2498	.1100	5.6343	.1125	6.0473

Interest Rate	.1000		.1025		.1050		.1075	
Annual Rent	.1023		.1046		.1068		.1091	
	Yield	Reversion	Yield	Reversion	Yield	Reversion	Yield	Reversion
	.1015	.4495	.1040	.4820	.1065	.5169	.1090	.5543
	.1030	.9363	.1055	1.0040	.1080	1.0768	.1105	1.1549
	.1045	1.4625	.1070	1.5686	.1095	1.6824	.1120	1.8047
	.1060	2.0309	.1085	2.1784	.1110	2.3369	.1135	2.5070
	.1075	2.6441	.1100	2.8365	.1125	3.0432	.1150	3.2652
	.1090	3.3051	.1115	3.5461	.1140	3.8049	.1165	4.0829
	.1105	4.0169	.1130	4.3103	.1155	4.6254	.1180	4.9639
	.1120	4.7828	.1145	5.1327	.1170	5.5086	.1195	5.9125
	.1135	5.6062	.1160	6.0171	.1185	6.4585	.1210	6.9328
	.1150	6.4908	.1175	6.9674	.1200	7.4793	.1225	8.0295

Index

Index